Culture-Infused Counselling

Second Edition

Editors

Nancy Arthur and Sandra Collins

Counselling Concepts
Calgary, AB

Culture-Infused Counselling
  - Second Edition
© 2010 Nancy Arthur and Sandra Collins

Library and Archives Canada Cataloguing in Publication

Culture-infused counselling / editors: Nancy Arthur and Sandra Collins. -- 2nd ed.

ISBN 978-0-9738085-1-3

1. Cross-cultural counseling--Canada. 2. Cultural awareness--Canada. 3. Multiculturalism--Canada. I. Arthur, Nancy, 1957- II. Collins, Sandra D. (Sandra Dawn), 1962-

BF636.7.C76C852 2009   361'.06089   C2009-903902-8

Counselling Concepts
917 Drury Ave NE
Calgary, Alberta T2E 0M3
www.counsellingconcepts.ca

Printed in Canada

Cover Design by Jennifer Lussier

Culture-Infused Counselling
Second Edition

CONTENTS

PREFACE
INTRODUCING CULTURE-INFUSED COUNSELLING

Nancy Arthur and Sandra Collins

Our intent in developing this book was to provide a resource to advance theoretical understanding about multicultural counselling and practical skills in a way that recognizes our uniqueness as Canadians as well as our connection to the broader international professional communities. The contributions of our Canadian colleagues showcase the growing national expertise in multicultural counselling. We wanted to highlight Canada's uniqueness while acknowledging the depth and breadth of research and practice considerations and resources beyond our national borders.

The title of the book, *Culture-Infused Counselling*, reflects the theoretical perspective we adopt in this book. It is our belief that culture is a fundamental component of human experience and that no person or group can be fully understood in the absence of a purposeful inquiry into culture. In keeping with the national political and professional stance in Canada, we broadly define culture to include ethnicity, national origin, gender, sexual orientation, age, ability, socio-economic status and social class, religion, and other salient dimensions of culture that are important for counsellor-client interactions. This broad conceptualization of culture is essential to ensuring that the multiple and dynamic dimensions of each individual's personal culture are honoured in the counselling process. Beyond counsellor-client interactions, cultural dimensions may be important considerations in other professional roles.

The risk of continuing to talk in terms of professional practice as multicultural counselling is that the underlying theoretical and practical models may be interpreted as applying only to certain groups in our society. Although Canadian public policy clearly supports the idea that we are part of a multicultural society in which all cultures are equally honoured, the reality is that many Canadians continue to see culture as something belonging to someone else. Our choice of the term *culture-infused counselling* reflects our belief that culture is a core construct for understanding all human beings. It follows that each of us is a cultural being and that we must approach our understanding of ourselves as professionals and each of our clients from this perspective. To this end, as writers, we have attempted to provide glimpses into our own experience of culture as a means of modelling both the diversity of experience and the importance of acknowledging the influence of our own cultural experiences on our roles as teachers, counsellors, and researchers.

This book is also based on the premise that cultural inquiry must be incorporated into all areas of professional practice of counselling and psychology. Much of the literature to date has focused on applied counselling practice. We will also use this as a starting point for developing our conceptual framework for enhancing multicultural counselling competence, but wish to broaden the focus to social justice. Multicultural competence extends to other critical areas of practice, such as teaching, research, consultation, and supervision. While it is impossible to address each of these areas effectively in one book, we hope that the coverage provided will serve as a starting point for students and practitioners to seek out additional resources to enhance their competence in these areas.

The emphasis on social justice in this book also provides part of the conceptual framework for our writing. It is our belief that the professions of counselling and psychology in Canada stand in a crucial position of influence at the grass roots level; in our work with individual clients, groups, and organizations; and at broader socio-political levels, with provincial or national forces. While we stand proud to be Canadians and attempt to highlight the globally recognized position of this country in terms of advanced multicultural policy, we also recognize that the reality of many non-dominant populations in Canada falls far short of the ideal of inclusiveness and mutual respect. It is our hope that reading this book will also inspire you to respond to your broader professional obligation to act on behalf of the less powerful in our society to effect lasting change.

The Editors

Nancy Arthur is a Professor in Applied Psychology, Faculty of Education, and holds a Tri-Faculty Canada Research Chair in Professional Education at the University of Calgary, Calgary, Alberta, Canada. She received her Masters degree in Sociology from the University of Alberta before specializing in counselling psychology in Masters and Ph.D. degrees from the University of Calgary. Prior to joining the faculty at the University of Calgary in 1996, Nancy worked in post-secondary education as a counsellor. During her 15 years as a counsellor with the Southern Alberta Institute of Technology (SAIT), she worked with a diverse range of adult learners from Canada and from other countries. Her involvement with international projects fostered a keen interest in the counselling and teaching implications of the internationalization of higher education. She is a chartered psychologist and continues to work with clients through consulting and private practice.

Nancy's current research interests include professional education for cultural diversity and social justice, cross-cultural transitions, and career development. She has developed curriculum for both classroom and online delivery of courses on career development and multicultural counselling. She has been an active member of the Canadian Counselling Association, serving as the President of the Career Development Chapter and an Associate Editor of the Canadian Journal of Counselling.

Nancy has published several books related to the topics of career development and multicultural counselling. The book, *Counseling International Students: Clients From Around the World,* examines the roles of counsellors for working with international students in higher education. Her co-edited book, with Dr. Sandra Collins, *Culture-Infused Counselling: Celebrating the Canadian Mosaic,* received the Canadian Counselling Association Book Award in 2006. Her book, *Case Incidents in Counselling for International Transitions,* co-edited with Dr. Pedersen, involved collaboration with authors from 12 countries. This book focuses on transition issues of international workers and students, immigrants and refugees, and military and peacekeeping personnel. Nancy has written extensively about professional education and practice issues regarding multicultural counselling, social justice, and career development.

Sandra Collins, Ph.D. R.Psych. (Alberta), is an Associate Professor and the Director of the Centre for Graduate Education in Applied Psychology at Athabasca University. She received her Masters and Doctoral degrees in Counselling Psychology from the University of Calgary. She began working for Athabasca University in 1998 and has been instrumental in the development of the university's graduate programs in Counselling Psychology. As part of her commitment to social justice and the mission of the university, she specializes in distributed delivery of graduate education to reduce barriers to education and professional development. The programs support students from rural areas, students with various forms of physical disability, women with multiple role demands, and mid-career practitioners who must balance work and learning. She is committed to making graduate education accessible in spite of geographic, cultural, and other system barriers.

Sandra's areas of research interest include cultural diversity, counselling women and lesbians, counsellor education and supervision, distributed and online learning, program planning and evaluation, and career development. One focus in her writing is the importance of culture in counselling and psychology. As a lesbian and hence a member of a non-dominant population in Canada, Sandra brings both personal and professional experiences to that writing. She also has a passion for creativity in the delivery of educational services and focuses much of her current writing and research in that area. She strives to promote the infusion of culture and social justice into all aspects of counsellor education.

Sandra is a chartered psychologist and has worked with a diverse range of clientele. She has been actively involved in both provincial and national counselling and psychology organizations. She has served on the board of directors and been president of the College of Alberta Psychologists, as well as a Director of the Canadian Career Development Foundation. She is currently the President of the Counsellors for Social Justice Chapter of the Canadian Counselling Association. Sandra is interested in the evolution of the professions of counselling and psychology in Canada and in the connection between shifts in the profession and the focus of university education. She is particularly interested in ensuring that the principles of social justice espoused for applied practice are effectively translated into the broader systems.

Contributing Writers

We have been privileged in writing this book to have worked with a number of colleagues who have provided a wealth of expertise in both the broad understanding of multicultural counseling and the specific application of culture-infused counselling to particular non-dominant populations in Canada. We have simply listed the credentials and professional affiliations of these writers here since each has provided a personal introduction at the beginning of her or his chapter. We asked writers to describe in those introductory sections of each chapter who they are and how they have come to write about the particular chapter content. It is our hope that these personal introductions will provide a glimpse into the personal cultural identity of the writers and the worldviews from which they write. This knowledge should provide a frame of reference for integrating your learning. We respectfully acknowledge the contributions of the following individuals:

Kevin Alderson, Ph.D., is an Associate Professor of Counselling Psychology at the University of Calgary. He is a registered psychologist and a member of the Canadian Psychological Association and the Canadian Society of Clinical Hypnosis, Alberta Division. He is the author of three books dealing with sexuality and two books focusing on self-hypnosis. Kevin is currently the Editor of the Canadian Journal of Counselling.

Arthur Blue is a retired professor of Native Studies at Brandon University. He was trained as a Clinical Psychologist and practiced at the Open Arrow Clinic. He was the first President of the Native Psychologists in Canada and Chairman of the Board of Editors for the Journal of Canadian Native Studies.

Wes Darou is Senior Risk Analyst at the Canadian International Development Agency. He holds a D.Ed. in educational counselling from McGill University and an MSc. in environmental engineering from the University of Waterloo. Dr. Darou has 25 years of experience in counselling, psychoeducation, and training. His other interests include vocational training in Africa, gender equality, and organizational counselling. Recent articles concern Ibrahima Sow's African personality model and violence against girls in southern African schools.

Ivana Djuraskovic is a doctoral student in the Division of Applied Psychology, Faculty of Education, University Calgary. She received a BA in Psychology and an MSc. in Counselling Psychology at the University of Calgary. She is currently working as a registered psychologist for Alberta Health Services. Ivana's research interests include acculturation and ethnic identity development, counselling immigrants and refugees, and multicultural counselling competencies.

Monica Justin, Ph.D., is an instructor, clinician, and trainer. She holds a Ph.D. in Counselling Psychology from McGill University and is a member of the Order of Quebec Psychologists. Her teaching, training, and research interests lie in the areas of multicultural counselling and diversity issues, ethnic women, ethnic and cultural identity, and biculturalism.

Vivian Lalande, Ph.D., is a consulting psychologist with interests including counselling women, career development and counselling, and program evaluation. She was formerly an Associate Professor in the Division of Applied Psychology at the University of Calgary and served as the Editor of the Canadian Journal of Counselling. She has worked in the mental health field for over 30 years, primarily in the area of post-secondary student counselling, and was awarded the Canadian Counselling Association Professional Contribution Award in 2008.

Ann Laverty, Ph.D., is a psychologist and Associate Director (Counselling) at the University of Calgary, SU Wellness Centre. Her practice focuses on individual and group counselling with areas of interest including counselling women, grief and bereavement, eating issues, and post-secondary student development. In addition to her counselling work, she is involved with supervision of practicum and internship students and applied research initiatives.

Noorfarah Merali, Ph.D., is an Associate Professor and the Coordinator/Director of the Counselling Psychology Graduate Program at the University of Alberta. She is a specialist in the areas of cross-cultural adjustment and immigrant and refugee mental health, and acts as a consultant to settlement agencies. She is a Registered Psychologist with the College of Alberta Psychologists and a member of the Canadian Psychological Association, American Psychological Association, and the Society for the Psychological Study of Social Issues (International).

Kathy Offet-Gartner, Ph.D., is a Registered Psychologist (AB) with Student Counselling Services at Mount Royal College in Calgary. Her practice interests include cross-cultural counselling, surviving personal trauma, improving communication and relationships, and career-life planning through a feminist, strengths-based lens. Her research interests and publications focus on the lived experience related to these counselling concerns, especially as they relate to Aboriginal peoples. Kathy has presented at provincial and national conferences on these topics. She also teaches in a variety of graduate programs.

Jane Oxenbury, M.Ed., R.Psych. (Alberta) has a private practice in Calgary, Alberta, where she works with individuals, couples, and families, specializing in the areas of family violence, sexual abuse, depression, and anxiety. She works extensively with the gay/lesbian/bisexual/transgendered communities, especially in the areas of same-sex domestic violence, the bullying and harassment of GLBT youth, and Gender Identity Disorder. She consults with and trains groups and professionals about the issues faced by this population and serves on many committees, working to increase knowledge and services for these communities.

Jean Pettifor, Ph.D., C.Psych. (Alberta), Past President of the Psychologists' Association of Alberta, the Canadian Psychological Association, and the College of Alberta Psychologists, and Adjunct Professor at the University of Calgary, has received many awards for her lifetime contributions to the profession of psychology. She has served in professional organizations as well as being a clinician, consultant, educator, and researcher. She continues to work provincially, nationally, and internationally to promote a value-based ethical decision-making model.

Carlos Ruano holds degrees in linguistics and history from the University of Ottawa and M.Sc. and Doctor of Education degrees in Sociology of Education from Georgia State University and the University of Toronto [OISE/UT]. His research centres around policy development, implementation, and assessment of learning processes in multicultural and multilingual societies, as well as the impact of administrative decision-making processes on students from bilingual and/or multicultural backgrounds. As an expert in international education, he has served as Senior Education Specialist and Program Manager with CIDA, ILO, UNESCO and the World Bank.

John Stewart, Ed.D., C.C.C., taught at the University of New Brunswick, in Fredericton, New Brunswick, as a professor of Counselling Psychology in the Faculty of Education. He retired in December 2007, but continues to teach graduate courses in counselling part-time. He has also worked as a high school teacher and school counsellor and has provided consultancy services in Asia. His research interests involve the career decision-making process and the role of culture in mediating interpersonal behaviour. He is a certified member of the Canadian Counselling Association. In 2009, John completed a Master of Theological Studies with a focus on Spirituality, awarded by the Toronto School of Theology.

Intended Audiences

We have received feedback from students and instructors across Canada who have used this book in graduate level counselling programs and undergraduate and college programs in other helping professions. This feedback has been extremely valuable in helping us to shape the direction of the second edition of this book. We continue to emphasize broad theoretical understanding of the role and importance of culture in professional practice and to target specific attitudes, knowledge, and skill development in working with particular non-dominant populations. However, we have placed more emphasis on multiple cultural identities to recognize the complexities through which many Canadians navigate the intersections of their identities across different contexts. We have also incorporated more writing about social justice as a foundation for culture-infused counselling.

Along with supporting preservice programs in counsellor education and as a resource for practicing counsellors, this book may be used as a foundation for professional development activities in organizations or professional associations. Many practitioners have told us that the book has been helpful in planning ways to enhance their competence for practice. This is encouraging, as we consider cultural competence to be something that is aspirational in nature, requiring ongoing learning and professional development.

Awards

We are very pleased that our first edition of the book, *Culture-Infused Counselling: Celebrating the Canadian Mosaic* (2005) was awarded the Canadian Counselling Association 2006 Annual Book Award. It was rewarding to see our work acknowledged by our professional colleagues at the joint conferences of the Canadian Counselling Association and American Counselling Association held in Montreal.

Organization of the Book

In this second edition of the book, we have left in foundation material and the classic sources that have informed our writing, teaching, research, and other professional practices. We have focused a major portion of the book on our expanded model of culture-infused counselling. Based on our experience in using the model in graduate education and training workshops, we have gained valuable feedback from students and practitioners. We continue to emphasize the importance of self-awareness and awareness of client cultural identities in the context of a culturally sensitive working alliance. However, we have enhanced our model with additional competencies related to social justice. This addition to our model shows our commitment to integrating social justice as a foundation for counselling practice. In this edition, we have also expanded our competency framework to help readers translate the concept of social justice to practical approaches in counselling. We invited our colleagues who contributed to the second edition to revisit their original chapters to decide what they wanted to include as foundational knowledge and to provide updates about current research and practice.

The book has been structured into four parts. Part I includes the first six chapters and focuses on the conceptual and theoretical foundations of culture-infused counselling. In Chapter 1 we begin by providing an overview of multiculturalism in Canada and defining our use of the key constructs that form a foundation for our approach to counselling. Chapter 2 provides a rationale for the infusion of culture into the practice of counselling and psychology. Chapter 3 then introduces our conceptual framework for culture-infused counselling competence, which is organized according to three core competence domains: (a) self-awareness of personal assumptions, values, and biases; (b) awareness of the cultural worldview of the client; and (c) development of a culturally sensitive working alliance. In chapters 3 through 5, we expand upon the core domains of competence, describing their unique features and their relationships in supporting cultural competence. The culture-infused model of counselling emphasizes the working alliance as the foundation for linking the first two competency domains to applied practice. Our purpose in these chapters is to address the *how to* of culture-infused counselling practice.

In Chapter 6, we expand our conceptual framework for infusing culture into professional practice by emphasizing social justice. We believe that it is critical for counsellors to work towards addressing the social conditions that lead to distress and towards making a positive difference in the lives of our clients. Whereas other writers have discussed social justice as an additional role of counsellors, we take the stand that social justice is a core value and responsibility for *all* counsellors. In Chapter 6, we introduce the process of cultural auditing as a form of reflective practice for working with *all* clients. The cultural auditing process demonstrates how the principles of culture-infused counselling connect with social justice in practice. These first six chapters form the theoretical foundation for all that follows in the book.

Part II of the book focuses on concepts and applications in counselling ethics, assessment, and research. Chapter 7 is devoted to exploring ethics and culture-infused counselling. Chapter 8 outlines some of the issues related specifically to assessment with client populations from diverse cultural backgrounds. Chapter 9 examines the process of conducting research across cultures. These chapters provide theoretical and practical information to support counsellors in applied practice and in research.

Part III focuses on culture-infused counselling with non-dominant populations in Canada. We introduce this section of the book with a chapter that addresses multiple and intersecting identities. This addition to the book positions our belief that clients cannot be defined solely by group membership. Counsellors require skills to assess worldview and the salience of various dimensions of culture considered by their clients as relevant for their presenting issues. Part of the challenge for us has been to honour the complexity of cultural identity while providing readers with content knowledge about common issues faced by many members of non-dominant populations in

Canada. It is impossible to do justice to the wide range of populations that forms part of the Canadian cultural mosaic. We have selected a number of areas of focus that we see as broad enough to enhance an overall understanding of approaching applied practice from a culture-infused perspective. At the same time we recognize the limitations of transferring culture-specific knowledge from one non-dominant group to another, and want to emphasize the importance of counsellors recognizing the heterogeneity of groups and need to assess individual identities. The contributions to these chapters by our Canadian colleagues illustrate the expertise required for becoming knowledgeable about working with specific populations, while honouring the core principles of culture-infused counselling.

The fourth and final section of the book contains our wrap-up chapter, in which we attempt to illuminate some of the potential implications of looking at counselling from a culture-infused perspective and to explore the future of culture-infused counselling in Canada. It is our hope that this final chapter will function both as a point of departure for your own continued professional development as a practitioner or student of counselling or psychology and as a guide for the profession in terms of future developments in research, practice, and education.

Acknowledgements

We wish to acknowledge the following individuals for their contributions of illustrative material for snapshots in some chapters of the book: Barbara Butchart, Pamela Dos Ramos, Carol McDonald, Marjorie McIntyre.

Both Athabasca University and the University of Calgary have played an important role in providing us with resources and time for academic writing and extensive library services that have facilitated our research.

The foundation for this book has developed from many sources of learning throughout our lives. In particular, countless students and clients have helped to shape our worldview and our views of professional practice.

We gratefully acknowledge Jennifer Lussier for her creativity, evidenced in our book cover design. We also wish to thank Jennifer Lussier for his visual design work on the book cover and the figures throughout the text, and Brenda Christians for copyediting,

Nancy Arthur
Sandra Collins

PART I

CONCEPTUAL AND THEORETICAL FOUNDATIONS OF CULTURE-INFUSED COUNSELLING

In the past several decades, multicultural counselling has become a major focus in psychology and counselling literature, both in Canada and in many other countries. New models for counselling members of non-dominant populations have emerged, challenges to the historical theories of counselling have been debated, and general principles for incorporating culture into a wide range of areas of professional practice have been developed. The plethora of writing in this area, however, has the potential to leave both current practitioners and students of counselling and psychology struggling to make sense out of how to incorporate the emergent emphasis on increasing multicultural competence into their own day-to-day practice. Important differences exist between countries in terms of the distribution of specific non-dominant populations in each country and the impact of national policies, practices, and socio-historical factors on the nature of multiculturalism.

In this book we are introducing a new term, *culture-infused counselling*, as a means of differentiating our particular perspective on multicultural counselling from the models and theories that have been developed to date. In this first section of the book, we will focus on situating this model within the context of Canadian culture (historical and current), within the professional practice of counselling and psychology in Canada, and within the breadth of existing literature on multicultural counselling and associated competence.

We have built our model for culture-infused counselling on the foundation of the multicultural counselling competencies that have emerged in the literature over the past several decades. We introduce a new conceptual model for integrating and further developing those competency frameworks. This conceptual model forms the foundation for our exploration of the attitudes, knowledge, and skills that we see as essential for competent practice. We do not differentiate between competent counselling practice and competent multicultural counselling practice. Rather, we take the position that culture-infused counselling is a model that applies to all clients and all areas of professional practice.

This first section of the book is intended to provide you with a solid foundation in both culture-infused counselling theory and practice and to integrate principles for social justice practices that are becoming more and more important as the demographics of our population and the professional and ethical expectations of counsellors and psychologists evolve.

CHAPTER 1
INTRODUCTION TO CULTURE-INFUSED COUNSELLING

Nancy Arthur and Sandra Collins

Key Terms and Concepts		
• Counselling • Culture • Culture-infused counselling • Cultural mosaic • Diversity	• Emic/group specific • Ethnicity • Etic/universal • Melting pot • Multicultural	• Multicultural policy • Non-dominant • Race • Salience of cultural dimensions

Introduction

As Canada embraces an increasingly diverse population, with individuals representing every major cultural group in the world forming part of our economic, social, and political systems, the need for respect, understanding, and communication across cultures becomes more and more important. As professionals involved with the psychological and emotional well-being of the Canadian people, counsellors and psychologists have a particularly crucial role to play in actively promoting health among members of non-dominant cultural groups and between members of these groups and the historically dominant populations.

This chapter introduces the concept of culture-infused counselling, drawing on the current literature on multicultural counselling. We begin, however, by providing an historical perspective on multiculturalism in Canada as a backdrop for understanding the rationale for and the nature of culture-infused counselling. It is important to understand this socio-political context in order to grasp the difference in perspectives on multiculturalism within Canada and between Canada and other countries and to appreciate the current conditions under which culture-infused practice is being promoted.

We will then examine some of the key constructs that form the foundation for understanding what we mean by culture-infused counselling. The questions that drive this discussion are: How do we define culture? Who counts as a *culturally diverse* client? What aspects of culture are salient to counselling practice? Where does the culture of the counsellor come into play? How do we embrace culture without losing sight of the commonalties across cultures? What is the relationship between multicultural counselling and counselling generally? What responsibilities do counsellors have in addressing adverse social conditions that contribute to mental health concerns? What roles can counsellors take to promote health and well-being among all members of Canadian society? It is our hope that by the end of this chapter you will have reflected on these and other questions that form the starting place for infusing culture into your own practice.

Many of you reading this book may immediately concur with us that culture is an essential and foundational construct for understanding the experience of all human beings. Although great strides forward have been made, we believe there is much work to do to infuse culture into current education, practice, and research in counselling psychology.

The Canadian Context

Recent Statistics Canada (2009) figures place the population of Canada at 33,311,400. Between 1996 and 2001, Canada's population increased by only 4%. During the 1990s, more than 2 million immigrants chose Canada as their home (Statistics Canada, 2005). 2006 census figures show that one in five people living in Canada are foreign-born (Statistics Canada, 2007a). Immigration continues to be the main source of population growth, making up half of the overall growth and compensating for a 30% decline in the number of births over deaths (Statistics Canada, 2002). The immigrant population continues to shift in terms of the diversity of countries of origin. Whereas early immigrants were predominantly British or French, the source countries of recent immigrants show increasing diversity from other parts of Europe and other continents around the world (Statistics Canada, 2007a). In 2008, Canada welcomed 247,202 permanent residents, approximately 70,000 more than in 1998. An additional 193,061 temporary foreign workers and 79,459 foreign students contributed to a combined total of 519,722 newcomers to Canada in 2008 (Citizenship and Immigration Canada [CIC], 2009b). Immigration is viewed as a national strategy to maintain and advance Canada's economic prosperity, compensating for declining birth rates and population projections regarding labour force requirements (Treasury Board of Canada Secretariat, 2008).

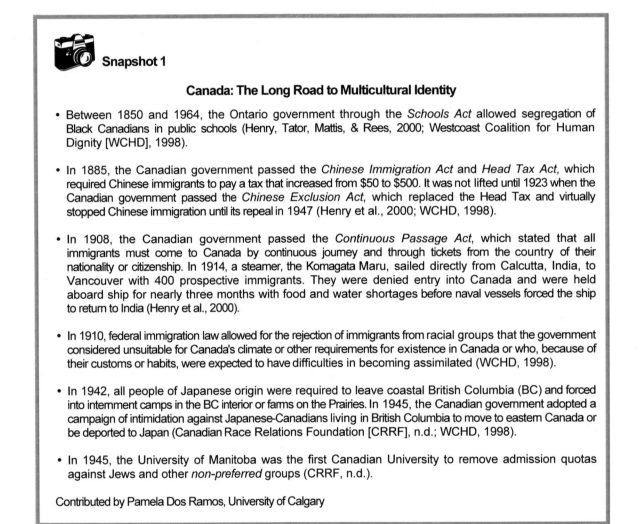

Snapshot 1

Canada: The Long Road to Multicultural Identity

- Between 1850 and 1964, the Ontario government through the *Schools Act* allowed segregation of Black Canadians in public schools (Henry, Tator, Mattis, & Rees, 2000; Westcoast Coalition for Human Dignity [WCHD], 1998).

- In 1885, the Canadian government passed the *Chinese Immigration Act* and *Head Tax Act*, which required Chinese immigrants to pay a tax that increased from $50 to $500. It was not lifted until 1923 when the Canadian government passed the *Chinese Exclusion Act*, which replaced the Head Tax and virtually stopped Chinese immigration until its repeal in 1947 (Henry et al., 2000; WCHD, 1998).

- In 1908, the Canadian government passed the *Continuous Passage Act*, which stated that all immigrants must come to Canada by continuous journey and through tickets from the country of their nationality or citizenship. In 1914, a steamer, the Komagata Maru, sailed directly from Calcutta, India, to Vancouver with 400 prospective immigrants. They were denied entry into Canada and were held aboard ship for nearly three months with food and water shortages before naval vessels forced the ship to return to India (Henry et al., 2000).

- In 1910, federal immigration law allowed for the rejection of immigrants from racial groups that the government considered unsuitable for Canada's climate or other requirements for existence in Canada or who, because of their customs or habits, were expected to have difficulties in becoming assimilated (WCHD, 1998).

- In 1942, all people of Japanese origin were required to leave coastal British Columbia (BC) and forced into internment camps in the BC interior or farms on the Prairies. In 1945, the Canadian government adopted a campaign of intimidation against Japanese-Canadians living in British Columbia to move to eastern Canada or be deported to Japan (Canadian Race Relations Foundation [CRRF], n.d.; WCHD, 1998).

- In 1945, the University of Manitoba was the first Canadian University to remove admission quotas against Jews and other *non-preferred* groups (CRRF, n.d.).

Contributed by Pamela Dos Ramos, University of Calgary

The dominant image currently used to describe the nature of Canada is a **multicultural mosaic** (Bowman, 2000; Canadian Task Force on Mental Health Issues Affecting Immigrants and Refugees [CTFMHI], 1988). The concept of the cultural mosaic is founded on *the acknowledgement of cultural diversity as a reality in this country, affirmation of the necessity of treating all people equally, regardless of culture-ethnic heritage, and encouragement of individuals and groups to maintain their cultural identity.* The emphasis in public policy is on the importance of providing all people with the opportunity to fully participate in Canadian life. Canadians have created a national identity based in large part on establishing an environment in which people of all cultural backgrounds are welcomed and encouraged to participate actively in society while openly maintaining their distinctiveness. Canada's position on multiculturalism is unique on the global scene, with the exception of the Australians, who have modelled much of their policy after Canadian policies (Kymlicka, 1997). Canada is viewed internationally as a pluralistic society and many see Canada's policies and practices in terms of immigration and multiculturalism as providing a model for much of the industrialized world (CTFMHI). In fact, in 1986, the United Nations awarded the Nansen Medal to the people of Canada for our response to the international refugee crisis and our national efforts to facilitate the integration of refugees into our society. This was the first time an entire nation had been identified for this type of recognition by the United Nations.

However, Canada's emphasis on cultural diversity is relatively recent. Like other industrialized nations, we have a long history of systemic racial and ethnic oppression (see Snapshot 1). It was not until 1967 that the final systemic racial and ethnic barriers to immigration were removed through immigration policy changes, which opened the door to those of non-European heritage. Since then, the visible diversity within Canada has dramatically increased. By 2002, people of non-European descent accounted for 13% of the population, or 2.9 million people (Statistics Canada, 2003d). Today, the majority of new immigrants from Canada are from countries other than Europe, thereby increasing the diversity of our population. The resultant shift in overall composition of Canadian residents continues to impact policies and practices related to multiculturalism.

Roots of Diversity: Canadian First Nations

Cultural diversity is not new to Canada, but it has characterized this country since its origins. When the first European colonialists arrived several hundred years ago, there were more than 56 Aboriginal nations speaking more than 30 languages. These peoples possessed a rich culture, with social, economic, and spiritual norms that had served them well for hundreds of years (Poonwassie & Charter, 2001).

Unfortunately, the human rights of these First Nations peoples have been infringed upon in various ways up to the present time. In spite of the fact that Aboriginal peoples were part of the Canadian scene long before the English and French arrived, the latter two have established the dominant institutions and social, political, and economic structures that have come to define Canadian culture (James, 1996). In establishing these systems, no attempt was made to reflect the traditional values and norms of the First Nations populations (Green, 1997). In fact, many of these structures and institutions were used to break down traditional social, political, economic, and cultural practices and systems that were more reflective of the Aboriginal worldview (Poonwassie & Charter, 2001).

First Nations peoples and European settlers peacefully coexisted and collaborated to a much larger degree in Canada than they did in the United States (Bowman, 2000). However, in spite of the treaties established, First Nations people were progressively blocked from access to traditional lands and were isolated and marginalized on reserves, where economic deprivation became the norm.

Many Aboriginal communities continue to struggle against the effects of the residential school system, which was no less dramatic than the attempts at cultural genocide we continue to witness in other parts of the world today. The goal was to purge children of their traditional language, values, and beliefs (Green, 1997; Robertson, 2006). It is estimated that 39% of current Aboriginal Elders attended residential schools (Statistics Canada, 1996). The impact on both individuals who attended the residential schools and subsequent generations has been profound and remains one of the darkest realities of Canadian history. Aboriginal Canadians continue to experience higher rates of poverty than other Canadians (Department of Canadian Heritage [DCH], 2002). In spite of changes in recent years, many social, economic, and political structures in Canada continue to perpetuate systemic racism and to foster assimilation of First Nations peoples rather than support for maintenance of their cultural heritage (Poonwassie & Charter, 2001).

Aboriginal peoples across Canada seem to have a defining sense of community and spirituality. In varying degrees they (may) see themselves as the appointed guardians of the land. Aboriginal peoples across Canada have banded together, particularly in the past several decades, to fight for their inherent rights as the First Nations of this country. Similar trends in self-assertion are visible in many other countries around the world in which colonialism has left similar marks on the cultural landscape, supported in part by the international efforts of the United Nations (UNESCO, 1995). Many are reclaiming their traditional cultural heritage and methods of healing. As explored later in the chapter on counselling First Nations peoples, the worldview and cultural practices of Aboriginal Canadians form an essential part of the Canadian cultural mosaic and offer much to traditional European ways of understanding health and healing.

In the last three decades, the Government of Canada has introduced legislation intended to acknowledge some of the wrongs committed against Aboriginal populations in Canada. The Supreme Court of Canada first acknowledged some land rights in 1973. The introduction of the *Canadian Charter of Rights and Freedoms* in 1982 included the rights of Aboriginal peoples to protection of their cultures and languages. In recent years, a report by Indian and Northern Affairs Canada [INAC] (1996) led to the development of the federal government's *Gathering Strength: Canada's Aboriginal Action Plan*, which is intended to facilitate collaboration with Aboriginal peoples in addressing health, social, economic, and political challenges. The overriding goal is to work in partnership with Canada's Aboriginal peoples to improve health, housing, and public safety; strengthen economic development; and assist with the implementation of self-government (DCH, 2002).

Aboriginal peoples are gradually regaining their traditional rights, their treaty rights, and their historical place in Canadian society. This is in sharp contrast to the historical oppression that has permeated government policies and practices. On June 11, 2008, Prime Minister Stephen Harper offered a fully apology on behalf of Canadians for the Indian Residential Schools system.

 **Snapshot 2**

Prime Minister Stephen Harper's Statement of Apology to Former Students of Indian Residential Schools

The treatment of children in Indian Residential Schools is a sad chapter in our history.

For more than a century, Indian Residential Schools separated over 150,000 Aboriginal children from their families and communities. In the 1870's, the federal government, partly in order to meet its obligation to educate Aboriginal children, began to play a role in the development and administration of these schools. Two primary objectives of the Residential Schools system were to remove and isolate children from the influence of their homes, families, traditions and cultures, and to assimilate them into the dominant culture. These objectives were based on the assumption that Aboriginal cultures and spiritual beliefs were inferior and unequal. Indeed, some sought, as it was infamously said, "to kill the Indian in the child." Today, we recognize that this policy of assimilation was wrong, has caused great harm, and has no place in our country.

One hundred and thirty-two federally-supported schools were located in every province and territory, except Newfoundland, New Brunswick and Prince Edward Island. Most schools were operated as "joint ventures" with Anglican, Catholic, Presbyterian or United Churches. The Government of Canada built an educational system in which very young children were often forcibly removed from their homes, often taken far from their communities. Many were inadequately fed, clothed and housed. All were deprived of the care and nurturing of their parents, grandparents and communities. First Nations, Inuit and Métis languages and cultural practices were prohibited in these schools. Tragically, some of these children died while attending residential schools and others never returned home.

The government now recognizes that the consequences of the Indian Residential Schools policy were profoundly negative and that this policy has had a lasting and damaging impact on Aboriginal culture, heritage and language. While some former students have spoken positively about their experiences at residential schools, these stories are far overshadowed by tragic accounts of the emotional, physical and sexual abuse and neglect of helpless children, and their separation from powerless families and communities.

The legacy of Indian Residential Schools has contributed to social problems that continue to exist in many communities today.

It has taken extraordinary courage for the thousands of survivors that have come forward to speak publicly about the abuse they suffered. It is a testament to their resilience as individuals and to the strength of their cultures. Regrettably, many former students are not with us today and died never having received a full apology from the Government of Canada.

The government recognizes that the absence of an apology has been an impediment to healing and reconciliation. Therefore, on behalf of the Government of Canada and all Canadians, I stand before you, in this Chamber so central to our life as a country, to apologize to Aboriginal peoples for Canada's role in the Indian Residential Schools system.

To the approximately 80,000 living former students, and all family members and communities, the Government of Canada now recognizes that it was wrong to forcibly remove children from their homes and we apologize for having done this. We now recognize that it was wrong to separate children from rich and vibrant cultures and traditions that it created a void in many lives and communities, and we apologize for having done this. We now recognize that, in separating children from their families, we undermined the ability of many to adequately parent their own children and sowed the seeds for generations to follow, and we apologize for having done this. We now recognize that, far too often, these institutions gave rise to abuse or neglect and were inadequately controlled, and we apologize for failing to protect you. Not only did you suffer these abuses as children, but as you became parents, you were powerless to protect your own children from suffering the same experience, and for this we are sorry.

The burden of this experience has been on your shoulders for far too long. The burden is properly ours as a Government, and as a country. There is no place in Canada for the attitudes that inspired the Indian Residential Schools system to ever prevail again. You have been working on recovering from this experience for a long time and in a very real sense, we are now joining you on this journey. The Government of Canada sincerely apologizes and asks the forgiveness of the Aboriginal peoples of this country for failing them so profoundly.

Nous le regrettons
We are sorry
Nimitataynan
Niminchinowesamin
Mamiattugut

In moving towards healing, reconciliation and resolution of the sad legacy of Indian Residential Schools, implementation of the Indian Residential Schools Settlement Agreement began on September 19, 2007. Years of work by survivors, communities, and Aboriginal organizations culminated in an agreement that gives us a new beginning and an opportunity to move forward together in partnership.

A cornerstone of the Settlement Agreement is the Indian Residential Schools Truth and Reconciliation Commission. This Commission presents a unique opportunity to educate all Canadians on the Indian Residential Schools system. It will be a positive step in forging a new relationship between Aboriginal peoples and other Canadians, a relationship based on the knowledge of our shared history, a respect for each other and a desire to move forward together with a renewed understanding that strong families, strong communities and vibrant cultures and traditions will contribute to a stronger Canada for all of us.

From the Office of the Prime Minister (2008). Prime Minister Harper offers full apology on behalf of Canadians for the Indian Residential Schools system. Retrieved April 25, 2009 from http://pm.gc.ca/eng/media.asp?id=2149

Canada as a Bilingual Nation

In spite of the presence of a very diverse population of First Nations, Canada has traditionally been described as a bicultural nation rather than a multicultural nation. The term biculturalism was first coined by Graham Spry in 1929 in reference to the two dominant cultural groups: English and French (Duffy Hutcheon, 1998). Beginning with the *Quebec Act* in 1774, Canadian policies have reflected a commitment to preserving the cultural heritage of Francophone Canadians (Bowman, 2000). The population distribution in Canada continues to be dominated by those of British and French heritage. According to Statistics Canada (2003d), approximately 46% of Canadians identify themselves as British, French, and/or Canadian, with 21% noting only British ancestry and 10% noting only French. Until quite recently, the expectation for newcomers to Canada was that they would assimilate into one of the two dominant cultures. In 1969, the *Official Languages Act* designated both English and French as official languages in Canada, mandating bilingualism for employees and services of the federal government (Duffy Hutcheon). Denis Coderre, Minister of Citizenship and Immigration Canada, stated that "linguistic duality is fundamental to our Canadian identity" (CIC, 2003, Message from the Minister, ¶3). It should be noted that the Northwest Territories has since declared six other official languages in recognition of Aboriginal populations in the north (UNESCO, 1995).

During the mid-1960s, the relationship between the two dominant cultural groups in Canada became increasingly tenuous as Francophone Canadians began to rebel against what they saw as the loss or marginalization of their distinct society. In 1963, the *Royal Commission on Bilingualism and Biculturalism* was appointed to explore the issues and provide the government with recommendations. What came out of the hearings held across the country, however, were not just recommendations related to French/English relations, but also an emphasis on the importance of cultural pluralism to the Canadian identity (Centre for Canadian Studies [CCS], n.d.). The earliest official use of the term *multiculturalism* appeared in this report (Duffy Hutcheon, 1998). The report reaffirmed the co-existence of two dominant cultures in Canada and encouraged the integration of other cultural groups into the pluralistic fabric of Canadian society (Duffy Hutcheon). In spite of the recognition of other ethnic groups, concerns continued to be raised that their importance to Canadian culture and society was seen as secondary to the role of the British and the French (Esses & Gardner, 1996).

Policy on Multiculturalism

In 1971, the federal government introduced its *Multiculturalism Policy*, making Canada the first country in the world to take that official step (DCH, 2003). The policy had two primary impacts: (a) it affirmed the pluralistic nature of Canadian society and (b) it changed the focus from assimilation of diverse populations into Canadian culture to a focus on maintaining cultural identity within the framework of integration into Canadian society. The policy introduced multiculturalism within a bilingual framework. English and French were affirmed as the two official languages of Canada, but a shift occurred from biculturalism to multiculturalism, with emphasis placed on the preservation and development of ethnic pluralism (CCS, n.d.; Esses & Gardner, 1996). Readers are referred to Leman (1999) for a fuller account of multiculturalism policy in Canada.

At the time these policies on multiculturalism emerged in Canada, the effort to distinguish Canadians from others on this basis was central to the national struggle for a unique Canadian identity (Esses & Gardner, 1996). The reception to Canada's new policy on multiculturalism was greeted with less warmth in Quebec, where many Francophone Canadians saw it as a federal government attempt to reduce the status of French-speaking Canadians from that of members of a *founding nation* to a status equal to that of many newer cultural subgroups within the population (UNESCO, 1995).

The *Canadian Bill of Rights*, set out in legislation during the 1960s, had established the fundamental right of every Canadian citizen as freedom from discrimination based on race, national origin, skin colour, religious belief, or gender (Duffy Hutcheon, 1998). The *Constitution Act* of 1982 added these protections to the Canadian constitution in the form of the *Charter of Rights and Freedoms* (see Snapshot 3). In 1988, the *Canadian Multiculturalism Act* (Bill C-93) came into existence, affirming the value of cultural diversity and formalizing Canada's **multicultural policy** into legislation (CCS, n.d.). In essence, that policy states that *the cultural and racial diversity of Canadians is part of Canada's core identity and an invaluable national resource. All members are free and encouraged to fully participate in Canadian society, while maintaining and sharing their cultural heritage* (see Snapshot 4). Many provinces introduced multiculturalism policies during the next decade. The *Canadian Charter of Rights and Freedoms* and the *Canadian Multiculturalism Act* reflect a national policy based on fairness and equity for all residents of Canada (CTFMHI, 1988).

Canada continues to attempt to build and maintain a national identity that simultaneously (a) recognizes and affirms the bilingual (and historically bicultural nature of the original colonialists who founded this country), (b) acknowledges and attempts to restore the rights of First Nations, and (c) takes an international leading role in promoting cultural pluralism. The following section will explore how well the national policies on bilingualism and multiculturalism are translating into the lived experience of non-dominant groups in our society.

 **Snapshot 3**

Excerpts from the Constitution Act, 1982
Part I: Canadian Charter of Rights and Freedoms

Fundamental freedoms

Everyone has the following fundamental freedoms:
(a) freedom of conscience and religion;
(b) freedom of thought, belief, opinion, and expression, including freedom of the press and other media of communication;
(c) freedom of peaceful assembly; and
(d) freedom of association.

Equality before and under the law and equal protection and benefit of the law

(1) Every individual is equal before and under the law and has the right to the equal protection and equal benefit of the law without discrimination and, in particular, without discrimination based on race, national or ethnic origin, colour, religion, sex, age, or mental or physical disability.

Affirmative action programs

(2) Subsection (1) does not preclude any law, program or activity that has as its object the amelioration of conditions of disadvantaged individuals or groups, including those who are disadvantaged because of race, national or ethnic origin, colour, religion, sex, age, or mental or physical disability.

From "*The Constitution Act,*" by Department of Justice Canada, 1982. Retrieved October 30, 2003, from http://laws.justice.gc.ca/en/const/annex_e.html#guarantee

---

Snapshot 4

Excerpts from the Canadian Multiculturalism Act, 1988
Multiculturalism Policy of Canada

Multiculturalism Policy

3. (1) It is hereby declared to be the policy of the Government of Canada to
(a) recognize and promote the understanding that multiculturalism reflects the cultural and racial diversity of Canadian society and acknowledges the freedom of all members of Canadian society to preserve, enhance, and share their cultural heritage;
(b) recognize and promote the understanding that multiculturalism is a fundamental characteristic of the Canadian heritage and identity and that it provides an invaluable resource in the shaping of Canada's future;
(c) promote the full and equitable participation of individuals and communities of all origins in the continuing evolution and shaping of all aspects of Canadian society and assist them in the elimination of any barrier to that participation;
(d) recognize the existence of communities whose members share a common origin and their historic contribution to Canadian society and enhance their development;
(e) ensure that all individuals receive equal treatment and equal protection under the law, while respecting and valuing their diversity;
(f) encourage and assist the social, cultural, economic and political institutions of Canada to be both respectful and inclusive of Canada's multicultural character;
(g) promote the understanding and creativity that arise from the interaction between individuals and communities of different origins;
(h) foster the recognition and appreciation of the diverse cultures of Canadian society and promote the reflection and the evolving expressions of those cultures;
(i) preserve and enhance the use of languages other than English and French, while strengthening the status and use of the official languages of Canada; and
(j) advance multiculturalism throughout Canada in harmony with the national commitment to the official languages of Canada.

From "*The Constitution Act,*" by Department of Justice Canada, 1982. Retrieved October 30, 2003, from http://laws.justice.gc.ca/en/const/annex_e.html#guarantee

Translating Policy into Practice

Canada's policy on multiculturalism takes a clear stand, but what is less clear is how effective that policy has been in facilitating the cultural mosaic that has become central to Canada's national identity. To what degree do non-dominant ethnic populations freely celebrate their cultural heritage while actively contributing to local, provincial, and national identities? How willing are Canadians of predominantly European heritage to relinquish their position of cultural dominance in favour of a more pluralistic society? How has the policy on multiculturalism enhanced or placed a barrier to the maintenance of Canada's bilingual national identity?

> The idea of building a multicultural and/or multiracial society generates a range of difficulties presented at times as challenges to be met and at other times as criticism of multiculturalism itself. Among these difficulties are those pertaining to the incorporation of immigrants in the "community of citizens," to civic equality, political participation, social inclusion, and economic integration, and finally to the maintenance of national unity and social cohesion. (Ulysse, n.d., Summary, ¶3)

Attitudes towards multiculturalism in Canada have varied across time, across rural and urban populations, across dominant language groups, and across provincial jurisdictions. According to the Department of Canadian Heritage (2003), Canadians are increasingly aware of Canada's multicultural policy and most support its objectives. Several surveys of Canadians conducted since the early 1990s (Angus Reid Group [ARG], 2000; DCH, 1998a, 2003) have identified the perceived benefits of Canada's policies on multiculturalism and immigration. Multiculturalism is believed by most to:

1. enhance Canadian society through appreciation of difference;
2. act as unifying force within the country;
3. contribute to Canada's economic growth, particularly in the global economy;
4. increase the sense of belonging to Canada by those from diverse cultural backgrounds;
5. lead to greater self-confidence among non-dominant populations;
6. increase tolerance for differences among both dominant and non-dominant populations;
7. facilitate a stronger sense of Canadian identity;
8. allow all Canadians to express that sense of identity with pride; and
9. facilitate the overall health and well-being of all Canadians.

In fact, 82% of Canadians viewed their multicultural nature as one of the best things about Canada (ARG, 2000).

However, the same survey (ARG, 2000) suggested that only about half of Canadians support current immigration policies. Canadians are also split almost equally in their preference for an assimilation approach to multiculturalism that encourages non-dominant populations to integrate into Canadian society by becoming more like the dominant groups versus the cultural mosaic approach that encourages them to maintain their cultural distinctiveness (ARG). Resistance to the concept of a multicultural mosaic is highest in Quebec and Alberta, and among older, male, and less educated individuals (ARG).

Although some see Canada's multicultural policy as actually threatening the integration of immigrants into society (Moodley, 2007), Kymlicka (1997) pointed out that the numbers applying for citizenship have increased since the introduction of the policy in 1971, in spite of the lack of economic advantage over remaining permanent residents. In addition, 98.6% of Canadians now speak either English or French, rates of intermarriage have steadily increased, and involvement in provincial and national politics has increased (Kymlicka). In fact, the French-English conflicts continue to be a much greater source of national divisiveness and threats to national identity than does the influx of other non-dominant ethnic populations (UNESCO, 1995).

The images of multiculturalism in Canada can be contrasted with the dominant image in the United States, which is that of a **melting pot**, where *members of all nationalities and cultures are to melt together into one culture.* Taken literally, one might assume this would mean the continuous evolution of a new culture as new components are added to the mix. In fact, historically, the major focus in the United States has been on *Americanization* of immigrant groups, which involves relinquishing their own cultural beliefs, norms, and practices in favour of the dominant culture (Atkinson, 2004). Historically, the French and the Aboriginal populations in Canada have both acted to oppose assimilation in favour of preserving their unique cultural identities (Bowman, 2000).

In the last couple of decades, the term *cultural pluralism* has come into favour by some in the United States as a way of acknowledging the importance of creating an environment in which members of non-dominant populations are free to maintain their cultural uniqueness while contributing to the overall evolution of society (Atkinson, 2004). Nonetheless, comparisons between Canada and the United States indicate that Canada remains significantly advanced on rates of integration and other measures of ethnic relations (Kymlicka, 1997). According to Kymlicka, Canada's multicultural policy:

> …is achieving what it set out to do: it is helping to ensure that those people who wish to express their ethnic identity are respected and accommodated, while simultaneously increasing the ability of immigrants to integrate into the larger society. Along with our fellow multiculturalists in Australia, Canada does a better job of respecting ethnic diversity while promoting societal integration than any other country. (The Comparative Evidence, ¶6)

While the benefits of multiculturalism to Canadian society may be widely espoused, the experiences of members of non-dominant populations in Canada are not always positive. As the contributing writers will point out in the various chapters on multicultural counselling with non-dominant populations in Canada, many individuals and groups continue to face cultural oppression and other forms of stigmatization on a regular basis.

As religious diversity increases within the Canadian population, counsellors are challenged to incorporate religion and spirituality as key dimensions of multicultural counselling (Fukuyama, Sevig, & Soet, 2008).

> Although the preamble to the *Canadian Multiculturalism Act* lists religion as one of the fundamental characteristics of Canadian diversity, some have argued that the public discourse around multiculturalism and immigration, and perhaps citizenship more broadly, has overlooked the importance for many Canadians of religious identities (as distinct from other cultural identity markers, such as ethnicity and language) and the needs of religious communities (Biles and Ibrahim, 2005). (CIC, 2009c, p. 1)

Significant public discourse on the place of religion in Canadian society has been going on for several decades. What is new in recent years is that our long-standing approach to accommodating religious differences must adapt to the increasing religious diversity in Canada. Uncertainty over whether and how to adapt private and public practice to this new reality has been evident in the significant attention that the media and the general public have paid to visible markers of religious diversity (e.g. head covers for Muslim women, turbans for Sikh men), faith-based arbitration, and incidents that have been perceived as signs of increased anti-Semitism and Islamophobia. Media attention has tended to perpetuate stereotypes about religious practices that diverge from mainstream Christian practices. Though Canada's religious minorities remain small, their continuing growth, coupled with increasing religious diversity, suggests that these issues will have a higher profile in the future (CIC, 2009c).

The extent to which multiculturalism stands as a viable model for guiding the practice of counselling and psychotherapy has been debated. Moodley (2007) argued that multiculturalism ignores critical questions of power relations, suggesting that it is important to look at the common experience of social oppression among non-dominant groups. In addition, he argued that multiculturalism does not provide useful information from which to determine assessment, diagnoses, and treatment. Counsellors interface with individuals and groups whose experience in daily life is far removed from the ideals of multicultural policies and acceptance of cultural diversity in Canadian society. As a result, we have positioned our model of culture-infused counselling to include social justice as a core value to guide counselling practices.

According to the Statistics Canada (2003d) *Ethnic Diversity Survey* completed in 2002, 8% of the Canadian population (1.8 million people) felt out of place or uncomfortable in Canada some of the time because of their ethnicity, culture, race, skin colour, language, accent, or religion. An additional 2% (330,000 people) reported that they felt this way most or all of the time. The rates were much higher for visible minorities; 24% (683,000 people) identified discomfort all, most, or some of the time. In addition, 20% of visible minorities reported sometimes or often experiencing discrimination or unfair treatment. Aboriginal people were not included in this survey.

 **Snapshot 5**

Calling on All Canadians: Our Work Has Just Begun

- Complaints filed by persons with disabilities with the Canadian Human Rights Commission [CHRC] (2003) increased by 85% in 2002 (compared with an overall increase in complaints of only 39%). In another survey, 36% of federal employees with disabilities reported being victims of harassment within the last two years. Thirty-seven percent had encountered at least one experience of discrimination.

- In November 2001, Aaron Webster, a gay man living in Vancouver, was beaten to death in Stanley Park. At that point, gays and lesbians were not protected under federal hate propaganda laws, even though they are one of the major groups targeted in hate crimes in Canada. In September 2003, passage of a private member's bill finally opened the door to inclusion of the sexual orientation category for protection under Canadian law (Egale Canada, 2003).

- Family violence continues to be a serious issue in Canada. In 2006, over 38,000 incidents of spousal violence were reported to police across Canada. Eighty-three percent of the victims were female and more than two thirds of the reported crimes were committed by current partners. Police-reported data show that for every 100,000 young persons, 334 were victims of physical or sexual violence by a friend or an acquaintance, 187 experienced violence by a family member, and 101 were victimized by a stranger (Canadian Centre for Justice Statistics, 2008).

- Non-dominant ethnic groups in Canada have less access to educational opportunities and are more likely to be unemployed or underemployed (James, 1996). Visible minority youth are less likely to pursue post-secondary education and they have higher levels of unemployment in comparison to non-visible minority youth (Bezanson et al., 2007). Adult immigrants from visible ethnic groups often have higher levels of education than their White counterparts and lower levels of both employment and income (Statistics Canada, 2003c). Furthermore, the higher one goes in the workplace, the *Whiter* it becomes (Canadian Council on Social Development, 2003; Esses & Gardner, 1996).

- There was little improvement in socio-economic well-being within Aboriginal communities between 1986 and 1996. A weak relationship exists between the employment, income, and housing of Aboriginal communities and the neighbouring non-Aboriginal communities, suggesting that these communities are not benefiting from general economic shifts (Armstrong, 1999).

- Disability decreases the probability of labour force participation, the number of hours worked, and, consequently, annual employment earnings. Disabled workers are more likely to be working in lower skill occupations due to having lower qualifications than the non-disabled. The lower earnings for persons with disabilities persist after controlling for differences in age, sex, education and occupation.... Our estimates show large earnings penalties associated with disability ranging from 21% for mild disabilities to over 50% for very severe disabilities. We also find that disability is associated with a 30 percentage point reduction in labour force participation (Emery & Brown, 2008).

- Statistics Canada's low income cut-off (LICO) scores are used to determine whether an individual or family may be considered low income (Statistics Canada, 2006a). In comparison to the average family or individual, those who fall below the LICO are expected to expend at least 20% more of their income on meeting basic needs such as food, shelter, and clothing (Statistics Canada, 2006b). In 2004, 41% of unattached women and 54% of single-mothers fell below LICO and were classified as low-income (Statistics Canada, 2006b). Individuals and families of low socio-economic status continue to be stigmatized and underserved by the psychological community (Pope & Arthur, 2009).

It is also important to remember that Canada's history of multiculturalism is relatively new. The 20th anniversary of the Canadian Multiculturalism Act occurred in 2008. Canada has a legacy of oppressive practices with populations such as non-dominant groups of immigrants and the Aboriginal population that leaves a heavy burden of care for the damage that has already been done. The dominant populations in Canada hold responsibility for both current forms of cultural oppression and past ills, which are carried forward in both the individual and collective memories of members of non-dominant populations. Ulysse (n.d., 1.2, ¶2) called for movement away from *equality of opportunity* to *equality of results*, noting that systemic barriers and cultural differences mean that "uniform treatment and application of *neutral laws*, blind to individual differences, are not necessarily guarantors of equality." The role of psychologists and counsellors in promoting social justice will be explored in more detail in Chapter 4.

Francophone communities across Canada, and particularly in Quebec, are facing an additional challenge that emerges from lower overall birth rates and lower rates of immigration. This is shifting the relatively equal population distribution of English- and French-speaking Canadians. In 2001, Canada received 250,346 immigrants. Most of these immigrants spoke English (114,775) or neither official language (111,229). Some spoke both French and English (13,027) and the least number spoke exclusively French (11,315). While two thirds of French-speaking immigrants settled in Quebec, only 3.1% of immigrants to other regions in Canada were French-speaking compared to the 4.4% of the population in these areas who are Francophone (CIC, 2007). Currently, both the federal and the Quebec provincial governments have initiatives under way to increase the number of French-speaking immigrants in Francophone communities across the country and to create a climate that will foster their effective integration (CIC, 2007).

Canada is also juggling changes related to the expanding definition of diversity. Canadians are being challenged to embrace other forms of diversity in the same way that we espouse our national respect for ethnic diversity. The *Canadian Charter of Rights and Freedoms* included race, national or ethnic origin, colour, religion, sex, age, or mental or physical disability in its call for equality rights for Canadians (DJC, 1982). It was not until 1996, however, that discrimination on the basis of sexual orientation became prohibited through Canadian legislation. Protected categories under current human rights legislation include race, national or ethnic origin, colour, religion, age, sex, sexual orientation, marital status, family status, disability, and conviction for an offence for which a pardon has been granted (DJC, 1976-77). Snapshot 5 is intended to serve as a reminder to us that the translation of policy into widespread practice in Canada is still in its initial stages.

As psychologists and counsellors we have a particularly important role to play in supporting the Canadian ideal of equality and freedom for all individuals and groups. With this backdrop of the nature and status of multiculturalism in Canada, we will now focus our attention on the impact of multiculturalism on counselling psychology and the implications for professional practice, research, and training. As a starting place, it is important to understand some of the core constructs that impact our understanding of multiculturalism in counselling and psychology.

Conceptualizing Culture and Multiculturalism

Before moving on to explore the concept of culture-infused counselling, it is important to clearly define our use of a number of key terms that are used in different ways in the counselling and psychology literature.

Race

We begin with defining the terms *race* and *ethnicity* since most of the literature on multicultural counselling focuses almost exclusively on those factors in identifying individuals or groups considered within the domain of cross-cultural or multicultural counselling. There are two basic positions in the literature related to definitions of race: (a) race as a biological factor and (b) race as a social construction (Atkinson, 2004; Hays, 2001). Historically, psychologists have tended to adopt the perspective that race is biologically determined, in spite of the lack of empirical evidence to support this assertion and the clearly non-biological selection of particular physical characteristics as defining features of racial identity (skin versus eye colour, for example) (Atkinson). Racial classification has been used as a means to label and "maintain separation between groups of people" (Henriksen & Paladino, 2009a, p. 13). Historically, such classifications have served the interests of the dominant White population and its practices of social division through colonization and oppression.

Currently, the position of most writers is that race is a socio-political concept (Helms & Cook, 1999; Monk, Winslade, & Sinclair, 2008; Norton & Coleman, 2003). The American Psychological Association [APA] (2003b, p. 9) defined **race** as "*the category to which others assign individuals on the basis of physical characteristics, such as skin colour or hair type, and the generalizations and stereotypes made as a result.*" A key factor in this definition is that race tends to be externally defined (i.e., defined by others) and often results in individuals or groups being treated *as if* certain group characteristics are then applicable to all.

At the heart of the discussion is the treatment of individuals and groups due to some individuals holding more power over others in our society. This is not an inherent right; rather, it is the product of social definitions of group categorizations and notions of superiority and inferiority. Unfortunately, the legacy of colonization lives on in attitudes towards certain populations in our society. However, a key point needs to be emphasized: "*Racism is a term that should be reserved for practices, not for people*" (Monk et al., 2008, p. 108). In other words, it is the stereotypes and actions directed towards others that are at the heart of racism.

Because the term *race* is a social construction based on variables that do not definitively assign individuals to a particular category, some authors argue that race is a term that is of little value in the discussions of multicultural counselling (Atkinson, 2004; Ho, 1995). The continued arbitrary categorization of people into racial subgroups is seen by some as simply a means of continuing to perpetuate inequality (Henriksen & Paladino, 2009a; Theron, 2002). In Canada, unlike the United States, interracial marriage has been common from the time of colonialization. Consequently, differentiation according to racial grouping is not feasible (Bowman, 2000). However, many continue to use the term *race* (Helms & Cook, 1999; Sue & Sue, 2003), arguing that it has a functional meaning in society in that physical appearance (particularly skin colour) will often supersede other variables in assigning individuals to particular groups with particular privileges. It also provides an important backdrop for understanding the concept of racism. It will be argued below that the term *ethnicity* is inclusive of the social meaning attached to race and is generally a preferable option for counsellors and psychologists.

Ethnicity

Ethnicity has also been defined in various ways in the literature to include physical characteristics (subsuming the term *race*), cultural characteristics (customs, rituals, practices), and origins (national, regional, or tribal) (Atkinson, 2004; Helms & Cook, 1999). The APA (2003b) defined **ethnicity** as "*the acceptance of the group mores and practices of one's culture of origin and the concomitant sense of belonging*" (p. 9). Unlike race, ethnicity tends to be assigned through self-identification rather than externally defined. Ethnicity is a more accurate and useful term than race and will be used throughout this book. Hays (2001) cautioned, however, that ethnicity should not be misconceptualized as setting up discrete categories. As in all other aspects of one's identity, the salience of one's ethnicity may vary across time and circumstance, and the factors that make up one's ethnic identity are idiosyncratic. James (1996) pointed out that, while many Canadians assert that they do not have an ethnic background, this is simply because they are so used to being in a position of cultural dominance as English or French-speaking Canadians of European descent that they fail to attend to ethnicity as a factor that applies as equally to them as it does to other non-dominant groups in society.

Culture

Culture may either be defined from an exclusionary perspective, where it is essentially equated with ethnicity, or from a more inclusive perspective (Daya, 2001; Pedersen, 2001). Some expand their definition somewhat to include other variables, such as gender, sexual orientation, and ability. However, most writers define culture more broadly and inclusively, including race or ethnicity as one of a range of factors that impact cultural identity. **Culture** includes shared clusters of:

- *worldview, beliefs, and values;*
- *rituals, practices, customs, or norms;*
- *social, religious, or spiritual traditions;*
- *language, history, ties to geographic locations; and*
- *social, economic, or political structures* (APA, 2003b; Atkinson, 2004; Harper & McFadden, 2003; Helms & Cook, 1999).

This definition of culture is based on the following assumptions: (a) each individual is a cultural being, (b) culture is learned and is transmitted through social interactions and from generation to generation, and (c) culture is dynamic and mutable (APA; Atkinson; Hays; Helms & Cook; Ho, 1995).

Culture is a more idiosyncratic concept than ethnicity, with each individual selecting, consciously or unconsciously, the components of their experience, history, context, and relational affiliation that define who they see themselves to be. This opens the door for individuals to hold multiple identities either simultaneously or concurrently. What is noteworthy for us in the use of the term *culture* is that it is both self-defined and inclusive of factors that are not necessarily connected to culture of origin. Individuals may have multiple cultural identities that evolve and change over the lifespan. As Paré (2008) noted, discourse about culture has tended to emphasize distinctions between people.

> Whereas "culture" reminds us that the persons who consult us come from distinct backgrounds, it's been less helpful in illuminating the many strands of often contradictory ideas and practices that converge simultaneously, like threads of alternate histories, in person's lives…. But *culture* falters in trying to capture how the myriad influences that surround us (someone once said, "We are fish; discourse is the water") are present *at the same* time, and recede in and out of the foreground as context shift. (p. 138)

The notion of cultural salience emphasizes hearing from the client which aspects of culture are relevant for defining personal identity and the fluidity of cultural identity across contexts. In other words, counsellors are cautioned about viewing clients as "rooted in particular cultures" (Paré, p. 138); instead, they must view culture and personal identity as a fluid process across contexts and over time. This point is particularly important as we examine the question of who is defined as a multicultural client. Readers are encouraged to consider the discussion of multiple cultural identities emphasized in chapters 10 and 13.

Multicultural

The term multicultural is often used interchangeably with the terms diverse or diversity (APA, 2003b). However, the term **diversity** is seen by some as *more inclusive than multicultural and is defined as including both culture (in its more narrow meaning related to ethnic identity) and other groups distinguished by sexual orientation, age, ability, gender, and so on* (Harper & McFadden, 2003). Arredondo and colleagues (1996), for example, make a distinction between the two terms, defining culture narrowly and reserving the term multicultural to include only racial and ethnic factors. The term diversity is used to refer to other factors that may impact an individual's sense of identity (age, gender, sexual orientation, etc.). They proposed the Personal Dimensions of Identity Model as a way of integrating these additional factors. Sue (2001) took a similar position.

We prefer to use the term **multicultural** to *include a wide range of identity factors, most commonly: ethnicity, gender, sexual orientation, mental and physical ability, socio-economic status, religion, and age* (APA, 2003b; Israel, 2006; Moodley, 2007; Sue & Sue, 2008). The risk identified by some writers in broadening the definition in this way is that the focus on non-dominant racial and ethnic populations may be diluted (Helms & Cook, 1999; Sue, 2001). This raises a valid caution in that we dare not forget the horrible offences perpetuated against certain ethnic groups in this country and become complacent about the need to have an active voice for equality. However, while it is very clear that racism continues to exist at the individual, community, and socio-political levels, there are other groups who share a common sense of identity and are targeted by society for negative attention and systemic oppression whose needs may be missed by narrowing our definition of multicultural in this way (Pope, 1995, 2008). Pedersen (2001) summarized this position:

> One advantage to the term multiculturalism is that it implies a wide range of multiple groups without grading, comparing, or making them as better or worse than one another and without denying the very distinct and complementary or even contradictory perspectives that each group brings with it. (p. 4)

While acknowledging that the term cultural is inclusive of other populations, the APA (2003b) guidelines define multicultural only as referring to non-dominant ethnic and racial groups in the United States. Other well-known writers take a similar position (Sue & Sue, 2003). In developing their multicultural competencies framework, Arredondo and colleagues (1996) and Sue, Arredondo, and McDavis (1992) limited the definition of multicultural to major racial/ethnic groups in the United States.

Defining culture and multiculturalism broadly, as we will do in this book, introduces new challenges into the development and application of multicultural competence, as we will discuss in a later section. However, it also facilitates development of a more comprehensive model that supports the idea that culture must be infused into the counselling process with all clients.

Whose Culture is Different?

Some writers use the terms *culturally different* or *culturally diverse* to refer to populations in Canada and the United States that stand apart from the European cultures that historically have dominated the social, political, and economic scene (Sue & Sue, 2003). This raises the critical question: different from whom? (Ho, 1995) and leads back to the dominant cultural groups as the reference point. Others continue to use the term minority (Atkinson, 2004; Atkinson & Hackett, 2004). We are choosing to use the term **non-dominant** to refer to *those groups who are commonly marginalized in society by virtue of their difference from the dominant Anglo-Saxon, male, heterosexual culture* for a number of reasons:

1. The term minority carries with it an inference that there is something *lesser than* inherent in the characteristics of a particular group. Our assertion is that the differential status is based on social, political, and economic power as opposed to inherent group characteristics, which is more clearly implied by the term non-dominant.

2. The term minority also places the focus of the power differential on the disadvantaged group rather than directing attention towards the oppressive social, political, and economic environments that are the root of the problem. The term non-dominant places a focus on the *dominant* population and shifts attention towards the change required at systemic levels to shift the balance of power.

3. Finally, the term minority implies that members of culturally diverse populations exist in fewer numbers than the dominant culture. This is not actually the case in many instances. In Canada, the increase in non-dominant racial and ethnic groups is tipping the balance in some areas. Women continue to make up more than half of the population in Canada and yet the balance of political and economic power remains with the men.

None of these terms are ideal, however, because they continue to define particular groups by comparing them to the dominant culture in Canada and the United States. Ideally, such groups should be defined in terms of what they are rather than what they are not or what someone else is. However, we are at a loss to offer a better term at this point. In addition, one of the major drivers behind the multicultural movement in counselling and in other disciplines is precisely the imbalance of power implied through the comparative terminology.

These non-dominant groups have not only been marginalized in Canadian society; they have also traditionally been either ignored or misrepresented in psychology (Hays, 2001). A major tenet of the work by Sue and Sue (2003) is that "counseling and psychotherapy have done great harm to culturally diverse groups by invalidating their life experiences, by defining their cultural values or differences as deviant and pathological, by denying them culturally appropriate care, and by imposing the values of a dominant culture upon them" (p. 8). By failing to attend to issues of cultural diversity, the professions of psychology and counselling have essentially become covert supporters of the status quo. Unfortunately, we must continue to examine how professional helpers and professional organizations may have contributed to the oppression and mistreatment of members of culturally diverse groups in the past and work towards culturally responsive professional practices.

At the outset of this book, we wish to address another common misconception associated with non-dominant groups that is particularly prevalent within the helping professions. It is often assumed that individuals who identify outside of the heterosexual, able-bodied, male, European, mainstream Canadian culture are simply disadvantaged. Counsellors in particular tend to develop a problem-focus in encountering clients from non-dominant populations. Rarely addressed in the psychological literature and the dialogues about multicultural counselling are the benefits of membership in sub-cultures. Before we continue to explore the challenges presented by non-dominant status in Canada, it is important to acknowledge the pride, sense of belonging and community, sense of identity, and other benefits that are derived from membership in non-dominant groups in our society. As we speak of the various populations addressed in this book, our intention is to both celebrate the uniqueness and value in those communities, while acknowledging the challenges that many community members face when they interact with the dominant culture.

Where Are My People?

One of the delightful experiences I have had since coming out as a lesbian is realizing that I now have a sense of community wherever I go. When I travel, there are symbols, body language, lingo, and other signs to indicate to me others who identify as part of the lesbian community. Before I became part of the community, however, much of this world was invisible to me, as it is to most members of Canadian society. I paid little attention then to what are now very important elements of the culture that I am immersed in. This experience has increased my awareness of the invisibility of other groups in our society, but it has also given me a sense of belonging and community. I am constantly attending to the presence of my people.

As I often travel with a particular colleague – male, heterosexual, of European descent – he has become attuned over time to the messages that I attend to around us, and much more adept at identifying my people as well. For him, however, this has prompted important questions about his own identity, raising the question for us of, who are his people? We haven't come up with the answer yet. I, on the other hand, am more aware than ever of how lucky I am to have this sense of belonging to community, however invisible to the rest of the world. I celebrate the privilege of membership within this very diverse, yet culturally distinct, group of women.

Personal reflection – Sandra Collins

Multicultural Counselling

The Multicultural Counselling Movement

In the past few decades, there has been an increased emphasis on attending to the broader systemic factors that influence an individual's perspective, behaviour, circumstances, relationships, and mental and emotional well-being. Some theorists have advocated for a focus in psychology *beyond the individual to the context and relationships that shape a person's life, self-perception, and ways of being in the world* (Cheatham et al., 1997; Ivey, D'Andrea, Bradford Ivey, & Simek-Morgan, 2002; Pedersen, 1991b, 2001). The importance of various factors that make up one's sense of cultural identity have come to the forefront and provide a lens through which individual or group experiences and meaning are understood.

At the same time, leaders in the counselling profession have been concerned about how well counsellor education programs prepare students for counselling clients who are from cultural groups different from their own. Research with graduates conducted in the past decade generally concluded that students were not sufficiently prepared for working with a diverse clientele and they struggle with ways of bridging cultural differences (Allison, Echemendia, Crawford, & Robinson, 1996; Arthur & Januszkowski, 2001; Pope-Davis & Ottavi, 1994; Zayas, Torres, Malcolm, & DesRosiers, 1996). Client experiences in counselling have also contributed to growing concerns about the adequacy of counsellor education for the realities of professional practice. Accounts of mislabelling and misdiagnosing client behaviour due to the lack of attention paid to cultural influences have left a legacy of negativity by many members of non-dominant groups towards the helping professions (Dana, 1998; Sue & Sue, 2008).

These concerns, coupled with the changing demographics of North America, have brought multicultural issues to the forefront, with some claiming that it should be regarded as a major paradigm shift and the fourth force of psychology and counselling (Pedersen, 2001, 2008). Ridley and Kleiner (2003) identified five themes that have come to dominate the literature on multicultural counselling competence (MCC) in recent years:

1. asserting the importance of MCC;
2. characteristics, features, dimensions, and parameters of MCC;
3. MCC training and supervision;
4. assessing MCC; and
5. specialized applications of MCC. (p. 5)

Multicultural counselling enhances earlier understanding of human behaviour and change processes introduced through the psychodynamic, behavioural, and humanistic forces (Ivey et al., 2002). Differences in worldview are acknowledged and the role of oppression and other socio-political forces on personal and collective well-being are emphasized. Pedersen (2001, 2008) claimed that we are in the midst of a paradigm shift that will see cultural variables integrated into the theory and practice of psychology as comprehensively as they have been excluded in the past, leading to a "culture-centred perspective in counselling" (Pedersen, 2001, p. 16) in which cultural values are attended to throughout every aspect of the counselling process. Although there continues to be debate about the direction of change and controversy about the ways that multicultural counselling should be practiced, this movement has gained considerable momentum. There is growing appreciation for the notion that the future of the counselling profession rests with the capacity to embrace multiculturalism as the fourth force to complement and strengthen theoretical understanding and practice of counselling (Pedersen, 1999).

Opponents of multiculturalism as a fourth force in psychology have levied challenges such as the scope of the movement and the viability of incorporating the Sue and colleagues (1982) competency framework into multicultural curriculum and counselling practice (e.g., Brown, 1996; Fowers & Richardson, 1996; Weinrach & Thomas, 1996, 2002). These debates highlight the fact that the field is in transition and offer valuable critique from which to examine the relative strengths of professional standards and from which to determine future directions (Arthur & Stewart, 2001; Sue et al., 1998).

Defining Culture-Infused Counselling

So what is culture-infused counselling and how does it differ from other forms of counselling? Just as there are multiple definitions of counselling in the literature, there is a range of definitions of multicultural counselling. Let's start with understanding what we mean by counselling. We define **counselling** as *a purposeful and collaborative relationship in which the counsellor draws on psychological, health promotion, developmental, and educational processes to facilitate wellness, personal growth, healing, problem-solving, and healthy personal and interpersonal development within individuals, groups, communities, or larger systems.* **Culture-infused counselling**, then, *is the conscious and purposeful infusion of cultural awareness and sensitivity into all aspects of the counselling process and all other roles assumed by the counsellor or psychologist.*

Several things are important in this definition:

1. It is our belief that culture is a fundamental component of human experience and that no person or group can be fully understood in the absence of a purposeful inquiry into culture. In keeping with the national political and professional stance in Canada, we define culture broadly to include ethnicity, gender, sexual orientation, ability, socio-economic status and social class, religion, age, and other dimensions of culture *that are relevant for each individual.* This broad conceptualization of culture is essential to ensure that the multiple and dynamic dimensions of each individual's personal culture are honoured in the counselling process.

2. Culture-infused counselling involves a purposeful interaction between counsellor and client in which culture is acknowledged as a critical factor. Failure to include cultural dimensions will likely introduce a barrier both between the counsellor and client and between the purpose of the interaction and the outcomes attained.

3. An awareness and appreciation of the impact of culture on all parties engaged in the counselling interaction is essential. This includes the counsellor's awareness of personal cultural influences as well as understanding of the impact of culture on the client and client systems.

4. The clients may be individuals and groups, or institutions and social systems. The role of the counsellor may range, therefore, from applied practice with individual clients or groups to organizational development or advocacy for social justice. At all levels, multicultural competence is essential.

5. In order to effectively infuse culture into all aspect of the counselling process, culture must be introduced as a central construct in research, counsellor education, supervision, accreditation and licensing, and other domains of psychology.

Our choice of the term *culture-infused counselling* reflects our belief that culture is a core construct for understanding all human beings. It follows that each of us is a cultural being and must approach our understanding of ourselves as professionals and each of our clients from this perspective. Effective culture-infused counselling requires counsellors and psychologists to expand the traditional range of competencies for professional practice to include specific attitudes, knowledge, and skills related to cultural competence (Arredondo et al., 1996; Sue & Sue, 2003).

It should be clear from our definition that we believe that all counselling is multicultural. Defining culture broadly and acknowledging that there are similarities and differences in cultural identities between counsellor and client in all interactions implies that there is, in fact, only one counselling process – the culture-infused counselling process. Sue and Sue (2003) argued that, rather than seeing multicultural competence as a subset of the skills required to be a competent practitioner, cultural competence should be viewed as "superordinate to counselling competency" (p. 9). Taking this approach ensures that culture has a central place in any definition of counselling competence. Our premise in this text, therefore, is that the core competencies for culture-infused counselling that will be discussed in chapters 3 through 6 must be considered foundational competencies for all counsellors.

Where Do Specific Cultural Groups Fit In?

In spite of our argument that culture must be infused into all aspects of counselling practice with all clients, there are particular cultural groups in Canada whose members are more likely to perceive larger gaps in cultural identity and experience between counsellor and client. We argue that it is important for practitioners to be knowledgeable about the needs, values, and worldviews of such identifiable groups.

During classes and workshops with hundreds of students and practicing counsellors and psychologists, we have asked the question, "Who do you think of when you think of a client who is culturally different from you?" This question is posed to identify the characteristics or dimensions that professionals use to define their clients. Although there are inevitably a variety of responses, many students and practitioners still hold assumptions that diversity is equated with the cultural dimensions of race and ethnicity. Discussion about additional defining characteristics of culture such as age, ability, socio-economic status, sexual orientation, and religion opens the scope of possibilities.

Research with counsellors in Canada confirms that a broader range of cultural dimensions should be considered (Arthur & Januszkowski, 2001). In this study, gender was the cultural dimension most often identified by counsellors, followed by ethnicity. Fewer respondents identified cultural dimensions of religion, ability, sexual orientation, race, gang membership, and refugee status. In a study of Canadian career development practitioners regarding their practices of social justice (Arthur, Collins, McMahon, & Marshall, 2009), we found that the majority of respondents commented on the importance of social justice for working with all clients. However, participants in this study noted the importance of considering the social and personal impacts of socio-economic status, race, gender, disability, immigration, sexual orientation, religion, and criminal activity. The results suggest that while the concepts of cultural diversity and social justice are important for all clients, there are members of particular groups who are marginalized in society. The call for social justice in professional practice draws attention to ways of improving our understanding of the experiences of such individuals and to enhance our strategies for mobilizing effective interventions.

Clearly there is a need to expand the perspective of counsellors and psychologists in Canada by revisiting the question of "Who counts?" in terms of the major cultural groups for whom particular multicultural competencies may be required. We have chosen to select a number of groups in this book for specific focus. We are defining these groups as non-dominant cultural groups in Canada based on the following factors:

1. Group members share a sense of collective culture (values, norms, practices, language, etc.).

2. Group members share some defining characteristics (behavioural, physical, and psychological). These characteristics may or may not be visible to others in society (e.g., gays or lesbians who attempt to *pass* as heterosexual, or members of ethnic groups who are not visibly distinct from the dominant culture but who nonetheless are impacted by social stigmatization and oppression). We make no distinction in this book, therefore, between visible and invisible cultural groups.

3. A power difference exists between members of the group and those defined by virtue of their cultural status as the dominant Canadian culture – able-bodied, heterosexual, males of European (English or French) descent.

4. Within Canadian society, these individuals or groups have experienced stereotyping, discrimination, or other forms of oppression by virtue of group membership.

5. Group members self-identify and associate with one another on the basis of group characteristics.

6. Federal legislation recognizes the need for protection of the rights of these groups as members of Canadian society.

7. Similar multicultural competencies are required of counsellors working with members of these groups as those identified in the literature for competent practice with non-dominant ethnic populations.

The groups we have chosen to highlight are non-dominant ethnic groups, women, gay males, lesbians, Aboriginal peoples, immigrants and refugees, and international students. We would also like to acknowledge persons who are differently abled as an important focus; however, we were unable to secure a Canadian writer to contribute a chapter specifically focused on that population for this edition of the book. As we did not feel qualified to provide guidance in that area ourselves through a separate chapter, we have attempted to be inclusive of persons with disabilities in our examples and illustrations.

Some writers treat older adults (Atkinson & Hackett, 2004), individuals from lower socio-economic groups, religions (Fukuyama et al., 2008; Smith, 2004b), and other groups as separate populations in their writings. The *Code of Ethics* of the Canadian Counselling Association [CCA] (2007) identifies these additional dimensions of culture: "Counsellors strive to understand and respect the diversity of their clients, including differences related to age, ethnicity, culture, gender, disability, religion, sexual orientation, and social-economic status" (A10. Sensitivity to Diversity, ¶a). Similarly, the Canadian Psychological Association [CPA] (2000) requires that "psychologists acknowledge that all persons have a right to have their innate worth as human beings appreciated and that this worth is not dependent upon their culture, nationality, ethnicity, colour, race, religion, sex, gender, marital status, sexual orientation, physical or mental abilities, age, socio-economic status, or any other preference or personal characteristic, condition, or status" (Principle I: Respect for the Dignity of Persons, Values Statement; ¶b). However, we have chosen to integrate a focus on age, ability, socio-economic status, language, religion, and rural-urban populations within the discussion of the groups highlighted in the text to emphasize within-group variability and the complexity and fluidity of each individual's cultural identity across time and context. We have also recognized gender as a core construct in multicultural counselling (Harkins, Hansen, & Gama, 2008). We invited the various writers in Part III of the book to attend to gender differences in their writing about particular populations.

The Emic Versus Etic Debate

While we have chosen to focus on particular non-dominant groups in this book, it is important to raise some cautions about defining clients by group membership. There are two theoretical models in the literature related to the importance of attending to cultural group membership and the impact that focus has on the counselling process. The central debate is between the culture-specific position (emic) and the universal position (etic). The **emic approach** argues that *specific cultural knowledge is required about the diverse groups counsellors work with (defined by ethnicity, sexual orientation, gender, ability, etc.), focuses on the uniqueness of each cultural group, and identifies specific theoretical models and strategies that are congruent with a particular cultural experience.* The **etic perspective** *defines culture more broadly and idiosyncratically, focuses on the commonalties across cultural groups, argues that all client encounters are multicultural in nature, and assumes that certain core constructs and processes regarding the theory and practice of psychology can be generalized to diverse populations.* Critical examination of this debate uncovers the values represented in each perspective and the implications for how counselling practice unfolds (Thomas & Weinrach, 1998). The position that you adopt will impact your definition and understanding of multicultural counselling, as it has affected our own. What is essential is a clear articulation of the assumptions you make about culture (Carter & Qureshi, 1995).

Group-specific views of multicultural counselling

Proponents of the emic position argue that the term culture should be used to refer to specific cultural variables such as ethnicity, race, gender, sexual orientation, ability, and age, rather than as a more inclusive reference to the unique set of values, beliefs, and worldview developed by each individual client. There are both advantages and disadvantages to targeting groups on the basis of a narrow definition of culture that is limited to a set of group characteristics. Some of the advantages are explored below.

1. Supporters of the emic position advocate that counsellors need to have knowledge specific to the client's culture in order to provide effective mental health services. Knowledge is recognized as a foundational domain of multicultural competence (Arredondo et al., 1996). One of the major issues in the provision of mental health services is that lack of knowledge about clients' cultural backgrounds leads counsellors to deliver services that are not meaningful for clients (Sue & Zane, 1987). The assumption is made that greater levels of knowledge about various cultures can help counsellors better understand their counselling issues and design culturally sensitive interventions.

2. A second major issue in the emic perspective has to do with the foundation of knowledge about counselling that counsellors bring to their work with clients from specific cultural groups. The point of contention is that the main theories instructed in counsellor education programs were developed in a particular cultural context (Arthur & McMahon, 2005; Daya, 2001; Nwachuku & Ivey, 1991). For example, psychodynamic, behavioural, and humanistic theories originate from Euro-North American cultural contexts. Theories reflect the values of the culture from which they originate, and those values are transmitted in the ways that counselling unfolds with clients. The controversial issue is whether theories can be adapted for use with specific cultural groups or whether theorizing should begin from the point of view of the host culture of clients (MacDougall, 2002; Nwachuku & Ivey; Young, Marshall, & Valach, 2007). Those taking an emic position would argue for specific models and techniques to be developed for application with clients from each cultural group.

3. Proponents of this position also argue that there is a continued need to bring attention to the particular issues of defined groups in our society. Otherwise, long-standing issues of racism and other forms of oppression will be ignored and there will be inadequate attention paid to the experiences of non-dominant groups in professional practice (Essandoh, 1996; Helms, 1994; Sue & Sue, 2008). This perspective advocates the need for a continued focus on specific groups in order to promote social equity. In Canada, employment equity legislation has focused on the experiences of women, Aboriginal peoples, persons with disabilities, and visible minorities (Employment Equity Act, 1995). Considerable efforts have been made through a variety of initiatives in the federal public service to address the employment needs of these groups (e.g., Arthur, Brodhead, Magnusson, & Redekopp, 2003). Although women and persons with disabilities have made notable gains in employment, this does not mean that efforts to address the needs of these populations should be discontinued. Visible minorities remain seriously under-represented in the public service as a whole, and have made few gains in occupational mobility within employment settings. Specific recommendations have been made to address organizational change that is needed to support long-term change (Task Force on the Participation of Visible Minorities in the Federal Public Service [TFPVM], 2000). This example illustrates the main premise of the emic position. Advocates of employment equity argue that continued and deliberate efforts are needed to improve the employment status of the four groups targeted through legislation.

There are also disadvantages associated with adhering strictly to an emic perspective in approaching clients who are culturally different from the counsellor:

1. The axiom *a little bit of knowledge is a dangerous thing* must be taken as a cautionary note to this approach. Group membership may actually tell us very little about individuals and their experiences in this world. Counsellors who define client needs on the basis of specific cultural variables run the risk of stereotyping based upon specific cultural characteristics, making assumptions about client experience, and marginalizing their clients (Ridley & Kleiner, 2003). Cautions are given against assuming that the needs of clients from specific cultural groups are uniform.

2. A focus on knowledge about specific cultural groups may be a starting point, but this approach is not sufficient for building multicultural competence. Group membership may have an influence on individual experience; however, individual experience may be unique and may be defined more

accurately outside of the group's perspectives. Although education about the general populations of our local communities has heuristic value, counsellors must also consider how processes such as acculturation, racial identity, and systemic influences are relevant for the experiences of individuals. These and other factors combine to produce a wide range of with-in group variability.

3. Cultural groups must not be considered as mutually exclusive. Many individuals identify with multiple non-dominant groups – for example, lesbian women of colour or Aboriginal individuals with a physical disability. There may be overlapping dimensions in the experience of clients that must be appreciated for their combined influences in the intersection of identities (e.g., Bowman et al., 2001; Constantine, 2002b; Javed, 1995; Pope-Davis & Coleman, 2001). It is also important to attend to the fact that some individuals will experience a compounding of oppression based on multiple non-dominant statuses in our society (Atkinson & Hackett, 2004). For others, the intersection of identities has been framed as a double positive (Leslie & MacNeil, 1995).

4. Counsellors are also reminded that they bring their personal culture to counselling and that a complete focus on client characteristics misses the dynamic interactions of culture that influence the counselling process. This point is elaborated upon in subsequent chapters that address the working alliance in multicultural counselling.

5. Critics of the emic perspective have also argued that the multicultural counselling movement continues to contribute to exclusionary practices. This occurs through limiting the scope of groups considered to be culturally diverse and failing to recognize the experience of dominance by a broader range of groups who are disenfranchised in our society (Pope, 1995, 2008).

6. In addition, there is a risk that counsellors will continue to consider multicultural counselling as something reserved for certain client populations, typically defined as clients from non-dominant racial or ethnic groups. This perspective limits when and how counsellors engage in multicultural counselling. It perpetuates the view of multicultural counselling as a specialist role in contrast to professional practice with all clients.

Universalistic views of multicultural counselling

Culture may also be considered as a central perspective from which each of us experience ourselves, other people, and the world around us (Daya, 2001; Draguns, 1996). When culture is defined in this broader way, all clients are defined as culturally diverse. The universalistic view of multicultural counselling argues that counselling must take into account the unique needs and circumstances of all clients. It follows that all counselling is multicultural to some extent (Pedersen, 1991c). The following have been identified as arguments for a more universal approach to culture and multicultural counselling.

1. Advocates of the universalistic position argue that each person has a unique cultural background and that all forms of counselling must be approached as multicultural (Patterson, 1996). The appeal of the etic position is that it recognizes the wide variety of experiences held by individuals within groups that are defined by cultural characteristics. Assumptions should not be made about the uniformity of group members' experiences; rather, heterogeneity of experiences is the assumption that predicates multicultural counselling. For example, it is presumptuous to assume that women of colour will have the same experiences as women in Canada of European descent. At the same time, it must be recognized that each woman carries her own experiences of being a woman that make her cultural identity unique. Considerations of culture need to extend beyond group membership to appreciate the culture internalized by the individual (Ho, 1995).

2. From this perspective, counsellors need to consider that every encounter with a client has the potential to be a cross-cultural one in that there will be relative similarities and differences in the worldviews between group members and differences between the worldviews of counsellor and clients (Pedersen, 1991c; Weinrach & Thomas, 1996). In essence, although clients may have similar backgrounds, their experiences, their worldview, and their needs are never identical.

3. This perspective also acknowledges that the cultural backgrounds of counsellors and their clients are comprised of unique experiences. Although counsellors can strive for cultural empathy (Ridley & Lingle, 1996), their experiences will never identically match those of their clients. Attention to one's own unique cultural identity is as important for the counsellor as understanding of the client's perspective.

4. The etic proponents argue that counsellors need to rethink their view of counselling as client-centred. Multicultural counselling means putting each client at the centre of defining cultural influences; each client experiences culture uniquely. Rather than utilizing group membership as a classifying variable, multicultural counsellors need to get beyond the visible characteristics of culture to consider the worldview and unique needs of clients (Lecca, Quervalú, Nunes, & Gonzales, 1998; Paré, 2008; Sue et al., 1998). In turn, counselling goals and processes need to be responsive to culture, as elaborated upon in Chapter 2.

5. This perspective shifts the focus to the interpersonal relationship between client and counsellor as the heart of multicultural counselling (Patterson, 1996; Sue & Zane, 1987). A priority in multicultural counselling, then, is the development of an effective working alliance in which counsellors are aware of themselves and their clients as cultural beings and strive to understand the unique cultural forces that influence people's needs in counselling.

Culture-Infused Counselling: Balancing the Emic and Etic Perspectives

Gaining background information about groups is important information to inform counselling practice. However, it is important to hold general knowledge about any group in tentative ways. Background information helps counsellors form cultural hypotheses against which to compare the experiences of individuals. Ultimately, however, counsellors need to establish a working relationship in which the worldview of the particular client is explored.

In assessing cultural influences on client issues, counsellors need to consider the **salience of cultural dimensions** such as race and gender in understanding a client's worldview (Toporek & Reza, 2001). The key question is *to what degree each dimension of a person's culture as experienced by that particular individual in the context of his/her life bears on the issues and themes that emerge in the counselling environment.* It must be recognized that the answer to this question will vary across time, context, and presenting concerns for each individual. Readers are encouraged to enhance their cultural competence for assessing the complexities, fluidity, and intersections of identities. Although it is conceptually easier to deal with one dimension of culture at a time, such as gender or social class, the realities of people's lives are such that these dimensions intersect into lived experience. The key is for counsellors to be mindful of looking more holistic at the client's worldview in order to assess, from the client's point of view, the dimensions of culture that are relevant. Chapter 10 provides a critical analysis of the concept of identity construction and provides readers with substantive discussion of multiple identities.

The culture-infused approach to counselling advocates a balance between the emic and etic perspectives. We recognize that membership in particular non-dominant groups may bring with it particular experiences and perspectives common to that group. We also recognize that such membership introduces the possibility of experiences of oppression and discrimination that may impact the client-counsellor relationship and the issues the client brings to the counselling process. At the same time, we acknowledge that group membership provides only one part of the picture and that there is often as much variation within groups as between groups. As such, the counselling process must be focused on the unique experiences and personal culture of each individual client. The task of the counsellor is to identify the relevant individual and group cultural variables that influence a client's counselling issues (Hays, 2001).

Like others, we argue for a culture-centred approach to counselling (Diller, 1999; Pedersen & Ivey, 1993) in which culture forms a foundation component of the counselling process. We believe that both the universal and the group-specific foci are of value and may be seen as complementary (Pedersen, 2001; Sue et al., 1992). Culture-infused counselling incorporates cultural diversity into the ongoing assessment, case planning, interventions, and evaluation of work with all clients. In subsequent chapters, we will explore in detail what this actually means in terms of developing multicultural competence and implementing a culture-infused counselling process.

Our position is that every client represents a unique culture and every counselling encounter needs to be considered as counselling across cultures. At the same time, our ability to fully appreciate the cultural experiences of our clients requires us to gain specific knowledge about traditionally under-serviced and marginalized populations (Ridley & Kleiner, 2003). Pedersen (2001) reminded us that: "No matter how similar we are, there will be differences. No matter how different we are, there will be similarities" (p. 19). More than 20 years ago, Vontress cautioned against placing too much emphasis on group affiliation, arguing that "humans are more alike than they are different. Therefore, counselors are advised to acknowledge the sameness of humanity and focus on similarities instead of cultural differences (Vontress, 1979)" (Vontress, 1986, p. 241). We believe that it is possible for counsellors to simultaneously analyze both similarities and differences with a view to seeing each individual as a unique cultural entity while building bridges between worldviews.

We end this chapter with an invitation for readers to consider their personal views of culture, who they position as members of non-dominant cultural groups, and how such views may permeate their professional interactions in counselling. As we explore the potential differences that exist between members of the population of Canada, and between nations, we are reminded of the cautions against overemphasizing group affiliation and assuming understanding of anyone's personal identity based on such limited information. In subsequent chapters, we explore the notion of personal identity and the importance of counsellor self-awareness and awareness of client cultural identities as fundamental for building an effective working alliance.

Chapter Summary

The purpose of Chapter 1 has been to paint a picture for you of the context of both the experience of non-dominant populations and the current practice of counselling and psychology in Canada. Canada leads the world in its policy on multiculturalism and offers members of all non-dominant groups an opportunity for full and unhindered participation in all aspects of Canadian social, economic, and political life. However, translating that policy into practice both at the community level and in professional practice in the mental health fields continues to present serious challenges. From the professional practice perspective, we have argued that what is required is a reframing of traditional models of counselling to a culture-infused counselling practice model that provides a general framework for multicultural counselling competence with a range of diverse client populations, as well as supporting integration of knowledge about specific non-dominant groups in Canada.

Conclusion: The Call for Multicultural Counselling Competence

Only during the past decade have graduate programs in Canada included coursework on multicultural counselling. This means that many practitioners (counsellors and psychologists) in Canada have not been exposed to specific training related to multicultural counselling during their formal education process. In addition, most counsellor educators will not have specific preparation in this area unless this is a focus of their professional development and research. It is often these earlier educated practitioners and academics who hold positions of influence within educational and professional practice organizations and who provide direction to the disciplines of counselling and psychology.

Research on multicultural counselling competencies demonstrates that most graduates do not feel prepared for the realities of professional practice (Allison et al., 1996; Arthur & Januszkowski, 2001; Pope-Davis & Ottavi, 1994). The wide range of issues experienced by clients from culturally diverse backgrounds challenges counsellors to provide culturally responsive services that recognize and incorporate culture as an essential influence in all dimensions of service provision. Higher levels of multicultural counselling competence have been attributed to direct exposure to people from particular cultural groups through training and casework (e.g., Allison, Crawford, Echemendia, Robinson, & Knepp, 1994; Allison et al., 1996; Pope-Davis & Ottavi, 1994; Zayas et al., 1996).

A survey of Canadian counsellors (Arthur & Januszkowski, 2001) provides some interesting insights into counselling practice. Many counsellors in this research study noted the importance of personal values in professional practice. However, they described a lack of knowledge about how to proceed in working with clients once value differences were recognized. Although 84% of the participants in this study completed a graduate degree, only 34% of the participants completed one or more courses in multicultural counselling during their post-secondary program. Approximately half of the sample completed their post-secondary education prior to 1990. Most of the curriculum in graduate education programs on multicultural counselling was introduced during the 1990s. Professionals who graduated earlier would have to take deliberate steps to access continuing education programming about multicultural counselling. In order to augment their training in multicultural counselling beyond course work, two thirds of this sample attended workshops or seminars that addressed multicultural counselling issues. It is noteworthy that two thirds of the counsellors surveyed in this study did not access supervision and that three quarters of the counsellors were not involved with other methods of case consultation when working with clients deemed culturally different from themselves.

Although these practices are not extreme in comparison to other studies of mental health professionals, they do raise some interesting questions about how professionals in the field engage in professional development pertaining to multicultural counselling competence. In this Canadian study of counsellors, the strongest predictors of multicultural competence were caseload of culturally diverse clients and completion of professional seminars on multicultural counselling. Experience working with clients is an avenue for increasing multicultural competencies. However, this needs to be more than trial-and-error practice. The next chapter will provide a rationale for attending to culture in all interactions with your clients. We hope that you will also see culture-infused counselling as an essential foundation for ethical and effective practice in counselling and psychology in Canada. According to Ridley and Kleiner (2003), multicultural counselling competence "is not a luxury; it is a necessity. In fact, we argue that part of what it means to be competent as a professional is to be multiculturally competent" (p. 15).

CHAPTER 2
RATIONALE FOR CULTURE-INFUSED COUNSELLING

Nancy Arthur and Sandra Collins

Key Terms and Concepts		
• Disability	• Ethics	• Socio-economic status
• Classism	• Hate crimes	• Systemic barriers
• Cultural malpractice	• Immigration trends	• Values
• Cultural tenets	• Religious diversity	• Worldview
• Demographic changes	• Social class	

Introduction

The discussion in Chapter 1 assumes that whether one takes an emic, an etic, or a combined approach, taking a culture-infused approach to counselling is important. However, this is a dramatic departure from the ways that counselling has been traditionally conceptualized. The culture-infused position requires a major shift in thinking by counsellors. In this chapter, we want to challenge readers to continue reflecting on their personal beliefs about culture and to examine their position on the influences of culture on professional practice. We will provide a rationale for culture-infused counselling and for the importance of integrating cultural competence into professional practice with all clients.

It is one thing to read about the importance of infusing culture as a central guiding concept for professional practice; it is quite another to practice from a culture-infused perspective. In our work in counsellor education and training, we have challenged students and practitioners to describe their beliefs about culture and to consider how they may directly or indirectly express their beliefs to clients, colleagues, supervisors, employers, funders, or other stakeholders. Likewise, we challenge readers to reflect on the reasons they consider important for adopting a culture-infused perspective for counselling.

Counsellors are often in a position to influence policies and practices within the agencies and institutions where they are employed. Working as an advocate for clients requires counsellors to have a clear understanding of the reasoning that supports adopting a culture-infused perspective. Counsellors may be called on to describe such a rationale to justify existing resources or to expand relevant programs and services. Diversity and social justice should be central considerations for services with all clients (Arthur & Lalande, 2009).

The ideas presented in this chapter are intended to help you to formulate your own positions and to articulate a rationale for culture-infused counselling to the various stakeholders involved in the planning and delivery of counselling services. We encourage readers to review the general points raised in the discussion and to articulate their own rationale for culture-infused counselling.

Rationale for Culture-Infused Counselling

Theories Guide Practice, For Better or For Worse

Prevailing theories of counselling that form the basis of counsellor education programs are primarily based on Western worldviews. Not only have these theories tended to provide a poor match with the worldview of non-dominant populations, but differences resulting from cultural diversity were often mislabelled as dysfunctional or pathological (American Psychological Association [APA], 2003b; Sue, Arredondo, & McDavis, 1992). Counselling practice needs to be grounded in theoretical perspectives. However, the dominant theories must be deconstructed to consider their embedded values, assumptions about clients, the role of counsellors, and the implications for counselling practice. Practitioners must take a critical look at the values and assumptions that drive their work with clients.

Theories are problematic when they are based on values that are not representative of the experiences of all clients. Sue, Ivey, & Pedersen (1996) discussed the **cultural tenets,** or *values embedded in Western theories of counselling*, that emphasize individualism and the development of a separate sense of self. These assumptions contrast with the more collective notion of identity that is held by the majority of societies in the world. Clients from collective societies may hold stronger values and a sense of commitment to upholding family and community relationships and responsibilities (Williams, 2003). Advocating a focus on self may be counterintuitive and in direct conflict with the dominant values held by a particular client's network of support (Daya, 2000). Flores (2009) provides additional examples of cultural tenets in career development theories that are instructive for evaluating other theories of counselling (see Snapshot 1).

Each practitioner, in making decisions about their own particular theoretical perspective, must reflect on who a counselling theory is written for, what the professional practice implications are, and how that theory can be modified or adapted in practice with a culturally diverse clientele (Arthur & McMahon, 2005; Sue et al., 1996; Young, Marshall, & Valach, 2007). Recent theories in the post-modern school have emerged in reaction to the biases inherent within Western views of counselling, questioning the explicit and implicit assumptions, and working towards a stronger client-centred perspective of counselling through the co-construction of meaning.

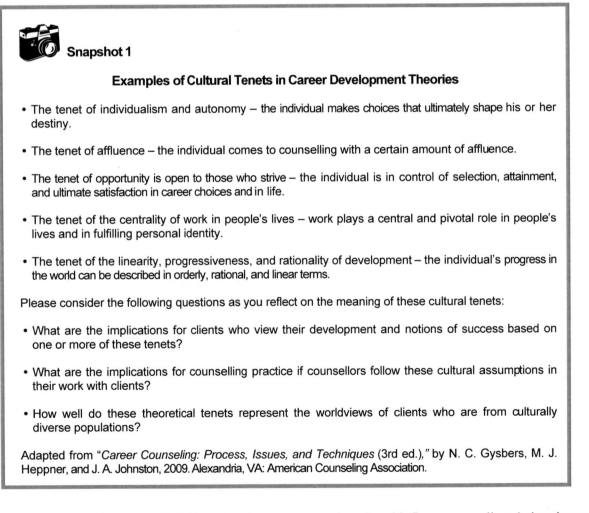

Snapshot 1

Examples of Cultural Tenets in Career Development Theories

- The tenet of individualism and autonomy – the individual makes choices that ultimately shape his or her destiny.

- The tenet of affluence – the individual comes to counselling with a certain amount of affluence.

- The tenet of opportunity is open to those who strive – the individual is in control of selection, attainment, and ultimate satisfaction in career choices and in life.

- The tenet of the centrality of work in people's lives – work plays a central and pivotal role in people's lives and in fulfilling personal identity.

- The tenet of the linearity, progressiveness, and rationality of development – the individual's progress in the world can be described in orderly, rational, and linear terms.

Please consider the following questions as you reflect on the meaning of these cultural tenets:

- What are the implications for clients who view their development and notions of success based on one or more of these tenets?

- What are the implications for counselling practice if counsellors follow these cultural assumptions in their work with clients?

- How well do these theoretical tenets represent the worldviews of clients who are from culturally diverse populations?

Adapted from *"Career Counseling: Process, Issues, and Techniques* (3rd ed.)," by N. C. Gysbers, M. J. Heppner, and J. A. Johnston, 2009. Alexandria, VA: American Counseling Association.

Theories that are more constructivist in nature incorporate socio-cultural influences on clients' situations and meanings, which in turn impact their personal beliefs. Through examining multiple systems of influence, counsellors work with clients to co-construct the meaning of client problems and to identify relevant strategies in counselling interventions. Interventions may be directed at the intrapersonal, interpersonal, or systemic levels or may include broader efforts that incorporate health promotion, prevention, or social change (Arthur & McMahon, 2005).

The main point in this discussion is that theories of counselling represent particular worldviews. For example, constructs of individuation, self, autonomy, and self-actualization contrast values such as collectivism, family and community responsibilities, and decision-making in light of tradition, destiny, or fate (Leong, Hardin, & Gupta, 2007; Williams, 2003). Interventions based on Western values and concepts may not always be appropriate for clients who adhere to collectivist values and norms for behaviour; imposing a worldview risks doing harm to clients. Imagine a client who, through counselling, is presented with a decision-making framework that emphasizes independence and autonomy. The client may feel conflicted about respecting family and community traditions, and decisions that do not take into account the perspectives of others could lead to conflict or loss of those relationships (Arthur & Popadiuk, in press). Readers are challenged to examine the cultural tenets and assumptions that underpin their professional practice.

A meta-theory of multicultural counselling has been developed by Sue and colleagues (1996) to address some of the limitations, challenges, and future directions that are essential in multicultural counselling. There are six basic propositions or tenets of their multicultural theory for counselling (Pedersen, 2001).

1. Each theory of counselling represents a different worldview that is expressed explicitly or implicitly in the details of the theory.

2. The client-counsellor relationship must be considered a priority in the focus of treatment.

3. Both the counsellor's and the client's personal cultural identities interact to influence how problems are defined, what goals are set, and which processes of counselling are most appropriate.

4. The overriding goal of multicultural counselling is to increase the repertoire of interventions available to counsellors.

5. Conventional counselling roles can be expanded to consider alternative ways of working that are culturally meaningful for clients.

6. Cultural contexts must be considered in developing an accurate understanding about individuals, families, groups, and organizations.

These propositions raise important points about how theories of counselling inform counselling practice. They also focus attention on many of the controversies that are raised in an examination of multicultural counselling (Pedersen, 1999, 2001). The models developed in this book for defining and enhancing multicultural competence and for implementing culture-infused counselling practice draw on these foundational principles.

Your Values Are Showing!

Values are defined as *the appraisals of worth, merit, desirability, usefulness, and so on that we place on people, objects, processes, or events.* Values permeate the ways that counsellor roles are constructed and how services are delivered. Counsellors are raised in social contexts where they are exposed to many messages about culture. These messages are transmitted through interactions with family, teachers, peers, and the media. *The internalization of these messages forms our* **worldview** *and the ways that we think about and behave around people from diverse cultural backgrounds.*

Some people argue that they separate their personal experiences from their professional roles. However, it is difficult to imagine leading such a compartmentalized life in which one's personal experiences and perceptions are put on hold. This is like taking off a coat of culture when practitioners leave their homes for work and enter their counselling offices. A more holistic view considers that our values influence all of our roles, including our professional role. There is also an issue of authenticity for counsellors and psychologists to behave in positive and congruent ways both within and outside of their counselling roles. Clients and students notice the behaviour of counsellors and teachers through watching their interactions with other people. What may be most impressive to the people we work with is our sense of genuineness and presentation as role models for the principles that we espouse in professional practice.

I was raised in a rural farming community. I attended a one-room school with separate entrances for boys and girls, as if something mysterious and dangerous would happen if we walked into the school together. I remember being 5 or 6 years old when the first Black family moved into our community. They were described as nice people, but nobody played with the kids outside of the schoolyard. The family moved away. The messages about Aboriginal people were scathingly negative. I honestly cannot remember a positive comment about them during the first 18 years of my life. The television show Bonanza was my only alternate source of information that suggested White people and Natives could actually talk together! People on welfare were described as lazy bums and it was their fault that they couldn't find work. I still shudder at the names I heard to describe migrant workers who picked fruit in the area – the N word. A family member was shunned with the disclosure that he was gay.

How much of this do I take on? There is a legacy of prejudice and racism that I have to own and figure out in terms of my own position and how I view the world.

Personal reflection – Nancy Arthur

The development of multicultural counselling competence was founded on the premise that counsellors need to be self-aware about the culture they bring to the counselling role. There is now general agreement that lack of understanding about the influence of culture in one's personal background contributes to problems of cultural encapsulation in training practices, research, and delivery of counselling services (Casas & Mann, 1996; Daniels & D'Andrea, 1996; Pedersen, 1995a). The need for counsellors to increase their self-awareness about the influences of their personal culture on professional practices is captured in the axiom "*Counsellor, know thyself!*" (Sue et al., 1998, p. 47). In essence, this requires awareness of self as a cultural being. Working as a culturally competent counsellor requires knowledge about the cultures of others as well as understanding of the influences of culture on self. Socialization processes are subtle and pervasive. It takes courage and honest reflection to consider how stereotypes of non-dominant groups in Canadian society may be internalized.

The discussion in Chapter 4 expands the exploration of cultural schemata in the context of the multicultural counselling competency of self-awareness. You are encouraged to reflect upon the messages that you received about culture when you were growing up and to explore how those have influenced your values about cultural diversity. The multicultural competency of self-awareness requires ongoing reflection about how personal values and beliefs influence our views of clients, client issues, and our notions about appropriate counselling interventions.

My upbringing led me to view individuals of other ethnic groups as heathens who were in need of the truth that I possessed. I lived most of my early life in a very sheltered environment where my information about people of different ethnic groups was limited to missionary presentations through the church. At that point, I didn't even consider the possibility of people holding different sexual orientations, but it is clear what category they would have fallen into.

This religious perspective that pervaded my thinking as a child and a young adult represented a considerable barrier for me as I encountered different value systems and beliefs. However, I held fast to my belief that my values were right and others were wrong. My personal exodus from this belief system didn't really begin until I encountered a situation in my own life where I personally could not fit within that value structure. In my early '20s I faced the choice of staying in an unhealthy marriage or accepting the judgment that accompanied making a healthier choice for myself.

The foundation of that closed belief system began to crack at that point and I began a long journey of redefining myself, my relationship to the world, and both the values I hold and the way in which I hold them.

Personal reflection – Sandra Collins

Demographic Changes

As introduced in Chapter 1, the population of Canada has changed from a relatively homogeneous group to a mosaic of people with diverse customs and cultures. Professional services such as counselling need to keep pace through taking into account the diversity of the populations living in our local communities. Changing demographics in Canada underscore the rationale for culture-infused counselling practice.

There has been a dramatic increase in both Aboriginal and immigrant populations over the last 50 years. The 2006 census counted 50,485 Inuit, 389,785 Métis and 698,025 First Nations people, surpassing the one million mark. It is notable that between 1996 and 2006, the Aboriginal population grew by 45%, compared with 8% for the non-Aboriginal population (Statistics Canada, 2008c). The discussion in Chapter 11 expands upon the diversity found within the Aboriginal population of Canada. In the following sections, we highlight changing demographics associated with immigration and ethnic diversity, international students, gay men and same-sex relationships, persons with disabilities, socio-economic status and social class, and religious and spiritual affiliations.

Immigration

Shifting immigration patterns during the past 30 years have resulted in people from a larger pool of source countries now living together in Canada (Esses & Gardner, 1996). The Canadian government has set a target of attracting at least 250,000 permanent immigrants per year. There are large numbers of temporary foreign workers and students from other countries attending schools in Canada. These combined groups culminated in 519,722 newcomers to Canada in 2008 (Citizenship and Immigration Canada [CIC], 2009b).

These trends result in more ethnic diversity within the population. Early migrants to Canada came primarily from European countries such as England and France. During the last three or four decades, fewer immigrants have migrated from Europe, and the main source countries have extended to other parts of the world. In 2006, the top four source countries (the People's Republic of China, India, the Philippines, and Pakistan) accounted for nearly 38% of all new immigrants. With the addition of immigrants from South Korea and Iran, 6 out of the 10 top source countries were in South Asia and the Middle East (Statistics Canada, 2007a). The remaining top source countries included the United States, Romania, the United Kingdom, and Colombia (Statistics Canada, 2007c).

Early immigrants faced many challenges in adapting to the Canadian environment, including language barriers, but were more closely connected to the dominant English-French population in terms of worldview. Many current immigrants from countries as diverse as those found in Southeast Asia and Africa, however, encounter more dramatic differences in terms of language structure, family systems, and political, social, and religious belief systems. The settlement and integration of new immigrants requires cultural adaptation by them as well as adaptation by members of the host society (Berry, 2001, 2005). The discussion in Chapter 12 focuses on social interaction between people who are newcomers and dominant groups in Canadian society.

Questions in the national census produce interesting insights into how people view their ethnic identity in Canada. Nearly 30% of the total population report multiple ethnic identities and approximately 30% report their ethnic affiliation with groups other than Canadian, French, or English categories. More than 200 different ethnic origins were reported in the 2006 census (Statistics Canada, 2008a).

There are growing numbers of people with multiple ethnic origins due to intermarriage between people whose families have lived in Canada for several generations (Statistics Canada, 1996). Another area of demographic change is the increase in the number of people who identify themselves as members of visible non-dominant groups. Since the 1970s, more than half of Canada's immigrant population have been members of a visible non-dominant group, increasing to more than three quarters of the immigrant population in the 1990s. In the 2006 census, more than 5 million people identified as members of a visible non-dominant group, representing more than 16% of the total population (Statistics Canada, 2008a). These numbers are expected to reach 20% of the adult population and 25% of children by the year 2016, estimated to be between 6.3 million to 8.5 million people (Statistics Canada, 2007a). In other words, it is estimated that within the next decade, about one Canadian in five could be a member of a visible minority group.

In addition, more and more Canadians are moving to urban centres, with 79.4% of Canadians living in centres with a population of at least 10,000 in 2001, compared with 78.5% in 1996 (Statistics Canada, 2003b). The majority of immigrants and refugees settle in Canada's major cities, with the heaviest population densities found in Toronto, Montreal, and Vancouver (Statistics Canada, 2008d). Recent immigrants prefer larger centres in Canada for reasons such as reuniting with family members in the city, living closer to friends, educational and employment opportunities, lifestyle, and housing (Statistics Canada, 2007a). Although there may be benefits for new Canadians living in urban centres, the impact of urbanization is often felt in the examples of breakdown of relations across cultures.

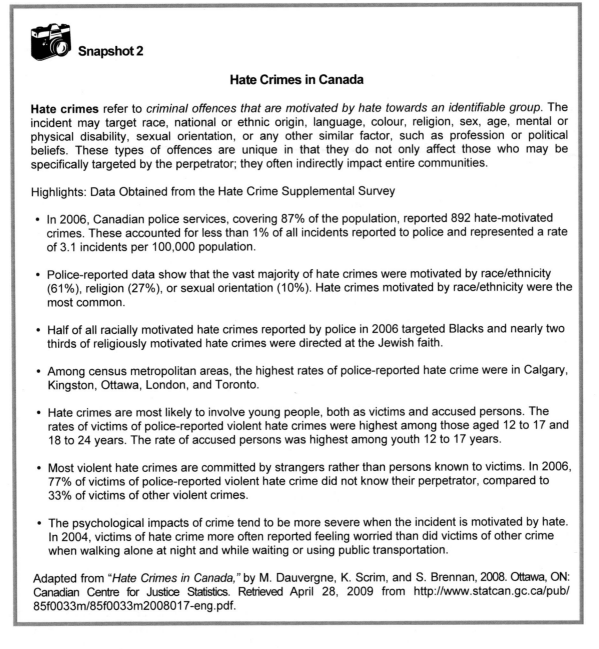

Snapshot 2

Hate Crimes in Canada

Hate crimes refer to *criminal offences that are motivated by hate towards an identifiable group.* The incident may target race, national or ethnic origin, language, colour, religion, sex, age, mental or physical disability, sexual orientation, or any other similar factor, such as profession or political beliefs. These types of offences are unique in that they do not only affect those who may be specifically targeted by the perpetrator; they often indirectly impact entire communities.

Highlights: Data Obtained from the Hate Crime Supplemental Survey

- In 2006, Canadian police services, covering 87% of the population, reported 892 hate-motivated crimes. These accounted for less than 1% of all incidents reported to police and represented a rate of 3.1 incidents per 100,000 population.

- Police-reported data show that the vast majority of hate crimes were motivated by race/ethnicity (61%), religion (27%), or sexual orientation (10%). Hate crimes motivated by race/ethnicity were the most common.

- Half of all racially motivated hate crimes reported by police in 2006 targeted Blacks and nearly two thirds of religiously motivated hate crimes were directed at the Jewish faith.

- Among census metropolitan areas, the highest rates of police-reported hate crime were in Calgary, Kingston, Ottawa, London, and Toronto.

- Hate crimes are most likely to involve young people, both as victims and accused persons. The rates of victims of police-reported violent hate crimes were highest among those aged 12 to 17 and 18 to 24 years. The rate of accused persons was highest among youth 12 to 17 years.

- Most violent hate crimes are committed by strangers rather than persons known to victims. In 2006, 77% of victims of police-reported violent hate crime did not know their perpetrator, compared to 33% of victims of other violent crimes.

- The psychological impacts of crime tend to be more severe when the incident is motivated by hate. In 2004, victims of hate crime more often reported feeling worried than did victims of other crime when walking alone at night and while waiting or using public transportation.

Adapted from *"Hate Crimes in Canada,"* by M. Dauvergne, K. Scrim, and S. Brennan, 2008. Ottawa, ON: Canadian Centre for Justice Statistics. Retrieved April 28, 2009 from http://www.statcan.gc.ca/pub/85f0033m/85f0033m2008017-eng.pdf.

International Students

Increasing cultural diversity is also represented in educational systems as more students from other countries live and learn in Canada. In 2006, there were more than 70,000 full-time and 13,000 part-time international students enrolled in higher education in Canada, representing 7% of full-time undergraduate and almost 20% of students enrolled in graduate programs (Association of Universities and Colleges of Canada [AUCC], 2007). Canadian universities attract international students from more than 200 countries. The focus on international students has expanded from their contributions as temporary immigrants to their human capital potential as permanent skilled immigrants (Hawthorne, 2006; Industry Canada, 2002). Canada's immigration policies are linked to our country's position in the new global economy, which is characterized by knowledge, information, and technology (Chen, 2008; Statistics Canada, 2005). In the global *skills race*, international students are ranked as attractive migrants (Ziguras & Law, 2006); they bring expertise regarding labour practices and customs from their home country and, as a result of studying in Canada, acquire valuable local experience. Immigration policy now permits international students to work in Canada while they are students and for three years post-graduation. Changes to employment visa policies were made to increase the qualifications of international students for immigration under the Canadian Experience Class. Readers are referred to Chapter 12 for details regarding immigration categories. As government policies are designed to encourage international students to stay in Canada, counsellors need to be well informed about such policy initiatives and be prepared to assist international students with career planning and decision-making (Arthur, 2007, 2008).

Sexual Orientation

The demographics for members of non-dominant sexual orientations in the population are not available through traditional sources such as census data. In 2001, for the first time, questions about sexual orientation were included in the Canadian national census. However, the questions asked were limited to those in a common-law relationship choosing to acknowledge either a same-sex or opposite-sex partner. The restriction to those in common-law relationships, coupled with fear of the consequences of disclosure of sexual identity, make the numbers suspect in terms of estimating actual population. In Chapter 16 Alderson cites research suggesting that the percentage is likely between 3% and 10% for both adults and adolescents (Frankowski, 2004; Savin-Williams, 2005b). These figures are tentative due to problems with the accuracy of information resulting from risks of disclosure. Research based in Calgary, Alberta, suggests that approximately 13% of males between 18 and 27 years of age identify as gay or bisexual (Bagley & Tremblay, 1998). It is speculated that this number may be a low estimate, as it is based on suburban dwellers and a high population of young gay men live in the inner city area. Census data indicates that the number of reported same-sex relationships increased by 33% in Canada between 2001 and 2006 (Statistics Canada, 2007c).

Although there has been increased recognition of the rights of these individuals, particularly through the legalization of same sex marriage in Canada, they continue to face stigmatization and various forms of social oppression. The estimate for gay and lesbian hate crimes is likely particularly low because of the increased stigmatization and risk associated with reporting (Roberts, 1995). Counsellors are challenged to consider their attitudes and practices towards the *invisible* populations of lesbian, gay, bisexual, transgendered (LGBT), and two-spirited people.

Persons with Disabilities

The dimensions of ability and disability have not received sufficient attention in the discussion of cultural influences on worldview (Brown, Reipe, & Coffey, 2005). It is our position that disability is a socially constructed term that segregates people into a less powerful position than able-bodied Canadians. It is important to remember that it is not disability, per se, that leads to cultural difference. Rather, it is people's views that serve to stigmatize and locate people in marginalized ways. We also remind readers that the *term disability is used to characterize individuals with a variety of distinct physical, intellectual, and emotional conditions.*

In 2006, there were 999,640 persons with disabilities aged 15 to 64 years, which accounted for 4.6% of the total population (Human Resources and Skills Development Canada, 2009). There is an increase in the number of adults with disabilities, primarily accounted for by the aging population and by more willingness of people to publicly report their disability status. The rate of disability among Aboriginal people over 15 years of age has been reported at 30%, over twice as high as the national average (Office for Disability Issues [ODI], 2002). Women with disabilities face almost twice the risk of physical, emotional, and sexual abuse than does the rest of the female population (Canadian Abilities Foundation, n.d.). There is contradictory evidence regarding the impact of disability on educational and occupational attainment. While progress has been made towards supporting the integration of persons with disabilities into educational, social, and work environments, the statistics reported in Chapter 1 show that people with both mild and moderate disabilities are significantly marginalized due to less educational preparation and lower paid occupations. It is important to recognize that such barriers have a significant impact on people's economic well-being, which ultimately impacts their social and psychological well-being (ODI, 2002). However, the statistics reported regarding disability do not take into account the varied nature of disabilities and the related impacts on health and functioning of many Canadian adults, children, and their families.

Concerns have been raised that the census process in Canada does not respect the needs and lives of deaf people (Canadian Association of the Deaf, 2002). The method of collecting information poses barriers for deaf people. Consequently, their under-representation in population statistics is problematic for policy-making in areas such as social security, taxation, education, and medical care, among other subjects.

Religious Diversity

As the source countries of Canada's population change, diverse customs and norms are introduced to Canadian society. There is a corresponding increase in religious diversity and practices within Canada. Although the majority of Canadians identify as Christians, there has been a decline in the mainline denominations, such as Catholic and Protestant, during the past decade, while members of other faith traditions have doubled (Fadden & Townsend, 2009). The trend of growth in the non-Christian population is expected to continue. Projections suggest that membership will increase for the Muslim, Hindu, and Sikh religions at the rate of 145%, 92% and 72% respectively (CIC, 2009a). However, there has been considerable public debate concerning the acceptance of various religions within Canadian society. The events of September 11 turned discussions to the problematic nature of such diversity, with many misunderstandings, stereotypes, and animosity directed against people of Muslim faith. The media contributed to a climate of fear (Chung, Bemak, Ortiz, & Sandoval-Perez, 2008) in which religious affiliation has increasingly become a misguided excuse for expressions of racism, discrimination, and social oppression (Racine, 2008).

There is growing recognition of the importance of considering religion and spirituality as key aspects of cultural identity (Fukuyama & Sevig, 1999; Fukuyama, Sevig, & Soet, 2008; Miller, 2003). Fukuyama et al. (2008) outlined several assumptions that support this focus in multicultural counselling:

1. In most cultures of the world, religious and spiritual beliefs and practices are connected to notions of health, illness, and methods of healing.
2. Although it is not possible for counsellors to be knowledgeable about all of the world's religions, it is possible to have a basic understanding of how religion and spirituality are related to people's worldviews, practices, issues they present in counselling, and their preferences for counselling process.
3. Counsellors can increase their awareness of diversity through exploring religious and spirituality beliefs, thereby increasing their competence for counselling across cultures.
4. Counsellors need to consider the notions of cultural salience and context in appreciating how religious and spiritual beliefs are integrated into multiple identities.
5. There are more sources of information available about religion and spirituality, including professional publications and conference presentations.

We emphasize the importance of counsellors gaining an appreciation of the potential influences of religious and spiritual beliefs for clients' worldviews. Readers are also reminded of the potential interaction of multiple dimensions of culture. For example, the influences of gender and feminist beliefs on women's experiences within patriarchal religions have been researched (Ali, Mahmood, Moel, Hudson, & Leathers, 2008).

It is important for counsellors to reflect on their own religious and spiritual beliefs as part of their personal worldview. This is an essential step for working with clients whose beliefs may be similar or different from those held by the counsellor. How accepting can you be of clients whose faith-based practices may pose value conflicts for you? Beyond personal reflection, it is a counsellor's responsibility to become acquainted with the main religions of clients who live in local communities. As part of community outreach, counsellors can exchange information with community and religious leaders that may help to open access for clients to pursue counselling and help counsellors to appreciate the ways in which religious and spiritual beliefs affect people's lives.

When I read the assumptions discussed by Fukuyama et al. (2008), I reflected about how new attitudes concerning religion and spirituality have been supported through the multicultural counselling movement. These assumptions are a striking contrast to earlier teaching in the field of psychology, which tended to avoid dealing with issues associated with clients' religious and spiritual beliefs. For example, as a graduate student, I was discouraged from such discussions and there appeared to be an unspoken taboo that counselling and religion simply "did not mix."

As a faculty member, I had the occasion to meet with a prospective student who was interested in applying to a graduate program in counselling psychology. She was very open about her religious beliefs and career goals to become a counsellor within her religious denomination. Her academic credentials and related counselling experience were very impressive. When she was not admitted to the graduate program, she asked to meet with me again to try to understand what she could do to improve a subsequent application. I could not see anything about her qualifications that would account for the admissions decision. However, I found myself in a dilemma regarding her letter of application, which exposed her strong religious affiliation. I was concerned that she was being discriminated against, although there was no concrete evidence of such action. Consequently, I suggested to her that she may want to reconsider the content of her letter of intent. She did so and was admitted to a graduate program the following year. We subsequently debriefed this outcome, including what it was like for me to provide such advice and what it was like for her to hide a part of herself that she considered to be central to her identity.

Personal reflection – Nancy Arthur

Socio-economic Status and Social Class

Socio-economic status and social class have been recognized as highly influential cultural dimensions in a person's life (Kosteniuk & Dickinson, 2003; Pope-Davis & Coleman, 2001; Smith, 2008). However, there has been a lack of attention paid to socio-economic status and class (SESC) in multicultural counselling in Canada (Pope & Arthur, 2009). This is surprising, given that the importance of SESC for everyday living and for its relationship with health and well-being (Kosteniuk & Dickinson). Counsellors need to be informed about the influences of SESC in relation to psychosocial well-being and psychological treatment.

The realities of many Canadians suggest that SESC is inextricably linked to their health and sense of well-being. Approximately 5.5% of Canadians are classified as low-income (Statistics Canada, 2006b). The picture of who falls into the low-income bracket positions paints a clearer picture about the intersection of poverty with people from non-dominant groups in Canadian society. There are much higher rates of low-income among unattached seniors, families led by single-parent mothers, members of visible minorities, and people with disabilities (National Council of Welfare, 2006). Almost 40% of individuals with low-income are deemed to be "working poor" (Fleury & Fortin, 2004). This accounts for 1.5 million Canadians. Working poor is defined as an individual who works over 910 hours per year but still falls below poverty cut-offs (Fleury & Fortin).

Although it may be easier to conjure up media images of poverty in other, less-developed countries, the experience of poverty in Canada should not be ignored. Canada's demographic profile shows relatively high poverty rates and also poverty persistence, when compared with other economically developed nations (Valetta, 2006). Low-income Canadians face major barriers for economic and social mobility; these barriers are determinants of poor physical and mental health (Canadian Institute for Health Information, 2004; Raphael, 2004). Pope and Arthur (2009) provided a summary of research that shows the adverse effects of low SES on physical and mental health. To recap, strong negative relationships are found between low SESC and health; this relationship strengthens with decreasing economic and social power. Researchers have discovered an inverse relationship between socio-economic status and depression, meaning the lower the socio-economic status, the higher the incidence of mental health concerns (Gallo & Matthews, 2003; Lorant et al., 2007).

The terms SES and class are often used interchangeably; however, the two concepts are not conceptually equivalent (Ostrove & Cole, 2003). SES organizes people according to social and economic dimensions and permits quantifiable stratification (e.g., income, occupation, education level). The components of SES are the basis upon which class hierarchies are constructed. However, class refers to particular relationships between social groups. In other words, dimensions of SES are used to socially segregate people based on their class membership. People positioned in the highest social class are afforded more privilege and resources in society. In contrast, people are positioned in the lower social class in ways that may be characterized by adversity, disparity, discrimination, power, and exploitation (Ostrove & Cole).

Criticisms levied against the profession of counselling psychology include **classism**, in which professionals *fail to consider the impact of economic power within society and treat individuals within that society as if they are classless* (Smith, 2008). This implies that helping professionals such as counsellors and psychologists need to be reflective about internalized classism (Smith, 2005) and stigma, which leads them to blame individuals for their lack of economic success. The model of culture-infused counselling expanded in the next chapter emphasizes the importance of reflection about personal attitudes towards culture and towards members of non-dominant groups in society. Pope and Arthur (2009) suggested that such reflection include addressing negative stereotyping of people from lower SESC and how such views may pose as barriers for effective service delivery. There is still considerable work to be done in the area of fostering changed attitudes and approaches towards people who are economically disadvantaged. Unfortunately, individuals and families of low SESC continue to be stigmatized and underserved by professionals in counselling psychology.

The Intersections of Culture

These examples of demographics highlight the increasing diversity of Canada's population. They are representative of changing consumer groups who require access to competent mental health services now and in the future. These demographic trends challenge counsellors to consider who is living in our local communities and how we can make counselling services an accessible and valuable resource for everyone who lives in Canada.

The selected examples illustrate the intersections of culture with the social and economic welling of people in Canadian society. Although not all members of non-dominant groups experience such hardships, the reality is that people located in the margins of our society are disproportionately from non-dominant groups. Although our model of culture-infused counselling emphasizes the importance of assessing individual worldview and circumstances, we also want to emphasize the importance of working towards building on the strengths of individuals from non-dominant groups and ameliorating the social conditions that lead to distress.

Meeting the Needs of Consumers

The existing research on usage rates suggests that persons from non-dominant groups seek counselling services for mental health issues at a rate that is lower than that of dominant groups in society and that they terminate counselling sooner, such as after one session (Arthur, 2004a; Leong, Wagner, & Tata, 1995; Sue et al., 1992). The need for multicultural competence is underscored by research that describes the negative effects for clients when cultural influences are not considered in assessment and treatment practices (Dana, 1998). These trends raise concerns about the quality of services offered to clients who are culturally diverse and how well counselling services meet the needs of consumers. Client mistrust of mental health systems and practitioners may be expressed through lower return rates, dissatisfaction with professional services, and preferences for informal sources of help (Allison, Echemendia, Crawford, & Robinson, 1996; Dana).

Two fundamental problems have been identified in the delivery of counselling services to clients who are culturally diverse. First, when counsellors fail to incorporate cultural influences into their views of clients' issues, they often miss critical information and do not form an effective working alliance. Clients may not feel that their presenting issues are appreciated. They may also feel misunderstood by counsellors when culture is underemphasized or ignored in counselling (Pedersen, 1995a; Ridley, 1995). Essentially, counsellors who work from a monocultural framework are not responsive to their clients. Second, when counsellors assume that clients' presenting issues are related to culture rather than other factors, there is a risk of cultural overgeneralization (Pedersen). The discussion in Chapter 4 elaborates on some of the problematic ways that culture is under- or over-represented in counselling.

The cultural issues surrounding client use and satisfaction with counselling services are complex and need to be examined from perspectives that consider multiple sources of influence (Constantine, 2002a). Cultural norms around help-seeking may be the greatest barrier for people from non-dominant groups in accessing counselling. Notions of privacy and family boundaries may prevent individuals from seeking services from an external agency (Bemak & Chung, 2008). Cultural norms also exist about seeking advice or help outside of subgroup communities. Counsellors need to be aware of the extra steps taken by individuals to contact counsellors and review issues that may be a source of pressure, such as confidentiality or access to client records.

Counselling international students provides an example of the complexity of understanding barriers to service provision. There is conflicting information about the utilization of counselling services and the reasons that account for usage rates (Raunic & Xenos, 2008). International students are generally less likely than local students to access counselling, and they typically go for only one session (Yoon & Jepsen, 2008). However, it has been suggested that research on ethnic group membership may provide more fruitful insights into ways of building connections with international students than may be provided by research that focuses only on comparisons between international students and local students (Raunic & Xenos).

There are several possible explanations for low usage rates of counselling services by some international students (Arthur, 2004a, 2008), including (a) preference for help-seeking with co-nationals or familiar persons such as instructors, (b) level of acculturation may determine comfort with using local support systems, (c) desire of international students for concrete problem-solving strategies to address pressing concerns, and (d) students' focus on academic studies may actually prohibit them from taking time to seek additional support. However, some international students would prefer to access counselling services so that their issues are separated from their social network or academic program. These examples underscore the importance of counsellors making the most of a single session to provide resources, support, and symptom relief. Especially when clients are looking for help with immediate demands, their sense of satisfaction with counselling is likely to be greater when interventions address their immediate needs.

There appear to be many factors that impact the motivation of clients to return to counselling. Additionally, the structures of counselling need to be examined to consider how well they match client expectations and needs. For example, office location, hours, and the ways that counselling services are organized are influential for usage patterns (Amundson, 1998). These issues are discussed in more detail in Chapter 5. Finally, there appears to be an underlying assumption that *effective counselling* only occurs through several sessions. Given the concern that clients will not return unless they find the first session to be meaningful, counsellors are advised to maximize that session for educating clients about counselling and for addressing client concerns.

In addition to norms for seeking help, individuals from non-dominant groups may have specific ideas about the kind of help they would like to receive. Counselling services have been constructed in cultural contexts that may appear to be very strange to people not familiar with professional helping services. For example, some people might find the idea of talking with a stranger about personal matters to be highly inappropriate. For other clients, the opportunity to move out of a closed system and tightly knit community network may be a welcome reprieve that allows them to gain support and access additional resources. Some clients may prefer traditional healing methods that are familiar to their culture (Moodley & West, 2005). Lack of access to usual methods of support may lead individuals to try counselling as an alternative. Counsellors need to be respectful of methods of helping that are culturally acceptable to clients and attempt to bridge cultural definitions of client issues and methods of providing help. These issues point to the importance of taking time early on to educate clients about the counselling process (Bemak, Chung, & Pedersen, 2003; Fuertes, Mueller, Chauhan, Walker, & Hadany, 2002; Sue & Sue, 2008). The discussion on counselling immigrants and refugees in Chapter 12 offers insight into the ways that counsellors can educate clients about the roles and purposes of counselling.

The review of available literature on client usage patterns and satisfaction with counselling services suggests that many clients simply do not like what they are offered. Testimonials from members of non-dominant groups are filled with examples of how they are turned off from returning for more sessions of counselling. Consider the examples from clients in Snapshot 3.

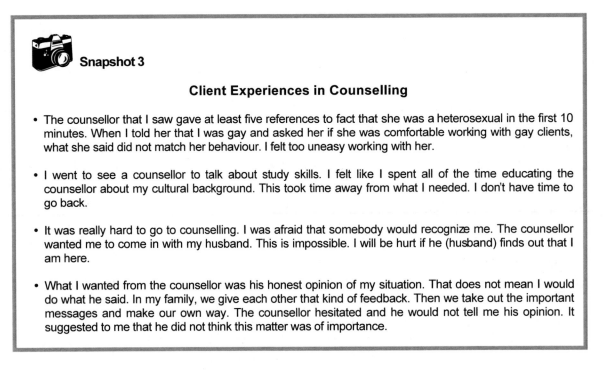

Snapshot 3

Client Experiences in Counselling

- The counsellor that I saw gave at least five references to fact that she was a heterosexual in the first 10 minutes. When I told her that I was gay and asked her if she was comfortable working with gay clients, what she said did not match her behaviour. I felt too uneasy working with her.

- I went to see a counsellor to talk about study skills. I felt like I spent all of the time educating the counsellor about my cultural background. This took time away from what I needed. I don't have time to go back.

- It was really hard to go to counselling. I was afraid that somebody would recognize me. The counsellor wanted me to come in with my husband. This is impossible. I will be hurt if he (husband) finds out that I am here.

- What I wanted from the counsellor was his honest opinion of my situation. That does not mean I would do what he said. In my family, we give each other that kind of feedback. Then we take out the important messages and make our own way. The counsellor hesitated and he would not tell me his opinion. It suggested to me that he did not think this matter was of importance.

Counselling across cultures is more complex, as misperceptions and misunderstandings can get in the way of building an effective working alliance and addressing client issues. Counsellors are challenged to consider the ways that multicultural competencies can help them examine potential biases and sources of client satisfaction and improve the level of culturally responsive counselling services offered to clients. In turn, evaluations of counselling services need to be designed to incorporate the experiences of diverse groups of clients (Arthur & Lalande, 2009).

Systemic Barriers

As illustrated by the many examples introduced into the discussion in this book, many clients face systemic barriers to both healthy living and access to appropriate services. These *social, economic, political, and religious systems surround clients and influence their personal, social, and career development.* Despite efforts to draw attention to *oppressive practices such as sexism, classism, racism, and heterosexism,* through formal laws and social reform, such practices continue to be pervasive social problems in society. For example, women still earn, on average, 72.5 cents for every dollar a man earns in Canada, regardless of their occupation, age or education. The wage gap is even greater for Aboriginal women, women with a disability, and women of colour (Canadian Feminist Alliance for International Action [FAFIA], 2007). Gender and race also intersect as multiple layers of oppression in accounting for the disparities of income earned by immigrant women in comparison to native-born Canadians (Kazemipur & Halli, 2003; Reitz, 2001).

Williams (2002), writing of mental health care systems in Canada, asserted that systemic racism continues to result in four dramatic impacts on members of non-dominant ethnic groups: (a) lack of opportunity to access mental health care; (b) inadequate care due to failure on the practitioner's part to establish a working alliance or to treat the client with respect; (c) improper and inappropriate care due to cultural stereotyping, language barriers, and misinformation; and (d) forced assimilation in order to receive adequate care. The Multicultural Coalition for Access to Family Services (2000) named systemic barriers based on racism as central factors in the lack of access to adequate services for newcomers to Canada.

Unfortunately, there are countless examples of systemic barriers that continue to impact the lives of many Canadians. The additional examples found in Snapshot 4 are not exhaustive, but are intended to highlight ways that peoples' lives are impacted by larger social, economic, or political systems. Clients may bring these issues to counselling as central concerns. Alternatively, counsellors may help clients examine their presenting issues in light of systemic issues that appear to impact their health and well-being. The implications are that counsellors need to be informed about the nature of systemic barriers and be familiar with systemic intervention strategies. Addressing these barriers may mean working directly with clients on an individual basis, working with organizations, advocacy in the community, or intervening directly with larger social, economic, or political systems.

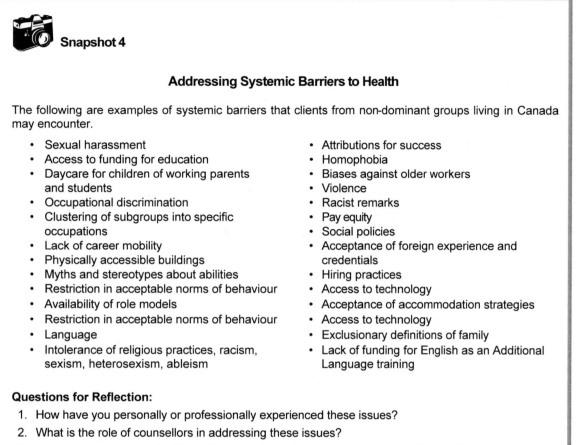

Snapshot 4

Addressing Systemic Barriers to Health

The following are examples of systemic barriers that clients from non-dominant groups living in Canada may encounter.

- Sexual harassment
- Access to funding for education
- Daycare for children of working parents and students
- Occupational discrimination
- Clustering of subgroups into specific occupations
- Lack of career mobility
- Physically accessible buildings
- Myths and stereotypes about abilities
- Restriction in acceptable norms of behaviour
- Availability of role models
- Restriction in acceptable norms of behaviour
- Language
- Intolerance of religious practices, racism, sexism, heterosexism, ableism

- Attributions for success
- Homophobia
- Biases against older workers
- Violence
- Racist remarks
- Pay equity
- Social policies
- Acceptance of foreign experience and credentials
- Hiring practices
- Access to technology
- Acceptance of accommodation strategies
- Access to technology
- Exclusionary definitions of family
- Lack of funding for English as an Additional Language training

Questions for Reflection:
1. How have you personally or professionally experienced these issues?
2. What is the role of counsellors in addressing these issues?
3. How can counsellors facilitate change related to systemic barriers with individual clients?
4. What strategies can counsellors use to directly impact systemic change?
5. What is the relationship between health promotion and working with systems?
6. Should we only intervene with individuals when there is a problem or should we create structures and environments that promote health for all clients?

In order to offer protection and advocacy for marginalized populations in our society, provincial and federal legislation has been enacted, such as landlord and tenant policies, codes of employee and student contact that include policies on discrimination, human rights legislation, and legislation on employment equity. Counsellors need to be familiar with these resources for the purposes of client education, client advocacy, and client referral. Some of the national resources available are listed in Snapshot 5. You are encouraged to also research provincial or territorial legislation and other resources that may be particularly applicable to your clients.

Snapshot 5

Canadian National Legislation and Commissions

- Access to Justice Network – http://www.acjnet.org
- Assembly of First Nations – http://www.afn.ca
- Canadian Charter of Rights and Freedoms – http://laws.justice.gc.ca/en/const/annex_e.html#guarantee
- Canadian Council on Rehabilitation – http://www.ccrw.org
- Canadian Human Rights Act – http://laws.justice.gc.ca/en/h-6/30599.html
- Canadian Human Rights Commission – http://www.chrc-ccdp.ca
- Canadian Labour Code – http://laws.justice.gc.ca/en/L-2
- Canadian Multiculturalism Act – http://laws.justice.gc.ca/en/C-18.7/30762.html
- Canadian Race Relations Foundation – http://www.crr.ca
- Citizenship and Immigration Canada – http://www.cic.gc.ca/english/index.asp
- Department of Canadian Heritage – http://www.canadianheritage.gc.ca
- Employment Equity Act – http://laws.justice.gc.ca/en/E-5.401
- Immigration and Refugee Board – http://www.irb-cisr.gc.ca
- Immigration and Refugee Protection Act – http://laws.justice.gc.ca/en/I-2.5
- Indian Act – http://laws.justice.gc.ca/en/I-5
- Indian and Northern Affairs Canada – http://www.ainc-inac.gc.ca
- National Council of Women of Canada – http://www.ncwc.ca
- Status of Women Canada – http://www.swc-cfc.gc.ca/index-eng.html

Snapshot 6

Canadian Standards and Guidelines for Ethical Practice with Members of Non-Dominant Populations

- Canadian Association of Rehabilitation Professionals, *Canadian Code of Ethics for Rehabilitation Professionals* – http://www.peakrehab.ca/CARPCode2002.pdf

- Canadian Counselling Association, *Code of Ethics* – http://www.ccacc.ca/ECOEJAN07.pdf

- Canadian Psychological Association, *Canadian Code of Ethics for Psychologists* – http://www.cpa.ca/cpasite/userfiles/Documents/Canadian%20Code%20of%20Ethics%20for%20Psycho.pdf

- Canadian Psychological Association, *Guidelines for Non-discriminatory Practice* – http://www.cpa.ca/cpasite/userfiles/Documents/publications/NonDiscPractrev%20cpa.pdf

- Canadian Standards and Guidelines for Career Development Practitioners, *Code of Ethics* – http://www.career-dev-guidelines.org/

- College of Alberta Psychologists, *Guidelines for Non-discriminatory Practice* – http://www.cap.ab.ca/pdfs/HPAPGFP-Non-discriminatoryPractice.pdf

- Medical Research Council of Canada, Natural Sciences and Engineering Research Council, and Social Sciences and Humanities Research Council, *Tri-Council Policy Statement: Ethical Conduct for Research Involving Humans* – http://pre.ethics.gc.ca/english/policystatement/policystatement.cfm

Check Your Codes of Ethics

One of the central arguments in our rationale for multicultural counselling is the provision of ethical counselling. As previously noted, professional bodies that regulate the practice of counselling have developed general standards for competent practice and specific guidelines for counselling clients from non-dominant populations (see Snapshot 6). The Canadian Counselling Association, the Canadian Psychological Association, and the Canadian Association of Rehabilitation Professionals have each developed codes of ethics that share fundamental principles while incorporating unique features. A central aspect addressed in of all codes of ethics is the provision of competent professional services.

Awareness and understanding of culture in relation to self and others facilitates ethical conduct (APA, 2003b; Chae, Foley, & Chae, 2006). Students and practicing counsellors and psychologists who join professional associations are required to be well informed about the codes of ethics that regulate their practice. As a condition of professional licensure or certification, psychologists and counsellors sign a membership form that states they are willing to abide by the code of ethical conduct endorsed by the regulatory body. This should not be taken lightly, for it has implications for professional practice on several levels.

1. Ethical codes provide practitioners with aspirational standards to strive towards in counselling practice. Consider, for example, the following statement about general responsibility from the Canadian Counselling Association *Code of Ethics*: "Counsellors maintain high standards of professional competence and ethical behaviour, and recognize the need for continuing education and personal care in order to meet this responsibility" (Sheppard, Schulz, & McMahon, 2007, p. 5). It is interesting to consider the cultural implications of this general responsibility statement. For example, how are high standards of professional competence in multicultural counselling defined? Do high standards of ethical behaviour translate equally well to counselling with all clients? What are the implications of securing continuing education and addressing personal care to meet multicultural counselling responsibilities? Adding a cultural lens to codes of ethics uncovers alternate meanings and challenges for professionals.

2. Ethical codes provide explicit clauses pertaining to anti-discriminatory practices. On one level, codes of ethics acknowledge that counsellors and psychologists are cultural beings and bring their personal experience to their professional roles. This necessitates ongoing reflection about personal biases that may influence counselling in negative ways. On a second level, although not as explicitly stated in most codes of ethics, it recognizes that counselling is organized in a cultural context. This addresses the need for counsellors to examine the structures of counselling services, including policies, procedures, and practices to consider cultural influences.

3. Ethical codes outline the scope of professional practice as being broader than individual services to include proactive roles and social advocacy to address discriminatory practices in the surrounding environment. Counsellors may benefit from additional training about ways to expand their counselling roles and how to engage in advocacy in order to improve the social, economic, and political systems that influence mental health.

4. Ethical codes provide guidelines for gaining specialist competencies and expertise with new client issues. Counsellors need to critically examine their definitions about who they consider to be culturally diverse. This helps counsellors identify specialist competencies for working with particular clients groups and for addressing client issues that cross group membership. Our position is that all counselling is multicultural counselling. It follows that all counsellors require specialist competencies in multicultural counselling in order to meet ethical standards of practice.

5. Ethical codes outline the benefits of supervised practice and encourage consultation about client issues. This makes it particularly important for counsellors who are unfamiliar with the cultural norms of non-dominant groups to become informed about possible interpretations of client behaviour and to understand culturally relevant interventions. Supervision may involve direct clinical work or it may involve consultation with community members regarding norms and customs that help to contextualize client behaviour.

6.   Ethical codes provide counsellors with guidelines for targeting and planning professional development to enhance counsellor competence. It is unrealistic to expect that graduates from counselling programs will be prepared in all areas of professional practice demanded by professional codes of ethics. Research attests to the need for counsellors to expand their repertoire of expertise to meet the needs of clientele who are culturally diverse (Arthur & Januszkowski, 2001; Sadeghi, Fischer, & House, 2003). Codes of ethics are designed to promote continuing education to enhance professional practice (Parham & Whitten, 2003).

7.   Finally, ethical codes are used to regulate the behaviour of members, including the adjudication of ethical behaviour. Failure to attend to the provisions for culturally competent practice leaves clients at risk for harmful practices and leaves counsellors and psychologists at risk for professional scrutiny and disciplinary action. Ethical codes serve as an earmark for clients about their own rights when they enter into the counselling process, including the types of attitudes and values, knowledge, and skills they can expect from practitioners operating under those codes. There is future potential for complaints against counsellors due to lack of multicultural competence.

Snapshot 7

Excerpts from the Canadian Counselling Association Code of Ethics, 2007

The following ethical principles are examples from the Code of Ethics of the Canadian Counselling Association. Some of the principles were developed as general practice guidelines, while others were developed to directly address the cultural diversity of clients. As you review these ethical principles, consider the points discussed in the rationale for culture-infused counselling.

Counsellors take reasonable steps to obtain supervision and/or consultation with respect to their counselling practices and, particularly, with respect to doubts or uncertainties which may arise during their professional work.

Counsellors strive to understand and respect the diversity of their clients, including differences related to age, ethnicity, culture, gender, disability, religion, sexual orientation, and socio-economic status.

Counsellors have a primary responsibility to respect the integrity and promote the welfare of their clients. They work collaboratively with their clients to devise integrated, individual counselling plans that offer reasonable promise of success and are consistent with the abilities and circumstances of clients.

Counsellors actively work to understand the diverse cultural background of the clients with whom they work, and do not condone or engage in discrimination based on age, colour, culture, ethnicity, disability, gender, religion, sexual orientation, marital, or socio-economic status.

Counsellors practice with caution when judging and interpreting the performance of minority group members and any other persons not represented in the group on which the evaluation and assessment instruments and procedures were standardized. They recognize and take into account the potential effects of age, ethnicity, disability, culture, gender, religion, sexual orientation, and socio-economic status on both the administration of, and the interpretation of data from, such instruments and procedures.

Counsellors are responsible for protecting the welfare of their research subjects during research, and avoid causing injurious psychological, physical, or social effects to persons who participate in their research activities.

From Sheppard, G., Schulz, W.E., & McMahon, S. (2007). Canadian Counselling Association Code of Ethics, January 2007. Retrieved April 29, 2009, from http://www.ccacc.ca/ECOEJAN07.pdf

---

There are a number of important questions that deserve careful reflection: What does it mean to be a culturally competent counsellor? How is competence defined and adjudicated through codes of ethics? Are ethical standards of practice universal and are they flexible enough to address specific situations that rise when counselling across cultures? Research suggests that counsellors experience many ethical dilemmas in their counselling across cultures (Sadeghi et al., 2003). There are many issues to be debated about the relevance of professional codes of ethics for multicultural counselling and how they can be adapted for such counselling (Garcia, Cartwright, Winston, & Borzuchowska, 2003; Pack-Brown & Williams, 2003; Pettifor, 2001a). Chapter 7 provides a historical account of the development of codes of ethics and expands upon these controversial issues in multicultural counselling. Codes of ethics can be augmented with recent writing on ethics and multicultural counselling, such as Pettifor's work in Chapter 7, Pedersen (2008), and Houser, Wilczenski, and Ham (2006). An overriding ethical principle is to strive towards continuous learning about culture in professional counselling practice.

In the diverse context of counselling practice in Canada, it would be difficult for most counsellors to practice ethically in the absence of continued development of multicultural competence (Arredondo & Toporek, 2004). Sue and colleagues (1992) asserted that "professionals without training or competence in working with clients from diverse cultural backgrounds are unethical and potentially harmful, which borders on a violation of human rights" (p. 480).

Culture IS Our Business

From purely a business perspective, the future of the counselling profession rests with our capacity to design and deliver professional services in which culture is effectively infused. Counsellors must consider who is living in their local communities and ensure that programs and services are meeting the needs of consumer groups. Clients in urban areas have many choices about whom they contact for professional services. The overlap in functions between helping professionals means that consumers have more choices about which profession to access for mental health services. The reputation of professions and individual counsellors quickly becomes known within consumer groups. Counsellors should consider their knowledge about who is living in local communities and increase their multicultural counselling competencies through networking and building positive relations with leaders and other community members. Chapter 5 details the importance of networking in building a positive community profile and suggests strategies for becoming more culturally informed about one's clientele.

The alternatives to culture-infused counselling portray an unappealing view of professional practice. If we think in terms of opposites, failure to integrate culture into counselling practice will result in more professional incompetence, less access for groups who are marginalized and disadvantaged, decreased satisfaction with counselling services, and counsellor-client interactions that are problematic by ethical standards. To continue as we have will result in increased underutilization of counselling services by the majority of people who will constitute Canadians in the future. The disparity between current practices and building mental health services that are responsive to the needs of culturally diverse clients is now well documented in the multicultural counselling literature. *Failure to take culture into account in the design and delivery of professional services* has been described as **cultural malpractice** (Hall, 1997). These possibilities are not in anyone's interests and are ultimately damaging to clients, practitioners, and professional bodies. In contrast, the professions of counselling and psychology can claim a key position within helping professions by providing leadership, education and training, and professional development opportunities that support culture-infused counselling.

Chapter Summary

The purpose of this chapter was to provide a rationale for culture-infused counselling. In education and training sessions, we have challenged students and participants to develop their own rationale and to be able to describe to others the importance of infusing culture into counselling. We have also invited discussion about the arguments against adopting culture and social justice as central concepts for professional practice. These exercises have clarified points of view and provided insights into what counsellors are willing to commit to in practice.

The rationale in this chapter focused on several arguments that can be made to support culture-infused counselling. The most obvious one highlights the changing demographics of the Canadian population. Counsellors need to look around at who is living in Canada and be informed about the demographics of their local communities. Culture-infused counselling requires counsellors to gain knowledge about the populations they serve and to work towards better access to counselling services. The theories and models that are used to inform counselling practice need to be deconstructed to consider how well frameworks of practice match the worldviews of client populations. Counsellors are challenged to consider how their personal and professional values may be similar or different from those of their clients and how to overcome potential conflicts. The extent to which counsellors can bridge cultural differences is a key for defining our profession as a viable means of professional support. In summary, the discussion of ethics in this chapter requires counsellors to look carefully at how principles and standards that guide our profession can be translated into effective practices across cultures.

Conclusion: The Call for Social Justice

The professions of counselling and psychology have their roots firmly planted in the social and political contexts of the Western world. As such, they have often been accused of supporting directly and indirectly the status quo (Sue et al., 1992; Smith, 2008; Vera & Speight, 2003). This means that subtle and blatant forms of discrimination and oppression continue to permeate the work of counsellors and psychologists in the ways that practices are organized, client issues are defined, and interventions are designed, delivered, and evaluated. Our profession has been challenged to not only identify existing biases in the assessment and treatment of persons from non-dominant groups, but to extend our roles to include a stronger social justice agenda (Arthur, Collins, McMahon, & Marshall, 2009; Constantine, Hage, Kindaichi, & Bryant, 2007; Lee, 2007; Toporek, Gerstein, Fouad, Roysircar, & Israel, 2006b).

The history of oppressive practices by professionals, including psychologists and counsellors, cannot be overlooked as something that simply *happened in the past*. Practices of colonization, attempts at conversion, assimilation, and exploitation of people from culturally diverse backgrounds in research and practice leave a legacy that must be used for the purpose of future improvements in professional practice (see Alderson, Chapter 16; O'Neill, 2004; Robertson, 2006). The culture-infused counselling competencies described in chapters 3, 4, and 5 are intended to support counsellors in their examination of personal beliefs and actions that may intentionally or unintentionally perpetuate oppressive and harmful practices (Pedersen, 1995a).

Reducing, overcoming, and eradicating social barriers require counsellors to be both proactive and reactive in their professional roles. Counsellors are challenged to consider how to improve the quality of life for clients and to effect social change. The examples of systemic barriers in chapters 1 and 2 highlight key relationships between cultural diversity and social justice. For many Canadians, social and political systems are inextricably tied to their experiences as members of non-dominant groups in Canadian society. Therefore, counsellors need to be prepared to examine the broader contextual influences on the lives of clients and to be skilled at influencing the systems that pose inequities in our society. The call for social justice requires the transformation of curriculum to help counsellors develop a stronger understanding of the relationships between culture and social justice and to prepare them to make a positive difference in the lives of all clients.

Culture-infused counselling requires broadening the network of resources available to clients, as well as the scope and function of counselling services. According to the APA, "psychologists are in a position to provide leadership as agents of prosocial change, advocacy, and social justice, thereby promoting societal understanding, affirmation, and appreciation of multiculturalism against the damaging effects of individual, institutional, and societal racism, prejudice, and all forms of oppression based on stereotyping and discrimination" (2003b, p. 16). In this edition of the book, we have attempted to strengthen the material addressing social justice and professional practice. In chapters 3 and 6, we describe our model of culture-infused counselling, which integrates competencies and practice principles to support the social justice agenda.

CHAPTER 3
CULTURE-INFUSED COUNSELLING:
A FRAMEWORK FOR MULTICULTURAL COMPETENCE

Sandra Collins and Nancy Arthur

Key Terms and Concepts		
• Culture-infused counselling • Culture-infused counselling competence	• Culture-infused counselling competencies	• Multicultural competencies • Working alliance

Introduction

The task of developing multicultural counselling competence may at first seem overwhelming when one explores the wide range of cultural populations in Canada and the degree of within-group variation. We have argued, however, that this is not an optional endeavour but a foundation for effective and ethical professional practice. Each of us faces the challenge of identifying our current level of multicultural competence and identifying the attitudes and beliefs, knowledge, and skills that we require to become competent in working with clients who are culturally different from ourselves. To make the goal of infusing culture effectively into counselling practice more manageable, counsellors require a starting place from which to review their current professional practices. Guidelines and standards of practice are a basis for targeting continuous learning through professional development. As noted in Chapter 2, codes of ethics provide an overarching view of counselling practices with culturally diverse clients. However, the details of how to improve standards of practice are not covered in most professional codes of ethics.

What have been developed in the counselling literature are collections of competencies for multicultural counselling practice organized according to various conceptual models. These models provide a framework to assist counsellors in beginning their journey of developing multicultural competence and incorporating new learning into professional practice as they acquire more experience working with clients. The purpose of this chapter is to review the conceptualizations of multicultural competence that have emerged in the literature over the past several decades and to propose a revised framework for identifying and applying multicultural competencies to professional practice. Our culture-infused counselling framework builds upon and develops further earlier conceptualizations. By the end of this chapter, you should have a more clear perspective on how the general call to become multiculturally competent translates into specific attitudes, knowledge, and skills for practice.

Multicultural Competence

Historical Development of the Multicultural Counselling Competencies

Over the past 25 years, a number of key documents have been produced in the United States that define competencies required for effective practice across cultures. A historical perspective on the development of the multicultural competencies provides the context for their current status in counselling practice. A brief overview is provided here and you are encouraged to review fuller accounts offered by Sue and colleagues (1998), Pedersen (2001), Ridley and Kleiner (2003), Arredondo and Perez (2006), and Arredondo, Tovar-Blank, and Parham (2008).

During the 1970s, members of the Division of Counseling Psychology (Division 17) of the American Psychological Association [APA] formed a committee for the purpose of developing culturally relevant counselling competencies (Sue et al., 1998). This initiative launched a framework for multicultural competencies that was initially published in *The Counseling Psychologist* (Sue et al., 1982). Ten years later, a set of revised competencies was jointly published in the *Journal for Multicultural Counseling and Development* and the *Journal for Counseling and Development* (Sue, Arredondo, & McDavis, 1992). The 31 competencies identified were endorsed by the Association for Multicultural Counseling and Development in the United States. In 1996, Arredondo and colleagues published a third document that attempted to operationalize the multicultural competencies. After more than 20 years of lobbying and refinement of the original document, the APA Council of Representatives endorsed and approved the *Guidelines on Multicultural Education, Training, Research, Practice and Organizational Change for Psychologists* (APA, 2003b). The articulation and publication of a multicultural counselling competency framework provided leadership that continues to influence the ways that we think about counsellor education in North America. The cultural contexts that prompted the development of the competencies in the United States, particularly in the area of race relations (Arredondo & Perez, 2003), are unique to the history of that country. However, the competencies have generally been assumed to be transferable and applicable across nations, as evidenced by the Canadian writings that draw heavily on the competency framework (Arthur & Stewart, 2001).

The original work by Sue and colleagues (1982) identified 11 competencies, organized according to beliefs and attitudes, knowledge, and skills. Sue and colleagues (1992) expanded the number of competencies to 31 and re-organized the **multicultural competencies** according to three core characteristics: (a) *"counsellor awareness of own assumptions, values, and biases;"* (b) *"understanding the worldview of the culturally different client;"* and (c) *"developing appropriate intervention strategies and techniques"* (p. 481). Each of these characteristics was defined along three dimensions: (a) beliefs and attitudes; (b) knowledge; and (c) skills. Arredondo and colleagues (1996) maintained the same structure, adding more detailed explanatory statements for each of the competencies identified. They identified additional counselling applications where further development work is required: assessment, evaluation, research, and career guidance. While the focus of the competency framework was on individual change, they also identified the need for attention to the systemic or organizational level. In recognition that counselling occurs in a cultural context, organizational development was added as a fourth domain of multicultural competence in the late 1990s (Sue et al., 1998).

Snapshot 1

Guidelines on Multicultural Education, Training, Research, Practice, and Organizational Change for Psychologists

Guideline #1: Psychologists are encouraged to recognize that, as cultural beings, they may hold attitudes and beliefs that can detrimentally influence their perceptions of and interactions with individuals who are ethnically and racially different from themselves.

Guideline #2: Psychologists are encouraged to recognize the importance of multicultural sensitivity/responsiveness, knowledge, and understanding about ethnically and racially different individuals.

Guideline #3: As educators, psychologists are encouraged to employ the constructs of multiculturalism and diversity in psychological education.

Guideline #4: Culturally sensitive psychological researchers are encouraged to recognize the importance of conducting culture-centered and ethical psychological research among persons from ethnic, linguistic, and racial minority backgrounds.

Guideline #5: Psychologists strive to apply culturally appropriate skills in clinical and other applied psychological practices.

Guideline #6: Psychologists are encouraged to use organizational change processes to support culturally informed organizational (policy) development and practices.

From *"Guidelines on Multicultural Education, Training, Research, Practice, and Organizational Change for Psychologists,"* by American Psychological Association, 2002. Washington, DC: Author.

The most recent document, the APA (2003b) *Guidelines on Multicultural Education, Training, Research, Practice, and Organization Change for Psychologists*, identified six core principles (see Snapshot 1). The writers set two principles as the foundation for the remaining four principles: (a) awareness of one's cultural self and (b) knowledge of the cultures of others. These two core principles parallel the first two characteristics identified in the original works. The assertion is that these foundational guidelines apply to all psychologists and the remaining four guidelines focus on specific practice contexts.

Critical Reflection on the Multicultural Counselling Competencies

The competencies developed by Sue and colleagues (1982, 1992) and Arredondo and colleagues (1996) have had a tremendous impact in the field of multicultural counselling over the past 20 years and have become the standard for counsellor training programs and accreditation processes. The multicultural competencies were developed through expert consensus and have not been submitted to careful empirical validation (Atkinson & Israel, 2003), although the volume of writing related to application of the competency framework in a wide range of context attests to its heuristic value. The multicultural competencies were introduced to the counselling community as a starting place for reflection and further development, and yet they have remained relatively stable over time in spite of the continued development of the construct of multicultural competence by others (D'Andrea, Daniels, & Noonan, 2003; Reynolds & Pope, 2003). Several factors suggest a need for some modifications to the current framework for understanding multicultural competence.

An Inclusive Definition of Culture

The definition of culture has been expanded to be inclusive of other personal identity factors. While a number of specific guidelines have been developed for working with particular populations, these have not been integrated into the overall framework nor has the language been modified to be more inclusive. The focus of the APA (2003b) document continues to be working with racial and ethnic minorities. Bowman and King (2003) described the diversity of experience between women and men of colour and asserted that gender is a critical factor in articulation of multicultural competencies. Leung (2003) pointed to the importance of clarifying the intersection between disability and the multicultural competencies. Other formal professional documents reference additional non-dominant groups, included in our definition of culture in Chapter 1; for example, the Guidelines for Psychotherapy with Lesbian, Gay, and Bisexual Clients (APA, 1998) and the Guidelines for Psychological Practice with Older Adults (APA, 2003a). Few attempts have been made to incorporate these other dimensions of culture into the articulations of multicultural competencies. The major models referenced in the literature remain exclusively focused on racial and ethnic minorities, a position that Mollen, Ridley, and Hill (2003) argued is no longer tenable.

The following competency, for example, highlights issues of race and ethnicity to the exclusion of cultural biases: "Culturally competent counselors are constantly seeking to understand themselves as racial and cultural beings and are actively seeking a non-racist identity (Arredondo et al., 1996, p. 60). Arredondo and Perez (2006) acknowledged that the multicultural competencies must be reframed to include these broader cultural dimensions. A noteworthy exception is the work of Hansen, Petitone-Arreola-Rockwell, and Greene (2000), who conducted a review of literature and identified 51 competencies that they then reduced to 12 core practice and 12 core research competencies. Of particular importance is the integration of focus on other non-dominant groups, identified by age, gender, race, ethnicity, religion, sexual orientation, ability, language, or socio-economic status. For example, they suggested that the self-awareness competency be reworded as: "Awareness of how one's own cultural heritage, gender, class, ethnic-racial identity, sexual orientation, disability, and age cohort help shape personal values, assumptions, and biases related to identified groups" (Hansen et al., p. 654).

The Intersection of Multiple Identities

One of the other criticisms of multicultural counselling competencies is that the primacy placed on race and ethnicity marginalizes the experiences of individuals with multiple non-dominant identities (Collins, in press a). So, for example, women of colour may have very different experiences than men of colour. In some situations, gender may have a more significant impact on their experiences, thoughts, or feelings than ethnicity. For the multicultural competencies to be truly reflective of the diversity of human experience, they need to be framed in such a way that careful attention is paid to the multiple identity factors that impact each client (Weinrach & Thomas, 2002), and there needs to be explicit attention on the part of the counsellor to how these impact the presenting problem and the resultant goals and tasks of counselling.

Unfortunately, the relative stability of the multicultural competencies over time has meant that they are not reflective of more recent emphasis on the intersection of gender and ethnicity or sexism and racism (Barret et al., 2005; Silverstein, 2006). Both bodies of literature have also been criticized for neglecting the interactional effects of other dimensions, such as sexual orientation, ability, or socio-economic status (Adair, 2005; Bowman et al., 2001; Brown, Reipe, & Coffey, 2005; Lowe & Mascher, 2001; Silverstein, 2006). Women of colour, lesbians with disabilities, and others who hold multiple cultural identities do not see themselves reflected in the traditional conceptualizations of culture and multicultural competence (Gustafson, 2007; Morrow, Hawxhurst, Montes de Vegas, Abouslesman, & Castaneda, 2006).

The Political and Ideological Nature of Culture

The treatment of culture in the multicultural literature has also served to perpetuate the idea that culture can be defined in terms of stable and essential attributes of individuals rather than as highly politicized ideological constructs (Gustafson, 2005; Weinrach & Thomas, 2002). Culture is not a neutral concept, and neither are any of the specific factors that we use to define cultural identity. Gender, ethnicity, sexual orientation, ability, and other cultural concepts reflect powerful social, historical, and political meanings (Anderson et al., 2003). Failure to attend to these broader systemic forces may mask the association of culture with issues of power and privilege (Gustafson, 2005). It may also lead to a tendency to mask cultural misrepresentations and biases and to facilitate the marginalization of particular perspectives and experiences (Anderson et al., 2003).

There has been a tendency to view the multicultural competencies as applicable only to work with culturally diverse individuals. Underlying this perspective is the assumption in much of the literature that culture is defined in terms of *otherness*, which sets up White, male, heterosexual, able-bodied, Christian, young, and middle class as the norm (Collins, in press a). Much of western psychological literature, including the multicultural competencies literature to some degree, remains infused with assumptions that reflect these larger cultural norms (Evans, Kincade, Marbley, & Seem, 2005; Morrow et al., 2006). There is also a tendency to treat culture as something that resides within the individual and influences their perceptions and behaviours rather than as something that is created and made meaningful through interaction (Knapik & Miloti, 2006). A post-modern and ideological view of culture requires us to define culture in the context of interaction and meaning making between counsellor and client.

The Social and Political Change Agenda

Applying cultural narrowly to particular individuals and groups has resulted in a tendency to focus the multicultural competencies on applied practice with individuals rather than the historical and social contexts that are responsible for both defining *otherness* and then supporting oppression based on this definition. It is essential that any reworking of the multicultural competencies integrate broader social and political analysis and systems change. To date the emphasis has been on personal and interpersonal awareness and sensitivity without an overt focus on promoting pluralism at social, economic, and political levels (Williams, 2007). There is a recognition of the impact of these broader systems of power and privilege on clients; however, the call to activism in promoting social, economic, and political change is much weaker than in the feminist literature (Morrow et al., 2006; Whalen et al., 2004).

In recent years, a strong social justice focus has emerged in the multicultural counselling literature and, with it, identification of additional competencies designed to actively challenge socio-cultural injustices (Lewis, Arnold, House, & Toporek, 2003). The recent *Handbook for Social Justice in Counselling Psychology* reflects a coalition between the APA sections for lesbian, gay, and bisexual awareness; ethnic and racial diversity; and advancement of women (Fouad, Gerstein, & Toporek, 2006). In our own work in recent years, we focused on identifying and assessing competencies for social justice in the area of career counselling (Arthur, Collins, Bisson, & McMahon, 2009; Arthur, Collins, McMahon, & Marshall, 2009).

Expanded Domains of Practice

In addition to the lack of competencies for promoting social justice, the current multicultural competencies focus primarily on applied practice, although both earlier (Arredondo et al., 1996) and more recent documents (APA, 2003b) identify additional areas of practice where new competencies need to be articulated. Other areas of practice have been introduced over time but have not been effectively integrated into the current models: organizational development, assessment, education and training, research, supervision, social justice, and consultation. Many authors are calling for the expansion of the competencies or development of additional sets of multicultural competencies in these additional areas of practice (Arredondo & Gordon Reinoso, 2003). In some cases, separate guidelines or lists of competencies have been developed for other areas of practice, such as the advocacy competencies introduced by Lewis and colleagues (2003). However, links to the overall framework have not been established and the framework itself has not been sufficiently modified over time to accommodate these additions.

Conceptual Clarity

Many current writers use two distinct frameworks for organizing the multicultural competencies as if the frameworks are conceptually interchangeable. The competencies are organized according to either Framework A or Framework B. Framework A consists of self-awareness, awareness of client culture, and intervention strategies and techniques. Framework B consists of attitudes and beliefs, knowledge, and skills. The three levels of competencies are treated as equivalent across frameworks: (a) self-awareness (with respect to counsellor's culture) = attitudes and beliefs; (b) awareness of client's culture = knowledge; and (c) intervention strategies and techniques = skills (Pedersen, 2001; Sue & Sue, 2003).

We would argue that these are not actually equivalent categories. Where this model breaks down is in the descriptions of the various competencies, which often contain components of attitudes and belief, knowledge, and skills, even though they are listed under one or the other category. This results in poor discrimination between items and reduces the meaningfulness of the organizational constructs.

One of the criticisms of earlier conceptualizations is that the competencies were difficult to operationalize, measure, and teach (Knapik & Miloti, 2006; Sue, 2006).There is a need to clarify the terminology and distinguish between a higher order concept such as self-awareness and the specific attitudes and beliefs, knowledge, and skills that may contribute to that awareness. The utility of competency frameworks depends, in part, on their simplicity, making it important to work towards discrete and non-overlapping items where possible.

Culture-Infused Counselling Competence

The theoretical and conceptual critiques of the traditional multicultural competencies lead us to introduce the working alliance as an overarching and pantheoretical construct to support a reconceptualization of the competency frameworks. In this edition of the text, we further expand our own conceptualization of culture-infused counselling competence to include a more direct focus on social justice as a core competency. These next few sections will review our rationale for these choices and introduce our own framework of culture-infused counselling competencies.

The Working Alliance as a Conceptual Framework for Culture-Infused Counselling Competence

The construct of the working alliance was first introduced by Borden in the 1970s, and it has endured the test of time in terms of its utility for understanding important elements of the relationship and process engaged in by counsellor and client. Building an effective working alliance is the core process in any counselling modality. An effective **working alliance** is defined as *a collaborative relationship between counsellor and client designed to facilitate change that involves three key components* (Castonguay, Constantino, & Holtforth, 2006; Hatcher & Barends, 2006):

   1.   co-construction of the goals to be accomplished through the relationship,

2.   *co-construction of the tasks to be fulfilled by each partner in the relationship, and*

3.   *a relationship characterized by mutual trust and respect that provides a solid foundation for facilitating the identification of culturally appropriate goals and tasks.*

Like Atkinson (2004), we are operating on the assumption that "culturally sensitive counsellors can establish the necessary and sufficient conditions of a productive helping relationship with clients who come from cultural backgrounds different from their own" (p. xxvi). The counsellor provides expertise in managing the working alliance in a way that ensures collaboration and client agreement on both goals of the counselling process and the activities that are engaged in to reach those goals. At the same time, clients provide expertise in their own experiences, cultural identity, context, and other factors that influence the nature of the relationship as well as the goals and tasks. Together they agree on the goals and processes that will enable them to do "purposeful and collaborative work" (Hatcher & Barends, 2006, p. 297). This agreement emerges from a co-construction of cultural meanings (Knapik & Miloti, 2006) and their application to the particular presenting concerns and context of the individual client. It should be clear from this description, then, that a culturally sensitive working alliance is impossible without attention to the first two core domains of multicultural competence: counsellor self-awareness and awareness of the client's cultural experience. As you will see later in this chapter, we are proposing that the working alliance replace the early construct of culturally appropriate intervention strategies (Arredondo et al., 1996) as the third core domain of multicultural competence.

Some empirical support for the inclusion of the working alliance in the conceptual framework of the multicultural counselling competencies is emerging in the literature (Roysircar, Hubbel, & Gard, 2003). Nonetheless, our inclusion of the working alliance as a central organizing feature of the multicultural competencies is based primarily on theoretical and conceptual grounds rather than on empirical research at this point. Several factors support this position.

1.   The existing models have been criticized for not placing sufficient emphasis on the counselling relationship, which some writers suggest should be added to the conceptual framework (Mollen et al., 2003; Ridley & Kleiner, 2003; Roysircar, Hubbell, & Gard, 2003). Sodowsky, Taffe, Gutkin, and Wise (1994) identified multicultural counselling relationships as a fourth competency domain through factor analysis of items on the Multicultural Counselling Inventory. Constantine and Ladany (2001) included an effective counselling alliance as one of six core competencies in their expanded model. It has been identified as a central change mechanism (Norton & Coleman, 2003). Sue, Ivey, and Pedersen (1996) included the client-counsellor relationship as one of their six basic tenets of their metatheory for multicultural counselling. In fact, Roysircar and colleagues (p. 263) asserted that "the relationship forms the center of the treatment."

2.   The working alliance is a pan-theoretical construct (Castonguay et al., 2006; Meissner, 2006) based on these three basic conditions: bonds between the counsellor and client, consensus on the tasks to be undertaken, and consensus on the goals or outcomes anticipated through engagement in those tasks (Horvath, 2000). In this sense, the working alliance construct, unlike early formulations of the therapeutic relationship, is not grounded in a particular theoretical orientation or worldview and is more culturally adaptive. Much of the newer literature points to the relationship as a common factor in therapeutic efficacy regardless of theoretical orientation (Goldfried & Davila, 2005).The working alliance is also robust in the sense that it is able to function as an organizing structure for the competencies currently identified under the *intervention strategies and techniques,* and it is inclusive of other factors that have emerged as relevant in the writings of others.

3.   There is considerable evidence that client and counsellor variables, especially the nature of the relationship between the two, are more significant predictors of outcomes than specific treatments (Coleman, 2004; Goldfried & Davila, 2005; Pope-Davis et al., 2002; Roysircar et al., 2003). This is reiterated in the APA task force on *Empirically Supported Therapy Relationships* (Ackerman et al., 2001). What this suggests is that the relationship is a more important variable than the interventions strategies and techniques construct identified in earlier writings (Horvath, 2006). According to Patterson (1996), the

preoccupation with intervention strategies in the earlier literature actually overshadowed the more appropriate emphasis on the relationship between counsellor and client as the core factor in promoting therapeutic change. According to Hatcher and Barends (2006): "Technique is an activity, alliance is a way to characterize an activity" (p. 294). The emphasis on skills also fails to elucidate the depth of personal engagement and transformation required for cultural competence (Fowers & Davidov, 2006). Introducing the working alliance as a backdrop for the multicultural competencies leads to a higher-order critical analysis of application of various intervention strategies and techniques (Collins & Arthur, in press a).

4. The pantheoretical construct of the working alliance opens the door to a more inclusive interface between the core competencies identified in the multicultural counselling literature and other bodies of theory and practice. For example, the collaborative relationship between counsellor and client is one of the commonalities between multicultural and feminist theories (Williams & Barber, 2004). In particular, the emphasis in feminist practice on openly addressing power differences in the therapeutic context (Morrow et al., 2006; Reynolds & Constantine, 2004) fits well with the working alliance model. It is important that any reconceptualization of these competencies be not only be inclusive of the broader definition of culture, noted in the previous section, but also of the therapeutic principles that have been developed by those working directly with women, persons with disabilities, gay, lesbian, bisexual, and transgendered clients, and so on.

5. The working alliance construct has also been shown to be applicable across practice areas. According to Hiebert (2001), the *client* in the working alliance may be an individual or group, an organization, or a broader social system that the professional is working with. The goals and purposes of the interactions may differ in each case, but each shares the need for a strong working alliance to support both parties in attaining their respective goals. Arthur and Collins (in press a) and Norton and Coleman (2003), for example, point to the working alliance as a central factor in multicultural supervision. Chapters 4 and 5 will expand on the culture-infused counselling competencies as they relate to applied professional practice with individuals, families, or groups. Chapter 6 will extend the concept of culture-infused counselling to social justice interventions designed to effect change at broader systems levels.

6. Finally, the working alliance provides the mechanism for gathering and translating self-awareness and conceptual cultural knowledge of the client into effective and culturally sensitive processes (Sodowsky et al., 1994). From a post-modern perspective, cultural meanings emerge in and through interaction (Knapik & Miloti, 2006); to apply cultural awareness outside of the context of relationship risks misinterpretation, presumption, and stereotyping. Fowers and Davidov (2006) emphasized the important of linking person, goal, and actions in the application of cultural knowledge and skills. In the absence of a virtue-driven interpersonal relationship characterized by openness to the other the same awareness may be used in manipulative, disrespectful, or exploitive ways (Fowers & Davidov). The first two core competencies are clearly insufficient until the knowledge, awareness, and skills are applied with a particular client, targeting change in a specific area, within a specific context. It is the collaborative and culturally sensitive working alliance that facilitates this application to practice. Some of the constructs identified in Chapter 4 as critical to multicultural competence, such as racial identity development of both counsellor and client, are only fully meaningful to the counselling process when considered in the context of the relationship between counsellor and client.

The Integration of Social Justice Competencies

Both feminist and multicultural literatures share an emphasis on the importance of environmental context to understanding individuals and groups (Williams & Barber, 2004). Recognition of the impact of systemic oppression and discrimination was foundational to the original multicultural competencies (Arredondo & Perez, 2006). However, the feminist literature placed more direct emphasis on socio-political analysis and on the role of the counsellor in directly influencing these broader social, economic, and political systems (Evans et al., 2005; Silverstein, 2006). As noted in Chapter 2, in the last decade a strong social justice movement has emerged within the psychological and counselling literature and with it a call to embrace facilitation of systems-level social justice as a central role for both individual practitioners and the professions as a whole.

The *Handbook for Social Justice in Counselling Psychology* (Toporek, Gerstein, Fouad, Roysircar, & Israel, 2006b) reflects the application of principles of social justice to training, work in schools, marginalized communities, career, health care, and policy and legislation. However, even though some of the original authors of the multicultural counselling competencies have contributed significantly to this work and there are multiple references to the competencies, there was no call for revision of that framework to be more inclusive of competencies for social justice. There is no other evidence in the literature to take a more inclusive and integrative stance.

Over the past several years, our own research has focused on the articulation and assessment of social justice competencies for career practitioners. The Social Justice and Career Development Survey (Collins, Arthur, & McMahon, 2006) was designed to gather information about the professional needs of career development practitioners and best practice examples in the area of social justice. The survey included a matrix of social justice competencies, organized by attitudes, knowledge, and skills, that was developed through a comprehensive review of the current literature. Ten content experts were then invited to provide feedback on the comprehensiveness and wording of the competency statements. The final online version of the questionnaire contained 41 competency statements and was conducted with practitioners in both Canada and Australia (Arthur, Collins, Bisson et al., 2009; McMahon, Arthur, & Collins, 2008). Based on this research we are able to articulate additional competencies for social justice that will be added to our framework for culture-infused counselling competency in an attempt to more fully integrate the social justice agenda.

A Revised Framework for Culture-Infused Counselling Competencies

Based on the observations above, we would like to propose a revised framework that is intended to be inclusive of the current and historical work in this area. We welcome the critical review of this work by students, practitioners, and colleagues who are educators and researchers. This is a work in progress and is considered a living document, open to incorporation of new ways of understanding culture-infused counselling competencies. The model proposed is based on the following assumptions.

1. The term culture is broadly defined to include diverse factors such as gender, sexual orientation, age, and ability. The language of the competencies must therefore be inclusive of factors beyond race and ethnicity that influence one's sense of cultural identity. Additional competencies may be required when working with specific cultural groups or within particular areas of practice. A means for integrating these competencies into the overall framework is essential to ensure full representation of diverse members of society.

2. Understanding the cultural identity of a particular client, however, must also take into account the broader factors that impact upon worldview. In this sense, every interaction between counsellor and client involves a multicultural encounter. Affiliation with a particular cultural group may, in fact, be less important to the counselling process than other aspects of personal identity. The model must therefore be based on the premise that it is applicable to all encounters between counsellors and clients. The key is in the assessment of the salience of various dimensions to the particular client context.

3. Some components of the multicultural competency domains are proposed as foundational to the wide range of functions that counsellors and psychologists perform. The two core principles noted in the APA (2003b) document and, in earlier writings, are reaffirmed as central constructs: (a) awareness of one's own cultural assumptions, values, and biases and (b) understanding of the cultural identities of the client. These constructs will be expanded upon in Chapter 4.

4. The construct of the working alliance provides an organizational framework for integrating the core multicultural competencies. This construct replaces the earlier, narrow focus on appropriate intervention strategies and techniques as the third core competency domain and provides, in our opinion, a more inclusive and broader framework for linking the competencies to the counselling process.

5. The various domains of practice of counsellors and psychologists extend beyond simply applied clinical practice, making it important to articulate additional competencies in other domains. Although the primary focus of this text is on applied practice, the focus on social justice interventions in Chapter 6 requires expansion of both roles and domains of practice for counsellors.

6. Within the intersection of competency domains, areas of practice, and cultural affiliations are specific multicultural competencies, which are defined at this more micro level according to the dimensions of attitudes and beliefs, knowledge, and skills. Personal or contextual identity factors are then used as means of assessing the salience of these factors to a particular client.

7. Since the first edition of this text was published in 2005, we have observed the burgeoning literature and increased emphasis at conferences and other professional venues on social justice. This has led us to prioritize social justice in this second edition. It has also facilitated a rethinking of the original presentation of the culture-infused counselling competencies to be more inclusive of social justice activities that extend beyond the interaction between counsellor and client.

Based on these assumptions we are proposing the following basic framework of culture-infused counselling competencies. The attitudes, knowledge, and skills that form each core competency will be described later in the chapter. For now, we would like to point out the three core competency domains, in particular the culturally sensitive working alliance. You will also notice that we have moved beyond the original formulation of the working alliance to include a fourth component: engagement in social justice activities to directly influence the systems that negatively affect the lives of non-dominant populations. Our rationale for integrated social justice under the working alliance construct is that it is in the context of work with our clients that we come to more fully understand the specific systemic factors that are leading to problems in their lives. This awareness becomes a call to action to promote social justice. In turn, our social justice interventions serve to positively impact the lives of our clients and to enhance our credibility and sensitivity within the working alliances we form.

Domain I: Cultural Self-Awareness **Active awareness of personal assumptions, values, and biases.**
Core Competency 1: Demonstrate awareness of your own cultural identities.
Core Competency 2: Demonstrate awareness of differences between your own cultural identities and those of individuals from other dominant or non-dominant groups.
Core Competency 3: Demonstrate awareness of the impact of culture on the theory and practice of counselling/psychology.
Core Competency 4: Demonstrate awareness of the personal and professional impact of the discrepancy between dominant and non-dominant cultural groups in North America.
Core Competency 5: Demonstrate awareness of your level of multicultural competence.
Domain II: Awareness of Client Cultural Identities **Understanding the worldview of the client.**
Core Competency 1: Demonstrate awareness of the cultural identities of your clients.
Core Competency 2: Demonstrate awareness of the relationship of personal culture to health and well-being.
Core Competency 3: Demonstrate awareness of the socio-political influences that impinge on the lives of non-dominant populations.
Domain III: Culturally Sensitive Working Alliance
Core Competency 1: Establish trusting and respectful relationships with clients that take into account cultural identities.
Core Competency 2: Collaborate with clients to establish counselling goals that are responsive to salient dimensions of cultural identity.
Core Competency 3: Collaborate with clients to establish client and counsellor tasks that are responsive to salient dimensions of cultural identity.
Core Competency 4: Engage in social justice activities to directly influence the systems that negatively affect the lives of non-dominant populations.

Figure 1. The culture-infused counselling competencies framework.

These same basic competencies may be applied with all clients regardless of their group affiliations or other dimensions of cultural identity and across various areas of practice (supervision, consultation, and so on). Although others have presented three-dimensional organizational structures for identifying competencies, intended to highlight the interaction across multiple dimensions (Sue, 2001), we do not actually see value in defining competencies in all of the potential areas of intersection. Nor do we see this as a feasible exercise, given the range of factors that can impact how each individual defines her or his own personal cultural identities (Collins, in press a). What we suggest is that the framework allows for those competencies that are foundational for working with all clients to be articulated, then additional competencies identified for working with particular clients in particular contexts. In most cases, the integration takes place at the level of the individual practitioner, as illustrated in figures 2 and 3.

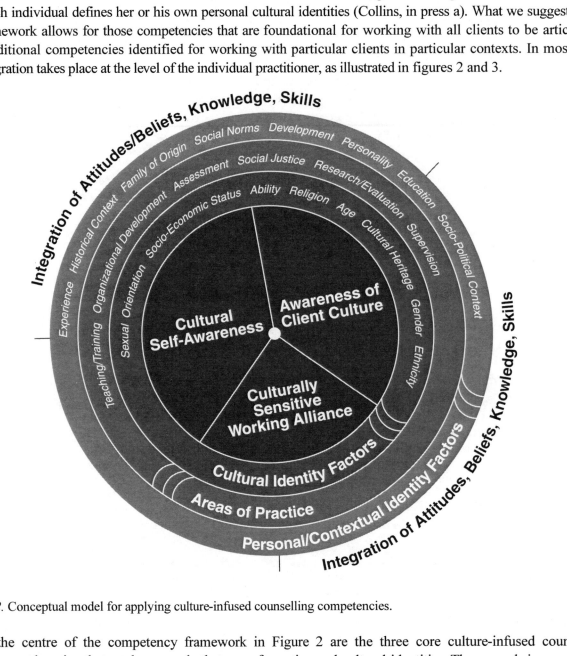

Figure 2. Conceptual model for applying culture-infused counselling competencies.

At the centre of the competency framework in Figure 2 are the three core culture-infused counselling competency domains that apply across both areas of practice and cultural identities. The second ring represents the group affiliations that are most commonly identified in discussions of non-dominant cultural status: ethnicity, gender, sexual orientation, age, ability, socio-economic status, and religion. Note that the ring of cultural identities can be rotated to line up those that are relevant in a particular counsellor-client interaction. Similarly, the areas of practice and personal identity factors rings can be rotated to create the combination of factors that a multiculturally competent counsellor would take into account in working with a particular client. The challenge for counsellors is to identify the various attitudes and beliefs, knowledge, and skills identified at each level and to integrate them effectively. Piecing together this puzzle provides a foundation for working with each client. Figure 3 illustrates the factors taken into account in working with a hypothetical client. One of the keys to such integration is assessment of salience of the various factors for the particular client.

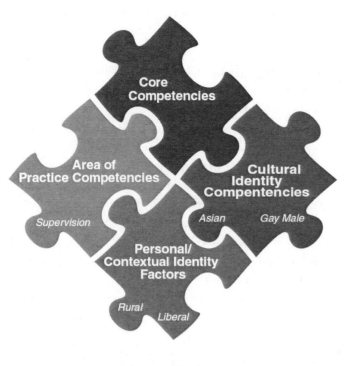

Figure 3. Hypothetical client application.

For some, the process of identifying and attaining core multicultural competencies, followed by the addition of specific competencies related to area of practice and salient cultural identities, and then effectively integrating these competencies based on the individual characteristics of the clients and the salience of the various factors may seem overwhelming. However, this is precisely the combination of factors that we are being asked to attend to in the current multicultural counselling literature. The weakness in the literature, at this point, is that there is no model for integrating these various components, so it becomes a conceptual nightmare for the practitioner. To simplify the process, we suggest that each of the core competency domains be described in terms of the attitudes and beliefs, knowledge, and skills that are common to all areas of practice. Then, additional or more specific competencies may be identified for specific practice areas or for working with particular non-dominant groups.

Since it would be impossible for any of us to develop expertise in addressing the needs of members of each of these groups in each of these professional practice areas (Hansen et al., 2000), practitioners are encouraged to define the areas of competency development according to their practice domains and the populations they most frequently encounter or choose to specialize with.

Defining Culture-Infused Counselling Competence

There have been numerous attempts to define multicultural counselling competence in the literature. While some suggest that a variety of definitions are feasible, Ridley and Kleiner (2003) strongly asserted that the field must eventually come to some consensus. A number of writers use the term culture-centred to describe the process of applying a cultural lens to all professional practice attitudes, behaviours, and interactions (APA, 2003b). While it may seem odd to wait until this point in our chapter to tackle this question, most definitions have involved some connection to articulated multicultural competencies. Sue and colleagues (1992), Pedersen (2001), and others draw on the three core competencies that form the basis of the traditional framework. In a similar way, we draw on the three core competency domains that form the foundation of our conceptual model:

1. Cultural Self-Awareness: Active awareness of personal assumptions, values, and biases.

2. Awareness of Client Cultural Identities: Understanding the worldview of the client.

3. Culturally Sensitive Working Alliance: Agreement on goals and tasks in the context of a trusting relationship.

Culture-infused counselling competence, then, is defined as *the integration of attitudes and beliefs, knowledge, and skills essential for awareness of the impact of culture on personal assumptions, values, and beliefs, understanding of the worldview of the client, coming to agreement on goals and tasks in the context of a trusting and culturally sensitive working alliance, and reinforcing that alliance by embracing a social justice agenda.* Embedded in this definition is the assumption that advanced integration includes attention to area of practice and the salience of the client's cultural affiliations and personal identity factors. What is important to competence is an appreciation of the broad brushstrokes that may enhance our understanding of particular groups combined with the unique, colourful, idiosyncratic experiences and self-definition of individual clients.

The position in much of the literature is that the competencies and guidelines are intended as recommendations rather than mandatory standards (APA, 2003b). However, as our population continues to change and evolve, it is our assertion that it will become increasingly difficult for counsellors to justify an approach to counselling that does not incorporate these guidelines (Watson, Herlihy, & Pierce, 2006). We would also argue that there should be no distinction between multicultural competence and professional competence since all encounters are, on some level, multicultural interactions. The basic assumption is that each individual or group (including the practitioner) is affected by historical, ecological, social, political, and other cultural contexts.

Advanced multicultural competence is conceptualized as the ability to integrate competencies identified across these various dimensions to establish an effective working alliance with a particular client, focused on a particular presenting concern, within a particular context. This is seen as a central focus of the model, since the real test for the counsellor is not in gaining specific competencies, but in the ability to apply those across contexts and with unique clients. This advanced integration involves judgment and diligence on the part of the counsellor. We draw on the definition of competence of the College of Alberta Psychologists (2003) in adding these two additional components to our definition of competence: **Culture-infused counselling competence** also *involves judgment (ability to assess when to apply particular knowledge or skills – e.g., with which client, under which circumstances, focused on which particular presenting concern) and diligence (consistent self-reflection and attention to both one's own level of multicultural competence and the appropriate application of the multicultural competencies in all areas of practice).*

The Culture-Infused Counselling Competencies

We would now like to introduce our framework of **culture-infused counselling competencies**. Figure 4 describes the *specific attitudes and beliefs, knowledge, and skills that are essential for demonstrating competence*. We have drawn heavily upon the earlier competency frameworks, but have reorganized the competencies to fit the proposed model and integrated additional components that have emerged in the literature over time. We wish to acknowledge, in particular, the work of Arredondo and colleagues (1996), the APA (1993, 2003b), Hansen and colleagues (2000), Sue and colleagues (1998), and Sue and Sue (2003) for their work in defining multicultural competencies that form a foundation for this revised framework. We have also drawn on competency guidelines related to specific non-dominant populations (APA, 1998, 2003a; Bowman & King, 2003). In this edition, we have also integrated our own research on defining competencies for social justice (Arthur, Collins, Bisson et al., 2009; McMahon et al., 2008) and the work of Lewis and colleagues (2003) in defining advocacy competencies for the *American Counselling Association*. In many cases, components of the competencies listed have been drawn directly from these sources.

We have introduced several core competencies in each of the three competency domains we have chosen, which are then broken down into distinct attitudes, knowledge, and skills required to demonstrate competence. We have added an additional column to link the competencies with the key terms and concepts introduced throughout this text. Our hope is that as you read the materials presented you will continue to cross-reference them with the culture-infused counselling competency framework to identify areas of strength and areas for further competence development. We hope that this model makes a clearer connection between the competencies described and the range of theoretical and conceptual issues addressed in the literature.

Please note that the competencies are described *as if* the counsellor is a member of the dominant population in Canada. We have done this simply because this is most often the case and because using a more generic wording tends to downplay the power differences among cultural populations. The wording can be easily adapted for counsellors who identify as members of non-dominant populations. In this case, it may be increased awareness and sensitivity in working with other non-dominant groups that is required. The attainment of multicultural counselling competence is equally important.

Domain I: Cultural Self-Awareness	
Active awareness of personal assumptions, values, and biases.	

Core Competency 1: Demonstrate awareness of your own cultural identities.

	Specific Knowledge, Attitude, and Skill Competencies	Key Concepts
Attitudes & Beliefs	• See yourself as a cultural being. • Be able and willing to self-reflect. • Value awareness of your own cultural identity or identities. • Acknowledge both positive and negative aspects of your own cultural group(s). • Acknowledge your tendency to view the world through your own cultural lens.	• Counsellor identity development (e.g., White, male, heterosexual) • Cultural identity • Cultural schemata • Culture • Disability • Diversity • Ethnicity • Internalized culture • Personal culture • Privilege • Race • Religious diversity • Social class • Socio-economic status • Values

Knowledge	• Define race, ethnicity, culture, and diversity.
	• Describe your own cultural identities.
	• Recognizes the factors that influence personal identity formation:
	  o personal factors (e.g., genetics, family, personality);
	  o cultural factors (e.g., gender, social class, ethnic identity, sexual orientation, ability, spirituality, or religion); and
	  o contextual factors (e.g., historical context, environment).
	• Explain the impact of these factors on your identity development.
	• List common phases of cultural identity development.
	• Identify your level of cultural identity development.
	• Describe the impact your identity development may have on the counselling process.	

Skills	• Actively pursue deeper cultural self-awareness. • Analyze cultural factors affecting self and others. • Actively support non-oppressive practices.	

Core Competency 2: Demonstrate awareness of differences between your own cultural identities and those of individuals from other dominant or non-dominant groups.

	Specific Knowledge, Attitude, and Skill Competencies	Key Concepts
Attitudes & Beliefs	• Recognize how your cultural identity affects your beliefs, values, and assumptions about members of non-dominant populations. • Be non-judgmental about differences between you and those of different heritage, ethnicity, gender, class, sexual orientation, ability, religion, and age. • Acknowledge personal discomfort or biases related to cultural differences. • Acknowledge personal biases about health, family, career, community, and other life experiences. • Assume responsibility for modifying your own attitudes and beliefs, knowledge, or skills.	• Cultural reciprocity • Culture shock (counsellor) • Difference versus deviance • Dominant and non-dominant groups • Imposition of values and standards • Multicultural policy • Multiculturalism • Professional codes of conduct
Knowledge	• Define multiculturalism. • Identify relevant professional and political guidelines. • Explain the benefits and limitations of multiculturalism policies. • Explain differences in culture and worldview between dominant and non-dominant groups in society. • Identify historical, socio-economic, political, and other contextual factors that impact these differences. • Explain the relationship between your own cultural group and other dominant or non-dominant groups in society. • Identify the potential impact of your cultural values and biases on clients from non-dominant groups.	
Skills	• Self-monitor negative emotional reactions, biases, or value judgments. • Actively challenge negative emotional reactions, biases, or value judgments. • Identify signs of personal culture shock. • Avoid withdrawing from engagement with clients or blaming clients for your emotional reactions.	

Figure 4. Culture-infused counselling competencies. Continues over several pages.

Core Competency 3: **Demonstrate awareness of the impact of culture on the theory and practice of counselling/psychology.**

Specific Knowledge, Attitude, and Skill Competencies		Key Concepts
Attitudes & Beliefs	• Acknowledge that counselling and psychology are culture-bound. • Recognize that a monocultural perspective does not fit for all clients. • Be open to alternative perspectives on health and healing.	• Cultural blindness • Cultural consciousness • Cultural encapsulation • Cultural malpractice • Culture-infused counselling • Ethnocentrism • Feminist counselling • Gay-affirmative counselling • Monoculturalism • Unintentional oppression • Western worldview
Knowledge	• Describe the historical and contextual factors that shape the theory and practice of counselling and psychology. • List the cultural tenets underlying Western theories of counselling. • Identify the impact of multicultural, feminist, and other diversity-sensitive movements on current theory and practice. • Describe Eastern psychological and healing practices. • Explain how your cultural identities affect your views of human nature, healthy functioning, and the change process.	
Skills	• Analyze the underlying values and assumptions in your theory of counselling. • Maintain theoretical flexibility. • Adapt Western theories and practices. • Incorporate non-Western theories and practices. • Analyze cultural biases in psychological literature and research. • Engage in culture-infused research practices. • Contribute to the knowledge base for working with non-dominant populations.	

Core Competency 4: **Demonstrate awareness of the personal and professional impact of the discrepancy between dominant and non-dominant cultural groups in North America.**

Specific Knowledge, Attitude, and Skill Competencies		Key Concepts
Attitudes & Beliefs	• Respect the dignity and equal worth of all individuals and cultural groups. • Uphold social justice and equity for all members of society. • Acknowledge racist, sexist, elitist, heterosexist, ableist, and ageist attitudes. • Be willing to work through any defensiveness or guilt.	• Cultural baggage • Cultural counter-transference • Empowerment • Cultural oppression • Hate Crimes • Overgeneraliz-ation/stereotypes • Power • Prejudice/discrimination • Privilege • Racism, sexism, heterosexism, classism, ableism, ageism, elitism • Unintentional racism
Knowledge	• Describe how oppression, discrimination, and stereotyping affect you personally and in your work. • Explain the nature of privilege. • Describe how you may have benefited directly or indirectly by societal oppression of members of non-dominant groups. • Discuss the impact of power differences on the counselling process. • Identify means of minimizing power differences. • Identify ways to promote social change.	
Skills	• Analyze overt and covert means of cultural oppression within your familial, social, work, community, and professional contexts. • Demonstrate non-racist, non-sexist, non-classist, non-heterosexist, non-ableist, and non-ageist practices. • Engage in professional and personal activities to promote social justice.	

Core Competency 5: **Demonstrate awareness of your level of multicultural competence.**

Specific Knowledge, Attitude, and Skill Competencies		Key Concepts
Attitudes & Beliefs	• View all encounters between counsellor and client as multicultural. • View multicultural competence as necessary for competent practice. • Value authenticity. • Demonstrate congruence between personal and professional roles. • Commit to continued development of multicultural counselling competence.	• Continued competency • Cultural reflection • Culture-infused counselling • Culture-infused counselling competence • Culture-infused counselling competencies • Ethical practice • Multicultural Case conceptualization • Nice counsellor syndrome
Knowledge	• Define culture-infused counselling. • Define multicultural counselling competence. • Identify specific competencies required for competent practice. • Identify potential ethics dilemmas involved in multicultural counselling. • Identify relevant standards and codes of ethics. • Explain the cultural limitations of these guidelines.	
Skills	• Infuse cultural inquiry into all dimensions of professional practice. • Assess your level of multicultural competence. • Identify the limits of your multicultural competence. • Implement a culturally sensitive model of ethical decision-making. • Implement strategies to manage situations beyond your level of competence. • Map out a process of continued professional development.	

Domain II: Awareness of Client Cultural Identities: Understanding the worldview of the client.

Core Competency 1: Demonstrate awareness of the cultural identities of your clients.

	Specific Knowledge, Attitude, and Skill Competencies	Key Concepts
Attitudes & Beliefs	• Value cultural diversity. • Be tolerant of ambiguity. • See worldviews as neither right nor wrong, good nor evil. • Acknowledge both healthy and unhealthy aspects of all cultural systems. • Believe that sensitivity to client cultural identities is necessary for competent practice.	• Cognitive complexity • Collective identity • Cultural hypotheses • Cultural identity factors

Knowledge	• Explain how cultural identities are shaped through historical, social, and cultural experiences and contexts.
	• Describe the basic tenets of the world's dominant religions.
	• Describe the cultural groups in your region.
	• List the cultural affiliations of your clients.
	• Identify the factors that influence client identity formation:
	   ○ personal factors (e.g., genetics, family, personality);
	   ○ cultural factors (e.g., gender, social class, ethnic identity, sexual orientation, religion, ability); and
	   ○ contextual factors (e.g., historical context, environment).
	• Explain how these factors influence the internalized culture of your client's values, beliefs, and worldview.
	• Recognize that within-group differences are sometimes as large as between-group differences.
		• Cultural relativism
		• Cultural schemata
		• Demographic changes
		• Gender identity
		• Immigration trends
		• Individualistic identity
		• Salience of cultural identity
		• Sexual identity
		• Sexual orientation
		• Worldview

Skills	• Implement strategies to increase your basic cultural knowledge. • Assess the unique cultural identities of your clients. • Assess the potential influences of cultural identity on counselling issues and interventions. • Hold tentatively to cultural hypotheses. • Avoid using general cultural knowledge in stereotypical ways. • Adjust your cultural lens in response to new information.	

Core Competency 2: Demonstrate awareness of the relationship of personal culture to health and well-being.

	Specific Knowledge, Attitude, and Skill Competencies	Key Concepts
Attitudes & Beliefs	• View culture as critical to fully understanding any individual or group. • Acknowledge the impact of cultural factors on healthy functioning, development and conceptualization of problems, and expressions of distress. • Respect alternative points of view about health, family, career, community, and other life experiences. • Respect the roles of family, community, social hierarchies, and religious or spiritual affiliations. • Believe in the interrelationship of all aspects of human nature and experience.	• Acculturation • Assimilation • Bicultural identity • Cross-cultural transition • Cultural blindness • Cultural consciousness • Cultural identity development models (non-dominant and dominant populations)
Knowledge	• Explain how cultural heritage, gender, social class, ethnic identity, sexual orientation, ability, religion, and age may impact well-being. • Identify the psychosocial health problems that commonly affect various non-dominant populations. • Explain how various non-dominant populations manage health issues. • Describe models of cultural identity development. • Explain the impact of culture shock on clients. • Define acculturation. • Explain the impact of different acculturation patterns on personal and social adjustment. • Describe the benefits of adopting a bicultural or hybrid identity. • Explain the potential impact of client identity development on the counselling process. • Describe supportive resources available within cultural communities.	• Cultural value conflicts • Culture shock (client) • Economic, psychological, social adaptation • Fluid identities • Hybrid identities • Intergenerational conflicts
Skills	• Assess your clients' assumptions and beliefs about healthy functioning and the change process. • Balance attention to culture with attention to factors unrelated to culture. • Differentiate between salient and non-salient aspects of culture. • Assess individual, family, or community barriers to seeking professional help. • Develop consultation and referral relationships with community members.	• Multiple and intersecting identities • Social locations • Situational ethnicity • Third space

Core Competency 3: Demonstrate awareness of the socio-political influences that impinge on the lives of non-dominant populations.

	Specific Knowledge, Attitude, and Skill Competencies	Key Concepts
Attitudes & Beliefs	• Oppose social, economic, and political oppression of members of non-dominant populations. • Be non-defensive about the historical oppression of non-dominant populations by your own cultural group. • Demonstrate commitment to change in social injustices.	• Cultural oppression • Cultural transference • Institutionalized racism, sexism, heterosexism, ableism, ageism, elitism
Knowledge	• Identify government policies and legislation on multiculturalism and equality. • Describe the social, economic, and political oppression of non-dominant populations. • Explain the psychological impact of oppression, prejudice, and discrimination. • Identify facilitative factors that mediate against the effects of oppression. • Identify discriminatory practices at the organizational, community, and regional levels that may impact the psychological welfare of your clients.	• Internalized racism, sexism, homophobia, etc. • Legislation and policy • Relationship between culture and power
Skills	• Facilitate client expression of negative reactions to social oppression, including oppression by your own cultural group. • Assess the impact of socio-political oppression. • Assess the internalization of negative stereotypes and biases. • Assess barriers to service at personal, familial, institutional, and social levels.	• Strengths-based model

Domain III: Culturally Sensitive Working Alliance.

Core Competency 1: Establish trusting and respectful relationships with clients that take into account cultural identities.

	Specific Knowledge, Attitude, and Skill Competencies	Key Concepts
Attitudes & Beliefs	• Demonstrate genuine interest in learning about your clients' cultures. • Recognize the potential impact of your emotional reactions towards clients from non-dominant groups on your working alliance. • Be sensitive to issues of oppression, sexism, heterosexism, elitism, ageism, religious discrimination, ableism, and racism. • Respect language differences. • Be open to referring clients to a member of their own cultural group.	• Central relationship paradox • Cognitive complexity • Communication style • Counselling conventions • Counsellor credibility
Knowledge	• Recognize that counselling skills, styles, and approaches may be culture-bound. • Explain how counselling styles and approaches may be modified to match client preferences and communication styles. • Recognize cultural norms embedded in office setting, appointment time, and other Western counselling conventions. • Identify cultural norms for both counsellor and client roles. • Discuss common challenges in establishing an effective working alliance across cultures.	• Cultural auditing • Cultural empathy • Cultural inquiry • Cultural sensitivity • Culture-in-action • Egalitarian relationships • Language barriers • Monolingualism
Skills	• Establish credibility with your clients. • Adapt your helping style to fit the particular client. • Engage in cultural inquiry to understand client perspectives. • Validate the cultural strengths of clients. • Use verbal and non-verbal skills to communicate empathy in culturally appropriate ways. • Tailor your relationship-building strategies to the stage of identity development of the client. • Monitor the impact of your own level of cultural identity development. • Be flexible about the setting, time, and other norms for counselling services. • Assess the impact of counsellor-client language differences. • Teach clients what to expect from the counselling process. • Identify and use appropriate referral services. • Facilitate strategic planning within counselling agencies to identify ways to enhance services for particular cultural groups. • Practice cultural auditing in ongoing work with clients.	• Mutual empathy • Power • Systemic barriers • Underutilization of mental health services • Verbal and non-verbal counselling skills

Core Competency 2: Collaborate with clients to establish counselling goals that are responsive to salient dimensions of cultural identity.		
	Specific Knowledge, Attitude, and Skill Competencies	Key Concepts
Attitudes & Beliefs	• Believe in the expertise of clients in their own experience and needs. • Believe in the importance of collaboration in the counselling process. • Acknowledge the strengths of clients from non-dominant groups in coping with various forms of oppression. • Value spiritual dimensions of client presenting concerns.	• Acculturation • Acculturative stress • Client-driven • Coping and survival behaviours • Counselling goals • Cultural auditing • Cultural reflection • Emic perspective (culture-specific) • Etic perspective (universal) • Identity management/ disclosure • Locus of control • Locus of responsibility • Multicultural • case conceptualization • Salience of cultural dimensions • Sex role socialization • Stages of identity development • Theoretical orientation
Knowledge	• Describe the impact of culture on your understandings of human nature, problem development, and appropriate targets for change. • Explain emic (culture-specific) and etic (universal) perspectives on client presenting concerns. • Identify the impact of level of cultural identity development on perceptions of problems and target outcomes. • Identify potential limitations and biases in common assessment practices and instruments. • Identify culture-specific assessment procedures and tools. • Describe systemic factors in assessment of client issues. • Identify signs that client distress results from external/systemic factors. • List possible goals for clients who are experiencing social injustices.	
Skills	• Accurately evaluate emic and etic hypotheses about the nature of client presenting concerns. • Assist clients to explore how social inequities have influenced their development. • Implement a multilevel, multimodal, and multisource approach to assessment to ensure accuracy and cultural relevance. • Draw on both traditional and culture-specific assessment instruments and procedures. • Challenge biases and discriminatory practices in assessment and evaluation. • Assess the client's level of acculturation, experience of culture shock or acculturative stress, and stage of cultural identity development. • Identify the impact of multiple non-dominant identities on clients. • Assess the salience of various aspects of client cultural identities to the presenting concerns. • Assess clients' strengths, coping strategies, support systems, and resources. • Identify contextual and systemic influences in case conceptualization and intervention planning. • Where appropriate, adapt your theoretical orientation to fit with clients' perceptions of the presenting concerns. • Assist clients to avoid inappropriately internalizing systemic oppression. • Assess the potential for clients to change external factors.	

Core Competency 3: Collaborate with clients to establish client and counsellor tasks that are responsive to salient dimensions of cultural identity.

Specific Knowledge, Attitude, and Skill Competencies		Key Concepts
Attitudes & Beliefs	<ul><li>Acknowledge the role of the client in identifying appropriate processes for goal attainment.</li><li>Reframe client 'resistance' as evidence of a poor working alliance or a mismatch between counsellor and client in terms of the goals and tasks of counselling.</li><li>Admit that Western practices may be of limited applicability across cultures.</li><li>Believe that clients have a right to draw on their own cultural practices to facilitate change.</li><li>Respect indigenous perspectives on health and healing practices.</li><li>Value the role of spirituality in the healing process.</li><li>Respect cultural healers and helping networks.</li><li>Commit to empowering clients to influence their environments.</li></ul>	<ul><li>Class-bound</li><li>Common change factors</li><li>Counselling processes</li><li>Cultural appropriation</li><li>Cultural auditing</li><li>Cultural reflection</li><li>Culturally responsive interventions</li><li>Culture-bound</li><li>Empowerment</li><li>Ethical decision-making</li><li>Gender role analysis</li><li>Indigenous support and healing systems</li><li>Interprofessional collaboration</li><li>Intraprofessional collaboration</li><li>Power analysis</li><li>Resistance</li><li>Salience of cultural identity</li><li>Universal healing conditions</li></ul>
Knowledge	<ul><li>Describe how professional practices are historically and culturally bound.</li><li>Explain how cultural heritage, gender, social class, ethnic identity, sexual orientation, religion, ability, and age may affect the appropriateness of counselling approaches.</li><li>Describe potential ethical dilemmas in supporting clients to influence their environments.</li><li>Describe potential ethical dilemmas in working collaboratively with clients to effect social change.</li><li>Describe the limits of your professional expertise.</li><li>List the advantages of collaborating with professionals from other fields.</li><li>Explain the ethical considerations of borrowing or using indigenous healing methods.</li><li>Recognize the cultural meanings of endings to self and to clients.</li></ul>	
Skills	<ul><li>Use cultural inquiry as a foundation for intervention planning.</li><li>Ensure a culturally responsive match between the goals and processes of counselling.</li><li>Demonstrate a process for ethical decision-making that recognizes social injustices.</li><li>Demonstrate competence with a broad repertoire of counselling interventions, strategies, and techniques that draw on both Western and culture-specific perspectives.</li><li>Design and implement intervention strategies that are free of cultural bias and respectful of client worldviews.</li><li>Facilitate indigenous support and healing systems.</li><li>Collaborate with professionals from other disciplines.</li><li>Make referrals where appropriate.</li><li>Recognize and work to eliminate biases, prejudices, and discriminatory intervention practices and contexts.</li><li>Implement strategies aimed at prevention of health problems.</li><li>Facilitate indigenous healing processes.</li><li>Empower clients to influence external factors that affect their well-being.</li><li>Teach clients the skills to advocate for themselves.</li><li>Support clients in carrying out self-advocacy interventions.</li><li>Negotiate appropriate timing and ways to end the counselling relationship with clients.</li></ul>	

Core Competency 4: Engage in social justice activities to directly influence the systems that negatively affect the lives of non-dominant populations.		
	Specific Knowledge, Attitude, and Skill Competencies	Key Concepts
Attitudes & Beliefs	• Believe that it is a professional responsibility to contribute to the elimination of social injustice. • Believe that counsellors should do more to help eliminate discrimination. • Acknowledge that counsellors have a role to play in influencing organizations, communities, and broader social, economic, and political systems.	• Advocacy • Advocacy competence • Advocacy competencies • Community capacity building • Consciousness raising • Consultation • Counsellor roles • Education • Evaluation • Networking • Organizational development • Organizational policy • Peacebuilding • Personal is political • Prevention • Professional is political • Research • Social justice • Structural violence • Systemic barriers
Knowledge	• Identify common social injustices encountered by your clients. • Explain why social justice is important to counselling practice. • Identify the expanded roles required of counsellors to effect social change. • Describe potential ethical dilemmas in intervening directly to facilitate change in systemic factors. • Identify barriers to social justice within organizations, communities, and broader social, economic, and political systems. • Identify facilitators of social justice within organizations, communities, and broader social, economic, and political systems. • Describe how to facilitate change in organizations, communities, and broader social, economic, and political systems. • Describe how to effectively evaluate social justice interventions.	
Skills	• Self-assess competence to facilitate activities that promote social justice. • Negotiate services and resources on clients' behalf. • Develop effective networks and establish allies within organizations, communities, and broader social, economic, and political systems. • Engage in prevention. • Facilitate educational activities related to social justice. • Engage in consciousness-raising with regard to social justice issues. • Engage in organizational consultation to promote social justice. • Build community capacity to effect change. • Advocate with those in positions of power. • Manage resistance to change at multiple levels. • Mobilize media to disseminate awareness of social injustices. • Lobby for changes in legislation. • Conduct evaluations to demonstrate the effectiveness of social justice interventions. • Engage in research to highlight social justice issues and change agendas. • Encourage other counsellors to examine social justice issues. • Encourage professional organizations to advocate for social justice.	

Applying the Competencies to Practice

Students and counselling practitioners frequently ask these two questions during courses and training workshops on multicultural counselling: "How do you *do* multicultural counselling?" and "How is multicultural counselling *different from* or *similar to* other counselling?" Now that we have mapped out the competencies involved in culture-infused counselling, we will turn our attention to the means by which counsellors can develop competence in each of these areas and the application of these competencies in practice.

The model presented in Figure 5 incorporates the core multicultural counselling competency domains into the overall counselling process, using the working alliance model as the organizational construct. The working alliance forms the foundation for the counselling process and the means for translating cultural self-awareness and awareness of the client's culture into a process designed to facilitate movement from where the client is now to where the client would like to be, emphasizing the client-driven nature of the process. The working alliance provides the mechanism for optimizing responsiveness to client needs within the context of their particular cultural experience. Focusing on the working alliance helps counsellors consider the unique needs of clients from culturally diverse backgrounds. It also helps counsellors bridge modalities of helping clients through the counselling process. The following discussion is intended to help counsellors understand the complexities of developing and maintaining an effective working alliance with clients.

Social justice has been incorporated as an additional component of the working alliance that emerged from and feeds back into the interaction between counsellor and client. Social justice activities that focus on empowerment, facilitate clients to advocate on their own behalf, or work with clients to effect change in contexts that affect their well-being are assumed to be part of the culture-infused counselling process. Running parallel to these are the efforts of the counsellor to directly influence organizations, community, and broader social, economic, and political systems.

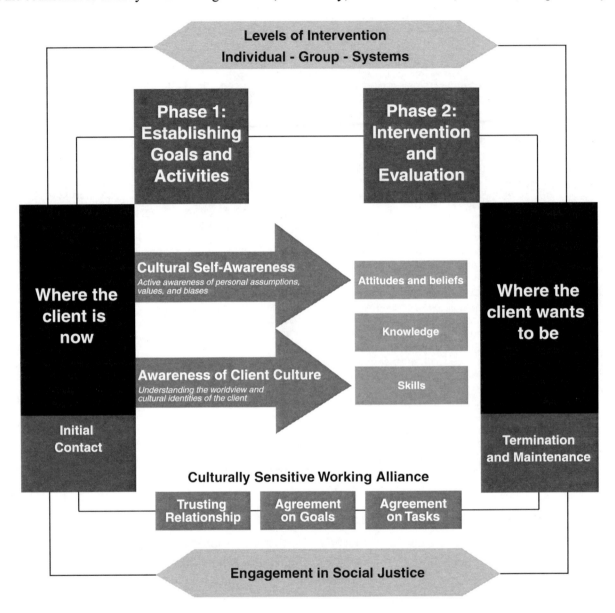

Figure 5. The working alliance as a foundation for a culture-infused counselling process.

This model for counselling practice will form the foundation for the next two chapters in which we begin to address the *how to* challenge noted above. In Chapter 4, we expand on the cultural self-awareness and awareness of client cultural identities components of the model. In Chapter 5, we turn our attention to the working alliance and to expanding on the key concepts involved in facilitating a culturally sensitive relationship and counselling process.

Chapter Summary

The purpose of this chapter was to introduce the culture-infused counselling competency framework as a means for counsellors to assess and build multicultural counselling competence. The framework builds on frameworks currently available in the literature to further refine the general and specific competencies essential for competent practice in all encounters between counsellor and client. It addresses weaknesses in early conceptual frameworks by introducing the working alliance as a pantheoretical umbrella designed to translate self-awareness and awareness of your clients into culturally sensitive practice. Competencies related to social justice are integrated throughout the competency framework, and those that extend beyond the defined work between counsellor and client are integrated into a fourth dimension of the working alliance construct.

Conclusion: Moving from Aspiration to Action

The original multicultural competencies were framed as recommendations and aspirational principles. The more recent APA (2003b) guidelines maintain the same aspiration focus through language that encourages psychologists to strive for self-awareness, knowledge of client culture, and culturally appropriate skill development. Although there are those who oppose strengthening the mandate of cultural sensitivity and social justice (Weinrach & Thomas, 2002, 2004), there is a stronger call in the current literature to integrate these foci into all aspects of professional practice (Arrendondo & Toporek, 2004; Fouad et al., 2006; Kaslow, 2004). According to Pedersen (2001), "the paradigm shift in counselling is changing the rules by which competent counsellors do counselling" (p. 4). Attending to culture is no longer an option; in fact, it is seen as essential component of what it means to practice counselling competently and ethically (Watson et al., 2006). We see these culture-infused counselling competencies as foundations for working with all clients.

At this point, you may feel overwhelmed by the breadth of attitude, knowledge, and skill that we are suggesting is required for culture-infused counselling competence. Pope-Davis, Coleman, Lui, & Toporek (2003) reminded us that "the path to attaining multicultural competence is difficult as it is a lifelong journey 'requiring' an open mind coupled with an adventuresome spirit" (p. xii). The focus of the next two chapters will be on enhancing your understanding of what it means to practice competent culture-infused counselling.

CHAPTER 4
SELF-AWARENESS AND AWARENESS OF CLIENT CULTURAL IDENTITIES

Sandra Collins and Nancy Arthur

Key Terms and Concepts

• Acculturation	• Cultural hypotheses	• Ethnocentrism
• Assimilation	• Cultural identity	• Internalized culture
• Bicultural or multicultural identities	• Cultural identity development	• Monoculturalism
• Cognitive complexity	• Cultural relativism	• Overgeneralization
• Cultural baggage	• Cultural schemata	• Privilege
• Cultural blindness	• Cultural sensitivity	• Power
• Cultural consciousness	• Cultural transference	• Stereotypes
• Cultural counter-transference	• Culture shock	• Unintentional oppression
• Cultural encapsulation	• Discrimination	• Worldview

Introduction

This chapter focuses on the conceptual and theoretical factors that support two of the core competency domains in the culture-infused counselling framework introduced in Chapter 3: (a) self-awareness of your own culture and (b) awareness of the client's cultural identities. We will highlight the concepts and principles that are the foundation of awareness of culture, with a view to encouraging self-exploration and motivating you to pursue ways to increase competence in these areas. Discussion of the final core competency domain, the culturally sensitive working alliance, is reserved for Chapter 5.

The focus in these chapters is on applied counselling / clinical practice. Our aim is to expand on the key concepts that were identified in the culture-infused counselling framework as a means of forming a foundation for what it means to be both self-aware and aware of culture as it relates to our direct work with clients. We hope that by the end of this chapter you will have developed a sense of what it really means to apply these principles in practice, explored your own cultural identities in more depth, and identified areas where you will pay more attention to the cultural contexts and experiences of the clients that you work with.

It is our assertion that the foundational competencies of awareness of self and others are necessary, although not sufficient, for all roles that counsellors and psychologists may engage in. It is impossible to be an effective teacher, consultant, advocate, and so on if you are not aware of your own cultural beliefs, values, and biases and are unable to assess and understand the worldviews of the organizations, communities, or other systems you are working with (Lee & Hipolito-Delgado, 2007). We will pick up this theme in Chapter 6, where we expand our focus beyond applied practice with individual and groups to social justice interventions aimed at changing conditions that often precipitate client distress.

Cultural Self-Awareness and Awareness of Client Culture

The main goal of the culture-infused counselling competency of self-awareness is to increase counsellors' **cultural sensitivity.** This is defined as *"the ability of counsellors to acquire, develop, and actively use an accurate cultural perceptual schemata in the course of multicultural counseling"* (Ridley, Mendoza, Kanitz, Angermeier, & Zenk, 1994, p. 36). Counsellors need to develop capacity for monitoring their personal reactions and for understanding how their socialization may influence their reactions to clients in potentially detrimental ways. The multicultural counselling competencies of self-awareness and awareness of client culture have been clustered in this chapter because they often operate in concert, with one influencing the other. When individuals are faced with cultural contrasts, they begin to appreciate the uniqueness of their personal culture. Conversely, increased self-awareness about culture fosters attunement to differences in client cultural experiences and identities. To be truly culturally sensitive, counsellors need to both acknowledge the importance of and take active steps to acquire cultural knowledge about themselves and others.

The rationale for multicultural counselling presented in Chapter 2 outlines many of the demographic changes that have occurred within Canada and that will continue to diversify our population in the future. The ethical guidelines of the Canadian Counselling Association (2007) and Canadian Psychological Association (2000) emphasize the importance of working with clients in a non-discriminatory manner. This requires counsellors to be aware of political, economic, historical, social, and psychological influences on the development of specific cultural groups within society. Such awareness prepares counsellors with a conceptual framework within which to understand the key influences on people's worldview, including cultural norms, values, perceived problems, and preferred interventions (Arthur & Stewart, 2001). Increased awareness also helps counsellors to appreciate the diversity of experiences within groups as a result of acculturation, cultural identity development, or the influence of multiple non-dominant identities (Berry, 2005; Collins, in press; D'Andrea & Heckman, 2008). These influences are important considerations in understanding the forces that shape the worldviews of people from non-dominant groups. When counsellors understand client worldviews, they have a solid basis from which to establish a culturally sensitive working alliance with clients, to better understand the nature of clients' counselling issues, and to design counselling interventions that are meaningful for clients (Lewis, 2006).

The challenge before each of us is to gain self-awareness and come to know others in a way that bypasses cultural barriers and stereotypes and allows us to connect in a real and meaningful way with each other. Senge (1990) described a greeting common among certain South African tribes. The expression *sawu bono* literally means *I see you.* A common response to this greeting is *sikhona* or *I am here.* The *I see you – you are there* exchange has important meaning for us as we strive for multicultural sensitivity and awareness. Many individuals in our society live with a continual sense of invisibility, stemming primarily from the experience of not being fully and openly seen for who they really are. In keeping with the belief system of these tribe members, by actually seeing others, we validate the reality of their experience and acknowledge their existence. Similarly, we might add to the greeting *I see me – I am here* to symbolize the importance of self-awareness to the active engagement and genuine presence of the counsellor in each encounter with clients. The challenge of this chapter is to open your eyes and really see yourself and your clients.

| **Domain I: Cultural Self-Awareness** |
| *Active awareness of personal assumptions, values, and biases.* |
| *Core Competency 1:* Demonstrate awareness of your own cultural identities. |
| *Core Competency 2:* Demonstrate awareness of differences between your own cultural identities and those of individuals from other dominant or non-dominant groups. |
| *Core Competency 3:* Demonstrate awareness of the impact of culture on the theory and practice of counselling/psychology. |
| *Core Competency 4:* Demonstrate awareness of the personal and professional impact of the discrepancy between dominant and non-dominant cultural groups in North America. |
| *Core Competency 5:* Demonstrate awareness of your level of multicultural competence. |
| **Domain II: Awareness of Client Cultural Identities** |
| *Understanding the worldview of the client.* |
| *Core Competency 1:* Demonstrate awareness of the cultural identities of your clients. |
| *Core Competency 2:* Demonstrate awareness of the relationship of personal culture to health and well-being. |
| *Core Competency 3:* Demonstrate awareness of the socio-political influences that impinge on the lives of non-dominant populations. |

Figure 1. Domains I and II of the culture-infused counselling competencies framework.

As you read this chapter, please use the *Culture-Infused Counselling Competency Framework* (see Chapter 3, Figure 4) as a reference point to link the concepts discussed to the essential attitudes and beliefs, knowledge, and skills outlined in the competency matrix. In this way, you will increase the meaningfulness of the constructs and identify areas in which your own level of culture-infused counselling competence may be strengthened. Figure 1 summarizes the core competencies related to self-awareness and awareness of client culture. You will notice that these core competencies share commonalities across the domains. The concepts explored in this chapter are intended to provide you with a foundation for building competence in each domain.

Cultural Identity

Our definition of culture and multiculturalism in Chapter 1 points to the kinds of factors that may influence one's sense of cultural identity. Various authors conceptualize personal and cultural identity differently. Several models of identity have been proposed in the multicultural literature (Arredondo & Glauner, 1992; Ho, 1995; Ivey, D'Andrea, Bradford Ivey, & Simek-Morgan, 2002; James, 1996; Sue & Sue, 2008). We have drawn from a number of these models to be inclusive of the range of factors that must be taken into account in understanding **cultural identity** (see Figure 2).

1. *Cultural factors* represent the group affiliations held by individuals, based on age, gender, culture, ethnicity, physical and mental ability, sexual orientation, and social class (Israel, 2006). The focus at this level is on between-group or intercultural differences (Ho, 1995). In both Canada and the United States, these factors are often identified for protection under various forms of equity and diversity legislation. Arredondo and Glauner (1992) asserted that it is these dimensions that are most likely to lead to stereotypes and discrimination.

2. *Personal identity factors* include idiosyncratic experiences, genetic make-up, developmental paths, socialization, and so on (Dana, 1998). We include in this dimension such factors as education, marital status, work experience, and other factors that are unique to the particular individual. At this level, attention is focused on within-group or intracultural differences (Ho, 1995).

3. *Contextual factors* refer to the historical, social, political, environmental, or economic context in which a particular individual lives. These broader factors can have an impact on personal experiences, worldview, values, and so on.

4. *Universal factors* include those elements of experience that are common to all and, to some degree, set human beings apart from other forms of life: self-awareness, ability to use symbols, common life experiences, and psychological and biological similarities (Sue, 2001). "All individuals are, in some respects, like all other individuals" (Sue, p. 793).

5. *Ideological factors* represent the assumptions and biases inherent in the dominant culture that lead to various forms of individual and group oppression: sexism, racism, heterosexism, and so on. The factors have not been included in other models of identity or have been subsumed under the contextual factors category (Arredondo & Glauner, 1992). The risks in doing so are that they are less prominent and their impact on the identities of members of non-dominant groups may be inadvertently minimized.

Sue (2001) pointed out that the primary focus of psychology has been on personal identity factors and universal factors. In the development of theoretical models and counselling processes, the cultural and contextual factors have virtually been ignored. With the emergence of multicultural counselling as the fourth force in psychology (Pedersen, 2001), the cultural and contextual factors have been given increased emphasis. There has been significant growth in research and theory in multicultural counselling that addresses the common concerns of individuals from non-dominant groups and of culture-specific resources. Ideological factors are also more strongly emphasized. As noted in Chapter 3, however, the traditional models of multicultural counselling have tended to focus predominantly on racism to the exclusion of sexism, ableism, heterosexism, elitism, and other expressions of social or institutional oppression. Similarly, early feminist writing was criticized for its emphasis on sexism to the exclusion of racism and other factors (Collins, in press). The more the profession argues over which of these factors is more important, the less likely it is that mainstream psychology will fully integrate attention to them into everyday practice (Williams & Barber, 2004). Fortunately, some of the core literature that has emerged in the last several decades calls for a more inclusive and collaborative approach to addressing systemic oppression of all individuals and groups. The influence of organizational, social, political, economic, and other broad systemic factors in Canada will be explored in this chapter as we examine issues of cultural oppression. Chapter 6 will address our responsibility as counsellors to directly influence these broader systems.

Figure 2 provides a visual representation of the kinds of cultural identity factors that may impact your own sense of personal and cultural identity as well as that of your clients. The image of the kaleidoscope was introduced by Collins (in press) to capture the fluid, dynamic, and interactive nature of the various factors. According to Merriam Webster's Online Dictionary (2008, ¶4), a kaleidoscope is defined as: "an instrument containing loose bits of colored material…between two flat plates and two plane mirrors so placed that changes of position of the bits of materials are reflected in an endless variety of patterns." Each individual reflects a unique combination of coloured glass as a result of heritage, social context, and life experience.

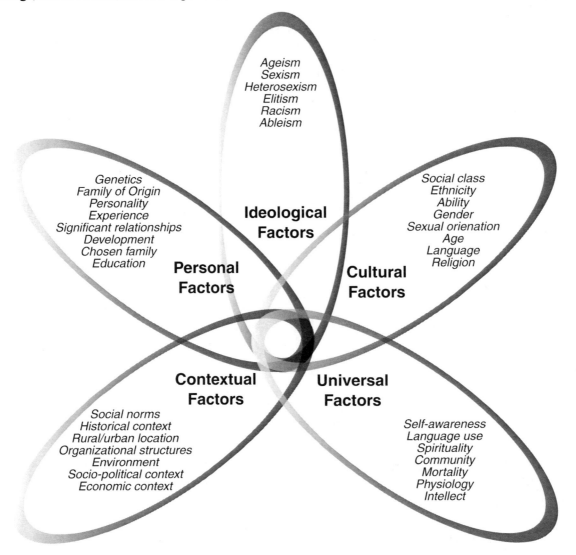

Figure 2. Factors influencing cultural identity.

Cultural identity may be expressed differently by individuals from similar groups because of the interaction with other identity factors. *Each individual internalizes various elements of culture from the five factors in the table to form their own unique kaleidoscope of cultural identities,* which is often referred to as **internalized culture** (Ho, 1995). It is the internalized culture of the individual that becomes significant at the psychological level. This internalized culture, however, does not reflect a static identity state. As individuals interact with the world around them, their values, perspectives, and behaviours evolve. They are active participants in the shaping of personal and collective culture, rather than passive products of external enculturation.

Culture is not defined only by the individual, however; it is internalized by individuals, but it evolves through the collective experience of a particular group (Gerstein, Rountree, and Orgonez, 2007). Cultures also change as they come into contact with one another. For the individual, each of these encounters can result in either subtle or dramatic repositioning of the coloured beads in the kaleidoscope, creating a new and unique expression of the individuals' cultural identities. The same image of a kaleidoscope is used by Gerstein and colleagues to refer to the macro level analysis of broad social patterns that emerge and evolve as cultures interact. The complexity of internalized culture highlights the importance of paying attention to the intersection of cultural dimensions such as ethnicity and gender, or ability and sexual orientation, to incorporate multiple layers of culture into our understanding of clients' worldviews (Ludvig, 2006; Pope-Davis & Coleman, 2001; Valentine, 2007). We will more fully address the complexity of working with clients with multiple non-dominant identities in Chapter 10.

While we will focus throughout this text on various dimensions of cultural identity, it is important to remember that within-group differences may sometimes be as significant as between-group differences (Fowers & Davidov, 2006). Counsellors must avoid treating cultural groups as homogenous without considering the individual perspectives of clients (Gerstein et al., 2007; Popadiuk & Arthur, 2004). Each client is unique and the salience of cultural identity factors must be constantly assessed. How individuals perceive and define themselves is dependent on the interpersonal and systemic factors present at a particular time and in a particular context. Taking all of these components of personal identity into account clearly supports the assertion that all interactions between counselling and client are multicultural.

> Culture is the context in which all behaviors are learned and displayed. Imagine yourself surrounded by thousands of people whom you have met, learned from, and come to appreciate in your lifetime. Each of these 'culture teachers' has taught you something that you have incorporated into your identity. You do not have just one cultural identity; rather there are thousands of different potentially salient identities in each of us. Imagine the thousands of culture teachers sitting in your seat with you, talking with you and talking among themselves about you as you interact actively or listen passively. These voices comprise the 'hidden messages' in culture-centred counseling. (Pedersen, 2001, p. 21)

Overgeneralization and Stereotyping

The concept of internalized culture is critical to avoiding the traps of overgeneralization or stereotyping. Ho (1995) defined **overgeneralizations** as *assigning particular characteristics inappropriately to a group based on the observations of a few individuals.* **Stereotyping** carries the assertion one step further *to characterize a whole group of people rigidly based only on group membership* (Ho). Often the individuals holding a particular stereotype actively resist disconfirming information and hold rigidly to the *correctness* of their beliefs (James, 1996). In either of these cases, the worldview and internalized culture of the individual is being defined externally and without active engagement in cultural exploration with that individual. Both the counsellor and the client may fall prey to these tendencies and may make assumptions based on cultural group membership that restrict understanding and appreciation of the uniqueness of the other person.

The quest to increase cultural awareness in multicultural counselling has to be tempered with a cautionary note. Counsellors have a responsibility to gain general cultural knowledge along with culture-specific information about the subgroups represented in their clientele. This background knowledge is important for establishing rapport with clients, helping clients feel more confident about your abilities, and bridging cultural differences. At the same time, counsellors need to hold tentatively to cultural knowledge to avoid stereotypic thinking (Gerstein et al., 2007). Cultural knowledge is best used in the form of **cultural hypotheses** that provide counsellors with *working understandings of client cultures as a starting point from which to assess and gain understanding about the experiences of individual clients.* It is recommended that counsellors hold cultural knowledge *loosely* while getting to know their clients and assessing the unique worldview of each one.

Internalization of Negative or Stereotypic Images

For members of non-dominant groups, there is a risk that the negative cultural stereotypes they are exposed to may be integrated into their own personal cultural identities. This phenomena finds expression in the terms internalized racism, internalized homophobia, and so on. In the absence of evidence to the contrary, individuals begin to define themselves based on their beliefs about how others perceive them, which derive in part from how they see their cultural groups defined by the dominant culture (Alvarez & Helms, 2001). Internalization of these negative messages can result in loss of self-esteem and damages to self-concept (McDougall &Arthur, 2001; Szymanski, 2005; Szymanski & Gupta, 2009). Internalization of these negative or stereotypic images impedes healthy identity development (Alvarez & Helms; Whitcomb & Loewy, 2006). It is important to actively listen for signs of internalized oppression, because these may not be operating consciously and they may affect the messages that clients send about desired changes and change processes. The inclusion of ideological factors in our model of cultural identities is intended to bring these issues to the forefront for both counsellors and clients. These issues are more fully explored in some of the chapters on particular non-dominant populations later in the book.

I am deeply saddened by the way that I see internalized homophobia play out in the lesbian community on a day-to-day basis. What are most troublesome, I think, are the opportunities that are missed for genuine connection with other people and for experiencing acceptance in work, school, and social situations. I often hear women describe their surprise at the positive reactions they receive from friends or colleagues when they open up about their sexual orientation or take the risk to bring their partner to a social function. Many of them realize that it was their own fear and internalized stigma that formed the largest barrier and carries over from situations of genuine risk to a more generalized approach to the world.

A friend of mine died several years ago after a battle with cancer. For the first time, in her obituary, she fully acknowledged her lesbian partnership of 15 years. She lost the opportunity to experience the acceptance and support of many of her colleagues, friends, and acquaintances, who likely knew that she was gay but waited for her to speak the words herself. She lost that opportunity because she had come to believe herself what others had told her throughout her life – that she was not normal and that her life path was not socially acceptable.

While I live my life openly as a lesbian, I am very aware that I also carry with me the negative connotations associated with my identity. Choosing not to listen to those internalized messages is a daily exercise that will likely continue throughout my life.

Personal reflection – Sandra Collins

Worldview

Personal, cultural, contextual, universal, and ideological factors merge to create each individual's **worldview** – the *looking glass through which one views the world* (Shebib, 2003). A worldview is essentially *a set of assumptions, values, and beliefs about how human beings and the world in which we live function that directly affect our responses to the world around us* (Kohl, 2006). Worldview is an expression of each individual's cultural identities. Worldviews serve an adaptive function by providing human beings with a conceptual framework with which to approach life. However, they may also create biases in perception and interpretation that limit the ability of individuals or groups to fully appreciate alternative perspectives (Eidelson & Eidelson, 2003). Components of worldviews are often shared within groups because of their basis in "culturally determined common experiences and shared frames of reference"(Eidelson & Eidelson, p. 183). Cultural and contextual influences on worldview often do not operate on a conscious level, which accounts for the fact that worldviews often are presumed as truths and are rarely the focus of personal or collective evaluation.

Where worldviews differ between the counsellor and the client, interactions are ripe for misunderstanding and miscommunication. For example, the collective values espoused in many Aboriginal cultures in Canada lead to the sharing of child-rearing by many adults who are significant in the lives of children. A traditional notion of parents and family may lead to confusion about who is responsible for the child and lead to accusations of child neglect. In contrast, insular families may resent involvement by others in matters pertaining to child-rearing, which leaves many Canadian children isolated and with insufficient support by other adult caregivers. The axiom *it takes a whole village to raise a child* and many other common cultural assertions need to be deconstructed to consider the underlying values and assumptions about who constitutes a family and who is responsible for children in Canadian society.

Components of Worldview	TRADITIONAL WESTERN-EUROPEAN PERSPECTIVE		
SOCIETY *Cultural Ideologies – Driven by Power*	Culture is an *ideology*, a social construction enforced through *power* (traced to both moral and materialistic roots; e.g., imperialistic and colonial endeavours). Specifically, *biological* (genetic deficiency model) and *philosophical* (Western Christianity) justifications led to oppressive political structures and clearly defined cultural boundaries. Cultural diversity became an invisible and silenced component of society (monocultural policies/practices).		
SCIENCE *Post-Positivism*	**Epistemology** *Objectivity* is important; researchers manipulate and observe in dispassionate, objective manner.	**Ontology** *One reality*; knowable within range of probability.	**Methodology** *Quantitative* (primarily); interventionist, decontextualized.
ETHICAL PRINCIPLES *Utilitarianism*	*Utilitarian principle* of the greatest good for the greatest number and optimum return on investment (human and financial) takes precedence over the *deontological* ethical principle of respect for the inherent value of human beings.		
ORGANIZED PSYCHOLOGY **Nature of Knowing** *Scientific - Absolutist, Value-Free*	Relies on knowledge attained through the traditional s*cientific method* – objectivity, empiricism, decontextualized, rational, and linear – plus the *absolutist* belief in the universality of psychological laws and theories. Methodology designed to produce uncontaminated factual knowledge on the nature of human behaviour. Science is *value-free* and assumes a knowable and singular reality.		
Human Nature *Reductionist, Dualistic, Intrapersonal*	Psychologists are *reductionists* and view the individual as divided into parts. The body and brain are separate and qualitatively different (*dualism*). "Higher" intellectual processes direct affect and action (*rational supremacy*). The study of individuals centres on the *intrapersonal* and the *intrapsychic*.		
Definitions of 'Normalcy' *Individualism, Action Orientation*	Western-European values, such as *individualism* and *action-orientation*, are institutionalized and viewed as the truth and the criteria from which others are judged (*one size fits all* perspective). Social constructs like racism and sexism reflect this assumed supremacy and are legitimized and institutionalized.		
Relationships Among People *Competitive, Power*	*Competitive* – commitment to groups is limited by individual interests. White, male-dominated, heterosexual relationships reflect positions of *power*. Self-referenced criteria are used to judge others and relationships are based on utilitarian principles.		
Relationship to Nature *Mastery*	The natural world is viewed as inferior and distinctly different from humankind. It is a commodity to be *mastered* – dominated, conquered, and controlled.		
Personality Development **Universalism, Privilege**	Personality develops according to common universal principles – inherent biological factors, the unconscious, socialization, and experience. Physical appearance and historical and familial lineage may afford a privileged position – the male, White, heterosexual majority often has higher education and earning power and more career choices. Race is misconstrued as a biological fact rather than a social construction.		
Health and Well-Being **Autonomy, Future-Focused, Independence**	Healthy functioning is linked to individualism, independence, and separation from the group. Healthy individuals strive for autonomy, potentiality, intellectual endeavours, and materialistic superiority. Healthy functioning reflects successful adaptation, conformity, and coping. Time orientation is future-focused.		

Figure 3. Dimensions of Western worldview, contributed by Barbara Butchart.

Components of Worldview	TRADITIONAL WESTERN-EUROPEAN PERSPECTIVE
Conceptualizations of Problems *Intrapsychic, Deficit/Dysfunction*	Individual problems derive from *intrapsychic processes* – unconscious conflict (psychodynamic perspective – Freud, Jung) or ineffective learned beliefs, emotions, and behaviours (cognitive-behavioural perspective – Adler, Ellis, Beck). Problems are *deficits/dysfunctions* to be controlled/eliminated. Status differences between individuals are maintained by locating problems within the person.
View of Causation *Determinism, Linear*	*Determinism* – there are direct *linear* causes and consequences for all events. The explanations for psychological problems rest with the individual's inability to cope, learn, or adapt (tendency to blame the victim).
Goal of Counselling *Individual, Prescriptive*	Focus is *individual* – insight, self-awareness, healthy functioning, ability to cope – and *prescriptive* – adaptation to values of society. Tendency is to trivialize cultural issues – minimize differences, assume similarities, and pathologize clients of diverse origins, thereby supporting the status quo.
Client-Counsellor Relationship *Hierarchical, Expert*	Control of knowledge rests with the dominant White community and the counsellor is viewed as the *expert*. Sessions are counsellor-centred and *hierarchical* in nature (power differentials). Counsellors are often either *colour blind* or *colour conscious*.
Nature of Change Process *Conformity, Mastery, Control*	*Action orientation, pragmatic* – The Protestant work ethic places emphasis on doing – hard work is the key to success. Individuals can control their environment (*internal locus of control*) and have primary responsibility for change (*internal locus of responsibility*). Interventions are diagnostic in nature, disorder specific, ahistorical, problem-focused, emphasize linear causality, foster coping, and function to maintain the status quo.

Figure 3. Dimensions of Western worldview (continued).

In the same way, current psychological theories need to be carefully examined because many are derived from monocultural, culturally encapsulated, and potentially oppressive cultural assumptions (Chae, Foley, & Chae, 2006; Kohl, 2006). Broad generalizations drawn from the classical research on male, middle-class college students of European descent may not apply well to clients from culturally diverse backgrounds. Figure 3 illustrates some of the components of the Western-European worldview as it applies to traditional psychological practice. We drew on these sources: Collins (1998), Cottone (1991), Enns (1993), Ho (1995), Katz (1985), Mertens (1998), Murphy and Davidshofer (2001), Palmer (1996), Peavy (1993), Pedersen (1995a), Pettifor (2001a), Sue and Sue (2008), and Tatar and Bekerman (2002). The perspectives presented are broad generalizations designed to be illustrative rather than definitive. We also recognize that through the impact of systems, feminist, and multicultural approaches, the assumptions underlying psychological practice are changing. Nonetheless, many of these cultural assumptions continue to pervade the practice of psychology in both subtle and not so subtle ways. The beliefs and assumptions underlying the Western-European perspective may differ dramatically from those of non-dominant cultural groups who form a significant portion of our counselling clientele. Gerstein and colleagues (2007) warned that even current multicultural models may fail to fully respect the cultural norms of diverse populations by continuing to use concepts that are tied to a Western cultural lens.

Ivey and colleagues (2002) discussed the link between worldview and counselling theories. Traditionally, most counselling theories have been based on the individualistic perspective represented by Figure 3 (psychodynamic, existential-humanistic, and cognitive-behavioural). In recent years, proponents of these models have begun to incorporate feedback from feminist and multicultural theorists and to modify the assumptions and tenets of the models to reflect an emphasis on larger social systems. In addition, distinct feminist and multicultural theories have emerged. More recently, there has been an attempt to bridge both feminist and multicultural perspectives and to see them more fully integrated into mainstream psychology (Reynolds & Constantine, 2004; Williams & Barber, 2004). Attention to culture makes it impossible to support a universal approach to counselling (Moodley, 2007). What is required is continued critical analysis and deconstruction of theory (Fowers & Davidov,

2006), which along with flexibility, eclecticism, and competence with multiple theoretical perspectives, will position the counsellor to be optimally responsive to the needs of all clients (Corey, 1996; Ivey et al.; Sue, Ivey, & Pedersen, 1996). Unexamined worldview differences are likely to lead to victim-blaming, mislabelling and misdiagnosis, stereotyping, and other forms of inappropriate and potentially harmful practices on the part of well-intentioned but culturally incompetent counsellors (Sue & Sue, 2008).

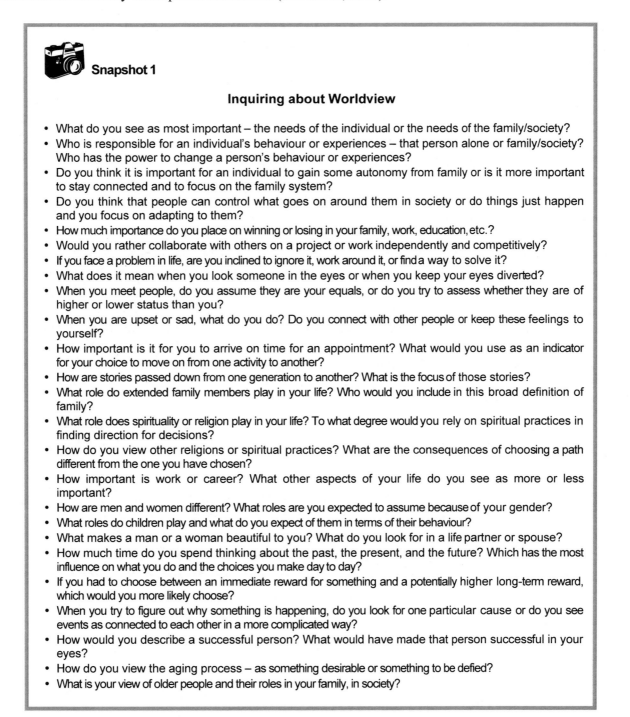

Snapshot 1

Inquiring about Worldview

- What do you see as most important – the needs of the individual or the needs of the family/society?
- Who is responsible for an individual's behaviour or experiences – that person alone or family/society? Who has the power to change a person's behaviour or experiences?
- Do you think it is important for an individual to gain some autonomy from family or is it more important to stay connected and to focus on the family system?
- Do you think that people can control what goes on around them in society or do things just happen and you focus on adapting to them?
- How much importance do you place on winning or losing in your family, work, education, etc.?
- Would you rather collaborate with others on a project or work independently and competitively?
- If you face a problem in life, are you inclined to ignore it, work around it, or find a way to solve it?
- What does it mean when you look someone in the eyes or when you keep your eyes diverted?
- When you meet people, do you assume they are your equals, or do you try to assess whether they are of higher or lower status than you?
- When you are upset or sad, what do you do? Do you connect with other people or keep these feelings to yourself?
- How important is it for you to arrive on time for an appointment? What would you use as an indicator for your choice to move on from one activity to another?
- How are stories passed down from one generation to another? What is the focus of those stories?
- What role do extended family members play in your life? Who would you include in this broad definition of family?
- What role does spirituality or religion play in your life? To what degree would you rely on spiritual practices in finding direction for decisions?
- How do you view other religions or spiritual practices? What are the consequences of choosing a path different from the one you have chosen?
- How important is work or career? What other aspects of your life do you see as more or less important?
- How are men and women different? What roles are you expected to assume because of your gender?
- What roles do children play and what do you expect of them in terms of their behaviour?
- What makes a man or a woman beautiful to you? What do you look for in a life partner or spouse?
- How much time do you spend thinking about the past, the present, and the future? Which has the most influence on what you do and the choices you make day to day?
- If you had to choose between an immediate reward for something and a potentially higher long-term reward, which would you more likely choose?
- When you try to figure out why something is happening, do you look for one particular cause or do you see events as connected to each other in a more complicated way?
- How would you describe a successful person? What would have made that person successful in your eyes?
- How do you view the aging process – as something desirable or something to be defied?
- What is your view of older people and their roles in your family, in society?

The tasks of counsellors are to identify clearly their own worldview and to carefully assess the worldviews of clients. The interaction of those worldviews will impact the quality, efficacy, and outcomes of the counselling relationship. It is important to remember that we are defining culture broadly and that gender, ability, sexual orientation, and so on may have as significant an effect on worldview as ethnicity. Lewis (2006) presented a model for working with persons with disabilities that centralized both self-awareness and awareness of client worldview. Counsellors need to be knowledgeable about the backgrounds of the main client groups they work with so that they have a general understanding of cultural influences. They must also be skilled in assessing the culture-specific behaviours of their clientele in order to gain insight and understanding of clients' unique worldviews. Snapshot 1 provides a list of questions that counsellors may consider in exploring the worldview of their clients.

Counsellor – Client Matching

Literature on the impact of matching or mismatching client and counsellor on cultural variables such as ethnicity and gender has suggested that some clients prefer counsellors who hold similar worldviews and values and that a culturally similar counsellor is anticipated to have more in common in these areas (Pope-Davis et al., 2002). There is also evidence that client-counsellor ethnic similarity, particularly combined with language pairing, leads to increased service usage and decreased attrition (D'Andrea & Heckman, 2008). The matching literature is limited, however, by the number of studies that focus on clinical outcomes, the samples selected, potential confounding variables, and the lack of attention to client variables (D'Andrea & Heckman; Pope-Davis et al.). Pope-Davis and colleagues noted a relationship between the salience of culture to the presenting problem and preference for counsellor-client cultural similarity. For clients who did not see culture as significant to their specific counselling issues, counsellor matching was less important. In addition, levels of acculturation and cultural identity development have an impact on preference for counsellor matching, suggesting that similarity in worldview rather than specific group identity is the key issue (Merali, 1999). Atkinson (2004) described the shifts in preference for cultural group versus worldview similarity according to stage of cultural identity development (see Figure 4 later in the chapter for more details). In many cases, matching counsellors with clients according to shared gender, ethnicity, sexual orientation, and other cultural factors is simply unrealistic, making a focus on understanding worldview and establishing points of commonality and difference essential. Fischer, Jerome, and Atkinson (1998), in their review of the literature on common factors in counselling efficacy, pointed to a match in worldview rather than a match in specific cultural group characteristics as the essential factor. It is only possible, however, to find commonalities across worldview when worldviews are explicitly examined as part of the counselling process.

Self-Awareness as the Starting Point

Counsellors need to gain understanding about clients' worldviews and the ways that those worldviews differ among clients. However, counsellors must also gain appreciation for how the worldviews of clients are similar to or different from their personal worldview. Counsellors must explore the cultural contexts that influence their own attitudes, beliefs, and behaviour (Arthur & Stewart, 2001; Hays, 2001). True cultural sensitivity requires counsellors to move from a position that assumes a singular, monocultural perspective to one that respectfully incorporates multiple belief systems (Chae et al., 2006; Williams, 2003). The multicultural competency of self-awareness challenges counsellors to consider who they are as cultural beings and how their socialization shapes their beliefs about themselves, their clients, and the world around them (Arthur & Stewart; Sue, 2006).

> ...the greater the cultural difference between counselor and counselee, the more critical multicultural awareness would be. More fundamentally, without multicultural awareness, self-understanding would be limited and incomplete, let alone other-understanding. This is why multicultural awareness figures prominently in any counseling process – more so than counselors have hitherto envisioned. (Ho, 1995, p. 21)

Ethnocentric monoculturalism

Self-awareness is the foundation of competency in multicultural counselling. It is the cornerstone from which counsellors gain an appreciation of the ways that cultural values and beliefs influence ways of operating in professional relationships. The importance of counsellor self-awareness is related to **cultural encapsulation.** This refers to *people's tendency to see the world through one set of assumptions based upon their own self-referenced experience* (Wrenn, 1962). Culturally encapsulated counsellors judge clients on the basis of prior experience with people who remind them of the client, view client issues through their own versus the client's definition of the situation, and impose interventions that are based upon the counsellor's notions about what is helpful. Even counsellors with the best of intentions introduce cultural bias into the counselling process in ways that are inadvertently harmful and, in so doing, contribute to the oppression of clients (Fowers & Davidov, 2006). This perspective can be contrasted with that of **cultural relativism**, in which *each culture is viewed as unique and inherently valuable. Each must be understood on its own without reference to another cultural framework.* This is a challenge for counsellors to step outside of their own conceptual lens to view client culture in a non-evaluative manner.

Ask most Canadians to describe the Canadian culture and they will likely find themselves at a loss for words. Some will fall back on the multicultural nature of Canada and assert that the cultural mosaic is what defines Canadian identity and culture. However, the experience of non-dominant groups within that cultural mosaic clearly attests to the fact that, however unconscious to most, the dominant culture in Canada includes very strong values, assumptions, or norms, as well as social, political, and economic structures and practices. James (1996) reminded us that this lack of collective awareness of dominant Canadian culture leads many to remain insensitive to the range of non-dominant cultures in our midst. "Despite the philosophy of multiculturalism, however, the English, and to a lesser extent the French, have continued to play a central role in defining Canadian society and culture" (James, p. 18).

Ethnocentrism is the *belief, conscious or unconscious, that one's own cultural experience, values, and assumptions are normal or foundational and that what is different is defined in relation to that self-referenced worldview.* Ethnocentric individuals are *culture-bound* and assume that all others share a similar set of assumptions, values, and beliefs. Taken a step further, culture-bound individuals assume that anything different is of less value (Eidelson & Eidelson, 2003; James, 1996; Shebib, 2003). Ethnocentrism forms the basis for the various *isms* – racism, heterosexism, sexism, and so on. In each case, the *other* is defined as *lesser than* in some way. The dynamics of **ethnocentric monoculturalism** (Fowers & Davidov, 2006; Sue, 2001, 2002) provide insight into the ways that counsellors inadvertently contribute to oppression through counselling:

1. *There is a strong belief in the superiority of one group's cultural heritage over the heritage of others.* In Canada, the dominant White, Anglo-Saxon, heterosexual population overtly or covertly functions *as if* their norms and values are more *right* than those of members of non-dominant groups. Because *White heterosexual* culture is largely unexamined and these assumptions are not explicitly stated, the belief in cultural superiority extends to members of the counselling profession whose training in predominantly Western paradigms is assumed to be superior.

2. *The counterpart to beliefs about cultural superiority is the inherent belief, held either consciously or unconsciously, about the inferiority of all other groups' cultural heritage.* This extends to their customs, values, traditions, and languages. Descriptions used to characterize people and practices from non-dominant cultures are filled with general pejorative perceptions such as *less developed.* Individual clients may be described as *pathological* or with labels that brand the person and take the focus off specific behaviours or systemic factors that impact well-being. Culture centre health practices may also be criticized or discounted.

3. *While most groups are prone to feeling a sense of allegiance to their cultural heritage, some groups hold more power to impose their values on other less powerful groups.* One of the defining features of ethnocentric monoculturalism is the unequal status and imposition of power in relationships between cultural groups. The group in power acts as though it is the only group that holds valid expertise and upholds regulatory and protective functions to maintain social power.

4. *The professionals who deliver counselling services are products of their cultural socialization.* Without deliberate efforts to gain self-awareness, we operate with the *myth of universality* – that everyone shares the same view of the world. This assumption needs to be challenged in multicultural counselling lest we perpetuate inequitable professional services.

5. *Ethnocentric values and beliefs are held by individuals and are also expressed in the organizational structures and institutional policies of societies.* Many practices are never reviewed because *this is the way*

we have always done things here. However, practices in organizations are determined by cultural beliefs that need to be exposed for their potential to continue the entrenchment in monocultural service provision. Otherwise, problems of access and service delivery continue to adversely impact members of non-dominant groups.

The helping professions have been criticized for their role in perpetuating the status quo, contributing to social oppression, and maintaining social power (Smith, 2008; Vera & Speight, 2003). There are growing concerns about the cultural competence of practitioners, evidence of intentional and unintentional oppression, and examples of failures to address structural inequalities in the delivery of professional services (Sue, 2002). Overcoming ethnocentric monoculturalism has been named as one of the main barriers to multicultural competence (Sue) and must be attended to at individual, organizational, and societal levels. According to Fowers and Davidov (2006, ¶3), the multicultural counselling movement is founded on the ethical premise that "a monocultural psychology is not simply less accurate or generalizable, but positively distortive and oppressive."

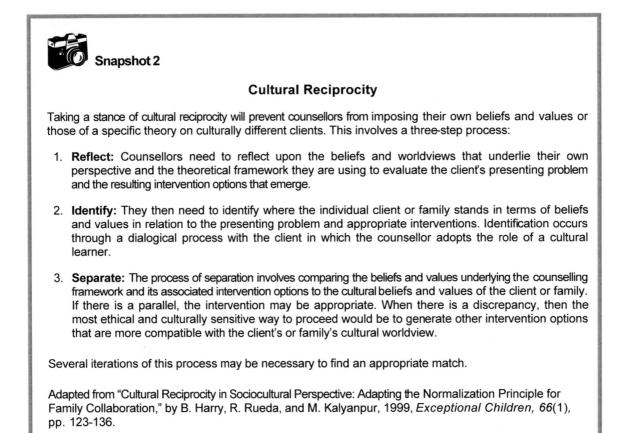

Snapshot 2

Cultural Reciprocity

Taking a stance of cultural reciprocity will prevent counsellors from imposing their own beliefs and values or those of a specific theory on culturally different clients. This involves a three-step process:

1. **Reflect:** Counsellors need to reflect upon the beliefs and worldviews that underlie their own perspective and the theoretical framework they are using to evaluate the client's presenting problem and the resulting intervention options that emerge.

2. **Identify:** They then need to identify where the individual client or family stands in terms of beliefs and values in relation to the presenting problem and appropriate interventions. Identification occurs through a dialogical process with the client in which the counsellor adopts the role of a cultural learner.

3. **Separate:** The process of separation involves comparing the beliefs and values underlying the counselling framework and its associated intervention options to the cultural beliefs and values of the client or family. If there is a parallel, the intervention may be appropriate. When there is a discrepancy, then the most ethical and culturally sensitive way to proceed would be to generate other intervention options that are more compatible with the client's or family's cultural worldview.

Several iterations of this process may be necessary to find an appropriate match.

Adapted from "Cultural Reciprocity in Sociocultural Perspective: Adapting the Normalization Principle for Family Collaboration," by B. Harry, R. Rueda, and M. Kalyanpur, 1999, *Exceptional Children, 66*(1), pp. 123-136.

Models of Identity Development

The focus on worldviews tends to be predominantly on between-group differences, although it is recognized that personal, cultural, contextual, and universal factors combine in each individual in unique ways. Self-awareness and awareness of the culture and worldview of others is only possible, however, through examination of some of the key factors that impact within-group differences. Beyond culture-specific information, counsellors need to be aware of the psychological processes that impact clients from culturally diverse backgrounds and lead to individual differences in worldview. Two psychological processes have been identified as core elements in counsellors' knowledge: cultural identity development and acculturation. The following sections will explore cultural identity development processes for both non-dominant and dominant populations and the impact of acculturation on sense of cultural identity.

Non-Dominant Cultural Identity Development

Recognition of cultural and contextual influences on identity development has led to the emergence of a number of models of identity development that focus on the interaction between the individual and the socio-cultural environment. The initial focus was on models of racial identity development specific to particular ethnic populations in the United States, particularly Black (e.g., Cross, 1995; Helms, 1995), Asian (e.g., Atkinson, Morton, & Sue, 1993; Sue & Sue, 1971), and Latino/Hispanic (e.g., Casas & Pytluk, 1995; Ruiz, 1990) racial identity. For a review of various ethnic identity development models, you are referred to Helms (1990c) and Sue and Sue (2008). More recently, models of women's identity development (Collings & Romans, 1998; Jordan, 1997; Petersen, 2000), feminist identity (Brabeck & Brown, 1997; Worell & Remer, 2003); lesbian/gay identity development (Barret & Logan, 2002; Cass, 1996; Fassinger, 1991; McCarn & Fassinger, 1996) emerged in the literature. Others have attempted to develop models that are more widely applicable across ethnic groups (Helms & Cook, 1999; Sue et al., 1998; Sue & Sue, 2008) or across populations experiencing cultural oppression (Atkinson, 2004; Highlen et al., 1988).

In this section, we will explore some of the general issues related to cultural identity development for members of non-dominant populations. Authors writing on specific non-dominant populations in later sections of the text will address the concept of identity development as it relates to that particular group. Two of the commonly referenced models of cultural identity development are summarized in Figure 4. **Cultural identity development** may be defined as *a dimension of self-concept that combines both awareness of self as part of an identifiable group with value judgments and corresponding affect towards both one's own group and an outside referent group (typically non-dominant and dominant populations).*

The two models demonstrate a fair amount of overlap in concepts. Central to both models is the assertion that cultural oppression results in internalized racism and that the identity development process involves coming to a personal resolution of self-identity in the context of non-dominant status in society. The focus at each stage is on individuals' attitudes towards their own cultural group, the dominant culture, and other non-dominant cultural groups. While these models are presented as stages, we stress the fluidity of development and note that some may begin the process at different stages, merge components of various stages, or loop back to earlier stages. Individuals may also remain at a particular stage (Atkinson, 2004; Helms & Cook, 1999). Nonetheless, some general sense of progression is implied in each model and the potential for interpersonal and intrapersonal problems exists where progression towards the final stage of cultural awareness is not achieved (Atkinson & Thompson, 1992). However, this does not infer that all clients at earlier stages of identity development are experiencing dysfunction (McDougall & Arthur, 2001).

These models have also been criticized for categorizing people on the basis of a single cultural dimension, such as race. Many researchers have noted the fluidity of identity across relationships and situation, preferring to emphasize an individual's multiple identities (Bridges, Selvidge, & Matthews, 2003; Garrett & Barret, 2003). Conversely, there are multiple sources of identity influences that are often not taken into account in stage theories (Yi & Shorter-Gooden, 1999). It has also been suggested that continuing to emphasize race, as is done in racial identity models, inadvertently perpetuates racism in psychological theorizing through overly emphasizing intrapersonal dynamics without sufficiently considering the influences of interpersonal, international, and structural dynamics (Theron, 2002). A key criticism levied is that, without racist ideology, race would not be pursued as a category (Hopkins, Reicher, & Levine, 1997). Theories in psychology, including racial identity models, need further critique to consider how social processes and power relationships position the object of study and support some people in positions of privilege while marginalizing others. We encourage you to apply the basic principles of these identity development models without locking individuals into particular categories of cultural identity.

Helms and Cook (1999) People of Colour Racial Identity	Atkinson (2004) Minority Identity Development Model	Atkinson (2004) Implications for Client in Counselling
Conformity • White culture is idealized. • Cultural stereotypes are internalized. • Attempts are made to assimilate. • One's own culture is denigrated. • Socio-racial concerns are minimized.	**Conformity** • Appreciation for the dominant culture and preferences for its values and norms. • Depreciation of self and one's own group.	• Cultural identity not identified as an issue or actively resisted. • Problems perceived as related to personal identity. • Preference for counsellor from dominant population. • Desire to please/appease.
Dissonance • Lack of fit with the dominant culture is acknowledged, resulting in confusion and ambivalence. • Idealization of the dominant culture wanes.	**Dissonance** • Circumstances arise that reduce denial and allow positive valuing of one's own cultural group. • Characterized by conflict and split allegiance between one's own cultural group and the dominant culture.	• Issues of identity are central and emotionally impactful. • Problems are viewed as related to cultural identity. • Counsellor's knowledge of the non-dominant population is seen as important.
Immersion • Search for positive cultural identity. • Idealization of one's own culture and denigration of the dominant culture. • Sensitivity to racism and other forms of cultural oppression. **Emersion** • Celebration of identity with one's own cultural group. • Characterized by solidarity, pride, exuberance.	**Resistance and Immersion** • Dominant culture becomes target of deprecation and rejection, while non-dominant cultural norms and values are embraced. • Vacillation between empathy for other oppressed groups and culturocentrism.	• Personal problems perceived as rooted in socio-cultural oppression. • Less likely to seek counselling or have strong preference for culturally similar counsellor. • Counsellor may be viewed as symbol of the status quo. • Distrust and anger common.
Internalization • Positive self and group identity. • Combined with ability to interact effectively and critically with members of both dominant and non-dominant populations.	**Introspection** • Loosening of the rigid inclusive/exclusive stance, accompanied by sense of personal autonomy. • Beginning to acknowledge value in both cultures.	• Preference for counsellor from own group, but openness to others who share similar worldviews and are culturally sensitive. • Tend to seek counselling to balance need for personal autonomy with strong cultural affiliation.
Integrated Awareness • Valuing of own identity. • Sense of connection with other non-dominant groups. • Integration of aspects of self drawn from other cultural influences.	**Synergistic Articulation and Awareness** • Self and cultural identity are affirmed and valued. • Open and thoughtful evaluation of cultural values of others and commitment to elimination of all forms of oppression.	• Similarity in worldview between counsellor and client is more important than group affiliation.

Figure 4. Models of cultural identity development.

The bottom line is that counsellors need to be sensitive to the cultural dimensions of identity that are important to clients. One would expect to find similarities across identity development models designed to address various aspects of culture (gender, ethnicity, sexual orientation, etc.). However, factors that may distinguish the experiences of some groups from others must also be taken into account when exploring identity development with clients. More research is required to explore the similarities and differences across cultural variables and to establish the impact of the following factors on identity development processes.

1. For ethnic populations, cultural identity is evident from birth and is likely supported by family and community contexts. It may take a period of time for children to begin to internalize the negative stereotypes that surround them in the social systems outside of family and cultural community. In contrast to this, gays and lesbians or persons with disabilities are likely to find few close role models and

may lack social support or experience active oppression from immediate family and friends (Pope, 1995). The potential loss of primary family and social connections is an additional factor for these individuals (Fassinger & Schlossberg, 1992).

2. Some non-dominant populations may also experience a change in cultural identities later in life, which introduces a change in developmental process at that point. For example, gay men and lesbians may come out to themselves as adolescents or adults, having already internalized many negative messages about their identities. Persons who experience sudden-onset disabilities may also face an identity development crisis at a later point in life.

3. Persons with multiple non-dominant identities may also find themselves at different points in their development process with respect to different aspects of their cultural identity. A lesbian woman of colour may feel secure in her ethnic identity, but may be struggling with internalized homophobia. She may also find herself in a position where she makes conscious or unconscious choices to validate one aspect of identity over another because of the potential loss of an ethnic cultural group. For example, if sexual identity is openly affirmed, connection to her ethnic community may be jeopardized.

4. There may also be differences in identity development processes for those of visible and invisible non-dominant groups. The process of disclosure of cultural identity is an added factor for persons with non-visible disabilities, those with non-dominant sexual orientations, and some members of non-dominant ethnic populations whose physical characteristics distinguish them less clearly from the European cultural roots of the dominant Canadian population (Pope, 1995).

Implications for counselling

Understanding the concept of cultural identity development is central to multicultural competence, as it highlights three important facets of client experience: (a) the impact of socio-cultural oppression, (b) within-group differences in worldview, and (c) the potential for ongoing development of cultural identity (Atkinson, 2004). Client cultural identity development may also have a direct impact on the client-counsellor relationship and the counselling process. The last column in Figure 4 highlights some of the potential impacts of client non-dominant identity development on the counselling process, based on the observations of Atkinson (2004). Client cultural identity development may impact: (a) perceived salience of cultural identity; (b) client perspective on the roots of the presenting concern (i.e., in the person or in the oppressive socio-cultural environment); (c) likelihood of seeking counselling; (d) preference for a counsellor of the same cultural group; and (e) orientation towards the counsellor (e.g., trust versus mistrust, desire to please versus anger and resistance). As with all other aspects of cultural identity, however, these must all be viewed as potential issues to be explored on an individual basis with each client as the counsellor's loosely held hypotheses about the role of culture are confirmed or disconfirmed through the counsellor-client interaction (Helms & Cook, 1999).

Dominant Cultural Identity Development

The majority of counsellors are from White, European backgrounds (Sue & Sue, 1990). This trend continues in spite of the changing demographics within Canada that show growing numbers of people who are members of non-dominant populations. There is a tendency for members of the dominant population to view the concept of cultural identity development as applicable only to non-dominant populations. The focus of identity development research has reflected this tendency (Sabnani, Ponterotto, & Borodovsky, 1991). There is also a tendency to view whiteness as a homogeneous category, which Moodley referred to as "an illusionary single white racial identity" (2007, p. 14). Cultural identity development is a process that all individuals engage in, albeit most commonly at an unconscious level.

Given the under-representation of professionals from non-dominant groups in psychology, most counsellors and psychologists hold cultural identities based predominantly on their European heritage and membership in the dominant Canadian culture. Many give thought to the implications of racism, sexism, heterosexism, and other factors on clients from non-dominant groups, but give less thought to the impact of cultural factors such as gender, sexual orientation, ethnicity, and ability on their own process of identity development. However, to become multiculturally competent, we must all work to overcome internalized racist, sexist, heterosexist, and other culturally oppressive attitudes and assumptions inherent in our identification with the dominant culture. Consequently, models have emerged to describe the identity development of dominant populations (e.g., Helms & Cook, 1999; Rowe, Bennett, & Atkinson, 1994; Sue et al., 1998), based on the assumption that unexamined identity status by definition is supportive of the status quo. While the focus of most writers has been exclusively on issues of White racial identity, the summary in Figure 5 attempts to expand the process to be inclusive of other aspects of identity that are often born without conscious reflection. The development of sexual identity awareness by a male heterosexual counsellor is illustrated in the sample self-dialogue. The conceptual framework is drawn from the model provided by Helms and Cook, with the suggested clustering of concepts provided by Richardson and Molinaro (1996).

Phase I: Abandonment of Culturally Oppressive Components of Identity		
Stage	**Description**	**Sample Self-Dialogue**
Contact	Satisfaction with the status quo and lack of awareness or denial of racism, sexism, heterosexism, ageism, ableism, and other forms of cultural oppression by the dominant population.	*"In my opinion, differences exist in society because people make different choices and set different priorities for themselves."*
Disintegration	Exposure to circumstances that make it difficult to continue to deny the existence of cultural oppression and one's role in that oppression; this leads to confusion, disorientation, and fractured loyalties.	*"George seemed really offended by that remark. Maybe being a gay guy in this counselling agency isn't that easy. How often do I make him feel uncomfortable?"*
Reintegration	Retreat into active valuing of dominant cultural identities and denigration of non-dominant populations with consequent reduction in anxiety and increase in socially acceptable forms of sexism, racism, etc.	*"I think George brings this on himself. Look at how flamboyant he is. We'd all get along fine if he just kept his sexual preferences to himself."*
Phase II: Development of Positive, Culturally Sensitive Identity		
Stage	**Description**	**Sample Self-Dialogue**
Pseudo-Independence	Rationalization of one's own group norms and designation of others as racist, sexist, homophobic, etc. Separation of self-identity from other group members who may be guilty of cultural oppression and expectation of non-dominant groups to conform with dominant cultural norms.	*"I can see that there are heterosexual male counsellors here who would deliberately make his life miserable given the opportunity. Perhaps I can give him some tips to help him draw less attention to himself when they are around."*
Immersion	Active, committed search for understanding of one's own identity as part of the dominant European, heterosexual, able-bodied, male culture. Honest quest for information, self-evaluation, and redefinition of self.	*"I've been really blind about my own heterosexuality. Why has it take me so long to actually get it? What do I do now to rid myself of these homophobic responses so I can be a supportive colleague and work effectively with my clients?"*
Emersion	Solidarity with like-minded individuals who are also seeking a culturally sensitive personal identity and searching for ways to oppose oppression.	*"I'm so excited to meet up with others who are learning about their own sexuality and redefining their heterosexuality in positive, nonexclusionary ways."*
Autonomy	Thoughtful analysis of cultural factors in self and others, in organization and systemic contexts, and actions that support non-oppressive practices.	*"I noticed that some of our agency materials still have a heterosexist bias in the language. Perhaps George and I can rework these materials together and set some policies for use of inclusive language."*

Figure 5. Dominant cultural identity development.

Whether one is part of the dominant Canadian culture or identifies with one or more non-dominant cultural subgroups in Canadian society, cultural identity development is likely to be a lifelong process. It may also be a painful and arduous process that involves significant self-transformation (Fowers & Davidov, 2006). Like the process of non-dominant cultural identity development, members of the dominant population may progress in a non-linear and cyclical fashion through these stages as they begin to open up to different aspects of their cultural identities. They are also likely triggered into this process by personal, contextual, or historical events that propel them to move beyond their current conceptual schemata. What is important to recognize is that the level of cultural identity development will likely impact one's receptivity to increasing multicultural counselling competencies (Sabnani et al., 1991).

As I reflect on my own cultural identity development, I'm aware of the ways in which the various aspects of my identity interact and have developed at different paces throughout my life. For me, the process of feminist identity development was one of the most profound identity transitions that I have experienced. As an adolescent and young woman, I internalized social and religious expectations about my role as a woman and chose paths for myself in keeping with those norms. I was unaware of my own internalized sexism and heterosexism.

In my mid '20s, I found myself caught in an unhealthy marriage and encouraged by those in the religious subculture that I was part of to simply accept my role as wife in spite of the attitudes and behaviours of my spouse. I felt trapped, isolated, and began to see more clearly the oppressive nature of the beliefs and values that I had internalized. My transition from that initial point of awareness to my current sense of feminist identity involved an agonizing decade of moving between my emergent solidarity with other women and feminist perspectives and the ingrained messages from my gendered socialization that lead me to rationalize to myself and others the choices I continued to make.

What I didn't consciously realize during this time period was that another parallel process of awakening was taking place related to my sexual identity development. Once the veil was lifted from my clouded sense of gender identity, my sexual orientation soon became clear to me. This time, the process of identity development was rapid and welcome. I had paved the way for my homosexual self to emerge through my previous feminist identity development process.

Personal reflection – Sandra Collins

Implications for counselling

The implications of cultural identity development for the counselling process, and specifically on the level of multicultural counselling competence, have been explored by a number of writers focused on racial-ethnic identity (Sue et al., 1998). For example, Vinson and Neimeyer (2000) found a positive correlation between level of racial identity development and level of multicultural counselling competencies for counsellors from both non-dominant and dominant groups. Counsellors who have not actively engaged in a process of identity development related to gender, sexual orientation, ethnicity, ability, and so on are less likely to be able to recognize the developmental processes that their clients are engaged in or to respond in culturally sensitive ways to their clients. Cultural identity is a central component of the worldview of both the client and counsellor, and the interaction between the two perspectives can have a dramatic impact on the relationship (McDougall & Arthur, 2001). Helms (1990a, 1990c) introduced a model for explaining the interactional patterns between counsellor and client at various stages in the racial-identity development process. Although this model has not been tested using varied non-dominant groups, the principles apply across other aspects of cultural identity.

Three possible combinations of interactions are outlined in Figure 6, along with some potential implications for the counselling process and a case example for each. The implications for counselling are explored in more detail in other writings (Carter & Akinsulure-Smith, 1996; Helms 1990a, 1990c; McDougall & Arthur, 2001; Sue et al., 1998; Sue & Sue, 2008). It is clear that the potential for a solid working alliance and facilitation of client development in counselling are dependent upon the level of cultural identity development of the counsellor, whether she or he is a member of dominant or non-dominant populations. Knowledge of the client identity development process will be insufficient if the counsellor is not also at a place in her or his own development to encourage insight and increased self-awareness on the part of the client. An important goal for all counsellors should be to reach the level of autonomy in their various cultural identities (gender, ethnicity, sexual orientation, ability, etc.), which may require significant attention to experiences that most do not actively acknowledge.

Interaction Pattern	Counsellor and Client Cultural Identity	Implications for Counselling	Case Example
Parallel	• Stages of development that reflect similar attitudes towards dominant and non-dominant groups.	• Both feel understood and relationship is stable and supportive. • At early stages of identity development, cultural issues may be ignored or avoided or, where acknowledged, not resolved, which reinforces the status quo. • At later stages, counselling process support for cultural identity development may be strong, but progress may be limited or capped at a certain stage of development.	• James entered counselling to deal with problems related to sexual intimacy with his wife. Although he has been attracted to a male colleague for a number of years, he does not mention this to his counsellor. Susan explores with James various factors that may be impacting his relationship. She assumes heterosexuality and does not question James about his affiliations towards men and women. Together they map out a plan for increasing his sexual intimacy with his wife.
Crossed Regressive	• Stages of development that reflect opposing attitudes towards dominant and non-dominant groups. • Client is at least one stage ahead of the counsellor	• Counsellor poses a barrier to the cultural identity development of the client. • Dysfunctional relationship characterized by tension and conflict. • Counsellor may avoid cultural identity issues, demonstrate lack of empathy, or react with discomfort and denial. • Client may experience increased anger, increased symptoms, and question counsellor competence. • Premature termination is more likely and potential for client harm exists.	• Chitra has joined an anti-racism group at her university. She is proud of her ethnic identity and is outspoken in counselling about her desire to continue reclaiming her roots. She complains about the lack of support from her friends and professors. Her counsellor, Rochelle, is concerned that Chitra may be setting herself up for social and academic struggles if she doesn't learn to tone down her passion a bit and recognize that racism is a two-way street. She encourages Chitra on her journey of self-exploration and suggests some alternative ways of self-expression that are more socially acceptable.
Crossed Progressive	• Stages of development that reflect opposing attitudes towards dominant and non-dominant groups. • Counsellor is at least one stage ahead of the client.	• Some tension may exist in the relationship, but it can be directed towards personal growth. • Counsellor may function as role model and facilitate insight, knowledge acquisition, and skill development on the part of the client. • Depending on the specific stages of counsellor and client, there may be a risk of lower empathy on the part of the counsellor, less significant progress towards counselling goals, and anger, guilt, or defensiveness on the part of the client.	• Alexis has been in an intimate relationship with her boyfriend for two years. She has recently begun hanging out with another couple who have a much more egalitarian relationship. She has been surprised at the way they share responsibilities and look out for each other's needs. She has raised this a few times with her boyfriend, but has backed down because he seems hurt that she doesn't care as much for him as she used to. Her counsellor, James, encourages her to read a couple of books on gender identity and invites her to imagine stepping outside of everyone else's expectations and to develop an image of her ideal relationship.

Figure 6. Interactional patterns between counsellor and client.

It is important for issues of cultural identity to be addressed early on in the counselling process with all clients to ensure that they do not become barriers to an effective working alliance. It is also important to recognize that cultural identity development is relevant regardless of the dominant or non-dominant status of the counsellor and the client (McDougall & Arthur, 2001). As we have asserted throughout this text, all counselling is multicultural in nature, and all human beings experience various aspects of cultural identity development. Although the majority of material on counsellor identity development has been written for members of the dominant population, counsellors from non-dominant groups should not take their self-awareness and understanding of cultural identity for granted. Cultural tensions do occur between various non-dominant groups in society; some purport there exists a hierarchy of colour that may be associated with discriminatory behaviour between members of non-dominant racial groups (Ridley, 1995). It is important for all counsellors to examine how their view of other dominant or non-dominant groups in Canadian society may reflect on their own cultural identity development and impact their interactions with clients.

Acculturation and Assimilation

Awareness of client culture must include an understanding of the individual's level of acculturation or assimilation (Sue, 2006). **Acculturation** is defined as *the process of integrating or assuming the worldview, values, customs, or norms of another cultural group, resulting in changes in thinking patterns, feelings, and behaviours. These changes that occur when two cultural groups encounter may be unidirectional or bidirectional* (Berry, 2005, 2008; Chung, Bemak, Ortiz, & Sandoval-Perez, 2008). As an ideal, our policy of multiculturalism suggests that Canadian culture is a unique combination of the cultural contributions of various members of society, with the patterns and norms of the dominant culture shifting over time as we learn from others with diverse worldviews. The more typical pattern in Canada, however, has been for the dominant group to exert overt and covert pressure on non-dominant groups to adapt to its norms, values, and practices (Atkinson, 2004; James, 1996). Supplementary allowance is made for retention of cultural identity.

While current multicultural policy may facilitate a more bilateral process of acculturation, historically, political, social, and economic forces in Canada have been used to force a process of assimilation on many non-dominant groups. **Assimilation** *implies both adoption of the dominant culture's worldview, values, and beliefs and integration into that culture through relationships that do not take into account ethnic or other cultural origins* (Atkinson, 2004; Chung et al., 2008). Assimilation implies change in only one direction. It is a component of acculturation, but it typically requires loss or denial of non-dominant culture in order to fit in (Berry, 2005). Complete assimilation may be blocked either by the dominant culture (who do not want to accept others as equals) or by the non-dominant population (who wish to maintain their own cultural heritage and practices) (Atkinson).

Acculturation is a key concept for understanding the experiences of people in cross-cultural transition (Berry, 2005). Counsellors need knowledge about the processes involved in acculturation in order to assess the relative influences of acculturation on clients' worldview. The degree of acculturation experienced by clients is not static; rather, there are bound to be both intergroup and intrapersonal changes over time. The extent to which clients align with their culture of origin and attempt to integrate with dominant groups in society has an impact on their mental health (Berry, 2001; Marsella & Yamada, 2000). In Chapter 11, the negative impact of forced assimilation on First Nations clients is examined. Chapter 13 details the tension experienced by members of non-dominant ethnic groups in their attempts to overcome racism in interactions with dominant members of society.

Clients may seek counselling in an effort to overcome conflicts they experience in trying to live biculturally. Acculturative stress results from the difficulties associated with acculturation and the resulting emotional strain (Diller, 1999). Intergenerational and gender conflicts within families are common sources of stress for individuals when family members adopt different positions in relation to the dominant values of a society (Bemak & Chung, 2008). The process of acculturation may be voluntary (immigrants) or involuntary (refugees or Aboriginal peoples). Arthur, Merali, and Djuraskovic (Chapter 12) and Arthur (Chapter 17) examine these issues in fuller detail in the discussions about counselling immigrants, refugees, and international students. Acculturation issues also surface in many areas of decision-making during adolescence and adulthood. The expectations of parents and significant others in a person's culture of origin can influence many lifestyle choices, such as partners, parenting practices, career decisions, religious practices, and relationships between men and women. Counsellors require background knowledge about acculturation and commonly related issues in order to sensitively support their clients with decision-making.

While the primary focus of acculturation research has been on non-dominant ethnic groups, members of other non-dominant cultural groups in Canadian society face similar processes of coming to terms with differences between cultural group norms and those of the dominant population. As noted in chapters 15 and 16, the process of coming out for gay and lesbian clients inevitably involves facing societal and family norms that are often in strong opposition to those of the gay culture. Counsellors must be careful about inadvertently imposing their values about how issues are defined or the desired solutions. Decisions made in one cultural context hold a variety of meanings and consequences in other cultural contexts (Merali, 1999). Counsellors need to be informed about acculturation to accurately understand the experiences of clients and to build relevant interventions to support people in resolving their concerns in light of competing cultural values.

Bicultural or Multicultural Identities

The outcomes of the acculturation process range from segregation from the dominant culture to the experience of marginalized existence within that culture to more full integration or assimilation (Berry, 2005, 2008). Successful acculturation often results in the assumption of a **bicultural** or **multicultural identity** in which *the individual embraces those aspects of dominant and non-dominant cultures that facilitate goal attainment and healthy functioning. Elements of two or more cultures are integrated and coexist within the individual's worldview, and the individual develops competence in functioning within each culture* (Berry, 2005, 2008). Members of non-dominant cultural groups in Canada are commonly bicultural or multicultural, adopting some of the behaviours and norms of the dominant (or other non-dominant) cultures in order to successfully function in society (James, 1996). Ho (1995) saw bienculturated or multienculturated individuals as having much to offer both dominant and non-dominant populations and as providing a model for promoting a balance between unity and diversity.

Cultural Schemata

The models of identity development reviewed above suggest that counsellors may initially resist the notion that they hold biases towards their clients. Some counsellors in training have argued that they separate their personal experiences and feelings from their professional roles. This conjures the image of people turning on and off part of themselves according to the roles they hold in life. It is our belief, however, that it is untenable for people to separate their worldview from their work as multicultural counsellors because values, beliefs, feelings, and experiences with people culminate in worldviews that are constant influences on how we define situations and view others (Pedersen, 2001). It is human nature to form perceptual schemata around culture, and counsellors' core beliefs strongly come into play in their work with clients from culturally diverse backgrounds (Lewis, 2006; Ridley et al., 1994). Counsellors are not immune to the influences of their socialization, including images and judgments about people from various cultural backgrounds. Consequently, prior experience with people from other cultures can be either an asset or a barrier in the delivery of counselling services, depending on the cognitive schema formed or reinforced during those encounters. A key question for counsellors to consider in culture-infused counselling is: *In what ways does my prior experience impact how I perceive and work with this client?* (Arthur, 2004a).

Self-awareness and awareness of client culture, worldview, cultural identity development, and level of acculturation are essential components of multicultural counselling competence. They also tend to be emotionally laden and difficult issues for counsellors to effectively address in themselves and in their clients. A counsellor's cultural sensitivity is related to perceptual schemata that are developed over time through cultural conditioning (Lewis, 2006; Ridley et al., 1994). **Cultural schemata** are defined as *the clusters of beliefs and assumptions formed around particular phenomena through social conditioning and experience that act as a kind of cultural filter through processing information in the environment, including how both counsellor and client behaviour is defined and interpreted.* Depending upon a counsellor's exposure to people who are culturally diverse, perceptual schemata may limit or expand culture-filtered meanings. The worldviews of counsellors and the meanings they assign to client behaviour are strongly influenced by previous experiences. Unfortunately, cultural differences between the counsellor and the client may be processed in ways that are overly limiting or contain distorted meanings that serve to misdiagnose or pathologize the behaviour of clients. Alternatively, prior experience may help counsellors to appreciate diversity and to engage in negotiation of shared meanings related to issues of counselling and culture-infused interventions.

The key question emerges: *How does one effect change in cultural schemata when the tendency is for incoming information to be interpreted through the lens of previous experience and learning?* We must all be open to examining our worldviews and reflective about the ways that culture influences our professional practice. Experiential learning provides a means for increasing self-awareness and providing a bridge between knowing about multicultural counselling competence and knowing how to be competent with clients (Arthur & Achenbach, 2002; Heppner & O'Brien, 1994). The goal of experiential learning is to remove cultural *blinders* that may limit the degree to which counsellors are able to perceive cultural information and use it effectively in working with diverse populations. Experiential learning appears to help counsellors broaden their cultural schemata through facilitating both cognitive and affective change (Arthur & Achenbach). Emotions appear to act as a gatekeeper in facilitating or blocking the extent to which the experience is processed. Engaging the emotions opens the door to shifting perceptual schemata. However, a strong emotional reaction might actually block an individual from fully processing incoming information. This can lead to the discarding of potentially relevant culture information or the information being processed by an alternate schema (Achenbach & Arthur).

One of the main means through which counsellors engage in experiential learning is in their day-to-day encounters with colleagues, clients, and others from cultural groups different from their own. Some of these experiences may be planned attempts to increase self-awareness and awareness of other cultures; however, most involve a less purposeful attempt at cultural learning. The literature on stress and coping is instructive for this discussion since many counsellors, when working across cultures, experience a stress reaction that can have an adverse effect on their ability to move beyond their current cultural schemata.

Coping with Stress in Culture-Infused Counselling

During situations that are novel or ambiguous, individuals are more likely to demonstrate strong personality characteristics (Folkman, Lazarus, & Dunkel-Schetter, 2000). In other words, when dealing with unfamiliar contexts, people *become more like themselves* and use familiar ways of behaving to introduce structure and control to the situation. There are several implications for multicultural counselling.

1. Counsellors are always working with clients whose backgrounds are different than their own. When working with clients where the degree of cultural differences is perceived to be great, the territory becomes less familiar. It may be more challenging for counsellors to establish a working relationship with clients who do not respond readily to a counsellor's usual way of working together. It may also be more difficult for counsellors to understand the nature of issues that clients bring to counselling and to make an intervention plan that is acceptable or workable from the client's point of view. There may be direct or indirect feedback from clients about how well the counsellor understands their issues and the cultural influences on their issues. All of these factors combine in multicultural counselling to add to the level of ambiguity involved in counsellor-client interactions.

2. Depending upon counsellors' tolerance for situations of ambiguity, they may experience strong emotional reactions when their efforts to work with clients are not readily successful. Counsellors need to be honest about their reactions to clients and engage in a process of self-reflection. When there is an imbalance between perceived demands in a situation and people's resources for coping with those demands, a stress reaction occurs (Folkman et al., 2000). This is often the reason that clients seek counselling assistance: to improve their resources for addressing perceived demands in their life. It follows that counsellors would experience a stress reaction when they perceive that their expertise and resources for working with clients are not meeting the clients' needs or their own expectations of how counselling should transpire.

3. The perceived stress of multicultural counselling may be increased or decreased by a counsellor's cultural schemata. An important skill for culture-centred counsellors is **cognitive complexity**

(Pedersen & Ivey, 1993), which is *the ability to deal with the ambiguity resulting from holding potentially conflicting or contrasting information simultaneously.* This skill enables counsellors to keep track of a number of cultural variables and counselling hypotheses concurrently, as well as the changes that occur as the counselling relationship unfolds. Counsellors with higher degrees of cognitive complexity may be able to hold loosely to cultural hypotheses, moderate their own reactions, and simultaneously consider competing influences on both counsellor and client perspectives. They will be able to incorporate new information and consider how it fits with their existing worldviews. Alternatively, counsellors with undeveloped cognitive complexity may become stuck in their own emotional reactions and block incoming information as a form of self-protection. This eliminates the possibility of examining culture on multiple levels. In essence, a strong stress reaction in multicultural counselling results in counsellors disengaging from the process of cultural learning.

4.   When counsellors are overly taxed by the demands of multicultural counselling, there are detrimental results for both clients and counsellors. On a personal level, counsellors may feel confused about their work and have a sense of unease about their capacity for helping certain clients. This can impact their sense of satisfaction and enjoyment of their work. These factors have been linked to the experience of counsellor burnout (e.g., Maslach, 1982). Alternatively, counsellors may adopt the stance that the problem lies with clients. This can lead to labelling clients as difficult or blaming clients for their problems (Pedersen, 1995a). Unfortunately, this defensiveness can add to stereotypical attitudes about working with clients from particular client groups. At minimum, when counsellors are uninformed or unwilling to examine their emotional reactions to clients, they withdraw from their engagement with clients. This shuts down further exploration of worldviews, examining alternate possibilities in defining client issues, and incorporating interventions that are centred in the client's cultural experience. At this point, the counselling that unfolds is likely to be ethnocentric, based in the worldview and preferences of counsellors.

It is important to recognize that stress in culture-infused counselling is normal and should be expected. Fully embracing culture in practice reduces our grip on the known and opens the door to multiple paths of action that may not fit the tidy pattern provided by traditional counselling models.

> How do we get it right in cultural matters? One of the most challenging aspects of learning cultural competence is that it is an open-ended process, with virtually no hard and fast rules about how to relate well to those who differ from one culturally.... We can become more capable of addressing cultural questions, but we will never have universally applicable rules for doing so because there are always many considerations and nuances associated with each situation. (Fowers & Davidov, 2006, ¶61)

Culture Shock in Culture-Infused Counselling

The reactions of counsellors in multicultural counselling contexts can also be examined in light of their experiences of crossing cultures. People who venture from their home culture to a host culture that is unfamiliar often experience a psychological reaction termed **culture shock**. "In a multicultural context, culture shock is *a more or less sudden immersion into a nonspecific state of uncertainty where the individuals are not certain what is expected of them or of what they can expect from the persons around them*" (Pedersen, 1995b). Originally introduced by Oberg (1960), culture shock describes the anxiety resulting from not knowing how to behave in a new cultural context. Culture shock has been studied primarily as the process of initial adjustment to an unfamiliar environment as people move between countries. However, the experiences of practitioners in Canada moving to settings in Northern Canada remind us that sharply contrasting cultural conditions exist within a country (Zapf, 1991, 1993). Simulation exercises have been developed to help counselling students gain insight into the experience that their clients have in crossing cultures (e.g., Achenbach & Arthur, 2002; Pedersen, 2003b). However, less attention has been paid to the culture shock of counsellors in multicultural contexts.

Culture shock has also been applied to the process of adjustment required by individuals when previous learning does not equip them for unfamiliar social systems (Pedersen, 1995b). This opens up the possibility of considering culture shock as a reaction by counsellors when their previous professional training has not sufficiently equipped them for the demands of working with clients across cultures. The usual cues for professional behaviour, meanings, and course of action may not exist (Arthur, 2004a). Consequently, counsellors experience ambiguity and uncertainty. The degree of cultural contrasts between counsellor and client worldviews influences the counsellor's experience of culture shock. When familiar ways of working do not work well, counsellors may experience a variety of reactions ranging from vague discomfort to a strong sense of disorientation, symptoms that have been previously associated with culture shock (Furnham & Bocher, 1986).

The experience of culture shock may be interpreted as a challenge to counsellors' sense of personal competence. Counsellors commonly respond in one of three ways:

1. They reduce their exposure to multicultural counselling and limit the types of clients and client issues that they deal with in counselling. From an ethical and practical perspective, this is not a viable option since it serves to restrict the settings and services available to non-dominant populations. The shifting demographic patterns of future clientele described in Chapter 2 suggest that a crisis in service will soon be reached if many counsellors adopt this approach (Arthur & Stewart, 2001; Hall, 1997).

2. They choose to operate in the same ways as they have in the past without making adjustments for the cultural diversity of their clientele. However comforting counselling from an ethnocentric worldview is for managing culture shock, it is a strategy fraught with difficulties from the point of view of effective services and ethical practices (Sue & Sue, 1990, 2003).

3. A desirable alternative is a commitment to ongoing cultural learning. Culture shock is an inevitable reaction for counsellors who actively engage with clients from culturally diverse backgrounds. A multicultural perspective requires counsellor role adjustment and change. A commitment to learning about culture can profoundly shape counsellors' sense of professional identity and support positive contributions to the health and well-being of clients. Culture shock is a reaction that may serve as an impetus for continuous learning about cultural influences on professional practice.

Self-awareness Supports Working Across Cultures

The construct of culture shock explains some of the dynamics that occur between counsellors and clients in multicultural counselling. As a general rule, the severity of culture shock is determined by the degree of similarity or difference between the worldviews of counsellor and clients (Arthur, 2004a). How counsellors manage the cognitive dissonance and emotional discomfort they experience in multicultural counselling is related to their level of self-awareness. Counsellors who have developed the basic competencies in the domain of self-awareness are better able to suspend their personal reactions and consider competing explanations of client behaviour (Pedersen & Ivey, 1993). This allows counsellors to search for similarities with clients and to negotiate shared meanings of the situation while demonstrating a tolerance of ambiguity (Pedersen, 2001).

Without self-awareness about culture, counsellors may be unsettled by the experience of culture shock. This leads them to focus on dissonance reduction (Stampley, 2008). Unfortunately, this process triggers mechanisms of self-protection, resulting in counsellors retreating to a position of cultural encapsulation. In order to end the sense of discomfort about cultural contrasts, counsellors increase their efforts to sustain the viability of their worldview. This leads to the imposition of personal views about clients. It then becomes easier for counsellors to impose labels on clients as they make attributions about the source of their discomfort. It is easy for client behaviour to be pathologized or labelled as *difficult* when an alternative explanation rests with the counsellor's difficulties in working across cultures. This is also the breeding ground for stereotyping, as counsellors add their negative experiences into their perceptual schemata about client groups (Stampley). Unfortunately, counsellors who have a difficult interaction with one client may filter that experience as a generalization about all people from that cultural subgroup (Arthur, 2004a). This is unfortunate because it detracts from the cultural learning that can occur from *difficult* interactions in multicultural counselling contexts.

Alternatively, counsellors can learn to use their metacognitive skills to monitor their emotional reactions to clients who are culturally diverse. If counsellors are self-aware, they can work with their emotional reaction of culture shock and move forward into a position of learning together with the client. They use their own reactions to prompt reflection: *What does this mean about the culture of the client?* and, equally important, *What does this mean about my personal culture?* (Arthur, 2004a). These situations are opportunities for counsellors to engage in a cultural audit in multicultural counselling, a concept elaborated upon in Chapter 6. This includes checking their personal expectations about standards for appropriate client behaviour and how a therapeutic encounter should unfold (Leong & Chou, 1996; Pedersen, 1995a). Counsellors build self-awareness through a willingness to examine when and why they *shut down* when faced with cultural differences. They can embrace their reactions to clients as challenges to find common ground and alternative ways of relating to clients. Multicultural counselling offers counsellors the opportunity to engage in continuous reflection and learning about others and about themselves (Arthur).

I had not thought much about racism, as it was not part of my personal experience – at least as the recipient of racism. I certainly had not thought much about being the perpetrator of racism. I am not sure whom I used to mean when I thought about racists; maybe it was the sensational stories portrayed in the media. When I began to read the multicultural counselling literature, a vague sense of discomfort began to become familiar. A feeling of uncertainty loomed and then the feelings started to get stronger.

I remember reading Pedersen's (1995a) article about counsellors as unintentional racists and I was quite upset when I read the article. I actually remember throwing the article into a pile of readings. I couldn't name it, but something in that article deeply disturbed me. At first, I was angry and resentful that all counsellors were accused of being racists.

After a while, I began to reconsider my reaction. What I was angry about was facing this topic. I couldn't live in the same way anymore. I had to take a look at it – I did not want to look, but neither could I turn away – not in the same way I could before. Once awareness begins, it seems to want to push through in turbulent waters. I have learned to let my emotions be my guide when reading material on multicultural counselling. If I am feeling something uncomfortable, that is the messenger telling me it is worth taking a second look – inside and outside.

Personal reflection – Nancy Arthur

The Risks of Cultural Oppression in Counselling

In the previous sections, it was suggested that counsellors' cultural sensitivity is related to perceptual schemata that are developed through cultural conditioning. Perceptual schemata influence how client behaviour is defined and interpreted (Ridley et al., 1994). Cultural schemata impact the degree to which counsellors explore the influences of culture on client behaviour and the relevance of culture for the counselling process. Ridley (1995) suggested that counsellors need to carefully examine their personal attitudes and beliefs about race, ethnicity, and other dimensions of culture that could lead to discrimination against clients from non-dominant groups. Many counsellors operate from a fundamental premise of *good intentions* and genuinely wanting to help others. However, their underlying beliefs need to be examined to consider how notions of help and helpfulness are constructed. For example, the axiom *Do unto others as you would have them do unto you* is intended as a cultural pejorative about treating others well. However, if counsellors treat clients in the same way that they would like to be treated, the counsellors' values are positioned as superior and there is little consideration of what clients want (Pedersen, 2001). This exemplifies the problematic nature of personal attitudes that have not been examined for their cultural biases. In this case, views of what is helpful stem from the counsellors' definition of *good treatment*. The worldview of clients is ignored, resulting in counselling that is biased according to the counsellors' prescriptions for mental health. Despite good intentions, there is a risk of oppressing clients through counselling practices that do not incorporate cultural influences. It may be difficult for well-intentioned counsellors to consider how their attitudes and behaviour can be potentially harmful to their clients. However, they need to examine how they intentionally or unintentionally engage in racism, sexism, heterosexism, ableism, or other forms of oppression against their clients (Crethar, Rivera, & Nash, 2008; Pedersen, 1995a; Ridley, 1995).

Power and Privilege

The preceding discussion suggests that the perceptual schemata of counsellors need to be expanded to appreciate their own cultural identities and the cultural identities of their clients. We would add that counsellors also need to develop awareness of the personal and professional impact of the discrepancy between dominant and non-dominant cultural groups in Canada. Two sets of related constructs are important in this regard: the existence of differential power and privilege based on group affiliation in Canadian society and the system of prejudice, oppression, and discrimination that serves to maintain that imbalance in power.

We begin with an exploration of the concepts of power and privilege. **Power** is defined as the *"capacity to produce desired effects on others...the capacity to influence, for one's own benefit, the forces that affect one's life"* (Pinderhughes, 1989, p. 109-110). Power, on its own, is not a negative commodity; in fact, some degree of personal power is essential to mental health. It is the differential distribution of power across various groups in society that leads to systemic forms of oppression and a sense of disempowerment among members of non-dominant populations. Ramsey (1997) pointed out that counsellors are often reticent about addressing issues of power because of their discomfort with being in a position of power both by virtue of their professional role and their membership in dominant groups. However, failure to actively assess and address issues of power could reinforce the status quo or promote further cultural oppression of clients from non-dominant groups.

Racism is a clear example of the use of power to enforce differential treatment or access to opportunity. Throughout our country, there are many examples of overt racism that most Canadians find appalling. Similarly, most Canadians would argue that discrimination on the basis of gender, ability, age, sexual orientation, and socio-economic status should not be tolerated in modern society. Most counsellors are able to identify the ways in which racism, sexism, heterosexism, and so on put certain members of the Canadian population at a disadvantage and impact healthy functioning. What is often more difficult for us to acknowledge and openly explore are the advantages that members of the dominant population reap on a day-to-day basis (Lowe & Mascher, 2001; Williams & Barber, 2004). Privilege is most often referred to as White privilege (McIntosh, 1988; Neville, Worthington, & Spanierman, 2001) or male privilege (Deutsch, 2001; McIntosh), but is expanded here to include other dominant cultural factors (Collins, in press; Lowe & Mascher). The concept of **privilege** refers to *the pervasive and both overt and covert ways in which White, male, heterosexual, able-bodied, middle class, Christian Canadians experience advantages, opportunities, entitlements, and immunities are conferred with dominance and control and are positioned at the top of the economic, political, and social hierarchy, often without conscious awareness or acknowledgement* (Atkinson, 2004; Crethar et al., 2008; Neville et al.). Although coveted by some, such privilege does not benefit society as a whole and leads to clear disadvantages for many (McIntosh).

> I have come to see white privilege as an invisible package of unearned assets that I can count on cashing in each day, but about which I was "meant" to remain oblivious. White privilege is like an invisible weightless knapsack of special provisions, assurances, tools, maps, guides, codebooks, passports, visas, clothes, compass, emergency gear, and blank checks. (McIntosh, 1988, p. 1)

From earliest childhood, those in the dominant groups are socialized to view the world through a lens that does not allow recognition of privilege (Kiselica, 1999; McIntosh, 1988). Privilege often remains invisible because we are taught to recognize acts of oppression only at the individual level and fail to recognize the ways in which institutionalized or systemic forces reinforce the unearned advantages of particular cultural groups (McIntosh). Just as members of non-dominant populations often experience compounded oppression, individuals may find themselves privy to various levels of privilege depending on their multiple identities. White heterosexual males, for example, hold a stronger position of privilege than White heterosexual females or White homosexual males (Neville et al., 2001). All counsellors function from a place of privilege by virtue of our education and social status (Arredondo, Tovar-Blank, & Parham, 2008). Kiselica described his painful journey of self-discovery of the privilege associated with his own Whiteness and ethnocentrism, providing an example to all of us of the value of such in-depth self-awareness. Snapshot 3 provides a series of statements designed to facilitate awareness of privilege based on cultural identities.

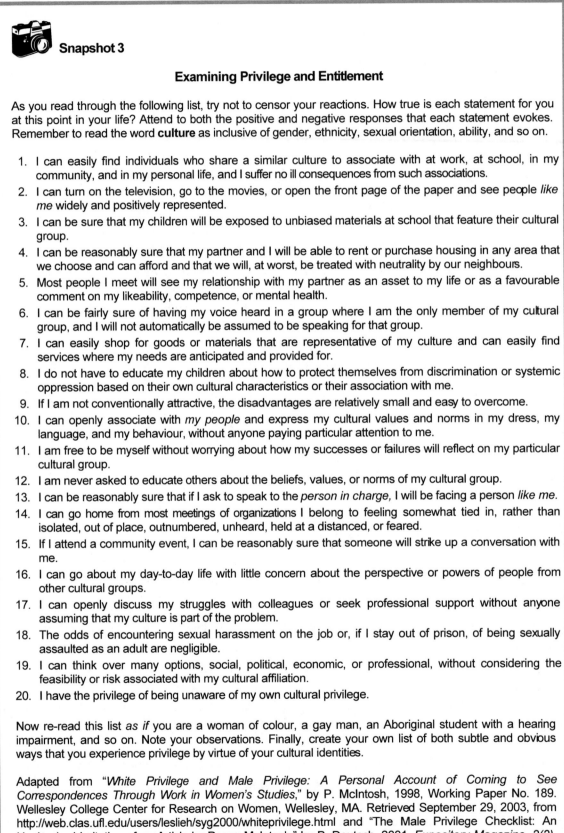

Snapshot 3

Examining Privilege and Entitlement

As you read through the following list, try not to censor your reactions. How true is each statement for you at this point in your life? Attend to both the positive and negative responses that each statement evokes. Remember to read the word **culture** as inclusive of gender, ethnicity, sexual orientation, ability, and so on.

1. I can easily find individuals who share a similar culture to associate with at work, at school, in my community, and in my personal life, and I suffer no ill consequences from such associations.
2. I can turn on the television, go to the movies, or open the front page of the paper and see people *like me* widely and positively represented.
3. I can be sure that my children will be exposed to unbiased materials at school that feature their cultural group.
4. I can be reasonably sure that my partner and I will be able to rent or purchase housing in any area that we choose and can afford and that we will, at worst, be treated with neutrality by our neighbours.
5. Most people I meet will see my relationship with my partner as an asset to my life or as a favourable comment on my likeability, competence, or mental health.
6. I can be fairly sure of having my voice heard in a group where I am the only member of my cultural group, and I will not automatically be assumed to be speaking for that group.
7. I can easily shop for goods or materials that are representative of my culture and can easily find services where my needs are anticipated and provided for.
8. I do not have to educate my children about how to protect themselves from discrimination or systemic oppression based on their own cultural characteristics or their association with me.
9. If I am not conventionally attractive, the disadvantages are relatively small and easy to overcome.
10. I can openly associate with *my people* and express my cultural values and norms in my dress, my language, and my behaviour, without anyone paying particular attention to me.
11. I am free to be myself without worrying about how my successes or failures will reflect on my particular cultural group.
12. I am never asked to educate others about the beliefs, values, or norms of my cultural group.
13. I can be reasonably sure that if I ask to speak to the *person in charge,* I will be facing a person *like me.*
14. I can go home from most meetings of organizations I belong to feeling somewhat tied in, rather than isolated, out of place, outnumbered, unheard, held at a distanced, or feared.
15. If I attend a community event, I can be reasonably sure that someone will strike up a conversation with me.
16. I can go about my day-to-day life with little concern about the perspective or powers of people from other cultural groups.
17. I can openly discuss my struggles with colleagues or seek professional support without anyone assuming that my culture is part of the problem.
18. The odds of encountering sexual harassment on the job or, if I stay out of prison, of being sexually assaulted as an adult are negligible.
19. I can think over many options, social, political, economic, or professional, without considering the feasibility or risk associated with my cultural affiliation.
20. I have the privilege of being unaware of my own cultural privilege.

Now re-read this list *as if* you are a woman of colour, a gay man, an Aboriginal student with a hearing impairment, and so on. Note your observations. Finally, create your own list of both subtle and obvious ways that you experience privilege by virtue of your cultural identities.

Adapted from "*White Privilege and Male Privilege: A Personal Account of Coming to See Correspondences Through Work in Women's Studies,*" by P. McIntosh, 1998, Working Paper No. 189. Wellesley College Center for Research on Women, Wellesley, MA. Retrieved September 29, 2003, from http://web.clas.ufl.edu/users/leslieh/syg2000/whiteprivilege.html and "The Male Privilege Checklist: An Unabashed Imitation of an Article by Peggy McIntosh," by B. Deutsch, 2001, *Expository Magazine, 2(2).* Retrieved October 29, 2003, from http://www.expositorymagazine.net/maleprivilege_checklist.htm

McIntosh (1988) pointed out that the position of privilege also brings with it disadvantages for the dominant group. Those in positions of privilege may not develop the strengths, coping mechanisms, and resources of non-dominant populations. The conscious or unconscious denial of privilege and uncritical examination of racism, sexism, or heterosexism is also evidence of cognitive distortions and misperceptions of self and others inconsistent with mental health and is likely to lead to irrational fears and anxiety (Neville et al., 2001). It would be interesting to see what would happen if racism and sexism were added as diagnostic categories of mental illness.

Privilege is reinforced by and reinforces the power of the dominant group. This power is expressed on individual, group, and systemic levels (Neville et al., 2001) and is institutionalized though language, symbols, and practices that reinforce and normalize differential access to social, economic, and political privileges. Common stereotypes, gendered and heteronormative language, and dominant images serve to maintain the status quo and create a sense of personal entitlement among the privileged that often serves as a blinder to awareness of inequities (Neville et al.). To be oblivious of privilege is to reinforce the status quo and to engage in unconscious cultural oppression (McIntosh, 1988; Arredondo et al., 2008).

A primary focus of dominant cultural identity development is the abandonment of the inherent entitlement and privilege, making this a critical development task for counsellors (Neville et al., 2001). Students and counsellors report that they find material on racial privilege difficult to process. They often experience strong feelings in reaction to readings, such as guilt, anger, and shame. Neville and colleagues and Ramsay (1997) noted similar emotional reactions. Such emotional reactions can motivate counsellors to gain a deeper level of self-understanding. This is an important prerequisite in improving one's conceptual and practical knowledge for working with material on cultural identity and privilege (Arminio, 2001). Counsellors need to fully understand how positions of power and privilege influence their interactions with clients from non-dominant groups (D'Andrea & Daniels, 2001a; Neville et al.; Lee & Hipolito-Delgado, 2007).

Prejudice and Discrimination

One of the common experiences of members of non-dominant groups is that of prejudice and discrimination. The power and privilege of the dominant cultural group are maintained though these processes (Neville et al., 2001). **Prejudice** may be defined as *preconceived ideas about individuals who are members of particular groups based on lack of information or misinformation* (James, 1996). Prejudice finds expression in the various *isms* – racism, heterosexism, sexism, ageism, and so on. What is important to note is that the source of prejudice is the irrational or unfounded beliefs on the part of the individual expressing the unreasonable affect or cognition. Prejudice does not reside in the object of the belief or cognition. **Discrimination** *is the active expression of prejudice in the unequal treatment of individuals, based on perceived group membership* (James, 1996).

Discrimination continues to be a common experience in the lives of many Canadians (Fassinger, 2003; Neville et al., 2001). The serious and debilitating impact of discrimination on health and social functioning must be taken into account in culture-infused counselling (Lott & Webster, 2006). Many counsellors are unaware of the degree of racial and other cultural tensions in Canadian history. There is often a comparison made to more serious cultural tensions in the United States and that is used to rationalize and minimize the severity of intercultural relations in Canada. The material presented in Chapter 13 provides examples of ethnic relations in a Canadian context and emphasizes the importance of anti-racist practices in multicultural counselling. Other chapters point to the impact of discrimination based on other cultural factors.

Counsellors need to understand how discrimination adversely impacts psychological well-being, social and emotional adjustment, and the personal and vocational development of individuals and groups. Discrimination in the form of racism, sexism, heterosexism, and so on exists on a number of different levels: (a) individual – negative attitudes included in the worldview of an individual; (b) institutional – inherent inequality in established norms and policies within organizations or institutions; and (c) societal – barriers to equal access and representation in major social structures that form the fabric of society (Israel, 2006; James, 1996). Counsellors have important roles to play in addressing discrimination on two levels. First, they help clients to gain a better understanding about discrimination, to resist the tendency to internalize and personalize societal messages about their self-worth, and to develop effective coping strategies. However, helping people adapt to noxious conditions in their employment, school, or social settings is insufficient (Vera & Speight, 2003). Counsellors also have a responsibility to work towards the prevention of discrimination at the individual, institutional, and societal levels (Toporek & Williams, 2006). Systems level intervention is the focus of Chapter 6.

The discussion in Chapter 12 outlines the importance of receptivity by the host culture for newly arriving immigrants and refugees in Canada. Discrimination is often a huge barrier for people who are crossing cultures. At a time when they are devoting considerable energy to the settlement process, discrimination is disruptive for their sense of belonging. Moving to Canada may be the first time in their lives that they are viewed as part of a non-dominant visible ethnic population. The discussion in Chapter 17 describes the experience of international students from visible non-dominant groups. Immersion into a new culture can trigger hyper-vigilant monitoring of visible differences and other people's reactions. This consumes personal energy, and many people find that the constant monitoring of ethnicity, whether performed consciously or unconsciously, results in symptoms of acculturative stress. There are few role models in education, employment, and leisure sectors. There continue to be problems with employment practices, such as recruitment and retention of visible ethnic group members, which are at least partially explained by experiences of discrimination (Task Force on the Participation of Visible Minorities in the Federal Public Service, 2000). As noted in Chapter 10, individuals who hold multiple non-dominant identities are even more likely to experience all levels of discrimination (Israel, 2006).

The behaviour of people in dominant groups in Canada continues to be both blatantly and discretely discriminatory. Members of non-dominant groups are more likely to be the victims of violence and other forms of aggression. Cultural differences such as ethnicity, religion, and sexual orientation have led to denigrating remarks, social exclusion, and other forms of oppressive practices. However, discrimination can be more subtle and not within the consciousness of perpetrators. It is as subtle as who is included in important discussions in the workplace, the pictures that are chosen for educational materials, the acceptance of different clothing styles, or the tolerance shown towards individuals speaking different languages. Each chapter in this book addresses some of the common problems that people from culturally diverse backgrounds experience in their lives through forms of individual and systemic discrimination. Counsellors who are familiar with these common issues are better prepared to address the realities of discrimination in the lives of their clients. It may take considerable courage for clients to bring up issues of discrimination due to fears about how they will be perceived. Counsellors must be prepared to validate clients' experiences. They also need to be comfortable about naming the situations that clients describe as discriminatory practices. This can help clients reframe the source of their problems from an internal to external base, which will facilitate appropriate action.

Discrimination is usually purposeful, albeit sometimes subconscious, behaviour that is designed to maintain the status quo and the power base of the dominant group (James, 1996). Counsellors' knowledge base about discrimination can be used to help them engage in anti-discrimination practices (Ridley, 1995). This requires counsellors to take a stand on what they consider discrimination and to set boundaries for their own behaviour and the behaviour of others. A guiding principle is that *doing nothing is not neutral.* This means that counsellors who refuse to engage in preventive practices contribute to the status quo. Counsellors have a responsibility for promoting social justice through consciousness-raising and other educational and advocacy practices. Chapter 6 focuses on who counsellors can get involved in the prevention of racism and other forms of discrimination (e.g., Ponterotto & Pedersen, 1993; Ridley).

> It is difficult...to conceive of anyone born and raised in [Canada] who has not inherited the racial biases of his or her forebears. These biases and prejudices are often expressed unintentionally and at an unconscious level.... One might even suggest that people are taught from the moment of birth to be culturally incompetent. (Sue, 2002, p. 803)

Personal and Professional Congruence and Authenticity

There is a tendency for individuals to focus primarily on themselves as professionals in the self-reflective process and to not delve deeply into the personal aspects of their experiences and worldviews (Toporek & Reza, 2001). Feminist therapy writers have contributed greatly in this area through their assertion that *the personal is political.* The *Feminist Therapy Code of Ethics* reminds practitioners that one cannot separate personal self from professional self since "each individual's personal experiences and situations are reflective of and an influence on society's institutionalized attitudes and values" (Feminist Therapy Institute, 2000, p. 1).

Toporek and Reza (2001) made an important point about power. As much as we may attempt to equalize power in our interactions with clients, the counsellor remains in a position of power within the counselling context. It may be easier in that context to behave as if one holds a particular value or belief about another's culture. In personal contexts, where the counsellor may be in a position of reduced power, those beliefs and values may be challenged on a deeper level. Increased awareness of privilege often brings with it a sense of loss and fear about giving up unearned status and opportunities and may result in conflict and negative social pressure from colleagues and friends who remain entrenched in their unconscious cultural superiority (Neville et al., 2001).

Challenging long-held perceptions of reality may also be more threatening in response to particular cultural factors (McIntosh, 1988) or when individuals see an impact on values, institutions, or norms they personally hold dear. For example, privilege based on sexual orientation remains a more threatening and controversial concept in Canada than inequalities based on gender and ethnicity. In spite of the legalization of gay marriage, this remains a hotly debated heterosexual privilege in some circles (Lahey & Alderson, 2004). Interethnic friendships and mixed marriages have increased over time, as has the openness of Canadians. In 1968, only 52% of Canadians approved of interethnic marriages, with this rate rising to 81% in 1995 (Department of Canadian Heritage, 1998b). In the last decade, the focus shifted to gay marriage, with many Canadians holding firmly to what they perceive as an entitlement that should be available to heterosexual couples alone. In 2002, the Supreme Court passed a ruling that legalized gay marriage in Canada and the federal government followed suit. However, the Canadian population remains divided in their recognition of and willingness to rescind their privilege in this area. While many justifications are provided for resistance to equal rights, counsellors are challenged to examine the incongruence between holding that position and taking a professional stand against cultural oppression.

Last year, in the emergency room in an urban hospital, I was told by the admitting clerk that she could not change my marital status from common law to married on my hospital records. I challenged her, and she asserted that this was hospital policy. On further pressure from me, she asserted that gay marriage wasn't recognized in Alberta. I pulled out my marriage license and, although I am unfortunately listed as the "groom," it was clearly a legal Alberta document. She finally relented and indicated that she had made the change; I remained unconvinced. This person was clearly both uninformed and operating from her own personal biases.

The next day, I sent an email to the regional health authority after carefully reviewing their policies on non-discriminatory practices so that I could use their own words in my complaint. My purpose was to ensure that others, who are in less of a position of privilege than I am, do not experience a similar discounting of their cultural identity and human rights. To the health authority's credit, the response was immediate, and I was provided with specific information about the steps taken to ensure that all front-line personnel are aware of their policies and to provide additional training in non-discriminatory practices.

This incident was rife with issues of power – my lack of power as a patient contrasted with the power that comes with listing my credentials in my complaint. It also reflects the inseparableness of personal and political power and privilege. Change happens when we all work together for value congruence and demand that of the broader systems we are part of.

Personal reflection – Sandra Collins

Unintentional Oppression in Counselling

Unintentional oppression manifests in several ways in counselling. First, counsellors may hold the illusion that a client from a non-dominant group is no different from a client from the dominant group. The term *colour blindness* is used to describe counsellors' lack of awareness about the influences of race on the experiences of clients from non-dominant groups (Neville et al., 2001; Ridley, 1995). Neville and colleagues (2001) referred to colour blindness as a new form of racial attitude that potentially results in shifting the focus away from oppressive systemic influences, provides a rationalization for racial oppression, and ends with blaming the victim. However, race is not the only issue at stake. We prefer the term **cultural blindness** to refer to *the lack of awareness and reluctance of counsellors to examine the influence of culture in counselling.* Recalling the discussion of cognitive schemata above, cultural blindness reflects a perceptual schema that distorts the interpretation of cultural information (Neville et al., 2001). This occurs because counsellors are unaware about cultural influences, because they are uninformed about how to incorporate culture into counselling, or because they feel awkward about ways to bring up culture with their clients. Regardless of the reasons, the outcome is the same: clients are short-changed in terms of examining some of the internal and external factors that influence their lives. On the broader level, cultural blindness serves to sustain the systems of cultural privilege that benefit the dominant population, but leads to emotional, social, psychological, and other forms of distress among non-dominant populations (Neville et al., 2001).

Imagine if we could access the internal dialogues of counsellors and clients to better understand their thoughts and feelings during a counselling session. This possibility has been elaborated in the Triad Training model (Pedersen, Crethar, & Carlson, 2008). The essence of the model is that there are three types of conversations going on in a counselling session. First, there is the overt conversation held between counsellor and client. Second, there is the covert conversation, or internal dialogue, that is going on inside the counsellor's head as the counselling session unfolds. Third, there is the internal dialogue that is going on in the client's mind in reaction to personal expectations of the counselling session and what is actually transpiring. As Pederson noted, the greater the cultural differences that exist between counsellor and client, the more challenging it will be for counsellors to appreciate hidden cultural messages and what a client might not be saying during a counselling session.

 **Snapshot 4**

Mary's Dilemma

Mary is a 35-year-old heterosexual woman who seeks counselling to discuss her growing concern about marital difficulties. She is thinking about leaving the marriage because of increased tension and her experience of emotional abuse. A confounding issue for Mary is her strong fundamentalist religion, which honours family as a central commitment in her life. She meets for the first session with Michelle, a counsellor who works as part of an employee assistance program in Mary's company. Michelle has practiced for 10 years and has a background in marital and family counselling. They meet for one session. Their internal dialogue at the end of the session is summarized here.

Michelle: "Mary seems really clear about what is going on for her and she is able to articulate her needs. She is in a good position financially and would not have to be dependent upon her spouse. I sensed that she is ready to leave the marriage and just needs to talk through an action plan. Women today are lucky to have that choice. I felt that encouraging her to honour her feelings and inner sense of knowing was an affirming action in this session. I invited her to come in with her husband for the next session as I think there is a lot of work that they could do together."

Mary: "Now I feel more confused than ever. The counsellor seemed to be emphasizing that I should do what I want to do – I wish it were that simple. I know how I feel about things with my husband and where I think things are going there. The counsellor kept bringing the discussion back to us as a couple. What I really wanted to talk about was my religious faith and how my church views marriage and divorce. I brought that up at least three times in the conversation, but the topic kept getting changed. I wonder if seeing a counsellor is the best option? I came here because it is difficult to talk to our church leaders about these matters and we are such a small community. My husband would turn everyone against me if he found out I was coming here. I really feel alone about where to turn."

A second source of unintentional oppression is exemplified when *counsellors go too far in emphasizing culture as the main source of clients' problems*. This is related to the *belief that the client's problems originate from being a member of a non-dominant group*. In the discussion of unintentional racism in counselling, this is termed colour consciousness (Pedersen, 1995a; Ridley, 1995), although we will use the broader term **cultural consciousness**. This is akin to shining a cultural spotlight on a client and viewing all of the client's issues according to cultural memberships. As discussed earlier in this chapter, defining client issues according to group membership may lead to stereotyping. The issues that clients bring to counselling may not be directly related to group membership.

It is important that counsellors refrain from an overzealous approach in their work and guard against turning client issues into cultural problems, which takes away from clients receiving help for the issues that matter most to them.

 **Snapshot 5**

Peter's Dilemma

Peter is a 24-year-old gay male. He seeks counselling assistance to help him make a decision about his career direction. Peter has worked as a computer programmer for his current company for three years and feels that he is not gaining the depth of experience that he would like and is considering looking for other sources of employment. However, he really likes the people he works with and there are a lot of positive benefits that his current employer provides. Peter was initially concerned about coming out at work, but found that most people were very accepting. He has met with a counsellor, Ron, for three sessions and they have explored some options for Peter if he stays with his current company or if he chooses to leave. In the third session, Ron feels that he has established enough rapport with Peter to explore the influence of his sexual identity on his vocational plans. Their internal dialogue at the end of the session is summarized here.

Ron: This was a difficult session for me. I have been wondering all along what to do with Peter's disclosure to me in the first session that he is gay. In fact, he seemed to open the session with that, so I figured that it must be really important to him. It seems that a lot of clients use one agenda to test the waters and I have been wondering if the vocational issues were a bit of a front for Peter to get to the issue that was really bothering him. Today, I decided to focus on his gay identity. This was a pretty intense session. Peter seemed to get upset when we talked about this and I am not sure what to make of his reaction. I asked him to think about this some more and we can take this up again in the next session.

Peter: Well, that was a piece of work. Ron is the third counsellor that I have seen in my life and I am pretty sick of the attitude, "He is gay and that must be the issue." I am out. I have been out for a long time. Can't somebody just need some help to decide what to do with a job? I told him up front that I was gay so that we could get that out in the open from the beginning and not dance around it. I thought we were pretty on track with the job stuff. Now I am not so sure that I want to work with somebody who pushes an agenda that isn't mine.

Counsellors may experience awkwardness about how to bring up cultural influences with the client. The result is often frustration on the part of clients and a growing mistrust of the counsellor. Clients feel that they are not heard and that an overemphasis on one aspect of their life overshadows attention paid to their immediate concerns. The adage *If you have a hammer, everything looks like a nail* can be rephrased as *As you gain competence in culture-infused counselling, don't make client issues all about culture.* Indeed, multicultural competencies are intended to help counsellors to be both selective and skillful about incorporating culture in ways that are respectful of clients' needs. There is a fine balance between exploring cultural hypotheses and overriding clients' agendas through making culture issues the central agenda.

A third potential window for unintentional oppression involves the ways that previous experiences impact the dynamics between clients and counsellors. It is prudent to remember that counsellors and clients bring their cumulative experiences with them to counselling sessions. Past encounters influence the socialization process and development of worldviews. Each of us has internalized thousands of *culture teachers* (Pedersen, 2001) that provide sources of personal identity and references for how to act across cultures. *When previous experience shapes clients' views of the counsellor in ways that are not directly connected to the here-and-now interactions between counsellor and client, they are likely engaged in a process of* **cultural transference** (Pedersen, 1995a). If clients are familiar with counselling and prior experience has produced positive results, they enter another counselling relationship with positive expectancies. However, if clients have difficult experiences with persons in authority, the counsellor may represent another authority figure. Clients may also bring cultural experience related to gender relations, views about the counsellors' age, ethnicity, or perceived socio-economic status. When previous cultural experience colours relations with the counsellor in negative ways, clients may resist engaging with the counsellor or have difficulties following through with change processes or new learning.

Rather than labelling clients as *difficult* or *problematic*, counsellors are advised to take extra time to examine the cultural representations that are blocking therapeutic relationships. This can be particularly difficult if historical cultural oppression is an issue in current contexts. Counsellors may feel confused about how to manage this dynamic in counselling or be resentful about having to address issues for which they do not assume personal responsibility. However, cultural transference can lead to major impasses in counselling and counsellors must be prepared to address these complex issues. Counsellors in positions of privilege also hold inherent responsibility for the historical processes that granted them privilege over other non-dominant groups.

The previous discussion highlighted cultural transference by clients. Counsellors also bring their cultural socialization and history of cross-cultural interactions to the counselling process. These can be influential in either positive or negative ways for building relationships with clients (Pedersen, 1995a). **Cultural counter-transference** was defined by Stampley (2008, p. 40) as *"clinicians' culturally held assumptions, values, attitudes, standards, worldviews, and intergenerational messages along with their feelings and thoughts about clients* [italics added]." In this instance, counsellors may have a tendency to project previously formed feelings and attitudes onto a client from a non-dominant group. In other words, experiences from the past colour the ways that counsellors interpret and react to the behaviour of clients. This shapes counsellors' behaviour in subtle ways.

Every counsellor will have areas of cultural bias and preferences for working with clients from some groups and not with others. There can also be biases or other negative reactions to working with particular issues related to culture. The name on an intake card can trigger thoughts about a particular ethnic group and prior experiences of working with clients from that group. Or, one member of a family may make a counselling appointment and other family members may show up for the session and speak for the client, which is likely to evoke the counsellors' cultural interpretations. Kohl (2006) described his experience of counter-transference in terms of over-interest and romantizing of his client's cultural identities. His case study provides a good reminder that both negative and positive feelings can emerge and the key issues is whose needs are being met in the moment through the therapeutic encounter. Attending carefully to both positive and negative reactions to clients can facilitate increased awareness of both self and others (Sue, 2006).

During the time period that I was coming out to myself and to others about my sexual orientation, I was working in a community counselling organization. I was so thrilled with my self-discovery and so ready to be out in the world as my new self that I could hardly contain myself. I'd been through a very long process to come to that point and had little concern about the perceptions and reactions of others.

Interestingly, the reaction I encountered from most of my counselling colleagues was to encourage me to slow down, not be too quick to tell others about my identity, etc. What I came to realize later in processing these reactions with them was that for many their only encounter with lesbians was through their clients – clients who often were experiencing negative personal and social consequences of coming out or were struggling with their own internalized homophobia. My colleagues had little contact with lesbian culture where identity was celebrated or with individuals who were happily and successfully living out in the day-to-day world. Hence, they carried with them a particular bias about lesbian experience based on their selective and limited window into the culture and community.

Personal reflection – Sandra Collins

The metaphor of **cultural baggage** helps to explain the processes of cultural transference and counter-transference. *Both clients and counsellors bring preconceived ideas about culture to their counselling process. Prior experience is either supportive of counselling or acts as a barrier in the establishment of an effective working alliance.* Clients and counsellors often resemble other people, prior relationships, or prior experiences that hold either a positive or negative emotional valence. The reasons for seeking counselling, expectations about how counselling should proceed, and the context where counselling occurs are potentially loaded with cultural meanings that influence the ways that both counsellors and clients react to each other. Where there is an alignment of cultural values, this is likely to enhance the development of a working alliance. However, diversity of perspectives and contrasting values may necessitate a bridging of worldviews (Arthur & Januszkowski, 2001). Culture-infused counselling competencies help counsellors to examine the cultural influences they bring to counselling and provide counsellors with a broader understanding about the cultural influences on clients' behaviour. Becoming a multiculturally competent counsellor requires a willingness to open the cultural baggage to see how personal experience impacts professional practices.

One of the most difficult experiences of cultural transference occurred for me in a training session involving members from various equity groups (e.g., women, Aboriginal people, persons with disabilities, and visible minorities). During the process of negotiating norms for the group to work together, I brought up the topic of time limits for group members' contributions in order to make sure that our training time was shared and that everyone could participate. This invoked an angry response from one participant, an Aboriginal woman, who interrupted the discussion with this statement, "Are you going to try to tell me when I can and cannot speak?" Despite my attempts to keep the focus on norms for group learning, this participant saw my actions as culturally offensive.

I chose to meet with this participant individually to discuss her reaction. She disclosed that her experience with teachers stemmed from residential school. My action hit a nerve that was raw and sore from previous experiences with teachers in a school where Aboriginal children were silenced. It was hard for us to move past this point in the training session. I tried to call upon her as much as possible. She made a point of interrupting me to make a point to me and to the group. What played out in our training session was historical oppression and I had to assume responsibility to try to make the current learning environment workable for her.

Another example of cultural transference occurred when I was working with a male student in counselling. The client had been referred by his program supervisor as he was not managing his academic program and this was his last chance to improve both attendance and exam performance. The student appeared motivated, even though I expressed concerns about the tight restrictions that were now placed upon his performance for academic success.

During five sessions of counselling, we talked about study skills and the client shared some of his views about life as a student, that it was a chance to party as much as he could before his impending marriage. His views about relationships and attitudes towards women were derogatory from my value system. I had to work hard to find something likable about this client and not impose my values in a judgment of his behaviour. Our last session was one of the most difficult I have ever encountered in working with hundreds of students. The client was belligerent, argumentative, and verbally abusive in his remarks about counselling, about women, and about me as a counsellor. I was initially stunned by this behaviour and had to step back from taking it personally. Finally, I said in a quiet voice, "I am not forcing you to be here, I am not trying to control your life. You can choose whether to be here or not. It seems that you are having difficulty with the terms of your academic contract. We can discuss that or you can decide that is not going to work for you."

The client calmed down and said that he would not be coming back because he had missed more days of classes because of partying. What seemed to be paramount for this client was his way of managing the ending of his school program and ending our counselling relationship. I was concerned about the gender issues that played out in this session and how representative this interaction was of the client's relationships with women. I also needed to reflect on how my reactions were based on gender issues and managing conflict across cultures.

Personal reflection – Nancy Arthur

Strategies for Increasing Self-Awareness and Awareness of Other Cultural Identities

Some counsellors have reacted strongly and negatively to the rationale for acquiring cultural awareness. The essence of the objection is that it is impossible to know everything about all cultures. This argument detracts from the benefits of gaining cultural knowledge and takes the focus off what is possible. Counsellors need to be knowledgeable about particular cultural groups in order to increase their cultural sensitivity (Jacob & Greggo, 2001). It may be overwhelming to consider expanding your knowledge, given the sheer magnitude of the number of cultural subgroups represented in Canada's population. However, you can set priorities for increasing competence through a number of means. Snapshot 6 lists some questions for reflection that may give you a place to start. These questions are relevant for each one of us, whether we are at the beginning of our journey towards multicultural competence or have been working in this area for many years. Cultural contexts continue to evolve, and each of us will continue to peel away the layers of our own cultural identities and biases over our professional lifetime – if we are willing to engage with ourselves and others on this level. In Chapter 18, you will find a detailed list of suggestions for how to continue to build your competency in the areas of self-awareness and awareness of client culture.

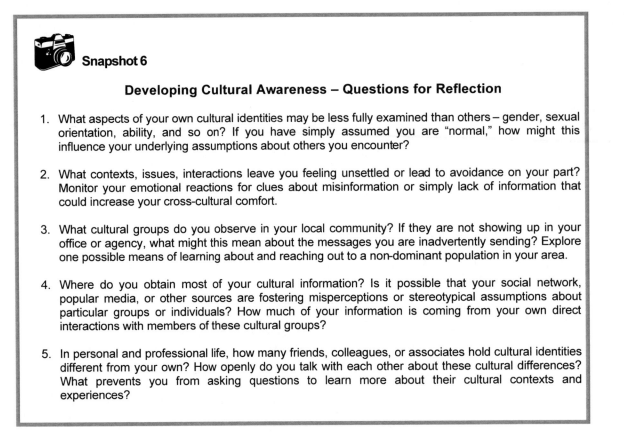

Snapshot 6

Developing Cultural Awareness – Questions for Reflection

1. What aspects of your own cultural identities may be less fully examined than others – gender, sexual orientation, ability, and so on? If you have simply assumed you are "normal," how might this influence your underlying assumptions about others you encounter?

2. What contexts, issues, interactions leave you feeling unsettled or lead to avoidance on your part? Monitor your emotional reactions for clues about misinformation or simply lack of information that could increase your cross-cultural comfort.

3. What cultural groups do you observe in your local community? If they are not showing up in your office or agency, what might this mean about the messages you are inadvertently sending? Explore one possible means of learning about and reaching out to a non-dominant population in your area.

4. Where do you obtain most of your cultural information? Is it possible that your social network, popular media, or other sources are fostering misperceptions or stereotypical assumptions about particular groups or individuals? How much of your information is coming from your own direct interactions with members of these cultural groups?

5. In personal and professional life, how many friends, colleagues, or associates hold cultural identities different from your own? How openly do you talk with each other about these cultural differences? What prevents you from asking questions to learn more about their cultural contexts and experiences?

Clients as Sources of Cultural Knowledge

One way that counsellors gain cultural knowledge is through their ongoing work with clients. Research confirms that caseloads and experience working with clients who are culturally diverse predict higher levels of multicultural competence (Allison, Crawford, Echemendia, Robinson, & Knepp, 1994; Allison, Echemendia, Crawford, & Robinson, 1996; Arthur & Januszkowski, 2001; Zayas, Torres, Malcolm, & DesRosiers, 1996). However, it is not the numbers of clients per se that contributes to the development of multicultural counselling competencies; rather, it is counsellors' willingness to be reflective about the stories that are shared by clients, to look for common patterns, and to incorporate learning into their repertoire of counselling expertise.

This does not mean that we should be reliant on our clients to inform us about culture. Although we invite clients to explain their culture to avoid stereotyping clients and imposing our ideas about best practice, it remains our responsibility to gain general background knowledge about the major cultural subgroups that are consumers of counselling services. Counsellors should engage in available professional development activities such as workshops, professional reading, and consultation activities that would increase their levels of cultural knowledge without having to solely rely on their clients (Arthur & Stewart, 2001; Roysircar, Hubbell, & Gard, 2003). The importance of self-responsibility in this area is mirrored in the frustration of clients who find that they are spending too much of their time (and money!) educating counsellors about basic cultural information that is readily available through other mediums. Clients find this particularly annoying when they do not perceive cultural factors as central to the presenting concern (Pope-Davis et al., 2002).

These comments should be read in light of the earlier discussion in this chapter about the importance of exploring personal cultural identity with clients and establishing the salience of particular components of identity to the presenting concerns. Each client develops an internalized culture based on personal, cultural, contextual, and universal factors, as well as cultural identity development processes. It is here that the counsellor should focus attention in the counselling process. However, this will be very difficult to effectively accomplish if you do not start from a point of solid cultural awareness of both your own and the client's culture. Once you establish competence in understanding other cultures, specific cultural information can be obtained through interactions with clients. The general background knowledge provides an orientation to culture from which to assess the worldviews of individual clients. Counsellors increase their level of collaboration with clients through encouraging them to be the experts about their situation, including the experts about their culture. However, boundaries need to be drawn to avoid exploiting clients as *cultural teachers* (Chung & Bemak, 2002). Clients quickly establish an impression about whether counsellors are likely to be able to understand their worldview and the issues for which they seek counselling. As consumer groups become more informed about professional practices, there will likely be more challenges directed to the professional competencies of counsellors in Canada.

Personal Transformation

As evidenced by the emphasis on self-awareness in this chapter, the multicultural counselling movement calls to counsellors to engage in a process of personal transformation (Fowers & Davidov, 2006). Fowers and Davidov, speaking from the perspective of virtue ethics, argued that to support the goals of multicultural counselling, it is important to focus on the cultivation of character strengths or virtues, which become the driving forces for action. These ideas reflect on the feminist principle of *the personal is political* discussed earlier in the chapter. We invite you, as you continue to read through this book, to engage in a process of personal transformation – to become the person and the professional you aspire to be.

Virtue is itself a culturally embedded concept (Fowers & Davidov, 2006); however, we have provided glimpses through this chapter of the kinds of personal/professional qualities that support culture-infused counselling. Many of these are also reflected in the culture-infused competency framework in Chapter 3. It is possible to behave according to particular attitude, knowledge, and skill competencies, however, and not actually engage in a process of personal transformation that results in a qualitative shift in *being* with oneself and others. One of the benchmarks suggested by Fowers and Davidov is that a virtue is something that is characteristic of an individual's attitudes and actions. One of the foundational character strengths required for culture-infused counselling competence is *openness to the other* (Fowers & Davidov). Chapter 5 will explore the ways in which this opening is expressed through the process of establishing a culturally sensitive working alliance.

Chapter Summary

The purpose of this chapter was to expand on the first two core competency domains for culture-infused counselling.

Domain I: Cultural Self-Awareness involves active awareness of one's own personal assumptions, values, and biases. There are five core competencies included in this domain, each described in terms of specific attitudes and beliefs, knowledge, and skills:

1. Demonstrate awareness of your own cultural identities.
2. Demonstrate awareness of differences between your own cultural identities and those of other dominant or non-dominant groups.
3. Demonstrate awareness of the impact of culture on the theory and practice of counselling/psychology.
4. Demonstrate awareness of the personal and professional impact of the discrepancy between dominant and non-dominant cultural groups in Canada.
5. Demonstrate awareness of your level of multicultural competence.

Domain II: Awareness of Client Cultural Identities involves understanding the worldview of the client and is divided into three core competencies, with subsequent attitudes and beliefs, knowledge, and skill competencies.

1. Demonstrate awareness of the cultural identities of your clients.
2. Demonstrate awareness of the relationship of personal culture to health and well-being.

3. Demonstrate awareness of the socio-political influences that impinge on the lives of non-dominant populations.

We have provided a glimpse into the kinds of concepts and process that will potentially enhance your competence in these areas through our exploration of cultural identity, worldview, models of identity development, acculturation and assimilation, cultural schemata, the risks of cultural oppression in counselling, and strategies for increasing awareness of culture. At this point in the book, you should be able to identify the areas of personal strength and weakness relative to these two core competencies.

Conclusion: Moving from Reflection to Engagement

The discussion in this chapter brings attention to the cultural issues that impact both counsellors and clients during every counselling interaction. No two individuals will present for counselling with identical worldviews or personal cultural identities, nor will there ever be a complete match between counsellor and client. It is from this foundation that we assert the importance of culture-infused counselling practices with all clientele. To be effective with a broad range of diverse clientele, counsellors must be willing to engage in continuous reflection about their cultural assumptions and their application of cultural knowledge. Failure to attend to specific cultural messages from clients risks stereotyping them and perpetuating their sense of marginalization in Canadian society (Arthur & Stewart, 2001). Viewing clients only as members of particular non-dominant groups homogenizes their experiences and ignores the tremendous cultural variability within any population (Popadiuk & Arthur, 2004). Individual differences need to be taken into account in the design and delivery of multicultural counselling services.

The culture-infused approach to counselling is designed to facilitate both general awareness of cultural differences alongside specific cultural inquiry, taking into account the relative similarities and differences between the worldviews of counsellors and clients (Pedersen, 2001; Weinrach & Thomas, 1996). Along with an assessment of worldview, counsellors are also encouraged to consider the influences of larger society that impact client behaviour. Unfortunately, forms of oppression such as racism, sexism, and homophobia continue to be evident in counselling practices and are reflected in the policies and procedures of organizations and other larger social systems (Helms, 1994; Sue et al., 1998). This culture-infused perspective balances the need for counsellors to appreciate salient cultural characteristics such as ethnicity, gender, or sexual orientation with other personal and contextual dimensions of experience (Hays, 2001; Pedersen & Ivey, 1993).

Gaining self-awareness and awareness of client cultures is not an end state; it is an ongoing developmental process. Whether one is a novice or an experienced counsellor, competency in this area includes continuous reflection on the potential influences of personal culture on one's professional role as a counsellor. Culture is complex, and our views of ourselves, others, and the world around us shift over time with additional life experience. Cultural awareness involves lifelong learning about who we are as cultural beings, how we are similar and different to others, and how we can bridge understandings of people's worldviews. Gaining cultural self-awareness and awareness of the cultural identities of others alone is not enough. The real challenge comes in moving from reflection to active engagement. The focus of Chapter 5 will be on translating the rationale for multicultural counselling from Chapter 2, the model of culture-infused counselling in Chapter 3, and the increased cultural awareness from Chapter 4 into effective counselling practices. The main mechanism for doing this is development of a culturally sensitive working alliance.

CHAPTER 5
CULTURALLY SENSITIVE WORKING ALLIANCE

Sandra Collins and Nancy Arthur

Key Terms and Concepts		
• Advocacy • Client-driven • Cognitive complexity • Consciousness-raising • Counselling conventions • Counselling microskills • Counsellor credibility • Cultural auditing	• Cultural empathy • Cultural inquiry • Culturally responsive intervention • Empirically supported treatments • Empowerment • Indigenous healing systems • Language barriers	• Multicultural case conceptualization • Mutual empathy • Resistance • Salience of cultural identity • Universal healing conditions • Working alliance

Introduction

One of the foundational premises of multicultural counselling is that the process needs to be centred in the cultural experience of clients (Moodley, 2007). Client issues must be viewed within the context of clients' life experience and worldview. This requires counsellors to be self-aware about the cultural conditioning that impacts their views of clients and counselling issues and to be knowledgeable about the worldviews of clients. However, multicultural competence also requires counsellors to define issues in ways that are meaningful for clients and to design interventions that are valued by their clients. Cultural awareness on its own is insufficient to ensure culturally responsive counselling services. This awareness must be translated into the specific tasks that facilitate attainment of counselling goals. The purpose of this chapter is to begin to translate these principles into practice by expanding on the culturally sensitive working alliance that forms the essential bridge between awareness and culture-infused practice.

Rather than developing a framework for culture-infused counselling for specific client groups, we will address core components of the counselling process to improve professional practice with all clients. We argue that the construct of the working alliance provides an inclusive framework to create a meaningful and respectful counselling process with all clients. We begin the chapter by reviewing the core principles related to the working alliance in light of some of the complexities of working across cultures. The focus of the subsequent discussion is on ways to incorporate cultural influences into counselling. This includes developing rapport between counsellors and clients, establishing goals and tasks of counselling, selecting and implementing interventions, and evaluating the effectiveness of counselling. In this chapter, we will approach the change process in the context of our work with individual clients, families, or groups. However, it is our premise that lasting change must also involve systems-level intervention, which will be more fully addressed in Chapter 6.

Connecting Multicultural Counselling to the Working Alliance

Students and counselling practitioners frequently ask these two questions: "How do you *do* multicultural counselling?" and "How is multicultural counselling *different from* or *similar to* other counselling?" There is no straightforward answer to these questions. As a starting point, let's revisit the discussion in Chapter 1 about *who counts* as a client in multicultural counselling. If counsellors take a culture-specific approach, they tend to define culture by specific dimensions of culture or group membership. This has implications for when and how counsellors engage in cultural inquiry with clients. If counsellors have the mindset that culturally diverse clients are equated to individuals from racial and ethnic groups different from their own, then they are likely to engage in cultural inquiry only with clients from those groups. In these cases, cultural inquiry is saved for designated client groups and remains an exceptional or separate part of counselling practice. Alternatively, counsellors who take a universalistic approach to multicultural counselling engage in cultural inquiry with all clients. Recall the discussion of cultural identities in Chapter 3; if you accept that each individual's internalized culture is reflective of a unique kaleidoscope of cultural, personal, contextual, universal, and ideological factors, then it is difficult to imagine a counsellor and client who would be a match on all of these factors. Our position locates culture at the centre of all work with clients (Pedersen & Ivey, 1993; Watson, Herlihy, & Pierce, 2006). The premise in this approach is that all counselling is multicultural in nature and that many of the same processes in counselling are relevant for working with all clients. If you accept this basic premise, then there is no difference between competent counselling and competent culture-infused counselling. However, this does not mean that *one size fits all*. Rather, it means that all counselling must be inclusive of culture and be flexible and responsive to the specific cultural experiences and needs of each client. Multicultural counselling is especially challenging when there are large differences between the worldviews of counsellors and clients. There are layers of complexity to culture that are constant considerations in the design and delivery of culture-infused counselling.

The emic/etic debate also applies to the theoretical frameworks counsellors select in their approach to working with clients from diverse cultural backgrounds. Several theoretical models exist for responding to culture in counselling (Mollen, Ridley, & Hill, 2003; Moodley, 2007). Some writers continue to assert that conventional counselling alone can serve the needs of all clients. There is little evidence to support this assertion. Many others call for modifications to conventional counselling through increased cultural sensitivity. Others focus on the development of culture-specific counselling interventions and techniques. These models can be distinguished based on their assumptions about the change process. The crux of the argument is whether the processes of change are universal or culture-specific (Mollen et al.). A number of authors have taken a common factors perspective, identifying what they see as universal healing elements or change processes (Daya, 2001; Fischer, Jerome, & Atkinson, 1998). Fischer and colleagues saw these approaches as providing a bridge between the culture-specific and universal approaches. The common factors approach supports the emphasis in this chapter on the development of a culturally sensitive working alliance (Lewis, 2006), identifying the client-counsellor relationship as primary among the potential common factors in therapeutic efficacy (Fischer et al.; Fukuyama 1990). The three other common factors identified by Fischer and colleagues are shared worldview between counsellor and client, expectations for change on the part of the client, and agreement on interventions that both counsellor and client believe will promote positive change. Each of these factors will be integrated into our exploration of the working alliance construct.

Although not explicitly acknowledged in the literature, the very existence of the multicultural competencies movement can be construed as reflective of an underlying belief in the universality of certain core factors in promoting change. The implicit assumption is that counsellors who become multiculturally competent based on a common set of competencies (broken down into specific attitudes and beliefs, knowledge, and skills) will be able to effect positive change with a range of clients who hold diverse cultural experiences and identities. Many current authors argue that the multicultural competence of the counsellor rather than the specific intervention protocol influences counselling outcomes (Coleman & Wampold, 2003; Fischer et al., 1998).

The culture-infused counselling competencies described in this book provide a framework for linking the emic and etic perspectives that we believe is more inclusive and responsive to cultural difference than the common factors approach. We are not suggesting that these competencies are all that is needed to serve the need of every client from every cultural background. What we are saying is that they provide the foundational tools for counsellors to approach clients with cultural sensitivity, to assess their needs, and to develop a plan to meet those needs or to provide clients with guidance on how to access resources that are more suited to their needs. A similar perspective is presented by Arredondo (1998).

The first two core domains of multicultural counselling competence were explored in Chapter 4: awareness of one's own culture and awareness of the client's culture. The purpose of this chapter is to help counsellors translate multicultural counselling competencies into the counselling process by exploring the third domain: establishing a culturally sensitive working alliance. As noted in Chapter 3, there are three core elements included in the traditional conceptualization of the working alliance. We have added a fourth component to build a stronger link between what happens in the counselling context and what is happening outside of that context to produce or perpetuate social injustices that negatively affect client well-being. The fourth competency in Figure 1 reflects this emphasis on social justice activities. Although we integrate social justice as a theme in this chapter, we will more fully expand on this particular core competency in Chapter 6.

Domain III: Culturally Sensitive Working Alliance.
Core Competency 1: Establish trusting and respectful relationships with clients that take into account cultural identities.
Core Competency 2: Collaborate with clients to establish counselling goals that are responsive to salient dimensions of cultural identity.
Core Competency 3: Collaborate with clients to establish client and counsellor tasks that are responsive to salient dimensions of cultural identity.
Core Competency 4: Engage in social justice activities to directly influence the systems that negatively affect the lives of non-dominant populations.

Figure 1. Domain III of the culture-infused counselling competencies framework.

As you read through this chapter, remember to use the *Culture-Infused Counselling Competency Framework* (see Chapter 3, Figure 4) as a reference point to link the concepts discussed to the essential attitudes and beliefs, knowledge, and skills outlined. In this way, you will increase the meaningfulness of the constructs and identify areas in which your own level of multicultural counselling competence may be strengthened.

Dilemmas in Building a Culturally Sensitive Working Alliance

At times, multicultural counselling feels like working on a *slippery slope.* There are tensions between adhering to the theoretical models and intervention strategies that are part of professional training and adapting practices to meet the contexts of clients' lives (Toporek & Reza, 2001). Some of the dilemmas surrounding multicultural counselling were introduced in Chapter 4 in the discussion of how counsellors may intentionally or unintentionally oppress clients. Many of these connect directly to the question of how one develops a culturally sensitive working alliance. Counsellors' concerns about offending clients may lead to reticence about introducing themes of culture into their discussion with clients. Taken to an extreme, counsellors avoid examining cultural influences on client issues. Overzealous counsellors committed to multicultural practices may overshoot the mark and turn up the cultural spotlight on client issues. Unfortunately, they may inadvertently miss issues that are a priority for clients. Counsellors may feel uncomfortable about issues of historical oppression and confused about how to deal with cultural transference issues that are projected from clients. Clients may be labelled as difficult due to perceived *difficult* cultural influences.

Counsellors need to recognize that their socialization and history of interacting with people from diverse cultures will influence their professional roles and how they perceive and respond to clients. Cultural currents are ever present in counselling and those currents influence forming and sustaining an effective working alliance with clients. The concept of the working alliance allows us to reframe some of the dilemmas encountered in terms of lack of congruity between counsellor and client perceptions of the goals, the tasks, or the nature of the counselling relationship (Collins, Arthur, & Wong-Wylie, in press). These barriers may reflect limitations in counsellor multicultural competence (e.g., discomfort with perceived cultural differences, insufficient knowledge of culture and culturally sensitive practices, or lack of expertise in managing a culture-infused counselling process), or they may reflect a client's level of cultural identity development, distrust of the counsellor or the counselling process, and other client factors.

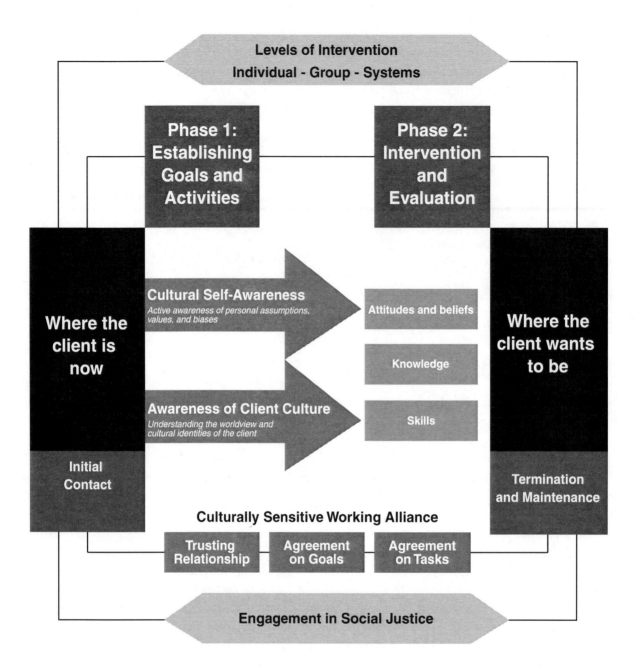

Figure 2. The working alliance as a foundation for a culture-infused counselling process.

Part of the challenge is that straightforward guidelines do not exist about ways to incorporate culture into counselling practices. More attention has been paid to how counsellors inadvertently make cultural faux pas and impose their worldview than on providing instruction about how to incorporate cultural influences in counselling. Figure 2 reflects our conceptual framework of the overall counselling process, first introduced in Chapter 3. By focusing on the working alliance as the foundation for the process of counselling, we are able to introduce concepts and strategies for establishing a collaborative, purposeful process that may be optimally responsive to the needs of all clients. The remaining sections of the chapter will be organized according to the first three core components of an effective working alliance: developing a trusting relationship and establishing agreement on goals and tasks. Like other writers in the multicultural counselling field, we are presenting culture-infused counselling as an orientation to practice that applies to all interactions with clients, not a specific model of counselling (Knapik & Miloti, 2006; Moodley, 2007).

Developing a Relationship of Trust and Respect

Roysircar, Hubbell, and Gard (2003) pointed out that one of the gaps in the literature on multicultural counselling is detailed exploration of the relationship between the counsellor and client. In the early 1950s, Carl Rogers introduced what have often been termed *necessary but not sufficient* healing conditions: empathy, congruence, and unconditional positive regard. Over time, a plethora of studies have assessed the impact of various aspects of the therapeutic alliance on counselling outcomes. One important theme that has emerged from these studies is that it is the client's subjective perception of the nature of the relationship rather than the counsellor's specific behaviours that impacts outcomes (Bachelor, 1995; Horvath, 2000). This is a particularly important observation in the context of multicultural counselling. What this implies is that counsellors may not be able to rely on a narrow set of skills for building an effective working alliance with all clients, but may need to incorporate other styles, approaches, and forms of communication so that what they intend to communicate is actually perceived by clients from culturally diverse backgrounds.

The development of an effective working alliance is an ongoing process in culture-infused counselling. An effective working alliance is built on a relationship that honours trust and respect. This is the glue between counsellors and clients in all counselling. Despite differences in worldview, establishing trust and demonstrating respect for clients forms a foundation for working together. In the late 1980s, Sue and Zane (1987) pointed to **counsellor credibility** as one of the central factors affecting client outcomes in counselling. Credibility was defined as *"the client's perception of the therapist as an effective and trustworthy helper"* (p. 40). Credibility is directly linked to culturally responsive and compatible conceptualization of client problems, counselling goals, and means for attaining those goals (Sue, 2006), all key components of the working alliance. Approaching clients in a way that is consistent with their culture is essential for building and maintaining credibility (Fowers & Richardson, 1996; Roysircar et al., 2003). Sue saw counsellor credibility as a significant factor in premature termination of counselling and encouraged counsellors to ensure that clients are able to identify a direct benefit from even the first counselling session.

Development of a working alliance does not occur at a single point in time, nor is it only a central concern at the beginning of counselling. As indicated in Figure 2, the working alliance is the foundation of the whole counselling process. However, there is evidence that if an effective alliance is not established within the first few encounters, the client is less likely to continue to engage in counselling (Horvath, 2000). Ongoing evaluation of the working alliance (Hiebert, 2001) is critical to ensuring that clients are adequately supported. Especially when the perceived gap between counsellor and client cultures is large, counsellors are advised to build in more frequent checks and indicators to assess the working alliance. This can be done through expressing interest and concern for understanding the cultural meanings of client behaviour (Chung & Bemak, 2002). Checking in with clients ensures that things are proceeding in ways that are meaningful for clients and that the manner of helping is viewed as supportive. When clients have a favourable view of helping professionals and find their services to be culturally relevant, they are more likely to access those services in the future.

Opening the Dialogue: Counsellor Experiences in Counselling Across Cultures

As a starting point, counsellors need to be willing to discuss some of the difficulties and tensions associated with working with clients across cultures. Open dialogue enables counsellors to identify key issues, increase confidence about working with clients from diverse backgrounds, and target specific domains of competency for professional development and growth. Supervision, consultation, and forums during professional development events offer counsellors opportunities for enhancing their competencies. The enhancement of competence and confidence for culture-infused counselling helps counsellors build an effective working alliance with clients.

Discussions about culture-infused counselling also need to draw attention to the positive aspects of working with clients from culturally diverse backgrounds. This helps to override the tendency, over time, to mislabel difficult counselling issues as *difficult clients* (Sue et al., 1998). Counsellors are encouraged to debrief with colleagues about the learning that they experience through working with clients across cultures. This leads to an exchange of expertise about practices that are meaningful to clients and ways to enhance the working alliance. This exchange of *best practices* helps counsellors acknowledge the positive aspects of their work with clients. It also affords an enriching professional development opportunity for peer supervision and sharing expertise with colleagues (Arthur & Stewart, 2001).

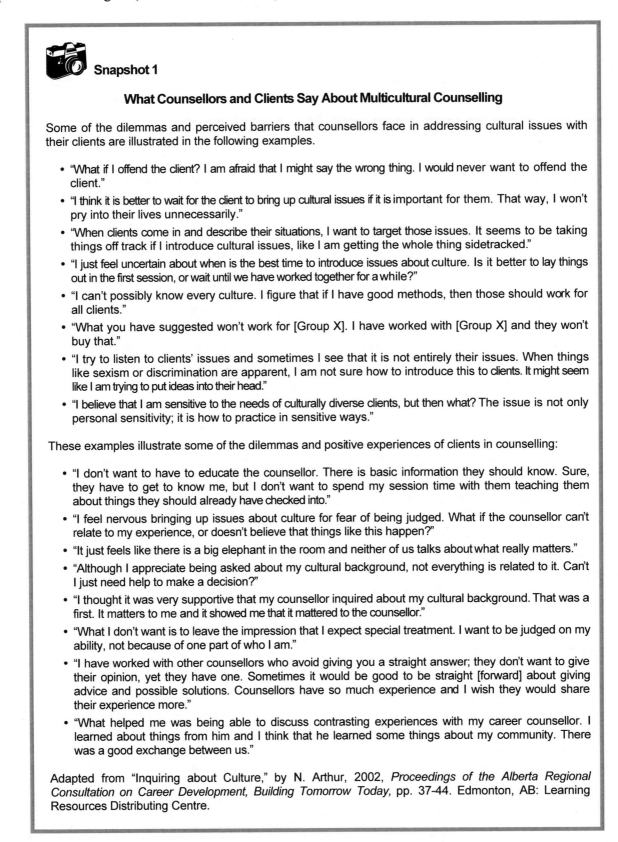

Snapshot 1

What Counsellors and Clients Say About Multicultural Counselling

Some of the dilemmas and perceived barriers that counsellors face in addressing cultural issues with their clients are illustrated in the following examples.

- "What if I offend the client? I am afraid that I might say the wrong thing. I would never want to offend the client."
- "I think it is better to wait for the client to bring up cultural issues if it is important for them. That way, I won't pry into their lives unnecessarily."
- "When clients come in and describe their situations, I want to target those issues. It seems to be taking things off track if I introduce cultural issues, like I am getting the whole thing sidetracked."
- "I just feel uncertain about when is the best time to introduce issues about culture. Is it better to lay things out in the first session, or wait until we have worked together for a while?"
- "I can't possibly know every culture. I figure that if I have good methods, then those should work for all clients."
- "What you have suggested won't work for [Group X]. I have worked with [Group X] and they won't buy that."
- "I try to listen to clients' issues and sometimes I see that it is not entirely their issues. When things like sexism or discrimination are apparent, I am not sure how to introduce this to clients. It might seem like I am trying to put ideas into their head."
- "I believe that I am sensitive to the needs of culturally diverse clients, but then what? The issue is not only personal sensitivity; it is how to practice in sensitive ways."

These examples illustrate some of the dilemmas and positive experiences of clients in counselling:

- "I don't want to have to educate the counsellor. There is basic information they should know. Sure, they have to get to know me, but I don't want to spend my session time with them teaching them about things they should already have checked into."
- "I feel nervous bringing up issues about culture for fear of being judged. What if the counsellor can't relate to my experience, or doesn't believe that things like this happen?"
- "It just feels like there is a big elephant in the room and neither of us talks about what really matters."
- "Although I appreciate being asked about my cultural background, not everything is related to it. Can't I just need help to make a decision?"
- "I thought it was very supportive that my counsellor inquired about my cultural background. That was a first. It matters to me and it showed me that it mattered to the counsellor."
- "What I don't want is to leave the impression that I expect special treatment. I want to be judged on my ability, not because of one part of who I am."
- "I have worked with other counsellors who avoid giving you a straight answer; they don't want to give their opinion, yet they have one. Sometimes it would be good to be straight [forward] about giving advice and possible solutions. Counsellors have so much experience and I wish they would share their experience more."
- "What helped me was being able to discuss contrasting experiences with my career counsellor. I learned about things from him and I think that he learned some things about my community. There was a good exchange between us."

Adapted from "Inquiring about Culture," by N. Arthur, 2002, *Proceedings of the Alberta Regional Consultation on Career Development, Building Tomorrow Today*, pp. 37-44. Edmonton, AB: Learning Resources Distributing Centre.

As we begin to explore how to develop a culturally sensitive working alliance, we encourage you to think about your own assumptions, fears, or misgivings about working with clients who differ from you in cultural identity. You may begin by listening to the voices of other counsellors and clients outlined in Snapshot 1.

Methods of Cultural Inquiry

One of the biggest dilemmas in counselling is how to open a dialogue about cultural influences with clients. One of the barriers to cultural inquiry is reluctance by counsellors to bring forward issues that they perceive to be *difficult topics*, such as ethnicity, socio-economic status, sexual orientation, religion, and disability. Fears about offending clients or introducing topics that might not be on clients' agenda lead to avoidance of cultural inquiry. A sense of uncertainty about how to discuss culture with clients may mean that salient cultural dimensions are never introduced. If counsellors think there are cultural influences on clients' presenting issues, it is important to bring forward the topic for verification through discussions with clients. There is an underlying principle for culture-infused counselling: *If in doubt, ask your client about her/his experience of culture!* Some clients may be confused by inferences and feel more comfortable responding to direct inquiries from counsellors. The main point of **cultural inquiry** is *to inquire about culture in a purposeful way to check out whether or not cultural influences are related to the clients' counselling issues.* Counsellors need to take the initiative to open discussion about culture in respectful ways. Clients are given choices about whether to pursue exploration about the influences of culture in their lives or to declare that cultural influences are not relevant (Arthur, 2002). Raising issues about cultural differences early in the counselling process is essential to establishing a sense of trust in the working alliance between counsellor and client (Fuertes, Mueller, Chauhan, Walker, & Hadany, 2002).

Direct methods of cultural inquiry

One way that counsellors manage cultural inquiry is to wait for the client to introduce topics, with the assumption that *if it is important, the client will bring it up.* However, this stance places the onus on clients to bring forward issues that may be ambiguous to them and that they have not fully considered as influential for counselling. When clients seek counselling, it is often at a time in their lives when they are facing a considerable amount of personal disruption. Clients who lack experience with professional helping relationships need guidance about what topics are considered as relevant content. Clients may also lack confidence about initiating conversations about culture for fear of being judged or for fear that their experiences will not be validated. This places the onus on the counsellor to gain competencies for engaging in cultural inquiry. Otherwise, counselling may proceed without important issues of culture being addressed.

Counsellors are advised to keep the purposes of cultural inquiry clearly in mind and to share with clients the purpose of their inquiry. The overriding goals of cultural inquiry are to express interest in understanding clients' perspectives and to gain greater insight into clients' issues. Counsellors must bear in mind whose needs are being served through cultural inquiry (Chung & Bemak, 2002). The focus is squarely placed on supporting clients. Although it is inevitable that counsellors will learn from clients, they should not be exploited as a source of cultural information. Otherwise, the purpose of cultural inquiry becomes misguided and an imposition on the client. Counsellors need to be astute enough to realize when discussion about culture is supportive for clients and reflects a direction the client wishes to pursue. It is possible that clients have resolved issues of culture, and persistence by counsellors may unnecessarily extend an agenda beyond what is in the clients' interests (Chung & Bemak).

Counsellors are reminded that clients are the experts on their lives. In turn, counsellors have responsibilities for assessing the potential influences of culture while letting client needs determine the agenda for counselling. Cultural inquiry can be as direct as asking clients about the salience of particular dimensions of culture on their lives, such as age, gender, race, socio-economic status, religion, sexual orientation, ethnicity, and disability (Hays, 2001) or creating exercises to facilitate exploration of various elements of cultural identity and their impact on the presenting concerns. The kaleidoscope model in Chapter 4 may provide a useful starting point for this discussion. In keeping with our model of culture-infused counselling, we recommend also integrating discussions of culture into intake interviews and case history processes with all clients. The more you enquire about culture as part of the *normal* process of counselling, the easier it will become and your clients will sense and respond to your comfort and ease.

Indirect methods of cultural inquiry

Cultural inquiry is also incorporated into multicultural counselling through indirect methods of assessment. A great deal of information can be gained about the influence of culture in a client's life without ever having to ask direct questions. This style may be chosen to match the communication styles of clients or used to complement information gained through direct methods of cultural inquiry. Indirect cultural inquiry requires counsellors to listen for cultural content as clients describe their lives and their current situations. Counsellors' multicultural knowledge about cultural groups is useful as a framework against which to compare individual client's experiences. The multicultural competency of cognitive complexity (Pedersen & Ivey, 1993), discussed in the next section, helps counsellors consider potential influences of culture in explaining clients' behaviour.

In a discussion of cultural inquiry in career counselling, Arthur (2002) provided examples of topics that provide a lot of information about cultural influences on clients' lives. These include:

- family history, roles, messages given by family members;
- beliefs about careers;
- resources accessible to the client;
- who else is impacted by decisions;
- conflicts in previous employment and work values;
- views of jobs in the family;
- values about work roles in comparison to other life roles;
- gender roles;
- sources of stress;
- clients' intuitive perspectives;
- beliefs about where the client should be in life;
- important role models; and
- what matters most to the client in life.

Culture-infused counselling requires deliberate efforts to incorporate cultural inquiry as a central process in counselling. Culture is a constant force in the lives of both clients and counsellors and a major influence on the therapeutic relationship. Incorporating cultural inquiry is essential for developing an effective working alliance.

Cognitive Complexity

One of the fundamental issues in multicultural counselling is counsellors' capacity and tolerance for ambiguity (Manese, Saito, & Rodolfa, 2004; Pedersen, 2001). As noted in the discussion of self-awareness, counsellors with low tolerance for ambiguity tend to retreat to ethnocentric approaches with clients. Alternatively, counsellors with greater tolerance for ambiguity are better able to stay engaged with their clients and seek new understandings of culture. **Cognitive complexity** is therefore *an essential competency that includes cognitive and affective skills for managing the ambiguities that emerge when working across culture, such as tolerance of ambiguity, ability to tentatively engage with multiple and sometimes competing perspectives, capacity for holding tentatively to interpretations of both client meanings and counsellor conceptual frameworks, assessment of the influence of personal values on judgments of client issues, and preferred treatment modalities.* Cognitive complexity skills are essential for counselling across cultural contexts (Pedersen & Ivey, 1993) and for establishing a solid working alliance with all clients. Cognitive complexity precludes premature assumptions, supports the ongoing examination of cultural influences through the counselling process, facilitates creative ways of testing these hypotheses, and helps counsellors to construct and revise cultural hypotheses as counselling unfolds (Sue, 2006). It also supports counsellors in examining cultural forces that occur in counselling relationships and their potential impact on the working alliance.

Cognitive complexity allows counsellors to consider a number of counselling hypotheses concurrently, including the salience of cultural dimensions for a client's presenting issues. This is not a static or one-time event; cognitive complexity skills are applied as an ongoing process in counselling. Cognitive complexity requires counsellors to simultaneously entertain a number of explanations, incorporating new information and discarding information that does not appear to be relevant for the client. It also requires counsellors to simultaneously monitor their personal reactions to clients and how their worldview may be compatible or incompatible with the worldview of clients. It supports reflective practice that considers the culture of both clients and counsellors.

Fischer and colleagues (1998) identified shared worldview between counsellor and client as one of the four key universal healing conditions. The worldviews of clients and counsellors come together in counselling, and counsellors require skills for monitoring the impacts of culture on the working alliance. The challenge of the working alliance is to bridge gaps in values, beliefs, and practices to establish common ground from which to build effective change processes. Ultimately, cognitive complexity skills help counsellors to stay engaged with their clients (Pedersen & Ivey, 1993) and avoid drawing premature conclusions about their clients and their presenting issues. These essential skills support counsellors in moving beyond a monocultural view to incorporating multiple belief systems in multicultural counselling. Counsellors are then able to expand their views of themselves, their clients, and the larger environment (Arthur & Stewart, 2001). This does not mean that counsellors must adopt the client's perspective as their own; rather, it suggests that points of connection must be established between worldviews so that clients feel understood and experience validation of their perspectives (Fischer et al.).

Cultural Empathy Enhances the Working Alliance

The hallmark of a working alliance is building an effective working relationship between counsellor and client throughout the entire counselling process. This requires counsellors to build rapport with people whose background and experiences may be quite different from their own (Fuertes et al., 2002). It takes considerable expertise and creativity to assess client worldviews, negotiate expectations, and build common goals and processes with clients from culturally diverse backgrounds. One of the most important aspects in building rapport is the demonstration of **cultural empathy** (Chung & Bemak, 2002; Ridley & Lingle, 1996). This extension of the term empathy recognizes the complexity of appreciating diverse worldviews, and is defined as *"the ability of counsellors to understand and communicate the concerns of clients from their cultural perspective"* (Ridley, 1995, p. 91). Cultural empathy is a dynamic process aimed at facilitating the development of shared worldviews in support of the overall multicultural counselling process.

There are two dimensions of cultural empathy: understanding the client's idiographic meaning and conveying an understanding of the client's idiographic experience (Ridley, Mendoza, Kanitz, Angermeier, & Zenk, 1994). Cultural empathy requires counsellors to be aware of their own worldview and to incorporate multiple perspectives. It supports counsellors in appreciating the worldviews of clients and in gaining a sense of understanding of the issues that they bring to counselling. The second component of empathy requires counsellors to have skills for intercultural communication. Counsellors must be able to communicate their understanding of counselling issues in ways that are culturally meaningful to clients. Culturally empathic counsellors are able to go beyond their perceptual filters of culture and work with the experiences and cultural meanings presented by clients. Cultural empathy in turn has been shown to increase the client's sense of counsellor credibility and hence strengthen the working alliance (Fischer et al., 1998).

Pedersen, Crethar, and Carlson (2008) suggested that empathy can be increased by counsellors in two ways. The concept of *perspective production* refers to the increase in attempts to understand another person from that person's point of view. At the same time as focusing on another person, counsellors need to be attuned to their personal reactions and interpretations. The concept of *perspective suppression* refers to the ability of counsellors to suppress their own perspectives in order to consider the perspectives of other people. These concepts point to useful strategies to help counsellors increase their abilities to empathize across cultures. The key is to be more open minded to multiple explanations and worldviews rather than limiting understanding to personal assumptions and worldview.

Cultural self-awareness and the working alliance

It is important to emphasize the link between cultural self-awareness and awareness of the cultural identities of clients, explored in Chapter 4, and the ability to establish a solid working alliance, examined in this chapter. Counsellor worldview may directly affect the ability of counsellors to effectively attend to and integrate cultural information. Constantine (2001a) found that counsellors with a more interdependent self-construal (defined as seeing a fundamental connection between self and others and valuing harmonious relationships) had better multicultural case conceptualization skills. Counsellors who reflected Western norms by viewing themselves as separate from others and valuing autonomy and independence showed less expertise for multicultural case conceptualization. Comstock and colleagues (2008), in their review of relational-cultural theory, used the term **mutual empathy** to refer to the *co-creation of shared understanding and connection that occurs as counsellor and client engage in a process of shared exploration of beliefs and worldview.* This concept of mutual empathy provides a better fit with the culture-infused competency model, in which self-awareness and awareness of client culture are intertwined. Developing cultural empathy may be more difficult for those who hold to traditional views of self in relation to others. Other monocultural perceptual schemata explored in Chapter 4 may function as barriers to both cognitive complexity and cultural empathy.

Another example of the impact of counsellor cultural awareness is reflected in the research on counsellor cultural identity development. Burkard, Ponterotto, Reynolds, and Alfonso (1999) explored the relationships between racial identity development and counsellors' ability to form a working alliance with clients. Although the results are limited by the use of counselling students as the sample, they clearly indicate that counsellors in the disintegration and reintegration stages may have more difficulty forming an effective working alliance with clients than those in later stages (pseudo-independent and autonomous). You are reminded to review the description of counsellor identity development and the implications for the counselling process in Chapter 4 and to take seriously the responsibility to openly examine your own level of identity development.

There is a misperception in some of the multicultural counselling literature that awareness of one's own cultural values and biases is the same as operating from a value-free perspective. Merali (1999) reminded us that, regardless of our theoretical orientation or degree of self-awareness, counselling is never a value-free activity. Counsellors are challenged to recognize and eliminate inappropriate cultural biases; however, this does not mean they are then without values and assumptions that will impact the counselling process. While cultural empathy involves communicating effectively to clients that their values and beliefs have been understood, it is also imperative that counsellor values be made explicit to clients. Where values are not made explicit, the working alliance between counsellor and client may be damaged, as those values find covert expression and reduce the level of trust on the part of the client (Merali).

Using cultural empathy in cultural inquiry

Cultural inquiry is best supported through counsellors' capacity for cultural empathy (Ridley & Lingle, 1996). Cultural empathy involves gaining understanding about the ways that culture has influenced a client's life and communicating that understanding back to clients in a meaningful way. The expression of cultural empathy gives clients the opportunity to confirm or disconfirm counsellors' portrayals of their issues. It is most useful in helping clients to gain a deeper understanding about cultural influences on their lives, their behaviour, and the issues that they bring to counselling. Cultural empathy is used to validate clients' strengths, to acknowledge values and beliefs, and to help clients understand how their issues might be seen from contrasting cultural perspectives (Arthur, 2002). Cultural empathy supports culture inquiry at different stages of the working alliance. It is fundamental for establishing rapport in the counselling relationship, it supports the establishment of counselling goals and tasks, and it supports collaboration in the selection and application of counselling interventions.

An initial step for cultural empathy is for counsellors to develop a mindset that culture matters. A second step requires them to deliberately incorporate cultural inquiry into their ongoing work with clients. Competent counsellors are able to incorporate their background knowledge about client cultures with new information provided by clients to appreciate their worldview and to define the unique needs of clients. In turn, clients may benefit from hearing feedback from counsellors about ways that their counselling issues may be impacted by cultural influences. This is particularly useful to shift the locus of client problems from solely intrapersonal sources to considering interpersonal, organizational, or systemic influences (Arthur, 2002). Some guidelines for establishing cultural empathy are provided in Snapshot 2, drawing on the work of Chung and Bemak (2002), Ridley (1995), and Ridley and Lingle (1996).

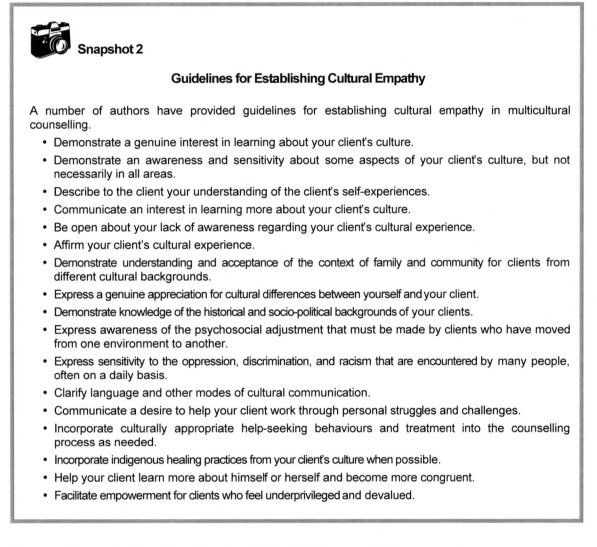

Snapshot 2

Guidelines for Establishing Cultural Empathy

A number of authors have provided guidelines for establishing cultural empathy in multicultural counselling.

- Demonstrate a genuine interest in learning about your client's culture.
- Demonstrate an awareness and sensitivity about some aspects of your client's culture, but not necessarily in all areas.
- Describe to the client your understanding of the client's self-experiences.
- Communicate an interest in learning more about your client's culture.
- Be open about your lack of awareness regarding your client's cultural experience.
- Affirm your client's cultural experience.
- Demonstrate understanding and acceptance of the context of family and community for clients from different cultural backgrounds.
- Express a genuine appreciation for cultural differences between yourself and your client.
- Demonstrate knowledge of the historical and socio-political backgrounds of your clients.
- Express awareness of the psychosocial adjustment that must be made by clients who have moved from one environment to another.
- Express sensitivity to the oppression, discrimination, and racism that are encountered by many people, often on a daily basis.
- Clarify language and other modes of cultural communication.
- Communicate a desire to help your client work through personal struggles and challenges.
- Incorporate culturally appropriate help-seeking behaviours and treatment into the counselling process as needed.
- Incorporate indigenous healing practices from your client's culture when possible.
- Help your client learn more about himself or herself and become more congruent.
- Facilitate empowerment for clients who feel underprivileged and devalued.

Equality and Power in the Counselling Relationship

Clients identify equality in the counselling relationship as a central factor in therapeutic success, particularly in multicultural contexts (Pope-Davis et al., 2002). Differential power can lead to distrust on both sides of the relationship. Both feminist and multicultural counselling models acknowledge the power differential in the counselling relationship and actively work to foster a collaborative relationship and a sense of empowerment in clients (Crethar, Rivera, & Nash, 2008; Goodman et al., 2004; Williams & Barber, 2004). Power is openly and actively analyzed to understand and reduce the impact of inherent power differences (Morrow, Hawxhurst, Montes de Vegas, Abousleman, & Castaneda, 2006; Reynolds & Constantine, 2004). Facilitating personal empowerment is more complex when working with clients from cultures where collective and familial values supersede individual interests. The challenge for the counsellor is to facilitate processes that enable the client to develop a sense of personal power that is culturally appropriate and allows them to move forward with their counselling goals (Ramsey, 1997).

Equality in the client-counsellor relationship is central to establishing trust as well as to the process of collaboration on the goals and tasks in the working alliance. Facilitating interpersonal empowerment may require the counsellor to release a personal hold on the power that comes from both position and group membership and to actively work to shift the balance of power in the interaction (Arredondo, Tovar-Blank, & Parham, 2008; Goodman et al., 2004). Traditional boundaries for the therapeutic relationship are re-examined in light of both cultural norms and social action agendas (Morrow et al., 2006). Roysircar and colleagues (2003) argued that, as counsellors engage fully in a process of increased self-awareness and awareness of the client's culture, power becomes a property of the relationship, a commodity that is shared between counsellor and client. A more egalitarian therapeutic relationship facilitates empowerment of clients to positively influence their own lives (Reynolds & Constantine, 2004).

Issues of expertise deserve special mention for their relevance in culture-infused counselling. Expertise should also be viewed as a shared commodity between counsellor and client. Clients from culturally diverse backgrounds are clearly the experts on their lives, their culture, and how their lives have been impacted through interaction with dominant groups in society (Crethar et al., 2008). As a professional resource, counsellors bring unique expertise about the counselling process. Counsellors need to take a leading role in educating clients about counselling and how this resource can enhance their lives (Crethar et al.). In some cases, the counsellor may assume the role of *cultural broker.* In this role, counsellors can help clients to better understand their lives in light of socio-political influences and to make informed decisions about accessing resources for their individual, family, or community needs.

Facilitating personal and interpersonal empowerment beyond the counselling relationship may be particularly challenging with clients who have experienced numerous forms of socio-cultural oppression and bring with them a sense of learned helplessness and disempowerment. In a later section of this chapter, we will explore the importance of moving the counselling agenda beyond the individual client to effect change in larger systems. This may include assisting clients from non-dominant populations to impact these social, economic, and political systems for their collective benefit (Lewis, Arnold, House, & Toporek, 2003). Lalande and Laverty, writing on feminist counselling in Chapter 14, discuss the important work of addressing systemic oppression of women as part of the counselling process. Similar positions are advocated by other contributors to this edited collection.

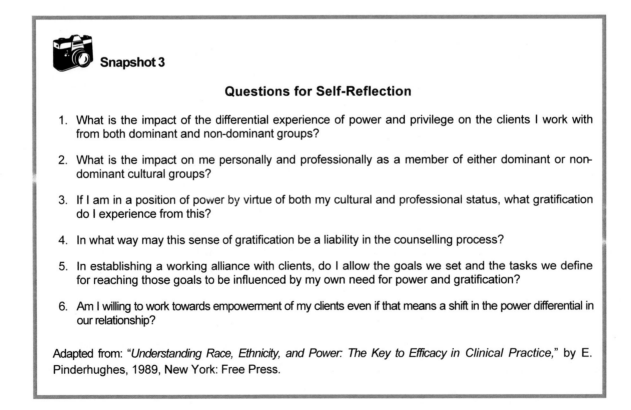

Snapshot 3

Questions for Self-Reflection

1. What is the impact of the differential experience of power and privilege on the clients I work with from both dominant and non-dominant groups?

2. What is the impact on me personally and professionally as a member of either dominant or non-dominant cultural groups?

3. If I am in a position of power by virtue of both my cultural and professional status, what gratification do I experience from this?

4. In what way may this sense of gratification be a liability in the counselling process?

5. In establishing a working alliance with clients, do I allow the goals we set and the tasks we define for reaching those goals to be influenced by my own need for power and gratification?

6. Am I willing to work towards empowerment of my clients even if that means a shift in the power differential in our relationship?

Adapted from: *"Understanding Race, Ethnicity, and Power: The Key to Efficacy in Clinical Practice,"* by E. Pinderhughes, 1989, New York: Free Press.

Communication Across Cultures

Effective communication skills are essential for culture-infused counselling, particularly in the expression of cultural empathy. It is challenging enough to maintain communication between people of similar cultural backgrounds. Communication is more complex across cultures due to the possibility of multiple meanings. Counsellors need to be able to communicate in ways that promote understanding of the worldview of clients and convey cultural understanding back to clients (Ridley & Lingle, 1996); effective communication itself is a critical intervention (Westwood & Ishiyama, 1990).

Counselling microskills

Various taxonomies for delineating and organizing communication skills have emerged in the counselling literature. In each case, **counselling microskills** are highlighted as *relatively discrete patterns of communication, each intended to accomplish a particular purpose in the counselling interaction. Typical examples include open questions or probes, reflections of meaning or affect, summaries, and other forms of structuring skills. Microskills also include non-verbal forms of communication such as silence and body language.* Counselling students are introduced to microskills as the foundation for developing more advanced helping techniques. The content of these courses typically relies on Western norms of communication and interviewing behaviour. Emphasis is placed on techniques such as direct eye contact, facing the client, open posture, and direct questions during counselling interviews. All of these techniques are culturally bound expressions of communication. These skills are also assumed to enable the counsellor to send and receive messages clearly and accurately (Knapik & Miloti, 2006). However, these concepts lose their meaningfulness if the complexity of cultural influences on each member of the interaction is not taken into account.

This doesn't mean that microskills are not important; rather, they must be understood within particular cultural contexts and their meanings must not be assumed to be universal. Although intended to foster behaviour that demonstrates interest during client interviews, microskills training can unintentionally introduce cultural barriers for working with clients from culturally diverse backgrounds if attention is not paid to the ways in which skill use must be tailored to meet the needs of the particular client. What is often lost in training processes is the link between skills (which in and of themselves are neutral tools) and the intended outcomes of using those skills. In working with clients from various cultural groups, different types or patterns of skills may be needed to effectively communicate the intended messages. Counsellors may also have to increase their repertoire of skills to reflect communication patterns consistent with clients' cultural experiences. For example, with some clients, a more significant use of silence as a core communication skill may be warranted.

It is essential that counsellors consider how meanings of communication are interpreted across cultures (Pedersen & Ivey, 1993). This includes consideration of verbal communication and non-verbal communication such as proxemics (use of personal and interpersonal space), kinesics (bodily movements), and paralanguage (vocal cues) (Sue & Sue, 1999). Evidence of competence in microskill use is in the ability to apply those skills differentially to achieve the desired results in a wide range of contexts with a wide variety of clients. To do this effectively the counsellor must have a vast repertoire of skills, possess awareness of cultural differences, and have sufficient mastery of the skill set in order to be responsive to the culture expectations of clients. Fischer and colleagues (1998) provided, as an example, a summary of the research on impact of counsellor self-disclosure on the working alliance. When ethnic identity was used as the independent variable, the studies revealed mixed results, with self-disclosure operating to facilitate or inhibit the relationship. Thus, even within a cultural group, attention to individual differences in style preferences is essential. Culturally competent counsellors are knowledgeable about a variety of interpretations that can be assigned to counsellor and client communication. They are also culturally flexible in tailoring their communication skills to support the development of an effective working alliance.

Counsellors may also assist clients through helping them understand the nuances of communication across cultures and the potential meanings that might be assigned to their own behaviour from other cultural viewpoints (Arthur, 2003a). This can help clients to better understand how they are perceived and responded to by others. Communication that appears to be straightforward in one cultural context might be very complex in others. For example, the seemingly simple response of *yes* has many meanings, ranging from clear agreement to total disagreement masked in an effort to save face for one or more of the people involved in the dialogue. Communication is complex, and counsellors require skills for understanding and conveying the meaning of communication with their clients. This requires counsellors to step outside their cultural context and develop skills for assessing the cultural nuances of communication.

Several years ago, I sustained a head injury that resulted in a year-long recovery process during which time my ability for certain types of complex cognitive processing slowly returned. I was a doctoral student at the time and, after several months away from school, I returned to classes and to some supervised practice in my practicum placement.

Before I was injured, I had been working with a relatively high-functioning client with a developmental disability. I had been doing acceptable work with her, but not exceptional from my perspective. The client was keen to return to counselling once I was back, and she became one of a few clients I continued to work with over those months of my own recovery. Within a few sessions, it was clear to me that something was dramatically different in our interaction and that she was responding to our interaction and showing progress in counselling in a new way. As I reflected on this change with my supervisory group, I came to understand that the shift I was noticing was, at least in part, the result of changes in me – particularly in the way in which I was communicating with her. My mind had slowed down. I was less inclined towards using language that was complex and difficult for her to understand. I was inclined to process things at a more concrete and less abstract level that was a better match for her level of functioning.

While I don't advise this means of enlightenment, the lesson has stuck with me in my interactions with others. We all tend to rely on language, ways of making meaning, or ways of processing information that are so familiar to us that we fail to see how that may be different for someone else. The tendency then becomes to rely on a change in the other person's level of understanding, when the responsibility for change often lies with us.

Personal reflection – Sandra Collins

Language proficiency

Communication in counselling is confounded by language proficiency. **Language barriers** may arise *when the counsellor and client are unable to communicate clearly in either the language of the counsellor or the language of the client.* This can be frustrating for both counsellors and their clients. When clients are experiencing psychological or other forms of distress, they can be overly taxed by limitations on their means of expression. When communication is perceived by clients to be difficult, it exacerbates a sense of anxiety about seeking professional services, and they become concerned about how they are judged by counsellors. At the same time, limited language proficiency inhibits the level of understanding that counsellors are able to acquire about their clients and their counselling issues. Counsellors may also feel discomfort about how best to overcome language barriers.

It is typical practice for clients to attempt communication in the language spoken by their counsellors. However, there is growing recognition of the rights of clients to be served in their first language, and counsellors need to be skilled about incorporating interpreters into the counselling process (Acevedo, Reyes, Annett, & Lopez, 2003; Sue, Arredondo, & McDavis, 1992). The following recommendations are offered for culture-infused counselling with clients who have limited capacity to communicate in the language of the counsellor (Arthur, 2003a):

- Gain information about the impact of language proficiency for clients' personal adjustment and mental health.
- Check your own discomfort or anxiety levels so this does not exacerbate the tensions experienced in the counselling relationship.
- Provide comfort and assurance to clients to help them feel more relaxed about communicating and to help clients feel they are accepted as they are.
- Provide feedback about the strengths of clients early in the interview so clients can overcome their sense of perceived weakness or deficits about language capacity.

- Encourage clients to take the time they need to formulate their words. Offer words to help with explanations and simplify the language used in interviews.

- Include more paraphrasing and perception checking to ensure understanding of clients.

- Use humour to let the client know how you might experience counselling if you had to communicate in the first language of the client!

Language proficiency issues also surface during group interventions with clients. Counsellors need to consider their group facilitation skills and how to incorporate language issues in ways that support fuller participation by clients. Several recommendations have been offered for group approaches to counselling (Arthur, 2003b):

- When negotiating norms about how the group will work together, introduce norms about language use.

- Encourage discussion between participants when clarification is needed.

- Invite a resource person who is fluent in the participants' first language to attend the workshop.

- Invite bilingual members of the group to assist with interpretation when needed.

- Translate key concepts for distribution to the group.

- Be tolerant, and encourage tolerance by other participants, of side conversations and disruptions to the flow of group interactions.

- Check your expectations for a quiet and controlled environment, and feel confident about facilitation with more than one or two people talking at once.

 Snapshot 4

Guidelines for Selecting an Interpreter

For individuals with low levels of English language proficiency, interpreters should be sought immediately upon receipt of the client's referral information. Interpreters should meet the following criteria.

1. Be proficient in the specific dialect of the target language that is spoken by the client (Santiago-Irizarry, 2001).

2. Be familiar with the communication norms and etiquette of the cultural group to which the client belongs (Pernice, 1994).

3. Be competently bilingual, with strong English skills, in order to respond to the frequent occurrence of code-switching among immigrant and refugee populations (Evans, Mejia-Maya, Zayas, Boothroyd, & Rodriguez, 2001; Santiago-Irizarry, 2001).

4. Be oriented to the nature of the counselling process, the issue of counsellor-client confidentiality, and the types of topics that may be discussed, as many of the simple terms for mental health concerns that tend to be used by counsellors such as *feeling down* or *blue* have no direct equivalents in immigrants' and refugees' native languages and may require thoughtful reframing (Dunnigan, McNall, & Mortimer, 1993; Rogler, 1999; Santiago-Irizarry, 2001).

In addition, the interpreter should be required to attend a post-session debriefing meeting with the counsellor after the first contact with the client to discuss any difficulties in the interpretation process (Pernice, 1994).

Contributed by Noorfarah Merali, University of Alberta

Clients' language proficiency should not pose a barrier to seeking professional services. Agencies where counselling services are offered need to develop policies and practices concerning the use of interpreters. Partnerships in the community, such as referrals to immigrant settlement agencies, can be helpful for securing interpreters for clients. Snapshot 4 provides guidelines for the use of professional interpreters. In cases where interpreters are not available, family members or friends often serve in the role of interpreter. Although this can facilitate communication, counsellors should be mindful of the potential impacts for clients and for their relationships. For example, because children often acquire fluency at a faster rate than their parents, children are sometimes asked to facilitate meetings on behalf of their parents. As noted in Chapter 13, this can result in a reversal of roles within the family. When community members serve in the role of interpreter during a counselling session, they are often in a position of gaining additional information about the client or the client's family that would not otherwise be available to them. Issues of confidentiality are heightened in these circumstances and need to be reviewed carefully with clients and their chosen interpreters.

The limitations of verbal communication

It is important for counsellors to recognize that language barriers may arise even if the counsellor and client speak the same language but identify with different cultural populations based on other identity factors such as gender, sexual orientation, or ability (Barret & Logan, 2002). Language norms are often defined by and in relation to the dominant male, heterosexual, able-bodied population, and subtle language barriers may emerge when counsellors fail to attend to the socio-cultural nature of communication and to recognize the importance of using terminology that fits for their particular client (Dorland & Fischer, 2001). Members of these non-dominant populations may also develop sub-cultural terminology that counsellors should become familiar with (Bridges, Selvidge, & Matthews, 2003). These issues are expanded upon further in the chapters on specific non-dominant populations in Canada.

Verbal communication itself may pose a barrier to the counselling process for clients who come from cultural groups where verbal articulation of thoughts and feelings is not the norm, particularly with someone outside of their cultural community (Chae, Foley, & Chae, 2006). Western approaches to counselling are based almost entirely on the *talking cure* model, including most models of multicultural counselling (Moodley, 2007). We will explores issues related to indigenous healing practices in a later section; it is important to recognize that our change processes remain very narrowly defined in spite of increased awareness of mind-body interface and alternative pathways to wellness.

To Be Directive or Not To Be Directive? Is That Really the Question?

Flexibility in counselling style has been identified by many writers as central to effective multicultural counselling. Some attempts have been made to link preferences for particular counselling styles to membership in specific non-dominant groups (Leong, 1993; Sue & Sue, 2003). However, we would argue that individual, within-group differences may be equally important considerations in establishing a good fit between counselling and client. It is critical for counsellors to develop a wide repertoire of counselling styles and responses to draw on in response to the cultural characteristics of particular clients (Sue & Sue, 1999).

One of the issues that counsellors often struggle with is the degree to which they should be directive in multicultural counselling contexts. Some clients specifically ask for their opinions or advice. Many counsellors have been trained to honour a cultural taboo from Western models of counselling about not giving advice to clients and avoiding the imposition of personal opinion. They are trained to let clients come to their own conclusions and to keep their opinions to themselves. This caution is useful to remind counsellors about the importance of letting clients be in charge of their own lives and about the hazards of imposing opinions on clients. However, the taboo about advice giving needs to be deconstructed for effective culture-infused counselling.

Part of the problem is that the multicultural counselling literature has stereotyped clients from non-dominant ethnic and racial groups as preferring directive counselling. In reality, counsellors must have skills for assessing levels of acculturation and negotiating a preferred style of counselling with clients. It is also presumptuous of counsellors to assume that their counselling is non-directive. We are always directive with our clients; it is a matter of degree. We are directive in choosing what parts of the conversation we attend to; we are directive through the tone of our feedback to clients; we are directive in punctuating client dialogue with acknowledgment, with praise, in honouring silence, and in choosing what to ignore.

It seems that the real issue is not about directiveness; rather, it is the counsellor's comfort level in operating on a continuum of directive behaviour in counselling. There are times when it is highly appropriate to share opinions with clients. These can offer clients new perspectives and help them to see how their behaviour might be viewed in another cultural context. There are potentially negative consequences when counsellors back away from being directive. To withhold opinion when asked by a client may be damaging to the working alliance. Clients may view the counsellor as evasive, feel their issues are not taken seriously, and wonder why a person they hold in esteem is not willing to share their professional opinions. The challenge for culture-infused counselling is to decide when sharing opinions and giving advice is supportive of the working alliance (Sue & Sue, 1999). There are fine lines between supporting a working alliance and imposing a worldview. Counsellors must examine the beliefs and assumptions upon which their professional training was based and have the courage to try working in ways that are based in client needs.

Cultural Influences on Counselling Conventions

The discussion of multicultural counselling competencies in Chapter 3 emphasized that counselling occurs in a context. **Counselling conventions** are *the structures of organizations that impact how counselling is designed and delivered. This includes things like the settings in which counsellors meet clients, the hours of service, the resources available for public use in waiting rooms, and the protocol that is used to set meeting times to meet with clients* (Fischer et al., 1998). Many of these structural issues are taken for granted by counsellors without considering the cultural norms that are embedded in social structures.

Amundson (1998) examined the social conventions embedded within the counselling relationship. These are instructive for making explicit the cultural norms that guide our relationships with clients. The cultural norms of counsellors become expectations about how counselling should unfold. Clients may be less familiar with these counselling conventions and need some assistance to understand the structures that surround counselling (Sue, 2006). Multicultural counsellors are challenged to examine the norms for counselling relationships in order to evaluate their utility for client access. What might be taken for granted is a strong message to clients about the way that counsellors are willing or not willing to provide services. The following examples of social conventions draw on Amundson.

- Counselling is structured by appointments that demand adherence to time restraints. The implication is that clients have to seek help when counsellors are available, which may not fit with their immediate needs. Some client issues and some preferred ways of relating might require drop-in services.

- The location of counselling is primarily an office setting designed for individual counselling, with some rooms allocated for family or group counselling. Limited space may prohibit the full and active participation of family members or other significant relations. It is not uncommon for one or more friends to accompany international students, and it is awkward to accommodate people when space is prohibitive.

- Counselling takes place only in these formal settings. The use of more informal settings, such as campus venues, other public places, parks, or client homes, is actively discouraged. Liability issues may need to be considered; however, the larger issue is our norms about where counselling should occur.

- Counselling relies primarily on verbal communication, and clients might not be highly verbal in expressing their needs.

- Counselling sessions normally involve continuous dialogue, which may seem overly intrusive and not be a good match for the communication style of some clients. Clients may benefit from time for reflection on content and consultation time. The use of silence can actually facilitate the change process.

- Most counselling follows a schedule of weekly appointments, unless special circumstances warrant alternative arrangements. However, weekly meetings might not serve clients' best interests; they may be disruptive to school or work schedules. Ideally, there needs to be flexibility about when sessions are scheduled and how often they occur.

- The length of time necessary for counselling reflects unspoken assumptions that counselling should extend beyond one session. When clients only attend one session, there are assumptions made about early termination and the ineffectiveness of the process. However, some clients benefit from an extended time frame for problem-solving within a single session. On the other hand, some clients need more time because of the complexity of their issues or because of their need to establish a solid relationship with their counsellor before discussing highly personal issues. Amundson (1998) recommended that counsellors approach each session with high levels of intensity in order to make the most of the time that is available.

- Evaluation of counselling services is also defined by cultural conventions. What counts as counselling is what happens in counsellors' offices and, more specifically, what falls under remedial interventions. Less appreciation and validation are given to outreach interventions focused on health promotion and illness prevention, effective counselling in informal settings, and so on. In many cases, numbers are the bottom line, whether they are clinically meaningful or socially responsible.

Taking the time to examine these conventions is an important step in culture-infused counselling. The process of cultural auditing, addressed in the next chapter, includes an examination of the policies and practices that surround the delivery of counselling. Ultimately, cultural auditing helps uncover barriers to access and helps strengthen the ways that counselling is responsive to all clients.

Trust and Respect as a Foundation for Engagement in Change Processes

The focus of this section has been on the development of an effective working alliance with all clients, both those similar and those quite different from the counsellor in terms of cultural identity and worldview. Engaging in both direct and indirect means of cultural inquiry with clients opens the door to understanding the lens through which they view the world. Such inquiry is facilitated by cultural empathy on the part of the counsellor and by cognitive complexity skills, which allow the counsellor to formulate and yet hold loosely to hypotheses about the impact of culture on client presenting concerns.

The working alliance in culture-infused counselling is based on the premises that both counsellor and client bring particular expertise to the relationship and that empowerment of clients is an essential component, especially for members of non-dominant populations who have experienced various forms of systemic oppression. To effectively build a relationship of trust and respect that will facilitate change on the part of the client, communication barriers, mismatches in counselling style, and changes to the traditional norms about how, where, and when counselling occurs may need to be considered. Once this type of relationship has been established the door is open wide for the counsellor and client to collaborate in setting appropriate goals and selecting culturally responsive means for reaching those goals, which is the focus of the next section.

Agreement on Goals and Tasks

One of the core elements of establishing a solid working alliance with clients is coming to agreement on goals and tasks. While we have listed goals and tasks as two separate elements in Figure 2, in practice there is a continual flow between these two elements throughout the counselling process, so they will be treated together in this section. Coming to agreement on goals and tasks involves more than simply arriving at a place where clients consent to following a particular path laid out for them by the counsellor. Rather, the focus is on establishment of a collaborative interaction in which all aspects of the counselling process are co-constructed and reflective of the unique cultural experiences and identities of both counsellor and client. The awareness of personal and client cultures provides the foundation for client and counsellor to work towards a shared definition of the problem, conceptualization of the various factors contributing to the problem, identification of the various means for addressing the problem, selection of an intervention strategy, and identification of the means by which success will be measured. The focus of this section will be on the various factors that facilitate or hinder this process, particularly in contexts where there are identifiable cultural differences between counsellor and client.

Cultural Flexibility in Assessment of Client Issues

Pedersen (2001) emphasized that definitions of problems and client diagnosis are strongly influenced by culture. The impact of culture is felt from the expression of symptoms, to the meaning attached to those symptoms, and the potential means for alleviating them (McCormick, 1996). What is *normal* is typically defined from a monocultural perspective, leaving many common experiences and adaptive behaviours of non-dominant populations open to interpretation as pathological, dysfunctional, or anti-social. As discussed above under the section on cognitive complexity, one important aspect of multicultural competence is the ability to entertain multiple hypotheses and to conceptualize client concerns by integrating and assessing the impact of cultural factors. Constantine (2001b) defined **multicultural case conceptualization** as *"the extent to which counsellors identify and integrate cultural factors into conceptualizations of client's presenting concerns"* (p. 34).

An important starting point may be an exploration of how members of a particular cultural group define health, what meaning they make of illness, and what factors they view as relevant to effecting change (American Psychological Association [APA], 2003b; Fischer et al., 1998; Sue, 2006). In keeping with this perspective, we have asked the writers of chapters later in the book to attend to the perspectives on health common among members of the non-dominant groups they write about. Similarly, a general understanding of human nature and goals of healing approaches may be essential.

 **Snapshot 5**

Principles of the Africentric Perspective as a Factor in Multicultural Case Conceptualization

- **The interconnectedness, interrelatedness, and unity of all things:** This principle is the foundation of the Africentric perspective. The spiritual, cognitive, affective, and behavioural dimensions of personality are all connected. People are connected to each other and to everything in their environment. An important aspect of this principle is a person's relationship with others.

- **The spiritual nature of human beings:** This principle of spirituality refers to the non-material or invisible spiritual essence or life force connecting all elements in the universe, with a holistic view of individuals in which mind, body, and spirit are inseparable. This principle is related to the principle of interconnectedness and contrasts with Eurocentrism, which stresses the material aspect of life. Integrated within this concept of spirituality is the important concept of morality, which, with its aspect of caring, could ideally help decrease human suffering. From a practice perspective, Africentrism stresses that everyone in society has the responsibility for helping ease adverse conditions that affect the quality of life of individuals, families, and communities.

- **Collective identity:** Also related to the principle of interconnectedness, this principle stresses the importance of the group or tribe over the individual. The group is responsible for the individual and the individual's responsibility is to the group. Group achievements are valued over individual achievements. It also manifests itself in the respect shown to elders by children and adults, and in the kinship and extended family system that includes not only the vertical family (grandparents, parents, and children), but also the horizontal family (aunts, uncles, cousins, and neighbours) (Cheboud & France, n.d.). Este and Bernard (2003) pointed out that "the presence of the extended family continues to be an important form of social support, assisting members of the community, who reside in a society where racism and discrimination are part of the daily reality" (p. 322).

- **The affective dimension:** The Africentric worldview considers a person's feelings and emotions essential to the process of self-examination and the acquisition of knowledge. Feelings and thoughts do not happen independently of each other. Este and Bernard (2003) suggested that in focusing on the relationship between feelings and thoughts, the Africentric perspective would assist helping professionals to gain a more holistic understanding of the experiences of clients and their world. This dimension would also include the perspective that time is fluid.

Contributed by Pamela Dos Ramos, University of Calgary.

Snapshot 6

Principles of the Inuit Perspective as a Factor in Multicultural Case Conceptualization

Inuit Qaujimajatuqangit (IQ) refers to Inuit traditional knowledge, culture, values, and language. Four Inuit IQ principles have been described by Wihak and Merali (2003) that directly relate to the counselling process:

The **principle of Pilimmaksarniq** [bold added] emphasizes valuing knowledge gained through observation and experience. It stems from the accepted fact among the Inuit community that the skills needed to ensure their success and survival in their own land were acquired by attending to both the nature of the land and other people's survival strategies, as well as through practice of various life skills.... This principle acknowledges that felt and revealed truth are more important and acceptable than logical/mathematical truth or scientific truth. (p. 244)

The **principle of Pijitsirniq** [bold added] emphasizes the need to serve one's community. It stipulates that an individual gains authority, leadership, and respect from the group through community participation, as well as by placing the needs and interests of the community above individual needs and goals. This principle also highlights the idea that authority and respect from community members comes from knowledge, skill, experience, and wisdom demonstrated in the context of community-based interactions, rather than from the position one holds.... (p. 247)

Stemming from the community orientation of the Inuit people, the **principle of Inuuqatigiittiarniq** [bold added] postulates that individual behaviour should be viewed within the larger community context. Respect, tolerance, and forbearance of others' actions are encouraged to promote peaceful coexistence among community members.... This principle therefore asserts the importance of non-interference in the Aboriginal worldview. (p. 249)

The **principle of Aajiiqatigiingniq** [bold added] addresses how decisions should be made in Inuit society. It encourages inclusive decision-making by all members of the family or community who may be affected by the outcome of a particular decision.... Therefore, this principle calls for a collaborative problem-solving approach that aims to create a climate where all parties in a situation understand each other and are relatively satisfied with decisions that may affect them. (p. 251)

From "Culturally Sensitive Counselling in Nunavut: Implications of Inuit Traditional Knowledge," by C. Wihak and N. Merali, 2003, *Canadian Journal of Counselling, 37*(4), 243-255.

Take, for example, African-Canadians and the components of worldview outlined in Snapshot 5. A counsellor coming from a Western perspective focused on independence and autonomy as symbols of healthy development and functioning may inadvertently frame an African Canadian student's struggle with career choices in a culturally inappropriate way unless the counsellor engages in a process of cultural inquiry to ascertain how closely that particular client holds to traditional cultural beliefs. McCormick (1996) provided a similar description of three core values of First Nations people in Canada: (a) balance among the physical, mental, emotional, and spiritual dimensions of human nature; (b) connectedness to family, community, nature, and spirit; and (c) transcendence of the individual ego. He argued that failure to attend to these core values will result in counselling processes that are not responsive to the unique goals of First Nations people. The four guiding principles of the Inuit worldview in Snapshot 6 provide yet another glimpse of the types of worldviews that are held by large portions of the Canadian population and that may not fit well with traditional foundations of Western counselling models. As you review these snapshots, reflect on the impact of these values and beliefs on the particular theoretical or conceptual framework that guides your counselling practice.

Based on the demographic changes in Canada noted in Chapter 2, it can be assumed that a large percentage of the Canadian population holds a collectivist worldview where interdependence is highly valued. Chung, Bemak, Ortiz, and Sandoval-Perez (2008) pointed to the risks of misdiagnosis of these individuals with the label of *dependent personality disorder*. To reinforce the point about the potential cultural bias of the *DSM-IV-R*, they suggested that we add the category of *independent personality disorder*, which would reflect Western cultural norms of self-responsibility and self-directedness and that could be seen as problematic to practitioners from other cultures.

Theoretical orientation

Conceptualization of client problems will be affected by the level of multicultural awareness and also by the theoretical orientation of the counsellor. It is important for counsellors to consider how their training represents particular cultural values, norms, and professional practices. There are serious limitations in the application of Western counselling theories and assessment practices with clients from culturally diverse backgrounds without considering their underlying assumptions about culture (APA, 2003b; Crethar et al., 2008; Moodley, 2007). Figure 3 in Chapter 4 delineates some of the cultural assumptions that typically underlie psychological practice and that may be damaging when working with clients from other cultures if simply applied without conscious awareness. Many of these assumptions are also tied to broader patriarchal models and cultural norms that are oppressive to women and members of other non-dominant populations (Evans, Kincade, Marbley, & Seem, 2005; Morrow et al., 2006). Many of the major theoretical forces in psychology have taken inadequate account of cultural differences in the understanding of human nature, healthy and unhealthy development, definitions of problems, and understanding of the change process (APA; Constantine, 2001b; Sue, Ivey, & Pedersen, 1996). Constantine examined the relationship between theoretical orientation and multicultural case conceptualization and found that counsellors with an eclectic or integrative theoretical stance were better able to incorporate multicultural knowledge into their understanding of client problems than those with a strictly psychodynamic or cognitive-behavioural perspective. Holding rigidly to a traditional Western perspective, on the other hand, puts one at risk of misdiagnosing or mislabelling clients from non-dominant populations (APA).

What any theoretical framework provides for counsellors is a template for organizing incoming information about a particular client. There is increased evidence that the choice of template may be less important than other variables in determining counselling outcomes (Atkinson, Wampold, Lowe, Matthews, & Aye, 1998; Fischer et al., 1998; Robinson & Howard-Hamilton, 2000; Sue, 1988). Each theoretical model provides a different way of conceptualizing client problems and intervention processes that may be equally effective if matched appropriately with a particular client's worldview and presenting concerns. It stands to reason that counsellors, who are adept at shifting conceptual frameworks among the traditional options available in psychology, will also be more adept at adding culture as an additional lens through which case conceptualization is viewed. What is most essential, however, is that the explanation for the problem arrived at by counsellor and client fit with the worldview and perspective of the client. The actual nature of the explanation (theoretical framework) appears to be less important than the credibility, salience, and acceptability of the conceptualization to both counsellor and client (Fischer et al.).

Cheatham and colleagues (2002a, 2002b) identified six theoretical principles that form a foundation for Multicultural Counselling and Therapy (MCT) and distinguished this approach from earlier conceptual frameworks. The first proposition is listed below; others are reflected in later sections of this chapter.

> *Proposition I.* MCT is a metatheory of counselling and psychotherapy. It is a theory about theories and offers an organizational framework for understanding the numerous helping approaches humankind has developed. It recognizes that theories of counseling and psychotherapy developed in the Western world, and those indigenous helping models intrinsic to other non-Western cultures, are neither inherently "right" or "wrong" or "good" or "bad." Rather, MCT holds that each theory represents a different world view. (p. 296)

Formal and informal assessment

An important area for consideration is the use of assessment and testing in the provision of psychological services. Problems associated with cultural bias in standardized testing are well documented (e.g., Chung et al., 2008; Paniagua, 2001). Many instruments, like the *DSM-IV-R*, are also based on a medical model that does not fit well with the counselling model of egalitarian working alliance between counsellor and client, attention to environmental and contextual factors in case conceptualization, and strengths-based, client-centred interventions (Zalaquett, Fuerth, Stein, Ivey, & Ivey, 2008). Counsellors must be skilled at incorporating culture into formal and informal assessment methods. This requires exploration of how client problems would be viewed in their home culture and the relative similarities and differences in the views of client issues from a dominant cultural point of view. It may also involve incorporating formal and informal assessment of racial identity development and acculturation (McDougall & Arthur, 2001). This doesn't mean that assessment measures like the *DSM-IV-TR* will never be used; however, they must be reconsidered from a multicultural/social justice perspective (Zalaquett et al.). Zalaquett and colleagues provided a model for reframing the use of the *DSM-IV-TR* from a tool for labeling diagnoses to the co-construction of culturally sensitive case formulations. Incorporating a cultural assessment of client issues is the first step in designing effective counselling interventions.

It is important to determine the limitations of formal assessment protocols and to eliminate those that are potentially damaging for clients from diverse cultural backgrounds (Crethar et al., 2008). Counsellors may feel torn between organizational demands for assessment services and professional knowledge about the potentially negative impact on particular clients. In these situations, counsellors must be prepared to discuss any problematic issues associated with assessment, to advocate for methods of assessment that are culturally fair, and to consult with their professional associations. Chapter 8 explores many of the issues related to assessment in multicultural counselling in more detail.

 **Snapshot 7**

Screening Culture Out

Jill is a counsellor working in a post-secondary institution that offers government-funded training programs to unemployed workers. Many of the applicants are from non-dominant racial and ethnic groups in the local community. The selection process includes administering achievement and aptitude tests that are offered only in English. Jill wonders about the disadvantage that this places on many applicants who seem to have a lot of expertise to bring to the program. She talks to the program coordinators and her supervisor about the problems associated with restrictions on the time taken to write the tests. They respond that they need a way to choose the best applicants and the testing process has always been used with timed tests. Her supervisor reminds her that partial funding for her position comes from the training programs and it is important to provide the assessment services. No changes are made.

Attending to Common Themes

While we emphasize throughout this book that each individual must be seen as a unique blend of cultural experience and identities, it is also important for counsellors working with clients from non-dominant populations to attend to some of the common experiences that have been identified in the literature that may be impacting on the particular client. There are two levels at which these common experiences or themes have been identified.

1. Fukuyama (1990) and others have pointed to shared concerns among members of diverse groups by virtue of their non-dominant status in society. Many of these themes were expanded upon on Chapter 4: cultural identity development, acculturation, cultural oppression, prejudice, stereotyping and discrimination, lack of privilege, and disempowerment. Counsellors working with clients from non-dominant groups are wise to include assessment of the personal relevance of these issues with all clients and to attend to the ways in which the experience of these factors may influence other presenting concerns.

2. The second level of common experience emerges in the literature related to specific non-dominant populations. One of the main contributions of the multicultural counselling movement has been the description of between-group differences, including conceptualization of health, development, and change processes (D'Andrea & Heckman, 2008). In Part II of this book, the invited authors identify some of the themes or common presenting concerns among lesbians, gay males, women, non-dominant ethnic groups, First Nations peoples, immigrants and refugees, and international students within Canada. Membership in each of these groups potentially includes a set of experiences or perspectives that may influence the counselling process. Counsellors must be cautious, of course, not to assume that these

issues are relevant for any particular client. Rather, they form another conceptual framework through which to approach the exploration of client presenting concerns and establishment of counselling goals.

The emphasis on common themes, combined with the ability to tolerate ambiguity and hold tentatively to cultural hypotheses, provides a foundation for counsellors to begin to build a sense of professional competence in working with a range of diverse clientele.

Applying a Social Justice Lens to Assessment

Many of the common themes that emerge in our work with clients from non-dominant populations involve some form of social injustice. The feminist, multicultural, and social justice movement in psychology share a common focus on the importance of environmental context to understanding individuals or groups (Crethar et al., 2008; Williams & Barber, 2004). Systemic oppression is asserted to impact all aspects of client experiences and to manifest in many symptoms of psychological unrest (Reynolds & Constantine, 2004; Whalen et al., 2004). The focus for both assessment and intervention must be expanded to include this oppressive environment. There is high potential for misdiagnosis when client cultural identities and contexts are not carefully considered (Crethar et al; Morrow et al., 2006).

Counsellors are encouraged to become informed about the socio-political contexts of their clients and to carefully analyze the existing power dynamics and the impact of oppression at both the interpersonal and socio-cultural levels (Bowman et al., 2001; Reynolds & Constantine, 2004; Whalen et al., 2004; Williams & Barber, 2004). In Chapter 6, we will provide some concrete strategies for approaching your work from a social justice perspective. In Chapter 10, we will revisit the interface of client experiences and identities with these systems of power (Morrow et al., 2006) and explore the implications of working with clients who hold multiple non-dominant identities. In the meantime, it is important to consider the impact of family, community, organizational structures, and social, economic, and political systems on the way in which each client describes and makes meaning of the issues they bring to the counselling process.

Matching Goals and Processes in Counselling

The working alliance needs to be **client-driven** in that both the *goals and tasks of multicultural counselling need to be understood and acceptable to clients, and they must derive from the synergistic and co-constructive contributions of both counsellor and client as cultural beings.* The danger of mismatches between goals and processes is higher when working across diverse cultures. It is important to ensure that clients and counsellors are working in the same direction and that they have negotiated the means of getting there. Shared perspective on defining the problem paves the way for the counsellor and client to come to agreement on the goals and tasks. Where such agreement exists, clients are more likely to hold expectations of positive change, a common factor in counselling efficacy identified by a number of authors (Fischer et al., 1998).

Leong (1993) detailed potential mismatches when the goals and processes of counselling are not well aligned. Figure 3 adapts Leong's model to the working alliance process and takes the constructs introduced a step further by arguing for a more idiosyncratic perspective of cultural identity. A culturally sensitive working alliance is built upon the congruence between counsellor and client perspectives on both goals and tasks. When counsellors do not negotiate mutually acceptable goals with their clients, counselling is less relevant to clients' presenting concerns. Mismatches in goals are more likely to occur when counsellors fail to see clients as unique cultural beings, either by assuming they are the same as the counsellor (ethnocentrism) or by classifying their needs according to misplaced assumptions about particular populations (stereotyping and prejudice). When goals have been mutually determined, counsellors need to ensure that the interventions that are chosen to reach counselling goals are culturally relevant for clients. This requires counsellors to have a wide repertoire of techniques and strategies that they can adapt to the needs of the particular client. Otherwise, clients may not see the relevance of counselling and may feel less motivated about trying interventions. In some cases, clients may be engaged with counselling interventions, but unable to articulate how they make a difference in their lives in relation to counselling goals. The risk of designing particular techniques for particular client groups is that group membership may not be the most salient factor in determining a particular client's needs and goals. Finally, when neither goals nor processes are matched in multicultural counselling, it is likely that counselling is proceeding from the monocultural view of the counsellor. This suggests the imposition of the counsellor's worldview and *what is best* for the client. Unfortunately, good intentions can lead to disastrous results in multicultural counselling.

**Agreement on
Goals**

Agreement on Tasks	**Cultural Sensitivity and Effective Working Alliance "I see you and I can help you"** • Negotiated and culturally responsive goals and tasks • Client feels understood and perceives the counsellor as trustworthy and credible • Client actively engages in culturally relevant interventions • Meaningful change likely to occur • Client satisfaction is high	**Limited Multicultural Competence "I see you, but I can't help you"** • Consensus on culturally relevant goals • Client feels understood but loses trust in the process and questions credibility of the counsellor • Counsellor is unable to translate goals into culturally appropriate and meaningful interventions • Lack of progress towards goals • Client satisfaction decreases	**Lack of Agreement on Tasks**
	Limited Multicultural Competence "I've learned a new technique; let's try it with you" • Goals derive from the counsellor's cultural perspective or stereotypic assumptions of client culture • Client feels misunderstood and distrustful • Counsellor may draw on culturally appropriate interventions, but they are not linked to the goals or salient cultural identity of the client • Change may occur, but may not be meaningful to the client	**Ethnocentric and Ineffective Working Alliance "I can help anyone if you just allow me to lead the way"** • Goals and tasks derive from the counsellor's cultural perspective • Client feels misunderstood and the counsellor lacks credibility and is seen as unworthy of trust • Counselling process is not relevant or meaningful for the client • Client is likely to become disillusioned and prematurely terminate • Distrust and cultural barriers to accessing service increase	

**Lack of
Agreement on
Goals**

Figure 3. Matching goals and processes in counselling.

What has commonly been referred to as **resistance** in traditional counselling models must be redefined in the context of our understanding of the culturally sensitive working alliance. Rather than being defined as a characteristic of the client that requires further intervention by the counsellor, *resistance is viewed as either a mismatch between counsellor and client in terms of the goals and tasks of counsellor or as evidence of a lack of trust and respect in the counselling relationship* (Hiebert & Jerry, 2002). It then becomes the counsellor's responsibility to manage the working alliance in a way that resolves these impasses rather than focusing on the client as the source of the problem. When clients feel they are not understood, they consider the services to have little utility and their opinions of professional helpers are adversely impacted. These examples underscore the importance of working collaboratively with clients in the determination of counselling goals and related counselling processes.

The points raised earlier in this discussion point to the necessity for counsellors to be reflective about how their personal agendas for clients are potentially biased. It also means using communication skills such as clarifying and perception checking throughout counselling to make sure that clients' agendas are the priority. Counsellors must also be careful to select interventions that are meaningful to clients and will ultimately serve their best interests (Merali, 1999). Counsellors require flexibility in selecting from a wide range of interventions and counselling styles used to deliver those interventions.

Respecting Counsellor Values and Responsible Caring

Ensuring cultural compatibility of goals and processes in counselling should not be misconstrued as blindly following the lead of the client or abandoning one's own value system in favour of that of the client (APA, 2003b; Ridley & Lingle, 1996). Rather, maturity as a counsellor involves being able to value and comfortably manage cultural difference (Fowers & Davidov, 2006). Merali (1999) contended that the premise of potential neutrality in some of the writing on multicultural counselling is both unrealistic and inappropriate. While we have challenged counsellors throughout this text to increase their awareness of personal and professional cultural biases and to work towards understanding of the clients' experience from within the perspective of their worldview, this should not be construed as meaning that the counsellor takes a value-neutral position or indiscriminately adopts the cultural values of the client.

Both counsellor and client have equally important roles to play in ensuring that the process of counselling enables the client to reach the desired outcomes and that the outcomes themselves will serve to enhance the healthy functioning of the client across a range of contexts. It is also important to recognize that client cultural frameworks may, in some cases, be limiting their potential for meaningful and healthy interactions, especially as cultures come into contact with one another. Counselling offers an opportunity for clients who are members of non-dominant cultural groups to also increase their awareness of the dominant culture (or sometimes other elements of their own culture as expressed within the Canadian context) and to expand their repertoire of communication and coping skills. It also offers them an opportunity to try on different conceptual frameworks for change. This may mean stepping outside of cultural comfort zones and engaging in new learning experiences (Sue & Zane, 1987). The key to client engagement in tasks that are less culturally familiar to them is their belief that the process will actually be effective in meeting their goals (Fischer et al., 1998). The ability of the counsellor to frame the process in terms that are meaningful to the client becomes critical.

There may also be circumstances in which the goals of the client are in direct conflict with the values of the counsellor or the ethical principles upon which the profession is founded. Merali (1999) pointed out that the principle of responsible caring in the *Canadian Code of Ethics for Psychologists,* which reflects the responsibility of the counsellor to promote the welfare of the client, may, in some cases where cultural worldviews clash, bring the counsellor into conflict with the principle of integrity in relationships, which promotes freedom from biases and respect for the client's perceived needs and goals. Particular attitudes, social norms, and behaviours within the client's culture may, in fact, reflect oppression or breaches of human rights. The call to cultural sensitivity must be balanced against the professional imperative to protect the welfare of both clients and society. Moodley (2007) argued that, to a large degree, the multicultural movement has ignored these issues of intracultural power and human rights. Multiculturalism has "failed to critique those ethnic minority cultural processes that are themselves hegemonic and oppressive, such as culturalism and fundamentalism (Moodley, p. 9). Chapter 7 will explore some of the issues that counsellors may need to grapple with in balancing the mandate of cultural sensitivity with their own boundaries or professional standards for competent and ethical practice.

An article in *Canadian Psychology* provided an example of the kinds of dilemmas that Canadian counsellors currently face as they struggle to balance an understanding of the impact of cultural oppression on clients with the expressed goals of clients and with their own values and demands of ethical practice. Fortier and Julien (2003) explored the ethical dilemmas surrounding the use of conversion therapy with gay, lesbian, and bisexual clients who want to function as heterosexuals. In spite of the recognition of the impact of widespread heterosexism and homophobia on the mental health of gays and lesbians in Canada and the current Canadian and American codes of ethics and guidelines for non-discriminatory practice, the writers conclude that the weight of the counsellor's decision to engage in conversion therapy should rest with the expressed needs of the particular client and their individual rights to establish their goals for counselling. Alderson in Chapter 16 and Collins and Oxenbury in Chapter 15 take exception to this conclusion on the basis that conversion therapy continues to reinforce the oppressive and discriminatory values of some members of Canadian society; the very existence of the continued debate is evidence of the complexity of the conflicts that may exist between personal, societal, and client value systems.

Merali (1999) pointed out that one of the most effective means of resolving ethical and value conflicts with clients is to explicitly explore the differences in values and the implications of those differences for the goals and tasks of counselling. "If values are considered to be an integral part of counselling, competence and skillfulness become equated with counsellors' ability to articulate and appropriately disclose the value system underlying their interventions preferences, and to critically examine the consequences of interventions stemming from different value positions" (Merali, p. 35). In this chapter, the emphasis on the working alliance as the umbrella construct for guiding the counselling process with all clients is motivated in part by our recognition of the fundamental collaborative nature of the counselling process. Such collaboration demands that the worldviews of all participants are understood, respected, and valued in each step of the process.

Designing Culturally Responsive Intervention Strategies

Sue and Zane (1987) pointed to the inability of counsellors to engage in culturally responsive intervention as the single most significant barrier to effective service provision to members of non-dominant cultural groups. This issue has continued to be highlighted by others over the past two decades (Dana, 1998; Sue & Sue, 2003). As a result, clients often see mental health services as unhelpful and either do not access these services in the first place or drop out early on (Arthur, 2003a; McCormick, 2000a).

Within the context of the working alliance model, we define **culturally responsive intervention** as *a purposeful activity or task that both client and counsellor agree to actively participate in, that fits with the worldview of both client and counsellor, and that both perceive as an effective means for attaining the goals they have mutually identified.* Others use the term *ritual* with similar meaning and have identified these rituals or interventions as another common factor in therapeutic efficacy (Fischer et al., 1998). As noted in the introduction to this chapter, however, a debate exists in the literature as to whether this means developing specific techniques for use with specific populations or viewing all counselling as multicultural in nature, as we have done, and requiring active adaptation of techniques from various models to fit with the cultural identity of each client.

The growing theoretical and research literature on multicultural counselling challenges counsellors to stay current with new developments that inform professional practice. Counsellors may choose to experiment with intervention strategies and techniques for working with specific client groups (e.g., Bingham & Ward, 1994; Casas & Vasquez, 1996; Leong, 1993; Prendes-Lintel, 2001). Alternatively, they may consider incorporating aspects of these models into their existing counselling frameworks. Although culture-specific techniques may form an important addition to a counsellor's repertoire, especially for clients who maintain the traditional values and beliefs of their culture (Fischer et al., 1998), caution is warranted. To judge the suitability of counselling methods based primarily upon the group affiliation risks masking the idiosyncrasies of the individual client and falling into the trap of applying stereotypes rather than seeing the individual for who he or she is (Coleman & Wampold, 2003; Patterson, 1996). The discussion of internalized culture in Chapter 4 reinforces the idea that each individual must be viewed as a unique combination of personal, cultural, contextual, universal, and ideological factors. Attempting to create specific treatment approaches for each combination of salient factors would result in an "unmanageable multiplicity of approaches to counselling. Let us beware of misguided multiculturalism leading us into the blind alley of particularism" (Ho, 1995, p. 17). The APA (2003b) guidelines favour culture-centred adaptations to development of a new and distinct repertoire of skills and strategies.

The importance of attending to cultural variables has been emphasized throughout this book. However, you are cautioned to pay careful attention to individual differences in assessing the impact of culture on client presenting concerns. The **salience of cultural identity** must be carefully assessed (Fowers & Davidov, 2006; Sue & Zane, 1987). Counsellors must answer the question: *To what degree do the various components of this particular client's cultural identity impact on the specific presenting concerns experienced in the particular contexts described?* There is wide variation within cultural groups based on level of cultural identity development and degree of acculturation, incorporation of multiple non-dominant identities, and degree of internalized oppression, for example (Dana, 1998; Sue & Zane, 1987). Once again, flexibility in adapting both style and process to the needs of the client emerges as a central multicultural competency. The task of the counsellor is to engage in a process of cultural inquiry that highlights the importance of cultural variables for a particular client. In some cases, culture may actually form the content of the problem and the tasks designed to address the problem. In other cases, it may be an important variable that impacts the presenting concern or it may have little or no bearing on the problem.

Within this approach, the working alliance between counsellor and client becomes the key to ensuring the cultural sensitivity and responsiveness of the counselling process. In the context of this relationship, the counsellor is able to assess "the appropriateness of the intervention to the specific client, with a unique cultural composition, experiencing a particular distress, in a particular moment" (Daya, 2001, p. 52). This approach fosters mutual respect and a collaborative dialogue between counsellor and client in which the cultural identity of both parties is recognized (Coleman & Wampold, 2003). The purpose of this section is to focus specifically on how counsellors might expand their repertoire of intervention strategies and techniques (counselling tasks) so they are better able to respond to the needs of a wide range of clientele from culturally diverse backgrounds (APA, 2003b). According to Cheatham and colleagues (2002b):

> *Proposition IV.* Counseling and therapy's effectiveness is enhanced when the counselor uses techniques, strategies, and goals consistent with the life experiences and cultural values of the client. No single helping approach or intervention strategy is equally effective across all populations and life situations. The ultimate goal of multicultural counselor and therapist training is to expand the repertoire of helping responses available to the professional, regardless of theoretical orientation. (p. 330)

Adapting Models of Counselling

As a starting point, counsellors trained in Western paradigms need to consider how those paradigms might be adapted for counselling across cultures (APA, 2003b; Tanaka-Matsumi & Higginbotham, 1996). This is only possible through a careful examination of the philosophical and theoretical assumptions that underlie these models to highlight how the fundamental values and practices found in Western models may be incompatible with the worldviews held by many clients (Crethar et al., 2008; Merali, 1999). Most counselling and psychology models are representative of Western European culture (Fukuyama, 1990; Merali). The values and assumptions associated with this cultural framework were outlined in Figure 3 in Chapter 4. This critical reflection should not be construed, however, as negating the contributions of these models to work with all clients, including those who hold non-dominant cultural identities. In fact, many recent conceptualizations of traditional theoretical models have been modified to attend more carefully to cultural differences (Merali). The multicultural counselling perspective is seen by most as supplementing rather than replacing the traditional psychodynamic, cognitive-behavioural, and humanist existential frameworks that make up the first three forces in Western psychology (APA, 2003b; Cheatham et al., 2002a, 2002b; Pedersen, 1991c).

Where problems arise is when counsellors hold indiscriminately to the tenets of a particular theoretical model without recognizing that model as simply one of many alternative perspectives for understanding human nature, healthy and unhealthy development, and the change process. This is where the art of counselling becomes important. Every moment of the counselling process is a creative and co-constructive endeavour that is shaped by the personalities, cultural identities, and experiences of both counsellor and client. For students and beginning counsellors, the prospect of letting go of the security of their favourite conceptual model may be tremendously intimidating. For this reason, they may choose to tread carefully in working with clients whose cultural identity is dramatically different from their own. Over time and through experience working with individuals different from themselves, they will increase their cognitive complexity and cultural empathy skills and be able to engage in cultural inquiry with clients in a way that facilitates adaptation of goals and tasks to fit with a broader range of clients.

The Search for Universal Healing Conditions

A number of authors writing from the common factors perspective have begun to identify what they see as **universal healing conditions**, defined as *fundamental change processes that may be tapped into through wide range of rituals or interventions as long as both counsellor and client hold positive expectations and view the task as culturally relevant and appropriate* (Fischer et al., 1998). The focus in this chapter on the working alliance is reflective of the themes that have emerged from the common factors research for promoting change in context where culture is a significant factor in the client-counsellor interaction. The assertion is that this approach may provide a unifying framework for the search for universal principles that apply across all counselling contexts and the aim of tailoring specific processes to the cultural context of a given client (Fischer et al., 1998; Fukuyama, 1990). We prefer the broader multicultural competencies model as the overarching framework for this unification, but recognize the contributions of the common factors approach to fleshing out the nature of those competencies. The common factors literature is limited in that it does not identify the kinds of cultural identity factors that can impact the client-counsellor relationship. For example, both counsellor and client expectations of change may be impacted by socio-political or historical contexts, experiences of oppression, and cultural perspectives on health and healing (Arredondo, 1998). In either framework the basic premise is "that the use of broad structures... does not imply reprieve from the need for specific knowledge" (Fischer et al., p. 541). Both culture-specific awareness and broad multicultural competence are essential.

Daya (2001) suggested that many of the common factors approaches fall short of providing counsellors with practical guidelines about how to approach the tasks of counselling with clients from diverse cultural backgrounds. She suggested that additional attention be paid to identification of universal processes for change that will facilitate the work of the multiculturally competent counsellor in implementing interventions that are meaningful for each client. While agreement on universal change processes remains elusive at this point, the responsibility falls to each counsellor to carefully examine the range of potential intervention processes and work with clients to select those that are most likely to lead to the desired outcomes.

A Comment on Empirically Supported Treatments

There is a movement in Canada focused on linking ethical and competent practice of psychology with **empirically supported treatments** [EST] (Hunsley, Dobson, Johnston, & Mikail, 1999; King, 1999; Pilkonis, 1999). A similar pressure exists within the multicultural literature generally (D'Andrea & Heckman, 2008; Fischer et al., 1998). The basic premise of the EST movement is that *it is possible to identify specific standardized treatment protocols for specific presenting problems based on empirical efficacy studies.* This has been referred to as the *unique factors* approach and is contrasted with the *common factors* approach discussed above (Fischer et al.). In the context of multicultural counselling, three challenges to or cautions about EST are warranted.

1. Much of the research used to support the implementation of certain treatment plans for certain presenting concerns has been conducted on clients representing the dominant cultural group. Little attention has been paid to variation across gender, ethnicity, sexual orientation, age, and so on (Coleman, 2004). "To assume universality of application to all groups is to make an unwarranted inferential leap" (Sue, 2001, p. 816). In their recent study, D'Andrea and Heckman identified 2,248 counselling outcomes articles compared to only 53 multicultural counselling outcomes articles. More culture-based outcomes research is clearly warranted.

2. As suggested above with reference to universal factors in counselling, there is compelling evidence that the key ingredients to success are factors common to many approaches and that the counsellor characteristics

and relationship between counsellor and client are central (Coleman & Wampold, 2003; Fischer et al., 1998; Horvath, 2000; Roysircar et al., 2003).

3. The premise of the empirically supported treatments movement runs counter to the argument posed in much of the multicultural literature that theoretical and practical flexibility on the part of the counsellor is essential in adapting the goals and tasks of the counselling process in response to the unique cultural identity and presenting concerns of the client. In fact, isolating specific cultural variables and determining the combination of variables that distinguish one individual from another in a way that allows for direct mapping onto relevant intervention strategies is an impossible task (Coleman & Wampold, 2003).

Counsellors are still responsible for ensuring that they draw on current counselling outcomes literature in designing appropriate interventions (D'Andrea & Heckman, 2008). However, all research must also be assessed for its cultural relevance, as elaborated on by Offet-Gartner in Chapter 9.

Impact of Cultural Identity Development and Level of Acculturation

Another important aspect of assessment of both goals and tasks in counselling is the level of cultural identity development and acculturation of both client and counsellor (Crethar et al., 2008; Sue, 2006). Cheatham and colleagues (2002a) acknowledged the importance of these factors in the core MCT propositions:

> *Proposition III.* Cultural identity development is a major determinant of both counselor and client attitudes toward the self, others of the same group, others of a different group, and the dominant group. These attitudes, which may be manifested in affective and behavioral dimensions, are strongly influenced not only by cultural variables, but by the dynamics of a dominant-subordinate relationship among culturally different groups. The level or stage of racial/cultural identity influences how clients and counselors define the problem and dictates what they believe to be appropriate counseling and therapy goals and processes. (p. 320)

The ability to assess a client's level of acculturation is essential for determining an appropriate course of action. A client may be from a visible non-dominant or ethnic group, but be highly acculturated to Western values and lifestyles (Sue, 2006). Alternatively, a client may hold strong beliefs about the traditions of her or his family and community and find interventions based upon Western models to be offensive, if not harmful. In the latter case, the counsellor needs to be skillful at assessing the type of culturally responsive intervention that is in the best interests of the client. Assessment of identity development must also extend to other factors beyond ethnicity. Being culturally sensitive may require going beyond the adaptation of traditional models of counselling to incorporate indigenous healing. Counsellors may be able to incorporate indigenous therapies into their own repertoire of interventions or build connections with local resource people who could assist in the facilitation of alternative counselling methods.

To establish an effective working alliance, the counsellor will also need to be aware of similarities and differences in stages of identity development between the client and counsellor (Crethar et al., 2008; Roysircar et al., 2003). Figure 6 in Chapter 4 illustrates several possible combinations of interactions, along with some potential implications for the counselling process and case examples. In the case of crossed regressive interactions, the counsellor's identity development may actually pose a barrier to client progress in counselling.

Multicultural competence is dependent upon counsellor self-awareness and active cultural identity development. Level of client cultural identity development may also affect the intervention tasks in two ways. First, cultural identity development itself may become a focus of the counselling process, with counsellor and client working towards enhancing client self-awareness and a more fully integrated identity status. Second, client cultural identity status may provide clues for the counsellor about barriers that may need to be overcome in addressing other counselling goals. For example, more effort may need to be invested in establishing trust between counsellor and client or interventions may be selected to focus on issues of alienation and isolation (McDougall & Arthur, 2001).

Addressing Spiritual Dimensions of Client Identity

Western paradigms of counselling have undervalued spiritual dimensions of problem definition and the ways that spirituality can be connected to client interventions. The neglect of spirituality in the multicultural literature, and the psychological literature generally, stands in stark contrast to the number of individuals in the population who hold some form of spiritual beliefs or practices (Berkel, Constantine, & Olson, 2007). There have been many biases, both implicit and explicit, about the role of religion and spirituality in counselling (Schlosser, 2003). Many counsellor training programs consider this topic to be too political to take on directly as part of the curriculum. However, there is a growing awareness that religion and spirituality may be central to many clients' healing processes (Fukuyama, Sevig, & Soet, 2008; McLennan, Rochow, & Arthur, 2001; Moodley, 2007) and that specific competencies may be required to work effectively with clients for whom spirituality is a salient cultural factor (Berkel et al.).

Spirituality and religion can play both a positive and a negative role in the lives of our clients. The chapters on gays and lesbians later in the book point to the struggles with personal spirituality that result from oppressive and identity-denying religious systems and the need to be prepared to address those issues in counselling. Counsellors must examine their own beliefs about religion and spirituality and be prepared to integrate spiritual dialogue into multicultural counselling (Berkel et al., 2007; Fukuyama, Murphy, & Siahpoush, 2003; Fukuyama & Sevig, 1999; McLennan et al., 2001). This includes reflection about Christian privilege and views of other religions practiced throughout the world (Schlosser, 2003).

Snapshot 8

Spiritual Competencies

The Association for Spiritual, Ethical, and Religious Values in Counseling (ASERVIC), a division of the American Counselling Association, asserts that professional counsellors must be able to:

1. Differentiate between religion and spirituality.

2. Contextualize religious and spiritual practices.

3. Increase self-awareness of beliefs and values to facilitate awareness and acceptance of those of others.

4. Examine personal belief systems in light of lifespan models of religious/spiritual development.

5. Demonstrate sensitivity and acceptance of client expressions of religion/spirituality.

6. Identify limits of understanding of spiritual/religious expressions and conduct appropriate referrals.

7. Assess the salience of religion/spirituality to the presenting concerns.

8. Be open to the client-driven integration of religious/spiritual themes in the counselling process.

9. Facilitate client-driven mobilization of religious/spiritual beliefs for goal attainment.

Adapted from "Spiritual Competencies," by ASERVIC, retrieved April 24, 2009, from http://www.aservic.org/competencies.

Spirituality also has healing potential (Moodley, 2007). Several models of counselling have been proposed that are more holistic in nature and that incorporate the spiritual dimension (e.g., Axelson, 1999; Diller, 1999; Lecca, Quervalu, Nenes, & Gonzales, 1998). Within the Canadian context, a number of writers have offered new ideas in this area. For example, McCormick and Amundson (1997) outlined a culturally relevant career-life planning model for use with First Nations people based on connectedness, balance, needs, roles, gifts, and aptitudes. This model acknowledges the importance of a holistic perspective in assessing client needs. It also incorporates the contexts of community and family in designing change processes and demonstrates how counsellors can enter those contexts to facilitate client growth within the context of relationships (Offet-Gartner, 2003a). Another model, suggested by Daya (2001), incorporates principles from Buddhist psychology, emphasizing views of human suffering, self, health, and disease into change processes with clients. These examples illustrate how counsellors can broaden their frame of references for working with clients across cultures.

The common thread in these approaches is the importance of initiating cultural inquiry about religion and spirituality (Berkel et al., 2007) and creating a space for clients to explore the meaning of their own experiences or beliefs for the issues at hand. Snapshot 8 illustrates some potential elements of enhanced cultural competence in this area; you will notice that, once again, awareness of the contextual, development, and other factors influencing one's own belief system is the starting point.

Facilitator of Indigenous Support and Healing Systems

Multicultural counselling requires counsellors to expand their knowledge about other modalities of helping and to be open to incorporating indigenous healing models (Coleman & Wampold, 2003; Moodley, 2007). Counsellors need to be able to make decisions that are in the best interests of their clients. This requires an ability to assess the nature of counselling issues from the worldview of the client and to design interventions that incorporate culture. In most cultures, there are **indigenous support and healing systems** that represent the *culturally embedded mechanisms for facilitating growth and change.* In Canada, these include *health care practices and traditional ways of healing of both First Nations peoples and immigrant communities* (Moodley). Counsellors need to take into account the role of traditional healing and the support systems that are meaningful for clients, which may lead to interventions outside of their usual realm of professional practice.

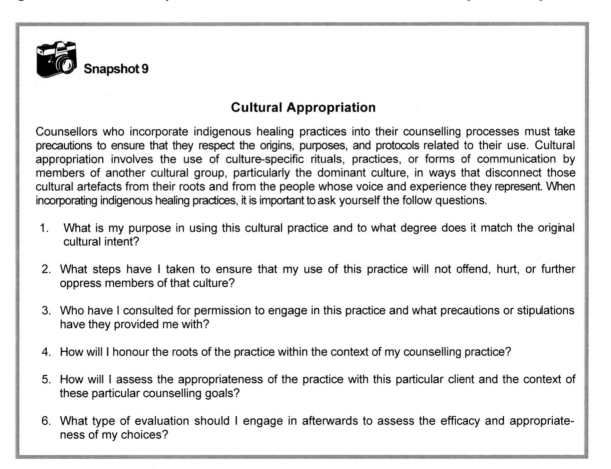

Snapshot 9

Cultural Appropriation

Counsellors who incorporate indigenous healing practices into their counselling processes must take precautions to ensure that they respect the origins, purposes, and protocols related to their use. Cultural appropriation involves the use of culture-specific rituals, practices, or forms of communication by members of another cultural group, particularly the dominant culture, in ways that disconnect those cultural artefacts from their roots and from the people whose voice and experience they represent. When incorporating indigenous healing practices, it is important to ask yourself the follow questions.

1. What is my purpose in using this cultural practice and to what degree does it match the original cultural intent?

2. What steps have I taken to ensure that my use of this practice will not offend, hurt, or further oppress members of that culture?

3. Who have I consulted for permission to engage in this practice and what precautions or stipulations have they provided me with?

4. How will I honour the roots of the practice within the context of my counselling practice?

5. How will I assess the appropriateness of the practice with this particular client and the context of these particular counselling goals?

6. What type of evaluation should I engage in afterwards to assess the efficacy and appropriateness of my choices?

From the worldview of some clients, traditional psychological interventions may be a foreign and inadequate way of addressing their concerns. Bankart (1997) reminded us that "everything we understand of the human condition and every assumption we make about human nature is ultimately a reflection of the historical, political, and cultural forces that have shaped our ways of seeing, and even being, in the world" (p. 5). He provided an interesting reflection on the evolution of the *talking cures* in Western psychology and contrasts these with a number of non-Western approaches built upon different philosophical foundations. Clients may respond better to indigenous support systems such as their extended family, community elders, church leaders, religious practices, as well as to indigenous healing methods (Sue, 2002). This requires counsellors to be familiar with the indigenous healing practices of culturally diverse groups who are living in their local communities. Gaining general familiarity with indigenous support and healing systems helps counsellors gain an appreciation of alternative models and facilitates client referral to and contact with the cultural resources in the local community. Collaboration with existing cultural and community resources broadens the basis for client support (Vera & Speight, 2007).

Counsellors may choose to extend their training to incorporate specific methods of indigenous healing. Clients may bring with them particular traditions and rituals related to cognitive, affective, or behavioural change that can be explored together in the counselling process. Counsellors who elect to treat their clients using indigenous healing methods are reminded of their ethical responsibilities to gain knowledge and skills in any new type of treatment prior to its application with clients. It is also advisable for counsellors to consider any cultural taboos against practicing some forms of indigenous healing by people considered to be *outsiders* to a cultural group. Respectful and ethical practices are important to facilitate indigenous healing systems (Sue & Sue, 1999).

Applying a Social Justice Lens to Intervention

The need to attend carefully to the salience of cultural identities and the impact of social injustices on client experiences is well established (Fouad, Gerstein, & Toporek, 2006). Current literature is focused on moving the focus of intervention beyond the individual client to the broader organizational, community, and social, economic, or political systems that foster social injustices (Crethar et al., 2008; Israel, 2006; Morrow et al., 2006). Drawing on their experience as anthropologists, Gerstein, Rountree, and Orgonez (2007) argued that counselling, even multicultural counselling, has tended to extract individual clients, both literally and figuratively, from their cultural contexts and in so doing has missed the opportunity to focus on system-level analysis and change. In some cases, this model furthers the isolation and sense of socio-cultural disconnection of these clients (Gerstein et al.). Insufficient focus has also been placed on power relations, social inequities, and the common experiences across non-dominant populations of various forms of cultural oppression (Moodley, 2007). According to Goodman and colleagues (2004):

> The target of intervention in social justice work is the social context in addition to or instead of the individual. Of course, the social context is not some abstract set of disembodied structures. Individuals compose a social context and shape policies, cultural practices, and social norms. The point here is that social justice-oriented psychologists locate the source of individual suffering in these social conditions and then work to change them. (p. 797)

This systems-level approach is essential if we are to truly honour the cultural norms, experiences, and social-political positioning of various cultural groups (Gerstein et al., 2007). The social justice agenda brings the multicultural counselling movement full circle to embrace its roots in the civil rights movement (Fouad et al., 2006). We will attend more fully to the issue of social justice in Chapter 6; however, it is important to note the implications of applying a social justice lens to the process of intervention with individual clients and groups. In this section, we briefly introduce systems-level intervention and then focus on consciousness-raising, empowerment, and direct advocacy for particular clients as examples of social justice interventions. In Chapter 6, we will expand upon on the counsellors' role in directly effecting social change.

Family, community, and larger social systems

One of the most significant implications of incorporating culture as a central factor in both the goals and tasks of counselling is the need to expand beyond the intrapsychic and individualistic focus of most traditional models to a more ecological perspective. Multiple layers of context must be attended to in both understanding the etiology of client problems and designing culturally responsive counselling processes (Coleman & Wampold, 2003; Crethar et al., 2008). The multicultural literature goes a long way in identifying some of those expanded contexts – families, organizations, social and political systems, and so on. From the initial assessment of client concerns to evaluation of counselling outcomes, counsellors are encouraged to take an ecological perspective and to attend to both intrapersonal and interpersonal or systemic factors. This principle is reflected in the following propositions by Cheatham and colleagues (2002a, 2002b):

> *Proposition II.* Counselor and client identities are formed and embedded in multiple levels of experiences (individual, group, and universal) and contexts (individual, family, and cultural). The totality and interrelationship of experiences and contexts need to be considered in any treatment. (p. 306)

> *Proposition V.* MCT stresses the importance of multiple helping roles developed by many culturally different groups and societies. Conventional counseling and psychotherapy are only one approach of many theoretical techniques and strategies available to the helping professional. These approaches extend beyond one-on-one therapy and involve helping strategies, systems intervention, and prevention approaches developed by the family, community, and larger social units. (p. 341)

Arredondo et al. (2008) pointed to the emergence or re-emergence of systemic approaches to counselling practice as a new wave multicultural practice that offers hope for the future. In recognizing these expanded contexts, there are two points for consideration. First, ecological contexts must be attended to in terms of their influence on the individual client or group that is the focus of intervention. Second, these broader systems may be targeted directly for intervention (Crethar et al., 2008). The phrase *the personal is political* was coined by feminist theorists to reinforce that social change is necessary for any lasting change at the individual level (Evans et al., 2005; Reynolds & Constantine, 2004). As counsellors, our primary focus may be on working directly with our individual clients; however, in many cases, change at the individual level is not sufficient to ensure lasting change (Williams & Barber, 2004). Social transformation is essential, and the locus of change must be broadened to include larger familial, organizational, social, and political systems (Crethar et al.; Gustafson, 2005; Israel, 2003, 2006; Reynolds & Constantine; Williams & Barber). The goal is to reduce inequities in power and privilege between dominant and non-dominant groups in society (Bowman et al., 2001; Williams & Barber).

Consciousness-raising

Consciousness-raising is central to both the feminist and multicultural counselling movements (Morrow et al., 2006; Reynolds & Constantine, 2004). In this context, **consciousness-raising** is defined as *the active engagement of client and counsellor in a critical analysis of the broader systemic factors that influence health and well-being, with a view to increasing awareness of the personal and interpersonal effects of systemic oppression and fostering shared commitment to social justice.* Part of the process of consciousness-raising is the demystifying of client experiences by opening dialogue about the impact of systemic discrimination and oppression (Morrow et al., 2006). Clients may not have consciously processed the connections between their problematic thoughts, feelings, or experiences and the broader contexts of their lives (Lewis et al., 2003). They may assume that the problem is theirs, when the problem is actually in the environment. The counselling process may involve analysis of gender and power relations, social injustices in access to resources and services, and other systemic barriers to health (Moodley, 2007). Awareness of the ways in which power and privilege are related to social location and cultural identities can illuminate the personal effects of various forms of oppression (Israel, 2003; Lowe & Mascher, 2001; Valentine, 2007) and open new avenues for intervention. Consciousness-raising itself functions as an intervention by fostering positive identity and empowerment (Crethar et al., 2008).

Social oppression of non-dominant groups often results in internalized racism, sexism, homophobia, and other misattributions. Consciousness-raising is an important means of assisting members of non-dominant populations to understand the role of oppression and discrimination in their lives and expand their conceptualization of both problems and solutions beyond themselves to the social, economic, and political contexts in which they live (Brabeck & Brown, 1997; Crethar et al., 2008; Fischer et al., 1998). Cheatham and colleagues (2002b) in their final proposition push the boundaries of traditional multicultural counselling to assert a similar position to the *personal is political* stance of feminist therapy writers:

> *Proposition VI.* The liberation of consciousness is a basic goal of MCT. Whereas self-actualization, discovery of how the past affects the present, or behavioral change have been traditional goals of

Western psychotherapy and counseling, MCT emphasizes the importance of expanding personal, family, group, and organizational consciousness of self-in-relation, family-in-relation, and organization-in-relation. Thus, MCT is ultimately contextual in orientation and also draws on traditional methods of healing from many cultures. (p. 351)

Empowerment

Crethar and colleagues (2008) identified empowerment as one of the cornerstones of feminist, multicultural, and social justice approaches. Bowman and colleagues (2001) defined **empowerment** as "*the process by which a marginalized person becomes aware of power dynamics and develops skills to gain control over his or her life without infringing on others' rights*" (p. 787). Client empowerment should be considered in three dimensions: *Personal empowerment – the sense of personal power and self-determination on the part of the individual; interpersonal empowerment – the sense that the individual can impact other people in a way that meets her or his needs and goals; and systemic empowerment – the sense of personal power for impacting the environment and conditions that affect individuals.*

As noted earlier in the chapter, client empowerment begins by establishing a collaborative and egalitarian working alliance (Goodman et al., 2004). A second key to empowerment is consciousness-raising (Crethar et al., 2008). Gaining an awareness of the impact of context on well-being opens up new avenues for change. However, awareness must be supplemented with the development of new skills required for clients to take control of their lives and to positively impact their environments (Crethar et al.; Lewis et al., 2003; Toporek & Williams, 2006). These new skills enable clients to take action to change the circumstances or systems in which they experience oppression (Morrow et al., 2006) and ultimately to model and encourage others in their communities to advocate for change (Crethar et al.). Israel (2006) noted that engaging in social action may support positive identity development for members of both non-dominant and dominant populations.

Advocacy

It is important to balance our belief in the power of our clients to define and shape their own lives with the constraints and barriers imposed by the power-laden contexts of their lived experiences (Valentine, 2007). There are times when it is simply unrealistic and potentially unsafe to expect clients to advocate on their own behalf. At this point, it becomes the counsellor's responsibility to take direct action on behalf of the client (Lewis et al., 2003). In this context, we define **advocacy** as a *twofold process that ranges from empowering and supporting clients to effect change in the external factors and systems that negatively impact health and well-being (client-led advocacy) to social justice actions on the part of the counsellor designed to effect change in these broader organizational community, social, economic, or political systems.* Toporek (2000) offered a useful theoretical framework in which empowerment and social action are considered as end points of a continuum. Counselling interventions with individuals or groups to support them in recognizing and addressing socio-political barriers to their health and well-being sit at one end of the continuum. Social action interventions in which the counsellor advocates on behalf of the client for social change in larger organizations or systems are located towards the other end. This framework is useful for considering the nature of client issues within social systems and helps counsellors to conceptualize relevant social action interventions.

Advocacy interventions may range from simply connecting clients to appropriate resources and paving the way for them to successfully meet their needs, to identifying and addressing barriers to effective and culturally sensitive service within organizations, to lobbying for change in social or political structures (Lewis et al., 2003). Bell and Goodman (2006) pointed out the necessity of taking a systems-level approach to the struggles of battered women, in which the counsellor actively works towards change in the social and economic situations that form barriers to change for these clients. A similar argument and model for systems-level intervention is presented by Palombi and Mundt (2006) in their work with women with disabilities. Counsellor advocacy will become a central focus of our discussion in the next chapter.

Planning For Endings in Culture-Infused Counselling

It is essential for counsellors to plan for endings in ways that maintain the integrity of the working alliance, especially where significant differences in cultural identities and worldview have been identified. There are general suggestions in the counselling literature about ways to bring closure and facilitate endings with clients (Arthur, 2002; Gysbers, Heppner, & Johnston, 1998; Kramer, 1990; Perlstein, 1998). However, there is little written about how culture might influence the process of finishing counselling. Cultural norms for relationships influence how counsellors and clients view endings in counselling. Counsellors need to be prepared to negotiate the terms of their relationship beyond counselling. Many clients value the relationship with a counsellor and wish to maintain contact after counselling. As noted in the examples in chapters 17 (Arthur) and 7 (Pettifor), counsellors need to examine their *rules* for boundaries in multicultural counselling, including contact with clients after the goals of counselling have been achieved. Dual relationships are more complex across cultures, and counsellors must carefully consider their decisions about when to sever relationships with clients. A *no contact rule* may not be appropriate for counsellors who have ongoing interactions with members of local community groups. It may also not be realistic for a member of a small non-dominant population (e.g., gays and lesbians) where social contact is often inevitable (Barret & Logan, 2002; Brown, 1985; Fassinger, 1991). Former clients may also be valuable cultural consultants for helping counsellors to understand the issues of future clients and for connecting to resources within the community. Regardless of the circumstances, counsellors need to take a lead role in negotiations with clients about when counselling will terminate and how future contact will be managed.

These issues underscore the importance of cultural reflection about the meaning of endings and the ways that endings will be facilitated. Of particular concern are premature endings by clients from under-represented groups who are discouraged by experiences of counselling (Gysbers et al., 1998; Sue & Sue, 1990). Unfortunately, counsellors may not be able to hear directly from clients about their reasons for choosing to end counselling before their goals have been attained. Additional research is needed to clarify the processes that support clients from culturally diverse groups to continue with counselling.

Chapter Summary

The purpose of this chapter was to explore the third core domain of the culture-infused counselling competency framework introduced in Chapter 3. The working alliance is proposed as an umbrella concept that provides the connection between cultural self-awareness and awareness of client cultural identities and the actual application of that awareness in applied professional practice. **Domain III: Culturally Sensitive Working Alliance** includes four core competencies, each described in terms of specific attitudes and beliefs, knowledge, and skills. This chapter expanded on the first three competencies. In Chapter 6, we will focus more directly on the fourth competency.

1. Establish trusting relationships with clients that take into account cultural identities.

2. Collaborate with clients to establish counselling goals that are responsive to salient dimensions of cultural identity.

3. Collaborate with clients to establish client and counsellor tasks that are responsive to salient dimensions of cultural identity.

4. Engage in social justice activities to directly influence the systems that negatively affect the lives of non-dominant populations.

It is in the context of the working alliance that counsellors communicate to clients that they understand and appreciate the cultural factors that impact on health and well-being and that they are able to mold the counselling process to suit culturally embedded meanings, needs, goals, and processes. We continue to argue that the same culture-infused counselling process is applicable to all client-counsellor interactions, but also recognize that, in working with members of many non-dominant populations in Canada, the knowledge, attitudes, and skills of the counsellor may be challenged to a greater degree and a broader range of counselling skills, conventions, styles, strategies, interventions, and resources may be required to be effective in meeting client needs.

The working alliance provides an overarching framework for linking the goals and tasks of counselling to the cultural awareness of self and other that forms the foundation for culture-infused counselling. This stretches beyond simply the selection of culturally appropriate strategies and techniques to flexibility in assessment processes, culturally responsive theoretical orientation, appropriate matching of goals and processes of counselling, identifying common change factors and universal healing conditions, incorporating indigenous healing practices and resources, and working to effect change in familial and social systems. While client retention remains a challenge in multicultural counselling contexts, attention to the working alliance from the point of initial contact through to termination and follow-up offers hope for engaging clients from a wide range of diverse backgrounds in an effective change process. For many practitioners, the translation of cultural awareness into practice through the working alliance will be the most challenging component of their pursuit of multicultural counselling competence.

Conclusion

Building multicultural counselling competencies requires a continuous process of reflection, knowledge acquisition, and practice of counselling skills. All of this needs to be managed in a deliberate way to help counsellors identify key areas for continued learning through professional development. Benchmarks for evaluation also help counsellors to review the competencies that they are incorporating into their individual and organizational practices. Application of the culture-infused counselling competencies framework supports counsellors in preparing for the increasing demands of providing services to clients who are from culturally diverse backgrounds.

For many years, the primary role of the counsellor has been in the direct professional practice of psychology with individuals, families, and groups. The culture-infused competencies framework begins from the perspective of this important role. However, as the demographics of Canada continue to shift and the clientele we meet are increasingly diverse in cultural background, themes begin to emerge that leave practitioners in a position of either continuing to covertly support the status quo or being called to action in roles that stretch beyond the boundaries of much of their professional training. Although it is important that we continue to mend the wounds of the disadvantaged, it is even more important that as counsellors we begin to take a more active role in preventing the social, economic, and political ills that lead to woundedness in the first place. In Chapter 6 we explore social justice issues as they relate to counselling and challenge you to consider ways in which you are able to effect change at broader systemic levels that will enhance the well-being of all clients, particularly those in positions of powerlessness by virtue of oppression in our society.

CHAPTER 6
SOCIAL JUSTICE AND CULTURE-INFUSED COUNSELLING

Nancy Arthur and Sandra Collins

Key Terms and Concepts		
• Advocacy	• Cultural auditing	• Expanded counselling roles
• Advocacy competence	• Cultural guides	• Nice Counsellor Syndrome
• Advocacy competencies	• Cultural reflection	• Oppression
• Counselling psychology	• Empowerment	• Social justice

Introduction

Chapter 5 focused on building an effective working alliance with clients to ensure that the goals and tasks of counselling are responsive to their cultural identities and worldviews. Our focus was predominantly on the first three core competences in Figure 1. We also emphasized the importance of looking beyond the individual client, family, or group to the broader systems they are part of to ensure appropriateness of both case conceptualization and intervention. The root of the problem for many clients may lie in community, organizational, social, economic, or political systems because these systems perpetuate the biases of the dominant culture – sexism, heterosexism, ageism, racism, classism, and so on. At the end of Chapter 5, we introduced some of the ways in which counsellors can work with clients to effect change in these broader systems through consciousness-raising, empowerment, and advocacy. The purpose of this chapter is to expand on the discussion of social justice and to provide more detailed information for counsellors on how to engage in social justice action to directly influence the systems that negatively affect the lives of non-dominant populations, the final core competency in Figure 1.

Domain III: Culturally Sensitive Working Alliance.	
Core Competency 1:	Establish trusting and respectful relationships with clients that take into account cultural identities.
Core Competency 2:	Collaborate with clients to establish counselling goals that are responsive to salient dimensions of cultural identity.
Core Competency 3:	Collaborate with clients to establish client and counsellor tasks that are responsive to salient dimensions of cultural identity.
Core Competency 4:	Engage in social justice activities to directly influence the systems that negatively affect the lives of non-dominant populations.

Figure 1. Domain III of the culture-infused counselling competencies framework.

As you read through this chapter, remember to use the *Culture-Infused Counselling Competency Framework* (see Chapter 3, Figure 4) as a reference point to link the concepts discussed to the essential attitudes and beliefs, knowledge, and skills outlined. In this way, you will increase the meaningfulness of the constructs and identify areas in which your own level of multicultural counselling competence may be strengthened.

This chapter expands upon the model of culture-infused counselling by discussing social justice as a core value for the practices of counsellors and psychologists. The themes expanded in the chapter include:

- exploring the ways in which counsellor roles and models for counselling delivery must be expanded to support social justice;

- examining the ways that culture and social justice are addressed in counselling theories and models of practice;
- reclaiming social change values in professional practice;
- reviewing perspectives on social justice that provide direction for culture-infused counselling;
- emphasizing the importance of community-capacity building and empowerment;
- describing social-justice advocacy;
- introducing the American Counselling Association (ACA) Advocacy Competencies (Lewis, Arnold, House, & Toporek, 2002);
- naming and overcoming barriers to social justice in professional practice;
- inviting dialogue about professional education for social justice;
- introducing cultural auditing as a tool for reflective practice; and
- applying cultural auditing through a case example.

The discussion in this chapter provides a rationale for infusing social justice advocacy as the foundation of multicultural counselling practice. The competency framework outlined in the previous chapters emphasized social justice as a core value that guides culture-infused counselling. In this chapter, the linkages between social justice and professional counselling practices are elaborated upon.

Expanding Roles in Culture-Infused Counselling

The American Psychological Association (APA) (2002b) *Guidelines on Multicultural Education, Training, Research, Practice, and Organizational Change for Psychologists* point to the "changing landscape of psychology" (p. 53). The demographics of the populations we serve are changing, but the roles and areas of practice are also changing. Counsellors and psychologists are increasingly involved in a variety of roles within government, health care systems, higher education, and the corporate and not-for-profit sectors (APA, 2002b). Sue's (2001) *Multiple Dimensions of Cultural Competence* model emphasizes the importance of expanding the focus of cultural competence beyond the level of applied practice with individuals or groups to the professional, organizational, and societal levels. This expanded focus introduces new roles and areas of practice for counsellors and psychologists that are not traditionally associated with the professions. "The development of cultural competence will only be successful if we take a systemic and holistic approach to infusing cultural competence throughout [the organizational and societal contexts]" (Sue, p. 817).

It is timely for counsellors to examine their professional beliefs about the delivery of counselling services. In addition to roles involving individual, group, and family counselling, there is growing recognition of the importance of roles that involve health promotion, prevention of illness, and social advocacy (Goodman, 2009; Sue, 2002; Toporek, Lewis, & Crethar, 2009). Counsellors are increasingly being asked to provide services to clients from diverse cultural backgrounds. A corresponding reality is that counsellors need to expand their views about what constitutes counselling, where counselling is delivered, and what constitutes effective service provision.

There are three forces driving these trends (Sue, 2002). First, conventional counselling roles may not be perceived as helpful for clients. Second, many client issues are caused by external forces. Although individual counselling may be helpful for a client, it is increasingly important to address environmental and systemic barriers. Third, there are many non-Western or indigenous forms of helping that are more compatible and effective for clients. Counsellors must be willing to expand their services to include alternate roles that are complementary to interventions dealing with symptoms of individual distress. This includes designing and delivering interventions for working with individuals, organizations, and promoting social change. The challenge for counsellors is to examine the traditional structures of counselling to see how well client issues are addressed. In turn, counsellors are encouraged to look at alternate ways of service delivery that expand their roles and methods of addressing the systems that surround client concerns.

Sue (2002) described the common characteristics of alternative roles for health providers that are instructive for counsellors:

- Counsellors are more active in these roles.

- Counsellors are working outside of their offices in settings such as homes, institutions, and other community settings.

- Counsellors are more focused on changing environmental conditions that impact their clientele. Interventions focus on the systems that adversely impact clients' daily lives or enhance their health and well-being.

- Counsellors view client problems as something experienced by clients as opposed to viewing clients as having problems. There is also more focus on conditions surrounding clients that contribute to the manifestation of problems experienced by clients.

- Counsellors shift their orientation from primary treatment and remediation of client problems to the prevention of problems and promotion of health.

- Counsellors increase their sense of responsibility for determining both the course and outcome of counselling. Ideally, this is determined in collaboration with clients who are involved in the selection of counselling interventions and in determining criteria for their effectiveness.

 **Snapshot 1**

Vignette

Thomas is a 30-year-old male who emigrated from Guatemala when he was 26. Thomas joined extended family in Canada, relatives who had fled to Canada as refugees in the early 1980s, so he did not remember these family members very well. Thomas was trained as an engineer in his home country and had gained two years' experience before immigration. He has been frustrated with his employment situation in Canada, as the only work offered to him is at the level of a technologist, and he feels underemployed. Recently, at work, he has had conflict with a co-worker. Thomas has discussed his experiences of working on a team. He feels like the engineers, who are also the bosses of the company, favour the other employees, who have more local experience. There is a lot of banter between employees, but Thomas feels it goes too far. He likes to bring dishes from his home country for lunch. After explaining about a dish that his aunt made for him, one of the other workers referred to him as "Tortilla Tom," a nickname that has stuck. Thomas seeks employee assistance counselling with the idea of returning to school, but he is not sure if there is really any point.

Questions for Discussion:

1. What dimensions of culture are relevant for working with this client? Please include dimensions that might be relevant for the client and dimensions that might be relevant for you as the counsellor.

2. Describe potential interventions that would be directed at social justice, through intervening with Thomas directly, and through intervening with the organization.

3. What are the ways that counsellors can build effective alliances for enhancing employment access and mobility for workers who are culturally diverse?

4. What competencies (attitudes, knowledge, and skills) would support counsellors for engaging in social justice interventions at the levels described in #3 and #4?

From Diversity to Social Justice in Culture-Infused Counselling

Views of multiculturalism are represented by "a continuum reflecting the varied ways in which 'difference' is understood or theorized" (Harris, 2001, p. 16). Harris suggested that the basic focus of multiculturalism is located in examining *differences between* cultural groups and *differences within* cultural groups and, in more complex ways, in seeking to examine *differences beneath* cultural groups. The multicultural counselling literature has alerted professionals to be cognizant about differences that exist between dominant and non-dominant groups in our society and to be sensitive about individual and within-group differences. Although sensitivity to the similarities and differences between counsellors and clients is a key focus in frameworks of multicultural competencies, it falls short of efforts to overcome some of the social inequities that adversely impact persons from non-dominant groups in Canada. From a culture-infused counselling perspective, it is important to examine the social structures *beneath and around people that perpetuate power differences* and to introduce efforts to ameliorate social inequities. This agenda extends from an emphasis on cultural diversity to incorporate an overarching value of social justice in the principles and practices that guide counsellors. For what is the point and purpose of counselling if it cannot deal with fundamental issues of injustice that adversely impact clients? The answer lies in the willingness of counselling psychologists to commit to an agenda of social justice (Fouad, Gerstein, & Toporek, 2006; Speight & Vera, 2008; Vera & Speight, 2003).

There are several reasons for psychologists and counsellors to become engaged in social justice goals and actions:

1. Millions of individuals in North America face barriers to the acquisition of resources that are necessary for human well-being (DeNavis-Walt, Procter, & Mills, 2005; Institute of Medicine, 2002; Schenk, 2001).

2. These barriers are often tied to cultural identities (gender, ethnicity, nationality, ability, religion, sexual orientation, etc.) (Vera & Speight, 2003).

3. Individuals with multiple non-dominant identities are more likely to experience cultural oppression and marginalization (Collins, in press).

4. Traditionally, the disciplines of psychology and counselling have functioned as instruments of the status quo and contributed to cultural oppression (Sue, 2001).

5. As a profession, we have not adequately recognized the impact of cultural oppression (racism, sexism, heterosexism, etc.) on non-dominant client groups and have not taken an active stance in addressing these issues on social and political fronts (Sue, 2001).

6. Too often we have focused on assisting clients to adjust to unjust circumstances rather than on empowering them and taking action ourselves to change the sources of their oppression (Pinderhughes, 1989).

7. Codes of ethics identify a range of professional roles and responsibilities that encourage counsellors to practice from a foundation of ethics and accountability (Toporek & Williams, 2006).

My own rationale for being involved in social justice is driven by my recognition that I, and other counsellors, psychologists, and helping professionals, are not only privileged by our education and positions in society, we also directly benefit as professionals from continued cultural oppression of particular marginalized groups in society. If we accept the premise that the broader systems influence, precipitate, and exacerbate client problems, then cultural oppression is a significant factor in the continued viability of the helping professions. I am conscious that I make my living, to a large degree, as a consequence of the emotional, social, and psychological impact of social inequities. This also applies to my role as a counsellor educator. The demand for counsellors and psychologists would dramatically decrease with the elimination of social injustices. There would be fewer students in our programs, less need for counsellor educators.

From my perspective, this puts an additional burden of responsibility on me to ensure that I do nothing to inadvertently support the status quo and, more so, that I take direct action to effect change at these broader systems levels. I'm not concerned about working myself out of a job, because the collective task before us is large and long term. What I am concerned about is not doing my part to move the social justice agenda forward and to tip the balance between my confrontation of and my professional profiting from social injustices!

Personal reflection – Sandra Collins

The focus on social justice is reflective also of the movement in psychology in recent years away from an individualistic worldview to a systemic worldview, which moves the focus of therapeutic attention to the larger systems of which the individual is a part. Individual clients are seen as reflections of the social and cultural systems that they are part of, and the role of the counsellor is expanded to focus on the systems that lead to clients experiencing mental health issues. The key point is that sometimes it is not the individual who needs to change; it is the system (Goodman et al., 2004; Ratts & Hutchins, 2009). Although counsellors may be more comfortable with interventions targeting individuals or small groups (Goodman, 2009; Sampson, 2009), it is vital that they get out of the comfort zones of their usual practice (Goodman et al.; Ratts & Hutchins). Through getting to know the needs of people in the local communities, counsellors are better positioned to use their advocacy expertise for addressing their clients' needs.

> If we counselors want to be fair to our students and clients, if we truly want to see a better world for them, if we truly believe that options arise from and are affected by interactions among individuals and the environments in which they find themselves, then we must be advocates. (Goodman, 2009, p. 259)

The call for social justice requires counsellors to develop competencies for addressing systems change in organizations, policies, and the larger public arena of social and political advocacy (Toporek et al., 2009).

Counsellors need to be prepared to intervene at multiple levels and through multiple roles in order to help improve the social conditions that continue to marginalize non-dominant groups and limit resources available to them in our society. Atkinson, Thompson, and Grant (1993) emphasized the roles of advisor, advocate, facilitator of indigenous support and healing systems, consultant, and change agent in counselling across cultures. Atkinson et al. identified the role of social or environmental change agent as the most frequently cited alternative to traditional applied practice roles in the literature. Snapshot 2 describes some of these additional intervention roles that fall within the practice domains related to social justice.

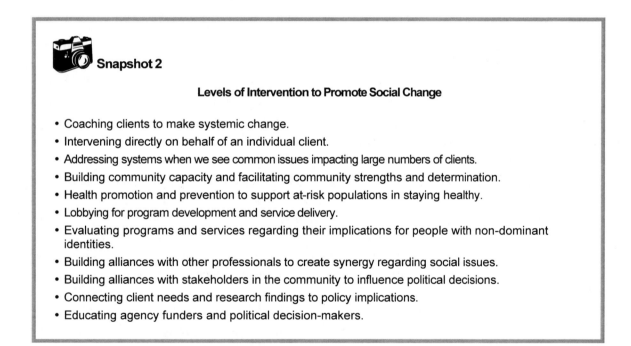

Snapshot 2

Levels of Intervention to Promote Social Change

- Coaching clients to make systemic change.
- Intervening directly on behalf of an individual client.
- Addressing systems when we see common issues impacting large numbers of clients.
- Building community capacity and facilitating community strengths and determination.
- Health promotion and prevention to support at-risk populations in staying healthy.
- Lobbying for program development and service delivery.
- Evaluating programs and services regarding their implications for people with non-dominant identities.
- Building alliances with other professionals to create synergy regarding social issues.
- Building alliances with stakeholders in the community to influence political decisions.
- Connecting client needs and research findings to policy implications.
- Educating agency funders and political decision-makers.

The vital importance of infusing social justice into multicultural counselling has led to the declaration that social justice is the *fifth force* in the field of counselling psychology (Ratts, D'Andrea, & Arredondo, 2004). However, along with support for social justice as the foundation of counselling, there are a number of controversies. First, concerns have been levied about the limitations of counselling theories and models of practice and the absence of attention paid to cultural influences. Second, there are debates regarding which core values should underpin models of professional service delivery and whose agenda is served by which values. Third, there has been more written about the importance of social justice than examples of best of practices to guide counsellors (Arthur, Collins, McMahon, & Marshall, 2009). Fourth, there are competing views about how well multicultural counselling competencies frameworks (i.e., Arredondo et al., 1996; Sue et al., 1998) incorporate competencies for social action (Arredondo, 1999; Arredondo & Perez, 2003; Vera & Speight, 2003). Fourth, the call for social justice must be matched by the transformation of curriculum to effectively prepare counsellors for social justice practices (Toporek et al., 2009). In the following sections, we elaborate upon these issues and consider how our model of culture-infused counselling incorporates social justice as a core value for professional practice.

Counselling Theories and Models of Practice: The Compass that Guides Us

Counselling theories need to explicate the interplay between individual client issues and systemic levels of cultural influences (Arthur & McMahon, 2004). As noted in the rationale for culture-infused counselling in Chapter 2, many theories of counselling are based on Western views of health and functioning, which locate the source of client concerns as an internal problem. Where cultural variables are introduced, they are often limited in their scope to dimensions such as race, gender, and ethnicity. Contemporary views of multicultural counselling have broadened the scope of client issues to consider the multiple and intersecting contextual forces that impact individuals (Ivey & Collins, 2003; Speight & Vera, 2008; Toporek & Reza, 2001). In our model of cultural identities in Chapter 4, we explicitly highlight the importance of contextual and ideological factors that impact client identities and affect both problem development and resolution. Rather than locating the source of client problems internally, counsellors need to consider problems as something experienced by clients. When client issues such as mental health or illness are defined through intrapersonal causes, there is a risk of blaming clients for their situations. This is not to exclude the importance of helping clients gain insight into their situation and to construct alternate perspectives or approaches to coping (Steenbarger, 1993). However, an over-focus on individual factors to explain behaviour decontextualizes the person from influential socio-historical contexts (Prilleltensky, 1997). Theories and models of counselling need to account for the interplay between individual and systemic levels of cultural influences and provide direction for counselling interventions (Arthur & McMahon).

With the growing recognition of the influences of environmental conditions on client well-being, counsellors need to examine their roles and methods of intervention to incorporate cultural influences on health and personal development. Vera and Speight (2003) challenged psychological practices that are based on helping clients to adapt to noxious social conditions. Unfortunately, the overriding role of remedial therapeutic interventions inadvertently perpetuates the status quo by encouraging individuals to *cope better* or *adjust* only after they have been harmed by destructive environments or oppressive policies (Prilleltensky, 1997; Sue, 1995). Avoiding discussions of oppression and *acting as if* contextual influences are unimportant influences on individual behaviour also perpetuate the status quo (Prilleltensky). The enterprise of counselling has drifted into essentially remedial approaches that focus on changing individuals instead of working to change their social contexts.

Greene (2005) offered a compelling argument to show how some people are treated as disposable and replaceable when they hold little social or economic power in our society. As noted in earlier chapters, this is often the experience of non-dominant groups in Canadian society, who are positioned on the basis of cultural group membership or individual identities related to ethnicity, gender, sexual orientation, ability, age, language, religion, or socio-economic status. Individuals from these groups may struggle with access to education and work or have limited opportunities due to power differences in our society and barriers, such as economic disparities, discrimination, or other forms of oppression. The greater the number of visible markers of difference, the greater the risk of cultural oppression and restricted access to resources and services (Pyles & Mee Kim, 2006). Rather than ignoring the plight of such individuals and groups, Greene stated that we need to recognize their circumstances and symptoms as a sign of social distress. Instead of viewing individuals with less power as somehow defective, we need to examine the toxic social conditions that lead them to experience debilitating symptoms of distress. From this point of view, social justice action directed towards those people in our society who suffer the most ultimately helps to improve the health and well-being of all members of society.

The implication is that counsellors require theories and models of practice that help to guide them towards ameliorating client concerns. However, theories and models of practice must also help counsellors to navigate the social structures and conditions that create problems for clients, such as discrimination, poverty, prejudice, and other forms of oppression. If social conditions are not addressed in our frameworks of practice, "counselors and psychologists will continue to work with victims of the system" (Ivey & Collins, 2003, p. 291). Culture-infused counselling incorporates the position that many client issues are better understood through explicating the social and political forces that impinge upon people's lives. Lack of social justice can be considered a risk factor for poor mental health. For example, the unequal distribution of health issues, such as depression, has been linked with social class, race, and gender (Ballou & Brown, 2002; Sheppard, 2002; Smith, 2008).

Power Plays at Work

In her writing on consultation, Pettifor (1994) illustrated how professionals and their work can be positioned in ways that serve the agendas of people with more social power. Professionals need to carefully consider the possibility of conflicting agendas between the more powerful and less powerful consumer groups. Consultants can be used as agents of social injustice when power differentials lead to the interests of managers or other persons in power being served instead of those of disempowered populations. For example, consultants may be placed in the difficult position of choosing between recommendations that are likely to be funded and those that could be unpopular with administrators and people in power who manage funding. Unfortunately, investments in preserving the status quo jeopardize the effectiveness of consultants who promote social justice through primary care, health prevention, or health promotion roles. Professionals need to be mindful of the tensions that can emerge when there are competing and conflicting agendas. Such situations require professionals to take a stand and voice their concerns while deciding what professional risks to take or to avoid in fostering a social justice agenda in service provision (Kiselica & Robinson, 2001; Lee & Rodgers, 2009).

In Chapter 7, Pettifor emphasizes the ethical prerogative that, above all, psychologists should do no harm in their work with clients. We concur that this is a *bottom line* in examining the roles of professionals for social justice. However, we align our work more closely with the feminist perspectives that include a social and political analysis of the problems of oppressed groups and individuals (Worell & Remer, 2003). The professional socialization of counsellors and psychologists has fostered more of an *apolitical stance* than the development of competencies that support active engagement with social change processes. However, counselling always contains political elements, and some would argue that those who favour a social justice perspective simply are more explicit about their political agenda (Sue & Sue, 1999; Watson, Collins, & Correia, 2004). The discussion in chapters 7 and 14 expand upon the feminist principle of *the personal is political*, implying that all action has an impact. We also support the notion that *the psychological is political* (Dworkin & Yi, 2003), which recognizes the overall impact of the profession on social, economic, and political norms. These principles challenge professionals to carefully examine their approaches to client issues and to actively work towards the equitable treatment of all people. They also challenge professionals to do more than engage in social justice as private citizens and to incorporate social advocacy more centrally in professional practice (Brown, 1997).

We believe that counsellors and psychologists are in a position to impact social change, and this is an integral part of professional practice in culture-infused counselling. From this perspective, counsellors and psychologists are charged with responsibilities for identifying and ameliorating the social conditions that contribute to the manifestation of problems experienced by clients. This implies that a clearer statement of social justice values needs to be explicated. It also implies that more proactive and preventative approaches must be used to address cultural bases of oppression, including interventions directed towards individuals, institutions, and social systems. As counselling psychology considers how best to promote mental health services for non-dominant populations, roles involving advocacy, public policy, community outreach, and facilitating indigenous support systems appear as viable alternatives for influencing social change.

Reclaiming Social Justice Values in Professional Practice

The call for counselling psychology to expand its focus from cultural diversity and difference to social justice is consistent with the major tenets of the profession. Helms (2003) and Gelso and Fretz (1992) reminded us that **counselling psychology** has traditionally held *a philosophy with three central tenets: (a) development of promotion of strengths and positive mental health over deficits and psychopathology; (b) prevention or use of psychoeducational interventions to teach principles of mental health as a means of avoiding problems and life crises; and (c) remediation, use of strategies, and interventions to alleviate mental health problems of individuals, dyads, and groups.* Social justice goals have long been associated with the counselling psychology profession (Toporek et al., 2009). Vera and Speight (2003) suggested that the practice of psychology needs to reclaim roles related to social change. The roots of professional practice have been eroded with the separation of individual and social action roles, with the focus of individual counselling and therapy in the former, and the latter delegated to other helping professions who are more involved with community-level interventions (Vera & Speight).

Counselling psychologists are challenged to think systemically about the nature of psychological issues and social forces that support personal growth. Culture-infused counselling requires professionals to expand their roles and methods of intervention to address cultural influences on people's development. This means moving beyond a focus on individual clients to addressing many of the organizational and systemic influences that impact clients. The *branding* or hallmarks of culture-infused counselling include counsellor competence to incorporate multiple helping roles and to incorporate multiple levels of interventions. Advocacy for social change is at the heart of culture-infused counselling. Vera and Speight (2003) argued that "multicultural competence includes the ability to function as a change agent at organizational, institutional, and societal levels" (p. 255). Models of service delivery have been developed that detail expanded professional roles that support advocacy interventions (Atkinson et al., 1993; Lewis et al., 2002). Counsellors need to be skilled at determining which professional role will best serve the needs of individual clients or consumer groups and hold competencies to adjust and expand their levels of intervention. Sampson (2009) suggested that we need to consider not only the individuals who become clients, but also the roles and responsibilities of professionals to address the needs of other citizens who may not be direct consumers of counselling, but whose well-being could be enhanced through our professional actions.

The Multiple Meanings of Social Justice

The main reason for advancing a social justice agenda in culture-infused counselling is that people's development is strongly influenced by the social systems that surround them. Unfortunately, for many individuals in Canada and other nations, social and political forces limit their educational and employment opportunities and compromise their health status. There are certain fundamentals that are required for human welfare that are not equitably distributed in our society: for example, adequate housing, nutrition, education, health and mental health care, childcare, and living wages (Lott & Webster, 2006). The examples provided in chapters 1 and 2 illustrate the ways in which cultural identity has been used to position many members of non-dominant groups in marginalized statuses within Canadian society. There are also inequities in terms of who can access professional services and in the relevancy and benefits of programs designed for culturally diverse populations (Arthur & Lalande, 2009). The bottom line is that we need to consider what counselling has to offer people who are socially or economically disadvantaged. Although counselling based on insight therapies and models of coping may be of assistance to individuals, it falls short of addressing the social and political conditions that foster many health concerns.

What is the extent to which counsellors should be addressing client symptoms of distress versus directing time and energy to the conditions that lead to distress? As noted previously, the counselling psychology profession has a history of advocacy in the work of counsellors (Toporek et al., 2009). However, due to pressures of policy and funding structures, as a profession, we have drifted away from a focus on action-based models of prevention, health promotion, and other forms of social action to interventions that primarily focus on the individual and the remediation of problems. Unfortunately, this direction does little to address the contextual and environmental forces that adversely impact people's health and well-being.

> A social justice approach to counseling (or any other endeavour) is based on (a) the acknowledgment of broad, systematic societal inequities and oppression and (b) the assumption of the inevitable, if unintentional, location of every individual (and every professional field) within this system. In turn, this assumption then obliges responsible action that contributes to the elimination of systematic oppression in the form of racism, sexism, heterosexism, classism, and other biases. This concept is closely related to multiculturalism, with its emphasis on cultural, racial, and ethnic issues, one of which is social injustice and oppression. (Smith, Baluch, Bernabei, Robohm, & Sheehy, 2003, p. 3)

The philosophy and meaning of social justice has been debated across academic disciplines for centuries (Reisch, 2002). Although discussions of social justice and social advocacy have resurfaced recently in the counselling psychology literature, we have noted that the concept is often not defined or the meaning of the concept is taken for granted as commonly understood. It is also problematic when multiple and contrasting meanings are suggested, as these may imply quite different principles and foci for counselling practice.

Crethar, Torres Rivera, and Nash (2008) discussed the key concepts that unite feminist, multicultural, and social justice counselling paradigms.

In a just society, opportunities, resources, and services are distributed equally and fairly. However, in most societies, some individuals or groups have greater access to educational, economic, and social mobility than others. This is because certain groups in society hold less power than others and may experience stereotyping, discrimination, or other forms of oppression. Social justice is a value that underpins an examination of societal concerns. According to Bell (1997), the overriding goal of social justice is:

> ...full and equal participation of all groups in a society that is mutually shaped to meet their needs. Social justice includes a vision of society in which the distribution of resources is equitable and all members are physically and psychologically safe and secure. (p. 3)

At the heart of social justice is an examination of social structure inequality and practices that involve unequal power distributions, determining those with power (i.e., privileged and dominant groups in our society) and those without power (i.e., the oppressed and non-dominant groups in our society) (Chizhik & Chizhik, 2002). Social justice involves "a fundamental valuing of fairness and equity" (Constantine, Hage, Kindaichi, & Bryant, 2007, p. 24). The term valuing implies more than simply knowledge; it requires a shift in attitudes, beliefs, and assumptions about justice and injustice.

Contemporary writers extend the meaning of social justice from addressing basic human needs and resources to providing opportunities for self-fulfillment (Reisch, 2002). Correspondingly, this view acknowledges the role that institutions play in allowing or preventing individuals from reaching their full human potential. For example, according to Young (1990), **oppression:**

> *...consists in systematic institutional processes, which prevent some people from learning and using satisfying and expansive skills in socially recognized settings, or institutionalized social processes which inhibit people's ability to play and communicate with others or to express their feelings and perspective on social life in contexts where others can listen.* [italics added] (p. 38)

From Young's perspective, a just society would be one in which the constraints of oppression and domination are eliminated, allowing people from all groups to develop and reach their full human potential. This would include lifting restrictions on participation in social institutions such as education, employment, and health care.

Current views of social justice also place increased emphasis on the importance of moving beyond acknowledgment of inequities to active interventions that challenge systems, institutions, and cultural norms that result in the oppression and marginalization of certain groups in society (Horne & Matthews, 2006). "This includes actively working to change social institutions, political and economic systems, and governmental structures that perpetuate unfair practices, structures, and policies in terms of accessibility, resource distribution, and human rights" (Fouad et al., 2006, p.1). It is no longer acceptable practice to acknowledge systemic barriers in the lives of our clients; it is considered a fundamental responsibility of counsellors to take action to promote structural and social change.

Young (1990) built on the emphasis placed on distribution of resources to examine the social structures that inhibit people's positive development. From this perspective:

> Justice should refer not only to distribution, but also to the institutional conditions necessary for the development and exercise of individual capacities and collective communication and cooperation. Under this conception of justice, injustice refers primarily to two forms of disabling constraints, oppression and domination. (p. 39)

Conditions of oppression may be overt, such as public laws and institutional policies, or more covert in terms of well-intentioned help that does not take into consideration the differential distribution of resources and opportunities available to our clients or the reality of social barriers for people's mental health and well-being.

Based on these definitions, four core components of **social justice** emerge: (a) *fair and equitable distribution of resources and opportunities, (b) direct action to ameliorate oppression and marginalization within society, and (c) full inclusion and participation of all members of society in a way that (d) enables them to reach their potential* (Arthur et al., 2009). The focus on human development and collaboration with clients is highly compatible with the foundations of counselling and psychology. The importance of engaging clients as active participants in decisions is a strong emphasis in emancipatory views of social justice, as noted in the following definition:

> A concept that advocates engaging individuals as coparticipants in decisions which directly affect their lives: it involves taking some action, and educating individuals in order to open possibilities, and to act with value and respect for individuals and their group identities, considering power differentials in all areas of counseling practice and research. (Blustein, Elman, & Gerstein, as cited in Toporek & Williams, 2006).

The intersections of power hierarchies and oppression in our society require counsellors to consider social justice from individual, organizational, and societal levels. These forces are complex and insidious by virtue of systems and structures that are unchallenged over time and become the *norm* for daily interactions and social relations. Counsellors are invited to examine the systems and structures that envelop their clients' lives, as well as their own. It may be a greater challenge to engage in reflective practice about how our personal views may perpetuate social injustice. According to Young (1990):

> Oppression refers to the vast and deep injustices some groups suffer as a consequence of often unconscious assumptions and reactions of well-meaning people in ordinary interactions, media and cultural stereotypes, and structural features of bureaucratic hierarchies and market mechanisms – in short, the normal processes of everyday life. (p. 41)

Readers are reminded of the importance of counsellor reflection about self outlined in the framework of culture-infused counselling, detailed in Chapter 3. The implication is that counsellors need to consider how their personal and professional socialization influences their views of people's development, the nature of their counselling issues, and their choices of interventions. Culture-infused counselling requires counsellors to examine how their worldviews may be similar or different to other people and also how counsellors may inadvertently perpetuate attitudes and actions that further disenfranchise some clients. The framework of culture-infused counselling outlined in Chapter 3 invites counsellors to move beyond supporting the status quo to addressing the social forces that pose as systemic barriers to people's growth and development .

Socal Justice and Empowerment

The discussion of social justice is closely linked to the concept of empowerment introduced in Chapter 5. To recap, interventions that are designed to be delivered directly to individuals may be conceived as having three levels to support client **empowerment:***(a) intrapersonal empowerment – facilitating the strengths and capacity of the individuals; (b) interpersonal empowerment – facilitating people's strengths and capacity for positively influencing others; and (c) systemic empowerment – facilitating people's strengths and capacities to influence organizations and other social structures in society.* Toporek (2000) offered a useful theoretical framework in which empowerment and social action are considered as end points of a continuum. Empowerment interventions target individuals or groups and aim to support and facilitate their efforts to change the social contexts that are negatively impacting their health and well-being. At the other end of the continuum is social action which targets direct change in larger organizations or systems. This framework is useful for considering the nature of client issues within social systems and helps counsellors to conceptualize relevant social action interventions.

Within the continuum of empowerment, counsellors serve as a cultural consultants or cultural guides. **Cultural guides** are defined as *professionals with expertise in multicultural counselling and consultation who function as liaisons between members of non-dominant populations and the dominant cultural or other helping professionals within that dominant culture.* When counsellors are in the role of cultural guides, they help clarify the cultural meanings embedded in situations or interpersonal interactions, help others bridge cultural differences by facilitating effective communication and establishment of common goals, help clients and practitioners negotiate ways of working together effectively, and help clients and practitioners access appropriate resources.

Apart from the specialization of community psychology, little attention has been paid to the roles of counsellors and psychologists in community capacity building. In order to advocate for common interests of client groups, the level of intervention that may be most appropriate is working directly with community members to support their group level of empowerment. Identifying community strengths is a key facet of empowerment as partnerships help to find solutions within the community (Fondacaro & Weinberg, 2002; Vera & Speight, 2003). In the field of career development, community capacity building has been recognized as a domain of specialization in competencies developed for the *Canadian Standards and Guidelines for Career Development Practitioners* (National Steering Committee for Career Development Guidelines and Standards, 2004). These types of interventions require professionals to develop and use their competencies related to consultation, group facilitation, needs assessment, and program evaluation (Vera & Speight). In the latter role of program evaluation, Pettifor (1994) discussed ethics and social justice in the context of professional responsibilities for the outcomes of actions so that the recipients of services receive benefit and avoid being harmed.

Social Justice Advocacy

It is timely to move forward from conceptual discussions of social justice to clarify the implications for practitioner roles and responsibilities. In practice, social justice action involves advocacy-related interventions that address issues of self-determination, social responsibility, and the equitable distribution of opportunities and resources in our society (Bell, 1997; Vera & Speight, 2003). Social justice practices such as advocacy counselling involve "helping clients challenge institutional and social barriers that impede academic, career or personal-social development" (Lee, 1998a, pp. 8-9). The emphasis here is placed on action that ultimately helps clients to reach their goals. As suggested by Toporek and Liu (2001), **advocacy** is defined as:

...action a mental health professional, counselor, or psychologist takes in assisting clients and client groups to achieve therapy goals through participating in clients' environments. Advocacy may be seen as an array of roles that counselling professionals adopt in the interest of clients, including empowerment, advocacy, and social action [italics added]. (p. 387)

 **Snapshot 4**

Advocacy Competencies

In 2003, the ACA Governing Council endorsed advocacy competencies (Lewis et al., 2002). The **advocacy competencies** are organized into *six domains, illustrating competencies for acting with clients and acting on behalf of clients. The competencies are also organized to illustrate a range of advocacy practices ranging from micro to macro levels.* A brief summary of each category is provided below. Many of the core advocacy competencies are reflected in the culture-infused competency framework; however, we encourage you to access the full ACA document and review the complete advocacy competency model.

A. Client/Student Empowerment

Starting at the micro level, counsellors empower their clients by raising their awareness of the impact of systemic factors on their well-being and providing them with the skills and resources to advocate for themselves within social, economic, political, or cultural systems. To be effective, counsellors must be able to capitalize on clients' strengths and resources, promote a systems level of analysis of problem and change processes, and provide clients with the skills to design and implement self-advocacy plans.

B. Client/Student Advocacy

In some cases, particularly with vulnerable populations, it is more appropriate to advocate directly on behalf of the client for access to resources and services or the elimination of barriers to health and well-being. Counsellors must be able to identify gaps and barriers and negotiate effectively, often in collaboration with other allies.

C. Community Collaboration

Over time, the counselling proces often brings to light common issues or challenges that affect members of specific client populations. In this case, it may be most appropriate to work with that cultural community to support their efforts at systemic change. Raising these issues appropriately, developing community-based alliance, and collaborating in a way that builds on the strengths and resources of the community are some of the key competencies identified.

D. Systems Advocacy

In other cases, counsellors act directly on behalf of a community to effect change that will ameliorate current concerns or prevent future problems from arising. Counsellors will be most effective if they are able to support their positions clearly, provide leadership and build alliances with those in positions of power, and design, implement, and evaluate systemic change processes.

E. Public Information

Counsellors can also use their advocacy skills to raise awareness in the general public about social injustices. Mobilizing media, matching information to specific target audiences, and capitalizing on interprofessional collaborators are some of the competencies identified.

F. Social/Political Advocacy

Certain barriers or social injustices have wide ranging effects that require direct social/political advocacy. Specialized competencies for influencing public policy include identifying the specific mechanisms for change, selecting and mobilizing allies, and lobbying for legislative and policy change.

Adapted from: Lewis, J., Arnold, M. S., House, R. O, & Toporek, R. L. (2002). *Advocacy competencies*. America Counselling Association. Retrieved May 28, 2009, from http://www.counseling.org/AboutUs//

Advocacy competence refers to *"the ability, understanding, and knowledge to carry out advocacy ethically and effectively"* (Toporek et al., 2009, p. 262). The overarching goals of social justice advocacy are to help to increase a client's sense of personal power and lead to socio-political changes that are more responsive to a client's personal needs (Kiselica & Robinson, 2001).

The model presented in Snapshot 4 provides a useful conceptual framework for counsellors to assess the level of intervention required in a particular situation (i.e., ranging from the client to community to broader social, economic, or political systems) and to distinguish between situations where it is most effective and culturally respectful to act in collaboration with the client, community, or system or to act directly on their behalf. As noted in the snapshot, different competencies may be required at different levels. Readers are referred to three articles that demonstrate applications of the ACA Advocacy Competencies. Ratts and Hutchins (2009) illustrated social justice advocacy at the client level with a case study involving a student. Lopez-Baez and Paylo (2009) provided a case example of social justice advocacy at the level of community collaboration and systems advocacy on behalf of a student. Lee and Rodgers (2009) challenged counsellors to take a personal stand in their roles and responsibilities to affect systemic change in the public arena. These articles provide rich examples of the positive differences that can be made for individuals and the surrounding systems through the advocacy actions of counsellors.

As part of a contract for an Employee Assistance Program, I was hired to provide outplacement services to a small manufacturing firm. With only a few hours' notice, I was asked to participate in a termination interview between a manager and an employee and to provide follow-up counselling services with the employee for the purpose of job search. As I met with the manager who would be handling the termination, it became obvious to me that he had not thought about how to tell the employee in a humane fashion, as his major emphasis was for me to "get him out of the plant as soon as possible with no fuss." The manager also had little information about the severance package and financial details of pension or benefits owed to the employee. I learned that the employee was 18 months away from receiving full pension. I was concerned about liability for the employer and about the upcoming interview with the employee. The interview was very difficult, as the manager basically berated the employee, told him he was no longer needed by the company, and asked him to leave the plant with all of his belongings as soon as possible. My job was then defined by the manager as damage control and cleaning up the mess.

I worked with the employee for three sessions and thought carefully about how to proceed through incorporating advocacy into the intervention at the level of working with the individual client. The client and I engaged in planning to clarify goals and processes that would support his job search. But we also developed strategies about ways for him to communicate with his previous company and seek appropriate legal, financial, and human rights consultation. The employee ultimately received a settlement that offset his loss of pension. The company that hired me to do job search got more than they bargained for.

Personal reflection – Nancy Arthur

One of my first experiences of social justice advocacy was when I worked in a group home for women and children escaping domestic violence. At one point, a new director was hired who had serious control issues and was manipulative and abusive with the clients. The staff initially felt quite disempowered, partly because we were also targets of her behaviour. Eventually we worked up the nerve to take our documentation to the board of directors. Unfortunately, the message we received was that we were all much easier to replace than she was. So the next week, she lined us up on a Friday afternoon to sign our prepared letters of resignation. I didn't sign and was escorted from the building. My colleagues were told that if they took any further action, she would ensure that they did not get re-employed in social services. Fortunately, I was leaving town for school and, although I had no experience or skills for social justice, I was stubborn, tenacious, and probably most significant, I was angry! I lobbied every person I could find from board members to MLA's to ministry representatives. After several months, I gave up. Then about three months after the incident, I was contacted by someone within the Ministry of Social Services and given the name of a lawyer to contact. The rest of the story happened mostly on their end, but five months after the incident, the staff who lost their jobs were reinstated, the board replaced, and the director removed.

I'd like to think that I would now be more respectful and skilful in my approach, recognizing that I was driven by my own anger and naïveté as much as by my sense of social justice. However, this experience instilled in me a sense of determination and hope that persistence and building connections with those in power can bring about positive change.

Personal reflection, Sandra Collins

Multicultural Competencies for Social Justice Advocacy

Counsellors are often called upon to advocate on behalf of their clients to ensure that they receive fair and equitable treatment. Clients may request this type of service directly, or counsellors may take a proactive stance to improve service delivery. Essential **advocacy skills** entail *representing an individual's or group's best interests to others*. Taking contextual influences into account requires professionals to have competencies for identifying and treating client issues with both individual and systemic approaches. As noted by Toporek et al. (2009):

> the importance of multicultural competence cannot be understated, particularly in understanding cultural relevance and appropriateness of advocacy interventions, sociopolitical histories and current context, as well as the counselor's own attitudes and beliefs. (p. 262)

In Chapter 3, we noted a number of criticisms about traditional models of multicultural counselling competencies that inspired us to develop our own model of culture-infused counselling. One concern levied is the scope of original multicultural counselling competencies. The main debate surrounds the conceptualization of the multicultural counselling and the implications for professional roles and practices. The level of intervention predominantly outlined in frameworks of multicultural counselling competencies involves individual counselling (Vera & Speight, 2003). It is obvious from the preceding discussion that multicultural competence must be expanded both within and beyond the context of individual counselling. This includes the ability of counsellors to promote social change at organizational, institutional, and societal levels (Ridley, Mendoza, Kanitz, Angermeier, & Zenk, 1994; Toporek & Reza, 2001). Sue's (2001) definition of cultural competence is reflective of an emphasis on social justice:

> Cultural competence is the ability to engage in actions or create conditions that maximize the optimal development of client and client systems. Multicultural counseling competence is defined as the counselor's acquisition of awareness, knowledge, and skills needed to function effectively in a pluralistic democratic society (ability to communicate, interact, negotiate, and intervene on behalf of clients from diverse backgrounds), and on an organizational/societal level, advocating effectively to develop new theories, practices, policies, and organizational structures that are more responsive to all groups. (p. 802)

Arredondo and Perez (2003) argued that social justice has been the foundation of the multicultural competency movement. The introductions provided to two of the multicultural counselling competencies frameworks (Arredondo et al., 1996; Sue et al., 1992) emphasize "recognition of the socio-cultural context, environmental stressors of oppression, and historical forces that impinge on the well-being of certain ethnic and racial groups" (Arredondo & Perez, 2003, p. 285). Although we have argued in previous chapters for expanding counsellor competencies to address a broader conceptualization of cultural groups, we agree with the central point that contextual forces must be considered in frameworks of multicultural counselling competencies.

We would encourage readers to revisit the competency framework outlined in Chapter 3. In this edition of the book, we have expanded the framework to further incorporate social justice competencies. In our model of culture-infused counselling, we have integrated social justice competencies as core to our work with clients, with organizations, and with social systems. The focus in this chapter is on expanding the fourth core competency under the *Culturally Sensitive Working Alliance* domain: Engage in social justice activities to directly influence the systems that negatively affect the lives of non-dominant populations. The list of attitudes, knowledge, and skills outlined in Chapter 3, Figure 4, provide a starting point; however, each competency can be expanded further to elucidate the underlying skills required for its implementation. Take, for example, *Lobby for changes in legislation*. Counsellors will require a cluster of related competencies to effectively implement lobbying efforts.

 **Snapshot 5**

Foundational Competencies for Social Justice

To engage effectively in social justice advocacy, counsellors must be familiar with client needs and be able to build alliances with others to work together. Advocacy work is facilitated when counsellors build positive working relationships so that their voices are heard when they bring up situations impacting their clients. Counsellors must be comfortable with the fact that their professional role is not a neutral one and that they hold political power. They are in a position to address individual or systemic biases that adversely impact clients from culturally diverse backgrounds. Below are some specific foundation competencies to support social justice advocacy.

- *The capacity for commitment and an appreciation for human suffering.* In other words, counsellors need to be humanitarians committed to improving the conditions that impact the health and well-being of their clients.
- *Nonverbal and verbal communication skills.* This entails communicating cultural empathy with clients in ways that show understanding about the social influences. It also entails competencies for effective communication with persons in power to negotiate resources for improving the quality of life for clients.
- *Maintaining a multisystems perspective.* The problems of individuals are often complex due to the different systems that influence an individual's life. Counsellors must have a general understanding of systems approaches and be able to entertain the influences of different systems and integrate their respective roles in contributing to client issues. In turn, interventions must be planned in light of systemic influences that target appropriate levels of change.
- *Individual, group, and organizational interventions.* Advocacy and social justice action involve interventions on multiple levels and counsellors must be skilled at intervening with individuals, groups, organizations, and larger social systems. This may entail helping clients navigate or negotiate with various systems, reaching out to groups, or intervening directly to change systems whose policies and practices have adverse effects on the personal development of clients. Consequently, counsellors must be skilled at integrating systemic interventions with individuals and facilitating group interventions and must be effective change agents with organizational interventions.
- *Knowledge and use of the media, technology, and the Internet.* Successful advocacy work depends upon counsellors' capacity to reach out to clients who may not have traditional access to services. In turn, counsellors need to be skilled at using media resources to draw public attention to social issues and utilize media effectively as a resource for public communication.
- *Assessment and research skills.* Beyond engaging in advocacy with clients, professionals need to document and evaluate their advocacy initiatives. This requires ongoing evaluation about whether professional services are making a positive difference in the lives of clients and what accounts for individual and social change. In turn, counselling research findings can be used to advance other social causes in the future.

Adapted from " Bringing advocacy counseling to life: The history, issues, and human dramas of social justice work in counseling," by M. S. Kiselica and M. Robinson, 2001, *Journal of Counseling and Development, 79*(4), pp. 387-397.

Several years ago, a woman that I know went missing. Her close friends had been searching her driving route to work, contacting her colleagues, and trying to trace her steps to no avail. They then began to branch out and contacted me and others for ideas on what else could be done. I realize in retrospect how the skills that I had developed as a counselling psychologist translate into the kinds of competencies required to mobilize community action. After brainstorming possibilities, several of us contacted a local non-profit agency that was closed for the weekend, set up a communications centre, printed hundreds of missing person flyers, and mobilized the women's community and others to canvas the city. I also prepared a press release and sent it to every local news agency I could find. One responded and met with us to profile this woman on the late night news. It turned out that she was sitting in a hotel room, where she had been for days, immobilized by depression. She saw herself on the evening news and called the front desk for help. I had more skills to draw on at this point in my life and had a network of friends and colleagues with other skills sets. Our collective efforts provide a good example of how quickly community resources and media can be mobilized by simply taking action.

Personal reflection, Sandra Collins

Identifying and Overcoming Barriers to Social Justice Advocacy

Attempts to change systems are frequently met with opposition as people holding power within social structures resist change to maintain the current status of the system (Lopez-Baez & Paylo, 2009). It is also possible that the persons identified with promoting change are responded to in ways that involve punitive action or social isolation. Counsellors may need to be prepared for difficult personal and professional circumstances when they make a decision to attempt systemic change (Lee & Rodgers, 2009). Helms (2003) noted several barriers to engagement in social justice activities:

- Interventions that threaten the status quo of high stakeholders in systems may be resisted and thwarted.

- Counselling psychologists tends not to be politically active in determining policy pertaining to positive mental health and broader based social justice interventions.

- Funding of fee-for-payment and third-party payments is typically centred on remediation rather than prevention or systemic interventions.

- The individuals and groups most in need of social justice based interventions are often disadvantaged financially.

- Administrators and policy-makers often do not understand or support social justice services either ideologically or economically.

In a recent study of career development practitioners in Canada (Arthur et al., 2009), the barriers to enacting social justice practices were examined in two ways. First, a check-list of barriers, conceptually driven from a review of the literature (e.g., Helms, 2003; Kiselica & Robinson, 2001) was administered in an on-line survey, and participants were asked to select all items that applied to their practice. Second, participants were asked to describe examples from actual counselling practice with a client whose career issues were influenced by social justice issues (e.g., lack of resources, inequity, discrimination, etc.). From those practice scenarios, participants were asked to identify any barriers to implementing their choice of intervention to address social justice. Using both methods enabled a comparison between the perceived barriers identified through the checklist and actual barriers that were experienced in the design and implementation of career-related interventions.

Participants in this study perceived a lack of training, time, funding, and power as barriers to implementing interventions related to social justice. Additional perceived barriers included fear of losing agency funding, fear of challenging the status quo, lack of support from supervisors and colleagues, fear of losing their job, and lack of interest. Collaborating evidence of barriers for implementing social justice interventions were found in practitioners' descriptions of their own efforts to implement social justice interventions. These included: lack of support from supervisors, lack of training, insufficient funding, and insufficient time to spend on social justice interventions. While the emphasis of writing about social justice has been placed on client's experience, Arthur et al. (2009) noted that counselling professionals face systemic barriers that seriously impact their capacity to provide interventions directed towards social justice. The results from this study suggest that lack of training and organizational restraints pose serious impediments for practitioners to implement interventions related to social justice.

Several implications emerge from the discussion of barriers to social justice practice. Bemak and Chung (2008) argue that one of the biggest hindrances to social justice action is the **Nice Counsellor Syndrome** (NCS). This term refers to the *tendency of counsellors to see themselves as positive, nice helpers who want to avoid rocking the boat or dealing with difficult circumstances that might lead to conflict* (Chung, Bemak, Ortiz, & Sandoval-Perez, 2008). Counsellor education programs support the development of qualities such as caring and empathy, and counsellor demeanour that is friendly and approachable. However, the risk is that counsellors actually turn into enablers because: a) they are not educated to address systemic and social change and b) to do so threatens the perception of counsellors as nice people. Unfortunately, the NCS and lack of social action may serve to perpetuate the very conditions that lead to client distress. Counsellors are encouraged to break out of the NCS and speak out against the difficult issues and circumstances faced by their clients.

Helms (2003) outlined additional considerations for barriers to social justice in counselling practice. First, there is strong danger that social justice may not be translated into professional roles if there are few systems in place to support a transformation of professional practice. There is a high risk in the current political and economic climate that social justice interventions will be relegated to *pro bono* or *volunteer* commitments by professionals and not be located centrally in the roles and responsibilities of paid professional practice. It seems that we must go beyond preparing graduates for expanded roles and interventions that support social justice to preparing them for engaging administrative and political support. Strategies such as negotiating, consultation, demonstrating efficacy of social justice activities, and ways to represent the benefits of sharing and redistributing power appear to be essential skills for meeting the realities of today's practice contexts. In order to implement an expanded view of social justice roles in counselling psychology, there is considerable work to be done to transform human service delivery systems to be more responsive to social justice interventions (Helms). However, the greatest barrier may not lie with external funders or persons who hold the power in administering mental health services; rather, the commitment to a social justice agenda within counsellor education may be one of the largest barriers to overcome.

Professional Education for Social Justice

Counsellors must be willing to act as change agents and deliberately target areas for improving conditions for their clients. This is an expanding counsellor role for which counsellor education programs need to match curriculum development. When asked about how counsellors can engage in advocacy services for their clients, many counselling students are unable to identify the types of actions that this may involve. Counsellor educators need to serve as role models and provide students with concrete examples of advocacy interventions, along with helping students build complementary culture-infused counselling competencies. It is important for counsellors to consider a scope of advocacy mandates. For example, actions range from crisis management for the more serious types of social injustices that unfortunately continue to impact clients to health promotion and prevention roles through striving to improve conditions so that they are welcoming and supportive for all clients.

Counsellors need to learn about ways to specifically advocate for social justice on behalf of their clients. This involves actions such as program planning, intervening to create organizational change, or lobbying for political decisions and/or economic resources that will positively influence programs and services for groups of clients. However, curriculum in counsellor education programs is only beginning to prepare students for social justice advocacy roles. Students often lack understanding about what it means to be an advocate for social justice and what kinds of action might lead to systemic and social change. Students may not even see social justice as part of their professional identity. A fundamental shift in the conceptualization of counsellor education programs is needed to help professionals see the importance of social justice as an underlying value for their work. Curriculum reform can help professionals translate the value of social justice into ethical practice through incorporating advocacy as "an integral part of every counsellor's role" (Lewis, Cheek, & Hendricks, 2000, p. 330). Toporek and McNally (2006) noted that social justice training in counselling psychology is developing in a parallel manner to the way that multicultural counselling curriculum unfolded over time. The introduction of the movement in more isolated and trial and error practice is gradually being informed by suggestions for more comprehensive approaches to curriculum reform (e.g., Talleyrand, Chung, & Bemak, 2006).

More than a decade ago, Lee (1998a) described three important functions of advocates that need to be matched by counsellor education curriculum. First, curriculum needs to prepare students to view client issues and professional roles from a systemic change perspective. Second, curriculum needs to prepare students to address systemic change directly and to help clients to build their skills and efficacy to advocate on their own behalf. The third point fundamentally supports the first two functions of advocates. Curriculum needs to prepare students with sufficient knowledge about principles of systemic change and sufficient skills to implement purposeful interventions.

To enhance culture-infused counselling competence, it is important for counsellors to be informed about groups in our society that are disenfranchised due to their social identities. However, this falls short of educating counsellors about how to integrate social justice into their professional roles. For example, it is a political decision to include content about counselling non-dominant groups in counsellor education curriculum and to decide which groups to highlight. The discussion in Chapter 12 focuses on counselling immigrants and refugees. However, counsellor education might go further and expose students to the contexts that lead to forced migration and issues such as torture and human rights violations. Arthur, Merali, and Djuraskovic encourage readers to become more familiar with groups of new Canadians who live in local communities and to become involved in outreach services. The involvement of professionals in settlement services programs and individual and family counselling is an important avenue for community capacity building. Social action at the local community, national, or international levels may be a more powerful way to improve the conditions that lead people to become refugees. Professionals can contribute to primary prevention approaches through participating in organizations that impact policy and program decisions regarding the health status of refugees (Arthur & Ramaliu, 2000).

There is concern that many counsellors are not sufficiently trained in advocacy approaches to shift their practices beyond remedial types of interventions to addressing contextual influences (Watson et al., 2004). This raises an interesting paradox: if counsellors are not trained with advocacy competencies, how can they teach clients to advocate on their own behalf? In turn, we fully expect counsellors to continue with a counselling agenda that supports the status quo if they are not equipped with competencies for advocacy roles. These concerns point to the necessity of strengthening counsellor education for social justice advocacy.

> Counselors can make great advocates. Training in human relationships, group dynamics, assessment, multicultural issues, and life span development provides counselor-advocates with a foundation to support clients who are facing barriers and systemic oppression. More attention, however, is needed to train counselors in systems-level issues and interventions as well as in ethical concerns regarding advocacy roles. To be effective, this training should be integrated throughout the curriculum and treated as part of counselors' roles, including relevant theory, skills, and applications in core and practicum courses. (Toporek et al., 2009, p. 265)

Counsellor educators also have a responsibility for helping students identify the risks associated with social justice advocacy. Lee and Rodgers (2009) discussed both the personal gains and personal costs associated with social justice advocacy. Counsellor educators can provide forums for discussing the importance of self-care and help counselling students build strategies for dealing with the time and energy that social advocacy entails (Roysircar, 2009). In turn, while students are learning about social advocacy roles, they can be encouraged to find allies who support their efforts towards change and a support network for consultation about their practices. The bottom line is that counsellor educators have a large role to play in preparing students to translate the concept of social justice into action. This includes preparing them for the realities of practice and strategies for overcoming barriers for their clients and those that they may face as professionals.

Advocacy as a counsellor educator can take many forms. It can mean making intentional decisions about what curriculum is included in a program and the kinds of experiential learning offered to students. Reading about issues is one thing; interaction with people who are impacted by social injustice and experience working for systemic change is where the real learning occurs.

Advocacy as a counsellor educator can also occur through applied research. A project that was particularly meaningful for me involved partnership with a local immigration agency. I had met the person who coordinated a host support program for refugees, and she told me she was having difficulty finding trained professionals to address the needs of survivors of torture. We subsequently partnered for a research project involving experienced clinicians. The results of the research informed a multidisciplinary professional development program which brought awareness to the issues faced by survivors of torture, enhanced clinical capacity through specialized training, and broadened the network of professionals available for referral.

One of the most rewarding courses that I have designed and instructed is about issues in social justice research. This course supports interdisciplinary discussion about the roles and responsibilities of researchers and how research is a political action. Students are encouraged to discover how they can incorporate principles related to social justice into their own research and how to be an informed consumer of research.

Personal reflection, Nancy Arthur

Helms (2003) raised questions about how far the field of counselling psychology is willing to go to commit to a social justice agenda. In responding to Vera and Speight's (2003) call for expanding counselling psychology's roles in social justice, Helms commented that, "In their view, social justice work is necessarily collaborative, action-oriented, socially relevant, and community focused and initiated. It is intriguing to think about how counseling psychology professors, students, training programs, and internship sites, as well as occupational opportunities, would have to change" (pp. 205-206). Toporek et al. (2009) noted that many counsellor educators have not received formal training in advocacy. Rather than relying solely on trial and error practices, continuing education opportunities for counsellor educators to engage in social justice and advocacy would help them to increase their capacity to provide leadership to students. In order to support the implementation and training, strategic planning within counsellor education programs, along with strengthening connections for licensing requirements are structural areas that deserve attention (Toporek et al.) The call for counsellors to respond to client needs through social justice advocacy needs to be supported through the curriculum and practices of counsellor educators and professional associations.

My experience of social justice advocacy as a counsellor educator has focused in large part on working towards justice within the profession of psychology for those students who face barriers to traditional models of psychological training. There continues to be a strong but unsupported bias against distributed learning, even though there is clear evidence in the literature for the effectiveness of interactive online learning and other non-traditional approaches to education. This bias undergirds an abuse of power within the profession aimed at excluding qualified applicants who don't fit the traditional educational mould. Full-time, classroom-based, on-campus graduate education models are designed for the economically and situationally privileged, and typically exclude individuals who need to work to support their families, cannot relocate for classes or internships, have physical limitations, or hold multiple roles and responsibilities that must be balanced with graduate work. In turn, these challenges are often connected to non-dominant cultural identities, particularly gender, ethnicity, socio-economic status, and ability.

I hope that through my efforts at negotiation, lobbying, research, and information sharing I am able to effect systemic change within the profession of psychology in Canada. I also hope that I am able to model through this process the kinds of advocacy and social justice competencies that students need to advocate for themselves and to work effectively on behalf of their clients to impact social injustices.

Personal reflection, Sandra Collins

Cultural Auditing as a Tool for Strengthening the Linkage Between Cultural Diversity and Social Justice Advocacy

Reflective Practice in Multicultural Counselling

We believe that social justice is a foundational value from which the professions of counselling and psychology can make a positive difference in the lives of clients who seek counselling and ameliorate the social conditions that lead to mental health concerns. As noted in the discussion above, social justice action often emerges from our awareness of the kinds of social injustices that impact the clients we work with. The ACA *Advocacy Competencies* (Lewis et al., 2002) highlight that this awareness may take several forms: a) understanding of the impact of systemic oppression on a particular client in a particular context, which may lead to client empowerment or client advocacy interventions; b) consciousness of recurrent themes that emerge as we work with individuals or groups from within a particular community, which can mobilize us to engage in community-level collaboration or advocacy to change the conditions affecting a particular group or groups; or c) more general awareness of systemic barriers or sources of cultural oppression that call for larger scale public consciousness-raising or social/political advocacy. At each of these levels, there is a visible link between what happens in the counselling session and the possible social justice activities that emerge.

We might ask then how it is that many counsellors and psychologists remain uncommitted to social justice action. In part the answer lies in a lack of awareness about the ways in which systemic and contextual factors impact their particular clients. The core culture-infused counselling competencies emphasize the importance of awareness of our own cultures and awareness of the cultures of our clients. This awareness necessarily entails an analysis of power and privilege at the systemic level. In this section we introduce a reflective practice model to facilitate this consciousness-raising as a foundation for: a) working with clients in traditional counselling settings and b) branching out in the types of social justice advocacy explored in this chapter.

Developing competence in working with clients who hold cultural identities different from your own requires continued learning and application of that learning. The foundation for such learning is in the process of **cultural reflection** – *focused and purposeful consideration of the influence of culture on all aspects of professional practice*. In a similar way, Toporek and Reza (2001) emphasized the importance of praxis – the "*continuous process of awareness, reflection, and action*" (pp. 17-18). To develop competence, counsellors must observe and reflect, but they must also put that learning into action. Culture-infused counselling involves active planning and initiative on the part of the counsellor to engage in reflective practice (Collins, Arthur, & Wong-Wylie, in press).

During interactions with clients, counsellors' skills for cognitive complexity allow them to hypothesize about the relevant influences of culture (Pedersen & Ivey, 1993). The questions are listed in Figure 2 and are linked conceptually to the core culture-infused counselling competency domains. The first two questions are linked to the domains of counsellor awareness of self and counsellor awareness of clients. The third question helps counsellors to be reflective about the influence of culture on the working alliance and ways to strengthen the professional relationship with clients. The fourth question helps counsellors to consider the possible influence of systems on client issues and concerns and any links with social justice. The fifth question cues counsellors to reflect upon and take action using appropriate levels of intervention linked to social justice advocacy.

"What does this mean about my personal culture?"	Counsellor self-awareness of culture
"What does this mean about the culture of the client?"	Counsellor awareness of the client's culture
"What does this mean for the working alliance?"	Culturally sensitive working alliance
"What does this mean for the ways in which clients are impacted by social systems?"	Social justice as a guiding value
"What does this mean for the level(s) of intervention that might make the most positive impact?"	Social justice advocacy

Figure 2. General questions for cultural reflection based on the competency framework.

While holding these questions in your mind as a general framework for approaching your work with clients from non-dominant populations is important, a more detailed audit of your counselling services generally and with individual clients will provide you with clear markers for continued competency development and service enhancement. The intent of **cultural auditing** is *to provide counsellors with focused reflection about the influences of culture on their work with individual clients, groups, and systems. Cultural audits may be formal processes embedded in formative and summative evaluation protocols but they are more often part of an individual practitioner's daily practice of cultural reflection.*

Cultural auditing is recommended as a process during interactions with clients and as a process for reviewing practices with clients. Counsellors need to be reflective about the potential confounding influences of culture in determining how counselling unfolds. This includes making sure that they have collaborated with clients about the indicators of change and when counselling will be terminated. The more skilled a counsellor becomes at noting, reflecting upon, and acting in accordance with her or his own observations about culture, the more cultural auditing becomes part of the counselling process itself. Cultural auditing is intended to enhance the therapeutic alliance and prevent early termination. It is also intended to help counsellors reflect about the influence of systems on clients' presenting issues and determine the level of appropriate intervention. The cultural auditing process encourages counsellors to consider whether there are social justice issues involved in the presenting concerns of clients and how social advocacy may be incorporated in intervention planning. Reflection about culture is also recommended following interviews with clients to identify common patterns and to consider where advocacy with organizations, community collaboration, and strategies for influencing social policy may be applied to promote the positive health and well-being of individual clients and non-dominant groups. As noted above in the section on barriers to social justice action, counsellors may experience resistance at the organizational or professional levels to social justice activities; careful cultural auditing also provides a documented rationale for action that may be required by supervisors, funding agencies, and so on.

The cultural auditing process is intended to provide a practical tool for reflection, learning, and action by counsellors. It is important to use the auditing process in a way that is not cumbersome and is part of everyday practice in culture-infused counselling. Collins et al. (in press) suggested the following ideas for integrating cultural auditing. It may be used: (a) as a prompt for dialogue with clients within the counselling session, allowing counsellor and client to collaborate in exploring the impact of culture on various aspects of the counselling process; (b) for counsellor personal reflection; (c) as a guide to note taking when counsellors review their sessions and engage in further case planning; (d) for client evaluation of counselling sessions; and (e) in the context of supervision and consultation.

Figure 3 provides guidelines and prompts for cultural auditing throughout the culture-infused counselling process. For the purpose of simplifying the language, the client is assumed to be female in this example. The first 11 steps of the cultural auditing process guide the counsellor from the point of intake and the initial meeting with the client through to termination and follow-up. The reflection questions in each step facilitate reflection on the application of both self-awareness and awareness of the client's culture through the working alliance. Some questions will inevitably have more or less relevance for working with individual clients and should be used flexibly for case planning. It is within the working alliance context that counsellors must infuse awareness of culture into their work with each particular client, with each particular presenting concern, and in each particular context (Collins et al., in press).

The last two steps in the culture auditing process emphasize continued competency development and social justice action. The reflective practice prompts in cultural auditing challenge counsellors to address their learning needs for working with similar client issues in the future. Additionally, the prompts encourage counsellors to be reflective about ways to increase their competencies for social justice advocacy. Reflection about each client encourages counsellors to shape their own practices in ways that are maximally responsive to client needs, identifying themes that emerge and noting processes that could lead to effective interventions at individual or systems levels (Lewis et al., 2002). Such learning can be shared through case conferences and strategic planning. It is through articulating and sharing experiences of cultural auditing with other practitioners that ideas can be shared and others can be encouraged to enhance their culture-infused competence for future practice and to work collectively on emergent social justice agendas. A case example involving the context of immigration and applying the cultural auditing process is offered by Collins and colleagues (in press).

Auditing Steps	Questions or Topics for Reflection
1. Reflect on the potential influences of culture on establishing initial rapport in the counselling relationship.	• How might gender dynamics and differences in age, sexual orientation, ethnicity, or range of ability between my client and I impact the counselling relationship? • What conflicts in values and beliefs might arise, including religious beliefs? • How might my prior history of working with clients from a similar cultural group impact my working with her? • What are her cultural norms about privacy and her preferences for informal versus formal relationships, degree of directiveness, and communication styles? • What have her previous experiences with people in authority been like? • What potential language barriers exist and how are those most effectively addressed?
2. Reflect on the potential influences of culture on the development of a relationship of trust and respect.	• What information about the counselling process might she require in order to understand the roles and processes involved? • Given my understanding of her cultural identity, how can I best highlight the ways that we share values, beliefs, and perspectives? • What style of counselling might best suit her particular cultural expectations and norms? • What types of cultural inquiry might fit best for her and ensure that all relevant factors are considered throughout the counselling process? • What can I do to enhance my credibility as someone who can help her reach her goals? • How do I best communicate to her that I understand and empathize with the experiences, thoughts, and feelings she has shared with me? • What aspects of her expressed needs can I address early on in our interaction that will increase her expectation for success in counselling? • How can I establish a collaborative interaction that equalizes power wherever possible?
3. Reflect on the potential influences of culture on counselling conventions.	• What can I do to structure the environment and the counselling session to enhance her trust and willingness to return to counselling? • What norms related to setting, time scheduling, frequency and length of appointments, or participants in the session might I want to consider adapting?
4. Reflect on the potential influences of your personal culture on how you view clients from this particular cultural group or groups.	• What assumptions am I making about this particular client and her culture? • In what ways do I assume we are similar and different because of our cultural backgrounds? • What aspects of my own beliefs, values, or worldview do I anticipate may be challenged or in conflict in my work with her? • What are my initial hypotheses about the impact of culture on her presenting concerns? How sure am I of the accuracy of those hypotheses? How open am I to considering new information and modifying those assumptions?
5. Reflect on the potential influences of your personal culture on how you view her presenting issues.	• What do I believe about human nature and healthy development? • What assumptions do I make about how problems arise and how change occurs? • What do I know about common presenting concerns among clients who identify with her cultural group(s)? • What assumptions do I make about the nature of her problems that may be a reflection of my own cultural encapsulation? • What stereotypes or biases might I need to watch out for in my assessment?
6. Reflect on the potential influences of her culture on how she views her presenting issues.	• What is her rationale for the problem and how does this fit with the ways that problems are conceptualized within her culture? • What is her view of causality, her sense of where the problem is located (internal or external), and her assessment of her ability to effect positive change? • How might her perspective on human nature, healthy development and functioning, and change processes differ from mine because of her cultural identity? • How might this alternative perspective fit or not fit with my theoretical orientation?
7. Reflect on the potential influences of broader social, economic, and political systems on her presenting concerns.	• How might her presenting problems be impacted by family, subcultural group, community, and larger social systems? • To what degree might socio-political oppression play a role in her presenting concerns? • How do the specific experiences of racism, sexism, heterosexism, ageism, ableism, and other forms of oppression impact her view of herself and of her social, familial, work, and community environments? • What expanded roles might be required for me to respond effectively to the multiple influences on her experiences?

Figure 3. Structure and prompts for conducting a cultural audit of counselling practices. Continued on next page.

Auditing Steps	Questions or Topics for Reflection
8. Reflect on the potential influences of culture on the definition and negotiation of client goals.	• How do the counselling goals appear to match her presenting issues? • What is the impact of her level of acculturation and cultural identity development on her goals for counselling? • How might my own level of identity development facilitate or hinder her in attaining those goals? • What methods have I used to ensure that the identified goals are consistent with the changes that she wishes to make? • Are her conceptualization of the problem and expectations about appropriate solutions compatible with my repertoire of intervention strategies? • What ethical considerations or personal and professional values may influence the boundaries I place on negotiating counselling goals?
9. Reflect on the potential influences of culture on associated tasks or subgoals and on the negotiation of counselling interventions.	• How well does my repertoire of intervention strategies and techniques prepare me to address her presenting concerns in a culturally respectful manner? • How are my choices of intervention influenced by my preferences for working with clients in particular ways? In what ways might those interventions need to be modified to work effectively with this client? • What levels of intervention could address her presenting concerns? • What interventions best match her preferred ways of help seeking and the goals we have established? • How open am I to incorporating indigenous healing practices or resources? • Who might be an appropriate cultural support or healer to involve in her counselling process?
10. Reflect on the best ways to evaluate her progress in counselling.	• What are the potential cultural influences on how I view desirable change made by clients? • What are the important indicators in her cultural context that demonstrate how counselling has made a difference in her life? • What indicators of success have been negotiated with her to determine that our work together is finished?
11. Reflect on the influence of culture on termination and follow-up.	• What are the cultural meanings of endings for me and for her? • What is the impact of her cultural context and my cultural context on the termination process? • What are the potential hazards and benefits of continuing contact with her in a non-counselling role? • What strategies should we put in place to ensure comfort and safety if we encounter each other in social settings?
12. Reflect on the links between her experience and the experience of other clients you encounter.	• What are the common concerns raised by clients from specific groups that are culturally diverse? • What are the common concerns raised by clients between groups that are culturally diverse? • What level of intervention would best address individual client issues? • What level of intervention would impact social change to ameliorate the conditions that lead to counselling concerns?
13. Reflect on the links between her experience in counselling and your continued competency development.	• Where did my current level of multicultural competence serve me well in the counselling process? • What feedback has she provided me about the working alliance, the counselling process, and the outcomes of counselling? • What barriers did I encounter in trying to support this client and how can they be overcome? • What attitudes, knowledge, and skills might I need to develop to work more effectively with a similar client in the future? • What attitudes, knowledge, and skills might I need to develop to increase my capacity for social justice advocacy for working with a similar client issue in the future?

Case Study

Marie has been working as a counsellor in post-secondary education for 5 years. She notices that there are rarely any international students who seek services for counselling. Recently, Chong, an international student from China came to the Counselling Centre for an appointment. Marie noticed that she was the counsellor assigned to see Chong the following week. She asked the receptionist if Chong was a male or female client as she could not tell from the name. This sparked an insight that she really did not know much about international students on the campus and was especially unfamiliar with Chinese culture. In preparation for the appointment, she decided to meet with the international student advisor. During that meeting she learned that the majority of the international students in Canada were from China. Recent changes in immigration had increased the number of students who were permitted student visas, and the campus had increased the number of students from China by more than double in the previous 3 years. Marie and the international student advisor talked about some of the common adjustment issues that international students face. The international student advisor suggested that Marie might want to talk to a member of the local Chinese community association who had been especially helpful in arranging social activities for the students. Initially, Marie wasn't sure that it was her job to do so, but asked the international student advisor to include her in the next meeting. Before the appointment with Chong, Marie also read some recent articles in professional journals about the common adjustment issues facing international students. Marie felt she had a stronger foundation of knowledge about international student transitions and looked forward to exploring relevant issues of concern with future clients.

When Chong arrived for the appointment, he seemed very nervous and would not look at Marie directly. He said that he wanted to talk to Marie about permanent immigration to Canada, but it was very important for him to know that she would not tell anybody about his plans. Marie made a point of emphasizing confidentiality and her record-keeping practices when she explained what counselling was and the types of services offered to students. She asked Chong about ways that he had approached seeking help in Canada and how that was the same as or different from how he would problem-solve in his home culture. She emphasized that she was a resource to Chong and would be willing to help him explore the decision to remain in Canada. She was honest in telling Chong that she was less familiar with the immigration rules, but she would help him find accurate information. She also made it clear that she had no influence with the immigration authorities in Canada.

Chong seemed to be engaged as Marie asked him to discuss how he came to the point of considering permanent immigration to Canada. He thoughtfully detailed his experience of studying and living in Canada. However, he became very distraught when Marie asked him what was holding him back from fully exploring his interests to stay in Canada. Quietly, Chong said that his family fully expected him to return home. As the eldest son, he was expected to play a key role in the family, including plans for caring for them in the future. His strong sense of family obligation was weighing heavily on him. It appeared that he felt a great deal of shame for considering a future direction that was different from the destiny prescribed by his family.

At one point in the interview, Chong looked up at Marie and asked, "What do you think I should do?" Marie was very uncomfortable with the question, as her professional training as a counsellor had emphasized not to give direct advice to clients. However, she was mindful that she had positioned herself as a resource to this student. She looked at him directly and said that although she could not tell him what to do, she would support him to make the best decision he could, considering both his family's needs and his own needs. She felt that it was important to let Chong know that she respected his capacity to make a decision while honouring his strong sense of family loyalty.

Marie noticed that her initial reaction to Chong's story was that his family was holding him back. She was conscious of this judgment during the session, cueing herself to be interested in his story and the circumstances that lead to his dilemma. Later, as she reflected on the session, she realized that her values of autonomy and independent decision-making were cultural biases that likely were in conflict with this client's strongly collectivist culture. She was less clear about the family obligations that this client described as the eldest son. As a result of the consultation with the international student advisor, she called the contact person in the community to ask if she could discuss some of the norms of family relations in traditional Chinese culture. This community consultation helped her to position some of the ways that she directly and indirectly explored Chong's concerns in subsequent sessions. She held the general cultural knowledge in tentative ways as she explored what seemed relevant for Chong, and what seemed relevant for exploring the context of his concerns.

When they were talking about how decisions were made in families, Marie decided to disclose the ways in which she had experienced decision-making in her family. This was done strategically to help Chong contrast the cultural learning he had experienced locally with the seemingly conflicting styles of his family. The counsellor's disclosure helped strengthen the therapeutic alliance in that there were points of commonality in their experiences and points where cultural contrasts were expanded in the discussion. As Marie learned more about Chong's family situation, she began to see Chong's situation as less about his inability to make a decision for himself, and more about how he was navigating his experience of acculturation. She also gained a deep appreciation for the dire economic circumstances facing his family and how his role as the eldest son and experience as an international student were keys for stabilizing their financial future. She was then able to contextualize his circumstances in terms of broader structural influences from his home culture and from the point of view of opportunities likely available to him in Canada. The goals and processes of their counselling work together shifted as Chong felt more comfortable about seeking counselling. His requests became less about specific information, and he engaged in discussion about his personal experiences of living biculturally. In turn, Marie adjusted her counselling style from more directive and problem-solving to a more constructivist exploration of meaning-making.

In reflecting about the counselling sessions, Marie wondered how gender dynamics between them may be a possible issue. She subsequently used the process of cultural inquiry to ask Chong about what it was like for him to discuss personal matters with a female and how that would be defined in his culture and by him. This cultural inquiry served to strengthen the alliance as it provided another way for Chong to explore his experience of living biculturally. In particular, it connected well to his preference to live a more Western lifestyle. He had been dating a woman in Canada. Although she was of Chinese ancestry, Chong believed his parents would not approve of the marriage because her family was not particularly affluent. This situation was intertwined with the larger issue of immigration as Chong explored lifestyle options and decision-making based on his choice to stay in Canada or return home. With mutual agreement, counselling sessions were terminated after six sessions when Chong felt that he had established a plan that included indicators he would use to make the final decision about permanent immigration to Canada.

Ultimately, this client decided that he needed to work in Canada for 1 year post-graduation to see how he felt about opportunities in that role versus the student role. He made a point of returning home to China to visit his family before commencing employment. That visit enabled him to discuss with his family the ways that his opportunities in Canada could better enhance their financial well-being in contrast to employment in China. He also decided to discuss with his family the possibility of remaining in Canada.

In reflecting about working with this student, Marie felt that although she recognized some of her cultural biases associated with Western and individualistic culture, she really did not know enough about collectivistic cultures. Along with accessing readings, she asked the international student advisor if she could arrange a meeting with two or three students who might be willing to talk about the similarities and differences in their cultures. This planted the seeds for an informal lunch-hour series in which staff and students from the institution were invited to meet to learn more about the countries and cultures of international students attending the institution. Marie used both formal and informal meetings with international students to document their presenting concerns. She invited two of the students to accompany her to a meeting with a manager to request resources for specific services.

Marie decided to be proactive about her learning to try to improve access to counselling for international students. She met with the coordinator of in-service training for new instructors. She and the international student advisor designed a workshop that became a regular part of the in-service training to help new instructors become informed about common issues faced by learners from other countries and how to access student support services. Marie also contacted the local school newspaper to see if they might be interested in a feature story about international students. She obtained permission from a colleague who taught a journalism course to ask for two volunteers to write some feature articles. Subsequently, articles about international students were incorporated as a regular column in the school newspaper. The focus on the positive achievements of international students and information about their host cultures provided education to the entire campus community.

Questions for reflection:

1. In what ways does this case example illustrate the steps of the cultural auditing process?

2. If you were offering peer consultation to Marie, what suggestions would you have for her to strengthen the application of the cultural auditing process?

3. How did the cultural auditing process increase Marie's awareness of broader systemic issues that might pose barriers to international students, both in terms of counselling services and integration into the university community generally?

4. How might this case scenario have played out differently if little or no cultural auditing occurred?

Chapter Summary

The multicultural counselling movement has created a paradigm shift from which to consider how client issues are defined and the appropriate roles and interventions that best serve populations that are culturally diverse. A renewed commitment to social justice suggests that we need to expand our notions of multicultural competence to include social action and advocacy-related interventions (Vera & Speight, 2003). Ultimately, this can lead to an integration of social justice into professional practice roles.

The focus of this chapter has been on the expanded areas of practice that counsellors and psychologists are increasingly being called upon to engage in as part of their professional roles, with a particular focus on social justice. Culture-infused counselling competencies also support counsellors in expanding their professional roles to include social justice advocacy. In organizational settings, this may means working to improve access to counselling and examining the responsiveness of policies and personnel towards clients who are culturally diverse. In the community and in larger social contexts, social justice advocacy can be directed towards actions that lead to social, economic, and/or political change. Social justice advocacy includes engaging in community consultation to encourage prevention practices and health promotion to support members of non-dominant populations to address social inequities.

The process of cultural auditing is one effective tool for heightening awareness of the impact of culture and systemic oppression based on cultural identities both individual clients and non-dominant populations more broadly. Culturally auditing not only supports continued development of culture-infused counselling competency; it also provides a solid foundation for a range of social justice activities and roles.

Conclusion

In this era of rapid demographic change, nationally and internationally, social justice has become the inevitable calling of the profession. A social justice perspective emphasizes societal concerns and seeks to eradicate inequities in society (Vera & Speight, 2003). Social justice advocacy requires counsellors to expand their practices to address change directly with clients, on behalf of their clients, and also within broader systems. Counsellors are challenged to expand their roles to function as change agents and to engage in systemic interventions to enhance the health and well-being of groups who are marginalized in our society. This requires counsellors to shift their views of themselves as apolitical and to leverage their positions and power to impact structural change. It requires counsellors to take responsibility to be role models for social justice advocacy (Arredondo & Perez, 2003). Similarly, counselling and psychological organizations are challenged to take an active role in promoting social justice by lobbying for changes in socio-political structures and ideological perspectives related to non-dominant populations (Neville, Worthington, & Spanierman, 2001).

Counsellor education programs will need to: (a) ensure that their own missions, policies, and practices are reflective of the cultural diversity of Canadian society; (b) expand curriculum to incorporate perspectives on social justice; and (c) to train counsellors to expand their roles to incorporate social justice advocacy (Toporek & McNally, 2006). Community outreach, participation on governing boards at municipal, provincial, and national levels, and strategies for influencing social policy in the public arena are important topics for counsellor education programs. Those in supervisor roles will also need to recognize social justice advocacy as a legitimate role for their supervisees and provide support and guidance in mentoring new counsellors and psychologists.

Professionals such as counsellors and psychologists are more familiar with working with individuals and their families through remedial interventions. However, they can be taught how to expand their focus to incorporate primary prevention approaches that address social inequities (Stone, 2003). This will only occur, however, if pre-service and continuing education opportunities exist for formal training. The bottom line is that adopting a culture-infused perspective requires a shift in perspective to incorporate professional practice for social justice.

PART II

CONCEPTS AND APPLICATIONS IN ETHICS, ASSESSMENT, AND RESEARCH

In the first part of the book, we provided an introduction to our model of culture-infused counselling and expanded on the core competency domains of cultural self-awareness, awareness of client culture, and development of a culturally sensitive working alliance. We also explored what it means to move beyond individual work with clients to impact the broader systems that impact wellness and provided a cultural auditing tool to support reflection on culture in practice and to bridge the work with individual clients and social justice actions.

In the second part of the book, we have invited several authors to contribute specific chapters that explore the impact of culture and social justice on ethical practice, assessment, and research. In Chapter 7, Pettifor introduces various professional codes of ethics and examines their implications for multicultural counselling. She provides a framework for addressing practical ethical dilemmas that counsellors are likely to encounter in their work with clients from diverse cultural backgrounds. In Chapter 8, Darou expands on the process of assessment in counselling, specifically addressing the impact of culture on both models of assessment and specific assessment tools. Failure to attend to cultural identities in the process of assessing client presenting concerns is likely to lead to cultural mismatches in case conceptualization and intervention planning. In Chapter 9, Offet-Gartner describes the evolution of psychological research in relation to culture and identifies some of the risks of failing to fully attend to culture in the design, implementation, and dissemination of research. She argues that ethical research must be culturally sensitive and provides principles for engaging in culture-infused research that aims to not only respect and explore the influence of culture on various psychological phenomena, but also to support the specific needs of cultural communities.

Our purpose in including these chapters is to provide further support for our assertion that culture must be a central consideration in all aspects of professional practice. The core principles of culture-infused counselling are transferable not only to these specific functions, but also to other areas of counselling practice such as supervision, counsellor education, or consultation not specifically addressed in this text. We invite you to consider each of these professional activities you are involved in as you read through these chapters and to reflect on the implications of adopting a culture-infused approach.

CHAPTER 7
ETHICS, DIVERSITY, AND RESPECT IN MULTICULTURAL COUNSELLING

Jean Pettifor

Key Terms and Concepts		
• Absolutist approach • Aspirational ethics • Deontological position • Diversity • Ethic of caring • Ethical decision-making	• Ethnocentric • Moral framework • Prescriptive ethics • Professional codes of ethics • Relativist approach • Respect	• Social action • Social justice • Universalist approach • Utilitarian/consequentialist position

Personal Introduction

How did I become involved in ethics? Looking back, I was probably born into ethical thinking, even if it was not so named. My parents were concerned about poverty, poor distribution of goods, exploitation of western farmers, racism, threat of annihilation through wars, inadequate medical and educational services, unequal opportunities for women, the criminality of birth control – in other words, social justice for all.

I became a psychologist still believing that I had, and others should have, a commitment to help people build a better life. I never adopted the position that my employment with the provincial government was just a job that required conformity to directions from management if such direction was harmful to clients. My belief was that the vulnerable should always be protected.

I became involved in psychology organizations provincially, nationally, and internationally. The primary focus of my professional activities was ethics – respect, caring, fairness, and quality services for everyone. After contributing to the development of the *Canadian Code of Ethics for Psychologists* (Canadian Psychological Association [CPA], 1986, 1991, 2000), I focused on spreading the good concepts of the Code, because the Code offers more respect for all persons than many other codes. I have looked for commonalities in other professional codes and I have looked at how the Code applies in special situations and with non-dominant populations, such as ethnic groups, women, persons with disabilities, recovered memories, and employee assistance programs. When I present internationally, psychologists respond most favourably to the articulation of ethical principles and the ethical decision-making steps.

My mission now is to promote value-based ethical decision-making that truly respects and cares for all persons. Understanding diversity enables counsellors to be more competent and respectful in serving the needs of others. I have learned that, internationally, counsellors must respect people collectively, not just as individuals; that they must take care that the language of communication does not carry unintended meanings; and that issues of social injustice may be major determinants of individual problems. The climate of social activism and the struggle for social justice into which I was born are still with me. My life's journey has given me opportunities to promote aspirational and relational ethics – reaching for the stars, but accepting that what one contributes to the journey may be more important in one's lifetime and more realistic than achieving Utopia.

What is Multicultural Counselling?

Multicultural counselling is counselling across cultures. What then is the meaning of culture? In Chapter 1, Arthur and Collins broadly defined culture as including "ethnicity, national origin, gender, sexual orientation, age, ability, socio-economic status and social class, religion, and other salient dimensions of culture that are important for counsellor-client interactions" (p. vi). They also argued that everyone is a cultural being and that therefore every human interaction is a cultural one. Hence, the expression *culture-infused counselling* implies that the core of competent counselling is multicultural. Pedersen (2001) saw a paradigm shift from multicultural counselling as engaging only persons who are obviously different to counselling all clients in the context of multiple identities. If these views of multiculturalism were widely accepted and practiced, there would be less need for special ethical guidelines for cultural and diversity-based counselling.

The driving force for special ethical and practice guidelines comes from groups who have suffered from oppression, discrimination, and injustice because our general standards documents have not sufficiently guided actual practice. The vast majority of literature on multicultural counselling that has come from the United States has focused on ethnicity and, more specifically, on the treatment of the black and Hispanic populations. Slowly, people with other types of "diversity" are receiving attention.

In our helping professions, and the contexts in which we work, we are slow to adopt a broader conceptualization of multicultural counselling. Therefore, in discussing ethics and multicultural counselling in this chapter I will reference both general codes of ethics and diversity-specific guidelines.

What Do We Need to Know About Professional Ethics?

Ethical principles are intended to guide our professional relationships with other persons, peoples, and organizations. Certain assumptions are especially relevant to working across cultures and diversities. Some of these assumptions are listed below.

1. Professional ethics deals with human relationships more than with specific codes of conduct.
2. Genuine respect among professionals and those with whom they interact is the foundation of ethical relationships.
3. Formal codes of ethics do not define multicultural competencies, such as the knowledge (what), skills (how), judgment (when), and diligence (commitment) required in serving the well-being of others.
4. Counsellors may focus less on diagnosing, prescribing, and treating than on facilitating, clarifying, understanding, encouraging, and helping others gain more power and satisfaction in their lives.
5. Formal codes of ethics and other practice guidelines are helpful, but are not sufficient to ensure that counsellors are sensitive to diversity issues in all of their practice roles.

Respect, caring, and integrity are the moral foundations for professional ethics. If we have respect and caring for human beings, individually and collectively, we have no choice but to include all sorts of **diversity**, *such as ethnicity, gender, abilities, age, and sexual orientation.* Moral principles of respect and caring are **aspirational** in *striving for optimal levels of car*e, address relationships among persons and peoples, and supersede **prescriptive** *behavioural standards that define correct conduc*t. The helping professions have made progress in acknowledging respect and caring for diversity, but injustice, prejudice, and suffering continue to thrive.

Multicultural counsellors are faced with a responsibility to advocate for individuals and groups. They have a responsibility to contribute to a just society through the reduction and elimination of unjust discriminatory practices. Appropriate strategies for social action vary tremendously at any given time and place. **Social action** *to change harmful or discriminatory aspects of society may include disseminating research results that are relevant to social policy-making, lobbying for individual clients, working to revise policies and practices within one's own work setting, and participating in community-based and political or professional groups to advocate, recommend, or protest.* Strategies are chosen to enhance success.

 **Snapshot 1**

Vignette

Mental Health Services hires an Asian-trained Vietnamese man to provide mental health services in the Vietnamese immigrant community in a large Canadian city. This man is a refugee himself, having barely escaped with his life, and is trying to obtain permission for his family to join him in Canada. He is deeply grateful for his job and for having a means of livelihood.

After he has been on the job for six weeks his supervisor reprimands him for visiting families in their homes and attending their community social functions. She says that he is in a conflict of interest because he is not maintaining professional boundaries. Moreover, she says that he can see more clients in a day if they come to the office for appointments.

The man is devastated. He has cultural respect for persons in authority, he cannot afford to lose his employment, and therefore he feels unable to defend his position. He also lives in the Vietnamese community. At the same time, he knows that, culturally, his people do not view mental health and illness in the North American way, and if he is aloof and not accepted, he cannot help them.

He comes to you as an understanding friend and colleague. How can you help?

The main purpose of this chapter is to consider the implications of professional codes of ethics for multicultural counselling and to provide a framework for addressing practical ethical dilemmas that are encountered by counsellors. Although multicultural counselling is relevant to all counselling, in this chapter special attention will be given to Canadian guidelines for working with persons who are from non-dominant or dissimilar groups. Multicultural counselling will be discussed under five headings:

1. Historical, philosophical, and moral foundations.
2. Codes of ethics for counselling practice.
3. Guidelines for cross-cultural research.
4. Responsibility to society.
5. Future considerations.

Cultural Criticisms of Professional Codes of Ethics

Professional codes of ethics are developed by professional associations to guide their members in providing ethical and competent services in practice, teaching, and research. Criticisms have been levelled against current codes of ethics for not recognizing or respecting cultural differences and against professional associations for not punishing professionals who discriminate against those who are different. Quotes from a number of authors are provided in Snapshot 2 as examples.

Historical, Philosophical, and Moral Foundations

History

Professional codes of ethics appear to have two lines of parentage: regulatory and philosophical. Historically, the need to define rules for appropriate behaviour and to distinguish appropriate from inappropriate behaviour seems to have been a strong driving force. Some of the impetus for developing codes of ethics resulted from the exposure of horrific violations of decency and respect for humans in Nazi Germany, some from the definition of rights in the *Universal Declaration of Human Rights* (United Nations, 1948), and some from the rapid development of professional psychology post-World War II with the establishment of regulatory legislation (Sinclair, Simon, & Pettifor, 1996). Regulatory bodies operating in the context of discipline value rules of conduct because, in adjudicating ethics complaints, it is easier to judge whether or not the rules have been violated. However, rules reflect cultural beliefs and, therefore, rules that are developed in one cultural context may be inappropriate in another context. The principle of respect for the dignity of persons and peoples is more universal. For example, a rule prohibiting professionals from accepting gifts may be seen as offensive and disrespectful in some cultures.

A philosophical foundation, or at least *an articulation of moral values*, provides a **moral framework** *to guide ethical behaviour*, and is the second and sometimes more obscure line of parentage for professional codes of ethics.

 **Snapshot 2**

Criticisms of Professional Codes of Ethics

"For too long we have deceived ourselves into believing that the practice of counseling and the data base that underlie the profession are morally, ethically, and politically neutral. The results have been (a) subjugation of the culturally different, (b) perpetuation of the view that minorities are inherently pathological, (c) perpetuation of racist practices in counseling, (d) provision of an excuse to the profession for not taking social action to rectify inequities in the system" (Sue & Sue, 1990, p. 24).

"The five moral themes that are problematic in the care of persons with disabilities are (a) the temptation of paternalism, (b) disability as an anomaly for traditional ethics, (c) medical versus environmental models of disability, (d) possessive individualism and independence versus interdependence, and (e) submitting to the care of strangers" (Gatens-Robinson & Tarvydas, 1992, p. 28).

"The professional field of counseling has tended to emphasize moral rules without identifying underlying cultural assumptions. This has resulted in ethical guidelines that direct counselors toward their own *self-reference criteria* to judge others' behaviour in a *one size fits all* perspective, focus on catching and punishing the wrongdoer rather than reconciliation, blur the boundaries between ethics and law, and finally institutionalize Euro-American values such as individualism as criteria of Truth" (Pedersen, 1997, p. 246).

"...the code treats culture, ethnicity, race, religion, gender, marital status, sexual preference, etc. as add-ons to the essential humanity of the person rather than acknowledging the social cultural relationships within which our humanity and individuality are constituted.... The individualized character of the rights, such as 'privacy, self determination, and autonomy' espoused in the code, provides an inadequate foundation for work with peoples to understand persons as being part of, or constituted, through their membership of a group or groups" (Nairn, 1998, p. 243).

"Ideally, a code of ethics (e.g., APA Code) should serve as a guide to resolving moral problems that confront members of the profession...with the primary emphasis on protecting the public.... Realistically, however, what a code of ethics does is validate the most recent views of a majority of professionals empowered by their colleagues to make decisions about ethical issues. Thus, a code of ethics is inevitably anachronistic, conservative, ethnocentric, and the product of political compromise" (Bersoff, 1999, p. 1).

"In fact, ethical codes have many limitations, the most serious perhaps being that they tend to reflect the dominant culture's values at the expense of minority values" (Ridley, Liddle, Hill, & Li, 2001, p. 186).

"...a dominant response to the poor by the non-poor is that of distancing, and examples of such distancing in the form of exclusion, separation, devaluing, and discounting, which operationalize classist discrimination have been drawn from many areas" (Lott, 2002, p. 108).

"If psychologists consider themselves leaders in providing competent and ethical mental health services, they must address the needs of all underrepresented groups and assure that all are acknowledged and provided with opportunities to empower their lives – including persons with disabilities" (Cornish et al., 2008, p. 495).

When rules are formulated prior to identifying a philosophical foundation, people may act on what feels okay, but without explicit reflection on moral values. Under these circumstances, it is easier to be guilty of unintentional racism and discrimination against any number of people and conditions that are seen as different and hence inferior. Pedersen (1997) maintained that the lack of a moral philosophical foundation encouraged unintentional racism and a trivialization of cultural issues. **Ethnocentric thinking** *judges others according to one's own ethnic perspectiv*e.

Today, a few professional codes articulate their ethical principles and link their standards directly to these principles. Others articulate their ethical principles without directly linking them to their standards. Professional codes of ethics place their highest values on respecting and serving the interests of clients equally and without discrimination. This point of view is compatible with the **deontological position** of Emmanuel Kant (1724-1804), which states that *ethical decisions are based on moral imperatives of intrinsic rightness -* that *each person must be treated as an end and never as means to an end.*

This position runs contrary to the **utilitarian** or **consequentialist position** of Mill (1806-1873) and Bentham (1748-1832): *that the ethical decision is the one that brings the greatest good, happiness, or outcome for the greatest number, or the least harm, and that sometimes the end may justify the mean*s. Today, economic agendas and budget cuts may push us towards more utilitarian thinking to judge who is more deserving than others to receive services. A utilitarian approach has negative implications for persons from non-dominant groups who are perceived as different. Despite the so-called Canadian "safety net," such concerns are real. It has been argued in some quarters that torture of suspected terrorists is justified in order to protect the greater good of the general population.

A **prescriptive approach to ethics** that *defines minimal standards of behaviour focuses on avoiding harm* more than on aspiring to serve the best interests of consumers. For example, a professional's refusal to engage in community activities in order to avoid dual relationships may be seen as aloof and uncaring. Rather than refusing on the basis of rules that prohibit dual relationships, it may be more respectful and caring to recognize the inevitability or even desirability of some overlapping relationships and to guard against the potential harm that could occur.

A Moral Framework for the Helping Professions

Professional codes are gradually beginning to articulate a moral framework before launching into the behavioural standards, but this in itself does not remove unintentional bias. The literature is beginning to demonstrate a reaction against rule-oriented ethics (Gergen, 2001; Jordan & Meara, 1999; Ray, 2001; Swim, St. George, & Wulff, 2001), and various authors have proposed a number of new descriptors for professional ethics, such as process, relational, reflective, virtue, contextual, and client-centred. These approaches reject a solely rule content model and instead advocate, in varying degrees, an emphasis on moral values and shared relationships between professionals and others with whom they interact. Gilligan (1982) is credited with describing an **ethic of caring** that *emphasizes interpersonal relationships within a specific context rather than abstract principles.* O'Neill (1998) described two approaches to teaching ethics as the overriding approach (i.e., the search for the fundamental rule) and the moral dilemma approach (i.e., the focus on context in finding the best fit between competing principles and the interests of different parties). Eberlein (1987) described these approaches as the correct answer approach (i.e., obedience and compliance) and the problem-solving approach (i.e., professional judgment and responsibility). Clearly, ethical practice in multicultural counselling must *address human relationships and specific contexts and be constantly aware of what others see as their own best interests.* A relationship based on mutual respect and caring is the foundation for the *working alliance* in culture-infused counselling to support competent and beneficial counselling.

One might wish for a utopian world of common values of equality, respect, and caring for all persons. In such a world there would be no need for special attention to diversity. In our world, unfortunately, discrimination and lack of respect for differences continue to flourish. Although we espouse respect for all persons, peoples, and cultures, there are some moral limitations on what we can accept of allegedly culturally appropriate beliefs. Where there are limitations, we need to know where to draw the line and with what moral justification. What is logically perceived to be seriously harmful to the dignity, safety, and well-being of persons and peoples is unacceptable, such as political terrorism, honour killings, genital mutilation, child sexual abuse, sex slavery, active euthanasia, infanticide, and widows burned alive on their husband's funeral pyre. **Respect** can be described as *an appreciation of the innate worth of all persons as human beings and the belief that they should be treated with dignity.*

Pedersen (1997) described the **relativist approach** as *accepting everything without a moral foundation,* while the **absolutist approach** says that *my way is the only way.* He recommended a **universalist approach** that *recognizes some values as universal in the interests of our common humanity and some values as specific to certain cultures.*

 **Snapshot 3**

Limitations on Respect and Relativism

We may find that some actions are completely offensive and unacceptable to us even though they are allegedly culturally appropriate. Think of three examples that bother you. What is your ethical rationale for not accepting them? How do you distinguish between sound ethical reasoning and personal bias? What does your reasoning have to do with concepts of relativism, absolutism, and universalism as described by Pedersen (1997)?

Social Action

Multicultural counsellors recognize that individual, family, or group counselling will not solve problems of extreme poverty, unemployment, violence, genocide, suicide, drug addiction, crime, or corruption, and that members of oppressed, depressed communities should not be diagnosed as pathological on the basis of privileged White professional standards. *Fixing* social problems related to cultural groupings requires social action and local empowerment that is often seen as beyond the scope of training and practice of counsellors. Professional training of health service providers focuses more on fixing individual problems than on removing the social determinants of problems. However, times are changing with increasing emphasis on the responsibilities of professionals to engage in changing those aspects of society that discriminate against some groups of people (Feminist Therapy Institute [FTI], 1999; Toporek, Gerstein, Fouad, Roysircar, & Israel, 2006b). Social action may also involve empowering clients to address social issues that impact on their lives. If counsellors do not accept an obligation to improve social conditions, then the allegations that they help clients to adjust and conform to an unjust status quo may be valid.

In today's multicultural society, cultures intermingle and we cannot assume that individuals fully represent values from their place of origin. Therefore, it is important to recognize those cultural characteristics that are important to the individual or family. In addition, individuals may simultaneously adopt two sets of values, one relevant to their "diversity"-community and another consistent with the mainstream society in which they are living. It is inappropriate to assume that persons of colour are recent immigrants or that new immigrants must have problems in our culture, as if they are deficient in some way. However, it is very appropriate for the counsellor and client to share information on values and beliefs that are relevant to the counselling situation.

Political Implications

The discussion so far has focused on ethical and moral issues around respect for diversity in multicultural counselling. All issues of equality, oppression, marginalization, or discrimination have strong political components. Groups may analyze issues of power, and they may struggle for power in order to achieve equality. Controversies around Aboriginal land claims are a combination of fighting for moral issues and for power against what has been perceived as an abuse of White power. A Maori woman in New Zealand told me that she had no concern for the rights of other ethnic groups until the Maori people first achieved equal power with the dominant White Europeans. Feminist activists fight for power against a perceived male patriarchy in order to achieve equality. The personal *is* political.

Most of us can accept the concept of respect and equality for diverse populations on an abstract moral level or when it is to our own advantage. Resistance increases when positions of privilege and power are threatened by the disenfranchised wanting to increase their social standing. For example, allegations are made in many countries that the poor in immigrant groups contribute to crime, welfare dependency, violence, and unemployment, while those who are successful take away *our* jobs or buy up *our* real estate. A psychologist at an international congress told me that their psychologists have traditionally avoided addressing professional ethics because to do so would necessitate embracing an ethnic-devalued minority group as well as taking a politically risky position of protesting against human rights violations by government. I do not expect to see this observation documented in the published literature.

Snapshot 4

Ethics and Power

Aboriginal groups in Canada demand ownership of large tracts of land. Employment equity laws require employers to actively recruit women, Aboriginal people, persons with disabilities, and persons of colour. What are the ethical arguments for these actions? What are the political arguments? What is the relationship between ethics and politics? What is your personal stand on these issues?

Codes of Ethics for Counselling Practice

Codes and Guidelines

Professional associations develop **codes of ethics** *to guide their members in providing ethical and competent services that serve and protect the public interest*. However, revisions to codes of ethics tend to be slow to catch up in addressing concerns of the day. This delay is seen in the development of guidelines for addressing diversity, for addressing recovered memories, for conducting research involving humans, and for providing services over the Internet. The American Psychological Association (APA) is often seen as a model for developing professional standards, including codes of ethics. It has also been seen as using codes of ethics to protect psychologists more than to protect the public (Bersoff, 1999). The APA was established in 1892, proposed its first code of ethics in 1953, its first *Guidelines for Research with Human Subjects* in 1973 (APA, 1973), and its first *Guidelines for Providers of Psychological Services to Ethnic, Linguistic, and Culturally Diverse Populations* in 1991 (APA, 1993).

The first statement in these guidelines on diverse populations consists of an admonition to educate clients to the processes of psychological interventions. This statement appears to reflect a policy of assimilation into mainstream processes rather than listening and respecting cultural differences. APA (2000) adopted *Guidelines for Psychotherapy with Lesbian, Gay, and Bisexual Client*s. Instead of using active verbs on what professionals *shall*, *will*, and *will not* do, this document uses more tentative phrases like *are cognizant, are aware, are knowledgeable, strive to understand, are encouraged to recognize, and make reasonable efforts*. One wonders if the weaker terminology indicates that the guidelines are not intended to be enforceable standards.

Pedersen (2001) believed that psychology and counselling are in a difficult process of making a paradigm change that focuses on multicultural perspectives. The APA strengthened its commitment to cultural diversity in 2002 by approving *Guidelines on Multicultural Education, Training, Research, Practice and Organizational Change for Psychologists* (APA, 2003b). In addition to culturally sensitive practice, psychologists are encouraged to use organizational change processes to support culturally informed organizational (policy) development and practices. Educational materials on ethics in multicultural counselling that reference American codes are increasingly available (e.g., Cory, Cory, & Callanan, 2003; Pack-Brown & Williams, 2003). However, Olkin and Pledger (2003) and Cornish et al. (2008) maintained that the APA does not recognize disabilities as a diversity and until it does it is not a truly a multicultural profession.

Pettifor (2001a) predicted that the articulation of moral principles and the use of a value-based decision-making process would promote greater respect and caring for non-dominant groups. Since 1986, the *Canadian Code of Ethics for Psychologists* has been on the leading edge among professions in defining a philosophical foundation for its code of ethics and in linking all standards to those ethical principles. The European Federation of Psychology Associations (EFPA) *Metacode of Ethics* (1995), the Psychological Society of Ireland *Code of Professional Ethics* (1999), the Canadian Association for Music Therapy *Code of Ethics* (Kerry & Sargent, 1999), the New Zealand Psychological Society (NZPS) *Code of Ethics* (2002), and the Vocational Rehabilitation Association of Canada (VRAC) (formerly the Canadian Association of Rehabilitation Professionals) *Canadian Code of Ethics for Rehabilitation Professionals* (2002) have followed suit.

In recent years, other associations have articulated their philosophical principles at the beginning of the code, but have made no attempt to link them to the specific standards that follow. This includes the APA (2002a), the Canadian Counselling Association (CCA) (2007); the Canadian Institutes of Health Research (CIHR), Natural Sciences and Engineering Research Council (NSERC), and Social Sciences and Humanities Research Council (SSHRC) (1998 with 2000, 2002, 2005 amendments). The advantage of making this linkage is that standards can be evaluated in terms of compliance with or demonstration of the longer lasting ethical principles and values.

Many professional codes of ethics are not explicit in articulating their ethical principles, although values may be implicit in their standards of behaviour. The disadvantage here is that it is more difficult to evaluate the rules in terms of demonstrating the overarching ethical principles. For example, we may believe that we respect and care for persons of other cultures, but our rules on obtaining informed consent, maintaining confidentiality, or avoiding dual relationships may not be seen in these cultures as demonstrating respect and caring. Where the moral framework is hidden, the criticisms that professionals are imposing dominant culture values, are unintentionally racist, or are trivializing cultural concerns are more likely to be valid.

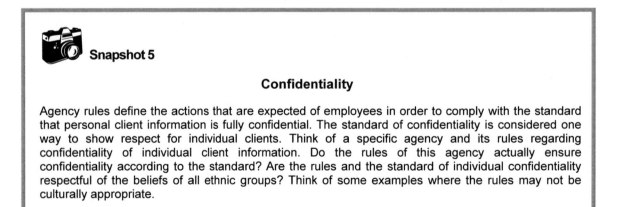

Snapshot 5

Confidentiality

Agency rules define the actions that are expected of employees in order to comply with the standard that personal client information is fully confidential. The standard of confidentiality is considered one way to show respect for individual clients. Think of a specific agency and its rules regarding confidentiality of individual client information. Do the rules of this agency actually ensure confidentiality according to the standard? Are the rules and the standard of individual confidentiality respectful of the beliefs of all ethnic groups? Think of some examples where the rules may not be culturally appropriate.

It is important from a cultural perspective to have ethical principles that are both named and defined. The *Canadian Code of Ethics for Psychologists, Third Edition* (CPA, 2000) names the ethical principles as Respect for the Dignity of Persons, Responsible Caring, Integrity in Relationships, and Responsibility to Society. Some codes name the principles as Autonomy, Beneficence, Nonmaleficence, Fidelity, and Justice. The *Canadian Code* defines respect as the positive valuing of human beings, which is more than simply accepting the decisions and wishes of the client or refraining from discriminatory behaviour. The *New Zealand Code* (NZPS, 2002) goes further in requiring psychologists to respect the dignity of persons and peoples and to be sensitive to their welfare and rights. This Code includes a commitment to social justice in its principle of Responsibility to Society. It also references the *Treaty of Waitangi* (the 1840 treaty between Queen Victoria and the Maori chiefs) as the basis of respect and equality between Maori and non-Maori in New Zealand. The principle of autonomy, defined as the promotion of individualism, independence, and self-determination (Corey et al., 2003), is grounded in Euro-North American thinking and is more restrictive than respect as a positive valuing of human beings.

Psychology's concept of responsible caring requires an active concern for the well-being of others, which means more than being competent or deciding what is of benefit and what is of harm. In addition, responsible caring requires a greater concern to protect the welfare of those in more vulnerable positions than those who are less vulnerable. Responsible caring is a commitment that is a characteristic of the professional and requires that knowledge and skills be applied in the service of others. *Others* includes all sorts of diversity and is not intended here to have racist implications. Hertzspring and Dobson (2000) recognized the Canadian psychology code's two principles of Respect for the Dignity of Persons and Responsible Caring as requiring psychologists to act in diversity-sensitive ways.

Snapshot 6

Sex Therapy

You have established a private practice limited solely to sex therapy. After a couple of years, you accept unmarried couples as clients, despite some vigorous criticism from a few individuals in the community. You discover that there is a need for therapy for gay and lesbian couples, but you anticipate that you will again receive widespread public disapproval from this community if you accept gays and lesbians as clients. How do you resolve this dilemma?

Adapted from Vignette #66, *Companion manual to the Canadian code of ethics for psychologists* (3rd ed.), by C. Sinclair and J. Pettifor, 2001. Ottawa, ON: Canadian Psychological Association.

The *Canadian Code of Ethics for Psychologists* (CPA, 2000) also serves as an umbrella document for more specific guidelines, such as the *Guidelines for Non-Discriminatory Practice* (CPA, 1996/2001a), *Guidelines for Psychologists Addressing Recovered Memories* (CPA, 1996/2001b), *Guidelines for Ethical Psychological Practice with Women* (CPA, 2007), and *Ethical Guidelines for Supervision in Psychology: Teaching, Research, Practice, and Administration* (CPA, 2009). In these documents, the four ethical principles of the *Canadian Code* are described as they apply to each topic and are followed by more specific standards. The guidelines support competent practice in serving clients and should also reduce the likelihood of disciplinary complaints being made against practitioners. Special guidelines are contained within a consistent moral framework through linking them to the ethical principles.

Many codes of ethics seem to limit their attention to diversity on admonitions to be competent and not to discriminate on the basis of age, colour, ethnicity, and so on. This has the appearance of being a minimalist legal interpretation of rights, as in the *Canadian Charter of Rights and Freedoms* (Department of Justice Canada [DJC], 1982), rather than an ethical commitment to respect and serve.

The *Feminist Therapy Code* (FTI, 1999) has special significance for ethical considerations because the philosophy and guidelines address the issues of power and oppression. The philosophy is outlined in the preamble rather than listing the moral principles.

> [Feminists believe in] the equal worth of all human beings, a recognition that each individual's personal experiences and situations are reflective of and an influence on society's institutionalized attitudes and values, and a commitment to political and social change that equalizes power among people.... Thus, a feminist analysis addresses the understanding of power and its interconnections among gender, race,

culture, class, physical ability, sexual orientation, age, and anti-Semitism as well as all forms of oppression based on religion, ethnicity, and heritage. (p. 1)

Substitute *multicultural counsellor* or *rehabilitation counsellor* for *feminist therapist*, and the standards are equally relevant.

In addressing diversity, the *Feminist Therapy Code* is more proactive than other codes in respecting people, monitoring one's own attitudes, empowering others, not abusing power, and actively working to change the oppressive aspects of society. While this code is rarely mentioned outside of feminist circles, it seems ready-made to assist professionals in infusing cultural diversity into professional practice.

Both CPA (2007) and APA (2007), in their guidelines for working with women, expanded their scope of services from therapy and counselling to all psychological services with women. The Canadian guidelines are linked to the four ethical principles of the *Canadian Code of Ethics for Psychologists*. Pettifor and Malone (in press) discussed the historical evolution of the Canadian guidelines from a focus on specific abuses to fostering respect, equality, and quality in services.

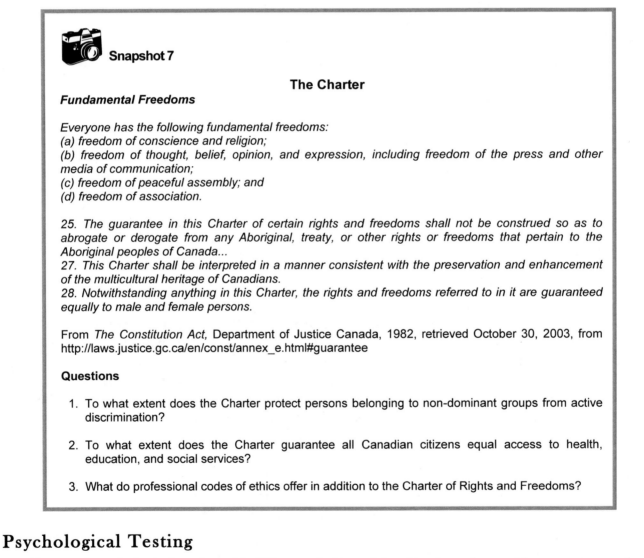

Snapshot 7

The Charter

Fundamental Freedoms

Everyone has the following fundamental freedoms:
(a) freedom of conscience and religion;
(b) freedom of thought, belief, opinion, and expression, including freedom of the press and other media of communication;
(c) freedom of peaceful assembly; and
(d) freedom of association.

25. The guarantee in this Charter of certain rights and freedoms shall not be construed so as to abrogate or derogate from any Aboriginal, treaty, or other rights or freedoms that pertain to the Aboriginal peoples of Canada...
27. This Charter shall be interpreted in a manner consistent with the preservation and enhancement of the multicultural heritage of Canadians.
28. Notwithstanding anything in this Charter, the rights and freedoms referred to in it are guaranteed equally to male and female persons.

From *The Constitution Act,* Department of Justice Canada, 1982, retrieved October 30, 2003, from http://laws.justice.gc.ca/en/const/annex_e.html#guarantee

Questions

1. To what extent does the Charter protect persons belonging to non-dominant groups from active discrimination?

2. To what extent does the Charter guarantee all Canadian citizens equal access to health, education, and social services?

3. What do professional codes of ethics offer in addition to the Charter of Rights and Freedoms?

Psychological Testing

Abuses of psychological testing with different ethnic, racial, cultural, gender, and language groups have been a major concern in the profession. The ethical concerns regarding harm to individuals from the inappropriate use and interpretation of tests has led to formal guidelines and practice standards for conducting psychological testing. Issues relative to testing and diversity are included in many national and international documents (American Educational Research Association, APA, and National Council on Measurement in

Education, 1999; CPA, 1987; International Test Commission, 2000; Turner, DeMers, Fox, & Reed, 2002). Issues pertaining to assessment in multicultural counselling are expanded upon in Chapter 8.

Ethics and the Law

Ethics and the law share the goals of regulating behaviour and protecting society. The laws of the land and professional ethics are usually complementary (Ogloff & Olley, 1996). Ethics and the law are sometimes in conflict. Psychologists and counsellors do not have privileged communication and therefore must disclose confidential information when so ordered by the courts. Reporting child abuse is mandatory regardless of whether the counsellor thinks that it is in the family's best interests. The law may be in conflict with Aboriginal beliefs about how justice is administered. Gay and lesbian couples may be prohibited from marrying or adopting children.

It is important to know the law as it affects one's practice and the lives of clients. Counsellors can help clients deal positively with situations in which the law impinges on their lives. Counsellors must keep clients informed about relevant legal matters and the choices that are available to them.

Snapshot 8

Reporting Child Abuse

You have a contract to provide mental health counselling for five days a month to a group of First Nations communities. In your work you become aware of children who have been sexually abused. In accordance with provincial law, you report the abuse to the proper authorities. Subsequently, social workers, police officers, and the courts become involved. One of the chiefs takes you aside and asks that you not make any further reports to the authorities "because the White system is racist, abusive, and disempowering to the Aboriginal people." He implies that your contract will be cancelled if you continue to report. How should you respond?

Adapted from Vignette #89, Companion manual to the *Canadian Code of Ethics for Psychologists* (3rd ed.), by C. Sinclair and J. Pettifor, 2001, Ottawa, ON: Canadian Psychological Association.

Ethical Decision-Making Steps

Professional codes of ethics generally do not provide **ethical decision-making** steps *as a process to assist professionals in taking a rational approach to resolving ethical dilemmas*, the exceptions being the codes of the CPA (1986, 1991, 2000), the Canadian Guidance and Counselling Association (1989; CCA, 1999), the Canadian Association for Music Therapy (Kerry & Sargent, 1999), the NZPS (2002), and the VRAC (2002). The above-mentioned codes have been influenced by the *Canadian Code of Ethics for Psychologists*.

Before looking at alternative decisions for action it is necessary to identify the ethical issues from the perspective of principles and values rather than only from that of rule compliance. Dilemmas usually involve a conflict between principles and rules or between interested parties. Value-based decision-making is more likely to address diversity than a strictly rule orientation. The third edition of the *Canadian Code of Ethics for Psychologists* has added some features to the ethical decision-making steps that make it more compatible to considering the needs of diverse populations (Sinclair & Pettifor, 2001):

- *The nature of the involvement of various partie*s. Identification of ethically relevant issues and practices, including the interests, rights, and any relevant characteristics of the individuals and groups involved and of the system or circumstances in which the ethical problem arose...
- *Self-awarenes*s. Consideration of how personal biases, stresses, or self-interest might influence the development of or choice between courses of action...
- *Systemic problem*s. Appropriate action, as warranted and feasible, to prevent future occurrences of the dilemma (e.g., communication and problem-solving with colleagues; changes in procedures and practices). (pp. 33-35)

The ethical decision-making steps provided by the VRAC (2002) allow for collaboration with persons with disabilities and other involved parties in arriving at decisions:

> Develop alternative courses of action remembering that you do not have to do this alone. (Where feasible, include interdisciplinary team members, clients, and others who may be affected by the decisions to share in the process. If the situation is difficult, consult with your professional association or other trusted professionals to maintain objectivity and increase your options for action.).... Act, with an individual or collective commitment, to assume responsibility for the consequences of the action (A collective commitment, as may occur within a multidisciplinary team, requires that someone be assigned the responsibility for follow-up.). (p. 3)

 **Snapshot 9**

Disability and Marriage

Betty is a 25-year-old woman with a disability who lives in a supported living situation and is 6 months pregnant. The baby's father is David, her boyfriend of 2 years. You are a rehabilitation career counsellor who assists Betty in maintaining employment. Her mother asks to see you, and you assume that it will be about how Betty's pregnancy affects her work situation. However, you soon find that her mother wants your assistance in preventing Betty from marrying David and in convincing Betty to be sterilized after the birth of the child. What are your counselling goals?

The *Feminist Model for Ethical Decision-Making* (Hill, Glaser, & Harden, 1995) emphasizes awareness of one's own emotional and intuitive reactions in resolving an ethical dilemma. It is intended to supplement, not to replace, the rational approach recommended by other professions. The increasing emphasis on the awareness of professionals of their own attitudes, feelings, biases, and early socialization is intended to achieve greater recognition and appreciation of persons with diverse beliefs, circumstances, and oppressions.

Regulation and Enforcement

Ideals may be inspired, but not enforced. However, criticisms are made that the professions do not enforce respectful, competent, non-discriminatory practice by their members and that they do not punish those who are guilty of unfair discrimination against persons of ethnic origin, or women, or persons with disabilities. Regulatory bodies are sometimes perceived to be negligent or deliberately protecting their members, contrary to the public interest.

In reality, regulatory bodies are limited in their ability to enforce high standards of practice. A regulatory body has the authority to use sanctions only against serious violations that have been reported, and it must abide by strict procedures to ensure that discipline hearings are fair and legally defensible. Behavioural standards or rules generally define acceptable behaviour specifically enough that it is clear when an individual has not obeyed the rules.

Increased respect and caring for diverse populations will not be achieved through disciplinary measures. Many professionals believe that diversity-sensitive practice is more likely to be achieved through education and *the promotion of optimal levels of practice that focus on positive interpersonal relationships and demonstrate respect and caring for all humans*. This **aspirational focus** is expected to enhance the quality of care provided.

Ethical Guidelines for Cross-Cultural Research

Criticisms of Ethical Guidelines and Practice in Cross-Cultural Research

Critics maintain that much cross-cultural research is neither respectful nor understanding of the culture under observation, and that research reports may be inaccurate and offensive.

 **Snapshot 10**

Vignette

You are a graduate student who wishes to conduct a qualitative study designed to explore and understand the experiences of physical and sexual abuse experienced by Aboriginal women living on a Canadian Indian reserve. You have taken graduate courses in research design, statistical analysis, and qualitative methods. You intend to publish your results and to make recommendations to the federal government on how to deal with the problem of violence against Aboriginal women.

What cultural issues must be addressed relative to informed consent, risk/benefit analysis, deception or "incomplete disclosure," confidentiality, and publication credits?

 **Snapshot 11**

Criticisms of Cross-Cultural Research

"The researcher cannot escape the moral and ethical implications of his/her research and must take responsibility for the outcome of his/her study. He/she should guard against misinterpretations and take into account cultural factors and the limitations of his/her instruments" (Sue & Sue, 1990, p. 25).

"Members of racial and ethnic minority groups understandably are wary of research comparing characteristics of their communities with those of members of White middle-class society" (Grisso et al., 1991, p. 762).

"People such as the homeless, runaways, unassimilated ethnic minorities, prostitutes, intravenous drug and crack users, dual-diagnosis mentally ill persons, and persons with alcoholism are involved in many problems that require research.... Many researchers...typically lack the cultural sensitivity required to adapt methodological and ethical principles to these settings" (Sieber, 1994, p. 372).

"One of the sources of inaccuracy in some areas of research has been the tendency to consider the male of the species as the norm and the female of the species as a deviation from the norm.... A considerable number of other identifiable groups in society have suffered the consequences of having been excluded from research samples and of having been misrepresented when included...persons with disabilities...the elderly...the very young...the economically disadvantaged, and...members of non-dominant cultures" (Stark, 1998, p. 205).

"Scientists as moral agents must integrate their caring and understanding of participant perspectives with a realistic sense of their own competencies to take responsibility for ethical decisions" (Fisher, 2000, p. 134).

"Several sources of reactivity were found. These include rigid protocol, differential treatment, non-Native researchers, threats to composure, lack of inherent social value for the participants and over publishing. In addition to these evident sources of reactivity, researchers need to show sensitivity about the simple workload on participants that are unfamiliar with testing and are working in their second language" (Darou, Kurtness, & Hum, 2000, p. 51). These authors discussed reasons for the James Bay Cree to eject psychology researchers from their land.

"Current ethics regulations, although critical, often disregard the unique ethical challenges that scientists confront in research with diverse ethnic populations" (Carpenter, 2001, p. 34).

Cross-Cultural Research Issues

The main purpose of research is the pursuit of scientific knowledge. Integrity in scholarship requires researchers to be competent, objective, and honest; to recognize the work of others; and to be open to sharing their work with the scientific community. The protection of human participants from harm is an important requirement in the process of pursuing scientific knowledge and is implemented by addressing informed consent, confidentiality, avoidance of risk, and, where feasible, the avoidance of deception. All of these concerns can be addressed in traditional research guidelines and still be lacking in respect for the different beliefs and the best interests of research participants.

Volumes of literature address how science should be conducted in both methodology and relationships with human participants. The concept of fully informed consent may be based on respect for individuals, but the signed consent form by an uninformed participant is neither respectful nor ethical.

Some cultures require consent from the governing bodies before considering consent from individuals. Today's codes do not prohibit but instead place restrictions or conditions on the use of deception and incomplete disclosure in order to balance respect for the research participants with the need to obtain data on important research questions. Honesty and a lack of deception are important in maintaining public confidence in funding research. Some cultural groups are distrustful of researchers. One strategy that is respectful of participants is to include them in planning and conducting the study, and to obtain their approval of the findings, including their consent, before making the report public.

Snapshot 12

Vignette

A government department has contracted you to conduct an empirical program evaluation of the effectiveness of a service program (such as an Aboriginal child welfare program, or a rehabilitation program for adults with acquired brain damage, or a career training program for the chronically unemployed). You are careful to fully respect guidelines for conducting research and you believe that it is respectful and helpful to establish a local advisory committee. At the conclusion of your study you make several recommendations for improving the effectiveness of the program. You check with the participants on the accuracy of your findings and you seek their approval to submit your report to the funding body. To your surprise they tell you to either change your findings or scrap the whole thing. They believe that you are providing grounds for the government department to discontinue their funding.

What are the key issues involved in who makes decisions about the results and dissemination of research? How should you proceed in negotiating what results, if any, can be distributed to the funder of this research and to the public? What steps could you take to protect the concerns raised by the research participants and their community?

Social justice concerns and protests of diverse populations have surfaced more frequently and more loudly in recent years. The denial of voice and of benefits of research for some non-dominant groups has led to recommendations for increased collaboration, benefits for participants and for society, promotion of social change for a just society, and attention to the uses and abuses of power. Various cultural groups believe that they are under-represented and misunderstood and suffer discrimination from insensitive, uncaring researchers. Changes to respect greater diversity, in both scientific methodology and in relationships between researchers and human participants, come gradually.

Historical Influences in Social Sciences Research

Science in modern society has often replaced older authorities as a respected source of knowledge and moral authority for decision-making. Yet scientists may be untutored in responding to ethical concerns intrinsic to their research and ideas or to the possible social applications of their work (Appleyard, 1992). House (1993) maintained that the perceived authority of science has come about as a result of the breakdown of traditional structures under advanced capitalism and the belief that science will contribute to the American dream of continuing progress and a better quality of life for all citizens.

Historically, the social sciences were based on the rigorous methodology of the natural sciences designed to produce uncontaminated factual knowledge on the nature of human behaviour for the ultimate betterment of humankind. Scientists aimed to discover laws that could be generalized in order to understand, predict, and control human behaviour. Personal beliefs and values were considered detrimental to conducting research because they introduced bias. Concern for the rights or well-being of the research subjects was often seen as an impediment to achieving scientific excellence. In the context of value-free science, scientists argued that social implications and human applications of research findings were not their responsibility. This approach is not compatible with a study of differences among peoples or the experience of belonging to a diversity-specific group in society.

Scientific and academic psychology has a much longer history than professional psychology, but the development of ethical principles for the conduct of research is more recent. External events contributed to changes in thinking about the values of science and the principles and rules for governing the conduct of research. Nuclear scientists faced a moral crisis when their science resulted in dropping atomic bombs on Japan in 1945. The discovery of atrocities committed in the name of science in Nazi Germany resulted in the development of the 1946 *Nuremberg Code of Ethics in Medical Research* for the adjudication of Nazi war crimes in human experimentation (Mappes & Zembaty, 1991). It is the first known code of ethics to incorporate the concept of informed consent, and is perhaps the first major challenge to the beneficence of the professions (Sinclair, 1993). The trust of the public in research diminished as reports of abuse of human participants in medical and social sciences surfaced in North America. Abuses in research involving both fraud and harm to human participants have regularly come to the public's attention over the past 50 years.

What did the post-World War II codes of research ethics address? The *Nuremberg Code of Ethics in Medical Research* (Mappes & Zembaty, 1991) addressed the importance of informed consent, protecting subjects from harm, and competence of researchers. The *Declaration of Helsinki* (World Medical Association, in Mappes & Zembaty) emphasized informed consent, competence, and a definitive statement that "the interest of science and society should never take precedence over considerations related to the well-being of the subject" (p. 213). The concerns following World War II were primarily for the protection of human subjects from harm, and informed consent was seen as the major means of protection, since competent subjects would not consent to be harmed.

Contemporary Codes Addressing Ethics in Research

Clearly, there is an evolution or revolution underway to expand the ethics of research (objective fact-finding and logical analysis) to include more proactive respect for the experiences of research participants and more proactive responsibility for the welfare of society. Both of these thrusts are value laden. Today, methodological changes in the study of social behaviour are more likely to include observations in natural and cultural surroundings and advanced correlational methods. These and other changes are seen as more respectful of participants and more relevant to the pursuit of knowledge. The ethic of responsibility and caring in relationships has been proposed as an alternative to the ethic of simply ensuring individual rights (Gilligan, 1982). Social action research and participatory action research have given research a social and political agenda to assist participants in improving the quality of their lives.

Although professional codes of ethics apply to practice, research, and teaching, a large number of guidelines have been formalized for conducting research. Examples are described below in terms of their relevance for cross-cultural research.

The APA's (1982) *Ethical Principles on the Conduct of Research with Human Participants* was first adopted in 1973 and revised in 1978 and 1981. The introduction to the *Ethical Principles in the Conduct of Research with Human Participants* reflects the perceived conflict between the scientist's obligation to expand knowledge for the sake of ultimate human betterment and an ethical requirement to not violate the rights of human participants. Many of the principles attempt to balance what are seen as conflicting responsibilities, such as the potential value of the research for human knowledge on the one hand and, on the other, the cost to the research participants. While there are admonitions to respect values of informed consent, avoidance of harm, and avoidance of deception, room is left to justify violations in the interests of the potential greater good. The discussion and ambivalence around the rights of human participants appear to be based on responses from a wide range of consultants who feared that stringent adherence to respecting the rights of research participants would restrict them from conducting valuable research.

The *Ethical Principles of Psychologists and Code of Conduct* (APA, 2002a) does not specifically address cross-cultural research. The general principles of (a) Beneficence and Nonmaleficence, (b) Fidelity and Responsibility, (c) Integrity, (d) Justice, and (e) Respect for People's Rights and Dignity clearly apply to both scientific and professional activities. The following statement appears under the section on competence.

> Where scientific or professional knowledge in the discipline of psychology establishes that an understanding of age, gender, race, ethnicity, culture, national origin, religion, sexual orientation, disability, language, or socioeconomic status is essential for effective implementation of services or research, psychologists have, or obtain the training, experience, consultation, or supervision necessary to ensure the competence of their services. (pp. 1063-1064)

The meaning of *establishes* in this context is unclear. However, psychologists are expected to recognize and respect human differences and to be competent in offering their services.

Ethics in Research with Human Participants (Sales & Folkman, 2000), published by the APA, appears to recognize special populations as only those that are legally incompetent; lack resources, such as persons who are homeless; are stigmatized, such as gay men and lesbians; or are institutionalized, such as prisoners and some people with mental disorders. Social Responsibility, as a principle in the 1991 code, does not appear in the 2002 revision. The APA guidelines appear to fall short of even a basic range of diversities discussed in the literature.

The *Tri-Council Policy Statement: Ethical Conduct for Research Involving Humans* (CIHR et al., 1998 with 2000, 2002, 2005 amendments), which was developed by Canada's three major federal research funding agencies, contains a chapter on *Context of an Ethics Framework* that, if applied, would serve diverse populations much better in the future than has been the case in the past. The chapter on moral framework discussed the importance of context, relationships, and commitment to social welfare. The Guiding Ethical Principles are (a) Respect for Human Dignity, (b) Respect for Free and Informed Consent, (c) Respect for Vulnerable Persons, (d) Respect for Privacy and Confidentiality, (e) Respect for Justice and Inclusiveness, (f) Balancing Harms and Benefits, (g) Minimizing Harm, and (h) Maximizing Benefit. A subject-centred perspective entails an active involvement by research subjects and ensures that their interests are central to the project or study and that they will not be treated simply as objects. The *Tri-Council Policy Statement: Ethical Conduct for Research Involving Humans* (CIHR et al., 1998) states:

- Good reasoning requires thought, insight and sensitivity to context, which in turn helps to refine the roles and application of norms that govern relationships. (Section G, ¶1)
- Beyond a keen appreciation for context, effective guiding principles also depend on procedures and policies for their implementation. (Section G, ¶5)
- An ethic of research involving human subjects should include two essential components: (1) the selection and achievement of morally acceptable ends, and (2) the morally acceptable means to those ends. (Section B, ¶1)

This document addresses the inclusion in research of women, Aboriginal persons, and those who are legally incompetent to consent, but does not otherwise discuss multiculturalism. Medical research and procedures for research ethics boards are given a great deal of attention. As of February 2009, this document is under review.

The *Canadian Code of Ethics for Psychologists, Third Edition* (CPA, 2000), places its highest value on respect for the dignity of persons and recognizes that as power differentials increase between psychologists and others, psychologists must accept a greater responsibility to protect the rights of vulnerable persons. The *Canadian Code* is explicit in requiring psychologists to be knowledgeable and self-aware of their own potential biases, as well as to take particular care to protect against misinterpretation and misuse when reporting the results of any work with vulnerable groups. The code recommends that psychologists be proactive, value-based, self-aware, and socially responsible for their actions.

All of the principles that apply to professional practice also apply to teaching and research. The steps for an ethical decision-making process are equally relevant for research and practice.

The Social Science Federation of Canada's *Ethical Decision-Making for Practicing Social Scientists: Putting Values into Practice* (Stark [-Adamec] & Pettifor, 1995) is a unique document in the evolution of guidelines for social scientists. In clearly articulating three overarching values to guide the activities of social scientists of various disciplines, it emphasizes integrity in relationships as essential to conducting good research and to contributing to social action. The three overarching principles are:

I. Integrity in scholarship and teaching. The conduct of social science involves the competent and responsible search for new knowledge and the accurate dissemination of this new knowledge. (p. B: 1)

II. Integrity in relationships. The conduct of social science is a social process involving relationships with others. In these relationships social scientists take care to demonstrate respect for individual and cultural differences, and respect for the dignity and rights of others. (p. B: 2)

III. Responsibility to society. Social scientists are engaged in a social contract with society. Society can reasonably expect to receive benefits in exchange for supporting the social sciences. (p. B: 2)

Steps for a problem-solving or an ethical decision-making process are provided to demonstrate adherence to principles and values in resolving ethical dilemmas. The last step of the decision-making process in the Canadian Code of Ethics (CPA, 2000) is to evaluate the systems within which the ethical issue arose, with a view to identifying and removing conditions that facilitate or reward unethical behaviour. This step recognizes that, while individuals are considered responsible for their own decisions, societal attitudes and organizational practices may encourage and reward unethical behaviour. Counsellors have a responsibility to attempt to change harmful aspects of society.

In reviewing the nearly 100 vignettes of real-life dilemmas submitted by social scientists (Stark [-Adamec] & Pettifor, 1995), integrity in relationships seemed to be the essential ingredient both in ensuring good scholarship and in contributing to the welfare of society. Many of the vignettes involve abuse of power and oppression or exploitation of those without power. Social justice is an underlying concept throughout the document.

Diversity-Specific Guidelines

Persons with disabilities

Social science literature addressing the needs of persons with disabilities is limited, although the social construction theory of disability describes social psychological barriers as more handicapping than biological and medical conditions. Gatens-Robinson and Tarvydas (1992) suggested five problematic moral themes within the disability context:

*   *The temptation of paternalism.* It is tempting for professionals to believe that they know the client's needs best and therefore to show little respect for client wishes and autonomy...

*   *Disability as an anomaly for traditional ethics.* Because persons with disabilities are perceived as less capable of rational decision-making, they are denied rights and privileges that are normally accorded competent adults...

*   *A medical model versus an environmental model of disability.* The medical model emphasizes fixing the object, disorder, deficit, or symptom more than enhancing the quality of life of persons within the natural community...

*   *Possessive individualism and independence versus interdependence.* Independence is unrealistically valued in society for all persons, which results in a devaluation of those who must depend on others.

*   *Submission to the care of strangers is too often viewed as charity beyond any moral obligation.* To be recipients of charity diminishes the value of persons with disabilities. (pp. 28-32)

According to these authors, research and practice in the field of disabilities should be based on (a) contextual deliberation, (b) non-hierarchical deliberations, (c) skilled communication with persons with disabilities as an essential prerequisite in addressing moral issues, and (d) movement away from impersonal interaction to more inclusive, person-centred types of interaction.

All of these observations and guidelines represent ways of showing genuine respect for the dignity and self-determination of persons with disabilities and a consideration of their quality of life within communities.

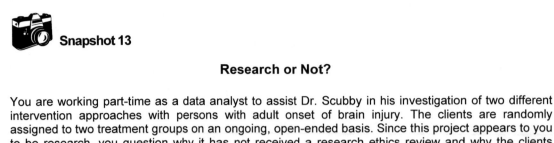

Snapshot 13

Research or Not?

You are working part-time as a data analyst to assist Dr. Scubby in his investigation of two different intervention approaches with persons with adult onset of brain injury. The clients are randomly assigned to two treatment groups on an ongoing, open-ended basis. Since this project appears to you to be research, you question why it has not received a research ethics review and why the clients have not been told and have not consented to be research participants. You also have questions about the adequacy of the research design. You are told that it is really just an internal quality assurance program, so it does not require review, and it makes no difference to the clients because no one is denied treatment and they might not understand anyway. You should just do your data analysis and not worry about these things. Later, Dr. Scubby presents the results of the study at a professional conference as research and publishes an article with no discussion of methodological limitations or of ethical implications. Do you have any further responsibilities?

First Nations/Cree

Darou et al. (2000), on the basis of their experience with the James Bay Cree in Northern Quebec, offered advice to researchers working with Aboriginal persons. The following suggestions are abridged from their discussion:

1. Be patient and accepting.

2. Be flexible, because you can never completely understand the cultural context.

3. Try to recuperate gracefully from your cultural gaffs. Do not pretend to be Native.

4. Learn something about the culture and the language.

5. Do not conduct research unless you have been invited and you have a clear and relevant purpose.

6. Obtain a local advisory committee, prepare culturally sensitive instruments, and provide feedback.

7. Consider non-experimental designs.

8. Remember that outside researchers put a great deal of strain on the community in terms of time, space, finances, and other sometimes scarce resources.

9. Put something valuable back into the community.

10. Share results with the community, debrief all parties, and seek approval from local authorities for publication.

11. Do not interfere with Native politics. (pp. 51-52)

All of these observations and guidelines represent ways of showing genuine respect for the culture, dignity, and self-determination of Aboriginal peoples and of correcting the errors of past researchers. Brant Castellano (2004) described the ongoing initiatives to develop codes of ethics for Aboriginal research that reflects Aboriginal culture worldview and the struggle for self-determination.

Feminist research guidelines

The purpose of feminist research is to provide knowledge that will promote equality in society. Issues of power and control influence all stages of the research and therefore must be addressed in every project. Freyd and Quina (2000, p. 119) provided guidelines for the ethical conduct and dissemination of scientific research that will minimize the power differential, respect the experience of participants, and serve their interests. Muzychka, Poulin, Cottrell, Miedema, and Roberts (1996) provided a guide to conducting feminist research. *Feminist Research Ethics: A Process* (Canadian Research Institute for the Advancement of Women, 1996, pp. 9-33) provided 189 questions that feminist researchers are asked to consider in conducting research. *Science Free of Sexism: A Psychologist's Guide to the Conduct of Nonsexist Research* (Stark-Adamec & Kimball, 1984) described the many ways that sexist bias can result in invalid research. It also provided a checklist of questions to guide researchers in conducting nonsexist research. Research guidelines have been developed for the protection of other special populations that may be subject to discrimination, such as *Ethical Principles for the Conduct for Research in the North* (Association of Canadian Universities for Northern Studies, 1982) and *Ethical Standards for Research with Children* (Society for Research in Child Development, 1990).

The diversity-specific guidelines for researchers emphasize showing respect for others through courtesy, honesty, understanding, egalitarianism, collaboration, sharing at all points in the research, benefit for the research participants, and seeking approval of reports or publications. The specific guidelines describe the characteristics that are essential in being respectful of other populations and the characteristics that are essential to remedy research abuses of the past. Generic codes of ethics are based on moral principles that apply to all situations and types of professional activity. However, generality may lead to ambiguity in addressing diversity-specific situations and thus may not be seen as a deterrent to unintentional discrimination against a variety of marginalized persons or to a trivialization of diversity issues. Some researchers still fear that being too considerate of research participants will be a barrier to conducting their studies, while others believe that not to do so invalidates the research. The theme of research across cultures is picked up again in Chapter 9.

Social Justice and Responsibility to Society

When the powerless and the poor are excluded, social justice is extremely limited. In Rawls' (1971) description of **social justice**, *(a) each person has an equal right to the most extensive basic liberty compatible with a similar liberty for others and (b) social and economic inequalities are arranged so that they are both (i) to the greatest benefit of the least advantaged (difference principle) and (ii) attached to offices and positions open to all under conditions of fair opportunity.*

House (1993) maintained that scientists and evaluators are reluctant to recognize the relevance of social and economic class in their findings of difference because to do so would question the fundamental tenets of American society of liberty, equality, and the good life for all. Instead, they tend to identify deficiencies in individuals, programs, expectations, or other external factors, thus devaluing others and placing blame on individuals rather than criticizing society. O'Neill (2004) maintained that how one defines a problem (individual or societal) determines what data one collects and what conclusions one makes.

By the 1960s and 1970s, there were many challenges to the concept that science was value-free as a source of knowledge and truth. Social science research, modelled on the experimental rigor of the natural sciences, faced a crisis of relevancy and credibility. Questionable research procedures were often rationalized in terms of potential long-term benefits to society (Dunbar, 1992), which should be no surprise, considering the ambivalence that scientists had about principles for the protection of human participants.

Demands for social justice come from many sources. The thrust of identity politics is the belief by many social groups (for example, those based on gender, sexual orientation, disability, and ethnicity) that they must strive to be liberated from the oppression and injustice they experience in society because of their specific identity (Heyes, 2002). Within this context, science is challenged to respond to the full diversity of human nature and to adhere to the ethics of respect and caring for all persons (Sampson, 1993b). Generalizable laws of human behaviour may not respect diversity except as deficiency.

In the last 10 years, another crisis has arisen for society: the challenge of balancing and adjudicating the allocation of resources to meet the social, health, and educational needs of the population. Research funding is also affected by budget cuts. Marginalized persons are more likely to suffer from restricted services. To some extent, the term "special interest group" has become a negative descriptor regarding the needs of non-dominant or minority groups instead of a call for respect of differences. Professionals may have difficulties caring for the most vulnerable when human values and virtue conflict with economic priorities and political agendas (Pettifor, 1996).

Snapshot 14

Diversity Implications for Access to Health, Education, and Social Services in a Climate of Economic Restraint and Privatization of Services

What do politicians mean when they say that they or the public must make *hard* decisions? Does this mean setting priorities about who will benefit and who will suffer by restricting services?

Identify a specific service in the area of health, education, or social services. Is it privately or publicly funded? Then think about the diversity of persons requiring services.

Questions

1. How will economic restraints generally affect citizens' access to services?
2. How much should access to services depend on what *I want, I need, I deserve*, or *I can pay*?
3. Will economic restrictions affect persons of some types of diversity more than others? Why or why not?
4. Will economic constraints affect the nature of your counselling clientele?
5. Will economic constraints affect primary prevention and social planning for the alleviation of social problems?
6. What social action strategies are appropriate for multicultural counsellors to embrace?

What Does the Future Hold?

Over the past decade or so there has been significantly increased attention paid to multicultural counselling in the professional literature, in professional training, and to standards for accreditation of training programs. As society becomes increasingly multicultural, and non-dominant populations become increasingly visible and vocal, there seems to be a greater acceptance of diversity in some domains of professional practice and greater rejection in others. Training, continuing education, publications, and conference presentations on competent and ethical multicultural counselling are still needed.

Some professionals are recommending that consumers of services should share in the development of codes of ethics, especially since they are the ones most affected by the nature of the services received. In a workshop on Ethics of Respect and Caring sponsored by a *Persons with Developmental Disabilities Board*, consumers, family members, service providers, and administrators were asked what it means for them to be respected and what it means for them to respect others. While each group endorsed the principle of respect for others, each felt that they were not sufficiently respected, understood, heard, or considered important by the others (Pettifor, 2001b). The direct exchange of views contributed to a better understanding. Whether or not consumers and other stakeholders are involved in the development of codes of ethics, there may be more dialogue in the future on what the ethical principles mean, and such dialogues will hopefully promote greater respect and understanding in practice.

A great deal of attention has been given in North America to defining competencies in multicultural counselling. Attempts are made to define the components of the knowledge, skills, and attitudes that are required. Competencies are not defined in codes of ethics, although adherence to ethics codes requires counsellors to be competent in their professional activities. Incompetent practice is unethical because it does harm. Collins and Arthur (2005) proposed the *working alliance* as an organizational construct to integrate core multicultural competencies. Various components of an effective counselling or therapeutic relationship (including competencies) have been proposed in the past, such as empathy, genuineness, trust, honesty, caring, and respect. All of these characteristics of good relationships contribute to the working alliance. If we extend the concept of cultural beings to all individuals and their individual identities, then what we propose about multicultural counselling can be applied to all counselling; there should be no need for special guidelines for special populations. Culture would be infused in all counselling. However, as long as non-dominant groups of people are treated unequally and marginalized there will be a need and a demand for special training and guidelines.

Two current issues in psychology may have an impact on multicultural counselling. The movement for professionals to adopt only empirically supported interventions must be monitored. If the professions, funders, and employers are rigid in requiring interventions that have been empirically matched to diagnostic categories, multicultural counsellors may face ethical dilemmas on to how to provide relevant services for clients. The inappropriate use of interventions could become a potential source of harm. The evidence used for supporting interventions must be relevant to non-dominant populations with their own cultural beliefs and living styles. Secondly, psychologists obtaining prescription privileges could be a benefit for professionals and clients, but it could also be a mistake if socially determined problems become *medicalized*, either for the convenience of professionals or because of insensitivity to culture and social issues.

International Association Codes of Ethics

Most of the literature on multicultural counselling addresses cross-cultural counselling within European and North American societies and therefore discusses the application of the values of Western societies. International associations, however, often develop ethical guidelines to guide members living and practicing anywhere in the world. These associations include the International Association of Educational and Vocational Guidance (2001), the International Association of Marriage and Family Counselors (2002), the International Association of Psychiatric Rehabilitation Services (2000), the International Federation of Social Workers (2002), the International School Psychology Association (Oakland, Goldman, & Bischoff, 1997), the World Medical Association (1994), and the World Psychiatric Association (2002). These guidelines all discuss such basic issues as respect for individuals (including informed consent, privacy, and confidentiality), competence, client well-being, and conflict of interest.

Some international ethical guidelines emphasize multicultural competency. For example, the International Association of Marriage and Family Counselors (2002) requires that members do not impose personal values on families, that members become multiculturally competent, and that they use indigenous healing practices when appropriate. The International School Psychology Association (Oakland et al., 1997) expects its members to respect the cultural environments within which they work and to provide appropriate ways to serve diverse populations.

Although international codes of ethics support non-discrimination and respect for diversity, few speak to responsibility to society or provide guidance when the cultural beliefs of clients, families, and communities are in sharp conflict with the requirements of professional codes of ethics. For example, respect for autonomy and self-determination of individuals is not desired in cultures that value interdependence and the collective good of families, communities, or nations or that see religious authority as more important than Western science in resolving problems. The international professional association-approved ethical guidelines appear to be strongly dominated by Western values, while still attempting to recognize and respect diversity. However, unintentional racism and trivialization of cultural differences are not yet things of the past.

In July 2008 the *Universal Declaration of Ethical Principles for Psychologists* was adopted by the International Union of Psychological Science (2008) and the International Association of Applied Psychology. This unique document, based on research and world-wide consultation, provides a moral framework of ethical principles that appear to be near-universal. The four overarching principles are described as: Respect for the Dignity of Persons and Peoples, Competent Caring for the Well-Being of Persons and Peoples, Integrity, and Professional and Scientific Responsibility to Society. Specific standards of behaviour to accompany each principle are deliberately not provided because how these principles and values are demonstrated in practice will be determined differently within the various cultural, regional, and political groups. The description of the Principle of Respect has been expanded beyond the usual definition in western codes of ethics:

> *All human beings, as well as being individuals are interdependent social beings that are born into and are a part of the history and ongoing evolution of their peoples. The different cultures, ethnicities, religions, histories, social structures, and other such characteristics of peoples are integral to the identity of their members and give meaning to their lives. The continuity of peoples and cultures over time connects the peoples of today with the peoples of past generations and the need to nurture future generations. As such, respect for the dignity of persons includes moral consideration of and respect for the dignity of peoples.* (International Union of Psychological Science, p. 2)

Despite signs of greater acceptance and understanding across cultures worldwide, political, economic, religious, and racial differences still underlie some of the worst violence, terrorism, genocide, and killing that the world has known. Science and technology have been used to augment the power to kill. Mutual respect among peoples calls for peaceful ways to address differences. Respect is the cornerstone of professional ethics.

Chapter Summary

The principles of good multicultural counselling should be the same principles for all counselling. However, multicultural counselling has traditionally addressed counselling with a range of persons from non-dominant or dissimilar groups in society. Respect, caring, and integrity are the moral foundations for professional ethics. Criticisms abound that professional codes and practitioners do not fully respect diverse populations. A review of recent revisions of ethics codes as they address multicultural counselling indicates an increased awareness and acceptance of differences. At the same time, some aspects of society are neglectful or oppressive. Ethical practice includes a responsibility to work for the betterment of society and the elimination of oppressive conditions. In addition to considering multicultural counselling within Euro-North American cultures, international professional associations are attempting to develop ethical guidelines that are appropriate across cultures worldwide. The challenges and the commitments are great.

Conclusion

Ethical guidelines must continue to evolve to reflect how we apply moral principles to our lives, and our lives must include those who are presently marginalized in society. The mainstream codes of ethics are good as far as they go, but they require proactive interpretation and implementation. Critics see them as falling short of meeting egalitarian and social justice aspirations. Ethical guidelines tend to lag behind progressive thinking in society. It is my contention that if we look at moral principles as the guiding lights for our interpretations, applications, and rules for conducting research and practice, then ethical principles and values should lead the way rather than follow.

To lead, we must address the diversity of people in all aspects of society with genuine respect and caring. Community psychology, feminist practice, and social construction theories of disability show significant leadership for developing more appropriate guidelines for professionals working cross-culturally. They address issues of power and oppression in society rather than limit attention to individual pathology and thus blame the *victim*. The counselling profession has been a leader in promoting multicultural sensitivity and practice. The *Universal Declaration of Ethical Principles for Psychologists* may be the next major accomplishment in including all persons and peoples as respected members of the human family. Culture may indeed need to be infused in all counselling.

CHAPTER 8
ASSESSMENT FROM A CONTEXTUAL PERSPECTIVE

John Stewart

Key Terms and Concepts		
• Acculturation • Assessment • Biculturalism • Constructivist perspective • Cultural identity • Idiographic information	• Item analysis • Item discrimination • Nomothetic information • Norm groups • Norms	• Qualitative assessment • Quantitative assessment • Random selection • Reliability • Validity

Personal Introduction

I grew up in rural Prince Edward Island in an agricultural community where my father owned a farm. My public school education took place in PEI and my university education was mostly in Atlantic Canada, with my doctoral studies in Counselling Psychology taking place at the University of Toronto. Within the rural agricultural context, I developed two perspectives that I have found to be similar to a collectivist worldview: an awareness of the need for interdependence and a decision-making style that revolved around what was best for the family in the short- and/or long-term. At the time, I did not know that my worldview was being shaped to reflect one shared by the majority of our global village.

After 20 years as a classroom teacher and school counsellor in the public school system in Prince Edward Island, I took a position in counsellor education at the University of New Brunswick. For my first sabbatical leave study, I had the opportunity to study with Dr. Paul Pedersen at the University of Alabama in Birmingham. It was there that I began a more detailed study on the topic of culture and its influence on behaviour. I learned that culture has a broad definition and includes many variables with a focus on ethnicity. Immediately after that sabbatical, I was asked to provide consultant support to the Ministry of Education in Bhutan, a small Himalayan kingdom in Asia. I spent three winters in Bhutan helping educators establish a school counselling program with a focus on career education. From this experience I learned that there is much commonality and yet diversity with [within] a culture and that ethnicity plays a part in cultural diversity.

Subsequent to these experiences, I travelled in Japan, Korea, and China. These experiences provided many experiential learning opportunities about the ways people whose cultural origins are different from mine behave interpersonally. As a member of the global village, I think the issue of social learning and the development of worldview is a fascinating area of study. Further, with the growing cultural diversity in Canadian society, we as helpers must learn to assess the culture within our clients if we are to meaningfully help those who request our services.

 **Snapshot 1**

Vignette

A young man who was in his last year of teacher education in Bhutan, Asia, shared this situation with me. It reflects some issues of ethnicity and culture as they influence behaviour.

The young man was a devout Hindu and respected the cultural practice of arranged marriages. His parents had arranged a marriage for him with a suitable woman who had completed Grade 12. However, he had only completed Grade 10 prior to entering preservice teacher education. He did not want to proceed with the marriage since his intended wife had a higher grade level achievement than he. He feared that he would not get respect from her or her parents due to his lower grade level attainment. He was highly anxious because he did not have a status similar to or greater than his intended wife. The time for the wedding was drawing near and he didn't want to go through with the marriage under the present circumstances. At the same time, he did not want to bring shame and dishonour to his parents by refusing to marry this woman.

This situation represents an intrapersonal problem for this individual. On one hand, he wants to respect his parents and follow their wishes. On the other hand, he expects to receive respect and honour from his wife and her family. In this situation, he would have a status unequal to that of his wife due to their differential grade level achievement. He was anxious about not knowing how to resolve his dilemma and was spending a lot of time ruminating about his situation. As well, he was not able to concentrate on his academic work.

Introduction

Assessment Defined

Assessment *involves using formal and/or informal techniques to describe the psychological, social, biological, and cultural factors that influence an individual's behaviour* (Ridley, Li, & Hill, 1998; Sattler, 2008; Whiston, 2005). It is a complex process and broader than diagnosis in that it involves both personality dispositions and contextual factors (Ridley et al.). During the assessment process, counsellors make a series of decisions and take a number of actions that culminate in a description of an individual. This assessment may take the form of a formal report or it may be the basis for developing counselling goals and planning interventions within the counselling process. Ideally, whether the assessment is formal or informal, the outcome should be an accurate and comprehensive description of the individual within the individual's context.

Perspectives on Assessment

When culture is defined from a broad perspective involving gender, sexual orientation, spirituality, ability, age, religion, and socio-economic status in addition to ethnicity, counsellors look within the individual's cultural group to find points of reference around which to make an assessment about the appropriateness of specific experiences (Dana, 1993). They note the personal and social variables that individuals use to make sense of their world. From a phenomenological perspective, collectively these variables comprise an individual's *culture within* (Pedersen, 1994) or their *personal culture* (Hogan-Garcia, 1999). This definition of culture lends itself to a view of assessment known as a constructivist perspective (McLeod, 2003; Neimeyer & Neimeyer, 1993; Sue, Ivey, & Pedersen, 1996).

A **constructivist perspective** maintains that *individuals are actively involved in developing a meaningful understanding of their world. That understanding is contextually embedded within the individual's personal and social environment.* This perspective is premised on three assumptions (McLeod, 2003): 1) individuals are purposeful learners engaged in interpreting their world, 2) language is the main means of shaping this interpretation, and 3) individuals' interpretations develop incrementally as they mature. A constructive perspective requires a phenomenological approach to exploring an individual's inner world or worldview (Day, 2004). The role of human experience plays a significant part in shaping this worldview. Additionally, one of the key tenets of this perspective is the notion of self as contextually embedded within the individual's cultural environment (Sue et al., 1996). A constructivist perspective helps account for the diversity of variables within and between cultural groups.

Culturally competent counsellors, working from a constructivist viewpoint, adopt a number of perspectives about culturally diverse groups to enhance their provision of competent and meaningful services (Fouad & Bingham, 1995; Ridley et al., 1998).

1. They acknowledge and value each cultural group for its uniqueness.

2. They recognize that all learning takes place within a cultural context.

3. To avoid stereotyping, they maintain that there is as much diversity within a group as there is between groups.

4. They acknowledge that the salient variables to consider in assessment may differ across cultural groups and that the weight placed on these variables may also differ across and within groups.

Chapter Focus

One of the principles for assessment in the Canadian Counselling Association Code of Ethics indicates that counsellors "proceed with caution" when interpreting data from minority group members and consider "the potential effects of age, ethnicity, disability, culture, gender, religion, sexual orientation, and socio-economic status on both the administration of, and the interpretation of data" from assessment instruments and procedures (Schulz, Sheppard, Lehr, & Shepard, 2006, p. 15). To this end then, the goal of this chapter is to acquaint counsellors with some of the significant cultural variables in assessment as well as the sources of bias that assessment instruments and procedures may have when working with diverse cultural groups. The chapter is intended for readers who already understand the theoretical and practical knowledge of assessment and its procedures. The following headings outline the content of the chapter: importance of culture, social and psychological dynamics in cultural understanding, counsellor assessment competencies, culture as a critical factor in assessment, the assessment process, collecting significant data, and methods of assessment.

Importance of Culture

The consideration of culture as a critical factor in the delivery of counselling services is widely accepted by practitioners (Arthur & Stewart, 2001). Culture, defined broadly, includes a number of variables that collectively influence the way an individual perceives the world (Diller, 2004; Ivey, D'Andrea, Ivey, & Simek-Morgan, 2007; Matsumoto, 1996). The integration of these variables into a conceptual network that forms the basis for the self-regulatory aspects of behaviour is an individual's personal culture. The idea of personal culture suggests that cultural groups have commonalities, but it does not preclude diversity within a group. Further, it highlights the role of social and historical influences on how and what is learned (Dana, 2000; Matsumoto).

Counsellors consider the influence of culture on behaviour as a critical variable in their assessment procedures because culture influences how individuals conceptualize, experience, and express intrapersonal and interpersonal behaviours. When counsellors neglect to use the cultural group as the standard, the assessment may be inaccurate and can lead to discrimination and stereotyping. The challenge then is for counsellors to use assessment procedures that provide accurate and appropriate information about their clients, particularly those from diverse cultural groups (Baruth & Manning, 2007).

Emic-Etic Continuum

Two approaches have influenced the concepts and attitudes professional counsellors have about how culture mediates behaviour. As noted in Chapter 1, although these approaches have similar content, such as the study of cultural values, there are differences between them (Baruth & Manning, 2007; Leong & Brown, 1995). The first approach is termed the cross-cultural approach or the etic approach. Typically, in North America, the etic approach focuses on understanding how the characteristics of the dominant cultural group may be generalized to those of other cultural groups. The goal of this approach is to understand the dimensions of culture that are universal. The second approach focuses on culture-specific components of human behaviour and is referred to as the emic approach. In North America, the emic approach focuses on understanding the determinants of behaviour by looking within a cultural group. While the etic approach is concerned with cultural validity, the emic approach is concerned with cultural specificity.

Both approaches are informative for counsellors, particularly for counsellors from one cultural background who work with clients from other cultural backgrounds. Combined, the two approaches provide cultural information both across and within groups. As noted in Chapter 4, counsellors need to understand their personal worldview as well as their cultural background and view themselves as a member of a cultural group. This self-understanding helps reduce the risk of counsellor bias when interpreting assessment results and increases the chances of accurate and non-discriminatory assessment outcomes (Baruth & Manning, 2007). Given this understanding, counsellors are prepared to help culturally diverse clients explore aspects of their personal culture during assessment. These variables will be discussed in the next section.

Social and Psychological Dynamics in Cultural Understanding

A number of variables influence peoples' perceptions, behaviours, and adjustment within the dominant culture (Ridley et al., 1998). Three variables will be considered here: worldview, acculturation, and identity formation. These variables are considered moderator variables because they influence the degree to which assessment procedures developed within one cultural context can be used appropriately with clients who embrace another cultural context (Dana, 1993).

Worldview

Worldview, or culturally specific cognition, helps individuals make sense of their life experiences (Dana, 1993). As noted in Chapter 4, worldview is a complex psychosocial construct. Four aspects of worldview are key to the assessment process (Dana):

1. The history and experiences of an individual's cultural group heritage result in a group identity. This heritage represents the collective experiences, memories, wisdom, and traditions of the group that influence their perceptions of the physical and social world. Within a culturally diverse society such as Canada, group members who retain the closest ties with their cultural group are more likely to hold values, beliefs, and assumptions that differ from those of other cultural groups. For example, given the history of discrimination of gay and lesbian groups, individuals from these cultural groups may be very reserved about expressing their sexual orientation in work contexts.

2. The self-perceptions organized around the psychocentric and sociocentric ideas of self form an individual's identity. In individualistic cultures, the self is more focused on psychocentric ideas, with the individual's self-interests at the core, whereas in collectivist cultures, the self is more focused on sociocentric ideas, with the social group's interests at the core. An individual's identity influences the number and types of variables considered in decision-making and problem-solving. For example, an individual with a collectivist worldview is likely to be more concerned with the views of the family in decision-making, while an individual with an individualistic worldview is likely to be more concerned about self-interests and aspirations.

3. Values involve ideals about such issues as human nature (i.e., good, evil, or a combination of both), time focus (i.e., past, present, or future), relationships with others, attitude towards the natural environment (i.e., mastery, harmony, or subservience), and human activity (i.e., sense of accomplishment, personal development, or spontaneous expressions of personality). Beliefs involve concepts about health and its expression, spirituality, and the extent of control one has over life events. For example, some religious groups promote a minimal involvement in society due to beliefs about the nature of evil present in the world and their need to maintain a focus on a strong relationship with the Divine.

4. The use of culturally specific language provides insight into an individual's behavioural, cognitive, and affective schemas. Together, values, beliefs, and language provide a basis for a number of perceptions. For example, the influence of popular advertising with its focus on fitness, attractiveness, and

youthfulness may promote feelings of unworthiness and low self-esteem among individuals who do not possess these characteristics. The absence of positive images for persons with disabilities sends a similar message.

Counsellors who acknowledge and discuss a client's cultural group and its heritage, as well as the client's personal identity, values, beliefs, and culturally specific language, maximize the client's full participation in the assessment process.

Cultural Adjustment

Acculturation is a term used to describe the *adjustment that individuals experience as they move from contact with their own cultural group to contact with a new cultural group*. Acculturation influences the behavioural, affective, and cognitive components of an individual's personality (Cuellar, Arnold, & Maldonado, 1995). As noted in Chapter 4, acculturation is a complex psychosocial phenomenon involving language usage, attitudes, identity, values, degree of awareness of the culture of origin and the new culture, and cultural group preferences (Kim & Abreu, 2001).

Acculturation status

Acculturation has been conceptualized along multilinear continua and in terms of different attitudes known individually as an acculturation status (Kim & Abreu, 2001; Sattler, 2008). Five such statuses are used to describe how ethnically different individuals adjust to the dominant culture in their new country. Traditional status is used to characterize individuals who value the traditions and people from their birth culture and who have little contact with people of the dominant culture. Marginality status is used to describe individuals who do not successfully meet the expectations of both their culture of origin and the dominant culture; consequently, these individuals often feel isolated from both cultures. Assimilation status is used to portray individuals who adopt the dominant cultural practices and reject the practices of their culture of origin. Integration status, or **biculturalism**, applies to *individuals who are successful in integrating the practices of both cultures and maintaining a strong sense of their personal identity*. A further status is termed *transitional* and describes individuals who participate in both their culture and the dominant culture but question the traditional values of both (Sattler, 2008). Recent research has suggested that all ethnic minority individuals can relate to issues of the dominant culture while retaining their ethnic identity within the dominant culture (Schmidt, 2006). This observation brings into question the usefulness of these statuses and the part they may play in stereotyping culturally diverse clients. Counsellors realize that there is much diversity between individual experiences when it comes to cultural adjustment.

Acculturation adjustment

A number of factors influence cultural group adjustment. Perceptual factors influence the degree and rate of adjustment within the dominant culture (Berry, 2003). If individuals adopt a positive stance towards the dominant culture, they adjust more quickly, whereas individuals who adopt a negative stance take longer and may manifest more difficulties during the adjustment period. Additionally, adjustment is influenced by the length of time an individual spends with people of the dominant cultural group (Paniagua, 2001). Intercultural experiences help individuals to develop their self-concepts, their view of others, and ultimately their worldview (Schmidt, 2006). When cross-cultural experiences are perceived positively, individuals increase their cultural sensitivity.

Acculturation may happen when individuals move within a society that is comprised of multiple cultures. When individuals move to another part of their country for work or school, they often feel out of place in the new location. To successfully adjust to this new environment, individuals typically adopt new behaviours and beliefs and yet retain some of the behaviours of their culture of origin. For example, I lived in rural Prince Edward Island where eye contact with individuals was an important interpersonal behaviour. However, I found that establishing eye contact with individuals in Toronto was not a behaviour that was always welcomed. I had to learn a new behaviour to look beyond people I met on streets or in the subway.

With immigrants, their age, the circumstances around migration, their place of residence in the country of origin, their socio-economic status, and the cultural similarity of the country of origin to the new country influence acculturation adjustment (Leong & Brown, 1995; Sattler, 2008). Typically, immigrants with a high level of socio-economic status who come from an urban area of a country similar to Canada will adjust more quickly to the Canadian culture than those who have a low socio-economic status and come from a rural area of a country whose culture is more unlike that of Canada. Intercultural group interaction in the new country influences acculturation adjustment among recent immigrants (Leong & Brown). If individuals relocate to a centre where they live with individuals of the same cultural background and have an opportunity to return frequently to their country of origin, they tend to maintain traditions within their culture of origin longer. Family issues, including language used at home, preference for cultural heritage, and cultural group pride and identity, also influence acculturation adjustment (Leong & Brown). Individuals with close ties to their immediate and extended family and whose parents insist on retaining their cultural customs and language will retain the traditions of the original culture longer.

Acculturation adjustment may produce stress for culturally diverse individuals (Sattler, 2008). Recent immigrants who leave family and friends behind may feel lonely. The use of language may be a source of stress. For example, individuals may experience stress if they have difficulty speaking and understanding English in North America, if they speak one language at home and another with friends, if they feel pressure to speak their cultural language at home, if they are teased about how they speak in the new culture, or if they have to serve as translators for family members who do not speak English. Further, family dynamics may be a source of stress. Children tend to adopt the ideas and behaviours of the dominant culture at a faster rate than their parents. Parents experience stress when their children adopt dominant group behaviours and ignore ethnic group behaviours. Acculturation is more of a concern with foreign-born recent immigrants, while identity is more of a concern for their children (Roysircar, 2003).

Identity Formation

Closely aligned with acculturation adjustment is cultural identity formation. Whereas acculturation refers to a group level process, **cultural identity** is considered *an individual psychological process concerned with the individual's retention of cultural characteristics.* Cultural identity formation may be viewed from three perspectives (Phinney, 1990). The first perspective focuses on a sense of belonging to one's cultural group that is assumed to help maintain a person's positive self-esteem. The second perspective focuses on a process of ego identity development that takes place over time, most notably during adolescence. The third perspective centres on the individual's involvement with and maintenance of behaviour acceptable to the individual's cultural group.

As noted in Chapter 4, most of the theoretical work on ethnic identity formation in North America has focused on African-American identity formation and on White identity formation (Fischer & Moradi, 2001). The conceptual work on the formation of these models comprises a developmental perspective involving a number of salient variables: cultural group loyalty, cultural identity and self-concept formation, personal conduct in the dominant culture, and feelings and attitudes about one's cultural group. It seems reasonable to assume that these variables would also influence clients' identity formation from other cultural groups. Further, gay and lesbian identity formation is often conceptualized from a developmental perspective and includes an awareness of sexual feelings for members of the same sex, exploration of sexuality and possible confusion from exploration, identification and acceptance of the orientation, and choosing a lifestyle that fits with one's evolving self-identity.

Recent theorizing has focused on models that address multiple dimensions of identity (Baruth & Manning, 2007; Howard-Hamilton & Frazier, 2005; Robinson, 2005). Traditionally, models of identity have focused on one dimension such as color, ethnicity, gender, or sexual orientation. One recent multi-dimensional model (Schmidt, 2006) highlighted a number of dimensions that influence identity, including sexual orientation, gender, race, religion, social class, and culture. These six influences, along with overall identity development, are influenced by socio-cultural contexts, family background, vocational and life planning, and daily life experiences. These dimensions intersect and can only be understood in relation to each other. These dynamics result in a multi-dimensional view of identity.

There are a number of implications for counselling services when clients' worldview is understood within the backdrop of their cultural group. This insight helps counsellors understand their clients' ideas about mental health and emotional difficulties, emotional expressiveness, beliefs about spirituality, expectations of authority figures, and the amount and type of information that can be shared outside the family unit (Aponte & Johnson, 2000). Similarly, understanding adjustment and identity formation helps counsellors to assess the degree to which clients from non-dominant cultural groups have integrated the components of their personal culture with that of the dominant culture. Further, understanding a person's degree of cultural integration has implications for the selection of instruments and procedures to use in assessment.

Illustrating the Constructs: Worldview, Acculturation, and Identity Formation

To illustrate how worldview, acculturation, and identity formation increase understanding of an individual, I will contrast some typical views from First Nations cultural groups with those of the dominant Canadian cultural group. You are cautioned, however, not to develop a stereotypical view of individuals from either cultural group, as any individual might hold some, all, or none of these views.

- Individuals from a First Nations group who may be considered traditional are likely to identify strongly with their cultural group. They tend to place a high value on cooperation in their relations with others within their cultural group. Individuals from the dominant Canadian group tend to value an individual focus.

- First Nations individuals tend to value brevity of speech and out of respect may not willingly share information about family issues. Individuals from the dominant Canadian group tend to engage in lengthy periods of discussion and trust professionals with their personal information.

- First Nations individuals are likely to see themselves as living in harmony with the environment. The dominant Canadian group would tend to value mastery over the environment.

- Illness from a First Nations perspective may be viewed as a disharmony in the family or cultural group and healing is accomplished when harmony is restored. Individuals from the dominant Canadian group tend to adopt the disease model of illness.

- Individuals from a First Nations group tend to hold a time orientation that is focused on the present, whereas the dominant Canadian group is more future focused. Individuals from the dominant cultural group tend to value activities such as planning, producing, and controlling. Individuals from First Nations groups tend to value being in the present. Additionally, individuals from First Nations groups tend not to value preciseness of time.

- Individuals from a First Nations group may view human nature as basically good and attribute positive motives to others. Such views may be expressed in the workplace as being helpful to others. However, this perspective may be viewed by the dominant Canadian group as gullible and in need of straightening up.

- In relation to work, individuals from First Nations groups tend to be more passive and process oriented in their attitudes towards getting a job. They may tend to wait for the job to present itself. Individuals from the dominant Canadian group tend to plan and be more active in their pursuit of work.

For further discussion of values and First Nations people, you are encouraged to read chapters 9 and 11. The above examples serve to illustrate some of the ways in which worldview, acculturation status, and identity formation are interrelated and how they influence an individual's behaviour. Counsellors who understand these interrelationships are able to provide assessment services that minimize discrimination and bias and help clients achieve their goals and aspirations. To achieve these outcomes, counsellors embrace a number of assessment skills and competencies, which will be discussed in the next section.

Counsellor Assessment Competencies

Skills in assessment are an important counsellor competency. Counsellors use standardized tests, checklists, inventories, observation protocols, and scales to gain pertinent information about their clients that is not easily obtained from other sources (Drummond & Jones, 2006; Hackney & Cormier, 2005; Sattler, 2008). Professional counsellors have an ethical responsibility to be knowledgeable about assessments and their procedures and limitations and to use them in a fair and objective manner with all individuals (Drummond & Jones; Schulz et al., 2006; Whiston, 2005). Counsellors providing services to individuals from culturally diverse backgrounds embrace a number of competencies (Drummond & Jones, 2006; Whiston, 2005).

1. They obtain knowledge of the culturally diverse group. This knowledge includes the client's cultural and linguistic characteristics and how the culture may affect such issues as personality development, career choice, manifestations of personality difficulties, expectations of helpers' behaviour, and appropriate assessment approaches.

2. They understand the social and psychological dynamics that influence the perceptions and behaviours of members of non-dominant groups as they function within and adjust to the dominant culture.

3. They seek training and experience in using assessment procedures with culturally diverse clients. This education includes an understanding of the technical aspects and cultural limitations of assessment procedures and an awareness of the sources of bias in them.

Culture as a Critical Factor in Assessment

Sources of Bias

In North America, most theorizing about assessment theory and practice has taken place in a European, middle-class, male context, a context that represents the dominant group in Canada. Given that all learning takes place in a cultural context (Pedersen & Ivey, 1993), these theories and practices reflect the dominant culture and its worldview and consequently may not be appropriate for individuals who maintain another cultural perspective and its worldview. This inappropriateness or bias originates from the characteristics of the population in which these theories and procedures were developed (Sandhu, 1995).

Assessment theory focuses on using a series of procedures to account for sources of error in assessment instruments and procedures through rigorous tests of validity, reliability, and item analysis (Anastasi & Urbina, 1997; Drummond & Jones, 2006; Sattler, 2008; Whiston, 2005). **Validity** is defined as *the degree to which tests actually measure the constructs they purport to measure*, while **reliability** is defined as *the consistency with which tests measure these constructs*. **Item analysis** refers to *the content and form of each item and its ability to distinguish between test takers' behaviour measured by the item*. These procedures begin with a defined group selected from a population, known as the **norm group**. The norm group is *the group of individuals on whom a test is standardized*. This group is selected using **random sampling**, which is *a procedure designed to select a norm group that is representative of the population from which the norm group was drawn*. In turn, this group is used to establish **norms** or *performance patterns on the instrument, and these norms are used to interpret the results of a client's performance*. Consequently, prior to selecting an instrument, counsellors must decide on the similarity of the client to the norm group so that the results of assessment can be interpreted appropriately.

In North America, most of the individuals who constitute these norm groups come from a European heritage and reflect an individualistic worldview (i.e., the dominant cultural group in Canada). Consequently, these instruments and procedures may not be appropriate for measuring characteristics of individuals from diverse groups who differ from the dominant Canadian group.

Implications for Assessment

An individual's level of cognitive integration and self-understanding influences the degree to which assessment procedures developed for the dominant cultural group are valid measures for clients who come from non-dominant groups. Counselling as a profession has its origins in a middle-class Eurocentric worldview (Ivey et al., 2007). For the principles and procedures of counselling to be valid (i.e., assessment procedures), clients must understand and be able to function within this worldview.

There are two broad approaches to assessment. **Quantitative approaches** *use assessment procedures that follow a standard set of administration procedures and produce results in numerical scores. The results are then* *interpreted as an amount or degree to which a client possesses or demonstrates a particular construct, such as aptitude, achievement, or vocational interest.* Conversely, **qualitative approaches** *use assessment procedures that do not follow a standard set of administration instructions and typically do not produce numerical scores.* Qualitative and quantitative assessment approaches may be appropriate for individuals who understand the dynamics of the dominant cultural group. However, qualitative assessment approaches are more appropriate for individuals who have not reached this level of understanding. Counsellors who understand the worldview, identity, and acculturation adjustment of their clients are able to employ culturally sensitive assessment procedures. Such procedures ensure that clients will volunteer valid and pertinent information.

Counsellors use nomothetic and idiographic information to interpret their clients' data in a culturally empathic manner, thus leading to accurate and culturally appropriate interpretations. **Nomothetic information** is defined as *information that is characteristic of the cultural group to which an individual belongs.* **Idiographic information** *is defined as information that is specific to the individual, such as age, level of aptitude, or gender.* In neglecting this information, counsellors might stereotype the client or engage in discriminatory action. Counsellors strive to reduce all sources of error and bias in the assessment process to ensure the validity of assessment interpretations.

The Assessment Process

Adopting a Culturally Relevant Perspective

During the assessment process, counsellors need to examine their views of non-dominant groups in order to avoid such reactions as excessive sympathy, overidentification, paternalism, and overconcern (Sattler, 2008). To avoid such reactions and to minimize assessment bias, counsellors should conceptualize the counsellor-client relationship on three interconnected levels (Paniagua, 1998; Smith, 2004a).

1. *The conceptual level.* This level is concerned with both the client's and the counsellor's perceptions of openness, honesty, empathy, sensitivity, and credibility of the other in the relationship. At this level, counsellors establish rapport through the use of culturally appropriate communication (Dana, 2000; Sattler, 2008). They demonstrate an openness to learn about the individual's cultural background. Further, counsellors consider the least biased assessment procedures to use (i.e., qualitative and/or quantitative).

2. *The behavioural level.* This level concerns the client's perception of the counsellor as competent and trustworthy and one who can provide something of worth in the assessment process. Counsellors understand and accept the client's point of view by using culturally appropriate questions and responses, sensitively exploring family issues pertinent to the assessment, demonstrating an understanding of the client's level of acculturation, and working to minimize socio-cultural gaps (Sattler, 2008).

3. *The cultural level.* The cultural level is concerned with the counsellor's awareness of the cultural variables that may influence assessment (Sattler, 2008). At this level, counsellors examine their biases and stereotypic views of the client's cultural group. They contact other professionals within the cultural group to gain an understanding of any cultural behaviour they do not understand. Lastly, counsellors gather knowledge of culturally relevant assessment procedures that are appropriate to their clients and the groups to which they belong.

Phases in the Assessment Process

One of the main difficulties for counsellors who work with culturally diverse clients is the lack of a coherent conceptual framework within which to conduct the assessment (Ridley et al., 1998). Many components of the process have been identified, but there have been few suggestions about how to link these pieces together in a coherent and culturally appropriate manner. The assessment process that follows addresses this issue. The process is conceived as a number of steps or phases in which the counsellor makes decisions about what procedures are most beneficial and will help minimize bias when collecting and interpreting the assessment data (Baruth & Manning, 2007; Dana, 2000; Paniagua, 1998; Ridley et al.). The assessment process involves collecting information about the client along a number of dimensions, including:

1. *Personal-psychological*: cognitions, affect, behaviour, mental pictures, sensations, values, spiritual perspective, language preference.

2. *Personal-demographic*: education, work experiences, economic status, age, marital status, length of time in the dominant culture.

3. *Interpersonal relationships*: family, others in the cultural community, individuals outside the cultural community.

4. *Personal history*: migration experiences, discrimination, ethnic history, socialization experiences.

5. *Type of cultural group*: first Nations group, immigrant, refugee, ethnic group, gay, lesbian, senior citizen.

6. *Acculturation status*: separation, bicultural, traditional, assimilation, marginal, transcultural.

While this list of dimensions is not meant to be exhaustive, it is meant to suggest that assessment from a cultural perspective involves considering a number of sources of information concerning the individual and the individual's personal cultural context.

Snapshot 2

Levels of the Client-Counsellor Relationship

Paniagua (1998) suggested that the client-counsellor relationship within a cultural diversity context should be understood from three distinct levels: the conceptual level, the behavioural level, and the cultural level. Typically, Canadian counsellors are conscious and skilled about relationship building on the first two levels, but may need further cultural information to accomplish relationship building at the third level. Using Asian clients as the cultural group, I will illustrate how counsellors can demonstrate relationship-building behaviours to ensure that a high quality of service is provided to clients from culturally diverse backgrounds. Readers are cautioned that Asian clients may display few or none of the expectations indicated in the following illustration, depending on the degree to which they hold to traditional cultural values.

Conceptual level: The relationship concerns centre on the client's and the counsellor's perceptions about issues of sincerity, honesty, empathy, motivation, credibility, and sensitivity. In essence, at this level counsellors should query themselves about their perceptions of their clients. They should be aware of any biases they may have towards a particular cultural group. Counsellors should use offices that are professionally decorated, display their diplomas, provide reasonable explanation and responses to client questions, and emphasize their prior experiences in working with members of their client's cultural group. These indicators help build trust and an expectation of competency, particularly with Asian clients.

Behavioural level: The relationship concerns centre on clients' perceptions of their counsellors as competent professionals with specialized education in assessment and intervention. Also, counsellors should be concerned about their perceptions of clients as individuals who have the ability to follow directions and implement intervention plans. With Asian clients, counsellors should use a formal and structured interview style and seek to maintain some distance between themselves and their Asian clients. This style is likely to enhance their credibility with Asian clients. Also, they should not expect an open discussion of personal issues immediately and should anticipate that Asian clients may express their cognitive and affective difficulties as bodily aches and pains. When counsellors understand these possible client behaviours, they are able to provide a facilitative style that suits the cultural expectations of the client.

Cultural level: Counsellors must be concerned with understanding the cultural group and its social and cultural expectations. For example, when dealing with Chinese Asian clients, counsellors should understand that such clients have had a history of prejudice and discrimination in Canada since the late 1800s. They tend to value family solidarity versus individual initiatives. Culturally, it is expected that children will be obedient and respectful of their parents and that women will marry, raise children, and respect the authority of their husbands. Asian clients will be hesitant to discuss personal problems outside the family unit because they do not want to bring shame and dishonour to their family. They will more often engage in indirect communication in that they tend to be passive, avoid eye contact and offending others, and will try to answer in the affirmative to be polite. Counsellors who have specific knowledge of their clients' cultural group will enhance their relationships with their clients. When such culturally specific behaviours are exhibited, counsellors will understand them as typical of a particular cultural group and not as resistance, which is how they might be interpreted relative to the dominant group in Canadian society.

Two useful frameworks that help to capture these dimensions use acronyms to identify the domains to be assessed. These two frameworks are particularly useful for culturally diverse clients (Ivey et al., 2007; Schmidt, 2006; Smith, 2004a). One such framework is ADDRESSING (Hays, 1996); other is RESPECTFUL (D'Andrea & Daniels, 2001b).The core concepts associated with these acronyms are introduced in Snapshot 3 below. The advantage of these two frameworks is that they identify additional dimensions to assess besides the psychological ones and present them in an easy-to-remember manner. These dimensions include such contexts as economic, family, spirituality, and past history. Readers are directed to the text box to see the domains suggested by these frameworks for assessment purposes.

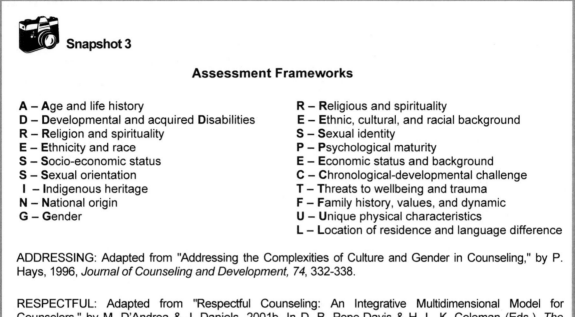

Snapshot 3

Assessment Frameworks

A – Age and life history	**R – R**eligious and spirituality
D – Developmental and acquired **D**isabilities	**E – E**thnic, cultural, and racial background
R – Religion and spirituality	**S – S**exual identity
E – Ethnicity and race	**P – P**sychological maturity
S – Socio-economic status	**E – E**conomic status and background
S – Sexual orientation	**C – C**hronological-developmental challenge
I – Indigenous heritage	**T – T**hreats to wellbeing and trauma
N – National origin	**F – F**amily history, values, and dynamic
G – Gender	**U – U**nique physical characteristics
	L – Location of residence and language difference

ADDRESSING: Adapted from "Addressing the Complexities of Culture and Gender in Counseling," by P. Hays, 1996, *Journal of Counseling and Development, 74*, 332-338.

RESPECTFUL: Adapted from "Respectful Counseling: An Integrative Multidimensional Model for Counselors," by M. D'Andrea & J. Daniels, 2001b. In D. B. Pope-Davis & H. L. K. Coleman (Eds.), *The intersection of Race, Class, and Gender in Multicultural Counseling* (pp. 417-466), Thousand Oaks, CA: Sage.

Developing Culturally Appropriate Rapport

Prior to beginning the assessment process, counsellors determine the culturally appropriate behaviours to use in the process. For example, traditional Asian clients might expect the counsellor to be more directive in the assessment process than clients of European descent might expect. Counsellors are cognizant of their use of questions, since different cultural group may perceive too many questions as intrusive. Counsellors assess the language skills of their clients and determine whether a translator is necessary. They should work in the language of the client's choice, if possible. Clients will feel understood if they can speak about themselves in their preferred language. Attending to these rapport-building behaviours, counsellors foster a relationship of trust and cooperation during the assessment process. During the early stages of the process, they seek to understand the content of the client's worldview. This information helps them develop a common language with their clients and works to promote a common understanding of the assessment process.

Collecting Significant Data

Counsellors adopt a collaborative stance when collecting information (Moreland, 1996). They may need to ask clients from cultural backgrounds different from their own what the significant issues are in the client's cultural group. Counsellors cannot be expected to be thoroughly familiar with all cultural groups, and, without using a collaborative approach, they risk asking irrelevant questions. Within this collaborative approach, counsellors collect data about the reasons for the assessment. This data may include medical, social, cultural, and psychological information. Other significant client information may include economic issues, experiences of discrimination, immigration/citizenship experiences, methods of parenting, religious and spiritual issues, and cultural values. For example, individuals with a gay or lesbian sexual orientation often experience discrimination and alienation in their job. When counsellors understand the typical behaviour for individuals with a gay or lesbian sexual orientation, they are able to assess the situation more accurately. Further, they are able to understand what behaviours are unique to the client. Other methods of collecting data include life histories and observations.

Organizing and Interpreting Data

Counsellors organize and interpret the information collected during initial interviews. This synthesis of information will lead to the formation of working hypotheses about the client and the assessment rationale. In forming these hypotheses, counsellors consider all data, both the idiosyncratic and cultural, and compare this information with their knowledge of this particular cultural group. At this point, counsellors share the hypotheses with their clients for the purpose of achieving a common understanding.

Using this collaborative approach, counsellors build client support for the subsequent activities and recommendations. As a result of this collaboration, they make decisions about what information can be attributed to personality dispositional factors and what information can be attributed to contextual factors.

Further, counsellors decide what data are relevant, including the client's strengths and resources, all of which have a significant impact on the assessment recommendations. They then reflect on these hypotheses using the following questions as a guide to determine what behaviours are typical or dysfunctional.

- Is the presenting issue self-defeating or self-enhancing?
- Do the client's cultural values contribute to the present impairment?
- Do the behaviours represent extremes in the cultural group?
- How does the client understand her or his presenting difficulty?

Using Assessment Procedures

After integrating the cultural data with the relevant clinical data, counsellors decide the assessment procedures that best test the hypotheses formed earlier in the assessment process. They rule out any medical basis for the presenting concern and decide whether to use the results of either standardized or non-standardized procedures to confirm or disconfirm their working hypotheses. The degree to which clients have integrated the culture of their group with that of the dominant group has implications for the selection of assessment procedures. All instruments used in the assessment process should be culturally valid and sensitive to the client's characteristics. Counsellors compare the data obtained to theoretical or categorical diagnostic information to determine whether the behaviours are appropriate or inappropriate for the client's cultural group.

Use of translators

If clients have difficulty with English, counsellors may use a translator to facilitate the assessment (Paniagua, 1998; Sattler, 2008). Prior to choosing a translator, counsellors discuss the use of a translator with their clients, seek permission to use a translator, and discuss how confidentiality will be maintained. Counsellors choose translators who are from the client's cultural background, have some training in mental health problems, are fluent in both the client's language and English, and are not family members. In preparation for the assessment phase, counsellors brief the translator about the goal of the assessment, explore the attitudes of the translator towards the client, and instruct the translator to attend to details such as the qualities of the client's language and paralinguistic voice qualities. During the interview, counsellors use a sequential manner of translation; for example, the client speaks, then the translator translates, and then the counsellor speaks. Counsellors avoid the use of technical terms, frequently summarize and negotiate meaning with their client, and observe the client's facial expressions, gestures, and reactions. After the assessment is completed, counsellors consider the potential influence of the translator's level of acculturation on the information provided and discuss any difficulties the translator had with the translation.

 **Snapshot 4**

Interview Protocol for Assessment with Clients from Non-Dominant Cultural Groups

The following questions are suggested for gaining an understanding of clients from culturally diverse backgrounds and their issues. It is not expected that a counsellor would ask all of these questions. To determine which questions are appropriate, counsellors need to assess their clients' cultural group expectations, explore the presenting client issues, and then proceed to ask questions that help them to understand their clients and their contexts.

Possible Questions

1. What is your country of origin?
2. What was your reason for coming to Canada?
3. How long have you been in Canada?
4. What is your generational status? (e.g., third-generation Asian, second-generation Indian)
5. Is your family in Canada?
6. Was any parent, grandparent, or relative living in this country before you came?
7. What language do you speak in your home? To your mother? To your father? To your brothers and sisters? To your grandparents (if applicable)? To your friends?
8. What languages can you speak? Read? Write? How well?
9. Do you have friends from your country here?
10. Are there people from your country living near you?
11. What are your thoughts and feelings about your religion? What are your personal religious views?
12. What is your sexual orientation? How does your cultural group relate to this orientation?
13. How does the dominant society feel about this orientation?
14. Where do you live? A house, apartment, or room?
15. What types of foods do you eat at home?
16. What ethnic or cultural holidays and traditions do you celebrate?
17. What culture do you feel most proud of?
18. What education or schooling do you have?
19. Are you currently going to school or taking classes somewhere?
20. Are you currently working? Where? What do you do on the job?
21. What type of work did you do before coming to this country?
22. What knowledge, skill, or other attributes do you bring to school, job, home, and home life?
23. What problems, if any, have you encountered since coming here?
24. What strengths, coping resources, or social supports have you drawn on?
25. What conflicts, if any, have emerged on the job, at school, or at home?
26. What strategies have you used to address those conflicts?
27. What have the easiest and the most difficult things been in adjusting to life in Canada?

The responses to these questions will provide counsellors with an indication of how positive or negative the client feels about each content area. These questions are intended to elicit responses in the following areas: background issues, current situation, family, language, cultural group contact, spiritual perspective, sexual orientation, social/economic status, cultural group identification, educational background, employment issues, and adjustment issues.

Adapted from "*Assessment of Children: Cognitive Applications* (4th ed.)," by J. M. Sattler, 2001, San Diego, CA: Author, and "*Appraisal Procedures for Counselors and Helping Professionals* (4th ed.)," by R. J. Drummond, 2000, Toronto, ON: Prentice-Hall.

To summarize, counsellors make every effort to reduce bias in their assessment procedures (Smith, 2004a). Bias can be avoided by using culturally appropriate ways to interact with the client, placing cultural variables prominently in the process, using translators if individuals prefer to express themselves in their original language, and using assessment methods that are culturally appropriate to the individual being assessed.

Methods of Assessment

There are four methods of assessment: quantitative instruments and three different forms of qualitative assessment methods (Sattler, 2008).

1. Quantitative instruments are termed norm-referenced. Such instruments as the Wide Range Achievement Test – Revision 3, the Differential Aptitude Test, the Strong Interest Inventory, and the Wechsler Intelligence Scale for Children – IV are used to measure achievement, aptitude, vocational interest, and intelligence, respectively. They provide scores that indicate how the person is functioning relative to other individuals in the same demographic cohort.

2. Qualitative interviews are useful for gaining information from clients and significant others in their social and cultural context.

3. Qualitative observation typically takes place in the natural setting.

4. Informal qualitative assessment procedures are used to obtain idiographic information from clients of culturally diverse backgrounds.

These methods can be used to collect a wide variety of data with which to describe the client (Diller, 2004; Lonner & Ibrahim, 2002; Sattler). Using these different methods to collect client information is termed the multi-method approach to assessment (Dana, 2000: Sattler). The use of a variety of methods to collect information ensures that pertinent and salient data will be available for the assessment. Each of these methods is explored here in more detail.

Quantitative Assessment

Quantitative assessment procedures tend to take an etic perspective; that is, they suggest that there are commonalities among humans and that the basis for the comparison can be from a position outside the cultural group (Dana, 1993). This perspective is essentially a between-group viewpoint. To use standardized instruments normed on the dominant cultural group within North America with a client from a non-dominant population would be an example of imposing an etic view from one cultural group on that of another cultural group

When considering the use of standardized instruments, counsellors make every effort to select the instrument that will yield the least biased results (Hinkle, 1994; Lonner & Ibrahim, 2002; Matsumoto, 1996; Paniagua, 2001). The majority of standardized assessment instruments developed in North America were normed on White middle-class students within the population. People of different cultural backgrounds may not have been represented within this norm group. However, this is not to say that such instruments are always inappropriate for other cultural groups. Counsellors should understand what the scales, scores, and categories mean for each instrument relative to a specific cultural group. Quantitative instruments are constructed based on an operational definition of a particular construct (Anastasi & Urbina, 1997; Sattler, 2008; Whiston, 2005). Behaviour that reflects a particular construct may vary across different cultural backgrounds. Each culture has its own unique set of traditions, idioms, myths, beliefs, and codes of behaviours. Consequently, an instrument normed using one set of cultural indicators may be inappropriate for measuring the construct within another culture. Counsellors recognize that there is no such thing as a culture-fair test.

If counsellors decide to use a standardized instrument, they evaluate its rigor to measure the construct for an individual whose cultural group was not represented in the norm group. In other words, they answer the question of whether the instrument items yield equivalent results for an individual from a different cultural background. There are four ways to consider equivalence (Lonner & Ibrahim, 2002).

1. Functional equivalence relates to whether a particular construct has the same function and indicators across cultures. For a test to measure a construct that is functionally equivalent across cultures, the counsellor must ensure that the functional prerequisite in one cultural context has its counterpart in another culture. An example is status and the behaviours that indicate status. In Asian cultures, one way that status is recognized between age groups is by a lack of eye contact; however, in North America, eye contact is not typically an indicator of status.

2. Conceptual equivalence is concerned with the meaning a person gives to a particular stimulus. For a test to be equivalent, the stimulus has to evoke the same conceptual schema in each culture. For a test item to measure ideas of human nature, the stimulus would have to evoke the same understanding of human nature in different cultures.

3. Linguistic equivalence suggests that the words used in tests, interviews, and questionnaires have the same meanings for everyone who responds to them. Some cultural groups may use the word *mad* to refer to someone who needs to be institutionalized due to high levels of anxiety, while North Americans tend to use the word to describe a person who is experiencing frustration.

4. Metric or scalar equivalence is concerned with the data and scales that result from completing the instrument. For a test to be metrically equivalent, it should demonstrate the same set of psychometric characteristics for different cultural groups; that is, each cultural group should demonstrate the same mean and item discrimination values. **Item discrimination** is defined as *the degree to which an individual test item discriminates on some criterion.*

Patterns in clients' responses to items on an instrument, known as response sets, can bias the outcome of assessment procedures (Hinkle, 1994; Lonner & Ibrahim, 2002). There are a number of different types of response sets. A response set of acquiescence suggests a tendency to agree with extremes. A response set of social desirability represents a tendency to respond in socially acceptable ways. A response set of evasiveness is a tendency to be noncommittal. A response set of carelessness is a tendency to make inconsistent responses to items measuring the same construct. A positional response set is a tendency to stick to one position all the time. Response styles vary both within and between cultures and, when used, influence assessment results. One way to offset the influence of response sets is to encourage clients to respond in a manner typical of what they think and feel. Further, counsellors should indicate who will have access to the results and how they will be used. Ensuring confidentiality helps clients know that the results will not bring dishonour to the family or cultural unit.

Qualitative Assessment

Qualitative assessment procedures do not involve comparing results with a norm group. In contrast to quantitative assessments, these procedures take an emic perspective that is culture specific and examines clients' behaviour using standards established within the culture (Dana, 1993). These procedures tend to be culture specific since the responses are typically idiographic and are used to develop narratives or categories for understanding clients from culturally diverse backgrounds. They help minimize the issues of cultural context and how meaning is construed within the culture because the client's cultural group is used as the standard for behaviour. However, to use such measures effectively, counsellors obtain specific knowledge of the cultural group to which the client belongs. Qualitative assessment procedures tend to take the form of open-ended questions and are usually administered informally through discussion or a structured interview (Lonner & Ibrahim, 2002). They tend not to be construct driven (Dana, 1993).

Interviewing

Interviewing is a procedure used by counsellors to collect information about their clients. It allows clients to respond using their own words (Ivey & Ivey, 2003). Interviews can be structured, semi-structured, or unstructured. In structured interviews there is a set list of questions to be answered. In semi-structured and unstructured interviews there is more flexibility in responding to questions and the focus of the interview may change as needed.

The assessment interview can cover a range of topics, including a description of the client's present situation, early memories, health, education, work, sexual development, marital status, family, self-description, and critical points in life (Dana, 1993; Hackney & Cormier, 2005). When conducting interviews with culturally diverse clients, counsellors decide how much information they should collect (Paniagua, 1998). One general guideline is to avoid collecting a large amount of information during the initial contact. Counsellors who collect too much information may be viewed by some culturally diverse clients as incompetent, as having little training in collecting significant data, and as offensive for asking too many questions about information that is not usually shared outside the family unit. This response might be typical of recent immigrants from Asia. For example, too many questions may provoke a response of distrust in the client, leading to hesitancy about answering questions (Ivey & Ivey, 2003).

During the assessment process, counsellors use culturally appropriate questions (Paniagua, 2001). To determine the appropriateness of such questions, counsellors obtain specific knowledge about life issues of the client's cultural group (Dana, 1993). For example, a female client may take a longer time than her male counterpart to make vocational decisions due to her need to balance and integrate family and work roles. Further, asking Asian clients to compare themselves to other Asians might be considered offensive. Asians typically do not like to compare themselves to others. However, to ask Asian clients to indicate whether their behaviours are culturally appropriate or inappropriate will lead to the same information. Questions, when used appropriately, can be a source of significant information.

Observation

Observation may be defined as *a method that involves recording overt behaviour as it occurs in its natural setting* (Longabaugh, 1980). Observation in natural settings, such as home or school, can be useful in evaluating cultural, economic, and experiential factors that influence the client's adjustment to the dominant culture (Wyatt, 1982). The time taken to observe the bicultural, bilingual, and dual value systems of a client from a non-dominant ethnic group and the impact of these systems on the client's cognitive, social, and emotional development can provide significant information. The main benefit of conducting assessment in naturalistic settings is to obtain information that is not readily available elsewhere (Dana, 1993; Longabaugh; Sattler, 2008; Wyatt). Clients tend to be more relaxed in their natural settings, and this degree of naturalness increases the validity of the information provided.

Prior to doing the observation, there are a number of decisions to be made. First, counsellors decide whether to focus on a broad series of behaviours or on specific behaviours. Generally, if counsellors observe a continuous series of interactions on the school playground, for example, they are able to observe a number of different behaviours, such as peer interaction or conflict resolution. Alternatively, using an in-depth observation procedure, counsellors might focus on specific behaviours, such as peer interactions in the classroom. Additionally, to give validity to the assessment, they decide on the quantity of behaviour to observe. Counsellors generally vary the quantity, time, and location of observations. Further, counsellors decide who and how many others will be observed. There are possible interaction effects between a person's behaviour and a particular setting. For example, a client's behaviour at home may differ somewhat from the client's behaviour at school.

Counsellors are careful to avoid generalizing behaviour from one setting to other settings without sufficient evidence to support the generalization. They distinguish between the intent of the behaviour, how the behaviour was exhibited, and its interpretation by the receiver. The intent of behaviour can include such motives as offering help, reprimanding, seeking dominance, acting sociably, offering support, and seeking attention. Counsellors note such aspects as interpersonal distance, verbal and nonverbal language, body posture and orientation, facial expressions, eye contact, and visual gaze.

When observing clients from non-dominant groups within the dominant cultural setting, there are a number of variables to consider (Sattler, 2008). There are cultural differences in the use of personal and interpersonal space, known as proxemics. For example, Europeans prefer a reasonable distance (about 3 feet) when in conversation with another person, while people from the Middle East may prefer to be closer than arm's length. There are differences in body movements, kinesics, and paralanguage (Sattler). Counsellors learn how to interpret these variables singularly and in combination in order to understand behaviour.

Informal procedures

There are a number of informal assessment procedures (Dana, 1993; Sattler, 2008). They can be criterion-referenced to determine whether the client has reached a particular standard using such sources as written language samples, prior or current records of work performance, or personal documents. They can involve self-assessment, where the client keeps a log of thoughts, feelings, and behaviours. They may also take the form of role play during which the counsellor observes how the client behaves in a mock situation.

Three procedures that allow counsellors to collect idiographic information when working with clients from culturally diverse backgrounds are the life history, the accounts procedure (Dana, 1993, 2000), and the culture grid (Pedersen & Pedersen, 1989; Stewart, 2002). The life history procedure permits clients to tell their stories from their personal and cultural perspectives.

 **Snapshot 4**

Life History

The life history technique permits clients to tell their story. The primary purpose of the life history is to enable the counsellor to collect information to describe the client's personality. Consequently, the counsellor may impose some parameters to direct the life history so that the needed information is obtained. Prior to using the life history technique, the counsellor reads published life histories about the cultural group represented by the client. Often these stories are published in the popular media or by anthropologists studying a particular ethnic group.

The life history has some features of an interview, but is different in that it is typically not structured in any direction. The life history has three phases. The beginning phase focuses on making contact with the client, establishing facilitative rapport, and clarifying the purpose of the interview and the expectations of the client during the interview. Also, the counsellor should address the client's affective needs to reduce anxiety and respond to any questions the client may have. During the middle phase, the focus is on listening to and collecting information about the person. In addition, the counsellor engages in understanding and clarifying the reasons for counselling and providing support by using empathic understanding. The counsellor may use paraphrasing and summarizing to demonstrate that the client's life history has been heard and understood. The closing phase focuses on bridging the gap between the present interview and a future interview. This forward-looking perspective is accomplished by providing support and reassurance to the client that services will be available. The counsellor engages in terminating the session by summarizing the issues raised during the telling of the life history and making another appointment to continue the dialogue.

During these three phases, the counsellor collects information in the following content areas. While this list is quite varied, the counsellor should assess the suitability of asking some of the questions due to client's cultural beliefs and practices about self-disclosure. The content areas are: reasons for the interview, family situation, physical and social development issues, health issues, education attainment and issues, work position and issues related to work, sexual orientation and experiences, marital data, self-description and critical incidents in the client's life, issues of ethnicity, language usage, and incidents around discrimination.

Using the results of the life history procedure, counsellors can describe a client's personality characteristics. This procedure is not based on a theoretical stance and permits counsellors to query clients about life events and their responses to them. The accounts method is used in conjunction with the life history approach. Working collaboratively with their clients, counsellors identify problems, specify both adaptive and maladaptive coping styles, and recommend appropriate interventions, using inputs from other significant members of the cultural group at appropriate points throughout the process. Counsellors record the actions, intentions, and goals of the behaviour underlying the presenting problem. The information provided by other members of the cultural group helps ensure cultural suitability by providing a context for the assessment recommendations.

The culture grid is a structured procedure conceptualized within two perspectives. The first perspective assumes that difficulties arise when there are differences in the behaviours, expectations, or values between two people or within a person. The second is that expectations, values, and behaviours are best understood as a product of social learning within a cultural context. The grid itself is composed of two broad categories. One category deals with social systems variables and includes such issues as ethnographic (e.g., nationality, ethnic background), demographic (e.g., age, gender), status (e.g., educational, social, and economic standing), and social affiliation (e.g., formal, involving professional groups, or informal, involving community groups). The other category includes cognitive variables including role behaviour, role expectations, and values. The presenting problem can either be interpersonal or intrapersonal. When the presenting problem is interpersonal, the counsellor must determine which behaviours actually took place and compare those behaviours to what would be expected within the culture. Additionally, this comparison helps determine the acculturation status of the client.

Snapshot 5

The Culture Grid

Social System Variables	Behaviour	Expectation	Values
Ethnographic Variables • Canadian • Irish heritage • English	He did not go on a school trip with his peers during March Break.	He worked hard to earn the extra money to participate in the trip. He wanted to see Montreal.	• Hard work • Cooperation • Education and schooling
Demographic Variables • Male • 11 years old • Heterosexual orientation • Good physical condition	He felt sad because he decided not to go on the trip at the last minute.	He felt that he should not discuss his feelings of inferiority with anyone.	• Wanted to appear strong as a male and didn't want to express any emotions
Status Variables • Low social status • Grade 6 education • Parents have little formal education	He felt inferior to his middle and upper socio-economic class peers.	He should have been able to go regardless of his socio-economic status.	• School expectations to participate • Educational value
Connections with Groups • Member of Grade 6 class • Low socio-economic status family • Attended church	He attended school regularly and earned good grades. He worked on weekends to earn extra money.	People who pay their way should be able to participate. His use of money should reflect family and personal needs.	• Strong work ethic • Meeting personal needs in the present

The information provided in the Culture Grid came from a student I worked with early in my career as a school counsellor. The issue is an intrapersonal one dealing with feelings of inferiority due to socio-economic status (SES) and financial issues.

I knew of his wish to participate in a school trip to Montreal as part of a cultural exchange with students in Quebec. I was able to help him raise some of the money he needed. After the students had returned, I met with the student. Initially he told me he did not participate because he did not have a suitcase to go on the trip. As we talked, he soon shared that due to his low SES context, he did not relate well to his classmates, who were richer than he was. He felt sad and disappointed that he decided not to go. He acknowledged that not having a suitcase was an excuse to preserve his dignity as a male because he could not share the real reasons for not going – feelings of inferiority.

To summarize, counsellors choose assessment procedures that reduce error and maximize the validity of their assessment findings. To accomplish this, counsellors understand the psychometric properties of standardized instruments and determine their suitability for use with clients from culturally diverse backgrounds. They obtain cultural knowledge about the appropriate use of questions when using an interview procedure and choose different locations to observe behaviours, collect culturally appropriate amounts of idiographic information, and determine culturally appropriate behavioural expectations using informal assessment procedures.

Case Study

Assume that the following information represents case notes taken during an initial assessment interview.

Peter was on his way home from the University of Toronto, where he was studying to be an aeronautical/astronautical engineer. He had been accepted into a co-op position with a large aeronautics firm in Ottawa. Peter was to begin his off-campus training in the summer. He did not arrive home. He was in an automobile accident that left him in a coma for three months and in rehabilitation therapy from 1991 to 1993.

Peter is a 33-year-old male, approximately 6' and weighs about 210 pounds. Due to his accident, Peter walks with a slight limp and holds his left hand up by his shoulder when he walks. He walks slowly, yet he is not physically limited. He is currently employed in a Mexican restaurant busing tables and conducting maintenance repairs. He lives alone in government-subsidized housing.

Peter grew up on a small farm in Peru with both of his parents and a sister who was two years younger than him. They came to Canada in 1986. His father works in the maintenance department of a large town in Quebec, and his mother works part-time doing laundry and house cleaning in Montreal. In Peru, they were farmers. They came to Canada as refugees who feared for their lives due to their political stance and open opposition to the totalitarian government in Peru. His father was connected to the Shining Path, a Marxist revolutionary group in favour of land reform.

Juan, as he was known in Peru, took the Canadian name of Peter soon after he came to Canada. He indicated that his parents were working-class people and that was the environment in which he was raised. His father's family emigrated from Northern Spain at the beginning of the century. His mother's side of the family was indigenous; they were Aboriginal people who lived in the country before the arrival of the Spanish.

Peter stated that he and his sister had always been supportive of one another, and it was difficult now that she was married and had a career. She had what he desperately wanted. Peter also talked about a grandmother who lived with his parents and who was very supportive and assisted him often. In general, Peter described his family as very close and supportive.

Peter attended high school in Quebec where, he laughingly stated, he excelled more in sports than in academics. He smiled and shared that he still holds the track record for the 400-metre dash at his school. It was Peter's high school academic advisor who suggested engineering as a possible college major because of his strengths in math and science. It was his love for spaceships and Star Trek that narrowed his choice to aeronautical/astronautically engineering.

Two years after his accident, Peter attempted to return to the University of Toronto, but he was physically, mentally, and emotionally unable to keep up with his rigorous schedule and course requirements.

Following this, he attended George Brown College and enrolled in introductory math courses. He continued to take classes part-time until four years ago, when he enrolled in a Computer-Aided Drafting and Design (CADD) course at Conestoga College in Kitchener, Ontario. He was able to successfully complete his diploma with a grade point average of 2.8.

Peter's employment history since his accident has been limited to temporary employment, primarily in fast food restaurants. His first work position was with Vocational Rehabilitation. He was placed in a rehabilitation facility where he was given assignments from local industries (e.g., putting parts together, counting screws and nuts, and packaging them). Peter stated that the work he was doing was "for handicapped and retarded people." His anger at being placed in the rehabilitation facility was quite apparent. He stated that he was not handicapped or like any of the people who worked there. He left the rehabilitation centre and found employment at Wendy's. He was in charge of cleaning and maintenance. He was not able to do the cooking because he was not physically fast enough. He worked for Wendy's and then for McDonald's doing cleaning and maintenance. He worked for three different McDonald's restaurants and he now has a position with a Mexican restaurant.

Your first impression of Peter came when he arrived for career counselling. He was sitting in the waiting area actively engaged in conversation with others in the room. He was wearing dress slacks, dress shirt, and a tie and appeared to have impeccable hygiene.

Peter's presenting issue was his frustration with obtaining full-time professional employment. Peter stated that because of his head injury, he has a difficult time remembering things he is told and sometimes what he did the day before. He said that he needs to be reminded of information several times to be able to remember it.

It has been two years since his CADD training and Peter stated that, due to the rapid changes in technology, he no longer felt qualified to obtain work and successfully complete the tasks involved in CADD employment. He seemed willing to learn a new occupation, but his willingness seemed limited to industrial or technical types of positions.

Peter's occupational interests lie in science and technology, and as a result he firmly believes that to be somebody he needs to be employed in an industrial or technical field. Although his social skills seemed to be above average, he perceives social service fields as less prestigious. He equates social service fields with low income and industrial or technical fields with high income and status.

Peter was very open to discussing his goals and abilities. He strongly expressed the desire to make a good living to support himself. He expressed anger at what has happened to him, but stated that he wants to work on the future, not the past. His family had suggested social service occupations because of his strong social skills, but he stated that he was afraid that he would not be able to make enough money, nor would he be a *real man* if he were not in a technical field.

Despite his memory limitations and unsuccessful employment attempts, Peter appeared to be optimistic and willing to make a strong commitment to career counselling. He stated that his head injury is not going to prevent him from obtaining employment and reaching his dreams of being a productive member of his family. He wants you to tell him what occupation he should pursue.

Assume that you are a career counsellor and Peter is your client. Answer the following questions:

1. How much information do you know about Latin Americans who settle in Canada?

2. Where or from whom can you locate further information about this cultural group?

3. What are your overall impressions of Peter? What are the themes that most interest you? Why?

4. What reasons can you offer to account for Peter's concern about obtaining a high-paying job?

5. What cultural variables might you consider in developing a working alliance with Peter?

6. How would you describe Peter's acculturation status? Ethnic identity? Worldview? What cultural values might be considered in your assessment of Peter?

7. Do you think it is important to invite his family to come for an interview? Why or why not?

8. If you were to conduct an observation, where would you conduct it, with whom, and for how long?

9. What standardized instruments might you consider using to collect further data? What qualitative procedures might you use?

Chapter Summary

To recapitulate, culture plays a significant part in mediating behaviour. Culture is multifaceted and includes a number of dimensions, such as gender, sexual orientation, religion, social and economic status, age, spirituality, ethnicity, and national origin. The synthesis of these variables into a worldview involves a number of psychological and social dynamics. When clients from culturally diverse backgrounds seek counselling services, counsellors engage in assessing the personal and cultural variables that are influencing the client's behaviour. Counsellors choose assessment procedures that are valid for the client. These assessment procedures fall into two categories: quantitative and qualitative. When counsellors use appropriate procedures, they minimize stereotyping and discriminating against culturally diverse clients. Counsellors who are knowledgeable about culture and its influence on behaviour are able to interpret assessment data in an accurate manner. They use the cultural context to assess the appropriateness of the behaviour.

Counsellors must synthesize the information gained from using one or a combination of procedures and formulate an assessment that is integrated, comprehensible, valid, and developmentally appropriate to the client. This approach to assessment is termed a multi-method approach and assumes a constructivist philosophy in which the emphasis is on understanding behaviour from a social and cultural perspective using both formal and informal assessment methods. Use of the multi-method approach reduces sources of error and increases the accuracy of the idiographic information collected during the assessment process. This accuracy leads to appropriate assessment conclusions and recommendations for clients from non-dominant populations.

CHAPTER 9
ENGAGING IN CULTURALLY COMPETENT RESEARCH

Kathy Offet-Gartner

Key Terms and Concepts		
• Acculturation	• Cultural location	• Member checks
• Colour blindness	• Cultural self-exploration	• Othering
• Cross-cultural research	• Culture	• Paradigm
• Cultural awareness	• Culture-infused research	• Privilege
• Cultural identity development	• Identity integration	• Self-reflexivity

Personal Introduction

Much that I have learned about conducting ethical, culturally infused research insists that researchers locate themselves, thereby identifying their cultural influences as well as their reasons for embarking on the project in question (Kincheloe & McLaren, 2005; Richards, 2005). Therefore, to share my ideas about conducting research across cultures, it is important to *locate* or *position* myself and my cultural influences. I am a White, heterosexual, well-educated, employed Canadian woman; as such, I have both earned and unearned *privilege*. Some might ask what I have to share on the topic of cross-cultural research. I have come to understand that I am a cultural being and that all of my encounters, including research, are cultural encounters. As such, I can share with you the deficits in my own education and life experience that failed to prepare me to work and research cross-culturally and the lessons I have learned along the way – lessons that have helped fill in the gaps and assist me in becoming more culturally competent.

Over the course of a long academic and professional career, I have been both a consumer and creator of research. Early on, psychology's quest to be considered as *valid* as the hard sciences (i.e., to offer consistent results, to generalize, and predict) was the primary driver in planning or conducting research. Issues of culture were rarely raised. Culture was thought of as synonymous with race. Issues of intersecting cultures, power, privilege, or socio-economic or political influences were virtually unheard of. Psychology prided itself in being a *value-neutral* science, where all individuals and their experience were treated as if all people were equal and had equal opportunities. Practitioners and researchers were taught to be *blank slates*; personal thoughts, values, and beliefs were to be left at the door of our offices. This trend of value-free, cultural-less psychology held fast through the first 15 years of my career. However, I began to have difficulty with this paradigm while working with various groups of children – autistic, Aboriginal, immigrant, rural – children whose experience did not necessarily fit this approach. I began to question, to search more closely for *other* knowledge sources that could assist me. Often my quests were futile. I was told that I should just adjust my way of thinking, treat the person the way that all others were treated or tested; after all, the results had been researched, normed, and *proven* to be true.

In the late nineties, I was introduced to the concept of multicultural influences – finally, something that accounted for many of the *anomalies* I struggled with for so many years. I began to feverishly seek out knowledge sources and to create my own research projects to fill in gaps when I could find no satisfactory assistance. I sought ways to incorporate what I had learned from *the field* – clients, families, real people, struggling with real issues that did not *fit* nicely into the *truths* described by earlier research. This led me to find the teachings of feminism, multiculturalism, and co-constructivism – the emergence of qualitative research. I learned about the complexity of the word *culture* and its many influences. I realized I had to discover a lot about my own self, my cultural influences, beliefs, and biases before I initiated research. I had to invest much more time and effort to get to know the influences and norms of the group I was interested in. I realized how time consuming and challenging culturally focused research can be. I also discovered how incredibly rewarding and meaningful it is. I now actively seek to consume and create culturally infused research to inform my practice and learning. I am still very much the learner. I now share my journey with you in the hopes that it will assist you in your quest to create culturally appropriate and inclusive research.

Introduction

> Culturally sensitive psychological researchers are encouraged to recognize the importance of conducting culture-centred and ethical psychological research among persons from ethnic, linguistic, and racial minority backgrounds. [American Psychological Association (APA), 2003b, Guideline #4, p. 1]

The earlier chapters of this book alerted readers to the complexities involved with the concept of *culture*. It is neither easy to define, describe, nor understand. Attempting a research project that includes cultural factors or that is truly culture-centred can prove to be even more complex and challenging. It is absolutely necessary that ethical, culturally appropriate research studies be conducted so that we can better understand and serve the populations that seek assistance from counselling professionals. As noted in the rationale for culture-infused counselling in Chapter 2, these populations are not only becoming more diverse, they are also becoming more culturally aware and demanding. It is imperative that students, professionals, and researchers heed the APA guideline that introduces the discussion in this chapter and learn as much as possible about how to better infuse culture into ethical research.

As with the first edition, this chapter is divided into four parts. The first part will introduce and examine some of the challenges, both historical and current, that have hampered former research projects from being culturally appropriate and responsive. The second part and main focus of this chapter will highlight some of the recent developments in culturally centred research and then offer an example, based on my own experience, of how to translate this theoretical information into practice. A number of concrete suggestions will be offered in an effort to assist others who seek to produce more culturally sensitive and ethical research. Part three examines some key ethical considerations that need to be explored when considering culturally infused research. The chapter concludes with a summary to condense the volume of information presented throughout the chapter and offers a checklist to assist those preparing to embark on a culturally infused research project of their own.

The principles and concepts presented in this chapter are designed to apply to research in a wide range of cultural contexts. However, for the purposes of more specific illustration, I will explore the application of these principles within the context of research with Aboriginal peoples. The intent is to make transparent my own process of my most recent major research project in the hopes that this example may demonstrate some of the complexities of applying the suggestions being made herein while assisting you to understand the concepts so that you might apply them to a broader range of cultural contexts.

The overarching aim of this chapter is to encourage those who perform, consume, or are benefactors of research to stop and consider things differently, to be more sensitive to *otherness*, and to own one's privileges, power, biases, and the effects these have on research. It is my hope to generate many more questions than answers. I encourage each of you to find the strength, courage, and desire to examine the cultural context and implications, defining your own culturally relevant question and answers, *before* attempting a research project. After all, *all* research is a cultural endeavour; ethically sound research is culturally infused research.

Identifying and Exploring the Problems

History of Research Across Cultures

Cross-cultural research has traditionally been defined as *research conducted by a member(s) of a dominant cultural group with and about members of a non-dominant cultural group(s)*. Throughout the years, a number of authors have shared their concern that much of the research with non-dominant populations is inaccurate, insensitive, and not overly practical for the people it studies (Bishop, 2005; Moradi, Mohr, Worthington, & Fassinger, 2009; Smith, 2005). In 1991, Ponterotto and Casas, two very prominent writers in the fields of cross-cultural counselling and research, developed the groundbreaking *Handbook of Racial/Ethnic Minority Counseling Research*. Although somewhat dated, their book identifies many problems *still* associated with culturally infused research and offers some practical and important things to consider before embarking on a research project. Although a number of resources have since been developed, it is interesting to note that a number of these issues still prevail. These include:

- lack of clear conceptual or theoretical frameworks that are respectful of cultural development to guide research projects;
- lack of a clear definition of culture, its many intersections, and influences;
- lack of understanding with regard to the researcher's own cultural development and how this might impact the research;
- lack of understanding of the culture being studied;
- lack of regard for within-group difference (assuming homogeneity);
- lack of attention paid to contextual influences (e.g., socio-economic status, gender, power, oppression);
- relatively small sample sizes, which were often compared with studies that were based on White, male, college students, with generalizations then made; and
- use of culturally encapsulated instruments, research questions, and methods.

Ponterotto and Casas were certainly not alone in their efforts to address these concerns. Many within the profession of psychology were beginning to take note of the dilemmas facing cross-cultural research, prompting the APA to host a symposium on the topic: *White Researcher in the Area of Cross-Cultural Issues* at their 1990 annual convention (Mio & Iwamasa, 1993). Some of the pertinent issues raised included:

- the lack of culturally relevant articles published in recognized journals;
- who completed and controlled most of the published research;
- lack of cultural awareness and definition;
- the impact of White privilege, especially when unacknowledged;
- the impact of worldviews;
- questions pertaining to which methodologies were most appropriate; and
- who should benefit from this type of research and how can that be ensured.

These concerns have guided writing and research since being articulated and will be addressed throughout this chapter.

What is Culture?

According to Pederson (2001), "culture is perhaps the most important and most misunderstood construct that has emerged from the social sciences in this century" (p. 20). He, like many authors since then, asserted that a number of factors contribute to this state; perhaps the most basic is the lack of consensus about how culture is *defined* (Fine, 2007; Palmer & Parish, 2008; Silverstein, 2006). No matter how much material you read, you will find a wide array of definitions for what is meant by the word *culture*. Perspectives on defining culture, ranging from a narrow focus on ethnicity to a broad, all-inclusive conceptualization, were explored in detail in Chapter 1. These wide variations in the meaning of culture have contributed to the criticism that much of early research held little meaning for most non-dominant populations (Bishop, 2005; Mihesuah, 2000; Moradi et al., 2009). Worse still, many early studies failed to define or even mention a cultural component, perhaps assuming that it was not a factor, further stripping it of value for some. Today, we realize that all behaviours are culturally constructed; therefore, culture cannot be excluded from research of any kind that involves the study of human lives (APA, 2003b; Denzin & Lincoln, 2005).

The *lack of focus on culture*, or what Pedersen (2001) called **colour blindness**, refers to the *assumption that one can apply all principles equally across all cultures*, a concept simply not possible and definitely dangerous in the realms of psychology and research. Culture must be accounted for in all psychological activities, including research. "Because all knowledge is socially situated (i.e., it arises from the culturally influenced cognitions of those who articulate it), the limitation of objectivity is unavoidable" (Henning-Stout & Meyers, 2000, p. 420).

Rather than ignoring or being blind to culture, we need to increase our awareness and understanding of cultural influences. **Cultural awareness** *requires us to acknowledge that culture lives in all our experience, language, and interpretation.* The old notion that a researcher can and should be an unbiased, objective observer needs to be discarded and replaced with an acknowledgement that researchers must declare their cultural selves and biases (Richards, 2005). This cannot begin unless researchers examine their own cultural development (Fleras, 2004). The need for this examination continues to be affirmed as the primary, most important step of culturally responsive and ethical research, yet it frequently remains the most overlooked step (APA, 2003b; Offet-Gartner, 2008; Ponterotto & Grieger, 2008).

I offer a story that launched my journey of learning about how power, privilege, culture, history, racism, and stereotypes influence and impact my ability to counsel and research with others.

Years ago, I was involved in doing some testing with a group of children from a rural school. I was assigned five children, all of whom were of Aboriginal descent. I thought growing up with Aboriginal friends and being included in traditional practices and events would assist me in working with these children. My formal training in psychology had taught me that all people were equal and that all treatment should reflect that premise. However, my interactions with these five youngsters, combined with my knowledge of the assessment instruments, raised concerns that the measurements that I would glean would not reflect the true ability of these children and that the instruments would be biased against them. This concern was not shared by my colleagues; it was a commonly held premise during this time that culture did not play a role in the practice of psychology or in the measurement of intelligence and ability. My desire was to not to "test" per se; rather, it was to provide assistance for the children to successfully transition to school. When I suggested contacting the parents to do some educational and enrichment programming, my supervisor thought I was going a bit overboard, but did not dissuade me. I arranged to meet with the parents of one of the little boys in their home and added that they could invite anyone they thought might like to join us. When I arrived at the family's house, I found over 20 people present and a celebration of sorts taking place. I wondered if I had interrupted something important or had gone to the wrong house. I did not know that these people were there because inadvertently I had invited them. My training did not prepare me for this experience, nor did it teach me the protocol necessary for a gathering such as this. I spoke when I thought the silence of the crowd was cueing me to do so; after all, I had asked for this gathering – I was the expert. It was not until several weeks later that I learned that the silence was not for me, but was out of respect for the Elder sitting in the corner. By speaking before her and not addressing her first, and only after a prayer and blessing had been offered, I had unknowingly been disrespectful and that Elder was not going to tolerate that. With the ease and swiftness of someone half her age, she was out of her chair, across the room, and slapped my face before I even knew what was happening. She told me to return 'when I had learned some manners' and then promptly turned and everyone left the room. I was stunned. The slap, more metaphoric than forceful, did not harm me; what pained me was that I had no idea what had just happened and worse still, I had failed to do anything to assist that young boy. It was the first time I became conscious that training and "good intentions" were not enough, that competent practice required more specific knowledge and could not be applied "carte blanche" across all situations and cultures. The realization that my limited worldview and lack of awareness might hinder my counselling, or worse, be harmful was overwhelming.

This experience led me to do much soul searching, about myself, my training, and my profession. I sought guidance from trusted Aboriginal friends, seeking to understand and learn. Then, I went back to find that Elder, to apologize for my naivety and ignorance, and to ask if she might help me learn what was necessary to work effectively in her community. She smiled and told me she had been waiting for me, thus beginning my real education into the world of culture-infused counselling, researching, and living. It is this story and the countless other faux pas committed along that way that have led me to study specifically in the area of culture-centred research and counselling practice.

Personal reflection – Kathy Offet-Gartner

Influence of Worldview

Many authors declare that a fundamental flaw with much of the earlier cultural research can be attributed to differences in worldviews between researchers and participants (Bishop, 2005; Pedersen, 2001; Ponterotto & Grieger, 2008; Smith 2005). It is believed that some researchers avoid cross-cultural studies or give cultural components only cursory mention because of these challenges (Pedersen; Rose, 1997). Other authors wonder about the utility of some of the research that has been completed across cultures (Mertens, 1998; Olesen, 2005; Saukko, 2005). Sue and Sundberg (1996) stated that "misinterpretations of research involving different cultural groups is common" (p. 324). Further, they stated that "cross-cultural research has been shaped primarily by the Euro-American standard, with little input from ethnic minorities" (Sue & Sundberg, p. 326), rendering it suspect or potentially invalid.

As an example, Darou, Kurtness, and Hum (2000) noted "that some research on First Nations has been misinformed or even harmful" (p. 47), and further postulated that non-Aboriginal people have compiled most of this research with little or no understanding of Aboriginal culture, values, or worldviews. They asserted that "the basic tenets of research are in conflict with Native values" (Darou et al., p. 44). This belief is shared by others who avow that research is a culturally constructed enterprise that has historically reflected a Eurocentric worldview as opposed to a culturally respectful one (Denzin & Lincoln, 2005; Richards, 2005; Saukko, 2005).

Sue and Sundberg (1996) pointed out that most research projects and practices have been designed by those who hold a Eurocentric worldview, and cautioned that the ensuing results may have led to misperceptions, improper assumptions, or invalid conclusions about the culture(s) being studied. They further declared that these biases are not conscious or intentional; rather, "our worldviews are so deeply ingrained that we rarely question our standards, and may not be consciously aware of the impact of our values on research" (Sue & Sundberg, p. 324). Stanfield (1994) included the statement that the paradigms that inform most research contain Eurocentric "cultural baggage" (p. 181) that can neither be fully accounted for nor completely divorced from the research project. He and other authors (Bishop, 2005; Kenny, 2000; Saukko, 2005; Wilson, 2007) called for the design of new paradigms of research that more accurately reflect the worldviews of those participating in the study and those who should benefit from the findings.

Historically, Who Published Cross-Cultural Research?

In 1993, Mio and Iwamasa published the results of a review they completed of prominent psychology journals with regard to cross-cultural research. They revealed that very few articles actually existed and, of those that did, the majority was authored by a handful of people, most from the dominant culture. They questioned how authors from the dominant culture would have any first-hand knowledge of what it is like to be oppressed or *othered*. Similarly, Graham (1992) revealed that much of the earlier research that was touted as multicultural relied heavily on White, middle-class, male college students as the primary participants. The question being raised by these authors is how research is relevant for people whose lives have been influenced, impacted, or altered by oppression and the lack of power to change the situation if the researcher does not even understand their concerns.

However, Mio and Iwamasa (1993) further noted that a number of authors from non-dominant cultures had attempted to be published in those same journals, but were unsuccessful. Atkinson (1993) and Parham (1993) affirmed this finding. Helms (1993) candidly explained that "White researchers have been the primary gatekeepers of cross-cultural research (e.g., journal editors, dissertation supervisors)" (p. 242). It became clear that change was needed or psychological research was going to fail to be of benefit for a rising portion of the population.

Addressing these concerns has been a major catalyst in advancing the development of ethical guidelines for conducting cross-cultural research [APA, 2003b; Canadian Psychological Association (CPA), 2000], as well as a number of good resource materials (Mertens, 1998; Ponterotto & Grieger, 2008; Saukko, 2005). What each of these sources implored as the first step in all competent, ethical cultural research is that researchers begin by examining their own cultural influences, especially if they come from the "White culture" where power and privilege is inherently accorded by birth. What is meant by the terms White culture, power, and privilege warrant further exploration.

Power of White Privilege

Those who are *White* continue to hold the majority of power and represent the most dominant group in many cultures (Bishop, 2005). Lynn (1994), in her powerful article on White culture and privilege, stated: "I live in the castle of my skin and accrue all of the implicit benefits of being white" (p. 149). Unfortunately, most members of the dominant population do not even realize that there exists a *White culture*, let alone an inherent, unearned privilege (Sue & Sue, 2007). Helms (1993) stated "that Whites are born the benefactors and beneficiaries of racism, although they may not be aware of their bequest" (p. 241). Others (Bishop, 2005; Smith, 2005) agreed that lack of awareness by Whites that they are cultural beings is a major contributor to the problems associated with research across cultures. Unexamined culture is likely to create an environment for racism and prejudice to grow, even unknowingly (Ridley, 2005; Saukko, 2005). McIntosh (1989) wrote the following revealing and impacting passage in her essay on culture, power, and privilege:

> I have come to see white privilege as an invisible package of unearned assets that I can count on cashing in each day, but about which I was "meant" to remain oblivious. . . I began to understand why we are justly seen as oppressive, even when we don't see ourselves that way. (p. 8)

In Chapter 4, Arthur and Collins expand the concept of **privilege** to include the *pervasive and both overt and covert ways in which European, male, heterosexual, able-bodied Canadians experience advantages, opportunities, entitlements, and immunities, are conferred dominance and control, and are positioned at the top of the economic, political, and social hierarchy, often without conscious awareness or acknowledgement.* Unexamined privilege accorded through one's culture often leads others to recognize the racism, sexism, heterosexism, and so on, and power dynamics at play long before the person who displays them (Ponterotto & Grieger, 2008). Frequently this leads to frustration, confusion, and resentment for both parties. Research that does not examine privilege is no different. It is limited in its applicability, causes misconceptions, and has, in the past, been used in damaging ways (Mertens, 1998; Sue & Sue, 2007). The danger with research that is steeped in a lack of cultural awareness is that the knowledge and interventions developed as a result may further affirm and perpetuate oppression through racism, unjust stereotypes, and hatred (Palmer & Parish, 2008; Sue & Sue, 1999).

It is not that the early producers of cross-cultural research did not have good intentions or sincere projects. Rather, understanding the impact of privilege implies that good intentions and worthy projects are simply not enough to address many of the concerns associated with cultural issues (Fleras, 2004; Mertens, 1998).

Whose Voice Is Heard Through Research?

Perhaps the greatest angst of *who* conducts cross-cultural research is the question of *whose voice* is represented within the study. Some authors (Chase, 2005; Mihesuah, 2000; Smith, 2005) have suggested that only members within a cultural group should conduct research pertaining to that group. These authors stated that only those close to the community can truly represent it without distortion. Cavender-Wilson (1998) felt that "the idea that scholars can 'sift through' the biases of non-Indian written sources sufficiently to get at the Indian perspective is presumptuous and erroneous" (p. 26). She further suggested that many researchers have written studies *about* groups of people without having a full understanding of the issues, worldview, or culture of those they are studying and without ever approaching them directly to learn about these constructs. She asked: "Would historians attempt to write a history of Germany without consulting any German sources? Would a scholar of Chinese history attempt to write Chinese history without consulting Chinese sources?" (Cavender-Wilson, p. 24).

Although this seems like a ludicrous suggestion, Cavender-Wilson (1998) is not alone in her questioning. Others (Smith, 2005; Tatar & Bekerman, 2002; Youngblood-Henderson, 2000) have suggested that researchers have described, defined, and drawn conclusions about groups of people without adequately gathering an understanding of the dynamics involved, or by only speaking to a small sample and then generalizing to all who identify as members of that group. Mihesuah (2000) emphatically stated her concern: "It is dangerous and unethical to presume to know what motivates Native women without talking to them, but scholars do it all the time" (p. 1248). Deloria (1998) echoed this sentiment in his essay on what he called the *Invented Indian*. He purported that much of the earlier research on Aboriginal people came *from afar*, that Aboriginal people not approached or consulted, and that they had no way to refute the messages that were being conveyed. He went on to say that "for most of the five centuries, whites have had unrestricted power to describe Indians in any way they chose" (Deloria, p. 66).

This problem has not been isolated to one group, but is experienced by all groups who identify as outside the norms of the dominant group. Stanfield (1993) called the major problem when only a few individuals are studied and what is learned then applied to all who hold similar membership the "fallacy of homogeneity" (p. 90). He recognized that no single voice represents any group and any attempt to essentialize people to a definitive *list* is unethical. Although a well-established limitation, the push to use research in ways that have small samples speak for entire groups continues (Bishop, 2005; D'Andrea & Heckman, 2008).

Brayboy (2000) admitted that it is not only *others* who essentialize and misrepresent. He said that this happens whenever assumptions are made regarding group identification, homogeneity, and generalizability. In his article on researching within his own cultural group he discovered, much to his chagrin, that he had fallen into the trap of making sweeping assumptions and categorizing according to some personally defined attribute, rather than asking people to define themselves. He shared: "Knowing that I have these biases of who counts as "real" and being critical of myself, and others who hold similar ones, does not preclude me from engaging in the very behavior to which I am opposed" (Brayboy, p. 421). He raised the issue of who gets to decide whether or not an individual *belongs* in the cultural group being studied and, consequently, whether their voice gets included or not. He was not alone in this concern. Mertens (1998) reminded us that participants, especially those of marginalized groups, have had their voices silenced or altered so much that the final research product no longer represents them. These impassioned words of hooks (1990) illustrate the problem of voice and representation in research across cultures:

> No need to hear your voice when I can talk about you better than you can speak about yourself. No need to hear your voice. Only tell about your pain. I want to know your story. And then I will tell it back to you in a new way. Tell it back to you in such a way that it has become mine, my own. Re-writing you, I write myself anew. I am still author, authority. I am still colonizer, the speak subject, and you now at the center of my talk. (pp. 151-152)

Historically, How Has Cross-Cultural Research Been Used?

Although the debate over who should conduct cross-cultural research continues, there is little debate over *how* the research ought to be used. A number of marginalized groups have expressed concern, and at times anger, over how research has been used in the past. Many believe that research has been used to further the roots and causes of racism rather than eradicate it (Bishop, 2005; Darou et al., 2000; Fleras, 2004; Kral, Burkhardt, & Kidd, 2002; Smith, 2005). A number of others (Deloria, 1998; Frank, 1997; Mihesuah, 2000; Robertson, 2006) noted that the anger and resentment felt by some members of non-dominant cultural groups towards researchers from dominant cultural groups is more than understandable when one considers the number of discriminatory acts that have been committed by this group, often in the name of education, that was supported by research. Although these events may have been historical, suspicions, fears, and resentments are not easily forgotten. As a result, dominant group researchers of today often end up facing repercussions for the behaviours of their predecessors (Sue & Sue, 2007). It is imperative to first have an awareness of the oppression that has been perpetuated by research and, second, to develop strategies for responding in more sensitive and effective ways if you are planning on conducting research across cultures (Goodman et al., 2004; Mertens, 1998; Ponterotto & Grieger, 2008).

Historically, Who Has Benefited From Research?

Another theme that was addressed by both the APA symposium (Ponterotto et al., 1990) and a number of more current sources (Bishop, 2005; Ponterotto & Grieger, 2008; Saukko, 2005; Sue & Sue, 2007) is: Who *benefits* as a result of cross-cultural research? These authors suggested that far too often the communities that so graciously allow research to take place receive little or nothing in return. Several authors (Darou et al., 2000; Parham, 1993; Smith, 2005) have said that the participants involved often do not recognize themselves or their community in the final product, if they were even privy to such a copy. Dickson and Green (2001) reported that all of their research participants regarded research negatively, as yet another form of exploitation and attempt at assimilation because, far too often, research "has quantified and described their reality but has done little to improve it" (p. 473). Gunn-Allen (1998) said that research often "objectified, explained, detailed, and analyzed their lives [participants] as though they were simply curios, artefacts, and fetishes" (p. 61). Others (Goodman et al., 2004; Mertens, 1998) stated that some marginalized people will not respond to research requests because they have been pathologized in the past or saw research as confirming existing stereotypes. With perceptions and realities such as these, it is no wonder that conducting ethical cultural research can be challenging.

Other authors (Mohatt & Thomas, 2006; Saukko, 2005) have pointed out that, all too often, the researchers have been the only ones who benefited, by way of grants, research positions, tenure, or further publishing. These factors have only added fuel to growing feelings of anger and resentment and are frequently barriers to any future research within a number of non-dominant communities (Kral et al., 2002). These negative feelings have, in fact, caused some communities to make blanket refusals to all research requests (Darou et al., 2000). This is a lose-lose situation that many fear will continue if researchers and the field of psychology do not change their focus to include a more culture-centred approach that celebrates both similarities and differences and ensures that research is used to equally benefit all people (Goodman et al., 2004; Pedersen, 2001; Sue & Sue, 2007). In that spirit, perhaps it is time to move from examining the many challenges that have plagued cultural research to date and to begin to explore some solutions.

Focusing on Solutions: A Culture-Infused Research Paradigm

> A **paradigm** is "a set of *beliefs*. . . . It represents a *worldview* that defines, for its holder, the nature of the "world," the individual's place in it, and the range of possible relationships to that world and its parts. (Guba & Lincoln, 1994, p. 107)

Recent work has begun to articulate new paradigms that are more reflective of culture as a central component (Bishop, 2005; Ponterotto & Grieger, 2008; Saukko, 2005; Smith, 2005; Wilson, 2007). The hope is that research compiled from these more inclusive, culture-centred research paradigms will more accurately reflect the experiences of the people they study, their culture, perspectives, and traditions, thereby increasing the utility and accuracy of the research.

This section will introduce the concept of **culture-infused research** as a means of *recognizing the centrality of culture in all research endeavours and ensuring that each step in the research process is reflective of and responsive to the cultural identities and experiences of all stakeholders in the process: researchers, participants, consumers, and so on.* The words *infused, inclusion,* and *centred* are used interchangeably throughout this chapter to denote that culture must be a core construct in all activity related to research. There are six defining features of culture-infused research; these will be explored in this section:

1. A broad and inclusive definition of culture.
2. Awareness of your own cultural identities as a researcher.
3. Understanding of the cultural identities of the researched.
4. Understanding of the historical context of the particular culture.
5. Understanding of the impact of acculturation on the group; and
6. Ensuring that the cultural group and individuals involved all benefit from the research.

Broadening the Definition of Culture and Cultural Research

> Culture should not be conceived as a gold standard currency with only so much to go around. It is more like the phonologies, in which each sound, each position of the mouth, is significant only as it is defined by the other sounds and no sound is any more real, any more rich, or more privileged than any other. (McDermott, 1993, p. 283)

To respond to earlier concerns about the limitations of narrow definitions of **culture**, many authors now suggest *broader definitions that include both individual and group identity, attitudes, beliefs, values, traditions and practices, worldview, language, as well as gender, socio-economic status, regionalism, age, and sexual orientation, to name a few* (Alberta & Wood, 2009; Sue & Sue, 2007). It presupposes that everyone has a number of cultural affiliations and therefore opportunities for a variety of intersecting identities (Silverstein, 2006). The salience of each is influenced by time, privilege, power, experience, language, economics, and socio-political events (Behring & Ingraham, 1998). Further, Ramsey (2000) stated that, "all cultural identifications are viewed as equivalent in importance, and there is no assumption of an identification hierarchy wherein one identification (e.g., ethnicity, gender, or sexual orientation) must take precedence over another" (p. 171). This broad definition allows for understanding culture as a multifaceted, complex, and very fluid construct. It assumes a multiplistic rather than an ethnocentric cultural identity where individuals are free to hold membership in a number of cultural groups that change and vary in importance and inclusion throughout one's life (Behrig & Ingraham). Hence, all activities, including research, *must* be viewed as cross-cultural activities because there will always be cultural factors at play (Sue & Sue).

Whatever definition you choose to embrace and work from, defining what you mean by *culture* is a crucial step in ensuring that your study is in fact culture-centred. Declaring your definition does not in and of itself make the study culture-infused, but it does make transparent one of the constructs that is informing and influencing your study (Mertens, 1998). Keeping it in the forefront will assist you throughout the process of the project to remember that "all knowledge is socially situated (i.e., it arises from the culturally influenced cognitions of those who articulate it)" (Henning-Stout & Meyers, 2000, p. 420). This behooves researchers to define culture as it applies philosophically and then to define the parameters of the group at the core of the study as well as their own cultural group (Goodman et al., 2004).

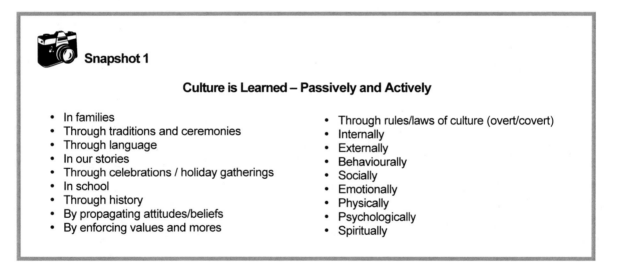

Snapshot 1

Culture is Learned – Passively and Actively

- In families
- Through traditions and ceremonies
- Through language
- In our stories
- Through celebrations / holiday gatherings
- In school
- Through history
- By propagating attitudes/beliefs
- By enforcing values and mores

- Through rules/laws of culture (overt/covert)
- Internally
- Externally
- Behaviourally
- Socially
- Emotionally
- Physically
- Psychologically
- Spiritually

Knowing Yourself as a Researcher

Once you have defined what you mean by culture, the next step in any study that is culture-infused is to know yourself as a cultural being and to understand how your cultural identities have evolved throughout your life span (Ponterotto & Grieger, 2008). **Cultural self-exploration** involves *inquiry into what attitudes, biases, beliefs, and values you hold, where they came from, their salience, and their potential to impact the research project you are contemplating.* Each of us is a cultural being who has *learned* their culture, often insidiously. This becomes problematic if the ensuing attitudes, beliefs, biases, and so on are not consciously re-examined throughout our lifetime to ensure current validity and utility. It is imperative for researchers to define how *they* see themselves as a cultural being, especially in relation to the group they are studying with. Researchers, like all individuals, have multiple selves and identities (e.g., gendered, ethnic, sexually orientated, religious, professional, educated) and "each of these selves should be acknowledged and examined to understand how they may be shaping the research narrative that emerges" (Goodman et al., 2004). This may sound like a step that can be glossed over, assuming that you know all you need to about your own heritage and cultural affiliations or by arguing that you are not the subject of study. However, as earlier stated, this may indeed be the most necessary and crucial step of all, and the least understood; it is therefore rarely completed. This step must be evident for cultural research to be considered ethical (Ponterotto & Grieger; Sue & Sue, 2007).

Little has been written to guide us on *how* to do this step, so I will attempt to assist with this process. This is not an exhaustive template. Rather, I encourage you to view this as an invitation for you to dive into your own heritage and affiliations and to get to know your history and your present well enough that you can examine and articulate their impact in a clear and concise way. Put particular emphasis on socio-historical factors. Start by asking:

- What is my lineage? Where did my relatives come from? What is my family history? Are there any secrets that we do not talk about still?

- What was the cultural atmosphere at the various times and places that I am reflecting on? Why might that have been so? How did it influence the lives and decisions of my relatives then? Does it continue to influence my family now? What attitudes, assumptions, beliefs, biases, and values do my family or I hold now as a result? Did those create any barriers for us then…and now?

- What family traditions do we observe…why? What purpose do they serve? How does this impact or influence my relationships with others…why?

- Has anyone in my family suffered oppression? Have I benefited from it?

- How were women, children, men, the elderly, the sick, and the *different* treated then…now?

- How were and are education, work, family, sexuality, religion, race, language, politics, and so on viewed and discussed? How are those of different groups considered?

- Is there any group I despise or fear…why? Where does that reaction come from? How does it impact me? What do I do with my thoughts and/or feelings regarding this?

- Is there any connection between me, my family and the cultural group I plan to study? How will that influence my study?

- How is my group viewed by other groups? What influence will this have on the research?

- Is there any connection between me, my family, and the cultural group I plan to study? How will that influence my study?

The point is to develop your own questions and guidelines and then search, ask, and learn, bringing into consciousness the many influences that make you who you are. What is important is that you get to know where you came from, how that influences you today, and how it might hinder or enhance your ability to complete the research you propose. Remember that "all interactions are cross-cultural, and that all of our life experiences are perceived and shaped from within our own cultural perspectives" (APA, 2003b, p. 1).

It is important to note that you will likely encounter some resistance, hesitancy, or maybe even shame about declaring all of the assumptions, biases, beliefs, and perhaps even stereotypes that you or members of your family hold or have held. Know that this is normal and that it may not be realistic to assume that you can change all of these, but it is crucial to determine how they might affect the study you are about to do (Ramsey, 2000). "Without such knowledge, they may do damage unwittingly" (Goodman et al., 2004, p. 800). Things to consider include:

- Will these beliefs keep you from seeking a certain type of participant?
- Will you formulate a hypothesis or conclusion from your beliefs?
- Will you ignore information that does not conform to your currently held belief?
- Will you treat participants differently?
- Will you know how your beliefs might be perceived as disrespectful to someone from another culture (e.g., if you address participants by their first name, look directly into their eyes, or not honour silence).

It is also critical to mention that you are not expected to change who you are to match who your participants are. Most would find this unattractive and, in fact, potentially damaging, perhaps even a form of appropriation (Saukko, 2005). The better alternative is to be comfortable with yourself and your culture and to be aware that others will likely pick up on any discomfort or ill regard you have of yourself or them, even if you think you are masking it (Darou et al., 2000; Sue & Sue, 1999, 2007). The following caution from the APA (2003b) *Guidelines on Multicultural Education, Training, Research, Practice, and Organizational Change for Psychologists* should be noted:

> Psychologists are urged to become more aware and sensitive to their own attitudes towards others, as these attitudes may be more biased and culturally limiting than they think. It is sobering to note that even those who consciously hold egalitarian beliefs have shown unconscious endorsement of negative attitudes toward and stereotypes about groups. (p. 3)

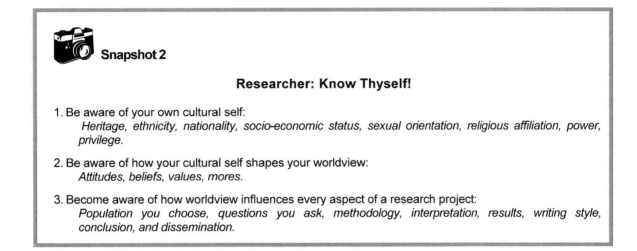

Snapshot 2

Researcher: Know Thyself!

1. Be aware of your own cultural self:
   Heritage, ethnicity, nationality, socio-economic status, sexual orientation, religious affiliation, power, privilege.

2. Be aware of how your cultural self shapes your worldview:
   Attitudes, beliefs, values, mores.

3. Become aware of how worldview influences every aspect of a research project:
   Population you choose, questions you ask, methodology, interpretation, results, writing style, conclusion, and dissemination.

Understanding Cultural Identity

There is general agreement among all of the authors reviewed for this chapter about the need for researchers, all researchers, especially those from dominant cultural groups, to examine their own cultural being. Worldviews and their ensuing biases are so ingrained that one rarely questions them (Lincoln & Cannella, 2009; Sue & Sue, 2007). This blindness or lack of awareness impacts the research question one chooses, the methodology and procedure one follows, the mannerism and attitudes displayed towards participants, and the way in which the final product is written (Fleras, 2004; Richards, 2005; Saukko, 2005). There is no way to completely strip culture from any research, since even the language used to report the findings is culturally bound (Chase, 2005). Therefore, all culture needs to be acknowledged and accounted for, including the typically unconsidered dominant culture (Goodman et al., 2004). To that end, various authors (Helms, 1990b, 1995; Ponterotto, 1988; Sabnani, Ponterotto, & Borodovsky, 1991) have created White identity models to help people become aware of, acknowledge, and feel comfortable with their dominant cultural identity. There are a number of other models of **cultural identity development** available (see Chapter 4), which I would encourage you to become familiar with as well. Although each of the models differ somewhat, they all have in common *the evolution of a culturally aware and sensitive cultural identity through a series of systematic stages.* For the purposes of this review, only one model will be summarized, as it is described as an integration of the models that have preceded it. While it refers only to ethnic identity, it is important to remember that gender, sexual orientation, and other cultural factors also involve an identity development process. Readers are reminded that these models, although presented in a systematic and linear way, are far more fluid and holistic. Movement back and forth throughout the stages is anticipated.

White identity stage model

The Sabnani and colleagues (1991) model consists of five stages. The first stage is the *Pre-Exposure/Pre-Contact* stage. It is characterized by a total lack of awareness on the part of White persons of their racial and/or cultural identity. Those in this stage do not recognize the role that being White plays in the oppression of others. *Conflict* begins when they begin to recognize the plight of other cultures and races, especially in contrast to their own. New awareness challenges the White person to examine and question his or her own cultural beliefs and biases. This frequently causes confusion, anger, guilt, anxiety, and sometimes depression, as they have to attempt to sort out their stance in society as a whole and the social acts that are constantly taking place within it. If they successfully resolve some of the strong emotional pressures of the previous stage, they will likely evolve to the *Pro-Minority/Anti-Racism* stage in which they actively work against racism and oppression. This often helps alleviate much of the assumed guilt felt in the previous stage. *Retreat into White Culture*, unfortunately, occurs when the emotions in stage two have not been resolved and proves to be too overwhelming for them so that they begin to avoid minorities and multicultural settings. People may not intentionally become racist, but they do not work to actively dispel it either. This leaves them vulnerable to becoming what Ridley (2005) described as an unintentional racist. Finally, *Redefinition and Integration* marks the point when people have successfully achieved a balance between their cultural identity and that of others. Individuals who achieve **identity integration** *acknowledge the concept of privilege, based on gender, ethnicity, ability, and so on, strive to use it in positive ways, and work conscientiously to become more aware of and sensitive to the rights and values of other cultures and cultural groups.*

Researchers who have reached the final stage of identity integration, and who are aware of themselves as cultural beings, have the greatest chance of compiling ethical and culturally sensitive research. Those who are not at this stage would likely produce work that is value-laden, subject to misunderstanding, and may even contribute to further oppression (Sue & Sue, 2007). Battiste (1998) warned that "Eurocentricism is not like a prejudice from which informed peoples can elevate themselves" (p. 23). She said that it does not happen alone, or overnight, and that it requires conscious thought and action to overcome. Battiste, along with Arthur and Collins in earler chapters of this book, and others prominent writers in this field (Goodman et al., 2004; Pedersen, 2001; Sue & Sue) suggested that individuals, academics, and communities alike must work together to eliminate biases and promote cultural awareness and acceptance.

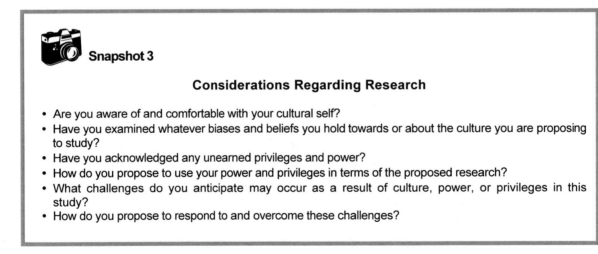

Snapshot 3

Considerations Regarding Research

- Are you aware of and comfortable with your cultural self?
- Have you examined whatever biases and beliefs you hold towards or about the culture you are proposing to study?
- Have you acknowledged any unearned privileges and power?
- How do you propose to use your power and privileges in terms of the proposed research?
- What challenges do you anticipate may occur as a result of culture, power, or privileges in this study?
- How do you propose to respond to and overcome these challenges?

Cultural Awareness of Research Participants

The third key to a culture-infused research paradigm is that the research must reflect the culture and traditions of the people being studied (Goodman et al., 2004; Smith, 2005). Consequently, it is imperative that investigators become familiar with the values and beliefs that are considered representative of the cultural group involved in the study. Care must be taken in doing so, as all cultural groups are both distinct and varied (Saukko, 2005). There is no single conclusive set of rules or values that can be utilized to guide the researcher in understanding exactly what constitutes *the* culture; homogeneity in any culture is more myth than reality (Sue & Sue, 2007). Researchers are encouraged to develop an understanding of the worldviews of those they intend to study with, their own worldviews, and those of any external stakeholders (e.g., university, sponsor), for each will have influence on the entire research process (Meadows, Lagendyk, Thurston, & Eisener, 2003). To accomplish this, investigators must develop an appreciation for the beliefs, values, and ways of life that are commonly held by each of these groups and then systematically determine how they may influence and/or impair the research that is being proposed (Alberta & Wood, 2009; Goodman et al., 2004).

In order to illustrate this concept, the following few pages are offered as examples of how commonly held values, in this case from an Aboriginal cultural perspective, may be important considerations for a research project. The concentration on Aboriginal culture reflects the focus of my research for a number of years now and, heeding the cautions of many authors (Goodman et al., 2004; Kincheloe & McLaren, 2005; Ponterotto & Grieger, 2008), I must declare what I know in the context that I know it. Your job as researchers, students, and practitioners is to use these examples to assist you to know *how* these constructs can affect the research process. It is certainly not an exclusive or exhaustive list, as there are a number of influences, contexts, and situations that might require additional consideration, depending on the culture and the stakeholders involved. This section of the chapter highlights additional points for reflection and contemplation about ways to infuse culture in research from an experiential standpoint.

Although there is diversity in the cultural heritage of Aboriginal people, there is agreement that some values and traditions are commonly held (Blue & Darou, 2005; McCormick, 1998). While a closer examination of some of the commonalities is warranted, it is essential to note that Aboriginal culture is far more complex and dynamic than can be described in the scope of this chapter. To ensure accuracy and relevancy, it is crucial to learn the specific cultural ways of the proposed research group. To maintain continuity and assist the reader in understanding the importance of developing awareness and sensitivity to these values and beliefs, some reflection is warranted. The nine main themes presented below reflect values ranging from spirituality to preferred learning style. Each is examined for its potential impact on research.

Balance

Aboriginal beliefs are holistic in nature, stressing the importance of balance between the spiritual, physical, emotional, and mental domains of life (Blue & Darou, 2005). Balance is symbolized by the medicine wheel, which represents the interrelatedness of these domains functioning together to create a whole (Poonwassie & Charter, 2001). It is believed the Creator bestows unique gifts on everyone and everything in the universe. For people, how the gift is used depends on how *in balance* the person is with the rest of the universe. If individuals are in balance, they are considered to be healthy, capable, and worthy of respect. Conversely, if individuals are out of balance, they are considered more susceptible to disease, ill temper, failure, and disrespect (Blue & Darou). In order to respect this cultural belief, researchers are encouraged to frame their projects in a holistic manner by including opportunities for exploration in all four aspects of the individual's experience (Mohatt & Thomas, 2006). This could include simple practices such as having refreshments and social time integrated throughout the project. It might also include use of more traditional practices such as asking an Elder to open and close a session with a prayer or inviting the burning of sweetgrass or sage (Stubben, 2001). This may stretch the non-Aboriginal and those trained in the more linear and concrete research designs that only incorporate rational, intellectual content. However, to be considered culturally competent, research must reflect and respect the values of the community(s) involved (Bishop, 2005).

Traditional healers

Healers are often the most respected members of their communities, and are typically regarded as having received extraordinary gifts from the Creator (McGraa, 1990). Healers must spend several years in training before being considered worthy of the title. Consequently, they are usually original residents of the community. Some authors recommend that researchers always seek the advice and counsel of traditional healers and invite them to act as advisory council or cultural guides (Mohatt & Thomas, 2006). Receiving approval from a healer can assist the researcher immensely. This is particularly true for learning the protocols appropriate for that community, increasing access to the people, and resolving potential dilemmas, such as how to incorporate respect for each of these values (Meadows et al., 2003). Conversely, angering or disrespecting a traditional healer will make trying to conduct a study with that community extraordinarily difficult, so it would be wise to avoid this situation (Gunn-Allen, 1998). Researchers are cautioned to respect protocols for approaching and requesting services from an Elder or healer. Gifts of money, tobacco, or some other form of tangible means may be required (Frank, 1997). Knowledge of these and other expectations is highly recommended before even attempting to approach anyone directly. Background preparation is a necessity before attempting culture-infused research (Ponterotto & Grieger, 2008; Meadows et al.).

Sacredness of the circle

Aboriginal people believe that the circle symbolizes the natural cycle of life and the interconnectedness of everything in life (Blue & Darou, 2005). Important or ceremonial events take place within a circle. "In these circles, the issues of expertise and authority are removed, and the quality of trust is nurtured" (Poonwassie & Charter, 2001, p. 67). Incorporating circle formations in any group activity will allow researchers to demonstrate respect for this traditional value. It is imperative that investigators acknowledge that all experience is valid and equal within the circle. Therefore, researchers must disengage from the role of *expert* and accept their place within the circle as an equal member who has knowledge and experience to share (Goodman et al., 2004). Approaching the community as a student as much as in the role of researcher will go a long way towards demonstrating respect for this value (Saukko, 2005). Further, some authors (Dickson & Green, 2001; McCormick & Amundson, 1997) have suggested that depicting data by means of circular models, graphs, and charts are ways to honour and respect this value.

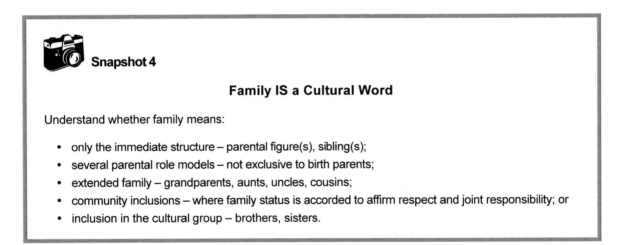

Snapshot 4

Family IS a Cultural Word

Understand whether family means:

- only the immediate structure – parental figure(s), sibling(s);
- several parental role models – not exclusive to birth parents;
- extended family – grandparents, aunts, uncles, cousins;
- community inclusions – where family status is accorded to affirm respect and joint responsibility; or
- inclusion in the cultural group – brothers, sisters.

Interconnectedness

A common traditional Aboriginal cultural belief is an orientation towards the collective as opposed to the individual. All things are connected and interrelated, with one never more important than another (Blue & Darou, 2005). This is often very confusing for non-Aboriginals to follow because of its multi-layered implications. *For example,* although unrelated, individuals within a community are frequently called by familial titles like as *auntie, grandmother,* or *brother.* This reminds individuals to treat all members of the community with the same respect and care they show to their family. To be considered a member of an individual's family is a sign of great respect and not necessarily a sign of blood relation (Frank, 1997). Conversely, "a common admonishment is to say of someone that they act as if they have no relations" (Haig-Brown & Archibald, 1996, p. 253). It is important to recognize that a person who refers to several mothers or grandmothers, for example, is not delusional, evasive, or untruthful; the person is being respectful and adhering to a central cultural value.

If understanding the individual's family structure is important to the study at hand, having the person map out family relationships is strongly encouraged (Wasserman, 1995). Mapping might also assist the researcher in building rapport with the participant and learning more about other cultural influences that might be involved. Inviting family and community members to take part in the research process is a wise plan, as it sends a respectful message, encourages participation, and provides an opportunity for your project to receive greater exposure (Meadows et al., 2003). This might facilitate a larger pool of participant selection, be more reflective of the community, and assist with retention (Ponterotto & Grieger, 2008).

Non-interference

Related values of not interfering and not competing with one another acknowledge the belief that every person must live their own life and learn from their own experience (McCormick, 1996, 2000a). "We do not have the right to judge others because of their beliefs, values or behaviors since we have not had their experiences and are not learning their life lessons" (Charter, 1994, p. 5). Showing off or believing that your way *is the only way* may bring embarrassment and dishonour from your peers and the community (Restoule, 1997). Understanding the impact of these values may assist researchers in understanding participants' behaviours. For example, in a group setting, it is usual for individuals to not volunteer an answer unless asked directly. Moreover, if an individual has been asked directly and chooses not to reply or offers an incorrect response, others are more likely to remain silent (Restoule). "Natives generally view questioning as interference" (Darou, 1987, p. 39).

If the research includes observing school-aged children, these values are frequently observed. Pepper and Henry (1991) found that Aboriginal children rarely put their hand up to volunteer answers and typically displayed discomfort when called on randomly, especially after a peer has already been called on. Avoid relying solely on question and answer, right/wrong types of inquiry. Dickson and Green (2001) found that even their participants – respected grandmothers – "had an aversion to being questioned directly" and that they "had learned a culture of silence" (p. 478) so as not to bring attention to themselves or be seen in a competitive way. This certainly impacts the research methodology you choose, since reliance on direct question and answer information gathering would seem to be at odds with this value. In addition, designing your study so that it does not overemphasize any individual or group in particular would be wise (Smith, 2005). Understand that participants may even be conscious of the amount of time you spend with each of them and see that as a form of competition (Mohatt & Thomas, 2006). Try to ensure that you are equally available to each participant and their families.

Role models

The importance of role models can be seen in almost every aspect of daily life among Aboriginal people (McCormick, 2000a; Rogers, 2001). Historically, there was an expectation that individuals would learn from one another experientially as the required skill became necessary (Stonechild, 2006). The community's survival depended on everyone contributing to the completion of tasks at the optimum time (Restoule, 1997). Although survival needs have changed considerably, the concept of learning by experience has not (Battiste, 1998). Being emulated as a role model in Aboriginal culture is a sign of utmost respect (Baldridge, 2001).

It would be wise to inquire about the participant's experience of role models with reference to what is being studied. This inclusion may invite a level of disclosure not likely achieved otherwise. It may also identify a variable not previously considered. Common experience with role models, one particular individual, or no experience at all might hold significance for your study and to the utility of the end-product (Offet-Gartner, 2008). Understanding this value will help researchers to include and value experiential learning. Utilizing group activities may allow participants to learn from each other in an accustomed way, perhaps making the study a more meaningful activity for them, thus increasing retention and better data (Goodman et al., 2004).

Connection to the land

"Our relationship to the Creator and to the land is a key component of the identity of many of us as First Nations people" (Calliou, 1997, p. 225). Some authors suggest that this connection to the land is common to all Indigenous people of the world, thereby connecting them spiritually (Bishop, 2005). France (1997) stated that those who want to work with Aboriginal people must understand that "the most important element is a respect and sensitivity to the land" (p. 8). Regardless of the nature of the study, this belief is likely to be held by the participants and it may be a factor in subtle ways. These might include needing to make an offering of tobacco, picking berries with your participant, holding sessions outdoors, or contributing to the beauty of the community in some tangible way to ensure that the message is clear – the land is sacred.

Storytelling

Poonwassie and Charter (2001) said that storytelling is one of the fundamental ways that cultural values, traditions, and histories are taught. They further suggested that stories are what connect the present to the past in a circular, fluid way. Akan (1999) said that "in giving this knowledge away to others we *keep* it" (p. 38). Stories are used to offer information in a way that is neither competitive nor seen as a sign of interference. The use of metaphor and reflection are intrinsically involved in this process (Wheaton, 2000). Take the time to listen and learn, realizing that the meaning behind the words, the story within the story, is closer to the *truth* than what is being offered on the surface. The following passage that Lightning (1992) recorded during his interview with Elder Louis Sunchild articulates this beautifully:

> The way to interpret those stories has never been clear to the literate, academic community until recently. The stories are not just "texts," or narratives that deal with sequences of events in a linear progression of events. There is a "surface" story: the text, and the things one has to know about the performance of it for others. The stories are metaphoric, but there are several levels of metaphor involved. The text, combined with the performance, contains a "key" or a "clue" to unlock the metaphor. When a hearer has that story, and knows the narrative sequence of it, there is another story contained within that story, like a completely different embedded or implicit text. The trick is this: that the implicit or embedded text, itself, contains clues, directions – better yet, specifications – for the interpretation of an implicit text embedded in it. (p. 229)

It is also important to know that not everyone is allowed to tell a full story or to talk about certain cultural things. Gunn-Allen (1998) cautioned that "a person is expected to know no more than is necessary, sufficient, and congruent with their spiritual and social place. One does not tell or enquire about matters that do not directly concern one" (p. 56). Therefore, ensuring that you have attracted the *right* participant for the question you are seeking to answer is crucial and takes preparation, sensitivity, patience, and cultural knowledge. Seeking advice from inside the cultural group cannot be understated (Meadows et al., 2003).

Designing a study that appreciates the richness of storytelling and avoids an emphasis on questions and answers would be respectful of this value (Fleras, 2004; Haig-Brown & Archibald, 1996). Again, this might prove difficult for researchers who are more traditionally trained or looking for brief, concise, or definitive responses.

Orientation of time

Although there are other values and traditions that could be examined, a final one that warrants discussion for its potential impact on research is the concept of time. Aboriginal people generally view time as a function of process rather than as a static, fixed event (Blue & Darou, 2005). If an individual gets involved in something, especially if it is with someone they respect, they are more likely to complete that task before moving on to another (Antone, 2000). This may have great implications for researchers when trying to schedule appointments. Lateness or a no-show should not be taken personally or as a sign of disinterest; rather, it might be seen as adherence to a cultural value (Stubben, 2001). Arranging to go *to* the participant, rather than them coming to you, and holding *come and go* sorts of forums are ways to minimize the effect that this value might have on your project (Meadows et al., 2003).

Furthermore, this value also behooves us as researchers and counsellors to invest greater amounts of time getting to know our participants than might be required in other settings (Alberta & Wood, 2009). Ethical research with Aboriginal peoples, as with other cultural groups, means committing yourself to building relationships (Lincoln & Canella, 2009). "It means spending precious time visiting with people at social functions such as community gatherings, ceremonies, local school events, and related activities" (Trimble &

Mohatt, 2006, p. 331). As Wax (1971) said, "You can't just drop in as if from Mars" (p. 15); the researcher must be prepared to participate, listen, and learn. Sadly, this is a luxury not all researchers have, even if they understand the benefit of it. This dilemma should be addressed *prior* to initiating any research project (Mohatt & Thomas, 2006).

Ignorance of these commonly held values or other cultural traditions on the part of a researcher can lead to alienation, resentment, and, quite possibly, expulsion from the community. Past research projects have been denied or terminated due to a lack of respect accorded to some of these values and beliefs (Frank, 1997). The importance of being guided by the values and beliefs of the individual community cannot be overstated. Short of examining one's own worldview, this may be the next most important step that you can take towards providing ethical and meaningful research (Fleras, 2004; Goodman, 2004).

 **Snapshot 5**

Common Aboriginal Values and the Potential Impact on Research

Value	Impact
Balance: Epitome of health, well-being, success.	Must consider all four domains of living: mental, physical, spiritual, and emotional.
Harmony: All things in balance seek harmonious relationships. All things/people hold equal value.	Strive for relational connections, respect for all forms of life and creation. May need to learn protocols, give offerings and gifts.
Traditional Healers: Most respected members of the community. Gift from the Creator.	Be open to their teachings. Their approval can mean the difference between success and failure. Usually well respected and known in the community. Great cultural guide.
Sacred Circle: All things in harmony are represented by a circle. It symbolizes the natural evolution of life. Equality is inherent.	This is a powerful concept. The circle is absolutely sacred and requires respect. Knowledge of directional patterns (clockwise) and protocols is strongly encouraged.
Relations: Family is of utmost importance. Family is not biologically determined; rather, a term of respect and endearment.	Can be very confusing! Ask the participants about the meaning of the relationship being referred to. Genograms are wise. Make no assumptions!
Non-Interference: Strong belief that everyone must learn their own lessons, at their own pace.	Help and charity are seen as a sign of failure and disrespect. Value placed on independence and mastery. Assistance needs to be given privately or anonymously.
Role Models: Preferred way of learning. Sign of honour and respect to be considered a role model.	Group work can naturally incorporate this concept and might increase participation and lower attrition.
Connection to the Land: A core belief that is essential to most Indigenous peoples. Mother Earth is sacred.	Incorporate an appreciation for this belief in all studies, especially those that directly involve the land. Ensure that your study is friendly to and contributes to the environment.
Storytelling: Often the way culture and history are taught. Storytelling is important.	Participants may prefer this style. Listen and be patient! Be comfortable with metaphors.
Orientation of Time: More relationship and process oriented than driven by a clock or future commitment.	Understand that time is relationally and process oriented. Do not take no-shows or tardiness personally. Make the most of each visit; going to your participants minimizes travel constraints.

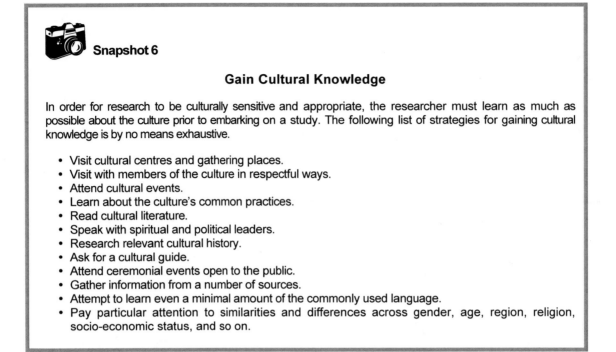

Snapshot 6

Gain Cultural Knowledge

In order for research to be culturally sensitive and appropriate, the researcher must learn as much as possible about the culture prior to embarking on a study. The following list of strategies for gaining cultural knowledge is by no means exhaustive.

- Visit cultural centres and gathering places.
- Visit with members of the culture in respectful ways.
- Attend cultural events.
- Learn about the culture's common practices.
- Read cultural literature.
- Speak with spiritual and political leaders.
- Research relevant cultural history.
- Ask for a cultural guide.
- Attend ceremonial events open to the public.
- Gather information from a number of sources.
- Attempt to learn even a minimal amount of the commonly used language.
- Pay particular attention to similarities and differences across gender, age, region, religion, socio-economic status, and so on.

The utilization of a cultural-centred and infused research paradigm depends on a basic understanding of relevant values and beliefs from the context of the community in which the study is proposed. I would caution that learning and appreciation of cultural values and ensuing worldviews be done in a number of ways; asking questions of one's own family, learning one's own history and cultural connections, and examining biases and beliefs and how they have been transcended throughout your life is the best place to start. Then ask the same sorts of questions with regard to the other invested parties or institutions, as even these have a distinct culture (Tatar & Bekerman, 2002). Once these influences, both current and historic, are better understood, turn the same sort of inquiries towards the culture you are planning to study with (Meadows et al., 2003). This can be achieved by opening yourself up to numerous and varied cultural opportunities, participating in cultural events, and visiting common cultural gathering places; read, listen, participate, ask questions, in polite and respectful ways, so that you can learn directly from the culture. Above all else, be open to and appreciate cultural diversity within *all* groups.

History of the Culture Involved

A fourth step that a researcher must take prior to embarking on a cultural inquiry is to learn about the realities of that culture's history (Ponterotto & Grieger, 2008). How has and is it being treated locally, nationally, and globally? I would caution that you do this with a critical and enquiring mind, remembering that history has often been *written* to serve the needs of the powerful and dominant group (Pedersen, 2001). We must remember that language is a cultural enterprise, whereby interpretations are culturally and socially located (Kincheloe & McLaren, 2005). As previously pointed out, those with the greatest power and privilege have provided the lens through which most history has been recorded. Be cautious about what you read (Gunn-Allen, 1998)! Seek out several sources, going as close to the margins as possible to find renditions closer to the *lived experience* of those you are seeking to understand (Chase, 2005). Broad knowledge of the history, as well as the stereotypes and myths of a group, along with a willingness to address them, to *hear* the experience of them *and* discuss their impact with your participants is paramount (Bishop, 2005; Smith, 2005). It is crucial that each researcher be prepared to go into a community as much a student as an academic and researcher (Goodman et al., 2004). Those in the community will watch and test you, judging your intentions by your behaviours, your words, your expressions, *and* your silence (Darou et al., 2000; McCormick, 2000a). Goodman and her colleagues suggested that to avoid this issue is similar to condoning and repeating the oppression and injustice the community may have encountered historically, even if the intent is not there.

Understanding the Impact of Acculturation

Prior to actually initiating the study, researchers using a culture-infused research paradigm must understand the concept of acculturation. Funk and Wagnall's *Canadian College Dictionary* (Avis, 1989) defined **acculturation** as "*the process by which one culture may be affected by another*" (p. 10). Arthur and Stewart (2001) wrote about cultural competence for counselling, which can be extended to the research that informs it, by warning that "counsellors [researchers] must also consider how processes such as acculturation to dominant and non-dominant groups in our societies influence individual clients [participants]" (p. 4). Since acculturation is a very real challenge for most non-dominant cultures, its impact and influence need to be understood as a factor in all research (Smith, 2005; Sue & Sue, 2007). Although acculturation scales have been created (Ryan & Ryan, 1980), ascertaining the impact of acculturation directly from each participant is the most appropriate choice to make (Youngblood-Henderson, 2000).

Who Benefits?

The final part of planning a culturally infused and competent study is to determine how the group(s) involved will benefit (Ponterotto & Grieger, 2008). These authors remind researchers that it is their responsibility "to bring the benefits of the research directly to the community in a tangible way" (p. 65). This means that the research must serve for more than just fulfillment of the researcher's agenda. The community should be able to reap the benefits in sustainable and obtainable ways. This will mean *beginning* the research project with the needs of the community in mind (Goodman et al., 2004), allowing them to articulate the questions they want answered and the goals they want to achieve, then designing the study with these goals in mind (Kral et al., 2002). Ensuring that the individuals in the community and their leaders have easy access to the information gathered means that researchers may have to create a separate document that provides the findings in a fashion that is consistent with how the community derives its knowledge (Smith, 2005). It may also mean that researchers have to assist communities, after the research is over, to obtain the supports they might need to ensure sustainability or to initiate the recommendations of the study (Kral et al.). "The purpose of research would no longer be to represent or know Others, but rather to examine and change the systems and discourses within which we function" (Lincoln & Cannella, 2009).

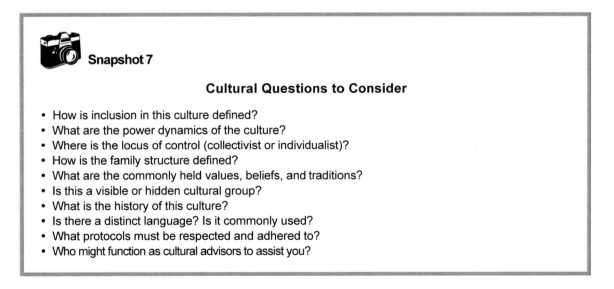

Snapshot 7

Cultural Questions to Consider

- How is inclusion in this culture defined?
- What are the power dynamics of the culture?
- Where is the locus of control (collectivist or individualist)?
- How is the family structure defined?
- What are the commonly held values, beliefs, and traditions?
- Is this a visible or hidden cultural group?
- What is the history of this culture?
- Is there a distinct language? Is it commonly used?
- What protocols must be respected and adhered to?
- Who might function as cultural advisors to assist you?

Who Should Conduct Cross-Cultural Research?

The previous section provided some insight into what it might mean to move towards a new culture-infused research paradigm. However, the question remains of who should do the much-needed research. Should members of dominant cultural groups be allowed to continue to write about issues for which they clearly do not have life experience (Silverstein, 2006; Sue & Sue, 2007)? Or, should research be completed only by members from within the cultural group of interest (Bishop, 2005)? Does any culture, or the members within it, have the right or the power to grant or deny permission to study multicultural issues (Mohatt & Thomas, 2006)?

Some might still want to limit research to those within the particular population. However, at this point there is general agreement that this is simply not practical or desirable (Mertens, 1998; Sue & Sue, 2007). It would surely mean that the number of research articles and projects would fall even lower, a circumstance that benefits no one. Ridley (1995) pointed out that to ask persons from non-dominant groups to do all of the work is not only unfair and undesirable, it is unethical as well. He said, "ironically, placing this heavy burden on minority professionals is yet another form of racism" (Ridley, p. 28). In addition, some authors (Brayboy, 2000; Mihesuah, 2000) have suggested that cultural similarity does not guarantee objectivity or true representation when it comes to research findings, as the researchers may, in fact, be too close to see the significance of everyday nuances or accepted practices. They may also believe that they need to protect information that they gather, or their participants may feel they are not as free to disclose certain information for fear of reprisal, recrimination, or loss of confidentiality.

There needs to be an appreciation for research as a process, which is influenced by a number of factors: who the researchers are, their philosophy, their methodology, their gender, their cultural identity, and a whole host of other factors make up these influences. So, limiting research based on *who* serves only to keep us stalemated in ongoing debate. It seems more appropriate to focus on *how* to conduct research from a culture-infused perspective that facilitates building bridges between cultures so that greater understanding and appreciation can evolve (Wilson, 2007).

Cultural Bridge Building

Sanders (2003) and Sue (1993) suggested that all researchers need to encourage the building of bridges to facilitate the production of more culturally appropriate and ethical research. Only with patience and true self-examination can bridges of trust and understanding be built. This is an active process, one that is not unidirectional. Sue further stated that he felt that, to date, people from non-dominant groups have done more than their fair share in building these bridges. A number of others would certainly agree with this statement (Bishop, 2005; Moradi et al., 2009). It is time for all who are interested in culture-infused, ethical research to step up, encouraging those around them to do the same. Introducing these concepts in the early education of potential researchers and counsellors is a step in the right direction (Palmer & Parish, 2008). Some suggestions are:

1. First and foremost, teaching the basic tenets of cultural competence and their applications to research (Ponterotto & Grieger, 2008).

2. As individuals become more culturally aware and competent, they will recognize "that all counseling and mental health research, is to some degree, cross-cultural, in that it is highly unlikely that the researcher and her or his participants represent precisely the same cultural matrix" (Ponterotto & Grieger, 2008, p. 58). Hence, we are cautioned to not view culture in an *add and stir* or purely intellectual, sterile way, but to seriously examine culture and diversity in relation to *real* issues that have meaning for *real* people as well as for ourselves (Mertens, 1998).

3. There are practical ways to assist with the generation of increased cultural knowledge by making education more accessible to minority students; mentoring students and researchers from diverse cultures; supervising dissertations that address cross-cultural issues, especially those being compiled by minority students; sitting on editorial review boards with the intent of aiding authors from non-dominant populations to successfully publish; and co-authoring with these authors (Alvarez, Blume, Cervantes, & Thomas, 2009; Fleras, 2004; Goodman, 2004).

4. Perhaps the technique easiest to achieve is one that Collins and Arthur in Chapter 4 and many other authors (Pedersen, 2001; Sanders, 2003; Sue & Sue, 2007) ask us all to learn, and that is to fully appreciate diversity, to not view *difference* as a *common enemy*, so that we might work together as

allies to ensure the continued growth of this important area. These authors not only acknowledge and celebrate difference and diversity; they take it one step further by preferring to emphasize culture-centred approaches that value all experience as equally valid and cultural in nature.

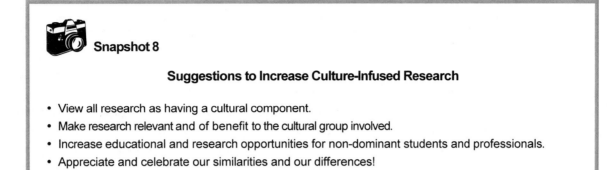

Snapshot 8

Suggestions to Increase Culture-Infused Research

- View all research as having a cultural component.
- Make research relevant and of benefit to the cultural group involved.
- Increase educational and research opportunities for non-dominant students and professionals.
- Appreciate and celebrate our similarities and our differences!

To Research or Not?

In the literature reviewed for this chapter, there is consensus of the need for more research in the area of multicultural issues. To call a moratorium on all cross-cultural counselling research would be both short-sighted and counter-productive (Fleras, 2004). "The multicultural problems are too large and the resources of persons from whatever group are too few to afford the luxury of fighting among ourselves. Our energy would be better used to educate one another and help all of us become more specific and accurate in our assessments" (Pedersen, 1993, p. 231). It would be unethical for members of dominant cultural groups to turn away from research across cultures or to leave this research solely up to members of non-dominant groups (McCormick, 2000a; Sue & Sue, 2007). We are reminded that we are either part of the problem or part of the solution; each of us has the responsibility to work together to actively transform our institutions and social groups to eradicate "isms," prejudice, and oppression (Lincoln & Cannella, 2009). Fleras asks us to learn new ways of "researching together differently" (p. 120). Developing sound, ethical, and culturally competent research practice is one way to assist in that process.

Conducting Culture-Infused Research

The previous sections provided an understanding of the foundations of culture-infused research and implored you to participate in increasing the availability of culturally responsive research with non-dominant populations in Canada. Even if you decide, however, that your research interests do not lie in areas where clearly defined cultural factors are evident, you are also reminded that to varying degrees all research is a cultural endeavour and the same basic principles and processes apply in all contexts and across all stakeholder groups. Once you have examined the impact of culture on your own perspectives, those of your participants, and any other stakeholders involved in the research project, you are encouraged to turn your cultural lens to the actual process of conducting culture-infused research. There are several steps in this process that will be outlined in this section:

1. selecting appropriate research methods,
2. building culturally sensitive relationships,
3. viewing data through the lens of culture,
4. interpreting the data and engaging in the writing, and
5. identifying and implementing potential benefits of the research.

What Methods Should be Used?

After all of the preliminary cultural exploration work described above has been done, the next step in conducting a research project is to choose the design and methodology that most appropriately fits the study and community involved. In selecting a research methodology, a number of variables must be considered (Ponterotto & Grieger, 2008). These include, but are not limited to, the question being asked, the skill of the person asking, what is already known, the size of the study, finances available, desired outcomes, participant pool, and the setting in which the study will take place.

The support for using qualitative rather than quantitative methods for cross-cultural research is extremely strong at present (Goodman et al., 2004; McCormick, 1998; Ponterotto & Grieger, 2008; Saukko, 2005; Smith, 2005). Osborne (1990) pointed out that this is not because qualitative research is better than quantitative methods; rather, it is because qualitative methods happen to be more experiential and flexible than experimental or objective methods. He believed that a focus on relationship, cultural context, and participants as the experts in their own experience makes it more congruent with the natural pedagogy found in most cultures. Many authors suggest this is because qualitative methods are more co-constructivist and collaborative and therefore has greater respect and provides a truer representation of participants' *lived experience*, making the findings much more meaningful for the community, as well as those who wish to deliver services to them (Fleras, 2004; Goodman et al.; Ponterotto & Grieger). Osborne believed that a qualitative method "stays closer to the meaning of human experience" and is like "coming home" (p. 79) for many counsellors and researchers who utilize the results of this type of enquiry to benefit their clients.

Furthermore, a plethora of authors have suggested the following ways that qualitative methods support ethical practices in culture-infused research (Goodman et al., 2004; Lincoln & Cannella, 2009; Mohatt & Thomas, 2006; Olesen, 2005; Ponterotto & Grieger, 2008; Richards, 2005; Saukko, 2005). Qualitative methods:

- include the researcher's biases and values upfront so that there is no question of where the interpretation of the results came from;
- promote understanding of the meaning of lived experience, generally the focus of most culturally inclusive research;
- are by nature collaborative and participatory, encouraging the researcher to include the participant and community in every step of the study;
- are concerned with issues of voice, authority, power, privilege, and oppression;
- allow for the inclusion of the participants as co-researchers;
- respect intuitive and indigenous knowledge, both frequently found in studies involving many non-dominant cultures;
- are concerned with the question of 'who benefits?'; and
- begin by designing applications within the community and seek to address social injustices.

Dudley (1992) stated that qualitative research "touches the heart, as well as the mind" (p. 341). Others have cautioned that quantitative methods are simply not conducive to research across cultures:

- Henning-Stout (1994) believed that, although quantitative methods can provide useful data, "it can provide only a partial view of any phenomenon to which it is applied" (p. 9).
- McCormick (1998) warned that "unless the researcher has a clear understanding of the variables involved in the cultural phenomena under study, quantitative analysis of such variables is a very risky venture" (p. 293).
- Frank (1997) stated that "traditional empirical research fails to recognize issues of values influence embedded in the research methodology" (p. 33).
- Fleras (2004) suggested that quantitative methods emphasize essentializing and prediction.
- Mohatt and Thomas (2006) stated that "random sampling procedures [a standard of quantitative

research] violate a fundamental principle of every indigenous group... it is exclusive rather than inclusive" (p. 110).

- Sohgn (1993) suggested that the use of traditional empirical methods is in fact culturally biased, blind, and perhaps even unethical.

Others advocate for the combined use of quantitative and qualitative methods (D'Andrea & Heckman, 2008; Haverkamp, Morrow, & Ponterotto, 2005; McCormick, 1998; Ponterotto & Grieger, 2007, 2008). Ponterotto and Grieger, in their 2008 review of the skills necessary for culturally competent research, stated "that a competent cross-cultural researcher has strong skills in *both* quantitative and qualitative methods and can select research approaches based on the research question under consideration and the needs of the community under study" (p. 66).

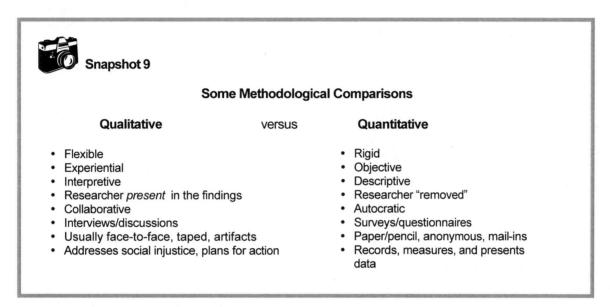

Snapshot 9

Some Methodological Comparisons

Qualitative	versus	**Quantitative**
• Flexible		• Rigid
• Experiential		• Objective
• Interpretive		• Descriptive
• Researcher *present* in the findings		• Researcher "removed"
• Collaborative		• Autocratic
• Interviews/discussions		• Surveys/questionnaires
• Usually face-to-face, taped, artifacts		• Paper/pencil, anonymous, mail-ins
• Addresses social injustice, plans for action		• Records, measures, and presents data

Although there is no clear consensus on this matter, the philosophical nature of qualitative methods, including the flexibility to draw from a variety of methods, the understanding that experience is contextually located, and the ability to self-locate does appear to lend itself to greater utility within a culture-infused research paradigm (McLeod, 2001; Richards, 2005).

Even this recommendation does not satisfy all who are invested in culturally inclusive research. Several authors have suggested that new methods of research are needed before culture-centred research can really be achieved (Bishop, 2005; Fleras, 2004; Kenny, 2000; Smith, 1999, 2005; Stanfield, 1994). "New ways of contemplating research are now needed that reveal the *intersections* of multiple, shifting subjectivities and historical contexts for each [participant]" (Tanaka, 2002, p. 288). Tanaka also said that "research methods can no longer afford to be 'timeless' or overlook the onrush of multiple cultural histories (p. 269). These authors stated their belief that trying to modify *old* methodologies will only water down or subjugate the centrality of culture in the research process.

Increasingly, authors are insisting that research reflect and respect the multiple cultural identities that are concurrently at play, each holding different salience depending on the context and dynamics of all the people involved in the research (Goodman et al., 2004; Lincoln & Canella, 2009; Silverstein, 2006). They contended that we need to include and locate all cultural voices, including that of the researcher in the research so that the entire process is culture-centred and makes transparent all of the known influences on the study. This means ensuring that the questions asked, regardless of methodology, include inquiries about the participant's *experience* of culture, race, gender, power, privilege, oppression, and so on so that a socio-cultural understanding of the influence these constructs have on the issue being studied can be acknowledged. Including these experiences increases the possibility of a rich and ethical study, while our understanding of the impact of these constructs increases with the hope of addressing any social injustice that may be revealed (Lincoln & Cannella).

If we know that power, privilege, and culture influence and often shape the lens through which we acquire knowledge and view the world, how then can we not include them in all studies that seek to further our understanding of something (Goodman et al., 2004)? Some authors (Bishop, 2005; Frank, 1997; Kenny, 2000; Smith, 2005) have felt so strongly about this issue that they have created new research protocols that are specific to the cultures they propose to study as a way to maximize cultural inclusion. Kirkness (1998) stated that the time for adapting old theories is gone. She wrote:

> We must begin by disestablishing many of our existing practices based on theories of the society that has dominated us for so many years. Then we must look within ourselves, within our communities, and our nations to determine which values are important to us, the content of what should be learned, and how it should be learned. This new direction must relate to theories firmly based on the traditions of our people. This means we must cut the shackles and make a new start. It is time for us to forget Band-Aiding; it is time for us to forget adapting; it is time for us to forget supplementing. (p. 11)

Other authors (Lincoln & Cannella, 2009; Pedersen, 2001; Ridley, 2005; Wilson, 2007) offered the observation that it is not so much the method researchers choose that makes the study more or less culture-centred; rather, it is the beliefs that researchers hold and the ways in which they *apply* the methodology that makes the difference. Whichever method is used, it is clear that more definition, description, participation in the process, ability to clarify, receive final drafts, and benefit from the process is wanted by the communities that find themselves the focus of cross-cultural research (Saukko, 2005).

Begin Research by Establishing Relationships

Beyond the primary importance of the preparatory steps of cultural examination (self and other) the second most important step is to begin building relationships with the participant group (Ponterotto & Grieger, 2008). This is best achieved by actively connecting with the intended research population, preferably in the same setting as the proposed research. Unlike the old, more objective, detached role of a researcher, this process requires the investigator to build relationships with potential participants *prior* to requesting their participation in a study (Fleras, 2004; Ponterotto & Grieger). "Spending time in the community will contribute to the practitioner's understanding of the unfamiliar culture or cultures and expedite the development of intercultural skills employed in the process of building relationships" (Alberta & Wood, 2009, p. 568). Activities such as visiting and participating in cultural events and joining in celebrations, may facilitate this process (Mohatt & Thomas, 2006). This nurtures the development of trust, understanding, and rapport in a more comfortable and natural way.

Effective communication skills, especially those of active and empathetic listening, are paramount (Haverkamp, 2005). Usher (1996) reminded us that "if the task is to represent the complexity of social reality, researchers need to form relationships which allow for those who are the researched to express what is significant in their everyday lives. It is this which provides for the validity of the research" (p. 134). Researchers are cautioned to be patient, as relationships may be slow to establish and barriers of mistrust may have to be broken down before true connections can occur (Smith, 2005). It is wise to remember that the cultural group you want to work with may be suspicious of all *outsiders*, especially ones who do research (Meadows et al., 2003). Building the research process from within the community through consultation, visits, and idea-generating conversations to determine what the group is interested in will aid in reducing these suspicions (Goodman et al., 2004). Lincoln and Cannella (2009) reminded us that "the practice of research involves relationships" (p. 274). Therefore, it should be clear that investing in building strong relationships is a necessity of ethical, culturally competent research. Simply stated: better relationships equal better research!

Engage with Your Data through the Lens of Culture

Once relationships have been formed and the focus and methodology have been chosen, the researcher can begin to collect data. As data begins to flow, the researcher has to begin to sift through reams of information in some organized fashion. Culture-infused research encourages the researcher to engage with the data in order to observe, reflect, and note any initial patterns or themes that may be present, keeping in mind the values and beliefs of the culture central throughout that process (Offet-Gartner, 2008). Kenny (2000) likened this process to that of a raven soaring high above the earth to get a broader understanding of the environment, coming in close to examine smaller details, and then back up again to watch, wait, and plan. Like the raven, it is important to remain aware of the relationship of self to the world at large. Other researchers have written about a similar process of viewing the data as a whole and as a sum of individual parts that interact with each other and the researcher in a fluid manner (Bishop, 2005; Goodman et al., 2004; Silverstein, 2006; Tatum, 1997; Usher, 1996). Each author described the relationship the researcher has with the data as being interactive and interpretive. This relationship places unique value on the *experience and voice* of each individual, *including those of the researcher* (McLeod, 2001; Richards, 2005). It recognizes the potential for new meanings, new learning, and growth to occur as a result of sharing one's experience: telling and retelling the story (Chase, 2005). According to Kenny (2000), "each time a story is told, there is new hope for positive change for our people. In this 'newness,' we can find 'renewal'" (p. 148). I would encourage all researchers to consider the wisdom of these sentiments, for all research tells a story, even if it was collected by anonymously circling numbers on a Likert-type scale or in other, more objective, quantifiable ways. Engaging with your data through this cultural lens is the necessary preparation for ethical interpretation (Ponterotto & Grieger, 2008).

Interpretation and Writing

"As with all scholarship, the observations and conclusions presented are necessarily limited by the worldviews of their authors" (Henning-Stout & Meyers, 2000, p. 420). Therefore, in order to infuse culture in research, Tanaka (2002) concluded that, "from now on researchers *must locate themselves* within their analysis or risk being perceived as ethnocentric *and* monological" (p. 289). Tanaka went on to say that "having voice means having culture" (p. 289). This concept is originally thought to have come out of feminism, especially the work of Gilligan (1982) and hooks (1984), who decreed that the realities of all forms of oppression (gender, orientation, race, religion, age, class, etc.) must be *acknowledged and talked about* before they can be arrested. In order for that to happen, everyone, especially the oppressed, must have a voice. Those who adhere to a culture-infused mindset agree that ***othering*** *or speaking for or generalizing to the norm* is contrary to useful ethical research (Lincoln & Cannella, 2009; Richards, 2005). Recall hooks' (1990) caution: "No need to hear my voice" (p. 151). Lincoln and Cannella concurred and warned that "impulses to represent the voices of others and to liberate the less fortunate are deeply embedded" (p. 276) in the traditions that inform research. The caution of these authors is not to stop compiling research; on the contrary, it is to *do research differently*.

Goodman and her colleagues (2004) reminded us that research can be used to "desilence the oppressed" (p. 802) by providing as many opportunities as possible to include the *voice* of the participants. Smith (2005) agreed and suggested staying as close to the original voice as possible, declaring your own voice and that of other stakeholders, and remaining transparent about agendas that may be operating overtly or covertly. Avoid generalizing, as it has typically meant comparing to White, middle-class, male, college students, which negates the experience of many and is simply another form of silencing and oppression (Silverstein, 2006). Culturally competent researchers are reminded that it is crucial not to essentialize by using monolithic definitions of culture or assuming homogeneity (Ponterotto & Grieger, 2008). Regardless of methodology, include the constructs of power, privilege, and culture-specific norms throughout the interpretive process to assist the study to be more culturally appropriate, inclusive, and ultimately more informative (Sue & Sue, 2007). Nowhere will this be more apparent than in your interpretation and writing.

Researcher's self-reflexivity

Throughout the interpretation and writing process, culture-infused research practice requires being **self-reflexive**, *stepping back from what is known, what is being said, and what can be learned several times throughout the process, paying close attention to similarities, differences, anomalies, and personal reactions.* "'Self-reflexivity' would be what happens when a *researcher uses what he learns about another culture to better understand all cultures, including his own* [italics added]" (Tanaka, 2002, p. 271). In turn, researchers use that knowledge to situate themselves and their understanding within the research process so that their learning becomes transparent to the reader and participant (Harrison, 2008). Marcus and Fischer (1986) cautioned that doing this requires researchers to view, read, and write research *differently*: with a sense of wonder, curiosity, and openness to being self-reflexive. The hope is to assist in an appreciation for all cultures and thereby in the inherent worth of all people (Pedersen, 2001). Tanaka called this possibility interculturalism and defined it as a "process of learning and sharing across difference where no one culture dominates" (p. 282). This sounds very similar to what Pedersen described as culture-centred research and to his call for a paradigm shift. Both support the notion of multiple cultural identities at play concurrently, each holding different significance and influence. Both advocate using a pluralist definition of culture and identity, as do many others (Silverstein, 2006; Sue & Sue, 2007). They proposed moving beyond the initial wave of calling for increased multicultural research to one that requests the inclusion and examination of all cultures, including Whites, which previously were not considered within the realm of cultural research. These authors raised the necessity of not assuming *identity* by overt or visible notions but inviting comfortable disclosure based on respect and acceptance (Moradi et al., 2009). This position recognizes that exclusion of any form is neither useful nor ethical and may in fact *do harm* (Ponterotto & Grieger, 2008). Ponterotto and Grieger encouraged researchers to maintain a self-reflexive journal throughout the entire process of research, regardless of methodological leanings. It is their premise that this step may increase the researcher's transparency and demonstrate an appreciation for the shifts that occur throughout the research process.

Cultural location of the interpretation

Interpreting the results of a study from a more culture-infused perspective requires you to attend to the **cultural location** of the experiences you are inquiring about. This means *understanding that all knowledge, language, and experience are socially, politically, historically, and culturally positioned* (Offet-Gartner, 2008). Taking them out of their original context changes them and renders them suspect and perhaps no longer valid (Smith, 2005). Mertens (1998) "cautioned researchers in cross-cultural studies to be careful in their interpretations of data and to base them on a thorough understanding of the culture that produced them" (p. 119). Many authors (Bishop, 2005; Kenny, 2000; Mohatt & Thomas, 2006) believe that the teachings, traditions, and language of the culture being studied should always be considered when interpreting data. Madak and MacDonald (2000) reminded us that "we are all products of our culture, and as such, are incapable of making absolute correct interpretations about behaviors observed in another culture" (p. 220). McLeod (2001) echoed the same sentiment, stating that there is no such thing as absolute truth, and that the language used to describe or report is always a representation and an interpretation that is subject to change. Therefore, he concluded that it is "inevitable whatever we find will be partial, open to re-interpretation by others, and both culturally and historically constructed" (p. 189). Many authors (Bishop; Chase, 2005; Fine, 2007; Lightning, 1992; McLeod; Richards, 2005) have warned that something is always lost in the writing of research because words can never truly capture all of the nuances of an experience or event, like notes on a sheet of music trying to represent the music you hear. This does not mean that you should exclude stating the results or making interpretations; rather, you should recognize the limitations and be open to the possibility that someone else may have a differing interpretation. "The data with which we work, regardless of how they are constructed and collected, cannot be presumed raw, uncontaminated, innocent, or authentic" (Fine, p. 471). Involving your participants, using as many of their own words, and culturally locating the research as much as possible are ways to arrive at the closest interpretation possible while realizing that you will never be able to fully capture the essence of an experience, simply a representation of it.

Use of member checks

There is growing support for the use of **member checks**, whereby *participants are asked to verify, clarify, and supplement the information or data that the researcher has gathered* (Bishop, 2005; McLeod, 2001; Meadows et al., 2003). With respect to qualitative research, Mertens (1998) stated that member checks are "the most important criteria in establishing credibility" (p. 182). Achieving this can be done formally or informally, through distribution and return of drafts, through first-hand conversations with participants, by allowing participants to hear the data with you and to comment, clarify, thicken, and create feedback loops, by using advisory councils and so on (Ponterotto & Grieger, 2008). Although this technique is clearly better suited for qualitative methods, it is just as imperative to incorporate the concept in more traditional methodologies because the intent is to ensure accuracy – a requirement of *all* research. If you do find yourself involved in a more traditional project, ask participants whether they would consider providing feedback on a preliminary summary. Studies that have pre/post tests allow for repeat contact with the participants. Including a follow-up session that allows for debriefing and verification does not compromise confidentiality or the original data; it simply allows for an opportunity to receive a commentary on what was suggested by the data (Ponterotto & Grieger). This is a relatively new concept that will require creativity on the part of researchers to decide the best way to include it in their studies.

Bloor (1997) chronicled some concerns associated with member checks. These include worry that researchers will have to alter their data, concern about participants changing their mind several times as to their meaning and making it difficult to decide which meaning to represent, struggles to determine at what point to put an end to the construction of the study, and a very real concern that the same issues that spurred researchers to use member checks are present in the subsequent interpretations. To address these concerns, researchers are encouraged to consult with their colleagues and other researchers in order to sort through these potential dilemmas (Mohatt & Thomas, 2006). Utilizing a cultural guide from the community involved *throughout* the research process is likely to reduce many of the concerns Bloor raised (Meadows et al., 2003). The benefits of going back to your participants to ensure that you *get it right*, to open up dialogue, and display that you *care whether you got it right,* rather than just assuming you did, far outweigh the negatives. In fact, in their recent overview of cultural competencies for counselling research, Ponterotto and Grieger (2008) affirmed that this practice is foundational for ethical cultural research.

Writing and representation

Once we are comfortable that we have adequate data, we need to interpret and record it in a way that others can receive it. Regardless of the methodology you use to do this, it will always be a cultural enterprise. Even language is a cultural interpretation and representation (i.e., words take on different meaning depending on who is using them, when, where, why, etc.). Gunn-Allen (1998) stated that "language does not merely describe reality, it creates it" (p. 390). Further, what we ask or chose not to ask, what we do or do not report, whom we include or exclude, and where and how the interpretations are positioned in the final product all convey a perspective that has been influenced by cultural factors (Fine, 2007). "Counsellor-researchers must be vigilant to ensure that they are not "seeing and interpreting" observed behaviour through lenses that have been tinted by their own cultural experiences" (Madak & MacDonald, 2000, p. 221). It can be argued that you cannot separate out your cultural lenses; rather, you must account for them and acknowledge how they may or may not be affecting the process and outcome of the research (Goodman et al., 2004). "The important point is that the researcher should develop a *self-reflexive* stance towards their own research: they must be accountable for their own cultural prejudices and disciplinary allegiance, and be alert to how these implicate them in the choices made in the research practice" (Usher, 1996, p. 134). Recognizing this may assist you in approaching your data as something fluid and vibrant rather than something static and absolute (Kenny, 2000; Newhouse, 2004). After all, it *represents something*; it holds meaning for living people and as such is as rich and varied as the people themselves.

Revisit your data and interpretations

"No matter what design, paradigm, or type of data collected researchers always need to consider competing explanations" (Mertens, 1998, p. 345). You are encouraged again to *step back* from your data, *look* at it, and *listen* to it. Do this several different times in a variety of ways, each visit listening for anything new or different from the time before. Each time you visit it will be a unique experience (McLeod, 2001). Ask yourself:

- How many competing influences are at play for each variable, person, and event?
- Would everyone have the same response as you at each viewing?
- How is your own experience influencing what you attend to and what you do not?
- What influence would time, location, experience, or familiarity have on the interpretation?

These premises are characteristics of culture-infused interpreting. Long and LaFrance (2004) challenged all researchers to "be as committed to listening *for* the truth as we are to speaking *about* the truth" (p. 4). To do this requires both vigilance and care. The purpose of this chapter is to provide some guidance on *how* to approach the task of research with cultural competence.

Include considerable contextual detail in the writing

Ponterotto and Grieger (2007) informed us that producing culturally competent material requires the researcher to provide as much detail and context as possible so that others can have a clearer picture of what, why, when, how, where, and with whom you did your study. They referred to this as *thick description*, and it provides rich details of all of the stages and influences of the research experience so that readers can make informed judgments of what is useful for them and what is not. Mertens (1998) stated that it is "the researcher's responsibility is to provide sufficient detail to enable the reader to make such a judgment" (p. 183). McLeod (2001) cautioned that "it is only by placing a study in a social and historical context that the reader can fully appreciate what has been found" (p. 205). Newhouse (2004) suggested that competent research must inform readers about the experiences of those who were involved so that we might learn to "grapple with each other's cognitive universes and learn how to see through the minds of others" (p. 154). This can only be done if we are given enough information – thick, situational, cultural context – to grapple with.

Who Should Benefit from Research?

The purpose of research is to generate knowledge and facilitate greater understanding. If a study is truly culture centred, then the entire project has to benefit more than just the researcher (Ponterotto & Grieger, 2008). Without exception, every resource reviewed for this chapter suggested that all research, and especially that of a cross-cultural nature, needs to benefit the community it originated from. Yvonna Lincoln (personal communication, August 8, 2004) reminded us that "we owe a debt to the persons whose lives we portray. We must do everything we can to repay them for assisting us." Haig-Brown and Archibald (1996) suggested asking the question: "*In what ways will the people (including me) and therefore the culture be changed and/or hurt by this research process?*" (p. 254). Trying to ensure that changes are positive requires special forethought and planning. All parties involved need to be considered in this and be given the opportunity to be heard, to reflect, and to grow as a result of being involved in the study (Goodman et al., 2004). Research must be used for more than just self-understanding, receiving a degree, funding, tenure, or publication credit. Focusing on the collective benefit *for* the community involved rather than that of the researcher or other stakeholders is a core competency that needs to be reflected in all ethical, culturally infused research (Ponterotto & Grieger).

Community considerations

Haig-Brown and Archibald (1996) felt that research should benefit the whole community, not just those directly involved in the study. They wanted researchers to acknowledge the wider audience and responsibility to others who might be involved peripherally, vicariously, or in very distinct ways. The adage *research is a living thing* suggests that research needs to contribute to the greater society, as all living things do (Lincoln & Cannella, 2009). Ponterotto & Grieger (2008) advocated incorporating the concept of care and benefit right from the beginning of your study, starting with the proposal and remaining evident throughout the entire process. To truly do this, we need to think *beyond* the confines of the study. Implicit in this statement is that competent cultural research needs to clearly articulate what it will leave behind. This includes building in sustainable programming as part of the actual project, assisting in the development of community advisory boards to begin the implementation of action items related to the study, and taking social action if necessary. In this way, research can be seen to enrich the lives of the participants and all those connected to them.

Practical suggestions include the following ways to invite a more positive view of research, which hopefully will encourage further collaborative efforts.

- Hire whatever assistance is required to complete the study from within the community, for it offers immediate employment and an opportunity to gain experience, and may help the research gain greater participation and validation from the rest of the community (Frank, 1997; Goodman et al., 2004; Meadows et al., 2003; Strickland, 1999).

- Teach research skills at the grassroots level, perhaps laying the foundation for more research, especially that of an in-group nature (Fleras, 2004; McCormick, 1998).

- Mentor and role model familiar practices that are intrinsic to many non-dominant communities (Alvarez et al., 2009; Meadows et al.).

- Focus on the strengths of the culture, as opposed to negative or pathological components, especially if they dispel previously held myths and stereotypes (Goodman et al.; Palmer & Parish, 2008).

- Use the research to confront social injustices and inequities. This may require researchers to advocate on behalf of the population and/or assist the community to do so along with them. The caution is for researchers to understand that social justice work comes with a cost; it is the researcher's responsibility to ensure that harm is not done to the participants or their community (Palmer & Parish; Ponterotto & Grieger).

Ideas such as these require new ways of viewing research. However, if we want to ensure that the ways we compile research are more culturally inclusive, we must examine *all* aspects of the research process. This requires a shift in thinking by a number of parties, perhaps none more apparent than academia (Alvarez et al., 2009; Fleras, 2004; Lincoln & Cannella, 2009; Smith, 2005).

Research as a catalyst for change

Schulz (2000) asked us to remember that research creates change, some of which will be beneficial, some perhaps not. Some changes are immediate and obvious; other changes are more subtle or happen long after the study is complete. Sometimes the change is not exactly what we hoped for or is negative in ways not considered in the preparation stage of the study (Goodman et al., 2004). There is no way of knowing the full extent of change that a study can invoke, for whom, or in what context, timeframe, or circumstance (Offet-Gartner, 2008). Research does not start and stop with the actual study (Lincoln & Canella, 2009). It lives on in experience, documentation, and knowledge, and, like all stories, it affects lives (Richards, 2005).

Research grounded in care and concern

We are reminded to ground research from a place of care and concern and to honour the people, the process, and the potential of research (Mertens, 1998; Ponterotto & Grieger, 2008). "When our research practices are informed by a caring attitude towards others, our decisions are based on what effect our actions will have on the relationship, on the development of the other as a caring person, and on our community of caring" (Schulz, 2000, p. 216). Schulz, like Lincoln and Cannella (2009), suggested treating research participants in the same way as we treat people in other relationships that we care about and, by doing so, creating better research. Caring should encourage us to invest in research that is of interest to our participants. Identifying a group that you want to work with and then asking them what queries they would like to explore demonstrates a respect for cultural competence and integrity that may reap enormous benefits for all involved (Ponterotto & Grieger).

This is a relatively new perspective that is reflective of the evolutional rise of the need to be more culturally inclusive and responsive to the communities that counselling psychology serves (Palmer & Parish, 2008). However, the simplicity is clear; the more invested all parties are, the more likely it is that the knowledge produced will hold deeper meanings and utility for all involved, thereby increasing the benefit of the inquiry (Offet-Gartner, 2008). This caring needs to be readily discernable throughout the entire process of research, but especially needs to be transparent in the final product because its reach is far and its audience wide. A study can be likened to a pebble that gets tossed into a lake. Its impact can create innumerable ripples that cannot be controlled, contained, nor completely predicted, the result of which extends far beyond the point of entry.

Whether you are conducting research where cultural differences are subtle or more obvious, taking a culture-infused approach to conducting your research will enhance your ability to contribute ethical and meaningful knowledge to the current body of knowledge. Selecting appropriate research methods, building culturally sensitive relationships, viewing and interpreting data through the lens of culture, engaging in a culturally responsive writing process, and identifying and implementing potential benefits of the research are keys to success.

Some Ethical Considerations and Potential Dilemmas

Engaging in culture-infused research not only requires a shift in conceptual framework and methodology; it also requires researchers to attend carefully to the types of ethical issues and dilemmas that may arise (Goodman et al., 2004; Haverkamp, 2005). The further apart the cultural reality of the research is from the researched, the greater the possibility for miscommunication or misinterpretation of behaviour (Mertens, 1998; Ponterotto & Grieger, 2008). This section will highlight some of the ethical considerations you may want to attend to in all research, particularly research *across* cultures.

Ethical Considerations

All researchers have an ethical responsibility to try to anticipate as many of the potential dilemmas as possible that may arise within or as a result of their study (Madak & McDonald, 2000). In Chapter 7, Pettifor provides several concrete examples that are linked to a number of ethical codes and culture-specific groups. The discussion in Chapter 7 outlines standards of practice that need to be included and considered for your study to be culture-centred and ethical, as does the information contained in Ponterotto and Grieger (2008). Familiarity with these as well as other sources of ethical considerations for the population you want to study with are strongly recommended. Notwithstanding, there is simply no way to predict each and every concern that might arise. Furthermore, there is not always a decisive *answer* to be found in the codes governing your research. McCormick (1998) reminded us that "although development of ethical codes is desirable, it is important to note that such guidelines are the product of the culture that created them. The guidelines, though necessary, reflect the beliefs and values of that culture" (p. 284). Therefore, the *codes,* simply deduced, reflect the culture of those who were empowered to write them. As such, they may not address the concerns of all other cultural interests and may in fact be frustrating, or worse, discriminatory. There is no way to avoid *this* dilemma, so developing an ethic of caring, of remaining open to conversation, and of mutual problem-solving and decision-making is the best ethical advice possible (Lincoln & Cannella, 2009; Nagy, 2005; Ponterotto & Grieger; Schulz, 2000).

Ethical decision-making

Madak and MacDonald (2000) noted that it is important to realize that there are many possible dilemmas, with "no clear-cut solutions" (p. 219). To try to rely on a template of right-wrong answers, even if one were available, would be far too limiting and would not acknowledge the uniqueness and creativity of the situation at hand. They suggested that ethics are more about a process of ethical decision-making than about right-wrong answers. It is their premise that researchers must develop their ethical reasoning *before* research begins because "waiting until an event or dilemma arises may place the counsellor-researcher in the difficult situation of trying to make a complex decision quickly without the luxury of having time to completely think out all the possible consequences of a particular option" (p. 225). Further, they stated that "once in the field, it is too late to say 'time-out while I go and get advice'" (p. 227). These authors did not suggest that knowledge of the codes is unnecessary. They simply wanted to remind us that rules and codes will not give us *the answer*. Ethics in research, as in every aspect of life, is about the way you *live* your life; ethics are a way of being, not just a way of reacting (Pettifor, 2005).

Snapshot 10

Basic Tenets of Ethical Cultural Research

Awareness	Know thy cultural self: be aware of and acknowledge all biases, values, beliefs, and attitudes.
Knowledge	Learn as much about the culture you are about to study from a variety of first-hand sources. Be prepared to *enter* the culture as respectfully as possible. Attendance at ceremonies, community events, and cultural centres or gathering places is highly recommended.
Skill	Increase your skills in counselling, interviewing, interpreting, and reporting. Demonstrate cultural awareness, sensitivity, and relevance in all skills within the research process.

Potential Dilemmas

Some examples of dilemmas that should be considered have been embedded throughout this chapter; a few others warrant highlighting. These include but are not limited to issues of relationship, counselling skill, closure, informed consent, uncovering negative constructs, who benefits, social action, political power, and collaboration.

Development of relationships

By opening yourself up to the community, you are likely to develop relationships, particularly with those who decide to directly participate in the study (Ponterotto & Grieger, 2008; Offet-Gartner, 2008). This raises all sorts of questions regarding boundaries, being *too close* to the situation, the role you will play in the community, and possible expectations to continue the relationship after the project is complete (Goodman et al., 2004). I cannot urge you enough to consider the impact of these before you start. After all, you are the instrument of your research (Lincoln & Cannella, 2009). Human beings, including you, are relational. Developing healthy, clear, and caring relationships will assist you and the participants to *all* benefit from the project you are mutually involved in (Richards, 2005). Recall the words of renowned research guru Yvonna Lincoln: "We owe a debt of gratitude to our participants" (personal communication, August 8, 2004). One way to repay them is to ensure that we treat them with respect, demonstrated by caring relationships.

Since much of the research suggests using qualitative methods, a special caution is offered to those who employ them. Relationship is integral to these methods, leading to a greater chance of *gray areas* (Chase, 2005; Mohatt & Thomas, 2006). Schulz (2000) cautioned that the closeness of the relationship between the researcher and the researched is what makes this research so valid; it also introduces the greatest ethical dilemmas. Madak and MacDonald (2000) obviously concurred, adding: "Therefore, the uses of qualitative research methods require a more diligent approach to the topic of ethical behavior" (p. 219). Both Chase (2005) and Richards (2005) reminded us to anticipate these relational challenges, remain diligent, and seek assistance when needed. Fleras (2004) stated that "researchers cannot possibly avoid participating with the people with whom they are studying" (p. 121). It was her premise, along with those of others in the field (Alvarez et al., 2009; Fisher & Ragsdale, 2006; Mohatt & Thomas, 2006; Ponterotto & Grieger, 2008), that if the participants and their communities are kept in the centre of the research, many potential dilemmas will not occur.

Anticipate potential changes

Schulz (2000) reminded us that "both researcher and participant change in the course of their work together" (p. 216). This change may not necessarily be positive. Either party might be forced to look at negative influences or patterns or reveal secrets that they no longer find acceptable. As Silverstein (2006) put it, to do cross-cultural work ethically, "all of us would be forced to admit our classism, racism, sexism, homophobia, and so forth – the parts of ourselves we like the least" (p. 27). These discoveries must be addressed and the impact worked through for the research to be truly ethical (Lincoln & Cannella, 2009). Miller (1996) and Osborne (1990) suggested that researchers must be prepared to finish whatever they start. For example, if questioning or interviewing causes the participant to emote strongly or delve deeper into the experience, it is the researcher's ethical responsibility to assist the participant to obtain closure or whatever intervention is appropriate. For this very reason, Miller suggested that researchers should possess some formal training in basic counselling skills and be familiar with a variety of referral sources, just in case. Additionally, Madak and MacDonald (2000) cautioned that "a researcher who is also a counsellor needs to be particularly cautious as she or he has specialized skills, which could be used to take advantage of a trusting volunteer" (p. 222). Conversely, Ponterotto and Grieger (2008) warned counsellors to maintain a clear boundary between the role of interviewer and that of counsellor; even though researchers may possess the skill, shifting roles would place the counsellors/researchers in a *dual* role, thereby contravening their ethical code. If researchers experience trauma as a result of the participant's experience, they too need to be debriefed and assisted. What is necessary is finding that healthy balance between connecting and inviting disclosure, knowing what to do with it once it is *out there*, and then representing it in ways that are as useful as possible. Above all else, our duty is to *do no harm!*

Informed consent

Another important issue for consideration is the *informed consent process*. Fisher and Ragsdale (2006) asked us to think about the language used to ascertain consent: is it the native tongue of the participant or researcher? Is the *in-group* language used, or is consent offered in more formal language? Smith (2005) asked us to consider how communities more used to oral tradition view written consent forms and requirements. An interesting dilemma raised by Madak and MacDonald (2000) is that of innocent bystanders, or those who are not directly involved as participants, but so close that they have become part of the study unknowingly or unwittingly (e.g., family members, colleagues, neighbours, other group members). They asked whether these folks need to be included in the informed consent or notified in any way that information about them is or has been recorded.

Along those same lines, do you have to find out all sides of an issue? If you get a strong opinion in one direction, is it necessary to balance it out with the other side? What if the *other* side is someone close to the participant (e.g., life partner, parent) and is not covered by your consent form? Do you now include that person in order to achieve this balance? What if the information offered from a participant represents cultural teachings? Who can give consent for it to be shared (Smith, 2005)? What if some respondents want to remain anonymous and others do not (Fleras, 2004)? Who has the right to make these decisions? How do you avoid losing something or someone in the process (Osborne, 1990)? These can become huge issues if they are not been considered prior to the study. Obviously, we cannot plan for every configuration, but to not consider any aberrations is to invite added anxiety along the way (Offet-Gartner, 2008).

Uncovering community issues

Every researcher, regardless of methodology, must be aware that the process of completing a study may uncover problems of a socio-economic or political nature at play in the community (Goodman et al., 2004). Darou and his colleagues (2000) cautioned specifically about Aboriginal politics; however, I think it would be fair to extend their wisdom across cultures: "it is ill advised to mess with Native politics. You are out of your league and you have the potential of doing enormous harm. Do not burn your bridges" (p. 52). This is not to suggest that glaring issues of oppression or mistreatment uncovered during the research process should be ignored, simply that they need to be considered from the cultural context from which they evolved. First and foremost, great care must be taken to ensure the *safety* and confidence of your participant (Fisher & Ragsdale, 2006). Involving them or your cultural guides in the examination of any injustice you sense will assist you in ensuring that your interpretation and reaction are accurate and then you can begin to consider possible remedial suggestions (Richards, 2005). Being able to discuss and address these issues with the participants, and with any governing leadership, can be a precarious endeavour and one that requires tact and diplomacy. Researchers must remember that they are ambassadors for their cultural group, their profession, and research as a whole. Whether bridges are built or burned will impact both current and future studies (Darou et al.). Involving the participants, their community, and, if present, community leaders throughout the entire research process should alleviate some of the difficulties with research across cultures and assist us to address some of the more obvious concerns in ways that are mutually acceptable and beneficial (Meadows et al., 2003; Mohatt & Thomas, 2006; Smith, 2005).

There is an increasing push for research to include a social justice component (Fouad, Gerstein, & Toporek, 2006; Goodman et al., 2004; Richards, 2005). This may include addressing issues of marginalization, inequality, poverty, social or political injustice, or maltreatment (Chase, 2005; Lincoln & Cannella, 2009). Since social action and benefit are often important catalysts within the research purpose, we must find respectful ways to bridge the gaps we find. As Pettifor (2001a) so aptly pointed out, "a sense of social justice and responsibility to society requires professionals to work in various ways to change political structures and power relationships that present barriers to a better quality life for people of all cultures and colours" (p. 33). I think it behooves us to not shirk this responsibility, all the while remembering to do this from a culturally informed and respectful stance, one that involves understanding, collaboration, and empowerment.

Research requirements

Academic requirements and protocols frequently place researchers in an *institutional press*, where the needs of the community may not be consistent with the requirements of academia or other sponsors (Kenny, 2000; Smith, 2005). These authors cite emphasis on written formats and contractual agreements, claiming ownership of *data*, storage of data away from a community, and copyright policies as examples. Others agree and believe this may be reason enough to ban cultural research (Battiste, 1998; Frank, 1997; Stubben, 2001). These authors advocated that all research data, including field notes, transcriptions, recordings, and photos be returned to the community studied or given to museums. This would ensure that any cultural language, history, stories, or traditions recorded remains available to that particular group, as well as to society at large (Bishop, 2005; Saukko, 2005; Smith). Both Smith and Frank suggested that academia's refusal to comply with these requests and the emphasis placed on publishing completed work in educational journals and papers are continued forms of acculturation and appropriation.

To respond to these concerns, it is highly recommended that the researcher negotiate ownership agreements, storage requirements, and publication formats prior to the initiation of any study (Frank, 1997; Haig-Brown & Archibald, 1996). Joyner (2003) said that "one of the greatest obstacles we face in this area is the lingering narrow definition of scholarship that pervades most institutions of higher education today" (p. 17). Approaching academic institutions to accept alternate forms of research that would be more congruent or representative of the culture being studied would be a step in the right direction (Palmer & Parish, 2008). These might include music or dance performances, live theatre, or displays of art. Joyner added that "the most important thing that faculty and administrators can do to encourage socially relevant research is to expand and celebrate diverse scholarly contributions" (p. 17).

Sharing power and voice

A final example of addressing potential dilemmas is in the area of collaboration and the commitment to share power and voice. These are important concepts; however, they are often far more aspirational than realistic. "Sharing power and crediting people's knowledge may be harder to practice than profess" (Dickson & Green, 2001, p. 481). These authors frankly discussed the realization that at times their participants were not willing or able to share the power with the researchers, other participants, and invested stakeholders. At other times, the participants simply did not have the time, energy, or resources to fully devote to the collaborative experience. This created a conundrum for them as believers in the necessity of this process. These authors, along with numerous others (Brayboy, 2000; Fine, 2007; Goodman et al., 2004; McLeod, 2001; Mertens, 1998; Richards, 2005), have discussed the difficulties associated with *knowing how to* conduct collaborative research and the struggle that can ensue when it proves to be a greater challenge in practice. Fully embracing this concept requires considerable commitment and desire of *all* parties within the project. Conflicts are bound to occur (Fisher & Ragsdale, 2006). It would be wise to consider some of these possibilities and some possible resolutions ahead of time. Reading broadly about the practice of research may assist you to escape the challenges of those who have attempted or completed projects. A great and often forgotten resource is simply to talk to others who have completed research (Meadows et al., 2003). They are a rich and readily available resource; as with all other areas of practice, the mantra is: *when in doubt, consult.*

As you can see, these dilemmas and the possible solutions vary and are rarely clear cut, right or wrong. Rather, they exist on a continuum of decision-making. This process involves looking at advantages versus disadvantages for a number of stakeholders, some more visible than others. Each case must be considered for its own merits and you must consider the amount of energy and resources available to make a solid judgment. "It is only through personal vigilance that each of us will avoid making ethical mistakes.... To avoid making errors in judgment, we must view research as a 'living practice'" (Madak & MacDonald, 2000, p. 229).

Additional Considerations in Culture-Infused Research

As illustrated in the preceding discussion, culturally appropriate and inclusive research can prove to be a greater challenge than it would seem on the surface. There a number of factors that have not been previously considered or accounted for sufficiently, yet they are absolutely necessary within the confines of a culture-infused research paradigm. Do not let those stop you from getting started on your own journey of exploration. May I recommend that you begin now, *before* someone is offended, before you find yourself being asked to leave a community, or before you are struggling to find or keep participants? Although I think templates are often like recipes in that they give us ideas, ingredients, instructions, and organize it all for us in a neat, step-by-step manner, the actual mastery of the dish comes from experience and from availability and freshness of the ingredients: adequate time, patience, ability, and individual tastes.

I thought offering a template or checklist of some of the things mentioned throughout this chapter might assist you to consider whether the recommendation is a *good fit* for your project (see Snapshot 11). In no way should it be seen as exhaustive. It is more a starting place to get you cooking. Although many authors have contributed to the creation of this *list*, Mertens (1998), Ponterotto and Grieger (2008), and Richards (2005) are highly recommended resources.

Chapter Summary

Several implications and guidelines for research using a culturally infused paradigm have been offered throughout this chapter. These include the importance of understanding oneself as a cultural being and being willing to examine and acknowledge the biases and beliefs that one holds as a result of cultural influences. Learning about culture from the specific community for the study is paramount for this paradigm (Saukko, 2005). Specific knowledge about the cultural values and beliefs that the proposed community subscribes to will assist the researcher in designing a more effective study (Smith, 2005). Including community leaders or Elders as advisors is advantageous to support the researcher in avoiding some of the cultural faux pas that are easy to commit (Mohatt & Thomas, 2006). These individuals can also serve as excellent resource people to facilitate introductions and assist with resolving potential difficulties. If designing a study within a community that has an existing political structure, gaining their approval is paramount (Darou et al., 2000). Having cultural advisers assist with this is very wise (Alberta & Wood, 2009). The importance of clear understandings for the storage of all research data and the manner in which the final product is disseminated are crucial steps for culturally inclusive research (Kenny, 2000). This may mean that the researcher has to facilitate discussions between the community involved and the sponsors of the project (Frank, 1997). This task may be difficult because there may be strong investments on both sides (Joyner, 2003).

Snapshot 11

Things to Consider for Culture-Infused Research

1. Get to know yourself as a cultural being.
2. Identify and acknowledge any stereotypes or biases that may negatively influence your study.
3. Consult with others who have compiled research with this group or similar groups.
4. Learn about the culture, in as many ways as you can.
5. Learn some of the language; even a simple phrase or local slang will show genuineness. Ensure that all written work reflects culturally inclusive or respectful language.
6. Explore areas of interest that might mutually benefit the community, yourself, and society.
7. Hold introductory meetings with as many invested parties as possible, in particular governing bodies if they exist. Be yourself, be prepared, and be open to answering questions and addressing concerns.
8. Clearly state the research purpose, intent, procedure, method for interpreting, dissemination, distribution of assets, and management of raw data in a variety of formats that can be given to participants and the community at large.
9. Prepare a handout or brochure outlining the details of your study that can be given out to community at large. Use conversational language (e.g., not "your informed consent").
10. Seek out the advice of cultural guides. Consider including advisory councils and choose wisely whom you entrust with this task.
11. Identify and involve the primary audience for the study, asking for their input throughout the research process.
12. Be guided by the cultural group to ensure that you use culturally inclusive and appropriate ways of relating.
13. Discuss expectations, level, and duration of participation commitment.
14. Consider and openly discuss the costs and benefits of participating in the study.
15. Negotiate what will be done with the findings and raw data once the study is complete. Be open to invitations to participate in community events, celebrations, or recreation. To turn these down may signal lack of acceptance, disrespect, or even distaste.
16. Do not be the *Expert*; rather, go as a learner and show interest in learning. This will go a long way towards showing good intentions.
17. Share your knowledge by way of mentorship, coaching, role modelling, and advocacy.
18. Be flexible! Sometimes things do not go the way we planned. Patience and creativity are imperative.
19. Create the least amount of disruption possible. Display your interest in THEM! Adjusting and accommodating to benefit them is wise.
20. Be aware that you will make mistakes. Admit them, learn from them, and share them in your final product so the rest of us can learn too and perhaps avoid the same mistake.
21. Ask participants to review the raw data and the subsequent interpretations for clarity and accuracy.
22. Take great care when you represent what you find. Carefully consider culturally appropriate or inappropriate ways to present your findings.
23. Hold debriefing sessions for participants and researchers to address topics related to ethics, possible trauma, or developing shared understandings.
24. Assist in any community change or social action that might evolve from the study. Your responsibility does not end with the granting of your degree or publication of your article. Research knowledge should be applied. Social justice requires action – act responsibly!
25. Work to resolve, in as positive a fashion as possible, any dilemmas or conflicts that arise and, of course, acknowledge them in the written product so the rest of us can learn.
26. Stick to what you said you were going to do or have ethical reasoning for why you deviated from your plan.

The need to preserve shareholder interests may challenge the researcher's commitment to the project. Ensuring that participants benefit from the research project is intrinsic in this paradigm and, some say, should be in all research (Ponterotto & Grieger, 2008). Being open to discussing historical trauma and experience is an important factor when working with marginalized groups (Sanders, 2003). A willingness to listen may increase the researcher's understanding of the participant's experience on a level that might not have been achieved had the topic been avoided (Fine, 2007). Designing studies that honour and incorporate cultural traditions and values, collaboration, and reciprocal relationships is of utmost importance (Mertens, 1998). In addition, personal traits such as patience, flexibility, effective communication skills, and a willingness to learn can add to the research being a positive experience for everyone (Richards, 2005).

Conclusion

Understanding culture is a complex task, even when it is one's own (Pedersen, 2001). Understanding another's culture is even more complicated. The recognition that we all possess a number of cultures that shape and influence our everyday experience, including all of our knowledge, feelings, and actions, is sobering to say the least (Tanaka, 2002). As noted in Chapter 4, culture is varied, multifaceted, dynamic, and diverse, making the understanding of it even more complicated. Despite the difficulties, we must forge ahead if we are to stay competent and relevant in addressing the needs of our society (Ponterotto & Grieger, 2008). One way to facilitate this understanding is to complete meaningful, culturally inclusive research.

In the earlier chapters of this book, Arthur and Collins suggested a framework for professional counselling practice that needs to be extended to all roles, including research. Fundamental to using a culture-infused research paradigm is, first and foremost, the understanding of one's own culture, including any power and privilege that inclusion in the particular culture affords us. This is not an easy or comfortable task. McIntosh (1989) and Lynn (1994) eloquently pointed out that we often benefit from remaining ignorant to the realities of these constructs. Resistance to their recognition is often deeply ingrained, subversive, and couched in good intentions (Ridley, 2005). Understanding one's own culture takes courage and a willingness to truly examine biases, beliefs, and values that may be so deeply entrenched in ethnocentrism that there is absolutely no awareness of them (Sue & Sue, 2007).

Understanding more about ourselves provides us with a greater capacity to understand *others* (Richards, 2005). If we want to research from a culturally inclusive and ethical perspective, we must invest the time to get to know the culture we want to study with, as well as the culture of any invested stakeholders, as each will have an impact on the study being proposed (Mohatt & Thomas, 2006). We need to examine the places where each of the cultures intersect and interplay with each other and then how that translates in our research (Mertens, 1998; Tanaka, 2002). Any efforts to minimize or ignore the effects of culture on the process of research will likely render the findings suspect and limit their utility (Frank, 1997).

Finally, we must conduct research from within paradigms that support and encourage the examination and inclusion of cultural factors (Smith, 2005). This may challenge some of the more traditional paradigms, as many authors believe that they cannot adequately reflect the experience of most marginalized people (Bishop, 2005, Goodman et al., 2004; Saukko, 2005; Smith). "Because a culture-centred perspective is complicated, it makes research, teaching, and direct service more inconvenient, which has caused cultural differences to be overlooked or viewed negatively" (Pedersen, 2001, p. 20). Stanfield (1994) advocated the creation of more culturally specific paradigms for research, but offered: "The purpose of creating the new baby is not to bury the old one, but instead to create a family" (p. 185). In order for a culture-infused research paradigm to become a member of the research family, it will require acceptance and recognition from other members of the family (Lincoln & Cannella, 2009). Directly or distantly, you are a member of this family. You therefore have some decisions to make as to whether or not you will acknowledge this new relative.

As with the birth of any baby, nurturance and healthy development requires time and considerable effort by a number of people. I implore you to make this investment. The family of psychology, including those who conduct, consume, and, most importantly, participate in and are affected by research will benefit from your commitment. This baby has an exciting future. We can all have a share in that future and its development!

PART III

CULTURE-INFUSED COUNSELLING WITH NON-DOMINANT POPULATIONS

The chapters included in Part II of this text focus on the experiences and needs of particular non-dominant groups in Canadian society. These chapters by Canadian scholars are intended to provide the broad brush strokes required to gain a preliminary understanding of particular populations. The personal and professional experiences of the writers allow them to provide insights for counsellors in working with individuals or groups whose cultural identities include one or more non-dominant cultural affiliations.

Before introducing the chapters on non-dominant populations, however, we have provided a chapter on multiple and intersection identities that we hope you will apply as a conceptual lens as you read each of the remaining chapters. A weakness in much of the writing on multicultural competencies, as well as on the experiences and needs of non-dominant populations, is the tendency to treat various cultural identities using an additive rather than an intersectional model (e.g., women plus disabilities, or lesbian plus black) (Bowleg, 2008). As noted in Chapter 10, the problem with this model is that it fails to recognize that an individual's identity can only be understood through the exploring the unique social spaces that emerge at the intersection of these multiple identities (Bowleg). What this means is that in reading the chapters on specific non-dominant populations in this book, you cannot assume (a) that the themes identified in a particular chapter fit for every person from a non-dominant cultural group or (b) that you can understand the experience of an individual by simply adding your cumulative knowledge of two non-dominant groups together.

Instead, these chapters form a backdrop for exploring the unique intersection of identities that each client brings to the counselling experience. You are encouraged to hypothesize as you read about how a particular strategy or approach might differ if the client(s) also identified other aspects of cultural identity as salient to the particular presenting concern. The authors have attempted to provide some examples themselves. In Chapter 13, Justin looks at the intersections of gender, first- and second-generation immigrant status, and ethnicity. In Chapter 12, Arthur, Merali, and Djuraskovic also explore the impact of gender and age on refugee immigrant experiences. Blue, Darou, and Ruano pay attention to the unique experiences and needs of First Nations women (Chapter 11). Lalande and Laverty include a section on examining the impact of socio-economic status on women's experiences (Chapter 14). Collins and Oxenbury highlight the impact of membership in non-dominant ethnic communities on the process of lesbian identity development and the specific needs of lesbian youth and older lesbians (Chapter 15).

In each of these cases, you will gain additional information about the potential intersections of multiple identities. However, it is important to remember that these only really come to full light through the process of cultural inquiry with a specific client. For example, Alderson's Chapter 16 case study focuses on a gay man from a conservative ethnic and religious background. Arthur's Chapter 17 case study includes an examination of how gender role conflict can emerge for international students through the process of acculturation. These examples provide only a snapshot of the kinds of issues that may emerge as clients integrate various aspects of their cultural identities within various contexts of their lives.

The challenge before you, as the counsellor reading these chapters, is to continually ask yourself how a particular situation, presenting concern, or practice principle might differ if affected by the intersection of gender and ability; ethnicity and sexual orientation; age, immigration, and socio-economic status; ability and First Nations membership; and so on. There can be no complete answer to these questions, of course, outside of the working alliance you build with a particular client, dealing with a particular presenting concern that is affected by specific elements of cultural identities and experienced within specific social and historical contexts. Although we have organized these chapters according to these broader categories of cultural identity, we want you to apply them in a bottom-up rather than a top-down fashion (Chao & Moon, 2005). Following the model in Chapter 10, we place the unique cultural identity of each client at the core of the cultural analysis and move out from there to draw in appropriate information from the broader cultural group affiliations. Together, counsellors and clients must "work out, from within an interaction, what distinctions (values, story forms, practices, identity categories, etc.) will be meaningful" (Knapik & Miloti, 2006, p. 382). Applying the lens of complex, multiple, intersecting, fluid, and contextual cultural identities reduces the risk of stereotyping clients based on group affiliation or assuming that you can simply add awareness of one cultural group to another to create a full and comprehensive understanding of client experiences and cultural identities.

Although we have attempted to be inclusive in our writing, our understanding and experience of any issue or phenomenon is affected by our own personal identities and professional contexts. For that reason, we wish to provide a lens through which you may view the following chapters. At the beginning of each of the population-specific chapters, we have asked the writers to provide a glimpse into their own lives as members of various cultural communities, of their professional roles, of the social and political contexts in which they write, or of the personal histories that have shaped their perspective and intent. Each chapter addresses issues of counselling members of a particular non-dominant population in a way that draws on literature from a wide range of sources and reflects the breadth of experience within the authors' own worlds. We hope that you will read them in a similar way and add to your overall understanding from the wealth of information that exists in the lives of the many people from culturally diverse backgrounds with whom you knowingly or unknowingly interact on a day-to-day basis.

In keeping with the model for culture-infused counselling and the competency framework presented in Chapter 3, we argue that the core competency domains are equally applicable across all non-dominant populations in Canada. The specific competencies, outlined in terms of attitudes and beliefs, knowledge, and skills and defined in chapters 4 through 6, form the foundation for multicultural counselling competence with members of each of these specific populations. What you will gain from reading these chapters is an appreciation of new competencies, or a refinement of the original competencies, that are considered by the authors as important when you engage with an individual, family, or community from one of these populations. As you read, attend to competencies that you may need to add to your repertoire to feel confident and competent in your own practice.

Each of the authors of these chapters was asked to follow the same general outline for the chapters, with a particular focus on application of the multicultural competencies to the population of interest. Although writing styles naturally vary among our content experts, the following basic content will be covered in each chapter:

- A description of healthy functioning and psychosocial well-being;

- An explanation of cultural identity and the relationship of the particular non-dominant population to the dominant culture;

- An introduction to key theoretical concepts and principles;

- A description of common presenting concerns;

- An analysis of the counselling process with members of that population;

- A case study to bring to life some of the concepts and principles for counselling described in the chapter; and

- Examples of emergent issues and future directions for counselling and research.

We hope that this structure will enable you to compare and contrast the content across chapters, paying particular attention to the impact on individuals of holding multiple non-dominant identities. We are grateful for the excellent contributions of our content expert authors. We invite you to read these chapters with a view to seeing more clearly the individuals who stand behind the words and to embrace the diversity of cultural experiences and expressions that we are fortunate to have in this country.

CHAPTER 10
THE COMPLEXITY OF IDENTITY: APPRECIATING MULTIPLICITY AND INTERSECTIONALITY

Sandra Collins

Key Terms and Concepts		
• Culture-in-action • Essentialized / fixed identities • Fluidity of identity	• Hybridity • Intersectionality • Multiple identities • Personal is political	• Situational ethnicity • Social locations • Third space

Introduction

Throughout this book, we have argued that each individual, counsellor or client, holds a unique cultural identity, making all interactions between counsellor and client multicultural in nature. No two individuals, no matter how similar their backgrounds, life experiences, or heritage, will internalize culture in the same way; there will always be differences in worldview, values, assumptions about human nature and the change process, and meaning making. These gaps in worldview will be more or less significant, depending on the nature of the presenting concern and the context in which the client lives out the particular issue or experience. The bottom line is that we must assume cultural differences with all of our clients and apply a culture-infused approach to practice to ensure that we treat them with respect and fully integrate their worldviews into the counselling process.

We all share commonalities that bind us together as human beings; however, psychology has most often overlooked the common experience of difference. Recall the quote, "No matter how similar we are, there will be differences. No matter how different we are, there will be similarities" (Pederson, 2001, p. 19). Culture-infused counselling is a way of approaching professional practice in counselling and psychology that emphasizes the relevance and essential role of culture in all interactions between counsellors and clients. In the first part of the book, we focused on some of the core concepts that apply in implementing a culture-infused perspective in applied practice. We provided a starting point for developing both self-awareness and awareness of client cultural identities and for engaging with clients in the context of a culturally sensitive working alliance. We then expanded that focus to include the domain of social justice. We also took a very close look at the impact of culture and multicultural contexts on assessment, professional ethics, and research.

As we have argued throughout this book, we see culture-infused counselling as providing a bridge between the emic (group specific) and etic (universal) perspectives. This model acknowledges that all counselling is multicultural and that all counsellors must possess foundational multicultural competencies for effective and ethical practice. Each individual presents with a unique set of personal cultural identities that impacts on her or his way of viewing and being in the world. Culture-infused counselling also recognizes, however, that group affiliation may provide valuable insights into the cultural identities of group members and that as counsellors and psychologists we are responsible for obtaining cultural information about the groups we work with. In the latter portion of the book, the chapters will focus on specific non-dominant populations and provide further insight into their cultural experiences and perspectives, as well as principles for effective culture-infused practice with members of these particular populations.

Before we proceed to these chapters on various non-dominant populations, it is important to revisit the concept of cultural identity in more depth. In Chapter 4, we introduced the metaphor of the kaleidoscope as a reflection of the complexity and fluidity of cultural identity. This chapter will pick up on that image and explore the challenge and privilege of working with individuals with multiple and intersecting cultural identities. There has been a tendency in the psychological literature for silos to be erected in an effort to ensure that the voices and needs of particular non-dominant groups are acknowledged. For example, the feminist and multicultural streams developed as relatively distinct and separate fields in spite of the synergies in their assumptions and principles for practice. Collins (in press) explored some of these commonalities and highlighted the shifts in recent years to a more inclusive stance that not only recognizes but, in some cases, centralizes the experiences of those with multiple non-dominant identities who tend to be most marginalized in society.

This chapter will take an in-depth look at cultural identity as a complex, fluid, intersectional, and dynamic phenomenon. It is intended to provide a contextual framework for critically analyzing and integrating the information on particular non-dominant populations in the second half of the book. The key question raised in this chapter is: What is the effect of holding multiple, intersecting, and sometimes conflicting cultural identities on clients' development, self-perception, and experiences? As counsellors, a secondary question then becomes: How do the multiple cultural identities of a particular client impact building a trusting and respectful working alliance, case conceptualization, establishment of the goals and tasks involved in the counselling process, and so on?

Viewing Diversity from a Multidimensional Perspective

We have attempted in our framework of culture-infused counselling competencies in Chapter 3 to reflect a broad definition of culture and to integrate principles of practice from feminist and other streams. We then included in the latter portion of this book chapters written by and about members of particular non-dominant populations. However, we recognized that taking this both/and approach – establishing common principles for infusing culture into practice with all clients and attending to the worldviews, historical contexts, and experiences of individuals from particular cultural groups – requires a delicate balancing act. It is easy to broaden our perspective in this way and still fail to truly account for and respect the complexity of identity within an individual by continuing to look at diversity from a unidimensional perspective and not fully appreciating the multiple and sometimes shifting identities that individuals hold over their lifetime (Bridges, Selvidge, & Matthews, 2003; Garrett & Barret, 2003). It is our belief that both general principles for culture-infused counselling and population-specific knowledge feed into our understanding and awareness of our own culture and the culture of clients, but is it through the working alliance with a particular client, facing a particular challenge, in a particular context, that the true impact of cultural identities can be appreciated. It is also in this context that the importance of full appreciation of the multiplicity and complexity of cultural identity emerges.

The exclusive focus on race and ethnicity in much of the earlier multicultural literature parallels the largely exclusive focus on gender in the early feminist literature (Collins, in press). Both fields have been criticized for failing to adopt a more inclusive and integrative perspective (Moodley, 2007; Reynolds & Constantine, 2004; Whalen et al., 2004; Williams & Barber, 2004). The tendency has been to focus on the commonalities among all members of a particular ethnic group or of all women without recognizing the intersection of multiple non-dominant identities (Arredondo, Tovar-Blank, & Parham, 2008; Ludvig, 2006; Valentine, 2007). Other dimensions of cultural experience have been marginalized or treated separately and poorly integrated – for example, sexual orientation, ability, and socio-economic status (Adair, 2005; Bowman et al., 2001; Brown, Reipe, & Coffey, 2005; Lowe & Mascher, 2001; Palombi & Mundt, 2006; Silverstein, 2006). The problem with this approach is that many of the individuals that these fields of research and practice were intended to support have been left out of the dialogue by virtue of the very thing that should have brought their voice to the surface – their complex cultural identities.

There have been significant developments in recent years, in feminist theory in particular, that have emphasized the importance of attending to multiple dimensions of women's experiences (Evans, Kincade, Marbley, & Seem, 2005; Gustafson, 2007) and to focusing attention on those women and girls with multiple non-dominant identities who are most marginalized in society (Anderson et al., 2003; Canadian Research Institute for the Advancement of Women [CRIAW], 2006; Dossa, 2008). Relational-cultural theory has emerged as a means of integrating the broader spectrum of cultural experience into current models of women's identity development (Jordan & Walker, 2004; Jordan, Walker, & Hartling, 2004). This model is addressed by Lalande and Laverty in Chapter 14. The strength of the feminist mandate, the **personal is political,** has become focused on *social transformation of the systems that continue to oppress and marginalize those most vulnerable* (Evans et al.; Morrow, Hawxhurst, Montes de Vegas,

Abousleman, & Castaneda, 2006). Much of the current feminist literature now leads the way in centralizing the voices and experiences of marginalized women and girls (Dossa; Gustafson; Jordan et al.; Suyemoto & Liem, 2007). Some argue that a new model of feminist multicultural counselling is required to appreciate the "braidings of racism; sexism; heterosexism; and other forms of privilege, power, and oppression (Morrow et al., p. 236).

As noted in Chapter 3, the relative stability of multicultural competencies over time has unfortunately meant that they are not reflective of more recent emphasis in both the multicultural and feminist literature on the intersection of gender and ethnicity or sexism and racism (Barret et al., 2005; Silverstein, 2006). One of the key points we have attempted to make in this book is that culture must be broadly defined to include dimensions of ethnicity, gender, sexual orientation, age, ability, socio-economic status, and religion (Israel, 2006; Moodley, 2007). Although most authors now argue that culture must be broadly defined to include all dimensions of cultural identity (Arredondo & Perez, 2006), and models have been introduced that take the multidimensionality of human development into account (D'Andrea & Heckman, 2008), we noted that the current American Psychological Association (APA) (2003b) *Guidelines on Multicultural Education, Training, Research, Practice, and Organizational Change for Psychologists* remain exclusively focused on racial and ethnic groups, to the exclusion even of gender. Instead, separate documents have been developed, such as the *Guidelines for Psychotherapy with Lesbian, Gay, and Bisexual Clients* (APA, 1998) and the *Guidelines for Psychological Practice with Older Adults* (APA, 2003a). We are not suggesting that these guidelines are inappropriate or unnecessary; in fact, we see them as providing essential information for working with these particular populations. The problem is in the lack of systematic integration and links to the concept of multicultural competence.

Recognizing and Valuing the Uniqueness of All Individuals

The cultural identity model introduced in Chapter 4 is revisited here to provide a conceptual framework for viewing the information on specific cultural groups in the latter portion of the book. Chapter 4 provided a detailed explanation of personal, contextual, universal, cultural, and ideological factors. The focus in this chapter is on what it actually means to incorporate multiple layers of culture into our understanding of clients' worldviews (Ludvig, 2006; Pope-Davis & Coleman, 2001; Valentine, 2007).

Collins (in press) introduced the metaphor of the kaleidoscope as a means of understanding the fluid, interactional, and multidimensional nature of cultural identity. If you hold a kaleidoscope steady, a beautiful pattern appears through the lens based on the positioning of the coloured beads and the flow of light through the reflective sides of the instrument. Shifting the kaleidoscope even slightly or changing the environment will result in a different, unique, but equally beautiful image. Opening the kaleidoscope and adding a different combination of coloured beads will again produce a new display. In the same way, each individual's cultural identity will evolve and change over time and in different contexts. In this section, we will explore some of the factors that must be taken into account as we work with individuals with multiple non-dominant identities. Speaking of the impact of these multiple factors on the landscape of society, Gerstein, Rountree, and Orgonez (2007) echoed this metaphor in their assertion that counselling needs to "shift its lens from an individual microscope to a vibrant, multicultural, kaleidoscope of social patterns" (p. 375). Others have used the metaphor of a *cultural mosaic* to describe the "multiple indicators of culture used to describe an individual" (Chao & Moon, 2005).

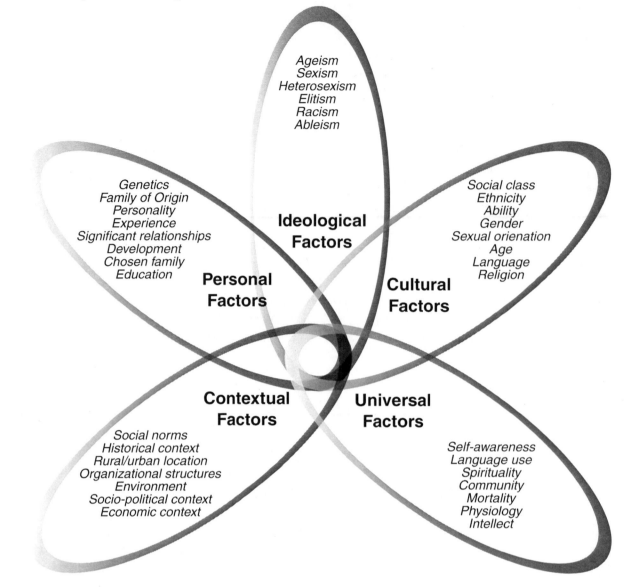

Ageism
Sexism
Heterosexism
Elitism
Racism
Ableism

Genetics
Family of Origin
Personality
Experience
Significant relationships
Development
Chosen family
Education

Ideological Factors

Social class
Ethnicity
Ability
Gender
Sexual orienation
Age
Language
Religion

Personal Factors

Cultural Factors

Contextual Factors

Universal Factors

Social norms
Historical context
Rural/urban location
Organizational structures
Environment
Socio-political context
Economic context

Self-awareness
Language use
Spirituality
Community
Mortality
Physiology
Intellect

Figure 1. Factors influencing cultural identity.

Multiple Intersecting Identities

One of the risks of simply adding new guidelines for various populations is that this approach fails to appreciate the well-known systems theory principle that the *whole is greater than the sum of the parts.* In other words, being female and having a disability cannot be understood by simply adding the dimension of ability to gender (Bowleg, 2008; Ludvig, 2006). An individual's identity can only be understood through exploring the unique social space that emerges at the intersection of these multiple identities (Bowleg; Moodley, 2007). The individual's experience of disability, for example, may be defined differently because of the intersection of gender; each must be viewed holistically, inclusively, and interactionally (Morris & Bunjun, 2007). Ludvig defined **intersectionality** as "*the merging and mingling of multiple markers of difference* [italics added]" (p. 246). If gender, for example, is represented by blue glass beads in the kaleidoscope, adding or deleting these glass beads will shift the entire pattern that emerges, potentially redefining other elements of the whole image. Yellow no longer shifts to show as green in some areas; red does not mute into shades of purple. Individuals do not experience various dimensions of their cultural identities separately or asynchronously (Valentine, 2007). Similarly, as counsellors, it is our responsibility to attend to the intersections and interactions of these multiple dimensions of cultural identity (Arredondo et al., 2008; Brown et al., 2005; Mahalingam & Leu, 2005; Silverstein, 2006).

Each individual also experiences and manages her or his cultural identities in a unique way (Collins, in press; Valentine, 2007). In Chapter 13, Justin explores the lives of second-generation East Indian women, identifying some of the common themes that emerge for members of this particular group. However, these still represent broad brushstrokes that can only be understood and applied in the context of the life of a particular woman of colour and her unique combination of intersecting and interacting cultural identities. In this case, treating gender and ethnicity as separate factors risks losing the meaning attached to being female within this particular ethnic context or the importance of East Indian or second-generation immigrant identity to the experience of gender. Counsellors must be open to exploring the unique self-identification of clients on each of the dimensions of their identities.

One of the criticisms of earlier feminist writing was that the focus was predominantly on White, western, middle-class, and able-bodied women (Evans et al., 2005; Silverstein, 2006); when ethnicity was included, it was most often treated as secondary to gender (Bowman et al., 2001). Although gender-based analysis is essential to challenging the lingering effects of patriarchal systems, prioritizing this aspect of identity over others can lead to ethnocentrism, marginalizing ethnicity and other important aspects of women's experience (CRIAW, 2006; Gustafson, 2007; Morrow et al., 2006). For some women and in some contexts, racism may have more impact than sexism (Zerbe Enns, Sinacore, Ancis, & Phillips, 2004). The same risk exists within the multicultural field where the exclusive emphasis on ethnicity has led to a marginalization of gender and a failure to attend to the intersections of gender and ethnicity, sexism and racism (Barret et al., 2005; Bowman & King, 2003; Silverstein, 2006). Although both fields are expanding to become more inclusive in their definitions and analysis of cultural identity, Lalande and Laverty raise concerns in Chapter 14 that the pendulum may have swung too far towards including all dimensions of identity under the umbrella of multiculturalism, which results in a weakening of the specific focus on gender. Their chapter provides an important contribution to this book by highlighting some of the key issues and principles in working with women. The continuing challenge for each of us is to ensure that the relative emphasis placed on any of these cultural identity factors is driven by the relationship with a particular client and her or his unique cultural identities.

Identity Conflict and Dissonance

The process of negotiating and maintaining multiple intersecting identities requires active and continuous effort on the part of many individuals. Each element not only affects the experience and definition of others, but the various elements may result in conflict and dissonance (Collins, in press; Lowe & Mascher, 2001; Riviere, 2004; Valentine, 2007). This discord emerges because cultural identities are closely tied to values and bringing together two or more cultural identities can result in values conflicts (Chao & Moon, 2005). In Chapter 15, Collins and Oxenbury challenge the assertion of some of the literature on lesbian identity development that holds up *living out* as the healthy end point for all lesbians. Conflict often emerges between sexual orientation and ethnic community affiliation, leaving individuals with the difficult choice of hiding an important aspect of their identity in order to maintain the support of their cultural community. For many, it may be more important to maintain family and cultural ties than to be able to freely express homosexual identity in all contexts. As counsellors, it is important that we not impose narrow assumptions about what constitutes healthy resolutions to the tensions across cultural identities because each individual must decide how to navigate complex cultural affiliations (Lowe & Mascher). Where these values conflicts occur, behaviour can become less consistent or predictable and context becomes even more influential on the expression of cultural identities (Chao & Moon). However, Moodley (2007) argued that these paradoxes and contradictions must be recognized as evidence of the resilience of these individuals in actively constructing and reconstructing cultural identities and not pathologized as part of the problem.

To some degree, this potential for tension between various aspects of cultural identity has supported the emergence of various silos within the profession (Collins, in press). The worldviews and values of feminism and multiculturalism may be pitted against one another, potentially creating tensions within the counsellor or client or even between them (Morrow et al., 2006; Reynolds & Constantine, 2004). For example, women of colour may have a strong allegiance to cultural and/or religious norms that include gendered roles and responsibilities. For some, cultural affiliations may be more important than issues of gender equality (Bowman et al., 2001). In fact, they may perceive challenges to gender inequity as fracturing the solidarity of the community in its attempts to take on racial oppression by the dominant culture (Evans et al., 2005). Counsellors must be careful to examine their own cultural affiliations and assumptions and to explore with each individual the potential losses and gains involved in prioritizing one cultural identity over the other. Raising challenges to cultural beliefs that are oppressive to women is completely appropriate in some contexts and with some clients; however, counsellors must carefully examine whether their own assumptions about gender and sexuality are culture-, class-, or ability-bound (Bowman et al.; Israel, 2003).

Creation of Hybrid Identities

In many cases, the tensions that emerge for individuals with multiple non-dominant identities are between their particular identities and those of the dominant culture. Several other chapters address the concepts of acculturation, assimilation, and bicultural identity development as they apply to the process of adjusting to encounters between one cultural identity and other (often non-dominant cultural identity and the dominant culture). See Chapter 4 for identity development models, chapters 15 and 16 for sexual identity models, and chapters 11, 12, and 13 for models related to encounters between non-dominant ethnic groups and the dominant culture. In some cases, individuals manage multiple identities so that they are relatively independent of one another or move between two or more cultural contexts, assimilating into the more dominant culture (Chao & Moon, 2005).

In other cases, however, individuals create a new identity that differs from either or any of the source identities. In Chapter 13, Justin emphasizes the active construction of personal identity as these second-generation women of colour negotiate the demands of intergenerational and intercultural contexts. What emerges for some individuals is a **third space,** defined as *the borders between cultural identities that reflect a blending of various cultural factors* (Barcinski & Kalia, 2005). These women navigate between traditional and non-traditional cultural contexts either simultaneously or sequentially, creating a new identity that combines elements of each context into a unique persona (Barcinski & Kalia). This *merging of identities to facilitate fluidity across contrasting social contexts* is referred to as **hybridity** (Bhabha, 1990). According to Racine (2008, p. 18), the third space "represents both a contradictory and ambivalent space where cultural differences are to be negotiated to produce hybrid cultures."

Fluidity of Cultural Identities

Another challenge to fully appreciating the complexity of cultural identity stems from the continued presentation of many aspects of identity in a dichotomous, polarized manner, as end points on a line or distinct categorical variables (Bepko & Johnson, 2000; Ludvig, 2006; Lowe & Mascher, 2001). Bridges and colleagues (2003) pointed to the Aboriginal cultural perspective as useful in assisting in reconceptualizing thinking about the various dimensions of culture to allow for both a more **fluid and continuous** understanding of **identity** and a means of integrating multiple components of identity. The First Nations worldview is further expanded on by Blue, Darou, and Ruano in Chapter 11. In this perspective, *various identity factors form points on a circle rather than on a line*, as illustrated in Figure 2. A client may identify as predominantly homosexual, but have a more androgynous sense of gender identity (A); alternatively, a client may have a clear sense of masculine identity, but be bisexual (B). The variability in expression of sexual orientation and gender are addressed more fully in Chapter 15 by Collins and Oxenbury and Chapter 16 by Alderson. As shown in the kaleidoscope in Figure 1, other dimensions can be added to this model to get a sense of the wholeness of a client's self-identification at a particular time. Individuals may also find themselves shifting over time in various aspects of their identity, a concept more easily accommodated through the circular intersecting identities model.

Embracing a more fluid and circular model of identity introduces an infinite number of possible points of identity intersection and normalizes variability in a way that may tend to reduce our human tendency to place value judgments on anything perceived as different from the norm (Garrett & Barret, 2003). This position may be challenged on socio-political grounds, however, by both non-dominant cultural communities and the dominant culture if there are benefits to holding to more distinct categorizations of identity that permit clarity about *us* and *them*. This phenomenon is sometimes evidenced in the lesbian community, for example, where bisexual women are characterized as sitting on the fence or holding on to heterosexual privilege (Rust, 2000). Likewise, the European majority in Canada continues to hold a vested interest in keeping persons of colour in a distinct category, in spite of the facts that inter-racial partnerships have existed in Canada since the time of colonialization and that there is little empirical support for the validity or utility of race as a category (Atkinson, 2004). What is required is a fundamental shift in attitudes and beliefs among Canadians that truly allows individuals to self-identify according to their own personal realities and embraces diversity in a way that no longer requires adherence to an *us* and *them* model.

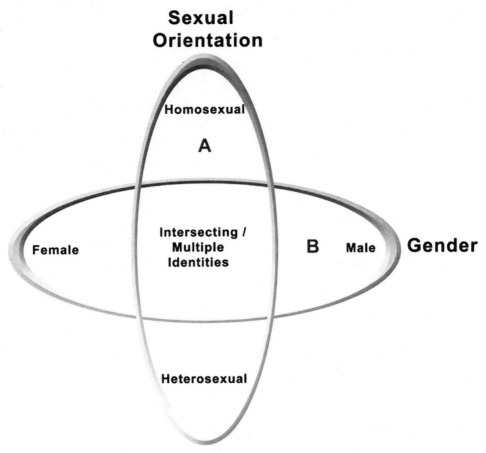

Figure 2. Multiple, fluid, and intersecting personal cultural identities.

Contextual Nature of Cultural Identities

Embracing a more fluid view of various dimensions of cultural identity requires us to release our hold on the existence of **essentialized or fixed identities** (Collins, in press; Racine, 2008). There is no such thing as *pure gender identity (male/female), sexuality orientation (gay/straight), ethnicity (White/Coloured),* and so on (Mahalingam & Leu, 2005). The interactions of various dimensions of identity, the fluidity of each element of identity, and the influence of context must all be taken into account (Barcinski & Kalia, 2005; Ludvig, 2006). Counsellors must attend to the **social locations** that influence individual identities, which are defined by *personal, familial, and professional situations; historical, social, economic, religious, and political contexts; and past and present forces* (Morris & Bunjun, 2007). This requires them to accept multiple influences on self-definition. It is also important to recognize that culture is expressed in different ways in different contexts and at different times. Meaning-making is context-specific and interaction-specific (Knapik & Miloti, 2006).

> ...culture as a thing is not 'discoverable' and 'knowable' in any final sense. What is interesting is how in particular counseling interactions certain descriptions of persons and lives are made relevant and not others; what meanings are used to make sense of what was going on; how alternate versions are undermined; or how explorations of cultural elements help to move counseling conversations forward. (Knapik & Miloti, 2006, p. 381)

In Chapter 12, Arthur, Merali, and Djuraskovic describe the experiences and challenges of immigrants and refugees. For individuals who are either gradually or suddenly, voluntarily or involuntarily, transported into a different cultural context, the perception and expression of cultural identity can undergo a dramatic transformation through the processes of acculturation and adaptation, which the authors explore in depth in that chapter. Using our image of the kaleidoscope, new coloured beads may be added to the mix, the background changes, and the positioning of light through the mirrors shifts to create a new image of self that may, at first, appear foreign even to the immigrant or refugee. It is essential that counsellors recognize the importance not only of the current expression of cultural identities but of the shifts in identity over time (Barcinski & Kalia, 2006).

In Chapter 13, Justin introduces the term **situational ethnicity** to refer to *the impact of context on the expression of personal identities of women of colour*. This principle applies for the expression of other forms of cultural identity. Depending on the social context, each individual draws on particular aspects or combinations of their cultural identities (Chao & Moon, 2005). In Chapter 16, Alderson introduces the ecological model of gay male identity, which emphasizes the individual, the environment, and the interaction between the two. The process of gay identity development often evolves over a long period of time, in large part due to the external constraints of familial and social contexts.

Within- Versus Between-Group Differences

One of the main reasons for providing you with this detailed analysis of the complex, fluid, contextual, and interactional nature of cultural identities is to reinforce the idea that within-group differences can be as significant (both in terms of magnitude and importance) as between-group differences (Collins, in press). The multicultural movement has contributed significantly to highlighting with-in group differences (D'Andrea & Heckman, 2008). In Chapter 11, Blue, Darou, and Ruano note that there are over 630 First Nations communities in Canada, speaking 53 different languages. They caution that, although their chapter provides insights into common values, experiences, and theoretical principles related to First Nations peoples, care must be taken not to make generalizations to all individuals. Not only do cultural differences exist among the various First Nations groups, but each individual will hold more or less tightly to Aboriginal cultural heritage based on social locations, personal and family history, age and generational impact, historical and cultural contexts, and so on. Similar within-group variability has been noted for persons with disabilities (Brown et al., 2005), women of colour (Bowman & King, 2003), sexual minority populations (Zerbe Enns et al., 2004), and others. Immigration and globalization have resulted in a blurring of boundaries across various ethnic communities (Barcinski & Kalia, 2005). Although Arthur provides some general principles for understanding cross-cultural transitions and supporting the success of international students in Chapter 17, she makes it clear that other identity factors such as gender, family norms, or nationality are important in understanding the experiences of individual students.

Although I've lived with chronic illness since my early 20's, I never fully incorporated my physical limitations into my sense of self. For many years, I treated illness as something outside of myself that I tried to control and compartmentalize – like an annoying but persistent extended family member. I transformed myself into a head on a stick for this, and other reasons, and lived my life with as little attention as possible to pain or physical challenges. This limited my ability to be fully knowable and present to myself and others.

At some point in my late 20's, I decided to befriend the beast and changed my internal strategies for managing my illness. However, my experiences remained largely invisible to those around me, and I chose to keep things that way. In retrospect, I realize that this had mostly to do with my own internalized fears and biases about being identified as someone with a physical disability. I didn't process at the time the implications of these internalized cultural messages for my sensitivity and openness to the experiences and identities of others who are also less able-bodied. I also limited my ability to hold appropriate personal and professional boundaries to maintain optional health.

As I reflect on the evolution of my own cultural identities, I recognize a number of core themes: shame, isolation, internalization of socio-cultural biases followed by freedom, celebration, and sense of well-being. Integrating my physical disabilities into my sense of self is likely not my final frontier and it remains one of my growing edges.

Personal reflection – Sandra Collins

Relationship of Cultural Identities to Power and Privilege

Although this chapter is focused on the individual's experience and active construction of a unique kaleidoscope of cultural identities, the "collective effects of social, political, and economical forces in shaping people's identities or multiple subjectivities" (Racine, 2008, p. 17) must also be taken into account. Counselling is criticized by anthropologists for taking culture and defining it as an individual phenomenon and, in so doing, disconnecting the individual from the broader cultural contexts that shape their identities (Gerstein et al., 2007). As noted in Chapter 4, the concepts of culture and cultural identities are highly politicized ideological constructs that cannot be separated from their association with social and economic power and privilege (Gustafson, 2005). There are still strongly held implicit (and sometimes explicit) assumptions that being White, male, heterosexual, able-bodied, Christian, young, and upper-middle class are *normal* and *desirable*.

The emergence of both feminist and multicultural movements have been in response, in part, to this patriarchal and ethnocentric paradigm that has lead to the oppression of particular groups in society and has also pervaded much of the traditional western psychological literature (Evans et al., 2005; Morrow et al., 2006). We see new waves of challenges and victories in the area of human rights over time that change the dominant discourses in society (Lowe & Mascher, 2001). The legalization of gay marriage in Canada is a good example. Nonetheless, it is important to keep clearly in mind that culture and cultural identities cannot be assumed to be neutral concepts.

Culture is most often defined in terms of *otherness*. We are aware in writing this book that we are attempting to walk a very fine line between: a) sending a clear message that everyone, every counsellor and every client, holds a cultural identity or identities that have a significant impact on the counselling process and b) there is important information to be gained by examining what is unique about particular cultural groups. Culture is not something that defines some groups in society and not others. Nonetheless, we have chosen to shine the spotlight on particular non-dominant groups in our efforts to address the continued potential for unintentional harm based on both ethnocentric and acultural practices in psychology (recall the discussion of colour consciousness and blindness in Chapter 4). The risk, of course, is that we reinforce the stereotypic belief that culture belongs only to non-dominant populations or that it is defined in relationship or in contrast to the dominant White, male, heterosexual, able-bodied, Christian, young, and upper-middle class cultural norms. On the flip side, to treat all cultural expressions as neutral and to fail to emphasize the continued reality that the definitions of normal, acceptable, and healthy are monopolized by the dominant culture does a disservice particularly to those with multiple non-dominant identities. As noted in Chapter 1, in spite of our public policies of inclusivity, culture, broadly defined, continues to have serious implications for social, economic, and political status. It is critical that we not lose sight of the negative meanings attached to various social locations (Gustafson, 2005). Our recognition of this leads to the emphasis on social justice in this book.

In addition, full awareness of counsellor and client cultural identities is limited, apart from an examination of the relationship of cultural identity to power and oppression (Bowman et al., 2001; Whalen et al., 2004). These broader ideological forces are noted in the kaleidoscope model of cultural identity in Figure 1. It is the counsellor's responsibility to examine both the specific impacts of these systems of power on client cultural identity development and the impacts of cultural identity on power and privilege or, more often, disempowerment and disprivilege (Morrow et al., 2006). Although we have suggested that each individual is an active architect in their unique and idiosyncratic expression of cultural identity, this must be balanced by an awareness of the limitations and barriers imposed on this self-definition by the contexts of each individual's lived experiences (Rivière, 2004; Valentine, 2007). Rivière noted the "multiple cycles of oppression" (p. 223) that have constrained her own self-definition as a black, female Canadian. Palombi and Mundt (2006) explored the relationship of women with disabilities to the dominant culture, noting that difficult choices have to be made about whether to stress sameness or difference and whether to aspire to integrate into the male-dominant/able-bodied society or to foster subcultural values and experiences that honour gender and differential ability. Examination of these layers of oppression must become part of our formulation of understanding of each client's presenting concerns (Israel, 2003; Lowe & Mascher, 2001).

What we have attempted to do in this book is to find a balance between providing general principles for culture-infused counselling that are applicable to both dominant and non-dominant cultural experiences while still arguing that categorizations of identity are important to understanding the common assumptions and general themes that reflect the experiences of particular non-dominant populations and to retain our commitment to fighting against social oppression. It is difficult to label and analyze systems of power and oppression without reference to more generalized categories of experience (Morris & Bunjun, 2007). This balancing act has been acknowledged by other writers (Razack, 1994; Valentine, 2007).

Moving Beyond Emic and Etic Perspectives

In Chapter 5, we highlighted the common factors approach (Fischer, Jerome, & Atkinson, 1998; Fukuyama, 1990) as one possible foundation for linking the emic and etic perspectives in multicultural counselling. We then argued that the framework for culture-infused counselling competencies provides a more comprehensive means of identifying the specific attitudes, knowledge, and skills that are essential to competent practice across cultures while honouring the differences in perspective and needs within various cultural groups. Others have argued that what need to be explored are the actual change processes that may be similar or different across cultures (Daya, 2001; Ridley & Kleiner, 2003). As we begin, however, to expand our view of cultural identities to a more fluid, interacting, and multidimensional perspective, it becomes clear that holding rigidly to cultural labels as the means for distinguishing particular group needs; preferences for counselling styles, skills, and strategies; or preferred counselling outcomes is simply not realistic or conceptually justifiable (Coleman &Wampold, 2003). How, for example, do we develop an intervention process or a set of specific counselling principles for working with lesbian women of colour who have experienced an adult-onset disability? To attempt to do so also ignores the social construction of culture, the meaning of which must be derived in the context of specific interactions (Knapik & Miloti, 2006).

There is considerable evidence that it is commonality in worldview rather than group affiliation that provides the foundation for establishment of a solid working alliance and ultimately for success in counselling (Fischer et al., 1998). However, there is little psychological or counselling literature that explores the essence of worldview differences and the implications of specific elements of worldview for counselling. For example, rather than designing an approach to counselling for First Nations Canadians per se, perhaps we are better off investing our time in developing an approach to counselling that honours a particular worldview commonly held by members of First Nations. In Chapter 11, Blue and colleagues provide a conceptual framework for tying the principles for counselling First Nations individuals to specific elements of worldview. This provides an opportunity for counsellors to explore the degree to which these underlying assumptions about human nature and the change process fit for a particular Aboriginal client, in a particular context, who potential holds other assumptions based on multiple and intersecting identities. This analysis of worldview may then provide evidence of who will benefit from a particular intervention strategy.

It is time to move beyond simply cultural group as the independent variable and look at components of worldview as the key factors that both provide the foundation for an effective working alliance and facilitate establishment of culturally responsive goals and tasks of counselling. This may mean revisiting specific interventions to articulate the components of worldview that form the core assumptions upon which the intervention is founded. It would also mean assessing client characteristics carefully for matches in worldview factors for various approaches or intervention strategies. This shift in perspective would allow us to hold less tightly to group affiliation generally and recognize the fluid and ambiguous nature of cultural identities, searching for commonalities across as well as between various cultural groups. This must be approached with caution, however, lest we create from worldview what has been done with culture in the past – some form of distinct and essentialized categories rather than constructs that find expression and meaning in new ways within the context of the therapeutic alliance. Knapik and Miloti (2006) introduced the term **culture-in-action**, which we interpret to mean that *culture exists and becomes meaningful to the counselling process only as it is explored, applied, and reflected upon in the immediate and bidirectional interaction between counsellor and client.*

As I write this section on fluidity of identities and encourage you to hold more tentatively to group affiliation, I acknowledge my own conflictual feelings about these statements. The conflict for me arises from the sense of potential loss of the strong sense of community that is supported by maintaining clear boundaries between homosexual and heterosexual worlds. I realize the tendency for me to organize my own life, at least my life outside of work, around an us and them perspective. I sometimes base my affiliations more on common non-dominant group status and less on commonalities in values, beliefs, and worldviews.

At the same time, I realize that there is a commonality of experience that creates the sense of community and that to a large degree it is the other-imposed us and them status that has lead to that collective mindset. I group together with other lesbians, in part, because we are not treated with equality in the world around us. It is the sense of disempowerment and experience of oppression that forms the glue that overrides the many differences in our ways of viewing and being in the world. I've pondered this often as I have struggled to understand the relationship of feminism to the lesbian community and have come to realize that women with women are not necessarily going to understand or hold a feminist perspective any more or less than women with men. The lesbian community is just as diverse as any other in perspectives on gender, ethnicity, and other cultural factors.

So what would it be like then if over time the heterosexual world let go of the need to maintain the façade of clear and distinct boundaries between us and them? How would the lesbian community change and evolve if terms like normal, family, marriage, etc. were actually redefined and embraced by all as inclusive rather than exclusive variables? I don't know the answer to these questions because there has never been a period in history where we were able as human beings to let go of our fear of difference, to release our hold on resources that belong to all people, and to give up the need to protect, sometimes with our lives, our own definitions of what is truly human.

And yet this may be the very challenge before us if we are to fully embrace the cultural mosaic that, as Canadians, we hold up as part of our national identity. The challenge is one that I also face as I look beyond cultural distinctions to find connections with people who share a commonality in perspective/worldview and simultaneously let go of the need for that perspective to be validated, supported, or mirrored by others in my world.

Personal reflection – Sandra Collins

Social Justice as a Common Thread

We need to be cautious that our approach is not interpreted to mean that group affiliation is not important or that we are placing the emphasis on the ways in which all human beings and human experiences are similar. In contrast, we are arguing that all human beings are to some degree different, even within the cultural group(s) that they affiliate with. Group membership provides one potential clue to understanding individual cultural identity, but it must be examined in the context of the individual client's worldview, identity formation, and social locations. Research on client perspectives clearly indicates that clients are looking for therapists to demonstrate awareness and openness to their specific needs and issues (Malley & Tasker, 2007).

One of the elements of worldview that emerges from this analysis is the common experience of cultural oppression (Brown et al., 2005) and the impact it has on self-definition, interpersonal relationships, career advancement, and overall well-being. Membership in a non-dominant group often results in experiences different from those of the dominant population (Malley & Tasker, 2007). The process of gender role analysis and power analysis described by Lalande and Laverty in Chapter 14 includes examples of the kinds of counselling processes that may support understanding of the impact of cultural oppression, leading to interventions tailored to meet the needs of clients who have internalized these experiences into their worldview.

The common experience of discrimination and disprivilege serve to energize and activate individuals and groups to take a stand against cultural oppression (Israel, 2006). Collins (in press) has argued that the social justice agenda provides one possibility for bridging the divide among various specializations in psychological practice, including the feminist and multicultural models. Morrow and colleagues (2006) introduced a new model of feminist multicultural counselling that explores the intersection of various forms of cultural oppression. The recent *Handbook for Social Justice in Counselling Psychology* is evidence of a move in this direction. It was developed through a coalition between the APA Section for Lesbian, Gay, and Bisexual Awareness, Section for Ethnic and Racial Diversity, and Section for the Advancement of Women (Fouad,

Gerstein, & Toporek, 2006). Silverstein (2006, p. 22) asserted that "feminism and multiculturalism are inextricably linked because the goal of both is social justice." "The dream of each ideology is to shape a world in which people can operate fairly and without biases" (Bowman et al., 2001, p. 797).

Savin-Williams (2006) hypothesized that the need for specific cultural labels will become less and less important as there is increased social and political acceptance of various non-dominant populations. He noted the rejection of the label *gay* among many youth in favour of a more fluid identity awareness, an openness to attraction to either sex, or a refusal to be labeled and placed in a particular box. All of the labels we apply to non-dominant and dominant populations are social constructions that serve a purpose in a particular context and point in history; over time, the need for these labels may fade into the history books (Savin-Williams). Unfortunately, we have a long way to go before this become a reality. In the short term, many labels are adopted by specific cultural groups, in part, as a means of standing together against social oppression. As you move into Part II of the book, we encourage you to read each chapter in the context of the principles outlined here and throughout the book and to find your own balance between learning from the cultural information provided by and about particular non-dominant groups and applying this in the context of real people with complex, idiosyncratic, and often multiple identities.

Chapter Summary

The principles of culture-infused counselling, which emphasize the idiosyncratic and contextual nature of cultural identity while still acknowledging the various cultures that make up the Canadian cultural mosaic, may offer a starting point for the professions of counselling and psychology to embrace this more fluid view of culture. However, we must all be willing to hold less tightly and exclusively to our cultural group affiliations and to embrace diversity in a new and more profound way. This chapter has provided further insight into the complex, fluid, intersectional, contextual, and often hybrid identities of individuals who hold multiple identities, particularly multiple non-dominant identities. Rather than treating these individuals as an exception to the rule, which has traditionally resulted in their marginalization, both in society and in psychological theory and practice, we have argued that understanding cultural identity from their perspective provides an important framework for approaching our work with all clients and offers to inform the practice of counselling and psychology generally.

The tendency historically has been for different streams of psychology to emerge in response to and as advocates for various non-dominant populations. For example, feminist, multicultural, queer, and other special interest groups continue to serve a vital role in providing insight into the needs and experiences of underserved populations. However, it is also vital for these movements to come together to: a) more fully address the needs of those with multiple, non-dominant identities; b) join forces to advocate for social justice; and c) demand a lasting transformation of mainstream theory and practice. We have argued in this chapter that fully recognizing the diversity of human experience and shifting cultural identity to the central core of counselling practice has the potential to move feminism and multiculturalism into the mainstream and to facilitate the application of the tenets of both to culture-infused practice with all clients (Silverstein, 2006; West, 2005; Williams & Barber, 2004).

Conclusion

Although some may argue that the attempts to merge the fields or at least the insights and practice guidelines of feminist, queer, multicultural, and other psychological streams may weaken the political agenda of each one, there are both practical and theoretical limitations to privileging one type of oppression over another, based primarily on the multiplicity and complexity of individual identities: "It is not possible to separate out the categories of gender, race, class, and sexuality, nor to explain inequities through a single framework" (Valentine, 2007, p. 12). In Chapter 13, Justin warns us that building our conceptualization of any person, particularly members of non-dominant populations, based on "monolithic and singular identity categories assumes a reductionist perspective that devalues all other dimensions of the individual" (p. 322). Further, the continued lack of dialogue and convergence of ideologies tends to leave the responsibility for the negotiation of multiple and complex identities with the individual, further marginalizing them from both mainstream society and mainstream psychological practice (Lowe & Mascher, 2001).

CHAPTER 11
ENGAGING THE ELDER WITHIN:
BRIDGING AND HONOURING THE CULTURAL SPACES
IN COUNSELLING WITH FIRST NATIONS

Art Blue, Wes Darou, and Carlos Ruano

Key Terms and Concepts		
• Biculturalism • Chronic stress deactivation effect • First Nations worldview • Generosity	• Healing circle • Interconnectedness • Medicine wheel • Mistapeo	• Rules of behaviour • Space and place • Storytelling • Strengths-based model

Personal Introduction – Arthur Blue

Many years ago at a southern Idaho mental hospital, newly won Master's degree in hand, I began an internship that initiated me into the art of patient contact and the practice of psychology. Many of the outpatients came from the nearby reservation, where a medicine man, known to me since my childhood simply as Hosie, also resided. I was soon to learn another lesson from this respected elder.

Half a century later, I can still see him as he visited me a few weeks into my internship. He knocked politely on my door, then entered my office and sat his bulky frame opposite me. Roughly cut shoulder-length grey hair framed his ruddy, aging, but chubby face. He did not speak or even look at me, just sat completely at one with the silence in the room.

I had been seeing people with the usual range of diagnoses: conduct disorder, depression, and alcohol abuse, to name a few. Very often, a client would refer to his relationships within his extended family as all or part of the problem. Since it seemed obvious and appropriate that this sort of difficulty lay in the domain of the medicine man, I suggested that these people gather a piece of cloth, some tobacco, and sage as a gift and in the evening visit my friend Hosie. Hosie now came to visit me.

I was pleasantly surprised to see him and thought, "Gee, this is the way that professionals work – good referrals, then case conferences."

Though I expected a case conference, I received a lesson instead. After 30 minutes of emptying, relaxing silence, Hosie spoke.

"I come to talk to you about all those people you bin sendin' me." He paused. I was expectant, thinking of diagnoses and treatments. Then he stated the lesson: "I can no longer handle all the people that you are sendin' me. Perhaps you should start dealin' with the problems that you are trained to work with and I will work with the spiritual problems that the people have. I can't do my work and your work too, not enough time to do both."

As we continued to talk, it became obvious that I was interpreting all problems as spiritual. To become an effective member of a treatment team, I needed to accept responsibility for the psychological aspects of the problems that patients presented and to aptly distinguish those from the truly spiritual. My work with medicine people has continued through the years, and Hosie's lesson many years ago expanded my awareness and increased my knowledge and effectiveness. He enabled me to become more comfortable in my work.

It is important for therapists to know that their space is different from that of the medicine men.

Personal Introduction – Wes Darou

When I was about five years old, we lived near an unregistered First Nations community. People derisively call the place Hollywood; my father said that it was not right to do that because life was difficult there, and the people had to work hard for what little they obtained. Later, I saw how happy he was when I brought home minority friends from university. My mother was not so open; she freaked out when she found out that I had a Jamaican girlfriend.

Having this background of general openness and interest in First Nations culture helped me when, as a counsellor in a group home, I began to work with an Algonquin teenager. Like many First Nations clients, as I was to later find out, he was stoic and quiet, and he did not normally talk about his feelings. From our point of view, he was a cooperative kid, but he had made no progress in his therapy (we were, of course, mistaken; he had made progress, but he did not get around to telling us about it).

The big breakthrough came when we did Volkswagen therapy. When he turned 16, I gave him driving lessons in my beat-up old Volkswagen. He would drive around the town and gradually begin to talk about the problems he had as a youth, his addiction, and finally about an illness that he had when he was five that wrenched him from his family and community and took him to a southern hospital. The driving lesson seemed to arouse his emotionality, and he would cry his eyes out as we careened around corners in the suburbs. He would literally spend hours sobbing about the complete culture shock he had lived through. By the time he got his license, he had completed his therapy and moved back to his home.

By that time, I was of course a nervous wreck. You could say this was my first experience in career counselling.

Personal Introduction – Carlos Ruano

I was raised in Guatemala, a country that can be seen as both a huge reservation and a case study in wall-to-wall denial. As a child with both Indigenous and African blood, with a twitch of European to add to my genetic salad, I sat at the Great Ethnic Divide – while not necessarily aware of its existence. By the time I reached puberty, I was confronted first hand with the wholesale slaughter that took place in the late 70s and early 80s. The Army was quite methodical in its Gestapo-like approach to dissent. We grew up very quickly under those circumstances. Of my preparatory teachers' class of 1980 there are very few left to tell the story, and all young people of my generation were deeply affected – regardless of cultural and ethnic background.

Today, more than 10 years after the war's end, the country is a study in full-blown denial, while lynching, murder, and constant fear have become an almost natural state of affairs. Absolutely none of the outstanding socio-economic issues that allowed the war to fester for almost 40 years have been dealt with and the psychological and social makeup of the society has the scars to prove it. To this day, the average Guatemalan is a study in psychosocial trauma and the country continues its rapid descent into a nightmarish scenario of self-mutilation, pathological anger, and fear. At the same time, community resilience and family support mechanisms have shown to be a potent counterweight to this chaotic state of affairs. From the war's ashes, a new Guatemalan identity is evolving, one that is no longer beholden to the old oppressive dichotomies or a hostage of its historic legacy. As individuals and communities grapple with their new emotional landscapes and look out the world beyond, the various approaches that we present in this chapter distill some of my experiences in educational settings with various differential intervention approaches that help us to seek out and engage our elder within.

 **Snapshot 1**

Vignette

The late Clare Brant was an eminent Mohawk psychiatrist. Early in his career, he interned at Moose Factory, a Cree village on James Bay. Clare was a gentle, small, unassuming man. When he arrived, he was almost immediately assigned the nickname Nodawa. He noticed that every time someone introduced him by this nickname, people laughed. As time went on, he also noticed that every time he asked for an explanation of his name, he got a different story. It was *the stranger,* the *guy from far away,* or the *Mohawk.* Finally, at the end of his year in Moose Factory, someone came clean with him. His nickname meant Mohawk all right, but more in the sense of *bloodthirsty enemy!*

Entering a First Nations community is not always an easy task, even if you are a First Nations person yourself. In general terms, a good strategy is to enter with patience, serenity, and a good sense of humour.

With respect to humour, the Crees in Moose Factory may not have been altogether mistaken in their view of Clare Brant. I once visited the Mohawk reserve of Akwesasne for a conference of the Native Physicians of Canada and the Native Psychologists of Canada. As I drove into town I saw a typical little First Nations house with a dog and a couple of old cars. The unique thing was the professionally printed sign that read, *Trespassers will be executed.* I mentioned it to one of the organizers. He said to look at the neighbour's sign. On the way out, I did. It read, *Survivors will be prosecuted!*

These signs represent a cultural difference; Mohawks do not of course execute each other any more than the rest of Canadian society. These cultural differences may be strange and even repulsive to some people. An important task of counsellors is to constantly try to open their spirit to people who are different from them.

Much of the counselling that happens with First Nations is cross-cultural, whether it is between two people of culturally different First Nations or between a First Nations and a *whitie.* Communication between First Nations and non-Natives can be a minefield. It is not easy between different First Nations, either. To add to this, a White North American counsellor may have to develop special skills for dealing with clients who are hostile because they perceive the counsellor as coming from the colonizing class. This is true in cross-cultural counselling with many different groups.

Clare Brant, after his experience in Moose Factory, organized an intercultural feast between the Crees and the Iroquois, traditional enemies from centuries past. He invited some Crees from Moose Factory on James Bay down to the Mohawk territory of Akwesasne on the St. Lawrence River. The feast was to last three days. It was well organized and the logistics worked out as planned. On the first night, a bounteous table was laid out. By the end of the evening, everybody wanted to go home and never come back. The Mohawks were saying that the Crees were absolute animals; the Crees were saying that the Mohawks were trying to kill them.

The next morning, before anybody could catch a plane, Clare called a council. There are many cultural differences between the two groups, and these were highlighted at the council. For example, the Crees are hunters and the Mohawks are agriculturalists. At a Cree feast, you must eat all of the food that is presented; otherwise you insult the animals that gave up their bodies to feed you. At a Mohawk feast, you must put out more food than can possibly be eaten so as to show your great generosity and respect for the visitors.

The people from Akwesasne had put out a huge table of food. The Crees ate it all. The Mohawks put out the reserve food. The Crees ate it all. The Mohawks went out and borrowed food from the neighbours, and the Crees, by now in pain, screwed up their famous courage, and ate it. By the end, the people from Akwesasne were running around to the all-night dépanneur (French for corner store), trying to buy up cartons of Mars bars. And the Crees ate everything, convinced the Mohawks were trying to kill them! Clare's diplomacy worked; the two groups were able to compromise on their differences, and everybody lived happily ever after.

Introduction

The purpose of this chapter is twofold. On the one hand, we aim to introduce both novice and experienced practitioners to cross-cultural models to support culture-infused counselling with First Nations in the North American context. On another level, we also wish to communicate to the reader how our life stories have informed our work and research in this complex field. In this sense, our stories are presented here to bring attention to those aspects of the evolving relationship that we all develop as counsellors and therapists with our clients.

We aim to place ourselves not so much at the centre of the chapter narrative, but rather as a complementary part to it. We wish to communicate our deep commitment and respect to all forms of Elder Wisdom, while trying to contribute useful insights from clinical research and practice. We recognize that this is neither always attainable nor desirable. At the same time, we feel that if cross-cultural psychology is to remain relevant to 21st-century communities, then we must always keep in mind the deep cultural and psychosocial roots that are embedded in the adjoining spaces of service to the community, competent research and clinical practice, and traditional knowledge.

We wish to thank all those who have, over the years, enriched our lives and professional practice with their remarkable narratives, not to mention tea and bannock. They are, and will always be, the centre of our efforts.

 **Snapshot 2**

Vignette

I knew a city woman, single, attractive, well off, and with a master's degree in psychology. She had a little trouble in adapting to the Native environment. One day the Dakota elder Eli Taylor took her aside and said, "Thank you, dear, for all the hard work you have done for the Native people in our community over the last three years." She thanked him profoundly; it's rare to get a direct compliment like that from an elder. "You have really added a lot to our community," Eli continued, "and we appreciate it very much." She thanked him even more profusely. Eli continued: "Now, however, it is time for you to go home and help your own people." She got the message; she found a new job.

There are two messages in this example. The first is that, to get in this much trouble, she must have missed many, many subtler messages that were sent her way. First Nations people often perceive Euro-Canadians as almost socially incompetent, missing even the most obvious messages. The White counsellor's greatest obstacle is probably arrogance. There is a tendency to think "I am a communications specialist; I am really skilled at listening." In fact, White counsellors miss most of the important messages given them. One method that is often used for non-Natives in the communities is to find a buddy who is familiar with your work and who can translate these messages into Euro-Canadian for you (e.g., you just messed up; don't do that again). The second message from this anecdote is to know when to leave.

An equally idiosyncratic but more encouraging response came when a life skills counsellor discretely asked an elder, Daniel Hall, why the community was "putting up with all the weird shit" the counsellor was doing. The elder answered, "Because when you walk home, you pet the dogs and play with the children." The complementary message here is that the community is very generous. You can miss a lot of messages and make a lot of mistakes if you show that you have a transparent, un-Machiavellian love for life. It also helps if you do excellent work, of course.

Healthy Functioning and Psychosocial Well-Being

It is a fundamental goal of a healthy First Nations person to invest a great deal of effort, research, and observation in developing a well-integrated sense of global functioning. Healthy function can be described as a medicine circle representing four aspects (physical, emotional, spiritual, and intellectual) in a complete balance. The physical and the spiritual are on opposite poles of the wheel (East-West), and this axis is the space of the traditional Native medicine person. The intellectual and emotional axis (North-South) is the space of the counsellor. Healthy functioning involves balancing all four aspects and resolving the conflicting ones.

Successfully Living in Both Worlds

According to acculturation theory (Born, 1970; Berry, 2008), coming into contact with a majority culture will result in acculturative or assimilation stress. Individuals under these conditions must end up choosing between several mutually exclusive strategies in dealing with the majority culture. Readers are referred to Chapters 4 and 12 for a discussion of acculturation models, and to Rudmin (2003) and Ward (2008) for critiques.

Bicultural people provide an important link to mainstream culture. The research of Kurtness (1991) shows that **biculturalism** is attainable for some and can provide an important bridge between integration and differentiation. *Successfully integrating two or more cultures* is very growth enhancing. It increases certain socio-cognitive skills (Tadmor, Tetlock, & Peng, 2009). This would apply to Native elders dealing with White society (Kurtness, 1991), but it applies just as much to non-Native counsellors integrating Native culture. According to Peavy (1995), however, "bicultural personhood is hard to come by" (p. 6).

People can choose to be traditional and have as little to do with the majority culture as they wish. At the other extreme, they can, in a free country, choose to be completely assimilated. In First Nations, the bicultural people are often, but not necessarily, elders, teachers, or community leaders.

Clearly there are major pressures from the dominant society to lose the heritage of First Nations people. In order to be bicultural, it is often essential for some people to regain traditional knowledge. Joe Hill, an educator from the Six Nations Mohawk, stated that "If you teach an Indian who he is, he will decide for himself where he is going" (personal communication, October 4, 1969).

 **Snapshot 3**

First Nations Humour

A sense of humour is certainly a sign of healthy functioning. Euro-Canadians need to keep in mind that First Nations humour is different from their own. The authors can speak with some knowledge about Algonquian, Iroquoian, Dene, and Siouxan humour. The other First Nations may very well have yet a different sense of humour. Below is a joke from *You're So Fat: Exploring Ojibwe Discourse,* by Spielmann (1998). If you tell this kind of joke in a mixed group, the non-Natives often look puzzled or may even be offended, and the Native people will break up in laughter.

> There was a nasty fur trader known for his temper and suspected of dishonesty. When he weighed furs, he would always lay his hand on the scales, pointing out that his hand weighed exactly one pound. One day a young trapper came in, and when the fur trader laid his hand on the scale, the trapper pulled out his own weights, which he'd bought in town, and announced that he would prefer to use them. The fur trader flew into a terrible rage and pulled his gun on the trapper. The trapper shot him dead on the spot. Afterwards, they cut off the trader's hand. They felt very sorry about the incident. His hand weighed exactly one pound. (p. 107)

Many non-Natives simply do not get this joke, yet most First Nations people consider it quite humourous. The jokes, like the Mohawk signs mentioned earlier, often contain an almost off-hand reference to violence. This is presumably done to mitigate the daily violence of living close to nature while maintaining a sense of harmony. Robert Jimiken, a Cree guide instructor, once told author Wes Darou, "You White people often have a naïve, idealistic idea about the bush life. In fact, it is very brutal" (personal communication, June 25, 1980).

Humour and teasing are important techniques that the traditional First Nations people use to give messages to others without imposing on them or causing them to lose face. If people gently tease you (as a counsellor) or make cute little jokes about you, they are probably trying to give you a deep and important message. A good exercise is to collect a series of First Nations jokes and analyze them to find out how they reflect something adaptive about community strength.

Cultural Identity and Relationship to the Dominant Culture

There are over 630 First Nations communities in Canada, with a total population of about 1,000,000, and speaking 53 languages (Indian and Northern Affairs Canada [INAC], 2002). These communities account for about 3% of Canada's population. It is often stated that First Nations people arrived in North America about 10,000 years ago. In fact, their history in the Americas appears to be much longer than that, possibly as much as 50,000 years (Zazula, 1999).

Canadian First Nations have a substantial international profile. In 1989, Amazonian Indians protested, in front of Canada's embassy in Washington, against low-level military flights over the Innu hunting territories in Labrador. The Crees of Quebec were major per capita contributors to Ethiopian famine aid. The Salish of British Columbia were able to block the filming of a high-budget film about the monster Ogopogo (actually *N'ha-a-itk* in Salish) being filmed in New Zealand. The Maori supported the Salish argument that the filming would be an act of cultural appropriation. White people were making a profit from a traditional Salish creature.

The indigenous peoples of Canada generally refer to themselves by the terms *First Nations* or *Native* people. This group includes 49 distinct Amerindian cultures such as the Dakota, Cree, and Haida (INAC, 2009). It usually does not include other Aboriginal people such as the Métis, Inuit, and Dene. It is difficult to make generalizations about counselling such a diverse group of people.

For example, the Algonquin language and the Mohawk language have literally as much in common as English and Mandarin, yet the two nations occupy adjoining territory. The two cultures are equally diverse. The Algonquins are traditionally hunters living in small villages and are more or less patriarchal, while the Mohawks are farmers living in larger towns and are clearly matriarchal.

Just choosing a name to describe the people can be a challenge. For example, the term *Aboriginal* is not acceptable in Europe; *indigenous* is not acceptable in China or South Africa; and the term *Indian,* while acceptable in the USA, is not acceptable in Canada. In this chapter, we follow the nomenclature used by First Nations themselves because we believe that it is an inherent right of peoples to choose their own name. Assimilationist processes have resulted in a loss of self-identification or collective awareness on the part of the Amerindian populations. For instance, of the estimated 60 Native languages that were spoken in Canada at first contact, 10 have disappeared and another dozen are on the brink of extinction (INAC, 2006; York, 1992). Nevertheless, during the last 20 years, some people have made an important effort to reverse this trend.

An important distinction is between people who are covered by treaties and those who are not. This often determines the positions people are obliged to take in negotiating with the government. The rights of the two groups are often different, for example, in determining who pays and who does not pay sales tax or who can or cannot live on certain reserves.

The *Métis* are an Aboriginal group that maintains another distinct identity. The nationalistic society was established in Manitoba under Louis Riel. Their language is different from that of other First Nations in that it is a marriage between French and different First Nations languages. They faced a very different and particularly challenging history of oppression that has tempered their negotiations and demands for land rights (Adams, 1995; Lussier & Sealey, 1975). McClanahan (2001) stated:

> Overly generalized labels, or ethnic glosses, are often used to identify and/or discuss ethnic, racial and cultural groups. I realize the inaccuracies inherent in the use of these ethnic glosses and do not mean to denigrate any group with their use. In this paper, the terms American Indian, Native American, Native, and Indian will be used interchangeably. The terms European American, Euro-Americans, Whites, and White Americans also are used synonymously. Whites and European Americans are descriptive terms appropriate in the mixed cultural environment of the southeastern United States where the study was conducted. The terms ethnic and cultural will be used interchangeably to avoid the ethnic glosses inherent in use of the terms race and racial. (p. 5)

Please note that in Canadian society there are a myriad of mistaken beliefs about First Nations, many of them based on a subtle variety of racism. Racist beliefs are almost always subconscious and as a result it is very difficult for counsellors to rid themselves of these beliefs. In fact, Ehrlinger, Gilovich, and Ross (2005) demonstrate that it is almost impossible to recognize bias in oneself. This phenomenon is known as the *bias blind spot.* It must be an ongoing exercise throughout the counsellor's career to question the things taken for granted (Kivel, 1995). As noted in Chapter 4, a first step is to develop an awareness of your own culture.

Values

Although First Nations cultures are diverse, Brant (1990) pointed out that most share certain **values** generally related to harmony, the community, and the earth. There are special rules about going into a Native person's home. Typically, you simply walk in and sit down. Your role is to wait patiently until the person there has finished what he or she is doing and is ready to meet with you. The host will bring you tea and will express pleasure in seeing you. When the host stops talking, it is your time to talk about why you came. You are essentially applying the same rules that would apply when people were in tents. By the way, it is not advisable for a White person to simply walk in without knocking unless that person is deeply imbedded in the community.

In some groups that are matrilineal, such as the Lakota and the Mohawk, the house is the woman's domain. A man would not normally invite you inside. This is not intended as a hard rule, but as an indication of what may be seen as respectful behaviour in a particular situation. As implied earlier, First Nations communities are full of rules, and the first rule is that none of the rules are stated directly.

Although they may share some values, First Nations cultures may differ from each other in many ways. In fact, the difference in values between some is larger than the difference between First Nations and Caucasians (Trimble, Fleming, Beauvais, & Jumper-Thurman, 1996). According to Trimble and colleagues (1996), "Indian clients undoubtedly will express values that are inconsistent with, if not disparate from, those of a non-Indian counsellor" (p. 188) or, we would add, a First Nations counsellor from a different culture.

The research of Trimble and colleagues (1996) found that Native people who had a positive self-perception tended to endorse kindness, honesty, self-control, social skills, social responsibility, and reciprocity. They pointed out that what is important then is to recognize one's own values, stay open to differing values, be able to recognize value conflicts, and be able to help clients deal with such conflicts. A White cook at a tourist camp on Lake Mistassini, Quebec, pointed out that it was not important that the Crees were Catholic, Protestant, Evangelical, or traditional. The key was simply that they had strong religious beliefs (personal communication, June 15, 1979).

The influence of elders is probably common to all First Nations and acts as a value overriding other values. The importance of this can be seen in the biography of Billy Diamond, the former Grand Chief of the Crees of Quebec. Although he was a successful student who wanted to complete his education, the elders pulled him back to his home community because they believed that he was essential to protecting the land from exploitation by Hydro Quebec (MacGregor, 1989).

The Anishinabek Educational Institute in North Bay, Ontario, has the mandate of providing quality community-based education and training for First Nations in Ontario. Its work is solidly based on seven teachings of the elders as explained in *The Mishomis Book: The Voice of the Ojibway* by Eddie Benton-Banai (1988). These values are love, respect, wisdom, bravery, honesty, humility, and truth. They provide a solid base for both our clients' lives and our own professional behaviour as counsellors (Morrissette, 2008).

By inductive reasoning, spirituality must be an important component of counselling because virtually all successful First Nations' services include a spiritual aspect (Trimble & Gonzalez, 2008). Some forms of therapy, such as psychosynthesis (Assagioli, 1983), believe that spirituality is a crucial and final step in a successful growth experience. Quoting one of Peavy's (1995) informants, "We have a special relationship with the land, with ancestors, with our community, and with nature. To achieve harmony is sometimes more important than anything else" (p. 3).

However, as Butson (1993) and Trimble and colleagues (1996) pointed out, recognizing value differences should not be the only concern; the strength and degree of endorsement of values must also be considered.

> Some therapists have made the assumption that all Native people are comfortable with traditional avenues of healing…. However, some Native clients have chosen not to follow these ways and may, in fact, reject them outright. Some are more comfortable with various Christian beliefs, Anglo institutions, or European ways. (Butson, 1993, p. 5)

There are times when non-Native counsellors should be strongly advised against using traditional spirituality practices. There is considerable interest internationally in North American First Nations spirituality, but this can easily become exploitation and cultural appropriation (Jenkins, 2004; Trimble & Gonzalez, 2008). To quote Jack Mitchell, an employability skills instructor from Regina: "Beware of spiritual leaders with business cards" (personal communication, February 2, 1998).

Residential Schools

The relationships between First Nations peoples and the dominant culture have not been easy. The residential school system is perhaps the clearest, best-documented experience of this. Residential schools were an unsuccessful attempt, over 350 years, to assimilate First Nations by *driving the Indianness out of them* (ironic statement). The effect of residential schools was to damage the identity of Aboriginal students (Robertson, 2006). This intentional act was done under the gloss of providing the gift of learning. The effects of what can reasonably be considered genocide will be felt for generations. This will be described later in the case study.

My [Wes's] first experience in really feeling the emotional horror of residential schools came when I was doing a life skills group at Stony Mountain Penitentiary. Inmates had spent 2 hours talking about the mind-numbing violence and depersonalization of prison life, and frankly, it was difficult and painful to listen to. At the end, everybody took a deep breath and prepared to get on with life. Then one of the Native guys said, "Sure, it's awful here in the joint, but at least it's not as bad as residential school. I've NEVER been beaten like I was at residential school." The point here is that it is very difficult for someone who has not lived it to understand the horror that these children lived through at residential school.

The book *Shingwauk's Vision* (Millar, 1996) describes the entire history of residential schools, from 1620 until their end in the 1980s. The original mission of the schools was to Christianize and educate. Millar's book recounts the efforts made by the elders in the last century to obtain schools so that their children could learn the powerful paper-writing skill that the colonizers used. The book explains how the mission later changed to rooting out this dangerous and powerful First Nations culture. It also shows why the real maliciousness of the schools became entrenched in the 1950s. A counsellor successfully working with First Nations must understand and appreciate the horror that Canadian institutions imposed on communities through intentionally assimilationist policies. The counsellor must also be prepared to deal discretely and compassionately with the anger and hate sometimes expressed towards the White majority. As noted in by Collins and Arthur in chapters 4 and 6, although counsellors may not have had a direct hand in oppression, they need to consider the impact of historical oppression and their responsibility for addressing social injustice.

There was a very satisfying period in the 1970s during which the students began to successfully sabotage the system and get their revenge. James Bay Cree youth, including Billy Diamond, Matthew Coon-Come, and Teddy Moses, produced a Cree-language Christmas pageant at the Sault Ste. Marie residential school that was so touching it even ran on provincial television. It was filled with words that cannot be found in the missionaries' Cree lexicon. They slipped in critical comments and bawdy stories in the Cree language not understood by the school staff. Both Diamond and Moses later became well-known chiefs and Coon-Come became the Director General of the Cree School Board.

The residential school system bears a striking resemblance with the *concentration camp* model. During the dictatorship of Franco in Spain (1939-1975), there were schools used to house orphan children and also children of suspected Republican opponents. Their treatment as semi-slave labourers closely resembles that of First Nations. The concentration camp model is intended to strip individuals of their identity, reduce their behaviour to automaton level, and force submission and obedience to a specific set of oppressive patterns or face extinction. Ruano's (1996, 1997, 2001, 2005, 2008) experiences in the case of indigenous communities and their treatment during counterinsurgency campaigns also show traits of the concentration camp model of schooling.

In the Canadian experience, it might be imagined that the school staff were trying to teach the children, but were perhaps misguided in their methods. It is difficult to explain widespread child sexual abuse and perennial violence as *misguided methods* (Dickason, 1992; Millar, 1996; Thomas, 2003). It should be noted that the Canadian experience of residential schools was quite different from that of the United States (Thomas, 2003).

The last Canadian residential school closed in 1976, ending an era of deprivation and abuse. Although the educators' efforts to assimilate First Nations students into the dominant culture were largely unsuccessful, they did separate children from their families and thereby deprived the communities of generations of shared knowledge. Such a void will be felt for generations to come.

In 2008, the Canadian Prime Minister, Steven Harper issued an Official Apology on behalf of all Canadians to former First Nations students of the Residential Schools system (INAC, 2008). A Final Settlement was reached that included monetary compensation and, perhaps more importantly, the establishment of a Truth and Reconciliation Commission that will hear testimony from various parties with a view to start the closing chapter in a long healing journey for those affected by the systemic abuses. It is too early to tell whether these measures will have a positive impact on the First Nations communities that were most affected.

Multigenerational Influences

So far in this section, we have seen the basic structure of First Nations in Canada and the particularly cruel and malicious experiences its people have survived at the hands of the dominant society. Poonwassie and Charter (2001) pointed out that, for First Nations, community development involves considering what the effects of any intervention will be for the next seven generations. Similarly, we can expect multigenerational trauma to take seven generations to heal. This particular mechanism has evolved in humans for perfectly adaptive reasons, as can be seen below.

Freud (1912) saw that society creates mechanisms to ensure social control of human instincts. He speculated that taboos had their genesis in guilt. For Freud, the past is not something that can be completely outgrown by either the individual or the society; rather, it is something that remains a vital and often disruptive part of existence. The emphasis on the past being alive in the present is a central theme in psychoanalytic approaches to the individual and society and has obvious applications to the situation of First Nations.

In *Totem and Taboo,* Freud (1912) set out to give an account of taboos and of prohibitions in general. He was guided by the idea that groups only prohibit what individuals really desire. Behind the laws that structure human society, he said, is the horror, and behind the horror is desire and the murderous capacity to act on desire. Freud was fascinated by ancient objects, as if they were witnesses to humanity's deepest impulses covered over by thousands of years of the civilizing process. The presence of these objects seemed to speak to him of the distant, yet still active, past.

So what does this have to do with the relationship with the dominant culture? There is a form of depression in First Nations that does not appear to respond to treatment. The focus seems to be associated with colonization, the loss of the country, or possibly major human losses that occurred during measles and smallpox epidemics. This association is passed on from generation to generation in the form of identification that takes place between parent and child. To look at things from a different perspective, we could speculate that the ravages First Nations faced could be traced back to the colonizers' unresolved trauma from the period in which they dealt with the great plagues of Europe.

Theoretical Principles and Conceptual Issues

First Nations' models about their own existence underlie the interconnectedness of First Nations psychological principles. Everything is smoothly linked, and it all begins from the original rootstock. A dependency exists between various orders of creation of the world. In the first place, God created the physical world, including the sun and moon. The physical world created the plant world in its own time, and the plant world in its own time created the animal world. The animals then created humans. Thus humans are the most dependent and have in their own right created nothing. One cannot wipe out the animal world and have man still exist; humans are completely dependent on the other orders (Johnston, 1990; McCormick, 1996).

European-based cultures have a hierarchical, individualist worldview. McCormick (2000b) pointed out that Euro-Western models of creation contain a hierarchy of God, humans, and nature. God dominates humans; humans master the animals; living beings exploit the land. The *First Nations worldview* from Western Canada is based on equality, connectedness, and harmony between humans and nature. The human is the least important and must serve the others. All parts must live in harmony.

Joseph B. Gone (2008) pointed out that it is not enough for counsellors to become *culturally competent*. They must also understand the deeply embedded and subliminal habits and orientations that cultural processes and practices furnish for meaning-full experience. In this section we will look at some of the conceptual principles and issues of the First Nations. This includes the medicine wheel, the Mistapeo, and the meaning of family. These concepts will in turn lead to a series of rules of behaviour for proper First Nations functioning.

The Medicine Wheel

The unity and balance of life are represented by the medicine wheel (Figure 1), a symbol that is found in several North American indigenous cultures (Bopp, Bopp, Brown, & Lane, 1984). It reflects life as a whole and is helpful in maintaining a balance between various aspects of existence. The Medicine Wheel also situates humans in relation to the universe as well as providing a terrestrial-based model of celestial phenomena (Faris, 1994)

The medicine wheel can, for example, structure problem-solving. The eagle of the East represents the vision and intellect (identifying issues), the mouse of the South represents relationships (what exists now for the group), the bear of the West represents knowledge and feelings (reactions to the current situation), and the buffalo of the North represents physical action (what can be done) (Chevrier, 1998). Even today, medicine wheels made of rocks aligned and placed in circles can be found all over western Canada, particularly on promontories and other prayer sites. These sites were and are used traditionally for a ceremony of self-discovery and rite of adulthood called the *vision quest*. Examples of ancient medicine wheels can be found in museums and on the Web.

Poonwassie and Charter (2001) described the importance of the medicine wheel in healing:

> The Medicine Wheel philosophy includes all stages of human development from birth to death and rebirth. It connects all stages with each other, with all living beings, and with all life in the universe, thus providing a place of centring for each person in the cosmos. An understanding of the Medicine Wheel is a starting point for helpers as well as those seeking healing. (p. 66)

Generosity

In most traditional First Nations societies, *status was gained by giving, not by hoarding. It was not the person who collected the greatest amount of goods who was respected, but the person (or family or clan) who gave away the most.* This is the essence of **generosity**. This is seen today in the sun dance ceremony, illegal for most of the 20th century, in which participants and their families give away large amounts of goods, even if they are of meager means. It is the central act of the West Coast Potlatch, another ceremony that was illegal for decades. The giveaway is an aspect of a generous society.

The importance of generosity seems surprisingly stable across contemporary First Nations. However, it can cause difficult value conflicts for people working in the wage system, particularly in urban environments.

Mistapeo and Its Relations to the Algonkian Unconscious

Joseph Kurtness, or Kakwa, granduncle of psychologist Jacques Kurtness, explained the relationship of the Mistapeo, literally *mista-napawo: great man*, to the religion of the Innu (James Bay Cree, Naskapi, Montagnais) (Speck, 1935). **Mistapeo** is *a small version of yourself that lives inside you and that represents your potential.* An ethical factor is present in Innu soul philosophy in which we learn that as the Great Man becomes more willing and more active in the interests of his material abode, the body of the individual, he requires the individual to be honest, practice no deception, and live a pure life. In particular, he is pleased with generosity, kindness, and help to others. Other ethical precepts are directed towards the care and respect of animal remains: ethics towards animals.

> Here we have the basis of noteworthy "good behaviour" of the "uncivilized nomads," which has caused travelers to remark upon native honesty and generosity before they have been spoiled by emulating the traders, whose examples tend to make them irreligious. (Speck, 1935, p. 25)

Marie-Lise Von Franz, in a book edited and co-authored by Jung and Henderson (1969), discussed the Jungian interpretation of the Mistapeo. In Jung's basic view of life, the soul of man is simply an *inner companion,* whom he calls *my friend* or Mistapeo. Mistapeo dwells in the heart and is immortal. In the moment of death, or shortly before, he leaves the individual and later may reincarnate himself. Innu who pay attention to their dreams and try to find their meaning and test their truth can enter into a deeper connection with the Great Man. He favours such people and sends them more and better dreams. Thus, the major obligation of an individual Innu is to follow the instructions given by dreams and then to give permanent form to their contents in art or music. Lies and dishonesty drive the Mistapeo away from one's inner realm, whereas generosity and love of one's neighbours and of animals attract him and give him life.

Kurtness (personal communication, May, 1989) explained that this is the Cree ego in the sense that it is the real *self.* It is also the *superego* in the sense that it will punish those who do not follow it.

George Daniels, a Saultaux/Anishinabe elder, gave an example of working from the unconscious (personal communication, June 21, 1978). As far as he was concerned, there is no contradiction in practicing and believing in both the Native religion and Christianity simultaneously. This can be extremely difficult for some non-Natives to reconcile. Levi-Strauss (1995) explained this problem as the difference between the non-Native's linear logic and the Native's logic of the senses (i.e., the unconscious). George said that the practice of having two religions at one time is particularly strong for the Métis of the plains. It also exists for some James Bay Crees who have a *town* religion and a *bush* religion.

In summary, in all traditional societies, an indigenous psychology exists that describes, from a slightly different perspective, the same phenomena as does European-based psychology. The examples given in this section underscore the core understandings that guide beliefs and values for First Nations people. These include a unity and connectedness of the spiritual and physical world, the importance of the unconscious, the meaning of dreams and the integration of art and creativity into First Nations belief systems.

Family

The extended family has central importance for traditional First Nations clients. The extended family cares for children when they are young and teaches them to survive. It is useful for a counsellor to include the extended family by asking how the various family members would see the client's problem or even by inviting some of them to some sessions. Attneave (1985) told of a psychiatric resident who complained "every time I want to talk about his mother, he starts in telling me about this aunt. I never encountered such resistance to therapy" (p. 139)! The resident did not understand that the client's extended family was a core part of his therapy and that the aunt was probably as much a mother to him as his biological mother. In McCormick and Amundson's (1997) model, interventions should incorporate core Aboriginal beliefs and values and involve significant others in helping youth understand their strengths and future directions. The implication is that family members need to be engaged in career planning and decision-making related to post-secondary education and vocational goals. The article by Halfe (1993) is dedicated to her "grandfathers and grandmothers, the elders...and all my relations."

Of all of the European psychologists, Jacques Lacan, a brilliant, radical, but controversial French psychoanalyst, seems to best grasp this concept.

> But some other objective traits: the organizational modes of this familial authority, the laws of its transmission, the concepts of progeny and of parenthood which are linked with it, the laws of inheritance and succession which combine with it, and finally its intimate links with the laws of marriage – these are entangled with psychological relationships and thus obscure them. (Lacan, 1966, p. iv)

First Nations people see perhaps more clearly than others that there are links among their nuclear family, the extended family and the family of society at large.

Rules of Behaviour

Clare Brant (1990) described a series of **rules of behaviour** of First Nations. Well-meaning but ethnocentric non-Natives may easily misinterpret these *ethical principles of an honest and upright Native person as pathology*. These rules are:

- Noninterference: Discouragement of coercion of any type.

- Noncompetitiveness: Management of intergroup dynamics to suppress rivalry and possible embarrassment.

- Emotional restraint: Promotion of self-control and discouragement of strong or violent feelings, common in many hunting societies. Brant (personal communication, May 15, 1995) commented that, "We (First Nations) repeatedly learn how clumsy White people are in reading apparently clear messages,"

- Sharing: Generosity that discourages hoarding, again a valuable trait in a remote, egalitarian community.

- Suppression of ambition: Related to the above.

- Flexibility with respect to the concept of time: Found in many groups that are in close harmony with nature;

- Not expressing gratitude or approval: The intrinsic reward of doing the deed is considered sufficient.

- Correction by teasing: Gentle teasing is used to comment on behaviour without causing the person to feel aggressed or humiliated. According to Brant, shaming and ridiculing are also used in more serious situations and may have long-term effects on how people develop the above behaviours.

- Projection of conflict: The above rules are promoted and reinforced by moving conflict to enemies or hypothetical or religious third parties.

- Native protocol: Native society appears loose and unstructured to a casual observer, but in fact there is a bewildering array (to the outsider) of rules about almost everything.

Restoule (1997) would add two rules to this: one regarding respect and the other regarding extended families. Respect is particularly important in relations with people of wisdom, such as elders. First Nations clients may have been taught to not look elders directly in the eyes, but to keep the eyes downcast. Direct eye contact may be perceived as confrontational or aggressive. Attneave (1985) associates this with the story of "He who kills with his eyes" (p. 138). Similarly, eye contact between men and women can be seen as a sexual gesture and can lead to perceived sexual transference or countertransference. Also, handshaking is generally sensitive and gentle as compared to the non-Native firm, energetic grasp.

In summary, these rules of behaviour for First Nations supply useful guidelines for counsellors. To the extent that they are believed and integrated by the particular people one is dealing with, counsellors may need to adapt their approach to building a collaborative approach by showing flexibility, supporting emotional restraint, and not interfering. On the other hand, if the counsellor comes from a different culture, the First Nations people will all know this, and the counsellor may wish to play with the rules or even strategically break them. In any event, just the simple fact of knowing that there are unwritten local rules may give the counsellor much-needed credibility.

Common Presenting Concerns in the Counselling Context

In a brief analysis, we cannot cover all presenting problems that a counsellor is likely to encounter. There is a high degree of uniqueness in client issues. However, an understanding of issues that may be common to many clients will provide a framework that allows one to more effectively explore individual issues.

Educational Stress and Posttraumatic Stress

Going south to get advanced education in a college or university is a particularly stressing event in the life of a northern First Nations youth. It can be quite difficult to move to a big city full of non-Natives, with its bad smells, constant noise, and disagreeable food. The attraction of a subway and a MacDonald's restaurant does not last long. A non-Native counsellor may have difficulty appreciating how stressful it is for a First Nations client to live in a milieu in which people have a completely different way of life. Students may have to overcome barriers in order to access higher education, including financial concerns, care for families, relevance of the curriculum for learning needs, and varying levels of emotional and instrumental support from family and community (Offet-Gartner, 2008).

It has been observed that Native students tend to deal with stress by reducing their activity level (*deactivation*). In similar circumstances, non-Native students tend to become hyperactive and talkative (*activation*) (Blue & Blue, 1981). A majority of First Nations students, particularly ones from traditional communities, tend to withdraw and deactivate in times of stress. After three months or so, this can become chronic. The effect can be seen in a university cafeteria around exam time. The non-Native students are generally agitated and loud. The Native students sit silent and frozen in their places.

There appears to be a neurological basis for this particular reaction involving the limbic system and neurotransmitters, although van der Kolk (1994) pointed out that the neurological links are not yet clear. According to van der Kolk's (1994) writings about posttraumatic stress, the concept of a **chronic stress deactivation effect** is supported by the fact that low levels of serotonin are found in inescapably shocked rats, an image many First Nations university students can identify with. In this *freeze response,* the brain releases opioids, which interfere with the storage of explicit memory and incidentally inhibit pain. Traumatized people often report being speechless; this represents a failure of the explicit semantic memory. When stressed, these people act as though they are being traumatized all over again and regularly revert to irrelevant or even non-adaptive emergency behaviour, often becoming partially amnesic.

There are some impressions of what mechanisms could cause this effect. Van der Kolk (1994) noted that norepinephrine affects memory storage in an inverted U function (i.e., high or low levels inhibit memory). The amygdala, which is involved in acquiring conditioned fear responses, may be overstimulated in people with chronic stress. Its function is to send memories of free-floating feelings to the hippocampus (e.g., "I am afraid"). The hippocampus links explicit memory to these feelings (e.g., "I am afraid of the exam"). If the hippocampus is in turn overstimulated, it inhibits exploratory behaviour. There is some suggestion that chronic stress may damage the hippocampus (Steinberg, 2001).

In the case of traditional First Nations people, these effects have some culturally adaptive aspects. The deactivation link with serotonin increases environmental monitoring, surely an advantage for a hunter who must not move for long periods. Also, deactivation is linked to pain inhibition; this will be recognized as an obvious benefit by anyone who has lived the bush life.

In summary, First Nations clients tend to experience educational stress and culture shock in a way that Euro-Canadians generally do not. They may deactivate, reducing their activity level to different degrees. This situation presents a dangerous and classic error that can be found with non-Native counsellors and Native clients: the counsellor will not notice that the client is in a major crisis state because the client looks calm and relaxed. If a client looks comfortable and stable in a situation that would drive anyone else wild, it is possible that the counsellor is misreading the nonverbal behaviours.

Drug and Alcohol Addiction

Despite the stereotypes, there is some evidence that addiction rates among First Nations are about the same as those for the majority culture when controlled for socio-economic status and educational level. In a survey comparing a large sample of White American adolescents, Hispanic adolescents, and American Indian adolescents, the White Americans exceeded both Hispanic and American Indian youth in their use of alcohol (Beauvais, Chavez, Oetting, Deffenbacher, & Cornell, 1996).

Philip May (personal communication, April 4, 2002) pointed out that serious problems are caused by a particular drinking style among American First Nations. That is, many people do not drink at all, but among those who do drink, the normative style is binge drinking. There is ample evidence to indicate that this is a continent-wide pattern. Among a subset of these binge drinkers are some very heavy drinkers who greatly elevate the public health consequences: fetal alcohol syndrome (FAS), mortality, crime, familial disruption, and general health morbidity (Ptasznik, 2008).

May (1994) pointed out several other stereotypes. Contrary to the stereotypes, Native people do not metabolize alcohol differently than other groups. "No basis at all for this myth is found in the scientific literature" (May, p. 124). There is not a higher prevalence of drinking. Prevalence varies widely; there are in fact more nondrinkers among American First Nations than among most other groups. The problem is destructive drinking style rather than prevalence. Among First Nations, alcoholism is not just a male problem; although women's addictions rates are lower than men's, their addictions can be just as chronic. FAS is not a major problem in the sense that FAS is an "equal opportunity birth defect" (May, p. 137); it affects all cultures. It is a major problem in the destruction that it causes to the individual First Nations people who are the victims. FAS prevention is a promising area for community development because, although the disease is particularly damaging, it is also preventable.

However, the whole issue of addictions is complex. Different drugs, different behaviours, and different individuals are likely to access different vulnerabilities (Redish, Jensen, & Johnson, 2008). Crabbe (2002) gave an outline of the major findings about the genetic contributions to addictions. At some level, there is clearly a genetic contribution, and this can be replicated, even among rats. The effect appears to be more at the level of a gene-environment interaction than a direct genetic link. "At least some contribution to substance abuse is likely to be the tendency of genetically susceptible individuals to remain in the risk-promoting environment" (p. 449). The most successful therapies appear to be those that advocate making radical changes in day-to-day living.

It is McCormick's (2000b) view that successful alcohol treatment must be based on connecting to meaning, family, spirituality, identity, and particularly culture. For example, the Round Lake Treatment Centre in British Columbia uses the motto *Culture is treatment.* Similarly, Stubben (1997), after interviewing 500 graduates of treatment centres, found that there were four key ingredients to successful treatment: 1) the presence of Native staff, 2) contact with elders that allowed clients to reclaim their identities, 3) aftercare in the community that included traditional healing and ceremonies, and 4) the existence of alternatives to an AA-only philosophy. Stubben found that programs with only Alcoholics Anonymous (AA) or Narcotics Anonymous (NA) had a 93% relapse rate, while programs that mixed AA or NA with tribal ceremonies had a 53% relapse rate.

Suicide Prevention

Suicide rates among First Nations are far higher than those for Canada in general: about 37 versus 13 per 100,000. First Nations male youth in Canada are eight times more likely to commit suicide than non-Native males of the same age (McCormick, 2002). Some of the demographic co-variables for suicide are age (the rates are particularly high for people aged 15 to 24, a group that represents 20% of the population), alcoholism (alcoholism, and not drugs, is involved in over half of the successful suicides), and education (Native Canadians who have not completed high school or who are unemployed have higher suicide rates).

Without understating the seriousness of the issue, again we find, on taking a closer look at the data, that if socioeconomic factors are taken into account, the rates are comparable with those of the rest of Canada (Ross, 1996). Note that the highest national suicide rates in the world tend to be in northern countries, and rates tend to be low in equatorial countries. Russia's rate is 34 per 100,000 and Finland's rate is 20 per 100,000; Mexico's is 4 per 100,000 and Costa Rica's is 6 per 100,000 (World Health Organization, 2008).

As a counsellor, it is valuable to know that three internal factors are important in the immediacy of suicide risk: loss, a trigger, and chemicals. We speak of loss in its broadest sense; that is, the person is truly in the process of mourning. It may be the loss of a loved one, a good friend, or an important aspect of the person's life. The chemical factor within the brain can be either external (alcohol) or internal (neurotransmitters). People can be high from psychoactive chemicals or may be affected by a long-term depression. There also has to be an immediate trigger. This may be a fight with a boyfriend or, on the other hand, the completion of a lifelong goal.

The demographic factors mentioned earlier are mostly extrapsychic and do not represent psychological problems. There is a tendency for counsellors to attribute intrapsychic causes when in many cases the problems have external sources out of the control of the client. In studying suicide risk, it has regularly been shown that hopelessness, and not suicidal ideation or depression, is the greatest predictor of completion (Cull & Gill, 1999). The best overall approach for dealing with these is to facilitate societal growth in First Nations so as to remove hopelessness, not to simply provide better counselling to suicidal clients. Ross (1996) pointed out that communities that move forward in their development inevitably show lower rates of suicide.

According to Ross (1996), a great number of actions could potentially improve the situation of suicide in First Nations: better management of access to prescription drugs, control of access to firearms, better access to quality care, effective treatment of alcohol dependence, reduction of the reluctance to make use of such care by promoting excellence in our First Nations' own services, and improving access to the basic necessities for good health, such as clean water, adequate sewage disposal, education, and opportunities for meaningful work.

Quality educational and vocational counselling allow people to develop important buffers against suicidal risk. Addicted women tend to be depressed. Some psychological treatments have been shown to be more effective than others in treating depression; we need to learn these approaches and adapt them to First Nations cultures. The simple act of practicing and supporting Aboriginal spirituality is therapeutic. Thus, we must develop holistic treatments that combine counselling with culturally appropriate healing, including social supports and traditional medicine. The recovery and healing of suicidal youth can be facilitated through practices such as increasing self-esteem, connecting with culture and tradition, becoming aware of the responsibility to others, expressing emotions appropriately, establishing future goals and hope, spiritual connection, role modeling and connecting with nature (McCormick, 2002).

Snapshot 4

M'KIZNUN

Upon your feet, my little one,
M'kiznun.
Yesterday
I made them.
          The deer gave up her hide for you,
A porcupine,
Quills. I prepared them.
               But see, these shoes are worn already,
A hole in each.
I put it there.
          No one starts a journey, little one, In
worn-out
M'kiznun.
Keep your feet from the Path of Souls.
          Stay in the lodge of your mother.
Grow
In strength.
Do not seek the Path of Souls.
          The world is good, little one. Live.
Grow up.
I will watch over you.

From: "M'kiznun [Moccasins]" by Wawaskone, 1977, *Tawow: Canadian Indian Cultural Magazine, 6(2)*, 27.

However crucial it is to build community strength, the counsellor is not well positioned to help in these efforts. Our role is to deal person-to-person with potential victims and their families. So are we simply giving Band-Aid solutions or, even worse, incorrectly placing the responsibility for the problem on the victims when in fact the problem is the sequelae of colonialization? The focus was correctly placed by Ross (1996) when she said, "We must remember that those who attempt or commit suicide are attempting to seek a solution to a problem that is causing intense suffering, a pain that is perceived as intolerable" (p. 253). As stated in the poem in Snapshot 4, we must encourage community members not to *seek the Path of Souls.*

Counselling Models

A wide range of counselling models exists. On one extreme, the typical Euro-American approach can be imposed without adaptation on First Nations. The vocational theories that were developed from White American subjects are applied whole (Darou, 2000; Kerr, 2001-2002, Morrissette, 2008). This model can be seen as unhelpful or even harmful to the individual and as eroding cultural integrity from the community (Darou, 1987). Used dogmatically, these approaches will break several of Brant's (1990) rules of behaviour, including noninterference, noncompetitiveness, emotional restraint, suppression of ambition, projection of conflict, and perhaps flexibility. The clearest example is the use of intelligence testing in an invalid and inappropriate environment (Chrisjohn & Young, 1998; Darou, 1992). The concept of testing is generally appropriate in itself. The inappropriate aspect comes when the answer is compared to an unsuitable group or norm and results are used in a way that systemically influences the individual or the community.

Another model is professional counselling (or any other professional specialty, for that matter) presented by a skilled and sympathetic non-Native counsellor (e.g., Couture, 1994). This model is an improvement, but considerable research shows that First Nations clients prefer First Nations counsellors where possible (Trimble & Gonzalez, 2008). This is particularly important in places such as cities in which First Nations are a minority. There, non-Native counsellors can inadvertently do more harm than good because their space as a role model interferes with people building their own cultural identity (Pedersen, 1995a). Also, from a structural point of view, even if the counselling helps an individual client, it adds little to the community and may inadvertently be deleterious.

Space is *the structural quality of the physical environment,* while **place** is *the notion of lived experience.* Regarding the differences in place and space between Euro-American psychology and First Nations therapeutic traditions, Gone (2008) explained that "the ethical and political costs associated with professional practice-as-usual in Native American communities amount to nothing less than an extension of the colonizing project" (p. 394).

Following the Hippocratic injunction of *do no harm,* a non-Native counsellor in an urban setting should be extremely hesitant in accepting a First Nations client if there are other resources available. In such a setting, a non-Native counsellor can actually harm the client by inadvertently eroding the person's self-concept. It is important to be sensitive to the circumstances that suggest referral to a First Nations resource. If this is not an option, some strategies are available.

The counsellor can work in collaboration with a Native elder, defer to a First Nations professional or manager who is hierarchically above the counsellor, see the person in group with other people of the same culture, or use the opportunity to do substantial amounts of collaborative cultural research on the person's home community. If as a counsellor you find yourself obliged to take on a Native client, it is your responsibility to vocally and unremittingly advocate for additional First Nations resources. Author Wes Darou, for example, shared readings from a newly released First Nations history text with his mixed group in a federal penitentiary. The clients were invited to share the information with the elders. Interestingly, the elders generally had oral history accounts of the same material, often handed down 200 years.

In communities where Native people are the majority, however, non-Native counsellors can be effective and are often sought out by clients. They may provide local children with an opportunity to interact with a person of a different culture whom they would not otherwise meet. In other words, community members have the opportunity to observe and practice skills for interacting with majority groups, such as White people, an all-important task when any person from a non-dominant group must deal with a majority group.

It is important to reiterate that non-Native counsellors need to be respectful of local practices. Failure to do so may simply be the result of cultural misunderstandings, but the potential for serious consequences should not be underscored. The results can lead to adverse results for clients and lack of acceptance of the professional within the community. For an account of such culture clash, see the case incident Wihak (2008) and responses offered by Blue, Rogers Blue, Couchie, Darou, & Kurtness (2008) and Deters & Lin (2008). To paraphrase Haaken (2008), White counsellors working in First Nations communities may feel the ghosts of the colonial past perpetually at their backs.

Multicultural Counselling Process

The following section begins with a discussion of general models and how to adapt them to the Native context, with particular emphasis on the importance of working from strength-based approaches rather than deficit- and victim-based models. The section then describes some counselling tools, such as the medicine wheel, storytelling, healing circles, and ceremonies, followed by more global issues, such as vocational counselling, the function of elders, the importance of values, counselling with Native women, and helping Native helpers.

First Nations Models Versus Euro-Canadian Models of Helping

According to Trimble and Gonzalez (2008), nondirective approaches may be ineffective because "many Indian clients, especially more culturally traditional ones, are likely to be reticent and taciturn during the early stages of counselling, if not throughout the entire course of treatment" (p. 193). The fluidity of the conversation seems to depend on the ability of the counsellor to listen and not on the client's ability to talk. Some clients treat counsellors with the respect that they normally reserve for elders (e.g., silence, no eye contact). This can be disconcerting to a Euro-Canadian using many contemporary counselling models and can be confounding for First Nations students in counselling programs.

Counsellors need to develop competencies in hearing nonverbal communication and particularly in dealing with silence. The counsellor's job is really to hear the meaning beyond the words and in the absence of the words. We typically understand silence when it indicates emphasis. We often misunderstand meaning when we toy with concepts inside our heads and reconstruct them to better express an experience or emotion. All things within the counselling session have meaning and need equal attention.

In a study by Trimble and colleagues (1996), taped counselling sessions were played to residential school students. The tapes included both Native and non-Native counsellors and three methods: directive, nondirective, Native culture based. The results showed that the Native counsellor was preferred and that nondirective counselling was rated as least effective. The conclusions made from this study are useful. All else being equal, Native counsellors who use some sort of concrete approach are perceived to be the best counsellors for Native clients, yet most counsellor training programs teach a more nondirective approach to counselling. The authors concluded that this is why Native people take a dim view of the usual counselling situation.

A survey study (Blue, 1977) also found that Native students generally took a dim view counselling services that were not adapted. The students tended to use the university counselling services for urban or guidance problems, such as finances and study skills. They used Native elders, however, for the really important stuff, such as alcoholism, religion and mental health. This particular study resulted in the hiring of a Sioux elder, Mary Hall, for the Brandon University counselling service.

The appreciative inquiry (Cooperrider & Srivastva, 1987) approach fits well with a First Nations model. In this approach, coming from the field of organizational development, interveners first use community members to list the strengths available to them. Next, the community members set out goals that they wish to move towards. Finally, they collaboratively find ways to use these strengths as tools to move towards the community's goals. Kerr (2001-2002) based her counselling program on principles of using strengths to build towards the client's goals. She strongly believed that this is more effective than a medical approach in which the counsellor attempts to heal the deficits and weaknesses of the client or of the community because this leads to blaming and victimization. Such **strengths-based approaches** that *highlight and draw on the strengths of the individual and the positive aspects of the community* (Chamberlin, 1998) will probably be more helpful for First Nations.

With children, a similar technique is to ask them to identify their favourite trickster story (e.g., Nanabush, Raven, Coyote). You, as the counsellor, listen closely, even if you have heard the story many times. Analyzing the themes, subjects, attributes, methods of the subject, and the outcomes can then give you some insight into the problems and into the strengths of the individual. The value of the technique is that it avoids personification of the problems. It allows you to work collaboratively to develop new ways to attack problems and build solutions.

Tolerance for ambiguity is an important competency for counsellors because Native people tend to structure systems differently or not structure them at all. A Native person's home may have objects placed in a seemingly random pattern. Similarly, clients will pull out information in a way that may appear random and confusing to the counsellor. However, this is more often due to the counsellor's lack of ability than to the pathology of the client. The counsellor's job is to be the one who hears the meaning that the client is presenting. Trimble and colleagues (1996) stated that:

> Counsellors must be adaptive and flexible in their personal orientation and use of conventional counselling techniques. Commitment to understanding the cultural context and unique cultural characteristics of clients also is essential. This often requires counsellors to extend their efforts beyond what is typical in a conventional office. (p. 196)

Counsellors need a deep understanding of their own values before they can become aware of their own biases and in turn understand the client's values. These are not always the values of trained counsellors. Because of the great variety of First Nations cultures in Canada, this statement applies as much to Native counsellors as to non-Native counsellors who are working with First Nations clients. A genuine sense of caring and understanding is the foundation of successful work.

Trimble and Gonzalez (2008) pointed out that counsellors of First Nations people can easily misunderstand their client's behaviour because of intercultural conflict. "Many clients…may not recognize the need for professional assistance when community-based helping networks are perceived as far more beneficial" (Trimble & Gonzalez, p. 196). On the other hand, counsellors can become so enchanted by the client's unique way of looking at the world that they fail to deal with the problem at hand. They need to focus on expressed values rather than on preconceived images or notions.

A similar example of how to manage White people is given by the Cree of James Bay, Quebec, who took control of their education system when they concluded the James Bay Agreement in 1974 (W. Darou, personal communication, June 15, 1982). At that time, the Cree began bringing in many non-Native teachers and administrators. The elders stated that the Whites whom they appreciated had the following motivations for moving to James Bay: fun, making money, fishing and hunting, and professional opportunity. They did not like people who came to escape, to transmit a philosophy, or for reasons of altruism. It may seem surprising that the elders did not like the do-gooders. But the elders have accurately noticed that the altruists regularly have underlying shadow sides of anger and mean-spiritedness. The professionals they liked came in with an appreciation of the strengths of Cree society: good humour, successful financial management, and pristine nature. The professionals they did not like came in with a deficit view of Cree society. Similarly, regarding Africans, Eugenie Aw, Africa's first female dean of journalism, stated that "African women face two major dangers: African men who want to oppress them, and Western women who want to 'maternalize' them" (Durand, 2008).

Interconnectedness

McCormick's (1996) research indicated that the successful practice of counselling for First Nations people differs from Euro-Canadian approaches. The aim of healing for First Nations is concerned with attaining and maintaining balance between the four dimensions of the person: intellectual, spiritual, emotional, and physical. In addition, First Nations healing focuses on **interconnectedness** rather than on autonomy. *First Nations people connect with the family, community, culture, nature, and spirituality for successful healing. This can be extended to connectedness with other First Nations.* Visiting other First Nations helps even First Nations people gain an understanding of origins, cultural influences, ways of life, and languages (Kerr, 2001-2002).

The theme of interconnectedness is common among most First Nations cultures. Clearly, there must be a connection with cultural values. However, it is also important to consider the individual in the context of the community (Lafromboise, Trimble, & Mohatt, 1990). Transcending the ego, bringing about harmony in the community, and completing the process with a community-based cleansing ceremony can be seen as a model for First Nations healing (McCormick, 1996). Cultural values may be reinforced by such community ceremonies as the sweat lodge, the vision quest, the shaking tent, and the sun dance (Mohatt & Eagle Elk, 2000). First Nations clients tend to turn to community elders for help with important personal problems (Blue, 1977).

The Advice of Elders

Counsellors can help empower their clients and the community by relinquishing their roles as experts and allowing community healing practices and elders to supply structure and the basis for learning. The advice a counsellor receives may at times be very powerful and often not what is expected. The advice given by elders is *agentive* in the sense that it places the advice as an instance of agency by the person and on the person. Elders have various roles, among them that of *guiding agents* through a journey of self-discovery and self-actualization. Therefore, it is clear that, out of respect, if you ask an elder for help, you are morally obligated to follow through with the advice.

This is not to say that psychologists must abrogate their position as professionals. The elders understand this situation and will generally try not to put the professional in a difficult situation. If the question is delicate, they will generally mitigate it by answering with an interpretable story, a riddle, or humour. Elders and counsellors simply have different cultural spaces.

Simply being old does not necessarily make one an elder, although all old people must be respected. Non-Native counsellors can recognize who are in fact elders by carefully observing to whom the Native population turns for wisdom or help in troubling situations. It must also be noted that the elders may have differing or even conflicting views about ways to help.

Storytelling

Storytelling *is a traditional way of transmitting healing messages.* Elders essentially *own* certain stories and use them to gently move people to new learning. It is a way of working that First Nations people are very comfortable with and are generally open to in the counselling setting. It also has the important role of establishing the value of the elders in transmitting key cultural information. Please note that it is important to gain permission to use an elder's stories, and it is important to follow the story as closely as possible. For an example of the use of stories based generally on the medicine wheel, see Storm (1985).

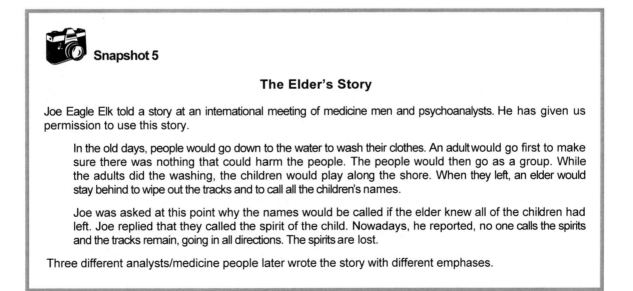

Snapshot 5

The Elder's Story

Joe Eagle Elk told a story at an international meeting of medicine men and psychoanalysts. He has given us permission to use this story.

> In the old days, people would go down to the water to wash their clothes. An adult would go first to make sure there was nothing that could harm the people. The people would then go as a group. While the adults did the washing, the children would play along the shore. When they left, an elder would stay behind to wipe out the tracks and to call all the children's names.

> Joe was asked at this point why the names would be called if the elder knew all of the children had left. Joe replied that they called the spirit of the child. Nowadays, he reported, no one calls the spirits and the tracks remain, going in all directions. The spirits are lost.

Three different analysts/medicine people later wrote the story with different emphases.

Healing Circles

An important tool in lifting pain and guilt is to use the healing circle. Its value can also be seen in less dramatic times when a facilitator wishes to ensure respect, openness and good listening. The **healing circle** *is a round robin, with several important rules of operation. A sacred stone or a feather is passed around the circle from right to left.* It is usually started by an elder, who explains what is to happen. This role could be filled by a counsellor, who would use this time to set some parameters on what to deal with, based on the counsellor's own experience. This sets the tone for the people who will speak. The holder of the stone can speak, and no one is to interrupt. Speakers can take as much time as they wish, or simply remain silent, or say nothing and pass on the stone. No one is to make comments or judgments on other speakers' statements, although statements of understanding can be given and further information can be requested. This process allows the freedom to speak and be respected and to have everyone's thoughts and point of view heard. It continues and goes around and around until the issue is resolved.

The healing circle in prisons is a great intervention that allows inmates a chance to speak about their experiences. The healing circle is also commonly used in treatment centres. In White society, there are great limitations of confidentiality. In Native society, there is often contact and sharing with the entire family that can be worked through and dealt with within a healing circle.

Ceremonies

Many people have different ways of understanding the effects of the intercultural contact that has impacted original societies. Over the 300 years of contact, many changes have occurred in both First Nations and Euro-Canadian peoples in North America. These differences have impacted on transportation, communication, education, and spiritual way of life. Few things in life have not changed drastically in that period. Halfe (1993) believed that colonization programmed First Nations for self-destruction. Programmed inferiority implies that "someone else has written the script" (Halfe, p. 7). The modern role of the ceremonies is to empower the community and make use of its strengths.

Many traditional ceremonies and practices have come to be recognized as beneficial in the treatment of a wide variety of personal and interpersonal issues. Elders in various social service agencies realize the healing of the spiritual self through gifts of the sweat lodge, vision quest, name giving, sun dance, medicine wheel, drumming, singing, dancing, pipe ceremony, storytelling, and sweetgrass purification.

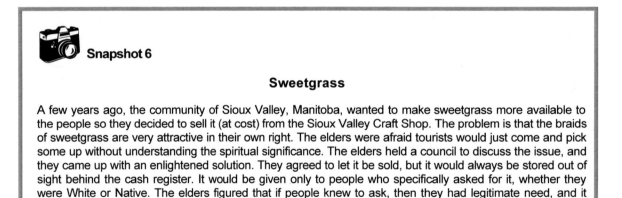

Snapshot 6

Sweetgrass

A few years ago, the community of Sioux Valley, Manitoba, wanted to make sweetgrass more available to the people so they decided to sell it (at cost) from the Sioux Valley Craft Shop. The problem is that the braids of sweetgrass are very attractive in their own right. The elders were afraid tourists would just come and pick some up without understanding the spiritual significance. The elders held a council to discuss the issue, and they came up with an enlightened solution. They agreed to let it be sold, but it would always be stored out of sight behind the cash register. It would be given only to people who specifically asked for it, whether they were White or Native. The elders figured that if people knew to ask, then they had legitimate need, and it was the elders' duty to make it available.

Sweetgrass or cedar ceremony

Important events often begin with a ceremony using sweetgrass (*Hierochloe odorata*), cedar, or sage, depending on the culture. This ceremony acts as a point of meditation and concentration before the beginning of a serious endeavour. A sweetgrass holder moves around the circle clockwise with smoking sweetgrass. The circle members wash their faces with the smoke to purify their thoughts and ask for the help of the ancestors. Note that you should not conduct this ceremony if you are not comfortable with the role. As for the authors, Blue, as an elder, does the ceremony regularly, but Darou is only comfortable doing it in private and Ruano does not do it at all. People will also use sweetgrass as a way of purifying a new house, welcoming a baby, or even blessing banal parts of one's life.

Vision quest

The vision quest is a traditional ceremony in which a person leaves the community for four days and nights or longer, without food, to meditate and seek out a guiding vision. After the quest, elders help the person understand the vision. Modern expressions of this ceremony include unstructured meditation in a quiet place without interruption or in a psychotherapy session.

Sweat lodge

This is a ceremony to enhance the power to dream and to give a sense of belongingness to a community. The sweat lodge ceremony is symbolic of purification, rebirth, and regaining old ways. There is a substantial level of preparation and a great deal of structure to both the construction and the ceremony. The lodge itself is a small structure in which hot rocks are placed and sprinkled with water to increase the sweathouse aspect of the experience. A gatekeeper sits outside and assists by bringing the rocks and opening the entrance at the proper times. Traditionally, the leader conducts the ceremony by song and prayers while the entrance is closed and indicates when individuals may make their own private prayers and when the entrance is to be opened.

Drumming

Drumming is a musical way of expressing the search for vision. Most people identify drumming as the Plains experience of it, but in fact it occurs in many Native cultures, including the Iroquoian and Inuit. The Iroquois have a song festival in the spring using a water drum that is tuned by the amount of water inside. The West Coast people also have a song ceremony that uses a hollowed-out cedar log.

Sun dance

The sun dance is one of the most spiritual of the rites and ceremonies. It was also illegal for 100 years. Because of its sacredness, it is not generally discussed in published works. If you ever have the good fortune to be invited to a sun dance, jump at the opportunity. However, you should make sure you have a guide who will explain the rules and the level of participation you may take; make an extra effort to remain respectful. The sun dance is traditionally done in the spring equinox as a ceremony of thanksgiving. Typically, one pledges to present a sun dance for good fortune.

Vocational Counselling

First Nations seem to find vocational counselling valuable despite the fact that some of the basic theoretical foundations do not seem to apply particularly to First Nations communities (Chevrier, 1998). Clients may not have the luxury of choosing their own occupation, the collectivism found in communities may not encourage the principle of pay for work, and ambition may be suppressed in order to reduce conflict in the community (Brant, 1990). As a result, it is important for counsellors to take into account several practical aspects of work with particular groups.

Northern communities tend to have insufficient people to fill the available work. There may be more work than the people can actually do to meet the day-to-day survival needs of the community. Other communities are in exactly the opposite situation and are time rich and information poor. As a result, in communities that do not have enough people for the work, individuals often fill more than one role. These roles may or may not be paid positions and might include a standard part-time job, trapping and hunting for food, bush construction, and caring for an elder. A counsellor must be respectful and careful not to treat clients who have no paid job as if they are unemployed. In addition, the counsellor may be confused when faced with resistance on the part of a client who, in the counsellor's mind, should be out looking for work. In fact, the client may be too busy, particularly in the seemingly slack winter months.

As part of healthy psychological functioning, many First Nations clients, particularly youth, have vocational aspirations that allow them to contribute to the welfare of their community (Offet-Gartner, 2008; Wintrob, 1969). Strong youth tend to have a solid connection with their family and to seek work that returns something to the community. If a client holds this value, it is unrealistic of the counsellor to suggest that the person take a job in sales, banking, or flower design, regardless of what an interest inventory score may indicate. The counsellor needs to be sensitive to the possibility that the client may need to take a profession that allows contact with kin, can fill an unmet community need, or will give value back value to the community.

Another important consideration has been known for half a century (Hallowell, 1955). For some traditional First Nations clients, social position is not gained from high professional status. Instead, social position and self-esteem are based mainly on personal power, global ability, and inner spiritual power. As a result, a client may receive the necessary education to practice a profession, but be unable to put it to use (Trimble et al., 1996). The counsellor must be aware that personal and even spiritual development may be prerequisites of successfully helping a client with a vocational problem.

A complete vocational model designed for working with First Nations clients can be found in McCormick (1996, 2000b, 2002) or in McCormick and Amundson (1997). Critique of this model and expansion of the application is provided by Offet-Gartner (2003b, 2008).

Counselling Native Women

According to Ross (1996), counsellors of Native women have some special needs and challenges. She stated that "Aboriginal women constitute a disadvantaged minority in the general population, relative to non-Aboriginal women and even Aboriginal men" (p. 249). Women tend to seek formal services less often than others and may put off their needs until they feel assured that others in their extended family have been served. Women also have lower earnings and higher unemployment.

Malone (2000) pointed out that women have been particularly affected by colonization, residential schools, and an oppressive child welfare system. She recommended learning about the great strengths of these women before embarking on a counselling practice with them. She suggested that counsellors take multicultural training and anti-racism training, review their reinforcements for this line of work, and consider doing their own therapy with a person from outside their culture. Her counselling methods are based on empowerment and have a focus on social causes. She gives clients permission to feel and express anger directly and effectively.

Traditional healing and holistic approaches appear to be particularly valuable (Ross, 1996). According to Malone (2000), in many First Nations societies, women are the owners of this information. For the Iroquoian people, herbal medicine was clearly the domain of women, particularly of the clan mothers. According to the research of Viau (2000), these women used 152 different medicinal herbs. Even today, some of the best herbalists available in Canada are Iroquoian women.

Much feminist therapy involves *walking the talk*. Malone (2000) said that clients can be encouraged to be educated and conscientious consumers. For example, they should be encouraged to negotiate the orientation, methods, and values of their counselling and to otherwise take an active part in it. For their part, counsellors need to be proactive and educated about women's issues.

For men helping women, the most important concern in establishing the relationship is acceptance. This has to be done in a very careful way. You cannot necessarily do it in the Euro-Canadian way because this may be perceived as sexual. Verbal following, direct eye contact, or pure silence are probably not appropriate; you need to respond with respect and positive acceptance. Virtually every situation will be seen as you rejecting them and not believing them. They expect to be treated as if nothing said is believable and as though, at some level, their problems are their own fault. They need to be treated constantly with respect and understanding.

Helping Native Helpers

Chrisjohn (1990) believed that First Nations helping professionals face an unusually high risk of burnout. Their workloads tend to be too high because of underfunding and multitasking. They are expected to be experts in their field of study, but also to be guest speakers, volunteers, cultural interpreters and translators, and even language teachers. Counsellors who have fewer paper qualifications than others may suffer from the classic impostor syndrome, but because of general underfunding, the impostor syndrome itself may become institutionalized. Next are built-in cultural conflicts. Principles of a given approach to psychotherapy may complicate the counsellor's own traditional principles (Pratt, 2007). The result may be that counsellors feel they are expending a lot of energy trying to fit clients into systems that are culturally inappropriate.

There are societal pressures on the First Nations counsellor to move things by bearing pressure on individuals in their own or other nations. This is not how things are done in First Nations communities. Power is implicit and gained by respect through hard work, time, and by "everybody knowing what it is you can do and cannot do" (Chrisjohn, 1990, p. 207). Prejudice is another issue. "Being an Indian in Canada is a stressful enterprise" (p. 209). First Nations counsellors thus have all the usual stressors of their profession plus a series of additional stressors.

Chrisjohn (1990) suggested several strategies. Change yourself in some ways; this can be empowering. Involve yourself elsewhere; stay with a hobby or something similar. Change the stress source in some way. Adopting a positive attitude can in fact be done directly as a choice, and you can reinterpret negative energy by positively reframing it. Personal growth can help you avoid burnout. The growth may be through individual classical therapy or through traditional First Nations methods. When you are involved in a large project, do not take for granted that the early stages will be easy or will even succeed at all. Be cooperative and get along with others at work. Similarly, use your network and share in it. Try to minimize spillover; that is, do not let stressors from one area of your life drain energy from the healing, refreshing areas. Avoid burnout by learning about it. Use cognitive-behavioural methods such as thought stopping and removal of cognitive distortions like generalization, emotional thinking, or denial of the positive. You can also use behavioural methods such as time management and assertiveness training.

 **Snapshot 7**

Repression and Empowerment

Ironically, political repression by the RCMP in the 1960s helped jumpstart First Nations organizations and provided opportunities for some of the country's most important First Nations leaders to develop. The Company of Young Canadians (CYC) was created by the federal government to tap young people's enthusiasm, idealism, and demands for social reform. Youth were given an orientation session and then sent across the country to help organize needy groups. The RCMP soon infiltrated the organization, but found that they "failed to achieve any appreciable results. The CYC...continues to be a relatively safe haven for subversive, criminal, and otherwise undesirable elements" (Valpey, 2002, p. A1). The RCMP saw the CYC as providing *cover, mobility, finances,* and *respectability* to these *subversive elements,* which included future First Nations leaders such as George Erasmus and Phil Fontaine! Parliament closed the CYC in 1976. Ironically, the empowerment of young leaders came about because of repressive efforts to shut them down.

Summary

We have provided here a large and sometimes complex or confusing body of information. In fact, the task of being an effective counsellor with First Nations is relatively simple. Once you have reached a level of self-understanding through your own therapy or some other structured process of personal growth, such as one of the First Nations processes mentioned, you simply need to be respectful, listen closely, be patient, and be yourself. The difficulty is, as always, in the process of self-observation.

We forget that the secrets of the culture are unknown to the culture. Jacques Lacan had a strong belief in the importance of truly listening to a patient, yet he walked around in his sessions, worked on articles, and made his patients attend his seminars. This kind of flexibility and integration into real life fits well with the model presented here. Lacan said that the greatest discovery that an analyst makes comes when he listens to the patient's experience (see, for example, Felman, 1987). This certainly is a rare experience. To effectively listen to First Nations clients, counsellors must do much more than use active listening and just repeat back to clients what they have already said.

Case Study

Melvin K. was referred to me by the court after a series of nuisance charges (drunk and disorderly conduct, etc.). He presented as depressed and with suicidal episodes with binge drinking. Melvin was born in a western province on a small reserve to parents who were out of control. He related his earliest childhood memories as drunken fighting between his parents.

At the age of 6, Melvin was placed in a residential school. Historically, his people lived in an area that government believed could become geopolitically unstable. The government moved this prosperous, well-structured, agrarian community to a mid-northern, isolated, small unfarmable area on the side of a highway. The people, who had been independent and self-supporting, were forced to go on welfare and become dependent on food banks. The children were removed from the homes and placed in residential schools. Some of the children were not even returned home during the summer.

While 8-year-old Melvin was home for the Christmas holiday, his parents became intoxicated during a party in the home. During an altercation Melvin's uncle stabbed his brother, Melvin's father. Melvin was given the responsibility of taking his father in a horse and wagon to the hospital in the nearest town. However, a storm and blizzard came up, and he only made it part of the way before the horses refused to move on. He spent the night with his father in the blizzard, and his father died. In the morning Melvin took him to town. He remembers his father as stiff and cold. He was returned to school, never got to attend the funeral, and did not return home for four years until he completed school at Grade 6.

Melvin worked for years on farms as a hired hand and entered the drinking crowd, barely getting by over a period of 10 years. He finally wound up in a small city as an assistant to a tradesman. His drinking and fighting continued. He spent his money when he had it and lived hand to mouth.

Melvin was reluctant to see me in therapy; however, he was in a position of either going to jail or doing something about his way of life. We spent many sessions in which he said that nothing happened. Sometimes he would get up and walk out; other times he would badmouth the courts, the law, and me. He would speak his language and cuss at me if I asked a question.

The turning point came after he became involved with a woman and had a child. She took off and left the baby as his responsibility. He was scared and didn't know what to do. He did not want welfare to take the baby, but didn't want the baby to live the life he had lived. Suddenly, he was a parent who wanted to know about his life, the baby's life, and how to deal with it. He wanted to know how to take care of a baby, but he had no experience of living in a family. I told him I was not going to tell him; he hit me and walked out. To my surprise, he returned the next day for another session. This was clearly the key moment and turning point in the case.

During the following period, Melvin spent a great deal of time explaining how he was responsible for all of the bad things that had happened in his life and that he was terrible. He had killed his father and been a no-good. He made very little progress in therapy; he spent the time beating up on himself. He slowly began to look at life in a way that started to mend the hurts that he had experienced in his childhood. He gradually began to see himself as someone who was giving life, not taking it.

This was not a case of a sudden insight; he was still a bit of a roustabout, but he still cared for the child. The principles and processes employed in working with Melvin are that therapy can be a long, slow process in which the counsellor is deeply authentic and the individual gradually moves forward. The counsellor takes the client's hand and walks through life with him or her. You, as the counsellor, become the person in whose presence clients can sort out their own problems.

The process is really no more complicated than that. As shown in this chapter, the various First Nations already have their own models of psychology, and their therapy is generally built on a model of consulting with the appropriate elder. Your job as a counsellor is to listen closely, be yourself, and be helpful.

(Please note that the authors are not recommending that counsellors tolerate violence from clients. This is an unusual circumstance, but something that can happen in particular cases.)

Emergent Issues and Future Research

The major forces in counselling with First Nations in Canada are First Nations professionals themselves (note that 60% of the references used in this paper are by First Nations writers). This fact has changed the power relationships and the focus of research in the field. Research is now being built on partnership and on answers to the research questions put forward by the First Nations involved (Boucher, 2002; Offet-Gartner, 2008), instead of addressing abstract issues that do more for the majority culture than for First Nations subjects. The following are several areas of research (largely coming out of the University of British Columbia) that would give added value to our work.

- Research in British Columbia has shown that an effective healing program for First Nations would invoke empowerment, cleansing, balance, discipline, and a sense of belonging. This research could be replicated with other First Nations across the country. An instrument could be developed to measure how non-Native counsellors or professionals develop a working alliance with First Nations. Additional narratives of First Nations healing stories could be recorded to further develop the concepts involved in First Nations healing (McCormick, 1995).

- Non-Native counselling approaches seldom deal with the spiritual aspects of people. There needs to be a reexamination of the transcendental ways of understanding the world and of communicating this in counselling. The effectiveness of the vision quest and of the medicine wheel could be examined (McCormick, 1996).

- Longitudinal studies could be developed to document the effectiveness of career planning models with First Nations clients from the point of view of First Nations people. It would be particularly interesting to determine what facilitates the attainment of career goals (Neumann, McCormick, Amundson, & McLean, 2000).

In general, research could look at evaluating the effectiveness of First Nations models, integrating spirituality and values-based approaches, and the long-term effectiveness of career development, although perhaps not to the seventh generation. There is a need for carefully controlled research, but also a blend of other qualitative approaches. Also, there are serious gaps in research on taking into account the heterogeneity of First Nations populations (Trimble & Gonzalez, 2008).

Conducting psychological research with First Nations is a delicate issue, especially if the researcher is Euro-Canadian. There is a long history of insensitively conducted research causing stress for communities (Darou, Kurtness, & Hum, 2000). Several recommendations can be made to reduce the chances of conducting disrespectful research:

1. Obtain informed consent and follow the directives of a local advisory group. Do not conduct research unless you have been invited in and you have a clear, relevant purpose.
2. Be patient and flexible. You may not be aware of things happening behind the scenes.
3. When you make gaffs, try to recuperate gracefully. The people are surprisingly forgiving.
4. Learn the culture, geography, and language of your community. Read the same documents that local First Nations professionals are expected to read.
5. Put something back into the community. Research often has a high social cost to the community, and it is important for researchers to put something back.
6. Consider the use of nonexperimental paradigms and be extremely cautious if you use any kind of testing.
7. Share your results with the community.
8. Use a brief questionnaire to judge the impact of your research on subjects.
9. Do not mess around in Native politics.

Research is helpful and important, but it is also a minefield of cultural conflict. Again, we refer to the Hippocratic injunction of *do no harm*. Review also Chapter 9 for an elaboration of issues and strategies for culturally sensitive research.

Chapter Summary

It is not appropriate to make generalizations about counselling and Canadian First Nations when the group is composed of 53 different cultures. However, there seem to be some commonalities based on religious beliefs that are tied to the land, common geography, and a common history based on colonization and the abuses that can go with it. The key forces of First Nations include sense of community, the elders, deep values, religious beliefs, respect for nature, and religious beliefs that promote growth. Some of the key issues that the communities would like to attack include assimilation stress, posttraumatic stress, cultural rupture, addictions, cultural identification, health, and other issues caused by societal disruptions.

The people may be wary of even well-meaning counsellors because they may be seen as unhelpful or even as potentially harmful to community strengths. As a result, counselling methods based on Euro-Canadian principles may be poorly received. Counselling methods need to be based on deep respect, benefit to the community, spirituality, and values. The key competencies are very simple: listen in a way that gives meaning to both verbal and nonverbal messages, grow personally from your own hardships so that you can be yourself during therapy, and instead of using good techniques, simply be helpful.

CHAPTER 12
FACILITATING THE JOURNEY BETWEEN CULTURES:
COUNSELLING IMMIGRANTS AND REFUGEES

Nancy Arthur, Noorfarah Merali, and Ivana Djuraskovic

Key Terms and Concepts		
• Acculturation	• Immigrant settlement services	• Psychological adaptation
• Adaptation	• Intergenerational conflict	• Refugees
• Cultural identity	• Minority identity development	• Socio-cultural adaptation
• Economic adaptation	• Psychological acculturation	• Torture

Personal Introduction – Nancy Arthur

When I joined the Faculty of Education at the University of Calgary, I was excited about teaching and researching about counselling issues with diverse populations. However, I realized that I needed more knowledge about community agencies that provided services to immigrants. During an orientation at a local immigration agency, I realized how unaware I was of issues pertaining to settlement and community integration for newly arriving immigrants and refugees. I was also humbled by the realization that my life was removed from working with these populations, despite my interest in cultural diversity.

Naively, I had never considered the link between war and organized violence in other countries and the impact of forced migration on the settlement experience. I participated with an interdisciplinary group of professionals to learn more about ways to support survivors of torture. The activities were educational in nature, providing cultural awareness, professional training, and consciousness-raising about service delivery to the survivors. I was exposed to people who were courageous in making public testimony about their experiences. I began reading about the mental health issues of survivors of torture. This was not easy reading; I fought to stay focused and engaged with the issues. I questioned how people could possibly recover from the atrocities inflicted by other human beings. I felt shame at the realization that health professionals were often in the role of torturer.

I began to wonder how we could engage other professionals in the local community to become involved with this unique population of refugees. The need for a multidisciplinary approach to addressing trauma appeared paramount. However, I had concerns about the health of professionals and volunteers who were being recruited to work with survivors of torture. The general literature on trauma was expanding upon the vicarious impacts for people in helping roles.

Consequently, I decided to research the experiences of mental health professionals who had worked with survivors of torture. Interviews shed light on both the horrors and the celebrations they had experienced with clients. A key theme emerged from these interviews. All participants talked about how their worldview had changed as a result of working with survivors of torture. There was an essential paradox in the portrayal of their work.

At one level, the mental health professionals had to come to terms with what they had heard from their clients and to confront the evil that can be inflicted on one person by another. They witnessed the pain and long-term suffering of their clients. At times, they questioned how well they were serving their clients in their culturally embedded notions of treatment. Yet the mental health professionals talked about the impact of working with survivors of torture at another level. They learned about profound human capacity for change and for finding new meaning in life.

The stories of immigration are highly individual in terms of what leads people to leave their host country to establish a new life in Canada. Counsellors have a pivotal role in helping to influence the quality of life for those who choose to call Canada home.

Personal Introduction - Noorfarah Merali

As a first-generation immigrant from Dares Salaam, Tanzania, I have directly experienced the challenges of integrating into Canadian society. Having arrived in Canada at a very young age, I constantly attempted to reconcile my own perspective with that of my parents, who were raised in East Africa. Many intergenerational differences emerged and required repeated family negotiation. The task of living in two worlds and establishing a bicultural identity has been a lifelong process. My status with respect to my home and host cultures has changed in each developmental stage and in reaction to various critical incidents.

As an adolescent, I identified most strongly with other Canadians. As a young adult searching to find out who I was, I found myself drawn to my own East African Muslim cultural community. Through this rejoining process, I experienced a sense of belonging, resulting in a more balanced attachment to members of my own group and other Canadians. As an adult, I have experienced the most significant impact on my identity through two recent events: the United States terrorist attacks and the backlash against Muslims that followed. As I watched the news coverage on the violence occurring towards Muslims in Montreal, Vancouver, Calgary, and Edmonton, my physical appearance as a member of a visible minority of Muslim descent became very salient. I realized that the same characteristics that led me to feel close to members of my own group could trigger negative reactions from members of other groups. The event sensitized me to the existence of varying levels of cultural tolerance and intolerance in Canada.

A more recent influence on my personal and professional development has been the opportunity I have had to work with my own cultural community to facilitate the integration of refugees from Afghanistan. Afghans currently represent the largest and most widely dispersed refugee group worldwide, having withstood the most long-standing political violence situation and the greatest length of internment in refugee camps. Their circumstances have led to prolonged interruptions in schooling and health care access, and exposure to multiple forms of trauma, which have contributed to various adjustment challenges in the Canadian context. The fact that the violence in Afghanistan continues and that family members left behind may be facing threat or persecution is a constant reminder to the refugees of their previous vulnerability and the ongoing impact on their loved ones. Organizing a multi-sector response within our community to respond to the mental health needs of the refugees in a way that acknowledges the relationship between these needs and the life stressors that perpetuate them (i.e., ongoing political turmoil, poverty, unemployment and underemployment, physical health problems, large family sizes, and language barriers) has been an incredibly challenging and gratifying experience. The focus on the adjustment challenges of the Afghan refugees has also been tempered by an understanding of the remarkable resilience of human beings against incredible odds, and the ways in which religion and spirituality in a faith community can assist in engendering hope for the future.

My personal and professional experiences have generated a passionate interest in multicultural counselling, particularly in the areas of immigrant and refugee mental health. In addition to teaching graduate-level courses in cross-cultural research and practice at the University of Alberta, I have counselled members of various cultural groups with diverse presenting problems, both with and without the assistance of interpreters. I have also been a consultant for immigrant-serving agencies. These experiences have been both incredibly complex and incredibly rewarding. I hope that, as you read this chapter, you come to the same conclusions about counselling immigrants and refugees.

Personal Introduction - Ivana Djuraskovic

I first became aware of the impact of being a refugee in Canada during my postgraduate training at the University of Calgary. At that time, I had already lived in Canada for eight years. Despite the resettlement challenges that my family and I experienced, I believed that I was not particularly affected by the immigration process. I was completely detached from my refugee experience until I watched a film about refugees from former Yugoslavia in a multicultural counselling class. I was so deeply affected by the refugee testimonies I heard that day that I knew I had to address the internal struggle that I was going through. I had to come to terms with the fact that my country no longer existed and that the life I once knew completely disappeared. What particularly captured my attention was a profound difference between refugees' and voluntary immigrants' experiences of acculturation and ethnic identity reconstruction. The more I became immersed in my own experience, the more I wanted to learn about the experiences of refugees who have undergone a journey similar to mine. My desire to find answers to my own struggle, as well as to the struggle of others, led me to conduct a study about acculturation and ethnic identity reconstruction experiences of former Yugoslavian refugees for my Master's thesis. The answers that I found during my research confirmed my belief that refugees do experience more challenges with acculturation and ethnic identity reconstruction and motivated me to continue to dedicate my academic and professional work to understanding and improving refugee mental health and functioning.

Since I completed my MSc. in Counselling Psychology, I have come to terms with my refugee journey. I managed to let go of some of the memories and accepted my developing bicultural identity. I still struggle from time to time trying to define where I belong and where my home is. In many ways, I see Canada as my home. However, I also know that I have another home that exists only in my mind and heart. When I look back at my own acculturation experience, I can say that I am still trying to integrate the two cultures. I view that process as a life-long and never-ending journey. I also view it as a journey that I embrace every day.

My personal and professional journey has led me to develop a strong interest in multicultural counselling of refugees and immigrants. Working as a registered psychologist in Calgary and pursuing my PhD at the same time allowed me to come in contact with various individuals from culturally diverse backgrounds. Their complex and unique life stories continue to enrich both my personal and my professional lives. I believe that we become richer when we open ourselves to others and invite them to tell their stories in ways that are healing for them. I hope that after reading this chapter, you too, will be able to do the same.

Snapshot 1

Vignette

Ross, an instructor in an engineering technology program, met with a counsellor about one of his students. Ross befriended a young man, Biyana, from Sudan, who had lived in Canada for five years. As the semester progressed, Ross became concerned because Biyana was missing classes. In class, Biyana was often distracted and would put his head down on his desk. Sometimes, he would just get up and walk out of the room, for no apparent reason. Ross mentioned that Biyana told him that conditions in his homeland were very bad before he came to Canada. Ross encouraged Biyana to see a counsellor, but Biyana replied, "Don't worry, I will be all right, this will pass." The counsellor asked Ross if he would be willing to accompany Biyana to the counselling centre at the end of his next class. He agreed, and the two of them came together to the counselling office reception area.

Biyana was very nervous meeting with the counsellor, but began to relax when the counsellor explained that their time together would be confidential, that she would not disclose any information to his instructors, and that Biyana could leave at any time. After sharing the concerns expressed by his instructor, the counsellor asked Biyana what he thought was going on. He replied, "I am not sleeping, and I am tired in class. I am having nightmares about my country. This happens when I am stressed. This will pass."

Introduction

Canada is a nation founded on cultural diversity. In addition to populations of Aboriginal people, immigration has changed the landscape of Canadian society so that it is one of the most diverse nations in the world. Approximately 30% of the total population reports their ethnic origin as belonging to groups other than British, French, or Canadian. Increasing numbers of immigrants from visible non-dominant ethnic groups have moved to

Canada during the past 30 years and represent more than three quarters of the immigrant population of the 1990s (Statistics Canada, 2003a). In 2001, 4.3 million people reported European origin other than British or French, 2.9 million reported non-European origins, and 3.3 million reported mixed origins, showing that 70% of Canada's visible minority population was foreign born (Statistics Canada, 2007). Changes in these demographics are accounted for by changes in the source countries from which Canada has accepted immigrants and refugees. In the early part of the 20th century, most immigrants came to Canada from European and North American source countries. From the 1960s forward, the source countries expanded to include Asian, Middle Eastern, Caribbean, Central American, and African countries (Statistics Canada, 2007). The majority of immigrants and refugees settle in Canada's major cities, with the heaviest population density found in Toronto, Montreal, and Vancouver (Statistics Canada, 2008d). It is estimated that by the year 2017, 20% of Canada's population could be of diverse origin, with 95% of the total immigrant and refugee population living in metropolitan areas (Statistics Canada, 2007).

Counsellors can first prepare for multicultural counselling by becoming informed about the culturally diverse groups that live in their local area and province. Second, counsellors can make contact with immigrant-serving agencies to familiarize themselves with settlement services and programs. Although counsellors have not traditionally been involved in settlement services, early exposure to mental health professionals may be a promising direction for health promotion and prevention, along with helping new Canadians feel comfortable about accessing treatment services. Third, counsellors will inevitably come into contact with immigrants and refugees through professional practice, even if they do not specialize in counselling this population. Knowledge of migration issues is important for appreciating the longer-term impact of cross-cultural transition.

Multicultural counselling with immigrant and refugee populations requires counsellors to develop cross-cultural competencies to address racism, oppressive practices, and social injustice, including knowledge about how political, economic, and social systems impact migration and settlement. Counsellors are exposed to messages about immigrants, refugees, and particular ethnocultural groups that may contain stereotypes and discriminatory views. As noted in the model of culture-infused counselling, it is imperative for counsellors to explore their attitudes towards immigrant and refugee populations. Higher ethnic tolerance attitudes and higher racism attitudes have been differentially associated with multicultural case conceptualization ability (Constantine & Gushue, 2003). As illustrated in Snapshot 1, a core competency is appreciating the sense of loss and trauma that can accompany migration, particularly in the case of refugee clients. Understanding the relationships between stages of migration and current issues of acculturation is paramount for framing client issues and for designing effective counselling interventions.

We hope that this chapter will encourage students to engage with immigrant and refugee populations, not as foreigners from another country, but as people who are seeking to establish a new life in the neighbourhoods and communities of Canada.

Definition of Healthy Functioning and Psychosocial Well-Being

As defined by the World Health Organization (1987), health is a "state of complete physical, mental and social well-being" (p. 1). In Western societies, health and illness are considered to be person-centred conditions caused by micro-level natural and etiological agents such as genes, viruses, and stress levels. In contrast, the health and illness schemata of many immigrant and refugee groups view both healthy and unhealthy functioning as interpersonal and continuously manifesting processes that are intricately linked to family harmony or dysfunction, one's status within and connection to the cultural community and members of the host society, relationships between human beings and nature, and religion and spirituality (Landrine & Klonoff, 1992).

The physical and mental health screening required by Canada's immigration policy results in the selection of the healthiest candidates for immigration out of a large group of applicants. Described as the *healthy migrant effect* (Kramer, Tracy, & Ivey, 1999), the health status of many immigrants upon arrival is better than that of many Canadian citizens (Statistics Canada, 2005). However, some documentation suggests that health status begins to deteriorate after migration (Ng, Wilkins, Gendron, & Berthelot, 2005) and recovery of personal well-being only occurs several years after resettlement once all required linguistic, cultural, economic, and interpersonal adaptations have been made (Health Canada, 1999). The decline in psychological adjustment has been attributed to a variety of factors, including language barriers that preclude access to health care, unemployment and underemployment, experiences of racism and discrimination, reactivation of previous trauma experiences, changes in family dynamics after migration, and challenges associated with acculturation (Ng et al.). Personal and social adjustment is strongly connected to how well immigrants adjust to new employment realities in the host country (Chen, 2008; Ngo & Este, 2006). Poverty and low socio-economic status have been implicated as predictors of health status, including mental health (Coburn, 2004). Despite the fact that children of foreign-born families are more than twice as likely to live in poor families compared to Canadian-born children, there are few disparities evident in health or levels of functioning. Using school performance as an indicator, immigrant children often outperform their host country counterparts. Although economic disruptions to families often occur during settlement, the longer-term implications of poverty need to be examined in relation to health status.

Changes in the socio-economic status of immigrants and refugees are paralleled by a cultural change process. **Acculturation** refers to a *twofold process of cultural and psychological changes in the values, behaviours, and interaction patterns of individuals as a result of cross-cultural contact* (Berry, 2005). Changes can occur within individuals or across people and situations. **Psychological acculturation** describes *changes in mental health, behaviours, and emotionality that are associated with the cross-cultural contact experience* (Berry, 2008), whereas **adaptation** refers to a *reasonably stable and multifaceted process and outcome of attempting to adjust to a new socio-cultural environment* (Berry, 2005).

After their arrival in Canadian society, immigrants and refugees are faced with two parallel decisions about their degree of emotional and behavioural investment in the home and host cultures: (a) a decision as to how much of their unique cultural identity they want to maintain and (b) a decision as to their desired level of interaction with people who do not share their cultural heritage. The specific acculturation strategies that result from these two decisions range from complete maintenance of one's identity and isolation from other groups (i.e., separation) to assimilation into the surrounding milieu. Biculturalism, the integration of home and host cultures in terms of both lifestyles and interaction patterns, represents the midpoint of these polarities. When an individual's decision-making process results in a lack of desire to retain unique cultural tenets paired with a lack of desire to socially integrate, the strategy of marginalization applies (Berry, 2003, 2005, 2006b). Berry (2005) reported that, across numerous studies, the strategy of biculturalism has been found to lead to the most positive mental health outcomes.

However, it appears that this is only the case when members of the surrounding society have favourable attitudes towards immigrants and refugees. For example, in a review of studies of various groups migrating to Quebec, Tousignant (1997) noted that East Indian and Haitian immigrants who used the strategy of biculturalism in adapting to life in French Canadian society experienced higher levels of psychological distress than those who fully retained their traditional heritage through the use of a separation strategy. These results are attributed to the lack of acceptance by French Canadians to support the integration of these immigrant groups; therefore, intercultural contact experiences produced instances of racism and intolerance.

Berry (2003, 2005) qualified his argument regarding biculturalism as the best mental health option for immigrants and refugees by stipulating that it must be accompanied by attitudes of acceptance by the host nation. Although Canada has adopted a multicultural policy of intercultural relations, it appears that the impact of the policy on attitudes towards various members of non-dominant groups may vary both with provincial jurisdictions and with immigrants' and refugees' degree of dissimilarity to members of the host group. For example, East Indians and Haitians are both highly visible minorities. Therefore, attitudes towards them may be different than attitudes towards less physically distinct or invisible non-dominant groups.

Taking these issues into account, Phinney, Horenczyk, Liebkind, and Vedder (2001) argued that the psychosocial well-being of immigrants and refugees is a function of the interaction between a combination of their selected acculturation strategies and attitudes towards the maintenance of their unique ethnic identities and the attitudes of the specific receiving community. These researchers also postulated that the specific characteristics and circumstances of the immigrant or refugee group moderate these relationships. Horenczyk (2000) further argued that immigrants' and refugees' acculturation does not occur in a vacuum, but is instead a result of both intragroup and intergroup relations that support as well as challenge immigrants' and refugees' ability to acculturate and reconstruct their sense of self.

Despite the difficulties associated with the migration experience, problem-focused literature on immigration is now beginning to be balanced by research suggesting that immigrants and refugees are resilient, healthy, and active participants in their acculturation (Berry, 2005; van Oudenhoven, 2006). Having frequent contact with more than one culture allows immigrants and refugees to adopt a cosmopolitan attitude towards resettlement and equips them with necessary skills to survive in increasingly larger multicultural societies (van Oudenhoven). The majority of immigrants and refugees manage the settlement experience and have a positive sense of cultural identity and positive views about the larger society (Berry, 2005; Phinney, 2003; Phinney et al., 2001).

Cultural Identity and Relationship to the Dominant Culture

Phinney (2003) described **cultural identity** as *consisting of the three interrelated components of a sense of belonging to particular ethnic group, the beliefs, attitudes, and values related to one's group membership, and feelings about the status of one's group within the larger society.* Development of cultural identity is a multifaceted and dynamic process that occurs over time and requires individuals to actively participate in successfully forming their ethnic identity (Phinney & Ong, 2007). There are significant discrepancies between the unique values and beliefs that form the basis of an immigrant or refugee client's cultural identity and the values and worldview of the dominant culture of Canadian society. There is also evidence suggesting that members of cultural groups that are dissimilar to the host group in physical appearance, language, or cultural norms may be treated as though they are of lower social status than other Canadians.

In a study of residents of 40 countries, including Canada and the United States, Hofstede (1980) identified four value dimensions in which national cultures vary: (a) the degree to which hierarchical relationships are emphasized as opposed to egalitarian relationships (Power Distance); (b) the level of sex-role differentiation that exists in the culture (Masculinity); (c) the extent to which personal needs and goals are assigned primacy in relation to those of the family, group, or collectivity (Individualism); and (d) the degree to which a national culture is bound by rules and rituals governing communication and interpersonal interaction (Uncertainty Avoidance).

According to Hofstede's (1980) taxonomy of national cultures, Canada is characterized by a relatively low degree of power distance and uncertainty avoidance, a high level of individualism, and an average degree of masculinity when compared to other cultures around the world. The values of many immigrants' and refugees' countries of origin are often incongruent with those of Canadian society. For example, adjustment issues may be better understood as challenges faced by some immigrants in trying to adapt their personal worldview from a collectivistic to individualistic society (Chung, Bemak, Ortiz, & Sandoval-Perez, 2008). In turn, adjustment may be more difficult when Canadians are less understanding of practices associated with collectivistic cultures.

Sue and Sue's (2008) synthesis of worldview differences between Western and non-Western cultures complements the model put forth by Hofstede (1980). They posited that the Western culture of North America is characterized by a focus on the future, a task orientation that emphasizes doing over being, and the mastery of humans over nature. This is contrasted with the worldviews of many non-Western cultures that have a past or present orientation and that value learning from history, emphasize the importance of being over doing, and reflect subjugation of humans to nature (i.e., life is determined by external forces, such as fate or God's will), or alternatively, harmony with nature. Ibrahim, Roysircar-Sodowsky, and Ohnishi (2001) also highlighted fundamental differences in how human nature is viewed across cultures. Their research shows that some non-Western groups view human nature to be neutral or inherently evil. This supports the need for direction and discipline to move people towards positive or prosocial behaviours. This view of human beings is the opposite of the positive appraisal of human nature in the Western worldview, which emphasizes people's innate potential for self-actualization.

The differences between various national cultures and Canadian culture outlined in Hofstede's (1980) classification system and implied by the work of Sue and Sue (2008) and Ibrahim et al. (2001) would only influence the counselling process with immigrants and refugees if they retained the values and practices of their countries of origin after immigrating. Canadian multicultural policy asserts that immigrants and refugees are free to retain their unique cultural values and behaviours as long as they display primary allegiance to Canadian society by acquiring one of the two official languages: English or French. The policy explicitly advocates a stance of mutual accommodation. On one hand, both government bodies and members of Canadian society are expected to promote the equal participation of newcomers in all aspects of Canadian life, including the provision of equal access to employment opportunities, housing, legal protections, and social networks. On the other hand, the policy encourages newcomers to share their cultural heritage with other members of Canadian society and to initiate efforts to preserve their native languages and cultures (Department of Canadian Heritage [DCH], 1988).

At first glance, the stance taken by Canadian multicultural policy appears to be superior to the philosophy held by other countries, which encourage newcomers to shed their differences and assimilate into the surrounding host society. Yet the Canadian reality falls short of the policy ideals. Consider the following examples.

Recall the work of Tousignant (1997) about the negative attitudes of people in Quebec society towards Indian immigrants. In reporting the findings of the Housing New Canadians Project in Toronto, Dion (2001) found similar results in the high rates of perceived discrimination among the most visible immigrant groups. Perceptions of discrimination in obtaining properties for rental or ownership purposes were reportedly based on race, accented speech, religion, and family size. Several studies (Mattu, 2002; Miraftab, 2000; Murdie, 2002; Novac, Darden, Haluchanski, Seguin, & Berneche, 2002) found that cultural and religious differences, large family size, and discrimination led to considerable problems in finding adequate housing for immigrants and refugees. Madariaga-Vignudo and Miladinovska-Blazevska (2005) also reported perceived discriminatory landlord practices towards refugees in Winnipeg, which contributed to considerably more struggles in finding adequate housing. Similarly, Bauder and Lusis (2008) reported negative perceptions of Filipino immigrants about their life due to a lack of employment, discrimination and violence, and their lack of social connections. Dion and Kawakami (1996) obtained a similar pattern of results in a study of perceived employment discrimination among visible and non-visible immigrant and refugee groups in Toronto.

In a study of the resettlement experiences of refugees in Alberta, the residents of seven cities were asked about their views of Canadian Multicultural Policy and Immigration Policy and about their degree of interaction with immigrants and refugees. Thirty-nine percent of the respondents expressed the opinion that too many immigrants are entering the country each year. Furthermore, among residents of some smaller Alberta cities, only 50% of individuals knew or interacted with an immigrant or refugee or included one in their support network (Prairie Centre of Excellence for Research on Immigration and Integration [PCERII], 1999).

This study also assessed experiences of racism and discrimination with respect to employment and housing in the Alberta context. In contrast with the findings of the Toronto study, reports of perceived housing discrimination were very low (4%). However, 14% of the sample reported experiencing discrimination in the pursuit of employment, and 17% reported experiences of racism or discrimination by service providers, such as members of the public service, agency staff, or ESL teachers (PCERII, 1999).

The differences between the Toronto and Alberta contexts may be due to differences in available housing. Because Toronto is a larger city and more overpopulated, housing may be scarcer there. Economic fluctuations also impact the availability of housing in different parts of Canada, leading homeowners to guard housing opportunities for people whom they perceive to be most worthy on the basis of race, ethnicity, and religious affiliation.

Experiences of racism and discrimination in the pursuit of housing, employment, and community services can affect the cultural and racial identity development of immigrants and refugees. These experiences may precipitate cultural changes geared towards increasing acceptance by others or protection from further maltreatment. **Minority identity development** *takes place through a reciprocal relationship between one's home culture and the culture of the new society; it is the continuous process of reflecting upon and deriving meaning from one's unique racial, cultural, and ethnic identity in response to the reactions and experiences produced by interaction with members of the dominant group in society, as well as members of other groups* (Atkinson, Morten, & Sue, 1993; Sue & Sue, 2008). The identity development process can affect the acculturation strategies that immigrants and refugees choose.

Perceived racial victimization can be the catalyst for people to enter the Dissonance or Resistance and Immersion Stages of the Minority Identity Development Model developed by Atkinson and colleagues (1993), which was discussed in Chapter 4. The Dissonance stage involves experiencing conflicting self-appreciating and self-depreciating attitudes paired with conflicting attitudes towards one's own cultural group or blaming the host cultural group for one's victimization. Ambivalence towards both the home and host cultures reflects a state of marginalization. In contrast, if individuals develop a stronger attachment towards their own group and a rejecting attitude towards the host group as a response to racism and discrimination, the individual would be in the Resistance and Immersion stage of the Minority Identity Development Model. The emphasis on immersing oneself in one's own culture suggests the use of a separation strategy of acculturation.

The specific acculturation strategy used by immigrants and refugees to respond to the realities of intercultural contact in Canada would affect the degree to which the cultural differences described in Hofstede's work and the work of others (Ibrahim et al., 2001; Sue & Sue, 2008) are likely to persist or to be reduced by value and behavioural shifts towards the dominant culture. For example, a person who is propelled into the Resistance and Immersion stage of the Minority Identity Development Model and who uses a separation strategy of acculturation to deal with an incident of racism would lean towards retaining unique values, worldviews, and behaviours. To prevent further victimization, this person may minimize contact with other Canadians. Therefore, the differences between the immigrant's or refugee's home culture and the host culture would be maximized by a reluctance to *mix* with and adopt the values and behaviours of other Canadians. It is important to note that even when immigrants and refugees show signs of external change, such as acquisition of English as a second language or the incorporation of Canadian social norms, their unique worldviews and values are often retained (Sue & Sue).

Theoretical Principles

Immigrant and Refugee Populations in Transition

There are important distinctions to recognize between those who migrate voluntarily (e.g., immigrants) and those who migrate involuntarily due to extenuating personal or political circumstances (e.g., refugees) (Bemak, Chung, & Pedersen, 2003). According to the definition adopted at the United Nations 1951 Geneva Convention, refugees are individuals who are outside of their country of origin and are unable to return due to the fear of persecution based on race, nationality, religion, and/or affiliation with a particular social group or political opinion (Amnesty International Canada, 2001). Due to the global humanitarian crisis in the 1990's, this long-standing definition has been widely criticized; it has been described as too narrow, not allowing for inclusion of people who leave their homes because of civil conflicts, organized violence, or other severe political, social, and economic factors (Bemak et al.; International Organization of Migrants, 1990). As a result, the definition of a refugee has been expanded to recognize and include individuals who are affected by the above-mentioned factors (Allen, Vaage, & Hauff, 2006).

In his kinetic model of the refugee in flight, Kunz (1973) described refugee migration and resettlement as an involuntary process, during which, if given a choice, refugees would most likely remain in their country, where they were living well-integrated lives. Thus, refugee migration is influenced by *push* factors in the country of origin, such as conditions of war, fear of political prosecution, and threats to safety of self, family, and community (Boyd, 1989). Kunz further distinguished between anticipatory and acute refugees and postulated that, while anticipatory refugees have limited time to prepare for their flight, acute refugees leave their home at the last moment. For example, one study of Vietnamese refugees found that 85% of individuals fled their home between two hours and two days of coming under severe threat (Liu et al., 1979).

Unlike refugee migration, immigrant migration is influenced by *pull* factors in the new country of settlement (Boyd, 1989; Kunz, 1973), such as educational and employment opportunities and security for one's family members. Thus, immigrant migration is of a voluntary nature and a result of immigrants' desire to build a better life in another country, remain in the country indefinitely, obtain employment, and enjoy benefits of citizenship (Mulder et al., 2001). Furthermore, voluntary immigrants often have optimistic expectations about their new lives and receive greater supports, which maximize the benefits of their immigration (Escobar et al., 2000).

 **Snapshot 2**

Citizenship and Immigration Canada has established categories of immigration under Canada's immigration policy. Broadly, these categories correspond with the economic, family reunification, and humanitarian objectives of the Immigration Act. Furthermore, Citizenship and Immigration Canada distinguishes between permanent and temporary residents. Temporary residents include foreign workers, foreign students, and visitors. Permanent residents are selected based on economic, family, and/or refugee class, or people become permanent residents on humanitarian and compassionate grounds (Citizenship & Immigration Canada, 2005).

The *economic* category includes assessment of the viability of immigrants to be successful in the labour market or in business. In response to Canadian immigration policy directives to attract immigrants who are highly educated and who can contribute skilled labour to the Canadian marketplace, economic immigrants now comprise approximately two-thirds of the total new immigrant population (Statistics Canada, 2005/2006). It is generally believed that immigrants from this category voluntarily move to Canada and have presumably prepared themselves for the transition. However, this does not preclude individual differences between family members and the possibility of adjustment issues surfacing through the process of acculturation. Also described as *independent immigrants,* applicants must demonstrate their capacity for financial stability through skilled work, entrepreneurship, investments, or self-employment. Canada's Business Immigration Program is based on the categories of entrepreneurs, self-employed persons, and investors. This category includes skilled workers, business immigrants, provincial nominees, and live-in caregivers (Citizenship and Immigration Canada, 2005).

Family class immigrants are close relatives who join family members already established in Canada, thus reuniting the family. The relative in Canada who is a Canadian citizen has the financial responsibility of providing support to relatives during their period of settlement. Reasons for moving are primarily focused on family matters, and economic reasons are less central to the application process. However, the relative who is a Canadian citizen may feel tremendous pressure to earn sufficient funds to sponsor one relative or several members of the family. *Assisted relatives* are immigrants who have at least one relative in Canada who demonstrates willingness to assist with integration.

The *refugee* category is defined by the United Nations Convention and Protocol Relating to the Status of Refugees. Essentially, **refugees** are *persons who require protection or relief, who most often have fled their countries involuntarily, and who have little if any time to prepare for moving to Canada.* Refugees may arrive directly in Canada from their country of origin; however, detention in temporary camps or seeking asylum in other countries prior to arriving to Canada is common.

The *Permanent Resident Status on Humanitarian and Compassionate Grounds* category includes all individuals who do not qualify for any other category and who are granted permanent status on humanitarian and compassionate grounds. The purpose of this category is to provide flexibility for cases that deserve to receive status in Canada (Statistics Canada, 2005/2006).

Adapted from:
"Immigrants and Ethnic Minorities on the Prairies: A Statistical Compendium," by N. Lamba, M. Mulder, and L. Wilkinson, 2000, Edmonton, AB: Prairie Centre of Excellence for Research on Immigration and Integration, p. 5.
"Recent Immigrants in the Calgary Metropolitan Area: A Comparative Portrait Based on the 1996 Census," by Informetrica Limited, 2000, Ottawa, ON: Citizenship and Immigration Canada, p. 13.
"Annual Report to Parliament on Immigration, 2005," by Citizenship and Immigration Canada, 2005, Ottawa, ON: Citizenship and Immigration Canada, pp. 1-14.
"Report on the Demographic Situation in Canada," by Statistics Canada 2005/2006, Ottawa, ON: Statistics Canada, pp. 1-108.

The pathways to immigration can have a profound effect on individuals' experiences of immigration. Even though voluntary migrants may have more time to prepare psychologically and practically for leaving their home country, this does not mean there will be no adjustment issues. Voluntary immigration often brings with it countless losses related to family, culture, and social life, which may negatively influence immigrants' resettlement (Djuraskovic & Arthur, 2009b). Ambivalence about the migration process within individuals and between family members adds complexity to the decision to migrate.

Other important considerations separate the refugee experience from that of *voluntary* immigrants. Forced displacement of refugees is in itself a traumatic event (Bemak et al., 2003). When choices about the relocation of refugees are severely limited, the experience of forced displacement and loss is significantly increased and refugees' difficulties are often further perpetuated. For example, Kunz (1973) pointed out that once refugees reach the place of first asylum, they are usually given three choices: to return to their country, to remain in the place of first asylum, or to resettle to another country. For most refugees, the return home is an impossibility; therefore, many choose to resettle to far away countries in order to survive. When such forced displacement and limited choice with regards to resettlement occur, refugees often experience psychological distress associated with an unexpected and very rapid resettlement process. When such a sudden process is paired with personal, social, economic, and cultural losses, refugees are placed in situations in which their physical and psychological well-being is severely compromised (Bemak et al.).

Regardless of the specific circumstances leading to migration, three stages have considerable potential for traumatic experiences and serious psychological distress: the premigration stage, the migration stage during transit to the new country, and the post-migration stage of settlement (Arredondo, 1986; Foster, 2001). A common feature in each stage is the occurrence of distressing events. In the premigration stage, there are threats to the safety or life of the individual or family as a result of war or other political campaigns. For example, many refugees witness genocide, killings, war, torture, hunger, homelessness, bombings, and other psychological and physical violence (Bemak et al., 2003; Bemak & Chung, 2005; Prendes-Lintel, 2001), placing them at risk for later developing serious difficulties such as post-traumatic stress, depression, anxiety, and other psychosocial problems (Bemak & Chung, 2002). Conditions of violence and trauma may be experienced by individuals, families, or the community as a whole. During the actual migration era, there is heightened fear related to the means of escaping and the possibility of being apprehended. Such fears often contribute to the lack of coping skills and place refugees at risk for experiencing more difficult and complex resettlement (Yakushko, Watson, & Thompson, 2008).

It is in the post-migration stage that refugees must simultaneously face the upheaval of adjustment in a new culture and the grieving process of the homeland, family, and life left behind. Premigration experiences and conditions are inextricably linked to mental health concerns that emerge during the post-migration period. It is the nature of the forced displacement and history of trauma that gives rise to refugees' problems, psychological distress, and disruption in normal functioning (Yakushko, Watson et al., 2008). When these circumstances are combined with acculturation stress, relational struggles, loss of social status, and oppression in the host society, the future for many refugees remains taxing. However, some immigrants and refugees may not experience such profound struggles with their adaptation. Understanding how resiliency factors influence acculturative success may help clarify specific strategies that immigrants and refugees use that help them with the integration process in a new culture (Djuraskovic & Arthur, 2009b).

The Psychology of Immigration

The most comprehensive model outlining the psychology of immigration has been proposed by Berry (e.g., Berry, 1997, 2001, 2003, 2005) based upon two domains of research. First, acculturation is viewed as a central process in cross-cultural psychology. Second, research on intergroup relations focuses on the experiences of immigrants as they interact with members of the dominant culture and on how group characteristics are maintained through contact between groups in society. Core constructs in the model proposed by Berry (2001, 2003, 2005) are provided to orient readers to contextual influences in the lives of immigrants and refugees. Additional acculturation models are also discussed.

Acculturation

Acculturation unfolds at both individual and group levels as members of two cultural groups interact in the settlement society. "Acculturation is a process involving two or more groups, with consequences for both; in effect, however, the contact experiences have much greater impact on the non-dominant group and its members" (Berry, 2001, p. 616). Psychological change at the individual level is referred to as *psychological acculturation* (Berry, 2003, 2008). The attitudes of the larger society represent a *multicultural ideology* (Berry & Kalin, 1995).

As a result of intercultural contact, individual immigrants and immigrant groups adopt one of four strategies discussed in the first section of this chapter for dealing with the receiving society: separation, assimilation, integration or biculturalism, and marginalization (Berry, 1997, 2001, 2005). The receiving society adopts parallel strategies for responding to immigrants. Similarly, other research focuses on describing different adjustment styles that immigrants and refugees use, including individual and socio-cultural factors such as age, language, education, job skills, religion, and kinship ties to explain how immigrants and refugees choose to adjust to the new culture (Khoa & VanDeusen, 1981; Meszaros, 1961; Westermeyer, 1989; Wong-Rieger & Quintana, 1987). Newer acculturation models; however, take into account the relevance of other acculturation domains (political, economic, occupational, family, social, religion, and diverse cognition), and include immigrants' and refugees' own perceptions of the acculturation process and ethnic identity reconstruction (Djuraskovic & Arthur, 2009b; Navas et al., 2005).

The acculturation strategies used by immigrants and refugees influence the development of their cultural identity. Development and redevelopment of ethnic identity is closely tied to the process of acculturation and it occurs parallel to the acculturation process (Djuraskovic & Arthur, 2009b). Cultural contrasts prompt people to become reflective about their personal cultural identity, often resulting in a change of worldviews (Arthur, 2000). The process of acculturation inevitably results in psychological changes and *behavioural shifts* (Berry, 2003). The greater the disparity between the home and host cultures, the greater the demands for *culture shedding* and *culture learning* (Berry, 1997, 2003). Culture shedding occurs when the demands of the new society require discarding familiar ways of operating because they are no longer viable. Individuals and groups are faced with learning new behaviour in order to be effective in new cultural contexts. Adaptation is impacted by the capacity of immigrants and refugees for cultural learning and the development of positive identities. As noted earlier, bicultural identities and attitudes of integration have been generally shown to support better psychological adaptation in immigrant populations (Berry, 2005) and to support favourable school adjustment for immigrant youth (Phinney et al., 2001). In contrast, the least favourable outcomes for adaptation have been associated with separated and marginalized identities (Berry, 2005).

Although bicultural identities and attitudes of integration have been deemed as more favourable strategies (Berry, 2005), immigrants and refugees may experience competing desires to assimilate and rebel against the host culture. Revisiting old acculturation patterns serves as a tool for resolving internal conflicts or challenges related to ongoing contact with the host culture (Djuraskovic & Arthur, 2009a). Therefore, evaluation of bicultural identities and strategies of integration is an ongoing and long-lasting process whereby immigrants and refugees recycle their acculturation experiences in order to strengthen the bond with both the original culture and the host society.

The context of intragroup and intergroup relations is important for understanding the acculturation attitudes of immigrants and refugees. It is through social interaction in the receiving society that immigrants define what is expected of them and what they believe is expected from them in the new society. Furthermore, acculturation may take various forms as individuals show high variability in how they experience changes provoked by cross-cultural interaction (Berry, 2005).

The interplay between personal acculturation expectations and perceived acculturation expectations of the host society is a complex process in which newcomers reconstruct and redefine their identity (Ben-Shalom & Horenczyk, 2003). Berry's recent writing (1997, 2003, 2005) has described acculturation as a process of mutual change through contact between new Canadians and the receiving culture. However, the degree of mutuality must be questioned. Non-dominant groups often have more invested in adapting to cultural norms and ways of living in the receiving country. Consequently, the nature of contact through acculturation may be more unidirectional than bidirectional.

Members of dominant groups need to be encouraged to examine the benefits that can occur through inclusive practices versus practices of domination and colonialism. However, contact alone between members of culturally diverse groups does not necessarily lead to mutual change. Dominant groups may strongly resist accommodating the culture of new groups and may direct their efforts to absorbing these groups into their own ways. Alternatively, contact may lead to a blending of cultures in which distinctive cultural practices and identity dissipate over time. Since the inception of the 1988 *Canadian Multiculturalism Act,* the federal government has sought "the full participation of all Canadians in the social, economic, cultural, and political facets of Canadian society"

(Government of Canada, 2003, p. 1). This notion was further extended through implementation of the *Immigration and Refugee Protection Act* in 2002, which recognized that "integration involves mutual obligations for new immigrants and Canadian society" (Government of Canada, p. 1). Consistent with the push towards mutual accommodation, Berry (2003) argued that national multicultural policies and the individual attempts of immigrants to integrate into the host society need to be matched by institutional change in the form of diversity and equity initiatives within mainstream organizations and systems. He argued that parallel acculturation strategies on all three levels (national, individual, and institutional) are prerequisites for effective inclusion of immigrants and refugees in Canada.

The social-psychological study of intergroup relations sheds light on the process of acculturation in the receiving culture (Berry, 2001). Many migrant groups are culturally defined by other groups according to specific dimensions of culture, such as race, religion, language, or geographical origin. Dimensions of culture can be the focus of stereotyping, negative attitudes, and prejudice to position newcomers as *outsiders* to the local culture. If the receiving culture is not open to pluralism and multiculturalism, acculturation may become a very difficult and challenging process for immigrants and refugees (Berry, 2005).

Attitudes of members of the dominant society towards particular immigrant and refugee groups range from a relative degree of acceptance to rejection. Conversely, immigrants' attitudes and behaviour towards the receiving society influence the attitudes held by members of the larger society towards them (Berry, 2001). For immigrants and refugees to successfully acculturate, a mutual accommodation between cultures must occur, including the right of all people to be accepted and live as culturally diverse individuals (Berry, 2005).

Ultimately, the result may be captured as a general *zero-sum* view of life (Esses, Dovidio, Jackson, & Armstrong, 2001). On one hand, people take pride in their appreciation for cultural diversity; on the other, they fear immigrants because of perceived threats to their economic and social stability. When resources in the larger society are limited, anti-immigration attitudes emerge as a protective stance against competition for commodities such as employment and social services (Berry, 2001; Palmer, 1996).

Adaptation

In general, "adaptation refers to the relatively stable changes that take place in an individual or group in response to external demands" (Berry, 2005, p. 709). Certain personal characteristics and conditions of migration are related to adaptation outcomes in the new society, including previous knowledge of the host culture, conditions of exodus from the country of origin, age of entry into the settlement country, employment, education, gender, and intergroup attitudes (Berry, 1997, 2003). Additionally, adaptation outcomes may turn out to be either positive or negative, showing high variability among individuals, and may range from being poorly adapted to well adapted in the new culture (Berry, 2005).

Adaptation occurs on three levels (Berry, 2003). First, **psychological adaptation** refers to *a general sense of satisfaction and well-being with one's life.* Psychological adaptation involves both an individual's psychological and physical well-being (Berry, 2005) and it occurs through a sense of satisfaction relative to other groups in the immigrant's country of origin and the settlement country. Psychological adaptation is optimized if immigrants perceive a match between the demands for linguistic, cultural, or social change placed upon them and their ability to meet these demands. When immigrants perceive discrepancies between the demands placed upon them by the host society and their ability to respond to these demands, they are likely to experience stress (Lazarus, 1997). Good psychological adaptation depends on the individual's personality, life changes, and supportive networks in the individual's social environment (Berry, 2005). In addition, there is some evidence that how successfully immigrants and refugees will adapt to the new culture largely depends on the acculturation strategies they choose for themselves (Kosic, 2002).

Second, **socio-cultural adaptation** refers to *progress in acquiring the requisite skills for managing daily life and for participating in society.* Many immigrants arrive in Canada with high levels of academic and professional qualifications, but lack social competencies for effectively integrating into a new society. Interventions such as skills coaching and training are integral aspects of settlement and employment programming (Westwood, Mak,

Barker, & Ishiyama, 2000). Individuals are said to have successfully adapted if they have increased cultural knowledge, increased the degree of contact with the host culture, and developed positive attitudes towards the groups they have come in contact with (Berry, 2005).

Although psychological and socio-cultural adaptation reflect two distinct theoretical concepts, they are interrelated in the process of adaptation. While psychological adaptation largely influences personal functioning, socio-cultural adaptation influences interactive activities in the new cultural environment (Berry, 2005). It is easier to manage the demands of interacting with members of the host culture if one is feeling psychologically well. Conversely, experiences of success and positive interactions with members of the host culture enhance a personal sense of health and satisfaction (Ataca & Berry, 2002).

Linked closely to both psychological and socio-cultural adaptation is the concept of **economic adaptation**, conceptualized as *a sense of accomplishment arising from participation in the economic spheres of life in Canada.* There are some disturbing patterns related to human capital that are relevant for the economic adaptation of Canadian immigrants. In comparison to the native-born population, immigrant women and men have lower rates of labour force participation and lower levels of earning (Reitz, 2001). There are also fewer returns on education for immigrants, as institutional barriers continue to be evident in the transfer of foreign credentials. Immigrants are screened in their host country for qualifications related to education and skilled labour. However, their expectations about securing suitable employment may sharply contrast their actual experiences of employment barriers (Chen, 2008). Employment status is strongly connected to economic stability. In comparison to native-born Canadians, immigrants are more likely to experience poverty, and poverty is most severely experienced by immigrants who are visible minorities (Kazemipur & Halli, 2000).

Immediate demands during initial entry to the settlement country can be disruptive and experienced as primarily negative; however, the demands of migration tend to shift in nature and be perceived in different ways as individuals gain new skills for coping in the settlement society (Berry, 1997, 2003; Lazarus, 1997). A sense of cultural competence and access to resources in the new culture can lead to long-term positive outcomes. Unfortunately, struggles to gain economic independence may exacerbate individual mental health problems at a time when individuals require a strong foundation from which to resolve traumatic experiences and integrate into the new culture (Bemak et al., 2003). Cultural adaptation is often complex and situationally dependent (Navas et al., 2005). In fact, how immigrants and refugees adapt constantly changes over time as their contact with the host culture and other cultural groups within the host culture changes.

Common Presenting Concerns in the Counselling Context

Immigrant and refugee populations have been described as "fractured, transitory, and diverse" (Pick, 1997, p. 50). Their experiences are highly individual, due to factors such as conditions in the country of origin, their motivations for seeking migration, the degree of difference between the cultural norms of the home and settlement countries, expectations about the host society, and receptivity of the host society towards new Canadians. This emphasis on the individual should not overshadow the fact that many intact families immigrate to Canada (Ataca & Berry, 2002). Family members will experience the demands of acculturation in various ways, resulting in reciprocal influences on the family unit. The reference points that clients use to compare themselves, including their peers and family back home, the majority community, and other immigrants from similar ethnocultural groups, are important considerations for understanding their sense of life satisfaction in Canada (Vohra & Adair, 2000).

Despite the diversity of experiences, a number of personal factors and common issues have been identified that impact the mental health of immigrants and refugees. Following the model of culture-infused counselling, counsellors have a responsibility to gain background knowledge as a basis from which to assess the unique circumstances and needs of individual clients.

Language

Language competency plays a critical role in the adjustment of immigrants and refugees in Canadian society. Fluency in the language that is spoken regionally is a tremendous advantage for entering Canadian society. Language skills are one of the major barriers to participation in the labour force (Chen, 2008). English language competency can also be a barrier for pursuing post-secondary education. In the authors' experience, applicants who are competent with technical and mathematical skills may be barred from pursuing training and educational opportunities due to difficulties with equivalency testing of English language skills.

Second-language programs may provide basic language skills, but they are not equivalent to the experience of learning language through development in a particular culture. Learning a new language can trigger feelings of loss of cultural identity, longing for one's homeland, and interaction with others who share language and other aspects of culture (Bemak et al., 2003). Frustrations can also lead individuals to question their capacity for mastering the language of the new culture, resulting in reduced feelings of competence and self-esteem. Beyond skills levels, the degree to which new Canadians feel confident about using English skills is related to their psychosocial and cultural adaptation (Dion, Dion, & Pak, 1990). Due to their increased contact with others through school, children frequently acquire language skills at a faster pace than adult members of the family. Role reversals can occur when children are placed in a position of translating for their parents or grandparents, creating an unusual shift in power in family relationships (Davidson, Murray, & Schweitzer, 2008).

Language skills can also be a barrier to seeking mental health services and deriving benefits from those services (Arthur, 2008). It is difficult to communicate distress in ways that are understandable to others and allow culturally sensitive helpers to appreciate the contexts of despair and loss (Alvarez, 1999). An example from a counselling session illustrates this point.

A male client, originally from China, became silent after he tried to explain an incident that had occurred in his life. When the counsellor inquired about this prolonged silence, the client quietly said, "I am tired of sounding like a baby when I talk. It is hard for me to show you who I am. It makes me so frustrated, I am angry and I can't even show that to you!" In this example, language proficiency was strongly related to the client's sense of personal identity and status in relating to other people. Apart from client frustrations about difficulty with expression, miscommunication due to limited English language ability can be the basis for misunderstandings, misdiagnoses, and mistreatment in mental health services.

Helping professionals may have varying levels of comfort in working with clients who speak English as a second language. When a counsellor is uncomfortable responding to foreign-accented speech, this may exacerbate clients' own discomfort in the use of English as a second language and the associated communication difficulties. Derwing and Rossiter (2002) found that helping professionals who received training in the characteristics of Vietnamese-accented English speech expressed greater confidence that they could interact successfully with individuals who spoke English as a second language than those who received only cross-cultural awareness training. These professionals also expressed greater empathy towards the immigrants they were working with than professionals who were less comfortable with foreign-accented speech.

Employment

The impact of employment is pervasive; it has a major influence on both the psychological well-being and adaptation of immigrants (Chen, 2008; Yakushko, Backhaus et al., 2008). In other words, better career transitions lead to better transitional experiences in personal and social domains (Chen, 2006, 2008). Unfortunately, many immigrants are less likely to secure employment at a comparable level in Canadian society for which training and education prepared them in their country of origin. The recognition of foreign experience and credentials for labour market entry and mobility are long-standing issues in Canadian society (Dolin & Young, 2004). It is estimated that more than half of professionally trained immigrants are not working in their field of specialization (Statistics Canada, 2005). Many others employed in their professional fields work at lower levels of employment than the positions held in their country of origin. The difficulties and sense of loss associated with unemployment or underemployment can manifest in psychological problems and difficulties with social and economic integration (Chen, 2008).

The underutilization of immigrant populations in the labour force can be accounted for by systemic factors. First, delays in the immigration processes of selection and admission can lag behind changes in the labour force. Consequently, immigrants' skills may be less in demand or become obsolete, and, during the same period of delay, opportunities for upgrading may be lost. Second, barriers to the recognition of credentials of trade and professional qualifications contribute to the underemployment and unemployment of immigrants (Chen, 2008; Foster, 2008). Conditions in the home country may also prevent some immigrants from obtaining documentation of their qualifications prior to leaving.

 **Snapshot 3**

The realities of work for many new Canadians challenge a common belief that Canada is a land of opportunity. The quality of life for immigrant women is strongly connected to their employment status. Consider the following points reported about immigrant women:

- After their arrival in Canada, three out of five women work in an occupation different from their field prior to immigrating.

- The vast majority of home-workers and contract shop employees in Canada's garment industry are immigrant women of colour. This sector is unregulated, with very low pay, irregular work, and no option for benefits.

- Domestic workers are almost exclusively immigrant women. Often living in the homes of their employers, they are particularly vulnerable to economic exploitation and human rights abuses.

- The numbers of non-status workers in Canada is unknown, but the vast majority are likely women and girls. They are at high risk of abuse because they have limited access to information, and contacting authorities puts them at risk of deportation.

- Language barriers and the transferability of foreign credentials are the most common challenges for both immigrant women and men as they seek employment.

- Immigrant women have difficulty accessing employment and training services due to eligibility criteria. Refugee women, in particular, are frequently denied access to services because they are not permanent residents.

- Lack of child care is a barrier for immigrant women trying to access employment and training services and a tremendous challenge for the many immigrant women employed in seasonal, irregular, and shift work positions.

From "*Immigrant Women: Employment Facts from ACTEW,*" by A Commitment to Training and Employment for Women (ACTEW), 2007, Retrieved February 3, 2009 from http://www.actew.org/pwp.

Immigrants experience at least two paradoxes in securing employment. They seek Canadian experience to improve their employment status, while their lack of Canadian experience is touted as a central reason for barring them from participation in the labour force. Second, they may be turned down from upper-level positions due to factors such as communication skills and lack of Canadian experience and subsequently rejected for lower-level positions because they are overqualified. Subtle biases exist in employment hiring practices that may fail to recognize the talents offered by highly-skilled immigrant applicants who are perceived to be less competent due to language and cultural differences (Purkiss, Perrewe, Gillespie, Mayes, & Ferris, 2006). When academic and employment credentials obtained in the country of origin are not accepted or are discredited by the settlement society, many immigrants and refugees face the painful realization that they must *start over* in order to obtain gainful employment. Entrance into the labour market and underemployment continue to be overriding issues for new

Canadians. In a comparison of new immigrants in the 1990s with previous cohorts, results from the 2001 census show an increasing gap between higher levels of education, lower employment rates, and lower earnings than the Canadian average (McIsaac, 2003). Barriers for the entrance of skilled immigrants into the Canadian labour force are receiving increased attention. As federal and provincial governments grapple with issues related to an aging workforce, there is increased motivation to incorporate an international labour pool. A disproportionate number of recent immigrants work in processing, sales, service, manufacturing, and hospitality jobs that require a low level of skill and may not be representative of the skills and potential that individuals have to offer Canada's labour market (Informetrica Limited, 2000).

Accessing suitable employment is a key factor for the integration of immigrant women and their families. In 2007, immigrant women continued to have higher rates of unemployment and lower rates of employment than immigrant men (Statistics Canada, 2008d). Professionally qualified immigrant women face many barriers to employment due to their newcomer status, their gender, and demands of employment that often conflict with family responsibilities (JobStart and Skills for Change, 2001). Health risks increase when women are marginalized to work in low-paying jobs in settings best described as *sweatshops* and unhealthy environments (Kramer et al., 1999).

The integration of immigrants and refugees into the labour force partially depends upon the felt sense of security in the lives of other Canadians. For example, fluctuations in the economy lead to intense competition for employment and other economic resources. During economic booms, temporary foreign workers have been recruited to fill gaps in the labour force, but they are often the first to be laid off due to economic downturns. Stereotypes and racist attitudes can be linked to economic fears and the belief that immigrants *take jobs* from other Canadians (Palmer, 1996). Without efforts to bridge cultural differences between workers from diverse backgrounds, problems of employment access and mobility will continue to be major barriers in the lives of many immigrants (Arthur, 2000).

Despite the multiculturalism agenda advanced by the Canadian government, employment issues faced by immigrants in Canada suggest that there are many discrepancies between policies and practice and that institutional racism impacts many newcomers. The downward mobility many immigrants face upon entry to Canada may reflect the dominant group's expectation that newcomers must occupy a lower social position. The downward trend in newcomers' employment success documented by Reitz (2001) supports the idea that Canadian society is a selective meritocracy that favours the Canadian-born.

Readers are encouraged to review Chen's (2008) depiction of challenges faced by immigrants in relation to life-career transitions. Chen's framework of Cross-Cultural Life-Career Development (CCLCD) provides counsellors with theoretical and applied suggestions for addressing the cross-cultural transition and multicultural counselling needs of new immigrants.

Intergenerational Differences

Intergenerational differences are frequently encountered in counselling immigrants and refugees (Darvishpour, 2002). Parents and children from other countries often disagree about how much they should become like other Canadians after immigrating. Through their school experiences, youth are saturated with the values and practices of the dominant culture. In contrast, their parents have the option of maintaining a certain level of social and psychological distance from other Canadians in order to preserve their unique cultural heritage. Therefore, many children and adolescents integrate into the host society to a greater degree than their parents. Changing family dynamics may result in considerable tension and anxiety for parents and children (Bemak & Chung, 2008).

Intergenerational conflict is *the rupture in parent-child relationships that may occur due to family members' differential levels of cultural integration in the new society* (Baptiste, 1993). Intergenerational gaps in host society integration between parents and youth can have three different consequences for immigrant and refugee families. First, they can create different expectations for adolescent behaviour in the home and school contexts. Adolescents may experience difficulty establishing a consolidated personal and ethnic identity as a result of incompatible and competing behavioural expectations (Pruegger, 1995; Segal, 1991). Although some youth experience identity confusion, the majority of immigrant and refugee adolescents successfully achieve a bicultural identity (Berry, Phinney, Sam, & Vedder, 2006; Phinney, 2003; Phinney et al., 2001).

Second, when the acculturation gap between parents and children causes familial disconnection, the quality of parent-child relationships may be greatly affected (Buki, Ma, Strom, & Strom, 2003). Immigrant parents are often more firm than other parents when it comes to controlling their children's behaviour. Children may rebel against traditional parental practices and experience challenges in balancing the traditional values they receive from their parents and the values of the host culture to which they are exposed through their daily interactions in school (Sam, 2006). Parents may experience feelings of personal inefficacy as a result of a perceived loss of parental authority and experience greater conflict with their children (Birman, 2006; Sam, 2006). These feelings can be heightened by family role reversals that occur when parents with low levels of English language proficiency rely on youth as translators (Davidson et al., 2008). There is an apparent paradox when parents hold high expectations of success for children but raise concerns about their children's adherence to cultural norms. For example, parental expectations have been identified as an important influence on immigrant children's school achievement (Li, 2001; Sam). Children and adolescents may be in a better position to adhere to parental expectations for success if they have higher levels of acculturation that allow them to successfully interpret the norms and expectations of local educational systems. Third, intergenerational conflicts regarding acceptable and unacceptable adolescent behaviour in the host society can create parent-adolescent acculturation disparity and reduce the level of perceived family support and cohesion from the perspective of both generations of family members (Baptiste, 1993; Gil & Vega, 1996; Noels, 1999).

Parent-adolescent acculturation disparity is only likely to be experienced if family members perceive the acculturation status of others to be incongruent with their own (Merali, 2002). When this is the case, adolescents may need assistance in making choices about their behaviour in the home and school contexts, in working through confusion about their ethnic and cultural identity, in renegotiating the family rules that are the source of intergenerational conflicts, and in becoming cognizant of the consequences – parental reactions – of making behavioural shifts towards Canadian norms. Parents may need counsellor assistance in mastering the childrearing role in a new society and in reframing adolescents' integration into the host society as an indicator of successful adaptation and upward socio-economic mobility for the family rather than as an indication of parental deficiency or defiance.

Older Family Members

The United Nations has recognized the health and well-being of older people as a pressing concern for the global community, since the aging population is growing worldwide (Antonucci, Okorodudu, & Akiyama, 2002). General research findings pertaining to aging across different countries are that: (a) elderly women are more likely to experience problems such as widowhood, physical illness, and financial hardship than elderly men; (b) social support from people that the elderly feel close to seems to be an important factor and resource for assisting older people to handle the changes associated with old age and maintain a sense of well-being; and (c) most elderly people around the world tend to build a sense of support and meaning through the contributions they make to their families (Antonucci et al.).

In the case of immigrant elderly, the contributions they make to their families may be diminished by the role reversal they experience due to difficulties in learning English as a second language at their late stage of life. They often become dependent on younger family members for translation and interpretation for access to health care and other supports. Furthermore, elderly immigrants and refugees often hold more traditional cultural values than other members of the host society. Paired with language and cultural barriers they experience, these value differences can instigate mental health problems (Lai, 2004). Also, they can become isolated due to having left other relatives or friends in the country of origin and being in the retirement phase of life with few opportunities for interaction outside of the home. Elderly immigrants and refugees often become marginalized and lose their sense of belonging, causing them to feel as if they are aging outside of a familiar environment (Lewis, 2009).

When lack of social support and financial difficulties occur in the lives of elderly immigrants and refugees, their risk for developing depression is significantly increased (Lai).

Silverstein and Chen (1999) found that elderly immigrants may face a second alienation process within their own families. They investigated the impact of differential rates of acculturation on relationships between youth and their grandparents. They found that youth who had high levels of integration into the host society tended to report less frequent interaction with their grandparents. They also reported declines in expressing affection towards them over time. Furthermore, the loss of social relations, familial ties, and overall support may cause both elderly immigrants and their families to experience various forms of stress (Ortiz & Cole, 2008). In addition, with having to care for their elderly family members, many immigrants and refugees report struggling with psychological issues (Gilliam, 2005) as well as sacrificing the time they have to spend with their spouses and children to engage in elder care (Brody, 2006).

Taking these findings into account, it appears that elderly immigrants may be left with limited resources and supports to manage the dual tasks of adapting to changes associated with old age and making the transition to a new socio-cultural environment. One possible solution to this problem is to identify strategies for reintegrating the elderly into their families by exploring ways that they can contribute to the family despite their limited English proficiency and cultural adaptation. For example, their contributions could take the form of assisting with childcare when traditional family systems are transformed into dual-career families in response to underemployment after immigration. Alternatively, they can share their wisdom or insights about cultural practices with youth who do not understand the meaning of specific customs that the family is trying to pass on from generation to generation. Finally, in light of the importance of social support in promoting the well-being of older people, it appears important to create support groups or to plan organized social activities for seniors to reduce isolation. The extent to which foreign-born elderly people in Canada perceive social support, their levels of social involvement, and the quality of their social contacts are important considerations for health (Wu & Hart, 2002).

Gender Issues

Regardless of age, the process of integrating into Canadian society may be different for males and females. Females have been found to be more receptive to adopting the values and practices of Canadian host society than their male counterparts (Dion & Dion, 2001). This has been attributed to the heightened restrictions placed on the behaviour and life options of females in most non-Western cultures; the acculturation process may offer women a certain degree of liberation from rigidly defined cultural role prescriptions. However, it has been found that immigrant women are less likely to be proficient in either of the official languages of Canada, and may be more vulnerable to psychological difficulties (Ataca & Berry, 2002). In addition, it is generally believed that women bear the majority of responsibilities for settlement and integration of family members into the receiving society (Naidoo, 2003). Value and behavioural shifts towards Western norms on the part of females often result in negative consequences for their interpersonal relationships and mental health, experienced as symptoms of depression and anxiety (Dion & Dion). In general, immigrant women tend to exhibit emotional disorders more frequently than men; this has been attributed to various factors such as power differences in the family system and role overload between family obligations and employment responsibilities. After the resettlement phase, marital changes often take place among immigrant couples. For example, women who are unemployed often become more dependent on their husbands, causing them to feel isolated, restricted, and left without support networks (Ataca & Berry). Another important consideration in how immigrant women define their health is in relation to their families' well-being (Meadows, Thurston, & Melton, 2001).

Consider the example of a woman from a traditional patriarchal family unit who was a stay-at-home mom in her country of origin. Due to socio-political warfare, the family suddenly fled to Canada for asylum. The husband's attempts to seek employment in Canada resulted in underemployment and an income that was insufficient to sustain the family. The woman therefore had to enter the workforce, increasing her responsibilities to include both mothering and breadwinner roles. Her husband's sense of power and authority in the family is challenged by his wife's role shift. His behaviour towards her becomes more controlling in an attempt to find other ways to exert his power and maintain his position as the man in the family. Dion and Dion (2001) suggest that, in such cases, the goal of counselling intervention should be to assist the couple in renegotiating family relationships and to explore different ways that each family member can achieve a sense of personal power.

This scenario also relates to the double burden and role overload that may be experienced by immigrant women. Although employment has been previously associated with better health outcomes for women, this finding is contradicted by research on female Korean immigrants (Noh, Wu, Speechley, & Kaspar, 1992). Female immigrants may have more responsibilities in the household and more responsibilities for socializing the next generation, and may not benefit in the same ways from social resources such as employment in comparison to male immigrants (Dion & Dion, 2001). In addition, when women decide not to seek employment, they risk becoming detached from Canadian society and only being connected to their own ethnic communities, which may considerably interfere with their adaptation process (Ataca & Berry, 2002).

Unfortunately, domestic violence is sometimes the outcome of unsatisfactory spousal roles and interaction patterns. Although there are controversies about whether domestic violence rates are higher among the immigrant population than among the native population, the circumstances of immigrant women often exacerbates their situation (Menjivar & Salcido, 2002). This includes issues such as limited host language skills, isolation or lack of contact with their families, and accessibility of employment. Furthermore, it appears that difficulties with the acculturation process increase the risk of domestic violence among immigrants and refugees (Firestone, Harris, & Vega, 2003). The process of acculturation often brings about changes in marital and family dynamics, and sometimes causes reversal in gender roles, increasing the risk of spousal abuse (Harris, Firestone, & Vega, 2005). Identifying and treating domestic violence can be complicated by the unique psychosocial and cultural needs of immigrant and refugee women (Srinivasan & Ivey, 1999). Due to cultural constructions of power and roles in the family, some women may not recognize their experiences as abuse (Merali, 1999). Women who remain in traditional gender roles seem to be less likely to report the abuse they are experiencing (Harris et al.). Fear of reprisal, a sense of failure about maintaining family harmony, feelings of guilt or shame, fear of disconnection from loved ones, and the belief in keeping personal affairs within the family are strong restraints against seeking help. Concerns for confidentiality may be paramount in working with immigrant and refugee women, along with acknowledging the courage that it has taken to seek support outside of the family.

Gender can also be a salient issue when female children feel that they are being treated differently from their male siblings. Females are often viewed as central figures in protecting sacred cultural values and behaviours and in transmitting their cultural heritage to children. Therefore, girls face more pressure to remain traditional in immigrant and refugee families than boys (Dion & Dion, 2001). In dealing with perceived double standards in childrearing or family rules, it is important for counsellors to assist clients in exploring the positive and negative consequences of departures from the family's behavioural and role prescriptions for both the individual and her interpersonal relationships.

 **Snapshot 4**

I argue that we are pushed to the margin for the purposes of maintaining the social structures that restrict our access to the privileges available to the dominant groups. We are the 'minority,' they are the 'majority.' This very minority/majority polarization reflects a power relation of domination and subordination. Our physical characteristics, our cultural, linguistic, and religious backgrounds are used to maintain our subordination and to protect the interest of the dominant groups and their sense of entitlement. Keeping us in the margin defends their location at the centre. The walls between margin and centre cause us to feel defeated, devalued, and homeless – defeated because our struggles to move to the centre are crushed; devalued because who we are and what we believe are rejected; and homeless because we are treated as outsiders. (Javed, 1995, p. 15)

Racism and Discrimination

The receptivity of the receiving country is generally believed to have a large impact on the mental health of immigrants and refugees (Chung et al., 2008). Despite Canada's pride in being a culturally pluralistic society, attitudes towards diverse groups continue to show a hierarchy of preferences (Berry, 2006c). Interaction with members of the host culture and their institutions provides daily reminders for some immigrants that they do not fit in with the prevailing cultural group.

Otherness is a social construction for the representation of those who are seen as *undesirable* (Javed, 1995). Otherness becomes an identity that has negative impacts for personal self-esteem and for a sense of belonging in Canada.

Oppression through racism is one of the most serious risk factors for negative impact on the mental health of immigrants and increase of immigrants' stress levels and decrease of immigrants' coping ability (Yakushko, Watson et al., 2008). The experience of racism and discrimination can have pervasive effects, such as depression and loss of self-esteem, on mental health during the acculturation process (Bemak & Chung, 2008). The impact of racism and discrimination is that people internalize the messages given to them by members of the dominant society; they may blame themselves and experience feelings of inferiority as self-esteem is eroded. In addition, biased media reports about immigrants and refugees increase negative stereotypes and prejudicial thinking (Chung et al., 2008). Ethic prejudice is now considered to be a universal characteristic of human behaviour in that all groups and all individuals hold attitudes that involve some form of prejudice against others. However, attitudes can extend to serious behaviour with deliberate actions to harm others. Immigrants and refugees may be targeted for hate crimes and violence.

In a pilot survey of 12 participating police departments in Canada in 2001 and 2002, it was found that 57% of all hate crimes were due to ethnicity/race, 43% were due to religion, and 10% were due to sexual orientation (Canadian Centre for Justice Statistics, 2004). Additional research is needed to determine the direct effects of racism and discrimination experienced by immigrants. Religion as a dimension of diversity has been increasing in Canada without corresponding research to examine challenges for integration (Biles & Burstein, 2003). There are also indirect effects to consider for the insidious impacts of racism and discrimination on areas such as housing, employment, and access to community services, including mental health services.

The evidence showing persistent levels of discrimination and racism in Canadian society challenges counsellors to address such practices in their direct work with clients and in roles to address social justice. Counsellors need to be skilled about addressing issues of systemic oppression such as racism and other forms of discrimination in relation to the presenting issues of clients and in designing appropriate interventions. As noted by Chung et al. (2008), it is not enough to be well intentioned; rather, working with immigrants and refugees requires advocacy skills and strategies for addressing environmental and social barriers.

 Snapshot 5

Canadians forget their history at their own risk. The names of religions taking root in Canada in the twenty-first century are different than those in the nineteenth. It is now Muslims, Hindus, Buddhists, and Sikhs who are, or have been, the immigrants building religious and community institutions. It is remarkable how consistent the patterns of citizenship building recur. While women and men participate in the structures of economic life, they do so for purposes which serve the well-being of families, friends, a whole range of communities and associations. It is those intersecting communities of attachment which shape the identities of Canadian citizenship in our time. It is then the recognition of religious and ethnic communities through policies like multiculturalism which define the practice of freedom, human rights, and, in the broadest sense, what being Canadian is becoming.... The bedrock of [the] future may be illustrated in how religious diversity in this country is given authentic recognition. (Bowlby, 2003, p. 46)

Trauma

Forced migration is associated with a sense of chaos, an inability to plan, concerns for personal safety, and disruption of life roles and processes that affirm a sense of personal identity and stability (Bemak et al., 2003). It is important for counsellors to have some background preparation regarding the conditions in the home country that manifest in health issues associated with trauma (Arthur & Ramaliu, 2000)

Premigration trauma has been categorized into four types: (a) deprivation (food, shelter, contact with other people); (b) physical injury, including torture; (c) incarceration and forced participation in re-education camps; and (d) witnessing the torture and killing of other people (Mollica, Wyshak, & Lavelle, 1987). According to the World Medical Association, **torture** is the *"deliberate, systematic, or wanton infliction of physical or mental suffering by one or more persons acting alone or on the orders of any authority to force another person to yield information, to make a confession, or for any other reason"* (Amnesty International, 1985, 9-10). Torture is one of the most common forms of interpersonal violence inflicted on human beings (Rasmussen, Rosenfeld, Reeves, & Keller, 2007), and the survivors of torture represent one of the most vulnerable clinical populations because of the despicable violence have they experienced (Jacobs & Iacopino, 2001).

The impact of torture and other traumatic events prior to migration may manifest in adverse psychological reactions and compound psychosocial adjustment challenges in the settlement process (Bemak et al., 2003). Survivors of torture experience such profound violence and loss that their life is thrown out of balance, and what used to be a familiar existence suddenly becomes an unchartered territory (Mollica, 2006). Grief issues concerning losses in their homeland and forced mobility can immobilize refugees from dealing with the tasks of daily living in a new culture. It is estimated that 5% to 35% of the world's 14 million refugees have experienced torture (Gerrity, Keane, & Tuma, 2001). Torture is a particular type of trauma resulting in complex and varied reactions that require specialized professional knowledge (Arthur & Ramaliu, 2000).

Refugee women may be at higher risk of experiencing sexual exploitation and violence (Koss & Kilpatrick, 2001). Rape has historically been used as an instrument of war, and sexual violence must be considered as a frequent, yet unspoken, experience of women refugees. Refugee women who have been raped or sexually violated in their countries may experience extreme difficulties in adjusting to life in the new country (Bemak et al., 2003). Their adjustment may be further hindered by lack of education, language difficulties, lack of support, and inaccessibility of community resources (Chung, 2000). During the migration process, there are few sources of protection from sexual violence, and mistrust of authorities may prevent the reporting of rape. Revealing the experience may have serious social consequences. Women's experiences of rape and other forms of sexual torture is complicated with particular patriarchal values that stem from their cultures of origin (Berman, Girón, & Marroquín, 2006). The discovery of rape can result in exile from family and community, with few alternative means of social or financial support. Consequently, counsellors must appreciate the significance of the rape experience within each woman's cultural perspective, including the individual, family, and community levels.

Due to the high risk of experiencing trauma directly or through witnessing acts of violence committed against other family or community members, posttraumatic stress disorder or PTSD (American Psychiatric Association, 2000) is a major concern with refugee populations. Although cultural variability in the expression of distress adds complexity to diagnosis and treatment, PTSD can be a response to political oppression and torture (Tracy, 1999). In fact, the symptoms that refugee survivors of torture present with may be viewed as appropriate given the severity of the traumatic experiences they have experienced in their countries (Gorman, 2001).

Reactions to trauma are highly individual and consideration must be made of the differing ways that trauma can impact family members. There are intergenerational effects for children who have been exposed to violence against their parents, causing children and families to respond differently to their circumstances depending on their developmental level, cultural background, and the attitudes of the host country (Pynoos, Kinzie, & Gordon, 2001; Walter & Bala, 2004). Premigration trauma that increases adverse health risks for parents during acculturation can manifest in emotional and behavioural problems in children. Survivor guilt and bereavement follow individuals through the course of forced migration (Bemak et al., 2003). Loss and uncertainly about the safety of family members in their country of origin can be a source of trauma that has longstanding effects for individuals as they attempt to make a life for themselves in a new country. How well refugees will adapt to the new country largely depends on their ability to make the sense of their situation and their ability to effectively cope with both pre- and post-migration circumstances (Walter & Bala). Refugees will ultimately decide how they want to approach their issues and healing. Exploring these decisions in a therapeutic setting allows the counsellor to understand and appreciate complex refugee experiences and organize the therapeutic process in a way that facilitates refugee healing (Walter & Bala).

Multicultural Counselling Process

Help-Seeking Patterns, Utilization Rates, Barriers to Seeking Counselling

The reluctance of migrants to seek help from mainstream mental health systems is well documented in the literature (Bemak & Chung, 2008). There are attitudes within immigrant and refugee populations that prohibit accessing services in the dominant culture. Likewise, issues in the design and delivery of mental health services pose barriers to accessibility.

Barriers to accessing community resources such as mental health programming may be material in nature or attitudinal. In a study of immigrant women's experiences as family caregivers (Neufeld, Harrison, Stewart, Hughes, & Spitzer, 2001), seven barriers were identified: (a) material circumstances, such as limited English language skills, inability to drive, or insufficient financial resources; (b) employment commitments, limited flexibility, or insufficient time to seek resources; (c) a sense of obligation to their family sponsor and limited economic resources; (d) personal and cultural values that conflict with the perspectives of community agencies; (e) the value placed on privacy and enforced by cultural sanctions about disclosing problems or showing strong emotions to a stranger; (f) conflicts between traditional healing practices and Western approaches; and (g) a sense of personal responsibility to care for family and viewing community support as a sign of personal failure.

Organized mental health services may be the last resort chosen by refugees, and their participation is by default rather than out of personal preference (Bemak & Chung, 2008). Cultural norms for seeking help may dictate efforts to seek assistance from other family members, elders, community leaders, and indigenous or religious healers. Accessing formalized mental health services may occur after problems have reached increased levels of severity and there is a sense of desperation for immediate action and relief from symptoms of distress.

It is important that counsellors recognize the additional efforts taken by many immigrant and refugee clients to seek professional mental health services. The reception during the first appointment may be pivotal for impressing upon clients how their problems are viewed and that the possibility of help is available in ways that are culturally compatible.

Interest shown towards the overall experience of settlement in Canada can serve to build rapport. This requires counsellors to be familiar not only with the general conditions of migration and common concerns, but also with issues that have impacted specific groups of immigrants and refugees. Counsellors need to take responsibility for learning about who is living in their local communities and the political and social circumstances that lead to migration. Most clients are astute at assessing the cultural biases and competencies of professionals with whom they interact in the settlement country.

Connecting with settlement agencies can greatly assist counsellors in understanding the immigration histories, settlement process, and needs of specific immigrant and refugee groups. **Immigrant settlement services** *provide assistance for the initial settlement and adaptation needs of immigrants and support newcomers to integrate into Canadian society*. Their functions include assisting with learning English as a second language, supporting immigrants in the job-finding process, and educating people about and helping them access the health care system, school system, transportation system, and legal services. Settlement counsellors in these agencies are usually members of the immigrant groups they serve and perform ongoing needs assessments based on their daily interactions with clients. Settlement services also connect new Canadians with volunteer and professional services that are vital sources of support for integration into the community (Behnam, 2002).

Acquiring information about refugee and immigrant groups can help counsellors feel more at ease in assessing the unique needs of individual clients while avoiding the stereotypical responses that come from limited knowledge about immigrant and refugee groups. An unstructured interview protocol developed by Prendes-Lintel (2001) is sensitive to various stages of refugee migration. This general assessment can be used to understand health issues related to migration and to build rapport to discuss health problems related to trauma.

A common assumption made in the literature is that clients from non-dominant ethnic populations terminate counselling after the initial interview (Arthur, 2008). This likely reflects the inappropriateness of conventional counselling approaches that have not been adapted to cross-cultural contexts, along with a lack of cultural sensitivity by counsellors who deliver mental health services. Counsellors typically have different ideas about both the nature of the mental health problem and effective intervention strategies than the perceptions held by immigrant and refugee clients. Misdiagnosis occurs and inappropriate interventions are selected because counsellors do not understand the cultural contexts that provide meaning to current signs of distress and mental health problems. For example, there are cultural differences in the expression of depression and other illnesses. It has been suggested in the literature that members of some ethnocultural groups express more somatic symptoms (Lee, Rodin, Devins, & Weiss, 2001; Zhang, 1995), whereas others favour individual strategies that contravene public intervention (Schreiber, Stern, & Wilson, 2000). Exploring cultural contexts is imperative for understanding client issues as a *normative* response to loss of relationships, identity diffusion, and oppressive social and economic conditions in a new country (Alvarez, 1999).

 **Snapshot 6**

Psychotherapy must facilitate the person's recognition of the connection between her/his losses and symptoms and the recurrence of these symptoms during significant developmental transitions. It is also essential to evaluate trauma experiences related to or pre-dating the migration experience. Helping people connect their symptoms with their losses and separations validates their experience in a nonpathological manner and empowers them to grieve and subsequently move to a position where they can begin to restore their sense of identity and build new emotional and interpersonal connections. (Alvarez, 1999, p. 15)

Counselling Immigrants and Refugees Using a Multilevel Model

The Multilevel Model (MLM) of counselling and psychotherapy (Bemak & Chung, 2002; Bemak et al., 2003) was designed for working with refugee clients. However, its general tenets can be adapted for working with immigrant clients. The model has been applied to several case studies of multicultural counselling with refugees (Bemak et al.).

There are several appealing aspects of this model: (a) it takes into account the complexity of the client's background, past and present stressors, and the psychosocial implications of acculturation to a new culture; (b) the MLM is a psychoeducational model that incorporates cognitive, affective, and behavioural interventions while considering the personal culture of clients and community and social processes; (c) it exemplifies the diversification of the roles that multicultural counsellors may need to use to help their clients; (d) it recognizes how clients' needs for assistance may require working on multiple levels of intervention; and (e) the model explicates the multicultural counselling competencies that are essential for employing the MLM effectively.

There are four levels represented in the model: (a) Level I: mental health education; (b) Level II: individual, group, and/or family psychotherapy; (c) Level III: cultural empowerment; and (d) Level IV: indigenous healing. Each level in the model contains individual goals and strategies for counselling refugees. It is important to note that the levels of the model are not fixed or sequential; the levels may be explored concurrently or particular levels may be worked on independently to address clients' needs (Bemak et al., 2003). It is essential that counsellors demonstrate cultural empathy (Chung & Bemak, 2002), regardless of which level is emphasized in counselling.

Level I: Mental health education

The focus of Level I is on providing clients with mental health education to increase their knowledge, familiarity, and acceptance of mental health practices and interventions in the dominant culture. Clients are prepared for the process of counselling through legitimizing the respective roles of counsellors, clients, and the helping process. Lack of contact with mental health professionals in the country of origin or differences in the types of counselling services available make this step essential to promoting client readiness for counselling. Many immigrants and refugees expect the counselling process to be similar to a doctor-patient relationship, where they receive concrete advice to facilitate problem solving (Sue & Sue, 2008). Attention to problem-solving strategies may be the priority for clients. Preparing clients for their role in the counselling relationship involves soliciting their expectations about the counselling process and having a general discussion about the counsellor's function and role (e.g., educator, client advocate, consultant, cultural broker), the various types of issues that can be brought up in counselling, what the counsellor expects from the client (depending on the counsellor's theoretical framework and proposed role), and communicating the types of help or assistance that the client can expect with respect to specific presenting problems. Discussion of *mental health basics* (Bemak et al., 2003) informs clients and ultimately aims to increase their sense of comfort about participating in counselling.

Although the presenting styles of counsellors are named as components of Level II of the model, some characteristics of these styles are relevant from the first point of contact. These characteristics include preferences for indirect and direct approaches, cultural norms regarding authority and help-seeking, and communication skills in counselling.

The use of questions, focus on emotions and strong feelings, probing cognitions, and asking for elaboration of details about personal matters are usual practices in Western models of counselling. However, this may be problematic for clients whose cultural norms value privacy, containment of emotional expression, and saving face during interpersonal interactions. The establishment of rapport and trust is paramount for inquiring about personal circumstances. Otherwise, questioning and probing into personal matters may seem too obtrusive to clients. In addition to cultural norms for communication, prior experience may leave refugees hypersensitive to the motives of people seeking personal information and may unintentionally raise levels of anxiety about professional services. At the same time as educating clients about fundamental mental health issues, assessment of clients during information sharing provides important clues for case conceptualization and intervention planning. For example, during Level I, the counsellor can monitor client reactions and gain important information about clients' mental health belief systems and attitudes towards help-seeking (Bemak et al., 2003).

Level II: Individual, group, and/or family counselling

Level II incorporates individual, group, and family therapy interventions found in Western perspectives on counselling. There is evidence that traditional approaches to individual and family therapy can be effective with culturally diverse populations (Zane & Sue, 1991). However, a pivotal point must be made: counselling approaches need to incorporate an appreciation of clients' cultural norms and practices in both the assessment and intervention processes.

Hwang (2006) developed the Psychotherapy Adaptation and Modification Framework (PAMF) to help guide counsellors in modification of empirically validated treatments for clients who are culturally diverse. This framework incorporates variability in definitions of mental health, expressions of psychological distress, and views about the cause of mental health problems, and acknowledges that clients may have varying degrees of confidence when it comes to the treatment they are receiving. The PAMF identifies six domains of possible adaptation of mental health interventions to suit the needs of specific client groups: (a) orientation, (b) addressing cultural complexities, (c) cultural beliefs, (d) client-therapist relationship, (e) cultural differences in expression and communication, and (f) cultural issues of salience.

Orientation involves providing general mental health education as addressed in Level I of the MLM as well as familiarizing clients with the specific counselling approach that is to be employed in assisting them with their presenting problems. Addressing cultural complexities involves assessing a client's racial/cultural identity or membership in a socially stigmatized or disadvantaged group, and incorporating a focus on identity development or resolution of identity concerns in the intervention process. Making adaptations related to cultural beliefs may involve matching the intervention approach or changing the intervention delivery to increase congruence with clients' perceptions of the causes of mental health problems or culturally appropriate healing strategies. Clients' religious or spiritual beliefs can be incorporated into the healing process. Modification of the client-counsellor relationship can involve matching counsellors to clients based on similarity in language or cultural backgrounds or level of acculturation into the host country. Alternatively, the adaptations made in this domain can focus on how the client-therapist relationship is structured, such as by adopting a more hierarchical relationship when working with clients who prefer the formality of a doctor-patient relationship, or using a more egalitarian approach when working with clients from collectivist cultures. Modifications to psychological interventions based on cultural differences in communication or expression can involve framing the mental health problem in a way that is consistent with how the client manifests distress (e.g., somatically), or altering communication styles to match those of the client's cultural group. Adapting the counselling process to incorporate cultural issues of salience requires attending to current stressors or practical problems in the lives of immigrant or refugee clients that may perpetuate their mental health problems. These life problems are addressed in Level III of the MLM: Cultural Empowerment.

Using the PAMF, counsellors have an opportunity to modify Western therapeutic approaches and increase their ecological validity. In addition, the PAMF may be used to improve clinical training. Hwang's framework represents a comprehensive model helpful in increasing the congruence between clients' backgrounds and Western therapeutic approaches, and as such has the potential for increasing therapeutic efficacy and clients' satisfaction with therapy.

Bemak, Chung, and Bornemann (1996) reviewed a growing body of literature that outlines the application of specific theoretical frameworks and counselling interventions with immigrants and refugees. The importance of integrating religion and spirituality into multicultural counselling has been emphasized (e.g., Fukuyama & Sevig, 1999; McLennan, Rochow, & Arthur, 2001), as these areas are often neglected in Western perspectives on counselling. One of the strengths of the PAMF (Hwang, 2006) is that it allows for incorporation of clients' spiritual beliefs into the problem conceptualization and intervention process.

Group and family therapy are viewed as important counselling modalities for facilitating positive adaptation during the acculturation process. Clients from collectivist cultures may especially benefit from the sense of interdependence that can be gained through group and family work (Bemak et al., 2003). The focus of group counselling is *cultural empowerment*, with the goal of assisting clients "to gain a better sense of environmental mastery" (p. 259) of the local culture. Curative factors with group work (Yalom & Leszcz, 2005), including corrective emotional experiences, can be powerful resources in facilitating the healing of painful psychological issues. Unfortunately, few guidelines are available to help counsellors make decisions on group composition.

There are generally two points of view. First, homogeneous groups of immigrants or refugees may share common experiences and foster a positive sense of group identity. However, counsellors are cautioned against assuming cultural homogeneity on the basis of country of origin. There can be many political and religious sectors within countries that have highly conflictual relationships. Knowledge of the political alliances within countries is essential knowledge for planning groups. A second point of view considers heterogeneity of group composition to be an asset. Common issues shared between cultural groups can help individuals see that their issues are normative within the experience of migration and acculturation. During group counselling, strategies for coping may be generated that offer clients alternative perspectives.

Due to the cultural importance of family bonds for many immigrants and refugees, family counselling appears to be a natural extension of program planning. Family adaptation is essential for family functioning, despite individual differences in the process of acculturation.

A framework for assessment of cultural worldview and acculturation can be applied to individual clients and their families (Grieger & Ponterotto, 1995). The family's attitudes towards conceptualizing problems in psychological terms and their willingness to support individual family members in their pursuit of counselling are important considerations in case conceptualization. Family counselling can address systemic issues rather than individual problems and strengthen the family unit for addressing cross-cultural difficulties.

It is imperative that counsellors have an understanding of the cultural norms in family relationships. Examples of critical cultural knowledge include how family power is distributed in the culture of origin (formally and informally, in public and in private), the role of elders, gender roles in marital relationships, and norms for child-rearing. Alternatively, counsellors might consider building partnerships with bicultural consultants to support multicultural counselling (Grant, Henley, & Kean, 2001).

The myriad of issues faced by immigrants and refugees are strongly connected to systemic barriers and gender biases. Although the processes of migration have an overarching impact on people's lives, cultural factors influence the ways in which people perceive their difficulties and make choices about whether to address their concerns and how they go about a resolution process. Feminist therapy can help clients gain empowerment by anchoring their experiences in the larger socio-political systems of which they are a part (Cheatham et al., 2002a). Helping clients define or redefine their issues in light of societal influences can relieve the sense of intrapersonal stress and failure that the clients experience. Solutions can be sought to mobilize resources that increase clients' sense of personal agency for penetrating systemic barriers and for mobilizing community resources.

A note of caution is in order pertaining to consciousness-raising for immigrant and refugee women. It is important for counsellors not to impose personal notions of relationship equity and disconnection from relationships that might appear to be unhealthy for women. Rather, issues such as gender role equity, family responsibilities, and even domestic abuse need to be seen in light of the realities of women's lives and with solutions that are culturally viable for them.

Level III: Cultural empowerment

Counsellors need to be cognizant that newcomers to Canada have predominant issues about understanding how local systems work and how to access services and resources pertaining to health, education, finances, and employment. Needs in these domains may take precedence over the resolution of psychological problems.

Assistance and guidance with systemic issues can be a major intervention. Hence, the role of *cultural systems information guide* (Bemak et al., 1996) is embedded in the interventions of multicultural counselling. Counsellors need to be comfortable addressing issues that clients deem to be a priority for daily living. Ultimately, helping clients build capacity for dealing with systems in the local culture can be an important direction for cultural empowerment and positive mental health.

The direct and mediating effect of social support on psychological well-being is well documented (e.g., Berry, 1997; Lazarus & Folkman, 1984). One of the key roles that counsellors can play is helping immigrants and refugees build support networks. Although it is important to increase the community integration of all immigrants and refugees, individuals who are isolated from family members due to death, displacement, or inability to make contact may be especially vulnerable to mental health problems.

Assuming the role of cultural broker can help clients broaden their resources for instrumental and emotional support. For example, counsellors can provide information about immigrant-serving agencies and programs in the local community where new Canadians can increase their positive contact with co-nationals. Host support programs where professionals and volunteers are involved in the settlement process are potent resources that support community integration of immigrants and refugees (Arthur & Ramaliu, 2000; Behnam, 2002). Assistance may be needed to connect with specific domains of the settlement culture, through contacts with employment services, family resources, or assistance to navigate the structures of education and training institutions.

Although this has traditionally been the domain of immigrant settlement workers, a stronger liaison and a presence during settlement orientation programs can increase the likelihood that newcomers will seek counselling services for mental health interventions (Prendes-Lintel, 2001). This bespeaks the need for counsellors to be well informed about resources and networks in the local community. Taking an instructional approach with clients can help them learn about resources that foster support, understand the connection between resource use and settlement issues, and build efficacy for accessing community resources and support networks. Beyond individual counselling, the establishment of a multidisciplinary professional team can bridge assessment, referral, and consultation services for clients who have experienced premigration trauma (Arthur & Ramaliu, 2000).

Social justice is an integral value embedded in the MLM (Bemak et al., 2003). Counsellors need to be proactively engaged in advocacy-related activities. Social justice may address the circumstances that lead people to become refugees and policies and practices regarding settlement in local communities, or it may help clients address unfair or discriminatory treatment. Although counsellors may choose to take on social advocacy roles in many ways, it is important for counsellors to learn how social justice can be integrated into counselling sessions. For example, helping clients write letters, making phone calls together, or coaching clients about how to address systemic barriers are valuable ways to use time in counselling sessions (Bemak et al.).

Level IV: Indigenous healing

Level IV of the MLM addresses the complementary use of Western traditional methodologies with indigenous healing. Unfortunately, lack of awareness about methods of healing that are used in clients' cultures or disregarding their authenticity leads to an over-reliance on Western traditional forms of counselling. Counsellors must be willing to explore how problems are viewed in the client's culture and to consider traditional health practices and indigenous healing. There is debate in the multicultural counselling literature about whether clients or counsellors should initiate discussion about indigenous healing. We believe there are advantages for counsellors to initiate discussions about traditional health practices and how health issues are addressed using indigenous healing. This may be an important door to open to help clients overcome fear of disapproval or beliefs held by clients that health care providers are uninformed or uninterested in their cultural practices.

Rogler (1987) described the use of indigenous methods in addressing the distress of Hispanic children. The approach of Cuento Therapy involves adapting folktales in the history of the Hispanic culture to the current problems experienced by Hispanic youth. Distressed children who acted out folktales that were made relevant to their experiences of inner-city living were found to experience significantly more improvement in their health status than those receiving Western traditional forms of help.

Despite their utility in counselling practice with immigrants and refugees, counsellors who only gain superficial levels of understanding about indigenous interventions are at risk of misapplying or abusing these methods of treatment. Like all areas of professional expertise, training in indigenous methods requires extensive knowledge and practice. Furthermore, it may be inappropriate for counsellors outside of clients' cultural groups to apply indigenous treatments in some circumstances, due to a lack of cultural credibility or due to religious or spiritual significance that is not recognized by the counsellor (Koss-Chioino, 2000). It is more realistic for most counsellors to channel their interests into the establishment of treatment partnerships (Bemak et al., 1996, p. 260) with people who are validated by cultural groups as indigenous healers, including religious leaders in the community.

Case Study

Mai was a 28-year-old woman who had lived in Canada for 15 years. She and her mother fled from Vietnam in the late 1970s due to fears of political prosecution. Her father had disappeared from the family after a raid on their town and had not been seen for 2 months. Mai's brother arranged for their passage out of the country on a boat, and he subsequently accompanied them to Canada. Mai and her mother were living together in Calgary and the brother had married and was living in Toronto.

Mai was a student in a training program designed to help women increase their marketable skills for entering the labour force. After a presentation in the class on counselling services, she made an appointment to see me in the office. On the intake sheet, she indicated academic issues as the reason for seeking counselling assistance. Mai presented as a friendly and well-spoken individual. It was difficult for me to tell how old she was, as I have typically underestimated the ages of clients from Asian cultures.

Mai smiled continually during the first interview and it was difficult from her physical presentation to assess any level of emotional distress. As a way to build rapport, I initially focused on her school program, what she liked about it, and areas of the program in the upcoming curriculum. She agreed that it was a good program, but hesitated when I inquired about the connection she saw for her future work life. When I commented on her uncertainty, she apologized to me, saying, "I am sorry, I know that I should have my life figured out by now."

Another clue to her presenting concerns arose when I asked her about her prior education and how long it had been since she studied in school. When she disclosed her current age, she added, "Don't you think that is old for me to be going to school and not be married?" After my attempt to reassure her that many women in Canadian society did not marry until later in life, Mai fell silent. I inquired whether this was a source of pressure for her, and she added, "I don't know whether to get married, or not."

Mai was feeling pressure from her mother to marry a friend of the family who had also immigrated to Canada. Mai said that she knew this was *the right thing to do.* After discussing the strengths of this relationship, I commented to Mai that she did not seem very excited about this relationship. She quickly defended her fiancé, noting that he was a good man. After a few minutes of silence, she commented that her "heart was not with him." Mai had been seeing another man for several months. She disclosed that she also loved him very much, but her mother would not want her to marry someone who did not understand her culture. The second man was Caucasian and Mai was concerned about her mother's view of a mixed marriage.

After working with Mai for three sessions to help her reduce her anxiety and increase her concentration for schoolwork, I asked her if there were any issues from her life in Vietnam or immigrating to Canada that were still difficult for her. I cautioned that she did not have to disclose details and that I did not want to press into painful areas of her life. Mai was silent for a few minutes and then said, "There are some things that you should know."

Mai described the fear and anxiety about being separated from her father and brother before leaving Vietnam. She described leaving suddenly in the night with clothes that her mother had selected, with pieces of jewelry and money sewn into the lining. Conditions on the boat were crowded. Pirates raided their boat. She disclosed that she had been raped during one of the attacks. Mai did not cry when she told me about her past, her voice was monotone, and she showed no expression. At the end of the story, she bowed her head and said, "I feel such shame, and I have told nobody else about this. My mother told me never to talk about it, to put it in the past."

In working with Mai, I made extra efforts to show my acceptance of her as a person. I told her that I felt honoured that she chose me to tell her life story. The direction of intervention involved a number of approaches.

First, it appeared that Mai was having symptoms of posttraumatic stress disorder. Her lack of concentration was compounded by nightmares and a number of somatic symptoms. I referred Mai to a trusted physician to check out any possible organic etiology to her bodily symptoms. I asked Mai to keep a diary of her thoughts, feelings, and the events that seemed to trigger her symptoms.

She noted that she found visits with her fiancé to be very stressful, especially when they visited his family. She would rarely sleep after spending time with his family. In exploring these relationships, Mai burst into tears and said, "They remind me too much of my home. They remind me too much of what has happened. How can I feel like a member of their family after what has happened to me?" When I asked her what would make her feel good about her future, she said, "I would not have to be reminded of the past. I hate it when people refer to us as boat people. I came to Canada on an airplane. I just want to get on with my life."

Another direction of counselling intervention was to explore Mai's sense of identity in being a Vietnamese Canadian. Her sense of being torn between two worlds was apparent in her indecision through relationships with two men, representing two cultural ideals. We explored the strengths of both cultures and the impact of potential choices for her personal future and for relationships with her mother.

A key component of this professional relationship was a close empathic connection. Mai monitored my reactions carefully, especially during the recounting of traumatic experiences. She often asked my opinions about aspects of life in Canada, and I decided to be open about issues and shared examples from my personal life. The intention of proceeding in these directions was to provide Mai with a strong interpersonal relationship where she would feel accepted, regardless of events in her past. I also felt that some level of personal disclosure and examples from working with other women clients would help normalize some aspects of her experience and bridge the dichotomy she was making between Vietnamese and Canadian culture.

Mai and I worked together for a total of 15 sessions. Her concentration increased, her sleeping patterns began to stabilize, and her manner of expression became fuller in sessions. As we terminated counselling at the end of her academic program, I asked her what was most meaningful for her about counselling. She replied that for the first time in years she *felt like herself.* She said that she knew she had to make a decision about her relationships and that, either way, she was determined to feel happiness in her life.

Cutting Edges in Multicultural Counselling

It is well established that migration is a risk factor for developing mental health problems, yet the majority of immigrants and refugees enjoy healthy lives in Canada. There tends to be a bias in the literature that portrays the problematic nature of migration, along with myriad problems experienced by immigrants and refugees. More attention is needed to highlight the strengths and contributions of newcomers to Canadian society.

In particular, what accounts for the strengths and resiliency of immigrants and refugees, despite social forces that press on their personal resources? What are the coping strategies that result in positive outcomes for mental health? How can social structures in Canadian society be reformed to support the settlement and integration processes? Investigations along these lines of inquiry could contribute to the general literature on multicultural counselling. They also have the potential to influence counselling and mental health services for *all* clients, if there is a willingness on the part of dominant health care systems to incorporate practices that have been introduced to Canadian society.

Unfortunately, there continue to be subpopulations of immigrants and refugees who are at greater risk for developing mental health concerns. Additional resources are required to examine the ways that multicultural counselling can support the acculturation experiences of adolescents, women, and elderly immigrants and refugees. These clients rarely stand alone in their settlement experiences; rather, their issues are connected to contexts within families and within the culture of their communities. Counsellors must have specialized knowledge about the cultural norms that influence the experiences of these populations and must be considerate of interventions that keep individuals connected to their family and community resources. Future research needs to incorporate a gender analysis of issues facing immigrants and refugees. Counselling issues and interventions are not well represented by research that is limited by a male reference group.

A subgroup that is beginning to receive increasing attention in the counselling literature includes immigrants with disabilities. This population risks multiple layers of oppression from the point of applying to Canada and being screened out due to health concerns. In turn, disabilities add to the complexities of integration within Canadian society. A major issue concerns the receptivity of Canadian society to persons with mental and physical disabilities and the levels of service available to support integration. Our review of specific immigrant populations must be tempered with a cautionary note. It should also be recognized that, within the groups identified as at risk, there is diversity of experience prior to coming to Canada and in their experience of integration.

Working with refugee clients inevitably means working with clients who have experienced trauma in their lives. The impact of trauma at premigration, migration, and settlement may be long-standing and may be acute upon arrival to Canada, or it may surface after several years of living in Canada. This bespeaks the need for counsellors to be informed about the conditions of migration that lead people to become refugees. It calls for multicultural counsellors to be familiar with assessment strategies for diagnosing trauma-related symptoms and with strategies for providing relief from symptoms that impact physical, mental, and social functioning. It speaks to the importance of multicultural counsellors' expanding their knowledge to worldwide scenes where political and social persecution leads to the plight of refugees. It also underscores the importance of multicultural counsellors expanding their roles to consider how their professional influence can be applied to matters of social justice.

Chapter Summary

Students do not often consider that their career path in multicultural counselling will involve working with immigrants and refugees. Without deliberate efforts, we are rarely privileged to meet people at the time of entry to Canada, as most counsellors work in settings removed from settlement services. However, the changing demographics of Canada point to the inevitability of coming into contact with new Canadians. The viability of our counselling profession depends upon the extension of culturally responsive services to people who have joined our communities through the experience of migration from other parts of the developing world.

A critical prerequisite for providing culturally responsive services is an awareness of the factors that affect the health and well-being of immigrants and refugees, including the impact of systemic conditions such as racism and discrimination on both their mental health status and their attempts to develop a consolidated bicultural identity.

The adjustment of immigrants and refugees in the new society is shaped by the nature of their premigration experiences, the degree of voluntariness of the move, and the acculturation and adaptation processes that are activated upon their arrival in Canada. Although the adaptation process can be characterized by many challenges due to language barriers, unemployment and underemployment, experiences of racism, activation of premigration trauma, and intergenerational conflicts in the family unit, the majority of newcomers to Canada are able to successfully integrate into the host society.

In the multicultural counselling process, it appears imperative that we expand our traditional view of the helping role to facilitate the cultural adaptation process for immigrants and refugees. Counsellors should establish liaisons with settlement agencies and other types of services to connect newcomers to existing supports in order to meet their basic needs. Collaboration between the counsellor and client is essential in the process of identifying appropriate goals and intervention strategies that are congruent with both voluntary immigrants' and refugees' stages of migration and cultural value systems.

CHAPTER 13
INTERSECTIONS OF IDENTITY: HYBRIDITY, SITUATIONAL ETHNICITY, AND IN-BETWEEN SPACES

Monica Justin

Key Terms and Concepts		
• Acculturation • Assimilation • Biculturalism • Cultural value conflicts	• First-generation immigrant • Hybrid identity • Multiple and intersecting identities	• Second-generation immigrant • Situational ethnicity • Third space • Worldview

Personal Introduction

As a second-generation East Indian woman, I immigrated to Canada with my family as a young child and my initiation into Canadian culture began with learning to speak English. Growing up in a suburb of Montreal, I was simultaneously immersed in both Anglophone and Francophone cultural milieus throughout my childhood and adolescence. This exposure often presented cultural messages that challenged and contradicted the values and gender role expectations presented in my traditional East Indian family. As a result, I often found myself caught somewhere in between two distinct cultural worlds, often questioning which fit me best. Ultimately, the advantage of learning to live with seemingly contradictory rules taught me to become attentive and competent in navigating and negotiating multiple cultural contexts.

As an adult, I have been fortunate to have a wide network of friends and colleagues from different racial, ethnic, and cultural backgrounds. These relationships have introduced me to a variety of cultural experiences, customs, and traditions that I might not otherwise have experienced.

Although I have always defined myself as East Indian, it was only in adulthood that I gained a deeper appreciation of the subtle ways that my ethnicity has informed my identity. As a result of a myriad of experiences, I have developed a bicultural and hybrid identity that enables me to situate and position myself in a variety of social and cultural contexts relatively easily. Nonetheless, this presents numerous paradoxes and contradictions connected to issues of identity, culture, gender role expectations, and cultural norms. The way I define and identify myself often completely contradicts the ways in which others perceive, define, and situate me. Although I define myself as an East Indian woman, that does not do justice to describe or qualify the multiple identities I possess.

My background has created the foundation for my interest and passion in multicultural counselling and diversity issues. Many of the themes that have emerged throughout my life represent cross-cultural issues that blur the boundaries of gender, race, ethnicity, and culture as distinct dimensions of my identity. Individuals such as me, meaning second- and later-generation individuals, constitute a new breed of Canadians. We are individuals who defy the traditional assumptions and conceptualizations of being immigrants, as well as what it means to be Canadian. Ironically, as Canadians we nonetheless continue to be perceived as minorities and members of a non-dominant ethnic group. Because we defy the traditional assumptions of being immigrants, our identity statuses also challenge traditional conceptualizations. As a result, traditional modes and models of counselling do not do justice to contextualizing the realities of our bicultural identities. Acknowledging the significance of identity issues connected to second-generation status necessitates incorporating multicultural counselling competency into counselling practice in order to work effectively with members of non-dominant ethnic groups within the Canadian cultural mosaic.

Introduction

Although this chapter will use the experience of second-generation East Indian Canadian women to highlight issues of ethnicity, cultural values, bicultural identity, and acculturation, it is important to note that these issues are also central themes in the lives of women from other non-dominant ethnic groups in Canada. As practitioners, researchers, and a counselling community, developing an awareness and understanding of the heterogeneity that exists within different segments of immigrant populations in Canadian society offers a lens through which to qualitatively understand how women from different non-dominant ethnic groups negotiate their daily lives.

Many non-Western cultures share similar value systems, such as a collectivist social orientation, hierarchical family structure, and traditional gender role expectations. Therefore, numerous parallels can be drawn from non-Western value systems and translated to understanding the experience of women from Asian, South East Asian, English and French West Indian, Latin, and African cultural backgrounds. While generalities can be drawn amongst these cultures, it is important to remember that a multitude of variables influence how individual value systems are expressed and represented. The following discussion will highlight how concepts of intersecting and overlapping identities need to be considered in establishing a more comprehensive understanding of Canadians from non-dominant ethnic groups within a counselling context.

Snapshot 1

Vignette

Manju was referred to the counselling centre by her professor. She is a fourth-year law student who until the past semester had been an excellent student. Her grades over the semester have progressively deteriorated, and her professors, colleagues, and friends have noted a dramatic change in her demeanor. They see her crying unexpectedly, missing classes, looking tired, and having difficulty concentrating. Manju was initially hesitant to seek counselling, but eventually came to the Centre with the hope that she might begin to find some answers for herself. She is an articulate and well-spoken young woman who described coming from a traditional Punjabi, Hindu family. As the session progressed she talked about the importance that her family and ethnic community placed on her becoming a lawyer. She described feeling depressed and anxious at times, seemingly for no apparent reason. Manju reported that she would be completing her studies in the upcoming year and, since she was 28 years old, her parents had eagerly begun the process of arranging her marriage. She reported being happy about this arrangement, since she had always envisioned getting married and having a family as well as a career.

Definition of Healthy Functioning and Psychosocial Well-Being

The contrast between Eastern and Western orientations, values, and cultural norms forms the basis of cultural value conflicts experienced by many women from non-dominant ethnic groups in Canada. Within the field of counselling, the inherent assumptions of health, psychological well-being, and normal developmental behaviour are primarily framed from a Western perspective (Ponterotto & Casas, 1991; Sue & Sue, 2008; Sue, Zane & Young, 1994).

Western psychology is considered to be a person- or individual-oriented phenomenon (Ponterotto, Casas, Suzuki, & Alexander, 2001; Sue & Sue, 2008). Conversely, Eastern philosophies and orientations view health and well-being as a complex balance of mind, body, spirituality, and nature, thus promoting the idea of living in harmony, respecting nature, and the interconnectedness of physical and metaphysical forces (Carter, 1990; Ibrahim, Ohnishi, & Sandhu, 1997).

Sue and Sue (2008) stated that Western culture emphasizes a task orientation, mastery over nature, and a focus on doing rather than being. Overall, this cultural system tends to be future oriented. In contrast, Eastern cultures focus on being present or past oriented, living in harmony with nature, and emphasize *being* rather than *doing*.

The majority of counselling theories affirm Western values and concepts of mental health, developmental stages, relationships, and family dynamics (Corsini & Wedding, 2000). For example, as adults, individuals are expected to become autonomous, self-sufficient, and independent. This is evidenced in the expectation that they live separate from their family and thereby become emotionally, psychologically, and financially independent from one another (Sue & Sue, 2008). A person-centred orientation is also evident in the promotion of individual qualities such as assertiveness, personal authority, power, success, informal personal relationships, and overt power dynamics in social interactions.

However, within an Eastern value system (such as an East Indian family or community), the aforementioned cultural values contradict and transgress the inherent cultural and societal values, norms, and expectations that create a foundation for the Indian family and Indian identity. For example, families believe in psychological, emotional, and financial interdependence (Lessinger, 1995). In addition, respecting the authority of elders, deference towards elders in all social interactions, living in extended family units before and after marriage, and teaching children (particularly girls) to be reserved and conservative in their demeanor and familiar with domestic tasks are commonly valued traits. Underlying some of these specific cultural values is a clear and unwritten understanding regarding the distinction between appropriate behaviour in public and private worlds. Family and home life are considered to be private domains; therefore, conflicts or problems within the family are kept within the family and dealt with by elders within the family.

Furthermore, Indian girls and women hold several cultural responsibilities. For example, girls are charged with the responsibility of transmitting cultural values to the next generation and maintaining the unity and cohesiveness of the family. Hence, their behaviour is often seen as a direct reflection of their upbringing. Consequently, they bear the task of honourably reflecting their family's reputation through their behaviour, making the issues of purity and innocence an important cultural imperative for girls. For these reasons, the social activities of girls are often supervised and monitored.

Several of the aforementioned characteristics represent values shared by other cultures and gendered expectations for females from other non-dominant ethnic groups. Traditional gender role expectations for women are described as common features in Japanese, Chinese, West Indian, and Latin family cultures (Comas-Diaz & Greene, 1994; McGoldrick, Giordano, & Pearce, 1996; Mindel, Habenstein, & Wright Jr., 1988; Waters, 1999).

Given the emphasis placed on a collectivist orientation, respect for elders, and the distinction between public and private spheres, there is often a stigma that continues to be connected to seeking formal counselling. Western counselling orientations assume and promote the value of talk therapy, which is grounded in freely articulating personal problems, family issues, and internal conflicts, thereby building an individual identity. According to a North American perspective, healthy and culturally appropriate functioning of individuals in an East Indian family might appear dysfunctional, enmeshed, and oppressive (Kwon, 2001).

Working with individuals from non-dominant groups such as second-generation East Indian Canadian women requires an awareness and understanding of the embedded nature of specific values, ideals, and beliefs that may inherently contradict normative values from a Western cultural framework.

Cultural Identity and Relationship to Dominant Culture

As noted in Chapter 1, the liberalization of immigration laws in 1967 has changed the face of the North American population through the settlement of an increasing number of ethnic immigrants. A clear example of this change is evident in the most recent census data; more than 200 different ethnic origins were reported (Statistics Canada, 2008b). There are now more than 5 million visible minorities in Canada, representing 16.2% of the country's total population. From 2001-2006, growth of the visible minority population was 26.2%, compared to total country population growth of 5.4%. Based on this trend, it is estimated that visible minorities will account for about one fifth of Canada's overall population by 2017. Visible minorities are defined by the Employment Equity Act as "persons, other than Aboriginal peoples, who are non-Caucasian in race or non-white in colour" (Statistics Canada, 2004b). Respectively, South Asians, Chinese, and Blacks represent the top three visible non-dominant ethnic groups in Canada (Statistics Canada, 2008b). Notably, South Asian Indians (East

Indians) now constitute the largest segment of the current immigrant population. Although there is a growing body of multicultural literature and research focusing on the experience of Asian and African Americans in the United States, literature focusing on the experience of East Indians is notably absent from the multicultural discourse, particularly from a Canadian perspective.

History

Documentation of East Indian immigrants to Canada dates back to 1904 when approximately 45 Punjabi-Sikh men immigrated to Vancouver, British Columbia. By 1908, approximately 5,200 East Indian immigrants had settled in British Columbia, and many of these labourers found employment in the lumber industry.

In 1908, due to political pressures and public outcry, the Federal government effectively banned East Indian immigration. New legislation cited a variety of reasons for the immigration ban, such as that East Indians were not suitable immigration candidates because they would have difficulty tolerating and habituating to the cold climate of Canada (Sampat-Mehta, 1984; Walker, 1992). Additional legislative dictates required that all immigrants arriving in Canada had to arrive via one continuous and uninterrupted voyage from their home country, something that was impossible for East Indian immigrants at the time due to established travel routes. In conjunction with the new immigration policies, East Indians who were established residents of Canada were subjected to discriminatory legislation that limited their social, economic, and political participation in Canadian society. For example, they were not allowed to own property or run private businesses, run for political office, or freely choose their place of residence. These measures further served to maintain East Indians in a lower economic and social position within Canadian society (Buchignani, 1984).

It was not until 1948 that East Indians gained the right to vote in British Columbia and it was only in 1967 that immigration laws were revised to remove all ethnic, racial, and national restrictions. As a result, a new wave of East Indian immigrants entered Canada. This second wave of immigrants is referred to as the post-1965 immigrants and they represented a different social and economic class of immigrants than the earlier European and Asian immigrants. Post-1965 immigrants were educated, middle-class, professionally qualified individuals who were actively sought by the Canadian government to fill professional positions in the labour market. Canada at that time lacked sufficient numbers of qualified professionals such as doctors, nurses, engineers, scientists, and professors; therefore, professionals from countries such as India, England, and Asia were actively recruited (Buchignani, 1984; Das & Kemp, 1997; Wakil, Siddique, & Wakil, 1981). These immigrants were often labelled a *model minority* because they were considered to be hard-working, educated professionals who were perceived as easily able to integrate into Canadian society. These dichotomous perceptions of East Indian immigrants have contributed to the contentious history and relationships this group has had with the dominant culture throughout their settlement in Canada.

This brief history of East Indian immigration is offered as a backdrop from which to begin to understand the complex and paradoxical relationship that exists between this ethnic group and Canadian society. On one hand, racial stereotypes continue to exist and infiltrate the perception of East Indians as a homogeneous group. Common assumptions include the idea that all East Indians are Hindu and therefore pray to animal deities, are socially distant and avoid integrating into Canadian society, have limited English skills, and are uneducated and unskilled labourers (e.g., taxi drivers, textile factory workers). In addition, cultural practices in terms of food, language, style of dress, family structure, social mannerisms, and arranged marriages continue to be perceived as norms that differ radically from those of mainstream society, thereby perpetuating a sense of social isolation and distancing. Ironically, the stereotype of model minority simultaneously continues to pervade the social consciousness and does not include images of the East Indian community as contributing to gang or inner city violence. One conclusion that can be drawn in spite of these perceptions is that the East Indian community is a heterogeneous group including individuals and groups from different social classes, levels of education, occupational status, language proficiency, immigration status, and countries of immigration. The degree of acculturation, desire to acculturate, and ability to integrate into mainstream society are markedly influenced by this range of factors.

Intergenerational Issues

The retention and maintenance of ethnic cultural values is of paramount importance in understanding cultural identity issues within the East Indian Canadian community (Das & Kemp, 1997; Dhruvarajan, 1993; Patel, Power, & Bhavnagri, 1996), as it is among other ethnic groups. The perceived loss of cultural identity is often a major source of tension and conflict between second-generation children and their parents (Pettys & Balgopal, 1998). First-generation parents often tend to strongly identify with their country and culture of origin (Akhtar, 1994; Aycan & Kanungo, 1998; Das Gupta, 1997, 1998; Wakil et al., 1981). However, second-generation individuals possess a bicultural identity based on their socialization within two cultural worlds (Ghuman, 1997; Lalonde & Giguère, 2008; Sandhu, 1992; Sodhi Kalsi, 2003). Jambunathan, Burts, and Pierce (2000) defined biculturalism as "a person's ability to function effectively in more than one culture and also to switch roles back and forth as the situation changes" (p. 396). Sue and Sue (1999) offered a similar point of view and emphasized that cultural value conflicts can arise for these individuals. They described biculturalism as the fact that minorities in North America inherit two cultural traditions. Therefore, bicultural conflicts can arise when an individual holds membership in two cultural groups that present conflicting value systems (societal norms, values, and attitudes). Lalonde and Giguère further supported this notion of bicultural conflicts in the context of "intercultural and intracultural conflicts" (p. 58) experienced by second-generation youth. Second-generation individuals may experience intercultural conflicts with parents or peers; intracultural conflicts may arise within the individual when they experience "feeling torn between two cultures" (p. 58). According to Lalonde and Giguère, intracultural conflicts are more likely to be experienced by the individual when the two cultural identities being negotiated are "equally and simultaneously salient" (p. 58) to the individual.

The conflict a person experiences may be related to positively emphasizing or implementing the specific values, behaviours, norms, or customs of one culture over another. Consequently, the central issue in negotiating a bicultural identity is possessing multiple identities that are informed by family, social, cultural, and environmental factors. For second-generation individuals, their sense of loyalty, connection, and identity lies in both their ethnic cultural heritage and within Canadian cultural context; they can simultaneously belong to both worlds, yet not fit in either (Asher, 2008; Lalonde & Giguère, 2008; Stroink & Lalonde, 2009). Second-generation women live in the margins that exemplify the reality of being a woman from a visible non-dominant ethnic group (Justin, 2003; Khan, 2002; Sodhi-Kalsi, 2003).

First-generation individuals can be understood as undergoing a selective acculturation process whereby they adopt varying degrees of social and behavioural practices in order to function and adapt to Canadian society (Das & Kemp, 1997; Lessinger, 1995). First-generation individuals may have been exposed to more overt forms of racial discrimination. The era in which these individuals immigrated, coupled with the absence of ethnic and racial diversity in the Canadian population, may have contributed to leaving them feeling more tentative about integrating more fully into Canadian society. The maintenance and retention of cultural practices, attitudes, and behaviours from their country of origin can be understood as creating a sense of familiarity, cultural affiliation, and community in an unfamiliar and foreign country (Lessinger).

Given their dual socialization, second-generation individuals have a different acculturative experience than their parents. They have been socialized and educated within Canadian society and therefore their identity is a bridge between two cultural worlds. In and of themselves, they possess knowledge, social skills, awareness, and the ability to move easily between these worlds. However, their racial status (visibility) may expose them to experiences of discrimination and racism. Although they may be perceived as *foreigners* by mainstream society, they typically define and identify themselves as Canadians.

In addition, second-generation individuals often tend to have a broader range of social relationships and exposure to North American social and cultural practices and customs. This contributes to the development of their ethnic and bicultural identity, and simultaneously contributes to intergenerational and cultural value conflicts. For example, East Indian families tend to be protective of their girls, limiting their personal and social freedom, particularly in adolescence. While their families may value limiting their personal freedom, Western attitudes take a more permissive stance in allowing personal and social freedom for adolescents, such as dating. Therefore, many girls may feel the push and pull of these opposing cultural values due to the influence of socializing in a Western culture that does not reinforce the same value system. Another example of this is traditional gender role expectations for girls, which require them to be more attentive to more domestic and family activities as well as to cultural practices. This is because girls and women are considered to be central in holding and transmitting cultural values to the next generation (Umana-Taylor & Yazedjian, 2006). Anticipating the potential loss and dilution of their cultural identity and heritage is seen as a significant factor in the emphasis that first-generation immigrant parents place on instilling a strong connection to cultural practices and traditions in their second-generation children. Because girls carry the primary responsibility for transmitting cultural values, they may encounter unique challenges as they negotiate a dual socialization process.

Several factors influence the relationship an individual from a non-dominant group has with the dominant culture. These include experiences of overt and covert discrimination, perception and attitude of the host society towards a particular ethnic or racial group, historical issues of oppression, and immigration status (Li, 2003; Sue & Sue, 2008). Although these variables may have stronger implications for first-generation immigrants, the children of immigrant parents are not completely immune to a similar evaluation by the dominant culture based on their racial status, skin colour, socio-economic status, acculturation level, and degree of anchoring and identification with their ethnic community.

Theoretical Principles and Conceptual Issues in Multicultural Practice

The past two decades have seen a proliferation of research on multicultural issues in the field of counselling psychology (Sue & Sue, 2008). Understanding how specific non-dominant groups and individuals position and situate themselves in the context of the larger North American population continues to be an area of interest for scholars, academics, and mental health practitioners. Fuertes and Gretchen (2001) asserted that several gaps remain in our understanding of the issues of non-dominant ethnic populations and advocated that "the significance of discerning the complexities of internalized aspects of cultural group membership and clients interpretations and meaning of their values and beliefs is emphasized beyond the simple appreciation of client group membership or affiliation" (p. 532). Therefore, clarifying how individuals construct, situate, and negotiate their cultural values and ethnic identity becomes a critical issue for the counselling profession as it continues to meet the needs of increasingly diverse clientele (Collins, in press).

Understanding salient constructs within the multicultural counselling literature, such as generational status, biculturalism, cultural value conflicts, multiple and intersecting identities as precursors to development of hybrid identities, situational ethnicity, and varying levels of acculturation, offers a general framework from which to begin to understand the lives of individuals from non-dominant ethnic groups, specifically second- and later-generation individuals. The aforementioned constructs are particularly meaningful in situating identity issues for second-generation women in the context of gender role expectations, cultural values tensions, the maintenance and retention of cultural values, and ultimately how they construct a bicultural identity. The following section will briefly describe these concepts and will proceed with a discussion of how these issues can be implicated in the common presenting issues for female clients.

Second-Generation Individuals

In recent years there has been growing awareness of the need for research on second-generation individuals (Abouguendia & Noels, 2001; Boyd & Grieco, 1998; Lalonde & Giguère, 2008; Waters, 1999). The importance of focusing on the experience of second-generation individuals as a *strategic research site* is highlighted by Portes (1997):

> The long-term effects of immigration on a host society depend less on the fate of first-generation immigrants than on their descendents [second and later generation children]...because they will determine the resilience and disappearance of culturally distinct ethnic enclaves...the decline or growth of ethnic intermarriages will be determined among it children and grandchildren. (p. 814)

The labels *first-* and *second-generation immigrant* or *first-* and *second-generation Canadian* are often used to denote the status of ethnic minorities in Canada. There is a lack of consensus in the literature regarding terminology, and therefore these labels are used interchangeably, creating some confusion and ambiguity in defining them. For the purpose of this chapter, **first-generation immigrant** is typically used to describe *individuals who immigrated to Canada as adults and literally represent the "new immigrant."* The label of **second-generation immigrant** refers to the *children of immigrant parents, meaning children who were either born in the host country or who arrived at preschool age* (Gans, 1992; Zhou, 1997). Hence, they are the second generation of immigrants in the host society. The same terminology can be applied to categorize each subsequent generation. For the purpose of clarity, first-generation Canadian is synonymous with second-generation immigrant status. It is beyond the scope of this discussion to delve into the various implications and implicit connotations connected to immigrant status or the categorizations that continue to classify successive generations of ethnic Canadians as immigrant. Nonetheless, it is important to note that race, ethnicity, status as a visible ethnic non-dominant group, and immigration status (refugee, naturalized citizen, landed immigrant) all carry implications for how individuals are perceived by the dominant culture (Li, 1999, 2003). For example, individuals from visible ethnic groups are often asked, "Where do you come from?" or "How long have you been in Canada?" Although these questions are not asked with ill intention, they implicitly convey the idea that being a person of colour does not equate to being Canadian; obviously being Canadian means being White (Justin, 2003). Therefore, the implication for second-generation individuals of visible minority status brings the issue of racial status to the forefront of identity issues connected to nationality.

Biculturalism

Jambunathan and colleagues (2000) defined **biculturalism** as *"a person's ability to function effectively in more than one culture and also to switch roles back and forth as the situation changes"* (p. 396). This concept is particularly meaningful for second-generation individuals because it describes the outcome of identity development defined by a socialization process that has demanded that they negotiate and assimilate two or more cultural milieus.

Ho (1995) referred to the same phenomenon as bienculturation or multienculturation, which suggests that "children of parents from diverse cultural backgrounds are enculturated in more than one culture" (p. 13). In their unique cases, "no one culture is regarded as the host or dominant... rather different cultural systems are internalized and coexist within the mind" (Ho, p. 13). Consequently, multienculturated individuals possess a plurality of cultural influences that enable them to have in-depth personal knowledge and experiences of multiple cultural contexts.

Cultural Value Conflicts

Sue and Sue (1999) described biculturalism as minorities in North America who inherit (at least) two cultural traditions; hence, **cultural value conflicts** are an inherent dimension of biculturalism. These value conflicts *arise for individuals when they hold membership in two cultural groups that present conflicting value systems.* The conflict they experience can be related to positively emphasizing or implementing the specific values, behaviours, norms, and customs of one culture over another. Hence, the dilemma that arises in constructing a bicultural identity is founded in being forced to constantly and actively choose specific cultural values to integrate into a congruent personal worldview. Ibrahim (1985) referred to **worldviews** as our *philosophy of life,* meaning that our worldviews are *comprised of our attitudes, values, and beliefs.* These in turn affect how we give meaning to our experiences, make decisions in our lives, think, and act. For second-generation individuals, cultural value conflicts can be a salient issue in their daily lives both in and outside of the home. These cultural tensions or conflicts can be expressed in contradictory gender role expectations, career-related issues, social restrictions, and religious practices that reflect the inherent differences between Eastern and Western social and cultural practices. For example, family allocentrism, described as "the expression of cultural collectivism at a family level" (Lay et al., 1998, as cited in Lalonde & Giguère, 2008, p. 60), can influence the degree of cultural tension experienced by second-generation individuals. For example, choice of life partner, traditional attributes of one's potential partner, and views of chastity and sexuality are all positively correlated to stronger adherence to heritage cultural values as opposed to preference for North American values and norms.

Multiple and Intersecting Identities

In examining the implications of cultural value conflicts and the concept of worldviews, it becomes important to consider the **multiple identities** we each possess as human beings. For example, *we each possess an identity connected to our gender, social class, age, ethnicity, race, and religion.* Traditionally, identity theories have prioritized a singular identity above all others, such as gender, race, or ethnicity (Collins, in press; Reynolds & Constantine, 2004; Williams & Barber, 2004). Conceptualizing individuals, particularly members of non-dominant populations, into monolithic and singular identity categories assumes a reductionist perspective that devalues all other dimensions of the individual (Valentine, 2007). Conceptualizing individuals as possessing multiple and intersecting identities that encompass variables such as age, gender, ethnicity, class, socio-economic status, religion, and immigration status offers a more comprehensive framework for understanding the complex and multifaceted phenomenon of identity and the challenges faced in negotiating broader issues of identity.

Hybrid Identity / Third Space

The notion of **hybrid identities** is a newer conceptualization that describes the paradoxical positioning of identity (Bhabha, 1990, 1994). This conceptualization *considers identity to be a fluid and dynamic phenomenon that is located across a range of contradictory social contexts.* This idea reinforces the notion that people live within multiple contexts and therefore possess multiple identities. Possessing multiple identities can give rise to paradoxical intersections and positioning of one's identity. It is important to pay careful attention to these intersections and interactions among multiple markers of identity (Arredondo, Tovar-Blank, & Parham, 2008; Ludvig, 2006; Silverstein, 2006). Through the process of cultural translation, individuals faced with dichotomous cultural influences merge these influences to create a **third space**: *a unique space that more appropriately defines their hybrid identity* (Barcinski & Kalia, 2005). Bhabha (1990) asserted that this "third space displaces the histories that constitute it and sets up new structures of authority, new political initiatives which are inadequately understood through conventional wisdom…the process of hybridity gives rise to something different, something new and unrecognizable, a new area of negotiation of meaning and presentation" (p. 211). Asher (2008) noted that "as individuals and communities craft hybrid identities and cultures by synthesizing the differences they encounter they may find themselves in in-between spaces or interstices. These interstitial locations can be sites of struggle and contradictions" (p. 15). Readers are referred to Chapter 10 in which Collins explores the implications of multiple non-dominant identities for identity development and the counselling process.

Superimposing this conceptualization to the experience of second-generation individuals depathologizes the seemingly contradictory and opposing cultural influences they must negotiate in constructing a congruent bicultural identity. Understanding that the contradictions and juxtapositions of identity are inherent in the process of identity development presents a different framework from which to understand an individual or group, particularly in considering their relationship to dominant societal norms and expectations.

Situational Ethnicity

Identity is also strongly influenced by the contexts or social locations, both past and present, that each individual encounters (Barcinski & Kalia, 2005; Ludvig, 2006). **Situational ethnicity** is a term that has evolved from the anthropological literature and is premised on the idea that *particular contexts may determine which of a person's identities or loyalties are appropriate at any given time.* With respect to identity, this concept highlights the fact that individuals' perceptions of a situation or context can influence the degree to which they reveal or affirm different dimensions of their ethnic identity (Knapik & Miloti, 2006). The decision to affirm one's ethnic identity can be influenced by how receptive others are perceived to be, social cues and signals, experiences of racism, and so forth (Okamura, 1981). Selectively self-disclosing personal information, or assessing the advantages and disadvantages of doing so, serves as a self-protective strategy, which can be the result of having experienced overt and covert instances of racism, discrimination, and oppression in one's life (Riviere, 2004; Valentine, 2007). For example, societal perceptions of what being *ethnic* or *immigrant* means usually reflect many negative stereotypical images. These include the common assumption that ethnic immigrants are uneducated, have limited English language proficiency, and are of lower socio-economic status. Given that these assumptions pervade the social consciousness and are reflected in biased attitudes towards individuals from visible non-dominant groups, it seems reasonable that individuals who are the subjects of these attitudes would actively assess and evaluate when, where, how, and with whom to share aspects of their personal life and cultural differences.

Situated identities are a concept that can be related to situational ethnicity. Clément and Noels (1992, as cited in Lalonde and Giguère, 2008) argued that immigrant children's behaviour at home and with their families is largely determined and defined by their heritage culture, while Canadian culture becomes the main determinant of behaviour at school or in public spheres. *Situated identities* refers to the phenomenon that "home represents the Indian end of the identity continuum and school as a public sphere represents the North American end of the identity continuum" (Asher, 2008, p. 15). The sense of ease individuals experience in choosing to express different aspects of their cultural identity does not preclude the fact that both the private and public spheres also present contradictory messages. For example, within the home environment, dressing in more North American style, or speaking back to elders can be perceived as disrespectful behaviour. Children may be clearly told they are *becoming too North American*. This message implies that they have lost connection and respect for their heritage culture. While at school, peers may make racial remarks and cultural assumptions, thus motivating the individual to correct the misassumptions or defend their culture of origin. Hence, choosing the degree to which children reveal or affirm different dimension of their ethnic identity is a dynamic process and requires constant negotiation of their social environment.

Acculturation

The construct of acculturation refers to a process of social change, not only at the individual and psychological levels, but also at the socio-cultural level. Originally, it was considered to be a unidimensional process that resulted in full assimilation of a newcomer or immigrant. It is important to note that assimilation and acculturation are interrelated processes and the terms are often used interchangeably in the literature and in common popular culture. Recent conceptualizations of the **acculturative process** refer to it as *a bidirectional and multifaceted process that refers to varying degrees of change in the values, behaviours, and interaction patterns as a result of cross-cultural contact* (Berry, 2003).

Berry's (1990, 2001, 2005) model of acculturation is a popular and frequently cited model. It proposes that as people move through an acculturation process they experience shifts in language, cognitive styles, personality, identity, attitudes, and acculturative stress. This model cites four main acculturative attitudes, described as (a) integration, (b) separation, (c) marginalization, and (d) assimilation. Integration represents individuals who maintain an active connection and interest in their culture of origin while simultaneously participating in the host culture. Individuals who present a separation attitude are seen as avoiding contact with the host culture and choosing to remain closely connected to their culture of origin. Marginalization occurs when individuals have no interest in participation in either their culture of origin or the host culture. Finally, assimilation represents people who actively engage in the host culture but ignore their culture of origin.

Considering Berry's acculturative attitudes, integration and assimilation appear to be the two strategies that reflect the inherent challenges of possessing a bicultural identity. They highlight the significance of cultural value conflicts and intergenerational conflicts that are cited in the literature as common issues for individuals from non-dominant ethnic groups (Ponterotto et al., 2001; Sue & Sue, 2003). These are also salient issues in considering the experience of second-generation East Indian women. For example, adopting a position of integration most closely represents a healthy and congruent bicultural identity. Conversely, assuming an assimilationist perspective can result in numerous and varied tensions for individuals in their family and ethnic community because they are perceived as having abandoned their ethnic identity and cultural values. Although an ethnic individual may feel more closely connected to a Western value system and lifestyle, this does not automatically assume that dominant culture will embrace that individual openly. The individual may still be perceived as an outsider based on racial differences and societal perceptions of desirability (Asher, 2008; Stroink & Lalonde, 2009).

Assimilation

Assimilation has been a popular concept used to describe how immigrants integrate into a host culture and society. This concept *assumes that individuals will progressively forego their ethnic heritage, values, and behaviour to adopt the values, customs, and traditions of a host culture* (Alba & Nee, 1997), hence the inherent assumption and expectation that immigrants comply with the cultural and normative standards of a host society, thereby abandoning their cultural distinctiveness and assimilating into dominant culture. One of the critiques in recent literature argues that the concept of assimilation is more representative of the societal expectations and personal objectives of early European immigrants to be accepted into a host culture (Gans, 1992; Zhou, 1997). Although assimilation may continue to covertly inform society's fundamental expectation of newer immigrants, it is expressed in different ways in today's society. An appreciation of multiculturalism is more readily apparent in today's society (if only superficially) in the form of ethnic food, fashion, and integration of Eastern philosophies of medicine, health, and spirituality. Therefore, in working with clients from non-dominant ethnic groups, it is important to consider a variety of theoretical and social factors that may have shaped their identity development and relationship to the dominant culture. The constructs popularly used to define the experience of individuals from non-dominant ethnic groups have often been conceptualized according to singular models and points of view. All individuals are dynamic and multifaceted beings; therefore, it becomes important to reorganize our theoretical frameworks within the context of multiple and intersecting identities. A perfect example of this is working with ethnic clients who possess a racial identity, ethnic identity, gender identity, cultural identity, and so forth. These identities do not exist in isolation; rather, they overlap and intersect.

Common Presenting Concerns

Clients seek counselling services for a variety of reasons. As practitioners, it is imperative to realize that clients from non-dominant ethnic groups are no different from the general population and may seek services for a range of personal or professional issues. This is also a critical consideration when working with second- and later-generation individuals because their social, cultural, and ethnic identities reflect a bicultural experience. As a result, they may not associate the same degree of stigma to seeking counselling services as their first-generation counterparts. Their bicultural status and identity become central considerations in the counselling context because this identity situates and positions them in a unique way as both insiders and outsiders within their families, ethnic communities, and mainstream society. Consequently, recognizing that their bicultural identity represents a constructed hybrid identity, uniquely representative of a variety of influences such as culture, ethnicity, race, gender role expectations, religion, education, social class, socio-economic status, and visible minority status, requires that counsellors avoid making stereotypical assumptions about the meaning and significance a client ascribes to any one of these influences.

As a practitioner, maintaining an awareness and consciousness about stereotypical assumptions and attitudes about individuals from non-dominant ethnic groups is one aspect of the counselling equation. As noted earlier in this chapter, concepts such as cultural value conflicts, ethnic, cultural and racial identity, and acculturation levels have been highlighted in the multicultural literature. These issues represent salient and recurrent themes in the lives of second-generation East Indian women as they negotiate and construct their bicultural identity over the course of their lives. While it is impossible to list a specific set of presenting concerns associated with clients from non-dominant ethnic populations, some broad generalizations can be made about common themes and issues that arise for second- or later-generation individuals. Although I will use examples focusing on second-generation East Indian women to highlight various concepts and constructs, these can be equally applied to understanding the experiences of women from other non-dominant ethnic groups. Some of these issues are (a) varying degrees of acculturation levels among family members, which result in intergenerational conflict; (b) cultural value conflicts, which emerge as a result of possessing a bicultural identity; (c) negotiating and constructing a personally defined identity that reflects hybrid influences; and (d) negotiating issues of discrimination, racism, and oppression.

This is not an exhaustive list of presenting concerns; nor are these issues mutually exclusive. Although each of these concepts is often discussed as a singular construct, in reality these issues represent multifaceted, multidimensional, and interconnected phenomenon. For example, it is impossible to engage clients in discussion about their ethnic identity without examining the implications of race and gender as closely connected variables. Similarly, we cannot talk about intergenerational conflicts and varying levels of acculturation among family members without addressing the concept of cultural values, gender role expectations, and the pressure of negotiating dichotomous social and cultural norms. By the same token, exploring cultural value conflicts requires examining issues connected to intergenerational conflicts, identity issues, ethnicity, social relationships, a sense of connection and disconnection from one's ethnic and cultural community, and so forth. Therefore, no one issue can be discussed as a single and separate variable without considering the influence of these additional overlapping denominators. It is the intersection and interplay of these multiple variables that is a notable consideration when working with individuals from non-dominant ethnic groups in a counselling context. The main point is that these issues and constructs are complex and embedded within each other, not only in the subjective experience of clients, but also in how they are defined by mainstream society.

Bicultural Identity

Identity development is a complex phenomenon that involves not only physiological and maturational development, but also requires that individuals actively engage in deconstructing and reconstructing their identity in order to create a sense of congruence. This personal engagement is a skill that is cultivated and refined with life experience and age (Justin, 2003). Repeatedly facing issues that challenge us to consciously evaluate, deconstruct, and reconstruct our sense of self and individual identity are often the motivating forces in our personal development. While these life events can be positive experiences, they also bring numerous challenges. In the case of second-generation women, these challenges can result in seeking counselling services for the purpose of support, personal growth, or crisis intervention. Although individuals can encounter numerous personal, social, and cultural challenges in facing overt and covert discrimination or questioning identity issues, it should not be assumed that this process is entirely negative. Understanding the process as a developmental issue that is repeatedly negotiated given one's status as *racial, ethnic,* or *cultural* minority contextualizes and normalizes the experience.

 **Snapshot 2**

Biculturalism

Leesa has always been told she is an attractive young woman with exotic features. She is often mistaken as of Mediterranean, Latin, or Spanish descent because of her dark hair, eyes, and olive skin. Many of her friends and colleagues have been surprised to learn she is East Indian, a reaction Leesa always finds curious. What did they expect? She sees herself as East Indian. Her mother always cooks Indian food at home, dresses in traditional dresses for different social and cultural events, and, most of all, her father still has an Indian accent, even after having been in Canada for 30 years. Growing up, Leesa often heard derogatory comments and jokes made about East Indians, names like Paki, Coolie, and so forth. She has never felt comfortable hearing these remarks, but at the same time has never really known how to react.

The mix of confusion, anger, and guilt she feels stems from questioning why Indians are so negatively labelled; after all, her family and friends in the Indian community certainly do not fit these stereotypes. Her father is a doctor and her mother a nurse. She and her three siblings were raised in upper middle class neighbourhoods and enjoyed many social and economic comforts and privileges. Her parents are also respected members in the larger community and in their church. Leesa has also noticed that she doesn't get the same reactions from people as her brother and younger sister, who are darker skinned. Even people in their ethnic community comment about Leesa's attractiveness and fair complexion in a positive way, usually commenting that she will easily find a suitable husband when the time comes. Leesa has always wondered where she fits into the grand scheme of things, being Indian but not really looking Indian, being a part of her ethnic community but also not fitting the negative stereotypes and images she has seen of Indians. This self-questioning and personal dilemma has been compounded by the fact that, although she feels connected to her ethnic and cultural heritage, she doesn't see herself living her life according to the same cultural rules as her parents.

Social Tensions and Disconnections

As an individual with a bicultural identity, living with different degrees of connection and disconnection within one's own ethnic community and within mainstream society can be a common experience (Justin, 2003; Lessinger, 1995). Give that second-generation women have learned to understand and navigate different cultural norms throughout their lives and developed skill in presenting a situational ethnicity, it is reasonable to expect that they have also been exposed to situations and contexts that present social challenges as a result of norms, etiquette, and expectations about appropriate social interactions.

 **Snapshot 3**

Social Tensions and Disconnection

Grace is 21 years old and lives at home with her parents and two younger siblings. She attends university full-time and her primary responsibility is to get good grades at school and successively complete her science degree. She is expected to help her mother around the house and look after her younger siblings on a regular basis. Grace has never dated or really socialized with boys. She has two distinct social networks, one made up of her Indian friends and the second composed of her White friends.

Although she likes both groups of friends, she describes a qualitative difference in these social relationships that leaves her questioning where she belongs and fits in. She's had these questions about herself for a long time and continues to struggle with understanding who she is. When she's with her Indian friends, they talk endlessly about the latest fights with their parents. They can all see the humor in the situation because their parents have the same ethnic mentality. So Grace has a comfort zone with these friends because she doesn't have to lie or try to explain all the rules in her family and culture because all her female friends live with the same rules. She has a lot of fun with her White friends, but doesn't always feel like she completely fits in with them or that they really understand her. They always invite her to go to clubs and bars, but she is not allowed to stay out that late, so she never really socializes with them on weekends. Her girlfriends talk about things like dating or having sex with their boyfriends. They also speak of their families and parents using derogatory language, something Grace never imagines doing. Grace often feels uncomfortable when these conversations arise, so she remains quiet and does not participate. The thing that bothers her most is when these friends tease her about not having a boyfriend and when they want to know her personal stories about dating and having sex.

Cultural Value Conflicts

An overarching theme in the lives of second-generation Indian women is cultural value conflicts. Possessing a bicultural identity inherently assumes the negotiation of cultural value conflicts. The cultural tensions that often emerge for these women are reflected in intergenerational conflicts between grandparents and second-generation children, or parents and second-generation children, particular female children (Inman, Ladany, Constantine, & Morano, 2001). As noted in an earlier section of this chapter, girls and women are seen as vessels through which cultural values are transmitted to successive generations. First-generation parents often hold a strong affiliation and connection to their country of origin and traditional cultural, social, and religious values and practices (Das & Kemp, 1997; Lessinger, 1995; Patel et al., 1996; Wakil et al., 1981). The tensions between older family members and the younger generation is grounded in the fact that their bicultural second-generation children have gained exposure to multiple social milieus, school, peers, and social activities and therefore have a broader repertoire of choices from which to selectively choose how to construct their identity. As a result, they may not hold the same alliances and sense of connection to traditional cultural practices, gender role expectations, or religious practices as older family members. The pressure they can experience from their family and ethnic community to conform can motivate these women to seek counselling services. While families can be a strong source of support for the individual, given the above issues, they can equally be a source of stress, especially for Indian girls and women (Das & Kemp).

Snapshot 4

Cultural Value Conflicts

Reena feels like she is always getting into fights with her parents. Whenever she goes out with her friends she comes home to a barrage of questions: Where have you been? Who did you go with? Why do you want to go out this late at night? Reena feels frustrated and annoyed. She is 23 years old and still needs to account for herself as if she were a child. Although she understands her parents' concern for her, it is hard to put up with the interrogation sessions. Her parents never harass her brother like that. He stays out all night sometimes, and he is two years younger than her. She always respects her parent's wishes and abides by the curfew they have set, but can't understand why they don't trust her. She feels frustrated and embarrassed with her friends because none of them go out before 10 pm on Friday night. By the time they meet at a club or bar, it is almost time for her to go home. And all the while she is getting ready to meet her friends, her parents are asking her: Why does she have to leave the house at this hour? It is unsafe for a girl to be out at night. Why can't she just stay at home with the rest of the family?

She is convinced that her White friends don't go through this same ritual every week and she knows they don't have a midnight curfew. They are always telling her to move out. After all, she is 23 years old and why is she still living at home anyways? She can't explain to her friends that moving out is not an option before she is married. Even suggesting something like that to her parents would start WWIII in her house. Truthfully, even though she fights with her parents, she can't imagine living on her own and away from them. Sometimes she thinks she is just too scared and afraid to take that step to become an independent person.

The snapshots in this section represent some examples of the identity issues, cultural value conflicts, and sense of social disconnection that second-generation women encounter in the context of their daily lives. The self-questioning and social dilemmas that permeate their experience often centre on examining, challenging, and making personal decisions on identity issues related to their ethnic and cultural backgrounds. Discovering ways of creating a sense of personal congruence within their biculturalism, struggling with the mixed messages, and internal and external contradictions that emerge from navigating different cultural norms and expectations are often the source of ongoing conflict in their lives. Unfortunately, this experience may leave adolescents at a greater risk for lower self-esteem and confusion as turmoil about their sense of personal identity and sense of belonging can be experienced as a heavy burden (Maxwell & Henriksen, 2009).

Multicultural Counselling Process

This section will highlight salient issues in the process of multicultural counselling, including implications for counsellor competencies and applications to the counselling process. The concept of worldview, components of multicultural competence, stigma connected to counselling, attrition, and identity as central issues to counselling will be discussed. Although the focus of this discussion will be on how the counselling process may be applied to second-generation Indian women, it is important to note that the aforementioned issues may be thoughtfully generalized to other non-dominant ethnic groups.

Worldview

Adopting a culture-centred perspective in counselling requires a fundamental awareness of clients' individual worldviews (Pedersen & Ivey, 1993; Sue & Sue, 2003). Worldview is a broad concept that encompasses issues such as language, assumptions, verbal and nonverbal behaviour, beliefs about human nature, social and cultural norms, and value orientations (Dana, 1998). Appreciating that each person is unique as a function of their individual worldview allows for the understanding that the worldview of a counsellor and client can be very similar or profoundly different. Differences can emerge as a result of many different variables, such as age, gender, or social class, and if we add increasingly complex variables to the equation such as race, ethnicity, and cultural variables, the likelihood of clashes of worldview becomes increasingly probable. Therefore, as counsellors, when we imagine sitting with a client from a different ethnic, racial, social, or cultural background from ourselves, we must acknowledge the significance and implications that differing worldviews may have in the counselling process. We must acknowledge this at all levels of communication and mutual understanding. As counsellors, our worldviews will influence our social mannerisms, verbal and nonverbal behaviour, level of formality or informality with our clients, style of communication, and mostly importantly the implicit and explicit expectations we have of our clients.

Remaining cognizant of these issues will enable counsellors to attend to the counselling process and interact with clients with sensitivity and respect. Although some general principles for working with members of non-dominant populations can be identified, we must not make blind assumptions that the counselling process must follow a specific series of sequential steps.

Components of Multicultural Competence

Three areas of counsellor competencies have traditionally been emphasized in multicultural counselling frameworks: awareness, knowledge, and skills (Arredondo et al., 1996; Collins & Arthur, in press a). In the culture-infused counseling framework, it is recognized that each of these components intersects in core competencies. Consequently, the competency framework outlined in Chapter 3 has been organized into three domains: counsellor self-awareness, awareness of client multiple identities, and a culturally sensitive working alliance. Cultivating competencies in these domains solidifies:

> … an understanding of multiculturalism and its implications for knowledge of self and others in a culturally pluralistic society; an understanding of the terms related to multiculturalism such as ethnicity, diversity, race, dominant and non-dominant groups; the ability to appropriately use counselling skills with clients from non-dominant groups; and a commitment to organizational development that reflects the values of multiculturalism. (Arredondo et al., 1996, p. 5)

The underlying tenet in the above mentioned competencies is a fundamental respect and valuing of cultural, personal, and contextual identity factors, which requires understanding each client as a unique human being whose identity and worldview have been influenced by a myriad of experiences (Collins & Arthur, in press b). Collins and Arthur (in press a) referred to this as *culture infused counseling,* which wholly represents the idea that each counselling interaction and the working alliance between counselor and therapist represents a distinct multicultural interaction. Hence, all counseling can be defined and understood as a multicultural encounter (Arthur & Collins, in press a; Pedersen, 2008).

Awareness of Client Culture

The demographic diversity of the Canadian population demands that counsellors possess knowledge about non-dominant ethnic groups, their immigration histories, cultural practices, general value systems, and relationship to mainstream society. Understanding that a wide spectrum of individual and groups differences exists in any population or community is critical. Heterogeneity within a community can be influenced by socio-economic status, education levels, occupation, social class, language proficiency, religious affiliations, geographical location from country of origin, native language or dialect, and so forth. Recognizing individual and group differences minimizes the tendency for misassumptions and the perpetuation of negative stereotypes within the counselling process. Awareness and sensitivity to a client's worldview requires a general knowledge base from which to ask informed questions and demonstrate an inherent respect towards a client. Counsellors can engage in a number of learning activities in order to meet this goal, such as remaining current with the literature (academic and non-academic), community cultural activities, social activities that encourage a respectful exposure and stance towards learning about different ethnic communities, and cultivating social and professional networks that facilitate personal growth (mentoring, formal supervision, etc.).

Das and Kemp (1997) outlined several broad values that permeate Indian culture and family values that can be useful for counsellors to remember:

- nonconfrontation or silence as a virtue,
- respect for older persons and the elderly,
- moderation in behaviour,
- devaluation of individualism,
- harmony between hierarchical roles,

- humility,
- obedience,
- high regard for learning,
- modesty about sexuality,
- not demonstrative with heterosexual affection,
- less need for dating,
- strong sense of duty to family,
- protection of family honour,
- marrying within versus outside of ethnic group, and
- importance attached to preserving the original religion. (p. 30)

Understanding that second-generation Indian women also live with different degrees of connection and disconnection to their family and extended family, ethnic community, religious traditions and customs, and in relation to mainstream society creates a situational context from which to explore the meaning and positioning of their identity issues. Therefore, recognizing the ways in which cultural, personal, and contextual identity factors intersect and situate the individual in a unique context becomes a significant consideration and has been highlighted by numerous scholars and multicultural researchers (Arthur & Collins, in press a, b; Pedersen, 2008; Sue & Sue, 2008). Striving to continually develop our skill and competence and becoming knowledgeable about various cultural traditions and practices further facilitates building the foundation of a genuine, respectful, and empathic working relationship with our clients. Snapshot 5 identifies some of the common issues that counsellors must be prepared to explore where appropriate with these clients.

Snapshot 5

Issues Connected to Second-Generation Individuals

- Levels of acculturation: behavioural, values, and cognitive.
- Role and implications of religion/spirituality/philosophy of life.
- Family/intergenerational relationships (areas of congruence and dissonance).
- Family's immigration history.
- Social relationships (social networks, dilemmas, and challenges).
- Gender role expectations.
- Cultural expectations.
- Experiences of overt and covert discrimination, racism, and oppression.
- Salience of race, ethnicity, culture, and so on as defining identity variables.

Counsellor Self-Awareness

As novice counsellors we often seek to understand *how to apply* the concepts we learn in the literature. Adopting a multicultural stance does not involve following a predetermined series of steps or interventions or applying a single counselling model or modality when working with clients from non-dominant ethnic groups. Instead, it requires engaging in a series of personal evaluations and reflections as a means of deconstructing and critically evaluating one's personal assumptions, values, and biases (Arthur & Collins, in press, a, b). As such it represents an ongoing effort and commitment by the counselor to pursue professional and personal activities and practices that promote and enable us to continually develop a deeper and richer awareness of how our personal assumptions operate and inform our thinking, attitudes, and behaviour. It is important to note that the aforementioned process is not static, but requires ongoing and continual personal assessment on the part of the counselor. Furthermore, examining how personal assumptions, values, and biases impact and translate to our professional practice and interactions with clients is a central aspect of developing deeper critical awareness and reflexivity. This personal awareness involves possessing an understanding of the inherent pitfalls that exist in traditional conceptualizations, modalities, interventions, and diagnostic tools that limit their applicability and effectiveness with diverse client populations. This process of reflexivity requires an openness to challenging personal belief systems as well as respectfully asking clients informed questions around the meaning of ethnicity, racial status, cultural values, attitudes, and cultural expectations. A counsellor's attitude and mentality are fundamental building blocks for developing multicultural competence when working with any client population. Snapshot 7 provides some prompts for you to explore your own attitudes and beliefs as they relate to non-dominant ethnic populations.

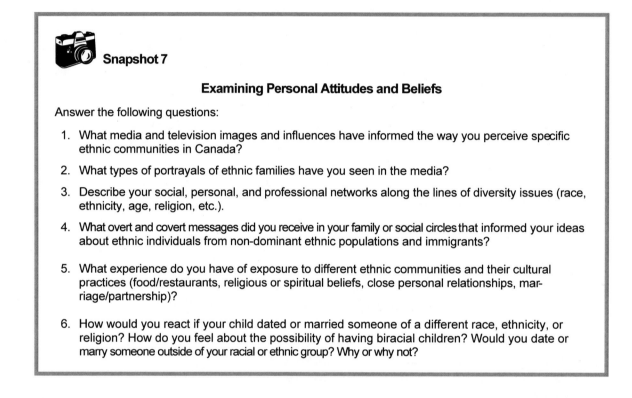

Snapshot 7

Examining Personal Attitudes and Beliefs

Answer the following questions:

1. What media and television images and influences have informed the way you perceive specific ethnic communities in Canada?

2. What types of portrayals of ethnic families have you seen in the media?

3. Describe your social, personal, and professional networks along the lines of diversity issues (race, ethnicity, age, religion, etc.).

4. What overt and covert messages did you receive in your family or social circles that informed your ideas about ethnic individuals from non-dominant ethnic populations and immigrants?

5. What experience do you have of exposure to different ethnic communities and their cultural practices (food/restaurants, religious or spiritual beliefs, close personal relationships, marriage/partnership)?

6. How would you react if your child dated or married someone of a different race, ethnicity, or religion? How do you feel about the possibility of having biracial children? Would you date or marry someone outside of your racial or ethnic group? Why or why not?

As a counsellor working with individuals and groups from non-dominant ethnic communities in Canadian society, understanding the multitude of factors that influence and determine the positioning of these individuals relative to mainstream culture is imperative in the delivery of effective services. Three levels of awareness must be considered in contextualizing experience: (a) the counsellor's own attitudes, biases, and values; (b) the client's definition of self, cultural, and ethnic identity; and (c) the way in which society perceives, treats, and positions individuals from non-dominant ethnic groups in relation to majority culture (Arthur & Stewart, 2001; Justin, 2003; Sue & Sue, 1999, 2003, 2008).

A Culturally Sensitive Working Alliance

Understanding that traditional modes of counselling and interventions have emerged from an ethnocentric and androcentric perspective founded in Western philosophies of health, well-being, and development requires re-examination of how they can be applied to clients from non-dominant ethnic groups (Arthur & Stewart, 2001; Comas-Diaz & Greene, 1994; Enns, 1997). Western psychotherapy is a talk therapy that requires clients to be verbally communicative and emotionally open and expressive. To this end, the objective of therapy is on acquiring personal insight and developing skills that allow clients to ultimately serve as their own counsellors.

It is important to acknowledge that not all cultures or individuals fit this mode of therapy. Seeking advice, guidance, or mentoring from a person perceived to be in a position of authority (i.e., an expert) is common among many cultures. Culturally speaking, Eastern cultures that emphasize the value of authority and deference to authority may be more inclined to seek more directive counselling services. For example, Sue and Sue (1999) talked about this attitude among Asian clients who may seek a more directive approach in counselling. Although Poonwassie and Charter (2001) also described Aboriginal culture as valuing the place of an elder as advice giver, they also asserted that Aboriginal clients may prefer a less directive and assertive approach in counselling.

Acknowledging that cultural variables may influence what individual clients seek from the process is important, but it is equally important to evaluate this understanding while maintaining the idea of individual differences (Barcinski & Kalia, 2005). Balancing cultural knowledge with individual difference (i.e., tentatively holding an etic and emic orientation) becomes a critical counselling skill. For example, a second-generation Indian client may simultaneously hold cultural values that are congruent with both an Indian identity and worldview and an identity that has integrated several Western values and beliefs. Given their unique bicultural identity, the ways in which they situate themselves within their family, ethnic community, social networks, and careers require understanding their unique identity construction. Working with this type of client requires exploring how they construct their identity and the ways they position themselves in different aspects of their lives. To do this, a counsellor needs to balance and integrate an etic and emic orientation in their work by attending to the concepts of internalized culture and cultural encapsulation in order to avoid making overgeneralizations and stereotyping clients (Ho, 1995).

The interventions provided in Snapshot 6 are some ways in which counsellors can begin to explore identity issues with their clients. It is important to note that the first priority in any counselling relationship is to establish a strong working alliance based on creating a safe, trusting, and respectful relationship between the counsellor and client. The working alliance represents a core competence and skill in all therapeutic endeavours, but is particularly meaningful when working with clients from diverse backgrounds. According to Arthur and Collins in Chapter 9 and Corey (2009), the working alliance represents an ongoing working relationship between counsellor and client throughout the therapeutic process. Counselling culturally diverse clients requires a genuine and skillful demonstration of cultural empathy; adopting a nonjudgmental stance in exploring, inquiring, and understanding the client's unique worldview and cultural perspective. As a counselor, demonstrating cultural sensitivity encourages a client to feel increasingly secure and trustful about sharing the uniquely personal and meaningful aspects of their cultural identity and realities. For a more extensive discussion on issues of working alliance, readers are referred to Chapter 5 of this text, as well as to the following resources: Brammer, Abrego, and Shostrom (1993), Corey (1991), Cormier and Nurius (2003), Corsini and Wedding (2000), Patterson (1980), and Sue and Sue (1999, 2003, 2008)

Exploratory questions and interventions should not be used indiscriminately, but rather with consideration to counselling objectives and intuitive evaluation of their appropriateness with any given client. Snapshot 6 provides some examples of culturally appropriate intervention strategies that may be helpful in working with second-generation East Indian women. You will notice that these strategies draw on concepts and theoretical principles discussed earlier in the chapter.

Reframing client issues and experiences through the lens of biculturalism and a strength-based orientation validates the complexity of their experience. It also enables clients to shift their self-perspective to one of competence versus incompetence. Pointing out the dilemmas and mixed messages they have internalized can facilitate creating a positive transformation in self-acceptance and developing a sense of congruence. This is an important consideration because young second-generation Indian women often struggle with fitting in and belonging. Their bicultural identity leaves them feeling like insiders and outsiders in their social, academic, family, and community environments. Facilitating the creation of a sense of personal fit, sense of congruence, and self-acceptance can serve to create helpful insights for clients.

Snapshot 6

Intervention Strategies for Working with Second-Generation East Indian Women

Reframing/normalizing internal struggles and dilemmas of identity as a normal process of negotiating and constructing a bicultural identity. Within the context of biculturalism, one critical element is offering clients a new conceptualization or framework to normalize and validate the contradictions they encounter in cultural and social messages. Reframing identity development as a dynamic and fluid process that exists on a continuum creates the possibility of (a) reframing client experience and perceptions of their internal and external experience and (b) presenting the idea that identity construction is an ongoing, lifelong process that does not conclude in resolution. Situating individuals as active agents in defining and constructing their identity, using a strength-based perspective versus deficit perspective, can further highlight the adaptation skills individuals have developed over their lifetime.

Objective: Create a new conceptualization and context for clients to understand and situate their experiences.

Gender role analysis explores messages about gender role expectations and the meaning individuals ascribe to lessons of gender learning from family, community, and society. For example, asking questions that examine the lessons of being a good woman, sanctions for transgressing gender expectations, taboo subjects and behaviours, and so forth offers a springboard for a deeper dialogue about gender issues. For a more detailed discussion about gender role analysis see Brown (1986) and Brown and Root (1990).

Objective: Create a critical dialogue and examination of values that inform and guide our thinking, choices, and behaviour as women.

Cultural analysis serves a similar function to conducting a gender role analysis; however, the focus is placed on cultural and racial messages. For example, exploratory questions can consist of asking: What ethnic group has most influenced your values and perception of yourself? What ethnic group do you identify with? How is your ethnic group perceived by mainstream society? What stereotypes or images are connected to your ethnic group? What messages have you received from within your ethnic community, family, or social network regarding dominant cultural norms?

Objective: Create a critical dialogue and analysis of ethnic, racial, and cultural perceptions and positioning in one's family, ethnic community, and society.

Translating, contextualizing, and normalizing multicultural concepts such as situational ethnicity, levels of acculturation, gender role expectations, and the juxtaposition of identity within different social and cultural contexts serves to situate a client's life experiences within a broad range of contexts (i.e., individual, family, community, and mainstream society). Engaging clients in a dialogue that (a) explores the meaning of these concepts in their lives, (b) compares and contrasts the different contexts in which these issues emerge, and (c) explores the ways congruence and dissonance are experienced by individuals relative to these issues offers a way to normalize the inherent tensions associated with racial, ethnic, and cultural identity issues.

Objective: Depathologize the complexity of navigating multiple identities and contexts and reinforce the development of adaptation skills that allow individuals to navigate the pitfalls and contradictions of bicultural identity development. Permits engaging clients in a dialogue about the influence of these concepts in their lives and examines how they can experience a sense of personal connection and disconnection.

Stigma of Counselling

Although seeking counselling is a fairly well-accepted source of support within a North American context, the multicultural literature draws attention to the fact that counselling continues to be stigmatized and viewed with skepticism by individuals within different ethnic and cultural communities (Lessinger, 1995; Sandhu, 1997; Sue & Sue, 2008). As noted earlier in this discussion, several factors may contribute to this phenomenon. One is the cultural assumption inherent among many Eastern and Latin cultural groups of the importance of maintaining family boundaries. This means adherence to the unwritten expectation that personal and family problems should be kept private and dealt with by the family or community.

Lessinger (1995) described this stigma within the East Indian community as "Indian immigrants may feel ashamed at having their shortcomings discussed among outsiders, pressure from concerned insiders is far more effective in changing attitudes and behaviour than the efforts of well-intentioned non-Indians" (p. 132). Lessinger also postulated that the hesitation and shame connected to seeking mental health services may also be connected to the ethnic community wanting to avoid undermining the public perception of East Indians as a *model minority*. Therefore, openly seeking counselling services contravenes the cultural value of saving face and protecting family honour and reputation. This attitude also reflects a pervasive cultural value among members of other non-dominant groups such as Asian, Latin, West Indian, and African cultural communities (McGoldrick et al., 1996; Sue & Sue, 1999). This value system may be more prevalent among first-generation immigrants for whom the concept of counselling may be completely foreign. This attitude of shame regarding counselling may be communicated in overt and covert ways to later-generation individuals through the transmission of cultural values focusing on family values and relational boundaries, thus exemplifying the internal dissonance reported by many ethnic clients when they seek counselling (Sodowsky & Carey, 1987; Sue & Sue, 1999, 2003; Sue et al., 1994). Remaining cognizant of the stigma and hesitation that many ethnic groups attach to Western counselling services, it also becomes important to consider individual differences in the process. While some second- and later-generation individuals may still shy away from counselling, others may not present with the same level of hesitation as their first-generation counterparts.

Attrition

High attrition rates among clients from non-dominant ethnic groups in counselling continue to be connected to the lack of cultural awareness and multicultural competence among practitioners working with diverse populations (Cardemil & Battle, 2003; Sue & Sue, 2003). Ethnic clients report that the ethnocentric attitudes and values frequently held by counsellors often leave them feeling misunderstood (Cardemil & Battle). A lack of cultural knowledge and awareness on the part of a well-intentioned counsellor can lead to ineffective communication between client and counsellor. This effect can be further compounded by a counsellor promoting Western conceptions of healthy functioning that result in distancing or alienating a client. A client who cannot either relate to or exercise the normative prescriptions offered by a counsellor would understandably see little value in pursuing counselling services. One-session attendance continues to be a persistent issue in working with individuals from non-dominant ethnic groups. If empathic communication is a central tenet in establishing an effective working alliance, then this communication first needs to be informed by counsellors' knowledge of the fundamental differences that may be connected to cultural values.

Cardemil and Battle (2003) presented several ways for counsellors to address issues of racial, cultural, and ethnic differences with clients. Their main proposition was to make these issues explicit and bring them to the table in the counselling process. Denying, avoiding, or maintaining a stance of colour blindness in the counselling process is a disservice to any client and may simply compound their sense of marginalization and distrust and reinforce the power hierarchy between client and counsellor. These authors also noted that not all clients may be willing to discuss the issue of race, cultural differences, or discrimination in their lives. Clients may react negatively or positively based on where they fall on a racial development scale. However, putting these concerns on the table in an honest and respectful manner conveys openness and sensitivity to the issues. It also permits a client to revisit these issues at a later point in the counselling process and contextualize their experience within these constructs, thereby allowing another lens from which to understand their experiences.

Identity as Central to the Counselling Process

A central premise of this chapter is how clients (particularly second-generation women) can possess multiple, intersecting, and paradoxical identities. Externalizing issues of racial and ethnic discrimination, facilitating the development of coping skills, and promoting a sense of personal insight and congruence can help clients negotiate the construction of their hybrid identity and the challenges they face in this process. Hence, identity issues become an overarching issue in the counselling process (Das & Kemp, 1997).

Facilitating clients' active construction of a unique and personal *third space* that validates their experience of identity challenges can contribute to creating a safe, respectful, and strong working alliance with clients. Furthermore, due to the distinct issues connected to bicultural identity issues for second-generation women, they may also lack positive role models from whom to learn effective coping skills as they learn to negotiate and navigate the personal and environmental challenges they encounter in their daily lives. Therefore, creating an empathic working alliance, one in which clients can explore, question, and voice their personal concerns, can become a powerful experience for clients who struggle to create a sense of personal acceptance in a context in which they do not fit the mould. By the same token, the research literature supports the notion that when ethnic clients feel misunderstood or alienated in the counselling process, their experience of marginalization is recapitulated (Ponterotto et al., 2001; Sue, Arredondo, & McDavis, 1992; Sue & Sue, 2003). As practitioners learning to juggle and balance personal values and expectations, understanding factors that are central to a client's worldview may be the springboard for creating an effective therapeutic relationship.

Case Study

Rea is a 25-year-old woman who immigrated to Canada with her family 22 years ago. She is currently completing a science degree and anticipates being accepted in the pre-med program of a well-known Canadian university. Rea's family immigrated to Canada because her father's older brother sponsored the family and had often described a good-quality standard of living in Canada. It was an opportunity the family did not want to miss. Rea's father was a doctor in India and, because he completed his medical training in England, he had no difficulty practicing medicine when he came to Canada. Rea describes growing up in an average suburban neighbourhood with her three younger sisters, attending good schools, and having a happy childhood. In India, her mother was an elementary school teacher, but when the family immigrated she decided to stay home to raise the family. Rea's sisters were all born in Canada. None of the children have travelled back to India in the past 22 years, although their mother has made several trips over the years. Rea describes herself as a happy person. She lives at home and gets along with her family, has a good network of friends and social relationships, and is involved in her community. She describes her father as fairly traditional and conservative, particularly when it comes to how his daughters should be raised. But at the same time, he has always been affectionate and loving, always telling them he is proud to have four daughters. He also encouraged each of them to be well-educated, self-sufficient, and independent thinkers. Rea describes her mother as a soft-spoken woman who is the heart of the family. She has always attended to all of the matters of the home and children and presents a strong role model for her daughters.

Listening to Rea describe her family in the first session, her reasons for seeking counselling were not immediately evident. However, as the session progressed, I encouraged her to tell me more about her home life, family, and friends. Rea began to slowly talk about struggling with several issues in her personal life, issues she could not really talk about with either her friends or family. Recently, she has begun to question whether she really wants to go into medicine and be a doctor like her father. She had attended a career workshop offered through the counselling centre several weeks ago in which they talked about following your passion, discovering your skills and abilities and intuition. She left the seminar feeling excited about what she had heard, but also anxious and stressed at the same time. Until that seminar she had never really considered any other career besides medicine. As far back as she can remember, she recalls being told that she would one day become a doctor; this simply became an accepted truth, not really a matter of personal choice. It's almost as if her parents wish for her has become her own personal career objective. Rea and I met over several more sessions and our conversations progressively evolved. The focus of the first two to three sessions was simply getting to know Rea and understanding who she is in different parts of her life. It slowly became more obvious that considering the possibility of changing her program of study was troubling to her. It seemed that considering the idea of career choice was destabilizing and unfamiliar in some ways.

By the third session, Rea also reported that she has been dating a boy at school for several months, something her family and friends did not know about. Over the past eight months, Rea has been living with the constant fear that she will be discovered or that news will somehow get back to her family. After eight months, she feels that her relationship is serious, but knows that her family would disapprove. She reports that the secrecy of their relationship has been taking its toll on her and on her relationship with her boyfriend. An added concern for Rea is that her boyfriend is Caucasian. He doesn't understand why she is hiding and at times questions whether she is ashamed of him because he has not met her family and they do not go out in public alone very often, only when there is a group of friends. Rea knows that her family would strongly disapprove and would be upset to find out that not only is she dating a boy, but he is not Indian. Her parents had an arranged marriage and Rea knows that they expect the same for her. Arranging the marriage of their eldest daughter is something her parents talk about fondly, even though they expect her to complete her education first. She describes feeling ashamed that she will deeply disappoint them on many levels, especially since she is the eldest daughter and she has always set an example for her sisters. The scandal and gossip that would erupt in her family and the community would be unbearable, and most of the blame for her actions would fall on her parents — they would be at the centre of the gossip. She has always been perceived as a good girl and expresses concern that her reputation would also be smeared. In addition, the idea of adding insult to injury by even considering not going to medical school would be too much for her parents. Rea describes feeling like she is living a lie and the energy it takes to keep this secret is becoming too much to bear.

Over the course of our sessions, our conversations tentatively explored the issues of cultural norms and gender role expectations. Several additional issues that surfaced were connected to the importance and meaning of family, family expectations and values, and the interrelationship of family and community on emotional, psychological, and cultural levels. One key aspect of working with Rea centred on developing an empathic and respectful dialogue about all these issues. Rea reported that she felt easier discussing these issues with another ethnic woman. We briefly discussed what made the experience more helpful for her. I also shared some elements of my own cultural and ethnic background with Rea and acknowledged the importance and influence of cultural values.

In self-disclosing this information, it also became important to remain mindful of not assuming that our life experiences were similar based on some shared cultural variables. Therefore, asking Rea to clarify, explain, and explore the meaning and impact of her ethnicity, race, culture, traditions and customs, and family connections required constant attention. Over the course of our sessions we moved to discussing the pros and cons of her disclosing her relationship to her friends and family, as well as the possible implications this might have. A secondary theme also revolved around her desire to explore other possible academic and career choices. We discussed whether a career in medicine fit her personal interests and skills and image of herself, and how this image compares to the aspirations and expectations her family hold for her. A key element in our work together focused on: (a) establishing an empathic and nonjudgmental relationship; (b) normalizing the personal dilemma of attempting to make personal choices in relation to cultural values that promoted a contrasting value system; (c) the meaning Rea gives to following and respecting cultural traditions and gender expectations; (d) the imagined and realistic implications of transgressing cultural rules and norms; (e) the ways in which she wants to live as an Indian woman and carry forward her cultural traditions, heritage, and customs; (f) realistic options for navigating the consequences of disclosing her relationship (partially or wholly) to either family or friends; and (g) what might happen if either of these groups become aware of her relationship.

We terminated our work together after 12 sessions. Although Rea did not overtly resolve or make a final decision about changing her academic program or disclosing her relationship to her family, she indicated that she had become more comfortable in living with the situation. She had taken steps to talk more openly with her boyfriend about the implications of their relationship and he had increasingly become a source of support in helping her negotiate and navigate the cultural value conflicts she was living with. He also expressed a strong emotional commitment to Rea that indicated he could wait to meet her family and in the meantime learn more about her culture, traditions, and customs.

Emerging Issues in Bicultural Identity Development

The majority of research in multicultural counselling in the past three decades has focused on issues of ethnic and racial identity development, cultural values, acculturation, and adaptation. First-generation immigrants and their experience of acculturation and adaptation have often been the focus of inquiry. These studies have highlighted the numerous obstacles these individuals encounter upon immigration. This research has contributed to broadening the depth and scope of multicultural literature in recent years and made multicultural counselling a significant force in the discipline of counselling (Pedersen, 1991c). It is now necessary to shift our attention to include issues of second-generation individuals in the current discourse on multicultural counselling. Second-generation individuals have been described as a "strategic research site" (Portes, 1997, p. 814) because they (more than their first-generation parents) are rapidly becoming a significant segment of the population. The increase in the number of biracial and multiracial individuals and interracial relationships and marriages and the disappearance of distinct ethnic enclaves are resulting in the merging of numerous cultural and ethnic groups, requiring a re-evaluation of the traditional ways in which we have defined and categorized race, ethnicity, and culture.

Although research has focused on a variety of non-dominant ethnic groups and individuals in recent years, we continue to have limited empirical data and research that highlights the experience of different segments of these communities. For example, the majority of research and literature has addressed issues pertinent to the African-American, Asian, and Latino communities in the United States (Ponterotto et al., 2001; Sue & Sue, 2003). Although these three groups represent a significant percentage of the population, we still need to broaden our awareness of issues relevant to other groups within our population. For example, the dearth of information regarding the East Indian community in North America represents a significant gap in the literature. Understanding how these individuals live and negotiate a bicultural identity in their personal and professional lives and the unique elements of their identity construction represents unchartered territory in multicultural literature.

Competence

Given the dearth of research literature on second and later generation individuals, numerous topics of inquiry can guide future research endeavours. The following issues do not represent an exhaustive list, but instead represent the idea of adopting a conceptual shift for future research endeavours focusing in second- and later-generation East Indian women. The first conceptual shift requires understanding the experience of these women and their bicultural identity development from a strength- and competency-based perspective.

As discussed through this chapter, the complexity and interaction of multiple variables come together to shape bicultural identity of second-generation women. Understanding that their identity development represents a multifaceted phenomenon also requires that this phenomenon be normalized and contextualized. Doing so demands that we understand these women as competent and active agents in their lives, individuals who since childhood have been faced with numerous questions about identity that have required them to consciously examine and construct a bicultural identity.

Having successfully faced repeated challenges and questions about their position as a cultural or ethnic minority relative to mainstream society often creates overt and covert coping skills that have allowed for successful negotiation of various dilemmas of identity and cultural value conflicts. Therefore, adopting a conceptual shift that views these women as resilient, healthy, and competent individuals enables us to reframe their lives and personal challenges and thereby also offers them a new way of understanding their experiences as normal developmental issues connected to bicultural identity development rather than framing them as being deficient in skills or dysfunctional for struggling with inherently cultural norms and expectations. Framing personal competence and authority by helping them draw upon the skills they have unknowingly cultivated throughout their lives becomes a reframing of cultural value conflicts as assets and skills.

Therapist's Attitudes

A second issue for consideration is recognizing the importance of a therapist's attitudes and not applying the concepts of multicultural counselling as a formula in the counselling process. Rather, gaining awareness and multicultural competence is a way of being in the world and does not merely represent a singular therapeutic orientation. It is a process of personal exploration that requires constant attention and mindfulness to one's attitudes, beliefs, and values and how we as individuals apply them to ourselves and our work as practitioners. This skill of personal awareness is highlighted in the model of culture-infused counselling as an attitude of critical personal reflection, showing respect for our clients by possessing knowledge and understanding about cultural issues and asking informed questions that demonstrate sensitivity and respect, rather than remaining passive and allowing our clients to educate us.

Although a counsellor cannot possess intimate knowledge about every non-dominant group, at the very least, understanding that Western culture is a minority value system in a global context demonstrates a receptivity and open-mindedness that is conducive to effective service delivery. Taking the initiative to integrate salient concepts from the multicultural literature as possible avenues for dialogue and discourse also demonstrates openness (Cardemil & Battle, 2003). As postulated by Sue and Sue (2003, 2008) and Cardemil and Battle (2003), making the issues of race, culture, and ethnicity explicit in the counselling process conveys that they are meaningful and important topics of discussion because they have implications in our lives on many levels.

Complexity of Multiple Identities

A third recommendation centres on awareness of meaning and implications of multiple identities and the implications of intersections as salient feature in the lives of second-generation women. Appreciating the paradoxical intersections created by possessing a bicultural identity requires reorganizing our conceptualizations and definitions because, historically, the literature talks about singular identities such as race, ethnicity, gender, and culture, thereby ignoring the notions of multiplicity, overlaps, and intersections (Ludvig, 2006; Morris & Bunjun, 2007). Choice for clients is not about choosing one identity, but rather about making seemingly contradictory identities and values work together cohesively to create a sense of personal congruence. Dissonance should not be understood as problematic and therefore requiring resolution, but rather as a normal process of learning to negotiate identity issues. A person becomes more skilled and masterful in negotiating and navigating identity challenges and dilemmas with experience. It is only in gaining that experience over time and life experience that skill and congruence can be achieved. Hence, it is critical to remember that variables such as cultural, racial, ethnic, and gender identity all come together in the construction of bicultural identity. Each dimension of identity is multifaceted and multilayered, thereby defying a simplistic and reductionist approach to understanding clients.

Chapter Summary

This chapter has attempted to highlight salient concepts and themes in the lives of second-generation Indian women. These broad themes can also be applied to understanding the lives of women from traditionally conservative and collectivist-oriented cultures. The main ideas to take away from this chapter include the following.

As multiculturally competent professionals it is imperative to adopt a stance of critical self-reflection in examining one's own personal attitudes, values, and beliefs about specific non-dominant ethnic groups. In working with these clients, it is imperative to understand their experience through a lens of cultural sensitivity, thereby adopting a competence perspective rather than a deficit perspective in understanding their abilities, skills, and personal challenges. Using criteria and normative standards based on mainstream cultural norms as the yardstick by which to assess normal and healthy functioning offers a narrow lens from which to understand and contextualize the experience of individuals from non-dominant groups. By these standards, they can only be seen as *deficient* or *less than*, thereby perpetuating common stereotypes of dysfunctional family structures and dynamics, enmeshed relational styles, and stunted identity development. Because the identity development of bicultural individuals may not follow the standard conceptions and may be constantly defined by negotiating identity conflicts, they can be misdiagnosed with any number of psychological problems. In order to avoid this pitfall, as ethical and competent professionals, it becomes critical to re-evaluate and question our perceptions and attitudes about healthy functioning to be more inclusive in nature.

Numerous models of identity development have been presented in the literature. For a comprehensive discussion of identity and acculturation models, see earlier chapters in this text and refer to the seminal work of Berry (1990); Cross (1971, 1995); Cuellar, Roberts, Nyberg, and Moldanado (1998); Feliz-Ortiz, Newcomb, and Myers (1994); Fisher and Moradi (2001); Helms (1984, 1990b); and Phinney (1989, 1990). Recent discussion of identity models and suggestions for counseling multiple-heritage individuals, couples, and families are offered by Henriksen and Paladino (2009b). It is important to note that competent multicultural counselling also requires attention to following guidelines for non-discriminatory practice and the professional code of ethics of the Canadian Counselling Association (2007) and the Canadian Psychological Association (2000). Readers are also encouraged to review the work of Pedersen (2008), Pettifor in Chapter 7, and Toporek and Williams (2006) regarding the applications of ethics in multicultural counselling.

The objective of this chapter is to promote an understanding of the subtle and overt complexities involved in developing, living, and negotiating a bicultural identity, a reality that often puts individuals at odds in many dimensions of their personal, academic, and professional lives. Paradoxical juxtapositions lie at the heart of understanding how individuals from marginalized groups construct their identity over the course of their lives.

CHAPTER 14
CREATING CONNECTIONS: BEST PRACTICES IN COUNSELLING GIRLS AND WOMEN

Vivian Lalande and Ann Laverty

<table>
<tr><td colspan="3" align="center">**Key Terms and Concepts**</td></tr>
<tr>
<td>
• Abuse
• Alpha bias
• Androgyny
• Assertiveness training
• Beta bias
• Central relationship paradox
• Egalitarian relationships
• Empathy
• Feminist counselling process
</td>
<td>
• Gender
• Gender-biased research
• Gender role analysis
• Gender stereotypes
• Mental health
• Multiple realities
• Mutual empathy
• Null environment
</td>
<td>
• Personal is political
• Power analysis
• Relational/cultural counselling
• Self-efficacy
• Sex
• Sex role socialization
• Structure of opportunity
• Voice
</td>
</tr>
</table>

Personal Introductions

As women counsellors, we know that relationships are central to our work. In particular, writing this text together has provided an opportunity to reflect about our interest in counselling girls and women.

Over the years, we have discussed our experiences as women, as women counsellors, and our work with women. We talk about our busy lives, juggling children, work, and other commitments. We share our feelings of frustration with the lack of significant progress related to women's issues and realize how our own experiences are often mirrored in the lives of the women we are helping and teaching.

We had the pleasure of attending a seminar at the Stone Center at Wellesley College a couple of years ago and were invigorated to share advancements in the field of counselling girls and women. We continue to discuss gender issues related to counselling, feminist supervision practices, and research. Although some of our professional interests are the same and some are different, we continue to work with issues regarding girls and women as colleagues and friends. Some of our best learning continues to come from our clients and students as we continually refine and expand our understanding in this area.

One of the challenges in capturing our knowledge is the recognition of how cultural identity and context limits our understanding of other women's lived experiences. While we work with and write about women, we are very aware that our representation is interpreted through the lens of our own lives and experiences. Knowing this, we acknowledge that gaps and questions remain within what we have written. Thankfully, feminist counselling philosophy and practice help us bridge these gaps by endorsing the value of developmental process, contextual knowing, and yet-to-be answered questions. In all of this, we recognize that the tension we experience in writing this chapter parallels the process we experience in counselling – the need to stay awake to new understandings or possibilities in the lives of girls and women similar to those of Harpreet, whose story follows.

Snapshot 1

Vignette

Harpreet stands at the reception desk crying. "I need to talk to someone right away," she murmurs. She is favouring her right leg as she enters my office and takes a chair. Sensing her reluctance to begin, I gently ask some questions about why she is crying. "I had a fight with my father last night and he kicked me out and disowned me," she said. "He was mad because I came in an hour late. I have nowhere to go, and no money or I.D. I tried to call home, but he won't let my mother or sisters talk to me. I am worried about my sisters because they count on me to protect them from my Dad. He gets mad sometimes and hits us, like he did to me last night. My mother might help me because we get along and she has money to give me, but if he finds out she is talking to me, she may get in trouble with him too. I can't go to my aunt's house, because I have been disowned and this means the family and my community will have nothing to do with me."

Listening to Harpreet, I begin to consider the complexity of her situation and the need to attend to the many layers of her experience. I decided to proceed by grounding our work in feminist counselling principles.

Introduction

Counselling girls and women like Harpreet invites counsellors to critique mainstream psychological research, theory, and practice. In doing this critique, counsellors draw upon knowledge of gender role socialization, psychosocial development, and cultural awareness of being female. Feminist principles and philosophy facilitate best practices in counselling girls and women, and two approaches (relational-cultural and multicultural) allow for the infusion of feminist practice with counselling theory.

Feminist counsellors utilize particular processes, interventions, and strategies during the stages of discovery/co-construction of goals and working together to achieve goals in both individual and group counselling. They also utilize ethical principles to guide their practice. In particular, there are effective approaches to assist women in dealing with depression, disordered eating, career development, and violence. Feminist practitioners continue to emphasize the importance of integrating culture and diversity and of respecting the many layers of experience that women bring to counselling. This chapter uses case examples and Canadian literature to illuminate issues and practices and elaborate on the above areas.

Cultural Identity and Relationship to the Dominant Culture

Current research and theory relevant to the psychology of girls and women is situated in a history of extensive work and struggle for knowledge representative of women's realities. In particular, this work provides a context and framework for counselling. While it is impossible to adequately represent this history in a brief overview, some key concepts and issues will be discussed.

The definitions of the terms *gender* and *sex* reflect and operationalize the relevance of the psychology of women for counsellors. **Sex** refers to *biological differences between males and females,* whereas **gender** refers to *the socially defined qualities and characteristics attributed to males and females* (Gilbert & Scher, 1999). **Sex role socialization** is *the process by which individuals learn and demonstrate female and male stereotypes.* Recent research suggested that gender identity is not static, but can change over one's lifetime, and is responsive to contextual influences (Diamond & Butterworth, 2008).

Gilbert and Scher (1999) identified four common assumptions about gender that can influence our thoughts and actions: (a) males and females are different or have opposite qualities; (b) gender can be used to organize and structure situations and experiences; for example, assuming that boys will prefer active experiences and girls will prefer passive activities; (c) language reflects and maintains assumptions about gender; and (d) gender is both a noun and a verb in that social interactions create gender. Such views are not only present in culture; they also profoundly influence our thoughts and actions towards men and women.

Deaux and Kite (1993) defined **gender stereotypes** as *people's perceptions of the traits possessed by a typical woman or man.* In their review, women were characterized as more expressive, communal, concerned with the welfare of others, and having more traits of affiliation, nurturance, and deference. Men were stereotyped as more assertive and controlling, with stronger attributes of achievement, dominance, autonomy, and aggression. Research findings indicated that gender stereotypes persist over time, are resistant to change, and "are not limited to the belief system of a few prejudiced individuals, but rather that they are part of the fabric of general societal beliefs and norms" (Deaux & Kite, p. 130). Expectations and behaviours associated with traditional male and female traits are seen in many life situations, such as partner roles in sexual relationships, and tend to favour men throughout the world (Beall, Eagly, & Sternberg, 2004). Males often assume positions of power, and characteristics associated with male gender stereotypes are valued over female gender stereotypes. The recognition of the existence of gender-linked traits contributes to valuing of the term **androgyny,** which refers to *the combination of male and female traits in one individual* (Finfgeld, 2001; Unger, 1992).

 **Snapshot 2**

Gender Role Socialization

Mrs. Flett reads every issue of *Good Housekeeping....* And every once in a while, between the cosmetic advertisements and the recipe columns, she comes across articles about ways a woman can please her husband in bed.... "There is no such thing as normal or abnormal sexual patterns. What goes on in the bedroom of married people is sacred." This advice struck Mrs. Flett as less than satisfactory; as a matter of fact, she isn't entirely sure what was meant. She does believe, though, that *every night* would be a lot to put up with. Nevertheless she always prepares herself, just in case – her diaphragm in position, though she is repelled by its yellow look of decay and the cold, sick-smelling jelly she smears around its edge. It's a bother, and nine times out of ten it isn't needed, but it seems this is something that has to be put up with. "Try to make your husband believe that you are always ready for his entreaties, even though his actual lovemaking may be sporadic and unpredictable." (pp. 185-86)

From *"The Stone Diaries,"* by C. Shields, 1993. Toronto, ON: Random House.

Although individuals may personally benefit from the development of both male and female traits, this does not imply that the culture of individuals will also value androgynous qualities and behaviours. For example, women who utilize the same assertive behaviours as men can be described as inappropriately aggressive.

Psychological Research

Historically, the majority of psychological research utilized a positivistic paradigm or view of knowledge that assumed that research could be objective, free of researcher bias, and generative of truths (Douglas & Walker, 1988; Unger, 1992). Feminist scholars challenged traditional **gender-biased research,** arguing that it *does not recognize that all knowledge occurs within a context and values guide the choice of research questions, how research is conducted, and how results are interpreted* (Bohan, 1992). Research citing support for the existence of biologically determined sex differences has been extensively critiqued for methodological and statistical problems leading to inaccurate conclusions (Sherif, 1992; Shields, 1992; Unger, 1992). Of note is the under-representation of women in research samples in much of the psychological research conducted until 1970. Research leading to conclusions regarding gender differences tended to focus on mean differences between males and females on measures of traits. Researchers ignored the potential variance in the expression of these traits that can be influenced by the setting and the varying norms and expectations for men and women in these settings (Hare-Mustin & Maracek, 1992). It is now more common to consider the similarities and differences between males and females as representing a continuum, and researchers are seeking a better understanding of why and how these similarities and differences exist, acknowledging the influence of both biological and contextual factors (Beall et al., 2004).

LaFrance, Paluck, and Brescoll (2004) summarized a number of recommendations for improving research on gender: (a) when sex differences are identified it is important to report the effect sizes, (b) multiple factor designs can best represent the complexity of the findings, (c) research needs to start with the assumption that "sex is a process" (p. 341), (c) fewer convenience samples are to be used in research so as to better understand how gender interacts with other cultural orientations, and (d) gender should be considered a complex construct that is impacted by and also impacts many other variables. Combining qualitative and quantitative methodologies will allow researchers to explore the complexity of how gender intersects with other cultural identities (Enns, 2008). An overview of feminist research methodologies can be accessed from Status of Women Canada (Demaris, 2001). In recognition of the greater influence that men have had on research practices and language, there is also a need to study language and its meaning in order for women to **voice** and generate new understandings of their reality (Hare-Mustin & Maracek, 1992). Gaps between experience and language are found in many contexts, such as that of menopause.

> "The women's network let me down. Nothing I've ever heard or read prepared me for this!" This particular yelp resulted from the plummet of energy and purpose I experienced with menopause and quickly led us to wider, livelier musings on what else had caught us unprepared, where else we had experienced gaps between female experience and expression. (Shields & Anderson, 2001, p. vii)

Research and knowledge of the psychology of women has been critiqued as having a tendency to reflect alpha and beta biases (Hare-Mustin & Maracek, 1992). **Alpha bias** *occurs when there are exaggerations of gender differences attributed to social inequities and power differentials.* This can be the inadvertent result of attempts to affirm positive female qualities such as relational skills. **Beta bias** is *the tendency to minimize differences between genders. This bias is more common in psychological theories that minimize the influence of social context and assume equality in the social system for men and women.* Both biases embody assumptions and have limitations in that neither fully represents the complexity of gender.

Principles of feminist research and therapy can assist practitioners in addressing the needs of clients from diverse backgrounds and to work against the oppression of women because it (McDowell & Fang, 2007): (a) allows their voices to be heard, (b) questions the "politics of knowledge production" (p. 549), (c) ensures that women benefit from research in which they are participants, (c) considers women's culture and context, (d) requires the researcher to have multicultural research competence, and (e) utilizes a variety of research methodologies.

Mentally Healthy Women

Women in Canada are more likely than men to be hospitalized for mental disorders and twice as many women reported being diagnosed with mood disorders than did men (Statistics Canada, 2006c). When 50% of the population has the power to identify health and illness according to their gender stereotype (men), the other 50% of the population (females) becomes over-represented in the total number of people treated for diagnosed mental disorders (Felipe Russo & Green, 1993). Diagnoses that share characteristics similar to the sex role stereotype of femininity, such as anxiety and depression, show higher rates of treatment. This reflects the tendency to perceive women's behaviour that goes against societal norms as illness. Women also receive more prescriptions for psychotropic drugs than do men (Travis & Compton, 2001).

Because the mental health of women is viewed within a social and political context, it is important to consider what women's mental health is not (Ballou & Brown, 2002). Women's mental health is not what is defined as normal by the dominant male culture and it is not the absence of pain and distress (Brabeck & Brown, 1997). It is also not adjustment to the dominant culture through the acquisition of skills or coping strategies more adaptive to male standards and situations (Finfgeld, 2001).

What is healthy functioning for a woman? The definition of **mental health** varies depending on a woman's context. In general, it *includes the skills and will to survive the experiences of powerlessness, dependency, and violence experienced by many women. Mental health is resistance and the pain that resistance can evoke* (Brabeck & Brown, 1997). *Women's mental health can be promoted by knowing which risk factors can be dealt with by the individual and which can be dealt with by social action (Finfgeld, 2004). Mentally healthy women are personally* *empowered to achieve their goals. Personal empowerment is the experience of agency, developing increased self-esteem, and valuing one's self as a woman of strength and resilience* (Worell & Remer, 2003).

Theoretical Principles

Psychosocial Development of Girls and Women

A surge of research and theory regarding the psychosocial development of women emerged during the late 1970s out of the recognition that previous developmental theory was primarily descriptive of males based on research of male subjects. This innovative perspective of how girls and women develop has been conceptualized as a "relational revolution" reflecting the political shift intrinsic to this work (Robb, 2006). Beginning with her research on women's moral development, Gilligan (1982) concluded that women and men experience moral development differently due to variations in the process of identity development. She built on the work of Chodorow (1978), which was critical of the psychoanalytic formulation of women's identity development as incomplete due to failure to resolve the oedipal conflict; that is, separation from mother. Chodorow argued that a girl's attachment to her mother is the basis for empathy, by which identity is defined.

Moral development model

Gilligan (1982) elaborated an interrelated model of women's moral and identity development. She described women's moral decisions as occurring out of consideration of responsibility in relationships and an ethic of care. This differs from the male conception of morality as problems of rights, rules, and fairness. Gilligan suggested that women develop an ethic of care through a three-stage process: (a) initially caring for self to ensure survival; (b) the criticism of selfishness, triggering a transition to an exclusion of self-care for the caring of others; and (c) a new understanding of self and others in which self and others are interdependent. These transitions occur in a society that values self-sacrifice in women, which is represented by the second stage of development. Gilligan proposed that women must overcome the opposition to self-development. An awareness of women's rights allows women to consider their own needs.

Women experience developmental transitions during life crises, such as the moral crisis of unwanted pregnancies. In studying these crises, Gilligan (1982) described a process of developmental transitions that provide an opportunity to return to a previously missed opportunity for growth. For example, if a woman has the experience of being abandoned by significant others, such as her partner, during a crisis, she will retreat to the stage of survival in which she will cut off feelings and not care for anyone but herself. If she does not experience abandonment, then the crisis has the potential for self-development. Through this process, women experience self-development within relationships.

Self-in-relation model

The theory of self-in-relation also emphasizes the centrality of relationships in women's self-development (Jordan, 1997; Jordan & Surrey, 1986). For women, the self is a relational self that is developed in the context of significant relationships. In this theory, self is defined as "a myriad of memory experiences that provide us with a sense of organization, coherence, and meaning" (p. 92).

Jordan and Surrey (1986) maintained that the capacity for relatedness is fundamental to women's development. They identified **empathy** as *"the process through which one's experienced sense of basic connection and similarity to other humans is established"* (p. 85). They emphasized that empathy is a two-way process of dialogue and communication. With empathy, intimacy in relationships is possible, and with mutual empathy, growth in the self is possible. There is a paradox within this process "in that in the joining process, one develops a more articulated and differentiated image of the other and hence responds in a more accurate way" (p. 85). Psychological growth occurs within mutually empathic relationships that are characterized when both participating individuals feel energized in the relationship, are active and motivated to be active outside of the relationship, and have more knowledge about themselves and the other, a greater sense of self worth, and a desire for more empathic relationships (Miller, 2008).

An "oscillation of images of self and other" (Jordan & Surrey, 1986, p. 92), which defines self in a dynamic process, occurs in relationships. Jordan and Surrey referred to this as the "oscillating self-structure" (p. 92). The process of self-definition is conceptualized as a continual differentiation of self from others within empathic relationships.

For women, Jordan and Surrey (1986) described the mother-daughter interaction as crucial to self-development in relationships. The mother-daughter relationship is described as one of mutual empathy and connectiveness that empowers both with mutual self-esteem. Within this relationship occurs oscillation of images of self and other.

Jordan and Surrey (1986) suggested that a women's self-development may also occur through a process of self-empathy (p. 100). This occurs when the observing and judging selves make understanding contact with the objective aspects of the self (recognized characteristics of self), thereby modifying the self. This process of self-empathy implies that the self-structure oscillates between objective self in relationship with experiencing self, as well as the self in relationship with other. This model of self-development has been further elaborated for diverse groups of women within the relational cultural model described below (Jordan, 1997; Jordan, Walker, & Hartling, 2004).

Jordan and Surrey (1986) noted that mutual empathy is difficult to establish in a society that values separateness and fails to value connection. This, they suggested, produces fragmentation and conflict in women in a number of ways. Women tend to adopt the two roles of behaving like a man outside the home and as a caregiver elsewhere, which produces a compartmentalization of functioning. With the loss or absence of close interpersonal relationships, women also "experience difficulty in delineating, articulating, and acting directly on their own needs and perceptions" (Jordan & Surrey, p. 99). This leads to the central relational paradox that occurs when it becomes more difficult to experience a true empathic relationship due to the fear of disconnection, preventing full participation in the kinds of relationships that are desired (Miller, 2008). For women, the absence of mutual empathy in relationships can also result in a loss of self-esteem because women value mutual empathy in relationships and feel guilt and shame if they cannot participate in these types of relationships. Disconnections that occur when women are not allowed to participate in mutually empathic relationships or when they experience abuse and violence include isolation, lack of psychological growth, and psychological problems (Miller, 2008).

Epistemological development model

Research also indicates that women's development of self-definition and epistemological perspectives are related (Belenky, Clinchy, Goldberger, & Tarule, 1986). Females often identify less with the authorities from whom knowledge is initially received than males do. They start at a position of silence, unable to voice the opinions of others or to speak the knowledge of authorities. This silent, selfless stance has been attributed to the tendency of women to occupy subordinate positions in society. For females, development as a thinker has been described as a process of attaining **voice**, *the process of coming to understand knowledge as personal or private and eventually arriving at the place of constructed knowledge.* Five categories of women's perspectives of knowledge have been identified, ranging from the perspective of no voice or self-definition to the perspective of a creator of knowledge.

Women integrate knowledge from others and self, utilizing empathy and the self as instruments of understanding in caring relationships. This is a process of connected knowing, in contrast to separate knowing, which is an impersonal, adversarial approach. In connected knowing, self-development and intellectual development are interrelated.

Future implications

Understanding of identity development in Caucasian women is improving, and research in the social neuroscience field supports that all development takes place in relationships (Banks, 2006). However, research is just beginning on how diversity and culture may affect women's psychosocial development. Feminist models of development for women, such as the self-in-relation model, have been criticized for not fully representing the cultural experiences of women in developing countries (Singh, 2007).

There is increasing support for the relevance of resistance in the process of identity development for women across cultures (Collins, 1991; Gilligan, Lyons, & Hammer, 1989; Petersen, 2000). Self-definition for many women involves resisting images defined by the dominant culture that are designed to maintain the status quo of women (Petersen, 2000). Women may consciously or unconsciously adopt a personality trait such as assertiveness rather than risk being stereotyped as a passive female. Central to the psychosocial development of women is the relationship between the external social and political context and the internal psychological domain (Collings & Romans, 1998).

Theoretical Principles of Feminist Counselling

As with research, theory, and knowledge developed about female experience, the field of counselling girls and women is shaped by feminist ideology and values. Feminist approaches to working with girls and women arose out of political, sociological, and philosophical perspectives rather than psychological theories. As such, the practice of feminist counselling involves intertwining feminist principles with a variety of counselling theories. Readers are referred to Worrel and Remer (2003) and Walker and Rosen (2004) for a more in-depth discussion of feminist counselling.

As with the culture-infused model, critique of counselling theory is an essential part of feminist counselling. Feminist practitioners view all counselling as a value-laden process in which counsellors are challenged to hold philosophical positionings guiding their practice in equal tension with the theory and techniques used in counselling (Brown & Walker, 1990; Sturdivant, 1980). Examples of philosophical positionings include the values, worldviews, and experiences the counsellor and client bring to the counselling setting. For feminist counsellors, the following philosophical tenets and beliefs are used to evaluate the goals, techniques, and theories that guide their counselling practice.

Personal is political

A key element in feminist therapy is that the **personal is political**. *The experience of human living is shaped and directed by social and political influences that intersect with personal spheres.* For example, issues such as traditional sex role stereotyping and institutional/societal gender-biased barriers are viewed as limiting to all individuals (Worell & Remer, 2003). Feminist counsellors recognize that much of the distress that brings people to therapy is socio-culturally based (Hill & Ballou, 1998). As such, counsellors must incorporate interpersonal, social, and political dimensions as well as intrapsychic analysis into their work with clients and they must think critically about the politics of power (Brabeck & Brown, 1997; Brown, 2006; Wyche & Rice, 1997). As Kitzinger and Perkins (1993) stated, "Whatever it pretends, psychology is never 'apolitical.' It always serves to obscure larger social and political issues (sexism, heterosexism, racism, classism), connecting them to individual pathologies by insistent focus on the person within therapy" (p. 6).

Perhaps the primary essential work of feminist counsellors is to assist clients in developing an ability to incorporate the principle of the personal is political into their understandings of themselves and their lives. In essence, working towards personal empowerment as well as social change are essential components of women's mental health (Funderbark & Fukuyama, 2001). For example, we have worked with women who have decided to not purchase fashion magazines that promote unhealthy attitudes and behaviours towards eating and body image.

Egalitarian relationships

Egalitarian relationships are *formed and maintained through an equal valuing and support of male and female perspectives.* While feminist counsellors believe that healthy relationships are egalitarian, they also recognize that power differentials related to gender and status exist in many relationships. In particular, power imbalances exist in many male/female relationships, majority/minority relationships, and in counselling practice. In some circles, those who oppose egalitarian relationships and want to eliminate efforts promoting equality view feminism is irrelevant and dangerous (Greenwood et al., 2008).

Feminist therapists refuse to accept that inequities between women and men are natural or inevitable, and they advocate that such beliefs must be constantly questioned (Jackson & Jones, 1998). Within the practice of therapy, clients are assisted in assessing their own experience, including sex role socialization and stereotyping and culturally oppressive and sexist practices, as central to their conceptualization of current issues in their lives. Change through therapy often involves individual and collective change and is a transformative movement within the therapeutic process and the client. Lerner (1993) described this process as:

> The awareness of women that they belong to a subordinate group; that they have suffered wrong as a group; that their condition of subordination is not natural, but is societally determined; that they must join with other women to remedy these wrongs; and finally, that they must and can provide an alternative vision of societal organization in which women as well as men will enjoy autonomy and self-determination. (p. 14)

In recent years, feminist counsellors have gained an increasing awareness of the limitations of their work and are now extending it to diverse populations to recognize all majority/minority relationships. For example, an emphasis on gender first and foremost may not speak to the lives of women of colour, lesbians, and women living in poverty (Russo & Vaz, 2001; Walker & Rosen, 2004). As such, power differentials based on ethnicity, sexual orientation, ability, and social class exist.

While feminist counsellors are beginning to address these issues (Jordan, 1997), there is a need to hear and integrate the knowledge of women of diversity, as they can offer an important corrective to psychological practice (Brabeck & Brown, 1997). In addition, while there is a need to empower the oppressed to speak for themselves; it is also necessary not to abandon the responsibility of the privileged to speak out against oppression. To not speak out is viewed as shirking the responsibility that is incurred by privilege (Forcey & Nash, 1998).

Finally, the practice of counselling must incorporate an awareness of the politics of psychology and counselling, which has historically been driven by traditional models of understanding that accentuate power differentials in counselling relationships (Worell & Remer, 2003). While feminist counsellors acknowledge that inevitable power differentials exist in counselling relationships, they attend to feminist principles by being sensitive to power in the structure and relationship of counselling, including attention to gender, ethnicity, class, sexual orientation, and ability (Brown, 2006). A more in-depth look at the application of these principles is provided later in this chapter.

Multiple realities

Feminist counsellors support **multiple realities**: *multiple, subjective viewpoints as viable and equally valid, rather than supporting positions authorizing the objectivity of knowledge and one universal truth* (Brabeck & Brown, 1997). As such, existing theories that are essentialist and individualistic must be critiqued to facilitate the development of new theoretical frameworks for counselling girls and women (Sampson, 1993a). For example, while psychoanalytic approaches have historically focussed on the inferiority of women, strength is noted in the importance placed on relationships (Jordan & Surrey, 1986; New, 1993). Similarly, humanistic approaches have focussed on personal experience and perceptions while failing to emphasize how external world influences, such as gender, class, and ethnicity, might be interrelated with the private self (Brown & Ballou, 1992; Enns, 1997). As well, cognitive behaviourism is criticized for implicitly supporting the standards of dominant social groups by encouraging clients to improve their adaptive capacities to meet environmental conditions rather than focusing on the need to change the situation (Kantrowitz & Ballou, 1992; Morawksi & Agronick, 1991; Worell & Remer, 2003). Narrative and constructivist approaches join feminist practice in objecting to claims of a singular truth, but fall short in advocating for societal change (Brown, 2006). These issues with current counselling models demonstrate the importance of creating frameworks for counselling practice that are more reflective of the realities of girls and women.

Emerging Models for Counselling Girls and Women

Amidst this criticism, counselling theory frameworks are emerging that address the diversity present through gender and through other lenses, such as race, ethnicity, religious affiliation, class, and sexual identity (Jordan, 1997; Russo & Vaz, 2001). In particular, these theorists are working to develop models that permit flexibility in attending to multiple realities while holding up feminist principles. In this venue, Brown (1990) suggested that counselling women must emerge from multi-paradigmatic perspectives and move towards non-linear causality models.

In light of these directions, it seems unlikely that counselling girls and women will be guided by a grand or meta-theory that explains a universalistic understanding of women or ways to improve their lives. Maynard (1995) stated: "There has been a move away from the assumption that theories need to be based on a fundamental core to which all elements of which they are comprised can be ultimately reduced" (p. 273). In other words, while all women share gender oppression, they experience it through their individual historical, social, political, economic, ecological, and psychophysical realities (Green & Sanchez-Hucles, 1997). As such, there is a need to find ways to include an understanding of women as a group and to attend to the particulars of their lives. As de Laurentis (1989) noted, *woman* is a unifying term, not necessarily a unified experience.

To this end, we have identified two theoretical frameworks that hold promise for bridging this gap. In essence, they typify middle-range theories that fall between meta-theories and the detailed descriptions of particulars not to be generalized (Merton, 1968).

Relational/cultural model

The relational/cultural model of feminist counselling evolved from the self-in-relation model of women's psychosocial development, which rejects the notion that women are mature when they achieve autonomy, independence, and self-sufficiency. This model was formulated from the research and writings of theorists at the Stone Center, Wellesley College (Jordan, 1997, 2000, 2003; Jordan, Kaplan, Miller, Stiver, & Surrey, 1991). In this model, the definition of a mentally healthy woman is one who experiences mutual empathy and empowerment in relationships. Jordan (2000) summarized the core ideas of the relational/cultural model as:

- people grow through and toward relationship throughout the life span;
- movement toward mutuality rather than movement toward separation characterizes mature functioning;
- relational differentiation and elaboration characterize growth;
- mutual empathy and mutual empowerment are at the core of growth-fostering relationships;
- in growth-fostering relationships, all people contribute and grow or benefit; development is not a one-way street;
- therapy relationships are characterized by a special kind of mutuality;
- mutual empathy is the vehicle for change in therapy; and
- real engagement and therapeutic authenticity are necessary for the development of mutual empathy. (p. 1007)

In **relational/cultural counselling**, the counsellor and the client work to better understand and rework the client's patterns of relationship connections and disconnections. From this perspective, the client learns to be inauthentic in relationships from her experiences of being hurt and without empathy in a relationship with someone in greater power than herself. The client develops patterns of relating in which she cannot be herself and may eventually be unable to clearly define herself. This experience, known as the **central relationship paradox**, *involves relating inauthentically within the relationship in order to sustain it.* The therapy relationship allows for corrective experiences through the development of mutual empathy. **Mutual empathy** is *"emotional responsiveness, understanding and being understood, expansive growth process for both people. Seeing another's empathic response"* (Jordan, personal communication, May, 2001).

Counsellors who use a relational/cultural model must be authentic and mutual through engaging with the client and being *real,* yet must remain aware of their possible impact on the client. This mutual empathy can be understood as the energy that drives the therapeutic interaction (Freedberg, 2007). Counsellors are open to learning from the client and offer genuine responsiveness that allows the client to develop an awareness of their impact on others in relationships. Turner (1997) emphasized the importance of using cross-cultural training interventions and strategies as an adjunct to relational counselling, encouraging counsellors to increase awareness of their own ethnicity and improve their capacity for understanding of a cultural worldview that may be different from their own.

Multicultural models

Attention is increasing with regard to the need to embed cultural awareness and sensitivity into counselling practice. A variety of models and research have emerged providing possible ways to address this concern by Collins and Arthur in Chapter 3 and others (Comstock et al., 2008; Goodman et al., 2004). Core competencies in the culture-infused model, introduced in Chapter 3, include: a) cultural self-awareness, b) awareness of other's cultural worldview, and c) culture-infused working alliance.

A number of authors have agreed that feminism shares many similarities to multiculturalism (Enns, 2008; Funderburk & Fukuyama, 2001; Goodman et al., 2004; McDowell & Fang, 2007). Goodman et al. (2004) highlighted six overlapping themes between multicultural and feminist counselling: a) ongoing self-examination, b) sharing power, c) giving voice, d) consciousness-raising, e) building on strengths, and f) empowering clients towards social change. Comstock et al. (2008) identified the relational-cultural model as attending to contextual and social-cultural impediments to individual change and growth-fostering relationships as well as attending to lifespan development issues. Counsellors are encouraged to attend to relational, multicultural, and social justice competencies by being attuned to disconnections on interpersonal and socio-political levels (Comstock et al., 2008).

Although multicultural models encompass women as one of the many cultures with which counsellors work, there is recognition of disadvantages to using this theoretical approach with women. Enns (2008) described this recent emphasis in the psychology of women as "multiplicity and intersectionality" (p. 449), considering gender identity to be one of many other social identities such as religion or race, all of which are defined by power differences. Some identities may be more salient at any one time, but as a whole are unique to each person. A more ecological model of gender is described as consisting of a number of subsystems of social experience that are impacted upon by factors such as gender and race. These more complex views of how gender interacts with other systems and experiences are similar to the culture-infused model, presented by Collins and Arthur in Chapter 4 and by Collins in Chapter 10. However, the focus is on the possibilities of the experience of gender rather than on the entire model of multiculturalism (McDowell & Fang, 2007). To exemplify this difference in emphasis, Enns (2008) provided a discussion of gender role conflict as one experience of gender that varies depending on other cultural identities such as the nationality of the individual.

Church, Pettifor, and Malone (2006) maintained that, although there have been improvements in the status of women, it is still important to highlight women's needs in counselling. Counsellors can be respectful of other cultural identities, but recognize problems and issues related to sexism (Church et al., 2006). Certain competencies, such as how to establish mutual empathy in a working alliance with women, may be important to address within the culturally sensitive working alliance competencies outlined by Collins & Arthur (in press b). In addition, multicultural models also include social change skills as competencies and could elaborate on how to empower clients to become agents of change (personal is political).

Although we do not want to enter into debates about the importance of one cultural group over another, we observe that with the increase in multicultural training there has been a decrease in training and professional psychology associations devoted to the psychology of women in Canada. It will be important for future research to explore the longitudinal implications that a multicultural approach has on social justice and activism activities, as well as the outcomes for individual cultural groups, including the status of women.

Feminist Counselling Process

Feminist counsellors support the belief that *counselling needs to move beyond traditional pathways of symptom reduction and exclusive emphasis on individual concerns.* As such, *they advocate for change to occur at a variety of levels, including prevention, education, remediation, empowerment, and community change* (McMullen & Stoppard, 2006; Worell, 2001). While each of these types of work can be distinct from one another, a great deal of counselling women from a feminist perspective involves interweaving these forms of intervention into individual and group counselling.

Individual Counselling Process

From the initial meeting with a client through to the final counselling session, feminist counsellors use a number of common strategies and interventions relevant to working individually with girls and women. These can be considered in terms of an initial discovery/goal-setting phase and a phase of working together to achieve the goals.

Discovery/co-construction of goals

The traditional model of assessment used to determine a diagnosis is widely criticized for its lack of relevance and potential harm for girls and women (Cammaert & Larsen, 1988; DeBarona & Dutton, 1997). Diagnostic labels imply that the counsellor has the power of an expert to define symptoms as intrapsychic problems, rather than viewing symptoms as an indication of how the social/political context may be the problem. Assessment does not consider an individual's cultural context, and diagnoses of pathology are given when women do not conform to culturally defined gender roles. The assessment process involves an imbalance of power between client and counsellor that parallels women's experiences of disempowerment and reinforce assumptions of pathology and inadequacy as client based. Rather than assessing clients, feminist counsellors prefer to use a process and focus to discover and co-construct goals with clients. In essence, this feminist-informed assessment focuses on a process of discovery beyond the individual woman and includes community, social and economic understandings and interventions determined in collaboration with the client (McMullen & Stoppard, 2006).

The process of discovery

Feminist counsellors create a context facilitative of a collaborative counselling process that starts in the discovery phase and continues throughout their work with clients. A number of strategies are suggested that allow feminist counsellors to establish a therapeutic alliance (Brown, 2006; Cummings, 2000; Gilbert & Scher, 1999; Worell & Remer, 2003).

Although counsellors will always have more power than their clients by the nature of their role, it is critical to strive for a more equitable client/counsellor relationship. Open communication about the counsellor's theoretical orientation, information about what the client can expect during counselling, and offering the client choices regarding the topics and direction for each session are all strategies that can demystify the counselling process and empower the client. Brown (2006) emphasized how clients will feel more satisfied and engaged in counselling when they experience respect, empathy, and connection. Feminist counsellors also tend to utilize increased levels of self-disclosure to appropriately show their *humanness* and offer role modeling. Consideration is given to the physical layout of the counselling office by feminist counsellors who are aware of how space and procedures can enforce power differentials between client and counsellor. The office of a feminist counsellor is often very welcoming, has a comfortable seating area apart from the desk or business space, and feminist counsellors openly involve clients when notes are made during sessions.

A feminist counsellor is aware of how nonverbal communication can convey assumptions or messages about gender. As women frequently experience violations of their personal boundaries through inappropriate touching or entering their personal space, it is important for counsellors to increase their awareness of nonverbal behaviours. Touching is usually avoided unless the client gives permission, and feminist counsellors monitor how their nonverbal behaviour may inadvertently reflect gender role assumptions. Personal reactions to client affect, focus of attention on particular topics or to appearance, and inattention are subtle nonverbal behaviours that can convey messages of what is appropriate and inappropriate to each client.

During the discovery process, feminist counsellors often avoid making judgments or providing opinions, but defer to the client as the expert on herself. The feminist counsellor takes the role of empathic listener, keeping an open, curious stance and attempting to fully understand the woman's experiences and concerns from a holistic perspective. The clients' interpretations of her experience are considered as equally valid as the interpretation of the counsellor. Clients can be encouraged to disagree with the counsellor, who acknowledges that the counsellor can be wrong at times. An example of this type of response is "I have tried to summarize what you experienced just now, but I may not fully understand your experience, yet. Let me know if I am off-track."

The focus of discovery

During the discovery phase, the counsellor and client work collaboratively to describe the client's experiences within the complex context of her life at that time (DeBarona & Dutton, 1997). Both client and counsellor gradually come to a more complete understanding of the client's experiences and together they identify goals for personal change. Rather than using standard diagnostic measures and approaches, a variety of strategies are recommended during the discovery phase (Brown, 2006; Cummings, 2000; Worell & Remer, 2003).

Experiences of pain and discomfort are recognized as possible indicators of victimization or the result of role conflict. If women sacrifice individual needs to conform to gender role stereotypes, they may develop symptoms in response to this conflict. Emotional distress or anger may be mislabeled as over-reaction or problematic by women if they adopt gender role expectations for themselves. Feminist counsellors explore symptoms in terms of how the woman's context may generate these symptoms. Brown (2006) advocated feminist diagnostic thinking that is a complex process, including describing the current distress, thinking about what informs that distress, understanding developmental factors related to the distress, exploring coping strategies within a feminist context, understanding current and past experiences of powerlessness and disempowerment, current and past factors of social location, possible biological vulnerabilities, and, finally, the strengths, competencies, and talents this woman brings to the table. Symptoms can be reinterpreted as healthy responses to the environment; for example, a woman's fear and anxiety can be a natural response to having been raped. Reframing symptoms as natural or healthy responses rather than as signals of the woman's problems prevents the woman from being victimized twice: once by her attacker and again by the counsellor, who implies that the woman is ill or unstable.

Working to achieve goals

With an emphasis on social action and empowerment, feminist counsellors move with their clients into the work of counselling in order to achieve previously established, co-constructed goals. It is here that feminist counselling can take on many faces, as counsellors use not only feminist principles, but also their own theoretical orientation of counselling. As such, counsellors may incorporate cognitive behavioural, interpersonal, constructivist, humanistic, or other theories of practice into a feminist framework.

While feminist counselling does predominately focus on philosophical tenets, a number of specific interventions have emerged to support this perspective that are unique to feminist approaches or that arise from other theories, yet are compatible with feminist principles. A common strategy is **gender role analysis** in which *attention is given to exploring how the woman has come to understand family values, life stage, and culture, and whether these understandings reflect gender role assumptions.* Questions regarding choices can indicate expectations for rewards or penalties for gender role compliance or non-compliance. Women who become aware of their gender role assumptions and biases through this process then have the choice to keep or reject these assumptions according to their individual values and needs.

Following gender role analysis, the counsellor may make summary responses, for example, to a client who feels guilt about being a working mother. "Although you believe that your children benefit from the extra income and the role modeling you provide, you still tend to define a 'good mother' in terms of how you were raised yourself. This conflict seems to create some feelings of guilt for you."

Power analysis is another strategy to use when working with women. The purpose of this strategy is to *increase awareness of power differentials between majority and minority groups and to empower clients to exact change in systems and situations that affect their lives* (Worell & Remer, 2003). Topics for discussion when engaging in power analysis could include defining power, recognizing different types of power, understanding different levels of access to power, and exploring how power can be extended to bring about change.

Assertiveness training can be a complementary strategy when using power analysis in counselling work. Once clients become aware of the presence of power, *communication skill development is often needed to increase* *access and mobilize resources.* Along with developing the belief that women have rights to power and opportunity, they need to develop an understanding of the differences among passive, assertive, and aggressive communication and have opportunity to practice skills through role-play situations (Alberti & Emmons, 1982). However, when making decisions about introducing feminist interventions such as assertiveness, it is important to consider the cultural background of the client and any potential risks in adopting these practices. Fortunately, culturally sensitive practices are being elaborated in the literature (Lambert, 2008).

Counsellors are cautioned to respect diversity in their use of the above principles, strategies, and interventions. Of significance is the potential for tension between a family's cultural norms and feminist principles of practice (Sparks & Park, 2000). For example, for Harpreet, the young woman introduced at the beginning of this chapter who had been kicked out and disowned by her family, learning communication skills to negotiate a later curfew with her father might be inappropriate. In her culture, the norm is often to give young women limited independence until marriage. As such, advocating for equal power between young men and women may be in direct conflict with cultural values that favour young men.

Minimizing power and authority in the therapeutic relationship may also be at odds with cultural assumptions regarding the authority of helping professionals. The feminist counselling process utilizes a variety of strategies to reduce power differentials between client and counsellor. For example, Mikako, an adolescent girl of Japanese heritage, may expect her career counsellor to provide expert knowledge on a suitable career goal. She may experience discomfort with a feminist counsellor who encourages her to be an active participant in the counselling process. Mikako may also assume that she cannot request a different style of counselling to better suit her needs.

Feminist counsellors cannot assume that gender is the most important organizing construct for Harpreet or Mikako. Of equal or greater significance may be their ethnicity or other frames of reference.

Group Counselling Process

The implications of the ways women come to think and learn are important when offering psychoeducational groups. Interpersonal group psychotherapy and consciousness-raising groups provide a context for positive social change as women reenact socio-political contexts and raise their social consciousness (Bender & Ewashen, 2000; Funderbark & Fukuyama, 2001). Women, particularly those from lower socio-economic or oppressed situations, may have difficulty finding their voice and expressing self-knowledge. In addition, feminist approaches to group counselling are being used in relational practice groups and psychoeducational multifamily group therapy (Jordan & Dooley, 2000; Tantillo, 2006).

Groups can facilitate the development of voice through the use of a connected teaching style (Belenky et al., 1986). Rather than lecturing to the group, information is generated through discussion that helps the participants to elaborate their own tacit knowledge. Uncertainty is welcomed during these types of discussions as women formulate ideas and opinions. As each woman is encouraged to express tentative thoughts and feelings and has the experience of being deeply heard, she will begin to carefully listen to herself and come to recognize herself as an important source of knowledge.

Connected classrooms (Belenky, 1994) also tend to evolve when groups of women meet over extended periods of time during which they learn to trust each other and gain the confidence to participate. The leader has a role to lead the group, but does not exert unnecessary power over the participants. Her role is to provide understanding, which is achieved through hearing women's stories rather than arguing opinions. Other strategies that encourage epistemological development are listed below.

1. Request that the participants write a journal of thoughts, ideas, and feelings after each session. This can facilitate further reflection on the information learned and personal insights.

2. During group discussions, write a summary of ideas expressed on posted flipchart paper. This can be typed and returned to the group during the next session. Participants may be surprised to see the value of their ideas and gain confidence in participating in further discussions.

3. When women are expressing personal opinions, acknowledge these ideas and validate this form of expression as important to the issue at hand.

4. Note that women may find cooperative structured exercises more supportive than competitive situations.

5. Frequently do rounds during the session so that everyone has an opportunity to express their thoughts or feelings at that moment. This can ensure that all participants have opportunities to become involved, even those women who find it difficult to interrupt or break into discussions.

6. Be aware of the physical space and how it can impede or encourage participation. Circles of chairs are always better than rows and the leader should have space as part of the group and should be at the group's physical level, when possible.

7. Provide a variety of participation levels for the participants. Not all people are comfortable speaking before a large group. Provide time for individual exploration and both small- and large-group discussion.

Ethical Practice

The professional training of feminist counsellors can arise from a variety of disciplines, including psychology, counselling, social work, and nursing. In any profession, the importance of ethical practice cannot be understated, and disciplines generally have a code of ethics to guide practitioners (Canadian Association of Social Workers, 2005; Canadian Counselling Association, 2007; Canadian Psychological Association, 2000). When working with female clients, counsellors are to adhere to the ethical principles of their professional body and to utilize the *Feminist Therapy Code of Ethics* (Feminist Therapy Institute, 1999) as well as the *Guidelines for Ethical Psychological Practice with Women* (Canadian Psychological Association, 2007). The Feminist Therapy Code of Ethics (Feminist Therapy Institute) outlines five main areas for non-sexist practice.

1. Counsellors acknowledge the influences of ethnicity/culture, gender, class, and sexual orientation and view them as inseparable elements in experiencing their own lives and the lives of clients. As such, they continually use self-reflexivity in their practice as they attend to issues of accessibility to counselling, uncovering and respecting differences, and confronting oppression.

2. Counsellors acknowledge power differentials between themselves and their clients and work to effectively use this dynamic to the benefit of clients. This can be demonstrated through appropriate self-disclosure, modeling healthy personal power, ongoing collaboration in working towards counselling goals, and informing clients of their rights as consumers of counselling services. In obtaining informed consent for videotaping of sessions, feminist counsellors ensure that the client fully understands the purpose of taping and that the client is fully capable of refusing to give consent without jeopardizing their counselling. The counsellor may delay videotaping and asking for consent before many sessions so as to empower the client in this regard.

3. Counsellors recognize the complexity of overlapping or dual relationships and accept responsibility for ensuring client safety through attending to confidentiality, not engaging in sexual behaviour with clients, and discussing with clients any concerns about possible overlaps in their relationships.

4. Counsellors attend to the importance of accountability in their work with clients. Taking time for self-care, working only in areas of professional competence, seeking out consultation opportunities with colleagues, and engaging in ongoing professional development and learning are key to this area.

5. Counsellors continually critique professional practices that are sexist or oppressive and work for continued social change at public, institutional, and individual levels. This is exemplified by the work we do in coordinating education initiatives to promote healthy body image and working towards women-friendly counselling practices within the Canadian Counselling Association.

As noted previously, feminist practitioners believe that feminist practice must emerge from the practice of counselling (Enns, 1997). This principle guides the development of non-sexist counselling practice and ethical decision-making. Feminist ethical practice also respects the autonomy of women, including those from different cultures, even when the counsellor may not agree with some client decisions that are guided by the client's culture (Saharso, 2007). Written materials continue to be produced to assist counsellors in the application of these ethical guidelines (Canadian Psychological Association, 2007; Hill, Glaser, & Harden, 1998). In these works, the process of ethical decision-making is supported through attending to rational and intuitive realms as well as through providing specific case examples where ethical decisions arise.

Women's Issues

Girls and women can come to counselling with a variety of presenting concerns. While a complete exploration of all possible concerns is not feasible within this chapter, a brief review of four common issues is provided.

Depression

Depression is a common presenting concern for women in counselling. Research indicates a 2:1 female to male gender ratio in depression (Statistics Canada, 2006c). Women, but not men, have a higher risk of depression if they experienced traumatic events as a child or young adult or have a low sense of mastery (Canadian Institute for Health Information, 2003).

The higher incidence of women who experience depression is attributed to their lack of power and social status (Nolen-Hoeksema & Keita, 2003). Psychosocial models focus on an interaction between psychological traits or attitudes and the presence of stressful life events (Jensen, 1994; Stoppard, 2000). Biological approaches emphasize genetics, biochemistry, and hormones, with particular attention to women premenstrually, postpartum, and during menopause (Brems, 1995; McGrath, Keita, Strickland, & Russo, 1990). Feminist approaches focus on how economic and political conditions, in tandem with gendered expectations, affect women (McMullen & Stoppard, 2006).

 **Snapshot 3**

Women's Depression in Context

"Good lord," said Richard, looking at me. "I thought you were freshening up. What happened to your eyes?" They must have been red. "Father's dead," I said. "They sent five telegrams. You didn't tell me." "Mea culpa," said Richard. "I know I ought to have, but I wanted to spare you the worry, darling. There was nothing to be done, and no way we could get back in time for the funeral, and I didn't want things to be ruined for you. I guess I was selfish, too – I wanted you all to myself, if only for a little while. Now sit down and buck up, and have your drink, and forgive me. We'll deal with all this in the morning." The heat was dizzying; where the sun hit the lawn it was a blinding green. The shadows under the trees were thick as tar. Richard's voice came through to me in staccato bursts, like Morse code; I heard only certain words. *Worry. Time. Ruined. Selfish. Forgive me.* What could I say to that? (p. 308)

From *The Blind Assassin* by M. Atwood, 2000, Toronto, ON: McClelland and Stewart.

Women-centred approaches examine both personality differences between men and women and the significance of relationship in women's lives. Some research suggests that while women may be reluctant to seek professional help, they prefer one-to-one support initially, followed by group interventions (Dennis & Chung-Lee, 2006; Letourneau et al., 2007). Some feminist theorists noted that key symptoms of depression, such as inhibition of activity and anger and low self-esteem, are encouraged in women's development and socialization (Stiver & Miller, 1997).

Perhaps most comprehensively, feminist approaches emphasize that while depression can be present in women's lives, it likely emerges from a complex variety of variables, including biological, societal/situational, and sex role socialization factors, rather than individual control (McMullen & Stoppard, 2003). This can be confusing for depressed women who recognize themselves as *sick* yet acknowledge how their situation contributes to their problems.

 **Snapshot 4**

Women and Depression

Surely no one would expect Mrs. Flett to come up with a theory about her own suffering – the poor thing's so emptied out and lost in her mind she can't summon sufficient energy to brush her hair, let alone organize a theory. Theorizing is done inside a neat calm head, and Mrs. Flett's head is crammed with rage and disappointment. She's given way. She's a mess, a nut case. In the morning light her hurt seems temporary and manageable, but at night she hears voices, which may just be the sound of her own soul thrashing. It sings along the seams of other hurts, especially the old unmediated terror of abandonment. Somewhere along the line she made the decision to live outside of events; or else that decision was made for her. (pp. 261-262)

From: *The Stone Diaries* by C. Shields, 1993, Toronto, ON: Random House.

In working with women experiencing depression, counsellors may begin by exploring these contributing factors in more depth. Biological connections may include postpartum depression, menopause, or other chemical/hormonal imbalances. Referral to a physician to assess for physical health contributors and possible use of medication can be essential at this stage. Societal/situational factors may include lifestyle factors, relationships, and multiple role conflicts. Sex role socialization factors may include learned helplessness and gender role stereotypes (Worell & Remer, 2003).

When counselling women with depression, best practices have emerged through the work of Canadian researchers. Hurst and Genest (1995) explored the use of a cognitive-behavioural approach with a feminist orientation in counselling women with depression. Through intertwining feminist principles about the socio-political environments in which women live with the tenets of cognitive-behavioural approaches, increased benefit is realized by clients. For example, a client may feel depressed due to pressures to get paid employment when she would prefer to maintain the more traditional roles of wife and mother. A feminist counsellor would acknowledge the stress inherent in managing this conflict and provide support in making choices congruent with the client's values.

Gammell and Stoppard (1999) interviewed women about their experiences of diagnosis and treatment of depression and found that a medicalized understanding and treatment of their depressive experiences did not co-exist with personal empowerment. With the label of depression, women can feel they are weak or flawed, which contributes to lower self-esteem. These researchers emphasized the importance of giving women choices in treatment options and of the need to continue to work towards greater integration between theoretical positions and the experience of depression in women's lives. Recently, researchers have become more vocal in critiquing traditional treatment approaches that simply advocate increasing pleasant activities, correcting negative thinking patterns and improving interpersonal patterns (LaFrance & Stoppard, 2006; McMullen & Stoppard, 2006). These can be gendered interventions that risk reinforcing female stereotypes that actually contributed to the development of the depression.

Eating and Body Image

Eating and body image issues are common concerns in the lives of girls and women. According to information released by Health and Welfare Canada, 1 to 2% of Canadian women between 14 and 25 years of age have anorexia, 3 to 5% experience bulimia, and another 10 to 20% engage in many of the behaviours associated with both of these eating disorders (National Eating Disorder Information Centre [NEDIC], personal communication, April 17, 2002). Earlier Canadian statistics indicated that 70% of women were weight preoccupied, 40% engaged in yoyo dieting, and 20% experienced disordered eating (NEDIC, personal communication, April 17, 2002). Jones, Bennett, Olmstead, Lawson and Rodin (2001) reported that 27% of girls aged 12 to 18 years experienced disordered eating attitudes and behaviours that gradually increased throughout adolescence. Given these realities, it is likely that women initiating counselling will experience concerns related to eating and body image issues as primary or secondary reasons for accessing assistance.

Extensive research is being conducted into the etiology of eating issues and is highlighting the socio-cultural, familial, biological, psychological, and genetic factors at play (Gordon, 2000; Polivy & Herman, 2002). We are coming to understand that single factors and simple linear models are inadequate, and greater hope is extended to models that focus on a combination of interacting factors (Stice, 2001). Feminist researchers support the use of multidimensional understandings of eating issues in women and attend to a number of important issues in this regard (Bryant-Waugh, 2000; Surrey, 1991).

While counselling women with eating concerns can proceed from a variety of theoretical orientations, use of a multidimensional model that attends to both psychosocial and physical health is paramount at present (Fairburn & Brownell, 2002). Cognitive behavioural and interpersonal approaches are being evaluated as holding particular promise in the treatment of eating issues and can be easily integrated into a feminist framework (Kotler, Boudreau, & Devlin, 2003; Wilson, Grilo, & Vitousek, 2007). A cognitive behavioural approach focuses on engaging the client by explaining a rationale for treatment, re-establishing regular patterns of eating, and combining cognitive and behavioural techniques to target both problematic cognitions (overevaluation of shape and weight) and behaviours such as dieting. An interpersonal approach focuses on identifying relationship issues that contribute to the eating concern, assisting the client in developing potential solutions, and supporting the client as she initiates change.

Motivational interviewing approaches are also being used extensively in treating eating disorders and these mesh with feminist approaches to counselling process. In particular, Canadians engaged in research and practice emphasize the use of these approaches in conjunction with a collaborative counselling process (Cassin, von Ranson, Heng, Brar, & Wojtowicz, 2008; Geller, Brown, Zaitsoff, Goodrich, & Hastings, 2003; Geller & Srikameswaran, 2006; Geller, Williams, & Srikameswaran, 2001). Geller et al. (2003) found that clients rate collaborative interventions as more acceptable and more likely to produce positive outcomes than directive interventions. Counsellors are encouraged to use strategies including being curious, valuing client self-knowledge, and being on the same side as the client to effect positive change (Geller et al., 2001).

In most instances, treatment will often include a team of health professionals, including a counsellor, a dietician, and a physician working with the woman and her social support system. Feminist counsellors working from either of these orientations will integrate discussion and critique of socio-cultural factors that pervasively influence the experience of girls and women related to eating and body image concerns (Cummins & Lehman, 2007; Irving & Cannon, 2000). Discussion may include a critique of media and advertising industries, cultural imperatives valuing thinness, and gender role socialization of girls. To this end, a counsellor may ask girls to create a collage from magazines reinforcing societal norms that promote thinness.

Women's Careers

No other topic so clearly demonstrates the relevance of feminist counselling than that of women's career development. Measurable inequities in occupational opportunities, wages, and workplace barriers continue to exist for women in many countries (Chope, 2008). A wage gap between women's and men's wages still exists. For example, on average, women who work full-time earn 70.5% of what men who work full-time earn (Statistics Canada, 2006c).

Astin (1985) labelled *the influence of societal forces on occupational decisions* as the **structure of opportunity**. Along with being socialized along gender lines, women's expectations about work are determined primarily by work opportunities. The structure of opportunity includes how jobs are distributed, sex typing of jobs, overt and covert discrimination, job requirements, the economy, family structure, and reproductive technology. These social and cultural barriers influence the type of work expectations women come to hold, along with their educational and occupational choices (Coogan & Chen, 2007).

Socialization experiences can reduce their expectations for **self-efficacy**: *the extent to which they believe they can perform a task or behaviour successfully* (Hackett & Betz, 1981) and can be an impediment to making and enacting career decisions (Sullivan & Mahalik, 2000). For example, in Canadian politics, women are subject to discrimination by the media and male colleagues.

 **Snapshot 5**

Women and Work

Sadly, I must state that I do not think there has been a great deal of improvement in the last fifteen years. The media are still writing stories about what female politicians are wearing. Hustler magazine recently tried to threaten the Honourable Sheila Copps into submission by sponsoring a contest surrounding sexual activity with her as the topic. The Honourable Anne McLellan's voice is called *piercing* and *grating* and *helium-dependent*. More significantly perhaps, the women who get most of the other media coverage are the ones who most frequently act like men. It is when women are raucous that they get publicity, not when they are sound and reasonable. The critics are quick to point out they do not like the raucous behaviour from woman politicians. Rarely, however, are men criticized for such behaviour. Consensus-building skills, which are so often part of a woman's attributes, are both underrated and undervalued. Yet woman parliamentarians quietly go about their work representing their constituents – work that frequently goes unnoticed by the media.... For many female politicians, the frustration remains. (p. 314)

From Politics: Is It a Woman's Game? by S. Carstairs, 2001. In C. Shields & M. Anderson (Eds.), *Dropped Threads: What We Aren't Told* (pp. 311-316). Toronto, ON: Vintage.

Women tend to have higher self-efficacy for traditional occupations and working with people and lower self-efficacy for male stereotyped occupations (Sharf, 2006). Women continue to be under-represented in some fields, such as physical science, applied mathematics, management, and engineering (Statistics Canada, 2006c).

For many women, a combination of work and family is a reality. The majority of women who have children work full-time and 65% of women with children under the age of 3 are employed (Statistics Canada, 2006c). Women have been described as having one of three types of career paths: (a) one without children, (b) a path that has periods of work alternating with periods of mothering, and (c) a path combining full-time employment with mothering (Whitmarsh, Brown, Cooper, Hawkins-Rodgers, & Wentworth, 2007). Rather than focusing on the issues related to managing multiple life roles, there is more of an emphasis in current research on elaborating possible benefits, such as increased social support and enrichment of self-concept (Enns, 2008). The centrality of relationships to women's career decisions is being identified as a critical factor in women's career development (Lalande, Crozier, & Davey, 2000), particularly for women in traditional occupations (Whitmarsh et al., 2007). There is a need for women's career models that include the interaction of career, relationships, social cultural contexts, and individual factors.

Research and literature on women's career development also calls for the development of career interventions and programs specifically designed for women and that recognize the complexity and barriers characterizing women's careers (Coogan & Chen, 2007). Women's career counselling needs to include relevant forms of role analysis, social analysis, therapist self-disclosure, role models, information, and interventions relevant to specific stages of career development and particular groups and offer strategies for dealing with barriers such as sexual harassment and job discrimination. Because women live in a society that presents barriers and may discourage and limit women's career development, it is important to counter these influences with proactive strategies, including affirmative action and training in the workplace (LaBeauf, Maples, D'Andrea, Watson, & Packman, 2007). As opposed to a **null environment** in which *the counsellor is neutral and unbiased,* women's career counsellors should be biased towards women's career development, providing encouragement, coaching, and validation when possible (Betz, 1989).

Poverty

Although a disproportionate number of women live at low income levels, little attention has been given to them in either research or practice. According to Statistics Canada (2006c), individuals are classified as in the low income category when a large proportion of their before-tax income is spent on food, shelter, and clothing. In Canada, twice as many women as men have low incomes after the age of 65. As well, 38% of single mothers have low income levels, compared to 13% of single fathers. Even though poverty has profound effects on well-being, the experiences of low income on women are poorly understood (Saris & Johnston-Robledo, 2000).

Low income or poverty involves the experience of scarcity, being poor, and "struggling over socially valued resources" (Weber, 1998, p. 18). Weber suggested that class, similar to gender, is understood in terms of the context of time and place. The meaning of class is socially constructed; for example, "middle class mothers who stay at home to care for their children are often viewed by the dominant culture as 'good mothers,' yet poor women who do the same are often considered lazy or 'welfare queens'"(Weber, 1998, p. 19). In addition, class represents another way that power is organized, with high-income women generally having more power than women with less income. Therefore, poverty is one more lens in addition, to gender, ethnicity, religious affiliation, and sexual identity, that shapes our understandings of the lives of girls and women such as Kit, who talks of how she feels about receiving gifts of food from her neighbours.

Snapshot 6

Poverty

It wasn't so much Margaret's lifting the lid of Shin's coffin and keeping the smell of his rotting corpse drifting across the nostrils of every soul in Haire's Hollow that bothered me the most, but her pointing out to me, every single solitary time that she visited, how poor I was. Others came too, besides old Joe with this truckloads of wood, and Margaret with her bottles of jam. Gert, Elsie, Maisie, Jimmy Randall's wife – they all came, bringing with them bottled moose, rabbit, seal, and salt water trout and salt water ducks. Plus the cellar was filled with turnip, potato, cabbage and carrots… It wasn't so much the cookies, but what the giving of them did for her that kept me noticing. Each time she passed over the brown paper bag… it felt as if I were receiving the bounty of her life's work, she passed them over with such reverence. She never came inside. Just held the bag out over the stoop and smiled a sad little smile which always seemed to be more for her than for me. (p. 239-240)

From "*Kit's Law*," by D. Morrissey, 1999, Toronto, ON: Penguin Books.

Women who have low income are at risk for a number of challenges. In general, individuals who are poor have lower levels of well-being (Todd & Worell, 2000). They tend to be at higher risk for problems in psychological functioning, have higher levels of stress, and experience more health issues (Belle & Doucet, 2003; Boisvert, 2002). For women who are single parents, the risks of low income have implications for their children, such as finding affordable housing and providing for nutritional needs. When considering women of diversity, it is important to note the high percentage of Aboriginal women (36%) and immigrant women (20%) who deal with low income as well as other layers of discrimination (Statistics Canada, 2006c).

The topic of counselling approaches for women living in poverty has been virtually unexplored through research. Upon realizing this, we identified a number of issues and strategies for counsellors working with this population. In considering a feminist approach to counselling women in poverty, counsellors need to recognize the role of systems in perpetuating poverty, rather than blame the woman herself. Low-income women have been found to have more psychiatric disorders than other women, but, in some instances, women with low incomes do not access human services as frequently as higher income women due to barriers such as stigma, prohibitive fees, or lack of childcare (Rosen, Warner, & Tolman, 2006). Feminist counsellors often include pro bono work as a proportion of their practice or offer a sliding fee scale that depends on the woman's income. Counsellors can also take the role of advocate, assisting women to access external resources or overcome existing barriers to additional funding or support. For example, women in prolonged legal divorce proceedings can be helped by timely referrals to competent lawyers, government housing, and childcare.

A woman who has experienced low income all her life may have difficulty attaining voice in counselling and may minimize or blame herself for problems. She may perceive class or power differences between herself and the counsellor that suggest socially prescribed patterns of interaction. It is particularly relevant to empower these women by validating their experiences, taking a collaborative approach, and recognizing the importance of their feelings and thoughts. Rather than focusing on the scarcity of resources and related problems in counselling, it is important to have the woman build on her strengths. This can be facilitated by helping her increase or maintain the use of the effective coping skills she has been using to survive while building new, more effective coping skills.

Interestingly, research indicates that resilience, or effective functioning in the face of stress, is diminished when low-income women have difficult social relationships. In addition, resilience can be improved by comparing one's self to those less fortunate (Todd & Worell, 2000). In light of this, expanding social support networks provide additional resources to rely upon; however, some women may need assistance in recognizing the value of depending on others in healthy ways rather than interpreting this as being overly dependent. As women improve their situations and level of income, it may be difficult to adjust from a *survival mode* to an *experience of plenty*. Poverty and survival usually mean that women have limited options, attend only to basic needs of food and shelter, and have limited time or energy for leisure and friends. Adjustment to the *experience of plenty* can be facilitated in counselling by considering options for changing assumptions and behaviours.

There is a significant demand for research and development of models of counselling for women with low income. Lack of attention to this population may be attributed to assumptions that middle-class women and low-income women are similar. Of question is whether prestigious journals value research on this topic (Saris & Johnston-Robledo, 2000). Finally, not only do we need to understand the problems and issues of low-income women, the strengths and everyday lives of these women also need to be recognized and explored.

Violence Against Women

Seventy percent of women who are victims of violence are attacked by relatives or acquaintances, and women are more likely than men to be victims of violence (Statistics Canada, 2006c). Women experience more serious, repeated spousal violence than men and are at greater risk of spousal homicide (Statistics Canada). **Abuse** can be broadly defined as "*any threats or acts of coercion (controlling another's behaviour), aggression (intent to cause harm to another), or violence (perpetration of damage or injury to another or to their belongings and property) that are unwanted by the victim*" (Worell & Remer, 2003, p. 248). Abuse is thought to be reflective of the norms and values of a culture and is consistent with the subordinate, powerless position of women. The effects of abuse include posttraumatic stress disorder along with profound emotional, physical, and sexual problems, including difficulties in cognitive processing (Koss, Bailey, Yuan, Herrera, & Lichter, 2003), depression, and anxiety (Statistics Canada, 2006c).

Women who experience abuse in a close relationship may feel unable to leave the abuser due to experiencing a cycle of violence in which each violent episode is followed by a period of remorse and apologies from the batterer along with a honeymoon period (Walker, 1984). The woman loses self-confidence from repeated acts of violence, while the possibility of the batterer changing encourages perseverance in the relationship. Counsellors who are not familiar with this model have a tendency to blame the victim for remaining in the abusive relationship. Worell and Remer (2003) described a three-stage model for intervention: (a) crisis intervention involving increasing the woman's safety, documenting the violence, and providing information and support; (b) exploration of possible options and decision-making; and (c) resolution and restructuring in which options are implemented and the woman can increase her levels of self-confidence and self-sufficiency.

Many women experience sexual assault in the form of rape or incest and struggle to integrate this experience of violence into their realities, as exemplified in Snapshot 7. As with other acts of violence against women, sexual assault is considered in terms of the culture within which it occurs. Research of societies that have rape and those who do not have rape has found that rape-prone societies tolerate violence, encourage men to be aggressive, isolate the sexes, devalue feminine traits, and promote male dominance over females (Worell & Remer, 2003).

Many survivors of sexual assault do not seek treatment, which is partially attributed to insensitive and uneducated counsellors who can inadvertently retraumatize the client (Russell & Davis, 2007). Part of living in a male society includes silence about experiences of incest, and it is important to encourage our clients to give voice to the *unspeakable* (Hyde, 1990). Along with trauma counselling and long-term counselling to facilitate healing, feminist counselling approaches for rape and incest victims acknowledge and provide correct information about the internalized societal myths about sexual assault that imply that the victim is somehow responsible for being sexually assaulted. Empowerment of survivors involves validating their experiences and the strengths they bring to coping with the trauma. Education is also provided about the reality and incidence of these crimes and how social structures and the power differentials between men and women contribute to these violent acts.

 **Snapshot 7**

Rape

Then I fell and he covered me with himself. There was something sharp against my cheek from one of his pockets. A pencil or maybe a stem of a pipe. The terrible stink of him and his hand was beneath my dress, tearing at my underclothes. Ripping them away from me. I was dizzy from all that turning and sick with the notion of what was happening. I said to the tramp, "You mustn't do this to me. You mustn't harm me like this." But he was only desperate and obscene. " Oh yes, Missus. Yes, Missus. I want to _ _ _ you so bad. I do. You'll like it, Missus. You'll like it." His words were something like that. Then I thought this. A terrible thing is going to happen and I can do nothing about it. It will be an ordeal, but I do not think they will kill me. They are not murdering men. They will run away as soon as this is over. My eyes were closed and I shuddered with the pain of his entrance into my body. (pp. 57-58)

From *"Clara Callan,"* by R. Wright, 2001, Toronto, ON: HarperCollins.

 **Snapshot 8**

Aging Women and Abuse

Margaret had lived a very long time without a rough hand on her body and now here it was. She moved permanently into Daphne's room, bought herself a new, firm mattress and a thick duvet, filled the empty closet and the dresser with her clothes and her mementos, with the few pieces of nice jewelry she hardly ever wore now, most of them gifts from the kids. She slipped away during a shopping trip to Sarnia with Andy to buy a deadbolt lock, which she kept in its box under the bed until one day she got the nerve to take the drill and the screwdriver upstairs. Bill followed her up, sat on her bed and watched her struggle with the instructions until the thing was secured on the door. She kept the key on a long string around her neck, wore it wet in the bathtub. He had struck her only once, otherwise. She'd told him she was taking the car down to the garage to get the oil changed, that she was going to leave the car and they would bring her back right away. When he called from his chair to say that it was his car, he would decide when the oil needed changing, she picked up the keys from the basket on the counter and said he mustn't worry about it, she had arranged that they would keep the car for only an hour or so, and then she heard him leave his chair. He came into the kitchen and charged her. When he grabbed the keys, she'd told him, only firmly, she thought, kindly, "I'll take those keys, thank you." And then the slap. (pp. 219-220)

From *"A Good House,"* by B. Burnard, 1999, Toronto, ON: HarperCollins.

Although couples counselling can be risky and often not recommended when there is spousal violence (Bograd & Mederos, 1999), if this service is provided, a systems approach is not recommended because of the assumption of equality of power in the systems approach (Bograd, 1988). Systems approaches do not recognize the inequities in relationships and can blame the victim by analyzing the relationship in terms of circular causality, whereby the victim is encouraged to consider how she has contributed to the abuse and the abuser does not take full responsibility for his actions.

Feminist family counsellors acknowledge that the family often mirrors societal constructions of gender and are careful not to perpetuate these in counselling. The full responsibility for the abuse is openly attributed to the abuser, with the expectation that the abuser is responsible for not being violent in the future.

Case Study

The following case study contrasts cognitive behavioural and feminist approaches to counselling a woman who experiences symptoms of depression. The column on the left provides a description of the case, while specific strategies and interventions are highlighted in the column on the right.

Mona is a 32-year-old wife and mother of an 8-year-old daughter. She came to counselling for help with her depression. The counsellor directs Mona to sit across the desk from him and picks up a pen to make notes while she speaks. Mona tearfully describes how she has experienced symptoms of depression for many months. She is very upset with herself because she cries uncontrollably and is unable to accomplish very much each day. She feels lazy because she sleeps approximately 13 hours a day and has not been able to cook the meals or care for her daughter. The counsellor diagnoses Mona as depressed and indicates that he will give her treatment for this illness.

> Counsellor as expert
>
> DSM-IV diagnosis

Mona says that she needs some strategies for overcoming her depression because she believes her husband, Bill, is running out of patience, although he has tried to be very tolerant with her until now. She thinks she is stupid and doubts whether she can get better. As treatment proceeds, the counsellor tries to teach Mona how to change her thinking from being so negative to being more positive. He tells her to monitor her use of time for a week and teaches her how to set goals and use positive reinforcement to reward herself for accomplishing her tasks. He tells her she needs to change her thinking and distract herself to control her tears. Mona becomes frustrated as her symptoms of depression decrease only slightly. Feeling like she has failed at therapy, she changes counsellors to try one more time.

> Cognitive restructuring
>
> Behaviour modification techniques

When Mona walks into the office of her new counsellor, she likes the inviting atmosphere and the fact that her counsellor does not sit behind her desk, but sits in a chair next to her to talk. Upon meeting Mona, the counsellor recognizes her from their community association meetings. She asks Mona whether she would feel awkward seeing her counsellor in the community meetings and Mona indicates that this does not bother her. They discuss how they would handle these meetings in a professional, respectful manner. Mona indicates that she does not mind if the counsellor says "hello," but wouldn't want to work on the same committees. The counsellor tells Mona a bit about her professional background and theoretical approach to counselling, and invites Mona to ask questions or express concerns about their work together at any time.

> Minimizing power differential
>
> Overlapping relationships
>
> Demystifying counselling and valuing client input

Mona's new counsellor asks Mona to describe her current life in more detail. Mona tells the counsellor she is depressed and unhappy. The counsellor invites her to talk about her daily routines. Mona describes how she tries so hard to be a good wife and mother but cannot achieve this. When asked for examples, Mona says she cooks elaborate meals, but is not able to find recipes that her husband likes. Bill often refuses to eat, even when she has spent two hours cooking a dish he has liked before.

> Understanding client's experience in context

Mona tearfully says he has been willing to give her a chance to improve her housekeeping and cooking skills, but he often criticizes her for spending too much money on groceries or for putting too much salt in a soup. The counsellor empathizes with Mona's feelings of distress and says she understands how Mona feels upset in this situation.

> Valuing client experiences

Mona is afraid to talk to Bill about what is wrong for fear that he will be less patient with her. She wants desperately to feel less depressed so she can work harder to make up for the problems she is causing at home. Despite having gone for counselling previously, she is upset with herself for not being able to learn how to control her feelings and stop her depression. The counsellor focuses on Mona's persistence in working to overcome the problems in her life.

Reframing problem as a strength

Utilizing feminist counselling principles, the counsellor and Mona begin to explore her assumptions and beliefs about her role as a wife and mother. Questions used to guide this exploration might include: How have you and Bill decided who is responsible for the various household chores, such as cooking and childcare? Who was responsible for these chores in your families when you were both growing up? What are other ways of deciding who is responsible for doing particular chores; for example, based on areas of expertise? What household chores do you prefer to do, and do you have a choice?

Gender role analysis

The counsellor also asks for more specific examples of when Mona feels upset and the preceding events or context for these symptoms. Over time, as Mona begins to recognize how problems in her life contribute to her feelings of frustration, inadequacy, and sadness, she feels less inadequate and more self-confident. Once she identifies problems in her life, she is encouraged to consider whether she wants to problem solve so as to be happier in her life. Problem-solving becomes a goal that Mona and the counsellor agree to work towards in future sessions. The counsellor explores when Mona has successfully problem-solved in other areas of her life, and suggests that she utilize her problem-solving skills to deal with the current identified issues.

Reframing from intrapsychic to societal/political

Collaborative goal setting

Building on strengths

Mona is concerned about how to talk to Bill about her dissatisfaction with their current situation and how to present her solutions that she has discovered from problem-solving. Through counselling, she has identified that one solution would be for her to cook half of the meals each week. She indicates that she has never told Bill what she wants and is concerned he may become angry or defensive, resulting in her backing down. The counsellor asks Mona if Bill has ever hit or hurt her and Mona says he just yells at her. Because Mona says she has never stood up to anyone in her life, the counsellor asks Mona if she would like to learn how to be more assertive. Mona says that she would like that. To assist Mona in becoming more assertive, the counsellor may suggest readings on assertiveness, discuss verbal and nonverbal communication, and engage in role plays with Mona to practice her skills. The counsellor also normalizes Mona's lack of assertiveness skills by disclosing how she herself has had to learn these skills and how many women are not taught assertiveness growing up.

Empowerment through increasing sense of choice

Learning assertiveness skills

Bibliotherapy

Counsellor self-disclosure to decrease power differential

Mona expresses frustration about the idea that women are not taught to be assertive and wishes this could be different. She indicates that she has talked about this with her sister before and doesn't want her own daughter to go through the same problems they've experienced as women. The counsellor talks with Mona about what she might do to make a difference and Mona indicates that she plans to share her reading and insights with her daughter and even to find out if she can give a talk to her daughter's Brownie group.

Personal is political / social change

Directions for Future Research

Although a feminist approach has much to offer, there are limitations within current knowledge and practices for women of diversity. There is concern that the current state of knowledge of the psychology of women and feminist psychology primarily represents White, Anglo-Saxon, middle-class women (Russo & Vaz, 2001). Women who represent various cultural/ethnic groups, sexual orientations, socio-economic standings, ranges of physical ability, and generations have not received adequate attention from researchers and theorists. With increasing recognition that the identity of woman may not be as central in the woman's conceptualization of self and other identities such as Black or poor, it will be important to develop models of theory and practice for diverse groups of women. While multicultural models attend to this concern, it will be important for future research and theory development to balance an emphasis on gender-related issues within more generic approaches and to determine the impact of culturally infused approaches on the status of women.

In our experience, feminists continually challenge assumptions of counselling research, theory, and practice, including the field of counselling girls and women. When counselling programs and services are developed for women, it is important that they be guided by relevant knowledge about the psychology of women. There is a need for more qualitative research about women's lives to inform our responses to their biological and mental health priorities (McMullen & Stoppard, 2006). In addition, there is a lack of appropriate evaluation models available to conduct meaningful evaluations of counselling programs and services involving cultural groups such as women (Arthur & Lalande, 2009).

In individual counselling, additional resources for effective, relevant interventions for women counselling women are needed. Brown (2006) highlighted the lack of psychological assessment tools to measure feminist constructs including resistance, empowerment, and regaining voice.

As we continually refine and elaborate upon the knowledge and practice of counselling girls and women, we will be better able to work with clients such as Harpreet, Mikako, and Mona. Perhaps equally significant is the work of counsellors in striving to eliminate the social and political inequities that create and maintain barriers to mental health for girls and women.

Chapter Summary

Counselling girls and women invites us to examine our notions of gender stereotypes and to critique psychological research findings from a feminist perspective. This perspective considers the context for women living with the barriers and biases inherent in a male-dominated culture. Our counselling goals and research need to be informed by current conceptualizations of women's development and their experiences of mental health.

Although a unified model or theory of feminist therapy does not exist, central tenets include: (a) the personal is political, (b) the valuing of egalitarian relationships, and (c) the presence of multiple realities. Two models of counselling girls and women are the relational/cultural and multicultural models. Feminist individual and group counselling strategies include the utilization of a collaborative counselling process, equalization of power between the counsellor and the client, consideration of the context in assessing symptoms, utilization of gender role and power analyses, formation of connected classrooms, and encouraging voice. Feminist ethics highlight attention to diversity issues, power differentials, dual relationships, and advocacy.

Feminist approaches include a variety of strategies and interventions effective in working with particular women's issues such as depression, eating and body image, career development, violence against women, and poverty. While significant progress has been made in articulating and applying emerging theories of counselling, inequities continue to exist, necessitating further research about the diverse lives of girls and women.

CHAPTER 15
AFFIRMING WOMEN WHO LOVE WOMEN: PRINCIPLES FOR COUNSELLING LESBIANS

Sandra Collins and Jane Oxenbury

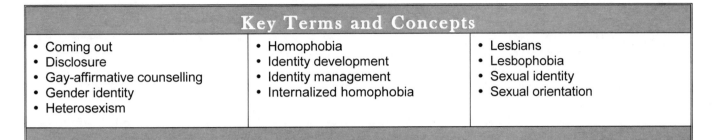

Key Terms and Concepts		
• Coming out • Disclosure • Gay-affirmative counselling • Gender identity • Heterosexism	• Homophobia • Identity development • Identity management • Internalized homophobia	• Lesbians • Lesbophobia • Sexual identity • Sexual orientation

Personal Introduction – Sandra Collins

The issues of power and privilege are emphasized throughout this book. As I write this chapter on counselling lesbians, I am very aware that I speak from a position of privilege about a subject that for many others brings loss of power and privilege and frequent experiences of discrimination and shame. I speak as a middle-class, educated, urban Caucasian woman who is well-established professionally as a psychologist and an academic. I experience the regular annoyances of heterosexism and homophobia in my personal and professional life, but I have the freedom to be out in every context of my life without fear of serious reprisal. This is not the experience of many lesbians! It has also not always been my experience.

The first 30 or so years of my life were a struggle to find myself amid the familial, religious, relational, and social confines that welcomed me into the world at birth and followed me for many years. The path from the fundamentalist religious context of my childhood and adolescence to my current feminist, women-centred world represented my first coming out. I am deeply grateful to those along the way who pointed to a different way of being in the world that honours the value and inherent worth of all people regardless of gender, class, ethnicity, or worldview.

Coming out to myself as lesbian was then a welcome homecoming that turned my life right side up! There was no lingering in the closet; I had waited too long for the discovery and was able to revel in its pleasure while the rest of my world either struggled to integrate this awareness or rejected it and drifted away. Like many others, I now go back and reconstruct those early years through a different lens. I wonder what my experiences may have been like if homosexuality had been recognized as a normal and healthy developmental path by parents, peers, teachers, preachers, counsellors, and others who have influenced my life along the way.

I delight in my current identity and am blessed with a wonderful life partner. Since the first edition of this book, we have joined many others in the gay community in Canada in celebrating our lives together through marriage. I feel very fortunate to live in one of the few countries in this world where my love for her is recognized in this way.

I see my role as an educator as extending into enhancing the understanding of others about the experiences, needs, and worldviews of lesbians. There are still those around me who are more comfortable with silence. I hope that, through the visible presence of lesbians in counselling roles in Canada, our unique experience will come to be respected rather than marginalized or feared.

Personal Introduction – Jane Oxenbury

As a White middle-class female, for most of my life I was virtually unaware of what it was like to be part of a non-dominant population – that is, until I began working with clients from both visible and invisible minorities and came out as part of an invisible minority group myself. Even now, I continue to learn each day, from personal and professional avenues, how discrimination and prejudice affect my life and those of others.

It hasn't all been painful and discouraging. Embracing all of the aspects of my identity has brought many joys and much growth. After many years, recognizing that I am, and always was, lesbian was like having all of the pieces of the puzzle finally fit. My life became even more complete with the discovery of my life partner and the beginning of our relationship. We have now been together many years and have raised three children – two boys and a girl.

As expected, homophobia and heterosexism have touched all of our lives in various direct and indirect ways. Far from causing irreparable harm, these instances have created growth and learning and have brought us closer together – not in a banding together against the world, but in an increasing acceptance of others and a willingness to fight for the rights of all.

Hopefully, my personal experience, along with my professional knowledge, will give you a balanced training in this area of cross-cultural learning that will serve you well with your current and future clients.

Snapshot 1

Vignette

Alison is a 33-year-old woman who teaches science at an inner-city high school in a large city in Alberta. For the past five years she has been in love with her best friend, who teaches in another school. They have travelled together, shared birthdays, holidays, and other significant events, talked frequently about plans for the future, and made plans to purchase a house together rather than maintaining two separate residences. They have not engaged in explicit sexual activity, although they spend a lot of time cuddling. They have not talked about being a couple or defined their relationship as lesbian, although Alison is beginning to tentatively question her own feelings and acknowledge her desires. They are careful to describe their activities as purely social when interacting with their work colleagues, and they don't attend work functions together.

Both women are members of an evangelical Christian church. In recent months, members of the congregation have begun to question the women about their relationship. Alison's friend has been talking regularly with the church pastor about it. Alison has noticed that her friend has begun to pull away from her and to spend more time with other people. Alison is feeling desperate for their relationship to continue, yet feels conflicted by the messages she is receiving from the church. A conference is being held in a few weeks for women from churches across the city to talk about appropriate expressions of sexuality for Christian women, and her friend is urging Alison to attend with her. Alison's stomach sinks every time she thinks about it.

Alison has begun to have migraine headaches on a regular basis and has talked to her doctor about going on an antidepressant to help her sleep. She has taken several sick days from work. She realizes that there is really no one to talk to outside of the church members, since most of her social life has revolved around that community. She tries to keep busy, but often finds herself overcome with an incredible sadness.

Introduction

In Canada, lesbians have traditionally been largely invisible and poorly understood (Stone, 1990). We live in a society in which everyone is assumed to be heterosexual. Disclosure is a theme that permeates each new encounter. Many counsellors, psychologists, educators, and other frontline service providers carry an image of *the lesbian* that is shaped almost exclusively by their experience with clients in pain (Bernstein, 2000). In addition, the psychological literature tends to paint a negative picture of lesbian, gay, bisexual, and transgendered (LGBT) persons through an overemphasis on the problematic nature of development and identity formation. There are far fewer studies that focus on LGBT individuals' strengths, resiliency, and positive identity development (Riggle, Whitman, Olson, Rostosky, & Strong, 2008). It is important for counsellors to recognize that not all lesbians are in pain! And for most, the pain experienced results not from internal, intrapsychic struggle, but from the relational, social, and political pressures to be something we are not. We hope that this chapter will provide a glimpse into why many lesbians openly celebrate their lives and into the common issues and stressors that emerge in the context of counselling lesbian clients. Your most valuable learning will likely occur, however, as you sit across the dinner table from your family member, friend, or colleague and listen carefully to her particular lesbian experience.

Lesbians are more likely to access counselling services than many other non-dominant populations (Reynolds, 2003) and heterosexuals (Szymanski, 2005). We have a professional obligation to ensure that the services we provide are sensitive and responsive to their particular needs. As part of an invisible non-dominant population, lesbians may access the services of counsellors and psychologists with or without actively identifying themselves as gay. Lesbians frequently find themselves faced with uninformed or negative responses from counsellors and psychologists (McCann, 2001). Such homonegativity exists in spite of the official non-discriminatory stance of the professions in Canada and the United States towards homosexuality and the growing body of literature related to gay-affirmative counselling practices (Barret & Logan, 2002; Crisp, 2006). **Gay-affirmative counselling** is based on *the assumption that homosexuality is a healthy, normal expression of sexual identity and specifically integrates theory and practice aimed at actively supporting lesbian and gay clients to optimize healthy functioning, while also addressing the systemic issues that are barriers to their health.* Including a specific focus on lesbian, gay, and bisexual issues in counsellor education is seen as a primary means for enacting change (Arnold et al., 2002; McCann, 2001; Monier & Lewis, 2000).

Defining Healthy Functioning and Psychosocial Well-Being

A fundamental premise in defining health is that lesbianism itself is a healthy, viable expression of relational and sexual identity (Eubanks-Carter, Burckell, & Goldfried, 2005). This does not mean that all lesbians are healthy; rather, it means that being unhealthy is not caused by being lesbian! Counsellors who do not accept this basic premise place themselves outside the boundaries of both ethical and competent practice of counselling and psychology.

Any definition of health is a reflection of cultural, social, and professional value systems. Therefore, defining healthy functioning and psychosocial well-being for lesbians requires disengagement from the traditional engendered and heterosexually biased literature within the field of psychology (Mencher, 1997). In the last 20 years, there has been a significant shift in how women's health and development are defined, initiated by writers like Gilligan (1982), Jordan, Kaplan, Miller, Stiver, and Surrey (1991), and Miller (1986). There are still barriers to overcome, however, in defining health for lesbians. Our preference is to look at health from the individual and the socio-cultural perspectives. What makes a lesbian healthy? What makes the world in which she lives healthy? From these perspectives, there are three basic components to health: (a) relationship to self, (b) relationship to significant others, and (c) relationship to the world.

Relationship to Self

Central to most definitions of health is the concept of self-acceptance, self-esteem, or self-empathy (Jordan, 1991). Lesbians face the challenge of integrating into their view of self a knowledge of self that is often viewed as deviant and unacceptable by the world around them. Movement from a place of dissonance to a sense of trust in one's personal reality is a foundation for establishing personal meaning, identity, and choice.

Relationship to Significant Others

The need for connection or belonging ties healthy functioning to relationships with others. Feminist literature redefined women's development to focus on a construction of self-in-relation rather than through the androcentric norms of autonomy and independence (Jordan, 2004). Connectedness and communal attachment are now seen as healthy and natural ways of being in the world. This literature provides a backdrop for reviewing models of lesbian identity development. For many lesbians, self-definition emerges and is crystallized in the context of a same-sex relationship. Reynolds (2003) pointed to the importance of romantic relationships in healthy human development. Lesbian health is severely compromised by external messages that the love they share is somehow less significant or is morally or socially wrong. Healthy functioning also often involves establishing mutually supportive connections to other women within the lesbian community.

Relationship to the World

The health of society has a major impact on the well-being of lesbians. Social stigmatization, prejudice, discrimination, and violence increase the risk of emotional and psychological distress (Twist, Murphy, Green, & Palmanteer, 2006). Many emotional and psychological struggles are directly related to interpersonal and social homophobia and intolerance (Fassinger, 1991; Hartmann, 1996). Counsellors have a role to play in actively contributing to the creation of a culture of acceptance and respect that will facilitate the health of all lesbians.

Figure 1. Lesbianism in Canada – A brief perspective.

In spite of the barriers to health that exist in the world around them, healthy lesbians abound. Many develop complex strategies for being in the world. These strategies range from *passing* as a heterosexual to *living out*. There is a tendency in the literature to associate maturity or health with open and public integration of lesbian identity in all realms of life. However, this ignores current social or systemic constraints against openly identifying as lesbian and assumes that there is only one path and one destination for healthy identity development. In reality, many healthy lesbians hold multiple and fluid identities and express them in a wide diversity of ways. In each case, a cornerstone of healthy functioning is the acknowledgement of personal choice and responsibility.

Cultural Identity and Relationship to the Dominant Culture

Popular views of lesbianism are often shaped by media portrayals of current events. The image in Figure 1 provides insight into how those events and images have changed over time in Canada by tracking headlines from Canadian media sources through the decades. Our cultural experience is not well represented in the dominant discourse in psychology in the same way that it is generally marginalized in society. A *true Canadian* is still often defined as White, male, heterosexual, able-bodied, Christian, young, and middle class. Psychological theory and practice are similarly infused with assumptions that reflect these cultural norms (Evans, Kincade, Marbley, & Seem, 2005; Reynolds & Constantine, 2004). This silence of the lesbian voice leaves a void that is often filled by misperception, stereotype, and fear. It may also result in an assumption of cultural homogeneity – a lesbian is a lesbian (Hays, 2001). While we will attempt to highlight some of the emergent themes in the lesbian culture, it is important to acknowledge that there is no single lesbian reality. Our realities include a range of socio-economic and cultural experiences, variations in feminine-androgynous-masculine identification, and a range of relationships to the heterosexual world (Laird, 2003). What we have in common is a primary affiliation with women that moves us outside of mainstream definitions of sexuality. It is important, therefore, not to make assumptions about individuals based on the broad brush strokes used in the chapter; rather, each lesbian must be understood based on her particular cultural context, experience, and self-identification.

Defining Sexuality

There are numerous views of the relationship between homosexuality and heterosexuality. Many models are based on the assumptions that gender can be classified neatly into dichotomous categories, that there are only one or two salient dimensions of sexuality, that sexual orientation is predominantly about genital activity, and that gender is related directly to biological sex (Nelson & Robinson, 1999; Rust, 2000). The definitions of sexuality in Snapshot 2 (Barret & Logan, 2002; Bem, 1993; Bernal & Coolhart, 2005; Edwards, 2000; Fassinger, 1991; Garrett & Barret, 2003; Hartmann, 1996; Nelson & Robinson, 1999) and the discussion below, however, illustrate the complexity of even the most basic concepts of sexuality.

The way in which lesbianism, and sexual orientation generally, is defined is reflective of personal, social, and historical contexts (Reynolds, 2003). The tendency to define lesbianism simply in terms of genital sexual activity is a reflection of the Canadian cultural preference for establishing well-defined categories of experience (Nelson & Robinson, 1999). From our perspective, such categorization stems, in part, from a homophobic need to clearly define what one is not. The reality of lesbian experience is much more complex and colourful. We prefer to define **lesbians** as *women who are women-defined and women-identified. When we speak of lesbians in this chapter, we refer to women whose primary emotional, social, and sexual affiliations are to other women* (Edwards, 2000).

It is important to take a moment to comment on the neglect of bisexual women's experience within this chapter. A number of writers have highlighted the importance of recognizing the unique experiences and needs of bisexual men and women in counsellor education (American Psychological Association [APA], 1998; Fox, 1996; Reynolds, 2003). Bisexual women often lack social support (Fox, 1996) and experience discrimination within the lesbian community, where they are seen as either denying their sexuality or attempting to maintain some level of privilege associated with heterosexuality (Rust, 2000). What is clear from these writings and from our own experience is that if bisexuality is subsumed under the category of homosexuality, bisexual women are further marginalized. We do not purport to address the topic of bisexuality in this chapter, but do affirm the need for counsellors working with this population to research their experiences and needs and to develop specific competencies.

Snapshot 2

Definitions of Sexuality

Sexuality is a complex and multifaceted dimension of human experience. Women self-identify according to a range of socially constructed concepts:

Sex is defined as the biological designation as male or female. The term *opposite sex* infers that whatever females are, males aren't, and vice versa.

Gender identity is a more recent term that reflects socio-cultural identification as masculine or feminine. While many cultures acknowledge additional androgynous or intermediate genders, most Canadians view gender as falling into two dichotomous categories. Canadians also tend to erroneously believe that sex (being born male or female) determines and is therefore consistent with gender (masculinity or femininity).

Two-spirited is a term used by some Aboriginal populations in Canada for individuals who embody both male and female spirits. Some consider two-spirited individuals to represent a third gender. These individuals have traditionally been socially valued and seen to possess magical powers not available to one-spirited individuals.

Sexual orientation refers to the sex (or sexes) of individuals we have feelings of emotional and physical attraction and affection towards and with whom we experience erotic energy or sexual arousal. The term **sexual preference** is less commonly used because of the social and political implications of inferring that sexuality is a matter of choice or volition. There is consensus in Canada for the existence of two sexualities: heterosexuality and homosexuality.

> **Heterosexuality** refers to an orientation towards members of the opposite sex. Heterosexual individuals are sometimes referred to as straight, although the inference that homosexuals are therefore crooked or deviant leads some to prefer the term **non-gay**.
> **Homosexuality** refers to an orientation towards members of the same sex. The term **homosexual** is rejected by some because of its historical association with a diagnosis of pathology. Others choose not to use the term for purposes of self-identification because of its exclusive focus on sexuality.
> **Bisexuality** is used to describe the orientation of a person who has feelings of affection and attraction towards both men and women. Some consider this a third sexual orientation.

Gay is a term that implies a subcultural lifestyle and social identity rather than simply a sexual orientation. A gay person's sexual identity is self-defined, affirmed, or acknowledged. This term is used more often than homosexual because of the positive emphasis on the multiple dimensions of sexual identity. It is also used to refer to a political movement. Some women see the use of the term gay to encompass lesbians and bisexuals, with gay men as androcentric, in the same way that the term mankind is used to include women. However, older women may use the term gay more frequently than the term lesbian.

> **Lesbian** is a term adopted by gay women to increase their visibility and sense of subcultural identity. The term is often associated with the community of women who share primary sexual or political affiliation with other women.
> **Dyke** is a synonym for lesbian that is usually considered a positive term if used among lesbians, but as a negative term if used by others. Younger women may be more inclined to adopt these terms.
> **Butch** and **femme** are terms that were used more frequently in the past, when the lesbian community tended to follow heterosexual norms in role definitions.
> **Queer** is a more inclusive term that is gaining popularity because it describes any individual that does not fit the cultural norm of heterosexuality. It recognizes that the boundaries between other categories above are fluid and not mutually exclusive.

Transgendered/trans-identified is an umbrella term relating to individuals who are transvestite (dress in the clothing of the opposite gender), those who are transsexual (believe that they were born the wrong sex and have a strong desire to change their sex, often resulting in sex reassignment surgery), or those aligned with neither gender or born with ambiguous genitalia.

LGBT – lesbian, gay, bisexual, transgendered.

Defining Lesbian Sexual Identity

Sexual identity is a *complex, fluid, and socially constructed concept (Reynolds, 2003) that involves several key components, as outlined in Figure 2. Sexual behaviour refers to what one does sexually, including lifestyle preferences; sexual orientation is defined as sexual and emotional attraction, desire, or affiliation towards members of a particular gender or genders; and self-identification refers to the label(s) that one uses to describe oneself* (Barret & Logan, 2002; Bridges, Selvidge, & Matthews, 2003; Fassinger, 1991; Savin-Williams, 2006).

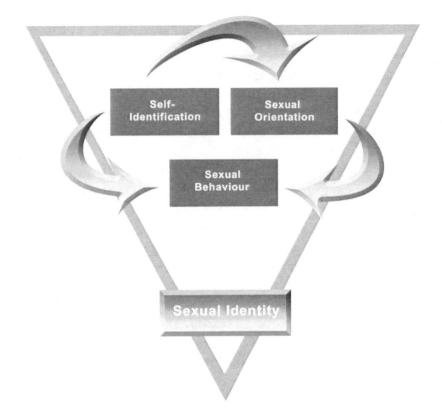

Figure 2. Components of sexual identity.

While these three components often evolve in concert with one another, this is not always the case. There is considerable evidence in Canadian and other cultures, for example, that many more individuals engage in same-sex behaviour than those who self-identify as homosexual (Savin-Williams, 2006). Likewise, a particular woman may experience attraction and desire for another woman, but never act on those feelings, or may engage in sexual activity, but not define herself as lesbian (Reynolds, 2003). Alternatively, she may self-identify as lesbian, but may continue to participate in her heterosexual marriage, at least for a period of time (Eubanks-Carter et al., 2005). Some women who are actively involved in feminist-lesbian politics may choose to self-identify as lesbian in the absence of either sexual desire or behaviour (Barret & Logan, 2002). Sexual attraction, behaviour, and self-identification appear to be relatively independent dimensions that may also shift over time (Savin-Williams, 2006). It is important for counsellors to not apply labels or to make assumptions based on any of these dimensions.

Heterosexism and Androcentrism – Formidable Barriers to Health

Canadian society is dominated by both sexist and heterosexist norms. Women continue to be propelled from early childhood towards traditional developmental markers, all steeped in the assumption of heterosexuality (Barret & Logan, 2002; Palma & Stanley, 2002; Reynolds, 2003). Only in the last several decades has writing on adult women's development expanded beyond a singular focus on stages in the childrearing process. Girls hear little about lesbians and what they do hear is often negative (Stone, 1990). Lesbian youth are left to struggle against the tide in defining themselves according to the norms of an invisible subculture for which few role models exist (Barret & Logan, 2002).

Although theorists are now calling into question the very nature of heterosexuality and defining it as an ideological and institutional construct rather than a biological norm, the heterosexual mandate remains institutionalized in our social, economic, legal, and political practices (Bem, 1993; Fassinger & Richie, 1996). As an *ideological position,* **heterosexism** *upholds heterosexuality as the norm and ignores, marginalizes, devalues, or pathologizes gay experiences. Heterosexism operates by means of two complementary processes: (a) invisibility and isolation and (b) overt attacks on expressions of lesbian identity* (Reynolds, 2003; Twist et al., 2006). It is reflected in active and overt discrimination as well as in subtle and unconscious assumptions of heteronormativity - the assumption that heterosexuality is the norm (Fassinger, 1991; Szymanski, 2005). It is also reflected in failure to adopt policies and laws that extend all civil rights to lesbians and gays (Palma & Stanley, 2002).

From the moment she awakes in the morning, a lesbian is surrounded by heterosexual norms. She is required to "swim in a sea of heterosexist language and practice, always marked by *difference* in many life settings, and always marginal and marginalized" (Laird, 2003, p. 177). For example, she listens to the radio or watches the morning news and sees no reflection of her relational or social experience, the images of advertisements on billboards portray only heterosexual couples, and conversations at work or school assume that she is heterosexual and marginalize her experience.

Canadian society also continues to be dominated by male privilege and male perspectives (Stone, 1990). To some degree, lesbians have a greater degree of freedom than their gay male counterparts. Women who assume more androgynous behaviour and appearance (e.g., more masculine) are more easily tolerated in an androcentric society than men who assume a more feminine persona (Bem, 1993). On the other hand, the fact that female sexuality continues to be defined almost exclusively in relation to men increases the invisibility of lesbians and leaves practitioners ill-prepared to address their particular needs (Bem, 1993). Many writers continue to lump together gay men and lesbians, ignoring entirely the fact that lesbians are women and that gender is a central construct in the understanding of experience (Stone, 1990).

Homophobia

Over time, popular views of homosexuality have shifted from classification as sin to criminal activity, to mental illness, and, in some spheres, to simply difference (Hartmann, 1996). In spite of changes in national and provincial legislation, many Canadians continue to resist shifting to the more inclusive stance of homosexuality as an equally valid expression of sexuality. Negative attitudes towards lesbians are most common among individuals who have not had personal contact with them, have conservative religious affiliation, support traditional gender roles, see sexual orientation as a choice, are older and less educated, or reside in rural areas (Herek, 1996). Increased visibility is one of the most effective means of countering prejudice and fear. Personal contact with gays or lesbians correlates strongly with gay positive attitudes in heterosexuals (Herek, 1996).

Homophobia refers to *the irrational fear of or discriminatory actions and attitudes towards individuals or groups identified as gay, lesbian, or transgendered* (Barret & Logan, 2002; Fassinger, 1991; Nelson & Robinson, 1999). Similar terms, preferred by some authors, are homonegativity and homoprejudice. Homophobia exists on both the individual and socio-cultural levels (Herek, 1996). Hartmann (1996) defined homophobia as "pathological and even quite dangerous, as it repeatedly harnesses untruths and fears to its cause" (p. xxx). The term **lesbophobia** is used by some to *specify fear and negative attitudes towards lesbians. It is coined as a means of recognizing that lesbians face sexist oppression as women in addition to heterosexist oppression* (Stone, 1990). For some lesbians, the homophobia in their social contexts is strong enough to prevent them from coming out to themselves (Palma & Stanley, 2002).

Considerable advances have been made in Canada in recent years that establish basic human rights for lesbians. The legalization of gay marriage in 2005 put Canada a huge step forward in terms of national support for gay rights. However, there continues to be considerable social and political resistance to the notion of equality. Lesbians still face discrimination, oppression, and threats of physical violence (Reynolds, 2003). As recently as 1999, over 50% of Canadians believed that homosexual couples should not be entitled to the same rights and roles in society as heterosexuals (Nelson & Robinson, 1999). Lesbians in other countries face greater challenges, with few legal rights in healthcare, property, child custody, and other areas. In many parts of the United States, homosexuality is a legal ground for firing someone from a job (Eubanks-Carter et al., 2005). In some countries, the consequences of homosexuality still include legalized violence and imprisonment.

Internalized Homophobia – A Double Whammy

In the face of both overt and covert messages about heteronormativity, each lesbian faces the risk of **internalized homophobia** in which she comes to *define herself, rather than identifying the culture, as pathological, and so internalizes negative beliefs, attitudes, and assumptions about herself* (Szymanski, 2005). A similar pattern of internalized racism has been identified in ethnic non-dominant populations in Canada (McDougall & Arthur, 2001). Fassinger and Richie (1996) referred to this as the *double whammy* of both externalized and internalized homophobia and oppression. Internalized homophobia complicates the process of coming to terms with one's own identity and increases the chance of experiencing psychological problems and assuming a negative view of self (Fassinger, 1991; Reynolds, 2003).

Theoretical Considerations

The Etiology of Lesbianism

Prior to the elimination of homosexuality as a diagnostic category by the American Psychiatric Association in 1973, psychological and psychiatric literature focused on the etiology and cure of homosexuality. However, the nature/nurture debate has limited application to counselling if one begins from the basic assumption that homosexuality is a form of healthy, normal human behaviour (Bernstein, 2000). Current literature reflects three primary themes: (a) exploration of the impact of external stressors (particularly heterosexism and homophobia), (b) psychological and emotional issues faced by lesbians (particularly in response to internalization of social stigmatization and oppression), and (c) gay-affirmative assessment and intervention models and techniques.

Prior to the 1980's, reparative therapy models designed to *cure* lesbians and gay men of their homosexuality were common (Davison, 2005). Such practices have since been condemned by the APA and other organizations because they begin from the assumption that homosexuality is deviant, abnormal, or morally wrong (a position that cannot be maintained by those practicing with current codes of professional conduct), lack evidence of their effectiveness, and are potentially harmful to clients (Crisp, 2006; Dworkin & Yi, 2003; Palma & Stanley, 2002). These practices essentially amount to designing an intervention to modify healthy normal functioning in favour of denial and oppression. While some clients may seek counselling with the express desire for such change, practitioners have an ethical obligation to recognize the impact of internalized homophobia and work with those clients on alternative, health-focused therapeutic agendas.

Lesbian Identity Development

A number of models of homosexual **identity development** have been proposed to describe *the process through which each individual establishes a sense of personal sexual identity. This process is often cyclical, inclusive of multiple identity factors, and continuous over the lifespan.* Many of these models are based exclusively on gay male experience and may not reflect lesbian identity development (Bringaze & White, 2001). The various models described in the literature differ in the starting point, the process, and the endpoint of identity development.

The point of departure

While most theorists agree that identity is formed through examination of similarities and differences between one's self-perception and the perceptions of others (Arthur & Stewart, 2001), some models focus predominantly on individual, intrapsychic awareness of difference as a starting point for development. The classic model proposed by Cass (1996), for example, focuses on self-image as the foundational construct and follows the individual's evolution from identity confusion through to identity synthesis. In this model, it is possible to establish gay identity quite apart from sexual intimacy with another woman.

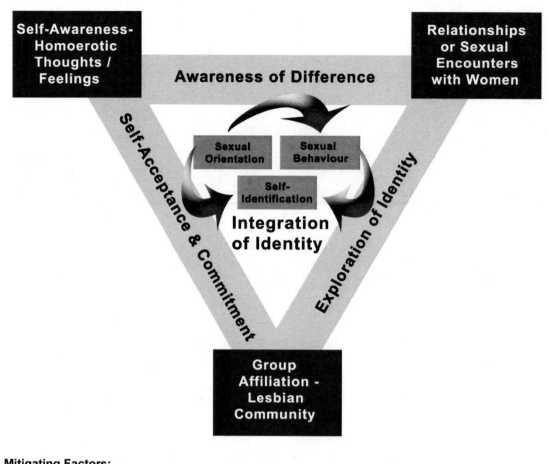

Mitigating Factors:
- Feminist affiliation
- Religious/spiritual affiliation
- Social/political activism
- Context: school, work, community
- Heterosexism and homophobia
- Internalized homophobia

- Cultural group identity
- Career choices and professional support
- Interpersonal and social relationships
- Gender identity: masculine – feminine
- Socio-economic status, age, rural/urban locale
- Family of origin

Figure 3. Lesbian identity development.

Although there is little exploration of gender differences in gay identity development in the literature, the logical extension of the self-in-relation model of women's overall development (Jordan, 2004) suggests that there may be significant differences in development paths for gay women and men. For example, women may be more likely to come out in the context of relationship, starting their identity development process from the point of intimacy and moving from there to a redefinition of self-identity.

A number of newer models take into account this relational focus in development (Barret & Logan, 2002; Fassinger, 1991). Women may enter into a relationship earlier in the development process and then look back over their lives and reconstruct an understanding of their behaviour, thoughts, and emotions that fits with their new view of themselves and their relational experiences (Rust, 1997). Another point of entry to the identity development process may be association with the lesbian community. For some women, particularly those engaged in feminist social and political, group identification may form a starting point (Fassinger, 1991; Laird, 2003). Barret and Logan (2002) followed the example of McCarn and Fassinger (1996) in proposing a model with two parallel developmental processes occurring simultaneously: individual psychosocial and group identity development. In her study of lesbian academics in Canada, Wine (1990) highlighted the diversity of paths leading to lesbian identity, with some women experiencing intimate relationships before coming out and others after establishing lesbian identity. The model of identity development proposed in Figure 3 reflects a more inclusive and flexible approach to identity development, with potential points of entry through self-awareness, relationships with women, or affiliation with the lesbian community.

The process of identity development

Earlier models of identity development assume a linear progression through a set of defined stages. Failure to move beyond a particular stage was seen as an arrest in development (Cass, 1996). These stage models present too rigid a picture of the identity development process (Degges-White, Rice, & Myers, 2000). Other models introduce more flexibility and fluidity into the development process (Bilodeau & Renn, 2005). What appears clear from the literature is that there is no single model of identity development that fits for all women (Laird, 2003). There are, however, a number of common elements that appear in most models.

1. *Awareness of difference.* This awareness may or may not be accompanied by feelings of confusion, self-rejection, rationalization, and so on (Bilodeau & Renn, 2005). For women exposed to feminist or lesbian communities prior to coming out, there may be no negative emotions associated with the evolution of self-identity. Following the model proposed in Figure 3, this awareness may emerge within the individual, as part of an intimate relationship, or through association with the lesbian community.

2. *Exploration of identity.* Some models suggest that there is a natural and essential progression from self-exploration to sexual encounters to participation in the lesbian community. However, there is evidence that older women, for example, may establish a women-centred identity in relationship without ever making a connection to the lesbian community or self-identifying as lesbian. The process is likely much more idiosyncratic and fluid, as reflected by the nonlinear and mutually interactive placement of the three core components in Figure 3.

3. *Self-acceptance and commitment to emergent identity.* In moving towards self-acceptance, some women may experience rejection or disaffiliation with the heterosexual world. In this sense, a woman may follow a similar pattern to the racial/cultural identity development process described by writers such as Sue and Sue (1999), in which a period of depreciation of the dominant culture occurs. Some women may remain fairly isolated in the process. Others may be actively involved in the lesbian community and may establish an identity of gay pride. For others, a separatist stance may emerge, in which identity is defined in part as a reaction against the heterosexual world, and deliberate action is taken to dissociate as much as possible from that world.

4. *Integration of identity.* The process of identity development facilitates increased congruence or integration between the various components of identity: self-identification, sexual behaviour, and sexual orientation (centre of the model in Figure 3). This may involve some form of group affiliation and integration into the lesbian culture as well as disclosure of identity to others.

These components of the identity development process are not linear or prescriptive. There is often a continuous construction of self-identity (or identities) in the context of interpersonal and social interactions over the lifespan (Edwards, 2000). Genest (2002), in her review of the literature on women's transitions in sexuality, pointed out that stage models fail to account for the complexity of women's experience and the importance of context in shaping the transitional process. Identity development is more likely to follow a fluid and cyclical process that shifts over time and in various contexts (Falco, 1996). The process of identity development may also be influenced by personal, interpersonal, and systemic factors such as those listed at the bottom of the diagram in Figure 3. These components may either facilitate or hinder the identity development process.

The endpoint of the identity development process

Some models of identity development suggest that the end result of the process is a fixed identity state that is integrated in some way into one's public persona. These models fail to account for differences associated with other cultural variables, multiple minority statuses, and social oppression, and for the fact that many individuals maintain a more fluid identity throughout their lifespan (Barret & Logan, 2002; Bringaze & White, 2001; Grov, Bimbi, Nanin, & Parsons, 2006; Reynolds, 2003). Each lesbian must face the challenge of integrating being lesbian with the other unique aspects of her identity, including ethnic, social, career, religious, and familial contexts (Eubanks-Carter et al., 2005). The proposed model is intended to suggest a continuous process of identity development over the lifespan without a predefined endpoint, recognizing that personal identity and group identification are two separate components.

Identity Management and Disclosure

Closely related to a lesbian's identity development is the process of **identity management**, which refers to *the patterns of disclosure in her relationship to the world around her.* The assumption that the final stage of development necessarily involves a merging of public and private identities may result from a confounding of these two potentially distinct processes. Each lesbian develops particular strategies to either maintain or dispel the assumption of heterosexuality. Whitman, Cormier, and Boyd (2000) referred to this process as identity management and emphasized the distinction between identity development and identity disclosure. **Disclosure** is the process of **coming out** or *revealing one's lesbian identity to others* (Wine, 1990).

While disclosure is not essential to development or health, one of the major factors that encourage lesbians to come out in various contexts of their lives is the need for an increased sense of internal congruence or personal integrity (Barret & Logan, 2002). Lesbians who come out to at least some others typically have a greater sense of psychological and emotional well-being (Herek, 1996; Marszalek, Dunn, & Cashwell, 2002). However, it is important that they engage in a cost-benefit analysis in each situation to determine the appropriateness of that choice (Green, 2000). The task for counsellors is to create a space in which each individual can establish her own sense of identity and make active and personal choices about how she manages that identity within her familial, social, career, and community contexts. For some, this may involve the establishment of multiple personas (Fassinger & Richie, 1996).

Lesbian and Racial Identity Development Models

A brief comment is warranted on the parallel between racial identity development models and lesbian identity development models. Some of the components of the development process are similar (Israel & Selvidge, 2003), and many lesbians establish what amounts to a bicultural identity that allows them to move fluidly between heterosexual and lesbian cultural contexts (Laird, 2003). However, there may be significant differences. As noted in the discussion of identity development models in Chapter 4, many non-dominant cultural groups experience strong social support as children in establishing a cultural identity; lesbians typically lack such recognition and validation (Eubanks-Carter et al., 2005). Lesbians are most often raised in non-gay families and communities where support and role models are lacking or where active discrimination and oppression occur (Israel & Selvidge, 2003). As a result, lesbian identity development may be delayed well into adulthood (Bringaze & White, 2001; Fassinger, 1991; Grov et al., 2006). There may also be differences stemming from the invisible nature of lesbian identity that warrant further exploration (Israel & Selvidge, 2003).

It is also important to attend to the impact of multiple non-dominant identities. Lesbians of colour or two-spirited Aboriginal people, for example, experience additional complications in negotiating a multiple identity development process (Bridges et al., 2003; Collins, in press; Davidson & Huenefeld, 2002; Garrett & Barret, 2003). Individuals from certain ethnic groups may engage in same-sex practices, but may self-identify predominantly according to the ethnic community, not to the gay/lesbian community. In some cultural contexts, the behaviour is deemed acceptable, while labelling oneself as lesbian is not (Bridges et al., 2003). The concepts associated with identity development in the proposed model should, therefore, not be viewed as normative truths that apply across all cultural contexts, nor should identity development be viewed as a one-dimensional process, since many women will manage multiple non-dominant identities over their lifetime (Collins, in press; Reynolds, 2003).

Common Presenting Concerns in the Counselling Context

The intent of this section is to provide a brief glimpse into the types of issues that may emerge in counselling lesbians and to identify the particular needs of certain sub-populations within lesbian communities. Gays and lesbians are making use of counselling services at a higher rate than heterosexual women (Eubanks-Carter et al., 2005; Twist et al., 2006). So, most therapists can expect to encounter lesbians throughout their careers. Because the presenting concerns of many lesbians reflect external rather than internal causes (Safren, 2005), we begin with a further look at the impact of heterosexism and homophobia.

You're Making Me Sick! The Impact of Heterosexism and Homophobia

In almost all social contexts, women are assumed to be heterosexual. The dominance of heterosexual norms in society fuels shame, secrecy, and alienation for those who step outside those boundaries (Bepko & Johnson, 2000). For the most part, lesbians remain invisible in our society precisely because of this heterosexual assumption (Whitman et al., 2000). Women have historically come to define themselves and to be defined by others predominantly in relation to men. The reconstruction of a sense of self in the absence of a male point of reference may be daunting. Lesbians face the complex task of finding a place in a society where their reality is ignored, devalued, and sometimes scorned.

Social and cultural realities either expand or limit a person's ability to create meaning and identity in life. The developmental challenges or life crises encountered by lesbians are often interpersonal or systemic, not intrapsychic in origin (Iwasaki & Ristock, 2007). A number of authors refer to the concept of *minority stress* to describe the impact of social oppression on members of non-dominant populations (Balsam & Szymanski, 2005; Savin-Williams, 2006). Stress-induced symptoms can include depression, anxiety, mood disorders, suicidal ideation, substance abuse, and others (Eubanks-Carter et al., 2005; Safren, 2005; Savin-Williams, 2006). The need to hide one's identity may result in feelings of inauthenticity (Herek, 1996). External messages and pressures to conform to *other-imposed* standards of living can lead to distrust in one's own feelings, perceptions, and intuition; a distorting or cutting off of part of one's self or one's experience; and a failure to integrate the past, present, and future into one's choices. The result may be a lack of integrity or congruence and interference with one's spontaneous ability to grow and change.

Coming Out, and Out, and Out . . .

The process of coming out refers to the acknowledgement of gay identity to oneself and the expression of that identity to others (Barret & Logan, 2002; Fassinger, 1991). Lesbians are often asked, "So when did you come out?" as if it were a singular event, as if once a lesbian is *out*, she is never *in* again. In fact, disclosure is a continuous process that characterizes lesbian experience throughout the lifespan (Herek, 1996; Reid, 1995; Reynolds, 2003). Most lesbians make active choices about the contexts in which they disclose. With each new relationship, friendship, or situation they make a decision about whether to come out, to whom, and when. Like the identity development process itself, the process of coming out is influenced by gender, ethnicity, socio-economic status, age, and so on (Fassinger, 1991).

The cost of passing

Many lesbians choose not to reveal their identity to those around them because of their fear of discrimination or the shame of internalized homophobia (Eubanks-Carter et al., 2005). As noted above in our discussion of androcentrism in Canadian society, it is much easier for a lesbian to don a straight mask and *pass* than it is for a gay man. She is freer to live with a woman, to express affection physically, and to dress in a more androgynous fashion. However, passing as heterosexual requires continual vigilance and may draw energy away from other aspects of her life. The constant self-censoring may result in less spontaneity, increased stress, guilt, low self-esteem, and increased rigidity that may generalize to other areas of her life (Eubanks-Carter et al., 2005; Falco, 1996; Palma & Stanley, 2002). It can also result in disruption to relationships with family and friends as she hides more and more of herself from them and can even make it difficult to establish new relationships (Herek, 1996). For lesbian couples, hiding their relationship from others may leave them isolated and lacking the relational supports often available to heterosexual couples (Herek, 1996; Herring & Furgerson, 2000).

The risks of disclosure

There is considerable evidence that regular exposure to diverse perspectives and experiences increases societal acceptance and appreciation of diversity. Social norms are shifting as more and more lesbians become visible members of society. However, each individual lesbian needs to carefully consider the consequences of disclosure. She may face risks in terms of economic and job security, personal safety, loss of significant relationships, child custody, and so on (Barret & Logan, 2002; Whitman et al., 2000). Family reactions can range from support to grief and confusion to overt hostility and rejection (Eubanks-Carter et al., 2005). Other cultural factors may confound the experience of disclosure. For some, embracing sexual identity may mean risking the loss of connection and support from their primary cultural communities (Bridges et al., 2003). It may also mean adding another layer to existing oppressions such as racism, sexism, and ableism (Hays, 2001).

Transitioning from heterosexuality

In many contexts, the question faced by the individual lesbian is not whether she should disclose, but when she should disclose. By disclosing early in relationships, she may risk rejection based on pre-established biases while choosing to delay disclosure opens her to accusations of dishonesty. Edwards (2000) explored the experiences of transition from heterosexual to homosexual identities for women over the age of 40, with particular attention to the ways in which women make meaning of these changes and redefine themselves through this experience. Many women who identify as lesbian have experienced multiple identities across their lifespans. Most have lived heterosexually defined lives at some point.

Living out

While there may be very good reasons for many lesbians to continue to pass in the heterosexual world or to selectively choose particular contexts in which to be out, *living out* offers many an increased sense of authenticity and identity synthesis (Barret & Logan, 2002; Herek, 1996). For some, living out may also mean involvement in the larger lesbian community or in political action. Each may provide an important source of social support, meaning, and identity. Living out also appears to be associated with overall emotional and physical well-being, Nonetheless, living out should not be seen as the climax of identity development processes or as evidence of self-actualization (Barret & Logan, 2002). To do so assumes that, in order to function at an optimal level of well-being, every lesbian must disclose her sexual orientation publicly. This is neither a practical nor an ethical expectation.

Even those individuals who chose to live out may continue to experience the effects of internalized homophobia because heterosexist and homophobic messages are so pervasive on our society. There is a direct relationship between internalized homophobia and psychological and emotional distress (Eubanks-Carter et al., 2005; Szymanski, 2005). In addition, internalized homophobia can have a negative impact on interpersonal relationships, often exacerbating or compounding other relational issues (Balsam & Syzmanski, 2005) and resulting in lower levels of relationship satisfaction (Spenser & Brown, 2007).

Lesbian Relationships

Throughout history, women have met and engaged intimately on many levels, although most would not have labelled themselves lesbian (Rupp, 1997). Today, lesbians come to know one another through the usual channels of social functions, work, common interests, friends, and, occasionally, advertisements for companions. However, since the community is small and often closeted, building relationships with one another can be challenging. There are also few role models or opportunities for feedback on relational issues, so it is easy for lesbians to assume a problem is related to sexual identity when it may simply be a normal relational or developmental challenge (Spitalnick & McNair, 2005). This section highlights some key issues in lesbian relationships.

Closeness and mutuality

The psychology of women's literature over the past several decades attests to the struggle to carve out a place for defining healthy development and functioning from a relational perspective (Jordan & Walker, 2004; Miller, 2008). Identity is seen as formed through connection and authentic relationships with others. It is no longer assumed that one must disconnect and sacrifice relationship as part of healthy self-development. To do so may, in fact, result in developmental problems (Jordan, 2004). Interestingly, the relational characteristics of authenticity, intimacy, and mutuality that are now embraced by women's literature were historically labelled as *fusion* or *enmeshment* in the literature on lesbian relationships (Ackbar, 2005). Many lesbian couples express a high degree of satisfaction in relationships and identify many of the characteristics previously labelled as fusion as important contributors to their sense of relational well-being: intense intimacy, interdependency, high levels of communication and emotional support, depth of mutuality, shared beliefs and goals, friendships, leisure activities, services accessed in common, and so on (Ackbar, 2005; Laird, 2003).

Women's capacity for emotional closeness and intimacy represents a relational strength. In lesbian relationships, this bond may be deepened through the shared experience of cultural oppression (Spenser & Brown, 2007). Health should be defined by the quality of such relational processes as mutual engagement, mutual empathy, and mutual empowerment. This is not to say that boundary issues do not emerge in lesbian relationships and that a potential loss of the sense of self is impossible. However, problems are more likely to arise when there is a mismatch between expectations of closeness rather than because there is something inherently pathological about women's ways of relating (Barret & Logan, 2002).

Building relationships

In the earlier stages of their relationships, lesbians may be challenged by homophobia, female role definitions, and/or religious beliefs about homosexuality. Perceived violations of expected social roles and rules can result in both internal and external pressure to conform (Reynolds, 2003). Adolescent sexual behaviour, fantasies or myths about relationships, or stereotypical beliefs about women in relationships may lead to unrealistic expectations. When entering a same-sex relationship for the first time, each lesbian may take some time to work out the new roles and expectations (Reynolds, 2003). There are no rituals and few models available to mark transitions or provide guidance. There is no standard language for her to use for her partnership or her partner. While she often develops an intense connection and sexual bond early on, she is faced with the challenge of hiding that affection and passion in public. Normal dating patterns (e.g., handholding, kissing, and affectionate touch) may be too risky, which limits casual foreplay. Consequently, most courtship takes place in the privacy of her home or at a lesbian function. This may lead to a shortened dating period and an attenuated courtship (Barret & Logan, 2002). It is not unusual to find couples moving in together after a short period of time. Throughout their relationship, lesbian couples may struggle with similar issues to most couples: sex, roles, abuse, parenting, money, and family or friendships. Breakdowns in communication may build further distance. However, most women in lesbian relationships learn effective modes of handling such conflict.

Cultural differences

Greene (1997) indicated that lesbian women of colour may find themselves in relationships that are largely unsupported outside of the lesbian community. They are usually accustomed to receiving family support for their struggles with racism and perhaps sexism, but cannot presume appropriate support for a same-sex relationship or during the dissolution of one (Reynolds, 2003). In fact, they risk losing the support of cultural community in other areas of their life if their sexual identity becomes known (Bridges et al., 2003; Palma & Stanley, 2002; Reynolds, 2003). The fact that lesbians of colour are most often in relationships with women not of their own ethnic group also introduces unique challenges. They are more visible than two women of the same ethnic group, and the racism of the dominant population is often reflected within the lesbian community (Bridges et al., 2003). Both partners may experience racism on a completely new level. On the other hand, a lesbian choosing someone from the same cultural group cannot presume that her partner will compensate for the loss of ethnic community or will show cultural loyalty. Many differences in experience or worldview may still exist. As with other areas of difference, these women may benefit from clarification of their expectations and assumptions about the relationship.

Sexual intimacy

Many lesbian couples establish healthy and satisfying emotional and sexual relationships with one another. There is some evidence that rates of sexual activity in lesbian relationships are similar to those of heterosexual relationships (Bepko & Johnson, 2000). However, sexual desire and activity may wane in a relationship due to lack of sexual knowledge and skills, affairs or outside attractions, unresolved couples issues, past abuse, and lack of communication. Women are generally socialized to feel uncomfortable expressing sexual desire or need and to play the less assertive role in sexual encounters (Spitalnick & McNair, 2005). Many lesbian couples express a desire for a more active sex life, which may suggest that they continue to struggle against the influences of female socialization in the context of intimacy with women (Herbert, 1996). The fact that there are two women involved may simply magnify the impact of that socialization.

A lesbian may struggle against the myth that she should automatically know how to please another woman sexually. However, we are all unique in our needs and desires, and since sexual expression is a learned response, new learning may need to occur. Internal homophobia, conflict about lesbian identity, past experiences, isolation, rigid roles, and the tension between taking the initiative, being passive, or striving for equality in sexual relating may also get in the way of a healthy sexual relationship (Clunis & Green, 1988). Rothblum (2000) indicated that a woman's definition of what constitutes sexual activity may differ with a male partner and a female partner. When she is with a male partner, she often separates sexual activity from her own sexual arousal and desire. Sex with a woman allows for a greater variety of sexual expressions, and the focus tends to be more broadly focused on love, affection, and romance than simply on genital sexual activity (Spitalnick & McNair, 2005). Like most women, lesbians often associate sexual satisfaction with the quality of the emotional connection rather than with physical sex (Herbert, 1996). However, if a couple disagrees on what constitutes *sex,* when they are *having sex,* or on frequency of sexual behaviour, they may experience other sexual conflicts.

In the area of sexual intimacy, several issues may arise. Sexual abuse and assault remain high risk factors for all women. Lesbian youth may be particularly vulnerable to repeated sexual abuse by virtue of their social isolation (Herring & Furgerson, 2000). This means there is a higher probability in lesbian relationships that at least one partner will have been victimized (Bepko & Johnson, 2000). Sometimes both are survivors of abuse. While these women may have more understanding and compassion for each other, the potential for sexual problems may also be magnified.

Monogamy

Many lesbians form long-term monogamous relationships. For some lesbians, however, a non-monogamous relationship is the norm (Simon, 1996). Open relationships allow for sexual expression with women other than the primary partner. This often involves sexual non-monogamy but emotional monogamy. This type of relationship is more common within the gay male population; however, it can present as an issue in lesbian couples therapy (Laird, 2003). If a couple desires to define their relationship this way, it is important that the counsellor help them weigh potential for growth against potential loss within the relationship, establish ways to keep the primary relationship central, and specify the details of the outside contacts.

Roles

In the past, many lesbian relationships mirrored traditional heterosexual roles. One woman took the role of the female, or *femme,* and the other took the role of the male, or *butch.* These roles defined everything from clothing to chores to sexual encounters. While a small butch/femme subculture continues to flourish, especially in large urban centres, most same-sex partners currently have non-traditional expectations about relational roles (Spitalnick & McNair, 2005). They have shared responsibilities for the household, mutuality in making decisions that affect their relationship, and flexibility in negotiating tasks (Laird, 2003). They are able to step outside of traditional gendered roles (Riggle et al., 2008). While experiencing more freedom, same-sex couples have to spend more time than heterosexual couples in negotiating relational roles, as there are no *appropriate* roles defined by society. The level of egalitarianism also seems to be impacted by other variables, such as class, ethnicity, and geographic location (Laird, 2003).

Ending relationships

There is less social pressure and support to maintain a lesbian relationship. There are also no rituals or institutions to help couples deal with the transition when relationships end. As a counsellor, it may be important for you to assist your client in creating her own rituals and markers during times of transition. Legal issues related to child custody, access, and division of property may be more complex for couples whose very existence is often denied. Counsellors should be aware of rapidly changing federal and provincial legislation so that they can assist clients in establishing agreements at the outset of a relationship and resolving issues of termination. Couples who are living out are more likely to be able to access resources to help them deal with the loss. If a woman has felt a need to hide her sexual orientation and her relationship from family and friends, little social support is available.

Lesbians have fewer alternatives for reestablishment of a network of social support and community than heterosexual women. The size of the lesbian community increases the likelihood that a woman will see her ex-partner at social events or will maintain common friendships (Reynolds, 2003). For this reason, there is a tendency in the lesbian community to move from breakup to some other form of social reconnection with former partners. At the very least, the subcultural expectation is for tolerance of each other's participation in the same circles. Many lesbians learn a whole new set of relational skills through this process.

Chosen Family

Counsellors are challenged to reflect on their personal values about what and who constitutes a family. One of the unique aspects of lesbian and gay culture is the *chosen family* (Bepko & Johnson, 2000). This was noted as one of the key positive aspects of being gay in a recent study (Riggle et al., 2008). In part because relationships with family of origin may be disrupted, many lesbians form a new extended family network that includes ex-lovers, friends, family of ex-lovers, and/or some members of their families of origin (Eubanks-Carter et al., 2005; Malley & Tasker, 2007). These relationships often last a lifetime and form a more significant source of security and social support than the family of origin (Green, 2000). It is important for counsellors to recognize the importance of chosen family and the complexity of negotiating issues such as time off work to support a chosen family member who is ill or recognition of these individuals in times of crisis. Chosen family members also have the potential to become important allies to the therapeutic process. Lesbians who have strong support from significant others for their sexual identity show higher overall levels of self-esteem, life satisfaction, and well-being (Beals & Peplau, 2005).

Domestic Violence

Although survey studies report widely varying rates of lesbian domestic violence (Ristock, 2002), lesbian couples are not immune from domestic violence, including physical, emotional, psychological, sexual, economic, and spiritual abuse. The root of such violence, as in heterosexual relationships, is the need for power and control; however, the forms of physical violence tend to be milder among lesbian couples (Rohrbaugh, 2006). There are other important differences.

The secrecy and isolation are greater for victims and perpetrators of same-sex violence, even within the lesbian community itself. The myth that women don't abuse women reinforces the silence (Ristock, 2002). Homophobia keeps both women from talking about the issue out of fear that they will not be believed or supported or will be discriminated against. Lesbians often find themselves blamed by medical, police, and legal personnel for an assault because of their sexual orientation and face the risks of public exposure if they report the assault (Fassinger, 1991; Herek, 1996). In addition, the perpetrator may use homophobia as a means of control. Threats of outing the victim to children, work or school colleagues, friends, or family can keep the cycle going and increase the sense of entrapment (Rohrbaugh, 2006). There can also be a threat to take stepchildren away from the relationship, and the victim may have no legal recourse (Rohrbaugh, 2006). Lastly, when it occurs, violence often occurs after a sexual encounter. This may be a reaction to the level of vulnerability involved. Rates of domestic violence are directly related to experiences of internalized homophobia (Balsam & Szymanski, 2005). If one partner is struggling with her own internalized homophobia, she may find it more difficult to maintain her own level of denial when she has just been sexual with another woman. This insecurity, self-doubt, and fear may lead to violent acts designed to reestablish control.

It is imperative that as a counsellor you always screen for domestic violence with each of your clients. Counsellors often overlook domestic violence, and this puts the victim at risk of having what they say in counselling used against them at home or colludes the therapist in the continuation of the abusive behaviour. We are fortunate in Canada that there is some legal protection and service available for same-sex couples; this is not the case in many other countries (Rohrbaugh, 2006).

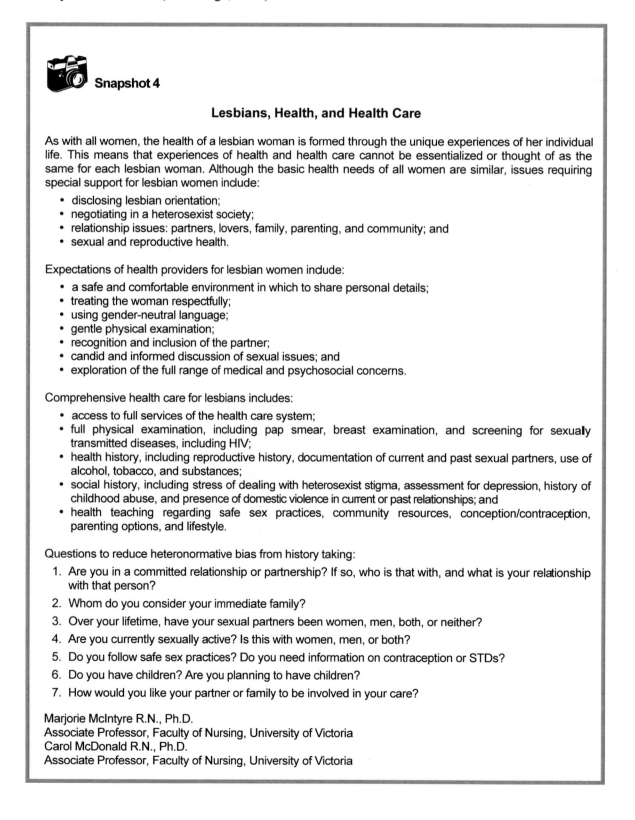

Snapshot 4

Lesbians, Health, and Health Care

As with all women, the health of a lesbian woman is formed through the unique experiences of her individual life. This means that experiences of health and health care cannot be essentialized or thought of as the same for each lesbian woman. Although the basic health needs of all women are similar, issues requiring special support for lesbian women include:

- disclosing lesbian orientation;
- negotiating in a heterosexist society;
- relationship issues: partners, lovers, family, parenting, and community; and
- sexual and reproductive health.

Expectations of health providers for lesbian women include:

- a safe and comfortable environment in which to share personal details;
- treating the woman respectfully;
- using gender-neutral language;
- gentle physical examination;
- recognition and inclusion of the partner;
- candid and informed discussion of sexual issues; and
- exploration of the full range of medical and psychosocial concerns.

Comprehensive health care for lesbians includes:

- access to full services of the health care system;
- full physical examination, including pap smear, breast examination, and screening for sexually transmitted diseases, including HIV;
- health history, including reproductive history, documentation of current and past sexual partners, use of alcohol, tobacco, and substances;
- social history, including stress of dealing with heterosexist stigma, assessment for depression, history of childhood abuse, and presence of domestic violence in current or past relationships; and
- health teaching regarding safe sex practices, community resources, conception/contraception, parenting options, and lifestyle.

Questions to reduce heteronormative bias from history taking:

1. Are you in a committed relationship or partnership? If so, who is that with, and what is your relationship with that person?
2. Whom do you consider your immediate family?
3. Over your lifetime, have your sexual partners been women, men, both, or neither?
4. Are you currently sexually active? Is this with women, men, or both?
5. Do you follow safe sex practices? Do you need information on contraception or STDs?
6. Do you have children? Are you planning to have children?
7. How would you like your partner or family to be involved in your care?

Marjorie McIntyre R.N., Ph.D.
Associate Professor, Faculty of Nursing, University of Victoria
Carol McDonald R.N., Ph.D.
Associate Professor, Faculty of Nursing, University of Victoria

Parenting

The lack of recognition of lesbian couples with children as *legitimate* families has led to under-representation of their needs and experiences in family research and in the family therapy literature (Laird, 2003). Lesbians often have children, either prior to or during a same-sex relationship, and they face unique circumstances and challenges as lesbian parents (APA, 1998; Reynolds, 2003). The inclusion in chosen families of both adults and children who are not legally or biologically related raises particular parenting issues.

Children raised in lesbian families are just as well adjusted as those raised in heterosexual families (Laird, 2003; Reynolds, 2003). This assertion is supported by all of the major medical, psychological, and psychiatric associations (Paccione-Dyszlewski, 2008). It is the nature of the specific family dynamics that determines the health of a child. However, children add a whole new dimension to the lives of lesbian couples. When children do become part of a relationship, they often bring a couple closer together, and they also take time away from that relationship (Brill, 2001). Counsellors may assist couples in planning ahead and making explicit decisions about parenting roles, division of tasks, parenting skills and strategies, how to handle extended family, and so on. Johnson and O'Connor (2001) recommended avoiding inequality in which one woman is seen as the expert parent, setting aside time to spend together as a couple, keeping some important rituals the couple shared before having children, and maintaining an intimate connection. There are few visible role models for lesbian mothers, so each couple must define for themselves the nature of their family system (Brill, 2001).

External and internal homophobia may exacerbate the normal trials of parenting. Children are more likely to experience harassment or bullying (Paccione-Dyszlewski, 2008). Guilt or shame about sexual identity may be expressed in a super-parent role. The non-biological parent may also experience jealousy or feel left out (Johnson & O'Connor, 2001). Other couples find that the arrival of a child or a relationship with a woman who has children actually lends legitimacy to the couple's relationship (Johnson & O'Connor, 2001). Some experience positive recognition and support from extended families that they had not previously experienced.

A major challenge for most lesbian couples is the choice of whether or when to come out to their children. Lesbian mothers must take into account perceived risks of discrimination, loss of custody, or rejection by their own children. If a couple decides not to come out to their children early on, the children may suspect and force the issue by asking direct questions. When questions do arise, parents need to be prepared to answer them in a way appropriate to age and circumstance. Once they do find out, children may feel angry and left out. Some children may react by asking their parents to *tone down* the expression of their sexuality (Brill, 2001). Johnson and O'Connor (2001) noted that while it is important to help children feel comfortable and not self-conscious, it is also important to model for children non-homophobic behaviour and to communicate to them that their family system is normal and healthy. Each couple will learn to draw their own boundaries in this area. Lesbian mothers should expect to be outed frequently and may need support in learning how to deal effectively with those situations. They should also be supported in identifying the advantages that their children have by virtue of being raised by a lesbian mother or lesbian parents.

Career Development Issues

Career and life choices for lesbians are affected by identity development, which in turn may be constrained by factors such as familial and social support, internalized homophobia, and community and job-related support (Rhieneck, 2005). A lesbian may feel less constrained by traditional gender norms and may pursue non-traditional career paths; however, she may remain closeted in order to access a broader range of career options (Herring & Furgerson, 2000). There is often an associated financial cost if she cannot tolerate oppressive work environments because of the correlation between earning potential and traditionally male-dominated occupations. Lesbian families also face challenges because women tend to earn lower wages (Perrone, 2005).

Since identity development is a lifelong process, and women often self-identify as lesbians in adulthood, career paths may be disrupted as they invest energy in their sexual identity development (Perrone, 2005; Reynolds, 2003; Rhieneck, 2005). There are potential costs associated with both remaining closeted and coming out in the work environment (Degges-White & Shoffner, 2002). Coming out may have a considerable impact on academic or career advancement, depending on the work environment (Green, 2000). For some, these effects may take the form of direct discrimination; for others, the impact is more subtle.

In the last several decades, the concepts of personal meaning and passion, integration of career and life planning, and a whole-being approach to career planning have dominated the career development literature (Collin & Young, 2000). Fear of discrimination may leave a woman feeling constrained to hide her authentic self from colleagues and employers. The internal conflict that results may impede healthy career development. This conflict may also be a barrier to participation in career counselling processes. Lesbian couples who remain closeted while navigating dual careers face even greater challenges (Fassinger & Richie, 1996; Herring & Furgerson, 2000). Career counsellors should familiarize themselves with professional networks, legal statutes, and resources supportive of lesbian clients as well as the careers in which active discrimination is most prevalent. Chung (2003) provided an excellent summary of the key themes emergent in the career development literature as they relate to competent practice with lesbian, gay, and bisexual individuals.

Lesbian Youth

The needs of lesbian youth are often marginalized, both generally in society and in the adult-oriented lesbian community. Counsellors also tend to view lesbianism as an adult phenomenon and are encouraged to pay more attention to the particular needs of girls and young women (APA, 1998; Barret & Logan, 2002). The establishment of personal identity or self has traditionally been associated with the developmental tasks of adolescence and early adulthood. For young lesbians, the task of coming out adds a new dimension to the developmental process as they establish a sense of self as different from peers and available role models. Lesbian youth often have to deal with these issues on their own because of their social isolation, their physical and financial dependence on parents, and the lack of appropriate supports and services (Barret & Logan, 2002; Bernal & Coolhart, 2005; Monier & Lewis, 2000).

There is some evidence that young people are becoming increasingly open and accepting of a wide range of sexual experiences and identities. There are many young lesbians who are self-confident, have high self-esteem, and find a supportive network of friends (Savin-Williams, 2005a). It is important, therefore, not to assume that all adolescent girls with sexual attractions to other girls will face crises. However, as in real estate, it's all about location! Adolescents still have even fewer places to safely explore their sexual orientation than adult women do. Those living in more conservative environments are more at risk. The collective culture in schools and communities often assumes that students are all heterosexual. There are few positive portrayals of alternative identities, and many lesbian youth feel pressured to hide their identities (Herring & Furgerson, 2000). The statistics on abuse and violence towards gay and lesbian youth within their families, peer groups, and school settings affirm the vulnerability that results from their invisibility and lack of support (Dworkin & Yi, 2003).

External pressures give rise to minority stress (Balsam & Szymanski, 2005; Savin-Williams, 2006), which may result in periods of depression, confusion, and anxiety, connected in many cases to a fear of exposure (Dworkin & Yi, 2003) or drug use, promiscuity, and other self-abusive behaviours to cope with the internal conflict or mask their homosexuality (Barret & Logan, 2002; Bridget, 2000; Monier & Lewis, 2000). Lesbian and gay youth are two to six times more likely to attempt suicide, with those who are isolated or homeless at highest risk (Bridget, 2000). Sexual minority youth of colour are at particularly high risk (Barret & Logan, 2002).

Lesbian youth cannot be expected to have developed the coping resources required to effectively confront societal prejudices (Monier & Lewis, 2000). School counsellors have a particularly important role to play, both in providing a safe environment for lesbian youth to explore issues of sexuality and in promoting a social context within school that is gay-friendly. Fostering development of solid sexual identity, self-esteem, positive internalized affirmations, and an ability to identify supportive resources in the midst of a hostile environment have been identified as essential to support youth through the coming-out process (Bernal & Coolhart, 2005).

Older Lesbians

Counsellors must also take into account the unique experience of older lesbians who may be less likely to define themselves personally or socially as lesbian and may be more at risk of having their experience marginalized by family, friends, or social systems (APA, 1998). Many of these individuals have endured times of much greater intolerance, stigma, and persecution (Reid, 1995; Shenk & Fullmer, 1996). The disproportionate level of alcohol abuse among older lesbians likely reflects a cohort effect from a generation when gay bars were the only point of social connection available to lesbians (Falco, 1996). Some older lesbians have also created a women-centred lifestyle in the absence of either personal or interpersonal identification as lesbian, which may increase their vulnerability and marginalization as they age and their affairs are managed by family or social services (Shenk & Fullmer, 1996). Reid (1995) also noted, however, that many older lesbians are less troubled by the pressures of life. They have acquired many strengths and coping resources.

Celebrating Being Lesbian

Even gay-affirmative counsellors are at a risk of focusing too heavily on the stressors associated with being lesbian in a heterosexual world and forgetting to balance these with the many positive features of lesbianism. Riggle and colleagues (2008), who claimed to have done one of the first comprehensive studies on the positive aspects of the lives of gay men and lesbians, noted that being lesbian often brings with it many of the benefits of non-dominant status, including a sense of culture and community, potential for a strong network of social support, and a sense of unique identity. Lesbians are also often committed to social justice and take active roles in their community to promote change (Riggle et al., 2008). The mock recruitment advertisement in Figure 4 highlights some of these features. It reflects a common myth that exposure to lesbians can result in others choosing this lifestyle; it also points out elements of our cultural experience that are treasured by many.

Women Seeking Women

Are you feeling stuck in traditional feminine roles, tired of struggling with your body image, worrying about birth control, or feeling dissatisfied with your sexual relationships? Do you wish you could freely choose a look that fits for you – sensible shoes and comfortable clothes, or lipstick and fancy footwear? Would you enjoy creating an innovative family structure and defining your roles based on talents, preferences, or skills? Do you long for the freedom to be yourself and to define yourself on your own terms?

The Lesbian Recruitment Force is the place for you! You may select from a wide range of diverse roles, participate in activities that highlight your strengths and preferences, and select whatever terms you wish to define yourself.

Call 1-800-les-be-in today!

Figure 4. Women seeking women.

One of the foundations of gay-affirmative therapy is the strengths-based approach (Crisp, 2006). The experience of confronting homophobia and actively defining one's sexuality often leads to the development of many strengths that can be capitalized on to face other life challenges: self-awareness, personal insight, strong sense of personal identity, authenticity, empowerment, resiliency, resourcefulness, and so on (Eubanks-Carter et al., 2005; Riggle et al., 2008). Lesbians' chosen family members are often strong and consistent sources of social support (Malley & Tasker, 2007; Riggle et al., 2008) and may in fact form a strong buffer in times of crisis or life transition.

Principles and Strategies for Working with Lesbian Clients

The current literature focuses little attention on the development of specific theoretical and practice models for use with lesbian clients. Instead, the focus is on identifying potential common stressors as well as on the strengths or assets that the client may bring to the counselling process. However, it is important not to assume that you can simply generalize existing counselling principles and strategies to effectively work with lesbian clients (Eubanks-Carter et al., 2005). A notable exception is feminist therapy, explored more fully by Lalande and Laverty in Chapter 14, which specifically addresses issues of oppression and social justice (Szymanski, 2005). Most writers agree that the foundation of gay-affirmative therapy rests in: (a) the beliefs and attitudes of the practitioner, specifically a positive and accepting view of homosexuality; (b) understanding of the issues and challenges commonly faced by lesbian and gay clients; and (c) principles for gay-affirmative practice (Crisp, 2006; Davison, 2005; Eubanks-Carter et al., 2005). These elements closely parallel the model of culture-infused counselling from Chapter 3, which highlights self-awareness, awareness of others, and development of a culturally sensitive working alliance as foundational competencies. The purpose of this section is to provide counsellors with some basic principles and strategies for counselling lesbians, organized according to the three core domains of culture-infused counselling competency, and to apply general culture-infused counselling competencies to specific practice with lesbian clients.

A. Self-Awareness

1. **Begin from the premise that lesbianism is a healthy, normal form** of love and sexuality. This is the foundation of gay-affirmative therapy (Crisp, 2006). The way in which practitioners look at a problem has a significant effect on how it comes to be understood in the therapeutic context. Homosexuality does not represent sexual deviance, development foreclosure, psychopathology, or sin! It is very important that counsellors explore the subtle influences of a pathological view of homosexuality on their view of clients and client problems (Eubanks-Carter et al., 2005).

   This is a fundamental point of departure for counselling lesbians, and it forms the foundation for each of the principles to follow. Women who love women lead healthy, productive, fulfilling lives. These women also face normal stressors and developmental challenges that may lead them to seek the services of counsellors and psychologists. If this is the lens that you bring to your assessment and intervention, then you are well positioned to facilitate health and growth in your LGBT clients. The focus must be on "the problems that homosexual individuals have rather than on the so-called problem of homosexuality" (Davison, 2005, p. 25). The absence of homophobia does not make for gay-affirmative therapy; it is defined by an active stance of validation, advocacy, and celebration of lesbian identity and experience (Crisp, 2006).

2. **Reflect on your own process of identity development and the various factors that have impacted your sexuality**. Self-awareness and, in particular, comfort with one's own sexual identity are critical to building an effective relationship with lesbian clients (Bringaze & White, 2001; Herring & Furgerson, 2000; Kocarek & Pelling, 2003). This may mean honest exploration of your own same-sex feelings and experiences. Or, it may involve actively exploring your heterosexual identity, perhaps for the first time. Writers in the area of multicultural counselling have developed models for White racial identity development, arguing that a specific process is required for counsellors to move from the point of being oblivious of their own inherent racism to the point of non-racist identity (McDougall & Arthur, 2001). Although little research has been done in this area, the same conceptual framework may be applied to heterosexual identity development. Heterosexual identity is often assumed, and counsellors spend little time reflecting on and exploring their own identity development. As a result, they may be unaware of their inherent heterosexist bias. Left unexamined, these factors may impact how you define what is *healthy* or *normal* (Arredondo et al., 1996).

3. **Recognize the inherent heteronormative biases in psychological theory and practice.** Although the professions of counselling and psychology have now taken an active stance in affirming the importance of a positive, strength-based approach to counselling lesbians, theory and practice remain embedded in a cultural context that is still biased and oppressive (Malley & Tasker, 2007) and heterosexism is still evident in research, education, and professional practice (Savage, Harley, & Nowak, 2005). It is important for counsellors to actively examine their own theoretical model for sexist, heterosexist, or androcentric biases.

4. **Pay attention to your own internalized homophobia and subtle tendencies to view heterosexuality as the norm.** Multicultural competence begins with awareness of your cultural values and biases (Arredondo et al., 1996). The Canadian Psychological Association's (2000) *Code of Ethics for Psychologists* points out the necessity of self-reflection on factors such as personal attitudes, worldview, life experience, and cultural background as a foundation for responsible caring. Due to the invisibility of the lesbian community, many heterosexual counsellors may have had little direct exposure to lesbians and may hold stereotypic or negative perspectives (Fassinger & Richie, 1996). There may also be a tendency to assume that all clients are heterosexual (Eubanks-Carter et al., 2005) rather than querying sexual orientation as a normal part of the assessment process. Subtle expressions of homophobia may emerge in counsellor attitudes towards parenting, intimacy, or other aspects of lesbian experience (Eubanks-Carter et al., 2005). Counsellors may also be inclined to overemphasize or minimize the role of sexual orientation in client presenting concerns (Crisp, 2006).

It is unlikely that any counsellor, gay or straight, is completely free of the influence of heterosexism and homophobia; however, the impact is reduced through thoughtful self-examination (Barret & Logan, 2002; Bridges et al., 2003; Fassinger, 1991; Reynolds, 2003). Understanding the prevalence of heterosexism and homophobia in Canadian society may assist you in identifying your own tendencies towards heteronormality. It is important to examine and minimize the effects of power differences and perceived privilege. You might also engage in a critical examination of how you may have benefited from institutional or cultural homophobia (Arredondo et al., 1996). To build an effective working alliance with lesbian clients, it is essential that counsellors deal with their own biases and move to a positive and affirmative stance on homosexuality (Eubanks-Carter et al., 2005).

5. **Engage in an honest self-appraisal of your competence to effectively counsel lesbian clients.** Your lesbian client deserves to work with someone who genuinely respects and values her experience. If you are not currently competent to counsel lesbian clients, find ways to increase your level of competence. Where knowledge or attitudes form a potential barrier, consultation, training, or referral may be indicated (APA, 1998; Arredondo et al., 1996). One of the ways in which heterosexism is displayed in counselling is in the unwillingness of the counsellor to refer lesbian clients to more gay-affirming resources (Fassinger & Richie, 1996). The most significant factor associated with positive attitudes towards lesbians is personal exposure, so invest in developing relationships with lesbians outside of the counselling environment. These relationships will also counter the tendency to generalize from your experience with lesbians in therapy to beliefs about all lesbians (Bernstein, 2000).

6. **Take active steps to ensure your continued competence in dealing with lesbian clients.** A common theme among non-dominant populations is frustration with educating the dominant culture about their particular worldview, experiences, values, and needs. While some embrace opportunities to impact the world around us by increasing the visibility of lesbian culture, you must remember that it is your responsibility to seek out learning opportunities; it is not appropriate to look to your client to educate you about the common experiences of lesbians in this culture. Take time to become more competent in addressing her needs through continuing education, training, supervision, and consultation (APA, 1998).

B. Awareness of the Experiences and Contexts of Lesbians

7. **Recognize that social, economic, and political factors are often at the root of client presenting concerns.** The feminist therapy principle of *the personal is political* is an important starting point for work with all lesbian clients (Szymanski, 2005). Your client has likely experienced a wide range of both subtle and overt forms of homophobia over her lifetime and continues to live out her day-to-day life in a world created and maintained by heterosexual norms. It is your responsibility to increase your own awareness of these systemic barriers to health and well-being and to ensure that they form a backdrop for your understanding of the issues she brings to the counselling process.

8. **Review the literature related to common presenting concerns among lesbian clients.** Competent counsellors take steps to familiarize themselves with the current literature related to counselling issues with

particular populations (Arredondo et. al., 1996; Eubanks-Carter et al., 2005). There is a growing body of literature that provides insight into some of the common presenting concerns of lesbian clients. Because clients often present with vague descriptions of the problem and may be reticent to openly discuss sexual orientation, counsellors must pay careful attention to integrating awareness of sexuality orientation and the associated experiences of lesbians into case conceptualization (Eubanks-Carter et al., 2005).

It is important to also become familiar with the literature on the psychology of women. Gender identity distinguishes developmental processes, presenting concerns, and appropriate counselling processes from those of homosexual men (Szymanski, 2005). Many of the issues faced by your lesbian client will mirror those of heterosexual women, but may be further exacerbated by the dual experience of sexism and heterosexism (Barret & Logan, 2002). The incidence of childhood abuse, rape, eating disorders, alcoholism, and other problems is similar to that of heterosexual women (Falco, 1996). What may differ are the risk factors that contribute to particular disorders. For example, while depression in heterosexual women may be associated with marriage, childrearing, and isolation, lesbians are more likely to struggle with a lack of social support or the impact of social oppression and discrimination.

9. **Recognize and respect the diversity of lesbian experience and self-expression**. As noted in the early chapters of this book, counsellors are expected to take active steps to understand the cultural background and worldview of their clients. Lesbians exist in all social classes, age ranges, cultural groups, and local communities in Canada. The invisibility of the lesbian population occurs in part because of social oppression and in part because of the wide diversity of expression of sexual identity and lesbian lifestyles (Barret & Logan, 2002; Fassinger, 1991; Reynolds, 2003). Be careful not to assume stereotypic behaviours or beliefs based on group affiliation because you may mask the individual uniqueness of your client.

10. **Attend to the impact of heterosexism, homophobia, and heteronormality**. It is important to assess your particular client's experience of various forms of victimization (Barret & Logan, 2002). You may also need to educate your client about her basic human rights as well as the specific social, political, and legal factors that may facilitate or impinge on those rights. The problems your client brings to counselling will often reflect the impact of social prejudice and discrimination (APA, 1998; Falco, 1996). Szymanski (2005) argues for an "integrated analysis of oppression" (p. 78) that focuses not only on gender and sexuality, but also on the impact of racism, ableism, or ageism, since your client may, over her lifetime, experience multiple forms of oppression that interact with each other (Bridges et al., 2003; Israel & Selvidge, 2003). Pay particular attention to the impact of socio-political factors on self-esteem and self-concept (Reynolds, 2003). Your client may have experienced rejection by family, friends, or religious, social, or cultural institutions. She may also need the space and freedom to grieve the loss of heterosexuality and the privileges that it affords (Arnold et al., 2002). This may be especially true during transitional phases in her identity development.

11. **Attend to the effects of internalized homophobia**. Many clients come to counselling having internalized the stigma, stereotypes, and negative assessments of lesbians prevalent in society (Szymanski, 2005). Shame and guilt often accompany expressions of lesbian identity, behaviour, and affiliation. In the absence of positive role models, your client may have a difficult time establishing a positive self-appraisal. It is your job to create an environment in which she can discuss her experiences without fear and shame. To do so, you must have a clear understanding of the complexity of identity development in a socially oppressive context.

Guilt and shame may even lead a client to express a desire to change sexual orientation. The problem lies in homophobia, not in sexual orientation (Crisp, 2006). It should be no surprise to counsellors that clients may experience dissonance, distress, and self-rejection in the face of social stigmatization and oppression, much of which becomes internalized over time. If common issues related to coming out are misinterpreted as pathology, you may inappropriately engage in gay-aversive strategies when a client is actually seeking and needing acceptance and support (Fassinger & Richie, 1996; McCann, 2001). Be prepared to recognize internalized homophobia and support her in reconstructing a sense of self that values her sexual expression (Crisp, 2006).

C. Development of a Gay-Affirmative Working Alliance

12. **Establish an inclusive physical and psychological environment.** Barret and Logan (2002) pointed to the importance of creating space for lesbian clients to feel both visible and affirmed. Take a look around your office space to see if images of gay and lesbian lifestyle are included. Do you have lesbian magazines in your waiting area? Do the posters on the walls reflect alternative lifestyles? Are the forms you use inclusive of same-sex relationships? Do you regularly include sexual orientation as part of initial assessment? Is gay-positive referral information visible (Herring & Furgerson, 2000)? Arredondo and colleagues (1996) also pointed to the importance of organizational cultural competence. The creation of an inclusive environment should extend to all levels of personnel, from support staff, who have direct or indirect contact with clients, through to board members, who establish policy. Counsellors who opt for silence in the face of sexist and homophobic remarks, images, practices, or policies reinforce the status quo.

13. **Pay attention to language.** It may not be obvious that you are working with a lesbian, which makes it even more important to attend to the language you use with all clients (Israel & Selvidge, 2003). Counsellor communication style and use of language can have a direct impact on the counselling relationship (Arredondo et al., 1996; Barret & Logan, 2002). Dorland and Fischer (2001) noted that heterosexist bias in language leads to decreased counsellor credibility, less willingness to return to counselling, and reticence to disclose personal information, particularly sexual orientation. It is also important to attend to the specific language used by lesbians of various ethnic groups and to select terms that are appropriate for the particular client (Bridges et al., 2003).

    Language is a powerful vehicle for self-identification and empowerment. One of the ways in which the lesbian community is reclaiming power is by adopting some of the language originally created as derogatory by the dominant culture. Such terms as *dyke* and *queer* are commonly used in affirmative self-labelling (Bernal & Coolhart, 2005). However, some terms may not be seen as positive when used outside of the lesbian community. As a general rule of thumb, you should create space for your lesbian client to use her own cultural expressions, but you should not use these terms yourself unless given permission by your client (Hays, 2001).

14. **Build an egalitarian relationship where power differences are minimized.** Although this general principle was discussed in the discussion of a culturally sensitive working alliance in Chapter 5, we are emphasizing it here as a central principle in feminist and gay-affirmative counselling. Your client is likely familiar with disempowerment and marginalization, and building a trusting relationship will depend in large part on your ability to foster her empowerment (Szymanski, 2005). Power must be openly and actively addressed in the therapeutic context to both understand and reduce the impact of inherent power differences (Reynolds & Constantine, 2004).

15. **Pay particular attention to issues of confidentiality, respecting your client's right to privacy in terms of her sexual identity.** Have you ever made a comment to a colleague about your *lesbian client* without thinking through the implications of the statement? Was the fact that she is lesbian salient to the issue you were consulting about or commenting on? Have you sought permission from your client to out her in this way? Counsellors must create a safe environment for their clients to disclose issues of sexual identity and provide assurance that such disclosures will be treated with respect and confidentiality (Fassinger, 1991). At the same time, it is important not to treat homosexual identity as a secret that carries with it a sense of shame (Bridges et al., 2003).

16. **Be aware of the factors that impact lesbian identity development.** There is no lockstep pattern of identity development, nor is there a clear final destination that applies equally well to all. Awareness of the various models of lesbian identity development, as well as women's development literature, will provide insight into the range of factors that may impact the process (Barret & Logan, 2002; Fassinger, 1991; Reynolds,

2003). Your client may wonder whether a lesbian orientation fits for her, whether she is comfortable with it, and whether she has enough knowledge about it. An important function for you is to normalize her same-sex feelings (Bringaze & White, 2001). She may not currently experience the level of congruence she desires between the various facets of her sexual identity. What is important is the meaning she attaches to the incongruence, the personal value placed on integration, and the factors that contribute to her current identity development (Falco, 1996). Take, for example, a woman who for a number of reasons decides to stay in a heterosexual marriage while identifying as lesbian and engaging in sexual relationships with women. She may find a place of subjective satisfaction in spite of an objective discrepancy between the labels she applies to herself, her sexual behaviour, and her affective and sexual affiliations. Since context plays such a critical role, she may be unable to find a more effective balance of all of the competing pressures. You must be prepared to support fluidity, idiosyncratic self-definition, and the maintenance of multiple identities in diverse contexts.

17. **Pay attention to gender identity in developmental processes.** Your client may also struggle with gender identity issues as she strives to redefine herself in reference to women rather than to men. Lesbians as a group tend to be more balanced in terms of masculine and feminine qualities than heterosexual women (Falco, 1996). However, your client may require support in defining her own gender identity. When she has her first same-sex relationship or sexual encounter, she may have questions about expected roles and behaviours or about the norms within a particular lesbian community. The basic principle that operates here is the right of every woman – straight, lesbian, bisexual, or asexual – to self-determination. Take care not to assume that you automatically understand what a woman means when she identifies as lesbian or when she describes her unique identity development process.

18. **Support clients in their coming-out process.** At some point, your client may struggle with whom she should come out to. Who will be first? What losses will she have to bear? She may also need to explore the costs of remaining closeted; for example, being treated as an individual rather than as a couple, living with secrecy, and lacking identity congruence. There is a natural tendency for the human mind to associate negative judgments with secrets or hidden aspects of the self. She may need your support to reframe nondisclosure as a positive, active coping strategy. Choosing the right time for disclosure is sometimes challenging. What are her motivators for coming out? What choices has her partner made about coming out? These are complex choices that are highly individualized (Falco, 1996). In a world where there are real risks to disclosure, personal identity integration may occur without coming out in all areas of one's life. Your role is to help your client develop strategies for coping effectively with these choices. While the types of strategies may change over time, the need for such strategies will follow her throughout her identity development process (Whitman et al., 2000).

Coming out to her family of origin may be of particular concern to your client (APA, 1998). Is she financially dependent on her family? If her culturally distinct family has functioned to protect her from a hostile or prejudicial world, is the potential loss of this support too much to risk (Greene, 1997)? Help her put appropriate supports and resources in place before she talks to her family and consider rehearsing the scene in advance. Prepare her for the possibility of reactions of shock, denial, or guilt and encourage her to allow time for them to digest the information and incorporate it into their view of her. Recognize also that not coming out to family may be an equally valid and healthy choice for her (Green, 2000).

19. **Take care not to assume that all lesbian clients will present with struggles related to identity development or that the fact that your client is lesbian necessarily has a bearing on the presenting concern.** Because of their lack of exposure to or ease in dealing with lesbian clients, heterosexual counsellors may either dismiss sexual orientation as a significant factor or magnify its importance in relation to the particular presenting concern (Crisp, 2006; Herring & Furgerson, 2000; Palma & Stanley, 2002). Working with lesbian clients involves putting aside assumptions about the salience of lesbian identity to a particular client in a particular situation (Eubanks-Carter et al., 2005) and recognizing the multiple identities of clients and the fluidity of identity salience across time and across contexts (Bridges et al., 2003; Hays, 2001). So, for example, while her lesbian identity may be a significant factor in the breakdown of

relationships with her family of origin, it may be of little relevance to your client's struggle to find meaningful work. A key question may be "What does your identity as a lesbian mean to you in this context?" It is important to support her in identifying such person-specific and context-specific meanings and to not assume that being lesbian is of relevance to a particular presenting concern.

20. **Be prepared to assist lesbians in developing healthy relational patterns where few non-gendered and non-heterosexist role models exist.** As with all human beings, the nature and quality of your client's intimate relationships have a tremendous impact on her emotional and psychological well-being. It is your responsibility to understand and take seriously the importance of these relationships (APA, 1998). She has an opportunity to be creative and to define her relationships without reference to the constraints of normative roles (Barret & Logan, 2002). However, she may find it very difficult to define herself in this relative vacuum and may look to you for support in this process.

21. **Be conscious of the multiple identities of lesbian clients and the unique challenges of dual or triple non-dominant status.** Other cultural factors (ethnicity, ability, socio-economic status, rural versus urban setting, etc.) may interact with lesbian identity and may function as more salient components of identity at any particular time (Bridges et al., 2003; Reynolds, 2003). If your client belongs to additional non-dominant groups, she may face the challenge of balancing multiple and often conflicting cultural norms, values, and beliefs and may find herself more isolated and lacking in social support (APA, 1998; Barret & Logan, 2002). Attending to the complexity of primary and extended family relationships is of particular importance in working with lesbians of colour (Bridges et al., 2003). There is considerable stress associated with managing multiple identities. Lesbian clients are often required to acknowledge one component of themselves over others in particular contexts. As a member of a visible non-dominant group, she may have developed a strong sense of cultural identity and may fear rejection and ostracism if she identifies as lesbian (Barret & Logan, 2002). Lesbians with physical, sensory, or cognitive/emotional disabilities may also face unique challenges (APA, 1998).

22. **Attend to the impact of negative messages and unmet needs in the area of spirituality.** Many lesbians have lasting effects from both internalized messages about the *sinfulness* of their identity and the rejection they experience in traditional religious contexts (Reynolds, 2003). Some may also have experienced harmful interventions in the form of *conversion* therapies that leave them with additional trauma to be overcome in the counselling process. It is important to recognize the spiritual needs your client may bring to counselling and to explore resources and processes for addressing those needs (Bridges et al., 2003). Finding a way to integrate lesbian identity with spiritual/religious beliefs may form an important aspect of the therapeutic process (Eubanks-Carter et al., 2005).

23. **Critically evaluate assessment and intervention strategies for their implicit values and assumptions.** Be sure that your counselling processes are gay-affirming. Counselling is both culture-bound and class-bound (Arredondo et al., 1996). Everything we do reflects implicit and often unexamined values. If you intend to work with lesbian clients, you should carefully examine all elements of the counselling process for both sexist and heterosexist biases. You will either take active steps to develop a gay-affirmative stance or, by default, fall into practices that passively or actively endorse social stigmatization (Fassinger, 1991). This default position may be evident in the wording of assessment instruments or in the assumptions underlying particular intervention strategies. While efforts have been made to address bias in assessment instruments with ethnically diverse clientele, little attention has been paid at this point to heterosexist bias (Chung, 2003). The lack of specific gay-friendly strategies and techniques leaves you to adapt existing models. Carefully examine your tools and procedures for assumptions of heterosexuality (Arnold et al., 2002). Choose your questions carefully to avoid subtle inferences that heterosexuality is the norm (Hays, 2001). Your assessment should include an exploration of the unique strengths and coping strategies that your client has likely developed on her journey towards a women-centred identity (Crisp, 2006). She may present with determination, independence, a sense of confidence in her own knowledge of self, and other assets that can be capitalized on in the counselling process.

24. **Expand intervention strategies beyond the individual to incorporate relational, systemic, and environmental factors and processes.** Part of your challenge in working with lesbian clients will be to expand your repertoire of assessment and intervention strategies to attend to factors beyond the individual, intrapsychic world of your client (Arredondo et al., 1996; Fassinger, 1991; Fassinger & Richie, 1996). The key is that the interventions play a deliberate and active role in counteracting the effects of discrimination and social stigmatization (Fassinger, 1991). Because of the isolation she may experience, psychoeducational and group approaches that link her with other lesbians may be particularly useful (Fassinger & Richie, 1996; Herring & Furgerson, 2000). Group work may decrease her sense of alienation, provide contact with positive role models, and normalize feelings and experiences (Arnold et al., 2002). Be aware of heterosexual bias or overt homophobic attitudes within community service agencies or other referral sources. Take responsibility to make careful referrals. In some cases, you may have to intervene on behalf of your client at the institutional level.

25. **Take an active stance in combating individual, social, and institutionalized oppression and become an agent for social change.** Both American and Canadian codes of ethics remain weak in the areas of advocacy and social activism (Carroll, Gilroy, & Murra, 2000). One exception is the *Feminist Therapy Code of Ethics,* which moves beyond a non-discrimination mandate to a call for explicit social action (Feminist Therapy Institute, 1999).

For many oppressed groups, engagement in social and political change processes can provide both a sense of group solidarity and a feeling of empowerment. Supporting your client in engaging in activist groups and taking a role yourself in advocating for social change models ways for her to combat disempowerment and social oppression (Barret & Logan, 2002; Israel & Selvidge, 2003; Reynolds, 2003). Fear of stigmatization keeps some counsellors from engaging in social action (Carroll et al., 2000). There may also be actual costs to an openly gay-affirming professional stance. However, until counsellors, psychologists, and other health professionals take an active role in social change, they will continue to contribute to heterosexist and homophobic norms (Reynolds, 2003). Social action may be as simple as providing in-service training to colleagues or expanding the literature on counselling lesbians by reporting case studies or group work (Herring & Furgerson, 2000).

Take an active stance in educating supervisees, colleagues, administrators, and others about the impact of social oppression on lesbians and other non-dominant groups (Bridges et al., 2003). Counsellor educators hold a particular responsibility for training new practitioners to be sensitive and responsive to the needs of lesbian clients, especially given the evidence that without specific training most maintain a strong heterosexist bias (Arnold et al., 2002).

26. **Assist clients in building social support networks.** Create a resource bank to link lesbian clients to the local community. Local feminist or lesbian communities can provide a valuable support base for clients, especially those who are feeling disempowered and disenfranchised (Barret & Logan, 2002; Falco, 1996). Your client may have spent many years hiding her self-identity and, as a result, may have broken ties with earlier support systems or failed to build new ones. Bringaze and White (2001), in their study of factors that facilitate lesbian identity development, found that association with other lesbians was the primary source of support. Your client may also have had little exposure to role models, cultural symbols, or images that reflect her emergent sense of self. Falco (1996) pointed out that "in schooling, in television, in history, in the arts, in printed sources, and in everyday culture, the absence of lesbian references is resounding, and quite consequential" (p. 402). Seek out available resources in the community, online, or within your own organization to connect clients with lesbian support groups, organizations, and other service providers (Barret & Logan, 2002; Bringaze & White, 2001; Fassinger & Richie, 1996; Herring & Furgerson, 2000).

Unique Issues for Lesbian Counsellors

Lesbian counsellors face a particular set of issues in their practice, which leads to two additional principles.

27. **Develop strategies to set boundaries with clients and maintain your own social freedom and privacy**. Lesbian counsellors often do not have the "boundary luxury of privacy and anonymity" assumed by heterosexual counsellors (Pearlman, 1996, p. 75). The smallness of the lesbian community often leads to encounters with clients in social situations. Clients and counsellors often have common social connections. Explore the potential zones of overlap with your client, establish a protocol for potential social encounters, and develop strategies for managing them (Barret & Logan, 2002; Fassinger, 1991). These strategies should include means for both protecting the client's privacy and respecting your boundaries.

28. **Use opportunities to come out to clients as a way to model healthy functioning and create safety for clients to explore their own identity issues**. Little attention is given in the literature or in counsellor training programs to the issue of counsellor identification as heterosexual. The lesbian counsellor, however, often finds herself addressing the question of disclosure in a more proactive fashion. Pearlman (1996) described some of the complexities of introducing her own sexual identity into the client-counsellor relationship. Your client will make her own assumptions about your sexuality based on the physical and psychological environment you create and the inclusiveness of your counselling style. You may also choose to explicitly self-identify in all encounters or to selectively come out to clients. A fundamental principle of self-disclosure is to base your judgments about degree and timing of disclosure on the therapeutic value to the client.

Counsellors who are public about their sexual orientation function as positive role models and open the door for peer consultation and professional education. They are sought out by members of the lesbian community, as well as by women who are exploring sexual identity. For a lesbian client, the advantages in working with a lesbian counsellor include both a depth of identification with lived experience and the possibility of role modelling and instillation of hope (Pearlman, 1996). It cannot be assumed, however, that all lesbians will want to see a lesbian counsellor. In fact, level of awareness and sensitivity to sexuality orientation is a stronger determinant of client satisfaction (Eubanks-Carter et al., 2005). A lesbian may also actively seek out a heterosexual counsellor based on issues of confidentiality within the lesbian community or her own comfort with her identity (Bernstein, 2000). Gay-affirmative heterosexual counsellors work effectively with lesbian clients.

Case Study

The following case study illustrates how to incorporate the principles outlined above into your daily interactions with your clients. We have chosen to highlight domestic violence because it can be a neglected area in training. Reference is provided to the numbered principles from the previous section.

You have been counselling Ann, a 37-year-old professional woman who is well-known in the community, for a month. She has had many ups and downs in her life (e.g., her marriage breakup several years ago and a major career change). She has two children, now 11 and 13. Lately she's been complaining of feeling on edge, jumpy, and tired. In the past, she has indicated that there is a lot of stress in her job. Today she tentatively implies that she has been in a relationship for two years and it's not going well. Rather than naming her partner, she uses non-gendered pronouns. When you recommend some family resources, she becomes anxious and minimizes the problems. You normalize that some relationships have differences that are hard to explain to others. Sometimes it's the form of the relationship, such as the couple both being of the same gender, or sometimes it's the type of problem in the relationship, such as a sexual issue (Principle #1). You make a mental note to ensure that your counselling facility echoes your accepting beliefs with visible posters, pamphlets, and non-gendered, non-heterosexist information and forms (#12). You also reevaluate how to be gay-affirming and welcoming in your practice and your space (#23). Perhaps Ann's hesitancy means that your personal values are not as transparent as you think.

Ann takes a breath and then discloses that her relationship is with a woman, the first relationship of this kind for her. You tell her that you realize that telling you this must be difficult for her. You let her know that you are prepared to work with women who are in relationships with women and explain your experience and knowledge in this area. You reinforce that she is the expert in her own experiences but that together you might be able to find new ways to look at what is happening for her (#14). You try to use the terms or language that Ann uses to describe her lifestyle and relationship. When you are unsure, you ask her what term she uses for herself, her partner, and her relationship (#13). You tell Ann about the struggles that many people go through as they make sense of their sexual identity (#11). If appropriate, you may share some of your own process and the impact of your own identity development on your relationships with others (#2).

You invite Ann to explore what she means when she says things aren't going very well with her partner. In the background, you constantly monitor any homophobic and heterosexist beliefs or attitudes you may have about relationships (#4). You feel relatively confident because you are current with the latest literature and training about counselling lesbians (#8). Ann reveals that her partner often gets very angry and responds by calling her names, swearing, and throwing things. You ask her for further details regarding this abusive behaviour, carefully assessing the risk to Ann and her children. You evaluate your competency to deal with same-sex domestic violence and are prepared to refer Ann elsewhere or to seek consultation if necessary (#5).

When the session is over, you look for various ways to update your competency regarding same-sex domestic violence (workshops, reading, research, newsletters, and Internet contacts) (#6). You also review resources and referral sources in your community (#26). Since there are insufficient services in your community for lesbians who are in abusive relationships, you take steps to advocate for their development (#25).

Ann is very concerned that her lifestyle and orientation will become public knowledge. She is well-known in your town and worries about her reputation and job security, the reaction of her family and friends, and the safety of her children. You assure her that any information she shares with you is bound by your oath of confidentiality, explaining any limitations (#15). She wonders why these things are happening to her this late in life. She thought she had her life figured out, and then she fell in love with a woman. She questions whether all lesbian relationships are like this. You reassure her that all relationships are complex and let her know that many women begin a same-sex relationship later in life (#16). However, you firmly establish with her that healthy lesbian relationships do not involve domestic violence and express your belief that abuse is unacceptable behaviour in any relationship. Ann recognizes that she may have some work to do to develop healthy relationships and expresses relief that she is not responsible for her present partner abusing her (#19). You explore Ann's relationship history and determine her needs, taking care to use non-gendered assessment tools (#23).

You reflect that many individuals in our society and your community believe that same-sex relationships are wrong. You acknowledge that living in a heterosexist and homophobic world may leave Ann questioning whether she is healthy, normal, or moral (#7). You discuss the impact this has on her fears and beliefs (#10). You query Ann about what effects internalized homophobia may have on her view of her orientation and this relationship. How has it impacted her views of domestic violence? You reflect back to her some of your inferences about her beliefs, revealing some of the myths she has internalized (#11). Like many lesbians, she is surprised that two women can be involved in an abusive relationship.

You explore the impact of Ann's environment and upbringing on her identity development. Family and cultural expectations can place undue pressure on women to take on traditional roles and be locked into limiting lifestyles (#17). Ann explores parts of her life that result in multiple discrimination (#21). Ann also indicates that her partner has threatened to out her to her work, family, and friends. She is afraid to end the relationship. You facilitate exploration of the consequences of staying in the relationship, such as the impact on her children, the impact on her physical and emotional well-being, and the message that this kind of behaviour is acceptable. You reassure her of her right to choose how and when she comes out to others. You encourage her to select one or two people in her support network that she can trust to fully support her (#18). You support her in her choices, as long as they do not hamper her growth as a healthy individual. You set up a safety plan with Ann to give her options and to keep her and her children safe. You assist her in beginning steps to leave the relationship and continue her growth and healing.

Future Directions

Historically, women's identity has been externally defined, with very little possibility of active self-definition. Even the writings on homosexuality tend to be focused on gay men. As women continue to access education, increase career choices, and attain personal, economic, and political freedom, lesbian culture and the experience of identity development will continue to evolve. Since many lesbians move outside of male-defined self-images and roles, the study of lesbian sexuality, relationships, career paths, and so on may actually provide insight into the emotional and psychological development of women in general by eliminating the confounding variable of male identification and influence. Further exploration of gender differences in identity development may be an important point of departure for research.

The study of lesbian relationships may offer a lens through which to further refine the theories of women's development in relationship. As Mencher (1997) pointed out: "Contrary to the notion that these relational patterns indicate something gone awry, these patterns may indicate movement towards the fulfillment of women's preferences for relational structures which feature mutual engagement, mutual empathy, mutual empowerment, and relational authenticity" (p. 324). The fact that women's sexuality has always been defined in relation to men, for example, leaves us wanting for a definition of sexuality that relates exclusively to women. In a similar vein, Laird (2003) suggested that lesbian and gay families may offer new insights into the definition and understanding of family structures generally, but this will require abandonment of the heterosexual norm as the point of comparison.

> With their relatively fluid boundaries and varied memberships, their patterns of non-hierarchical decision-making, their innovative divisions of labor, and the relative weight given to friendship as well as blood relatedness, such families offer further challenge to the dominant notions of family structure and function, and present an opportunity for mental health professionals to assess the limitations in current definitions of family and kinship. (Laird, 2003, p. 179)

The links between the experiences of lesbians and gays as members of non-dominant populations in Canada and those of other non-dominant groups warrant further study. Further research is needed to explore differences within the lesbian population across ethnicity, class, geographic location, and so on (Laird, 2003). This research will be most effective if it approaches the lived experiences of lesbians from an intersectional perspective, exploring the complex, dynamic, and unique identities of women who manage multiple non-dominant identities (Collins, in press; Iwasaki & Ristock, 2007; Suyemoto & Liem, 2007). Experiencing multiple cultural affiliations may dramatically alter the meaning and significance of any one cultural factor to the individual (Valentine, 2007). From a postcolonial feminist perspective, "the intersections of gender, class, race, age, and other social relations are…necessary axes of analyses to explicate the complex nexus of everyday meanings and realities" (Anderson et al., 2003, p. 200).

Unlike many other non-dominant groups, lesbians are quite likely to access counselling services (Eubanks-Carter et al., 2005; Twist et al., 2006). Ironically, the likelihood of encountering lesbian clientele is not reflective of research interest in mental health issues for lesbians (Reynolds, 2003). The research that has been conducted has also tended to take a problem focus rather than emphasizing strengths, coping resources and strategies, resiliency, and protective factors (Reynolds, 2003). There is a growing body of literature that highlights the importance of training counsellors to work effectively with gay and lesbian clients, as well as the need to address the social and systemic barriers to health within the counselling context (McCann, 2001). However, little research exists on the impact of counsellor heterosexism and homophobia on therapeutic efficacy and client well-being. In addition, little research has been done on the heterosexual assumptions or biases in current counselling practices or theories, although writers are acknowledging the need for such analysis.

Chapter Summary

While many healthy, adaptive lesbians exist in Canada, many others continue to struggle against the tide of social prejudice and marginalization. Heterosexism, androcentrism, and homophobia continue to be formidable barriers to wellness. Ultimately, change in the health status of lesbians depends, to a large degree, upon social change. It is incumbent upon counsellors to be active agents of social justice.

The complex experiences of identity development and identity management are lifelong processes that are expressed in idiosyncratic and context-specific ways by each woman. Each woman will weigh relational, economic, career, familial, and other consequences each time she makes a choice to come out in the heterosexual world. She may develop very effective strategies for selective disclosure or she may choose to live out in most areas of her life.

In the counselling setting, a client may choose to address issues related to building healthy relationships with women in the absence of cultural norms or role models. She may present with concerns about domestic violence or she may want to explore how to effectively parent children with her same-sex partner. She may look for support in making career choices that allow her to express her authentic self. She may also present with concerns that have little to do with her lesbian identity. The effective counsellor will begin to work with the client from the basic premise of lesbianism as a healthy normal identity and will attend to the impact of social oppression on her view of self and her presenting concerns. The counselling process will be carefully monitored for inherent biases and will reflect active gay-affirming processes.

CHAPTER 16
FROM MADNESS TO MAINSTREAM:
COUNSELLING GAY MEN TODAY

Kevin Alderson

<table>
<tr><td colspan="3" align="center">Key Terms and Concepts</td></tr>
<tr>
<td>
• Coming out
• Conversion therapy
• Closeted
• Disclosing
• Ecological model of gay male identity
</td>
<td>
• Gay-affirmative therapy
• Gay identity
• Heterosexism
• Homonegativity
• Homophobia
</td>
<td>
• Homosexual orientation
• Internalized homophobia
• Philia
• Positive gay identity
• Sexual orientation
</td>
</tr>
</table>

Personal Introduction

It's still easier to be a Caucasian male in Canada than it is to be part of a non-dominant group. I know this is changing, but genuine acceptance for all individuals is more an ideal than a current reality. Most non-dominant groups are visible – you can't easily hide the fact that you're a woman, a person of colour, or a person who is physically or mentally challenged. You can, however, hide the fact that you're gay.

I became an expert in this, as most gay men do before they come out, so expert, in fact, that I wouldn't acknowledge to myself the deep longing that bore a hole daily into my heart, a longing that spoke of attraction and affiliation towards men. People can only deny themselves for so long before symptoms develop. My symptoms were that I had lost all passion in my life, and from this, I continued a journey that left me further and further removed from who I am. In 1985, I married a woman for whom I still hold the greatest respect. She is also the mother of our two children.

In 1992, I began losing my grip. Shockingly, I was falling in love with one of my clients and simultaneously with a student I was teaching. Both were young men. Intoxicating myself almost nightly didn't seem to change these feelings and neither did getting angry with my young son for not eating all of his dinner. Why was I so angry? All I knew was that I needed help.

My cocky psychiatrist told me at the end of our second session that he knew what was wrong with me. I laughed inside, thinking he was completely nuts. How could anyone figure me out that fast? He said I was gay, and that I had never come to accept this about myself. My heart sank and a part of me died; yet, another part of me began to rejoice.

Through the emotional highs and lows that followed during the ensuing months, I came to accept myself as a loving person, a gay person, who is still alive thanks to this psychiatrist's efforts in helping me integrate the many scattered fragments of identity.

I pray, God, that no one else will ever have to go through this. But I know many will.

Sixteen Years Later - February 9, 2009

How do I describe the feeling I have right now – part fear and anxiety, and part vulnerability that comes from being subjugated? Waiting at the Calgary airport, I realize I am fully at the mercy of an immigration officer as to whether Manuel will be let into Canada. I have been here since 1:50 pm and now it is 2:45. I feel – we feel – so helpless. We are gay, and he is a Mexican citizen, denied a work permit twice while I was with him: once because his Labour Market Opinion had expired and once because his medical report used vague language. My only prior experience with Canadian Immigration was when I arrived back in Canada after visiting another country. They were always smiling and so polite that I came to see these people as typical of my Canadian stereotype. I never knew they had another side, the side where they interrogate someone whose second language isn't English with words launched in a quick attack that would probably make even me ask, "What did you just say?" No, my image of them has changed forever. Their kindness matched with Jekyll and Hyde harshness, waiting for the flip of a coin to dictate who or what emerges. These are mostly my feelings speaking now as I ask myself, "What is happening to him? Will he be deported?"

As I sit experiencing varying degrees of purgatory, the doors swing open and before me exits the most beautiful man I have ever met. His middle name is Valentin, and in his honour, I decided to marry him on Valentine's Day.

As I type this now on Friday the 13th, I am again awestruck by the juxtapositions of life. The day Canadian and American societies most correlate with horror (and some of my feelings before coming out) with tomorrow is also the day we most associate with love (and where my heart now lies). The only scattered fragments now are the many tears that flow in every direction as I thank God for saving me. I've waited more than 30 years for this Valentine.

I observe first that characteristically the client shows a tendency to move away, hesitantly and fearfully, from a self that he is not.... It will be clear that the very expression of this fear is a part of becoming what he is. Instead of simply being a facade, as if it were himself, he is coming closer to being himself, namely a frightened person hiding behind a facade because he regards himself as too awful to be seen. (Rogers, 1961, pp. 167-168)

Introduction

For the first time in history, people with gay identities are receiving varying degrees of support around the globe. For example, in 1989, Denmark became the first country in the world to legalize same-sex domestic partnerships, offering these couples the same rights and privileges as those with opposite-sex marriages, except for the right to adopt a child who is not the biological offspring of at least one parent (Wood, n.d.). By 2001, this had extended to Norway, Sweden, and Iceland. In the same year, the Netherlands, Italy, Spain, and Israel were looking at bringing in similar legislation (Wood). These contractual and legal arrangements, however, were still not considered analogous to marriage, and partakers were placed on a separate list from heterosexual couples who became legally married.

The Netherlands took legislation and social justice a step further, however, and on April 1, 2001, became the first country in the world to offer same-sex marriage (Lahey & Alderson, 2004). Same-sex marriage provides equivalent rights and status compared to heterosexual marriage. From there, the dominos toppled as several countries and states legalized same-sex marriage (Same-Sex Marriage, 2009): Belgium (2003), the State of Massachusetts (2004), Spain (2005), Canada (the bill received royal assent and consequently became federal law on July 20, 2005), South Africa (2006), the State of Connecticut (2008), and most recently Norway (January 1, 2009). The state of California granted 18,000 same-sex marriages between June 2008 and November 2008, but voters overturned the law by requiring that the state's Constitution be rewritten to only recognize marriages between a man and a woman. Although California's Supreme Court heard arguments regarding the ban on March 5, 2009 (Cherry, 2009), the court has 90 days to rule in the case (Schwartz & McKinley, 2009). Same-sex couples living anywhere in the world can marry in Belgium and Canada, which are the only two countries offering same-sex marriages that do not have restrictions regarding nationality (Stritof & Stritof, n.d.).

Adoption rights in Canada are under provincial/territorial jurisdiction, and therefore the laws may differ by region. Reportedly, most regions in Canada allow legal adoption by same-sex couples (LGBT Adoption, 2009). Several Canadian cities have had openly gay aldermen (Spence, n.d.). The first openly gay mayor of a large North American city was Glen Murray, mayor of Winnipeg, Manitoba, between 1998 and 2004 (Glen Murray - Politician, 2009). Canada has also had a cable television station dedicated to the gay, lesbian, bisexual, and transgendered community since 2001 (OUTtv, 2008-2009; Rau, 2006).

Snapshot 1

Vignette

It certainly isn't the first time, and it won't be the last either. Most gay adolescents wouldn't dare come out in high school. If they did, could they walk hand in hand with their partner down the hallways without drawing unwelcome attention and criticism upon themselves? Could they embrace each other and show their affection in ways similar to their heterosexual counterparts? Could they attend school dances together? Could they dance once they got there?

In early May 2002, the answer at Monsignor John Pereyma Catholic High School in Oshawa, Ontario was a resounding NO. Marc Hall was 17 years old and, like other adolescents, he wanted to take his partner to his graduation. It should have been a time to celebrate. It wasn't. The Catholic School Board rejected his plea to attend the dance with his boyfriend (*Canadian Press,* 2002).

In a last-minute decision, however, an Ontario Superior Court judge granted an injunction that allowed Marc and his boyfriend to attend the prom. The school board obeyed the ruling, and on the evening of May 10, 2002, the two of them made history. The school board, however, intends to continue the court battle, which will likely end up in the Supreme Court of Canada (Smith, 2002). We live in a country that purports to respect diversity, yet a school tried to decide whom a student could or could not take to his graduation. I remember the theme slogan from my own high school graduation – *"You only pass this way once."*

Marc will remember his graduation with the dignity and respect awarded to non-gay students. He passed this way once, epitomizing incredible courage and determination to be himself – lessons to be remembered.

Queer as Folk was a popular gay sitcom. The television station Showcase reported that it was their second-highest rated show, next to the soft-core *Red Shoe Diaries,* and that it had a large heterosexual following (Underwood, 2002). Since then, many television series and films have incorporated lesbian, gay, bisexual, and/or transgendered (LGBT) characters and themes into their screenplays (List of Television Shows with LGBT Characters, 2009). These are just a few of the global changes occurring.

But don't think for a minute that gay people – men and women, children and adults – have not been affected by the prejudice and discrimination levied against them by acquaintances, employers, family, and others. Some have suffered such deleterious effects that many have contemplated and some have succumbed to suicide. This chapter is about understanding and helping gay men through counselling.

Definition of Healthy Functioning and Psychosocial Well-Being

The definition of a healthy functioning gay male that was provided in *Beyond Coming Out* (Alderson, 2000) is still appropriate:

> Individuals who have attained a **positive gay identity** have developed *a high self-regard for themselves as gay persons. They view their gay status as equal to straight status. If given a choice, they would not prefer to be straight over gay, for they have come to value their uniqueness, and the richness of life that comes from being themselves. They have integrated their gay identity with their other identities, and having accomplished this, they are* out *in most areas of their lives, wherever and whenever it is not highly disadvantageous to do so. They have largely overcome their own internalized homophobia, which frees them to fully love others of the same gender* [bold and italics added]. (p. 189)

Gay men with healthy identities are proud of who they are, and they have overcome negative emotions, such as guilt and shame for being gay, and problems, such as internalized homophobia and spiritual conflicts. Psychologically healthy gay men do not use any more defense mechanisms than psychologically healthy heterosexual men and do not have a greater likelihood of suffering from mental disorders than heterosexual men.

Healthy gay men can and do establish meaningful relationships with people who have differing sexual orientations. They can and do establish intimate relationships with other gay men. They have largely broken free of heterosexist conditioning, which allows them to become liberated in many respects, including the numerous ways in which they establish significant relationships with other people.

As suggested in the definition of *positive gay identity*, psychologically healthy gay men want to be out with as many people and in as many venues as possible. Their intent is not to flaunt their sexuality, but to feel free to express it. This requires honesty in how they live their lives. Consequently, they become, either consciously or inadvertently, role models and change agents to other gay men, gay youth, and society in general.

Cultural Identity and Relationship to the Dominant Culture

This is a time of incredible change and challenge within Canadian society. In *Future Shock*, Alvin Toffler (1970) described the stresses we were about to face in trying to cope with the changes created by rapid-fire advances in technology. The computerization of our nation has affected everyone. Within the field of counselling psychology, conducting research and providing counselling services over the Internet has become a reality.

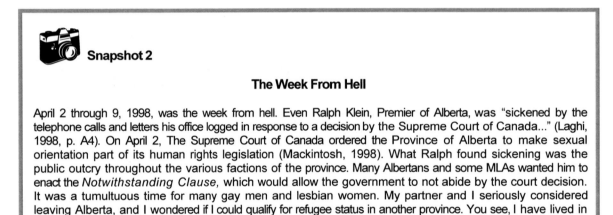

Snapshot 2

The Week From Hell

April 2 through 9, 1998, was the week from hell. Even Ralph Klein, Premier of Alberta, was "sickened by the telephone calls and letters his office logged in response to a decision by the Supreme Court of Canada..." (Laghi, 1998, p. A4). On April 2, The Supreme Court of Canada ordered the Province of Alberta to make sexual orientation part of its human rights legislation (Mackintosh, 1998). What Ralph found sickening was the public outcry throughout the various factions of the province. Many Albertans and some MLAs wanted him to enact the *Notwithstanding Clause,* which would allow the government to not abide by the court decision. It was a tumultuous time for many gay men and lesbian women. My partner and I seriously considered leaving Alberta, and I wondered if I could qualify for refugee status in another province. You see, I have lived in Alberta all of my life, and I felt I couldn't live where my basic rights were not upheld.

On April 9, the 63-member Conservative caucus voted by a two-to-one margin in favour of protecting gay rights (Chase, 1998). I was supposed to be placated, but I knew that a third of the caucus wanted to deny my rights. I still live in Alberta. Sometimes I think I must be mad. And I am mad.

Another change is occurring that follows from a Canadian ideology that respects diversity: the implementation of laws and policies aimed at protecting the rights and freedoms of the culturally diverse. One of these is the culture of gay males. Following a 1998 Supreme Court of Canada decision, the Alberta Government decided to revoke its threat to use the *Notwithstanding Clause* contained within the *Canadian Charter of Rights* against gay individuals (Laghi, 1998). If invoked, the clause would have denied gay people the right to employment and rental accommodation. The week leading up to this decision was tumultuous, as the news reported both sides of the debate, revealing that a sizable number of Albertans were deeply opposed to equal rights legislation for gay men and lesbian women (Laghi). Some American writers (Sapp, 2001; Unks, 1995) have stated that gay individuals are the most hated group in the United States. Canadian writers have not been so bold, but in 1998, it seemed clear that gay people were not a well-loved group in Alberta (Laghi). A few years later, the Alberta government was the only provincial/territorial jurisdiction that sent a legal representative to oppose same-sex marriage before the Supreme Court of Canada while the Court was preparing a reference regarding same-sex marriage after being asked to do so by the federal government (Larocque, 2006). In similar fashion to their actions in 1998, the Alberta government also threatened to use the Notwithstanding Clause to avoid recognizing same-sex marriage in Alberta (Filax, 2004).

The culture of gay males (and lesbian women, for that matter) has, for the most part, been one of secrecy. The code of silence has been honoured by virtually everyone, a tightness of lip that has made representative sampling for research purposes impossible. Consequently, gay and lesbian research has primarily been based on well-educated Caucasian samples of individuals who are relatively accepting of their homosexual orientation (Croteau, Anderson, Distefano, & Kampa-Kokesch, 2000). We still do not know the actual size of the gay population, although various representative American studies have suggested that the percentage is likely between 3% and 10% for both adults and adolescents (Frankowski, 2004; Savin-Williams, 2005b). Research done in Calgary, Alberta (Bagley & Tremblay, 1998), found that approximately 10% of the men in their sample had homosexual orientations, but because many gay men relocate to cities to live more open lives, this figure is likely inflated. We know very little about uneducated gay people, about those who have not yet come to identify as gay, and about bisexual individuals.

 **Snapshot 3**

Playing Truth or Dare

One of my friends has been out for 29 years, but his mom still doesn't know. Neither did his dad, who passed away a few years ago. He never really knew his son, and his mom probably won't either. My friend will probably never talk about the men he has loved, and his current love will be only a secret within his heart. He will diligently honour the code of silence that forever keeps his voice muted. No voice and no truth. Where does this lie end and the next one begin?

It's easy to be dishonest when society and family reward you for doing so. No one really wants to hear that you're gay. At best, they're happy for you. But how do they really feel? How do *you* really feel? What if your son was gay? Could you celebrate his joy in dating his first boyfriend? Could you hold him and tell him how much you love him? I hope you would know that he would need to hear it from you more than ever before.

You see, my friend doesn't believe his mom, or his late dad, would have loved him as he is. And what's worse, I think he may be right.

Gay men establish unique identities (Alderson, 2000); hence, there is a great deal of diversity within the gay male population. Many myths abound regarding the characteristics of gay men, and the majority of them, based on heterosexist thinking, are pejorative. For example, gay men have been described as "mentally ill, emotionally crippled, neurotic, sexually confused, promiscuous, unfulfilled, parentally fixated, unhappy, obsessed, lonely, depressed, [and] incapable of relationships" (DuBay, 1987, p. 102). They are seen as undependable, with overly strong libidos and defective genes (Hart, 1981). They are also supposedly narcissistic, shallow, overly critical of others (Beard & Glickauf-Hughes, 1994), effeminate, and overly talkative (Lee, 1977). The love of the colour green is supposedly common among gay males (Paul, 1985).

Hetrick and Martin (1984) have provided some less commonly held beliefs about gay people. For example, in the past, homosexuals were blamed for destroying civilizations, a well-respected sexologist reported that they could not *whistle,* apparently lacked body hair, caused the Second World War and the American defeat in Vietnam, were child molesters, and could not form mature nonsexual friendships with either sex. They also supposedly caused anorexia nervosa and crime in the streets (Hetrick & Martin).

Hetrick and Martin (1987) reported some frequently asked questions that were posed by homosexual youth at their gay youth outreach program in New York City:

"Does this mean I have to be a hairdresser or something like that?"
"Will I start messing around with little kids?"

"Am I going to get AIDS?"
"The Pope hates homosexuals! How can I be queer?" (p. 32)

The youth reported that they were afraid they would be found out, wanted to run away because the pressures of hiding were too much, and, perhaps most frightening, wanted to kill themselves rather than be queer.

Even gay men and lesbians are subject to believing some of these stereotypes. A study by Saghir and Robins (as cited in Dunkle & Francis, 1996) revealed that although 71% of male homosexuals and 44% of female homosexuals sampled believed they could recognize other gay people from their appearance, they were unable to distinguish pictures of homosexuals from heterosexuals beyond chance levels. A study by Dunkle and Francis (1996) revealed that both male and female undergraduates assigned higher homosexuality ratings to pictures of unattractive males and females than to their attractive counterparts, suggesting that university students are still subject to stereotyping. Bell and Weinberg (1978) conducted a large-scale study of homosexual men and women in the San Francisco Bay area that amply demonstrated that relatively few conformed to any of the stereotypes that people have of them.

The adult gay community has also suffered tremendously from homophobia and heterosexism. **Homophobia** *is the fear, dislike, or intolerance of gay individuals.* **Heterosexism,** on the other hand, refers to *the many ways in which individuals in our society consciously or unconsciously minimize gay people, either by assuming that they don't exist or by projecting a belief that they are somehow inferior to their heterosexual counterparts.*

Many adults do not come out until they are in their thirties, and they then suffer something akin to a *delayed adolescence* (Malyon, 1982). This is analogous to being a teenager trapped inside an adult's body. Sexual desire is no longer repressed, which can seem a bit overwhelming. Emotional development has been delayed, as gay relationships have not had the opportunity to develop. The awareness that their feelings are chronologically misplaced creates great psychic pain. Recent research indicates that gay men are somewhat more inclined to suffer from mood disorders and anxiety disorders, both of which are viewed as stress-related maladies (Cochran, 2001). Mays and Cochran (2001) have also provided evidence suggesting that the greater elevation of these stress-related conditions may be due to discrimination.

Largely through the work of activists and the improved social landscape that has resulted, adolescents are self-identifying as gay or lesbian at increasingly younger ages (D'Augelli, 2006; Savin-Williams, 2005b) and they are also disclosing their identities at younger ages than in the past (D'Augelli; Platt, 2001; Taylor, 2000). On the other hand, representative American studies have shown that lesbian, gay, and bisexual youths continue to experience adjustment problems (D'Augelli). A recent Canadian study revealed that lesbians and gay men experience minority stress arising from (a) self-identification issues, (b) relationship and family problems, (c) conflict regarding one's sexuality, and (d) society's continuing antigay attitude towards them (Iwasaki & Ristock, 2007). Yet another study focused on the relationship stress that same-sex couples continue to experience as they navigate their personal lives and interact with families, coworkers, and communities (Rostosky, Riggle, Gray, & Hatton, 2007).

The gay community has been plagued by some of the same problems that affect many Aboriginal communities. Gay adolescents are at least three times more likely to attempt suicide than heterosexual youth (Cooley, 1998; Morrison & L'Heureux, 2001; Radkowsky & Siegel, 1997), as many as 40 to 60% of street youth may be gay (Kunreuther, as cited in Radkowsky & Siegel, 1997), and alcohol and substance abuse problems are estimated to be three times over-represented in the gay community as compared to the heterosexual community (Ratner, 1993). In general, parents are not delighted to find out their child is gay (Goldfried & Goldfried, 2001; Savin-Williams & Dube, 1998), whereas children from nearly every other non-dominant group have parents who share their group status and are therefore most often supportive of the non-dominant group and their son or daughter. Most churches and world religions are not accepting of gay individuals (Birken, 1997; Herdt, 1997). Prejudice towards gays and lesbians remains "firmly entrenched throughout the United States" (Lehavot & Lambert, 2007, p. 279) and in Canada (Alderson, Orzeck, & McEwen, 2009). Given society's abhorrence of homosexuality, particularly in the past, gay people have been victimized by pervasive anti-gay sentiment. In effect, the majority of them have been emotionally abused and spiritually raped on a global level.

 **Snapshot 4**

The Feeling of *Being Stuffed*

Many of us learn to stuff our feelings, sometimes for years. So how do we learn to unstuff them? I know a gay man who developed bulimia around the same time he decided to stop receiving conversion therapy and begin accepting himself as gay. To do so meant he had to give up his fundamentalist Christian beliefs, leaving a spiritual void and emptiness. Everyone needs acceptance from others and a spiritual belief system that is inclusive of who we are. What are the many ways that we can punish ourselves, consciously and subconsciously, for being excluded from our family of origin or from the family of God? Think about it.

The situation for gay men (and lesbians) is not as bleak as all of the above sounds, however. Savin-Williams (2005b) stressed that the majority of sexual minority youth are resilient and they come through their adolescence unscathed. Riggle, Whitman, Olson, Rostosky, and Strong's (2008) research focused on the positive aspects of being gay/lesbian and, from their online survey of 203 men and 350 women, they found themes of (a) having greater empathy and compassion for others who are oppressed (most common theme mentioned by gay men), (b) sense of belonging to a community, (c) forming strong relationships with people other than immediate family, (d) feeling more connected to their true selves, (e) freedom from societal norms regarding relationships and gender typical roles, and (f) having the ability to role model to others and be involved in social justice issues.

Furthermore, the future for gay people in Canada appears to be more promising than ever, and despite the pervasive abuse they have suffered, the evidence supporting the mental health of gay individuals is voluminous (e.g., Brady & Busse, 1994; Chang & Block, 1960; Garnets, Herek, & Levy, 1990; Gonsiorek, 1982; Haldeman, 1994; Hammersmith & Weinberg, 1973; Hooker, 1957; Leserman, DiSantostefano, Perkins, & Evans, 1994; Miranda & Storms, 1989; Morin & Rothblum, 1991; Ross, Paulsen, & Stalstrom, 1988; Rothblum, 1994; Schmitt & Kurdek, 1987; Watters, 1986; Weinberg, 1970). Gays do not differ significantly from straight individuals in their upbringing (Martin, 1982b), and most gay men believe that they differ from heterosexuals only in their sexual behaviour and preference (Troiden, 1979). Gay men generally value relationships more than casual sex (Connell, 1992), and comparable to heterosexuals, are capable of establishing and maintaining meaningful long-term relationships (Martin, 1982a; Schmitt & Kurdek; Troiden). Available research suggests that between 40 and 60% of gay men are currently in a committed relationship with a same-sex partner (Peplau, 1993).

The next section provides an overview of Cass's (1979, 1996) theory of sexual identity development before advancing a new theory that includes all environmental factors that affect gay men in their sexual identity development. The new theory also expands current understanding of what constitutes the components of having a positive gay identity.

Theoretical Principles and Conceptual Issues

Without self-labeling, sexual feelings are partitioned from sexual identity, causing a lack of continuity and integration of self-images. (Miranda & Storms, 1989, p. 41)

The development of a positive gay identity is not easy (Alderson, 2000, 2002; Beane, 1981; Obear & Reynolds, as cited in Pope, Prince, & Mitchell, 2000), but one that is necessary if a gay person is to become psychologically healthy (Alderson, 2000, 2002; Brady & Busse, 1994; Coleman, 1987; Leserman et al., 1994). Since the 1970s, a number of theories have been proposed, especially developmental stage models of identity development (Cass, 1979; Coleman, 1981-82; Cooper, 2008; Dank, 1971; Hencken & O'Dowd, 1977; Lee, 1977; McCarn & Fassinger, 1996; Minton & McDonald, 1983-84; Plummer, 1975; Troiden, 1993) and a social-psychological theory (Cox & Gallois, 1996).

Cass's (1979) theory has received the most recognition in the published literature (Eliason, 1996), and some have described her model as exceptionally comprehensive and grounded, with some empirical support (Levine & Evans, as cited in Chojnacki & Gelberg, 1995). Cass (1996) revised her theory in the mid-1990s, retaining her six stages of homosexual development, but changing the theoretical perspective from interpersonal congruency theory to social constructionism (Barber & Mobley, 1999).

The stages begin with *identity confusion*, in which individuals label their behaviour (defined in a global sense as either actual behaviour or inclusive of thoughts and emotions) as homosexual, which creates a deeper question of whether the person is homosexual. "Who am I?" becomes the most salient question. Stage 2, called *identity comparison*, focuses on the social alienation resulting from the individual's feeling a lack of belonging. The person is aware of feeling different from others, and the task of Stage 2 is to deal with the social alienation that results.

In Stage 3, *identity tolerance*, the individual has moved towards a self-image that is more closely aligned with homosexual, expressed in the statement "I probably am a homosexual." At this stage the individual seeks out homosexuals and their subculture. Next, the person may move on to *identity acceptance*, now accepting rather than simply tolerating a gay identity. Increased contact with other homosexuals occurs. In Stage 5, *identity pride*, the person feels a strong commitment to the gay community and apparently seeks out other homosexuals as the only *true* companions. It is suggested that individuals at this stage negatively view heterosexuals and positively view homosexuals. I suspect that many gay individuals today would find this stage objectionable and, for the most part, invalid. Although people often feel anger when overcoming heterosexist thinking and conditioning, the amount of generalization suggested by Cass (1979) is suspect. Sophie (1985-86) commented that the role of anger and pride in Cass's theory is a reflection of the importance of historical changes that have occurred in the gay liberation movement.

Stage 6 results in *identity synthesis*. Gayness becomes viewed as only one part of identity. The person is again able to see both homosexuals and heterosexuals as individuals. Cass (1983-84) reiterated her stance that identity formation is not complete until this stage is attained.

Eliason (1996) criticized Cass's model in that research has shown that not all women pass through the stages, or in the order specified. Furthermore, Cass's last stage of identity synthesis suggests that one's gay identity becomes less important in relation to other personal identities. This would imply that gay activists, for example, who likely emphasize their gay identities, are deficient or stuck at an earlier level of gay identity development (Eliason).

The developmental stage theories have been recently criticized in the literature because of their over-reliance on the experience of Caucasian gay males, the dichotomous treatment of *homosexuals* versus *heterosexuals*, and the implication that the final stage of development in each theory is the attainment of a positive gay identity across all situations (Dworkin, 2000). The rigidity of the stage models does not explain the developmental trajectories of all gay individuals, which for some is back and forth through various aspects of the stages, and the models fail to incorporate the fluid and dynamic nature of gay identity (Dworkin; Eliason, 1996).

I propose a theory of development called the **Ecological Model of Gay Male Identity**. According to Bubolz and Sontag (1993, p. 419), "human ecology theory is unique in its focus on humans as both biological organisms and social beings in interaction with their environment." As an applied discipline, human ecology attempts to identify the influences that enhance human development in hopes that this knowledge can be used to optimize human functioning (Westney, Brabble, & Edwards, 1988). Westney and colleagues suggested that the core concepts in human ecology have three foci: (a) the individuals, (b) their environment, and (c) the interaction between the two.

The ecological model advanced here is holistic in that it seeks to identify all influences affecting the person (Bubolz & Sontag, 1993)*, including internal factors (physical and psychological) and external factors (social and environmental).* References to the physical factors that may affect development of a gay identity are not discussed, as this would necessitate reviewing the theorized causes of homosexuality. This would serve no useful purpose, as the heated debate between the essentialists and the constructionists is ongoing (Halwani, 1998) and likely irresolvable (Kitzinger & Wilkinson, 1995).

The ecological model contains both developmental stages and process components. The three stages are: (a) *before coming out,* (b) *during coming out,* and (c) *beyond coming out.* **Coming out** can mean one of two things, and usually the context provides the appropriate connotation. *First, coming out can be used to refer to the process of self-identifying as gay. Second, coming out can refer to* **disclosing** *one's gay identity to others.* Coming out here refers to self-identifying as gay. Each stage has its own processes, and these are outlined below. Figure 1 is a graphical depiction of the ecological model.

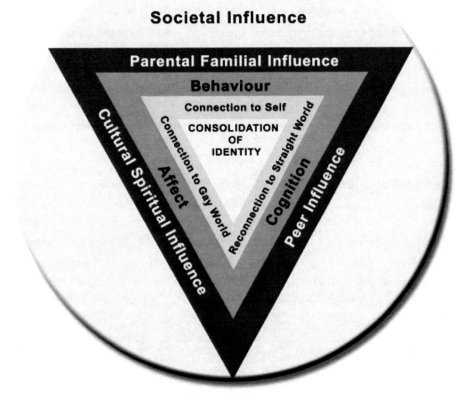

Figure 1. Ecological model of gay male identity.

Before Coming Out

Before a gay male self-identifies as gay, he experiences intrapsychic conflict between catalysts, which serve to inform him that he might have a homosexual orientation, and hindrances, which serve to either suppress or repress his homoerotic and homoaffiliative feelings (Alderson, 2000; Alderson & Jevne, 2003). Examples of catalysts are having dreams with homosexual content, feeling sexually attracted to males, and falling in love with a male. Examples of hindrances are having deeply entrenched internalized homophobia and witnessing how gay people are minimized and denigrated in society. A full description of the catalysts and hindrances is contained in both *Beyond Coming Out* (Alderson) and in a published article (Alderson & Jevne).

Some influences can act as either catalysts or hindrances, including (a) parental/familial, (b) cultural/spiritual, (c) peer, and (d) societal. Some families are supportive of their gay sons (Goldfried & Goldfried, 2001; Savin-Williams & Dube, 1998); some cultures are more supportive than others, like American Caucasians compared to African Americans (Barber & Mobley, 1999); some churches, such as the Unitarian-Universalists, Society of Friends (also known as Quakers), Ethical Humanists (Herrman, 1990), the United Church, the Metropolitan Community Church (Blumenfeld & Raymond, 1993), and some religions, like Buddhism, are supportive of gay people; some friends are more accepting than others of gay individuals; and finally, some societies are more tolerant or accepting, such as Canada, which is more supportive than Vietnam (Dong, 1999).

Furthermore, many societies are becoming increasingly supportive over time. For example, compare Canada and the United States between 1950 and 2009.

In South East Asian societies, for example, the importance of belonging to family is more important than one's individual identity. In such societies, one's sexual identity (or other individual identities for that matter) is generally not considered important. Instead, the focus is on one's place in the family, and on how one conducts oneself within it. Most gay men living in Asia will conform by becoming married to a woman and fulfilling their responsibility of having children. Sexual relations are a private matter, regardless of the gender of one's partner, and often a gay man's means of having a male lover is one similar to the American military dictate of *don't ask, don't tell* (Laurent, 2005). Despite the silence around same-sex sexuality, South East Asian countries are generally much less overly homophobic than North American cultures (Laurent). South East Asia provides a good example of how a different society from our own shapes the expression (or lack thereof) of a gay identity.

The intensity of the intrapsychic battle depends on an individual's particular configuration of catalysts and hindrances. Theoretically, the intrapsychic battle occurs because of cognitive dissonance (Festinger, 1957), which results when two beliefs or cognitions, or a belief and a behaviour, are viewed or experienced as incompatible. When there is enough psychic press to push the catalysts above the hindrances, a gay male is able to come out and self-identify as gay. In Figure 1, before coming out is primarily represented graphically by the outer circle of societal influence and by the largest triangle representing cultural/spiritual influence, and so forth.

During Coming Out

The hallmark of this phase is the acquisition of a gay identity. **Gay identity** is defined as *an identity status denoting those individuals who have come to identify themselves as having primarily homosexual cognition, affect, and/or behaviour, and who have adopted the construct of gay as having personal significance to them.* The theory underlying this definition is *symbolic interactionism,* which posits that our identities emerge within a particular social context, and it is the context that provides meaning to our experience (Minton & McDonald, 1983-84).

During the *coming out* phase, most gay men experience many conflicting emotions, both positive and negative (Alderson, 2000). The degree of tumultuousness will depend on the relative weighting between the catalysts and hindrances. For example, an individual raised within an accepting environment at all levels (societal, parental/familial, cultural/spiritual, peer influence) will have a much easier time coming out than someone raised within an intolerant environment at every level. During the coming out phase, the individual will need to reduce internalized homophobia and begin learning what it means to be gay and to act in a manner that seems appropriate to him. **Internalized homophobia** refers to *gay individuals fearing, disliking, or hating themselves. The term also applies to gay individuals fearing, disliking, or hating other gay people, or those whom they perceive as gay.*

Before moving on to the next phase, which not all gay men are likely to attain (Beane, 1981; McDonald, 1982), the individual needs to become certain that he is in fact gay and not bisexual or heterosexual. Becoming certain will depend to some extent on the individual's assessment of the components comprising the second largest triangle in Figure 1; that is, an assessment of the extent of homosexual cognition (e.g., thoughts, images, and fantasies with homoerotic or homoaffiliative content), homosexual behaviour (e.g., sensual or sexual body contact with others of the same gender, including necking, touching, holding, caressing, fondling, petting, and other more intimate sexual acts), and homoaffiliative affect (e.g., encompasses erotic and passionate feelings, including love, towards others of the same gender). As defined here, **sexual orientation** is *the interaction between affect and cognition such that it produces attraction, erotic desire, and ultimately philia for members of the opposite gender, the same gender, or both.* **Philia** is *the propensity to fall in love romantically with members of a particular gender* (or both, as in the case of *biphilia).*

It is also hypothesized that individuals who have a clear direction for their opposite gender, same gender, or bi-gender affinity in these three domains of behaviour, cognition, and affect will have a clearer sense of their sexual identity than those who are still exploring the direction of their affinity. Furthermore, it seems likely that those who have all three domains (behaviour, cognition, and affect) focused in the same direction, whether towards males, females, or both, will experience the least cognitive dissonance and confusion. As an example, men who have sex with men (behaviour), who experience homosexual fantasies (cognition), and who are sexually attracted to men (affect) will feel a greater sense of identity integration than those who have sex with men, but experience mostly sexual fantasies and lust for women.

Most males who self-identify as gay do so because they have made an assessment that their homosexual orientation is stronger than their heterosexual orientation. This is not necessarily the case (Ellis & Mitchell, 2000; Rosario et al., 1996), but it is postulated that those who do not primarily have a homosexual orientation will not do the necessary psychological and emotional work required of the next stage. The coming out phase is represented diagrammatically in Figure 1 by movement from the second largest triangle to the third largest triangle.

Beyond Coming Out

Most gay men develop a positive gay identity, but the process used to take 16 years on average from the point of coming out to oneself (Obear & Reynolds, as cited in Pope et al., 2000). Savin-Williams (2005b), however, reported that the vast majority of gay teenagers today develop positive gay identities within a few years after self-identifying.

The third largest triangle of Figure 1 represents the three areas that need to become further integrated in order for a gay man to feel positive about who he is becoming: connecting with self, connecting with the gay world, and reconnecting with the straight world. Some of the work involved in connecting with self involves embracing self-love, developing a positive view of being gay, and developing a sense of wholeness and authenticity (Alderson, 2000). Connecting with the gay world includes feeling a sense of community with other gay individuals and pursuing the development of intimate relationships. The final achievement, which often occurs simultaneously with the other two, consists of the many ways one learns to reconnect and cope with the generally homophobic heterosexual community. The final consolidation of identity, which includes an integration of the self, the gay world, and the straight world, will not be the same for any two individuals. Becoming a positive gay man is about an individual's unique way of constructing a viable, healthy identity (Alderson). The inner triangle represents the highest achievement in the ecological model – the attainment and consolidation of a positive gay identity.

Common Presenting Concerns in the Counselling Context

Despite the fact that the American Psychiatric Association removed homosexuality as a mental disorder from the DSM in 1973 (Bayer, 1981) and that the American Psychological Association went a step further two years later by strongly urging psychologists to help reduce stigma (Conger, 1975), a recent survey of 139 clinical psychologists reported that 11% supported conversion therapy (Jordan & Deluty, 1995). In fact, heterosexist thinking and homonegativity continue to be common amongst psychologists (Phillips & Silling, as cited in Morrison & L'Heureux, 2001).

Although many gay people remain suspicious of the psychological profession due to its history of treating homosexuality as a mental disorder (Dworkin, 2000), proportionally more gay individuals use mental health services than heterosexual individuals (Dworkin). Their concerns are as varied as those of non-gay individuals. Eight of the main counselling issues in which the therapist will require specialized knowledge and skills in working with gay men are sexual orientation confusion, coming out and disclosing to others, identity fragmentation, internalized homophobia, relationship problems, religious conflicts, HIV and AIDS, and managing the consequences of external homophobia (including victims of gay bashing).

Sexual Orientation Confusion

Conflict about sexual orientation is a common concern for gay individuals, at least in the early stages of coming out (Jones & Gabriel, 1999). Sexuality is complex, and three areas need to be understood in order for effective work to occur: sexual behaviour, sexual identity, and sexual orientation. Sexual behaviour itself is a relatively poor predictor of eventual sexual identity (Hewitt, 1995; Richardson, 1993; Vare & Norton, 1998). Anyone can enjoy the feelings associated with sexual relations (e.g., touch, caring, orgasm) with any person, regardless of gender, so long as homophobia is absent or negligible. For that matter, people enjoy sexual activity by themselves or with inanimate objects. The majority of gay men and lesbian women have experienced sexual intercourse with the opposite gender (Betz & Fitzgerald, 1993), and many male adolescents and prisoners have had same-gender sexual relations without identifying as gay (Blumstein & Schwartz, 1993; Green, 1998; Vare & Norton). Sex is only sex, particularly for men (Townsend, 1998), and by itself says very little about one's identity.

Sexual identity is a label that we give ourselves, and the main choices are heterosexual (or *straight*), gay or lesbian, bisexual, transsexual, or queer. The label *queer* reflects an ideology that is noncommittal and suggests an openness to sexual experience or relationship with either gender. But identity labels can change. Most gay people define themselves as heterosexual before they self-identify as gay. Some may first consider themselves to be bisexual and later identify as gay (Rosario et al., 1996), or they may think they are gay and later identify as heterosexual.

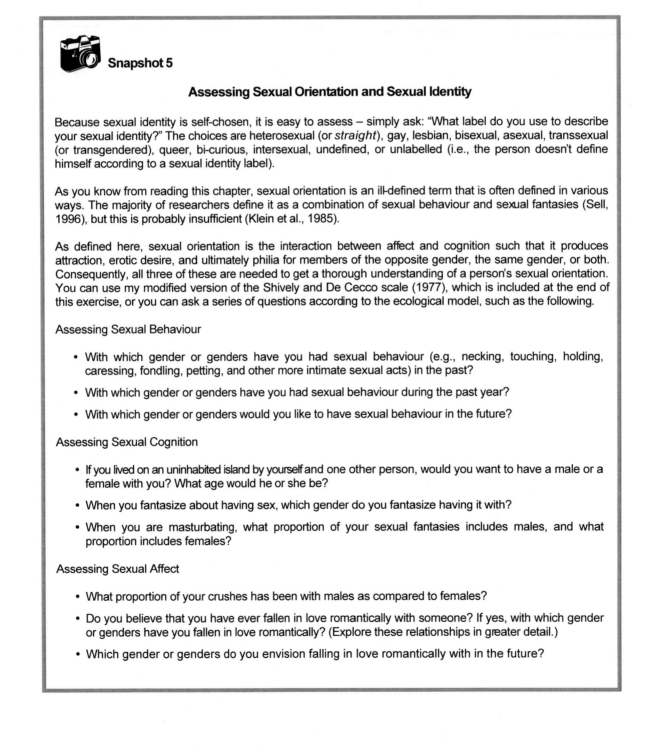

Snapshot 5

Assessing Sexual Orientation and Sexual Identity

Because sexual identity is self-chosen, it is easy to assess – simply ask: "What label do you use to describe your sexual identity?" The choices are heterosexual (or *straight*), gay, lesbian, bisexual, asexual, transsexual (or transgendered), queer, bi-curious, intersexual, undefined, or unlabelled (i.e., the person doesn't define himself according to a sexual identity label).

As you know from reading this chapter, sexual orientation is an ill-defined term that is often defined in various ways. The majority of researchers define it as a combination of sexual behaviour and sexual fantasies (Sell, 1996), but this is probably insufficient (Klein et al., 1985).

As defined here, sexual orientation is the interaction between affect and cognition such that it produces attraction, erotic desire, and ultimately philia for members of the opposite gender, the same gender, or both. Consequently, all three of these are needed to get a thorough understanding of a person's sexual orientation. You can use my modified version of the Shively and De Cecco scale (1977), which is included at the end of this exercise, or you can ask a series of questions according to the ecological model, such as the following.

Assessing Sexual Behaviour

- With which gender or genders have you had sexual behaviour (e.g., necking, touching, holding, caressing, fondling, petting, and other more intimate sexual acts) in the past?

- With which gender or genders have you had sexual behaviour during the past year?

- With which gender or genders would you like to have sexual behaviour in the future?

Assessing Sexual Cognition

- If you lived on an uninhabited island by yourself and one other person, would you want to have a male or a female with you? What age would he or she be?

- When you fantasize about having sex, which gender do you fantasize having it with?

- When you are masturbating, what proportion of your sexual fantasies includes males, and what proportion includes females?

Assessing Sexual Affect

- What proportion of your crushes has been with males as compared to females?

- Do you believe that you have ever fallen in love romantically with someone? If yes, with which gender or genders have you fallen in love romantically? (Explore these relationships in greater detail.)

- Which gender or genders do you envision falling in love romantically with in the future?

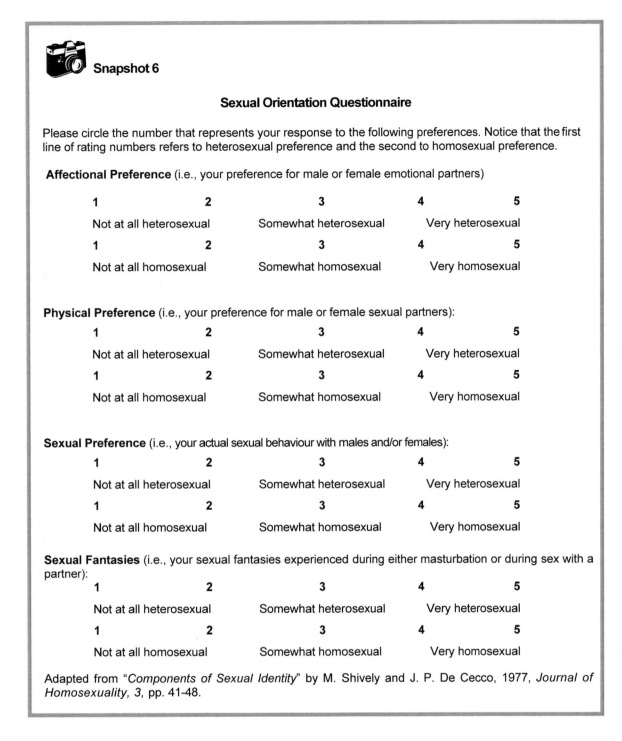

Snapshot 6

Sexual Orientation Questionnaire

Please circle the number that represents your response to the following preferences. Notice that the first line of rating numbers refers to heterosexual preference and the second to homosexual preference.

Affectional Preference (i.e., your preference for male or female emotional partners)

1	2	3	4	5
Not at all heterosexual		Somewhat heterosexual		Very heterosexual

1	2	3	4	5
Not at all homosexual		Somewhat homosexual		Very homosexual

Physical Preference (i.e., your preference for male or female sexual partners):

1	2	3	4	5
Not at all heterosexual		Somewhat heterosexual		Very heterosexual

1	2	3	4	5
Not at all homosexual		Somewhat homosexual		Very homosexual

Sexual Preference (i.e., your actual sexual behaviour with males and/or females):

1	2	3	4	5
Not at all heterosexual		Somewhat heterosexual		Very heterosexual

1	2	3	4	5
Not at all homosexual		Somewhat homosexual		Very homosexual

Sexual Fantasies (i.e., your sexual fantasies experienced during either masturbation or during sex with a partner):

1	2	3	4	5
Not at all heterosexual		Somewhat heterosexual		Very heterosexual

1	2	3	4	5
Not at all homosexual		Somewhat homosexual		Very homosexual

Adapted from "*Components of Sexual Identity*" by M. Shively and J. P. De Cecco, 1977, *Journal of Homosexuality, 3*, pp. 41-48.

Sexual orientation is a controversial term. The majority of researchers have defined it according to sexual behaviour, sexual fantasies, sexual attractions, affectional preferences, or some combination thereof (Klein, Sepekoff, & Wolf, 1985; Russell, Seif, & Truong, 2001; Sell, 1996). I concur with Money (1988) that the defining feature of sexual orientation is who one is capable of falling romantically in love with – in other words, philia. The propensity to fall in love romantically only with members of the opposite gender, the same gender, or both genders is respectively called *heterophilia*, *homophilia*, or *biphilia*.

Clinicians who attempt to change a homosexual or bisexual orientation into a heterosexual orientation are called **conversion therapists.** They have demonstrated that, at least for some individuals, sexual behaviour and sexual fantasies can be behaviourally modified (Nicolosi, Byrd, & Potts, 2000b; Throckmorton, 1998). We also know that it is easy enough to get someone to change their sexual identity label, particularly if one is made to feel shameful and guilty for defining as gay or bisexual. Perhaps sexual attraction can be modified as well (Nicolosi et al., 2000b; Throckmorton). But can philia be changed? I don't believe so, and no one has yet provided any conclusive empirical research to demonstrate this (Drescher, 1998; Ellis & Mitchell, 2000; Haldeman, 1994). Conversion therapists believe they can change all aspects of sexual orientation (Nicolosi, Byrd, & Potts, 2000a), but they have not yet demonstrated this (Drescher; Ellis & Mitchell; Haldeman). A study published by Nicolosi and colleagues (2000b) suggested that, even in cases where Nicolosi's form of conversion therapy is effective, the average length of treatment is three to four years.

Robert Spitzer (2003), a world-renowned researcher who had a significant influence on the American Psychiatric Associations' decision to remove homosexuality from the DSM in 1973 (Bayer, 1981), however, has provided recent data that suggest that sexual orientation conversion may be possible for some highly motivated gay men (usually motivated due to religious beliefs). His published study was based on 200 telephone interviews with men who reported that they changed their sexual orientations – to varying degrees – from homosexual to heterosexual. His findings are considered highly contestable by researchers who do not believe that conversion is possible for men with strong homosexual orientations. Criticisms focused on sampling bias and the fact that the study was retrospective. Furthermore, one could argue that these individuals may have had a bisexual orientation despite their identity labels of heterosexual before commencing conversion therapy (which itself was completed, on average, 12 years before Spitzer interviewed them). Several of the criticisms of his study can be found in *Peer Commentaries on Spitzer* (2003). In addition, "the current literature fails to support CT [conversion therapy] as an EST [empirically supported treatment] based on the criteria outlined by Chambless and Ollendick (2001)" (Cramer, Golom, LoPresto, & Kirkley, 2008, p. 102).

Regardless of whether conversion therapy is possible, there is the bigger concern about ethical and professional considerations. Mental health practitioners are ethically bound to "avoid bringing harm to the client" (Cramer et al., 2008, p. 110), and conversion therapy has amply demonstrated its harmful effects to clients, including: (a) increased suicidal ideation and suicide attempts; (b) elevated anxiety and depression; (c) decreased self-esteem and increased feelings of shame and self-loathing; (d) increased feelings of internalized homophobia and distorted perceptions of homosexuality; (e) intrusive imagery; (f) sexual dysfunction; (g) preoccupation with speech, mannerisms, and gender role expression; (h) loss of family, religiosity, and spirituality; (i) phobic anxiety towards attractive men; (j) increased aggression and hostility; (k) feelings of being inauthentic; (l) slowing of the self-identification process; (m) social isolation and loss of same-sex partners; (n) irrational fear of being a child abuser; and (o) difficulty in establishing intimate relationships (Blackwell, 2008; Cramer et al.). Interestingly, many of the groups that have touted the benefits of conversion therapy have seen their own leaders return to their previous lives as gay men and lesbian women (Jenkins & Johnston, 2004).

Aside from the harm that conversion therapy has caused many clients, Tye (2003) concluded that there are three ethical-philosophical underpinnings to it: (a) the focus is on changing clients' nondysfunctional sexual orientation because of the discomfort it causes them rather than work on changing the societal norms that are judgmental towards it (similar to the idea of trying to change skin colour rather than deal with society's attitudes towards those of other races); (b) advocates are unwilling to recommend gay-affirmative therapy, despite the effectiveness of cognitive behaviour therapy in helping individuals modify cognitive distortions and irrational beliefs; and (c) therapists offering it implicitly deny that non-heterosexual orientations can be healthy and instead reinforce the idea that any deviation from heterosexuality is defective, inferior, and/or immoral. Clinicians should note that most mental health professional organizations stipulate that offering conversion therapy in its various forms constitutes unethical practice (Blackwell, 2008).

Coming Out to Self and Others

More youth are coming out than ever before (Savin-Williams, 1998, 2005b), despite the emotional turmoil they may feel in developing a gay identity (McFarland, 1993). Self-identifying as gay can be extremely tumultuous (Alderson, 2000), perhaps especially for older individuals. For example, Isay (1996) warned that middle-aged married men who come out "pose a serious suicide risk" (p. 109). Disclosing to others can be equally difficult. Half of the gay bashing that occurs is at the hands of family members (Bohan, 1996), and the number of street youth who are gay speaks volumes to the nonacceptance that many receive at home.

Gay adults who disclose to others may also face numerous consequences. Harassment in the workplace is pervasive for gay individuals (Croteau et al., 2000). Many face the *lavender ceiling* (Conklin, 2000), which is commonly referred to as the *glass ceiling* when applied to women or members of other visible non-dominant groups, meaning that they will not be promoted within their employment settings. The loss of friendships and family ties is also a real threat for many gay individuals.

Fragmentation of Identity

Cornett (1995) suggested that the primary issue for gay men is the need to achieve an integrated identity. Most gay people have been raised amid much homophobia and heterosexism. Consequently, they could have learned to denigrate their sexual orientation. To avoid the painful anxiety that results when unwanted thoughts and feelings rise to the surface, gay men become expert at using defense mechanisms. Denial is common (Beane, 1981; de Monteflores & Schultz, 1978; Malyon, 1982); other defenses often employed include compartmentalization, overcompensation, repression, reaction formation, and rationalization (Coleman, 1981-82; Gonsiorek, 1993; Malyon). The defense mechanisms serve to shut off or fragment the parts of identity that are considered unacceptable, which is the very essence that defines a homosexual orientation. This splitting off of libido, or sexual desire, reduces energy and enthusiasm for life, thus leaving the conflicted gay person especially vulnerable to depression and reduced or negated passion (Helminiak, 1994; Isay, 1996; Napier, 1990; Vargo, 1998). In turn, this can arguably increase the likelihood of suicidal ideation.

Internalized Homophobia

Every gay person experiences internalized homophobia to some extent, and some to a very high degree (Allen & Oleson, 1999; Fassinger, 1991). We have all been raised with many scripts that help to define us. Traditional gender roles, for example, expected men to be providers and women to be nurturers (Weiten & Lloyd, 2000). These messages can be very difficult to overcome in adulthood. Likewise, virtually every society in the world has viewed homosexual acts as immoral (Batchelor, as cited in O'Donohue & Caselles, 1993), and those who deviate from the heterosexual script spend their lives attempting to overcome the psychological damage created by varying degrees of intolerance.

Gay people grow up learning the same social and sexual scripts as the majority culture, and most cultures, both past and present, have denigrated those who act upon their homosexual desires or homosexual orientation. School-age children levy anti-gay slurs at one another (Russell et al., 2001; Sapp, 2001), and everyone who hears them knows that these words do not describe a sought-after and respected sexual orientation. Working through internalized homophobia is a lifelong process for many gay people (Martin, 1982a). Recent research has also shown that internalized homophobia is associated with greater relationship problems in lesbian, gay, and bisexual individuals (Frost & Meyer, 2009).

Relationship Problems

Relationship problems are a common presenting concern for individuals seeking counselling services. For gay men, relationships can be particularly difficult to navigate for any or all of the following reasons.

1. Our society is unsupportive of men dating one another. Most parents are not delighted to hear that their son is gay or that he has a same-sex partner. Gay couples who publicly display signs of physical affection towards one another run the risk of harassment or assault (Garnets & Kimmel, 1993; Klinger, 1995; McKirnan & Peterson, 1989). Most print and video media have traditionally included very few gay characters (Kielwasser & Wolf, 1993-94). Even today, my observation is that most gay characters in television series and movies are stereotyped.

2. Males have been socialized with scripts that are not conducive to intimacy. Although being raised with androgynous attitudes is theoretically freeing to both men and women, the majority of men are raised to not touch one another, except in aggression. Men are also raised to be competitive, a stance perhaps helpful in business, but problematic in relationship building (Weiten & Lloyd, 2000).

3. Gay male relationships often follow different rules than heterosexual relationships. Most heterosexual relationships have a clearly defined trajectory, with possible marriage and childbearing as clear demarcations of commitment.

4. Gay men do not have formalized relationship scripts to follow or role models that inform them of how to construct their relationship (Garnets & Kimmel, 1993). Consequently, the rules that apply to heterosexual relationships may not apply to gay couples (Dworkin, 2000; Risman & Schwartz, 1988). For example, many if not most gay male couples eventually develop sexually open relationships (Bell & Weinberg, 1978; Bohan, 1996). This may create special challenges for how the couple preserves integrity and commitment within their primary relationship.

Religious Conflicts

Religious conflicts are common for individuals with sexual minority identities (Dworkin, 2000). Because most world religions are disapproving of homosexual behaviour (Birken, 1997; Herdt, 1997), those who are gay must find ways to come to terms with the religious conflict this often creates for them. These conflicts are often derivatives of the belief that they are sinful if they experience homosexual attraction, fantasies, or behaviour.

The Koran does not condemn homosexuality per se, and does not recommend specific punishments (Blumenfeld & Raymond, 1993). The gospels of the New Testament do not indicate that Jesus of Nazareth had anything to say about homosexuality, although some letters in the New Testament and some references in the Old Testament certainly speak against homosexual acts between two heterosexual individuals, particularly when sex occurs out of lust or as an act of domination and power (Helminiak, 1994).

Although the answers are inconclusive, they generally tend to support the idea that heterosexualism and power hierarchies of all types derive at least some of their force from organized religion (Herdt, 1997).

HIV/AIDS

The rate of HIV infection in Canada is increasing among men who have sex with men (Patrick, Wong, & Jordan, 2000; Public Health Agency of Canada, 2006), and gay men throughout Canada and the United States have been the primary victims of the virus (Birken, 1997; Jones, 1997). Counselling related to HIV/AIDS is an area of focus with infected gay men.

HIV infection can be transmitted sexually through sexual intercourse (vaginal and anal) and through oral sex (mouth-penis, mouth-vagina). Although the mouth is considered an inhospitable environment for the HIV virus, there are documented cases in which HIV was transmitted orally (SF AIDS Foundation, 2008.

To date, there is no cure for HIV/AIDS. The available *drug cocktails* prolong life, but do not kill the virus that eventually causes AIDS. If you are not thoroughly familiar with HIV/AIDS and how to prevent it, detailed information is available from the Centers for Disease Control and Prevention (2009) and the SF AIDS Foundation (2008).

Managing the consequences of external homophobia is also a problem for which gay men seek help. The more one discloses one's sexual identity status to others, the more opportunities there are for negative consequences to occur. At the other end of the spectrum are those who remain closeted. The term **closeted** refers to *gay people who have not disclosed their sexual identity to others.* These consequences can affect any area of the gay person's existence, including job or career life, home life, family relationships, peer relationships, and physical safety. Griffin (1992) proposed four levels of being out.

1. The most closeted level involves using *passing* strategies, which means leading others to believe that one is heterosexual.

2. The next level involves using *covering* strategies, which means that the gay person takes actions to help prevent others from finding out, but does not pretend to be heterosexual.

3. The third level is being *implicitly out*, and involves gay people being themselves and not attempting to pretend or avoid identity disclosure, but not actually telling others that one is gay or lesbian either.

4. The most *explicitly out* level involves telling others that one is gay or lesbian.

Most research suggests that about 20 to 25% of gay men have been physically assaulted because of their perceived sexual orientation (Carragher & Rivers, 2002; Ratner, 1993; Wells & Tsutsumi, 2005), and such assaults leave emotional scars (Dworkin, 2000). The treatment of posttraumatic stress disorder is not an uncommon counselling need for those who have been gay bashed (Dworkin). The above list is not exhaustive; it is only suggestive of the multitude of problems for which gay males may seek help. The next section looks at assessment and intervention strategies with gay men.

Assessment and Counselling Practice with Gay Males

On Becoming a Gay-Affirmative Therapist

As I mentioned earlier, many gay people are skeptical of receiving help from psychologists, yet they face many psychological issues and stresses as a result of society's condemnation of them (Connolly, 2004; Garnets et al., 1990). Some gay individuals refuse to seek counselling from those who are not gay (Dworkin, 2000), but the majority are open to receiving help from non-gay therapists (Dworkin).

Before working with gay men, therapists need to ensure that they can provide competent care. Most psychologists received little to no training or exposure to gay and lesbian issues while they were graduate students (Alderson, 2004; Buhrke, Ben-Ezra, Hurley, & Ruprecht, 1992).

The model of culture-infused counselling presented in this text emphasizes the importance of self-awareness as a foundation for competent practice. By virtue of living in a society that is strongly heterosexual, even gay positive therapists must carefully examine their beliefs, values, and assumptions for the ways in which they have internalized these heteronormative biases. Therapists need assistance in overcoming their own homophobia and heterosexism if they are to work effectively with gay persons (Dworkin & Gutierrez, 1989; Martin, 1982a; Richardson, 1993; Russell, 1989).

The second core competency domain in culture-infused counselling is awareness of the experiences, perspectives, and worldview of the client. Besides overcoming homophobia and heterosexism, which is no easy task, therapists require knowledge of how lesbian and gay culture is different from the heterosexual world, and how it is similar (Elliott, 1993). This requires extensive reading and association with gay people. The supervision of a gay-affirmative therapist is highly recommended, if available. **Gay-affirmative therapists** *view gay status as equal to heterosexual status.* The gay-affirmative therapist needs to be familiar with the oppression that gay males have experienced and how this invisible minority has suffered psychologically and spiritually; first, from learning to hide their feelings from themselves, and then how most continue to hide their identities from many who know them. Their reliance on defense mechanisms (Beane, 1981; Coleman, 1981-82; de Monteflores & Schultz, 1978; Gonsiorek, 1993; Malyon, 1982) to help soften emotional pain and ease societal stigma is something to which the gay-affirmative therapist needs to be sensitive.

Armed with their increased awareness of themselves and of the gay population, therapists must then develop a culturally sensitive working alliance with clients. In the case of gay-affirmative therapists, this begins with the creation of work environments that are welcoming to gay individuals. Their use of verbal and written language is inclusive and non-heterosexist. Ask the question, "How would I talk about this differently if I knew this client was lesbian or gay?" (Morrow, 1997, p. 10). The office setting itself should have signs of gay affirmation, such as a visible small rainbow flag or inverted pink triangle (both are symbols of gay acceptance), and books or posters from local or national gay organizations (Croteau & Thiel, 1993). Last, gay-affirmative therapists cannot afford to honour the code of silence, which effectively minimizes the existence of gay people; discussions about sexual orientation and professional development sessions aimed at increasing understanding of sexual minorities need to occur (Sailer, Korschgen, & Lokken, 1994).

In the sections that follow, other aspects involved in developing a culturally sensitive working alliance with gay men will be explored, such as the impact on assessment and intervention strategies. This includes assessment of sexual orientation and published instruments that contain bias towards gay men.

Assessment of Gay Men

Many clients, especially soon after coming out, wonder if they are in fact gay, lesbian, or bisexual (Dworkin, 2000). Remember that *gay* and *lesbian* are identity labels (i.e., sexual identity), while *bisexual* might refer to identity, behaviour, or sexual orientation. Most clients who are unsure about their sexual identity are really asking whether their sexual orientation is consistent with their label. Not that their label is generally self-chosen, but sometimes our clients become confused because of other people's perceptions of their sexual orientation (e.g., the client thinks he is heterosexual, but others think he has mostly a homosexual orientation).

The ecological model of gay male identity will prove helpful in assisting both you and the client in making this assessment. A complete appraisal of sexual orientation will include taking a history of the following, including information from both the past and the present: (a) sexual fantasies, both those that are conscious and those that occur during sleep; (b) erotic or sexual attraction; (c) *crushes* or infatuations; (d) sexual behaviour; (e) preference for male or female sexual partners; (f) preference for male or female emotional partners (i.e., the gender with which they form the closest friendships); (g) sexual identity labels used to define oneself; and, most importantly, (h) propensity to fall in love romantically with which gender, or actual experiences of falling in love romantically.

According to Sell (1996), the main scales used to measure sexual orientation are the Kinsey Scale (Kinsey, Pomeroy, & Martin, 1948), dichotomous measures (which simply ask the person to identify himself as gay or heterosexual), the Klein Sexual Orientation Grid (Klein et al., 1985), and the Shively & De Cecco Scale (Shively & De Cecco, 1977). I have included a modified version of the Shively & De Cecco Scale in Snapshot 6 in this chapter.

Snapshot 7

Overcoming Your Own Homonegativity

Complete the following scale to get a sense of your own level of homonegativity.

THE HOMONEGATIVITY SCALE

1 = strongly agree   2 = disagree   3 = don't know   4 = agree   5 = strongly agree

I believe that . . .

1. Homosexuals should not be allowed to work with children.   1 2 3 4 5

2. Homosexuality is a mental disorder.   1 2 3 4 5

3. Homosexuals should not have the same rights as heterosexuals.   1 2 3 4 5

4. Homosexuals are immoral.   1 2 3 4 5

5. People who support homosexual rights are probably homosexual themselves.   1 2 3 4 5

6. Homosexuals should be avoided whenever possible.   1 2 3 4 5

Adapted from "The Psychometric Properties of the Homonegativity Scale" by T. G. Morrison, A. V. Parriag, and M. A. Morrison, 1999, *Journal of Homosexuality, 37*(4), 111-126.

The higher your score, the greater your current level of homonegativity. Few of us have escaped the negative environmental influence of homonegativity. **Homonegativity** is a more specific term than homophobia and *refers to having negative views of gay people, regardless of the reason.* Think about the negative terms you heard in grade school to describe gay people of either gender; perhaps you used some yourself on occasion. I don't think most people really mean anything by these terms; nonetheless, they become effective insults.

In the minds of young people, these words later become associated with the construct of gay, so already in their minds there is a negative connotation, called an *antilocution* (Allport, 1958). Antilocutions are negative verbal messages directed against the hated group. They form the beginnings of homonegativity and homophobia. According to Allport, antilocutions are the first stage of negative actions directed against a non-dominant group, followed by discrimination and violence.

How can you reduce your own homonegativity? There is no substitute for getting to know gay people. Reading about gay men and lesbian women may help, but it's probably not going to be enough. It is easy to believe that all gay people are this or that if you don't have an accurate reference group. For example, if your only exposure to Inuit people has been with those who live in igloos, you might find it hard to believe that most now live in modern dwellings. Similarly, if your only exposure to gay men has been noticing and avoiding an effeminate and flamboyant gay teenager when you were in high school, you might believe most gay men are effeminate and flamboyant.

Frequent a gay bar a few times until you have had a chance to observe plenty of gay people, male and female. You can't assume they all are gay, so spend some time talking to them. In my opinion, gay people want one thing from heterosexual individuals more than anything – acceptance.
Better yet, begin associating with a gay person who has admirable qualities, the kind you look for in a friend. As your friendship develops, don't be surprised if you stop seeing him or her as gay after awhile.

Another method I believe works well is to write out a number of gay affirmations you would like to incorporate into your belief system. You will find a number of possibilities from your reading of this chapter. Here are some examples:

> *"Gay people are similar to heterosexual people, except they experience homophilia instead of heterophilia."*
> *"Gay people are unique like everyone else. Some I would like because of their traits or characteristics, and others I wouldn't."*
> *"Gay people are of equal worth compared to heterosexual individuals."*
> *"I love people – who they love doesn't matter."*

Then spend some quiet time reading your affirmations to yourself, reflecting on them for a few minutes. Continue doing this daily until you become aware that your views have changed.

My ex-wife is Filipina, and I remember when we went looking for our first house. Two of our married friends joined us, and when they saw the townhouse we were planning to buy, the woman spoke up and said, "You don't want to live here – there are a lot of immigrants in this neighbourhood." My wife spoke up and said, "Have you forgotten that I am an immigrant myself?" With that, our friend turned red, and so did I – with anger.

Sell (1996) concluded that each measure is unsophisticated and inadequate. He created his own measure of sexual orientation (Sell), which is also inadequate due to its focus on only three factors and its limited time frame in asking respondents only about the past year. Since gay males request therapy for more than just questions of sexual orientation or sexual identity, the gay-affirmative therapist also needs to be cognizant of other problems that often constitute the presenting complaint (see earlier section in this chapter).

Clinicians trained in the use of psychometrics must be cautious when using some of the available measures with gay clients. The Edwards Personal Preference Schedule, which is still widely used in career assessment (Prince, 1997), contains examples of heterosexism. Two of the items on the test are "I like to kiss attractive members of the opposite sex" and "I like to be in love with members of the opposite sex." Other tests that have been found to contain some form of heterosexist bias include the Social Readjustment Rating Scale, the Minnesota Multiphasic Personality Inventory-2, the Sexual Addiction Screening Inventory, the Symptom Checklist Revised, and the Multimodal Life History Inventory (Prince, 1997). Although the Strong Interest Inventory is exemplary in not containing heterosexist bias, the test relies on Holland's theory of occupational choice, a theory based on the concept of congruence between self and environment (Prince, 1995). Because it takes many gay men years to achieve an integrated identity, and some never achieve one, Holland's theory may not apply to all gay men (Prince, 1995).

Clinicians should also remain skeptical of the Myers-Briggs Type Indicator (MBTI). In my experience with this instrument, many individuals respond to the questions with how they wish to be seen by themselves or others (their *ideal* self), rather than with traits that actually define them (their *real* self). Before gay men develop a positive gay identity, many wish they were or could have been heterosexual (Alderson, 2000). I have coined the term *heterofacsimile* to denote a gay person's conscious and unconscious efforts to become heterosexual, and to appear heterosexual. Such attempts may occur through use of language and through appearance and deportment. As is generally true of defense mechanisms, gay men who indulge in heterofacsimile are less in touch with themselves. Consequently, there may be even less congruence between the real self and the ideal self of gay men as compared to heterosexual men, thus calling into question the validity of using the MBTI with gay men.

Intervention Strategies and Techniques Based on the Ecological Model

This section looks at the eight problem areas for gay men described in the previous section, ordered within categories defined by the Ecological Model of Gay Male Identity.

Combination of Sexual Affect, Cognition, and Behaviour

Sexual orientation confusion occurs when there is perceived disparity between sexual affect, cognition, and behaviour. An individual who has sexual fantasies for both men and women (cognitive component), who enjoys having sex with both genders (behavioural component), but who only falls in love with women (affective component) will probably question his sexual orientation. He will likely call himself a bisexual and think of this as an identity label. According to the ecological model, however, he has only demonstrated bisexual behaviour and cognition, not sexual affect (i.e., falling in love romantically with either or both genders), which is defined by the Ecological Model as the quintessential feature of sexual orientation. Depending on the individual's age, it may not be possible to properly assess his sexual orientation. We know that young men tend to have high sex drives, and we know that many young men will have sexual interests in both genders for a period of time (Green, 1998; Savin-Williams, 2005b; Sobocinski, 1990). For example, if he is 18 years of age he is likely not ready to give himself an accurate identity label. According to Marcia's (1966) theory of identity statuses, this individual is in an identity moratorium. It would be a mistake for him to foreclose on his identity, which would mean that he decides prematurely that he is either *heterosexual* or *bisexual.*

Using the same example, if the individual is 30 years of age and his heart has never gone out to other men, it is unlikely to ever do so. His sexual orientation is therefore *heterosexual,* despite the fact that he enjoys sex with both genders. Using now a different example, if a 30-year-old man had only fallen in love romantically with men, but had some sexual attraction towards women and had sex with women, this individual has a homosexual orientation, which he is currently denying to himself. Counselling this individual will be challenging, as his defense mechanisms are keeping the catalysts from outweighing the hindrances. Such a client probably has deep-seated reasons for not coming to terms with his sexuality.

As mentioned earlier, an individual comes out to himself when the catalysts outweigh the hindrances. Once this occurs, counselling focused on helping him affirm his feelings and working through cognitive dissonance will prove helpful. Other work that needs to be done includes helping the individual reduce internalized homophobia by helping him correct his stereotypes about gay men and resolve inner conflicts by restructuring some of his beliefs (Alderson, 2000). Helping or encouraging him to learn social and sexual gay roles is also important. For example, learning to become sexual with another man will be a different experience for him, as will learning to deal with men pursuing him for either sex or a date.

Helping Gay Men Connect with Self

Becoming whole and authentic

Helping a gay man develop a sense of being whole and authentic is an important therapeutic undertaking (Alderson, 2000, 2002; Hanley-Hackenbruck, 1988; Malyon, 1982). This means helping him reclaim the parts of himself that have been repressed or denied due to guilt and shame (Cornett, 1995). There is no substitute for providing him with Roger's (1957) core conditions of therapeutic effectiveness: unconditional positive regard, empathy, and congruence. An atmosphere of safety, warmth, and reflection will help him see the various fragments of identity and give meaning to them. Furthermore, the use of cognitive restructuring techniques will simultaneously prove invaluable in reducing cognitive dissonance and helping him accept the parts of himself that he finds disdainful.

Underlying much of the fragmentation is internalized homophobia. Helping the gay man accept his fragmented parts, which have been egodystonic to this point, will significantly reduce internalized homophobia. Helping him to love himself fully as a gay person will reduce it still further.

Religious conflicts

Many gay men experience religious conflicts, and referring them to gay-affirmative clergy or books on this topic can be helpful. Dworkin (2000, p. 172) recommended the following books: *"Twice Blessed: On Being Lesbian, Gay, and Jewish* (Balka & Rose, 1989), *Coming Out Within: Stages of Spiritual Awakening for Lesbians and Gay Men* (O'Neill & Ritter, 1992), and *Just as I Am: A Practical Guide to Being Out, Proud, and Christian* (Williams, 1992)." Another suggested reading is *What the Bible Really Says about Homosexuality* (Helminiak, 1994). Religious conflicts can be particularly challenging because, in some cases, the individual experiencing them may feel that he needs to reject his religion in its entirety. This is certainly an option, but not necessarily the best one. Other options include helping him: (a) focus more on spirituality than religion (Shannon & Woods, 1991); (b) accept that some parts of his faith will remain in disparity with those of others in his congregation; (c) understand that the written word is often different from people's interpretations of the written word (therefore, the religion may have adopted some beliefs and practices that provide only one interpretation of scripture); and (d) appreciate that although a text may be perceived as sacred, it may still contain errors, particularly as it applies to modern life, where we now have a deeper psychological understanding of homosexuality.

Living with HIV/AIDS

Working with gay men living with HIV/AIDS will depend on the stage of the infection, their level of acceptance of their serostatus, and how much they know about HIV/AIDS. Those at the early stages of knowing they are HIV positive will likely experience stages similar to Kubler-Ross's stages of dying (Kubler-Ross, 1969). One HIV-positive individual interviewed for *Beyond Coming Out* (Alderson, 2000) described his disclosure of his serostatus as a third form of coming out: first one comes out to self, then one comes out to others as a gay man, and then one comes out as a gay man who is HIV positive. Individuals with HIV/AIDS need to make decisions about whom to disclose their status to, when, and how. The result of doing so is often emotionally difficult for both the infected person and the one receiving the news. Individuals who have developed symptoms of AIDS have concerns about diminishing health, and some have diminished mental abilities to cope with the changes (Kalichman, 1998).

Helping Gay Men Connect with the Gay World

Encouraging gay men to associate with other gay men is important for the development of a positive gay identity (Frable, Wortman, & Joseph, 1997). Through interactions with others, one learns many of the things that gay-affirmative therapists try to teach. Besides involvement in the gay community to a greater or lesser degree, the vast majority of gay men want to be in a committed relationship (Troiden, 1979), and approximately half are already in such relationships (Peplau, 1993). Relationships between any two people are challenging, and coupled gay men are no exception. Nonetheless, research indicates that having relationships is good for gay men's psychological health (Simonsen, Blazina, & Watkins, 2000).

Besides typical relationship problems, other issues that may come up include negotiating the degree of sexual freedom that will be permitted in the relationship, dealing with each other's family, the career challenges that each faces (including relocation possibilities and possible emigration problems for the partner), and other problems created by each having been raised with the same heterosexual gender roles. Those who want to begin dating other men may need help with all aspects of deportment, including how to show interest in someone, how to ask the other out on a date, how to deal with rejection, how to deal with others approaching them, and how to act appropriately once on a date. Gay men often become sexual very early on in dating (Garnets & Kimmel, 1993; Slater, 1988), but this is not a predetermined eventuality. The client may need help in deciding such matters. Also, as in other relationship constellations, individuals are not always looking for the same outcome, so the gay person may need help in distinguishing what the other person wants from either the date or the developing relationship.

Helping Gay Men Reconnect with the Straight World

Disclosing to others is a never-ending challenge. Gay men must decide who, when, and how to tell. If a gay man is completely honest with people, he will face varied reactions in response to his disclosure, and he may find that he needs to explain himself and tell his coming-out story far more than he desires. Most gay men are discerning about who they tell, and a focus in therapy might be looking at who, when, and how to disclose. Telling family is often particularly difficult (Goldfried & Goldfried, 2001), and although most parents eventually do adjust in some manner to their son's telling them he is gay (Savin-Williams & Dube, 1998), full acceptance is still the exception rather than the rule (Ben-Ari, 1995).

Learning to manage and in some instances minimize external homophobia may be another treatment concern for gay men. The important thing to remember is that there are consequences to being gay in today's society. A gay person needs to be properly armed with the skills required to cope with external homophobia. Dealing with people who have been gay bashed is similar to dealing with other victims of violence. A longitudinal study looking at hate crimes committed against lesbian, gay, and bisexual individuals (Herek, as cited in Dworkin, 2000) provided evidence that anger, stress, and depression can last for up to five years following the attack. Doubts about one's sexual identity can also occur following an attack (Bridgewater, 1992, as cited in Dworkin). Part of proper assessment is looking for signs of posttraumatic stress disorder.

Three excellent resources that can help you design appropriate interventions for gay men and lesbian women are *Breaking Out* (Alderson, 2002), the *Handbook of Affirmative Psychotherapy with Lesbians and Gay Men* (Ritter & Terndrup, 2002), and the *Handbook of Counseling and Psychotherapy with Lesbian, Gay, Bisexual, and Transgender Clients* (Bieschke, Perez, & Debord, 2006). *Breaking Out* is designed as a self-help, how-to book for lesbians and gay men using a cognitive behavioural approach. The topics and exercises within it are very helpful in designing treatment plans. The remaining two books contain highly referenced coverage regarding affirmative counselling practice.

Dealing with Diverse Populations

Counselling individuals with multiple non-dominant identity statuses

Those who have multiple non-dominant identities experience a special challenge. For example, gay men who are also non-Caucasian, non-Christian, physically challenged, or mentally challenged may face other obstacles. A common dilemma for non-Caucasian gay men is deciding which identity status will have the greatest significance (Garnets & Kimmel, 1993). A recent study with Asian gay men found that situational factors (i.e., familial, cultural, societal influences) determined the importance and relevance of their minority identities (Operario, Han, & Choi, 2008).

Gay men of colour generally receive little support from others of their racial/ethnic background, whether Asian (Han, 2006, 2007; Mao, McCormick, & Van de Ven, 2002; Operario et al., 2008), Black (Crawford, Allison, Zamboni, & Soto, 2002; Savage & Harley, 2005), or Latino (Ramirez-Valles, 2007). Furthermore, the gay media and the gay community idealize and sexualize White, physically beautiful young men (Han, 2006). Those who don't fit the stereotype are often ignored and rendered invisible by those searching for the White ideal, including by other gay men of the same racial/ethnic background who themselves have internalized this desire for a White partner (Han, 2007). When Asians, Blacks, and Latinos are cruised sexually, they are often pursued by others having a stereotypical view of them: For example, Asians are stereotyped as effeminate *bottoms* (those preferring to be penetrated), Blacks are assumed to have large penises and to be masculine *tops* (those preferring to penetrate), and Latinos are labelled somewhere in between (Han, 2007).

> Gay men of color don't simply experience racism because they are racial minorities and homophobia because they are sexual minorities. Instead, they experience a unique type of racism and homophobia because they are gay and of color.... Within this framework, gay men and women of color are relegated to the bottom of the hierarchy in both communities. (Han, 2007, p. 66)

Many gay men of colour experience a third form of disparity compared to their heterosexual White counterparts: that of poverty (Iwaski & Ristock, 2007). Although all of these forms of social oppression create minority stress (Iwaski & Ristock), some individuals are able to transform these "experiences into behaviours leading to resiliency and even optimal functioning" (Riggle et al., 2008). There are no easy solutions to these problems, but therapists can provide support and encourage clients to look at ways to best manage their various identities.

Counselling aging gay men

Research indicates that aging gay men are as well-adjusted psychologically as their heterosexual counterparts (Bohan, 1996). A study conducted between 1997 and 1998 of 416 lesbian, gay, and bisexual adults between 60 and 91 years of age found that most reported good self-esteem and mental health. However, 27% said they lacked companionship and 13% reported feeling isolated. The participants, however, did average six people in their support networks, and those who were living with domestic partners were less lonely (Grossman, D'Augelli, & O'Connell, 2001). Other research has shown that gay men are *not* [italics mine] more isolated than older men in general (Shippy, Cantor, & Brennan, 2004). Gay men are not socially isolated from the gay community (a common stereotype), although understandably many prefer the company of other aging gay men who have had similar experiences (Kean, 2006).

Clinical concerns of aging gay men are similar to those of other older people (Garnets & Kimmel, 1993). Aging gay men may have skills that will help them better cope with the increasing possibility that they may be alone someday. For example, because most have not had women who helped take care of them, they have learned to "cook, clean iron, shop, do their own laundry, [and] make their own social arrangements" (McDonald & Steinhorn, 1990, p. 110). Nonetheless, one can speculate that those who are forced to live in nursing homes may face special challenges if they encounter prejudice and discrimination from other residents or nursing staff (Kean, 2006).

Counselling gay men living in rural communities

Feeling isolated is a common experience for gay men living in rural communities (Cody & Welch, 1997). Studies suggest that heterosexual individuals living in rural areas are generally more homophobic and heterosexist than those living in urban settings (Bohan, 1996). Despite the finding that exposure to gay people helps decrease homonegativity for most individuals (Goldfried & Goldfried, 2001), many if not most gay individuals migrate to cities to find greater acceptance and a sense of community (Bagley & Tremblay, 1998). For those who remain in rural settings, a counselling goal may be to help them establish a community network with other rural gay men, similar to what some did in northern New England (Cody & Welch).

Counselling gay students

Gay and lesbian students request help from school counsellors for problems of depression, poor self-esteem, social isolation, and suicidal ideation (Fontaine, 1998). Schools continue to be homophobic environments (Russell et al., 2001). On a typical day, high school students hear 26 anti-gay comments; 97% of the time teachers do not intervene (Sapp, 2001). Research has clearly established that schools (i.e., kindergarten to grade 12, or 13 in some jurisdictions) remain one of the most heterosexist and homophobic institutions in Canada (Totten, Quigley, & Morgan, 2004; Williams, Connolly, Pepler, & Craig, 2003). Homophobic remarks are frequently heard in Canadian schools (Totten et al.). University settings also remain largely homophobic and heterosexist (Buhrke et al., 1992; Wills & Crawford, 2000), including programs focused on continuing adult education (Hill, 2006). These concerns are addressed in the next section.

Counselling gay male adolescents

More young people are coming out than ever before (Savin-Williams, 1998, 2005b), despite how challenging it is for many of them to develop a gay identity (McFarland, 1993). Most who believe they are gay probably are gay – after all, there is no social pressure for people to be gay in our society (Ashkinazy, 1984). Remember, however, that many adolescents experience attraction to the same gender, and this is sometimes transitory (Malyon, 1981; Richardson & Hart, 1981).

The most common concern brought to the Hetrick-Martin Institute in New York, an organization that works with lesbian and gay youth, is a sense of isolation (Hetrick & Martin, 1987). Whereas those 18 years or older can frequent gay bars (at least in Alberta), which remain the most common meeting place for gay people (Shannon & Woods, 1991), minors cannot. Most gay adolescents are not out in high school, so meeting other gay youth is nearly impossible. Most large cities have a gay youth group offered by a gay information resource service, but any particular gay adolescent may not connect to those who attend it.

The second most common concern brought to the Hetrick-Martin Institute in New York is problems with family members (Hetrick & Martin, 1987). Both individual and family therapy may be indicated to help a gay adolescent through turbulence at home. Helping gay youth is a special challenge for therapists for at least two reasons:

1. If the youth is under 18 or 19 years of age in Canada, he is still a minor under the law (note: the age of majority varies from province to province). This means that parents have the legal right to full disclosure of what occurs in counselling sessions, if requested.

2. Particularly if the therapist is gay, some may perceive that the therapist is *recruiting* the client into the gay world, implying that being gay is a choice (which it is; remember that it is sexual orientation that is theorized to be immutable). Consequently, many therapists may be uncomfortable with helping a young person come out to self and others.

When working with minors, it is important to get agreement from legal guardians during the first session as to what information will and will not be kept confidential. My practice has generally been to have the legal guardian(s) attend at least the beginning of the first session with their child or adolescent. I ask for their agreement to complete confidentiality, with the provision that if I think the minor is getting into something that is harmful to self or others, I will break confidence to the legal guardian(s). I have found that both parents and their son or daughter respect this approach.

Integrating the Ecological Model with Culture-Infused Counselling

The ecological model and culture-infused counselling are complementary approaches to working with gay male clients; every encounter with a client is culture infused. You are your own person, complete with the attitudes, beliefs, and values you were raised with and the ones you rejected and changed as you came to differentiate your identity from that of your early caregivers.

I hope this chapter has helped you to open your mind and your heart to the humanness that defines each one of us, including those of us who are gay. As you have come to understand the culture of gay men, you have also learned that the concept of a positive gay identity is not identical for any two individuals. Gay men, too, are differentiated because they have challenged their attitudes, beliefs, and values from their early caregivers and they have needed to question their own perceptions of what it means to be gay both within and outside of the gay community. How you establish a strong working alliance with a gay client will be an extension of your knowledge of yourself and the other. Ultimately, it will come down to the respect and love that you genuinely feel and project: two emotions that many gay men have not experienced nearly enough in their lives.

 **Snapshot 8**

Designing Interventions

Your client, John, is a 40-year-old married man with three children. He works as a petroleum engineer, earning approximately $100,000 per year. Judy, his wife, stays home and cares for the children, aged 2, 4, and 5. Judy is trained as a legal secretary, and she plans to return to work once all of the children are in school.

John tells you he is worried because lately he has had increasing fantasies of being sexual with men. As you take his history, you discover that he was in love romantically with another man once when he was 22 years old. It didn't work out because both were homophobic and afraid it would interfere with their careers. John believes he was in love romantically with three women in the past, including Judy in the early stages of their relationship. Now, however, the relationship seems mundane – no pizzazz, no fun, no sex. In fact, they rarely talk to one another, and when they do, it is often about uncompleted tasks or childcare matters. Since the sex ended two years ago, John has had a few sexual encounters with men. He finds them exciting and enjoyable, but they often occur after drinking excessively. Consequently, John sometimes is unaware of whether the other guy is wearing a condom when he gets anally penetrated. Judy knows nothing of John's proclivities or his *extracurricular activities*.

Based on this scenario, take some time to reflect on and make decisions about the following.

Further Assessment

- What else do you want to know before setting therapeutic goals?
- How would you go about establishing John's sexual identity?
- How would you go about establishing John's sexual orientation?
- What meaning would you ascribe to his sexual behaviour with men?

Setting Goals

Therapeutic goals are generally set in collaboration with the client. In this example, if you were setting goals yourself as the therapist, what would you deem to be appropriate therapeutic goals?

Designing Interventions

Assume goals have been set with John to address the following.

- How would you go about helping John and Judy re-establish a sex life together?
- What suggestions do you have for improving their relationship in general?
- If John decided he wanted to disclose everything to his wife, how would you help prepare him for this?
- If John ended up coming out as a gay man, what would the next steps look like in counselling?
- How would you help John develop a positive gay identity (if it is established that John is in fact gay)?
- How would you teach John about safer sex?
- If John decides he is going to divorce Judy, how would you help him achieve this goal?

General Questions

- What do you think is the most fitting identity label for John?
- Do you think their marriage can sustain itself?
- What is your current understanding of safer sex? Are condoms necessary if engaging in oral sex?
- If John doesn't intend to tell his wife about his risky sexual behaviours, what are your ethical responsibilities, if any?
- What strategies or approach would you use to encourage John to inform his wife or to at least protect her sexually? (Assume they never use condoms with each other.)
- What therapeutic approach do you believe will be most helpful in John's situation? Why?

Case Study

The following case study of a 20-year-old male I call Hamed will help you begin thinking about the complexity of sexuality. The Ecological Model is applied to this fictitious case to show how an assessment can be conducted and how a treatment plan can be formulated around the client's presentation.

Hamed, a 20-year-old Lebanese man, comes to see you for personal counselling. As you greet him, you can tell that he is feeling a great deal of turmoil. As he sits in your office, you see that he is visibly shaking and highly anxious. Your first thought is that Hamed is a sensitive man who feels guilty about something he has done. Your first priority is to help him feel more comfortable. You ask if he would like a glass of water or coffee; he declines, so you begin to tell him a little about yourself. This seems to help, as he starts to look more relaxed. You begin asking him some innocuous questions:

"Where were you born?"
I was born in Lebanon.

"How long have you lived in Canada?"
It's going on 13 years.

"Do you have family here?"
Yes, I live with my dad. My mom passed away a few years ago. I also have other relatives living here: two aunts and uncles, and my grandmother.

[Building rapport.] "I have lived here for 10 years. My family lives in Saskatchewan. How would you describe your relationship with your dad?"
Well, he is very strict, and often overcontrolling. At my age, I feel I should have more freedom. He is from the old school, if you know what I mean. He believes children are children until they get married. I am supposed to get married too, but I haven't met a woman that seems at all suitable for me.

[Probing this further.] "Given your father's control, have you had much opportunity to date?"
Yes, he lets me go on many dates; in fact, he pushes me to date. I have little interest, but he keeps introducing me to more and more young women. Some of them are beautiful, and kind, but I'm just not that interested.

[Creating a comfort zone.] "I know many people who are not that interested in the opposite sex. Some of my friends, in fact, are more interested in others of the same gender. Have you been attracted to other people?" *[Client begins blushing, hesitates, and begins looking anxious again, says nothing.]*

[Creating greater comfort, probing.] "I can tell that talking about this is uncomfortable for you. Many young men, like you, have attractions to other guys, and this is perfectly normal. I might think you were a bit odd if you had never had some attraction to another guy."
Really…? I've had strong attraction to guys since I was 15 years old. I've tried very hard to get rid of these feelings, but I can't. My culture and religion [Muslim] expect me to marry, and my dad is pushing it on me. I don't feel ready. I don't know what to do. Can you help me?

Using the ecological model, you first look at societal influence. Islam religion expects men to marry (Blumenfeld & Raymond, 1993). The social environment in Lebanon is also extremely homophobic (Halwani, 1998). Hamed has spent most of his life in Canada, so he may be experiencing some conflict between the two societal expectations. Regarding religious influence, the Islam faith is opposed to homosexuality (Blumenfeld & Raymond, 1993). His father is probably opposed to the expression of homosexuality, and you would want to verify this with Hamed.

You don't know yet if Hamed has any siblings; if he has, you want to understand their views as well. Next, you want to find out about Hamed's friends. What are they like? Do they have tolerant or intolerant views on a number of topics, including homosexuality?

It's important to note that at this juncture, you don't know whether Hamed has a homosexual orientation or an undeveloped heterosexual one. Chances are, however, that he is more homosexually inclined. You might begin by asking Hamed about his sexual self-identity (heterosexual, gay, etc.). If he acknowledges an identity label as gay or bisexual, you already know that he has some openness to further exploring sexual minority statuses. If he believes he is heterosexual, you might hypothesize for the moment that he may be in denial of homosexual affect, cognition, or behaviour. You need to explore this further by asking about *crushes* he has had on girls, boys, women, and men, asking about sexual content in dreams and fantasies, sexual behaviour (if any), and emotional preference for male or female friendships. Lastly, and most importantly, you want to find out if he believes he has a propensity to fall in love romantically with men or women or both, if he ever has fallen in love, and with whom.

He may not have fallen in love and may not know his propensity. If this is the case, you know it would be premature for Hamed to give himself an identity label. If Hamed tells you he has in fact fallen in love before, with two different guys, then you can be certain he at least has a bisexual orientation. He could have a primarily homosexual orientation, but at his age, you don't know whether he might fall in love romantically with the right woman at a later time.

If Hamed's entire constellation of sexual affect, cognition, and behaviour are in accord with homosexuality, there is a greater likelihood that he has a homosexual orientation, which then suggests that he is in denial of it for reasons of societal influence, church and cultural influence, familial influence, and possibly peer influence.

Working with him to help him accept his homosexual desire will be difficult because of the huge amount of conditioning that will need to be challenged. Beyond this, helping him identify as gay will be even more difficult. If this can be attained, however, you can begin helping him develop a positive gay identity by moving into the inner triangle of the ecological model (i.e., helping him consolidate self, gay world, and straight world).

Working with people like Hamed is common. I have learned to never underestimate the fears that such clients harbour within themselves. To come out to themselves is a huge accomplishment, but disclosing to family is sometimes contraindicated. Remember my definition of positive gay identity stated earlier: they are out in most areas of their lives, wherever and whenever it is not highly disadvantageous to do so. Disclosing to family needs to be carefully assessed, and the client must decide whether it is ever appropriate. Not everyone can live without the closeness that family of origin sometimes provides, even if this means forever lying to them.

Cutting Edges in Counselling Gay Men

> For every action there is an equal and opposite reaction. – Sir Isaac Newton

Areas for Future Research

It is amazing how Sir Isaac Newton's famous third law applies not only to motion, but also to so much in human psychology. As lesbian, gay, and bisexual (LGB) individuals attain greater acknowledgement, understanding, rights, and privileges, an undercurrent exists that may serve to undermine the positive changes that are occurring in Canadian society. Conversion therapy remains alive and well in the United States (Alexander, 1999; Associated Press, 2001; Gonsiorek, 2004; Nicolosi et al., 2000a, 2000b), and it remains to be seen whether this movement will surface in Canada.

Along with social constructionism, *queer theory* has evolved, a philosophy that questions and challenges the identity constructs of gay, heterosexual, or bisexual. There are no identity labels in queer theory (Eardley, 2002), only the indefinite label of *queer*. The word *queer* was traditionally used in a derogatory manner against LGB individuals (Blumenfeld & Raymond, 1993); queer theorists have reclaimed the term and attempted to give it a positive connotation. Eardley indicated that queer theory has been criticized because its meaning constantly shifts, along with other social constructs, and the term therefore loses its meaning. If the meaning constantly changes, it cannot be all that freeing or radical. Eardley also suggested that the word *queer* was and is generally applied to gay men, not women, thereby ignoring gender politics.

If there is no immutable quality to sexual orientation, conversion therapy can be argued as an ethical therapeutic practice. In fact, some have already argued that conversion therapy is ethical (Nicolosi et al., 2000a, 2000b; Throckmorton, 1998). The result of ongoing conversion therapy based on social constructionist philosophy will only produce one societal effect: the ongoing emotional abuse and spiritual rape of those who are gay and those who are attempting to come out. As this chapter has clearly articulated, there are many aspects to human sexuality, and *sexual orientation* as a term has been poorly defined, if defined, in research that supposedly addresses it and its conversion, whatever it is.

The cutting edge of research, therefore, needs to more clearly define the construct of sexual orientation and in further investigating the aspects that change naturally, the aspects that can change through intervention strategies, and the aspects that are immutable. Likewise, it is difficult to do research on a construct until a good measure of it exists. To date, no such measure exists.

A more recent cutting edge concerns the legalization of same-sex marriage throughout Canada. This is already having global implications (Lahey & Alderson, 2004). Of the three countries that permit same-sex marriage (i.e., the Netherlands, Belgium, and Ontario and British Columbia in Canada), the two Canadian provinces are the only places where same-sex couples can marry without either partner needing to be a resident of Canada. Consequently, couples are coming to Ontario and British Columbia from other countries to marry there and then returning to their homeland to begin the challenge of having their marriage legally recognized (Lahey & Alderson). Same-sex marriage will bring with it: (a) new understandings of the construct of marriage, (b) marriage and premarital counselling for gay couples, and (c) same-sex divorce and its sequelae. Same-sex marriage is likely creating greater visibility for gays and lesbians, and this means, in turn, that counsellors will need to be equipped to deal with gay clients and their issues more so than in the past.

The Future of Counselling Gay Men

> As long as you are alive, that which is your uniqueness is also alive. All of the pain you are going through, all of your past mistakes are fertilizer that will make your plant bloom stronger and brighter. The great sadness is dying, never having enjoyed the happiness of being yourself. (Herrman, 1990, p. 89)

The future of counselling gay men is that there is a future. Gay men are here to stay. We always have been here, we still are, and we aren't going anywhere. Future work in counselling research will be in looking at how to further help gay men with their identity development and the issues that are unique to them. A great deal of work still needs to be done by individuals who are not afraid to be labelled as gay (even if they aren't). Those who have conducted any form of gay research have traditionally been assumed to be gay themselves (Warren, 1977). If you think about it, it isn't much different today. It's no wonder that the state of research in gay and lesbian studies is seriously flawed and of questionable validity.

The invisible minority must be helped to become visible if research is to advance significantly. Before that can happen, however, gay people must feel safe. But they don't. That's why you probably know so few gay people beyond your own gay friends. Gay physicians, gay dentists, gay engineers, gay geologists, gay schoolteachers, even gay professors; how many of them do you know? Where are they? They are in hiding, and don't think for a minute that they choose this path because they believe their sexual orientation is irrelevant to their everyday working lives. Every day I hear someone tell me something about their significant other, including comments from physicians, dentists, engineers, geologists, teachers, and professors. Gay people also have relationships; most are simply afraid to tell you for fear of repercussions. Fear has never helped people be honest.

Chapter Summary

The Canadian mosaic is changing, and gay individuals are beginning to secure equal rights and privileges. The psychological and spiritual damage that has been done through years of global homophobia and heterosexism, however, remains a problem for many who are trying to attain a positive gay identity. Without question, many still remain in the closet, a cold dark place that feels safer than escape. This chapter has advocated helping gay men move from darkness into light, from the misery of cold to a place of accepting and loving one's uniqueness. Besides gay men, gay youth clearly need our help. If they don't receive it, we may end up reading about them in the obituaries. Consequently, we need to hear them and help them learn to be true to themselves, even if this perceived self may change over time. Perhaps most important, we need to love them, because they may believe we are the only ones who do right now.

Regardless of age, religion, gender, or locale, gay individuals continue to live in societies throughout the world, including Canada, that do not fully accept them. Our job as therapists is to give voice to those who have had their voices diminished. But our job as citizens is to end the prejudice and discrimination once and for all.

CHAPTER 17
LEARNERS IN CROSS-CULTURAL TRANSITION: COUNSELLING INTERNATIONAL STUDENTS

Nancy Arthur

Key Terms and Concepts		
• Acculturation • Acculturation stress • Cross-cultural transition	• Culture shock • Foreign student • International student	• Internalization • Re-entry transition

Personal Introduction

"Was this counselling session helpful for that client?" I began to think about this question, and it gained a louder voice. After several years of working as a counsellor in post-secondary education, the question took on new meaning. It surfaced more and more as I reflected on the ways in which counselling was delivered and on what counts as counselling. It was on my mind as a result of an intuitive feeling at the end of some sessions – that the connection with clients was not as strong as it could be. It reared its head when I worked with new Canadians who were seeking access to counselling programs and services. It was loudest when I was asked to work with international students, although those clients rarely came to our counselling office.

The institution where I worked was trying to attract more international students, and I was asked to examine the student services infrastructure for this student population. I first looked at the literature and found few resources for counselling international students. Several articles were available that discussed the students' concerns, but few suggested how to counsel them.

The view of international students was very negative; they were portrayed as students with a myriad of problems. This did not fit my conceptualization of the students I had met – most were incredibly resourceful and successful, motivated to study and to learn about our local culture. I began to receive phone calls from faculty members who said, "We have a student from X or Y country – how should we work with that student?" What we all seemed to be looking for was a manual that would tell us what to do, as if students would neatly fit into the moulds that we created.

Prior to joining the faculty at the University of Calgary, I counselled and taught adult learners at the Southern Alberta Institute of Technology for 15 years. For the last two years, I worked exclusively with international students, a rare opportunity for a counsellor. I worked with students from more than 30 different countries who were enrolled in regular academic programs or customized training programs. Many of our students were skilled professionals who were selected from their country to further their education and bring new innovations to their country's labour force. I also had the opportunity to work on international projects in which faculty were involved in instructional roles in both domestic and international settings.

It was a time when close relationships with international students, academic faculty, and Canadian students were formed through informal and formal partnerships, all with a common goal – we were interested in proactively supporting international students. I have also been involved with programming and research on preparing international students for returning home. Working with Canadian students who have studied in other countries has opened up the scope of career planning through incorporating international experience. I have shifted my perspective about cross-cultural transitions to see it more as an unfolding process that extends well beyond the initial stage of adjustment to returning home.

In retrospect, I realize how ethnocentric my counselling has been with students from other countries and cultures. I have worried that my personal biases and the biases of the counselling paradigms that I have studied are not compatible with the needs of clients. However, I am grateful for the experience of working closely with international students – the times that we have celebrated successes and the times when, in not so subtle ways, they have let me know that "this counselling session was not helpful." It challenged me to learn more about adapting counselling services. This is an ongoing learning process that I invite you to join through your counselling work with clients who are culturally diverse.

 **Snapshot 1**

Vignette

I am sitting in class wondering what is going on here. Everybody seems to be talking at once. I can't believe how the students treat their professors here. They are often late for class. It seems so rude. They interrupt the professor and each other. People just talk when they want to. Back home that would show disrespect for the teacher. We are careful not to ask questions that suggest the person is not a good teacher. Here, students seem to be criticizing the teacher with their questions.

I am having difficulty knowing what to do in class. I sit and wait for the professor to ask me a question, but I am scared to say anything in case it is wrong. I don't want other students to think that I am stupid. I don't always agree with their answers and wonder what the right answer is. We are given class readings, but there is too much to do. It takes me a long time to read the material. It is frustrating when I stay up late to review something the professor says is important, and then we don't talk about it in class. Do you think that I will be able to pass this course? What should I do?

Amy, first-year student

Introduction

At the beginning of this decade, an estimated 1.8 million international students were enrolled in educational institutions around the world, and those numbers were expected to quadruple by 2025 (Bohm, Davis, Meares, & Pearce, 2002). The mobility of students between countries is a key priority for the internationalization of educational institutions (Association of Universities and Colleges of Canada [AUCC], 2007). **Internationalization** has been defined as "*a process that prepares the community for successful participation in an increasingly interdependent world*" (Francis, 1993, p. 5). In 2006, there were 70,000 full-time and 13,000 part-time international students enrolled in higher education in Canada, representing 7% of full-time undergraduate and almost 20% of students enrolled in graduate programs (AUCC, 2007). Canadian universities attract international students from more than 200 countries; the top 10 source countries are China, the United States, France, India, South Korea, Iran, Japan, Hong Kong, Mexico, and Pakistan (AUCC, 2007). International students need to be treated as more than sources of revenue for academic institutions. International students provide resources for internationalization of curriculum, contacts for future recruitment and alumni projects, and build a foundation for longer-term international relations (Francis, 1993; Knight, 1994). However, the emphasis on recruitment is not always matched with fostering the full potential of international students "as catalysts and agents for internationalization" (Knight, 1994, p. 7).

In designing services for international students, a key question must be addressed: "Are we doing a good job of integrating international students on our campuses and in our communities, or are we simply enrolling them and then leaving them to cope on their own?" (Cunningham, 1991, p. 2). Counsellors can play key roles in directly assisting international students, intervening on their behalf with other members of the campus community, and providing consultation about programs and policies. In addition to helping international students with common adjustment problems, counsellors also need to be prepared to address more serious mental health issues. The experience of cross-cultural transition may exacerbate psychiatric issues and psychological problems, which are estimated to be as high as 20% in the general population (Leong & Chou, 2002). Counsellors have considerable expertise to contribute to a coordinated and systematic approach to the design and delivery of services to international students (Arthur, 2004a, 2008).

Counselling international students inevitably requires counselling across cultures. Counsellors can do several things to enhance and improve their practice with international students:

- gain familiarity with the common demands that international students face when living and learning in a foreign country,

- examine their own multicultural competencies for working with students from different countries and cultures,

- acquire knowledge about the nature of cross-cultural transitions,

- be proactive about engaging this student population so that they access counselling services, and

- advocate for ways to address issues in service delivery or larger educational structures that pose barriers.

A framework for counselling international students that incorporates campus internationalization and multicultural counselling competencies is discussed by Arthur (2004a). Many of the topics introduced in this chapter, as well as considerations for multicultural counselling with specific international student populations, are expanded upon in Pope & Singaravelu (2007). Additional examples of case studies and perspectives on counselling international students are found in Arthur & Pedersen (2008). In this chapter, counsellors are invited to consider ways of applying the cultural-infused approach introduced in Chapters 3 through 6 to counselling international students.

The Mental Health of International Students

The terms *foreign student* and *international student* have been used to describe the student population that studies in other countries. Objections have been raised against using the term **foreign student** due to its negative connotations (Pedersen, 1991a). This focus on the *foreigner* detracts from the reality that all countries, cultures, and people can be considered as *foreign,* depending upon one's cultural point of view: it may be difficult for people in their home culture to view themselves as others may see them. The term **international student** includes *those students who study at an educational institution outside of their home country.* The focus of this chapter is on students from other countries who choose to live and learn in Canada.

Cross-cultural transition refers to *the process of psychological change that occurs over time as a result of exposure to cultural contrasts that differ from one's personal culture, through which individuals shift their view of self or the world around them* (Arthur, 2004a, 2008). International students are in a process of cross-cultural transition that includes leaving their home country and entering and adjusting to the host culture in which they are living and learning, followed by the transition home. Exposure to cultural contrasts and inadequate coping resources can exacerbate difficult issues of adjustment and have serious consequences for mental health. This creates a paradox: experiences that have potential for personal and cultural learning can also be sources of difficult adjustment problems.

Defining healthy functioning for this population is directly linked to students' capacity to manage cross-cultural transitions (Arthur, 2008). Healthy functioning occurs when international students can navigate through the demands of living and learning in new cultural contexts and is dependent upon students developing a repertoire of coping strategies that can be applied to transition demands. Students may possess many strengths upon entering a new culture; however, positive adaptation is highly dependent upon their capacity for cultural learning.

It is very important for counsellors to have an understanding of cross-cultural transitions and the related process of acculturation. **Acculturation** refers to *the psychological changes that result from efforts to adapt during cross-cultural transition.* **Acculturative stress** results when *the demands of a new cultural context exceed personal coping resources* (Berry, 1997; Lazarus, 1997). These processes are fundamental for appreciating the issues faced by international students and for designing appropriate counselling interventions (Johnson & Sandhu, 2007).

International students attempt to manage many of the same demands faced by local students. However, the demands faced by international students are compounded by the simultaneous demands of cultural transition (Alexander & Shaw, 2001; Leong & Chou, 2002). At the same time that international students face cultural differences in teaching and learning methodology, they must master changes in lifestyle, communication, and roles of daily living in the local culture. As a general rule, major differences between the local norms and the customs of a student's home culture lead to greater adjustment difficulties (Pedersen, 1991a). Given the sheer number of countries and cultures involved in international education, it should not be assumed that students experience cross-cultural transitions as equally stressful (Tanaka, Takai, Kohyama, & Fujihara, 1994; Wan, Chapman, & Biggs, 1992).

Psychological stress is influenced by students' cultural backgrounds, the length of time they spend in the host country, and their levels of acculturation and intercultural competence (Wilton & Constantine, 2003).

Snapshot 2

Myths about International Students

1. **Myth:** Canadians subsidize international students.

   Fact: Canadian students are subsidized through provincial and federal government funding, so they directly pay only a portion of their actual tuition costs. International students do not receive this benefit. Their tuition costs are typically two to three times more than those paid by local students.

2. **Myth:** Foreign students take *seats* in educational programs away from Canadian students.

   Fact: Educational programs establish the number of seats available in academic programs. In most cases, international students are *extra to program* quotas.

3. **Myth:** International students are the academically best students from their country.

   Fact: Some students are awarded sponsorship due to their excellent record of academic achievement. However, there is wide variation in the background preparation and motivation for studying in a foreign educational program.

4. **Myth:** All foreign students have access to Canadian education.

   Fact: All prospective students must receive immigration authorization from their home country as well as from immigration authorities in Canada for student visas. Beyond immigration relationships between countries, the costs of a foreign education are prohibitive for students from poor families in many countries.

5. **Myth:** International students come from wealthy families.

   Fact: Financial resources are a critical factor in accessing foreign education. In addition to private funding, some students receive sponsorship through their government, employer, or international development programs.

6. **Myth:** International students who have previous travel experience will not experience culture shock.

   Fact: Culture shock is a normal reaction for all people who are faced with cultural contrasts. It may be difficult for adult students who perceive themselves as competent to reconcile their reactions to transition demands. Education about transitions can help students be proactive in developing coping strategies.

7. **Myth:** International students prefer single-session counselling, as reflected in their usage rates.

   Fact: Like all clients, international students prefer counselling that is meaningful to them. Their need for immediate resources to solve emerging problems may transfer to fewer sessions spaced over the period of cross-cultural transition. Usage rates may be an indicator of service access and levels of satisfaction or dissatisfaction.

8. **Myth:** International students are difficult to work with, as they do not view counselling as valuable.

   Fact: Many international students are not familiar with Western constructs of counselling and need assistance to understand the relevance of counselling to academic and personal success. Cultural views of help-seeking and addressing problems, along with the cultural competencies of counsellors, are important considerations.

Most international students appear to resolve adjustment issues through time and experience in the new culture. Immediate demands for cultural adaptation lead students to operate in *survival mode,* responding to cultural demands as best they can. When a student's usual ways of coping do not match demands in the new environment, there can be serious consequences for the student's personal and academic adjustments (Arthur, 2004a; Chen, 1999). The rapid pace and the sheer volume of new demands, along with pressing needs for cultural competency, can lead to serious stress reactions in the form of anxiety or depression (Reynolds & Constantine, 2007; Rosenthal, Russell, & Thomson, 2008).

Despite these considerations, international students should not be viewed only in light of their problems of transition. Most manage exceedingly well in the face of cultural adversity and never access the services of professional counsellors. The counselling literature is full of platitudes about the strength and resiliency of this population and pays less attention to the huge variations in experiences between international students from similar and differing nations (Popadiuk & Arthur, 2004). More attention is needed to understand ways to make counselling services more responsive to international students from diverse backgrounds. Counsellors could also be more proactive in facilitating the positive adaptation of students through health promotion and illness prevention programming (Popadiuk & Arthur, 2004).

Before exploring common adjustment issues, it is important for you to have an understanding of the nature of cross-cultural transition. This is the context for appreciating cultural influences on the mental health and adjustment experiences of international students (Arthur, 2008).

Perspectives on Cross-Cultural Transition

Research on international students has emphasized adjustment problems, paid less attention to the resiliency of this population, and generally ignored dynamics of cross-cultural adjustment (Popadiuk & Arthur, 2004). As noted earlier, a hallmark characteristic of international students is that they are in cross-cultural transition (Pedersen, 1991a). They are temporary sojourners to a foreign country for the duration of their academic program, as determined by the conditions of their immigration status. Navigating differences between home and host cultures is a fundamental aspect of their transition experience. It is important to note that international students face two pivotal transitions: the transition from home to host culture and the re-entry transition home.

Cross-cultural transition involves a process that unfolds over time, as international students are faced with cultural contrasts between their home country and the culture of the host country. The essence of transition is that individuals experience a shift in their personal assumptions or ways in which they view themselves, relationships, and the world around them (Schlossberg, 1984, 1992). Even when transitions are generally viewed as positive and desirable, international students may simultaneously experience a profound sense of loss as familiar ways of behaving, routines, customs, and relationships also change (Johnson & Sandhu, 2007).

People in cross-cultural transition are immediately faced with learning and adjusting to new role demands. For example, international students must rapidly acquire cultural knowledge about local educational systems, interpersonal relationships, and the demands of daily living, such as transportation, changes in diet, and personal routines. Exposure to norms and behaviour that contrasts with one's personal culture can trigger dissonance about prior understandings of self, assumptions about others, or beliefs about the world (Ishiyama, 1995a, 1995b). Cross-cultural transitions result from exposure to external changes and differences in the physical environment, such as climate, food, and housing, as well as to internal changes, such as role changes and shifts in social status.

Role adjustment has been proposed as one perspective for understanding cross-cultural transition (Ishiyama, 1995a, 1995b; Pedersen, 1991a). International students may have to shed some prior roles and usual ways of operating in those roles and build new sources of identity. Immediately upon entering the host culture, role demands can create pressure for learning appropriate behaviour and adjusting to new ways of behaviour. The capacity for rapid role learning is a pivotal influence on international student's adjustment (Pedersen). Disruptions to roles that provided sources of self-validation and social support can be experienced as very stressful (Ishiyama, 1995a, 1995b). Role changes during transition may create opportunities for trying new ways of behaving, such as gender role expectations (Popadiuk, 2008). However, role changes may also lead to confusion about personal identity and how to reconcile role expectations between home and host cultures (Arthur & Popadiuk, in press).

Along with role adjustment, international students may experience debilitating stress if their coping strategies, including social support, are inadequate to manage the demands of the new culture (Mallinckrodt & Leong, 1992; Wan et al., 1992). Taxonomies of coping skills that have been developed for a variety of life transitions (Lazarus &

Folkman, 1984; Schlossberg, 1984, 1992), career transitions (Brammer & Abrego, 1992), and cross-cultural transitions (Arthur, 2000; Winkelman, 1994) can be applied to the transition needs of international students.

Culture Shock

Culture shock refers to *the process of adjustment during cross-cultural transitions that manifest in psychological or physiological reactions of stress* (Oberg, 1960; Ward, Bochner, & Furnham, 2001; Winkelman, 1994). Culture shock was originally portrayed as a stage model (Lysgaard, 1955) including contact with the host culture, conflict with the host culture, and adaptation to the host culture. Patterns of adjustment were represented as a U-curve with upward and downward shifts in morale along the three stages. A W-curve model represented an additional stage of adjustment when people returned to their home culture (Gullahorn & Gullahorn, 1963).

The major contribution of these early models is that they depict changes in cross-cultural adjustment over time. The static nature of these models and the lack of attention paid to individual differences have been criticized (Furnham & Bochner, 1986; Leong & Chou, 2002). Research has indicated that there is variation in people's cross-cultural experiences, accounted for by factors such as personal adjustment at the time of entering the new culture, the cultural novelty found in the host country, perceptions about aspects of the new culture that are stressful, and the coping resources available for people to use during cross-cultural transition (Furnham & Bochner, 1986; Ward & Kennedy, 1993). The heuristic value of the original models of culture shock must not overshadow the need for counsellors to explore the personal circumstances and reactions of international students at different stages of cross-cultural transition (Arthur, 2004a).

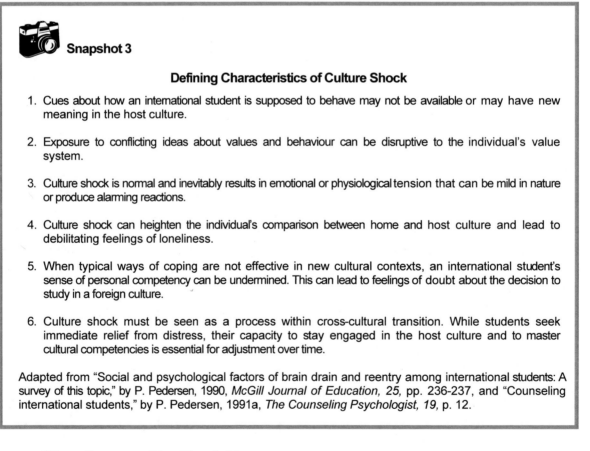

Snapshot 3

Defining Characteristics of Culture Shock

1. Cues about how an international student is supposed to behave may not be available or may have new meaning in the host culture.

2. Exposure to conflicting ideas about values and behaviour can be disruptive to the individual's value system.

3. Culture shock is normal and inevitably results in emotional or physiological tension that can be mild in nature or produce alarming reactions.

4. Culture shock can heighten the individual's comparison between home and host culture and lead to debilitating feelings of loneliness.

5. When typical ways of coping are not effective in new cultural contexts, an international student's sense of personal competency can be undermined. This can lead to feelings of doubt about the decision to study in a foreign culture.

6. Culture shock must be seen as a process within cross-cultural transition. While students seek immediate relief from distress, their capacity to stay engaged in the host culture and to master cultural competencies is essential for adjustment over time.

Adapted from "Social and psychological factors of brain drain and reentry among international students: A survey of this topic," by P. Pedersen, 1990, *McGill Journal of Education, 25,* pp. 236-237, and "Counseling international students," by P. Pedersen, 1991a, *The Counseling Psychologist, 19,* p. 12.

Culture Shock as a Cyclical Process

Contemporary views of culture shock (Pedersen, 1995b; Winkelman, 1994) address many of the shortcomings of earlier models. Four phases are outlined, with the premise that they are both sequential and cyclical. The first phase, characterized as the *honeymoon* or *tourist phase,* assumes that people who enter other cultures have positive expectations and that they are intrigued with learning about cultural differences. The stress associated with cross-cultural transition is usually viewed in positive ways during this phase.

The second phase of *crisis* or *disintegration* occurs with the experience of dissatisfaction with the host culture. This may occur at different points in the cross-cultural transition, ranging from immediately upon arrival to after several months of residency. What was formerly perceived as fascinating and exciting becomes perceived as a source of irritation and disappointment. When the stage of crisis is entered early in the cross-cultural transition and is prolonged over time, students may cope through shutting themselves off from the host culture. Preoccupation with returning home can disrupt a focus on academic achievement and efforts to be successful in the host culture. Counsellors can have an important role as *cultural therapists* (Dei, 1992) in assisting international students to resolve difficult issues, particularly those that are experienced as crisis, and to prevent issues from escalating to the point where the student sees no other option than to return home. Although research is lacking on international students, studies of employees have indicated that it is difficult to resolve the sense of personal failure that accompanies early termination of a cross-cultural work experience (Harrison, Chadwick, & Scales, 1996).

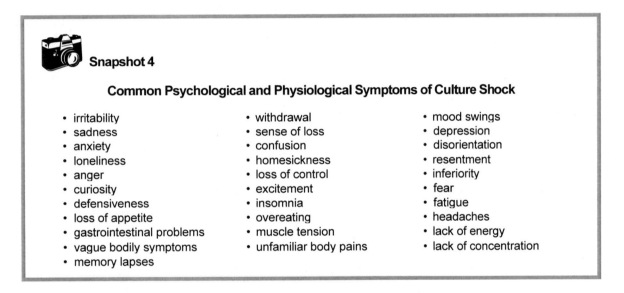

Snapshot 4

Common Psychological and Physiological Symptoms of Culture Shock

• irritability	• withdrawal	• mood swings
• sadness	• sense of loss	• depression
• anxiety	• confusion	• disorientation
• loneliness	• homesickness	• resentment
• anger	• loss of control	• inferiority
• curiosity	• excitement	• fear
• defensiveness	• insomnia	• fatigue
• loss of appetite	• overeating	• headaches
• gastrointestinal problems	• muscle tension	• lack of energy
• vague bodily symptoms	• unfamiliar body pains	• lack of concentration
• memory lapses		

The *adjustment* and *reorientation phase* (Pedersen, 1995b; Winkelman, 1994) is characterized by a large degree of learning and trying new ways of coping with contrasts found in the host culture. International students move from a position of cultural and personal crisis to one of cultural learning and appreciation. This reorientation does not mean that all problems with culture shock end; international students develop the attitudes and skills needed for effective problem solving.

The fourth phase of culture shock depicts the *adaptation, resolution,* or *acculturation* processes of cross-cultural transition (Pedersen, 1995b; Winkelman, 1994). International students feel a greater sense of stability as their sense of self-efficacy increases and they experience success in the host culture. Despite earlier difficulties and ongoing challenges of living in a foreign culture, cultural learning is experienced as highly rewarding. In this phase, international students experience a greater sense of stability as they experience success in navigating through the new culture.

Acculturation and Cross-Cultural Transition

Another framework that has been applied to populations in cross-cultural transition is the process of acculturation (Berry, 1997, 2001, 2008). Strengths of this model are that it avoids describing cross-cultural transition as a linear process and incorporates both common patterns of adjustment and individual differences. Acculturation focuses on the psychological changes that result from efforts to adapt during cross-cultural transition. Factors such as the scope and severity of demands in the new culture and the individual's capacity for learning are viewed as important influences. Acculturative stress may be experienced as minor problems of adjustment or may manifest in serious psychological disturbances (Berry, 2006a). This model also considers acculturation as a multidimensional process involving newcomers and the host society. The receptiveness of the host society to international students is seen to play a large part in the integration and acculturation process (Johnson & Sandhu, 2007).

Berry's model of acculturation emphasizes the complexity of cross-cultural transition, noting the interrelationships between psychological, socio-cultural, and economic adaptations. *Psychological adaptation* refers to internal psychological outcomes, such as a positive sense of personal identity, mental health, and a sense of personal satisfaction in the new culture (Berry, 1997). *Socio-cultural adaptation* refers to external matters that impact acculturative stress, such as the individual's capacity for managing social demands such as family, work, or student roles (Berry, 1997; Ward & Kennedy, 1993). The emphasis on financial support and financial stability in *economic adaptation* is relevant for international students (Berry, 1997).

The dimensions of voluntariness, mobility, and permanency are also important for understanding acculturation (Berry, 1997). There are variations in the degree to which international students *volunteer* to study in another country. The motivation to study abroad is influential for international student adjustment (Chirkov, Safdar, de Guzman, & Playford, 2008). According to Chirkov et al. (2008), students' motivations to study abroad may be classified according to *preservation* or *autonomous* goals. In the former case, international students' motivations to study abroad are strongly connected to adverse conditions in their home country. Safety or security issues can be paramount or pressures from family members to study abroad may be the primary consideration. In contrast, international students with autonomous goals strive towards self-determination and mastery of their goals, including academic and occupational pursuits. These students have typically invested considerable time and energy into pursuing foreign education prior to arriving in the host country. Students' motivations for international study are predictive of adjustment outcomes, and may provide important clues for helping some students to clarify their academic goals and build positive motivation for attaining them.

Regardless of their motivations for studying in another country, international students are temporary sojourners who will inevitably be returning home. From the point of arriving in the host country, students should be preparing for their eventual return home, including future academic and occupational plans (NAFSA, 1996).

Adaptation to cross-cultural transition can be depicted as four essential styles or strategies of acculturation. These are based upon the degree to which people maintain their original cultural identity and the extent to which they actively participate with other groups in the new culture (Berry, 1997, 2008). *Assimilation* occurs when international students do not want or are unable to hold on to their original cultural identity. The onus is on international students to bridge the distance between cultures, as there may be less interest expressed by members of the host culture to learn about the students' culture of origin. The efforts needed for international students to *fit into* the local culture to support academic success may necessitate suspending or giving up some elements of their cultural identity.

Alternatively, international students who resist immersion into the new culture and hang onto their original cultural identity adopt a position of *separation*. This may be a preferred choice in which contact with members of the host culture is minimized. There may be barriers in the host culture that prevent international students from establishing meaningful relationships, while, at the same time, students may not have sources of support to maintain their original cultural identity. This can lead to a profound sense of *exclusion* or *marginality*.

The strategy of *integration* occurs when it is possible for international students to actively engage with the local culture and to maintain some degree of their original culture (Berry, 1997). The development of a bicultural identity (Helms, 1995) is generally considered to be a significant achievement in adapting to cross-cultural transition (Berry, 2008). As a result of cultural learning, international students incorporate aspects of the new culture into their personal identity. This allows them greater flexibility in navigating between both home and host cultures. However, this process is subtle and the amount of change in personal identity may not be apparent until students return to their home culture. It is through feedback from family and friends that many international students recognize the degree to which they have acquired a bicultural identity.

Readers are encouraged to consider other models of acculturation reviewed by Arthur, Merali, and Djuraskovic, which can be found in Chapter 12 on counselling immigrants and refugees.

A Model of Stress and Coping

Lazarus and Folkman's (1984) model of stress has been applied to international students to understand their experience of psychological stress (Chen, 1999). The transactional model of stress considers the reciprocal interaction between person and environment in determining how demands are perceived, how people cope, and their experience of negative and positive emotions (Folkman & Moskowitz, 2004; Lazarus, 1990, 1993, 2006).

At the heart of the model is the concept of *appraisal*. When faced with demands in the environment, the individual simultaneously engages in two facets of appraisal. During *primary appraisal*, the person evaluates the situation for personal relevancy; that is, what is at stake here? At the same time, through *secondary appraisal*, the person evaluates resources available to manage the situation; that is, how can I cope with this situation? Depending upon the degree of congruence between these levels of appraisal, the individual may evaluate the demands of a situation as benign or stressful. Appraisals of stress include harm, threat, and challenge. *Harm* refers to the psychological harm that has already occurred to the individual. *Threat* refers to the anticipation of unwelcome consequences. *Challenge* may be a more positive aspect of stress; however, the person still appraises that the coping resources available for deployment are inadequate.

Upon encountering a new cultural environment, international students are faced with many new demands or situations that require coping in new ways. When a student perceives that prior experience may not be applied in the new culture and is unfamiliar with acceptable ways of behaving, a stress reaction is inevitable. Even when students deliberately seek out new experiences, they may feel stressed about the challenges that they appraise to be part of living and learning in a new culture. Even when aspects of cross-cultural transitions are perceived as stressful, international students can simultaneously experience negative and positive emotions (Folkman, 2008). Counsellors can utilize research on stress and coping to explore international students' appraisal of demand characteristics in the environment and their perceptions about available coping resources (Ryan & Twibell, 2000). Interventions may involve learning about local resources and skill training for utilizing those resources.

Common Transition Issues of International Students

Sandhu (1994) organized the common concerns of international students into two domains: (a) interpersonal factors related to their environment and surroundings and (b) intrapersonal factors related to internal processes. In reality, there is tremendous overlap between these issues. The capacity of international students to resolve stress associated with one domain can be pivotal for success in other domains. For example, international students with higher amounts of general life stress and lower levels of social support are more likely to experience greater stress associated with academic demands (Misra, Melanee, & Burant, 2003). It is important to emphasize that each international student will have a unique cross-cultural experience. However, familiarity with the common concerns of international students provides a foundation from which to explore individual experiences.

Academic Performance

Academic concerns represent the major transition issue faced by international students (Walker, 1999). Consequently, the stress experienced by international students frequently pivots around academic concerns (Wan et al., 1992). Counsellors need to be aware that academic concerns may have complex meanings. First, there are many investments made in academic success prior to beginning an academic program. Most students leave family and friends behind and often leave positions of employment. Financial sponsors, including family, corporate, and government stakeholders, have a vested interest in student success. A student's immigration status is contingent upon academic success, and the threat of failure can be experienced as an overwhelming pressure (Arthur, 1997).

International students may also experience academic concerns due to prior academic preparation, discrepancies between the teaching and learning methodologies of home and host cultures, expectations of performance, curriculum content, and workload issues. These demands may be experienced as either understimulation or overstimulation, depending upon the prior experience and preparation of students. Students who are accustomed to didactic methods, a high degree of structure, and formal lines of authority in the teacher-student relationship may struggle to respond to the local learning norms based on constructivist and discovery methodology (Barker, Child, Gallois, Jones, & Callan, 1991; Sheehan & Pearson, 1995). International graduate students may feel stressed about conflicts in the relationship with their faculty supervisors. Perceived lack of openness, time to discuss academic issues, the quality of feedback, unclear and unmet expectations, and poor English proficiency are sources of potential conflict in student-supervisory relationships (Adrian-Taylor, Noels, & Tischler, 2007). A systemic issue is the degree to which faculty members are prepared for supervising international students.

Instructors and peers may misinterpret an international student's lack of participation in classroom learning as a sign of disinterest or lack of language proficiency. However, when classroom discussions and learning assignments are restricted to local contexts, international students may struggle to find relevant points of entry into the learning process (Huxur, Mansfield, Nnazor, Schuetze, & Segawa, 1996). International students become discouraged if they doubt their competencies or the extent to which new learning can be transferred to their home environment. These examples illustrate the types of influences on whether international students feel included or excluded in their academic programs.

Communication Problems

Language proficiency is a critical factor in the academic and social adjustment of international students (Hayes & Lin, 1994; Jochems, Snippe, Smid, & Verweij, 1996; Tanaka, Takai, Kohyama, Fujihara, & Minami, 1997). Students with high proficiency to study in the dominant language of the host environment are less likely to view academic demands as stressful (Wan et al., 1992). When students lack language proficiency, they struggle to understand new content in their academic program and lack the language to fully engage in learning processes. Language capacity has also been implicated as a barrier in the career choices made by international students because some students may pursue occupations that do not require high levels of English language competence (Reynolds & Constantine, 2007).

Six components of language competency have been identified in the intercultural communication literature (Redmond & Bunyi, 1993). First, *social decentring* refers to the capacity of international students to understand and adapt to others who are culturally different. Communication from a monocultural perspective may lack the flexibility of communicating in ways that make sense to others. Second, knowledge of the host culture builds capacity for social decentring. Familiarity with the history, norms, and cues for nonverbal behaviour can reduce anxiety about social appropriateness and minimize intercultural misunderstanding. Third, language competency is rated as the single most important factor in international students' adjustment (Ying & Liese, 1990). This is inextricably tied to the fourth component of intercultural adaptation: language competency supports students in becoming interpersonally flexible, as they can transcend their personal focus and concentrate on adapting to different points of view. Fifth, there is a reciprocal relationship between communication effectiveness and intercultural competence: language competency helps international students feel more confident about engaging in interactions with people in the local culture and improves the quality of social interactions (Huxur et al., 1996). In turn, individual differences in adjustment are strongly associated with confidence in using language skills (Swagler & Ellis, 2003; Yang, Noels, & Saumure, 2006). Ultimately, the capacity for intercultural communication impacts social integration and how well international students are able to participate in local social networks (Redmond & Bunyi, 1993). Correspondingly, intercultural competence influences the acculturation process and international students' experience of stress (Wilton & Constantine, 2003).

Accessing Social Support

The availability of social support during cross-cultural transition is pivotal for positive adaptation. In the transition to a new country, international students lose immediate access to their established social network of family, friends, and community contacts, except what is possible through technology such as e-mail. This loss can result in severe feelings of homesickness (McKinlay, Pattison, & Gross, 1996; Sandhu & Asrabadi, 1994). Without their usual sources of personal validation (Ishiyama, 1995a, 1995b), international students are at risk for debilitating stress if they are unable to establish adequate social support in the host culture. The role of social support as a powerful coping resource during life transitions is well-established (e.g., Schlossberg, 1984), and it is considered essential for managing the stress associated with cross-cultural transition (Ward & Kennedy, 1993).

International students may be reticent about their need to access social support in the host culture. This is usually connected to concerns about language competency, social appropriateness, and a sense of social isolation in the host culture. They may be more likely to approach faculty members or students from similar cultural backgrounds for assistance with academic and personal issues (Mallinckrodt & Leong, 1992).

Caution is advised about grouping international students together and assuming that there will be compatibility. It should also not be assumed that bringing international and local students together automatically results in cross-cultural friendships. The *contact* approach must be supported with interventions to overcome language barriers and diverse values (Arthur, 2004a). Students in the host culture are often inexperienced in bridging cross-cultural friendships and lack sensitivity about ways to include international students in their social and academic networks (Hayes & Lin, 1994). Programs designed to facilitate international friendships are helpful to prepare students for sustaining cross-cultural relationships (Nesdale & Todd, 2000; Saidla & Grant, 1993). Although international students may desire more contact with local students, negative or unfulfilling experiences may lead them to seek out a common source of identity through other international students who share language and other cultural similarities (Arthur, 2004a; Schmitt, Spears, & Branscombe, 2003). Students who enjoy friendships in social networks involving local and international students from other countries experience more positive adjustment (Kahima & Loh, 2005).

Financial Concerns

Financial assistance for international students through host educational institutions is limited. With increasing financial constraints, post-secondary institutions are examining ways to recruit more international students, yet are reluctant to subsidize their academic programs, particularly those of undergraduate students (Lambert, 1992). Differential tuition fees can be thousands of dollars more for international students in comparison to the fees of local students.

Changes in the standard of living can be a major factor in cross-cultural transitions. For some students, crossing cultures may offer financial advantages. However, higher costs of living in the host culture can threaten the financial and social status previously enjoyed by international students and their family members in their home country (Chittooran & Sankar-Gomes, 2007).

It should not be assumed that international students come from wealthy families. Certainly, there are students whose personal circumstances permit expenditure on foreign education and a generous lifestyle in the host culture. For others, a foreign education is only possible through sponsorship from government, foreign aid, or considerable financial drain on the resources of immediate and extended family (Pedersen, 1991a). In the latter case, students may feel additional pressure to succeed academically as they realize what has been invested in their future. There may be reluctance to request additional assistance from family resources, even in cases where students lack basic items such as food and clothing. Concerns about finances are a major distraction for international students. Assistance with budgeting and information about local resources may be essential to helping international students maintain their focus on academic achievement.

Discrimination and Racism

Living in a foreign country may bring unexpected experiences of discrimination and racism (Dei, 1992; Sandhu & Asrabadi, 1994). Life as an international student may represent a change of social status; that is, it may be the first time a student has been in a minority group (Schmitt et al., 2003) or even the first time a student has confronted racism (Constantine, Anderson, Berkel, Caldwell, & Utsey, 2005). Negative stereotypes held against members of racial and ethnic minorities can spill over into negative interactions with international students.

Institutional racism may be insidiously woven into campus policies and procedures. For example, student visa restrictions typically limit the employment opportunities of international students (Dei, 1992). Even when international students are eligible for employment, employer preferences for local experience may be a barrier. Educational curriculum may also inadvertently be sources of discrimination. There may be biases in curriculum about the *right* way of understanding the world, based on Eurocentric experiences (Dei, 1992). This can silence international students and restrict the degree to which diverse practices are validated. A key issue concerns whether or not the expertise of international students is invited and/or considered valid.

Curriculum can also be problematic when portrayals of people, norms, and practices in other countries are outdated, generalized, or focused on problematic features of that society, as is often reported in the media. These uninformed and outdated views of international students and their countries can extend to the views of student services personnel and materials used in international student programming. Problems of discrimination and racism may be represented in blatant forms of interpersonal relations, in subtle ways, or through lack of action in responding to student needs.

Gender Role Expectations

Transition to a country with more liberal gender norms can be disruptive to belief systems and challenge notions of appropriate behaviour (Arthur & Popadiuk, in press; Popadiuk, 2008). Students from countries where notions of patriarchy are firmly entrenched may be exposed to notions about egalitarian relationships or the acceptability of public expressions of affection. In general, female international students hold more liberal attitudes than males about the rights and roles of women (Gibbons, Stiles, & Shkodriani, 1991). Female international students may see the advantages of more freedom and personal rights, whereas males may be reluctant to give up perceived power and associated male privileges. Yet, research on gender differences in the experiences of international students shows that females experience greater levels of distress (Mallinckrodt & Leong, 1992). This may be partially explained by role confusion and expectations for role behaviour, role conflicts with family expectations, and lack of programming to address women's experiences (Popadiuk, 2008).

Most of the literature on gender role expectations assumes that international students will be travelling from more *traditional* countries to the more *liberal* countries of Europe and the United States and to Commonwealth countries. Increased opportunities are available for students to study in countries that are more conservative in their depictions of gender norms. In these instances, international students may need to temper their judgments about differential treatment between men and women and modify their typical ways of dressing or behaving in public places. Regardless of the direction of student mobility, cross-cultural transitions may pose an opportunity to examine new ways of thinking about our gendered world.

Exposure to new ways of behaving in gender roles can be confusing for international students at a time when they are trying to understand the nuances of social interaction. The complexity of explicit and implicit norms of behaviour can lead to misunderstandings and behaviour considered beyond the boundaries of acceptance in local contexts. The interpretation of verbal and nonverbal behaviour between cultures includes the expression of sexual behaviour (Tyler & Boxer, 1996). Cross-cultural miscommunication can have serious consequences for international students if it is deemed to be sexual harassment or assault, regardless of the intent. With the implementation of policies regarding the prevention and adjudication of sexual harassment on most campuses, international students need to be educated about appropriate and inappropriate behaviour.

Family Issues

The adjustment of international students during their cross-cultural transition to a foreign country may be strongly impacted by their relationships with family members. An inability to participate in family relations and access a family support system can be a major source of stress for students (Parr, Bradley, & Bingi, 1992). International students miss family rites of passage, rituals, and their role in fulfilling family-related responsibilities. Students may feel like they are living with two separate identities – who they are as a family member and who they are in the new culture. Attempts to resolve these differences can lead international students to question their identity as they realize they have shifted in their values and beliefs away from their family of origin. For others, experience in the foreign culture provides a firmer grasp and appreciation of the values and practices of their family (Arthur & Popadiuk, in press).

It is important to consider family members who accompany international students (Chittooran & Sankar-Gomes, 2007). Family members may experience issues related to social and economic status, role changes, language proficiency, ability to be gainfully employed, and social isolation. It is also important to consider the differential rates of acculturation for family members as a consequence of varying levels of participation in the host culture. Exposure to a new culture can result in tension and debate about the desirability of incorporating new cultural practices into the family unit. Concern with family matters can be a serious distraction for international students.

Career Issues

There is limited research on the career development needs of international students (Arthur, 2007; Reynolds & Constantine, 2007; Singaravelu, White, & Bringaze, 2005; Yang, Wong, Hwang, & Heppner, 2002). Some research has suggested that international students' primary concerns are with job search and placement (Shen & Herr, 2004; Spencer-Rodgers, 2000). Undergraduate and graduate students have different career-related needs due to the stage and specialization and focus in their career preparation (Mallinckrodt & Leong, 1992; Shen & Herr, 2004). Research is only beginning to identify the variables that are relevant for career counselling with international students. For example, variables such as vocational identity, developing a stable understanding of aspirations, interests, and abilities may be impacted by international students' acculturation levels (Shih & Brown, 2000). Recent research has suggested that higher acculturation stress is associated with lower career aspirations (Reynolds & Constantine, 2007). Preoccupation with cross-cultural adjustment may distract students from focusing on their career goals.

A common theme found in the available literature is that international students would benefit from career and life planning skills. The term *career* may have different meanings across cultures and the content and relevance of career counselling services may be unfamiliar to international students. Arthur (2007) organized international students' career planning and decision-making needs around three phases of cross-cultural transition: a) managing the cross-cultural transition of entering a new culture, b) learning in a new cultural context, and c) transferring international expertise to work settings in either the host or home countries.

For most international students, the motivation to study abroad is inextricably linked to the enhancement of qualifications and future employment prospects. Yet, academic and vocational choices may not be consolidated when they begin their foreign education. Students' interests may change or they may discover that their original plans are no longer realistic (Singaravelu et al., 2005). As students live and learn in a new cultural context, it is possible they will discover new career options or reconsider their original plans.

Exposure to cross-cultural transition often results in shifts in personal identity in which international students experience dissonance about their values and beliefs. For some students, this experience helps them to gain a stronger appreciation for their host cultural identity (Arthur & Popadiuk, in press). Other students may experience a sense of personal crisis as they attempt to come to terms with new understandings about themselves or about their roles and relationships. Values clarification can be integrated into career counselling to help students gain clarity about their career goals.

As international students progress towards the end of their international education experience, career counselling may be utilized to help them explore new educational or vocational options and to debrief ways of incorporating international experience into future career planning (Arthur, 2003, 2007). Many students decide to pursue employment in the host country and benefit from exploring the implications of such decisions and from exploring resources for job search (Shen & Herr, 2004). The Canadian government has targeted international students in a strategy to attract increased numbers of skilled immigrants (Industry Canada, 2002). As a result of changes in immigration policy, career planning may pivot around a key decision about pursuing immigration to Canada or returning home.

Re-entry Transition Issues

Re-entry transition is defined as *the re-acculturation of the individual to the home culture after an extended period of exposure to another culture* (Adler, 1981). There are three important distinctions between the initial stage of transition and re-entry (Martin, 1984). The first distinction pertains to expectations about the degree of adjustment required. International students, their families and friends, and members of the host culture usually expect some degree of adjustment required when entering a new culture. However, international students and their families may operate with the assumption that the home environment will be the same and they do not believe they will have adjustment problems. Lack of preparation for the re-entry transition can leave students ill-prepared and without the benefits of anticipatory coping (Arthur, 2003).

A second distinction between the stages of cross-cultural transition is the amount of change (Martin & Harrell, 1996). Upon immersion into a new culture, international students immediately face contrasts and changes. However, the degree of change in the home culture may be more subtle, cumulative, and not expected. A lack of appreciation for the degree of change that occurs during cross-cultural transition increases the risk of adjustment problems and *reverse culture shock* (Gaw, 2000; Leung, 2007). Alternatively, lack of change in the home environment may be experienced as a difficult adjustment. The third distinction pertains to international students gaining awareness about the changes that have occurred (Adler, 1981). It may only be upon returning to the home culture and receiving feedback from family and friends that international students recognize how much change has occurred; this includes change in the environment around them and personal change that has resulted from their experience as an international student.

Snapshot 5

Vignette

Rene is a Canadian student who participated in the international option of her degree in education. She worked in South Korea teaching English for a semester. The initial transition was difficult as she found she had to adjust her teaching methods to meet cultural expectations and she missed her friends and family in Canada. However, Rene quickly became fond of her students and new life in Korea. She was able to travel throughout the country and tried her best to immerse herself in the local culture. However, when Rene returned to Canada, her enthusiasm for the international experience was quickly replaced with a sense of discouragement. She missed many things about Korean culture, such as the pace of life she had experienced, and her interactions with students and their families. Although she was glad to reunite with her family and friends, she found that they had little interest in her international experience. When she applied for a job teaching in Canada, she found that employers did not consider her overseas teaching experience as valuable. In fact, one employer interrupted her during an interview and said, "Rene, traveling to Korea sounds very nice, but what is your teaching experience in Canada?" Rene began to second-guess her choice to study abroad.

International students have reported a wide range of re-entry concerns, including loss of the host culture, values conflicts, transferability of educational and language expertise, career mobility, economic and political conditions in their home country, and resuming prior relationship or employment roles (Arthur, 2003). Experience in the foreign culture may also create dissonance about returning home. Despite the positive associations made about reuniting with friends, family, and other aspects of the home environment, international students may have mixed feelings about leaving the foreign culture and returning home. This can be prompted through recognition of changes in identity through personal learning and lifestyle changes in the new culture (Wang, 1997). Beyond physically relocating home, the re-entry transition involves a psychological process of adapting to the home culture. Students may be surprised that they feel conflicted about the home and host culture and may wonder how they will ever feel at home again. It may be beneficial to reframe re-entry as a time of *new* discoveries about the home culture, rather than as returning to an *old* familiar culture (Arthur, 2008). Psychoeducational interventions about the re-entry transition can be designed and delivered in various formats, such as web-based information, workshops, and presentations by international students who have experienced reverse culture shock (Arthur, 2003; Leung, 2007). Students who experience higher levels of anxiety about leaving the host culture and returning home may benefit from individual counselling.

Counselling Considerations for Working with International Students

As noted in the model of culture-infused counselling overviewed in Chapter 3, counsellors are inevitably involved in multicultural counselling when they work with international students. The importance of cultural competencies and flexibility for working with a diverse student population are paramount (Arthur, 2004a). Readers are encouraged to review the culture-infused counselling competencies detailed in Chapter 3 and consider their application with international students. First, counsellors are challenged to consider their attitudes towards international students, both as a group and as individual clients. Perceptions about working with international students may be biased, depending upon the institutional climate that is prevalent towards this group of students. Stereotypes of international students as *difficult to work with* may be based upon specific student situations or lack of experience by counsellors. International students have reported problems of discrimination and racism in academic curriculum during interactions with other students and staff of educational institutions (Dei, 1992). Ultimately, counsellors need to be reflective about sources of bias that are rooted in personal value systems (Collins, Arthur, & Wong-Wylie, in press). Perceptions about life in other countries can be based on limited exposure or on a negative bias portrayed in the media. Counsellors are subjected to those influences during the course of their daily lives.

One argument made against multicultural counselling is the impossibility of learning about the cultures of people from all different countries. Adopting a culture-infused counselling orientation emphasizes what is possible through reflective practice and cultural learning (Collins & Arthur, in press a, in press b). For example, the culturally aware counsellor will have considered how personal values and beliefs may adversely impact professional relationships. Counsellors can also become informed about the main source countries of international students at their local educational institutions. Reading about those countries, meeting with students on an informal basis, and connecting with local community groups are important ways to gain cultural knowledge that can assist in fostering positive perspectives. The following sections outline considerations for designing effective counselling services for international students.

Negotiating Understanding about Counselling

International students, like many other client groups, may be unfamiliar with what counselling services have to offer, what they can expect from counselling, and the ways that counselling can be linked to their transition concerns. International students who have previously accessed formal helping services might take the offer of counselling in stride. In contrast, students who hold beliefs about maintaining personal control of problems or not disclosing personal concerns may feel conflicted about seeking counselling services due to stigma or a sense of shame (Yoon & Jepsen, 2008). Cultural norms for problem-solving and help-seeking can serve as either prohibitive or enhancing factors (Brinson & Kottler, 1995; Sandhu, 1994).

It is very important for counsellors to consider the potential conflicts that emerge for some students through seeking professional services (Arthur, 2004a). Additional attention may need to be paid to issues of confidentiality, assurance about the legitimacy of seeking assistance, and acknowledgement of negative feelings about going outside the family or cultural group for assistance. It may be a case of *double jeopardy* as students feel overtaxed by transition demands and feel like they are betraying their sense of family obligations.

Given these potential issues and the inevitability of working across cultures, counselling should proceed as a negotiated process. The identification and interpretation of client problems varies across cultures. The use of cultural auditing, outlined in Chapter 6, suggests ways in which the working alliance, including both the goals and processes of counselling, can be strengthened. Roles of counsellor and client, approach to counselling, ways of conceptualizing client concerns, and the design of counselling interventions need to be made as transparent as possible. This avoids the risk of applying services that do not fit the expectations of clients or that do not fall within the client's repertoire of acceptable paths for ameliorating concerns. It is critical that counsellors take the lead in exploring students' expectations of counselling to negotiate a common framework from which to respond appropriately to clients (Arthur, 2008).

International Student Use and Satisfaction with Counselling Services

Access to counselling services is strongly dependent upon the profile that counsellors build with the international student population. Depending upon the availability of counselling services in their home country, international students may be unfamiliar with the nature of counselling and how services can provide support. Ironically, the confusion of a new culture and need to spend more time on academic work may act as barriers to participating in student programs. It is important that reticence about accessing services not be construed as indifference. Rather, international students may not feel that their problems are important enough to warrant counselling (Russell, Thomson, & Rosenthal, 2008). They need clear information about the purpose of counselling and how it can enhance their personal and academic success (Arthur, 2008).

Research on counselling services utilization by international students shows conflicting results (Raunic & Xenos, 2008). Research on usage rates suggests that international students are generally less likely than local students to access counselling (Yoon & Jepsen, 2008) and the majority go for one session (Arthur, 2004a; Russell et al., 2008). It is important to consider the factors that might lead to these conclusions. First, seeking assistance from a stranger is a foreign idea in many cultures! Second, international students may be seeking immediate solutions for problem-solving aspects of cross-cultural transition and exhaust other avenues of support before accessing counselling. Third, misinformation and misunderstandings about counselling services may be problematic. Fourth, cultural norms regarding help-seeking may deter students from accessing counselling services or continuing counselling services. Fifth, usage rates vary according to nationality (Flathman, Davidson, & Sanford, 2001; Walker, 1999). Research is needed to verify the suggestion that ethnic group membership may be a more important variable for counselling utilization than comparisons between international and local students (Raunic & Xenos, 2008).

Several factors have been associated with positive views of seeking counselling by international students. These include length of time in the host country and level of acculturation, being female, having greater openness to emotions, and prior experience with counselling (Komiya & Eells, 2001). Gender differences in utilization rates have been challenged due to the fact that females outnumber males on many campuses and this factor is often not taken into account in research (Raunic & Xenos, 2008). There is evidence that international students have a low level of satisfaction with counselling services (Pedersen, 1991a). Counselling style has been identified as an influential factor with clients, with some generalizations made in the literature suggesting that international students prefer directive approaches (Arthur, 2004a). Drawing general conclusions about the entire international student population, or even subgroups (e.g., Asian students), is risky. There is contrasting evidence that some groups of international students may prefer a nondirective style of counsellor expertise (D'Rozario & Romano, 2000). Caution is warranted about stereotyping international students as preferring one particular style (e.g., directive or nondirective counselling). What can be gleaned from limited research is the importance of counsellor flexibility when working with international students. Based on cultural values and experience working with people in positions of authority, some clients may prefer a more directive approach than is typically taught in Western paradigms of counselling theories and interventions (Yoon & Jepsen, 2008). However, as students gain more experience and comfort with counselling, some may prefer to shift from directive to more collaborative approaches. Based on the culture-infused counselling model outlined in earlier chapters, it is important to consider general cultural knowledge in tentative ways and negotiate preferred counselling style with individual clients.

Views of the counsellor may also be influential for accessing services as well as satisfaction with those services. Counsellors may be viewed more informally, with a strong emphasis on the relationship component (i.e., counsellor as local friend) or in a strongly formal sense as a local authority with expectations for directive and concrete advice (i.e., counsellor as expert). The counselling relationship may be strongly influenced by the previous experience of international students with hierarchical relationships (Mori, 2000). Cultural norms may dictate that the student behaves towards the counsellor as an *expert* or *authority*.

Corresponding expectations may be that the style of counselling unfolds in more directive and active ways, at least during the initial stages of counselling, until rapport is established to sufficient levels to explore other ways of interacting together. This poses challenges to professionals whose counselling education has emphasized mutuality, collaboration, and the sharing of power. Yet enacting those professional practice values may actually conflict with the expectations of students and influence evaluations about the effectiveness of services. Counsellors need to be flexible about considering the counselling styles that will help students to feel more comfortable at the beginning of counselling and shift interpersonal styles as the counselling process unfolds. Again, readers are encouraged to consider the cultural auditing process outlined in Chapter 6 for ways of enhancing the working alliance with international students.

Psychoeducational Approaches to Counselling

A psychoeducational approach to counselling services can help students feel more comfortable about accessing services. With a focus on instruction and learning, psychoeducational programming can be used to introduce topics related to cross-cultural transition and help students self-assess the need for additional counselling support. A group counselling approach, such as psychoeducational workshops, engages participants in the exchange of ideas and in learning from the experiences of other international students. Students may benefit from identifying potential demands that they had not previously considered and from hearing about the strategies that other students have applied to manage cross-cultural demands (Arthur, 2003). Group experiences can stimulate affective reactions that may lead to new learning or reframing ideas about transitions (Westwood, Lawrence, & Paul, 1986). The collective identification of issues and strategies makes group interventions a valuable resource in discussing ways to manage cross-cultural transitions.

Orientation programs are an effective way to educate international students about commonly experienced adjustment concerns and about the student services designed to support their success (Walton, 1990). Beyond orientation programming offered at the beginning of the transition to the host country, counselling about re-entry transition can assist with the closure experience of leaving the host country (LaBrack, 1993; Wang, 1997). An example of group counselling using a psychoeducational approach has been applied to counselling international students for the re-entry home (Arthur, 2003). The premise of this type of programming is that psychoeducational groups can provide *cultural inoculation* for leaving life in the host culture and focusing on the transition to home. Considerations for organizing and facilitating group work with international students are provided by Arthur (2004a) and Walker and Conyne (2007).

Counsellors as Cultural Therapists

The role of counsellors in working with international students has been described as that of a *cultural therapist* (Dei, 1992). Counsellors must be adept at appreciating students' worldviews and how that can be challenged through contact with the host culture. At times, this means helping students reconcile conflicts about giving away or denying aspects of their home culture in order to function effectively in the host environment. Alternatively, it may mean helping students reconcile the ambivalence they feel about returning home to aspects of their culture that they deem to be undesirable. It is important to remember that decisions made in one cultural context can have a major impact on roles and relationships defined by contrasting cultural values (Arthur, 2007).

Communication during cross-cultural transitions requires competencies for interpreting meanings and responding in culturally appropriate ways (Arthur & Collins, 2005). Counsellors can also take an instructional approach with individual clients to help them better understand the cultural meanings of communication and interpersonal dynamics in the host culture. This requires counsellors to be astute at understanding situations from the point of view of international students and to be able to analyze and describe the cultural significance of specific interactions in their own culture. What may be taken for granted in day-to-day interactions locally can be a source of confusion and frustration for those who lack the context for interpreting behaviour.

Counsellors may also be called upon to mediate serious conflicts between international students and other members of the educational community. Cross-cultural conflicts are complex in several ways. First, the potential for conflict escalates between people who hold divergent beliefs and values. Second, misunderstandings and miscommunication can add to volatile situations. Third, competing perspectives can contribute to barriers for identifying mutual interests and avenues for conflict resolution.

Counselling skills for mediating cross-cultural skills are typically beyond the interpersonal skills taught in counsellor education curriculum. A useful resource for counsellors is the Interpersonal Cultural Grid (Singelis & Pedersen, 1997; Stewart, 2002). The premise of the grid is to overcome the misunderstandings about behaviour that can occur during cross-cultural interactions and that become a source of distraction that further deteriorates effective communication. Focus is redirected towards the intent of behaviour and shared positive expectations. This common ground is then used as a foundation from which to generate alternative solutions. Focus is kept on areas of similarity and mutually beneficial actions. This process can help in moving beyond blame and viewing the cultural norms of the other person as the source of conflict.

Language Proficiency and Counselling

In general, international students with better language proficiency report fewer adjustment problems than students who rate themselves as having weak language abilities (Wan et al., 1992). The impact of language in cultural adjustment has been described as *language shock* (Smalley, 1963). When international students do not understand the nuances of the local language, many of the cues to social interaction are missed.

Many international students are studying in their second language, and issues of language shock can emerge in counselling. A limited vocabulary can inhibit the level of understanding that counsellors can gain with respect to client issues. International students may have a limited vocabulary from which to describe their concerns and associated symptoms. Combined with the anxiety of seeking counselling services, international students may feel both a sense of embarrassment and a sense of inadequacy about their need for assistance (Yoon & Jepsen, 2008).

Counsellors need to be aware of the complications of second language issues in counselling. Students may experience further frustrations about not being able to express, in fuller ways, *who they are.* Counsellors can encourage clients and put them at ease about communicating in a second language. Students are often better prepared to speak the counsellor's first language than vice versa! It is important to allow for sufficient silences for students to formulate their words, to offer words to support their explanation, and to build in perception checks to make sure that shared meanings are understood. Counsellors' expressed sincerity about wanting to help students and the quality of their contributions to the conversation are salient factors in overcoming language barriers (Hayes & Lin, 1994). Language proficiency is also an important consideration for group interventions and counsellors need to be skilled at facilitating groups across cultures (Arthur, 2003, 2004a; Walker & Conyne, 2007).

Examining Cultural Norms in Counselling Services

"It is important for counsellors working with international students to broaden their understanding of counselling beyond narrowly defined methods and contexts" (Pedersen, 1991a, p. 29). Working from a model of culture-infused counselling is an opportunity to consider how counselling practices are organized around particular cultural norms. It is also an opportunity to consider how the organization of counselling services may inadvertently pose barriers for clients (Arthur & Collins, 2005).

For example, the *50-minute hour* may be convenient for office management in a Western culture, but some people may find it overly restrictive. Flexibility to spend more time with students in fewer sessions may better match student needs. This is particularly relevant for transition concerns of international students, who may need immediate assistance with crisis management or immediate action strategies to deal with demands before they turn into crisis (Hayes & Lin, 1994).

Another example of how norms of professional practice may contrast with accessibility issues for international students is the setting in which counselling occurs. Informal settings may be more appealing and it is not uncommon for international students to approach counsellors in more casual settings such as hallways or when walking on campus. Students may feel reticent about making formal appointments, but may gain a lot from contact with a counsellor during more informal contacts on campus. The hesitancy of international students to seek services on their own means that it is crucial for counsellors to take proactive approaches outside of the counselling office (Sandhu, 1994). Counsellors need to recognize the extra effort expended by international students to seek help and acknowledge these steps through responsive services (Hayes & Lin, 1994).

Notions of privacy and confidentiality can also be challenging across cultural contexts. Some students may welcome the privacy and formality of counselling services because it helps them avoid identification by others. Alternatively, students from collective cultures may feel more comfortable with one or more friends accompanying them to a session. Counselling offices may be more crowded than usual, and this may challenge your comfort level about who is the client and who has access to information. A representative of an international student group may also approach a counsellor on behalf of the issues experienced by a group. Along with discussing issues and solutions, the student will undoubtedly have information to pass on to peers about the approachability and the utility of working with a counsellor.

Cognitive Restructuring and Coping Resources

International students who are overwhelmed with transition demands may benefit from reframing their comparisons between home and host cultures. This can be problematic when students dichotomize their experiences with all-or-nothing thinking, in which home and host cultures are labelled as *good* or *bad.* Comparison between cultures is a natural process as students experience contrasts. For example, students may want to try out new styles of dress, food, and social interaction in the initial phase of transition. Students may view adaptation as the extent to which they can disguise their *differences* and blend in locally. However, aspects of either the home or host culture that were once attractive may eventually be questioned or criticized. Counsellors need to be familiar with the shifting influences of acculturation on presenting client issues, as introduced earlier in this chapter.

International students may also dichotomize their evaluations of how they are coping in the host culture. The experience of acculturative stress or culture shock can threaten students to the point where they feel that they are not managing anything well and their success as a student is at risk (Arthur, 2004a). Counsellors can help international students shift from global evaluations to making reference to specific aspects of cross-cultural transition. For example, the W-curve model of culture shock (Gullahorn & Gullahorn, 1963) can be introduced to students to generate discussion about their experience of transition. Specific domains of transition can be identified through introducing characteristics of transition (Schlossberg, 1984) or a validationgram exercise (Ishiyama, 1995a). Breaking down cross-cultural transitions into specific areas, such as academic, work, making new friends, using local transportation, speaking in a second language, and participating in campus activities, can help students identify the progress that they have made and gain clarity about which areas require intervention.

The goal of counselling is not to eliminate culture shock. Students may need assistance to reduce severe stress reactions such as anxiety or depression that are related to culture shock. Helping students develop a systematic way of examining their learning in cross-cultural contexts supports their overall adjustment. For example, a cultural learning journal can encourage individual reflection about transition demands. Students are encouraged to identify, on an ongoing basis, critical situations and events in the host culture that can be used to assess the adequacy of their coping strategies. As referred to earlier in this chapter, students may experience both negative and positive emotions related to the same situation (Folkman, 2008) and benefit from strategies directed at increasing their coping capacity. International students often want more than to be listened to; they seek solutions and suggestions for immediate concerns, which are often related to their academic programs.

International students may place a priority on their academic success, and they may feel more motivated to seek resources that they believe can enhance their academic situation. International students who are reluctant to seek counselling for a mental health issue due to the perceived *loss of face* or social stigma may be more responsive to discussing their academic concerns. A positive connection with a counsellor about academic matters can build rapport for discussing issues in other life areas. Counsellors can leverage the focus on academic success by clarifying the ways in which counselling services are connected to academic success.

Enhancing Social Support

Helping international students build social support on campus is a key goal of counselling interventions with this student population (Chen, 1999). Counsellors are an integral source of support for helping students to connect with other campus services and programs to increase their support network. In order to help students build the confidence they need to reach out to others, extra steps taken by the counsellor make a huge difference. For example, rather than merely describing services on campus to students, walking with the student to campus venues and making introductions to other staff members can make the difference between student confidence in using or not using campus services. Encouraging students to take on volunteer roles or paid jobs, often found through campus international centres, can help students learn new skills and meet other students.

The counsellor's connections and reputation among international student groups are essential for peer referral. More confident international students have the potential to become peer helpers and role models for helping other international students (Parr et al., 1992). Partnership programs with local students can be valuable assets for building social support. Peer tutoring, language training, and programs designed to enhance cultural exchanges can assist international students in integrating with campus life. Programs based on the premise of peer pairing can help international students adjust to the local culture, while local students gain a valuable cross-cultural experience (Westwood & Barker, 1990).

The role of counselling with family members of international students is an important aspect of service provision (Chittooran & Sankar-Gomes, 2007). Many international students are accompanied by their spouse and children. The well-being of family members influences international students' capacity to focus on academic achievement and their sense of satisfaction in the host country. Expanding counselling services could include support groups and initiatives through which family members can connect with one another (Mori, 2000). Counsellors may also help to interface with school and parent interactions involving children (Chittooran & Sankar-Gomes, 1997)

Counsellors may not directly offer services in these types of campus programs, but they are often called upon to help with the design of such programs. Assistance in accessing both formal and informal resources on campus can be an effective intervention for international students. Counselling interventions may be maximally effective if they are centred on developing a strong social support network. Consequently, counsellors need to have a campus network of resource people who have demonstrated cross-cultural sensitivity and an interest in international students (Arthur, 2004a).

Ethical Issues

Ethical issues that surface with international students are centred in counsellor competencies for working across cultures and for becoming knowledgeable about the unique concerns and issues of this population. International students' views of the counsellor may, at times, pose ethical considerations in terms of dual roles and boundary issues. For example, counsellors may be involved in the instruction of psychoeducational programs, have informal contacts with students, and work with students for individual counselling.

International students may also define the relationship with counsellors in ways that extend beyond a professional relationship. In cases where the counsellor is one of few sources of support, demands for time and interaction outside of the formal counselling role may press beyond clarity about roles. At the same time, it is recommended that counsellors gain a profile among international students, and a building block for this is informal interaction. Counsellors may need to be cognizant of boundary issues. Definitions of helping relationships are built in a cultural context. Someone who is helpful may be viewed not only as an authority figure, but more as a close friend. It may be confusing for international students that counsellors are not interested in or available to pursue interaction beyond defined campus roles. To avoid potential conflicts, counsellors must be prepared to explain the limits of their relationships with international students so that misunderstandings and misattributions can be avoided (Arthur, 2004a).

Another area that can be contentious is the giving and receiving of gifts. It is common practice in many cultures for gifts to be given as a token of appreciation. Counsellors must carefully consider the meaning of gift giving. To adopt a *no gifts* policy risks offending international students who offer gifts as a cultural courtesy. This must be balanced with implications regarding future obligations and expectations for favours. Each situation requires a judgment call by the counsellor in weighing the potential risks and benefits in multicultural counselling.

Case Study

Nigel was a student from one of the South Pacific Islands, considered to be a developing country. At the age of 27, Nigel traveled to Canada to pursue studies in an engineering technology program. This was the first time that he had ever been off the island and away from his family. His education was sponsored by winning a scholarship from an employer, with the condition that he return home for employment for a minimum of two years following his studies. Nigel described this achievement as an honour for himself, his family, and his country.

I met Nigel initially through an orientation for new students. My participation in that program was to make an introduction to the types of resources available to students through counselling services. Because of the physical proximity of my office to the area in which international student services were housed, I often met students on their way to or from that office. Remembering Nigel from the orientation session, saying hello was the beginning of a meaningful relationship with this student. In the two years that I knew Nigel on campus, he came only once to my office for a formal counselling session. However, this was one of my closest counselling relationships with an international student. Nigel and I met together in the international student centre several times and conversed at one of the tables. He would often come early or stay after planned events for international students to talk to me about his life in Canada.

Nigel was one of two children in his family. His father died when Nigel was only 9 and his sister was 2. Nigel described a very close relationship with his mother. I was initially struck by the intensity of feelings that he expressed towards his mother. At some level, I wondered if this was appropriate for a man of his age, wondered about his capacity for individuation from the family and whether this was an issue for him to resolve. This immediate reaction was more about my values than about the values of the collective culture in which this student was raised. I shared this reaction with Nigel, noting that it was rare for me to hear such fondness and centrality of the mother-son relationship when I worked with Canadian students. As he laughed, he said, "In my country, mothers are the heart of the home, and you listen to them all of your life, or else!" We explored his sense of loneliness from his mother, as he had always lived at home with his mother and his sister. As a strategy in counselling, I often asked Nigel what he thought his mother would say or do if he could ask her advice. Despite the miles between them, his mother's presence and his internal dialogue with her appeared to be a major source of social support.

My early conversations with Nigel were focused on lifestyles in his country. He was delighted to learn that I had traveled to his home country, but I quickly clarified that my knowledge of his country was limited as a tourist. I was also concerned about Nigel spending too much time educating me about his home country, instead of discussing personal matters that were of concern. However, this seemed to be a source of connection for us. He would use this as a reason to seek me out on campus, often bringing me a picture or other objects that he had brought from home.

I faced a dilemma when Nigel offered to cook for me. What was the meaning of this gesture? Was this overly personal and did it have connotations that might not be seen as a counselling agenda? I was faced with having to make a decision that had implications for boundaries and also for offending him. I chose to proceed by agreeing to meet him for lunch so that we could talk about how things were going for him. If he would bring one of his favourite foods to share with me, I would do the same. This turned out to be a turning point in the depth of our counselling relationship.

Nigel's adjustment to academic studies was minimal. His academic background was strong and with good study habits he experienced few gaps between the curriculum he learned in school and expectations for academic achievement in Canada. English was his first language. His first realization that language could be a barrier occurred when he exclaimed, "I have been told that I have a strong accent. I have never thought of myself having an accent. You Canadians also have an accent that can be difficult to understand." Nigel described an embarrassing incident in class when one of his instructors asked him to repeat an answer because he could not understand his accent. This cultural learning reminded him to slow down and take his time with conversation.

Nigel underwent a major transformation in terms of his identity development during the process of acculturation. During the first three months he was in Canada, he embraced symbols of Canadian culture. He stopped wearing clothes made in his native country. He bought clothes with designer labels and adopted a look that was fashionable in North America. He was fascinated with learning phrases and expressions that he had never heard before. He exclaimed that he never felt freer in his life and wanted to become Canadian.

This was an opportunity for us to talk about some of the restrictions in his life at home that had not previously been apparent to him. This included an obligation to family that required many hours every week. This was an interesting contrast to the picture of family relations and positive sense of obligation and respect that he had described during his initial entry to Canada.

I also noticed a shift in the ways that Nigel presented himself to women. During initial meetings with other students, Nigel was always friendly, but always reserved, emphasizing good manners and a *proper* presentation. His style changed to the point where some female students complained about his behaviour. I was concerned that Nigel was misinterpreting social cues that he was observing during interactions between Canadian students. I was also concerned that he could risk offending a female student to the point where a situation could constitute harassment or sexual assault. As an entry point for discussing the changes that I observed, I asked Nigel to tell me about gender relations in his country.

This invitation led to us exploring his sense of loneliness and the fact that he had given up a relationship to travel to Canada. He asked me a direct question: "Don't you think that 27 is old not to be married?" He also disclosed his sense of confusion about interactions with Canadian women. "At home, you know where you stand with women. Here you don't. One minute they are nice and the next, they are not. I am not sure what they want." We were then able to explore levels of social interaction between women and men in Canadian culture and how some of his behaviour might be construed. I made sure that I gave Nigel lots of positive feedback about who he was as person and that he did not have to turn into someone he was not in order to be liked by others. I asked him to consider which Canadian women he had met with whom he might consider developing friendships. He agreed that this might be important for him to gain the confidence to pursue any romantic relationships.

In the second semester of his program, Nigel experienced a period of demoralization. This was very consistent with models of culture shock, which describe a downward spiral once the initial fascination with culture is experienced with a more critical view. When Nigel told me he was not feeling well, I asked him to make an appointment with me at the office. He reluctantly agreed and came for the appointment.

His appearance was disheveled, his tone of voice lacked enthusiasm, and he was distant in our relationship. It was difficult to engage him in conversation. In assessing the degree of this stress, I learned that his sleep patterns were interrupted and he was having headaches on a daily basis. He was also experiencing a problem with lack of concentration on his schoolwork and he was worried about impending exams. When I inquired about his correspondence with his mother, he indicated that he had not been in touch with her for several weeks. When I inquired about the delay in contacting her, he averted his eye contact from me, and said in a quiet voice, "I am ashamed to contact my mother. I am ashamed of how you see me today."

Nigel recounted a specific experience that seemed to be the catalyst for his current state of distress. He said, "I am confessing to you that I ate beef. I have gone against everything my culture stands for, and I am ashamed." This event seemed to touch the core of Nigel's values and it was obvious that he was having difficulties reconciling the values and lifestyles that he was experiencing in Canada with the behaviour that would be expected of him at home.

In that session, there were three directions that I felt were priorities. First, I believed that it was paramount that I convey to Nigel that I accepted him for who he was, regardless of his recent behaviour. His sense of shame could erode our relationship if he felt that I was not tolerant of his recent actions. Second, I felt that this could be a turning point for Nigel to reclaim the values that he said he had abandoned. Third, I was concerned about this student's potential level of depression, as the intensity of his symptoms had persevered for several weeks.

Nigel initiated a conversation about depression, saying that he had heard about it, even though that was a term that was not used in his country. I asked him if he would like to learn more about depression, that I could describe some of the symptoms and how it could be treated through counselling. I was also careful to add that many international students had symptoms of culture shock that felt like depression, that this did not represent something wrong with them, but that their bodies were reacting to the stress of living and learning in a new culture. Nigel seemed surprised that others had these symptoms. I invited him to keep in closer touch with me over the next month so that we could work on his feeling better. I also suggested that he meet with a campus physician to make sure there were no physical conditions related to his symptoms. He agreed to make an appointment and let me know the result of this examination.

At the end of this appointment, Nigel turned to me and said, "I don't like meeting you here. You are different here in your office." I took this an indication of Nigel's discomfort with meeting me formally for counselling. This was a challenge for me, as I had previous concerns about the type of information that Nigel disclosed to me in public places.

However, it seemed that what was needed was follow-up in a location that was more comfortable for him. We agreed to meet in the international student centre the following week.

Nigel's stress level dissipated over the next month. Several levels of intervention seemed to make a difference for this student. First, a strong connection with a counsellor offered him support in the absence of other interpersonal relationships. Second, I challenged Nigel to consider aspects of his culture in which he took pride, even if they were different from the values and behaviours he was experiencing in Canada. As a specific homework task, he agreed to go to the Devonian Gardens and think about what mattered to him about his culture. This setting is a place where the plants and flowers offer a stark contrast to winter weather. Third, I invited Nigel to participate as one of our student volunteers in organizing programs for other international students. This gave him a reason to keep in touch with me and provided him with contact with other students. Fourth, I invited him to give a presentation about his culture to other students and staff. He brightened at that idea, asking if he could serve kava at the event!

Over the course of the next two months, Nigel's appearance changed and he began to wear clothing brought from home. He helped organize a trip for other students and played host at that successful event. We kept in touch, less frequently, as his life became fuller with activity and friendships formed with other international students. In my mailbox one day, I found a packet of cooking spices, with a note scribbled, "Thank you, these are from my mother to you."

Future Directions in Counselling International Students

We are just beginning to understand the complex ways in which culture influences international students' experiences of transition. In a review of American counselling literature, Yoon and Portman (2004) reported five dominant themes in research related to counselling international students: universal versus subgroup characteristics, environmental versus personal factors, developmental versus pathological perspectives, counselling goals, and methodological problems. From the review of literature for this chapter, several areas are highlighted for future research:

1. Although most of the counselling literature is directed towards international students in higher education, attention must also be paid to the growing number of adolescent students who study abroad (Kuo & Roysircar, 2006).

2. The literature on international students has focused on adjustment issues and the problems that are faced by students in adapting to life in a new country. Unfortunately, this tendency leads to a problem-based view of this population, with less attention paid to their resiliency, strengths, and the coping resources that they find to be effective (Popadiuk & Arthur, 2004). What is largely ignored in research is an explanation of how and why some international students experience their study abroad life in positive ways (Tseng & Newton, 2002).

3. In a review of literature on counselling international students, Leong and Chou (2002) noted that attention has been concentrated on client variables. They called for a shift of emphasis in both theory and practice to focus on therapist and counselling process variables.

4. Emphasis on the initial stage of transition has not been balanced by research addressing the stage of re-entry transition. Further research is needed to appreciate the issues faced by international students as they depart from Canada and move to other countries or return to life at home.

5. Research is needed to identify the factors that influence international students' career decisions, the stability of their career choices, and what factors help them to persist in attaining their academic and career goals (Singaravelu et al., 2005). Additionally, a better understanding about the ways that students integrate their international experience into their career development, including facilitators and barriers, would inform career counselling (Arthur, 2004b).

Evaluation of services to international students needs to include representation from the general population as well as from specific groups of international students. Focus groups have been identified as a useful methodology to complement survey questionnaires about the responsiveness of student services (Luzzo, Henao, & Wilson, 1996). It is important that institutions engage international students in ongoing evaluations about the quality of existing services and the extent to which those services meet the unique needs of this diverse student population.

Lastly, counsellors are challenged to expand their view of international students. Although the focus of this discussion has been centred on students from other countries who study in Canada, this ignores Canadian students as international learners. Canadian students have opportunities to participate in student exchange, terms abroad, internships, co-op placements, research and fieldwork, and international development projects, many of which can be undertaken for academic credit (Knight, 2000). Although study abroad programs are a key facet of internationalization, these programs remain an underutilized source of cross-cultural learning for students. In 2006, 17,850 Canadian students participated in study abroad programs, representing more than double the participation rate from 2002 (AUCC, 2007). However, these rates are modest in comparison to other countries and lack of financial support and a federal strategy to support Canadian student mobility are cited as the main barriers (AUCC, 2007). Counsellors can incorporate international experience as a strategy in career planning, become involved with orientation programs to prepare students for studying abroad, and support returning students with the re-entry transition (Arthur, 2004b; MacDonald & Arthur, 2004).

Chapter Summary

Attention to multicultural issues in counsellor education programs has increased the amount of information available on working with clients from other cultures. However, general knowledge about multicultural counselling falls short of equipping counsellors to work with specific populations such as international students. Counsellors also need to be knowledgeable about the nature of cross-cultural transitions and apply multicultural counselling competencies (Arthur, 2008; Lin & Pedersen, 2007). The culture-infused counselling model presented in Chapter 3 provides counsellors with ways to enhance their competence for working with international students. Counsellors are invited to examine cultural influences on defining client issues, the therapeutic relationship, and the selection and application of counselling interventions.

International students are not a homogenous group. Counsellors need to consider both the common experiences and unique circumstances of international students. Lack of attention to the cultural variability within this student population perpetuates the marginalization of students (Popadiuk & Arthur, 2004). Through acknowledging that the population of international students encompasses many countries and many cultures from around the world, counsellors take a big step towards respecting the diversity of students who choose to study in Canada.

Counsellors have instrumental roles in working with students to help them problem-solve transition issues and develop effective coping skills. Counselling roles need to be broadened from direct contact with students to advocacy and educational roles that foster a responsive campus environment. Counsellors can also be consultants and resource people in programming designed to support international students. In the larger campus community, counsellors can advocate for ways to overcome systemic and organizational barriers that have negative influences on student adjustment. The examples provided in this chapter illustrate the ways that taking a culture-infused approach to counselling can help international students achieve academic and personal success.

In return, international students will be deeply grateful for the assistance that you provide. They will remember you as a Canadian who took an interest in them when they were living away from home, and who helped them navigate their journey of cross-cultural transition.

PART IV

THE FUTURE OF CULTURE-INFUSED COUNSELLING

Canada is one of the most culturally diverse countries in the world and is recognized by most for its advanced policies on multiculturalism. In fact, this has become one of the defining features of our national identity (Reza, 2006). A study in the early 1990s revealed that a large portion of Canadians favour the country's policy on multiculturalism, which encourages full participation of non-dominant groups in social, economic, and political life while encouraging the maintenance of cultural distinctiveness (Gauthier & Phillips, 1997). The report also found that 95% of Canadians had pride in both their national and ethnic identities. However, a quarter of Canadians were unaware of the national policies on multiculturalism and another quarter opposed them. More recent information from the Department of Canadian Heritage (2003) suggested that Canadians are increasingly aware of Canada's multicultural policy and most support its objectives.

On the professional level, Pettifor in Chapter 7 points out that Canadian psychology, through the *Canadian Code of Ethics for Psychologists* (Canadian Psychological Association [CPA], 2000), has been on the leading edge among professions in Canada, and within psychology internationally, in founding the code of ethics on a set of clear philosophical and ethical principles. Foremost among these is respect, defined as the positive valuing of all human beings. However, as we have pointed out in Chapter 6, counselling and psychology in Canada have some distance to go in expanding the responsibilities of individual psychologists and of the professions as a whole to engage in social justice. The New Zealand Psychological Society (2002) *Code of Ethics*, although built upon the Canadian code, goes further in requiring psychologists to respect the dignity of persons and peoples and to be sensitive to their welfare and rights. The North American *Feminist Therapy Code* (Feminist Therapy Institute, 1999) takes the strongest position in addressing the issues of power and oppression directly and calls on practitioners to take an active stance in promoting social justice for all people.

In spite of the increase in awareness and public support for multicultural diversity, there is evidence of continued oppression of non-dominant groups in Canada at the individual, organizational, social, and systemic levels. We presented some of the current statistics on various non-dominant populations in Canada in Chapters 1 and 2 as evidence that, in spite of our national identity and policies on multiculturalism, many ethnic and other non-dominant group members continue to struggle to obtain access to resources, services, and opportunities for advancement readily available to the dominant populations. Reza (2006) drew on several recent national surveys to reaffirm these inequities for immigrant populations, particularly those who are more recent immigrants and members of visible non-dominant ethnic groups. In spite of these inequities, most immigrants express a strong sense of belonging and attachment to Canada as their new country of residence (Reza).

We are also facing challenging economic times on a global level, and consequently we are witnessing an international rise in anti-immigration sentiment. Several countries in the European Union have seen a resurgence in right wing, conservative political parties that hold as a primary mission not only restrictions on future immigration, but the expectation that immigrants and refugees currently in those countries return to their homelands. Although Canada has been buffered to some degree from the most devastating effects of the economic downturn, competition for employment and scarce economic resources is leading to a surge of negative sentiments about government policies to increase the number of immigrants as a way of addressing the longer-term labour market needs. We have witnessed an increase in anti-immigration comments within our own professional circles, which suggests that it is even more important now to be vigilant and explicitly committed to maintaining a global perspective, eliminating social injustices and inequities based in cultural group affiliation, and supporting a sense of national culture that is inclusive and recognizes diversity as a strength and a resource.

The nature of the Canadian population, our national government policy on multiculturalism, and the principles and guidelines for practice established through our professional associations provide a foundation for

Canadians to continue to take the lead internationally in further developing the field of multicultural counselling. The place to begin is in ensuring that counsellors and psychologists in Canada embrace the principles of culture-infused counselling and actively work to apply those principles in their individual practices, in the expanded areas of practice and roles they engage in, and as a collective through professional bodies, educational institutions, and health service organizations. In this final section of the book we look forward at these aspiration goals and present some ideas about how we can work together effectively to build a better community locally, nationally, and globally for all people.

CHAPTER 18
FUTURE DIRECTIONS IN CULTURE-INFUSED COUNSELLING

Sandra Collins and Nancy Arthur

Key Terms and Concepts		
• Collaborative client-centred practice • Collaborative patient-centred practice • Continued competence	• Interdisciplinary approaches • Interprofessional collaboration • Intraprofessional collaboration • Nice Counsellor Syndrome • Peacebuilding	• Personal is political • Professional is political • Structural violence • Universal principles of culture-infused counselling

Introduction

Millions of individuals in North America face barriers to the acquisition of resources that are necessary for human well-being (DeNavis-Walt, Procter, & Mills, 2005; Institute of Medicine, 2002; Schenk, 2001). As noted throughout the book, these barriers are often tied to cultural identities of individuals and groups, based on gender, ethnicity, nationality, ability, religion, sexual orientation, socio-economic status, age, and the intersections of those identities (Vera & Speight, 2003). In Chapter 10, Collins noted that individuals with multiple non-dominant identities are more likely to experience cultural oppression and marginalization (Collins, in press). We have proposed that the model of culture-infused counselling provides a foundation for counsellors, psychologists, and other mental health professionals to begin to more fully appreciate the interaction of cultural identities and wellness. The model also encourages professionals to recognize and address the impact of systemic oppression on individuals and groups and to effect change in the broader organizational, community, social, political, and economic systems that differentially impact the health of all members of Canadian society.

In this final chapter, we will explore a number of key issues related to the future of culture-infused counselling. We begin by returning to the *how to* question from Chapter 5 in terms of continued development of culture-infused counselling competency and provide some specific strategies for continued professional development. We then explore some of the barriers to engaging in culture-infused practice and to adopting a professional stance that leads to social justice action. We recognize that infusing culture into practice is not easy – it requires personal and professional transformation. And it likely cannot be accomplished in isolation. We complete the chapter with an exploration of the effects of globalization and the implications for multicultural competence and principles of culture-infused counselling at the national and international levels. Particular attention will be paid to the issues of interprofessional collaboration and international collaboration for social justice.

We hope that you will walk away from this final chapter inspired and equipped to expand your personal and professional roles in working for dignity, respect, and equality for all people within our national borders and beyond.

A Framework for Continued Culture-Infused Competence Development

The multicultural movement in the counselling field has gained considerable momentum. Although there are many controversies to be addressed, this is a sign that the field is in a process of transformation (Pedersen, 2001). This includes the recent attention paid to social justice advocacy competencies as key facets of counselling practice (Toporek, Lewis, & Crethar, 2009). The model of culture-infused counselling provides counsellors with a way to ground their theoretical approaches and practices in respect and appreciation of cultural diversity. The competencies framework described in chapters 3 through 6 is intended to provide a comprehensive and systematic presentation of the myriad of factors that have emerged in the multicultural literature about the requisite attitudes, knowledge, and skills for working effectively with members of diverse cultural populations. We have strengthened our model by incorporating competencies for social justice advocacy.

Toporek and Reza (2001) emphasized the need for **continued competence** development and the integration of a focus on multicultural competence into supervision and consultation. They suggested a model that incorporates *assessment of current competence, identification of competency development needs (knowledge, awareness, skills), and development of a strategic plan (goals and activities) designed to meet those competency needs.* We encourage you to carefully review the culture-infused counselling competencies framework (Chapter 3, Figure 4) to identify areas where you sense a need for continued competency development. Students may use this resource to define and develop competent practices. Experienced counsellors may find the culture-infused counselling competencies to be a useful resource for designing professional development programs. Counsellors can self-assess their current levels of competence and target areas for growth and development, using a template similar to the one provided in Figure 1. You will notice that we have added an additional column to the model suggested by Toporek and Reza that describes the specific evidence of goal attainment for each target area. Being very clear and descriptive about what positive change will look like is an important process for linking goals and outcomes in counselling, and it applies equally well to the continued professional development of the counsellor.

Where individuals often experience the most difficulty is in completing the third column, the *Strategies for Enhancing Level of Competence*. Students are often able to identity a gap in attitude, knowledge, and skill, but struggle to identify things they can do in their personal and professional lives to increase their multicultural competence in those areas. Arredondo and colleagues (1996) included as an appendix to their article a set of strategies for increasing one's multicultural competence, following the general competency framework they designed. We have expanded on that contribution by pulling on suggestions from other authors (Alvarez & Miville, 2003; Ancis, 1998; Pope-Davis, Breaux, & Liu, 1997; Vazquez & Garcia-Vazquez, 2003) and our own experience in teaching multicultural counselling at the graduate level to provide the suggestions outlined in Figure 2. We were very careful in the design of our competency framework to describe each competency as a discrete attitude, knowledge, or skill to make it easier to operationalize, develop, and assess the competencies.

It is easy to become overwhelmed when you look at a list like the one provided in Figure 2 and think about all the possibilities for learning about culture, examining the effects of culture on access to resources and services, and exploring ways of promoting cultural respect and social justice. We are very aware that this is a huge task and that many practitioners, students, researchers, and academics are already stretched to capacity. However, we also recognize our ethical and moral obligation to move the professions of counselling and psychology in the direction of culture-infused practice and the active promotion of social justice. Like any other movement this begins by developing a critical mass of individuals and groups who are conscious of the issues, passionate about change, and willing to take even small steps individually and collectively to promote social justice. We encourage each of you to consider how you might engage in the types of social justice advocacy roles suggested in Chapter 6.

***Domain I: Cultural Self-Awareness:* Active awareness of personal assumptions, values, and biases.**

Core Competencies	Specific Targets for Professional Development (Attitudes and Beliefs, Knowledge, Skills)	Strategies for Enhancing Level of Competence	Evidence of Increased Competency
Demonstrate awareness of your own cultural identities.	1. 2. 3.	1. 2. 3.	1. 2. 3.
Demonstrate awareness of differences between your own cultural identities and those of individuals from other dominant or non-dominant groups.	1. 2. 3.	1. 2. 3.	1. 2. 3.
Demonstrate awareness of the impact of culture on the theory and practice of counselling/psychology.	1. 2. 3.	1. 2. 3.	1. 2. 3.
Demonstrate awareness of the personal and professional impact of the discrepancy between dominant and non-dominant cultural groups in Canada.	1. 2. 3.	1. 2. 3.	1. 2. 3.
Demonstrate awareness of your level of multicultural competence.	1. 2. 3.	1. 2. 3.	1. 2. 3.

Figure 1. A framework for continued competency.

Domain I: Cultural Self-Awareness: **Active awareness of personal assumptions, values, and biases**
Strategies for Developing Competency

***Core Competency 1:* Demonstrate awareness of your own cultural identities.**

- Create a personal cultural genogram (family tree).
  - Include generation perceptions towards members of diverse cultural groups, including issues of gender and sexual orientation.
  - Note messages received about the dimensions of your personal cultural identity from members of your family.
- Interview extended family members for insights into your cultural heritage.
  - Identify factors influencing your cultural heritage and conduct further research into the history of ancestral ethnic and other cultural affiliations.
- Develop a model of your cultural identity or identities, drawing on personal, cultural, and contextual dimensions.
  - Introduce yourself to individuals or groups according to salient dimensions of personal culture.
- Create a developmental timeline of your experiences from childhood through to adulthood, highlighting significant events that have impacted your worldview, values, and assumptions.
- Analyze your level of cultural identity development (bearing in mind that you may have different levels and processes of identity development across ethnicity, gender, sexual orientation, etc.).
- Write your personal cultural story, highlighting socialization and contextual influences.

***Core Competency 2:* Demonstrate awareness of differences between your own cultural identities and those of other dominant or non-dominant groups.**

- Research a cultural group in the community where you grew up or where you now live.
- Write a fictitious letter to a cultural group in your community outlining your opinions of the group, your perceptions of its strengths, and your concerns about the group.
- Immerse yourself in an environment in which you are the only person who is non-White, female, able-bodied, heterosexual, or other applicable cultural dimension.
  - Record your experiences and debrief them with a trusted colleague or supervisor.
- Write a fictional narrative or create a piece of art or music designed to express your understanding of the experience of racism, sexism, heterosexism, ageism, ableism, and other forms of cultural oppression.

***Core Competency 3:* Demonstrate awareness of the impact of culture on the theory and practice of counselling/psychology.**

- Describe the values and assumptions underlying the theories you personally use in counselling.
- Critically evaluate a theory based upon its cultural assumptions and implications for counselling practice.
- Prepare a written statement for distribution to clients about the theories that inform your work
- Read theoretical and applied practice books and articles written from other cultural perspectives.
  - Access resources that describe feminist and gay-affirmative counselling.
- Interview counsellors and other healers who adopt a non-Western or non-traditional theoretical perspective.

***Core Competency 4:* Demonstrate awareness of the personal and professional impact of the discrepancy between dominant and non-dominant cultural groups in Canada.**

- Analyze newspapers, magazines, TV commercials, and other popular media sources for incidents of racism, sexism, heterosexism, ableism, ageism, or elitism.
- Conduct a cultural audit of services and resources available in your community to assess for barriers to access for members of non-dominant populations.
- Create a list of the privileges you have experienced throughout your life by virtue of your cultural identity (identities).
  - Discuss the emotional reactions that you have to this list with a colleague or supervisor.
- Identify one or two areas in your personal and professional life where you can take an active stance against racism, sexism, heterosexism, ableism, ageism, or elitism.
  - Develop an action plan, implement that plan, and reflect on both your personal reactions and the outcomes of your actions.

***Core Competency 5:* Demonstrate awareness of your level of multicultural competence.**

- Journal about your experiences with counselling clients, noting highlights, successes, and areas for future learning.
- Develop a plan for continued competency development, specifying attitude, knowledge, and skill targets, strategies for increasing competence in those areas, and outcomes evaluation criteria.
- Develop a multicultural competence portfolio to track your progress.
- Work with a mentor who is culturally similar to yourself and who can serve as a model and source of feedback for multicultural competence.
- Engage in multicultural supervision.
- Incorporate cultural auditing in work with all clients.
- Debrief regularly with colleagues to share your learning with clients.

Figure 2. Strategies for continued competency development. Continued on the next two pages.

Domain II: Awareness of Client Cultural Identities: Understanding the worldview of the client

Strategies for Developing Competency

Core Competency 1: Demonstrate awareness of the cultural identities of your clients.

- Become actively involved with individuals from non-dominant groups outside the counselling setting (e.g., community events, social and political functions, celebrations, friendships).
- Find opportunities to interact with individuals and groups in healthy contexts to gain a balanced perspective.
- Consult with cultural guides from within non-dominant populations.
- Enroll in a cultural anthropology, ethnic studies, human sexuality, rehabilitation, or gender studies course.
- Read newspapers, magazines, or novels specific to particular non-dominant populations.
- Participate in cultural film festivals or rent culture-specific or international films.
- Access information about various cultural groups via the Internet, paying particular attention to websites generated by rather than simply about various non-dominant populations.
- Examine current statistics on regional distributions and issues affecting particular populations.
- Analyze usage patterns in your organization to determine major consumer groups and identify underserved populations.
- Advocate for training opportunities through professional associations, educational institutions, and so on.
- Organize a workshop or session at a conference for discussions about multicultural counselling.

Core Competency 2: Demonstrate awareness of the relationship of personal culture to health and well-being.

- Analyze characters in film or literature according to some of the key concepts related to cultural identity development, cross-cultural transition, culture shock, acculturation, assimilation, bicultural identity, and so on.
  - o Apply this analysis to members of both dominant and non-dominant groups.
  - o Assess your personal reactions to each character in terms of your cultural identity development.
  - o Compare your observations with others who have done a similar assessment.
- Videotape your sessions with clients and then analyze the tapes for examples of cultural blindness and cultural consciousness.
  - o Invite feedback from others on your attention to salient cultural factors.
  - o Obtain training videos for counsellors and conduct a similar analysis.
- Select a client who presents with multiple cultural identities and develop a diagram to conceptualize the intersection and interplay of these factors.
- Interview members of non-dominant groups on their views of healthy human development and functioning.
  - o Note the relationship of culture to health.
  - o Identify differences in worldview and the impact those might have on how they approach change.

Core Competency 3: Demonstrate awareness of the socio-political influences that impinge on the lives of non-dominant populations.

- Research provincial and federal legislation that affects the client groups you commonly encounter.
- Talk to your municipal, provincial, or federal government representatives about their views on cultural diversity and their political platform in this regard.
  - o Join a social or political organization to fight for the rights of non-dominant populations in Canada.
- Visit a school, health centre, or community group in an impoverished area of your town or city.
  - o Volunteer to participate in an event in the school or community aimed at improving social, economic, or educational conditions. Take a follower rather than a leadership role.
- Select one client population or counselling issue to devote professional time to for social advocacy.

Domain III: Culturally Sensitive Working Alliance
Strategies for Developing Competency

Core Competency 1: Establish trusting relationships with clients that take into account cultural identities.

- Work with a cultural mentor from a non-dominant group and solicit feedback on your attitudes, knowledge, and skills.
- Engage in counselling services as a client and actively seek out a counsellor with a different ethnic background, sexual orientation, gender, age, or other cultural identity variables.
  - Track your experiences as a client, noting the counsellor attitudes, behaviours, and skills that are helpful to your personal growth.
- Participate in other forms of culture-specific healing processes or practices to gain experience from the perspective of the client.
- Initiate case conferences and discussions in peer supervision about cultural influences on the working alliance.
- Videotape a client session and solicit feedback from your cultural guide/supervisor on verbal and nonverbal behaviours.
- Solicit direct feedback about your credibility, ability to communicate empathy, empowerment of others, and other issues of communication and counselling style from clients who are similar and dissimilar to you in cultural background.
  - This may be done informally as part of debriefing individual sessions or as part of an exit interview or questionnaire with clients who are terminating counselling.
  - This may also be done informally as part of a consultation session with leaders of community groups in learning how to increase your professional credibility and work effectively.
- Conduct an environmental and organizational cultural audit to assess the monocultural, ethnocentric messages communicated through office décor, marketing or intake materials, service norms, and so on.
- Learn another language common to your client populations.
- Research service provision patterns in local organizations to identify barriers to access for non-dominant populations.
  - Conduct surveys or interviews with clients and potential clients to assess facilitators and barriers to service provision.
- Visit community agencies to learn more about client needs and potential sources of resources and referral.

Core Competency 2: Collaborate with clients to establish counselling goals that are responsive to salient dimensions of cultural identity.

- Use role plays and simulated counselling interviews to obtain feedback on your ability to match counselling goals and processes to client worldview and needs.
  - Engage a colleague from another cultural group or a cultural guide to play the role of the client and to exaggerate points of cultural difference to enhance your learning.
  - Transcribe the interview to further analyze your areas of strength and weakness.
- Read case studies developed by practitioners who are from or working with non-dominant populations to explore differences in case conceptualization.
- Request information during professional training sessions or from marketing representatives about the cultural relevance of assessment tools and procedures.
  - Conduct a cultural audit of your personal or agency assessment policies and procedures to identify cultural limitations.
- Attend various religious or spiritual ceremonies and rituals to expand your understanding of the impact of cultural belief systems on conceptualization of problems and change processes.
- Present case studies to colleagues and supervisors with a view to expanding your perspectives on the multiple and often systemic factors impacting clients from non-dominant groups.
  - Seek out opportunities for consultation with members of other professional groups who may also be involved in client care.

Core Competency 3: Collaborate with clients to establish client and counsellor tasks that are responsive to salient dimensions of cultural identity.

- Seek out professional training in the use of non-Western, indigenous healing practices or interventions designed to work effectively with other non-dominant populations.
  - Provide opportunities for client feedback related to intervention strategies and outcomes of the counselling process, specifically addressing issues related to the fit with client worldview.
  - Engage in gender role analysis and power analysis of your work with clients.
- Develop relationships with members of non-dominant populations in the community or profession who may function as cultural informants and consultants.
- Meet with organizations servicing non-dominant groups to see how to support and learn from their services.
  - Create a resource and referral bank for your personal work with clients or for your organization as a whole.
- Actively recruit colleagues, students, and paraprofessionals from non-dominant cultural groups to work with on a daily basis.
  - Seek out volunteer, practicum, internship, or continued professional development opportunities that allow you to work directly with clients from cultural backgrounds different from your own.
- Engage in a continuous process of cultural auditing at all levels and in all areas of professional practice.

Domain III: Culturally Sensitive Working Alliance (Continued)
Strategies for Developing Competency
Core Competency 4: Engage in social justice actions to directly influence the systems that negatively affect the lives of non-dominant populations.

- Engage in activities to promote consciousness of social justice issues.
  - o Read, observe, and participate in activities that increase your understanding of local, national, and global economic, social, and political trends.
  - o Explore research and writing from other disciplines that have a history of social action.
- Become active in your local community to increase your awareness of social inequities and local resources and initiatives targeting social justice.
- Discuss with community leaders what they see as important changes for improving the health and well-being of their members.
- Advocate for multicultural training within your organization.
  - o Start an advisory group aimed at promoting multicultural competence at the organizational level.
  - o Seek out training to support the adoption of other roles – consultation, advocacy, education, facilitator of indigenous healing processes – as culturally appropriate.
- Travel to other parts of the world to meet with practitioners and lay healers.
  - o Request opportunities to directly observe their work with clients.
- Join organizations or chapters within organizations that have a social justice agenda.
  - o Encourage conference themes and keynote speakers with expertise and experience in social justice action.
  - o Engage in shared activities to promote social justice locally, nationally, or internationally.
  - o Participate in activities that expose to you others who are actively engaged in social justice.
- Look for opportunities to engage in social advocacy at multiple levels, including:
  - o helping clients advocate for their circumstances,
  - o advocating directly on behalf of a client in a specific context,
  - o advocating on behalf of a group of clients,
  - o advocating to change situations that impact clients with common issues, and
  - o advocating for broader social change.
- Build connections with professionals from other disciplines around social justice themes.
- Write a letter to your local newspaper drawing public attention to a social justice issue.
- Build alliances with community members who have influence over social policy.
- Ask questions about how well programs and services address the needs of diverse populations.
- Focus your research on issues of social injustice or strategies to promote social justice.
- Practice how to tell others about the role of counsellors in promoting social change.

Overcoming Resistance to Culture-Infused Counselling

Arredondo, Tovar-Blank, and Parham (2008) identified a number of factors that contributed to the continued resistance of some counsellors and psychologists to accepting the need for cultural competence. First, we need to object to comments that suggest addressing diversity was something done in the past and is no longer needed. Cultural diversity is not a phase; it is a reality of the social fabric of Canadian society and many nations around the world. Counselling psychology must be prepared as a profession to address the needs of populations that are increasingly adding diverse practices and customs to Canadian society (Young & Nichol, 2007). Second, the changing nature of our world and the portrayal of certain groups in the media have created an undercurrent of fear that often is associated with the *other* (Arredondo et al.). A third factor is continued unexamined cultural privilege (Arredondo et al.) as explored in Chapter 4, which leaves some arguing that increased cultural competence is unnecessary. Finally, some continue to argue that we should adopt an approach to counselling that assumes that all individuals are similar enough to engage in the same processes of assessment and intervention without special attention to culture. The argument goes something like this: Good counselling is good for everyone. We would suggest that good counselling needs to be defined from the point of view of consumers and through taking into account the ways that culture intersects with the goals and processes of counselling.

Bemak and Chung (2008) introduced the concept of the **Nice Counsellor Syndrome** (NCS) as another point of resistance to embracing the challenge of cultural competence, particularly as the full appreciation of client cultural identities and their context moves the counsellor into realms of social justice action. NCS counsellors *may, in fact, believe in the importance of social justice, but their actions are driven by the more* *immediate need to preserve the peace, mediate among diverse perspectives, and be perceived as nice people.* This syndrome can result not only in impotence in the face of social injustices, but also in unintentional oppression through the suppression of the needs of those who experience social injustices and the affirmation of the status quo (Bemak & Chung; Chung, Bemak, Ortiz, & Sandoval-Perez, 2008). It is important to recognize that social justice cannot be achieved without conflict, upsetting the status quo, or stepping on the toes of those in positions of power or dominance.

There is not an infinite pool of social privilege – distributing resources, services, and access comes with a cost to those currently in positions of privilege. Our current observations of the relationship between economic hard times and the rise of intergroup tensions and anti-immigration sentiments bear this out. It becomes increasingly more difficult to encourage people to examine their positions of privilege and to inspire them to consider a redistribution of resources and status when they are personally experiencing the adverse impact of social and economic forces. However, it is in this context that the popular interpretation of the Chinese character 危 for *crisis* as *danger plus opportunity* becomes meaningful.

Another risk emerges from the impact of increased awareness of social injustices on the counsellor. If counsellors are not presented with hope and possibilities for change or given tools and empowerment to implement changes, counsellors can fall prey to guilt over their own ineffectiveness and eventually succumb to apathy (Bemak & Chung, 2008). Our own research brought to light the barriers that career practitioners face in promoting social justice (Arthur, Collins, McMahon, & Marshall, 2009; McMahon, Arthur, & Collins, 2008). These barriers were described in more detail in Chapter 6 and included: insufficient time and resources, lack of training and personal empowerment, lack of support from colleagues and supervisors, and fears of losing funding or jobs or of challenging the status quo. The latter fits with the NCS noted by Bemak and Chung above.

Recent discussions of social justice emphasize the rights of all individuals to full participation in society and to obtain the resources and supports required for self-actualization (Arthur et al., 2009). Johan Galtung (1969), writing on peace, introduced the concept of **structural violence** to refer to *the systematic ways in which the political, legal, economic, or cultural traditions or systems of power and privilege prevent individuals and groups from achieving their full potential.* In Figure 3, Stoltz, Collins, Arthur, and Audet (2009) summarized the essence of Gultung's arguments in the distinctions between episodic and structural violence and then, consequently, between peacemaking and peacebuilding. We have argued throughout this text that social justice action is an essential professional response to structural violence. What is important in relation to the NCS is that this action engages us in **peacebuilding**, which by its very nature may result in increased tensions, negative reactions from colleagues and supervisors, or labeling of social justice focused counsellors as *troublemakers.*

Episodic (Direct Violence)	Structural (Indirect Violence)
• Typically kills or harms people *quickly*. • *Intermittently* kills or harms people. • *Acute* insult to well-being. • Dramatic; visible.	• Typically kills or harms people *slowly*. • *Continuously* deprives people of basic needs. • *Chronic* insult to well-being. • Normalized; invisible.
Peacemaking	Peacebuilding
• Reduces violent episodes. • Emphasizes nonviolence. • Seeks to prevent violent episodes. • Produces intergroup tension reduction.	• Reduces structural violence. • Emphasizes social justice. • Seeks to ameliorate structural violence. • Produces intergroup tension enhancement.

Figure 3. Episodic/structural violence and peacemaking/peacebuilding.

Counsellors need to be well prepared with a solid rationale for culture-infused counselling and social justice. They may need to let go of their own misperceptions about what it means to be a counsellor and their own need for affirmation. One of the best ways that we have discovered for moving forward in this direction is finding like-minded people who will remind you of what is important and support you in engaging in social justice individually or collectively. In both Canada and the United States, social justice chapters have been formed as part of the national counselling associations. The *Counsellors for Social Justice* (CSJ) chapter of the *Canadian Counselling Association* states as its mission:

> To advocate for social justice and social change through the role of the professional counsellor. The Chapter promotes equity and human rights for individuals and societies through action, education, training, consciousness-raising, advocacy, and conscientious objection. The Chapter is dedicated to working across borders, boundaries, professional disciplines, and differences in the pursuit of peace and wellness for all. (CSJ, 2008, ¶ 1)

These types of organizations provide an opportunity to connect with others who are exploring ways to increase their cultural competence and positively impact the profession and those we serve.

I have come to recognize a familiar and unpleasant feeling in my gut when I'm confronted with resistance or backlash as a result of my efforts to promote social justice. There was a time, not long ago, when I was tired of sticking my neck out and had turned in on myself in a self-protective stance. What pulled me out of this position was finding others who held similar values and beliefs and finding both social support and collective energy to continue to engage with our environments in a way that promotes change. I've come to realize just how important it is to foster these relationships and to carefully select individuals and groups who will counterbalance the fully anticipatable reactions to social justice work from both within and outside of the professions of psychology and counselling.

I still get that sick feeling in my gut when I open an email or engage in a dialogue that challenges the status quo or pushes back against my efforts to promote justice. But I have now learned not to ignore it, but to simply process it as useful information about the situation I am facing and about caring for my own needs. In some ways, it is an unenviable measure of whether I am on track or not. I understand from this place in my gut the temptation of the Nice Counsellor Syndrome. It would be great to feel respected and valued all of the time. But I also recognize this as part of my privilege that I choose to set aside in support of the more important goal of eliminating social injustices and promoting access to services, resources, and other supports necessary for each member of the Canadian and global cultures to achieve their full potential.

Personal reflection – Sandra Collins

I could really relate to Sandra's reflection when she mentioned that sick feeling, which I also get when I experience disapproving reactions from others. It might be the action of dismissing my comment, attributing a good idea to someone else, the rolling of the eyes, the heated silence, or the e-mail that is strategically circulated to show the repercussions to me or to my colleagues for stepping out of line or speaking up about less popular issues. I wonder what it is like for other colleagues who are far more vocal and who take action more often or more intensely than I do. At times, I wonder if it is just me, but I never wonder anymore if it is worth the price – perhaps that comes with experience and with more integration of my beliefs about social justice into more congruent personal and professional identity. What has made a difference for me in having courage to speak up and to stand up against the status quo has been a support network - just having someone else to consult with and trust, to say, "No, it is not you that is the problem; it is the system that is the problem." What I have learned to do is choose my battles and take small steps against big issues. It is difficult to predict when and how systems will change. However, what I have witnessed is the profound ways in which even small changes can make life so much easier for other people who were burdened by systems that were not working for them. I have enjoyed the role of advocate most of all when it involved problem-solving with colleagues who had the same goals of working with clients, with students, or with other groups in our local community. I feel a compelling need to be able to walk the talk and provide students with real-life examples of how counsellors have enacted social justice advocacy. If we all take small steps, then the journey is not nearly as long nor difficult as walking alone.

Personal reflection – Nancy Arthur

Collaborating For Wellness and Social Change

"Contemporary counselling is markedly deficient in linking the field to the larger society and world as a social change agent and/or advocate to address the social, political, cultural, and economic problems faced by hundreds of millions of people" (Bemak, 1998, p. 280). Despite the call for counsellors to engage in social and political change that is embedded in professional standards of practice, social activism is absent from the daily practices of most counsellors. As emphasized in chapters 5 and 6, a focus on individual counselling and the remediation of clients' symptoms should not mean ignoring the social and political contexts that contribute to their problems. The changing world in which we are living demands that we rethink our approaches to professional practice. The scope and depth of social transformation has led to complex social issues that manifest in mental health concerns. Bemak noted: "It is apparent that to keep up with the complexity and depth of these changes new roles and competencies will be required of counsellors" (p. 280). More than 10 years later, we are beginning to see the results of counsellor educators who have taken a stand in calling for a return to social justice as a foundation for counselling practice. The movement forward is seen in the growing attention paid to ways of engaging students and practitioners in expanded roles, including social justice advocacy (Toporek et al., 2009; Toporek, Gerstein, Fouad, Roysircar, & Israel, 2006a). Collaborative efforts are needed to address the complexity of client issues and this includes investing time and energy towards social action at the local, national, and international levels.

The Movement from Interdisciplinary to Interprofessional Education and Practice

Social justice has been described as collaborative, action-oriented initiatives aimed at eradicating the social inequities that adversely affect health and human development (Crethar, Rivera, & Nash, 2008; Helms, 2003; Vera & Speight, 2003). One of the key elements of this definition is collaboration. Interdisciplinary collaboration is gaining increased attention for its potential to reform approaches to counselling interventions and research. It is also proposed that interdisciplinary approaches have the potential to impact social change through challenging dominant ways that mental health services are organized and delivered.

There is debate about the similarities and differences in the use of *interdisciplinary* versus *interprofessional* practice. **Interdisciplinary approaches** *imply that more than one professional perspective is used to influence client services.* Interdisciplinary practices may occur naturally in counsellor education through practicum placements where students and supervisors from multiple mental health professions interact. However, it should not be assumed that bringing multiple professions together necessarily leads to collaboration and co-operation for the mutual goals of improved client care. Entrenchment in one's professional discipline and hierarchies of power between professionals and between professionals and paraprofessionals continue to dominate health care services. We prefer an emphasis on the term interprofessional, in which the goals of learning from and about each profession are honoured to improve collaboration and the quality of care provided to clients. Arredondo, Shealy-Neal, and Winfrey (2004) provided a useful definition of interprofessional collaboration:

> **Interprofessional Collaboration** *refers to education, training, scholarship, practice, and other professional activities that prepare and call for psychologists to work: (a) in a respectful, collaborative, integrative, and informed manner with other psychologists and members of other disciplines and professions; and (b) with individuals, groups, systems, and organizations that may have diverse values, ethical perspectives, or worldviews, and accountability to different constituencies.* [bold and italics added] (p. 789)

The shared knowledge and skills of mental health providers from multiple disciplines may positively influence the ways in which client issues are defined and client care is provided. A 2004 Health Canada report suggested that we must change the fundamental ways that health care professionals are educated. The emphasis on **collaborative patient-centred practice** "*is designed to promote the active participation of each discipline in patient care. It enhances patient and family centred goals and values, provides mechanisms for continuous communication among care givers, optimizes staff participation in clinical decision making within and across disciplines and fosters respect for disciplinary contributions by all professionals* [italics added]" (Health Canada, 2004, p. ii). We prefer the term **collaborative client-centred practice** to acknowledge that *health care services, including mental health services, are offered in a number of settings beyond traditional medical systems where the use of the term patient is not* *always appropriate. It also de-emphasizes the power relationship between practitioners and clients and recognizes that the client may be defined as more than an individual (e.g., organization, community group).*

It is important to take a moment in this discussion to reflect back on our emphasis throughout this book that clients are the experts in their own cultural identites and in determining the change processes that are a best fit for their particular presenting concerns and cultural interpretations of health, problem development, and change processes (Toporek et al., 2006a). The concept of collaborative client-centred practice is founded on this principle; although our focus in this section is on interprofessional practice, the primary collaborator in any change process is the individual, family, or community whose needs are being addressed. The whole reason for collaboration is to improve service delivery for clients, and they have a vital role to play in determining the direction of such services (Pyle & Arthur, in press). This client collaboration extends to existing cultural and community supports, which can be very valuable resources in building an effective collaborative team (Vera & Speight, 2007).

The rationale for collaborative practice is that the combined synergy of professional perspectives can improve the quality of health care. We have argued throughout this book that the changing demographics of Canadian society and shifting national and international social, economic, and political climate necessitate new ways of approaching our work with clients. The complexity of client cultural identities and health care needs in contemporary society provides a rationale for making changes to the way health care services are delivered (Johnson, Stewart, Brabeck, Huber, & Rubin, 2004). An increasing number of health care agencies and professionals are working from an interprofessional collaborative model out of the necessity to blend expertise, employ multidimensional approaches, and pool resources to address complex health issues (Slattery & Knapp, 2003; Toporek et al., 2006a).

Several professionals and their professional associations (e.g., social work, nursing, and counselling psychology) are endorsing the importance of interprofessional collaboration for the provision of quality health care (Johnson et al., 2004). These interdisciplinary teams can form powerful and formidable alliances in promoting systems level change (Toporek et al., 2006a). However, like any change process, new models of interprofessional collaboration will challenge those professions and individuals who have traditionally held positions of power to consider the benefits of collaborative approaches in which power is shared, decision-making is collaborative, and authority is equalized between team members (Arredondo et al., 2004; Baxter & Brumfitt, 2008). It is precisely issues of power, stereotypes, and misunderstandings about other disciplines that make it imperative that professionals have opportunities to share perspectives about the common and unique contributions to be made to mental health services. Ideally, this will lead to improved methods and interventions available to clients. However, concerted efforts must be made to shift from valuing the potential contributions of interprofessional collaboration to making it standard *best practice* in counselling psychology and other disciplines concerned with the provision of mental health services (Johnson et al.).

The movement towards interprofessional collaboration suggests four essential directions for the education of counsellors and psychologists:

1. Students will require learning settings and curriculum that are conducive to participating on interdisciplinary teams. Research is beginning to uncover models that can be used in curriculum for interprofessional education, to articulate the competencies of effective interprofessional teams, the enablers and barriers to working collaboratively, and the ways client outcomes are favourably influenced (Health Canada, 2004; Suter, Arndt, Arthur, Parboosing, & Taylor, 2009).

2. As noted by Arredondo and colleagues (2004), "psychologists need to acquire and demonstrate the knowledge, skills, attitudes, and values necessary to work in a collegial, integrative, and informed manner across specialty and practice areas" (p. 791). This requires a fundamental value shift in curriculum models to honour and support interprofessional collaboration (Toporek et al., 2006a). Although the attention paid to interprofessional collaboration paints a promising picture of the shared benefits to consumers, interprofessional education and practice need to be fostered in counsellor education and supervision (Arthur & Russell-Mayhew, in press).

 **Snapshot 1**

Promoting Interdisciplinary Collaboration

Bemak (1998) outlines 17 guiding principles to promote interdisciplinary collaboration aimed at social change:

1. Identify with counseling as a profession to understand the similarities and differences between other mental health professions.

2. Overcome interprofessional hostility and phobia and seek common goals based on trust and respect.

3. Remember counseling solutions are not always the answer and be open to alternative ways of approaching client issues.

4. Establish mutually defined projects and goals to promote social change and share responsibility for planning and implementation.

5. Design mutual projects to meet those goals through working cooperatively on the process and procedures that culminate in shared achievements.

6. Redefine professional roles, functions, and boundaries within the framework of interdisciplinary teams.

7. Share power and decision making to enhance the knowledge and expertise of all team members.

8. Set up interprofessional exchanges to afford learning about professional discipline, their programs, and services.

9. Reconstruct incentives to reward interdisciplinary collaboration aimed at social change.

10. Restructure offices to reflect a team approach.

11. Redesign funding schemata to address allocation of resources to meet the needs of interprofessional collaboration.

12. Conduct whole team training to define roles, tasks, functions, and relationships.

13. Establish graduate interdisciplinary training to foster socialization of new professionals.

14. Understand change theory to support organizational and social change.

15. Encourage interdisciplinary publications and cross-fertilization of knowledge available to readers.

16. Make collaborative cross-discipline presentations to model working together and to share collaborative perspectives.

17. Cooperate in documentation and research to help document the ways that social change can be achieved and the benefits of interprofessional collaboration.

From: "Interdisciplinary Collaboration for Social Change: Redefining the Counseling Profession," by R. Bemak, 1998. In C. Lee & G. R. Walz (Eds.), *Social action: A mandate for counselors* (pp. 279-304). Alexandria, VA: American Counseling Association.

3. Curriculum must address some of the major barriers to collaboration with other professionals. Paproski and Haverkamp (2000) have identified six issues that impede collaboration:

    a. Clients must be protected in the sharing of any information. The ethics of informed consent must be re-examined in light of multiple professions and multiple people involved in client services.

    b. Mental health teams will increasingly involve collaboration between professionals and paraprofessionals. There is variation in training and standards of practice that must be examined to ensure high standards of care.

    c. Collaboration is time-consuming. With constraints on time and resources, there are challenges to coordinating meetings and mental health team members must be comfortable with variety in communication mediums.

    d. Reluctance may be the greatest barrier of all for collaborative practice. Misunderstandings and tensions between professional groups require skillful negotiation about the roles and responsibilities of team members.

e. Training needs to include knowledge and awareness to foster interprofessional collaboration. Students and practicing professionals require training about the purposes of collaboration, about who are potential partners for collaboration, and processes that foster effective team relationships.

f. Coordination and case management issues may pose a strain when a designated case manager or coordinator is not assigned or when one is assigned who has not traditionally served in this role. There may also be reluctance to work with family members who are proactive about taking charge of case management.

4. Counsellors need to become more familiar with the role of social change agents or advocates and must be provided with opportunities to learn the requisite competencies that support this role. Collaboration across professions is an essential direction for addressing complex issues in local settings and for adopting a global perspective to address social and psychological issues that cross cultures and transcend national borders. Gaining an international perspective is essential to prepare counsellors to respond to local needs and issues that are common in countries throughout the world.

Starting in Our Own Backyard – The Importance of Intradisciplinary Collaboration

In chapters 3 and 10, we noted the tendency within the disciplines of counselling and psychology for various streams of theory and practice to emerge around particular non-dominant populations, such as multicultural, feminist, and queer. In spite of commonalities of perspective and goals, feminist and multicultural theory, for example, have developed as relatively independent streams within psychology (Reynolds & Constantine, 2004; Whalen et al., 2004). Separate professional groups or chapters within professional associations have also emerged that tend to focus predominantly on one element of cultural identity (Israel, 2003). Attempts to more fully integrate the feminist and multicultural streams are fairly recent (Morrow, Hawxhurst, Montes de Vegas, Abousleman, & Castaneda, 2006). Much of the writing in this area has been generated by and centred on women whose lived experiences and identities do not fit neatly into any of the professional silos erected around ethnicity, gender, sexual orientation, ability, and so on.

As noted in Chapter 10, the social justice movement in psychology is now providing a umbrella for linking the perspectives, change agendas, and collective efforts of members of these professional groups and streams of research and literature. According to Bowman et al. (2001), "The dream of each ideology is to shape a world in which people can operate fairly and without biases" (p. 797). It is unlikely that the current social justice movement in psychology will thrive without the integration of feminist, multicultural, LGBTT, and other streams of theory and practice that reflect the interests of particular non-dominant populations. From a purely practical perspective, however, there is a tendency for researchers and theorists to be more aware of one field of psychology and not the other(s) (Reynolds & Constantine, 2004). We have ourselves certainly been more fully emersed and fluent in the multicultural counselling literature over the years than in the feminist and other bodies of literature. In this second edition of the text, we have attempted to be more inclusive in our own writing, drawing more heavily from feminist and other sources.

Fouad, Gerstein, and Toporek (2006) argued that social justice has been the core of the practice of counselling psychology from its outset, but they noted that other issues have distracted researchers and theorists from this central goal. Achieving the goals of social justice requires those with power and privilege to give up these assets. This applies specifically to those of us who practice the professions of counselling and psychology. Williams and Barber (2004) ask the question: "Are feminists and multiculturalists ready to both let go of privileged status *and* to share in the acknowledgement of different kinds of oppression?" (p. 393). This is certainly a critical starting point for **intraprofessional collaboration**. As we build *bridges across various areas of professional theory and practice we will no doubt be able to strengthen our understanding of and ability to effectively address cultural diversity and social injustices.* This intraprofessional collaboration is an important starting point from which we will be better able to collaborate across professions on both national and international change agendas.

Expanding Culture-Infused Counselling to the Global Level

The current American Psychological Association (APA) (2002) guidelines, as well as much of the other writing on multicultural counselling, make reference only to interactions that occur within our own countries (Canada and the United States). With the globalization of education, economics, and other social systems, it is increasingly important to look more carefully at both the application of multicultural counselling in other countries and the types of universal competencies that may apply across countries.

It is also important for counsellors and psychologists to extend the call for social action to the global level (Dworkin & Yi, 2003; Marsella, 2006). Canada has gained a reputation for advanced policies on multiculturalism and, in spite of continued internal struggles with racism, sexism, heterosexism, and so on, Canadians still stand at the leading edge of human rights legislation and policy. Canada has an opportunity, through its international policies and through the impact of its professional groups, to act as a leader in bridging cultural differences and enhancing appreciation for diversity on the global level. For example, Dworkin and Yi pointed out the particular plight of gays, lesbians, and transgendered persons across the world and called upon psychologists to engage in social action at the international level.

Interprofessional Collaboration for Global Issues and Social Change

In crafting a vision for the global future of professional counselling at the end of the last century, Lee (1997) emphasized the importance of an agenda for social change:

> As the world enters a new century, counseling professionals have the opportunity to assess the philosophy and scope of mental health intervention. The philosophy of counseling in the 21st century must encompass a commitment to social change that focuses on helping to empower individuals to meet the challenges of global transformation. The scope of this commitment must entail a global collaboration of counseling and related mental health professionals who have the awareness, knowledge, and skills to promote human development locally, nationally, and internationally. (p. 285)

Beyond using remedial interventions to work with individuals, interprofessional collaboration holds great potential to impact social change in our local communities and to address global issues. The importance of international linkages for the exchange of professional expertise is emphasized (Lee, 1997, 1998b). A goal of international forums is to exchange ideas and research on counselling and human development. Ultimately, international perspectives should focus on addressing the mental health of citizens within individual countries, along with addressing global social change. When professional groups work together, strategies can be developed to address conditions in many parts of the world through an emphasis on human development and actualization of each individuals' full potential.

Lee (1998b) provided examples of significant transformations that have occurred throughout the world that are relevant for a global social action agenda. "These transformations can be found in such areas as the nature of employment, cultural diversity, migration and refugees, the roles of men and women, increasing rates of innovation and expanding technology, and major changes in patterns of local, regional, and national identity" (p. 297). Similarly, broad global patterns, such as the current economic recessions, can quickly act to turn back the clock on social advancements, resulting in increased social injustices worldwide. Social transformation has impacted individuals as well as the institutions that have traditionally been responsible for public services. As institutions redefine their social roles and responsibilities, they can benefit from consultation processes that help connect their services to the needs of individuals and communities. Human rights violations, violence towards women, children's poverty, anti-racism, and access to education are examples of a myriad of issues that can be taken up in proactive international partnerships to benefit people who are marginalized around the world. The disciplines of counselling and psychology have considerable potential to influence individuals, communities, governments, and other institutions that are directly responsible for human development.

Sharing information about best practices related to professional interventions for social change builds upon the collective strengths of individuals, professions, and nations. Pedersen and Leong (1997) provided compelling reasons for why counselling psychologists should be concerned with other countries and cultures.

1. Interactions with colleagues in other countries offer cultural contrasts through which we can gain increased insights and understandings about our country and cultural backgrounds. In essence, working internationally helps us overcome cultural encapsulation.

2. Learning about how counselling psychology is practiced in other countries can inform and reform our local practices. Although many health issues transcend national borders, the approaches taken to increase the health and welfare of clients vary between cultures and between countries. Although Western models and practices may be sought after, professionals need to be open to ways that alternate views and methods may be imported to improve practices in Canada and the United States.

3. Although the discussion here focuses on practices shared between countries, we cannot lose sight of the fact that Canada is becoming an increasingly multicultural nation, as newcomers arrive from many nations. It is imperative that we continually test and revise our methods and measures of professional practice to assess their cultural validity and limitations in local contexts and between nations.

4. The exchange of knowledge need not be limited to specializations within the discipline of psychology. Researchers and practitioners from other social science fields have common interests that can be addressed through sharing approaches that ultimately inform the practice of psychology.

Cautions are levied against the domination of psychology and of mental health practices by Western perspectives (Norsworthy, 2006). Placing the emphasis on the exportation of Western perspectives reflects a flagrant disregard for the cultural traditions and expertise found in other nations, particularly emerging countries (Lynch, 2002; Norsworthy). At minimum, we must guard against lack of multicultural awareness and assumptions that what works with one cultural group in one part of the world is effective in other contexts. We must make sure that our efforts for international collaboration involve partnerships for learning about the methods and contexts in which mental health services are provided in specific countries and in specific cultures. At best, international collaboration leads to exposure to multiple worldviews and ways of approaching research and applied practice that enhances our roles with all clients (Leong & Ponterotto, 2003; Leung, 2003; Stevens & Gielen, 2007). At worst, they have the potential to reinforce the experience of domination and colonialization (Norsworthy). As Pedersen (2003a) reminded us, "We must learn to become followers as well as leaders in the global context of psychology" (p. 397). This requires us to be patient with the pace of change, particularly since sustainable change comes from within rather than being imposed through well-meaning but culturally myopic change agendas (Toporek et al., 2006a).

In order to expand psychology's horizons, we must be willing to look at shared concerns in various parts of the world and the methods and resource people who contribute to solutions. Professionals need to respect, learn from, and collaborate with indigenous healers. A huge variety of *healers*, as well as many complementary therapies, that can make significant contributions to our understanding of health and healing must be included in global collaborations (Moodley & West, 2005; Takooshian, 2003). Additionally, the roles of paraprofessionals in promoting culture-infused health care have received insufficient attention (Health Canada, 2004). Cultural diversity among client groups, among health care providers in various parts of our nation, and in other developing nations must be incorporated into health care planning and delivery. Increased international professional collaboration among counsellors offers the possibility of setting a strategic view of counselling and human development. It also supports a new level of social activism through which counsellors can address the social transformations that have adversely impacted the lives of many people. It is particularly important for counsellors to unite in efforts to create new and innovative ways of empowering individuals and groups with a history of social and economic marginalization (Lee, 1997). In turn, global collaboration can facilitate human development through an emphasis on counselling psychology's roots in health promotion and illness prevention. Advancing psychosocial development may include designing educational or occupational programming that improves their sense of personal empowerment.

These directions suggest that counsellor education needs to also expand its horizons to prepare students to work from a global perspective. The rationale for internationalizing counselling psychology curriculum is essentially to be responsive to the increasingly global nature of our lives and the increasing interdependence of the world in which we live (Leong & Leach, 2007; Marsella & Pedersen, 2004; Savickas, 2007). The multicultural counselling competency movement offers a foundation from which to incorporate international perspectives on mental health and the roles of counsellors for impacting social change in local, national, and international contexts.

In Chapter 7, Pettifor talked about the movement for international psychology associations to develop a *Universal Declaration of Ethical Principles for Psychologists* that reflects common principles applicable across cultures and contexts. A similar challenge is before us in terms of the multicultural counselling competencies and the process of culture-infused counselling. What might we learn from examining culture and counselling from within the cultures of origin rather than as transplanted subcultures within our own countries? What common principles might emerge that are applicable across cultural, national, and socio-political contexts? The *Universal Declaration of Ethical Principles for Psychologists* may pave the way for the exploration of **universal principles of culture-infused counselling.** *These principles would represent common factors for establishing an effective working alliance in any cultural context and for facilitating effective and culturally sensitive processes of change.* It may be in exploring this issue by moving beyond the borders of North American culture that we are able to actually begin to identify those factors that are truly universal and to clarify the variables that underlie similarities and differences in experiences and needs in counselling.

Chapter Summary

We have attempted in this final chapter to pull together some of the themes have emerged throughout this book and to leave you with a sense of where we feel the professions of counselling and psychology must head in the years to come if we are to continue to develop and fully embrace the reality of multiculturalism nationally and internationally.

The framework for culture-infused counselling competencies proposed in this book represents one of the few attempts in the literature to challenge the traditional models that have been the focus of the multicultural counselling movement for a number of decades. This challenge comes from both a theoretical and a practical perspective, the latter driven by the need to be more inclusive of developments that have appeared in the literature since the multicultural counselling competencies were first introduced. We acknowledge the criticisms levied against earlier models for their lack of empirical validation and invite others to include our conceptualization of competence in future validation studies. In the meantime, the need remains for counsellors and psychologists to develop competence in responding to the needs of clients from diverse cultural backgrounds. Students and practitioners both express a desire for support in addressing the *how-to* of competency development. To this end, we have provided a structure for a continued competence plan based on the framework proposed in this book and have provided strategies for enhancement of culture-infused counselling competence.

We also recognize that even with all of the attitude, knowledge, and skill competencies that we have developed over the years, it is still a daily challenge to approach our lives and our practices with cultural sensitivity and to continue to challenge social injustices as we encounter them. We have reviewed some of the potential barriers to adopting a culture-infused and social justice focused approach to practice and have introduced the idea of peacebuilding as a central process in confronting structural violence against individuals and groups.

Finally, one of the most important messages that we have to bring to the professions of counselling and psychology is the need to expand the parameters of practice to include actions and roles that will impact the larger systems in which our clients function and that impact their health and well-being on a daily basis. The emphasis on social justice from Chapter 6 was expanded in this final chapter with a particular focus on the need for interprofessional and international collaboration. The importance of moving beyond our ethnocentric perspectives to embrace the global reality of multiculturalism cannot be overstated. Counsellors and psychologists are challenged to embrace the call for social action through their relationships with clients, colleagues, professional organizations, and broader systems both nationally and internationally.

Conclusion: Think Big - Creating a Truly Multicultural Nation

Canadians have 30 years of experience with the current multicultural policy and, while we stand at the cutting edge on the international front, there is still much to be done to fully embrace diversity within this country. Although we are proud to be Canadian and have emphasized throughout this book the uniqueness of Canadian policies on multiculturalism, we also recognize the discrepancies between policy and practice, ideology and reality. Reza (2006) suggested that part of the problem in reaching our national goals is our failure to recognize the weakness of our Western worldview as a foundation for a truly multicultural nation. In Chapter 4, we noted how the individualistic model upon which much of our psychological theory and practice is based may be limited in its application across cultures. Reza made the same argument at the national policy level. She saw a direct correlation between adherence to a dominant ideology of individualism/corporatism and support (or rather lack thereof) of ethno-racial minorities. In contrast, she saw the collectivist perspective of many of these groups as more conducive to supporting social justice, precisely because it focuses on the well-being of the whole – community, organization, nation, and so on.

In our current economic times, as competition for resources increases, the willingness of individuals and groups in positions of privilege to relinquish some of the monopoly on resources and power may decrease even further. The professions of psychology and counselling are better equipped than most to have a positive impact on the progression of our society towards the goals of equity, respect, and dignity for all. Now, perhaps more than ever before, we are faced with choices on the local, national, and international levels about how willing we are as Canadians to be fully inclusive of all others. A philosophical shift in counselling and psychology is required to: a) redefine the norm in human experience by the richness, complexity, and diversity of cultural identity and worldview (Barret et al., 2005); b) centralize rather than marginalize the experiences of individuals with multiple non-dominant identities as an essential avenue to a more full appreciation of human experience (Canadian Research Institute for the Advancement of Women, 2006; Morris & Bunjun, 2007); and c) assume a more proactive stance towards societal contexts of power and privilege (Lowe & Mascher, 2001). Cultural competence, as counsellors and as a profession, must include both a more complete appreciation of the cultural contexts, experiences, and perspectives of clients and a multi-level, multidisciplinary, and potentially multinational response to the common experience of cultural oppression that moves beyond the individual to organizations, communities, and broader systems (Williams, 2007).

Reynolds and Constantine (2004) argued that to really transform the profession, we must move beyond first-order change, the integration of new information, to second-order change, which "fundamentally alters the structure and practices of a system" (p. 352). Second-order change requires changes in core values and assumptions, which then drive theory and practice (Reynolds & Constantine). It has been our assertion throughout the book that the starting place for transformation is the person of the counsellor. To be culturally competent requires this high level of introspection and honesty. We invite you to continue to explore your own cultural identities and examine your own privilege or dis-privilege and the implications they hold for your assumptions about theory and practice.

For a number of decades the **personal is political** cry of feminist therapists has served as a reminder to us that *we cannot separate our personal lives from our professional lives but must act to promote justice and equality in both realms.* Where counselling and psychology as professions fall short is in leaving this call with the individual practitioner and failing to recognize the important role of the profession as a whole in the political arena (Dworkin & Yi, 2003). It is time to add a new call to recognize that the **professional is political** and to hold *expectations of leaders and professional organizations to take a stance on political issues that impact the disadvantaged in our society.*

Moving the focus of counselling and psychology to a political level will force the professions to take a stronger stand on the principles and standards that have been set forth in codes of ethics and guidelines for professional practice. Atkinson and Israel (2003) noted what they considered to be a backlash against multiculturalism within the profession of psychology in the United States. There are those who argue that the professions must maintain more breadth in perspective, allowing for inclusion of those who hold values and worldviews that do not respect the dignity, worth, and equality of all. We would argue that the collective identity and potential voice of the profession for the oppressed of this world is compromised by our failure to demand of each other adherence to our stated codes of conduct, which include requisite attitudes, knowledge, and skills. As Canadians, we may be uniquely positioned to support the continued infusion of culture into all areas of professional practice.

While the multicultural competencies explored in this book and in other professional writings do not have the status of code of conduct and do not represent enforceable guidelines, we invite you to see them as aspirations for the profession that may offer a foundation for us as a collective body to impact the very nature of Canadian society and to positively affect the lives of non-dominant or oppressed populations worldwide.

As I reflect on the process of writing this book and the lessons that I have learned along the way, I am reminded of my own developmental process as a researcher, educator, and practitioner. We speak throughout this book of the importance of awareness of the worldviews of others in every aspect of our lives and our work. I have certainly expanded my level of awareness throughout this writing process. I have a clearer sense of the questions to ask, the complexity of fully understanding the personal cultural identity or identities of another person, and the importance of setting aside my own cultural lens if I am to fully engage with another person(s) in the counselling process.

Where I find myself struggling is in finding the line between acceptance of differences in worldview and the social justice agenda emphasized throughout this book. Where is the boundary between non-evaluative acknowledgement of and respect for differences and actively promoting values that underscore equality and justice for all human beings? I have often stated that my own growing edge in this area is my intolerance for intolerance. As we finalize the material for this second edition, I am faced again with this question of where I draw this line and how I hold both of these important personal and professional values simultaneously.

I find myself on firmer ground, however, as I flip this question around to explore my responsibility as counsellor, educator, supervisor, consultant, and social advocate. My responsibility lies in protecting and advancing the cause of the under-serviced, underprivileged, and under-represented. This may mean challenging the values and assumptions of others who wish to maintain the status quo and, in so doing, protect their sense of ownership and power over resources, institutions, and statuses that rightfully belong to all. It will certainly mean taking an active stand against all forms of racism, sexism, heterosexism, ableism, ageism, and other forms of oppression in both my personal and professional lives. And it will likely mean continually learning to hold a social justice agenda while simultaneously deepening my awareness of the worldview of those who oppose that agenda so that I can facilitate building bridges to promote mutual understanding rather than walls that continue to perpetuate misunderstanding.

Personal reflection – Sandra Collins

REFERENCE LIST

Abouguendia, M., & Noels, K. A. (2001). General and acculturation related hassles and psychological adjustment in first and second generation South Asian immigrants to Canada. *International Journal of Psychology, 36*(3), 163-173.

Acevedo, M. C., Reyes, C. J., Annett, R. D., & Lopez, E. M. (2003). Assessing language competence: Guidelines for assessing persons with limited English proficiency in research and clinical settings. *Journal of Multicultural Counseling & Development, 31*(3), 192-205.

Achenbach, K., & Arthur, N. (2002). Experiential learning: Bridging theory to practice in multicultural counselling. *Guidance & Counselling, 17,* 39-45.

Ackbar, S. (2005). Re-defining fusion in lesbian relationships: Relating attachment, social support, and outness to intrusiveness and closeness-caregiving. *Society for the Psychological Study of Lesbian, Gay, and Bisexual Issues Newsletter, 21*(3), 9-11.

Ackerman, S. J., Smith Benjamin, L., Beutler, L. E., Gelso, C. J., Goldfried, M. R., Hill, C., et al. (2001). Empirically supported therapy relationships: Conclusions and recommendations of the Division 29 Task Force [Electronic version]. *Psychotherapy: Theory, Research, Practice, Training, 38*(4), 495-497.

Adair, V. C. (2005). Class absences: Cutting class in feminist studies. *Feminist Studies, 31*(3), 575-603.

Adams, H. (1995). *A tortured people: The politics of colonization.* Penticton, BC: Theytus Books.

Adler, N. J. (1981). Re-entry: Managing cross-cultural transitions. *Group and Organizational Studies, 6,* 341-356.

Adrian-Taylor, S., Noels, K. A., & Tischler, K. (2007). Conflict between international graduate students and faculty supervisors: Towards effective conflict prevention and management strategies. *Journal of Studies in International Education, 11,* 90-117.

Akan, L. (1999). *Pimosatamowin Sikaw Kakeequaywin:* Walking and talking: A Saulteaux Elder's view of Native education. *Canadian Journal of Native Education, 23*(1), 16-39.

Akhtar, S. (1994). A third individuation: Immigration identity and the psychoanalytic process. *Journal of American Psychoanalytic Association, 43*(4), 1051-1084.

Alba, R., & Nee, V. (1997). Rethinking assimilation theory for a new era of immigration. *International Migration Review, 31*(4), 826-874.

Alberta, A. J., & Wood, A. H. (2009). A practical skills model for effectively engaging clients in multicultural settings. *The Counseling Psychologist, 37*(4), 564-579.

Alberti, R., & Emmons, M. (1982). *A guide to assertive living: Your perfect right.* San Luis Obispo, CA: Impact.

Alderson, K. (2002). *Breaking out: The complete guide to building and enhancing a positive gay identity for men and women.* Toronto, ON: Insomniac Press.

Alderson, K. G. (2000). *Beyond coming out: Experiences of positive gay identity.* Toronto, ON: Insomniac Press.

Alderson, K. G., & Jevne, R. F. J. (2003). Yin and yang in mortal combat: The psychic conflict beneath the coming-out process for gay males. *Guidance and Counselling, 18,* 128-141.

Alderson, K. G. (2004). A different kind of outing: Training counsellors to work with sexual minority clients. *Canadian Journal of Counselling, 38,* 193-210.

Alderson, K. G., Orzeck, T. L., & McEwen, S. C. (2009). Alberta high school counsellors' knowledge of homosexuality and their attitudes toward gay males. *Canadian Journal of Education, 32*(1), 85-116.

Alexander, C. J. (1999). Reparative therapy for gays and lesbians. *Journal of Gay and Lesbian Social Services, 9*(4), 115-118.

Alexander, M. A., & Shaw, E. (1991). International students at a college of nursing: Concerns and coping. *Journal of American College Health, 39,* 245-247.

Ali, S. R., Mahmood, A., Moel, J., Hudson, C., & Leathers, L. (2008). A qualitative investigation of Muslim and Christian women's views of religion and feminism in their lives. *Cultural Diversity and Ethnic Minority Psychology, 14*(1), 38-46.

Allen, D. J., & Oleson, T. (1999). Shame and internalized homophobia in gay men. *Journal of Homosexuality, 37*(3), 33-43.

Allen, J., Vaage, A. B., & Hauff, E. (2006). Refugees and asylum seekers in societies. In D. L. Sam & J. W. Berry (Eds.), *The Cambridge handbook of acculturation psychology* (pp. 198-217). New York: Cambridge University Press.

Allison, K., Crawford, I., Echemendia, R., Robinson, L., & Knepp, D. (1994). Human diversity and professional competence: Training in clinical and counseling psychology revisited. *American Psychologist, 49,* 792-796.

Allison, K., Echemendia, R., Crawford, I., & Robinson, W. (1996). Predicting cultural competence: Implications for practice and training. *Professional Psychology: Research and Practice, 27,* 386-393.

Allport, G. (1958). *The nature of prejudice.* Garden City, NY: Doubleday.

Alvarez, A. N., Blume, A. W., Cervantes, J. M., & Thomas, L. R. (2009). Tapping the wisdom tradition: Essential elements to mentoring students of color. *Professional Psychology: Research and Practice, 40*(2), 181-188.

Alvarez, A. N., & Helms, J. E. (2001). Racial identity and reflected appraisals as influences on Asian Americans' racial adjustment. *Cultural Diversity & Ethnic Minority Psychology, 7*(3), 217-231.

Alvarez, A. N., & Miville, M. L. (2003). Walking a tightrope: Strategies for teaching undergraduate multicultural counselling courses. In D. B. Pope-Davis, H. L. K. Coleman, W. M. Lui, & R. L. Toporek (Eds.), *Handbook of multicultural competencies in counseling and psychology* (pp. 528-545). Thousand Oaks, CA: Sage.

Alvarez, M. (1999). The experience of migration: A relational approach in therapy. *Journal of Feminist Family Therapy, 11,* 1-29.

American Educational Research Association, American Psychological Association, & National Council on Measurement in Education. (1999). *Standards for educational and psychological testing.* Washington, DC: Authors.

American Psychiatric Association. (2000). *Diagnostic and statistical manual for mental disorders* (4th ed., text rev.). Washington, DC: Author.

American Psychological Association. (1973). *Ethical principles in the conduct of research with human participants.* Washington, DC: Author.

American Psychological Association. (1982). *Ethical principles on the conduct of research with human participants.* Washington, DC: Author.

American Psychological Association. (1993). *Guidelines for providers of psychological services to ethnic, linguistic, and culturally diverse populations.* Washington, DC: Author.

American Psychological Association. (1998). *Guidelines for psychotherapy with lesbian, gay, and bisexual clients.* Retrieved April 15, 2002, from http://www.apa.org/divisions/div44/guidelines.html

American Psychological Association. (2000). Guidelines for psychotherapy with lesbian, gay, and bisexual clients. *American Psychologist, 55,* 1440-1451.

American Psychological Association. (2002a). Ethical principles for psychologists and code of conduct. *American Psychologist, 57,* 1060-1973.

American Psychological Association. (2002b). *Guidelines and principles for accreditation of programs in professional psychology.* Retrieved September 29, 2004, from http://www.apa.org/ed/G&P2.pdf

American Psychological Association. (2003a). *Guidelines for psychological practice with older adults.* Retrieved September 15, 2003, from http://www.apa.org/practice/Guidelines_for_ Psychological_Practice_ with_Older_Adults .pdf

American Psychological Association. (2003b). Guidelines on multicultural education, training, research, practice, and organizational change for psychologists. *American Psychologist, 58,* 377-402.

American Psychological Association. (2007). *Guidelines for psychological practice with girls and women: A joint task force of APA Divisions 17 and 35.* Washington, DC: Author.

Amnesty International. (1985). The declaration of Tokyo (World Medical Association). In Amnesty International Secretariat (Ed.), *Ethical codes and declarations relevant to the health professions* (2nd ed .). London: Author.

Amnesty International Canada. (2001). *Refugees.* Retrieved October 10, 2004, from http://www.amnesty.ca/Refugee/who.php

Amundson, N. E. (1998). *Active engagement: Enhancing the career counselling process.* Richmond, BC: Ergon Communications.

Anastasi, A., & Urbina, S. (1997). *Psychological testing* (7th ed.). Toronto, ON: Prentice-Hall.

Ancis, J. R. (1998, Spring). Cultural competency training at a distance: Challenges and strategies. *Journal of Counseling and Development, 76,* 134-142

Anderson, J., Perry, J., Blue, C., Browne, A., Henderson, A., Khan, K. B., et al. (2003). "Rewriting" cultural safety within the postcolonial and postnational feminist project. *Advances in Nursing Science, 26*(3), 196-214.

Angus Reid Group. (2000, May 6). Canadians and immigration. Retrieved October 1, 2003, from http://www.ipsos-reid.com/search/pdf/media/mr000506.pdf

Antone, E. M. (2000). Empowering Aboriginal voice in Aboriginal education. *Canadian Journal of Native Education, 24*(2), 92-101.

Antonucci, T. C., Okorodudu, C., & Akiyama, H. (2002). Well-being among older adults on different continents. *Journal of Social Issues, 58,* 617-626.

Aponte, J. F., & Johnson, L. R. (2000). The impact of culture on intervention and treatment of ethnic populations. In J. F. Aponte & J. Wohl (Eds.), *Psychological intervention and cultural diversity* (pp. 18-39). Toronto, ON: Allyn and Bacon.

Appleyard, B. (1992). *Understanding the present.* London, UK: Pan Books.

Arminio, J. (2001). Exploring the nature of race-related guilt. *Journal of Multicultural Counseling & Development, 29*(4), 239-252.

Armstrong, R. P. (1999, June). Geographic patterns of socio-economic well-being of First Nations Communities. *Statistics Canada: Rural and Small Town Canada Analysis Bulletin, 1(8),* 1-13. Retrieved April 12, 2004, from http://www.stat-can.ca/english/freepub/21-006-XIE/19990821-006-XIE.pdf

Arnold, M. F., Cutler, H. A., Myers, J. E., Campbell, T., Long, J., & Davis, W. (2002). Infusing gay, lesbian, & bisexual issues into counselor preparation programs. *Q The Online Journal, 2*(1). Retrieved April 30, 2002, from http://www.aglbic. org/Q/Vol2Num1/Arnold.htm

Arredondo, P. (1986). Immigration as a historical moment leading to an identity crisis. *Journal of Counseling and Human Service Professions, 1*(1), 79-85.

Arredondo, P. (1998). Integrating multicultural competencies and universal helping conditions in culture-specific contexts (Reconceptualizing multicultural counselling). *The Counseling Psychologist, 26,* 592-301.

Arredondo, P. (1999). Multicultural counseling competencies as tools to address oppression and racism. *Journal of Counseling & Development, 77*(1), 102-108.

Arredondo, P., & Glauner, T. (1992). *Personal dimensions of identity model.* Boston: Empowerment Workshops.

Arredondo, P., & Gordon Reinoso, J. (2003). Challenges to the development of culturally relevant, empirically supported treatment. In D. B. Pope-Davis, H. L. K. Coleman, W. M. Lui, & R. L. Toporek (Eds.), *Handbook of multicultural competencies in counseling and psychology* (pp. 330-346). Thousand Oaks, CA: Sage.

Arredondo, P., & Perez, P. (2003). Expanding multicultural competence through social justice leadership. *The Counseling Psychologist, 31*(3), 282-289.

Arredondo, P., & Perez, P. (2006). Historical perspectives on the multicultural guidelines and contemporary applications. *Professional Psychology: Research and Practice, 37*(1), 1-5.

Arredondo, P., Shealy, C. Neale, M., & Winfrey, L. L. (2004). Consultation and interprofessional collaboration: Modelling for the future. *Journal of Clinical Psychology, 60*(7), 787-800.

Arredondo, P., & Toporek, R. (2004). Multicultural competencies = ethical practice. *Journal of Mental Health Counselling, 26*(1), 44-55.

Arredondo, P., Toporek, R., Brown, S. P., Jones, J., Locke, D. C., Sanchez, J., et al. (1996). Operationalization of the multicultural counseling competencies. *Journal of Multicultural Counseling and Development, 24*, 42-78.

Arredondo, P., Tovar-Blank, Z. G., & Parham, T. A. (2008). Challenges and promises of becoming a culturally-competent counselor in a sociopolitical era of change and empowerment. *Journal of Counseling & Development, 86*, 261-268.

Arthur, N. (1997). Counselling issues with international students. *Canadian Journal of Counselling, 31*, 259-274.

Arthur, N. (2000). Career competencies for managing cross-cultural transitions. *Canadian Journal of Counselling, 34*, 204-217.

Arthur, N. (2002). Inquiring about culture. *Proceedings of the Alberta Regional Consultation on Career Development, Building Tomorrow Today,* 37-44. Edmonton, AB: Learning Resources Distributing Centre.

Arthur, N. (2003). Preparing international students for the re-entry transition. *Canadian Journal of Counselling, 37*(3), 173-185.

Arthur, N. (2004a). *Counseling international students: Clients from around the world.* New York: Kluwer/Plenum.

Arthur, N. (2004b, January). *Show off your international experience.* Paper presented at The National Consultation on Career Development (NATCON), Ottawa, ON.

Arthur, N. (2007). Career planning and decision-making needs of international students. In H. Singaravelu & M. Pope (Eds.), *A handbook for counselling international students in the United States* (pp. 37-56). Alexandria, VA: American Counseling Association.

Arthur, N. (2008). Counseling international students. In P. Pedersen, J. G. Draguns, W. J. Lonner, & J. E. Trimble (Eds.), *Counseling across cultures* (6th ed., pp. 275-290). Thousand Oaks, CA: Sage.

Arthur, N., & Achenbach, K. (2002). Developing multicultural counselling competencies through experiential learning. *Counselor Education and Supervision, 42*, 2-14.

Arthur, N., Brodhead, M., Magnusson, K., & Redekopp, D. (2003). Employment equity career counselling in Canada. *Guidance & Counselling, 18*(2), 52-58.

Arthur, N., & Collins, S. (2005). *Culture-infused counselling: Celebrating the Canadian mosaic.* Calgary, AB: Counselling Concepts.

Arthur, N., & Collins, S. (in press). Culture-infused counsellor supervision. In N. Pelling, J. Barletta, & P. Armstrong (Eds.), *Practice of Supervision.* Bowen Hills, QLD: Australian Academic Press.

Arthur, N., Collins, S., Bisson, S., & McMahon, M. (2009). *The assessment of career practitioners' social justice competencies.* Manuscript in preparation.

Arthur, N., Collins, S., McMahon, M., & Marshall, C. (2009). Career practitioners' views of social justice and barriers for practice. *Canadian Journal of Career Development, 8*(1), 22-31.

Arthur, N., & Januszkowski, T. (2001). Multicultural competencies of Canadian counsellors. *Canadian Journal of Counselling, 35*(1), 36-48.

Arthur, N., & Lalande, V. (2009). Diversity and social justice implications for outcome approaches to evaluation. *International Journal for the Advancement of Counselling, 31*(1), 1-16 .

Arthur, N., & McMahon, M. (2004). *Multicultural career counseling: Theoretical applications of the Systems Theory Framework.* Manuscript submitted for publication.

Arthur, N., & McMahon, M. (2005). A systems theory framework for multicultural career counseling. *The Career Development Quarterly, 53*(3), 208-222.

Arthur, N., & Pedersen, P. (Eds.). (2008). *Case incidents in counseling for international transitions.* Alexandria, VA: American Counseling Association.

Arthur, N., & Popadiuk, P. (in press). A cultural formulation approach to career counseling with international students. *Journal of Career Development.*

Arthur, N., & Ramaliu, A. (2000). Crisis interventions with survivors of torture. *Crisis Intervention and Time Limited Treatment, 6*(1), 51-63.

Arthur, N., & Russell-Mayhew, S. (in press). Preparing counsellors for interprofessional collaboration through supervision and lateral mentoring. *Canadian Journal of Counselling.*

Arthur, N., & Stewart, J. (2001). Multicultural counselling in the new millennium: Introduction to the special theme issue. *Canadian Journal of Counselling, 35*(1), 3-14.

ASERVIC. (2009). *Spiritual competencies*. Retrieved April 24, 2009, from http://www.aservic.org/competencies.html

Asher, N. (2008). Listening to hyphenated Americans: Hybrid identities of youth from immigrant families. *Theory into Practice, 47,* 12-19.

Ashkinazy, S. (1984). Working with gay and lesbian youth. *Practice Digest, 7*(1), 21-23.

Assagioli, R. (1983). *Psychosynthèse: Principes et techniques* [Psychosynthesis: Principles and techniques]. Paris: ÉPI.

Associated Press. (2001, May 9). Study says some gays can switch. *Calgary Herald,* p. A5.

Association of Canadian Universities for Northern Studies. (1982). *Ethical principles for the conduct of research in the north.* Ottawa, ON: Author.

Association of Universities and Colleges of Canada. (2007). *Canadian universities and student mobility.* Ottawa, ON: Author.

Astin, H. A. (1985). The meaning of work in women's lives: A sociopsychological model of career choice and work behavior. *The Counselling Psychologist, 12*(4), 117-126.

Ataca, B., & Berry, J. W. (2002). Psychological, sociocultural, and marital adaptation of Turkish immigrant couples in Canada. *International Journal of Psychology, 37,* 13-26.

Atkinson, D. R. (1993). Who speaks for cross-cultural counseling research? *The Counseling Psychologist, 21*(2), 218-224.

Atkinson, D. R. (2004). *Counselling American minorities* (6th ed.). New York: McGraw-Hill.

Atkinson, D. R., & Hackett, G. (2004). *Counselling diverse populations* (3rd ed.). New York: McGraw-Hill.

Atkinson, D. R., & Israel, T. (2003). The future of multicultural counselling competence. In D. B. Pope-Davis, H. L. K. Coleman, W. M. Lui, & R. L. Toporek (Eds.), *Handbook of multicultural competencies in counseling and psychology* (pp. 591-606). Thousand Oaks, CA: Sage.

Atkinson, D. R., Morten, G., & Sue, D. W. (1993). *Counseling American minorities.* Dubuque, IA: Brown & Benchmark.

Atkinson, D. R., & Thompson, C. E. (1992). Racial, ethnic, and cultural variables in counseling. In S. D. Brown and R. W. Lent (Eds.), *Handbook of counseling psychology* (2nd ed., pp. 349-382), New York: John Wiley & Sons.

Atkinson, D. R., Thompson, C. E., & Grant, S. K. (1993). A three-dimensional model for counseling racial/ethnic minorities. *The Counseling Psychologist, 21,* 257-277.

Atkinson, D. R., Wampold, B. E., Lowe, S., Matthews, L., & Aye, H. (1998). Asian American preferences for counselor characteristics. *The Counseling Psychologist, 26,* 101-123.

Attneave, C. L. (1985). Practical counseling with American Indian and Alaska Native clients. In P. Pedersen (Ed.), *Handbook of cross-cultural counseling and therapy* (pp. 135-140). Westport, CT: Greenwood.

Atwood, M. (2000). *The blind assassin.* Toronto, ON: McClelland and Stewart.

Avis, W. S. (Ed.). (1989). *Funk and Wagnall's Canadian college dictionary.* Vancouver, BC: Fitzhenry & Whiteside.

Axelson, J. A. (1999). *Counseling and development in a multicultural society* (3rd ed.). Toronto, ON: Brooks/Cole.

Aycan, Z., & Kanungo, R. K. (1998). Impact of acculturation and socialization beliefs and behavioral occurrences among Indo-Canadian immigrants. *Journal of Comparative Family Studies, 29*(3), 451-467.

Bachelor, A. (1995). Clients' perceptions of the therapeutic alliance: A qualitative analysis. *Journal of Counseling Psychology, 42*(3), 323-337.

Bagley, C., & Tremblay, P. (1998). On the prevalence of homosexuality and bisexuality, in a random community survey of 750 men aged 18-27. Journal of Homosexuality, 36(2), 1-18.

Baldridge, D. (2001). Indian elders: Family traditions in crisis. *American Behavioral Scientist, 44*(9), 1515-1527.

Balka, C., & Rose, A. (Eds.). (1989). *Twice blessed: On being lesbian, gay and Jewish.* Boston: Houghton Mifflin.

Ballou, M., & Brown, L. (Eds.). (2002). *Rethinking mental health and disorder: Feminist perspectives.* New York: Guilford Press.

Balsam, K. F., & Szymanski, D. M. (2005). Relationship quality and domestic violence in women's same-sex relationships: The role of minority stress. *Psychology of Women Quarterly, 29,* 258-269.

Bankart, P. (1997). *Talking cures: A history of Western and Eastern psychotherapies.* Pacific Grove, CA: Brooks/Cole.

Banks, A. (2006). Relational therapy for trauma. Journal of Psychological Trauma, 5(1), 25-47.

Baptiste, D. A. (1993). Immigrant families, adolescents, and acculturation: Insights for therapists. *Marriage and Family Review, 19,* 341-363.

Barber, J. S., & Mobley, M. (1999). Counseling gay adolescents. In A. M. Horne & M. S. Kiselica (Eds.), *Handbook of counseling boys and adolescent males: A practitioner's guide* (pp. 161-178). Thousand Oaks, CA: Sage.

Barcinski, M., & Kalia, V. (2005). Extending the boundaries of the dialogical self: Speaking from within the feminist perspective. *Culture & Psychology, 11*(1), 101-109.

Barker, M., Child, C., Gallois, C., Jones, E., & Callan, V. J. (1991). Difficulties of overseas students in social and academic situations. *Australian Journal of Psychology, 43*(2), 79-84.

Barret, B., & Logan, C. (2002). *Counseling gay men and lesbians: A practice primer.* Pacific Grove, CA: Brooks/Cole.

Barret, S. E., Chin, J. L., Comas-Diaz, L., Espin, O., Greene, B., & McGoldrick, M. (2005). Multicultural feminist therapy: Theory in context. *Women & Therapy, 28*(3/4), 27-61.

Baruth, L. G., & Manning, M. (2007). *Multicultural counseling and psychotherapy: A lifespan perspective* (4th ed.). Toronto, ON: Pearson Education.

Battiste, M. (1998). Enabling the autumn seed: Toward a decolonized approach to Aboriginal knowledge, language, and education. *Canadian Journal of Native Education, 22*(1), 16-27.

Bauder, H., & Lusis, T. (2008). *"Provincial" immigrants: The social, economic, and transnational experiences of the Filipino Canadian Community in three Ontario second-tier cities.* Retrieved January 10, 2009, from http://ceris.metropolis.net/Virtual%20Library/WKPP%20List/WKPP2008/CWP62.pdf

Baxter, S. K., & Brumfitt, S. M. (2008). Professional differences in interprofessional working. *Journal of Interprofessional Care, 22*(3), 239-251.

Bayer, R. (1981). *Homosexuality and American psychiatry.* New York: Basic Books.

Beall, A. E., Eagly, A. H., & Stearnberg, R. J. (2004). Introduction. In A. H. Eagley, A. E. Beall & R. J. Sternberg (Eds.) *The psychology of gender* (pp. 1-8). New York: Guilford Press.

Beals, K. P., & Peplau, L. A. (2005). Identity support, identity devaluation, and well-being among lesbians. *Psychology of Women Quarterly, 29,* 140-148.

Beane, J. (1981). "I'd rather be dead than gay": Counseling gay men who are coming out. *The Personnel and Guidance Journal, 60,* 222-226.

Beard, J., & Glickauf-Hughes, C. (1994). Gay identity and sense of self: Rethinking male homosexuality. *Journal of Gay & Lesbian Psychotherapy, 2*(2), 21-37.

Beauvais, F., Chavez, E., Oetting, E., Deffenbacher, J., & Cornell, G. (1996). Drug use, violence, and victimization among White American, Mexican American, and American Indian dropouts, students with academic problems, and students in good academic standing. *Journal of Counseling Psychology, 43,* 292-299.

Behnam, B. (2002). Friends and caring professionals as important support for survivors of war and torture. *International Journal of Mental Health, 30*(4), 3-18.

Behring, S. T., & Ingraham, C. L. (1998). Culture as a central component of consultation: A call to the field. *Journal of Educational and Psychological Consultation, 9*(1), 57-72.

Belenky, M. F. (1994). Ways of knowing and the empowerment of women. In J. Gallivan, S. D. Crozier, & V. Lalande (Eds.), *Women, girls, and achievement* (pp. 1-17). North York, ON: Captus Press.

Belenky, M., Clinchy, B., Goldberger, N. R., & Tarule, J. M. (1986). *Women's ways of knowing: The development of self, voice and mind.* New York: Basic Books.

Bell, A. P., & Weinberg, M. S. (1978). *Homosexualities: A study of diversity among men and women.* New York: Simon and Schuster.

Bell, L. A. (1997). Theoretical foundations for social justice education. In M. Adams, L. A. Bell, & P. Griffin (Eds.), *Teaching for diversity and social justice: A sourcebook* (pp. 3-15). New York: Routledge.

Bell, M. E., & Goodman, L. A. (2006). Seeking social justice for victims of intimate partner violence: Real-world struggles in pursuit of systemic change. In R. L. Toporek, L. H. Gerstein, N. A. Fouad, G. Roysircar, & T. Israel (Eds.), *Handbook for social justice in counseling psychology: Leadership, vision, and action* (pp. 155-169). Thousand Oaks, CA: Sage.

Belle, D., & Doucet, J. (2003). Poverty, inequality, and discrimination as sources of depression among U.S. women. *Psychology of Women Quarterly, 27*(2), 101-114.

Bem, S. L. (1993). *The lenses of gender: Transforming the debate on sexual inequality.* New Haven, CT: Yale University Press.

Bemak, R. (1998). Interdisciplinary collaboration for social change: Redefining the counseling profession. In C. Lee & G. R. Walz (Eds.), *Social action: A mandate for counselors* (pp. 279-304). Alexandria, VA: American Counseling Association.

Bemak, F., & Chung, R. (2005). Advocacy as a critical role for urban school counselors: Working toward equity and social justice. *Professional School Counseling, 8,* 196-202.

Bemak, F., & Chung, R. C. (2002). Counseling and psychotherapy with refugees. In P. B. Pedersen, H. G. Draguns, W. J. Lonner, & J. E. Trimble (Eds.), *Counseling across cultures* (5th ed., pp. 209-232). Thousand Oaks, CA: Sage.

Bemak, F., & Chung, R. C. (2008). Counseling and psychotherapy with refugees. In P. B. Pedersen, J. G. Draguns, W. J. Lonner, & J. E. Trimble (Eds.), *Counseling across cultures* (6th ed., pp. 307–324). Thousand Oaks, CA: Sage.

Bemak, F., & Chung, R. C. (2008). New professional roles and advocacy strategies for school counselors: A multicultural/social justice perspective to move beyond the Nice Counselor Syndrome. *Journal of Counseling & Development, 86,* 372-381.

Bemak, F., Chung, R. C., & Bornemann, T. H. (1996). Counseling and psychotherapy with refugees. In P. B. Pedersen, J. G. Draguns, W. J. Lonner, & J. E. Trimble (Eds.), *Counseling across cultures* (4th ed., pp. 243-265). Thousand Oaks, CA: Sage.

Bemak, F., Chung, R. C., & Pedersen, P. B. (2003). *Counseling refugees: A psychosocial approach to innovative multicultural interventions.* Westport, CT: Greenwood Press.

Ben-Ari, A. (1995). The discovery that an offspring is gay: Parents', gay men's, and lesbians' perspectives. *Journal of Homosexuality, 30*(1), 89-112.

Ben-Shalom, U., & Horenczyk, G. (2003). Acculturation orientations: A facet theory perspective on the bidimensional model. *Journal of Cross-Cultural Psychology, 34*(2), 176-188.

Bender, A., & Ewashen, C. (2000). Groupwork is political work: A feminist perspective of interpersonal group psychotherapy. *Issues in Mental Health Nursing, 21*(3), 297-308.

Benton-Banai, E. (1988). *The Mishomis book: The voice of the Ojibway.* St. Paul, MN: Red School House.

Bepko, C., & Johnson, T. (2000). Gay and lesbian couples in therapy: Perspectives for the contemporary family therapist. *Journal of Marital and Family Therapy, 26*(4), 409-419.

Berkel, L. A., Constantine, M. G., & Olson, E. A. (2007). Supervisor multicultural competence: Addressing religious and spiritual issues with counseling students in supervision. *The Clinical Supervisor, 26*(1/2), 3-15.

Berman, H., Girón, E. R. I., & Marroquín, A. P. (2006). A narrative study of refugee women who have experienced violence in the context of war. *Canadian Journal of Nursing Research, 38,* 32-53.

Bernal, A. T., & Coolhart, D. (2005). Learning from sexual minorities: Adolescents and the coming out process. *Guidance & Counseling, 20*(3/4), 128-138.

Bernstein, A. C. (2000). Straight therapists working with lesbians and gays in family therapy. *Journal of Marital and Family Therapy, 26*(4), 433-454.

Berry, J. W. (1990). Psychology of acculturation: Understanding individuals moving between cultures. In R. W. Brislin (Ed.), *Applied cross-cultural psychology* (pp. 232-253). Newbury Park, CA: Sage.

Berry, J. W. (1997). Immigration, acculturation, and adaptation. *Applied Psychology: An International Review, 46*(1), 5-68.

Berry, J. W. (2001). A psychology of immigration. *Journal of Social Issues, 57,* 615-631.

Berry, J. W. (2003). Conceptual approaches to acculturation. In K. M. Chun, P. B. Organista, & G. Marin (Eds.), *Acculturation: Advances in theory, measurement, and applied research* (pp. 17-37). Washington, DC: American Psychological Association.

Berry, J. W. (2005). Acculturation: Living successfully in two cultures. *International Journal of Intercultural Relations, 29,* 697-712.

Berry, J. W. (2006a). Acculturative stress. In P. T. P. Wong & L. C. J. Wong (Eds.), *Handbook of multicultural perspectives on stress and coping* (pp. 287-298). Dallas, TX: Springer.

Berry, J. W. (2006b). Mutual attitudes among immigrants and ethnocultural groups in Canada. *International Journal of Intercultural Relations, 30,* 712-734.

Berry, J. W. (2006c). Stress perspectives on acculturation. In D. L. Sam & J. W. Berry (Eds.), *The Cambridge handbook of acculturation psychology* (pp. 43-57). New York: Cambridge University Press.

Berry, J. W. (2008). Globalisation and acculturation. *International Journal of Intercultural Relations, 32,* 328-336.

Berry, J. W., & Kalin, R. (1995). Multicultural and ethnic attitudes in Canada. *Canadian Journal of Behavioural Science, 27,* 301-320.

Berry, J. W., Phinney, J. S., Sam, D. L., & Vedder, P. (2006). *Immigrant youth in cultural transition: Acculturation, identity, and adaptation across national contexts.* Mahwah, NJ: Lawrence Erlbaum.

Bersoff, D. (1999). *Ethical conflicts in psychology* (2nd ed.). Washington, DC: American Psychological Association.

Betz, N. E. (1989). Implications of the null environment hypothesis for women's career development and for counselling psychology. *The Counselling Psychologist, 17,* 136-144.

Betz, N. E., & Fitzgerald, L. F. (1993). Individuality and diversity: Theory and research in counseling psychology. *Annual Review of Psychology, 44,* 343-381.

Bezanson, L., Arthur, N., Saunders, R., Hughes, D., Browne, V., Watts, T., et al. (2007, December). *Career development from under-represented to inclusive: Opening doors to post-secondary participation.* Research paper submitted to the Canadian Millennium Scholarship Foundation for the Neither a Moment nor a Mind to Waste International Symposium, Ottawa, ON.

Bhabha, H. K. (1990). The third space (interview with Homi Bhabha). In J. Rutherford (Ed.), *Identity, community, culture, difference* (pp. 207-221). London, UK: Lawrence & Wishart.

Bhabha, H. K. (1994). *The location of culture.* New York: Routledge.

Bieschke, K. J., Perez, R. M., & Debord, K. A. (Eds.). (2006). *Handbook of counseling and psychotherapy with lesbian, gay, bisexual, and transgender clients* (2nd ed.). Washington, DC: American Psychological Association.

Gil, A. G., & Vega, W. A. (1996). Two different worlds: Acculturation stress and adaptation among Cuban and Nicaraguan families. *Journal of Social and Personal Relationships, 13,* 435-456.

Biles, J., & Burstein, M. (2003, April). Immigration: Economics and more. *Canadian Issues,* 13-15.

Biles, J., & Ibrahim, J. (2005). Religion and public policy: Immigration, citizenship, and multiculturalism – Guess who's coming to dinner? In P. Bramadat & D. Seljak (Eds.), *Religion and ethnicity in Canada* (pp. 154-177). Toronto, ON: Pearson Longman.

Bilodeau, B. L., & Renn, K. A. (2005). Analysis of LGBT identity development models and implications for practice. *New Directions for Student Services, 111,* 25-39.

Bingham, R. P., & Ward, C. M. (1994). Career counselling with ethnic minority women. In W. B. Walsh & S. H. Osipow (Eds.), *Career counselling for women.* Hillsdale, NJ: Erlbaum.

Birken, L. (1997). Homosexuality and totalitarianism. *Journal of Homosexuality, 33*(1), 1-16.

Birman, D. (2006). Acculturation gap and family adjustment: Findings with Soviet Jewish refugees in the United States and implications for measurement. *Journal of Cross-Cultural Psychology, 37,* 568-589.

Bishop, R. (2005). Freeing ourselves from neocolonial domination in research: A Kaupapa Maori approach to creating knowledge. In N. K. Denzin & Y. S. Lincoln (Eds.), *Handbook of qualitative research* (3rd ed., pp. 65-84). Thousand Oaks, CA: Sage.

Blackwell, C. W. (2008). Nursing implications in the application of conversion therapies on gay, lesbian, bisexual, and transgender clients. *Issues in Mental Health Nursing, 29*(6), 651-665.

Blue, A. W. (1977). A study of Native elders and student needs. *United States Bureau of Indian Affairs Educational Research Bulletin, 5,* 15-24.

Blue, A. W., & Darou, W. (2005). Counselling First Nations peoples. In N. Arthur & S. Collins (Eds.), *Culture-infused counselling: Celebrating the Canadian mosaic* (pp. 303-330). Calgary, AB: Counselling Concepts.

Blue, A. W., & Rogers-Blue, M. A. (1981). The trail of stress. *The Canadian Journal of Native Studies, 1,* 311-330.

Blue, A. W., Rogers-Blue, M. A., Couchie, L., Darou, W., & Kurtness (2008). When cultures clash: Response 1. In N. Arthur & P. Pedersen (Eds.), *Case incidents in counseling for international transitions* (pp. 40-43). Alexandria, VA: American Counseling Association.

Blumenfeld, W. J., & Raymond, D. (1993). *Looking at gay and lesbian life* (updated and expanded ed.). Boston: Beacon Press.

Blumstein, P. W., & Schwartz, P. (1993). Bisexuality: Some social psychological issues. In L. D. Garnets & D. C. Kimmel (Eds.), *Psychological perspectives on lesbian and gay male experiences* (pp. 168-183). New York: Columbia University Press.

Bograd, M. (1988). Power, gender, and the family: Feminist perspectives on family systems theory. In M. A. Dutton-Douglas & L. E. A. Walker (Eds.), *Feminist psychotherapies: Integration of therapeutic and feminist system* (pp. 118-133). Norwood, NJ: Ablex.

Bograd, M., & Mederos, F. (1999). Battering and couples therapy: Universal screening and selection of treatment modality. *Journal of Marital & Family Therapy, 25*(3), 291-312.

Bohan, J. S. (1996). *Psychology and sexual orientation: Coming to terms.* New York: Routledge.

Bohm, A., Davis, D., Meares, D., & Pearce, D. (2002). *Global student mobility 2025: Forecasts of the global demand for international higher education.* Sydney, NSW: IDP Education Australia.

Boisvert, J. A. (2002). Associations of subjective socioeconomic status and women's psychological health. *Psymposium, 12*(1), 11-12.

Bopp, J., Bopp, M., Brown, M., & Lane, P. (1984). *The sacred tree.* Lethbridge, AB: Four Worlds Development Press.

Born, D. O. (1970). Psychological adaptation and development under acculturative stress. *Social Science and Medicine, 3,* 529-547.

Boucher, G. (2002, May 12). Les Amérindiens ne sont plus des sujets d'étude, maisz des partenaires [Amerindians are no longer subjects of research; instead they are partners]. *Le Devoir,* G8.

Bowman, M. L. (2000). The diversity of diversity: Canadian-American differences and their implications for clinical training and APA accreditation. *Canadian Psychology, 41*(1), 230-243.

Bowman, S. L., & King, K. D. (2003). Gender, feminism, and multicultural competencies. In D. B. Pope-Davis, H. L. K. Coleman, W. M. Liu, & R. L. Toporek (Eds.), *Handbook of multicultural competencies in counseling and psychology* (pp. 59-71). Thousand Oaks, CA: Sage.

Bowman, S. L., Rasheed, S., Ferris, J., Thompson, D. A., McRae, J., & Weitzman, L. (2001). Interface of feminism and multiculturalism: Where are the women of colour? In J. G. Ponterotto, J. M. Casis, L. A. Suzuki, & C. M. Alexander (Eds.), *Handbook of multicultural counseling* (2nd ed., pp. 779-798). Thousand Oaks, CA: Sage.

Bowlby, P. W. (2003, April). Diasporic religions in Canada: Opportunities and challenges. *Canadian Issues,* 45-46.

Bowleg, L. (2008). When black + lesbian + woman = black lesbian woman: The methodological challenges of qualitative and quantitative intersectionality research. *Sex Roles, 59,* 312-359.

Boyd, M. (1989). Family and personal networks in international migration: recent developments and new agendas. *International Migration Review, 23,* 638-670.

Boyd, M., & Grieco, E. M. (1998). Triumphant transitions: Socio-economic achievements of the second-generation in Canada. *International Migration Review, 32*(4), 853-876.

Brant, C. (1990). Native ethics and rules of behavior. *Canadian Journal of Psychiatry, 35,* 534-539.

Brant Castellano, M. (2004). Ethics of aboriginal research. *Journal of Aboriginal Health, 1*(1), 98-114.

Brabeck, M., & Brown, L. (1997). Feminist theory and psychological practice. In J. Worell & N. G. Johnson (Eds.), *Shaping the future of feminist psychology: Education, research and practice* (pp. 15-35). Washington, DC: American Psychological Association.

Brady, S., & Busse, W. J. (1994). The gay identity questionnaire: A brief measure of homosexual identity formation. *Journal of Homosexuality, 26,* 1-22.

Brammer, L., & Abrego, P. (1992). Counseling adults for career change. In H. D. Lea & Z. B. Leibowitz (Eds.), *Adult career development: Concepts, issues, and practices* (2nd ed., pp. 90-101). Alexandria, VA: National Career Development Association.

Brammer, L. M., Abrego, P. L., & Shostrom, E. L. (1993). *Therapeutic counselling and psychotherapy* (6th ed.). Englewood Cliffs: NJ: Prentice Hall.

Brayboy, B. M. (2000). The Indian and the researcher: Tales from the field. *International Journal of Qualitative Studies in Education, 13*(4), 415-427.

Brems, C. (1995). Women and depression: A comprehensive analysis. In E. Beckham & W. Leber (Eds.), Handbook of depression (2nd ed., pp. 539-566). New York: Guilford Press.

Bridges, S. K., Selvidge, M. M. D., & Matthews, C. R. (2003). Lesbian women of color: Therapeutic issues and challenges. *Journal of Multicultural Counseling and Development, 31,* 113-130.

Bridget, J. (2000). *Lesbian, gays, and suicide research findings.* Retrieved May 24, 2002, from http://www.lesbianinformationservice.org/suicide.htm

Brill, S. A. (2001). *The queer parent's primer: A lesbian and gay families' guide to navigating the straight world.* Oakland, CA: New Harbinger.

Bringaze, T. B., & White, L. J. (2001). Living out proud: Factors contributing to healthy identity development in lesbian leaders. *Journal of Mental Health Counseling, 23*(2), 162-173.

Brinson, J. A., & Kottler, J. (1995). International students in counseling: Some alternative models. *Journal of College Student Psychotherapy, 9*(3), 57-70.

Brody, E. M. (2006). *Women in the middle: Their parent care years* (2nd ed.). New York: Springer.

Brown, D. (1996). Reply to Derald Wing Sue. *Spectrum, 57*(2), 5-7.

Brown, L. (1985). Power, responsibility, boundaries: Ethical concerns for the lesbian feminist therapist. *Lesbian Ethics, 1,* 30-45.

Brown, L. (1990). The meaning of a multi-cultural perspective for theory-building in feminist therapy. In L. Brown & M. Root (Eds.), *Diversity and complexity in feminist therapy* (pp. 1-21). New York: Harrington Press.

Brown, L. (2006) Still subversive after all these years: The relevance of feminist therapy in the age of evidence-based practice. *Psychology of Women Quarterly, 30,* 15-24.

Brown, L., & Ballou, M. (Eds.). (1992). *Personality and psychopathology: Feminist reappraisals.* New York: Guilford Press.

Brown, L., & Walker, L. E. A. (1990). Feminist therapy perspectives on self-disclosure. In G. Stricker & M. Fisher (Eds.), *Self-disclosure in the therapeutic relationship* (pp. 135-154). New York: Plenum Press.

Brown, L. S. (1986). Gender role analysis: A neglected component of psychological assessment. *Psychotherapy: Research, Practice, Training, 23,* 243-248.

Brown, L. S. (1997). The private practice of subversion: Psychology as tikkun olam. *American Psychologist, 52,* 449-462.

Brown, L. S., Reipe, L. E., & Coffey, R. L. (2005). Beyond color and culture: Feminist contributions to paradigms of human difference. *Women & Therapy, 28*(3/4), 63-92.

Brown, L. S., & Root, M. P. P. (1990). *Diversity and complexity in feminist therapy.* New York: Harrington Park Press.

Bryant-Waugh, R. (2000). Developmental-systemic-feminist therapy. In K. Miller & J. Mizes (Eds.), *Comparative treatments for eating disorders* (pp. 168-181). New York: Springer.

Bubolz, M. M., & Sontag, M. S. (1993). Human ecology theory. In P. G. Boss, W. J. Doherty, R. LaRossa, W. R. Schumm, & S. K. Steinmetz (Eds.), *Sourcebook of family theories and methods: A contextual approach* (pp. 419-448). New York: Plenum Press.

Buchignani, N. (1984). South Asians in Canada: Accommodation and adaptation. In R. N. Kanungo (Ed.), *South Asians in the Canadian mosaic* (pp. 157-180). Montreal, QC: Kala Bharati Foundation.

Buhrke, R. A., Ben-Ezra, L. A., Hurley, M. E., & Ruprecht, L. J. (1992). Content analysis and methodological critique of articles concerning lesbian and gay male issues in counseling journals. *Journal of Counseling Psychology, 39,* 91-99.

Buki, L. P., Ma, T. C., Strom, R. D., & Strom, S. K. (2003). Chinese immigrant mothers of adolescents: Self-perceptions of acculturation effects on parenting. *Cultural Diversity & Ethnic Minority Psychology, 9,* 127-140 .

Burkard, A. W., Ponterotto, J. G., Reynolds, A. L., & Alfonso, V. C. (1999). White counselor trainees' racial identity and working alliance perceptions. *Journal of Counseling & Development, 77*(3), 324-330.

Burnard, B. (1999). *A good house.* Toronto, ON: HarperCollins.

Butson, S. (1993). Native community counselling. *Cognica, 26*(2), 3-7.

Calliou, S. (1997). "Us/them, me/you: Who?" (Re)thinking the binary of First Nations and non-First Nations. *Canadian Journal of Native Education, 22*(1), 1.

Cammaert, L., & Larsen, C. (1988). Feminist frameworks of psychotherapy. In A. A. Dutton-Douglas & L. E. A. Walker (Eds.), *Feminist psychotherapies: Integration of therapeutic and feminist systems* (pp. 12-36). Norwood, NJ: Ablex.

Canadian Abilities Foundation. (n.d.). Women with disabilities violence prevention resource guide. Retrieved April 12, 2004, from http://www.enablelink.org/women/WOMEN.html

Canadian Association of the Deaf. (2002). *The Canadian census.* Ottawa, ON: Author. Retrieved April 27, 2009, from http://www.cad.ca/en/issues/canada_census.asp

Canadian Association of Social Workers. (2005). *Social work code of ethics.* Ottawa, ON: Author.

Canadian Bureau for International Education. (2002). *The national report of international students in Canada, 2000/01.* Ottawa, ON: Author.

Canadian Centre for Justice Statistics. (2004). *Hate crime in Canada.* Retrieved March 1, 2009, from http://www.statcan.gc.ca/pub/85-002-x/85-002-x2004004-eng.pdf

Canadian Centre for Justice Statistics. (2008). *Family violence in Canada: A statistical profile 2008.* Catalogue 85-244-X. Retrieved April 26, 2009, from http://www.statcan.gc.ca/pub/85-224-x/85-224-x2008000-eng.pdf

Canadian Council on Social Development. (2003). *Unequal access: A Canadian profile of racial difference in education, employment, and income.* Retrieved November 30, 2003, from http://www.crr.ca/EN/Publications/ResearchReports/pdf/ ePub_UneqlAcc_full.pdf

Canadian Counselling Association. (1999). *Code of ethics.* Ottawa, ON: Author.

Canadian Counselling Association. (2007). *Code of ethics.* Ottawa, ON: Author.

Canadian Feminist Alliance for International Action. (2007). *Pay equity and women in Canada.* Retrieved April 29, 2009, from http://www.fafia-afai.org/en/ pay_equity_and_women_in_canada

Canadian Guidance and Counselling Association. (1989). *Guidelines for ethical behaviour.* Ottawa, ON: Author.

Canadian Human Rights Commission. (2003). *2000 annual report.* Ottawa, ON: Minister of Public Works and Government Services.

Canadian Institute for Health Information. (2003). *Women's health surveillance report: A multi-dimensional look at the health of Canadian women.* Retrieved February 17, 2004, from http://www.cihi.ca

Canadian Institute for Health Information. (2004). *Improving the health of Canadians.* Retrieved October 28, 2006, from http://secure.cihi.ca/cihiweb/products/IHC2004_ch6_e.pdf

Canadian Institutes of Health Research, Natural Sciences and Engineering Research Council, and Social Sciences and Humanities Research Council. (1998, with 2000, 2002, 2005 amendments). *Tri-Council policy statement: Ethical conduct for research involving humans.* Retrieved January 21, 2009, from http://pre.ethics.gc.ca/english/policystatement/policystatement.cfm

Canadian Press. (2002, April 4). Gay teen fights school board. *Calgary Herald,* p. A12.

Canadian Psychological Association. (1986). *Canadian code of ethics for psychologists.* Ottawa, ON: Author.

Canadian Psychological Association. (1987). *Guidelines for educational and psychological testing.* Ottawa, ON: Author.

Canadian Psychological Association. (1991). *Canadian code of ethics for psychologists.* Ottawa, ON: Author.

Canadian Psychological Association. (1996/2001a). *Guidelines for non-discriminatory practice.* Ottawa, ON: Author.

Canadian Psychological Association. (1996/2001b). *Guidelines for psychologists addressing recovered memories.* Ottawa, ON: Author.

Canadian Psychological Association. (2000). *Canadian code of ethics for psychologists* (3rd ed.). Retrieved October 2, 2003, from http://www.cpa.ca/ethics2000.html

Canadian Psychological Association. (2007). *Guidelines for ethical psychological practice with women.* Ottawa, ON: Author.

Canadian Psychological Association. (2009). *Ethical guidelines for supervision in psychology: Teaching, research, practice, and administration.* Ottawa, ON: Author.

Canadian Race Relations Foundation. (n.d.). *Facts about acknowledging and defining racism.* Toronto, ON: Author.

Canadian Research Institute for the Advancement of Women. (1996). *Feminist research ethics: A process* (2nd ed.). Ottawa, ON: Author.

Canadian Research Institute for the Advancement of Women. (2006). *Intersectional feminist frameworks: An emerging vision.* Ottawa, ON: Author. Retrieved November 12, 2008, from http://www.criaw-icref.ca/IFF/The IFFs- An Emerging Vision.pdf

Canadian Task Force on Mental Health Issues Affecting Immigrants and Refugees. (1988). *After the door has been opened: Mental health issues affecting immigrants and refugees in Canada.* Ottawa, ON: Multiculturalism and Citizenship Canada.

Cardemil, E. V., & Battle, C. L. (2003). Guess who's coming to therapy? Getting comfortable with conversations about race and ethnicity in psychotherapy. *Professional Psychology: Research and Practice, 34*(3), 278-286.

Carpenter, S. (2001). Experts with ethical issues in research with ethnic-minority youth. *Monitor in Psychology, 32,* 34-35.

Carragher, D. J., & Rivers, I. (2002). Trying to hide: A cross-national study of growing up for non-identified gay and bisexual male youth. *Clinical Child Psychology and Psychiatry, 7,* 457-474.

Carroll, L., Gilroy, P. J., & Murra, J. (2000). Advocating for gay, lesbian, bisexual, and transgendered persons: Overcoming barriers and resistances. Q The Online Journal, 1(1). Retrieved April 30, 2002, from http://www.aglbic.org /Q/Vol1Num1/Carroll.htm

Carstairs, S. (2001). Is it a woman's game? In C. Shields & M. Anderson (Eds.), *Dropped threads: What we aren't told.* Toronto, ON: Vintage.

Carter, R., & Qureshi, A. (1995). A typology of philosophical assumptions in multicultural counseling and training. In J. Ponterotto, J. Casas, L. Suzuki, & C. Alexander (Eds.), *Handbook of multicultural counseling* (pp. 239-262). London, UK: Sage.

Carter, R. T. (1990). Cultural value differences between African American and White Americans. *Journal of College Student Development, 31,* 71-79.

Carter, R. T., & Akinsulure-Smith, A. M. (1996). White racial identity and expectations about counseling. *Journal of Multicultural Counseling and Development, 24,* 218-228.

Casas, J., & Mann, D. (1996). MCT theory and implications for research. In D. W. Sue, A. Ivey, & P. Pedersen (Eds.), *A theory of multicultural counseling and therapy* (pp. 139-154). Pacific Grove, CA: Brooks/Cole.

Casas, J. M., & Pytluk, S. D. (1995). Hispanic identity development. In J. G. Ponterotto, J. M. Casas, L. A. Suzuki, & C. M. Alexander (Eds.), *Handbook of multicultural counseling* (pp. 155-180). Thousand Oaks, CA: Sage.

Casas, J. M., & Vasquez, M. J. T. (1996). Counseling the Hispanic: A guiding framework for a diverse population. In P. B. Pedersen, J. G. Draguns, W. J. Lonner, & J. E. Trimble (Eds.), *Counseling across cultures* (4th ed., pp. 146-176). Thousand Oaks, CA: Sage.

Cass, V. (1996). Sexual orientation identity formation: A Western phenomenon. In R. P. Cabaj & T. S. Stein (Eds.), *Textbook of homosexuality and mental health* (pp. 227-252). Washington, DC: American Psychiatric Press.

Cass, V. C. (1979). Homosexual identity formation: A theoretical model. *Journal of Homosexuality, 4,* 219-235.

Cass, V. C. (1983-84). Homosexual identity: A concept in need of definition. *Journal of Homosexuality, 9,* 105-126.

Cassin, S., von Ranson, K., Heng, K., Brar, J., & Wojtowicz, A. (2008). Adapted motivational interviewing for women with binge eating disorder: A randomized controlled trial. *Psychology of Addictive Behaviour* 22(3), 417-425.

Castonguay, L. G., Constantino, M. J., & Holtforth, M. G. (2006). The working alliance: Where are we and where should we go? [Electronic version]. *Psychotherapy: Theory, Research, Practice, Training, 43*(3), 271-279.

Cavender-Wilson, A. (1998). American Indian history or non-Indian perceptions of American Indian history? In D. A. Mihesuah (Ed.), *Natives and academics: Researching & writing about American Indians* (pp. 23-26). Lincoln, NB: University of Nebraska Press.

Centers for Disease Control and Prevention. (2009). *National Center for HIV, Viral Hepatitis, STD, and TB Prevention.* Retrieved April 29, 2009, from http://www.cdc.gov/nchhstp/

Centre for Canadian Studies. (n.d.). *About Canada: Multiculturalism in Canada.* Retrieved September 20, 2003, from http://www.mta.ca/faculty/arts/canadian_studies/english/about/multi/index.htm

Chae, M. H., Foley, P. F., & Chae, S. Y. (2006). Multicultural competence and training: An ethical responsibility. *Counseling and Clinical Psychology Journal, 3*(2), 71-80.

Chamberlin, J. (1998). People need help finding what makes them happy. *APA Monitor, 20*(1), 1. Retrieved May 31, 2002, from http://www.apa.org/monitor/oct98/happy.html

Chang, J., & Block, J. (1960). A study of identification in male homosexuals. *Journal of Consulting Psychology, 24,* 307-310.

Chao, G. T., & Moon, H. (2005). The cultural mosaic: A metatheory for understanding the complexity of culture. *Journal of Applied Psychology, 90,* 1128-1140.

Charter, G. A. (1994). *A medicine wheel approach to working with men who batter. A commissioned paper for the WUNSKA network.* Ottawa, ON: Canadian Association of Schools of Social Work.

Chase, S. (1998, April 10). Caucus accepts gay rights ruling. *Calgary Herald,* A1.

Chase, S. E. (2005). Narrative inquiry: Multiple lenses, approaches, voices. In N. K. Denzin & Y. S. Lincoln (Eds.), *Handbook of qualitative research* (3rd ed., pp. 651-680). Thousand Oaks, CA: Sage.

Cheatham, H., Ivey, A. E., Ivey, M. B., Pedersen, P., Rigazio-DiGilio, S., Simek-Morgan, L., et al. (1997). Multicultural counseling and therapy: The fourth force. In A. E. Ivey, M. B. Ivey, & L. Simek-Morgan (Eds.), *Counseling and psychotherapy: A multicultural perspective* (4th ed., pp. 133-205). Toronto, ON: Allyn and Bacon.

Cheatham, H., D'Andrea, M., Ivey, A. E., Ivey, M. B., Pedersen, P., Rigazio-DiGilio, S., et al. (2002a). Multicultural counseling and therapy I: Metatheory – Taking theory into practice. In A. E. Ivey, M. D'Andrea, M. B. Ivey, & L. Simek-Morgan (Eds.), *Theories of counseling and psychotherapy: A multicultural perspective* (5th ed., pp. 291-328). Toronto, ON: Allyn and Bacon.

Cheatham, H., D'Andrea, M., Ivey, A. E., Ivey, M. B., Pedersen, P., Rigazio-DiGilio, S., et al. (2002b). Multicultural counseling and therapy II: Integrative practice. In A. E. Ivey, M. D'Andrea, M. B. Ivey, & L. Simek-Morgan (Eds.), *Theories of counseling and psychotherapy: A multicultural perspective* (5th ed., pp. 329-362). Toronto, ON: Allyn and Bacon.

Cheboud, E., & France, H. (n.d.). Counseling African-Canadians: Issues and challenges. Retrieved February 17, 2003, from http://www.educ.uvic.ca/faculty/hfrance/african-canadian.htm

Chen, C. (2006). *Career endeavour: Pursuing a cross-cultural life transition.* Aldershot, UK: Ashgate.

Chen, C. (2008). Career guidance with immigrants. In J. Athanasou & R. Van Esbroeck (Eds.), *International handbook of career guidance* (pp. 419-442). New York: Springer.

Chen, C. P. (1999). Common stressors among international college students: Research and counseling implications. *Journal of College Counseling, 2,* 49-65.

Cherry, T. (2009, February 11). *California high court to hear case on gay marriage ban.* Retrieved February 11, 2009, from http://www.wiredprnews.com/2009/02/11/california-high-court-to-hear-case-on-gay-marriage-ban_200902112336.html

Chevrier, M. (1998). *Niijaanhzinaanig-Waaniniigaanhzijig Anishinabek youth gathering 1998: Final report.* North Bay, ON: Anishinabek Educational Institute.

Chirkov, V. I., Safdar, S., de Guzman, J., & Playford, K. (2008). Further examining the role motivation to study abroad plays in the adaptation of international students in Canada. *International Journal of Intercultural Relations, 32,* 427-440.

Chittooran, M. M., & Sankar-Gomes, A. (2007). The families of international students in U.S. universities: Adjustment issues and implications for counselors. In M. Pope & H. Singaravelu (Eds.), *A handbook for counselling international students in the United States* (pp. 113-136). Alexandria, VA: American Counseling Association.

Chizhik, E., & Chizhik, A. (2002). Decoding the language of social justice. *Journal of College Student Development, 43*(6), 792-808.

Chodorow, N. (1978). *The reproduction of mothering.* Berkeley, CA: University of California Press.

Chojnacki, J. T., & Gelberg, S. (1995). The facilitation of a gay/lesbian/bisexual support-therapy group by heterosexual counselors. *Journal of Counseling & Development, 73,* 352-354.

Chope, R. C. (2008). Practice and research in career counseling and development – 2007. The Career Development Quarterly, 57(2), 98-173.

Chrisjohn, R. (1990). *Burnout and stress management. Helping Native helpers.* Proceedings of the conference of the Native Mental Health Association of Canada, Toronto, ON.

Chrisjohn, R., & Young, S. (1998). *The circle game: Shadows and substance in the Indian residential school experience in Canada.* Penticton, BC: Theytus Books.

Chung, R. C. (2000). Psychosocial adjustment of Cambodian refugee women: Implications for mental health counselling. *Journal of Mental Health Counseling, 23,* 115-126.

Chung, R. C., & Bemak, F. (2002). The relationship of culture and empathy in cross-cultural counseling. *Journal of Counseling & Development, 80,* 154-159.

Chung, R. C., Bemak, F., Ortiz, D. P., & Sandoval-Perez, P. A. (2008, Summer). Promoting the mental health of immigrants: A multicultural/social justice perspective. *Journal of Counseling & Development, 86,* 310-317.

Chung, Y. B. (2003). Ethical and professional issues in career assessment with lesbian, gay, and bisexual persons. *Journal of Career Assessment, 11*(1), 96-112.

Church, E., Pettifor, J., & Malone, J. (2006). Evolving Canadian guidelines for therapy and counselling with women. *Feminism & Psychology, 16*(3), 259-271.

Citizenship and Immigration Canada. (2003, November). *Strategic framework to foster immigration to Francophone minority communities.* Retrieved April 1, 2004, from http://www.cic.gc.ca/english/pub/framework-minorities.html

Citizenship and Immigration Canada. (2005). *Annual report to Parliament on immigration, 2005.* Retrieved January 24, 2009, from http://www.cic.gc.ca/english/resources/publications/annual-report2005

Citizenship and Immigration Canada. (2007). *Annual report to Parliament on immigration, 2007.* Retrieved April 25, 2009, from http://www.cic.gc.ca/ENGLISH/RESOURCES/PUBLICATIONS/annual-report2007/section5.asp

Citizenship and Immigration Canada. (2009a). *Annual report on the operation of the Canadian Multiculturalism Act 2007-2008.* Retrieved April 28, 2009, from http://www.cic.gc.ca/ENGLISH/RESOURCES/PUBLICATIONS/multi-report2008/part1.asp

Citizenship and Immigration Canada. (2009b). *News release: Canada welcomes a record high number of newcomers in 2008.* Retrieved April 25, 2009, from http://www.cic.gc.ca/english/department/media/releases/2009/2009-02-20.asp

Citizenship and Immigration Canada. (2009c). *A survey of recent research on religious diversity and implications for multiculturalism policy.* Retrieved April 26, 2009, from http://www.policyresearch.gc.ca/page.asp?pagenm=2009-0008_15

Clunis, D. M., & Green, G. D. (1988). *Lesbian couples.* Seattle, WA: Seal Press.

Coburn, D. (2004). Beyond the income inequality hypothesis: Globalization, neo-liberalism, and health inequalities. *Social Science & Medicine, 58,* 41-56.

Cochran, S. D. (2001). Emerging issues in research on lesbians' and gay men's health: Does sexual orientation really matter? *American Psychologist, 56,* 931-947.

Cody, P. J., & Welch, P. L. (1997). Rural gay men in northern New England: Life experiences and coping styles. *Journal of Homosexuality, 33*(1), 51-67.

Coleman, E. (1981-82). Developmental stages of the coming out process. *Journal of Homosexuality, 7*(2-3), 31-43.

Coleman, E. (1987). Assessment of sexual orientation. *Journal of Homosexuality, 14*(1-2), 9-24.

Coleman, H. K., & Wampold, B. E. (2003). Challenges to the development of culturally relevant, empirically supported treatment. In D. B. Pope-Davis, H. L. K. Coleman, W. M. Lui, & R. L. Toporek (Eds.), *Handbook of multicultural competencies in counseling and psychology* (pp. 227-246). Thousand Oaks, CA: Sage.

Coleman, H. L. K. (2004). Multicultural counselling competencies in a pluralistic society. *Journal of Mental Health Counseling, 26*(1), 56-66.

College of Alberta Psychologists. (2003). *Bylaws.* Edmonton, AB: Author.

Collin, A., & Young, R. (Eds.). (2000). *The future of career.* Cambridge, UK: Cambridge University Press.

Collings, S. C. D., & Romans, S. E. (1998). Women and psychotherapy. In S. E. Romans (Ed.), *Folding back the shadows: A perspective on women's mental health* (pp. 231-250). Ortego, NZ: University of Ortego Press.

Collins, P. (1991). Learning from the outsider-within: The sociological significance of Black feminist thought. In M. Fonow & J. Cook (Eds.), *Beyond mythology: Feminist scholarship as lived research* (pp. 35-59). Bloomington, IN: Indiana University Press.

Collins, S. (1998). *A multi-site exploration of adolescent health-related needs: Student and adult perceptions.* Unpublished doctoral dissertation. University of Calgary, Alberta, Canada.

Collins, S. (in press). Women on the margins: Honouring multiple and intersecting cultural identities. In L. Ross (Ed.), *Counselling women: Feminist issues, theory, and practice.* Canadian Scholars' Press / Women's Press.

Collins, S., & Arthur, N. (2005). Enhancing the therapeutic alliance in culture-infused counseling. In N. Arthur & S. Collins (Eds.), *Culture-infused counseling: Celebrating the Canadian mosaic* (pp. 103-150). Calgary, AB: Counselling Concepts.

Collins, S., & Arthur, N. (in press a). Culture-infused counseling: A fresh look at a classic framework of multicultural counseling competencies. *Counselling Psychology Quarterly.*

Collins, S., & Arthur, N. (in press b). Culture-infused counseling: A model for developing multicultural competence. *Counselling Psychology Quarterly.*

Collins, S., Arthur, N., & McMahon, M. (2006). *Social justice and career development survey.* Unpublished document.

Collins, S., Arthur, N., & Wong-Wylie, G. (in press). Enhancing reflective practice in multicultural counseling through cultural auditing. *Journal of Counseling & Development.*

Comas-Diaz, L., & Greene, B. (1994). Women of colour with professional status. In L. Comas-Diaz & B. Greene (Eds.), *Women of colour: Integrating ethnic and gender identities in psychotherapy* (pp. 347-388). New York: Guilford Press.

Comstock, D., Hammer, T., Strentzsch, J., Cannon, K., Parsons, J., & Salazar II, G. (2008). Relational-cultural theory: A framework for bridging relational, multicultural, and social justice competencies. *Journal of Counselling Psychology 86,* 279-287.

Conger, J. J. (1975). Proceedings of the American Psychological Association for the year 1974: Minutes of the annual meeting of the Council of Representatives. *American Psychologist, 30,* 620-651.

Conklin, W. (2000). Employee resource groups: A foundation for support and change. *Diversity Factor, 9*(1), 12-25.

Connell, R. W. (1992). A very straight gay: Masculinity, homosexual experience, and the dynamics of gender. *American Sociological Review, 57,* 735-751.

Connolly, C. M. (2004). Clinical issues with same-sex couples: A review of the literature. In J. J. Bigner & J. L. Wetchler (Eds.), *Relationship therapy with same-sex couples* (pp. 3-12). New York: Haworth Press.

Constantine, M. (2002a). Predictors of satisfaction with counseling: Racial and ethnic minority clients' attitudes towards counseling and ratings of their counselors' general and multicultural counseling competence. *Journal of Counseling Psychology, 49*(2), 255-264.

Constantine, M. (2002b). The intersection of race, ethnicity, gender, and social class in counseling: Examining selves in cultural contexts. *Journal of Multicultural Counseling & Development, 30*(4), 210-216.

Constantine, M. G. (2001a). Independent and interdependent self-construals as predictors of multicultural case conceptualisation ability in counsellor trainees. *Counseling Psychology Quarterly, 14*(1), 33-42.

Constantine, M. G. (2001b). Multicultural training, theoretical orientation, empathy, and multicultural case conceptualization ability in counsellors. *Journal of Mental Health Counselling, 23*(4), 357-372.

Constantine, M. G., Anderson, G. M., Berkel, L. A., Caldwell, L. D., & Utsey, S. O. (2005). Examining the cultural adjustment experiences of African international college students: A qualitative analysis. *Journal of Counseling Psychology, 52,* 57–66.

Constantine, M. G., & Gushue, G. V. (2003). School counsellors' ethnic tolerance attitudes and racism attitudes as predictors of their multicultural case conceptualisation of an immigrant student. *Journal of Counseling and Development, 81*(2), 185-193.

Constantine, M. G., Hage, M., Kindaichi, M. M., & Bryant, R. M. (2007). Social justice and multicultural issues: Implications for the practice and training of counselors and counseling psychologists. *Journal of Counseling and Development, 85,* 24-29.

Constantine, M. G., & Ladany, N. (2001). New visions for defining and assessing multicultural counselling competence. In J. G. Ponterotto, J. M. Casas, L. A. Suzuki, & C. M. Alexander (Eds.), *Handbook of multicultural counseling* (2nd ed., pp. 482-498). Thousand Oaks, CA: Sage.

Coogan, P. A., & Chen, P. C. (2007). Career development and counselling for women: Connecting theories to practice. *Counselling Psychology Quarterly, 20*(2), 191-204.

Cooley, J. J. (1998). Gay and lesbian adolescents: Presenting problems and the counselor's role. *Professional School Counseling, 1*(3), 30-34.

Cooper, L. (2008). On the other side: Supporting sexual minority students. *British Journal of Guidance & Counselling, 36*(4), 425-440.

Cooperrider, D. L., & Srivastva, S. (1987). Appreciative inquiry in organizational life. *Research in organizational change and development, 1,* 129-169.

Corey, G. (1991). *Theory and practice of counselling and psychotherapy* (4th ed.). Pacific Grove, CA: Brooks/Cole.

Corey, G. (1996). Theoretical implications of MCT theory. In D. W. Sue, A. E. Ivey, & P. B. Pedersen (Eds.), *A theory of multicultural counselling and therapy* (pp. 99-111). Pacific Grove, CA: Brooks/Cole.

Corey, G. (2009). *The art of integrative counseling* (2nd ed.). Pacific Grove, CA: Brooks/Cole.

Corey, G., Corey, M. S., & Callanan, P. (2003). *Issues and ethics in the helping professions* (6th ed.). Pacific Grove, CA: Brooks/Cole.

Cormier, S., & Nurius, P. S. (2003). *Interviewing and change strategies for helpers.* Pacific Grove, CA: Brooks/Cole.

Cornish, J. A. E., Gorgens, K. A., Monson, S. P., Olkin, R., Palombi, B. J., & Abels, A. V. (2008). Perspectives on ethical practice with people who have disabilities. *Professional Psychology: Research and Practice, 39*(5), 488-497.

Cornett, C. (1995). *Reclaiming the authentic self: Dynamic psychotherapy with gay men.* Northvale, NJ: Jason Aronson.

Corsini, R. J., & Wedding, D. (2000). *Current psychotherapies.* Itasca, IL: Peacock.

Cottone, R. R. (1991). Counselor roles according to two counseling worldviews. *Journal of Counseling and Development, 69,* 398-401.

Counsellors for Social Justice. (2008). *Social Justice chapter.* Retrieved May 30, 2009, from http://www.ccacc.ca/e_SJ.html

Couture, L. (1994). *L'homme qui comprend les dessins d'enfants* [The man who understands children's drawings]. Montreal, QC: Vaugeois Éditeur.

Cox, S., & Gallois, C. (1996). Gay and lesbian identity development: A social identity perspective. *Journal of Homosexuality, 30*(4), 1-30.

Crabbe, J. C. (2002). Genetic contributions to addiction. *Annual Review of Psychology, 53*, 435-462.

Cramer, R. J., Golom, F. D., LoPresto, C. T., & Kirkley, S. M. (2008). Weighing the evidence: Empirical assessment and ethical implications of conversion therapy. *Ethics & Behavior, 18*(1) , 93-114.

Crawford, I., Allison, K. W., Zamboni, B. D., & Soto, T. (2002). The influence of dual-identity development on the psychosocial functioning of African-American gay and bisexual men. *Journal of Sex Research, 39*(3), 179-189.

Crethar, H. C., Rivera, E. T., & Nash, S. (2008, Summer). In search of common threads: Linking multicultural, feminist, and social justice paradigms. *Journal of Counseling & Development, 86*, 269-278.

Crethar, H. C., Torres Rivera, E., & Nash, S. (2008). In search of common threads: Concepts that unite multicultural, feminist, and social justice counseling paradigms. *Journal of Counseling & Development, 86*, 269-278.

Crisp, C. (2006). The gay affirmative practice scale (GAP): A new measure for assessing cultural competence with gay and lesbian clients. *Social Work, 51*(2), 115-126.

Cross, W. E. (1995). The psychology of nigrescence: Revising the Cross model. In J. G. Ponterotto, J. M. Casas, L. A. Suzuki, & C. M. Alexander (Eds.), *Handbook of multicultural counseling* (pp. 93-122). Thousand Oaks, CA: Sage.

Cross, W. E., Jr. (1971). The Negro to Black conversion experience: Toward a psychology of Black liberation. *Black World, 20*, 13-27.

Croteau, J. M., Anderson, M. Z., Distefano, T. M., & Kampa-Kokesch, S. (2000). Lesbian, gay, and bisexual vocational psychology: Reviewing foundations and planning construction. In R. M. Perez, K. A. DeBord, & K. J. Bieschke (Eds.), *Handbook of counseling and psychotherapy with lesbian, gay, and bisexual clients* (pp. 383-408). Washington, DC: American Psychological Association.

Croteau, J. M., & Thiel, M. J. (1993). Integrating sexual orientation in career counseling: Acting to end a form of the personal-career dichotomy. *The Career Development Quarterly, 42*, 174-179.

Cuéllar, I., Arnold, B., & Maldonado, R. (1995). An acculturation scale for Mexican American normal and clinical populations. *Hispanic Journal of Behavioral Sciences, 2*(3), 199-217.

Cuellar, I., Roberts, R. E., Nyberg, B., & Moldanado, R. E. (1998). Ethnic identity and acculturation in a young adult Mexican origin population. *Journal of Contemporary Psychology, 25*, 535-549.

Cull, J. G., & Gill, W. S. (1999). *Manual for the Suicide Probability Scale.* Los Angeles: Western Psychological Services.

Cummings, A. L. (2000). Teaching feminist counselor responses to novice female counselors. *Counselor Education and Supervision, 40*, 47-54.

Cummins, L., & Lehman, J. (2007). Eating disorders and body image concerns in Asian American women: Assessment and treatment from a multicultural and feminist perspective. *Eating Disorders 15*, 217-230.

Cunningham, C. G. (1991). *The integration of international students on Canadian post-secondary campuses.* Ottawa, ON: Canadian Bureau for International Education.

Dana, R. H. (1993). *Multicultural assessment perspectives for professional psychology.* Toronto, ON: Allyn and Bacon.

Dana, R. H. (1998). *Understanding cultural identity in intervention and assessment.* Thousand Oaks, CA: Sage.

Dana, R. H. (2000). Psychological assessment in the diagnosis and treatment of ethnic group members. In J. E. Aponte & J. Wohl (Eds.), *Psychological intervention and cultural diversity* (pp. 59-74). Toronto, ON: Allyn and Bacon.

D'Andrea, M., & Daniels, J. (2001a). Expanding our thinking about White racism: Facing the challenge of multicultural counseling in the 21st century. In J. G. Ponterotto, J. M. Casas, L. A. Suzuki, & C. M. Alexander (Eds.), *Handbook of multicultural counseling* (2nd ed., pp. 289-310). Thousand Oaks, CA: Sage.

D'Andrea, M., & Daniels, J. (2001b). Respectful counseling: An integrative multidimensional model for counselors. In D. Pope-Davis & H. Coleman (Eds.), *The intersection of race, class, and gender in multicultural counseling* (pp. 417-466). Thousand Oaks, CA: Sage.

D'Andrea, M., Daniels, J., & Noonan, M. J. (2003). New developments in the assessment of multicultural competencies. In D. B. Pope-Davis, H. L. K. Coleman, W. M. Lui, & R. L. Toporek (Eds.), *Handbook of multicultural competencies in counseling and psychology* (pp. 154-167). Thousand Oaks, CA: Sage.

D'Andrea, M., & Heckman, E. F. (2008, Summer). A 40-year review of multicultural counselling outcome research: Outlining a future research agenda for the multicultural counseling movement. *Journal of Counseling & Development, 86*, 356-363.

Daniels, J., & D'Andrea, M. (1996). MCT theory and ethnocentrism in counseling. In D. W. Sue, A. Ivey, & P. Pedersen (Eds.), *A theory of multicultural counseling and therapy* (pp. 155-174). Pacific Grove, CA: Brooks/Cole.

Dank, B. M. (1971). Coming out in the gay world. *Psychiatry, 34*, 180-197.

Darou, W. G. (1987). Counselling and the northern Native. *Canadian Journal of Counselling, 21*(1), 33-41.

Darou, W. G. (1992). Native Canadians and intelligence testing. *Canadian Journal of Counselling, 26*, 96-99.

Darou, W. G. (2000, January 1). Vocational counselling and First Nations. *Pimohtewin*. Retrieved May 31, 2002, from http://www.ualberta.ca/~pimohte/W_Darou_manuscript.htm

Darou, W. G., Kurtness, J., & Hum, A. (2000). The impact of conducting research with a first nation. *Canadian Journal of Counselling, 34*(1), 43-54.

Darvishpour, M. (2002). Immigrant women challenge the role of men: How the changing power relationship within Iranian families in Sweden intensifies family conflicts after immigration. *Journal of Comparative Family Studies, 33,* 270-296.

Das, A. K., & Kemp, S. F. (1997). Between two worlds: Counselling South Asian Americans. *Journal of Multicultural Counselling and Development, 25,* 23-33.

Das Gupta, M. (1997). What is East Indian about you? A gendered, transnational approach to ethnicity. *Gender & Society, 11*(5), 572-596.

Das Gupta, S. (1998). Gender roles and cultural continuity in the Asian East Indian immigrant community in the US. *Sex Roles, 38*(11/12), 953-974.

D'Augelli, A. R. (2006). Developmental and contextual factors and mental health among lesbian, gay, and bisexual youths. In A. M. Omoto & H. S. Kurtzman (Eds.), *Sexual orientation and mental health: Examining identity and development in lesbian, gay and bisexual people* (pp. 37-53). Washington, DC: American Psychological Association.

Dauvergne, M., Scrim, K., & Brennan, S. (2008). *Hate crimes in Canada 2006.* Ottawa, ON: Canadian Centre for Justice Statistics. Retrieved April 28, 2009, from http://www.statcan.gc.ca/pub/85f0033m/85f0033m2008017-eng.pdf

Davidson, G. R., Murray, K. E., & Schweitzer, R. (2008). Review of refugee mental health and wellbeing: Australian perspectives. *Australian Psychologist, 43,* 160-174.

Davidson, M. M., & Huenefeld, N. (2002). Struggling with two identities: The case of Eileen. *The Career Development Quarterly, 50,* 306-310.

Davison, G. C. (2005). Issues and nonissues in the gay-affirmative treatment of patients who are gay, lesbian, or bisexual. *Clinical Psychology: Science and Practice, 12*(1), 25-28.

Day, S. X. (2004). *Theory and design in counseling and psychotherapy.* Boston: Houghton Mifflin.

Daya, R. (2000). Buddhist psychology, a theory of change processes: Implications for counsellors. *International Journal for the Advancement of Counselling, 22*(4), 257-271.

Daya, R. (2001). Changing the face of multicultural counselling with principles of change. *Canadian Journal of Counselling, 35,* 49-62.

de Monteflores, C., & Schultz, S. J. (1978). Coming out: Similarities and differences for lesbians and gay men. *Journal of Social Issues, 34,* 59-72.

Deaux, K., & Kite, M. (1993). Gender stereotypes. In F. L. Denmark & M. A. Paludi (Eds.), *Psychology of women: A handbook of issues and theories* (pp. 107-139). Westport, CT: Greenwood Press.

DeBarona, M., & Dutton, M. A. (1997). Feminist perspectives on assessment. In J. Worell & N. G. Johnson (Eds.), *Shaping the future of feminist psychology: Education, research and practice* (pp. 37-56). Washington, DC: American Psychological Association.

Degges-White, S., Rice, B., & Myers, J. E. (2000). Revisiting Cass' theory of sexual identity formation: A study of lesbian development. *Journal of Mental Health Counseling, 22*(4), 318-333.

Degges-White, S., & Shoffner, M. F. (2002). Career counseling with lesbian clients: Using the theory of work adjustment as a framework. *The Career Development Quarterly, 51,* 87-96.

Dei, G. J. (1992). *The social reality of international post-secondary students in Canada.* Ottawa, ON: Canadian Bureau for International Education.

Deloria, V., Jr. (1998). Comfortable fictions and the struggle for turf: An essay review of the Invented Indian: Cultural fictions and government policies. In D. A. Mihesuah (Ed.), *Natives and academics: Researching & writing about American Indians* (pp. 65-83). Lincoln, NB: University of Nebraska Press.

Demaris, D. (2001). Revisiting feminist research methodologies: A working paper. Retrieved February 17, 2004, from http://www.swc-cfc.gc.ca/pubs/revisiting/index_e.html

DeNavis-Walt, C., Procter, B. D., & Mills, R. J. (2005). *Income, poverty, and health insurance coverage in the United States: 2004.* Retrieved June 30, 2008, from http://www.census. gov/prod/2005pubs/p60-229.pdf

Dennis, C., & Chung-Lee, L. (2006). Postpartum depression help-seeking barriers and maternal treatment preferences: A qualitative systematic review. *Birth: Issues in Perinatal Care, 33*(4), 323-331.

Denzin, N. K., & Lincoln, Y. S. (2005). Paradigms and perspectives in contention. In N. K. Denzin & Y. S. Lincoln (Eds.), *Handbook of qualitative research* (3rd ed., pp. 183-190). Thousand Oaks, CA: Sage.

Department of Canadian Heritage. (1988). *Canadian Multiculturalism Act.* Retrieved October 8, 2002, from http://www.pch.gc.ca/multi/policy/act_e.shtml

Department of Canadian Heritage. (1998). *Evidence series: Facts about multiculturalism: Vol. 1. Ethnic identity reinforces attachment to Canada.* Retrieved September 30, 2003, from http://www.pch.gc.ca/progs/multi/evidence/series1_e.cfm

Department of Canadian Heritage. (1998). *Evidence series: Facts about multiculturalism: Vol. 3. Multiculturalism promotes integration and citizenship.* Retrieved September 30, 2003, from http://www.pch.gc.ca/progs/multi/evidence/series3_e.cfm

Department of Canadian Heritage. (2002). *Canadian diversity: Respecting our differences.* Retrieved October 7, 2003, from http://www.pch.gc.ca/progs/multi/respect_e.cfm

Department of Canadian Heritage. (2003). *Annual report on the operation of the Canadian Multiculturalism Act 2001-2002.* Retrieved September 30, 2003, from http://www.pch.gc.ca/progs/multi/reports/ann01-2002/contents_e.cfm

Department of Justice Canada. (1976-77). *The Canadian Human Rights Act.* Retrieved October 30, 2003, from http://laws.justice.gc.ca/en/h-6/30599.html

Department of Justice Canada. (1982). *The Constitution Act.* Retrieved October 30, 2003, from http://laws.justice.gc.ca /en/const/annex_e.html#guarantee

Derwing, T. M., & Rossiter, M. (2002). Teaching native speakers to listen to foreign-accented speech. *Journal of Multilingual and Multicultural Development, 23,* 245-259.

Deters, P., & Lin, S-P. (2008). When cultures clash: Response 2: In N. Arthur & P. Pedersen (Eds.), *Case incidents in counseling for international transitions* (pp. 43-49). Alexandria (VA): American Counseling Association.

Deutsch, B. (2001). The male privilege checklist: An unabashed imitation of an article by Peggy McIntosh. *Expository Magazine, 2*(2). Retrieved October 29, 2003, from http://www.expositorymagazine.net/maleprivilege_checklist.htm

Dhruvarajan, V. (1993). Ethnic cultural retention and transmission among first generation Hindu Asian East Indians in a Canadian prairie city. *Journal of Comparative Family Studies, 24*(1), 63-79.

Diamond, L. M., & Butterworth, M. (2008). Questioning gender and sexual identity: Dynamic links over time. Sex Roles, 59, 365-376.

Dickason, O. P. (1992). *Canada's First Nations: A history of founding peoples from earliest times.* Toronto, ON: McClelland and Stewart.

Dickson, G., & Green, K. L. (2001). Participatory action research: Lessons learned with Aboriginal grandmothers. *Health Care for Women International, 22,* 471-482.

Diller, J. V. (1999). *Cultural diversity: A primer for the human services.* Toronto, ON: Brooks/Cole-Wadsworth.

Diller, J. V. (2004). *Cultural diversity: A primer for the human services* (2nd ed.). Toronto, ON: Nelson.

Dion, K. K., & Dion, K. L. (2001). Gender and cultural adaptation in immigrant families. *Journal of Social Issues, 57,* 511-522.

Dion, K. K., Dion, K. L., & Pak, A. W. (1990). The role of self-reported language proficiencies in the cultural and psychosocial adaptation among members of Toronto, Canada's Chinese community. *Journal of Asian Pacific Communication, 1*(1), 173-189.

Dion, K. L. (2001). Immigrants' perceptions of housing discrimination in Toronto: The housing new Canadians project. *Journal of Social Issues, 57,* 523-540.

Dion, K. L., & Kawakami, K. (1996). Ethnicity and perceived discrimination in Toronto. *Canadian Journal of Behavioral Science, 28,* 203-213.

Djuraskovic, I., & Arthur, N. (2009a). *Heuristic inquiry: A personal journey of acculturation and identity reconstruction.* Manuscript submitted for publication.

Djuraskovic, I., & Arthur, N. (2009b). The acculturation of former Yugoslavian refugees. *Canadian Journal of Counselling, 43,* 18-34.

Dolin, B. R., & Young, M. (2004). *Recognition of the foreign experience and credentials of immigrants*: PRB 04-29E. Retrieved February 3, 2009, from http://dsp-psd.pwgsc.gc.ca/Collection-R/LoPBdP/PRB-e/PRB0429-e.pdf

Dong, T. B. (1999). Foreword. *Journal of Homosexuality, 36*(3-4), xxiii-xxvi.

Dorland, J. M., & Fischer, A. R. (2001). Gay, lesbian, and bisexual individuals' perceptions: An analogue study. *The Counseling Psychologist, 29*(4), 532-547.

Dossa, P. (2008). Creating alternative and demedicalized spaces: Testimonial narrative on disability, culture, and racialization. *Journal of International Women's Studies, 9*(3), 79-98.

Douglas, M. A., & Walker, L. E. A. (1988). Introduction to feminist therapies. In M. A. Dutton-Douglas & L. E. A. Walker (Eds.), *Feminist psychotherapies: Integration of therapeutic and feminist systems* (pp. 3-11). Norwood, NJ: Ablex.

Draguns, J. G. (1996). Humanly universal and culturally distinctive: Charting the course of cultural counselling. In P. B. Pedersen, J. G. Draguns, W. J. Lonner, & J. E. Trimble (Eds.), *Counseling across cultures* (pp. 1-20). Thousand Oaks, CA: Sage.

Drescher, J. (1998). I'm your handyman: A history of reparative therapies. *Journal of Homosexuality, 36*(1), 19-42.

D'Rozario, V., & Romano, J. L. (2000). Perceptions of counselor effectiveness: A study of two country groups. *Counseling Psychology Quarterly, 13,* 51-63.

Drummond, R. J. (2000). *Appraisal procedures for counselors and helping professionals* (4th ed.). Toronto, ON: Prentice-Hall.

Drummond, R. J., & Jones, K. D. (2006). *Assessment procedures for counselors and helping professionals* (6th ed.). Toronto, ON: Pearson Education.

DuBay, W. H. (1987). *Gay identity: The self under ban.* Jefferson, NC: McFarland.

Dudley, N. Q. (1992). Participatory principles in human inquiry: Ethics and methods in a study of the paradigm shift experience. *Qualitative Studies in Education, 5*(4), 325-344.

Duffy Hutcheon, P. (1998, July). *Multiculturalism in Canada.* Paper presented at the World Congress of the International Sociological Association in Montreal. Retrieved September 30, 2003, from http://patduffyhutcheon.com/Papers%20and%20Presentations/Multiculturalism%20in%20Canada.htm#1

Dunbar, J. (1992). *A critical history of codes of ethics: Canadian Psychological Association, 1939-1986.* Unpublished doctoral dissertation, York University, Toronto, Ontario.

Dunkle, J. H., & Francis, P. L. (1996). "Physical attractiveness stereotype" and the attribution of homosexuality revisited. *Journal of Homosexuality, 30*(3), 13-29.

Dunnigan, T., McNall, M., & Mortimer, J. T. (1993). The problem of metaphorical non-equivalence in cross-cultural survey research: Comparing the mental health status of Hmong refugee and general population adolescents. *Journal of Cross-Cultural Psychology, 24,* 344-365.

Durand, M. (2008, December 30). Retour au bercail: Du Labrador à Dakar [Back to the fold: From Labrador to Dakar]. Le Devoir. Retrieved June 22, 2009+B483, from http://ledevoir.com

Dworkin, S. H. (2000). Individual therapy with lesbian, gay, and bisexual clients. In R. M. Perez, K. A. Debord, & K. J. Bieschke (Eds.), *Handbook of counseling and psychotherapy with lesbian, gay, and bisexual clients* (pp. 157-182). Washington, DC: American Psychological Association.

Dworkin, S. H., & Gutierrez, F. (1989). Introduction to special issue. Counselors be aware: Clients come in every size, shape, colour, and sexual orientation. *Journal of Counseling and Development, 68,* 6-8.

Dworkin, S. H., & Yi, H. (2003). LGBT identity, violence, and social justice: The psychological is political. *International Journal for the Advancement of Counselling, 25*(4), 269-279.

Eardley, E. (2002). "Queer's" near absence in academic and student service websites. *International Journal of Sexuality and Gender Studies, 7,* 39-50.

Eberlein, L. (1987). Introducing ethics to beginning psychologists: A problem-solving approach. *Professional Psychology: Research and Practice, 18,* 353-359.

Edwards, N. K. (2000). *Works in progress: Women's transitional journeys in the realm of sexuality.* Unpublished doctoral dissertation, University of Minnesota, Twin Cities, Minnesota.

Egale Canada. (2003). *Make your voice heard in the struggle against hatred!* Retrieved October 1, 2003, from http://www.egale.ca/index.asp?lang=E&menu=38&item=157

Ehrlinger, J., Gilovich, T., & Ross, L. Peering into the bias blind spot: People's assessment of bias in themselves and others. *Personality and Social Psychology Bulletin, 31,* 1-13.

Eidelson, R. J., & Eidelson, J. I. (2003). Dangerous ideas: Five beliefs that propel groups toward conflict. *American Psychologist, 58*(1), 182-192.

Eliason, M. J. (1996). Identity formation for lesbian, bisexual, and gay persons: Beyond a "minoritizing" view. *Journal of Homosexuality, 30,* 31-58.

Elliott, J. E. (1993). Career development with lesbian and gay clients. *The Career Development Quarterly, 41,* 210-226.

Ellis, A. L., & Mitchell, R. W. (2000). Sexual orientation. In L. T. Szuchman & F. Muscarella (Eds.), *Psychological perspectives on human sexuality* (pp. 196-231). New York: John Wiley & Sons.

Emery, H., & Brown, C.L. (2008). *The impact of disability on earnings and labour force participation in Canada: Evidence from the 2001 PALS.* Working Paper 2008-26. Calgary, AB: Department of Economics, University of Calgary.

Employment Equity Act. (1995). *Canada gazette part II, 130(23),* 2970-3034. Ottawa, ON: Queen's Printer for Canada.

Enns, C. Z. (1993). Twenty years of feminist counselling and therapy: From naming biases to implementing multifaceted practice. *The Counseling Psychologist, 21,* 3-87.

Enns, C. Z. (1997). *Feminist theories and feminist psychotherapies: Origins, themes, and variations.* New York: Harrington Park Press.

Enns, C. Z. (2008). Toward a complexity paradigm for understanding gender role conflict. *The Counseling Psychologist, 36*(3), 446-454.

Escobar, J. I., Nervi, C. H., & Gara, M. A. (2000). Immigration and mental health: Mexican Americans in the United States. *Harvard Review of Psychiatry, 8,* 64-72.

Essandoh, P. K. (1996). Multicultural counselling as the "fourth force": A call to arms. *Counseling Psychologist, 24*(1), 126-137.

Esses, V. M., Dovidio, J. F., Jackson, L. M., & Armstrong, T. L. (2001). The immigration dilemma: The role of perceived group competition, ethnic prejudice, and national identity. *Journal of Social Issues, 57,* 389-412.

Esses, V. M., & Gardner, R. C. (1996). Multiculturalism in Canada: Context and current status. *Canadian Journal of Behavioral Sciences, 28,* 145-52.

Este, D., & Bernard, W. T. (2003). Social work practice with African Canadians: An examination of the African-Nova Scotia community. In A. Al-Krenawi & J. R. Graham (Eds.), Multicultural social work in Canada: Working with diverse ethno-racial communities (pp. 306-337). Don Mills, ON: Oxford University Press.

Eubanks-Carter, C., Burckell, L. A., & Goldfried, M. R. (2005). Enhancing therapeutic effectiveness with lesbian, gay, and bisexual clients. *Clinical Psychology: Science and Practice, 12*(1), 1-18.

European Federation of Psychology Associations. (1995). *Metacode of ethics.* Brussels, Belgium: Author.

Evans, K. M., Kincade, E. A., Marbley, A. F., & Seem, S. R. (2005). Feminism and feminist therapy: Lessons from the past and hopes for the future. *Journal of Counseling & Development, 83,* 269-277.

Evans, M. E., Mejia-Maya, L. J., Zayas, L. H., Boothroyd, R. A., & Rodriguez, O. (2001). Conducting research in culturally diverse inner city neighborhoods: Some lessons learned. *Journal of Transcultural Nursing, 12*(1), 6-14.

Fadden, R., & Townsend, T. (2009). *Dealing with religious diversity: Opportunities and challenges.* Retrieved April 28, 2009, from http://www.policyresearch.gc.ca/page.asp?pagenm=2009-0008_03

Fairburn, C. G., & Brownell, K. D. (Eds.). (2002). *Eating disorders and obesity: A comprehensive handbook.* New York: Guilford Press.

Falco, K. L. (1996). Psychotherapy with women who love women. In R. P. Cabaj & T. S. Stein (Eds.), *Textbook of homosexuality and mental health* (pp. 397-412). Washington, DC: American Psychiatric Press.

Faris, J. C. (1994). *The Nightway: A history and a history of a Navajo ceremonial book.* Albuquerque, NM: University of New Mexico Press.

Fassinger, R. E. (1991). The hidden minority: Issues and challenges in working with lesbian women and gay men. *The Counseling Psychologist, 19*(2), 157-176.

Fassinger, R. E. (2003). Introduction to the special issue. *Journal of Multicultural Counseling and Development, 31*(2), 82-84.

Fassinger, R. E., & Richie, B. S. (1996). Sex matters: Gender and sexual orientation in training for multicultural counseling competency. In D. Pope-Davis & H. C. Coleman (Eds.), *Multicultural counseling competencies: Assessment, education and training, and supervision* (pp. 83-110). Thousand Oaks, CA: Sage.

Fassinger, R. E., & Schlossberg, N. K. (1992). Understanding the adult years: Perspectives and implications. In S. D. Brown & R. W. Lent (Eds.), *Handbook of counseling psychology* (2nd ed., pp. 217-249). New York: John Wiley & Sons.

Felipe Russo, N., & Green, B. L. (1993). Women and mental health. In F. L. Denmark & M. A. Paludi (Eds.), *Psychology of women: A handbook of issues and theories* (pp. 379-436). Westport, CT: Greenwood Press.

Feliz-Ortiz, M., Newcomb, M. D., & Myers, H. (1994). A multidimensional measure of cultural identity for Latino and Latina adolescence. *Hispanic Journal of Behavioral Science, 16,* 99-115.

Felman, S. (1987). *Jacques Lacan and the adventure of insight: Psychoanalysis in contemporary culture.* Cambridge, MS: Harvard University Press.

Feminist Therapy Institute, The. (1999). *Feminist therapy code of ethics.* San Francisco: Author.

Festinger, L. (1957). *A theory of cognitive dissonance.* Stanford, CA: Stanford University Press.

Filax, G. (2004). Queer youth and strange representations in the province of the "severely normal": Alberta in the 1990s. In J. McNinch & M. Cronin (Eds.), *I could not speak my heart: Education and social justice for gay and lesbian youth* (pp. 139-162). Regina, SK: Canadian Plains Research Center, University of Regina.

Fine, M. (2007). Expanding the methodological imagination. *The Counseling Psychologist, 35*(3), 459-473.

Finfgeld, D. (2004). Empowerment of individuals with enduring mental health problems: Results for concept analyses and qualitative investigations. *Advances in Nursing Science 27*(1), 44-52.

Finfgeld, D. L. (2001). New directions for feminist therapy based on social constructionism. *Archives of Psychiatric Nursing, 15*(3), 148-154.

Firestone, J. M., Harris, R. J., & Vega, W. A. (2003). The impact of gender role ideology, male expectancies, and acculturation on wife abuse. *International Journal of Law and Psychiatry, 26,* 549-564.

Fischer, A. R., Jerome, J. M., & Atkinson, D. R. (1998). Reconceptualizing multicultural counselling: Universal healing conditions in a culturally specific context. *The Counseling Psychologist, 26,* 525-588.

Fischer, A. R., & Moradi, B. (2001). Racial and ethnic identity: Recent developments and needed directions. In J. G. Ponterotto, J. M. Casas, L. A. Suzuki, & C. M. Alexander (Eds.), *Handbook of multicultural counseling* (2nd ed., pp. 341-370). Thousand Oaks, CA: Sage.

Fisher, C. (2000). Relational ethics in psychological research: One feminist's journey. In M. Brabeck (Ed.), *Practicing feminist ethics in psychology* (pp. 125-142). Washington, DC: American Psychological Association.

Fisher, C. B., & Ragsdale, K. (2006). Goodness-of-fit ethics for multicultural research. In J. E. Trimble & C. B. Fisher (Eds.), *The handbook of ethical research with ethnocultural populations & communities* (pp. 3-25). Thousand Oaks, CA: Sage.

Flathman, O. Y., Davidson, M., & Sanford, T. (2001, March). *International students at American counseling centers: A study of utilization patterns.* Poster presented at the Division 17 Counseling Psychology Conference, Houston, TX.

Fleras, A. (2004). "Researching together differently": Bridging the research paradigm gap. *Native Studies Review, 15*(2), 117-129.

Fleury, D., & Fortin, M. (2004). Canada's working poor. *Horizons, 7*(2), 51-57.

Flores, L. Y. (2009). Empowering life choices: Career counseling in the contexts of race and class. In N. Gysbers, M. Heppner, & J. Johnston (Eds.), *Career counseling: Contexts, processes and techniques* (3rd ed., pp. 49-74). Alexandria, VA: American Counseling Association.

Folkman, S. (2008). The case for positive emotion in the stress process. *Anxiety, Stress, and Coping, 21,* 3-14.

Folkman, S., Lazarus, R. S., & Dunkel-Schetter, C. (2000). The dynamics of a stressful encounter. In E. T. Higgins & A. W. Kruglanski (Eds.), *Motivational science: Social and personality perspectives* (pp. 111-127). Philadelphia: Psychology Press.

Folkman, S., & Moskowitz, J.T. (2004). Coping: Pitfalls and promise. *Annual Review of Psychology, 55,* 745-774.

Fondacaro, M. R., & Weinberg, D. (2002). Concepts of social justice in community psychology: Toward a social ecological epistemology. *American Journal of Community Psychology, 30*(4), 473-492.

Fontaine, J. H. (1998). Evidencing a need: School counselors' experiences with gay and lesbian students. *Professional School Counseling, 1*(3), 8-14.

Forcey, L., & Nash, M. (1998). Rethinking feminist theory and social work therapy. *Women and Therapy, 21*(4), 85-99.

Fortier, C., & Julien, D. (2003). Les psychotherapies de conversion pour les personnes gaies, lesbiennes et bisexuelles: Enjeux ethiques et deontologique. *Canadian Psychology, 44*(4), 332-350.

Foster, L. (2008). Foreign credentials in Canada's multicultural society. In M. A. Wallis & S. Kwok (Eds.), *Daily struggles: The deepening racialization and feminization of poverty in Canada* (pp. 129-142). Toronto, ON: Canadian Scholars' Press.

Foster, R. P. (2001). When immigration is trauma: Guidelines for the individual and family clinician. *American Journal of Orthopsychiatry, 71,* 153-170.

Fouad, N. A., & Bingham, R. P. (1995). Career counselling with racial and ethnic minorities. In W. B. Walsh & S. H. Osipow (Eds.), *Handbook of vocational psychology* (pp. 331-365). Mahwah, NJ: Lawrence Erlbaum.

Fouad, N. A., Gerstein, L. H., & Toporek, R. L. (2006). Social justice and counselling psychology in context. In R. L. Toporek, L. H. Gerstein, N. A. Fouad, G. Roysircar, & T. Israel (Eds.), *Handbook for social justice in counselling psychology: Leadership, vision, and action* (pp. 1-16). Thousand Oaks, CA: Sage.

Fowers, B. J., & Davidov, B. J. (2006). The virtue of multiculturalism: Personal transformation, character, and openness to the other. *American Psychologist, 61*(6), 581-594.

Fowers, B. J., & Richardson, F. C. (1996). Why is multiculturalism good? *American Psychologist, 51,* 609-621.

Fox, R. C. (1996). Bisexuality: An examination of theory and research. In R. P. Cabaj & T. S. Stein (Eds.), *Textbook of homosexuality and mental health* (pp. 147-171). Washington, DC: American Psychiatric Press.

Frable, D. E. S., Wortman, C., & Joseph, J. (1997). Predicting self-esteem, well-being, and distress in a cohort of gay men: The importance of cultural stigma, personal visibility, community networks, and positive identity. *Journal of Personality, 65*(3), 599-624.

France, M. H. (1997). First Nations: Helping and learning in the Aboriginal community. *Guidance & Counselling, 12*(2), 3-8.

Francis, A. (1993). *Facing the future: The internationalization of post-secondary institutions in British Columbia.* Vancouver, BC: British Columbia Centre for International Education.

Frank, L. (1997). *The protection of Aboriginal culture: A resource and information guide on cultural appropriation.* Westbank, BC: Association of Aboriginal Post-Secondary Institutes Education Resource Centre.

Frankowski, B. L. (2004). Sexual orientation and adolescents. *Pediatrics, 113,* 1827-1832.

Freedberg, S. (2007). Re-examining empathy: A relational-feminist point of view. *Social Work, 52*(3), 251-259.

Freud, S. (1912). *Totem and taboo: Psychic lives of savages and neurotics.* New York: Prometheus Books.

Freyd, J., & Quina, K. (2000). Feminist ethics in the practice of science: The contested memory controversy as an example. In M. Brabeck (Ed.), *Practicing feminist ethics in psychology* (pp. 101-123). Washington, DC: American Psychological Association.

Frost, D. M., & Meyer, I. H. (2009). Internalized homophobia and relationship quality among lesbians, gay men, and bisexuals. *Journal of Counseling Psychology, 56*(1), 97-109.

Fuertes, J. N., & Gretchen, D. (2001). Emerging theories of multicultural counselling. In J. Ponterotto, J. M. Casas, L. Suzuki, & C. M. Alexander (Eds.), *Handbook of multicultural counselling* (pp. 509-541). Thousand Oaks, CA: Sage.

Fuertes, J. N., Mueller, L. N., Chauhan, R. V., Walker, J. A., & Hadany, N. (2002). An investigation of Euro-American therapists' approach to counseling African-American clients. *The Counseling Psychologist, 30,* 763-789.

Fukuyama, M. A. (1990). Taking a universal approach to multicultural counselling. *Counselor Education and Supervision, 30,* 6-17.

Fukuyama, M. A., Murphy, M., & Siahpoush, F. (2003). Bridging the gaps: Weaving multicultural and humanistic perspectives into transpersonal education. *Humanistic Psychologist, 31,* 182-200.

Fukuyama, M. A., & Sevig, T. (1999). *Integrating spirituality into multicultural counseling.* Thousand Oaks, CA: Sage.

Fukuyama, M. A., Sevig, T., & Soet, J. (2008). Spirituality in counseling across cultures: Many rivers to the sea. In P. B. Pedersen, J. G. Draguns, W. J. Lonner, & J. E. Trimble (Eds.), *Counseling across cultures* (pp. 345-361). Thousand Oaks, CA: Sage.

Funderburk, J., & Fukuyama, M. (2001). Feminism, multiculturalism and spirituality: Convergent and divergent forces in psychotherapy. *Women & Therapy 24*(3/4), 1-18.

Furnham, A., & Bochner, S. (1986). *Culture shock: Psychological reactions to unfamiliar environments.* London, UK+B565: Methuen.

Gallo, L. C., & Matthews, K. A. (2003). Understanding the association between socioeconomic status and physical health: Do negative emotions play a role? *Psychological Bulletin, 129*(1), 10-51.

Galtung, J. (1969). Violence, peace, and peace research. *Journal of Peace Research, 6*(3), 167-191.

Gammell, D., & Stoppard, J. (1999). Women's experience of treatment of depression: Medicalization or empowerment? *Canadian Psychology, 40*(2), 112-128.

Gans, H. (1992). Second-generation decline: Scenarios for the economic and ethnic future of the post-1965 American immigrants. *Ethnic and Racial Studies, 15*(2), 173-192.

Garcia, J., Cartwright, B., Winston, S. M., & Borzuchowska, B. (2003). A transcultural integrative model for ethical decision making in counseling. *Journal of Counseling & Development, 81,* 268-278.

Garnets, L., Herek, G. M., & Levy, B. (1990). Violence and victimization of lesbians and gay men: Mental health consequences. *Journal of Interpersonal Violence, 5,* 366-383.

Garnets, L. D., & Kimmel, D. C. (1993). Introduction: Lesbian and gay male dimensions in the psychological study of human diversity. In L. D. Garnets & D. C. Kimmel (Eds.), *Psychological perspectives on lesbian and gay male experiences* (pp. 1-51). New York: Columbia University Press.

Garrett, M. T., & Barret, B. (2003). Two spirit: Counseling Native American gay, lesbian, and bisexual people. *Journal of Multicultural Counseling and Development, 31,* 131-142.

Gatens-Robinson, E., & Tarvydas, V. (1992). Ethics of care, women's perspectives, and the status of the mainstream rehabilitation ethical analysis. *Journal of Applied Rehabilitation Counseling, 23,* 26-33.

Gauthier, J. G., & Phillips, A. G. (Eds.). (1997). *Canada's multicultural society, report of the National Conference on Psychology as a Science.* Retrieved Sept. 19, 2003, from http://www.cpa.ca/science/contents.htm

Gaw, K. F. (2000). Reverse culture shock in students returning from overseas. *International Journal of Intercultural Relations, 24,* 83-104.

Geller, J., Brown, K., Zaitsoff, S., Goodrich, S., & Hastings, F. (2003). Collaborative versus directive interventions in the treatment of eating disorders: Implications for care providers. *Professional Psychology: Research and Practice, 34*(4), 406-413.

Geller, J., & Srikameswaran, S. (2006). Treatment non-negotiables: Why we need them and how to make them work. European Eating Disorders Review 14, 212-217.

Geller, J., Williams, K., & Srikameswaran, S. (2001). Clinician stance in the treatment of chronic eating disorders. *European Eating Disorders Review, 9,* 365-373.

Gelso, C. J., & Fretz, B. R. (1992). *Counseling psychology.* Fort Worth, TX: Holt, Rinehart, & Winston.

Genest, S. (2002). *Transition of sexuality for adult women.* Unpublished manuscript. Calgary, AB: University of Calgary.

Gergen, K. (2001). Relational process for ethical outcomes. *Journal of Systemic Therapies, 20,* 7-10.

Gerrity, E., Keane, T. M., & Tuma, F. (2001). *The mental health consequences of torture.* New York: Plenum.

Gerstein, L. H., Rountree, C., & Orgonez, A. (2007). An anthropological perspective on multicultural counselling. *Counselling Psychology Quarterly, 20*(4), 375-400.

Ghuman, P. A. S. (1997). Assimilation or integration? A study of Asian adolescents. *Educational Review, 39*(1), 23-35.

Gibbons, J. L., Stiles, D. A., & Shkodriani, G. M. (1991). Adolescents' attitudes toward family and gender roles: An international comparison. *Sex Roles, 25,* 625-643.

Gilbert, L. A., & Scher, M. (1999). *Gender and sex in counseling and psychotherapy.* Boston: Allyn and Bacon.

Gilliam, V. L. (2005). Caregiving: Taking care of them, taking care of you. *Delta Kappa Gamma Bulletin, 71,* 9-13.

Gilligan, C. (1982). *In a different voice: Psychological theory and women's development.* Cambridge, MA: Harvard University Press.

Gilligan, C., Lyons, N., & Hammer, T. (1989). *Making connections: The relational worlds of adolescent girls at the Emma Willard School.* Troy, NY: Emma Willard School.

Glen Murray (Politician). (2009). Retrieved February 13, 2009, from http://en.wikipedia.org/wiki/Glen_Murray_(politician)

Goldfried, M. R., & Davila, J. (2005). The role of relationship and technique in therapeutic change. *Psychotherapy: Theory, Research, Practice, Training, 42,* 421-430

Goldfried, M. R., & Goldfried, A. P. (2001). The importance of parental support in the lives of gay, lesbian, and bisexual individuals. *In Session: Psychotherapy in Practice, 57,* 681-693.

Gone, J. P. (2008). 'So I can be like a Whiteman': The cultural psychology of space and place in American Indian mental health. *Culture and Psychology, 14,* 369-399.

Gonsiorek, J. C. (1982). Results of psychological testing on homosexual populations. *American Behavioral Scientist, 25,* 385-396.

Gonsiorek, J. C. (1993). Mental health issues of gay and lesbian adolescents. In L. D. Garnets & D. C. Kimmel (Eds.), *Psychological perspectives on lesbian and gay male experiences* (pp. 469-485). New York: Columbia University Press.

Gonsiorek, J. C. (2004). Reflections from the conversion therapy battlefield. *Counseling Psychologist, 32*(5), 750-759.

Goodman, J. (2009). Starfish, salmon, and whales: An introduction to the special section. *Journal of Counseling & Development, 87,* 259.

Goodman, L. A., Liang, B., Helms, J. E., Latta, R. E., Sparks, E., & Weintraub, S. R. (2004). Training counseling psychologists as social justice agents: Feminist and multicultural theories in action. *The Counseling Psychologist, 32*(6), 793-837.

Gordon, R. A. (2000). *Eating disorders: Anatomy of a social epidemic* (2nd ed.). Malden, MA: Blackwell.

Gorman, W. (2001). Refugee survivors of torture: Trauma and treatment. *Professional Psychology: Research and Practice, 32,* 443-451.

Government of Canada. (2003, March). Inclusion and exclusion in Canada. *Metropolis,* 1-27.

Graham, S. (1992). "Most of the subjects were White and middleclass:" Trends in published research on African Americans in selected APA journals, 1970-1989. *American Psychologist, 47,* 629-639.

Grant, K. J., Henley, A., & Kean, M. (2001). The journey after the journey: Family counselling in the context of immigration and ethnic diversity. *Canadian Journal of Counselling, 35,* 89-100.

Green, B., & Sanchez-Hucles, J. (1997). In J. Worell & N. G. Johnson (Eds.), *Shaping the future of feminist psychology: Education, research and practice* (pp. 173-202). Washington, DC: American Psychological Association.

Green, B. C. (1998). Thinking about students who do not identity as gay, lesbian, or bisexual, but…. *Journal of American College Health, 47*(2), 89-91.

Green, H. (1997). May I walk in beauty: First Nations and self-esteem. *Guidance and Counselling, 12*(2), 22-26.

Green, R. J. (2000). "Lesbians, gay men, and their parents": A critique of LaSala and the prevailing clinical "wisdom." *Family Process, 39*(2), 257-266.

Greene, B. (1997). Lesbian women of colour: Triple jeopardy. In E. D. Rothblum (Ed.), *Classics in lesbian studies* (pp. 109-147). Binghamton, NY: Harrington Park Press.

Greene, B. (2005). Psychology, diversity, and social justice: Beyond heterosexism and across the cultural divide. *Counselling Psychology Quarterly, 18*(4), 295-306.

Greenwood, R., Zeedyk, S., Bowe, M., Stell, C.., Wakefield, J., & Webber, E. (2008). Toward a new psychology of women: Still relevant after all these years? *Feminism & Psychology, 18*(3), 358-367.

Grieger, I., & Ponterotto, J. G. (1995). A framework for assessment in multicultural counseling. In J. G. Ponterotto, J. M. Casas, L. A. Suzuki, & C. M. Alexander (Eds.), *Handbook of multicultural counselling* (pp. 357-374). Thousand Oaks, CA: Sage.

Griffin, P. (1992). From hiding out to coming out: Empowering lesbian and gay educators. In K. M. Harbeck (Ed.), *Coming out of the classroom closet* (pp. 167-196). Binghamton, NY: Harrington Park Press.

Grisso, T., Baldwin, E., Blanck, P., Rotheram-Borus, M., Schooler, N., & Thompson, T. (1991). APA's mechanism for monitoring the challenges. *American Psychologist, 46,* 758-766.

Grossman, A. H., D'Augelli, A. R., & O'Connell, T. S. (2001). Being lesbian, gay, bisexual, and 60 or older in North America. *Journal of Gay & Lesbian Social Services: Issues in Practice, Policy, & Research, 13*(4), 23-40.

Grov, C., Bimbi, D. S., Nanin, J. E., & Parsons, J. T. (2006). Race, ethnicity, gender, and generational factors associated with the coming-out process among gay, lesbian, and bisexual individuals. *The Journal of Sex Research, 43*(2), 115-121.

Guba, E. G., & Lincoln, Y. S. (1994). Competing paradigms in qualitative research. In N. K. Denzin & Y. S. Lincoln (Eds.), *Handbook of qualitative research* (pp. 105-117). Thousand Oaks, CA: Sage.

Gullahorn, J., & Gullahorn, J. (1963). An extension of the U-curve hypothesis. *Social Issues, 19,* 33-47.

Gunn-Allen, P. (1998). Problems in teaching Silko's ceremony. In D. A. Mihesuah (Ed.), *Natives and academics: Researching and writing about American Indians* (pp. 55-64). Lincoln, NB: University of Nebraska Press.

Gustafson, D. L. (2005). Transcultural nursing theory from a critical cultural perspective. *Advances in Nursing Sciences, 28*(1), 2-16.

Gustafson, D. L. (2007). White on whiteness: Becoming radicalized about race. *Nursing Inquiry, 14*(2), 153-161.

Gysbers, N. C., Heppner, M. J., & Johnston, J. A. (1998). *Career counseling: Process, issues, and techniques.* Needham Heights, MA: Allyn & Bacon.

Gysbers, N. C., Heppner, M. J., & Johnston, J. A. (2009). *Career counseling: Processes, issues, and techniques* (3rd ed.). Alexandria, VA: American Counseling Association.

Haaken, J. (2008). When White Buffalo Calf Woman meets Oedipus on the road: Lakota psychology, feminist psychoanalysis, and male violence. *Theory and Psychology, 18,* 195-208.

Hackett, G., & Betz, N. E. (1981). A self-efficacy approach to the career development of women. *Journal of Vocational Behavior, 18,* 326-339.

Hackney, H. L., & Cormier, L. S. (2005). *The professional counselor: A process guide to helping* (5th ed.). Toronto, ON: Pearson Education.

Haig-Brown, C., & Archibald, J. (1996). Transforming First Nations research with respect and power. *Qualitative Studies in Education, 9*(3), 245-267.

Haldeman, D. C. (1994). The practice and ethics of sexual orientation conversion therapy. *Journal of Consulting and Clinical Psychology, 62*(2), 221-227.

Halfe, L. (1993). Healing from a Native perspective. *Cognica, 26,* 7-10.

Hall, C. I. (1997). Cultural malpractice: The growing obsolescence of psychology with the changing U.S. population. *American Psychologist, 52,* 642-651.

Hallowell, A. I. (1955). *Culture and experience.* Philadelphia: University of Pennsylvania.

Halwani, R. (1998). Essentialism, social constructionism, and the history of homosexuality. *Journal of Homosexuality, 35*(1), 25-51.

Hammersmith, S. K., & Weinberg, M. S. (1973). Homosexual identity: Commitment, adjustments, and significant others. *Sociometry, 36*(1), 56-78.

Han, C. S. (2006). Geisha of a different kind: Gay Asian men and the gendering of sexual identity. *Sexuality & Culture: An Interdisciplinary Quarterly, 10*(3), 3-28.

Han, C. S. (2007). They don't want to cruise your type: Gay men of color and the racial politics of exclusion. *Social Identities: Journal for the Study of Race, Nation and Culture, 13*(1), 51-67.

Hanley-Hackenbruck, P. (1988). "Coming out" and psychotherapy. *Psychiatric Annals, 18,* 29-32.

Hansen, N. D., Petitone-Arreola-Rockwell, F., & Greene, A. F. (2000). Multicultural competence: Criteria and case examples. *Professional Psychology: Research and Practice, 31*(6), 652-660.

Hare-Mustin, R. T., & Maracek, J. (1992). The meaning of difference: Gender theory, postmodernism, and psychology. In J. S. Brohan (Ed.), *Seldom seen, rarely heard: Women's place in psychology* (pp. 227- 249). Boulder, CO: Westview Press.

Harkins, A., Hansen, S., & Gama, E. (2008). Updating gender issues in multicultural counseling. In P. Pedersen, J. Draguns, W. Lonner, & J. Trimble (Eds.), *Counseling across cultures* (6th ed., pp. 185-200). Thousand Oaks, CA: Sage.

Harper, F. D., & McFadden, J. (2003). *Culture and counseling: New approaches.* Boston: Pearson Education.

Harris, C. (2001). Beyond multiculturalism? Difference, recognition, and social justice. *Patterns of Prejudice, 35*(1), 13-34.

Harris, R. J., Firestone, J. M., & Vega, W. A. (2005). The interaction of country of origin, acculturation, and gender role ideology on wife abuse. *Social Science Quarterly, 86,* 463-483.

Harrison, R. L. (2008). Scaling the ivory tower: Engaging emergent identity as researcher. *Canadian Journal of Counselling, 42*(4), 237-248.

Harrison, J. K., Chadwick, M., & Scales, M. (1996). The relationship between cross-cultural adjustment and the personality variables of self-efficacy and self-monitoring. *International Journal of Intercultural Relations, 20,* 167-188.

Harry, B., Rueda, R., & Kalyanpur, M. (1999). Cultural reciprocity in sociocultural perspective: Adapting the normalization principle for family collaboration. *Exceptional Children, 66*(1), 123-136.

Hart, J. (1981). Self and professional help. In J. Hart & D. Richardson (Eds.), *The theory and practice of homosexuality* (pp. 128-138). Boston: Routledge & Kegan Paul.

Hartmann, L. (1996). Foreword. In R. P. Cabaj & T. S. Stein (Eds.), *Textbook of homosexuality and mental health* (pp. xxv-xxxi). Washington, DC: American Psychiatric Press.

Hatcher, R. L., & Barends, A. W. (2006). How a return to theory could help alliance research [Electronic version]. *Psychotherapy: Theory, Research, Practice, Training, 43*(3), 292-299.

Haverkamp, B. E. (2005). Ethical perspectives on qualitative research in applied psychology. *Journal of Counseling Psychology, 52*(2), 146-155.

Haverkamp, B. E., Morrow, S. L., & Ponterotto, J. G. (2005). A time and place for qualitative and mixed methods in counselling psychology research. *Journal of Counseling Psychology, 52*(2), 123-125.

Hawthorne, L. (2006). *Labour market outcomes for migrant professionals: Canada and Australia compared – executive summary.* Retrieved April 15, 2009, from http://www.cic.gc.ca/english/resources/research/2006-canada-australia.asp

Hayes, R. L., & Lin, H. (1994). Coming to America: Developing social support systems for international students. *Journal of Multicultural Counseling and Development, 22,* 7-16.

Hays, P. (1996). Addressing the complexities of culture and gender in counseling. *Journal of Counseling and Development, 74,* 332-338.

Hays, P. A. (2001). *Addressing cultural complexities in practice: A framework for clinicians and counselors.* Washington, DC: American Psychological Association.

Health Canada. (1999). *Canadian research on immigration and health: An overview.* Ottawa, ON: Author.

Health Canada. (2004, February). *Interdisciplinary education for collaborative, patient-centred practice: Research and findings report.* Ottawa, ON: Author.

Helminiak, D. A. (1994). *What the Bible really says about homosexuality.* San Francisco: Alamo Square Press.

Helms, J. E. (1984). Toward a theoretical explanation of the effects of race on counselling: A Black and White model. *The Counseling Psychologist, 12,* 153-165.

Helms, J. E. (1990a). Applying the interaction model to social dyads. In J. E. Helms (Ed.), *Black and White racial identity: Theory, research, and practice* (pp. 177-185). Westport, CT: Praeger.

Helms, J. E. (1990b). *Black and white racial identity: Theory, research and practice.* Westport, CT: Greenwood Press.

Helms, J. E. (1990c). Counseling attitudinal and behavioral predispositions: The Black/White interaction model. In J. E. Helms (Ed.), *Black and White racial identity: Theory, research, and practice* (pp. 135-163). Westport, CT: Praeger.

Helms, J. E. (1993). I also said, "White racial identity influences White researchers." *The Counseling Psychologist, 21*(2), 240-243.

Helms, J. E. (1994). How multiculturalism obscures racial factors in the therapy process: Comment on Ridley et al. (1994), Sodowsky et al. (1994), Ottavi et al. (1994), and Thompson et al. (1994). *Journal of Counseling Psychology, 41,* 162-165.

Helms, J. E. (1995). An update of Helm's White and People of Color racial identity models. In J. G. Ponterotto, J. M. Casas, L. A. Suzuki, & C. M. Alexander (Eds.), *Handbook of multicultural counseling* (pp. 181-198). London, UK: Sage.

Helms, J. E. (2003). A pragmatic view of social justice. *The Counseling Psychologist, 31*(3), 305-313.

Helms, J. E., & Cook, D. A. (1999). *Using race and culture in counselling and psychotherapy: Theory and process.* Needham Heights, MA: Allyn & Bacon.

Hencken, J., & O'Dowd, W. (1977). Coming out as an aspect of identity formation. *Gay Academic Union, 1,* 18-22.

Henning-Stout, M., & Meyers, J. (2000). Consultation and human diversity: First things first. *School Psychology Review, 29*(3), 419-426.

Henriksen, R. C., & Paladino, D. A. (2009a). History of racial classification. In R. C. Henriksen & D. A. Paladino (Eds.), *Counseling multiple heritage individuals, couples, and families* (pp. 1-16). Alexandria, VA: American Counselling Association.

Henriksen, R. C., & Paladino, D. A. (Eds.). (2009b). *Counseling multiple heritage individuals, couples, and families.* Alexandria, VA: American Counselling Association.

Henry, F., Tator, C., Mattis, W., & Rees, T. (2000). *The colour of democracy: Racism in Canadian society* (2nd ed.). Toronto, ON: Harcourt Brace Canada.

Heppner, M. J., & O'Brien, K. M. (1994). Multicultural counsellor training: Students' perceptions of helpful and hindering events. *Counsellor Education and Supervision, 34*(1), 4-18.

Herbert, S. E. (1996). Lesbian sexuality. In R. P. Cabaj & T. S. Stein (Eds.), *Textbook of homosexuality and mental health* (pp. 723-742). Washington, DC: American Psychiatric Press.

Herdt, G. (1997). *Same sex, different cultures.* Boulder, CO: Westview Press.

Herek, G. M. (1996). Heterosexism and homophobia. In R. P. Cabaj & T. S. Stein (Eds.), *Textbook of homosexuality and mental health* (pp. 101-114). Washington, DC: American Psychiatric Press.

Herring, R. D., & Furgerson, K. (2000). Counseling issues with sexual minority populations: An invisible minority school population. *Q The Online Journal, 1*(1). Retrieved April 30, 2002, from http://www.aglbic.org/Q/Vol1 Num1/Herring.htm

Herrman, B. (1990). *Being - Being happy - Being gay.* San Francisco: Alamo Square Press.

Hertzspring, E. A., & Dobson, K. (2000). Diversity training: Conceptual issues and practices for Canadian clinical psychology programs. *Canadian Psychology, 41,* 184-191.

Hetrick, E. S., & Martin, A. D. (1984). Ego-dystonic homosexuality: A developmental view. In E. S. Herrick & T. S. Stein (Eds.), *Innovations in psychotherapy with homosexuals* (pp. 1-21). Washington, DC: American Psychiatric Press.

Hetrick, E. S., & Martin, A. D. (1987). Developmental issues and their resolution for gay and lesbian adolescents. *Journal of Homosexuality, 14*(1-2), 25-43.

Hewitt, C. (1995). The socioeconomic position of gay men: A review of the evidence. *American Journal of Economics and Sociology, 54,* 461-479.

Heyes, C. (2002, Fall). Identity politics. In E. M. Zata (Ed.), *The Stanford encyclopedia of philosophy.* Retrieved January 13, 2004, from http://plato.stanford.edu/archives/fall20022/entries/identity-politics/

Hiebert, B. A. (2001). *Creating a working alliance: Generic interpersonal skills and concepts.* Unpublished manuscript.

Hiebert, B. A., & Jerry, P. (2002). *The working alliance concept.* Unpublished manuscript.

Highlen, P. S., Reynolds, A. L., Adams, E. M., Hanley, T. C., Myers, J., Cox, C., et al. (1988, August). Self-identity development model of oppressed people: Inclusive model for all? Symposium presented at the American Psychological Association Convention, Atlanta, GA.

Hill, M., & Ballou, M. (1998). Making feminist therapy: A practice survey. *Women and Therapy, 21*(2), 1-16.

Hill, M., Glaser, K., & Harden, J. (1995). A feminist model for ethical decision making. In E. Rave & C. Larsen (Eds.), *Ethical decision making in therapy: Feminist perspectives* (pp. 18-37). New York: Guilford Press.

Hill, M., Glaser, K., & Harden, J. (1998). A feminist model of ethical decision making. *Women and Therapy, 21*(3), 101-121.

Hill, R. J. (2006). What's it like to be queer here? *New Directions for Adult and Continuing Education, 112,* 7-16.

Hinkle, J. S. (1994). Practitioners and cross-cultural assessment: A practical guide to information and training. *Measurement and Evaluation in Counseling and Development, 27,* 103-115.

Ho, D. Y. F. (1995). Internalized culture, culturocentrism, and transcendence. *The Counseling Psychologist, 23*(1), 4-24.

Hofstede, G. (1980). *Culture's consequences: International differences in work-related values.* Beverly Hills, CA: Sage.

Hogan-Garcia, M. (1999). *The four skills of cultural diversity competence.* Toronto, ON: Brooks/Cole–Wadsworth.

Hooker, E. (1957). The adjustment of the male overt homosexual. *Journal of Projective Techniques, 21,* 18-31.

hooks, b. (1984). *Feminist theory: From margin to center.* Boston: South End Press.

hooks, b. (1990). *Yearning: Race, gender, and cultural politics.* Boston: South End Press.

Hopkins, N., Reicher, S., & Levine, M. (1997). On the parallels between social cognition and the 'new racism'. *British Journal of Social Psychology, 36,* 306-329.

Horenczyk, G. (2000). Conflicted identities: Acculturation attitudes and immigrants' construction of their social worlds. In E. Olshtain & G. Horenczyk (Eds.), *Language, identity, and immigration* (pp. 13-30). Jerusalem: Magnes.

Horne, S. G., & Mathews, S. S. (2006). A social justice approach to international collaborative consultation. In R. L. Toporek, L. H. Gerstein, N. A. Fouad, G. Roysircar, & T. Israel (Eds.), *Handbook for social justice in counseling psychology: Leadership, vision, and action* (pp. 388-405). Thousand Oaks, CA: Sage.

Horvath, A. O. (2000). The therapeutic relationship: From transference to alliance. *JCLP/In Session: Psychotherapy in Practice, 56*(2), 163-173.

Horvath, A. O. (2006). The alliance in context: Accomplishments, challenges, and future directions [Electronic version]. *Psychotherapy: Theory, Research, Practice, Training, 43*(3), 258-263.

House, E. (1993). *Professional evaluation: Social impact and political consequences.* Newberry Park, CA: Sage.

Houser, R., Wilczenski, F. L., & Ham, M. (2006). *Culturally relevant ethical decision-making in counseling.* Thousand Oaks, CA: Sage.

Howard-Hamilton, M. F., & Frazier, K. (2005). Identity development and the convergence of race, ethnicity, and gender. In D. Comstock (Ed.), Diversity and development: Critical contexts that shape our lives and relationships (pp. 67-90). Toronto, ON: Nelson.

Human Resources and Skills Development Canada. (2009). 2006 employment equity data report. Ottawa, ON: Government of Canda. Retrieved April 27, 2009, from http://www.hrsdc.gc.ca/eng/labour/publications/equality/eedr/2006/page07.shtml

Hunsley, J., Dobson, K. S., Johnston, C., & Mikail, S. F. (1999). Empirically supported treatments in psychology: Implications for Canadian professional psychology. *Canadian Psychology, 40*(4), 289-301.

Hurst, S., & Genest, M. (1995). Cognitive-behavioral therapy with a feminist orientation: A perspective for therapy with depressed women. *Canadian Psychology, 36*(3), 236-257.

Huxur, G., Mansfield, E., Nnazor, R., Schuetze, H., & Segawa, M. (1996). Learning needs and adaptation problems of foreign graduate students. *Canadian Society for the Study of Higher Education, 15,* 1-16.

Hwang, W. (2006). The psychotherapy adaptation and modification framework: Application to Asian Americans. *American Psychologist, 61,* 702-715.

Hyde, N. D. (1990). Voices from the silence: Use of imagery with incest survivors. In T. A. Laidlaw & C. Malmo (Eds.), *Healing voices: Feminist therapy approaches to therapy with women* (pp. 163-193). San Francisco: Jossey-Bass.

Ibrahim, F. A. (1985). Effective cross-cultural counselling and psychotherapy: A framework. *The Counseling Psychologist, 13,* 625-638.

Ibrahim, F., Ohnishi, H., & Sandhu, D. S. (1997). Asian American identity development: A culture-specific model for South Asian Americans. *Journal of Multicultural Counselling and Development, 25,* 34-50.

Ibrahim, F. A., Roysircar-Sodowsky, G., & Ohnishi, F. (2001). Worldview: Recent developments and needed directions. In J. G. Ponterotto, J. M. Casas, L. A. Suzuki, & C. M. Alexander (Eds.), *Handbook of multicultural counseling* (2nd ed., pp. 425-456). Thousand Oaks, CA: Sage.

Indian and Northern Affairs Canada. (1996). Report of the Royal Commission on Aboriginal Peoples. Retrieved October 25, 2003, from http://www.ainc-inac.gc.ca/ch/rcap/sg/cg_e.html

Indian and Northern Affairs Canada. (2008). *Statement of apology.* Retrieved Feb. 18, 2009, from http://www.ainc-inac.gc.ca/ap/fn/index-eng.asp

Indian and Northern Affairs Canada. (2009). *First Nations.* Retrieved June 22, 2009, from http://www.ainc-inac.gc.ca/ap/fn/index-eng.asp

Industry Canada. (2002). *Achieving excellence: Investing in people, knowledge, and opportunity. Canada's innovative strategy.* Ottawa, ON: Government of Canada.

Informetrica Limited. (2000). *Recent immigrants in the Calgary metropolitan area: A comparative portrait based on the 1996 Census.* Ottawa, ON: Citizenship and Immigration Canada.

Inman, A. G., Ladany, N., Constantine, M. G., & Morano, C. K., (2001). Development and preliminary validation of the cultural values conflict scale for South Asian women. *Journal of Counselling Psychology, 48*(1), 17-27.

Institute of Medicine. (2002). *Care without coverage: Too little, too late.* Washington, DC: National Academy Press.

International Association of Educational and Vocational Guidance. (2001). *Ethical standards.* Retrieved December 6, 2003, from http://www.iaevg.org.English/html/about standards.html

International Association of Marriage and Family Counselors. (2002). *Ethical standards.* Retrieved December 8, 2003, from http://www.iamfc.com/ethicalcodes.html

International Association of Psychiatric Rehabilitation Services. (2000). *Code of ethics.* Retrieved September 10, 2003, from http://www.ifsw.org/application_manual.1

International Federation of Social Workers. (2002). *Second draft document: Ethics in social work statement of principles.* Retrieved December 8, 2003, from http://www.ifsw.org/GM-Ethics-2draf.html

International Organization of Migrants. (1990). *International roundtable on the movement of people: New developments.* Geneva, Switzerland: International Institute of Humanitarian Law.

International Test Commission. (2000). *International guidelines for test use: Version 2000.* Retrieved April 20, 2002, from http://www.intestcom.org/test_use.htm

International Union of Psychological Science. (2008). *Universal declaration of ethical principles for psychologists.* Retrieved February 25, 2009, from www.am.org/ethics/univdec2008.html

Irving, L., & Cannon, R. (2000). Starving for hope: Goals, agency, and pathways in the development and treatment of eating disorders. In C. R. Snyder (Ed.), *Handbook of hope: Theory, measures, and applications* (pp. 261-283). New York: Academic Press.

Isay, R. A. (1996). *Becoming gay: The journey to self-acceptance.* New York: Pantheon Books.

Ishiyama, F. I. (1995a). Culturally dislocated clients: Self-validation and cultural conflict issues and counselling implications. *Canadian Journal of Counselling, 29,* 262-275.

Ishiyama, F. I. (1995b). Use of validationgram in counselling: Exploring sources of self-validation and impact in personal transition. *Canadian Journal of Counselling, 29,* 134-146.

Israel, T. (2003). Integrating gender and sexual orientation into multicultural counseling competencies. In G. Roysircar, P. Arredondo, J. N. Fuertes, J. G. Ponterotto, & R. L. Toporek (Eds.), *Multicultural counseling competencies 2003: Association for Multicultural Counseling and Development* (pp. 69-78). Alexandria, VA: American Counseling Association.

Israel, T. (2006). Marginalized communities in the United States: Oppression, social justice, and the role of counseling psychologists. In R. L. Toporek, L. H. Gerstein, N. A. Fouad, G. Roysircar, & T. Israel (Eds.), *Handbook for social justice in counseling psychology: Leadership, vision, and action* (pp. 149-154). Thousand Oaks, CA: Sage.

Israel, T., & Selvidge, M. M. D. (2003). Contributions of multicultural counseling to counselor competence with lesbian, gay, and bisexual clients. *Journal of Multicultural Counseling & Development, 31*, 84-98.

Ivey, A. E., & Collins, N. M. (2003). Social justice: A long-term challenge for counseling psychology. *The Counseling Psychologist, 31*(3), 290-298.

Ivey, A. E., D'Andrea, M., Bradford Ivey, M., & Simek-Morgan, L. (Eds.). (2002). *Theories of counseling and psychotherapy: A multicultural perspective* (5th ed.). Boston: Allyn & Bacon.

Ivey, A. E., D'Andrea, M., Ivey, M. B., & Simek-Morgan, L. (2007). *Theories of counseling and psychotherapy: A multicultural perspective* (6th ed.). Toronto, ON: Pearson Education.

Ivey, A. E., & Ivey, M. B. (2003). *Intentional interviewing and counselling: Facilitating client development in a multicultural society* (5th ed.). Toronto, ON: Brooks/Cole, Thomson Learning.

Iwasaki, Y., & Ristock, J. L. (2007). The nature of stress experienced by lesbians and gay men. *Anxiety, Stress, & Coping, 20*(3), 299-319.

Jackson, S., & Jones, J. (1998). *Contemporary feminist theories.* New York: New York University Press.

Jacob, E. J., & Greggo, J. W. (2001). Using counselor training and collaborative programming strategies in working with international students. *Journal of Multicultural Counseling & Development, 29*(1), 73-88.

Jacobs, U., & Iacopino, V. (2001). Torture and its consequences: A challenge to clinical neuropsychology. *Professional Psychology: Research and Practice, 32*, 458-464.

Jambunathan, S., Burts, D., & Pierce, S. (2000). Comparison of parenting attitudes among five ethnic groups in the United States. *Journal of Comparative Family Studies, 31*(4), 395-406.

James, C. E. (1996). Race, culture, and identity. In C. E. James (Ed.), *Perspectives on racism and the human services sector: A case for change* (pp. 5-35). Toronto, ON: University of Toronto Press.

Javed, N. S. (1995). Salience of loss and marginality: Life themes of "immigrant women of color" in Canada. In J. Adleman & G. M. Enguidanos (Eds.), *Racism in the lives of women: Testimony, theory, and guides to antiracist practice* (pp. 13-23). Binghamton, NY: Haworth Press.

Jenkins, D., & Johnston, L. B. (2004). Unethical treatment of gay and lesbian people with conversion therapy. *Families in Society, 85*(4), 557-561.

Jenkins, P. (2004). *Dream catchers: How mainstream America discovered Native spirituality.* New York: Oxford.

Jensen, C. (1994). Psychosocial treatment of depression in women: Nine single-subject evaluations. *Research on Social Work Practice, 4*(3), 267-282.

JobStart and Skills for Change. (2001). *Access for foreign-trained IT professionals: An exploration of systemic barriers to employment.* Ottawa, ON: Department of Canadian Heritage, Multicultural Program.

Jochems, W., Snippe, J., Smid, H. J., & Verweij, A. (1996).The academic progress of foreign students: Study achievement and study behavior. *Higher Education, 31*, 325-340.

Johnson, C. E., Stewart, A. L., Brabeck, M. M., Huber, V. S., & Rubin, H. (2004). Interprofessional collaboration: Implications for combined-integrated doctoral training in professional psychology. *Journal of Clinical Psychology, 60*(10), 995-1010.

Johnson, L. R., & Sandhu, D. S. (2007). Isolation, adjustment, and acculturation issues of international students: Intervention strategies for counselors. In M. Pope & H. Singaravelu (Eds.), *A handbook for counselling international students in the United States* (pp. 13-36). Alexandria, VA: American Counseling Association.

Johnson, S. M., & O'Connor, E. (2001). *For lesbian parents: Your guide to helping your family grow up happy, healthy, and proud.* New York: Guilford Press.

Johnston, B. (1990). *Ojibway heritage.* Lincoln, NB: University of Nebraska Press.

Jones, A. J. (1997). Truth and deception in AIDS information brochures. *Journal of Homosexuality, 32*(3-4), 37-75.

Jones, J., Bennett, S., Olmstead, M., Lawson, M., & Rodin, G. (2001). Disordered eating attitudes and behaviors in teenaged girls: A school-based study. *Canadian Medical Association Journal, 165*(5), 547-552.

Jones, M. A., & Gabriel, M. A. (1999). Utilization of psychotherapy by lesbians, gay men, and bisexuals: Findings from a nationwide survey. *American Journal of Orthopsychiatry, 69*, 209-219.

Jordan, A., & Meara, N. (1999). Ethics and professional practice of psychologists: The role of virtues and principles. *Professional Psychology: Research and Practice, 21*, 107-114.

Jordan, J. V. (1991). Empathy and self boundaries. In J. V. Jordan, A. G. Kaplan, J. B. Miller, I. P. Stiver, & J. L. Surrey (Eds.), *Women's growth in connection* (pp. 67-80). New York: Guilford Press.

Jordan, J. V. (Ed.). (1997). *Women's growth in diversity.* New York: Guilford Press

Jordan, J. V. (2000). The role of mutual empathy in relational/cultural therapy. *JCLP/In Session: Psychotherapy in Practice, 56*(8), 1005-1016.

Jordan, J. V. (2001). *Challenges to connection: New directions in a relational approach to therapy.* Professional Workshop, Calgary, AB.

Jordan, J. V. (2003). Relational-cultural therapy. In M. Kopala & M. Keitel (Eds.), *Handbook of counselling women* (pp. 2230). Thousand Oaks, CA: Sage.

Jordan, J. V. (2004). Toward competence and connection. In J. V. Jordan, M. Walker, & L. M. Hartling (Eds.), *The complexity of connection* (pp. 11-27). New York: Guilford Press.

Jordan, J. V., & Dooley, C. (2000). *Relational practice in action: A group manual (No. 6)*. Wellesley, MA: Stone Center.

Jordan, J. V, Kaplan, A. G., Miller, J. B., Stiver, I. P., & Surrey, J. L. (1991). *Women's growth in connection*. New York: Guilford Press.

Jordan, J. V., & Surrey, J. L. (1986). The self-in-relation: Empathy and the mother-daughter relationship. In T. Bernay & D. W. Cantor (Eds.), *The psychology of today's woman: New psychoanalytic visions* (pp. 81-104). Hillsdale, N.J.: Analytic Press.

Jordan, J. V., & Walker, M. (2004). Introduction. In J. V. Jordan, M. Walker, & L. M. Hartling (Eds.), *The complexity of connection: Writings from the Stone Center's Jean Baker Miller Training Institute* (pp. 1-8). New York: Guilford Press.

Jordan, J. V., Walker, M., & Hartling, L. M. (Eds.). (2004). *The complexity of connection: Writings from the Stone Center's Jean Baker Miller Training Institute*. New York: Guilford Press.

Jordan, K. M., & Deluty, R. H. (1995). Clinical interventions by psychologists with lesbians and gay men. *Journal of Clinical Psychology, 51,* 448-456.

Joyner, L. M. (2003). Applied research in the pursuit of justice: Creating change in the community and the academy. *Social Justice, 30*(4), 5-20.

Jung, C., Von Franz, M-L, & Henderson, J. (1964). *Man and his symbols*. New York: Doubleday.

Justin, M. (2003). *Walking between two worlds: The bicultural experience of second-generation East Indian Canadian women*. Unpublished doctoral dissertation, McGill University, Montreal, Quebec, Canada.

Kahima, E. S., & Loh, E. (2005). International students' acculturation: Effects of international, conational, and local ties and need for closure. *International Journal of Intercultural Relations, 30,* 471-485.

Kalichman, S. C. (1998). *Understanding AIDS: Advances in research and treatment* (2nd ed.). Washington, DC: American Psychological Association.

Kantrowitz, R., & Ballou, M. (1992). A feminist critique of cognitive behavioral therapy. In L. Brown & M. Ballou (Eds.), *Personality and psychopathology: Feminist reappraisals* (pp. 70-87). New York: Guilford Press.

Kaslow, N. J. (2004, November). Competencies in professional psychology. *American Psychologist*, 774-781.

Katz, J. (1985). The sociopolitical nature of counseling. *The Counseling Psychologist, 13,* 615-624.

Kazemipur, A., & Halli, S. (2003, April). Poverty experiences of immigrants: Some reflections. *Canadian Issues*, 18-20.

Kazemipur, A., & Halli, S. S. (2000). *The new poverty in Canada: Ethnic groups and ghetto neighbourhoods*. Toronto, ON: Thompson Educational.

Kean, R. (2006). Understanding the lives of older gay people. *Gerontological Care and Practice, 18*(8), 31-36.

Kenny, C. (2000). A sense of place: Aboriginal research as ritual practice. In R. Neil (Ed.), *Voice of the drum* (pp. 139-150). Brandon, MN: Kingfisher.

Kerr, L. (2001-2002). Career counselling in a culturally diverse setting. *Contact Point Bulletin, 5*(3). Retrieved May 31, 2002, from http://www.contactpoint.ca/bulletin/v5-n3/v5-n3s.html - anchor_3

Kerry, J., & Sargent, J. (1999). *Canadian Association for Music Therapy code of ethics*. Waterloo, ON: Canadian Association for Music Therapy.

Khan, S. (2002). *Aversion and desire: Negotiating Muslim female identity in the diaspora*. Toronto, ON: Women's Press.

Khoa, L. X., & VanDeusen, J. M. (1981). Social and cultural customs: Their contribution to resettlement. *Journal of Refugee Resettlement, 1,* 48-51.

Kielwasser, A. P., & Wolf, M. A. (1993-94). Silence, difference, and annihilation: Understanding the impact of mediated heterosexism on high school students. *High School Journal, 77*(1-2), 58-79.

Kim, B. S. K., & Abreu, J. M. (2001). Acculturation measurement: Theory, current instruments, and future directions. In J. G. Ponterotto, J. M. Casas, L. A. Suzuki, & C. M. Alexandra (Eds.), *Handbook of multicultural counseling* (2nd ed., pp. 394-424). Thousand Oaks, CA: Sage.

Kincheloe, J. L., & McLaren, P. (2005). Rethinking critical theory and qualitative research. In N. K. Denzin & Y. S. Lincoln (Eds.), *Handbook of qualitative research* (3rd ed., pp. 303-342). Thousand Oaks, CA: Sage.

King, M. (1999). Realpolitik and the empirically validated treatment debate. *Canadian Psychology, 40*(4), 306-307.

Kinsey, A. C., Pomeroy, W. B., & Martin, C. E. (1948). *Sexual behavior in the human male*. Philadelphia: W. B. Saunders.

Kirkness, V. J. (1998). Our people's education: Cut the shackles; cut the crap; cut the mustard. *Canadian Journal of Native Education, 22*(1), 10-16.

Kiselica, M. S. (1999). Confronting my own ethnocentrism and racism: A process of pain and growth. *Journal of Counseling and Development, 77*(1), 14-17.

Kiselica, M. S., & Robinson, M. (2001). Bringing advocacy counseling to life: The history, issues, and human dramas of social justice work in counseling. *Journal of Counseling and Development, 79*(4), 387-397.

Kitzinger, C., & Perkins, R. (1993). *Changing our minds: Lesbian feminism and psychology*. New York: New York University Press.

Kitzinger, C., & Wilkinson, S. (1995). Transitions from heterosexuality to lesbianism: The discursive production of lesbian identities. *Developmental Psychology, 31,* 95-104.

Kivel, P. (1995). *Uprooting racism: How White people can work for racial justice*. Gabriola Island, BC: New Society.

Klein, F., Sepekoff, B., & Wolf, T. J. (1985). Sexual orientation: A multi-variable dynamic process. *Journal of Homosexuality, 11*(1-2), 35-49.

Klinger, R. L. (1995). Gay violence. *Journal of Gay & Lesbian Psychotherapy, 2*(3), 119-134.

Knapik, M., & Miloti, A. (2006). Conceptualizations of competence and culture: Taking up the postmodern interest in social interaction. *International Journal for the Advancement of Counselling, 28,* 375–387.

Knight, J. (1994). Internationalization: Elements and checkpoints. *CBIE Research, 7,* 1-15.

Knight, J. (2000). *Progress & promise: The AUCC report on internationalization at Canadian universities.* Ottawa, ON: Association of Universities and Colleges of Canada.

Kocarek, C. E., & Pelling, N. J. (2003). Beyond knowledge and awareness: Enhancing counsellor skills for work with gay, lesbian, and bisexual clients. *Journal of Multicultural Counseling & Development, 31,* 99-112.

Kohl, B. G. (2006). Can you feel me now? Worldview, empathy, and racial identity in a therapy dyad. *Journal of Emotional Abuse, 6*(2/3), 173-196.

Komiya, N., & Eells, G. T. (2001). Predictors of attitudes toward seeking counseling among international students. *Journal of College Counseling, 4*(2), 153-160.

Kosic, A. (2002). Acculturation attitudes, need for cognitive closure, and adaptation of immigrants. *The Journal of Social Psychology, 142,* 179-201.B885

Koss-Chioino, J. D. (2000). Traditional and folk approaches among ethnic minorities. In J. F. Aponte & J. Wohl (Eds.), *Psychological intervention and cultural diversity* (2nd ed., pp. 149-166). Needham Heights, MA: Allyn & Bacon.

Koss, M. P., & Kilpatrick, D. G. (2001). Rape and sexual assault. In E. T. Gerity, R. M. Keane, & F. Tuma (Eds.), *The mental health consequences of torture* (pp. 178-194). New York: Plenum.

Koss, M., Bailey, J., Yuan, N., Herrera, V., & Lichter, E. (2003). Depression and PTSD in survivors of male violence: Research and training initiatives to facilitate recovery. *Psychology of Women Quarterly, 27*(2), 130-142.

Kosteniuk, J. G., & Dickinson, H. G. (2003). Tracing the social gradient in the health of Canadians: Primary and secondary determinants. *Social Science and Medicine, 57,* 263-276.

Kottler, L., Boudreau, G., & Devlin, M. (2003). Emerging psychotherapies for eating disorders. *Journal of Psychiatric Practice, 9*(6), 431-441.

Kral, M. J., Burkhardt, K. J., & Kidd, S. (2002). The new research agenda for a cultural psychology. *Canadian Psychology, 43*(3), 154-162.

Kramer, E. J., Tracy, L. C., & Ivey, S. L. (1999). Demographics, definitions, and data limitations. In D. J. Kramer, S. L. Ivey, & Y. Ying (Eds.), *Immigrant women's health: Problems and solutions* (pp. 3-18). San Francisco: Jossey-Bass.

Kramer, S. A. (1990). *Positive endings in psychotherapy: Bringing meaningful closure to therapeutic relationships.* San Francisco: Jossey-Bass.

Kubler-Ross, E. (1969). *On death and dying.* New York: MacMillan.

Kunz, E. F. (1973). The refugee in flight: Kinetic model and forms of displacement. *International Migration Review, 7,* 125-146.

Kuo, B. C. H., & Roysircar, G. (2006). An exploratory study of cross-cultural adaptation of adolescent Taiwanese unaccompanied sojourners in Canada. *International Journal of Intercultural Relations, 30*(2), 159-183.

Kurtness, J. (1991). Trois phases-clé dans l'acculturation des Montagnais du Québec [Three key phases in the acculturation of the Montagnais of Quebec]. In M. Lavallée, F. Ouellet, & F. Larose (Eds.), *Identité, culture et changement social* [Identity, culture, and social change] (pp. 72-81). Paris: L'Harmattan.

Kwon, S. (2001). Codependence and interdependence: Cross-cultural reappraisal of boundaries and relationality. *Pastoral Psychology, 50*(1), 39-52.

Kymlicka, W. (1997). Immigrants, multiculturalism, and Canadian citizenship. Retrieved October 1, 2003, from http://www.pearson-shoyama.ca/Hot_Button/immigran.htm

Lambert, R. D. (1992). Foreign student flows and the internationalization of higher education: NAFSA Working Paper #37. Evans City, PA: NAFSA.

LaBeauf, I., Maples, M. E., D'Andrea, L., Watson, Z., & Packman, J. (2007). Is affirmative action still necessary? Journal of Employment Counseling, 44, 98-114.

LaBrack, B. (1993). The missing linkage: The process of integrating orientation and reentry. In R. M. Paige (Ed.), *Education for the intercultural experience* (pp. 241-280). Yarmouth, ME: Intercultural Press.

Lacan, J. (1966). *Écrits* [Writings]. Paris: Seuil.

LaFrance, M., Paluck, E. L., & Brescoll, V. (2004). Sex changes: A current perspective on the psychology of gender. In A. H. Eagley, A. E. Beall, & R. J. Sternberg (Eds.) *The psychology of gender* (pp. 328-344). New York: Guilford Press.

Lafrance, M., & Stoppard, J. (2006). Constructing a non-depressed self: Women's accounts of recovery from depression. *Feminism & Psychology, 16*(3), 307-325.

Lafromboise, T., Trimble, J., & Mohatt, G. (1990). Counseling intervention and American Indian tradition: An integrative approach. *The Counseling Psychologist, 18,* 628-654.

Laghi, B. (1998, April 11). Rage finds its voice in Alberta. *The Globe and Mail,* A1, A4.

Lahey, K. A., & Alderson, K. (2004). *Same-sex marriage: The personal and the political.* Toronto, ON: Insomniac Press.

Lai, D. W. L. (2004). Impact of culture on depressive symptoms of elderly Chinese immigrants. *Canadian Journal of Psychiatry, 49,* 820-827.

Laird, J. (2003). Lesbian and gay families. In F. Walsh (Ed.), *Normal family processes: Growing diversity and complexity* (3rd ed., pp. 176-209). New York: Guilford Press.

Lalande, V., Crozier, S. D., & Davey, H. (2000). Women's career development and relationships. *Canadian Journal of Counselling, 34*(3), 193-203.

Lalonde, R. N., & Giguère, B. (2008). When might the two cultural worlds of second generation biculturals collide? *Canadian Diversity – Diversité Canadienne, 6*(2), 58-62.

Lambert, L. (2008). A counselling model for young women in the United Arab Emirates: Cultural considerations. *Canadian Journal of Counselling, 42*(2), 101-117.

Landrine, H., & Klonoff, E. A. (1992). Culture and health-related schemata: A review and proposal for interdisciplinary integration. *Health Psychology, 11,* 267-276.

Larocque, S. (2006). *Gay marriage: The story of a Canadian social revolution* (R. Chodos, L. Blair, & B. Waterhouse, Trans.). Toronto, ON: James Lorimer.

Laurent, E. (2005). Sexuality and human rights: An Asian perspective. *Journal of Homosexuality, 48*(3/4), 163-225.

Lazarus, R. (1990). Theory-based stress measurement. *Psychological Inquiry, 1*(1), 3-13.

Lazarus, R. (1993). From psychological stress to the emotions: A history of changing outlooks. *Annual Review of Psychology, 44,* 1-21.

Lazarus, R. (1997). Acculturation isn't everything. *Applied Psychology: An International Review, 46*(1), 39-43.

Lazarus, R., & Folkman, S. (1984). *Stress, appraisal, and coping.* New York: Springer.

Lazarus, R. S. (2006). Emotions and interpersonal relationships: Towards a person-centered conceptualization of emotions and coping. *Journal of Personality, 74,* 9-46.

Lecca, P. J., Quervalú, I., Nunes, J. V., & Gonzales, H. F. (1998). Cultural competency in health, social, & human services: Directions for the twenty-first century. New York: Garland.

Lee, C. C. (1997). The global future of professional counseling: Collaboration for international social change. *International Journal of Intercultural Relations, 21*(2), 279-285.

Lee, C. C. (1998). Counselors as agents of social change. In C. C. Lee & G. R. Walz (Eds.), *Social action: A mandate for counselors* (pp. 3-14). Alexandria, VA: American Counseling Association.

Lee, C. C. (1998). Professional counseling in a global context: Collaboration for international social action. In C. Lee & G. R. Walz (Eds.), *Social action: A mandate for counsellors* (pp. 293-304). Alexandria, VA: American Counseling Association.

Lee, C.C (Ed.). (2007). Counseling for social justice. Alexandria, VA: American Counseling Association.

Lee, C. C., & Hipolito-Delgado, C. P. (2007). Introduction: Counselors as social justice agents. In C. C. Lee & C. P. Hipolito-Delgado (Eds.), *Counselling for social justice* (pp. xiii-xxviii). Alexandria, VA: American Counselling Association.

Lee, C. C., & Rodgers, R. A. (2009). Counselor advocacy: Affecting systemic change in the public arena. *Journal of Counseling & Development, 87,* 284-287.

Lee, J. A. (1977). Going public: A study in the sociology of homosexual liberation. *Journal of Homosexuality, 3,* 49-78.

Lee, R., Rodin, G., Devins, G., & Weiss, M. G. (2001). Illness experience, meaning, and help-seeking among Chinese immigrants in Canada with chronic fatigue and weakness. *Anthropology & Medicine, 8*(1), 89-107.

Lehavot, K., & Lambert, A. J. (2007). Toward a greater understanding of antigay prejudice: On the role of sexual orientation and gender role violation. *Basic and Applied Social Psychology, 29*(3), 279-292.

Leman, M. (1999). *Canadian multiculturalism.* Retrieved May 25, 2009, from http://dsp-psd.pwgsc.gc.ca/Collection-R/LoPBdP/CIR/936-e.htm

Leong, F. T. L. (1993). The career counselling process with racial-ethnic minorities. *The Career Development Quarterly, 42,* 26-41.

Leong, F. T. L., & Brown, M. T. (1995). Theoretical issues in cross-cultural career development: Cultural validity and cultural specificity. In W. B. Walsh & S. H. Osipow (Eds.), *Handbook of vocational psychology* (pp. 143-180). Mahwah, NJ: Lawrence Erlbaum.

Leong, F. T. L, & Chou, E. L. (1996). Counseling international students. In P. B. Pedersen, J. G. Draguns, W. J. Lonner, & J. E. Trimble (Eds.), *Counseling across cultures* (4th ed., pp. 210-242). Thousand Oaks, CA: Sage.

Leong, F. T. L., & Chou, E. L. (2002). Counseling international students and sojourners. In P. B. Pedersen, J. G. Dragun, W. J. Lonner, & J. E. Trimble (Eds.), *Counseling across cultures* (5th ed., pp. 185-207). Thousand Oaks, CA: Sage.

Leong, F. T. L., Hardin, E., & Gupta, A. (2007, May). *Culture and self in vocational psychology: A cultural formulations approach to career assessment and career counseling.* An invited paper presented at the Society for Vocational Psychology Biennial Conference, University of Akron, Ohio.

Leong, F. T. L., & Leach, M. M. (2007). Internationalising counseling psychology in the United States: A SWOT analysis. *Applied Psychology: An International Review, 56*(1), 165-181.

Leong, F. T. L., & Ponterotto, J. G. (2003). A proposal for internationalizing counseling psychology in the United States: Rationale, recommendations, and challenges. *The Counseling Psychologist, 31*(4), 381-395.

Leong, T. L., Wagner, N. S., & Tata, S. P. (1995). Racial and ethnic variations in help-seeking attitudes. In J. G. Ponterotto, J. M. Casas, L. A. Suzuki, & C. M. Alexander (Eds.), *Handbook of multicultural counselling* (pp. 415-438). Thousand Oaks, CA: Sage.

Lerner, G. (1993). *The creation of feminist consciousness.* New York: Oxford University Press.

Leserman, J., DiSantostefano, R., Perkins, D. O., & Evans, D. L. (1994). Gay identification and psychological health in HIV-positive and HIV-negative gay men. *Journal of Applied Social Psychology, 24,* 2193-2208.

Leslie, D., & MacNeill, L. (1995). Double positive: Lesbians and race. In J. Adleman & G. M. Enguidanos (Eds.), *Racism in the lives of women: Testimony, theory, and guides to antiracist practice* (pp. 161-170). Binghamton, NY: Haworth Press.

Lessinger, J. (1995). *From the Ganges to the Hudson: East Indian immigrants in New York City.* Boston: Allyn & Bacon.

Letourneau, N., Duffett-Leger, L., Stewart, M., Hegadoren, K., Dennis, C., Rinaldi, C., et al. (2007). Canadian mothers' perceived support needs during postpartum depression. *Journal of Obstetric, Gynecologic, & Neonatal Nursing, 36*(5), 441-449.

Leung, A. (2007). Returning home and issues related to reverse culture shock. In M. Pope & H. Singaravelu (Eds.), *A handbook for counselling international students in the United States* (pp. 137-154). Alexandria, VA: American Counseling Association.

Leung, P. (2003). Multicultural competencies and rehabilitation counseling/psychology. In D. B. Pope-Davis, H. L. K. Coleman, W. M. Lui, & R. L. Toporek (Eds.), *Handbook of multicultural competencies in counseling and psychology* (pp. 439-455). Thousand Oaks, CA: Sage.

Leung, S. A. (2003). A journey worth traveling: Globalization of counseling psychology. *The Counseling Psychologist, 31*(4), 412-419.

Levi-Strauss, C. (1995). *Myth and meaning.* New York: Schocken.

Lewis, A. N. (2006). Three-factor model of multicultural counseling for consumers with disabilities. *Journal of Vocational Rehabilitation, 24,* 151-159.

Lewis, D. C. (2009). Aging out of place: Cambodian refugee elders in the United States. *Family and Consumer Sciences Journal, 37,* 376-393.

Lewis, J., Arnold, M. S., House, R. O., & Toporek, R. L. (2002). *Advocacy competencies.* Retrieved May 28, 2009, from http://www.counseling.org/AboutUs/

Lewis, J. A., Arnold, M. S., House, R., & Toporek, R. L. (2003). *Advocacy competencies.* Alexandria, VA: American Counselling Association.

Lewis, J. A., Cheek, J. R., & Hendricks, C. B. (2000). Advocacy in supervision. In L. J. Bradley & N. Ladany (Eds.), *Counselor supervision: Principles, process, and practice* (3rd ed., pp. 330-341). Philadelphia: Brunner-Routledge.

LGBT adoption. (2009). Retrieved February 11, 2009, from http://en.wikipedia.org/wiki/LGBT_adoption

Li, J. (2001). Expectations of Chinese immigrant parents for their children's education: The interplay of Chinese tradition and the Canadian context. *Canadian Journal of Education, 26*(4), 477-494.

Li, P. S. (1999). *Race and ethnic relations in Canada* (2nd ed.). Don Mills, ON: Oxford University Press.

Li, P. S. (2003). *Destination Canada: Immigration debates and issues.* Don Mills, ON: Oxford University Press.

Lightning, W. C. (1992). Compassionate mind: Implications of a text written by Elder Louis Sunchild. *Canadian Journal of Native Education, 19*(2), 153-215.

Lin, S., & Pedersen, P. (2007). Multinational competencies of international student service providers. In M. Pope & H. Singaravelu (Eds.), *A handbook for counselling international students in the United States* (pp. 285-298). Alexandria, VA: American Counseling Association.

Lincoln, Y. S., & Cannella, G. S. (2009). Ethics and the broader rethinking/reconceptualization of research as construct. *Cultural Studies ↔ Critical Methodologies, 9*(2), 273-285.

List of television shows with LGBT characters. (2009, February 8). Wikipedia, the free encyclopedia. Retrieved February 11, 2009, from http://en.wikipedia.org/wiki/List_of_television_shows_with_LGBT_characters

Liu, W. T., Lamanna, M., & Murata, A. (1979). *Transition to nowhere: Vietnamese refugees in America.* Nashville, TN: Charter House.

Long, D., & LaFrance, B. (2004). Speaking the truth with care: Introduction to a dialogue on Aboriginal research issues. *Native Studies Review, 15*(2), 1-5.

Longabough, R. (1980). The systematic observation of behavior in naturalistic settings. In H. C. Triandis & J. W. Berry (Eds.), *Handbook of cross-cultural psychology* (pp. 57-126). Boston: Allyn and Bacon.

Lonner, W. J., & Ibrahim, F. A. (2002). Appraisal and assessment in cross-cultural counselling. In P. B. Pedersen, J. G. Draguns, W. K. Lonner, & J. W. Trimble (Eds.), *Counseling across cultures* (5th ed., pp. 355-379). Thousand Oaks, CA: Sage.

Lopez-Baez, S. I., & Paylo, M. (2009). Social justice advocacy: Community collaboration and systems advocacy. *Journal of Counseling and Development, 87,* 276-283.

Lorant, V., Croux, C., Weich, S., Deliege, D., Mackenbach, J., & Ansseau, M. (2007). Depression and socio-economic risk factors: 7-year longitudinal study. *British Journal of Psychiatry, 190,* 293-298.

Lott, B. (2002). Cognitive and behavioral distancing from the poor. *American Psychologist, 57,* 100-110.

Lott, B., & Webster, K. (2006). Carry the banner where it can be seen: Small wins for social justice. *Social Justice Research, 19*(1), 123-133.

Lowe, S. M., & Mascher, J. (2001). The role of sexual orientation in multicultural counseling: Integrating bodies of knowledge. In J. G. Ponterotto, J. M. Casis, L. A. Suzuki, & C. M. Alexander (Eds.), *Handbook of multicultural counseling* (2nd ed., pp. 755-778). Thousand Oaks, CA: Sage.

Ludvig, A. (2006). Differences between women? Intersecting voices in a female narrative. *European Journal of Women's Studies, 13*(3), 245-258.

Lussier, A. S., & Sealey, D. B. (1975). *The Métis: Canada's forgotten people.* Winnipeg, MB: MMF Press.

Luzzo, D. A., Henao, C., & Wilson, M. (1996). An innovative approach to assessing the academic and social needs of international students. *Journal of College Student Development, 37,* 351-352.

Lynch, M. F. (2002). The dilemma of international counsellor education: Attending to cultural and professional fits and misfits. *International Journal for the Advancement of Counselling, 24,* 89-100.

Lynn, K. (1994). White privilege: What's in it for me? In C. James & A. Shadd (Eds.), *Talking about difference* (pp. 149-173). Toronto, ON: Between the Lines.

Lysgaard, S. (1955). Adjustment in a foreign society: Norwegian Fulbright grantees visiting the United States. *International Social Science Bulletin, 10,* 45-51.

MacDonald, S., & Arthur, N. (2004, January). *When international experience throws a career curve.* Paper presented at the National Consultation on Career Development (NATCON), Ottawa, ON.

MacDougall, C. (2002). Rogers' person-centered approach: Consideration for use in multicultural counseling. *Journal of Humanistic Psychology, 49*(2), 255-264.

MacGregor, R. (1989). *Chief: The fearless vision of Billy Diamond.* Markham, ON: Viking.

Mackintosh, C. (1998, January-March). Sexual orientation now a matter of law. *The Citizen* (publication of the Alberta Human Rights Commission), p. 1.

Madak, P. R., & MacDonald, S. L. (2000). The question of ethics in qualitative research. In W. E. Schulz (Ed.), *Counselling ethics casebook 2000* (pp. 219-273). Ottawa, ON: Canadian Counselling Association.

Madariaga-Vignudo, L., & Miladinovska-Blazevska, T. (2005). *Housing experiences: The case of refugees in Winnipeg.* Retrieved January 12, 2009, from http://ceris.metropolis.net/9thMetropolisConference/WorkshopPresentations

Mahalingam, R., & Leu, J. (2005). Culture, essentialism, immigration, and representations of gender. *Theory & Psychology, 15*(6), 839-860.

Malley, M., & Tasker, F. (2007). "The difference that makes a difference": What matters to lesbians and gay men in psychotherapy. *Journal of Gay & Lesbian Psychotherapy, 11*(1/2), 93-109.

Mallinckrodt, B., & Leong, F. T. (1992). International graduate students, stress, and social support. *Journal of College Student Development, 33,* 71-78.

Malone, J. L. (2000). Working with Aboriginal women: Applying feminist therapy in a multicultural counselling context. *Canadian Journal of Counselling, 34*(1), 33-42.

Malyon, A. K. (1981). The homosexual adolescent: Developmental issues and social bias. *Child Welfare, 60,* 321-330.

Malyon, A. K. (1982). Biphasic aspects of homosexual identity formation. *Psychotherapy: Theory, Research, and Practice, 19,* 335-340.

Manese, J., Saito, G., & Rodolfa, E. (2004, January). Diversity-based psychology: What practitioners and trainers need to know. *Board of Psychology Update, 11*(1), 16-19.

Mao, L., McCormick, J., & Van de Ven, P. (2002). Ethnic and gay identification: Gay Asian men dealing with the divide. *Culture, Health, & Sexuality, 4*(4), 419-430.

Mappes, T., & Zembaty, J. (1991). *Biomedical ethics* (3rd ed.). Toronto, ON: McGraw Hill.

Marcia, J. E. (1966). Development and validation of ego-identity status. *Journal of Personality and Social Psychology, 3,* 551-559.

Marcus, G. E., & Fischer, M. J. (1986). *Anthropology as cultural critique.* Chicago: University of Chicago Press.

Marsella, A. (2006). Justice in a global age: Becoming counsellors to the world. *Counseling Psychology Quarterly, 19,* 121-132.

Marsella, A. J., & Pedersen, P. (2004). Internationalizing the counseling psychology curriculum: Toward new values, competencies, and directions. *Counseling Psychology Quarterly, 17*(4), 413-423.

Marsella, A. J., & Yamada, A. M. (2000). Culture and mental health: An introduction and overview of foundations, concepts, and issues. In I. Cuellar & F. A. Paniagua (Eds.), *Multicultural mental health: Assessment and treatment of diverse populations* (pp. 3-24). San Diego: Academic Press.

Marszalek, J. F., Dunn, M. S., & Cashwell, C. S. (2002). The relationship between gay and lesbian identity development and psychological adjustment. *Q The Online Journal, 2*(1). Retrieved April 30, 2002, from http://www.aglbic.org/Q/Vol2 Num1/Marszalek.htm

Martin, A. D. (1982a). Learning to hide: The socialization of the gay adolescent. *Adolescent Psychiatry, 10,* 52-65.

Martin, A. D. (1982b). Some issues in the treatment of gay and lesbian patients. *Psychotherapy: Theory, Research, and Practice, 19,* 341-348.

Martin, J. N. (1984). The intercultural reentry: Conceptualization and directions for future research. *International Journal of Intercultural Relations, 8,* 115-134.

Martin, J. N., & Harrell, T. (1996). Reentry training for intercultural sojourners. In D. Landis & R. S. Bhagat (Eds.), *Handbook of intercultural training* (2nd ed., pp. 307-326). Thousand Oaks, CA: Sage.

Maslach, C. (1982). *Burnout: The cost of caring.* Englewood Cliffs, NJ: Prentice-Hall.

Matsumoto, D. (1996). *Culture and psychology.* Scarborough, ON: Nelson.

Mattu, P. (2002). *A survey on the extent of substandard housing problems faced by immigrants and refugees in the lower mainland of British Columbia.* Retrieved January 12, 2009, from http://www.mosaicbc.com/PDF_files/SCPI%20Summary%20Report.pdf

Maxwell, M., & Henriksen, R. C. (2009). Counseling multiple heritage adolescents. In R. C Henriksen & D. A. Paladino (Eds.), *Counseling multiple heritage individuals, couples, and families* (pp. B92965-82). Alexandria, VA: American Counselling Association.

May, P. A. (1994). The epidemiology of alcohol abuse among American Indians: The mythical and real properties. *American Indian Culture and Research Journal, 18,* 121-143.

Maynard, M. (1995). Beyond the 'Big Three': The development of feminist theory into the 1990's. *Women's History Review, 4*(3), 259-281.

Mays, V. M., & Cochran, S. D. (2001). Mental health correlates of perceived discrimination among lesbian, gay, and bisexual adults in the United States. *American Journal of Public Health, 91,* 1869-1876.

McCann, D. (2001). Lesbians, gay men, their families and counselling: Implications for training and practice. *Educational & Child Psychology, 18*(1), 78-88.

McCarn, S. R., & Fassinger, R. E. (1996). Re-visioning sexual minority identity formation: A new model of lesbian identity and its implications of counseling and research. *The Counseling Psychologist, 24*(3), 508-534.

McClanahan, P. W. (2001). *The associations among receptive nonverbal decoding accuracy, cultural identification, and personal functioning in Southeastern American Indian adults.* Unpublished doctoral dissertation, Emory University, Atlanta, GA.

McCormick, R. M. (1995). The facilitation of healing for the First Nations people of British Columbia. *Canadian Journal of Native Education, 21,* 251-322.

McCormick, R. M. (1996). Culturally appropriate means and ends of counseling as described by the First Nations people of British Columbia. *International Journal for the Advancement of Counselling, 18*(3), 163-172.

McCormick, R. M. (1998). Ethical considerations in First Nations counselling and research. *Canadian Journal of Counselling, 32*(4), 284-297.

McCormick, R. M. (2000a). Aboriginal traditions in the treatment of substance abuse. *Canadian Journal of Counselling, 34*(1), 25-32.

McCormick, R. M. (2000b, January). *The relationship of Aboriginal people with nature.* Paper presented at the National Consultation on Vocational Counselling, Ottawa, ON.

McCormick, R. M. (2002). *The facilitation of healing for American Indian youth who are suicidal: An exploratory study.* Unpublished manuscript, University of British Columbia at Vancouver.

McCormick, R. M., & Amundson, N. E. (1997). A career-life planning model for First Nations people. *Journal of Employment Counseling, 34,* 171-179.

McDermott, R. (1993). The acquisition of a child by a learning disability. In S. Chaiklin & J. Lave (Eds.), *Understanding practice: Perspectives on activity and context* (pp. 269-305). Cambridge, UK: Cambridge University Press.

McDonald, G. J. (1982). Individual differences in the coming out process for gay men: Implications for theoretical models. *Journal of Homosexuality, 8*(1), 47-60.

McDonald, H. B., & Steinhorn, A. I. (1990). *Homosexuality: A practical guide to counseling lesbians, gay men, and their families.* New York: Continuum.

McDougall, C., & Arthur, N. (2001). Applying models of racial identity in multicultural counselling. *Canadian Journal of Counselling, 35*(2), 122-136.

McDowell, T., & Fang, S. R.S. (2007). Feminist informed critical multiculturalism. *Journal of Family Issues, 28*(4), 549-566.

McFarland, W. P. (1993). A developmental approach to gay and lesbian youth. *Journal of Humanistic Education and Development, 32,* 17-29.

McGoldrick, M., Giordano, J., & Pearce, J. K. (1996). *Ethnicity and family therapy.* New York: Guilford Press.

McGraa, E. (1990). *Mother Earth spirituality: Native American paths to healing ourselves and our world.* San Francisco: Harper.

McGrath, E., Keita, G. P., Strickland, B. R., & Russo, N. F. (1990). *Women and depression: Risk factors and treatment issues.* Washington DC: American Psychological Association.

McIntosh, P. (1988). *White privilege and male privilege: A personal account of coming to see correspondences through work in women's studies. Working paper no. 189.* B952Retrieved September 29, 2003, from http://web.clas.ufl.edu/users/leslieh/syg2000/whiteprivilege.html

McIntosh, P. (1989, July/August). White privilege: Unpacking the invisible knapsack. *Peace and Freedom,* 8-10.

McIsaac, E. (2003, May). Immigrants in Canadian cities: Census 2001 – What do the data tell us? *Policy Options,* 58-63.

McKinlay, H. J, Pattison, H. M., & Gross, H. (1996). An exploratory investigation of the effects of a cultural orientation programme on the psychological well-being of international university students. *Higher Education, 31,* 379-395.

McKirnan, D. J., & Peterson, P. L. (1989). Alcohol and drug use among homosexual men and women: Epidemiology and population characteristics. *Addictive Behaviors, 14,* 545-553.

McLennan, N., Rochow, S., & Arthur, N. (2001). Religious and spiritual diversity in counselling. *Guidance and Counselling, 16,* 132-137.

McLeod, J. (2001). *Qualitative research in counselling and psychotherapy.* Thousand Oaks, CA: Sage.

McLeod, J. (2003). *An introduction to counseling* (3rd ed.). Maidenhead, UK: Open University Press.

McMahon, M., Arthur, N., & Collins, S. (2008). Social justice and career development: Views and experiences of Australian career development practitioners. *Australian Journal of Career Development, 17*(3), 15-25 .

McMullen, L., & Stoppard, J. (2003). Conclusion. In J. Stoppard & L. McMullen (Eds.), *Situating sadness: Women and depression in social context* (pp. 207-215). New York: New York University Press.

McMullen, L., & Stoppard, J. (2006). Women and depression: A case study of the influence of feminism in Canadian psychology. *Feminism & Psychology, 16*(3), 273-288.

Meadows, L. M., Lagendyk, L. E., Thurston, W. E., & Eisner, A. C. (2003). Balancing culture, ethics, and methods in qualitative health research with Aboriginal peoples. *International Journal of Qualitative Methods, 2*(4). Retrieved February, 13, 2009, from http:www.ualberta.ca/~iiqm/backissues/2_4/pdf/meadows.pdf

Meadows, L. M., Thurston, W. E., & Melton, C. (2001). Immigrant women's health. *Social Science & Medicine, 52,* 1451-1458.

Meissner, W. W. (2006). The therapeutic alliance – A proteus in disguise [Electronic version]. *Psychotherapy: Theory, Research, Practice, Training, 43*(3), 264-270.

Mencher, J. (1997). Intimacy in lesbian relationships: A critical reexamination of fusion. In J. V. Jordan (Ed.), *Women's growth in diversity: More writings from the Stone Center* (pp. 311-330). New York: Guilford Press.

Menjivar, C., & Salcido, O. (2002). Immigrant women and domestic violence: Common experiences in different countries. *Gender and Society, 16,* 898-920.

Merali, N. (1999). Resolution of value conflicts in multicultural counselling. *Canadian Journal of Counselling, 33*(1), 57-66.

Merali, N. (2002). Perceived versus actual parent-adolescent assimilation disparity among Hispanic refugee families. *International Journal for the Advancement of Counseling, 24,* 57-68.

Merriam-Webster OnLine. (2008). *Kaleidoscope.* Retrieved June 3, 2009, from http://www.merriam-webster.com/dictionary/kaleidoscope

Mertens, D. M. (1998). *Research methods in education and psychology: Integrating diversity with quantitative and qualitative approaches.* Thousand Oaks, CA: Sage

Merton, R. (1968). *Social theory and social structure.* London, UK: Macmillan.

Meszaros, A. F. (1961). Types of displacement reactions among the post-revolution Hungarian immigrants. *Journal of Canadian Psychiatric Association, 6,* 9-19.

Mihesuah, D. (2000). A few cautions at the millennium on the merging of feminist studies with American Indian women's studies. *Signs: Journal of Women in Culture and Society, 25*(4), 1247-1251.

Millar, J. R. (1996). *Shingwauk's vision: A history of Native residential schools.* Toronto, ON: University of Toronto Press.

Miller, G. (2003). *Incorporating spirituality in counseling and psychotherapy.* Hoboken, NJ: John Wiley & Sons.

Miller, J. B. (1986). *Toward a new psychology of women* (2nd ed.). Boston: Beacon.

Miller, J. B. (2008). Connections, disconnections, and violations. *Feminism and Psychology, 18*(3), 368-380.

Miller, M. E. (1996). Ethics and understanding through interrelationship: I and thou in dialogue. In R. Josselson (Ed.), *Ethics and process in the narrative study of lives: Vol. 4* (pp. 129-147). Thousand Oaks, CA: Sage.

Mindel, C. H., Habenstein, R. W., & Wright Jr., R. (1988). *Ethnic families in America: Patterns and variations* (3rd ed). New York: Elsevier.

Minton, H. L., & McDonald, G. J. (1983-84). Homosexual identity formation as a developmental process. *Journal of Homosexuality, 9*(2-3), 91-104.

Mio, J. S., & Iwamasa, G. (1993). To do or not to do: That is the question for white cross-cultural researchers. *The Counseling Psychologist, 21*(2), 197-212.

Miraftab, F. (2000). Sheltering refugees: The experience of refugees in Metropolitan Vancouver. *Canadian Journal of Urban Research, 9,* 42-63.

Miranda, J., & Storms, M. (1989). Psychological adjustment of lesbians and gay men. *Journal of Counseling and Development, 68,* 41-45.

Misra, R., Melanee, C., & Burant, C. J. (2003). Relationships among life stress, social support, academic stressors, and reactions to stressors of international students in the United States. *International Journal of Stress Management, 10*(2), 137-157.

Mohatt, G., & Eagle Elk, J. (2000). *The price of a gift.* Lincoln, NB: University of Nebraska.

Mohatt, G. V., & Thomas, L. R. (2006). "I wonder why you would do it that way?" Ethical dilemmas in doing participatory research with Alaska Native communities. In J. E. Trimble & C. B. Fisher (Eds.), *The handbook of ethical research with ethnocultural populations & communities* (pp. 93-110). Thousand Oaks, CA: Sage.

Mollen, D., Ridley, C. R., & Hill, C. L. (2003). Models of multicultural counseling competence. In D. B. Pope-Davis, H. L. K. Coleman, W. M. Lui, & R. L. Toporek (Eds.), *Handbook of multicultural competencies in counseling and psychology* (pp. 21-37). Thousand Oaks, CA: Sage.

Mollica, R. F. (2006). *Healing invisible wounds: Paths to hope and recovery in a violent world.* Nashville, TN: Vanderbilt University Press.

Mollica, R. F., Wyshak, G., & Lavelle, J. (1987). The psychosocial impact of war trauma and torture on Southeast Asian refugees. *American Journal of Psychiatry, 144,* 1567-1572.

Money, J. (1988). *Gay, straight, and in-between: The sexology of erotic orientation.* New York: Oxford University Press.

Monier, S. S., & Lewis, A. C. (2000). School counselors and sexual minority students. *Q The Online Journal, 1*(1). Retrieved April 30, 2002, from http://www.aglbic.org/Q/Vol1Num1/Monier.htm

Monk, G., Winslade, J. M., & Sinclair, S. L. (Eds.). (2008). *New horizons in multicultural counseling.* Thousand Oaks, CA: Sage.

Moodley, R. (2007). (Re)placing multiculturalism in counselling and psychotherapy. *British Journal of Guidance & Counselling, 35*(1), 1-22.

Moodley, R., & West, W. (Eds.). (2005). *Integrating traditional healing practices into counseling and psychotherapy.* Thousand Oaks, CA: Sage.

Moradi, B., Mohr, J. J., Worthington, R. L., & Fassinger, R. E. (2009). Counseling psychology research on sexual (orientation) minority issues: Conceptual and methodological challenges and opportunities. *Journal of Counseling Psychology, 56*(1), 5-22.

Morawski, J., & Agronick, G. (1991). A restive legacy: The history of feminist work in experimental and cognitive psychology. *Psychology of Women Quarterly, 15,* 567-579.

Moreland, K. (1996). Persistent issues in multicultural assessment of social and emotional functioning. In L. Suzuki, P. Meller, & J. Ponterotto (Eds.), *Handbook of multicultural assessment: Clinical, psychological, and educational applications* (pp. 57-74). San Francisco: Jossey-Bass.

Mori, S. (2000). Addressing the mental health concerns of international students. *Journal of Counseling & Development, 78,* 137-144.

Morin, S. F., & Rothblum, E. D. (1991). Removing the stigma: Fifteen years of progress. *American Psychologist, 9,* 947-949.

Morris, M., & Bunjun, B. (2007). *Using intersectional feminist frameworks in research: A resource for embracing the complexities of women's lives in the stages of research.* Retrieved November 12, 2008, from http://www.criaw-icref.ca/IFF/Final layout of report with front cover.pdf

Morrison, L. L., & L'Heureux, J. (2001). Suicide and gay/lesbian/bisexual youth: Implications for clinicians. *Journal of Adolescence, 24,* 39-49.

Morrison, T. G., Parriag, A. V., & Morrison, M. A. (1999). The psychometric properties of the homonegativity scale. *Journal of Homosexuality, 37*(4), 111-126.

Morrissette, P. (2008). Clinical engagement of Canadian First Nations couples. *Journal of Family Therapy, 30,* 60-77.

Morrow, S. L. (1997). Career development of lesbian and gay youth: Effects of sexual orientation, coming out, and homophobia. *Journal of Gay and Lesbian Social Services, 7*(4), 1-15.

Morrow, S. L., Hawxhurst, D. M., Montes de Vegas, A. Y., Abousleman, T. M., & Castaneda, C. L. (2006). Toward a radical feminist multicultural therapy: Renewing a commitment to activism. In R. L. Toporek, L .H. Gerstein, N. A. Fouad, G. Roysircar, & T. Israel (Eds.), *Handbook for social justice in counseling psychology: Leadership, vision, and action* (pp. 231-247). Thousand Oaks, CA: Sage.

Mulder, T. J., Hollmann, F. W., Lollock, L. R., Cassidy, R. C., Constanzo, J. M., & Baker, J. D. (2001). *US Census Bureau measurement of net international migration to the United States: 1990-2000.* Retrieved February 6, 2009, from http://www.census.gov/population

Murdie, R. (2002). The housing careers of Polish and Somali newcomers in Toronto's rental market. *Housing Studies, 17,* 423-443.

Murphy, K. R., & Davidshofer, C. O. (2001). *Psychological testing: Principles and applications* (5th ed.). Toronto, ON: Prentice Hall.

Muzychka, M., Poulin, C., Cottrell, B., Miedema, B., & Roberts B. (1996). *B1009.* Ottawa, ON: Canadian Research Institute for the Advancement of Women.

NAFSA: Association of International Educators. (1996). *NAFSA's international student handbook.* Washington, DC: Author.

Nagy, T. F. (2005). *Ethics in plain English: An illustrative casebook for psychologists* (2nd ed.). Washington, DC: American Psychological Association.

Naidoo, J. (2003). South Asian Canadian women: A contemporary portrait. *Psychology & Developing Societies, 15*(1), 51-67.

Nairn, R. (1998). NSCBI and the Canadian Code of Ethics. Excerpt from an article published in The Bulletin of the New Zealand Psychological Society, 87(1995, December), 13-14. *Canadian Psychology, 39,* 243.

Napier, N. J. (1990). *Recreating yourself: Building self-esteem through imaging and self-hypnosis.* New York: Norton.

National Council of Welfare. (2006). *Poverty profile 2002 and 2003.* Retrieved October 28, 2006, from http://www.ncwcnbes.net/htmdocument/reportPovertyProfile20022003/ PP20022003Eng.pdf

National Steering Committee for Career Development Guidelines and Standards. (2004). *Canadian standards and guidelines for career development practitioners.* Retrieved July 31, 2004, from http://www.career-dev-guidelines.org

Navas, M., Garcia, M. C., Sanchez, J., Rojas, A. J., Pumares, P., & Fernandez, J. S., (2005). Relative Acculturation Extended Model (RAEM): New contributions with regard to the study of acculturation. *International Journal of Intercultural Relations, 29,* 21-37.

Neimeyer, G. J., & Neimeyer, R. A. (1993). Defining the boundaries of constructive assessment. In G. J. Neimeyer (Ed.), *Constructivist assessment* (pp. 1-29). Newbury Park, CA: Sage.

Nelson, E. D., & Robinson, B. W. (1999). *Gender in Canada.* Scarborough, ON: Prentice Hall.

Nesdale, D., & Todd, P. (2000). Effect of contact on intercultural acceptance: A field study. *International Journal of Intercultural Relations, 24,* 341-360.

Neufeld, A., Harrison, M. J., Stewart, M. J., Hughes, K. D., & Spitzer, D. L. (2001). *Immigrant women's experience as family caregivers: Support and barriers.* Edmonton, AB: Prairie Centre of Excellence for Research on Immigration and Integration.

Neumann, H., McCormick, R., Amundson, N., & McLean, H. (2000). Career counselling First Nations youth: Applying the First Nations Career/Life Planning Model. *Canadian Journal of Counselling, 34,* 172-185.

Neville, H. A., Worthington, R. L., & Spanierman, L. B. (2001). Race, power, and multicultural counseling psychology: Understanding White privilege and color-blind racial attitudes. In J. G. Ponterotto, J. M. Casas, L. A. Suzuki, & C. M. Alexander (Eds.), *Handbook of multicultural counselling* (2nd ed., pp. 257-288). Thousand Oaks, CA: Sage.

New, C. (1993). The power of lies and the project of feminist therapy, Part 2. *Free Associations, 4*(30), 191-209.

New Zealand Psychological Society. (2002). *Code of ethics.* Auckland, NZ: Author.

Newhouse, D. (2004). Indigenous knowledge in a multicultural world. *Native Studies Review, 15*(2), 139-154.

Ng, E., Wilkins R., Gendron, F., & Berthelot, J. M. (2005). *Dynamics of immigrants' health in Canada: Evidence from the National Population Health Survey.* Retrieved January 15, 2009, from http://www.statcan.gc.ca/pub/82-618-m/2005002/pdf

Ngo, H., & Este, D. (2006). Professional re-entry for foreign-trained immigrants. *Journal of International Migration and Integration, 7*(1), 27-50.

Nicolosi, J., Byrd, A. D., & Potts, R. W. (2000a). Beliefs and practices of therapists who practice sexual reorientation psychotherapy. *Psychological Reports, 86,* 689-702.

Nicolosi, J., Byrd, A. D., & Potts, R. W. (2000b). Retrospective self-reports of changes in homosexual orientation: A consumer survey of conversion therapy clients. *Psychological Reports, 86,* 1071-1088.

Noels, K. A. (1999, August). *General and acculturation-related daily hassles and psychological adjustment in first- and second-generation South Asian immigrants to Canada.* Paper presented at the International Conference on Immigration and Integration sponsored by the Society for the Psychological Study of Social Issues, Toronto, ON.

Noh, S., Wu, Z., Speechley, M., & Kaspar, V. (1992). Depression in Korean immigrants in Canada: II. Correlates of gender, work and marriage. *Journal of Nervous and Mental Disease, 180,* 578-582.

Nolen-Hoeksema, S., & Keita, G. (2003). Women and depression: Introduction. *Psychology of Women Quarterly, 27*(2), 89-90.

Norsworthy, K. L. (2006). Bringing social justice to international practices of counseling psychology. In R. L. Toporek, L. H. Gerstein, N. A. Fouad, G. Roysircar, & T. Israel (Eds.), *Handbook for social justice in counselling psychology: Leadership, vision, and action* (pp. 421-441). Thousand Oaks, CA: Sage.

Norton, R. A., & Coleman, H. L. K. (2003). The influence of race-related issues in supervision process and outcome. In D. B. Pope-Davis, H. L. K. Coleman, W. M. Lui, & R. L. Toporek (Eds.), *Handbook of multicultural competencies in counseling and psychology* (pp. 114-134). Thousand Oaks, CA: Sage.

Novac, S., Darden, J., Haluchanski, D., Seguin, A., & Berneche, F. (2002). *Housing discrimination in Canada: The state of knowledge* (Research Report). Ottawa, ON: Canadian Mortgage and Housing Corporation.

Nwachuku, U. T., & Ivey, A. E. (1991). Culture specific counseling: An alternative training model. *Journal of Counseling and Development, 70,* 106-111 .

Oakland, T., Goldman, S., & Bischoff, H. (1997). Code of the International School Psychology Association. *School Psychology International, 18,* 291-298.

Oberg, K. (1960). Cultural shock: Adjustment to new cultural environments. *Practical Anthropology, 7,* 177-182.

O'Donohue, W., & Caselles, C. E. (1993). Homophobia: Conceptual, definitional, and value issues. *Journal of Psychopathology and Behavioral Assessment, 15*(3), 177-195.

Offet-Gartner, K. (2003a). Career-life planning for First Nations people. *What Works – Alberta: Effective Practices for Social, Workplace, and Labour Market Programs and Services, 1*(4), 6-7.

Offet-Gartner, K. (2003b). Career-life planning with First Nations people. Consultation Proceeding from Building Tomorrow Today, Edmonton, AB: Consultation for Career Development in Alberta, 2002, 85-97.

Offet-Gartner, K. (2008). *Sharing the story: Education as the key to opening the door of career possibilities with First Nations women.* Unpublished doctoral dissertation, University of Calgary, Calgary, Alberta, Canada.

Office for Disability Issues. (2002). Strategic plan 2002-2007: Leadership, engagement, results. Retrieved April 12, 2004, from http://www.sdc.gc.ca/en/hip/odi/documents/strategicPlan/strategicPlan.pdf

Ogloff, J., & Olley, M. (1996). The interaction between ethics and the law: The ongoing refinement of ethical standards for psychologists in Canada. *Canadian Psychology, 39,* 221-230.

Okamura, J. Y. (1981). Situational ethnicity. *Ethnic and Racial Studies, 4*(4), 453-465.

Olesen, V. (2005). Early millennial feminist qualitative research: Challenges and contours. In N. K. Denzin & Y. S. Lincoln (Eds.), *Handbook of qualitative research* (3rd ed., pp. 235-278). Thousand Oaks, CA: Sage

Olkin, R., & Pledger, C. (2003). Can disability studies and psychology join hands? *American Psychologist, 58,* 296-304.

O'Neill, C., & Ritter, K. (1992). Coming out within: Stages of spiritual awakening for lesbians and gay men. San Francisco: Harper.

O'Neill, P. (1998). Teaching ethics: The utility of the CPA code. *Canadian Psychology, 39,* 194-201.

O'Neill, P. (2004). The ethics of problem definition. Canadian Psychology, 46(1), 13-20.

Operario, D., Han, C. S., & Choi, K. H. (2008). Dual identity among gay Asian Pacific Islander men. *Culture, Health, & Sexuality, 10*(5), 447-461.

Ortiz, D. V., & Cole, S. A. (2008). Culture, place of origin, and service delivery for Latino older adult immigrants: The case of Puerto Rican older adults. *Journal of Gerontological Social Work, 51,* 300-314.

Osborne, J. W. (1990). Some basic existential-phenomenological research methodologies for counsellors. *Canadian Journal of Counselling, 24*(2), 79-91.

Ostrove, J. M., & Cole, E. R. (2003). Privileging class: Toward a critical psychology of social class in the context of education. *Journal of Social Issues, 59,* 677-692.

OUTtv. (2008-2009). *Homepage.* Retrieved February 13, 2009, from http://www.outtv.ca/

Paccione-Dyszlewski, M. (2008). Children of same gender parents: What is known. *The Brown University Child and Adolescent Behavior Letter, 24*(2), 4-6.

Pack-Brown, S. P., & Williams, C. B. (2003). *Ethics in a multicultural context.* Thousand Oaks, CA: Sage.

Palma, T. V., & Stanley, J. L. (2002). Effective counseling with lesbian, gay, and bisexual clients. *Journal of College Counseling, 5,* 74-89.

Palmer, A., & Parish, J. (2008). Social justice and counselling psychology: Situating the role of graduate student research, education, and training. *Canadian Journal of Counselling, 42*(2), 278-292.

Palmer, D. L. (1996). B1070*Canadian Journal of Behavioral Science, 28,* 180-192. Retrieved October 22, 2003, from http://www.cpa.ca/cjbsnew/1996/abs%5Fpalmer.html

Palombi, B. J., & Mundt, A. M. (2006). Achieving social justice for college women with disabilities: A model for inclusion. In R. L. Toporek, L. G. Gerstein, N. A. Fouad, G. Roysircar, & T. Israel (Eds.), *Handbook for social justice in counseling psychology: Leadership, vision, and action* (pp. 170-184). Thousand Oaks, CA: Sage.

Paniagua, F. A. (1998). *Assessing and treating culturally diverse clients: A practical guide.* Thousand Oaks, CA: Sage.

Paniagua, F. A. (2001). *Diagnosis in a multicultural context: A casebook for mental health professionals.* Thousand Oaks, CA: Sage.

Paproski, D. L., & Haverkamp, B. E. (2000). Interdisciplinary collaboration: Ethical issues and recommendations. *Canadian Journal of Counselling, 34*(2), 85-97.

Paré, D. (2008). Discourse, positioning and deconstruction: Response to chapter 5. In G. Monk, J. Winslade, & S. Sinclair (Eds.), *New horizons in multicultural counseling* (pp. 137-140). Thousand Oaks, CA: Sage.

Parham, T. A. (1993). White researchers conducting multicultural counseling research: Can their efforts be "mo betta"? *The Counseling Psychologist, 21*(2), 250-256.

Parham, T. A., & Whitten, L. (2003). Teaching multicultural competencies in continuing education for psychologists. In D. B. Pope-Davis, H. L. K. Coleman, W. M. Liu, & R. L. Toporek (Eds.), Handbook of multicultural competencies in counselling & psychology (pp. 562-605). Thousand Oaks, CA: Sage.

Parr, G., Bradley, L., & Bingi, R. (1992). Concerns and feelings of international students. *Journal of College Student Development, 33,* 20-25.

Patel, N., Power, T. G., & Bhavnagri, N. P. (1996). Socialization values and practices of East Indian immigrant parents: Correlates of modernity and acculturation. *Child Development, 67,* 302-313.

Patrick, D. M., Wong, T., & Jordan, R. A. (2000). Sexually transmitted infections in Canada: Recent resurgence threatens national goals. *The Canadian Journal of Human Sexuality, 9,* 149-165.

Patterson, C. H. (1980). *Theories of counseling and psychotherapy* (3rd ed.). New York: Harper & Row.

Patterson, C. H. (1996). Multicultural counseling: From diversity to universality. *Journal of Counseling & Development, 74*(3), 227-231.

Paul, J. P. (1985). Bisexuality: Reassessing our paradigms of sexuality. *Journal of Homosexuality, 11*(1-2), 21-34.

Pearlman, S. F. (1996). Lesbian therapists and their therapy: From both sides of the couch. *Women & Therapy, 18*(2), 7-180.

Peavy, R. V. (1993). *Development of Aboriginal counselling: A brief submitted to Royal Commission on Aboriginal Peoples.* Law Commission of Canada. Retrieved October 23, 2002, from http://www.lcc.fc.ca

Peavy, V. (1995). *Career counselling for Native youth: What kind and by whom?* (Report No. RR93002004). Washington, DC: Office of Educational Research and Improvement. (ERIC Document Reproduction Service No. EDO-CG-95-46).

Pedersen, A., & Pedersen, P. (1989). The culture grid: A framework for multicultural counselling. *International Journal for the Advancement of Counselling, 12,* 299-307.

Pedersen, P. (1990). Social and psychological factors of brain drain and reentry among international students: A survey of this topic. *McGill Journal of Education, 25,* 229-243.

Pedersen, P. (1991a). Counseling international students. *The Counseling Psychologist, 19,* 10-58.

Pedersen, P. (Ed.). (1991b). Introduction to the special issue on multiculturalism as a fourth force in counselling: Multiculturalism as a fourth force in counselling [Special issue]. *Journal of Counseling & Development, 70*(1), 4.

Pedersen, P. (Ed.). (1991c). Multiculturalism as a generic approach to counseling: Multiculturalism as a fourth force in counselling [Special issue]. *Journal of Counseling & Development, 70(1),* 6-12.

Pedersen, P. (1994). *A handbook for developing multicultural awareness* (2nd ed.). Alexandria, VA: American Counseling Association.

Pedersen, P. (1995a). The culture-bound counselor as an unintentional racist. *Canadian Journal of Counseling, 29,* 197-205.

Pedersen, P. (1995b). *The five stages of culture shock.* Westport, CN: Greenwood Press.

Pedersen, P. (1997). *Counselor centered counseling interventions: Striving for accuracy.* London, UK: Sage.

Pedersen, P. (1999). *Multiculturalism as a fourth force.* Philadelphia: Bruner/Mazel.

Pedersen, P. (2001). Multiculturalism and the paradigm shift in counselling: Controversies and alternative futures. *Canadian Journal of Counselling, 35*(1), 15- 25.

Pedersen, P. (2003a). Culturally biased assumptions in counseling psychology. *The Counseling Psychologist, 31*(4), 396-403.

Pedersen, P. (2003b). "Walking the talk": Simulations in multicultural training. In G. Roysircar (Ed.), *Multicultural competencies: A guidebook of practices* (pp. 29-38). Alexandra, VA: Association for Multicultural Counseling & Development.

Pedersen, P. (2008). Ethics, competence, and professional issues in cross-cultural counseling. In P. Pedersen, J. Draguns, W. Lonner, & J. Trimble (Eds.), *Counseling across cultures* (6th ed., pp. 5-20). Thousand Oaks, CA: Sage.

Pedersen, P., & Ivey, A. (1993). *Culture-centered counseling and interviewing skills: A practical guide.* Westport, CT: Praeger.

Pedersen, P., & Leong, F. (1997). Counseling in an international context. *The Counseling Psychologist, 25*(1), 117-122.

Pedersen, P. B. (1993). The multicultural dilemma of White cross-cultural researchers. *The Counseling Psychologist, 21*(2), 229-232.

Pedersen, P. B., Crethar, H. C., & Carlson, J. (2008). *Inclusive cultural empathy.* Washington, D.C.: American Psychological Association.

Peplau, L. A. (1993). Lesbian and gay relationships. In L. D. Garnets & D. C. Kimmel (Eds.), *Psychological perspectives on lesbian and gay male experiences* (pp. 395-419). New York: Columbia University Press.

Pepper, F. C., & Henry, S. L. (1991). An Indian perspective of self-esteem. *Canadian Journal of Education, 18*(2), 145-160.

Perlstein, M. (1998). Where, oh where, has the therapeutic alliance gone? Disquieting log-jams in the therapeutic relationship. *Women & Therapy, 21*(3), 63-68.

Pernice, R. (1994). Methodological issues in research with refugees and immigrants. *Professional Psychology, Research, & Practice, 25,* 207-213.

Perrone, K. M. (2005). Work-family interface for same-sex, dual-earner couples: Implications for counsellors. *The Career Development Quarterly, 53,* 317-324.

Petersen, S. (2000). Multicultural perspective on middle-class women's identity development. *Journal of Counselling and Development, 78,* 63-71.

Pettifor, J. (1994). Ethics and social justice in program evaluation: Are evaluators value-free? *Canadian Journal of School Psychology, 10*(2), 138-146.

Pettifor, J. (1996). Ethics: Virtue and politics in the science and practice of psychology. *Canadian Psychology, 31,* 1-12.

Pettifor, J. (2001a). Are professional codes of ethics relevant for multicultural counselling? *Canadian Journal of Counselling, 35*(1), 26-35.

Pettifor, J. (2001b). *Report on workshop on the ethics of respect and caring.* Unpublished manuscript.

Pettifor, J. (2005). Ethics and multicultural counselling. In N. Arthur & S. Collins (Eds.), *Culture-infused counselling: Celebrating the Canadian mosaic* (pp. 213-238). Calgary, AB: Counselling Concepts.

Pettifor, J., & Malone, J. (in press). Counselling women: Ethics for diversity and social justice. In L. Ross (Ed.), *Counselling women: Feminist issues, theory and practice.*

Pettys, G. L., & Balgopal, P. R. (1998). Multigenerational conflicts and new immigrants: An Indo-American experience. Families in Society. *The Journal of Contemporary Human Services, 79*(4), 410-423.

Phillips, S. D., & Imhoff, A. R. (1997). Women and career development: A decade of research. *Annual Review of Psychology, 48,* 31-59.

Phinney, J. (2003). Ethnic identity and acculturation. In K. M. Chun, P. B. Organista, & G. Marin (Eds.), *Acculturation: Advances in theory, measurement, and applied research* (pp. 63-82). Washington, DC: American Psychological Association.

Phinney, J. S. (1989). Stages of ethnic identity development in minority adolescents. *Journal of Early Adolescence, 9,* 34-49.

Phinney, J. S. (1990). Ethnic identity in adolescence and adults: Review of research. *Psychological Bulletin, 108,* 499-514.

Phinney, J. S., Horenczyk, G., Liebkind, K., & Vedder, P. (2001). Ethnic identity, immigration, and well-being: An interactional perspective. *Journal of Social Issues, 57,* 493-510.

Phinney, J. S., & Ong, A. D. (2007). Conceptualization and measurement of ethnic identity: Current status and future directions. *Journal of Counseling Psychology, 54,* 271-281.

Pick, S. (1997). Berry in Legoland. *Applied Psychology: An International Review, 46,* 49-52.

Pilkonis, P. A. (1999). Let us move ahead, together: Commentary on "Empirically supported treatments in psychology: Implications for Canadian professional psychology." *Canadian Psychology, 40*(4), 302-305.

Pinderhughes, E. (1989). *Understanding race, ethnicity, and power: The key to efficacy in clinical practice.* New York: Free Press.

Platt, L. (2001, January 1). Not your father's high school club. *The American Prospect, 1.*

Plummer, K. (1975). *Sexual stigma: An interactionist account.* Boston: Routledge & Kegan Paul.

Polivy, J., & Herman, C. P. (2002). Causes of eating disorders. *Annual Review of Psychology, 53,* 187-204.

Ponterotto, J., & Pedersen, P. B. (1993). *Preventing prejudice: A guide for counselors and educators.* Thousand Oaks, CA: Sage.

Ponterotto, J. G. (1988). Racial consciousness development among White counselor trainees: A stage model. *Journal of Multicultural Counseling and Development, 16,* 146-156.

Ponterotto, J. G., Atkinson, D. R., Casas, J. M., Helms, J. E., Ivey, A. E., Parham, T. A., et al. (1990, August). *The White American researcher in multicultural counseling: Significance and challenges.* Symposium presented at the 98th Annual Convention of the American Psychological Association, Boston, MA.

Ponterotto, J. G., & Casas, J. M. (1991). *Handbook of racial/ethnic minority counselling research.* Springfield, IL: Charles C. Thomas.

Ponterotto, J. G., Casas, J. M., Suzuki, L. A., & Alexander, C. M. (2001). *Handbook of multicultural counselling* (2nd ed). Thousand Oaks, CA: Sage.

Ponterotto, J. G., & Grieger, I. (2007). Effectively communicating qualitative research. *The Counseling Psychologist, 35*(3), 404-430.

Ponterotto, J. G., & Grieger, I. (2008). Guidelines and competencies for research in cross-cultural counseling research. In P. B. Pedersen, J. G. Draguns, W. J. Lonner, & J. E. Trimble (Eds.), *Counseling across cultures* (6th ed., pp. 57-72). Thousand Oaks, CA: Sage.

Poonwassie, A., & Charter, A. (2001). An Aboriginal worldview of helping: Empowering approaches. *Canadian Journal of Counselling, 35*(1), 63-73.

Popadiuk, N., & Arthur, N. (2004). Counseling international students in Canadian schools. *International Journal for the Advancement of Counselling, 26*(2), 125-145.

Popadiuk, N. E. (2008). Managing multiple identities: Response 2. In N. Arthur & P. Pedersen (Eds.), *Case incidents in counselling for international transitions* (pp. 140-148). Alexandria, VA: American Counseling Association.

Pope-Davis, D. B., Breaux, C., & Liu, W. M. (1997). A multicultural immersion experience: Filling a void in multicultural training. In D. B. Pope-Davis & H. L. K. Coleman (Eds.), *Multicultural counseling competencies: Assessment, education, and training, and supervision* (pp. 237-241). Thousand Oaks, CA: Sage.

Pope-Davis, D. B., & Coleman, H. L. K. (2000). *The intersection of race, class, and gender in multicultural counseling.* Thousand Oaks, CA: Sage.

Pope-Davis, D. B., & Coleman, H. L. K. (2001). *The intersection of race, class, and gender in multicultural counseling.* Thousand Oaks, CA: Sage.

Pope-Davis, D. B., Coleman, H. L. K., Lui, W. M., & Toporek, R. L. (2003). *Handbook of multicultural competencies in counseling and psychology.* Thousand Oaks, CA: Sage.

Pope-Davis, D., & Ottavi, T. (1994). Examining the association between self-reported multicultural counselling competencies and demographic variables among counsellors. *Journal of Counseling and Development, 72,* 651-654.

Pope-Davis, D. B., Toporek, R. L., Ortega-Villalobos, L. D., Ligiero, D., Brittan-Powell, C. S., Liu, W. M., et al. (2002). Client perspectives of multicultural counselling competence: A qualitative examination. *The Counseling Psychologist, 30*(3), 355-393.

Pope, J., & Arthur, N. (2009). Socioeconomic status and class: A challenge for the practice of psychology in Canada. *Canadian Psychology, 50*(2), 55-66.

Pope, M. (1995). The "salad bowl" is big enough for us all: An argument for the inclusion of lesbians and gay men in any definition of multiculturalism. *Journal of Counseling and Development, 73,* 301-304.

Pope, M. (2008). Culturally appropriate counseling considerations for lesbian and gay clients. In P. Pedersen, J. Draguns, W. Lonner, & J. Trimble (Eds.), *Counseling across cultures* (6th ed., pp. 201-222). Thousand Oaks, CA: Sage.

Pope, M., & Singaravelu, H. (Eds.). (2007). A handbook for counselling international students in the United States. Alexandria, VA: American Counseling Association.

Pope, M. S., Prince, J. P., & Mitchell, K. (2000). Responsible career counseling with lesbian and gay students. In D. A. Luzzo (Ed.), *Career counseling of college students: An empirical guide to strategies that work* (pp. 267-282). Washington, DC: American Psychological Association.

Portes, A. (1997). Immigration theory for a new century: Some problems and opportunities. *International Migration Review, 31*(4), 799-825.

Prairie Centre of Excellence for Research on Immigration and Integration. (1999). *The settlement experiences of refugees in Alberta.* Edmonton, AB: Author.

Pratt, G. (2007). Reflections of an Indigenous counselor: Sharing the journey, therapist, or person. *Australasian Psychiatry, 15,* 54-57.

Prendes-Lintel, M. (2001). A working model in counselling recent refugees. In J. G. Ponterotto, J. M. Casas, L. A. Suzuki, & C. M. Alexander (Eds.), *Handbook of multicultural counselling* (2nd ed., pp. 729-752). Thousand Oaks, CA: Sage.

Prilleltensky, I. (1997). Values, assumptions, and practices: Assessing the moral implications of psychological discourse and action. *American Psychologist, 52,* 517-535.

Prince, J. P. (1995). Influences on the career development of gay men. *The Career Development Quarterly, 44,* 168-177.

Prince, J. P. (1997). Career assessment with lesbian, gay, and bisexual individuals. *Journal of Career Assessment, 5,* 225-238.

Pruegger, V. (1995). *Immigrant youth symposium '95: Building tomorrow today.* Calgary, AB: Youth Symposium Committee.

Psychological Society of Ireland. (1999). *Code of professional ethics.* Dublin, Ireland: Author.

Ptasznik, A. (2008). Confronting the negative spirit: Does harm reduction have a place in Aboriginal communities? *Cross Currents.* Retrieved January 6, 2009, from http://www.camh.net/Publications/Cross_Currents/Winter2008-09/negativespirit_crcuwinter2008_09.html

Public Health Agency of Canada. (2006, August). *HIV/AIDS Epi update: HIV infections among MSM in Canada.* Centre for Infectious Disease Prevention and Control. Retrieved July 22, 2007, from http://www.phac-aspc.gc.ca/publicat/epiu-aepi/epi-06/pdf/epi06_e.pdf

Purkiss, S. L., Perrewe, P. L., Gillespie, T. L., Mayes, B. T., & Ferris, G. T. (2006). Implicit sources of bias in employment interview judgments and decisions. *Organizational Behavior and Human Decision Processes, 101*(2), 152-167.

Pyle, N., & Arthur, N. (in press). Clients' perspectives on interprofessional collaboration. *Journal of Interprofessional Care.*

Pyles, L., & Mee Kim, K. (2006). A multilevel approach to cultural competence: A study of the community response to underserved domestic violence victims. *Families in Society: The Journal of Contemporary Social Services, 87*(2), 221-229

Pynoos, R. S., Kinzie, J. D., & Gordon, M. (2001). Children, adolescents, and families exposed to torture and related trauma. In E. T. Gerity, R. M. Keane, & F. Tuma (Eds.), *The mental health consequences of torture* (pp. 211-226). New York: Plenum.

Rabinowitz, V. C., & Sechzer, J. A. (1993). Feminist perspectives on research methods. In F. L. Denmark & M. A. Paludi (Eds.), *Psychology of women: A handbook of issues and theories* (pp. 23-66). Westport, CT: Greenwood Press.

Racine, L. (2008). Examining the conflation of multiculturalism, sexism, and religious fundamentalism through Taylor and Bakhtin: Expanding post-colonial feminist epistemology. *Nursing Philosophy, 10,* 14-25.

Radkowsky, M., & Siegel, L. J. (1997). The gay adolescent: Stressors, adaptations, and psychosocial interventions. *Clinical Psychology Review, 17*(2), 191-216.

Ramirez-Valles, J. (2007). "I don't fit anywhere": How race and sexuality shape Latino gay and bisexual men's health. In I. H. Meyer & M. E. Northridge (Eds.), *The health of sexual minorities: Public health perspectives on lesbian, gay, bisexual, and transgender populations* (pp. 301-319). New York: Springer Science + Business Media.

Ramsey, M. (1997). Exploring power in multicultural counselling encounters. *International Journal for the Advancement of Counselling, 19*(3), 277-291.

Ramsey, M. L. (2000). Monocultural versus multicultural teaching: How to practice what we preach. *Journal of Humanistic Counseling, Education, & Development, 38*(3), 170-184.

Raphael, D. (2004). Introduction to the social determinants of health. In D. Raphael (Ed.), *Social determinants of health: Canadian perspectives* (pp. 1-18). Toronto, ON: Canadian Scholars Press.

Rasmussen, A., Rosenfeld, B., Reeves, K., & Keller, A. S. (2007). The effects of torture-related injuries on long-term psychological distress in a Punjabi Sikh sample. *Journal of Abnormal Psychology, 116,* 734-740.

Ratner, E. F. (1993). Treatment issues for chemically dependent lesbians and gay men. In L. D. Garnets & D. C. Kimmel (Eds.), *Psychological perspectives on lesbian and gay male experiences* (pp. 567-578). New York: Columbia University Press.

Ratts, M., D'Andrea, M., & Arredondo, P. (2004, July). Social justice in counselling: 'Fifth force" in field. *Counseling Today,* 28-30.

Ratts, M. J., & Hutchins, A. M. (2009). ACA advocacy competencies: Social justice advocacy at the client/student level. *Journal of Counseling & Development, 87,* 269-275.

Rau, K. (2006, July 20). *Gay TV station changes hands – again.* Retrieved February 13, 2009, from http://www.xtra.ca/public/Toronto/Gay_TV_station_changes_hands_again-1903.aspx

Raunic, A., & Xenos, S. (2008). University counselling service utilisation by local and international students and user characteristics: A review. *International Journal for the Advancement of Counselling, 30,* 262-267.

Rawls, J. (1971). *A theory of justice.* Cambridge, MA: Belkamp.

Ray, F. K. (2001). Ethics in therapy: Moving from the mind to the heart. *Journal of Systemic Therapies, 20*, 25-36.

Ryan, M. E., & Twibell, R. S. (2000). Concerns, values, stress, coping, health and educational outcomes of college students who studied abroad. *International Journal of Intercultural Relations, 24*, 409-435.

Razack, S. (1994). What is to be gained by looking White people in the eye? Culture, race, and gender in cases of sexual violence. *Signs: Journal of Women in Culture and Society, 19*(4), 894-921.

Redish, D., Jensen, S., & Johnson, A. (2008). A unified framework for addiction: Vulnerabilities in the decision process. *Behavioral and Brain Sciences, 31*, 415-437.

Redmond, M. V., & Bunyi, J. M. (1993). The relationship of intercultural communication competence with stress and the handling of stress as reported by international students. *International Journal of Intercultural Relations, 17*, 235-254.

Reid, J. D. (1995). Development in late life: Older lesbian and gay lives. In A. R. D'Augelli & C. J. Patterson (Eds.), *Lesbian, gay, and bisexual identities over the lifespan: Psychological perspectives* (pp. 215-240). New York: Oxford Press.

Reisch, M. (2002). Defining social justice in a socially unjust world. *Families in Society: The Journal of Contemporary Human Services, 83*(4), 343-354.

Reitz, J. G. (2001). Immigrant success in the knowledge economy: Institutional change and the immigrant experience in Canada, 1970-1995. *Journal of Social Issues, 57*, 579-614.

Restoule, B. (1997). Providing services to Aboriginal clients. *Guidance & Counselling, 12*(2), 13-17.

Reynolds, A. L. (2003). Counseling issues for lesbian and bisexual women. In M. Kopala & M. A. Keitel (Eds.), *Handbook of counselling women* (pp. 53-73). Thousand Oaks, CA: Sage.

Reynolds, A. L., & Constantine, M. G. (2004). Feminism and multiculturalism: Parallels and intersections. *Journal of Multicultural Counseling and Development, 32*, 346-357.

Reynolds, A. L., & Constantine, M. G. (2007). Cultural adjustment difficulties and career development of international college students. *Journal of Career Assessment, 15*, 338-350.

Reynolds, A. L., & Pope, R. L. (2003). Multicultural competence in counseling centers. In D. B. Pope-Davis, H. L. K. Coleman, W. M. Lui, & R. L. Toporek (Eds.), *Handbook of multicultural competencies in counseling and psychology* (pp. 365-382). Thousand Oaks, CA: Sage.

Reza, N. M. (2006). Contemporary realities and future visions: Enhancing multiculturalism in Canada. *Canadian Ethnic Studies, 38*(1), 149-158.

Rhieneck, J. E. (2005). Career decision self-efficacy of lesbians throughout the lifespan. *Adultspan Journal, 4*(2), 79-91.

Richards, L. (2005). *Handling qualitative data: A practical guide.* Thousand Oaks, CA: Sage.

Richardson, D. (1993). Recent challenges to traditional assumptions about homosexuality: Some implications for practice. In L. D. Garnets & D. C. Kimmel (Eds.), *Psychological perspectives on lesbian and gay male experiences* (pp. 117-129). New York: Columbia University Press.

Richardson, D., & Hart, J. (1981). The development and maintenance of a homosexual identity. In J. Hart & D. Richardson (Eds.), *The theory and practice of homosexuality* (pp. 73-92). Boston: Routledge & Kegan Paul.

Richardson, T. Q., & Molinaro, K. L. (1996). White counsellor self-awareness: A prerequisite for developing cultural competence. *Journal of Counseling and Development, 74*, 238-242.

Ridley, C., Liddle, M., Hill, C., & Li, L. (2001). Ethical decision making in multicultural counseling. In J. Ponterotto, J. Casas, L. Suzuki, & C. Alexander (Eds.), *Handbook of multicultural counseling* (2nd ed., pp.165-188). Thousand Oaks, CA: Sage.

Ridley, C. R. (1995). *Overcoming unintentional racism in counseling and therapy: A practitioner's guide to intentional intervention.* Thousand Oaks, CA: Sage.

Ridley, C. R. (2005). *Overcoming unintentional racism in counselling and therapy: A practitioner's guide to intentional intervention* (2nd ed.). Thousand Oaks, CA: Sage.

Ridley, C. R., & Kleiner, A. J. (2003). Multicultural counselling competencies: History, themes, and issues. In D. B. Pope-Davis, H. L. K. Coleman, W. M. Lui, & R. L. Toporek (Eds.), *Handbook of multicultural competencies in counseling and psychology* (pp. 3-20). Thousand Oaks, CA: Sage.

Ridley, C. R., Li, L. C., & Hill, C. L. (1998). Multicultural assessment: Reexamination, reconceptualization, and practical application. *The Counseling Psychologist, 26*(6), 827-910.

Ridley, C. R., & Lingle, D. W. (1996). Cultural empathy in multicultural counseling: A multidimensional process model. In P. Pedersen, W. Lonner, & J. Draguns (Eds.), *Counseling across cultures* (pp. 21-45). Thousand Oaks, CA: Sage.

Ridley, C. R., Mendoza, D. W., Kanitz, B. E., Angermeier, L., & Zenk, R. (1994). Cultural sensitivity in multicultural counseling: A perceptual schema model. *Journal of Counseling Psychology, 41*(3), 125-136.

Riggle, E. D. B., Whitman, J. S., Olson, A., Rostosky, S. S., & Strong, S. (2008). The positive aspects of being a lesbian or gay man. *Professional Psychology: Research and Practice, 39*(2), 210-217.

Risman, B., & Schwartz, P. (1988). Sociological research on male and female homosexuality. *Annual Review of Sociology, 14*, 125-147.

Ristock, J. L. (2002). *No more secrets: Violence in lesbian relationships.* New York: Routledge.

Ritter, K. Y., & Terndrup, A. I. (2002). *Handbook of affirmative psychotherapy with lesbians and gay men.* New York: Guilford Press.

Rivière, D. (2004). Adventures of a Black girl in search of herself: Some thoughts on Canadian feminism. *Hecate: An Interdisciplinary Journal of Women's Liberation, 30*(1), 222-230.

Robb, C. (2006). *This changes everything: The relational revolution in psychology.* New York: Farrar, Straus, and Giroux.

Roberts, J. V. (1995). *Disproportionate harm: Hate crime in Canada – An analysis of recent statistics.* Retrieved November 12, 2003, from http://www.nizkor.org/hweb/orgs/canadian/canada/justice/disproportionate-harm/

Robertson, L. H. (2006). The residential school experience: Syndrome or historic trauma. *Pimatisiwin: A Journal of Aboriginal and Indigenous Community Health, 4*(1), 1-28.

Robinson, T. L. (2005). *The convergence of race, ethnicity, and gender: Multiple identities in counseling* (2nd ed.). Toronto, ON: Pearson Education.

Robinson, T. L., & Howard-Hamilton, M. F. (2000). *The convergence of race, ethnicity, and gender: Multiple identities in counselling.* Upper Saddle River, NJ: Merrill-Prentice Hall.

Rogers, B. (2001). A path of healing and wellness for Native families. *American Behavioral Scientist, 44*(9), 1512-1514.

Rogers, C. (1957). *Client centered counseling.* Boston: Houghton Mifflin.

Rogers, C. (1961). *On becoming a person.* Boston: Houghton Mifflin.

Rogler, L. H. (1987). What do culturally sensitive mental health services mean? The case of Hispanics. *American Psychologist, 42,* 565-570.

Rogler, L. H. (1999). Methodological sources of cultural insensitivity in mental health research. *American Psychologist, 54,* 424-433.

Rohrbaugh, J. B. (2006). Domestic violence in same-gender relationships. *Family Court Review, 44*(2), 287-299.

Rosario, M., Meyer-Bahlburg, H. F. L., Hunter, J., Exner, T. M., Gwadz, M., & Keller, A. M. (1996). The psychosexual development of urban lesbian, gay, and bisexual youths. *Journal of Sex Research, 33*(2), 113-126.

Rose, G. (1997). Situating knowledges: Positionality, reflexivities, and other tactics. *Progress in Human Geography, 21*(3), 305-320.

Rosen, D., Warner, L. A., & Toman, R. M. (2006). Comparing psychiatric serves use among low-income women and women in a general household population. *Social Work Research, 30*(4), 223-232.

Rosenthal, D. A., Russell, J., & Thomson, G. (2008). The health and wellbeing of international students at an Australian university. Higher Education, 55, 51-67.

Ross, M. (1996, March). The relationship between addiction and suicide in Aboriginal women. *Journal of the Society of Obstetricians and Gynaecologists of Canada,* 245-253.

Ross, M. W., Paulsen, J. A., & Stalstrom, O. W. (1988). Homosexuality and mental health: A cross-cultural review. *Journal of Homosexuality, 15,* 131-152.

Rostosky, S. S., Riggle, E. D. B., Gray, B. E., & Hatton, R. L. (2007). Minority stress experiences in committed same-sex couple relationships. *Professional Psychology: Research and Practice, 38*(4), 392-400.

Rothblum, E. D. (1994). "I only read about myself on bathroom walls": The need for research on the mental health of lesbians and gay men. *Journal of Consulting and Clinical Psychology, 62,* 213-220.

Rothblum, E. D. (2000). Sexual orientation and sex in women's lives: Conceptual and methodological issues. *Journal of Social Issues, 56,* 193-204.

Rowe, W., Bennett, S., & Atkinson, D. R. (1994). White racial identity models: A critique and alternative proposal. *Counseling Psychologist, 22,* 120-146.

Roysircar, G. (2003). Understanding immigrants: Acculturation theory and research. In F. D. Harper & J. McFadden (Eds.), *Culture and counseling: New approaches* (pp. 164-185). Toronto, ON: Allyn and Bacon.

Roysircar, G. (2009). The big picture of advocacy: Counselor, heal society and thyself. *Journal of Counseling & Development, 87,* 288-294.

Roysircar, G., Hubbell, R., & Gard, G. (2003). Multicultural research on counselor and client variables. In D. B. Pope-Davis, H. L. K. Coleman, W. M. Lui, & R. L. Toporek (Eds.), *Handbook of multicultural competencies in counseling and psychology* (pp. 247-266). Thousand Oaks, CA: Sage.

Ruano, C. R. (1996). From Cholo to terrorist: Ethnicity as illness in Peruvian society. *Student papers from the Sociology of Knowledge Doctoral Seminar,* University of Toronto, ON.

Ruano, C. R. (1997). Living the truth in Guatemala. *Outlook Magazine, 35*(3), 8, 30.

Ruano, C. R. (2001). La participación de Minorias Nacionales dentro de Sistemas Educativos Pre-Modernos: El caso de los Garífunas de la costa Atlantica de Guatemala. *Education Policy and Evaluation Archives, 9*(23) [Electronic version].

Ruano, C. R. (2005). Understanding the cultural construction of wealth and power differentials through ethnographic narrative analysis in Colombia. *Teaching in Higher Education, 10*(4), 519-526.

Ruano, C. R. (2008, June 10). New schools, collective knowledge, and individual learning: The possibilities of the Latin American pedagogical practice [La nueva escuela ante los aprendizajes individuales y los saberes colectivos: culturas, escolarizaciones y las posibilidades del modelo educativo] latinoamericano. *Revista Iberoamericana de Educación, 46,* 4.

Rudmin, F. W. (2003). Critical history of the acculturation psychology of assimilation, separation, integration, and marginalization. *Review of General Psychology, 7,* 3-37.

Ruiz, A. S. (1990). Ethnic identity: Crisis and resolution. *Journal of Multicultural Counseling and Development, 18,* 29-40.

Rupp, L. J. (1997). "Imagine my surprise": Women's relationships in historical perspective. *Journal of Lesbian Studies, 1*(2) 155-176.

Russell, J., Thomson, G., & Rosenthal, D. A. (2008). International student use of university health and counselling services. *Higher Education, 56,* 59-75.

Russell, P. L., & Davis, C. (2007). Twenty-five years of clinical research on treatment following sexual assault. *Best Practices in Mental Health, 3*(2), 21-37.

Russell, S. T., Seif, H., & Truong, N. L. (2001). School outcomes of sexual minority youth in the United States: Evidence from a national study. *Journal of Adolescence, 24,* 111-127.

Russell, T. G. (1989). AIDS education, homosexuality, and the counselor's role. *The School Counsellor, 36,* 333-337.

Russo, N. F., & Vaz, K. (2001). Addressing diversity in the decade of color. *Psychology of Women Quarterly, 25,* 280-294.

Rust, P. C. R. (1997). "Coming out" in the age of social constructionism: Sexual identity formation among lesbian and bisexual women. In E. D. Rothblum (Ed.), *Classics in lesbian studies* (pp. 25-54). Binghamton, NY: Haworth Press.

Rust, P. C. R. (2000). Bisexuality: A contemporary paradox for women. *Journal of Social Issues, 56*(2), 205-221.

Ryan, L., & Ryan, R. (1980). *Mental health and the urban Indian.* Unpublished manuscript.

Sabnani, H. B., Ponterotto, J. G., & Borodovsky, L. G. (1991). White racial identity development and cross-cultural counsellor training: A stage model. *The Counseling Psychologist, 19*(1), 76-102.

Sadeghi, M., Fischer, J. M., & House, S. G. (2003). Ethical dilemmas in multicultural counseling. *Journal of Multicultural Counseling & Development, 31*(3), 179-191.

Safren, S. A. (2005). Affirmative, evidence-based, and ethically sound psychotherapy with lesbian, gay, and bisexual clients. *Clinical Psychology: Science and Practice, 12*(1), 292.

Saharso, S. (2007). Feminist ethics, autonomy, and the politics of multiculturalism. Feminist Theory, 4(2), 199-215.

Saidla, D. D., & Grant, S. (1993). Roommate understanding and rapport between international and American roommates. *Journal of College Student Development, 34,* 335-340.

Sailer, D. D., Korschgen, A. J., & Lokken, J. M. (1994). Responding to the career needs of gays, lesbians, and bisexuals. *Journal of Career Planning and Employment, 54*(3), 39-42.

Sales, B., & Folkman, S. (Eds.). (2000). *Ethics in research with human participants.* Washington, DC: American Psychological Association.

Sam, D. L. (2006). Acculturation of immigrant children and women. In D. L. Sam+B1251 & J. W. Berry (Eds.), *The Cambridge handbook of acculturation psychology* (pp. 403-418). New York: Cambridge University Press.

Same-sex marriage. (2009). Retrieved February 11, 2009, from http://en.wikipedia.org/wiki/Same-sex_marriage

Sampat-Mehta, R. (1984). First fifty years of South Asian immigration: A historical perspective. In R. N. Kanungo (Ed.), *South Asians in the Canadian mosaic* (pp. 13-31). Montreal, QC: Kala Bharati Foundation.

Sampson, E. (1993a). *Celebrating the other: A dialogic account of human nature.* Boulder, CO: Westview Press.

Sampson, E. (1993b). Identity politics: Challenges to psychology's understanding. *American Psychologist, 48,* 1219-1230.

Sampson, J. P. (2009, June). *Translating career theory to practice: The risk of unintentional social injustice.* Keynote presentation to the International Association of Educational and Vocational Guidance conference, Jyväskylä, Finland.

Sanders, M. (2003). Building bridges instead of walls: Effective cross-cultural counselling. *Corrections Today, 65*(1), 58-60.

Sandhu, D. S. (1994). An examination of the psychological needs of students: Implications for counselling and psychotherapy. *International Journal for the Advancement of Counselling, 17,* 229-239.

Sandhu, D. S. (1995). Pioneers of multicultural counselling: An interview with Paul B. Pedersen. *Journal of Multicultural Counseling and Development, 23,* 198-211.

Sandhu, D. S. (1997). Psychocultural profiles of Asian and Pacific Islander Americans: Implications for counselling and psychotherapy. *Journal of Multicultural Counseling and Development, 25,* 7-22.

Sandhu, D. S., & Asrabadi, B. R. (1994). Development of an acculturative stress scale for international students: Preliminary findings. *Psychological Reports, 75,* 435-448.

Sandhu, R. S. (1992). *Sikhs in America: Stress and survival.* Retrieved July 24, 2003, from http://www.lib.ucdavis.edu/punjab/assim.html

Santiago-Irizarry, V. (2001). *Medicalizing ethnicity: The construction of Latino identity in a psychiatric setting.* Ithaca, NY: Cornell University Press.

Sapp, J. (2001). Self-knowing as social justice: The impact of a gay professor on ending homophobia in education. *Encounter: Education for Meaning and Social Justice, 14*(4), 17-28.

Saris, R., & Johnston-Robledo, I. (2000). Poor women are still shut out of mainstream psychology. *Psychology of Women Quarterly, 24,* 233-235.

Sattler, J. M. (2001). *Assessment of children: Cognitive applications* (4th ed.). San Diego: Author.

Sattler, J. M. (2008). *Assessment of children: Cognitive foundations* (5th ed.). La Mesa, CA: Author.

Saukko, P. (2005). Methodologies for cultural studies: An integrative approach. In N. K. Denzin & Y. S. Lincoln (Eds.), *Handbook of qualitative research* (3rd ed., pp. 343-356). Thousand Oaks, CA: Sage.

Savage, T. A., & Harley, D. A. (2005). African American lesbian, gay, and bisexual persons. In D. A. Harley & J. M. Dillard (Eds.), *Contemporary mental health issues among African Americans* (pp. 91-105). Alexandria, VA: American Counseling Association.

Savage, T. A., Harley, D. A., & Nowak, T. M. (2005). Applying social empowerment strategies as tools for self-advocacy in counseling lesbian and gay mail clients. *Journal of Counseling & Development, 83*, 131-137.

Savickas, M. L. (2007). Internationalisation of counseling psychology: Constructing cross-national consensus and collaboration. *Applied Psychology: An International Review, 56*(1), 182-188.

Savin-Williams, R. C. (1998). The disclosure to families of same-sex attraction by lesbian, gay, and bisexual youths. *Journal of Research on Adolescence, 8*(1), 49-68.

Savin-Williams, R. C. (2005a, November-December). The new gay teen: Shunning labels. *The Gay & Lesbian Review,* 16-19.

Savin-Williams, R. C. (2005b). *The new gay teenager.* Cambridge, MA: Harvard University Press.

Savin-Williams, R. C. (2006). Who's gay? Does it matter? *Current Directions in Psychological Science, 15*(1), 40-44.

Savin-Williams, R. C., & Dube, E. M. (1998). Parental reactions to their child's disclosure of a gay/lesbian identity. *Family Relations, 47*(1), 7-13.

Schenk, C. (2001). *From poverty wages to a living wage.* Toronto, ON: Ontario Federation of Labour.

Schlossberg, N. (1984). *Counseling adults in transition: Linking practice with theory.* New York: Springer.

Schlossberg, N. (1992). Adult development theories: Ways to illuminate the adult development experience. In H. D. Lea & Z. B. Leibowitz (Eds.), *Adult career development: Concepts, issues, and practices* (2nd ed., pp. 2-16). Alexandria, VA: National Career Development Association.

Schlosser, L. Z. (2003). Christian privilege: Breaking a sacred taboo. *Journal of Multicultural Counseling & Development, 31,* 44-52.

Schmidt, J. J. (2006). *Social and cultural foundations of counseling and human services: Multiple influences on self-concept development.* Toronto, ON: Pearson Education.

Schmitt, J. P., & Kurdek, L. A. (1987). Personality correlates of positive identity and relationship involvement in gay men. *Journal of Homosexuality, 13*(4), 101-109.

Schmitt, M. T., Spears, R., & Branscombe, N. T. (2003). Constructing a minority group identity out of shared rejection: The case of international students. *European Journal of Social Psychology, 33*(1), 1-12.

Schreiber, R., Stern, P. N., & Wilson, C. (2000). Being strong. How Black West-Indian women manage depression and its stigma. *Journal of Nursing Scholarship, 32*(1), 39-51.

Schulz, R. (2000). Collaborative narrative inquiry and the ethic of caring. In W. E. Schulz (Ed.), *Counselling ethics casebook 2000* (2nd ed., pp. 212-218). Ottawa, ON: Canadian Counselling Association.

Schulz, W., Sheppard, G., Lehr, R., & Shepard, B. (2006). *Counselling ethics: Issues and cases.* Ottawa, ON: Canadian Counselling Association.

Schwartz, J., & McKinley, J. (2009, March 5). California court weighing gay marriage ban. *New York Times.* Retrieved March 18, 2009, from http://www.nytimes.com/2009/03/06/us/06marriage.html?_r=1

Segal, U. A. (1991). Cultural variables in Asian Indian families. *Families in Society, 72,* 233-241.

Sell, R. L. (1996). The Sell assessment of sexual orientation: Background and scoring. *Journal of Gay, Lesbian, and Bisexual Identity, 1,* 295-309.

Senge, P. (1990). *The fifth discipline: The art and practice of the learning organization.* New York: Currency Doubleday.

SF AIDS Foundation. (2008, August 25). AIDS 101: What Is AIDS, HIV, and HIV disease? Retrieved April 29, 2009, from http://www.sfaf.org/aids101

Shannon, J. W., & Woods, W. J. (1991). Affirmative psychotherapy for gay men. *The Counseling Psychologist, 19*(2), 197-215.

Sharf, R. F. (2006). *Applying career development theory to counseling* (4th ed.). Pacific Grove, CA: Brooks/Cole.

Shebib, B. (2003). *Choices: Interviewing and counselling skills for Canadians.* Toronto, ON: Prentice Hall.

Sheehan, O. T., & Pearson, F. (1995). Asian international and American students' psychosocial development. *Journal of College Student Development, 36*(6), 522-530.

Shen, Y., & Herr, E. L. (2004). Career placement concerns of international graduate students: A qualitative study. *Journal of Career Development, 31*(1), 15-29.

Shenk, D., & Fullmer, E. (1996). Significant relationships among older women: Cultural and personal constructions of lesbianism. *Journal of Women and Aging, 8*(3/4), 75-89.

Sheppard, G., Shulz, W., & McMahon, S. (2007). *Canadian Counselling Association code of ethics.* Ottawa, ON: Canadian Counselling Association. Retrieved May 25, 2009, from http://www.ccacc.ca/ECOEJAN07.pdf

Sheppard, M. (2002). Mental health and social justice: Gender, race, and psychological consequences of unfairness. *British Journal of Social Work, 32,* 779-797.

Sherif, C. W. (1992). Bias in psychology. In J. S. Bohan (Ed.), *Seldom seen, rarely heard: Women's place in psychology* (pp. 107-146). Boulder, CO: Westview.

Shields, C., & Anderson, M. (2001). *Dropped threads: What we aren't told.* Toronto, ON: Vintage.

Shields, S. A. (1992). Functionalism, Darwinism, and the psychology of women. In J. S. Brohan (Ed.), *Seldom seen, rarely heard: Women's place in psychology* (pp. 79-106). Boulder, CO: Westview Press.

Shih, S., & Brown, C. (2000). Taiwanese international students: Acculturation level and vocational identity. *Journal of Career Development, 27*(1), 35-47.

Shippy, R. A., Cantor, M. H., & Brennan, M. (2004). Social networks of aging gay men. *Journal of Men's Studies, 13*(1), 107-120.

Shively, M., & De Cecco, J. P. (1977). Components of sexual identity. *Journal of Homosexuality, 3,* 41-48.

Sieber, J. (1994). Will the new code help researchers to be more ethical? *Professional Psychology: Research and Practice, 25,* 369-375.

Silverstein, L. B. (2006). Integrating feminism and multiculturalism: Scientific fact or science fiction? *Professional Psychology: Research and Practice, 37*(1), 21-28.

Silverstein, M., & Chen, X. (1999). The impact of acculturation in Mexican American families on the quality of adult grandchild-grandparent relationships. *Journal of Marriage and the Family, 61,* 188-198.

Simon, G. (1996). Working with people in relationships. In D. Davies & C. Neal (Eds.), *Pink therapy: A guide for counsellors and therapists working with lesbian, gay, and bisexual clients* (pp. 101-115). Bristol, PA: Open University Press.

Simonsen, G., Blazina, C., & Watkins, C. E. (2000). Gender role conflict and psychological well-being among gay men. *Journal of Counseling Psychology, 47,* 85-89.

Sinclair, C. (1993). Codes of ethics and standards of practice. In K. Dobson & D. Dobson (Eds.), *Professional psychology in Canada.* Toronto, ON: Hogref & Huber.

Sinclair, C., & Pettifor, J. (2001). *Companion manual to the Canadian Code of Ethics for Psychologists* (3rd ed). Ottawa, ON: Canadian Psychological Association.

Sinclair, C., Simon, N., & Pettifor, J. (1996). The history of ethical codes and licensure. In L. Bass, S. DeMers, J. Ogloff, C. Peterson, J. Pettifor, R. Reaves, et al. (Eds.), *Professional conduct and discipline in psychology* (pp. 1-15). Washington, DC: American Psychological Association, and Montgomery, AL: Association of State and Provincial Psychology Boards.

Singaravelu, H., White, L., & Bringaze, T. (2005). Factors influencing international students' career choice: A comparative study. *Journal of Career Development, 32,* 46-59.

Singelis, T. M., & Pedersen, P. (1997). *Conflict and mediation across cultures.* In K. Cushner & R. W. Brislin (Eds.), *Improving intercultural interactions: Modules for cross-cultural training programs, Vol. 2* (pp. 184-204). Thousand Oaks, CA: Sage.

Singh, S. (2007). Deconstructing 'gender' and 'development' for 'identities of women'. *International Journal of Social Welfare, 16,* 100-109.

Slater, B. R. (1988). Essential issues in working with lesbian and gay male youths. *Professional Psychology: Research and Practice, 19*(2), 226-235.

Slattery, J. M., & Knapp, S. (2003). In-home family therapy and wraparound services for working with seriously at-risk children and adolescents. In L. VandeCreek & T. Jackson (Ed.), *Innovations in clinical practice: Focus on children & adolescents* (pp. 135-149). Sarasota, FL: Professional Resource Press / Professional Resource Exchange.

Smalley, W. A. (1963). Culture shock, language shock, and the shock of self-discovery. *Practical Anthropology, 10,* 49-56.

Smith, G. (2002, May 11). Gay teen wins prom fight. *The Globe and Mail,* pp. A1, A9.

Smith, L. (2005). Psychotherapy, classism, and the poor: Conspicuous by their absence. *American Psychologist, 60,* 687-696.

Smith, L., Baluch, S., Bernabei, S., Robohm, J., & Sheehy, J. (2003). Applying a social justice framework to college counseling center practice. *Journal of College Counseling, 6,* 3-13.

Smith, L. S. (2008). Positioning classism within counseling psychology's social justice agenda. *The Counseling Psychologist, 36,* 895-924.

Smith, L. T. (1999). *Decolonizing methodologies: Research and indigenous peoples.* Dunedin, NZ: University of Otago Press.

Smith, L. T. (2005). On tricky ground: Researching the native in the age of uncertainty. In N. K. Denzin & Y. S. Lincoln (Eds.), *Handbook of qualitative research* (3rd ed., pp.85-108).Thousand Oaks, CA: Sage.

Smith, T. B. (2004a). A contextual approach to assessment. In T. Smith (Ed.), *Practicing multiculturalism: Affirming diversity in counseling and psychology* (pp. 97-120). Toronto, ON: Pearson Education.

Smith, T. B. (2004b). Practicing multiculturalism: Affirming diversity in counseling and psychology. Boston: Pearson.

Sobocinski, M. R. (1990). Ethical principles in the counseling of gay and lesbian adolescents: Issues of autonomy, competence, and confidentiality. *Professional Psychology: Research and Practice, 21*(4), 240-247.

Society for Research in Child Development. (1990, Winter). SRCD ethical standards for research with children. *SRDC Newsletter,* 5-7.

Sodhi Kalsi, P. (2003, January). Ethnic identity: Examining impact of the school and home environments on second-generation Sikhs in Canada. *The Sikh Review.* Retrieved June 24, 2003, from http://www.sikhreview.org/january2003/social2.htm

Sodowsky, G., Taffe, R., Gutkin, T., & Wise, S. (1994). Development of the Multicultural Counseling Inventory: A self-report measure of multicultural competencies. *Journal of Counseling Psychology, 41,* 137-148.

Sodowsky, G. R., & Carey, J. C. (1987). Asian East Indian immigrants in America: Factors related to adjustment. *Journal of Multicultural Counselling and Development, 15,* 129-141.

Sohgn, S. S. (1993). Are traditional empirical research methods inherently biased against people of color? In W. W. Hudson & P. S. Nurius (Eds.), *Issues in social work* (pp. 22-36). Toronto, ON: Allyn and Bacon.

Sophie, J. (1985-86). A critical examination of stage theories of lesbian identity development. *Journal of Homosexuality, 12*(2), 39-51.

Sparks, E. E., & Park, A. H. (2000). The integration of feminism and multiculturalism: Ethical dilemmas at the border. In M. M. Brabeck (Ed.), *Practicing feminist ethics in psychology* (pp. 203-224). Washington, DC: American Psychological Association.

Speck, F. (1935). *Naskapi: The savage hunters of the North.* Norman, OK: University of Oklahoma Press.

Speight, S. L., & Vera, E. M. (2008). Social justice and counseling psychology: A challenge to the specialty. In S. D. Brown & R. Lent (Eds.), *The handbook of counseling psychology* (4th ed., pp. 54-67). Hoboken, NJ: John Wiley & Sons.

Spence, A. (n.d.). *Perceptions: The first twenty-two years, 1983-2004: An index to the Canadian gay & lesbian newsmagazine. Politicians.* Retrieved April 29, 2009, from http://library2.usask.ca/srsd/perceptions/1875.html

Spencer-Rodgers, J. (2000). The vocational situation and country of orientation of international students. *Journal of Multicultural Counseling and Development, 28,* 32-49.

Spenser, B., & Brown, J. (2007). Fusion or internalized homophobia? A pilot study of Bowen's differentiation of self hypothesis with lesbian couples. *Family Process, 46*(2), 257-268.

Spielmann, R. (1998) *You're so fat: Exploring Ojibwe discourse.* Toronto, ON: University of Toronto Press.

Spitalnick, J. S., & McNair, L. D. (2005). Couples therapy with gay and lesbian clients: An analysis of important clinical issues. *Journal of Sex & Marital Therapy, 31,* 43-56.

Spitzer, R. L. (2003). Can some gay men and lesbians change their sexual orientation? 200 participants reporting a change from homosexual to heterosexual orientation. *Archives of Sexual Behavior, 32*(5), 403-417.

Srinivasan, S., & Ivey, S. L. (1999). Domestic violence. In D. J. Kramer, S. L. Ivey, & Y. Ying (Eds.), *Immigrant women's health: Problems and solutions* (pp. 178-189). San Francisco: Jossey-Bass.

Stampley, C. D. (2008). Social workers' culture-based countertransferences. *Journal of Ethnic & Cultural Diversity in Social Work, 17*(1), 37-59.

Stanfield, J. H., II. (1993). Epistomological considerations. In J. H. Stanfield & R. M. Dennis (Eds.), *Race and ethnicity in research methods* (pp. 16-36). Newbury Park, CA: Sage.

Stanfield, J. H., II. (1994). Ethnic modeling in qualitative research. In N. K. Denzin & Y. S. Lincoln (Eds.), *Handbook of qualitative research* (pp. 175-188). Thousand Oaks, CA: Sage.

Stark, C. (1998). Ethics in the research context: Misinterpretations and misplaced misgivings. *Canadian Psychology, 39,* 202-211.

Stark-Adamec, C., & Kimball, M. (1984). Science free of sexism: A psychologist's guide to the conduct of nonsexist research. *Canadian Psychology, 25,* 23-25.

Stark (-Adamec), C., & Pettifor, J. (1995). *Ethical decision making for practicing social scientists: Putting values into practice.* Retrieved January 8, 2004, from http://uregina.ca/ ~starkc/ethical_decision_making_1.html

Statistics Canada. (1996). 1996 census. Retrieved October 1, 2003, from http://www12.statcan.ca/english/census01/info/census96.cfm

Statistics Canada. (2002). A profile of the Canadian population: Where we live. Retrieved September 30, 2003, from http://geodepot.statcan.ca/Diss/Highlights/Index_e.cfm

Statistics Canada. (2003a). *2001 census: Visible minority population, provinces and territories.* Retrieved August 8, 2003, from http://www.statcan.ca/english/Pgdb/defdemo40a.htm

Statistics Canada. (2003b). *Average earnings by sex and work pattern.* Retrieved August 1, 2003, from http://www.statcan.ca/english/Pgdb/labor01b.htm

Statistics Canada. (2003c). *Educational standards.* Retrieved September 30, 2003, from http://www.statcan.ca/english/census01/Products/Analytic/companion/educ/pdf/96F0030XIE2001012.pdf

Statistics Canada. (2003d). *Ethnic diversity survey: Portrait of a multicultural society.* Retrieved September 30, 2003, from http://www.statcan.ca/english/freepub/89-593-XIE/free.htm

Statistics Canada. (2004a). *The daily.* Retrieved May 15, 2004, from http://www.statcan.ca/Daily/English/030121/d030121a.htm

Statistics Canada. (2004b). *Visible minority populations, 2001 Census Canada.* Retrieved March 24, 2004, from http://www.cic.gc.ca

Statistics Canada. (2005). *Longitudinal survey of immigrants to Canada: A portrait of early settlement experiences.* Ottawa, ON: Ministry of Industry.

Statistics Canada. (2005/2006). *Report on the demographic situation in Canada.* Retrieved February 10, 2009, from http://www.statcan.gc.ca/pub/91-209-x/91-209-x2004000-eng.pdf

Statistics Canada. (2006a). *Low income cut-offs for 2005 and low income measures for 2004* (Statistics Canada Catalogue no. 75F0002MIE, Vol. 4). Retrieved November 2, 2006, from http://www.statcan.ca/english/research/75F0002MIE/75F0002MIE2006004.pdf

Statistics Canada. (2006b). *Persons in low income before tax by prevalence in percent (2000-2004).* Statistics Canada Catalogue no. 75-202-X. Retrieved October 28, 2006, from http://www40.statcan.ca/l01/cst01/famil41a.htm

Statistics Canada. (2006c). *Women in Canada: A gender-based statistical report* (5th ed.). Ottawa, ON: Author.

Statistics Canada. (2007a). *Ethnic diversity and immigration.* Retrieved January 30, 2009, from http://www41.statcan.ca/2007/30000/ceb30000_000_e.htm

Statistics Canada. (2007b). *Family portrait: Continuity and change in Canadian families and households in 2006: 2006 census.* Statistics Canada catalogue no. 97-562-XWE2006002. Ottawa, ON: Government of Canada.

Statistics Canada. (2007c). *Immigration in Canada: A portrait of the foreign-born population, 2006 census: Immigrants came from many countries.* Ottawa, ON: Government of Canada. Retrieved April 28, 2009 from http://www12.statcan.ca/english/census06/analysis/immcit/asia.cfm

Statistics Canada. (2008a). *2006 census: Ethnic origin and visible minorities.* Ottawa, ON: Government of Canada. Retrieved April 28, 2009, from http://www12.statcan.ca/census-recensement/2006/rt-td/eth-eng.cfm

Statistics Canada. (2008b). 2006 census: Ethnic origin, visible minorities, place of work and mode of transportation. Ottawa, ON: Government of Canada. Retrieved April 25, 2009, from http://www.statcan.gc.ca/daily-quotidien/080402/dq080402a-eng.htm

Statistics Canada. (2008c). *Aboriginal peoples in Canada in 2006: Inuit, Métis and First Nations, 2006 census: Findings.* Ottawa, ON: Government of Canada. Retrieved April 27, 2009, from http://www12.statcan.ca/english/census06/analysis/aboriginal/index.cfm

Statistics Canada. (2008d, May 18). *The daily: Canada's immigrant labour market, Tuesday.* Retrieved February 3, 2009, from http://www.statcan.gc.ca/daily-quotidien/080513/dq080513a-eng.htm

Statistics Canada. (2009). *Summary table: Population by year, by province and territory.* Retrieved April 25, 2009, from http://www40.statcan.gc.ca/l01/cst01/demo02a-eng.htm.

Steenbarger, B. N. (1993). A multicontextual model of counseling: Bridging brevity and diversity. *Journal of Counseling & Development, 72,* 8-15.

Steinberg, D. (2001). Understanding stress disorder takes on urgency. *The Scientist, 15*(22), 1. Retrieved May 31, 2002, from http://www.the-scientist.com

Stevens, M. J., & Gielen, U. P. (Eds.). (2007). *Toward a global psychology: Theory, research, intervention, and pedagogy.* Mahwah, NJ: Lawrence Erlbaum.

Stewart, J. (2002). Using the culture-grid in culture-centered assessment. *Guidance & Counselling, 18*(1), 10-16.

Stice, E. (2001). Risk factors for eating pathology: Recent advances and future direction. In R. H. Streigel-Moore & L. Smolak (Eds.), *Eating disorders: Innovative directions in research and practice* (pp. 51-73). Washington, DC: American Psychological Association.

Stiver I., & Miller, J. B. (1997). From depression to sadness in women's psychotherapy. In J. Jordan (Ed.), *Women's growth in diversity* (pp. 217-238). New York: Guilford Press.

Stolz, J., Collins, S., Audet, C., & Arthur, N. (2009, May). *Stories from the field: Integrating social justice awareness and action into counselling practice.* Canadian Counselling Association Annual Conference, Saskatoon, Saskatchewan, Canada.

Stone, C. B. (2003). Counselors as advocates for gay, lesbian, and bisexual youth: A call for equity and action. *Journal of Multicultural Counseling & Development, 31*(2), 143-155.

Stone, G. L. (1997). Multiculturalism as a context for supervision: Perspectives, limitations, and implications. In D. B. Pope-Davis & H. L. K. Coleman (Eds.), *Multicultural counselling competencies: Assessment, education and training, and supervision* (pp. 263-289). Thousand Oaks, CA: Sage.

Stone, S. D. (Ed.). (1990). *Lesbians in Canada.* Toronto, ON: Between the Lines.

Stonechild, B. (2006). *The new white buffalo: The struggle for Aboriginal post-secondary education in Canada.* Winnipeg, MB: University of Manitoba Press.

Stoppard, J. (2000). *Understanding depression: Feminist social constructionist approaches.* New York: Routledge.

Storm, H. (1985). *Seven arrows.* New York: Ballantine.

Strickland, C. J. (1999). The importance of qualitative research in addressing cultural relevance: Experiences from research with Pacific Northwest Indian women. *Health Care for Women International, 20,* 517-525.

Stritof, S., & Stritof, B. (n.d.). Same-sex marriage FAQ – gender – neutral marriage laws. Retrieved February 11, 2009, from the About.com website: http://marriage.about.com/cs/samesexmarriage/a/samesex.htm

Stroink, M. L., & Lalonde, R. N. (2009). Bicultural identity conflict in second-generation Asian Canadians. *The Journal of Social Psychology, 149*(1), 44-65.

Stubben, J. (1997). Culturally competent substance abuse prevention research among rural American Indian communities. In *Rural substance abuse: State of knowledge and issues* (NIDA Research Monograph, No. 168, pp. 459-483). Retrieved May 31, 2002, from http://www.nida.nih.gov/PDF/Monographs/Monograph168/Download168.html

Stubben, J. D. (2001). Working with and conducting research among American Indian families. *American Behavorial Scientist, 44*(9), 1466-1481.

Sturdivant, S. (1980). *Therapy with women: A feminist philosophy of treatment.* New York: Springer.

Sue, D., & Sundberg, N. D. (1996). Research and research hypotheses about effectiveness in intercultural counseling. In P. Pedersen, J. Draguns, W. Lonner, & J. Trimble (Eds.), *Counseling across cultures* (4th ed., pp. 323-352). Thousand Oaks, CA: Sage.

Sue, D. W. (1993). Confronting ourselves: The White and racial/ethnic-minority researcher. *The Counseling Psychologist, 21*(2), 244-249.

Sue, D. W. (1995). Multicultural organizational development: Implications for the counseling profession. In J. G. Ponterotto, J. M. Casas, L. A. Suzuki, & C. M. Alexander (Eds.), *Handbook of multicultural counseling* (pp. 474-492). Thousand Oaks, CA: Sage.

Sue, D. W. (2001). Multidimensional facets of cultural competence. *The Counseling Psychologist, 29,* 790-821.

Sue, D. W. (2002). Cultural competence in behavioral health care. In J. C. Chunn (Ed.), *The health behavioral change imperative: Theory, education, and practice in diverse populations* (pp. 41-50). New York: Kluwer Academic/Plenum.

Sue, D. W., Arredondo, P., & McDavis, R. J. (1992). Multicultural counseling competencies and standards: A call to the profession. *Journal of Counseling and Development, 70,* 477-483.

Sue, D. W., Bernier, J. B., Durran, M., Feinberg, L., Pedersen, P., Smith, E., et al. (1982). Position paper: Cross-cultural counseling competencies. *Counseling Psychologist, 10,* 45-52.

Sue, D. W., Carter, R. T., Casas, J. M., Fouad, N. A., Ivey, A. E., Jensen, M., et al. (1998). *Multicultural counseling competencies: Individual and organizational development.* Thousand Oaks, CA: Sage.

Sue, D. W., Ivey, A. E., & Pedersen, P. B. (1996). *A theory of multicultural counselling and therapy.* Pacific Grove, CA: Brooks/Cole.

Sue, D. W., & Sue, D. (1990). *Counseling the culturally different: Theory and practice.* New York: Wiley.

Sue, D. W., & Sue, D. (1999). *Counseling the culturally different: Theory and practice* (3rd ed.). New York: John Wiley & Sons.

Sue, D. W., & Sue, D. (2003). *Counseling the culturally different: Theory and practice* (4th ed.). New York: John Wiley & Sons.

Sue, D. W., & Sue, D. (2007). *Counseling the culturally diverse: Theory and practice* (5th ed.). New York: John Wiley & Sons.

Sue, D. W., & Sue, D. S. (2008). *Counseling the culturally diverse: Theory and practice* (5th ed.). Hoboken, NJ: John Wiley & Sons.

Sue, S. (1988). Psychotherapeutic services for ethnic minorities: Two decades of research findings. *American Psychologist, 43,* 301-308.

Sue, S. (2006). Cultural competency: From philosophy to research and practice. *Journal of Community Psychology, 34*(2), 237-245.

Sue, S., & Sue, D. W. (1971). Chinese American personality and mental health. *Amerasian Journal, 1,* 36-49.

Sue, S., & Zane, N. (1987). The role of culture and cultural techniques in psychotherapy. *American Psychologist, 42*(1), 37-45.

Sue, S., Zane, N., & Young, K. (1994). Research on psychotherapy with culturally diverse populations. In A. E. Bergin & S. L. Garfield (Eds.), *Handbook of psychotherapy and behaviour change* (pp. 783-847). New York: John Wiley & Sons.

Sullivan, K., & Mahalik, J. (2000). Increasing career self efficacy for women: Evaluating a group intervention. *Journal of Counselling and Development, 78,* 54-62.

Surrey, J. L. (1991). The "self-in relation": A theory of women's development. In J. V. Jordan, A. G. Kaplan, J. B. Miller, I. P. Stiver, & J. L. Surrey (Eds.), *Women's growth in connection: Writings from the Stone Center* (pp. 51-66). New York: Guilford Press.

Suter, E., Arndt, J., Arthur, N., Parboosing, J., & Taylor, E. (2009). Role understanding and effective communication as core competencies for interprofessional collaborative practice. *Journal of Interprofessional Care, 23,* 21-41.

Suyemoto, K. L., & Liem, J. H. (2007). Training therapists to be culturally sensitive with Asian American women clients. *Women & Therapy, 30*(3/4), 209-227.

Swagler, M. A., & Ellis, M. V. (2003). Crossing the distance: Adjustment of Taiwanese graduate students in the United States. *Journal of Counseling Psychology, 50,* 420-437.

Swim, M. A., St. George, S. A., & Wulff, D. (2001). Process ethics: A collaborative partnership. *Journal of Systemic Therapies, 20,* 14-24.

Szymanski, D. M., & Gupta, A. (2009). Examining the relationship between multiple internalized oppressions and African American lesbian, gay, bisexual, and questioning persons' self-esteem and psychological distress. *Journal of Counseling Psychology, 56*(1), 110-118.

Szymanski, D. (2005). A feminist approach to working with internalized heterosexism in lesbians. *Journal of College Counseling, 8,* 74-85.

Tadmor, C. T., Tetlock, P. E., & Peng, K. (2009). Acculturation strategies and integrative complexity: The cognitive implications of biculturalism. *Journal of Cross-Cultural Psychology, 40,* 105-139.

Takooshian, H. (2003). Counseling psychology's wide new horizons. *The Counseling Psychologist, 31*(4), 420-426.

Talleyrand, R. M., Chung, R. C., & Bemak, F. (2006). Incorporating social justice in counselor training programs. In R. L. Toporek, L. H. Gerstein, N. A. Fouad, G. Roysircar, & T. Israel (Eds.), *Handbook for social justice in counseling psychology: Leadership, vision, and action* (pp. 44-58). Thousand Oaks, CA: Sage.

Tanaka, G. (2002). Higher education's self-reflexive turn: Toward an intercultural theory of student development. *Journal of Higher Education, 73*(2), 264-296.

Tanaka-Matsumi, J., & Higginbotham, H. N. (1996). Behavioral approaches to counseling across cultures. In P. B. Pedersen, J. G. Draguns, W. J. Lonner, & J. E. Trimble (Eds.), *Counseling across cultures* (4th ed., pp. 205-241). Honolulu: University of Hawaii Press.

Tanaka, T., Takai, J., Kohyama, T., & Fujihara, T. (1994). Adjustment patterns of international students in Japan. *International Journal of Intercultural Relations, 18,* 55-75.

Tanaka, T., Takai, J., Kohyama, T., Fujihara, T., & Minami, H. (1997). Effects of social networks on cross-cultural adjustment. *Japanese Psychological Research, 39*(1), 12-24.

Tantillo, M. (2006). A relational approach to eating disorders multifamily therapy group: Moving from difference and disconnection to mutual connection. *Families, Systems, & Health, 24*(1), 82-102.

Task Force on the Participation of Visible Minorities in the Federal Public Service. (2000). *Embracing change in the Federal Public Service* [Catalogue No. BT22-67/2000].Ottawa, ON: Author.

Tatar, M., & Bekerman, Z. (2002). The concept of culture in the contexts and practice of professional counselling: A constructivist perspective. *Counselling Psychology Quarterly, 15*(4), 375-384.

Tatum, B. D. (1997). Racial identity development and relational theory: The case of Black women in White communities. In J. Jordan (Ed.), *Women's growth in diversity: More writings from the Stone Center* (pp. 91-106). New York: Guilford Press.

Taylor, H. E. (2000). Meeting the needs of lesbian and gay young adolescents. *The Clearing House, 73,* 221-224.

The Multicultural Coalition for Access to Family Services. (2000). *Settlement services for newcomers and access to family services.* Retrieved April 1, 2004, from http://www.settlement.org/downloads/Access_Family_Services.pdf

Theron, G. (2002). *A hermeneutic exploration of the self-understanding of the racialized other in Canadian society.* Unpublished doctoral dissertation, University of Calgary, Alberta, Canada.

Thomas, K. R., & Weinrach, S. G. (1998). Diversity-sensitive counseling today: A postmodern clash of values. *Journal of Counseling Psychology, 76,* 115-122.

Thomas, R. M. (2003). Can money undo the past? A Canadian example. *Comparative Education, 39,* 331-343.

Throckmorton, W. (1998). Efforts to modify sexual orientation: A review of outcome literature and ethical issues. *Journal of Mental Health Counseling, 20*(4), 283-304.

Todd, J. L., & Worell, J. (2000). Resilience in low income, employed African American women. *Psychology of Women Quarterly, 24,* 119-128.

Toffler, A. (1970). *Future shock.* New York: Random House.

Toporek, R. L. (2000). Developing a common language and framework for understanding advocacy counselling. In J. Lewis & L. Bradley (Eds.), *Advocacy in counselling: Counselors, clients, and community* (pp. 5-14). Greensboro, NC: CAPS.

Toporek, R. L., Gerstein, L. H., Fouad, N. A., Roysircar, G., & Israel, T. (2006a). Future directions for counselling psychology: Enhancing leadership, vision, and action in social justice. In R. L. Toporek, L. H. Gerstein, N. A. Fouad, G. Roysircar, & T. Israel (Eds.), *Handbook for social justice in counselling psychology: Leadership, vision, and action* (pp. 533-552). Thousand Oaks, CA: Sage.

Toporek, R. L., Gerstein, L. H., Fouad, N. A., Roysircar, G., & Israel, R. (2006b). *Handbook for social justice in counseling psychology: Leadership, vision, and action.* Thousand Oaks, CA: Sage.

Toporek, R. L., Lewis, J. A., & Crethar, H. C. (2009). Promoting systemic change through the ACA advocacy competencies. *Journal of Counseling & Development, 87,* 260-268.

Toporek, R. L., & Liu, W. M. (2001). Advocacy in counseling: Addressing race, class, and gender oppression. In D. B. Pope-Davis & H. L. K. Coleman (Eds.), *The intersection of race, class, and gender in multicultural counseling* (pp. 285-413). Thousand Oaks, CA: Sage.

Toporek, R. L., & McNally, C. J. (2006). Social justice training in counseling psychology: Needs and innovations. In R. L. Toporek, L. H. Gerstein, N. A. Fouad, G. Roysircar, & T. Israel (Eds.), *Handbook for social justice in counseling psychology: Leadership, vision, and action* (pp. 37-43). Thousand Oaks, CA: Sage.

Toporek, R. L., & Reza, J. V. (2001). Context as a critical dimension of multicultural counseling: Articulating personal, professional, and institutional competence. *Journal of Multicultural Counseling & Development, 29*(1), 13-30.

Toporek, R. L., & Williams, R. A. (2006). Ethics and professional issues related to the practice of social justice in counseling psychology. In R. L. Toporek, L. H. Gerstein, N. A. Fouad, G. Roysircar, & T. Israel (Eds.), *Handbook for social justice in counseling psychology: Leadership, vision, and action* (pp. 17-34). Thousand Oaks, CA: Sage.

Totten, M., Quigley, P., & Morgan, M. (2004). *CPHA safe school study.* Retrieved February 18, 2009, from http://www.ysb.on.ca/english/pdf/LE/Safe%20School%20Study%202004.pdf

Tousignant, M. (1997). Refugees and immigrants in Quebec. In A. Al-Issa & M. Tousignant (Eds.), *Ethnicity, immigration, and psychopathology* (pp. 57-70). New York: Plenum Press.

Townsend, J. M. (1998). *What women want - what men want: Why the sexes still see love and commitment so differently.* New York: Oxford University Press.

Tracy, L. C. (1999). Posttraumatic stress disorder. In D. J. Kramer, S. L. Ivey, & Y. Ying (Eds.), *Immigrant women's health: Problems and solutions* (pp. 220-231). San Francisco: Jossey-Bass.

Travis, C. B., & Compton, J. (2001). Feminism and health in the decade of behavior. *Psychology of Women Quarterly, 25,* 312-323.

Treasury Board of Canada Secretariat. (2008). *Section II: Analysis of program activities by strategic outcome.* Retrieved April 25, 2009, from http://www.tbs-sct.gc.ca/rpp/2008-2009/inst/imc/imc02-eng.asp

Trimble, J., Fleming, C., Beauvais, F., & Jumper-Thurman, P. (1996). Essential cultural and social strategies for counseling Native American Indians. In P. B. Pedersen, J. G. Draguns, W. J. Lonner, & J. Trimble (Eds.). *Counseling across cultures* (4th ed., pp. 177-249). Thousand Oaks, CA: Sage.

Trimble, J. E., & Gonzalez, J. (2008). Cultural considerations and perspectives for providing psychological counselling for Native American Indians. In P. B. Pedersen, J. G. Draguns, W. J. Lonner, & J. Trimble (Eds.), *Counselling across cultures* (6th ed., pp. 93-111). Thousand Oaks, CA: Sage.

Trimble, J. E., & Mohatt, G. V. (2006). Coda: The virtuous and responsible researcher in another culture. In J. E. Trimble & C. B. Fisher (Eds.), *The handbook of ethical research with ethnocultural populations & communities* (pp. 325-334). Thousand Oaks, CA: Sage.B1450

Troiden, R. R. (1979). Becoming homosexual: A model of gay identity acquisition. *Psychiatry, 42,* 362-373.

Troiden, R. R. (1993). The formation of homosexual identities. In L. D. Garnets & D. C. Kimmel (Eds.), *Psychological perspectives on lesbian and gay male experiences* (pp. 191-217). New York: Columbia University Press.

Tseng, W., & Newton, F. B. (2002). International students' strategies for well-being. *College Student Journal, 36*(4), 591-597.

Turner, C. W. (1997). Clinical applications of the Stone Center theoretical approach to minority women. In J. V. Jordan (Ed.), *Women's growth in diversity: More writings from the Stone Center* (pp. 74-90). New York: Guilford Press.

Turner, S., DeMers, S., Fox, H., & Reed, G. (2002). APA's guidelines for test user qualifications: An executive summary. *American Psychologist, 56,* 1099-1113.

Twist, M., Murphy, M., Green, M. S., & Palmanteer, D. (2006). Therapists' support for gay and lesbian human rights. *Guidance & Counseling, 21*(2), 107-113.

Tye, M. C. (2003). Spitzer's oversight: Ethical-philosophical underpinnings of "reparative therapy." *Archives of Sexual Behavior, 32*(5), 452-453.

Tyler, A., & Boxer, D. (1996). Sexual harassment? Cross-cultural/cross-linguistic perspectives. *Discourse Society, 7*(1), 107-133.

Ulysse, P. J. (n.d.). *Social justice, exclusion, and citizenship: The ethnic minorities in Canada – A review of the literature.* Retrieved April 1, 2004, from http://www.canada.metropolis.net/events/socialjustice /ulysse_e.html#Footnotes

Umana-Taylor, A. J., & Yazedjian, A. (2006). Generational differences and similarities among Puerto Rican and Mexican mothers' experiences with familial ethnic socialization. *Journal of Social and Personal Relationships, 23*(3), 445-464.

Underwood, N. (2002, January 21). Queer as mainstream: Returning for season two, Queer as Folk has a long heterosexual following. *Maclean's, 115*(3), 42, 44.

UNESCO. (1995). *Multiculturalism: A policy response to diversity.* Retrieved April 1, 2004, from http://www.unesco.org/most/sydpaper.htm

Unger, R. K. (1992). Through the looking glass: No Wonderland yet! In J. S. Brohan (Ed.), *Seldom seen, rarely heard: Women's place in psychology* (pp. 147-170). Boulder, CO: Westview Press.

United Nations. (1948). *United Nations universal declaration of human rights.* New York: Author.

Unks, G. (Ed.). (1995). *The gay teen: Educational practice and theory for lesbian, gay, and bisexual adolescents.* New York: Routledge.

Usher, P. (1996). Feminist approaches to research. In D. Scott & R. Usher (Eds.), *Understanding educational research* (pp. 120-142). London, UK: Routledge.

Valentine, G. (2007). Theorizing and researching intersectionality: A challenge for feminist geography. *The Professional Geographer, 59*(1), 10-21.

Valetta, R. (2006). The ins and outs of poverty in advanced economies: Poverty dynamics in Canada, Germany, Great Britain, and the United States. *Review of Income and Wealth, 52,* 261-284.

Valpey, M. (2002, March 18). RCMP infiltrated agency that spawned future star politicians. *Globe & Mail,* p. A-1. Retrieved May 31, 2002, from http://www.globeandmail.com/servlet/ArticleNews/printarticle/gam/20020318/UCOMPN

van der Kolk, B. A. (1994). The body keeps the score: Memory and the evolving psychobiology of posttraumatic stress. *Harvard Review of Psychiatry, 1,* 235-263.

van Oudenhoven, J. P. (2006). Immigrants. In D. L. Sam & J. W. Berry (Eds.), *The Cambridge handbook of acculturation psychology* (pp. 163-180). New York: Cambridge University Press.

Vare, J. W., & Norton, T. L. (1998). Understanding gay and lesbian youth: Sticks, stones, and silence. *The Clearing House, 71*(6), 327-331.

Vargo, M. E. (1998). *Acts of disclosure: The coming-out process of contemporary gay men.* Binghamton, NY: Harrington Park Press.

Vazquez, L. A., & Garcia-Vazquez, E. (2003). Teaching multicultural competence in the counseling curriculum. In D. B. Pope-Davis, H. L. K. Coleman, W. M. Lui, & R. L. Toporek (Eds.), *Handbook of multicultural competencies in counseling and psychology* (pp. 546-561). Thousand Oaks, CA: Sage.

Vera, E. M., & Speight, S. L. (2003). Multicultural competence, social justice, and counselling psychology: Expanding our roles. *The Counseling Psychologist, 31,* 253-272.

Vera, E. M., & Speight, S. L. (2007). Advocacy, outreach, and prevention: Integrating social action roles into professional training. In E. Aldarondos (Ed.), *Advancing social justice through clinical practice* (pp. 373-388). Mahwah, NJ: Lawrence Erlbaum.

Viau, R. (2000). *Femmes personnes: Sexes, genres et pouvoirs en Iroquoisie ancienne* [I'm nobody's woman: Sex, gender, and power in ancient Iroquois society]. Montreal, QC: Boréal.

Vinson, R. S., & Neimeyer, G. J. (2000). The relationship between racial identity development and multicultural counseling competency [Electronic version]. *Journal of Multicultural Counseling and Development, 28*(3), 177-192.

Vocational Rehabilitation Association of Canada. (2002). *Canadian code of ethics for rehabilitation professionals.* Toronto, ON: Author.

Vohra, N., & Adair, J. (2000). Life satisfaction of Indian immigrants in Canada. *Psychology and Developing Societies, 12*(2), 109-37.

Vontress, C. E. (1986). Social and cultural foundations. In M. D. Lewis, R. Hayes, & J. Lewis (Eds.), *Introduction to the counseling profession* (pp. 215-250). Itasca, IL: Peacock.

Wakil, S. P., Siddique, C. M., & Wakil, F. A. (1981). Between two cultures: A study in socialization of children of immigrants. *Journal of Marriage and Family, 43,* 929- 940.

Walker, J. (1992). South Asians in Canadian immigration policy: An historical overview. In R. Ghosh & R. Kanungo (Eds.), *South Asian Canadians: Current issues in the politics of culture* (pp. 1-34). Montreal, QB: Shastri Indo-Canadian Institute.

Walker, J. L. (1999). *Canada first: The 1999 survey of international students.* Ottawa, ON: Canadian Bureau for International Education.

Walker, L. (1984). *The battered woman syndrome.* New York: Springer.

Walker, L. A., & Conyne, R. K. (2007). Group work with international students. In M. Pope & H. Singaravelu (Eds.), *A handbook for counselling international students in the United States* (pp. 299-310). Alexandria, VA: American Counseling Association.

Walker, M., & Rosen, W. (Eds.). (2004). *How connections heal: Stories from relational-cultural therapy.* B1489

Walter, J., & Bala, J. (2004). Where meanings, sorrow, and hope have a resident permit: Treatment of families and children. In J. P. Wilson & B. Drožđek (Eds.), *Broken spirits: The treatment of traumatized asylum seekers, refugees, war and torture victims.* New York: Brunner-Routledge.

Walton, S. J. (1990). Stress management training for overseas effectiveness. *International Journal of Intercultural Relations, 14,* 507-527.

Wan, T., Chapman, D. W., & Biggs, D. A. (1992). Academic stress of international students attending US universities. *Research in Higher Education, 33,* 607-623.

Wang, M. M. (1997). Reentry and reverse culture shock. In K. Cushner & R. W. Brislin (Eds.), *Improving intercultural interactions: Modules for cross-cultural training programs: Volume 2* (pp. 109-128). Thousand Oaks, CA: Sage.

Ward, C. (2008). Thinking outside the Berry boxes. New perspectives on identity, acculturation, and intercultural relations. *International Journal of Intercultural Relations, 32,* 105-114.

Ward, C., Bochner, S., & Furnham, A. (2001). *The psychology of culture shock* (2nd ed.). Hove, East Sussex, UK: Routledge.

Ward, C., & Kennedy, A. (1993). Where's the "culture" in cross-cultural transition? Comparative studies of sojourner adjustment. *Journal of Cross-Cultural Psychology, 24,* 221-249.

Warren, C. A. B. (1977). Fieldwork in the gay world: Issues in phenomenological research. *Journal of Social Issues, 33*(4), 93-107.

Wasserman, E. (1995). Personal reflections of an Anglo therapist in Indian country. In J. Adleman & G. Enguidanos (Eds.), *Racism in the lives of women: Testimony, theory, and guides to antiracist practice* (pp. 23-32). New York: Harrington Press.

Waters, M. C. (1999). *Black identities: West East Indian immigrant dreams and American realities.* New York: Russell Sage Foundation.

Watson, A. L., Collins, R. L., & Correia, F. C. (2004). Advocacy and social action in the context of ecological counseling. In R. K. Conyne & E. P. Cook (Eds.), *Ecological counseling: An innovative approach to conceptualizing person-environment interaction* (pp. 289-314). Alexandria, VA: American Counseling Association.

Watson, Z. E. P., Herlihy, B. R., & Pierce, L. A. (2006, January). Forging the link between multicultural competence and ethical counseling practice: A historical perspective. *Counseling and Values, 50,* 99-107.

Watters, A. T. (1986). Heterosexual bias in psychological research on lesbianism and male homosexuality (1979-1983) utilizing the bibliographic and taxonomic system of Morin (1977). *Journal of Homosexuality, 13,* 35-58.

Wawaskone. (1977). M'kiznun [Moccasins]. *Tawow: Canadian Indian Cultural Magazine, 6*(2), 27.

Wax, R. (1971). *Doing field work.* Chicago: The University of Chicago Press.

Weber, L. (1998). A conceptual framework for understanding race, class, gender and sexuality. *Psychology of Women Quarterly, 22,* 13-32.

Weinberg, M. S. (1970). Homosexual samples: Differences and similarities. *Journal of Sex Research, 6,* 312-325.

Weinrach, S. G., & Thomas, K. R. (1996). The counseling profession's commitment to diversity-sensitive counseling: A critical assessment. *Journal of Counseling and Development, 74,* 472-477.

Weinrach, S. G., & Thomas, K. R. (2002). A critical analysis of the multicultural counseling competencies: Implications for the practice of mental health counseling. *Journal of Mental Health Counseling, 24*(1), 20-35.

Weinrach, S. G., & Thomas, K. R. (2004). The AMCD multicultural counseling competencies: A critically flawed initiative. *Journal of Mental Health Counseling, 26*(1), 20-35.

Weiten, W., & Lloyd, M. (2000). *Psychology applied to modern life: Adjustment at the turn of the century.* Stamford, CT: Wadsworth.

Wells, K., & Tsutsumi, L. M. (2005). *Creating safe and caring schools for lesbian, gay, bisexual, and trans-identified students: A guide for counsellors.* Retrieved August 12, 2006, from the Society for Safe and Caring Schools and Communities website:
http://www.sacsc.ca/PDF%20files/Resources/LGBTQ%20guide%20for%20counsellors%20unbooked.pdf

West, C. K. (2005). The map of relational-cultural theory. *Women & Therapy, 28*(3/4), 93-110.

Westcoast Coalition for Human Dignity. (1998). *Choose dignity: A kit for fighting hate.* Vancouver, BC: Author.

Westermeyer, J. (1989). *Mental health for refugees and other migrants: Social and preventive approaches.* Springfield, IL: Charles C. Thomas.

Westney, O. E., Brabble, E. W., & Edwards, C. H. (1988). Human ecology: Concepts and perspectives. In R. J. Borden & J. Jacobs (Eds.), *Human ecology: Research and applications* (pp. 129-137). College Park, MD: Society for Human Ecology.

Westwood, M. J., & Barker, M. (1990). Academic achievement and social adaptation among international students: A comparison group study of the peer-pairing program. *International Journal of Intercultural Relations, 14*, 251-263.

Westwood, M. J., & Ishiyama, F. I. (1990). The communication process as a critical intervention. *Journal of Multicultural Counseling & Development, 18*(4), 163-172.

Westwood, M. J., Lawrence, W. S., & Paul, D. (1986). Preparing for re-entry: A program for the sojourning student. *International Journal for the Advancement of Counselling, 9*, 221-230.

Westwood, M., Mak, A., Barker, M., & Ishiyama, I. (2000). Group procedures and applications for developing socio-cultural competencies among immigrants. *International Journal for the Advancement of Counselling, 22*, 317-330.

Whalen, M., Fowler-Lese, K. P., Barber, J. S., Williams, E. N., Judge, A. B., Nilsson, J. E., et al. (2004). Counseling practice with feminist-multicultural perspectives. *Journal of Multicultural Counseling and Development, 32*, 379-389.

Wheaton, C. (2000). An Aboriginal pedagogical model: Recovering an Aboriginal pedagogy from the Woodlands Cree. In R. Neil (Ed.), *Voice of the drum* (pp. 151-167). Brandon, MN: Kingfisher.

Wihak, C. (2008). Case incident 3: When cultures clash. In N. Arthur & P. Pedersen (Eds.), *Case incidents in counseling for international transitions* (pp. 37-40). Alexandria, VA: American Counseling Association.

Wihak, C., & Merali, N. (2003). Culturally sensitive counselling in Nunavut: Implications of Inuit traditional knowledge, *Canadian Journal of Counselling, 37*(4), 243-255.

Whiston, S. C. (2005). *Principles and applications of assessment in counseling* (2nd ed.).Toronto, ON: Thomson, Brooks/Cole.

Whitcomb, D. H., & Loewy, M. I. (2006). Diving into the hornet's nest: Situating counseling psychologists in LGB social justice work. In R. L. Toporek, L. H. Gerstein, N. A. Fouad, G. Roysircar, & T. Israel (Eds.), *Handbook for social justice in counseling psychology: Leadership, vision, and action* (pp. 215-230). Thousand Oaks, CA: Sage.

Whitman, J. S., Cormier, S., & Boyd, C. J. (2000). Lesbian identity management at various stages of the coming out process: A qualitative study. *International Journal of Sexuality and Gender Studies, 5*(1), 3-18.

Whitmarsh, L., Brown, D., Cooper, J., Hawkins-Rodgers, Y., & Wentworth, D. K. (2007). Choices and challenges: A qualitative exploration of professional women's career patterns. *The Career Development Quarterly, 56*, 85-94.

Williams, B. (2003). The worldview dimensions of individualism and collectivism: Implications for counseling. *Journal of Counseling & Development, 81*, 370-374.

Williams, C. C. (2002). A rationale for an anti-racist entry point to anti-oppressive social work in mental health services. *Critical Social Work, 2*(2), 20-31. Retrieved April 1, 2004, from http://www.criticalsocialwork.com/CSW_V2_N2_WILL.pdf

Williams, C. C. (2007). Mixed-method evaluation of continuing professional development: Applications in cultural competence training. *Social Work Education, 26*(2), 121-135.

Williams, E. N., & Barber, J. S. (2004). Power and responsibility in therapy: Integrating feminism and multiculturalism. *Journal of Multicultural Counseling and Development, 32*, 390-401.

Williams, R. (1992). *Just as I am: A practical guide to begin out, proud, and Christian.* New York: Harper Collins.

Williams, T., Connolly, J., Pepler, D., & Craig, W. (2003). Questioning and sexual minority adolescents: High school experiences of bullying, sexual harassment, and physical abuse. *Canadian Journal of Community Mental Health, 22*(2), 47-58.

Wills, G., & Crawford, R. (2000). Attitudes toward homosexuality in Shreveport-Bossier City, Louisiana. *Journal of Homosexuality, 38*(3), 97-116.

Wilson, S. (2007). Guest editorial: What is an Indigenist research paradigm? *Canadian Journal of Native Education, 30*(2), 193-195.

Wilson,T., Grilo, C., & Vitousek, K. (2007). Psychological treatment of eating disorders. *American Psychologist, 62*(3), 199-216.

Wilton, L., & Constantine, M. G. (2003). Length of residence, cultural adjustment difficulties, and psychological distress symptoms in Asian and Latin American international college students. *Journal of College Counseling, 6*(2), 177-187.

Wine, J. D. (1990). Outsiders on the inside: Lesbians in Canadian academe. In S. D. Stone (Ed.), *Lesbians in Canada* (pp. 157-171). Toronto, ON: Between the Lines.

Winkelman, M. (1994). Cultural shock and adaptation. *Journal of Counseling and Development, 73,* 121-126.

Wintrob, R. W. (1969). The Cree: Education, identity conflict, and psychopathology. *McGill Journal of Education, 4,* 25-34.

Wong-Rieger, D., & Quintana, D. (1987). Comparative acculturation of Southeast Asian and Hispanic immigrants and sojourners. *Journal of Cross-Cultural Psychology, 18,* 345-362.

Wood, O. (n.d.). *The fight for gay rights: World timeline.* Retrieved June 15, 2002, from http://cbc.ca/news/indepth/background/gayrights2.html

Worell, J. (2001). Feminist interventions: Accountability beyond symptom reduction. *Psychology of Women Quarterly, 25,* 335-343.

Worell, J., & Remer, P. (2003). *Feminist perspectives in therapy: Empowering diverse women.* Hoboken, NJ: John Wiley and Sons.

World Health Organization. (1987). *Care for the mentally ill: Components of mental health policies governing the provision of psychiatric services.* Geneva: Author.

World Health Organization. (2008). Suicide rates per 100,000 by country, year, and sex (Table). Retrieved January 29, 2009, from http://www.who.int/mental_health/prevention/suicide_rates/en/index.html

World Medical Association. (1994). *International code of medical ethics.* Retrieved December 8, 2003, from http://www.wma.net/e/policy/c8.htm

World Psychiatric Association. (2002). *Madrid declaration on ethical standards for psychiatric practice.* Retrieved December 8, 2003, from http://www.wpanet.org/generalinfo/ethicl.html

Wrenn, C. G. (1962). The culturally encapsulated counsellor. *Harvard Educational Review, 32,* 444-449.

Wright, R. (2001). *Clara Callan.* Toronto, ON: HarperCollins.

Wu, Z., & Hart, R. (2002). Social and health factors associated with support among elderly immigrants in Canada. *Research On Aging, 24,* 391-412.

Wyatt, G. E. (1982). Sociocultural assessment of home and school visits in psychiatric evaluations of Afro-American children and families. In B. A. Bass, G. E. Wyatt, & G. J. Powell (Eds.), *Sociocultural assessment of home and school visits in psychiatric evaluations* (pp. 137-151). New York: Grune & Stratton.

Wyche, K., & Rice, J. (1997). Feminist therapy: From dialogue to tenets. In J. Worell & N. Johnson (Eds.), *Shaping the future of feminist psychology: Education, research, and practice* (pp. 57-71). Washington, DC: American Psychological Association.

Yakushko, O., Backhaus, A., Watson, M., Ngaruya, K., & Gonzalez, J. (2008). Career development concerns of recent immigrants and refugees. *Journal of Career Development, 34*(4), 362-396.

Yakushko, O., Watson, M., & Thompson, S. (2008). Stress and coping in the lives of recent immigrants and refugees: Considerations for counseling. *International Journal for the Advancement of Counseling, 30,* 167-178.

Yalom, I. D., & Leszcz, M. (2005). *The theory and practice of group psychotherapy* (5th ed.). New York: Basic Books.

Yang, E., Wong, S. C., Hwang, M., & Heppner, M. J. (2002). Widening our global view: The development of career counseling services for international students. *Journal of Career Development, 28*(3), 203-213.

Yang, R. P., Noels, K. A., & Saumure, K. D. (2006). Multiple routes to cross-cultural adaptation for international students: Mapping the paths between self-construals, English language confidence, and adjustment. *International Journal of Intercultural Relations, 30,* 487-506.

Yi, K., & Shorter-Gooden, K. (1999). Ethnic identity formation: From stage theory to a constructivist narrative model. *Psychotherapy, 36,* 16-26.

Ying, Y. W., & Liese, L. H. (1990). Initial adaptation of Taiwan foreign students to the United States: The impact of prearrival variables. *American Journal of Community Psychology, 18,* 825-845.

Yoon, E., & Jepsen, D. A. (2008). Expectations of and attitudes toward counseling: A comparison of Asian international and U.S. graduate students. *International Journal for the Advancement of Counselling, 30,* 116-127.

Yoon, E., & Portman, T. A. (2004). Critical issues of literature on counselling international students. *Journal of Multicultural Counseling & Development, 32*(1), 33-44.

York, G. (1992). *The dispossessed: Life and death in Native Canada.* Toronto, ON: Little Brown and Co.

Young, I. M. (1990). *Justice and the politics of difference.* Princeton, NJ: Princeton University Press.

Young, R., Marshall, S., & Valach, L. (2007). Making career theories more culturally sensitive: Implications for counseling. *Career Development Quarterly, 56,* 4-18.

Young, R. A., & Nicol, J. J. (2007). Counselling psychology in Canada: Advancing psychology for all. *Applied Psychology: An International Review, 56*(1), 20-32.

Youngblood-Henderson, J. (2000). Challenges of respecting Indigenous world views in Eurocentric education. In R. Neil (Ed.), *Voice of the drum* (pp. 59-80). Brandon, MN: Kingfisher.

Zalaquett, C. P., Fuerth, K. M., Stein, C., Ivey, A. E., & Ivey M. B. (2008, Summer). Reframing the DSM-IV-TR from a multicultural/social justice perspective. *Journal of Counseling & Development, 86,* 364-371.

Zane, N., & Sue, S. (1991). Culturally responsive mental health services for Asian Americans: Treatment and training issues. In H. Myers, P. Wohlford, P. Guzman, & R. Echemendia (Eds.), *Ethnic minority perspectives on clinical training and services in psychology* (pp. 49-59). Washington, DC: American Psychological Association.

Zapf, M. K. (1991). Cross-cultural transitions and wellness: Dealing with culture shock. *International Journal for the Advancement of Counselling, 142,* 105-119.

Zapf, M. K. (1993). Remote practice and culture shock: Social workers moving from isolated northern regions. *Social Work, 38*(6), 694-704.

Zayas, L., Torres, L., Malcolm, J., & DesRosiers, F. (1996). Clinicians' definitions of ethically sensitive therapy. *Professional Psychology: Research and Practice, 27,* 78-82.

Zazula, G. D. (1999, February). The role of linguistics within a multidisciplinary framework for studying the initial peopling of the Americas. Pimohtewin. Retrieved May 31, 2002, from http://www.ualberta.ca/~pimohte/zazula.html

Zerbe Enns, C., Sinacore, A. L., Ancis, J. R., & Phillips, J. (2004). Toward integrating feminist and multicultural pedagogies. *Journal of Multicultural Counseling and Development, 32,* 414-427.

Zhang, D. (1995). Depression and culture – A Chinese perspective. *Canadian Journal of Counseling, 29,* 227-233.

Zhou, M. (1997). Segmented assimilation: Issues, controversies and recent research on the new second generation. *International Migration Review, 31*(4), 975-1008.

Ziguras, C., & Law, S. (2006). Recruiting international students as skilled immigrants: the global 'skills race' as viewed from Australia and Malaysia. *Globalisation, Societies, and Education, 4,* 59-76.

SUBJECT INDEX

Ableism, 39, 58, 60, 82
Aboriginal peoples (see First Nations)
Abuse (see also Addiction, Power)
    child, 67, 172, 177, 266, 386
    definition, 358
    emotional/psychological, 33, 96, 400, 421
    First Nations, 6, 177, 266, 283
    lesbian/gay, 377-382, 401
    physical, 33, 96, 358-360, 379
    relationship, 303, 310, 344, 358-360, 377-379
    research, 176, 181-185, 213
    sexual, 6, 33, 42, 172, 177, 266, 378
    spiritual, 379, 400, 421
Acculturation/adaptation/assimilation (see also Assessment, Transition), 85, 193, 227, 289, 294-297, 323, 425, 429-431
    definition, 85
    reacculturation, 31, 252, 263
    status/level, 131, 193-195, 206, 301, 320-325, 435
    strategies, 289-296
Addiction, 172, 271, 284, 375, 382, 400
Advocacy, 136, 149
    barriers, 39, 136, 154
    competencies/competence, 139-152
    definition, 136, 149
    interventions, 136, 146, 152-157
    social justice, 149-162
    skills, 150-157, 304
Affirmative action, 9, 356
Africentrism, 121
Age/ageism/aging, 58-60
Androcentrism, 369
Antilocution, 413
Appropriation, cultural, 62, 133, 264-266
Assessment (see also Acculturation; Culture-infused counselling), 189-208, 411-414
    approaches, 196
    bias, 44, 196
    client, 54, 121-126
    competencies, 195
    cultural understanding/flexibility/sensitivity, 192, 196
    definition, 190
    ethics of psychological testing, 176
    formal/informal, 123, 216
    frameworks, 199, 249
    item discrimination, 203
    methods/instruments/tools, 202-208
    nomothetic/idiographic information, 197
    norm groups, 189-203
    procedures/processes, 196-200
    protocols, 201
    qualitative/quantitative, 196, 202
    social justice lens, 125
    worldview, 182, 192
Assimilation (see Acculturation)
Associations (see Professional associations)
Assumptions
    bias, 55-57, 69
    client/client experience, 21, 27-29
    counsellor, 37, 71, 104
    theoretical, 46-58, 74-77, 104, 119-129
Attitudes, 54, 59, 92, 336
Auditing, cultural, 120, 157-163, 437-439
Authenticity, 94-99
Awareness
    blindness, cultural, 95
    client culture, 67-69, 328
    cultural, 18, 212

    self/self and others, 67-102, 112, 217-219, 329
    strategies for increasing, 99-101, 217-219
    working across cultures, 89

Baggage, cultural, 58, 98, 213
Bias (see Assessment, Assumptions)
Biculturalism, 193, 263, 321
Bilingualism, 7
Bisexuality, 367-368

Canada/Canadian context (see also Oppression, Identity), 3, 93, 127-132, 176, 286
    legislation and policy, 9, 13, 40, 462
Career development, 28, 279-280, 355-356, 381-382
    structure of opportunity, 355
Ceremonies (see First Nations, Healing)
Change
    social and political agenda, 48
    processes, 120, 130-132, 150, 173, 256, 390, 459
Classism / Socio-economic status, 35-38, 194, 272, 289
Client
    as sources of cultural knowledge, 100
    common themes, 124
    context, 134
    experiences, 38, 108
Closeted (see Identity management)
Code of ethics/conduct (see Ethics)
Cognition
    cognitive complexity, 87, 110-112, 158
    cognitive dissonance, 89, 404, 414
    cognitive restructuring, 360-415
    cognitive/cultural schemata 57, 59, 86, 90
Colour blindness, 211
Collaboration, 458-465
    collaborative approach, 70, 199, 270, 358, 458-461
    intraprofessional, 62, 461
    interprofessional/interdisciplinary, 150, 178, 449, 458-465
    international/global, 449, 462-464
Coming out (see Identity management)
Communication (see also Ethics)
    cultural/intercultural, 111-118, 432
    heteronormative language, 93
    language barriers, 38, 60, 116-118, 289, 299, 440
    language proficiency, 116, 298, 301, 432, 440
    skills, 115, 127, 153, 233, 308
    style, 60, 110, 119, 309, 387
    translators/interpreters, 117, 194, 199-202, 301
    verbal/nonverbal, 116-119, 15, 275, 349
Community resources (see also Immigrant), 134, 305, 313, 381
Competence/competency (see Culture-infused counselling competence)
Congruence, 94-99
Connection/connectedness, 121, 222, 267-276, 365, 415-416
Consciousness
    cultural, 96
    raising, 63, 135, 157, 310, 348-351
Consultation, 59, 63, 145, 149, 164, 463
Consumer groups/needs, 36, 43, 101, 145, 453
Coping (see Stress and Coping)
Counselling/counsellors (see also Culture-infused / Multicultural counselling; Specific populations, such as First Nations, lesbian, gay; Interventions; Organizational development; Stress; Working Alliance)
    agreement, 120, 126
    assertiveness training, 350
    attrition, 76, 225, 327, 333